Fifth Edition

CONTEMPORARY
MORAL PROBLEMS

James E. White
St. Cloud State University

West Publishing Company

Minneapolis/St. Paul   New York   Los Angeles   San Francisco

Cover Image: Juan Miró, *Personnage Oiseaux II.*
Photograph provided by Christie's
Images. © 1996 Artists Rights Society
(ARS), NY/ADAP, Paris.
Copyeditor: Deborah Drolen Jones
Compositor: Parkwood Composition Service, Inc.
Permissions Coordinator: Lynn Reichel
Proofreader: Emily P. McNamara
Indexer: Schroeder Indexing Services

Library of Congress Cataloging-in-Publication Data

Contemporary moral problems / [edited by]
James E. White.—5th ed.   p.   cm.
   Includes bibliographical references and index.
   ISBN 0–314–08523–8 (soft : alk. paper)
   1. Applied ethics.   2. Ethical
problems.   3. Civilization, Modern—1950–
I. White, James E.
BJ1031.C6   1997   96–12277
170–dc20   CIP

∞

WEST'S COMMITMENT TO THE ENVIRONMENT

In 1906, West Publishing Company began recycling materials left over from the production of books. This began a tradition of efficient and responsible use of resources. Today, 100% of our legal bound volumes are printed on acid-free, recycled paper consisting of 50% new fibers. West recycles nearly 27,700,000 pounds of scrap paper annually—the equivalent of 229,300 trees. Since the 1960s, West has devised ways to capture and recycle waste inks, solvents, oils, and vapors created in the printing process. We also recycle plastics of all kinds, wood, glass, corrugated cardboard, and batteries, and have eliminated the use of polystyrene book packaging. We at West are proud of the longevity and the scope of our commitment to the environment.

West pocket parts and advance sheets are printed on recyclable paper and can be collected and recycled with newspapers. Staples do not have to be removed. Bound volumes can be recycled after removing the cover.

Production, Prepress, Printing and Binding by West Publishing Company.

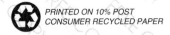
PRINTED ON 10% POST CONSUMER RECYCLED PAPER

CONTENTS

Chapter Five
Hunger and Welfare 269

Chapter Six
Discrimination and Affirmative
Action 349

Chapter Seven
Corporate Responsibility 417

Chapter Eight
Animals and the
Environment 453

Chapter Nine
War and Violence 527

PREFACE

The choice of topics for the fifth edition was determined mostly by student surveys and suggestions from instructors who have used the book. There is renewed interest in affirmative action and welfare, perhaps because Newt Gingrich and his followers have attacked these programs. There is a return to the topic of corporate responsibility, a matter of increasing concern as we see corporations increasing their profits by questionable actions such as laying off thousands of workers, reducing retirement benefits, and eliminating health insurance. Students continue to be interested in the topics of abortion, suicide, euthanasia, and capital punishment. War remains on the center stage as long as the war in Bosnia continues and as long as Russia and other countries are perceived to be threats. Wars have been going on throughout human history, and there seems to be no end in sight. A chapter on animals and the environment is included even though interest in these topics seems to have declined. There is a chapter on ethical theories for instructors who want it, and feminist theory is still represented in several chapters.

The choice of particular readings for each topic was influenced by a variety of considerations. First there was an attempt to find readings of high quality. As a result, almost all of the articles have been previously published, and some are regarded as "classics," such as Mary Anne Warren's "On the Moral and Legal Status of Abortion." Some of the readings were chosen for their historical importance—for example, the Supreme Court decisions on abortion and the death penalty. Also, there was an attempt to balance the readings, to have different points of view expressed. On most of these issues, one can discern a conservative view and a more liberal view opposed to it. For example, in the chapter on abortion, John T. Noonan defends the conservative view that abortion is the killing of an innocent human being and as such it is

almost always wrong, whereas Mary Anne Warren expounds the liberal view that abortion is not the killing of a person with a right to life and that women have a right to get an abortion. Whenever possible, a moderate view has been included. In the chapter on abortion, for instance, L. W. Sumner defends the moderate view that the fetus does not have moral standing until it is conscious. Finally, a feminist perspective has been added in some chapters. The feminist article on abortion is Susan Sherwin's "Abortion Through a Feminist Ethics Lens."

Suitability for students was another important consideration. The book is intended to be an introductory-level textbook that can be read and understood by most college students. Many of the readings were assigned in class, and students were tested for comprehension. Some students had difficulty. Sometimes they did not know the meanings of words. Most of the time this problem can be solved by having the student consult a good dictionary, or if necessary, a philosophical dictionary. Sometimes the students could not follow the reading or missed the point. To alleviate such problems, several student aids have been provided:

1. **Chapter Introductions.** Each chapter begins with a general introduction that explains the issue and supplies background information. When it is necessary, there is a brief survey of the main philosophical issues, arguments, and theories relevant to the moral issue.

2. **Reading Introductions.** An author biography and a brief summary of the author's main conclusions and arguments precede each reading.

3. **Study Questions.** Two types of study questions follow each reading. First are rather detailed and pedestrian review questions that test the student's grasp of the main points in the reading. These are intended for students who may have had difficulty following the text. Second are more difficult discussion questions that

probe deeper into the subject. These are aimed at the student who has understood the reading and is ready to discuss it.

4. *Problem Cases.* The problem cases at the end of each chapter require the student to apply the arguments and theories discussed in the chapter to hard cases, either actual or hypothetical. This case-study method, as they call it in law schools and business schools, can produce lively discussion and is a good way to get students to think about issues from a moral point of view. The problem cases can also be assigned as short paper topics or used for essay tests. A booklet containing additional problem cases is available to instructors and can be shrink-wrapped with student copies of the text.

5. *Suggested Readings.* At the end of each chapter is a list of specific suggestions for further reading. Usually this consists of books and articles that might have been included in the chapter. It is not intended to take the place of a comprehensive bibliography.

6. *Glossary.* A glossary of philosophical terms located at the end of the book defines words that might not be found in an ordinary dictionary, such as those in Arabic language or technical philosophical terms. It is not meant to take the place of a standard dictionary, but simply to supplement it.

In revising the book for the fifth edition, I have benefited from the help and advice of many people. As usual, my friend and colleague Myron Anderson answered all my questions. Jordan Curnutt made several useful suggestions and provided an article for Chapter 8. Clark Baxter, my editor at West Publishing Company, was an unfailing source of good advice and encouragement. Linda Poirier helped on many details, too many to mention here. Finally, I am grateful to the following reviewers for their detailed criticisms and suggestions for improving the text: Professor Ken Aizawa, Central Michigan University; Professor Alan Cunningham, Johnson County Community College; Professor Allen Hance, University of Illinois; Dr. Eric Hoffman, University of Delaware; Professor Melodee Lambert, Salt Lake Community College; Dr. Peter Mehl, University of Central Arkansas; Professor Jacob Pinnolis, University of Florida; Professor John Sarnecki, Rutgers University; Professor Bonnie Steinbock; SUNY/Albany; Professor Thomas Tracy, Bates College; Professor Harold Wicks, Troy State University.

Chapter One

ETHICAL THEORIES

Introduction

This chapter presents the basic moral theories that are the background for the subsequent readings in the book. For the sake of discussion, we can divide the theories into five types: theory of the right, theory of the good, virtue theory, rights theory, theory of justice, and feminist theory. We will consider each in turn.

Theory of the Right   A theory of the right tries to tell us what is morally right and what is morally wrong. Such a theory is obviously relevant to moral problems in the book such as abortion, suicide, or the death penalty.

Theories of the right are usually subdivided into two different types: teleological and deontological theories. **Teleological theories** focus on the consequences of an act or rule; they can be said to be forward-looking. **Deontological theories** do not do this, but rather look backward at some nonconsequential feature such as a motive or God's commands.

Perhaps the most famous teleological theory is **Utilitarianism**. The standard formulation of this theory is presented by John Stuart Mill in the third reading for the chapter. The most basic principle in Utilitarianism is the Principle of Utility, which Mill states as follows: "Actions are right in proportion as they tend to promote happiness, wrong as they tend to produce the reverse of happiness." But what is happiness? Mill's answer is that happiness (or what is good) is pleasure and the absence of pain. Here Mill adopts an important theory of the good, called **Hedonism**, the view that the good is pleasure. We will examine this theory and alternatives to it in the next section.

In considering the happiness or unhappiness (or the good or evil) produced, Utilitarianism counts everyone equally. But who counts? The answer of Mill and his followers is radical and important: We should consider everyone who is capable of suffering, including nonhuman animals and fetuses in the later stages of development. In the next chapter we find Sumner arguing that fetuses deserve our moral attention when they become conscious or sentient, and in Chapter 8 we see Singer and others arguing that it is wrong to discriminate against animals. This is in sharp contrast to the conventional view (defended by Noonan in Chapter 2) that only human beings count, or at least that human beings count more than nonhumans.

Another alternative is to only consider yourself. The teleological theory that holds that people should consider only their own good or self-interest is called **Ethical Egoism**. More precisely, the theory is usually stated as follows: Everyone ought to act in his or her own self-interest. The theory is supposed to apply to everyone equally, as distinguished from a merely personal egoism where I believe that only I ought to act in my self-interest. Universal Ethical Egoism (as distinguished from personal egoism) is not represented in the readings. It may have popular appeal, but few philosophers adopt it when discussing moral problems. One standard criticism is that it is just selfish or immoral to consider only yourself; to be a moral person you have to be concerned about the welfare of others. Another complaint is that the theory involves some sort of inconsistency when it comes to giving advice to others. If John and Mary have a fight, an egoist will tell both to try to win. But there is something odd about this advice since they both can't win. Or suppose I am in a conflict with you such that it is contrary to my self-interest for you to act in your self-interest. Should I still advise you to act in your self-interest? It seems that egoism requires me to advise others *not* to be egoists but to be altruistic and help me. A feminist criticism is that the theory promotes competition rather than cooperation. None of these criticisms is decisive, however, for a determined egoist can reply that the objections ei-

ther **beg the question** or do not refute the theory.

Now let us turn to the other main kind of theory of the right, Deontological Theory; it determines rightness or wrongness by appealing to something other than consequences. One such a theory is the **Divine Command Theory** discussed by Arthur in the first reading for the chapter. This theory says that an act is right if it is commanded by God and wrong if God forbids it. This theory is accepted by many religious people, and it has been defended by a few philosophers. But according to Arthur, it faces a host of difficulties. First, it assumes that there is a personal God who issues commands, and this is very difficult to prove. Next, there is the problem of discovering God's commands. Do we accept Moses, the Biblical prophets, Jesus, or Mohammed as the prophet of God? Do we read the Old Testament, the New Testament, or the Koran? Then there is the problem of interpreting a given command. Consider the commandment "Thou shalt not kill." As Brandt points out in Chapter 3 in the reading on suicide, it is not clear how this commandment is to be interpreted. Finally, there is the famous question posed by Socrates in Plato's dialogue Euthyphro: Is something holy (or right) because God commands it, or does God command it because it is holy (or right)? As Arthur demonstrates in his discussion, this question raises some fundamental difficulties for the Divine Command Theory.

Another standard deontological theory is Relativism. This theory is examined by Shaw in the second reading for the chapter. Shaw distinguishes between two versions of Relativism. One version holds that moral rightness is relative to the beliefs of a culture. This theory is sometimes called **Cultural Relativism**, since it makes values relative to a culture's beliefs. The other version says that what is right is relative to a person's belief. This second version is sometimes called **Subjectivism**, since it makes values relative to a person's subjective opinions or beliefs. Shaw raises various difficulties for Cultural Relativism. Subjectivism is defeated by an apparently decisive objection, the objection that a person can be simply mistaken in his or her moral belief, and admit it. If so, a person's belief that an action is right does not make it right. A similar objection seems to defeat cultural relativism as well. Is it not obvious that societies or cultures have held mistaken moral beliefs? For example, the United States before the Civil War allowed the practice of slavery, but now we agree that slavery is wrong. Wasn't slavery a moral mistake that we have now corrected? Aren't racism and sexism morally mistaken views that have been correctly repudiated? For example, in World War II, the Germans tried to exterminate the Jews, but now they grant that this was a tragic mistake. Before 1920 women were not allowed to vote, but now we agree that women should have the right to vote.

The most influential deontological theory in the readings of the book is Kant's theory. Kant believes that by pure reasoning we can discover one supreme moral principle that is binding on all rational beings. By "pure reasoning" he means reasoning that does not appeal to anything else such as religious faith or popular opinion; it is like reasoning in geometry and mathematics. The category of "rational beings" excludes animals (at least on Kant's view) and includes not just human beings but also God and angels. The supreme moral principle is called the **Categorical Imperative** because it commands absolutely, as distinguished from hypothetical imperatives that command only if you have certain desires.

Kant formulates the Categorical Imperative in several different ways, but commentators usually focus on two distinct versions. The first one is that you should "act only on that maxim through which you can at the same time will that it should become a universal law." This principle gives you a way of deciding whether an act is wrong or not. You ask yourself what rule you would be following if you did something; this rule is the "maxim" of your act. If you are not willing to have this rule become a universal law that everyone follows, then the act is wrong. To take one of Kant's examples, suppose you want to lie to someone. The rule you would be proposing

(the "maxim" of your act) would be "It is not wrong to lie to someone." But you would not be willing to have everyone follow this rule, Kant claims, because it would be self-defeating. If everyone lied at will, then your lie would be pointless because nobody would believe you. According to Kant, these considerations prove that lying is always wrong. In Kant's terminology it is a **perfect duty** that admits no exceptions.

Many philosophers have thought that this first formulation of the Categorical Imperative is problematic. One problem is that you can formulate the rule under which an act falls in different ways. Some of these rules could be made universal and others not. For example, instead of a general rule about lying, you could have a more specific rule about lying, such as "It is not wrong to lie to save someone's life." This seems to be a rule about lying that we would be willing to have as a universal law.

Another and related objection is made in the reading by Ross. The objection is that there are no perfect duties because there are always possible exceptions, exceptions that arise when there is a conflict between duties. Suppose, for example, there is a conflict between the duty to not lie and the duty to not harm others. A terrorist asks you for a loaded gun to use in killing innocent hostages. You know where there is a gun handy, but should you tell the truth? It is intuitively obvious (Ross would say) that you should not tell the truth in this case because the duty to not harm others overrides the duty to not lie.

Kant formulated the Categorical Imperative in a second way that commentators such as O'Neill (in the reading following Kant's reading) find more plausible. This second formulation, called the Formula of the End in Itself, recommends that you should "act in such a way that you always treat humanity, whether in your own person or in the person of any other, never simply as a means, but always at the same time as an end." According to O'Neill, treating others as a mere means is to engage them in an activity to which they could not, in principle, consent, e.g., a deception. Treating people as ends in themselves requires that we treat them not as mere means, but that we help them with their plans and activities. This gives us a duty to help or a duty of beneficence, but this duty is only imperfect. That is, it is a duty that cannot always be satisfied (like a perfect duty), but requires us to exercise judgment and discretion.

Kant's theory has had an important impact on three of the moral problems covered in the book. First, Kant is a stern defender of capital punishment. In the reading in Chapter 4, Kant condemns the "serpent-windings of Utilitarianism" and insists that murderers must die because they deserve to die. They must be paid back for their crimes, and the consequences of the punishment are irrelevant. Kant is one of the main sources of the retributive theory of punishment, which holds that guilty people ought to be punished and the punishment should fit the crime.

Second, Kant believes that we do not have any direct duties to animals but only indirect duties based on the effect the treatment of animals has on our treatment of humans. We should not be cruel to animals because this makes us likely to be cruel to humans. Animals are not subjects of direct moral concern because they are not rational beings. Kant's view, then, stands in vivid contrast to the utilitarians such as Mill and Singer who believe that animals do have the status of moral subjects who deserve moral considerations.

Third, there is the abortion controversy. Kant does not discuss abortion. However, it seems clear that fetuses are not rational beings, and thus an implication of Kant's view is that they have no more moral status than animals. This is the position that Warren takes in the reading in Chapter 2.

The last theory to be discussed in this section is Ross's **Intuitionism**. His theory is usually classified as deontological even though it includes consequences as one of the features that can make an act right. In the reading, Ross argues that there are various features of an act that can make it right, and not just one, as in Utilitarianism and Kant's theory. An example of a backward-looking feature, as distinguished from forward-looking consequences, is the fact that a person has made a promise. This fact is a good reason for saying that the promise-maker ought to keep the promise. In Ross' terminology (which is found throughout the book), the person has a **prima facie duty** to keep the promise, even if doing so will not produce good consequences. Ross' theory is classified as Intuitionism because he holds that moral intuition or judgment has to be used to resolve conflicts between prima facie duties, if, for example, keeping the promise results in harming someone. Also, intuition is supposed to reveal general principles of duty that are just as self-evident as the axioms and postulates of geometry.

Theory of the Good   A theory of the good tries to tell us what is good and what is bad. Teleological theories seem to require some theory of the good in order to evaluate consequences. We noted above that Mill accepts Hedonism, the theory that the good is pleasure. Hedonism is usually defended by making two important distinctions. First, there is a distinction between intrinsic and instrumental value. Something has **intrinsic value** if it is good or bad in itself apart from its use or consequences. By contrast, something has **instrumental value** if it is good or bad depending on how it is used. Hedonists allow that other things such as knowledge or beauty can be instrumentally good but insist that only pleasure is intrinsically good. Similarly, other things besides pain such as ignorance or ugliness can be instrumentally bad, but hedonists maintain that only pain is intrinsically bad.

Critics of Mill and Hedonism such as Rachels (in the fourth reading for the chapter) argue, however, that other things besides pleasure can be intrinsically good—for example, unexperienced beauty that is not instrumentally good because no one experiences it. And other things besides pain can be intrinsically bad—for example, injustice. Indeed, the fact that Utilitarianism does not seem to give a satisfactory account of justice leads to the formulation of theories of justice independent of

Utilitarianism such as Rawls' Theory of Justice (discussed below).

Another criticism of Hedonism (which can be found in the reading by Aristotle) is that pleasure is an appropriate goal for animals but not for humans. According to Aristotle, the highest good for humans is found in contemplation because this involves the use of reason, and reasoning is what humans are naturally suited to do. The reply that Mill makes to this objection rests on a second distinction made by hedonists, a distinction between higher and lower pleasures. Roughly, higher pleasures involve the use of the intellect, whereas lower pleasures involve the senses. The higher pleasures are better than the lower pleasures, Mill argues, because the person who has experienced both will prefer the higher pleasures. Whether this is true or not is a matter of debate. In any event, Mill's view about the good life turns out to be not much different than Aristotle's view; on both views intellectual activities have a central role.

Another alternative to Hedonism is to grant that a variety of things can be good. This leads to a form of Utilitarianism called **Ideal Utilitarianism**. This theory was defended by the British philosopher G. E. Moore and is discussed by W. D. Ross in the reading for this chapter.

Other alternatives to Hedonism are found in religion where the highest good is some religious goal such as **Nirvana** (in Buddhism), harmony with the **Tao** (in Taoism), or union with God (in Hinduism and mystical Christianity, Judaism, and Islam). Although we will not be concerned with religion as such, there is no doubt that religion has played an important role in ethics. Arthur discusses some of the connections between ethics and religion in the reading. We have already discussed the Divine Command Theory, which is tacitly adopted in the monotheistic religions of Judaism, Christianity, and Islam. Other religious doctrines come up in various contexts. For example, in the abortion controversy some people appeal to the Doctrine of Ensoulment (mentioned by Noonan in Chapter 2); this is the doctrine that a soul enters the fetus (or technically the zygote) at the moment of conception. Traditionally, philosophers have defended our lack of moral concern for animals by maintaining that animals do not have souls; for that matter western religions have not thought that trees, rocks, and other natural objects have souls either. In Chapter 9, the Doctrine of Jihad is a very important religious doctrine about war.

Virtue Theory Virtue theory is included in this chapter because it offers an important alternative to the theories presented so far, all of which dwell on moral rightness and duty. As Mayo notes in the reading, the writings of Plato and Aristotle do not contain an ethics of duty that tells us what to do, but rather an ethics of virtue that tells us what to be. In the reading, Aristotle makes several important points about virtues. First, there is a distinction between intellectual and moral virtue. Intellectual virtue involves the use of what is best in humans, namely reasoning, and the highest form of reasoning is self-sufficient pure contemplation. Moral virtues involve a mean between extremes of excess and deficiency. To use one of Aristotle's examples, courage is a mean between the excess of foolhardiness and the deficiency of cowardliness. Second, Aristotle claims that some actions do not involve any mean but are always wrong. This is an important point, for if there are such actions, then it seems to follow that some of the theories we have just discussed are false. Consider, for example, the action of torturing a small child to death. It seems obvious that this is wrong even if a person or a culture believes it is right, and even if God commands it, and even if it produces good consequences for others. If so, then Cultural Relativism, Subjectivism, the Divine Command Theory, and Utilitarianism all have a problem.

According to Mayo, the important contribution of virtue theory is that it switches our attention from principles and rules to ideal moral heroes such as Aristotle's person of moral wisdom, Plato's just person, or Augustine's citizen of the City of God, or to actual moral saints such as Jesus, Confucius, the Buddha, and St. Francis. Instead of trying to formulate and follow abstract rules about right action, we should try to be more like these people.

Rights Theory   Many of the readings in the book do not appeal to virtues or to duties, but to rights. We find references to the rights of fetuses, newborn infants, the terminally ill, animals, the needy, and the environment. Writers appeal to the rights of life, liberty, and property. But what exactly is a right? In the reading, Feinberg explains personal rights in terms of claims; he calls them "claim-rights," and distinguishes them from other liberties, immunities, and powers. Let us consider an example, the moral right to life. On Feinberg's analysis, when people have a right to life, they have a legal claim-right to life such that they have no duty to relinquish their lives, and other people have a duty to not interfere with their lives. Notice that on Feinberg's analysis, rights logically entail other people's duties, so in an indirect way rights theory does include duties.

What other rights do people have? According to Dworkin (in the reading following Feinberg), United States citizens have certain fundamental rights that they hold against other people as well as the government; these rights include the right to free speech, free press, the right to bear arms, and so on. The basis for these rights is the Constitution; they are moral rights that have been turned into legal rights.

What is the basis for moral rights? On Dworkin's view, the basis of moral rights is the Kantian idea that humans who are members of the moral community should be treated with respect; Dworkin also appeals to the utilitarian idea of political equality.

The traditional basis for moral rights, however, is not utility or respect for persons, but rather the fact that they are given to us by God. Locke and Jefferson talk about God-given rights that are inalienable, that cannot be taken away by other people or the government. But most philosophers today do not want to appeal to God; they want a theory that appeals to nonbelievers too. The traditional secular view that is used to provide a foundation for rights is the **Social Contract Theory** of Hobbes and Rousseau. According to this theory, it is in everyone's self-interest to live together in a society rather than alone in a state of nature. Life in a state of nature would be short, nasty, and brutish. But to live in a society, people must agree to follow certain rules (don't steal, don't murder, etc.), and these rules imply corresponding rights. Every citizen tacitly makes such an agreement (the social contract) to get the benefits of living in society. Without this social contract, society would be impossible.

Theory of Justice   We will consider only one theory of justice, the influential theory of John Rawls. This theory is relevant to moral problems about the distribution of goods and resources, such as world hunger, welfare, and affirmative action. It is also relevant to problems involving the rights of citizens.

Rawls' theory is a kind of social contract theory. He imagines that the social contract is made by self-interested but free and rational persons. To ensure impartiality or fairness, the original contractors make the agreement in a hypothetical, original position where they are ignorant of all the particular facts about themselves but are aware of general facts about social theory and psychology. According to Rawls, the original contractors in the original position would agree upon two basic Principles of Justice: that "each person is to have an equal right to the most extensive basic liberty compatible with a similar liberty for others," and that "social and economic inequalities are to be arranged so that they are both (a) reasonably expected to be to everyone's advantage, and (b) attached to positions and offices open to all." Whether these principles are acceptable as they stand, and just how they should be applied to problems such as welfare, are matters of lively debate among philosophers.

Feminist Theory   In general, feminist theory is critical of all the ethical theories discussed so far. They display a male bias that ignores the experience of women and contributes to the oppression of women in a male-dominated society. Furthermore, feminist theory challenges many of the basic assumptions and concerns of traditional male ethical theory. According to Annette Baier (see her reading), the male theories in ethics, which take obligation to be the central concern, fail to show why parents have any obligation to love and care for their children and other members of the family. As Baier puts it, these so-called liberal male theories such as Rawls' theory (which she mentions several times) make "only hand waves concerning our proper attitude toward our children, toward the ill, toward our relatives, friends, and lovers." Baier thinks that the Ethics of Love best captures women's insights and concerns, but it fails to give any account

of obligation. As a third alternative, Baier proposes a theory of appropriate trust which includes both love and obligation.

In the last reading for the chapter, Virginia Held presents another feminist theory, the Ethics of Care. She agrees with many feminists that an adequate moral theory is not based on abstract principles such as Mill's Principle of Utility, Kant's Categorical Imperative, or Rawls' Principles of Justice. Instead what is needed in the late twentieth century is a feminist theory based on women's experiences in birthing and mothering, which emphasizes caring and trusting relationships with particular people.

John Arthur

Religion, Morality, and Conscience

What is morality? Does it need religion in some way? Or is it purely social? In this essay, John Arthur first discusses, and rejects, three ways morality has been thought to depend on religion: that without religious motivation people could not be expected to do the right thing; that religion is necessary to provide guidance to people in their search for the correct course of action; and that religion is essential for there even to be a right and wrong. Arthur then considers another conception of morality, suggested by John Dewey, which claims "morality is social." He concludes with some brief comments on the importance of these reflections for moral deliberation and for education. John Arthur is professor of philosophy and director of the Program in Philosophy, Politics, and Law at Binghamton University.

My first and prime concern in this paper is to explore the connections, if any, between moral-

ity and religion. I will argue that although there are a variety of ways the two can be connected, in fact religion is not necessary for morality. Despite the lack of any logical or other necessary connection, I will claim, there remain important respects in which the two are related. In the concluding section I will discuss the notion of moral conscience, and then look briefly at the various respects in which morality is "social" and the implications of that idea for moral education. First, however, I want to say something about the subjects: Just what are we referring to when we speak of morality and of religion?

1. MORALITY AND RELIGION

A useful way to approach the first question—the nature of morality—is to ask what it would mean for a society to exist without a social moral code. How would such people think and behave? What would that society look like? First, it seems clear that such people would never feel guilt or resentment. For example, the notions that I ought to remember my parents' anniversary, that he has a moral responsibility to help care for his children after the divorce, that she has a right to equal pay for equal work, and that discrimination on the basis of race is unfair would be absent in such a society. Notions of duty, rights, and obligations would not be present, except perhaps in the legal sense; concepts of justice and fairness would also be foreign to these people. In short, people would have no tendency to evaluate or criticize the behavior of others, nor to feel remorse about their own behavior. Children would not be taught to be ashamed when they steal or hurt others, nor would they be allowed to complain when others treat them badly. (People might, however, feel regret at a decision that didn't turn out as they had hoped; but that would only be because their expectations were frustrated, not because they feel guilty.)

Such a society lacks a moral code. What, then, of religion? Is it possible that a society such as the one I have described would have religious beliefs? It seems clear that it is possible. Suppose every day these same people file into their place of worship to pay homage to God (they may believe in many gods or in one all-powerful creator of heaven and earth). Often they can be heard praying to God for help in dealing with their problems and thanking Him for their good fortune. Frequently they give sacrifices to God, sometimes in the form of money spent to build beautiful temples and churches, other times by performing actions they believe God would approve, such as helping those in need. These practices might also be institutionalized, in the sense that certain people are assigned important leadership roles. Specific texts might also be taken as authoritative, indicating the ways God has acted in history and His role in their lives or the lives of their ancestors.

To have a moral code, then, is to tend to evaluate (perhaps without even expressing it) the behavior of others and to feel guilt at certain actions when we perform them. Religion, on the other hand, involves beliefs in supernatural power(s) that created and perhaps also control nature, the tendency to worship and pray to those supernatural forces or beings, and the presence of organizational structures and authoritative texts. The practices of morality and religion are thus importantly different. One involves our attitudes toward various forms of behavior (lying and killing, for example), typically expressed using the notions of rules, rights, and obligations. The other, religion, typically involves prayer, worship, beliefs about the supernatural, institutional forms, and authoritative texts.

We come, then, to the central question: What is the connection, if any, between a society's moral code and its religious practices and beliefs? Many people have felt that morality is in some way dependent on religion or religious truths. But what sort of "dependence" might there be? In what follows, I distinguish various ways in which one might claim that religion is necessary for morality, arguing against those who claim morality depends in some way on religion. I will also suggest, however, some other important ways in which the two are related, concluding with a brief discussion of conscience and moral education.

2. RELIGIOUS MOTIVATION AND GUIDANCE

One possible role which religion might play in morality relates to motives people have. Religion, it is often said, is necessary so that people will DO right. Typically, the argument begins with the important point that doing what is right often has costs: refusing to shoplift or cheat can mean people go without some good or fail a test; returning a billfold means they don't get the contents. Religion is therefore said to be necessary in that it provides motivation to do the right thing. God rewards those who follow His commands by providing for them a place in heaven or by ensuring that they prosper and are happy on earth. He also punishes those who violate the moral law. Others emphasize less self-interested ways in which religious motives may encourage people to act rightly. Since God is the creator of the universe and has ordained that His plan should be followed, they point out, it is important to live one's life in accord with this divinely ordained plan. Only by living a moral life, it is said, can people live in harmony with the larger, divinely created order.

The first claim, then, is that religion is necessary to provide moral motivation. The problem with that argument, however, is that religious motives are far from the only ones people have. For most of us, a decision to do the right thing (if that is our decision) is made for a variety of reasons: "What if I get caught? What if somebody sees me—what will he or she think? How will I feel afterwards? Will I regret it?" Or maybe the thought of cheating just doesn't arise. We were raised to be a decent person, and that's what we are—period. Behaving fairly and treating others well is more important than whatever we might gain from stealing or cheating, let alone seriously harming another person. So it seems clear that many motives for doing the right thing have nothing whatsoever to do with religion. Most of us, in fact, do worry about getting caught, being blamed, and being looked down on by others. We also may do what is right just because it's right, or because we don't want to hurt others or embarrass family and friends. To say that we need religion to act morally is mistaken; indeed, it seems to me that many of us, when it really gets down to it, don't give much of a thought to religion when making moral decisions. All those other reasons are the ones that we tend to consider, or else we just don't consider cheating and stealing at all. So far, then, there seems to be no reason to suppose that people can't be moral yet irreligious at the same time.

A second argument that is available for those who think religion is necessary to morality, however, focuses on moral guidance and knowledge rather than on people's motives. However much people may want to do the right thing, according to this view, we cannot ever know for certain what is right without the guidance of religious teaching. Human understanding is simply inadequate to this difficult and controversial task; morality involves immensely complex problems, and so we must consult religious revelation for help.

Again, however, this argument fails. First, consider how much we would need to know about religion and revelation in order for religion to provide moral guidance. Besides being aware that there is a God, we'd also have to think about which of the many religions is true. How can anybody be sure his or her religion is the right one? But even if we assume the Judeo-Christian God is the real one, we still need to find out just what it is He wants us to do, which means we must think about revelation.

Revelation comes in at least two forms, and not even all Christians agree on which is the best way to understand revelation. Some hold that revelation occurs when God tells us what he wants by providing us with His words: the Ten Commandments are an example. Many even believe, as evangelist Billy Graham once said, that the entire *Bible* was written by God using thirty-nine secretaries. Others, however, doubt that the "word of God" refers literally to the words God has spoken, but believe instead that the *Bible* is an historical document, written by human beings, of the events or occasions in which God revealed himself. It is an especially important document, of course, but nothing more than that. So on this second view, revelation is not understood as *statements* made by God but rather as His *acts,* such as leading His people from Egypt, testing Job, and sending His son as an example of the ideal life. The *Bible* is not itself revelation, it's the historical account of revelatory actions.

If we are to use revelation as a moral guide, then, we must first know what is to count as revelation—words given us by God, historical events, or both? But even supposing that we could somehow answer those questions, the problems of relying on revelation are still not over since we still must interpret that revelation. Some feel, for example, that the *Bible* justifies various forms of killing, including war and capital punishment, on the basis of such statements as "An eye for an eye." Others, emphasizing such sayings as "Judge not lest ye be judged" and "Thou shalt not kill," believe the *Bible* demands absolute pacifism. How are we to know which interpretation is correct? It is likely, of course, that the answer people give to such religious questions will be influenced in part at least by their moral beliefs; if capital punishment is thought to be unjust, for example, then an interpreter will seek to read the *Bible* in a way that is consistent with that moral truth. That is not, however, a happy conclusion for those wishing to rest morality on revelation, for it means that their understanding of what God has revealed is itself dependent on their prior moral views. Rather than revelation serving as a guide for morality, morality is serving as a guide for how we interpret revelation.

So my general conclusion is that far from providing a short-cut to moral understanding, looking to revelation for guidance often creates more questions and problems. It seems wiser under the circumstances to address complex moral problems like abortion, capital punishment, and affirmative action directly, considering the pros and cons of each side, rather than to seek answers through the much more controversial and difficult route of revelation.

3. THE DIVINE COMMAND THEORY

It may seem, however, that we have still not really gotten to the heart of the matter. Even if religion is not necessary for moral motivation or guidance, it is often claimed, religion is necessary in another more fundamental sense. According to this view, religion is necessary for morality because without God there could BE no right or wrong. God, in other words, provides the foundation or bedrock on which morality is grounded. This idea was expressed by Bishop R. C. Mortimer:

God made us and all the world. Because of that He has an absolute claim on our obedience. . . . From [this] it follows that a thing is not right simply because we think it is. It is right because God commands it.[1]

What Bishop Mortimer has in mind can be seen by comparing moral rules with legal ones. Legal statutes, we know, are created by legislatures; if the state assembly of New York had not passed a law limiting the speed people can travel, then there would be no such legal obligation. Without the statutory enactments, such a law simply would not exist. Mortimer's view, the *divine command theory,* would mean that God has the same sort of relation to moral law as the legislature has to statutes it enacts: without God's commands there would be no moral rules, just as without a legislature there would be no statutes.

Defenders of the divine command theory often add to this a further claim, that only by assuming God sits at the foundation of morality can we explain the objective difference between right and wrong. This point was forcefully argued by F. C. Copleston in a 1948 British Broadcasting Corporation radio debate with Bertrand Russell.

COPLESTON: . . . The validity of such an interpretation of man's conduct depends on the recognition of God's existence, obviously. . . . Let's take a look at the Commandant of the [Nazi] concentration camp at Belsen. That appears to you as undesirable and evil and to me too. To Adolph Hitler we suppose it appeared as something good and desirable. I suppose you'd have to admit that for Hitler it was good and for you it is evil.

RUSSELL: No, I shouldn't go so far as that. I mean, I think people can make mistakes in that as they can in other things. If you have jaundice you see things yellow that are not yellow. You're making a mistake.

COPLESTON: Yes, one can make mistakes, but can you make a mistake if it's simply a question of reference to a feeling or emotion? Surely Hitler would be the only possible judge of what appealed to his emotions.

RUSSELL: . . . You can say various things about that; among others, that if that sort of thing makes that sort of appeal to Hitler's emotions, then Hitler makes quite a different appeal to my emotions.

COPLESTON: Granted. But there's no objective criterion outside feeling then for condemning the conduct of the Commandant of Belsen, in your view. . . . The human being's idea of the content of the moral law depends certainly to a large extent on education and environment, and a man has to use his reason in assessing the validity of the actual moral ideas of his social group. But the possibility of criticizing the accepted moral code presupposes that there is an objective standard, that there is an ideal moral order, which imposes itself. . . . It implies the existence of a real foundation of God.[2]

Against those who, like Bertrand Russell, seek to ground morality in feelings and attitudes, Copleston argues that there must be a more solid foundation if we are to be able to claim truly that the Nazis were evil. God, according to Copleston, is able to provide the objective basis for the distinction, which we all know to exist, between right and wrong. Without divine commands at the root of human obligations, we would have no real reason for condemning the behavior of anybody, even Nazis. Morality, Copleston thinks, would then be nothing more than an expression of personal feeling.

To begin assessing the divine command theory, let's first consider this last point. Is it really true that only the commands of God can provide an objective basis for moral judgments? Certainly many philosophers have felt that morality rests on its own perfectly sound footing, be it reason, human nature, or natural sentiments. It seems wrong to conclude, automatically, that morality cannot rest on anything but religion. And it is also possible that morality doesn't have any foundation or basis at all, so that its claims should be ignored in favor of whatever serves our own self-interest.

In addition to these problems with Copleston's argument, the divine command theory faces other problems as well. First, we would need to say much more about the relationship between morality and divine commands. Certainly the expressions "is commanded by God" and "is morally required" do not *mean* the same thing. People and even whole societies can use moral concepts without understanding them to make any reference to God. And while it is true that God (or any other moral being for that matter) would tend to want others to do the right thing, this hardly shows that being right and being commanded by God are the same thing. Parents want their children to do the right thing, too, but that doesn't mean parents, or anybody else, can make a thing right just by commanding it!

I think that, in fact, theists should reject the divine command theory. One reason is what it implies. Suppose we were to grant (just for the sake of argument) that the divine command theory is correct, so that actions are right just because they are commanded by God. The same, of course, can be said about those deeds that we believe are wrong. If God hadn't commanded us not to do them, they would not be wrong.

But now notice this consequence of the divine command theory. Since God is all-powerful, and since right is determined solely by His commands, is it not possible that He might change the rules and make what we now think of as wrong into right? It would seem that according to the divine command theory the answer is "yes": it is theoretically possible that tomorrow God would decree that virtues such as kindness and courage have become vices while actions that show cruelty and cowardice will henceforth be the right actions. (Recall the analogy with a legislature and the power it has to change law.) So now rather than it being right for people to help each other out and prevent innocent people from suffering unnecessarily, it would be

right (God having changed His mind) to create as much pain among innocent children as we possibly can! To adopt the divine command theory therefore commits its advocate to the seemingly absurd position that even the greatest atrocities might be not only acceptable but morally required if God were to command them.

Plato made a similar point in the dialogue *Euthyphro*. Socrates is asking Euthyphro what it is that makes the virtue of holiness a virtue, just as we have been asking what makes kindness and courage virtues. Euthyphro has suggested that holiness is just whatever all the gods love.

SOCRATES: Well, then, Euthyphro, what do we say about holiness? Is it not loved by all the gods, according to your definition?

EUTHYPHRO: Yes.

SOCRATES: Because it is holy, or for some other reason?

EUTHYPHRO: No, because it is holy.

SOCRATES: Then it is loved by the gods because it is holy: it is not holy because it is loved by them?

EUTHYPHRO: It seems so.

SOCRATES: . . . Then holiness is not what is pleasing to the gods, and what is pleasing to the gods is not holy as you say, Euthyphro. They are different things.

EUTHYPHRO: And why, Socrates?

SOCRATES: Because we are agreed that the gods love holiness because it is holy: and that it is not holy because they love it.[3]

This raises an interesting question. Why, having claimed at first that virtues are merely what is loved (or commanded) by the gods, would Euthyphro contradict this and agree that the gods love holiness *because* it's holy, rather than the reverse? One likely possibility is that Euthyphro believes that whenever the gods love something, they do so with good reason, not without justification and arbitrarily. To deny this and say that it is merely the gods' love that makes holiness a virtue would mean that the gods have no basis for their attitudes, that they are arbitrary in what they love. Yet—and this is the crucial point—it's far from clear that a religious person would want to say that God is arbitrary in that way. If we say that it is simply God's loving something that makes it right, then what sense would it make to say God wants us to do right? All that could mean, it seems, is that God wants us to do what He wants us to do; He would have no reason for wanting it. Similarly, "God is good" would mean little more than "God does what He pleases." The divine command theory therefore leads us to the results that God is morally arbitrary, and that His wishing us to do good or even God's being just mean nothing more than that God does what He does and wants whatever He wants. Religious people who reject that consequence would also, I am suggesting, have reason to reject the divine command theory itself, seeking a different understanding of morality.

This now raises another problem, however. If God approves kindness because it is a virtue and hates the Nazis because they were evil, then it seems that God discovers morality rather than inventing it. So haven't we then identified a limitation on God's power, since He now, being a good God, must love kindness and command us not to be cruel? Without the divine command theory, in other words, what is left of God's omnipotence?

But why, we may ask, is such a limitation on God unacceptable? It is not at all clear that God really can do anything at all. Can God, for example, destroy Himself? Or make a rock so heavy that He cannot lift it? Or create a universe that was never created by Him? Many have thought that God cannot do these things, but also that His inability to do them does not constitute a serious limitation on His power since these are things that cannot be done at all: to do them would violate the laws of logic. Christianity's most influential theologian, Thomas Aquinas, wrote in this regard that "whatever implies contradiction does not come within the scope of divine omnipotence, because it cannot have the aspect of possibility. Hence it is more appropriate to say that such things cannot be done than that God cannot do them." [4]

How, then, ought we to understand God's relationship to morality if we reject the divine command theory? Can religious people consistently maintain their faith in God the Creator and yet deny that what is right is right because He commands it? I think the answer to this is "yes." Making cruelty good is not like making a universe that wasn't made, of course. It's a moral limit on God rather than a logical one. But why suppose that God's limits are only logical?

One final point about this. Even if we agree that God loves justice or kindness because of their nature, not arbitrarily, there still remains a sense in which God could change morality even having rejected the divine command theory. That's because if we assume, plausibly, I think, that morality depends in part on how we reason, what we desire and need, and the circumstances in which we find ourselves, then morality will still be under God's control since God could have constructed us or our environment very differently. Suppose, for instance, that he created us so that we couldn't be hurt by others or didn't care about freedom. Or perhaps our natural environment were created differently, so that all we have to do is ask and anything we want is given to us. If God had created either nature or us that way, then it seems likely our morality might also be different in important ways from the one we now think correct. In that sense, then, morality depends on God whether or not one supports the divine command theory.

4. "Morality Is Social"

I have argued here that religion is not necessary in providing moral motivation or guidance, and that the religious person should not subscribe to the divine command theory's claim that God is necessary for there to be morality. In this last section, I want first to look briefly at how religion and morality sometimes *do* influence each other. Then I will consider briefly the important ways in which morality might correctly be thought to be "social."

Nothing I have said so far means that morality and religion are independent of each other. But in what ways are they related, assuming I am correct in claiming morality does not *depend* on religion? First, of course, we should note the historical influence religions have had on the development of morality as well as on politics and law. Many of the important leaders of the abolitionist and civil rights movements were religious leaders, as are many current members of the pro-life movement. The relationship is not, however, one-sided: morality has also influenced religion, as the current debate within the Catholic [C]hurch over the role of women, abortion, and other social issues shows. In reality, then, it seems clear that the practices of morality and religion have historically each exerted an influence on the other.

But just as the two have shaped each other historically, so, too, do they interact at the personal level. I have already suggested how people's understanding of revelation, for instance, is often shaped by morality as they seek the best interpretations of revealed texts. Whether trying to understand a work of art, a legal statute, or a religious text, interpreters regularly seek to understand them in the best light—to make them as good as they can be, which requires that they bring moral judgment to the task of religious interpretation and understanding.

The relationship can go the other direction as well, however, as people's moral views are shaped by their religious training and their current religious beliefs. These relationships are often complex, hidden even from ourselves, but it does seem clear that our views on important moral issues, from sexual morality and war to welfare and capital punishment, are often influenced by our religious outlook. So not only are religious and moral practices and understandings historically linked, but for many religious people the relationship extends to the personal level—to their understanding of moral obligations as well as their sense of who they are and their vision of who they wish to be.

Morality, then, is influenced by religion (as is religion by morality), but morality's social character extends deeper even than that, I want to argue. First, of course, the existence of morality assumes that we possess a socially acquired language within which we think about our choices and which alternatives we ought to follow. Second, morality is social in that it governs relationships among people, defining our responsibilities to others and theirs to us. Morality provides the standards we rely on in gauging our interactions with family, lovers, friends, fellow citizens, and even strangers. Third, morality is social in the sense that we are, in fact, subject to criticism by others for our actions. We discuss with others what we should do, and often hear from them

concerning whether our decisions were acceptable. Blame and praise are a central feature of morality.

While not disputing any of this, John Dewey has suggested another important sense in which morality is social. Consider the following comments about the origins of morality and conscience taken from an article he titled "Morality Is Social":

In language and imagination we rehearse the responses of others just as we dramatically enact other consequences. We foreknow how others will act, and the foreknowledge is the beginning of judgment passed on action. We know *with* them; there is conscience. An assembly is formed within our breast which discusses and appraises proposed and performed acts. The community without becomes a forum and tribunal within, a judgment-seat of charges, assessments and exculpations. Our thoughts of our own actions are saturated with the ideas that others entertain about them. . . . Explicit recognition of this fact is a prerequisite of improvement in moral education. . . . Reflection is morally indispensable.[5]

So in addition to the three points I already mentioned, Dewey also wants to make another, and in some ways more important suggestion about morality's social character. This fourth idea depends on appreciating the fact that to think from the moral point of view, as opposed to the selfish one, for instance, demands that we reject our private, subjective perspective in favor of the perspective of others, envisioning how they might respond to various choices we might make. Far from being private and unrelated to others, moral conscience is in that sense "public." To consider a decision from the moral perspective requires envisioning what Dewey terms an "assembly of others" that is "formed within our breast." In that way, conscience cannot even be distinguished from the social: conscience invariably brings with it, or constitutes, the perspective of the other. "Is this right?" and "What would this look like were I to have to defend it to others?" are not separable questions.[6]

It is important not to confuse Dewey's point here, however. He is *not* saying that what is right is finally to be determined by the reactions of actually existing other people, or even by the reaction of society as a whole. To the contrary, what is right, and accords with the true dictates of conscience, might in fact not meet the approval of others. Conscience is "social" not in the sense that morality is determined by surveying what others in society think. Understood as the voice of an "assembly" of others within each of us, conscience cannot be reduced to the expected reaction of any existing individual or group. But what then does Dewey mean? The answer is that the assembly Dewey is describing is not an actual one but instead an hypothetical, "ideal" one; the actual "community without" is transformed into a "forum and tribunal within, a judgment seat of charges, assessments and exculpations." Only through the powers of imagination can we exercise our moral powers, envisioning with the powers of judgment what conscience requires.

Morality is therefore *inherently* social, in a variety of ways. It depends on socially learned language, is learned from interactions with others, and governs our interactions with others in society. But it also demands, as Dewey put it, that we know "with" others, envisioning for ourselves what their points of view would require along with our own. Conscience demands we occupy the positions of others.

Viewed in this light, God might play a role in moral reflection and conscience. That is because it is unlikely a religious person would wish to exclude God from the "forum and tribunal" that constitutes conscience. Rather, for the religious person conscience would almost certainly include the imagined reaction of God along with the reactions of others who might be affected by the action. So it seems that for a religious person morality and God's will cannot be separated, though the connection between them is not as envisioned by the divine command theory.

This leads to my final point, about moral education. If Dewey is correct, then it seems clear there is an important sense in which morality not only can be taught but must be. Besides early moral training, moral thinking depends on our ability to imagine others' reactions and to imaginatively put ourselves into their shoes. "What would somebody (including, perhaps, God) think if this got out?" expresses more than a concern with being embarrassed or punished; it is also the voice of conscience and indeed of morality itself.

But that would mean, thinking of education, that listening to others, reading about what others think and do, and reflecting within ourselves about our actions and whether we could defend them to others are part of the practice of morality itself. Morality cannot exist without the broader, social perspective introduced by others, and this social nature ties it, in that way, with education and with public discussion, both actual and imagined. "Private" moral reflection taking place independently of the social world would be no moral reflection at all; and moral education is not only possible, but essential.

Endnotes

1. R. C. Mortimer, *Christian Ethics* (London: Hutchinson's University Library, 1950), pp. 7–8.
2. This debate was broadcast on the Third Program of the British Broadcasting Corporation in 1948.
3. Plato, *Euthyphro,* trans. H. N. Fowler (Cambridge, MA: Harvard University Press, 1947).
4. Thomas Aquinas, *Summa Theologica,* Part I, Q. 25, Art. 3.
5. John Dewey, "Morality Is Social" in *The Moral Writings of John Dewey,* rev. ed., ed. James Gouinlock (Amherst, NY: Prometheus Books, 1994), pp. 182–4.
6. Obligations to animals raise an interesting problem for this conception of morality. Is it wrong to torture animals only because other *people* could be expected to disapprove? Or is it that the animal itself would disapprove? Or, perhaps, that duties to animals rest on sympathy and compassion while human moral relations are more like Dewey describes, resting on morality's inherently social nature and on the dictates of conscience viewed as an assembly of others?

REVIEW QUESTIONS

1. According to Arthur, how are morality and religion different?
2. Why isn't religion necessary for moral motivation?
3. Why isn't religion necessary as a source of moral knowledge?
4. What is the divine command theory? Why does Arthur reject this theory?
5. According to Arthur, how are morality and religion connected?
6. Dewey says that morality is social. What does this mean according to Arthur?

DISCUSSION QUESTIONS

1. Has Arthur refuted the divine command theory? If not, how can it be defended?

2. If morality is social, as Dewey says, then how can we have any obligations to nonhuman animals? (Arthur mentions this problem and some possible solutions to it in endnote 6).

3. What does Dewey mean by moral education? Does a college ethics class count as moral education?

William H. Shaw

Relativism in Ethics

William H. Shaw teaches philosophy at the University of California, Santa Cruz. He is the editor of Social and Personal Ethics *(1993).*

Shaw distinguishes between two forms of Relativism. One version says that what is right is relative to the beliefs of a culture, whereas the second version makes rightness relative to a person's beliefs. Shaw thinks that the second version is implausible; he argues that the first version is subject to various puzzles and objections.

The peoples and societies of the world are diverse; their institutions, fashions, ideas, manners, and mores vary tremendously. This is a simple truth. Sometimes an awareness of this diversity and of the degree to which our own beliefs and habits mirror those of the culture around us stimulates self-examination. In the realm of ethics, familiarity with strikingly different cultures has led many people to suppose that morality itself is relative to particular societies, that right and wrong vary from culture to culture.

This view is generally called "ethical relativism"; it is the normative theory that what is right is what the culture says is right. What is right in one place may be wrong in another, because the only criterion for distinguishing right from wrong—the only ethical standard for judging an action—is the moral system of the

society in which the act occurs. Abortion, for example, is condemned as immoral in Catholic Spain, but practiced as a morally neutral form of birth control in Japan. According to the ethical relativist, then, abortion is wrong in Spain but morally permissible in Japan. The relativist is not saying merely that the Spanish believe abortion is abominable and the Japanese do not; that is acknowledged by everyone. Rather, the ethical relativist contends that abortion is immoral in Spain because the Spanish believe it to be immoral and morally permissible in Japan because the Japanese believe it to be so. There is no absolute ethical standard, independent of cultural context, no criterion of right and wrong by which to judge other than that of particular societies. In short, morality is relative to society.

A different sort of relativist might hold that morality is relative, not to the culture, but to the individual. The theory that what is right and wrong is determined by what a person thinks is right and wrong, however, is not very plausible. The main reason is that it collapses the distinction between thinking something is right and its actually being right. We have all done things we thought were right at the time, but later decided were wrong. Our normal view is that we were mistaken in our original thinking; we believed the action to have been right, but it was not. In the relativist view under consideration, one would have to say that the action in question was originally right, but later wrong as our thinking changed—surely a confused and confusing thing to say! Furthermore, if we accept this view, there would be no point in debating ethics with anyone, for whatever he thought right would automatically be right for him, and whatever we thought right would be right for us. Indeed, if right were determined solely by what we took to be right, then it would not be at all clear what we are doing when we try to decide whether something is right or wrong in the first place—since we could never be mistaken! Certainly this is a muddled doctrine. Most likely its proponents have meant to emphasize that each person must determine for himself as best he can what actually is right or to argue that we ought not to blame people for acting according to their sincere moral judgments. These points are plausible, and with some qualifications, perhaps everyone would accept them, but they are not relativistic in the least.

The theory that morality is relative to society, however, is more plausible, and those who endorse this type of ethical relativism point to the diverseness of human values and the multiformity of moral codes to support their case. From our own cultural perspective, some seemingly "immoral" moralities have been adopted: polygamy, homosexuality, stealing, slavery, infanticide, and the eating of strangers have all been tolerated or even encouraged by the moral system of one society or another. In light of this, the ethical relativist feels that there can be no nonethnocentric standard by which to judge actions. We feel the individuals in some remote tribe are wrong to practice infanticide, while other cultures are scandalized that we eat animals. Different societies have different rules; what moral authority other than society, asks the relativist, can there be? Morality is just like fashion in clothes, beauty in persons, and legality in action—all of which are relative to, and determined by, the standards of a particular culture.

In some cases this seems to make sense. Imagine that Betty is raised in a society in which one is thought to have a special obligation to look after one's maternal aunts and uncles in their old age, and Sarah lives in a society in which no such obligation is supposed. Certainly we are inclined to say that Betty really does have an obligation that Sarah does not. Sarah's culture, on the other hand, may hold that if someone keeps a certain kind of promise to you, you owe him or her a favor, or that children are not required to tell the truth to adults. Again, it seems plausible that different sorts of obligations arise in Sarah's society; in her society, promisees really do owe their promisors and children are not wrong to lie, whereas this might not be so in other cultures.

Ethical relativism explains these cases by saying that right and wrong are determined solely by the standards of the society in question, but there are other, nonrelativistic ways of accounting for these examples. In Betty's society, people live with the expectation that their sister's offspring will look after them; for Betty to behave contrary to this institution and to thwart these expectations may produce bad consequences—so there is a reason to think she has this obligation other than the fact that her society thinks she has it. In Sarah's world, on the other hand, no adult expects children to tell the truth; far from deceiving people, children only amuse them with their tall tales. Thus, we are not required to be ethical relativists in order to explain why moral obligations may differ according to the social context. And there are other cases in which ethical relativism seems implausible. Suppose Betty's society thinks that it is wicked to engage in intercourse on Sundays. We do not believe it wrong of her to do so just because her society thinks such conduct is impermissible. Or suppose her culture thinks that it is morally reprehensible to wear the fur of rare animals. Here we may be inclined to concur, but if we think it is wrong of her to do this, we do not think it so because her society says so. In this example and the previous one, we look for some reason why her conduct should be considered immoral. The fact that her society thinks it so is not enough.

Ethical relativism undermines any moral criticism of the practices of other societies as long as their actions conform to their own standards. We cannot say that slavery in a slave society like that of the American South of the last century was immoral and unjust as long as that society held it to be morally permissible. Slavery was right for them, although it is wrong for us today. To condemn slave owners as immoral, says the relativist, is to attempt to extend the standards of our society illegitimately to another culture. But this is not the way we usually think. Not only do we wish to say that a society is mistaken if it thinks that slavery (or cannibalism, cruelty, racial bigotry) is morally permissible, but we also think we have justification for so saying and are not simply projecting ethno-centrically the standards of our own culture. Indeed, far from mirroring those standards in all our moral judgments, we sometimes criticize certain principles or practices accepted by our own society. None of this makes sense from the relativist's point of view. People can be censured for not living up to their society's moral code, but that is all; the moral code itself cannot be criticized. Whatever a society takes to be morally right really is right for it. Reformers who campaign against the "injustices" of their society are only encouraging people to be immoral—that is, to depart from the moral standards of their society—unless or until the majority of society agrees with the reformers. The minority can never be right in moral matters; to be right it must become the majority.

This raises some puzzles for the theory of ethical relativism. What proportion of a society must believe, say, that abortion is permissible for it to be morally acceptable in that society—90 percent? 75 percent? 51 percent? If the figure is set high (say 75 percent) and only 60 percent of the society condone abortion, then it would not be permissible; yet it would seem odd for the relativist to say that abortion was therefore wrong, given that a majority of the population believes otherwise. Without a sufficient majority either way, abortion would be neither morally permissible nor impermissible. On the other hand, if the figure is set lower, then there will be frequent moral flip-flops. Imagine that last year abortion was thought wrong by 51 percent of the populace, but this year only 49 percent are of that opinion; that means, according to the relativist, that it was wrong last year, but is now morally permissible—and things may change again. Surely, though, something is wrong with majority rule in matters of morality. In addition one might wonder what is to count, for the relativist, as a society. In a large and heterogeneous nation like the United States, are right and wrong determined by the whole country; or do smaller societies like Harlem, San Francisco, rural Iowa, or the Chicano community in Los Angeles set their own moral standards? But if these are cohesive enough to count as morality generating societies, what about such "societies" as outlaw bikers, the drug cul-

ture, or the underworld? And what, then, does the relativist say about conflicts between these group moralities or between them and the morality of the overall society? Since an individual may be in several overlapping "societies" at the same time, he may well be receiving conflicting moral instructions—all of which, it would seem, are correct according to the relativist.

These are all questions the relativist must answer if he is to make his theory coherent. To raise them is not to refute relativism, of course, since the relativist may be able to explain satisfactorily what he means by "society," how its standards relate to those of other groups, and what is to count as moral approval by a given society. However the relativist attempts to refine his theory, he will still be maintaining that what is right is determined by what the particular society, culture, or group takes to be right and that this is the only standard by which an individual's actions can be judged. Not only does the relativist neglect to give us a reason for believing that a society's own views about morality are conclusive as to what is actually right and wrong, but also his theory does not square with our understanding of morality and the nature of ethical discourse. By contending that the moralities of different societies are all equally valid, the relativist holds that there can be no nonethnocentric ground for preferring one moral code to another, that one cannot speak of moral progress. Moralities may change, but they do not get better or worse. If words mean anything, however, it seems clear that a society that applauded the random torture of children would be immoral, even if it thought such a practice were right. It would simply be mistaken, and disastrously so. Since this is the case, ethical relativism must be false as a theory of normative ethics. . . .

Reason-giving is essential to the nature of morality, at least as we understand it. Suppose that Smith and Jones both think that incest is immoral. Smith, when challenged, argues that it is unnatural, harmful to the family unit, and psychologically destructive to the individuals involved. Each of these reasons can be pursued in greater detail: For example, what is "unnatural," and is the unnatural always immoral? And we can raise other relevant issues with Smith about, say, consent, age, or individual rights. Jones, on the other hand, offers no reasons and does not assent to those Smith gives. When pressed, Jones merely says, "I don't need to give a reason; incest is simply wrong." At this point, one may doubt that Jones is making a moral judgment. He may well be troubled by the thought of incest; it may agitate him; he may be adamant in condemning it. But if he resists offering a justification for his opinion, we shall very likely refuse to recognize it as a moral position at all.[1] Instead, we would suspect that he is only expressing a personal quirk or emotional reaction. The point I am making about our practice of morality—namely, that reason-giving and argumentation are essential to it—is attested to by the fact that prejudice frequently dresses itself in the language of reason. We recognize that the racist is only rationalizing his visceral bias when he attempts to justify segregation with spurious theories of racial differences, but his effort to so justify his prejudice at least acknowledges the fact that one must have reasons to back one's views if they are to count as a moral position in the first place—let alone be taken seriously.

Two related points are relevant here. The first is that not only are reasoning and argumentation basic to our practice of morality, but only certain sorts of reasons are countenanced by it. If Jones were to offer, as a justification of his judgment that incest is immoral, the reason that the idea is too gross for him to contemplate, or if a racist were to try to justify segregation by pointing to the skin color of the group he disdains, their "arguments" would simply be ruled out of bounds. By contrast, appeals to other sorts of considerations—for example, the rights of the persons involved, fairness, or the happiness produced—are perfectly appropriate and often suffice to establish at least the **prima facie rightness** or wrongness of the action. In other words, within moral discourse there are certain standard moves and relevant considerations—acknowledged by the vast majority of those who engage in it—just as there is an accepted framework of legal principles, policies, rules, and precedents on which a lawyer can and must draw in making his case.

The second point is that the relevant standards are fairly clear and can be applied with a reasonable claim to objectivity. Within the complex institution of morality it is not the case that it is all subjective, that all judgments are equal. There are criteria, and they can be interpreted and applied with a substantial degree of objectivity—just as judges can decide cases, teachers grade essays, or referees call penalties with a legitimate claim to be doing so correctly and objectively. And mistakes can be made: the fact that a judge's decision can be appealed implies that there are accepted standards against which it can be measured. Within our society we do not see eye to eye on everything, but our considered and reflective moral judgments do enjoy extensive agreement. Moral life is, to a large extent, a common life. We have a feel for morality; we understand what constitutes a legitimate moral position and what counts as a moral argument; we share certain institutional practices as well as paradigms of moral and immoral, just and unjust, conduct. There are agreed-upon standards in our moral practice, and within limits most moral determinations can be said to be correct or incorrect, justified or unjustified. . . .

Endnote

1. Reasons are construed broadly here, so that one who claimed such a judgment was self-evident, axiomatic, or an intuitive moral insight would be offering a kind of justification for it. How plausible the justification is, is another matter.

REVIEW QUESTIONS

1. Distinguish between the two versions of Ethical Relativism.
2. Why is the second version implausible according to Shaw?
3. What are the problems and difficulties for the first version?
4. What does Shaw mean when he says that reason-giving is essential to morality?

DISCUSSION QUESTIONS

1. Has Shaw refuted both versions of Ethical Relativism? Why or why not?

2. The torture of children is immoral, Shaw says, even if a society approves of it. Has any society actually approved of this? Suppose there is such a society; is the torture of children still wrong in that society?

3. People do say that incest is wrong without giving any reason. Does this fail to be a moral judgment?

John Stuart Mill

Utilitarianism

John Stuart Mill (1806–1873) was one of the most important and influential British philosophers. His most important works in ethics are On Liberty *(1859) and* Utilitarianism *(1861), from which the reading is taken.*

Mill sets forth the basic principles of Utilitarianism including the Principle of Utility (or the Greatest Happiness Principle) and the hedonistic principle that happiness is pleasure. He explains the theory by replying to various objections, and concludes with an attempt to prove the Principle of Utility.

The creed which accepts as the foundation of morals, Utility, or the Greatest Happiness Principle, holds that actions are right in proportion as they tend to promote happiness, wrong as they tend to produce the reverse of happiness. By happiness is intended pleasure, and the absence of pain; by unhappiness, pain, and the privation of pleasure. To give a clear view of the moral standard set up by the theory, much more requires to be said; in particular, what things it includes in the ideas of pain and pleasure; and to what extent this is left an open question. But these supplementary explanations do not affect the theory of life on which this theory of morality is grounded—namely, that pleasure, and freedom from pain, are the only things desirable as ends; and that all desirable things (which are as numerous in the utilitarian as in any other

From John Stuart Mill, *Utilitarianism* (1861), chapters 12 and 17.

scheme) are desirable either for the pleasure inherent in themselves, or as means to the promotion of pleasure and the prevention of pain.

Now, such a theory of life excites in many minds, and among them in some of the most estimable in feeling and purpose, inveterate dislike. To suppose that life has (as they express it) no higher end than pleasure—no better and nobler object of desire and pursuit—they designate as utterly mean and grovelling; as a doctrine worthy only of swine, to whom the followers of Epicurus were, at a very early period, contemptuously likened; and modern holders of the doctrine are occasionally made the subject of equally polite comparisons by its German, French, and English assailants.

When thus attacked, the Epicureans have always answered, that it is not they, but their accusers, who represent human nature in a degrading light; since the accusation supposes human beings to be capable of no pleasures except those of which swine are capable. If this supposition were true, the charge could not be gainsaid, but would then be no longer an imputation; for if the sources of pleasure were precisely the same to human beings and to swine, the rule of life which is good enough for the one would be good enough for the other. The comparison of the Epicurean life to that of beasts is felt as degrading, precisely because a beast's pleasures do not satisfy a human being's conceptions of happiness. Human beings have faculties more elevated than the animal appetites, and when once made conscious of them, do not regard anything as happiness which does not include their gratification. I do not, indeed, consider the Epicureans to have been by any means faultless in drawing out their scheme of consequences from the utilitarian principle. To do this in any sufficient manner, many Stoic, as well as Christian elements require to be included. But there is no known Epicurean theory of life which does not assign to the pleasures of the intellect, of the feelings and imagination, and of the moral sentiments, a much higher value as pleasures than to those of mere sensation. It must be admitted, however, that utilitarian writers in general have placed the superiority of mental over bodily pleasures chiefly in the greater permanency, safety, uncostliness, etc., of the former—that is, in their circumstantial advantages rather than in their intrinsic nature. And on all these points utilitarians have fully proved their case; but they might have taken the other, and, as it may be called, higher ground, with entire consistency. It is quite compatible with the principle of utility to recognize the fact, that some *kinds* of pleasure are more desirable and more valuable than others. It would be absurd that while, in estimating all other things, quality is considered as well as quantity, the estimation of pleasures should be supposed to depend on quantity alone.

If I am asked, what I mean by difference of quality in pleasures, or what makes one pleasure more valuable than another, merely as a pleasure, except its being greater in amount, there is but one possible answer. Of two pleasures, if there be one to which all or almost all who have experience of both give a decided preference, irrespective of any feeling of moral obligation to prefer it, that is the more desirable pleasure. If one of the two is, by those who are competently acquainted with both, placed so far above the other that they prefer it, even though knowing it to be attended with a greater amount of discontent, and would not resign it for any quantity of the other pleasure which their nature is capable of, we are justified in ascribing to the preferred enjoyment a superiority in quality, so far outweighing quantity as to render it, in comparison, of small account.

Now it is an unquestionable fact that those who are equally acquainted with, and equally capable of appreciating and enjoying, both, do give a most marked preference to the manner of existence which employs their higher faculties. Few human creatures would consent to be changed into any of the lower animals, for a promise of the fullest allowance of a beast's pleasures; no intelligent human being would consent to be a fool, no instructed person would be an ignoramus, no person of feeling and conscience would be selfish and base, even though they should be persuaded that the fool, the dunce, or the rascal is better satisfied with his lot than they are with theirs. They would not resign what they possess more than he for the most complete satisfaction of all the desires which they have in common with him. If they ever fancy they would, it is only in cases of unhappiness so extreme, that to escape from it they would exchange their lot for almost any other, however undesirable in their own eyes. A being of higher faculties requires more to make him happy, is capable probably of more acute suffering, and certainly accessible to it at more points, than one of an inferior type; but in spite of these liabilities, he can never really wish to sink into what he feels to be a lower grade of existence. We may give what explanation we pleasure of this unwillingness; we may attribute it to pride, a name which is given indiscriminately to some of the most and to some of the least estimable feelings of which mankind are capable; we may refer it to the love of liberty and personal independence, an appeal to which was with the Stoics one of the most effective means for the inculcation of it; to the love of power, or to the love of excitement, both of which do really enter into and contribute to it: but its most appropriate appellation is a sense of dignity, which all human beings possess in one form or other, and in some, though by no means in exact, proportion to their higher faculties, and which is so essential a part of the happiness of those in whom it is strong, that nothing which conflicts with it could be, otherwise than momentarily, an object of desire to them. Whoever supposes that this preference takes place at a sacrifice of happiness—that the superior being, in anything like equal circumstances, is not happier than the inferior—confounds the two very different ideas, of happiness, and content. It is undisputable that the being whose capacities of enjoyment are low, has the greatest chance of having them fully satisfied; and a highly endowed being will always feel that any happiness which he can look for, as the world is constituted, is imperfect. But he can learn to bear its imperfections, if they are at all bearable; and they will not make him envy the being who is indeed unconscious of the imperfections, but only because he feels not at all the good which those imperfections qualify. It is better to be a human being dissatisfied than a pig satisfied; better to be Socrates dissatisfied than a fool satisfied. And if the fool, or the pig, are of a different opinion, it is because they only know their own side of the question. The other party to the comparison knows both sides.

It may be objected, that many who are capable of the higher pleasures, occasionally, under the influence of temptation, postpone them to the lower. But this is quite compatible with a full appreciation of the intrinsic superiority of the higher. Men often, from infirmity of character, make their election for the nearer good, though they know it to be the less valuable; and this no less when the choice is between two bodily pleasures, than when it is between bodily and mental. They pursue sensual indulgences to the injury of health, though perfectly aware that health is the greater good. It may be further objected, that many who begin with youthful enthusiasm for everything noble, as they advance in years sink into indolence and selfishness. But I do not believe that those who undergo this very common change, voluntarily choose the lower description of pleasures in preference to the higher. I believe that before they devote themselves exclusively to the one, they have already become incapable of the other. Capacity for the nobler feelings is in most natures a very tender plant, easily killed, not only by hostile influences, but by mere want of sustenance; and in the majority of young persons it speedily dies away if the occupation to which their position in life has devoted them, and the society into which it has thrown them, are not favourable to keeping that higher capacity in exercise. Men lose their high aspirations as they lose their intellectual tastes, because they have not time or opportunity for indulging them; and they addict themselves to inferior pleasures, not because they deliberately prefer them, but because they are either the only ones to which they have access, or the only ones which they are any longer capable of enjoying. It may be questioned whether any one who has remained equally susceptible to both classes of pleasures, ever knowingly and calmly preferred the lower; though many, in all ages, have broken down in an ineffectual attempt to combine both.

From this verdict of the only competent judges, I apprehend there can be no appeal. On a question which is the best worth having of two pleasures, or which of two modes of existence is the most grateful to the feelings, apart from its moral attributes and from its consequences, the judgment of those who are qualified by knowledge of both, or, if they differ, that of the majority among them, must be admitted as final. And there needs be the less hesitation to accept this judgment respecting the quality of pleasures, since there is no other tribunal to be referred to even on the question of quantity. What means are there of determining which is the acutest of two pains, or the intensest of two pleasurable sensations, except the general suffrage of those who are familiar with both? Neither pains nor pleasures are homogeneous, and pain is always heterogeneous with pleasure. What is there to decide whether a particular pleasure is worth purchasing at the cost of a particular pain, except the feelings and judgment of the experienced? When, therefore, those feelings and judgment declare the pleasures derived from the higher faculties to be preferable *in kind,* apart from the question of intensity, to those of which the animal nature, disjoined from the higher faculties, is susceptible, they are entitled on this subject to the same regard.

I have dwelt on this point, as being a necessary part of a perfectly just conception of Utility or Happiness, considered as the directive rule of human conduct. But it is by no means an indispensable condition to the acceptance of the utilitarian stand; for that standard is not the agent's own greatest happiness, but the greatest amount of happiness altogether; and if it may possibly be doubted whether a noble character is always the happier for its nobleness, there can be no doubt that it makes other people happier, and that the world in general is immensely a gainer by it. Utilitarianism, therefore, could only attain its end by the general cultivation of nobleness of character, even if each individual were only benefited by the nobleness of others, and his own, so far as happiness is concerned, were a sheer deduction from the benefit. But the bare enunciation of such an absurdity as this last, renders refutation superfluous.

According to the Greatest Happiness Principle, as above explained, the ultimate end, with reference to and for the sake of which all other things are desirable (whether we are considering our own good or that of other people), is an existence exempt as far as possible from pain, and as rich as possible in enjoyments, both in point of quantity and quality; the test of quality, and the rule for measuring it against quantity, being the preference felt by those who in their opportunities of experience, to which must be added their habits of self-consciousness and self-observation, are best furnished with the means of comparison. This, being, according to the utilitarian opinion, the end of human action, is necessarily also the standard of morality; which may accordingly be defined, the rules and precepts for human conduct, by the observance of which an existence such as has been described might be, to the greatest extent possible, secured to all mankind; and not to them only, but, so far as the nature of things admits, to the whole sentient creation. . . .

I must again repeat, what the assailants of utilitarianism seldom have the justice to acknowledge, that the happiness which forms the utilitarian standard of what is right in conduct, is not the agent's own happiness, but that of all concerned. As between his own happiness and that of others, utilitarianism requires him to be as strictly impartial as a disinterested and benevolent spectator. In the golden rule of Jesus of Nazareth, we read the complete spirit of the ethics of utility. To do as you would be done by, and to love your neighbour as yourself, constitute the ideal perfection of utilitarian morality. As the means of making the nearest approach to this ideal, utility would enjoin, first, that laws and social arrangements should place the happiness, or (as speaking practically it may be called) the interest, of every individual, as nearly as possible in harmony with the interest of the whole; and secondly, that education and opinion, which have so vast a power over human character, should so use that power as to

establish in the mind of every individual an indissoluble association between his own happiness and the good of the whole; especially between his own happiness and the practice of such modes of conduct, negative and positive, as regard for the universal happiness prescribes; so that not only he may be unable to conceive the possibility of happiness to himself, consistently with conduct opposed to the general good, but also that a direct impulse to promote the general good may be in every individual one of the habitual motives of action, and the sentiments connected therewith may fill a large and prominent place in every human being's sentient existence. If the impugners of the utilitarian morality represented it to their own minds in this its true character, I know not what recommendation possessed by any other morality they could possibly affirm to be wanting to it; what more beautiful or more exalted developments of human nature any other ethical system can be supposed to foster, or what springs of action, not accessible to the utilitarian, such systems rely on for giving effect to their mandates. . . .

OF WHAT SORT OF PROOF THE PRINCIPLE OF UTILITY IS SUSCEPTIBLE

It has already been remarked, that questions of ultimate ends do not admit of proof, in the ordinary acceptation of the term. To be incapable of proof by reasoning is common to all first principles; to the first premises of our knowledge, as well as to those of our conduct. But the former, being matters of fact, may be the subject of a direct appeal to the faculties which judge of fact—namely, our senses, and our internal consciousness. Can an appeal be made to the same faculties on questions of practical ends? Or by what other faculty is cognizance taken of them?

Questions about ends, in other words, question what things are desirable. The utilitarian doctrine is, that happiness is desirable, and the only thing desirable, as an end; all other things being only desirable as means to that end. What ought to be required of this doctrine— what conditions is it requisite that the doctrine should fulfil—to make good its claim to be believed?

The only proof capable of being given that an object is visible, is that people actually see it. The only proof that a sound is audible, is that people hear it: and so of the other sources of our experience. In like manner, I apprehend, the sole evidence it is possible to produce that anything is desirable, is that people do actually desire it. If the end which the utilitarian doctrine proposes to itself were not, in theory and in practice, acknowledged to be an end, nothing could ever convince any person that it was so. No reason can be given why the general happiness is desirable, except that each person, so far as he believes it to be attainable, desires his own happiness. This, however, being a fact, we have not only all the proof which the case admits of, but all which it is possible to require, that happiness is a good: that each person's happiness is a good to that person, and the general happiness, therefore, a good to the aggregate of all persons. Happiness has made out its title as one of the ends of conduct, and consequently one of the criteria of morality.

But it has not, by this alone, proved itself to be the sole criterion. To do that, it would seem, by the same rule, necessary to show, not only that people desire happiness, but that they never desire anything else. Now it is palpable that they do desire things which, in common language, are decidedly distinguished from happiness. They desire, for example, virtue, and the absence of vice, no less really than pleasure and the absence of pain. The desire of virtue is not as universal, but it is as authentic a fact, as the desire of happiness. And hence the opponents of the utilitarian standard deem that they have a right to infer that there are other ends of human action besides happiness, and that happiness is not the standard of approbation and disapprobation.

But does the utilitarian doctrine deny that people desire virtue, or maintain that virtue is not a thing to be desired? The very reverse. It maintains not only that virtue is to be desired, but that it is to be desired disinterestedly, for itself. Whatever may be the opinion of utilitarian moralists as to the original conditions by which virtue is made virtue; however they may

believe (as they do) that actions and dispositions are only virtuous because they promote another end than virtue; yet this being granted, and it having been decided, form considerations of this description, what *is* virtuous, they not only place virtue at the very head of the things which are good as means to the ultimate end, but they also recognise as a psychological fact that possibility of its being, to the individual, a good in itself, without looking to any end beyond it; and hold, that the mind is not in a right state, not in a state conformable to Utility, not in the state most conducive to the general happiness, unless it does love virtue in this manner—as a thing desirable in itself, even although, in the individual instance, it should not produce those other desirable consequences which it tends to produce, and on account of which it is held to be virtue. This opinion is not, in the smallest degree, a departure from the Happiness principle. The ingredients of happiness are very various, and each of them is desirable in itself, and not merely when considered as swelling an aggregate. The principle of utility does not mean that any given pleasure, as music, for instance, or any given exemption from pain, as for example health, is to be looked upon as means to a collective something termed happiness, and to be desired on that account. They are desired and desirable in and for themselves; besides being means, they are a part of the end. Virtue, according to the utilitarian doctrine, is not naturally and originally part of the end, but it is capable of becoming so; and in those who love it disinterestedly it has become so, and is desired and cherished, not as a means to happiness, but as a part of their happiness.

To illustrate this farther, we may remember that virtue is not the only thing, originally a means, and which if it were not a means to anything else, would be and remain indifferent, but which by association with what it is a means to, comes to be desired for itself, and that too with the utmost intensity. What, for example, shall we say of the love of money? There is nothing originally more desirable about money than about any heap of glittering pebbles. Its worth is solely that of the things which it will buy; the desires for other things than itself, which it is a means of gratifying. Yet the love of money is not only one of the strongest moving forces of human life, but money is, in many cases, desired in and for itself; the desire to possess it is often stronger than the desire to use it, and goes on increasing when all the desires which point to ends beyond it, to be compassed by it, are falling off. It may, then, be said truly, that money is desired not for the sake of an end, but as part of the end. From being a means to happiness, it has come to be itself a principal ingredient of the individual's conception of happiness. The same may be said of the majority of the great objects of human life—power, for example, or fame; except that to each of these there is a certain amount of immediate pleasure annexed, which has at least the semblance of being naturally inherent in them; a thing which cannot be said of money. Still, however, the strongest natural attraction, both of power and of fame, is the immense aid they give to the attainment of our other wishes; and it is the strong association thus generated between them and all our objects of desire, which gives to the direct desire of them the intensity it often assumes, so as in some characters to surpass in strength all other desires. In these cases the means have become a part of the end, and a more important part of it than any of the things which they are means to.

What was once desired as an instrument for the attainment of happiness, has come to be desired for its own sake. In being desired for its own sake it is, however, desired as *part* of happiness. The person is made, or thinks he would be made, happy by its mere possession; and is made unhappy by failure to obtain it. The desire of it is not a different thing from the desire of happiness, any more than the love of music, or the desire of health. They are included in happiness. They are some of the elements of which the desire of happiness is made up. Happiness is not an abstract idea, but a concrete whole; and these are some of its parts. And the utilitarian standard sanctions and approves their being so. Life would be a poor thing, very ill provided with sources of happiness, if there were not this provision of nature, by which things originally indifferent, but conducive to, or otherwise associated with, the satisfaction of our primitive desires, become in themselves sources of pleasure more valuable than the primitive pleasures, both in permanency, in the space of human existence that they are capable of covering, and even in intensity.

Virtue, according to the utilitarian conception, is a good of this description. There was no original desire of it, or motive to it, save its conduciveness to pleasure, and especially to protection from pain. But through the association thus formed, it may be felt a good in itself, and desired as such with as great intensity as any other good; and with this difference between it and the love of money, of power, or of fame, that all of these may, and often do, render the individual noxious to the other members of the society to which he belongs, whereas there is nothing which makes him so much a blessing to them as the cultivation of the disinterested love of virtue. And consequently, the utilitarian standard, while it tolerates and approves those other acquired desires, up to the point beyond which they would be more injurious to the general happiness than promotive of it, enjoins and requires the cultivation of the love of virtue up to the greatest strength possible, as being above all things important to the general happiness.

It results from the preceding considerations, that there is in reality nothing desired except happiness. Whatever is desired otherwise than as a means to some end beyond itself, and ultimately to happiness, is desired as itself a part of happiness, and is not desired for itself until it has become so. Those who desire virtue for its own sake, desire it either because the consciousness of it is a pleasure, or because the consciousness of being without it is a pain, or for both reasons united; as in truth the pleasure and pain seldom exist separately, but almost always together, the same person feeling pleasure in the degree of virtue attained, and pain in not having attained more. If one of these gave him no pleasure, and the other no pain, he would not love or desire virtue, or would desire it only for the other benefits which it might produce to himself or to persons whom he cared for. . . .

REVIEW QUESTIONS

1. State and explain the Principle of Utility. Show how it could be used to justify actions that are

conventionally viewed as wrong, such as lying and stealing.

2. How does Mill reply to the objection that Epicureanism is a doctrine only worthy of swine?
3. How does Mill distinguish between higher and lower pleasures?
4. According to Mill, whose happiness must be considered?
5. Carefully reconstruct Mill's proof of the Principle of Utility.

DISCUSSION QUESTIONS

1. Is happiness nothing more than pleasure, and the absence of pain? What do you think?

2. Does Mill convince you that the so-called higher pleasures are better than the lower ones? What about the person of experience who prefers the lower pleasures over the higher ones?
3. Mill says, "In the golden rule of Jesus of Nazareth, we read the complete spirit of the ethics of utility." Is this true or not?
4. Many commentators have thought that Mill's proof of the Principle of Utility is defective. Do you agree? If so, then what mistake or mistakes does he make? Is there any way to reformulate the proof so that it is not defective?

James Rachels

The Debate over Utilitarianism

James Rachels is university professor of philosophy at the University of Alabama of Birmingham. He is the author of The End of Life: Euthanasia and Morality *(1986) and articles on the right to privacy, reverse discrimination, and the treatment of non-human animals. The reading is taken from his textbook* The Elements of Moral Philosophy *(1986).*

Rachels presents the main objections to Utilitarianism and the replies given by defenders of Utilitarianism. His own view is that Utilitarianism is correct in telling us to consider the consequences of actions and in advising us to be impartial, but incorrect in ignoring other important moral considerations such as merit.

The utilitarian doctrine is that happiness is desirable, and the only thing desirable, as an end; all other things being desirable as means to that end.
John Stuart Mill, *Utilitarianism* (1861)

From James Rachels, *The Elements of Moral Philosophy*, (New York: McGraw-Hill Publishing Company, 1986). Reprinted by permission of The McGraw-Hill Companies.

Man does not strive after happiness; only the Englishman does that.
Friedrich Nietzsche, *Twilight of the Idols* (1889)

THE RESILIENCE OF THE THEORY

Classical Utilitarianism—the theory defended by Bentham and Mill—can be summarized in three propositions:

First, actions are to be judged right or wrong solely in virtue of their consequences. Nothing else matters. Right actions are, simply, those that have the best consequences.

Second, in assessing consequences, the only thing that matters is the amount of happiness or unhappiness that is caused. Everything else is irrelevant. Thus right actions are those that produce the greatest balance of happiness over unhappiness.

Third, in calculating the happiness or unhappiness that will be caused, no one's happiness is to be counted as more important than anyone else's. Each person's welfare is equally important. As Mill put it in his *Utilitarianism,*

the happiness which forms the utilitarian standard of what is right in conduct, is not the agent's own happiness, but that of all concerned. As between his own happiness and that of others, utilitarianism requires him to be as strictly impartial as a disinterested and benevolent spectator.

Thus right actions are those that produce the greatest possible balance of happiness over unhappiness, with each person's happiness counted as equally important.

The appeal of this theory to philosophers, economists, and others who theorize about human decision making has been enormous. The theory continues to be widely accepted, even though it has been challenged by a number of apparently devastating arguments. These antiutilitarian arguments are so numerous, and so persuasive, that many have concluded the theory must be abandoned. But the remarkable thing is that so many have *not* abandoned it. Despite the arguments, a great many thinkers refuse to let the theory go. According to these contemporary utilitarians, the antiutilitarian arguments show only that the classical theory needs to be *modified*; they say the basic idea is correct and should be preserved, but recast into a more satisfactory form.

In what follows, we will examine some of these arguments against Utilitarianism, and consider whether the classical version of the theory may be revised satisfactorily to meet them. These arguments are of interest not only for the assessment of Utilitarianism but for their own sakes, as they raise some additional fundamental issues of moral philosophy.

Is Happiness the Only Thing That Matters?

The question *What things are good?* is different from the question *What actions are right?* and Utilitarianism answers the second question by referring back to the first one. Right actions, it says, are the ones that produce the most good. But what is good? The classical utilitarian reply is: one thing, and one thing only, namely happiness. As Mill put it, "The utilitarian doctrine is that happiness is desirable, and the only thing desirable, as an end; all other things being desirable as means to that end."

The idea that happiness is the one ultimate good (and unhappiness the one ultimate evil) is known as Hedonism. Hedonism is a perennially popular theory that goes back at least as far as the ancient Greeks. It has always been an at-tractive theory because of its beautiful simplicity, and because it expresses the intuitively plausible notion that things are good or bad only on account of the way they make us *feel*. Yet a little reflection reveals serious flaws in the theory. The flaws stand out when we consider examples like these:

1. A promising young pianist's hands are injured in an automobile accident so that she can no longer play. Why is this a bad thing for her? Hedonism would say it is bad because it causes her unhappiness. She will feel frustrated and upset whenever she thinks of what might have been, and *that* is her misfortune. But this way of explaining the misfortune seems to get things the wrong way around. It is not as though, by feeling unhappy, she has made an otherwise neutral situation into a bad one. On the contrary, her unhappiness is a rational response to a situation that *is* unfortunate. She could have had a career as a concert pianist, and now she cannot. *That* is the tragedy. We could not eliminate the tragedy just by getting her to cheer up.

2. You think someone is your friend, but really he ridicules you behind your back. No one ever tells you, so you never know. Is this situation unfortunate for you? Hedonism would have to say no, because you are never caused any unhappiness by the situation. Yet we do feel that there is something bad going on here. You *think* he is your friend, and you are "being made a fool," even though you are not aware of it and so suffer no unhappiness.

Both these examples make the same basic point. We value all sorts of things, including artistic creativity and friendship, for their own sakes. It makes us happy to have them, but only because we *already* think them good. (We do not think them good *because* they make us happy—this is what I meant when I said that Hedonism "gets things the wrong way around.") Therefore we think it a misfortune to lose them, independently of whether or not the loss is accompanied by unhappiness.

In this way, Hedonism misunderstands the nature of happiness. Happiness is not something that is recognized as good and sought for its own sake, with other things appreciated only as means of bringing it about. Instead, happiness is a response we have to the attainment of things that we recognize *as* goods, independently and in their own right. We think that friendship is a good thing, and so having friends makes us happy. That is very different from first setting out after happiness, then deciding that having friends might make us happy, and then seeking friends as a means to this end.

Today, most philosophers recognize the truth of this. There are not many contemporary hedonists. Those sympathetic to Utilitarianism have therefore sought a way to formulate their view without assuming a hedonistic account of good and evil. Some, such as the English philosopher G. E. Moore (1873–1958), have tried to compile short lists of things to be regarded as good in themselves. Moore suggested that there are three obvious intrinsic goods—pleasure, friendship, and aesthetic enjoyment—and that right actions are those that increase the world's supply of such things. Other utilitarians have tried to bypass the question of how many things are good in themselves, leaving it an open question and saying only that right actions are the ones that have the best results, *however* goodness is measured. (This is sometimes called Ideal Utilitarianism.) Still others try to bypass the question in another way, holding only that we should act so as to maximize the satisfaction of people's *preferences*. (This is called **Preference Utilitarianism.**) It is beyond the scope of this book to discuss the merits or demerits of these varieties of Utilitarianism. I mention them only in order to note that although the hedonistic assumption of the classical utilitarians has largely been rejected, contemporary utilitarians have not found it difficult to carry on. They do so by urging that Hedonism was never a necessary part of the theory in the first place.

ARE CONSEQUENCES ALL THAT MATTER?

The claim that only consequences matter *is,* however, a necessary part of Utilitarianism. The most fundamental idea underlying the theory is that in order to determine whether an action would be right, we should look at *what will happen as a result of doing it.* If it were to turn out that some *other* matter is also important in determining rightness, then Utilitarianism would be undermined at its very foundation.

The most serious antiutilitarian arguments attack the theory at just this point: they urge that various other considerations, in addition to utility, are important in determining whether actions are right. We will look briefly at three such arguments.

1. *Justice.* Writing in the academic journal *Inquiry* in 1965, H. J. McCloskey asks us to consider the following case:

Suppose a utilitarian were visiting an area in which there was racial strife, and that, during his visit, a Negro rapes a white woman, and that race riots occur as a result of the crime, white mobs, with the connivance of the police, bashing and killing Negroes, etc. Suppose too that our utilitarian is in the area of the crime when it is committed such that his testimony would bring about the conviction of a particular Negro. If he knows that a quick arrest will stop the riots and lynchings, surely, as a utilitarian, he must conclude that he has a duty to bear false witness in order to bring about the punishment of an innocent person.

This is a fictitious example, but that makes no difference. The argument is only that *if* someone were in this position, then on utilitarian grounds he should bear false witness against the innocent person. This might have some bad consequences—the innocent man might be executed—but there would be enough good consequences to outweigh them: the riots and lynchings would be stopped. The best consequences would be achieved by lying; therefore, according to Utilitarianism, lying is the thing to do. But, the argument continues, it would be wrong to bring about the execution of the innocent man. Therefore, Utilitarianism, which implies it would be right, must be incorrect.

According to the critics of Utilitarianism, this argument illustrates one of the theory's most serious shortcomings: namely, that it is incompatible with the ideal of justice. Justice requires that we treat people fairly, according to their individual needs and merits. The innocent man has done nothing wrong; he did not commit the rape and so he does not deserve to be punished for it. Therefore, punishing him would be unjust. The example illustrates how the demands of justice and the demands of utility can come into conflict, and so a theory that says utility is the *whole* story cannot be right.

2. *Rights.* Here is a case that is *not* fictitious; it is from the records of the U.S. Court of Appeals, Ninth Circuit (Southern District of California), 1963, in the case of *York v. Story:*

In October, 1958, appellant [Ms. Angelynn York] went to the police department of Chino for the purpose of filing charges in connection with an assault upon her. Appellee Ron Story, an officer of that police department, then acting under color of his authority as such, advised appellant that it was necessary to take photographs of her. Story then took appellant to a room in the police station, locked the door, and directed her to undress, which she did. Story then directed appellant to assume various indecent positions, and photographed her in those positions. These photographs were not made for any lawful purpose.

Appellant objected to undressing. She stated to Story that there was no need to take photographs of her in the nude, or in the positions she was directed to take, because the bruises would not show in any photograph. . . .

Later that month, Story advised appellant that the pictures did not come out and that he had destroyed them. Instead, Story circulated these photographs among the personnel of the Chino police department. In April, 1960, two other officers of that police department, appellee Louis Moreno and defendant Henry Grote, acting under color of their authority as such, and using police photographic equipment located at the police station made additional prints of the photographs taken by Story. Moreno and Grote then circulated these prints among the personnel of the Chino police department. . . .

Ms. York brought suit against these officers and won. Her *legal* rights had clearly been violated. But what of the *morality* of the officers' behavior?

Utilitarianism says that actions are defensible if they produce a favorable balance of happiness over unhappiness. This suggests that we consider the amount of unhappiness caused to Ms. York and compare it with the amount of pleasure taken in the photographs by Officer Story and his cohorts. It is at least possible that more happiness than unhappiness was caused. In that case, the utilitarian conclusion apparently would be that their actions were morally all right. But this seems to be a perverse way to approach the case. Why should the pleasure afforded Story and his cohorts matter at all? Why should it even count? They had no right to treat Ms. York in that way, and the fact that they enjoyed doing so hardly seems a relevant defense.

To make the point even clearer, consider an (imaginary) related case. Suppose a Peeping Tom spied on Ms. York by peering through her bedroom window, and secretly took pictures of her undressed. Further suppose that he did this without ever being detected and that he used the photographs entirely for his own amusement, without showing them to anyone. Now under these circumstances, it seems clear that the *only* consequence of his action is an increase in his own happiness. No one else, including Ms. York, is caused any unhappiness at all. How, then, could Utilitarianism deny that the Peeping Tom's actions are right? But it is evident to moral common sense that they are not right. Thus, Utilitarianism appears to be an incorrect moral view.

The moral to be drawn from this argument is that Utilitarianism is at odds with the idea that people have *rights* that may not be trampled on merely because one anticipates good results. This is an extremely important notion, which explains why a great many philosophers have rejected Utilitarianism. In the above cases, it is Ms. York's right to privacy that is violated; but it would not be difficult to think of similar cases in which other rights are at issue—the right to freedom of religion, to free speech, or even the right to life itself. It may happen that good purposes are served, from time to time, by ignoring these rights. But we do not think that our rights *should* be set aside so easily. The notion of a personal right is not a utilitarian notion. Quite the reverse: it is a notion that places limits on how an individual may be treated, regardless of the good purposes that might be accomplished.

3. *Backward-Looking Reasons.* Suppose you have promised someone you will do something—say, you promised to meet him downtown this afternoon. But when the time comes

to go, you don't want to do it—you need to do some work and would rather stay home. What should you do? Suppose you judge that the utility of getting your work accomplished slightly outweighs the inconvenience your friend would be caused. Appealing to the utilitarian standard, you might then conclude that it is right to stay home. However, this does not seem correct. The fact that *you promised* imposes an obligation on you that you cannot escape so easily. Of course, if the consequences of not breaking the promise were *great*—if, for example, your mother had just been stricken with a heart attack and you had to rush her to the hospital—you would be justified in breaking it. But a *small* gain in utility cannot overcome the obligation imposed by the fact that you promised. Thus Utilitarianism, which says that consequences are the only things that matter, seems mistaken.

There is an important general lesson to be learned from this argument. Why is Utilitarianism vulnerable to this sort of criticism? It is because the only kinds of considerations that the theory holds relevant to determining the rightness of actions are considerations having to do with the *future*. Because of its exclusive concern with consequences, Utilitarianism has us confine our attention to what *will happen* as a result of our actions. However, we normally think that considerations about the *past* also have some importance. The fact that you promised your friend to meet him is a fact about the past, not the future. Therefore, the general point to be made about Utilitarianism is that it seems to be an inadequate moral theory because it excludes what we might call backward-looking considerations.

Once we understand this point, other examples of backward-looking considerations come easily to mind. The fact that someone did not commit a crime is a good reason why he should not be punished. The fact that someone once did you a favor may be a good reason why you should now do him a favor. The fact that you did something to hurt someone may be a reason why you should now make it up to her. These are all facts about the past that are relevant to determining our obligations. But Utilitarianism makes the past irrelevant, and so it seems deficient for just that reason.

THE DEFENSE OF UTILITARIANISM

Taken together, the above arguments form an impressive indictment of Utilitarianism. The theory, which at first seemed so progressive and commonsensical, now seems indefensible: it is at odds with such fundamental moral notions as justice and individual rights, and seems unable to account for the place of backward-looking reasons in justifying conduct. The combined weight of these arguments has prompted many philosophers to abandon the theory altogether.

Many thinkers, however, continue to believe that Utilitarianism, in some form, is true. In reply to the arguments, three general defenses have been offered.

The First Line of Defense

The first line of defense is to point out that the examples used in the antiutilitarian arguments are unrealistic and do not describe situations that come up in the real world. Since Utilitarianism is designed as a guide for decision making in the situations we actually face, the fanciful examples are dismissed as irrelevant. . . .

The Second Line of Defense

The first line of defense contains more bluster than substance While it can plausibly be maintained that *most* acts of false witness and the like have bad consequences in the real world, it cannot reasonably be asserted that *all* such acts have bad consequences. Surely, in at least some real-life cases, one can bring about good results by doing things that moral common sense condemns. Therefore, in at least some real-life cases Utilitarianism will come into conflict with common sense. Moreover, even if the antiutilitarian arguments had to rely exclusively on fictitious examples, those arguments would nevertheless retain their power; for showing that Utilitarianism has unacceptable consequences in hypothetical cases is a perfectly valid way of pointing up its theoretical defects. The first line of defense, then, is weak.

The second line of defense admits all this and proposes to save Utilitarianism by giving it a new formulation. In revising a theory to meet criticism, the trick is to identify precisely the feature of the theory that is causing the trouble and to change *that,* leaving the rest of the theory undisturbed as much as possible.

The troublesome aspect of the theory was this: the classical version of Utilitarianism implied that *each individual action* is to be evaluated by reference to its own particular consequences. If on a certain occasion you are tempted to lie, whether it would be wrong is determined by the consequences of *that particular lie.* This, the theory's defenders said, is the point that causes all the trouble; even though we know that *in general* lying has bad consequences, it is obvious that sometimes particular acts of lying can have good consequences.

Therefore, the new version of Utilitarianism modifies the theory so that individual actions will no longer be judged by the Principle of Utility. Instead, *rules* will be established by reference to the principle, and individual acts will then be judged right or wrong by reference to the rules. This new version of the theory is called *Rule-Utilitarianism,* to contrast it with the original theory, now commonly called *Act-Utilitarianism.*

Rule-Utilitarianism has no difficulty coping with the three antiutilitarian arguments. An act-utilitarian, faced with the situation described by McCloskey, would be tempted to bear false witness against the innocent man because the consequences of *that particular act* would be good. But the rule-utilitarian would not reason in that way. He would first ask, "What *general rules of conduct* tend to promote the greatest happiness?" Suppose we imagine two societies, one in which the rule "Don't bear false witness against the innocent" is faithfully adhered to, and one in which this rule is not followed. In which society are people likely to be better off? Clearly, from the point of view of utility, the first society is preferable. Therefore, the rule against incriminating the innocent should be accepted, and *by appealing to this rule,* the rule-utilitarian concludes that the person in McCloskey's example should not testify against the innocent man.

Analogous arguments can be used to establish rules against violating people's rights, breaking promises, lying, and so on. We should accept such rules because following them, as a regular practice, promotes the general welfare. But once having appealed to the Principle of Utility to establish the rules, we do not have to invoke the principle again to determine the rightness of particular actions. Individual actions are justified simply by appeal to the already-established rules.

Thus Rule-Utilitarianism cannot be convicted of violating our moral common sense, or of conflicting with ordinary ideas of justice, personal rights, and the rest. In shifting emphasis from the justification of acts to the justification of rules, the theory has been brought into line with our intuitive judgments to a remarkable degree.

The Third Line of Defense

Finally, a small group of contemporary utilitarians has had a very different response to the anti-utilitarian arguments. Those arguments point out that the classical theory is at odds with ordinary notions of justice, individual rights, and so on; to this, their response is, essentially, "So what?" In 1961 the Australian philosopher J. J. C. Smart published a monograph entitled *An Outline of a System of Utilitarian Ethics;* reflecting on his position in that book, Smart said:

Admittedly utilitarianism does have consequences which are incompatible with the common moral consciousness, but I tended to take the view "so much the worse for the common moral consciousness." That is, I was inclined to reject the common methodology of testing general ethical principles by seeing how they square with our feelings in particular instances.

Our moral common sense is, after all, not necessarily reliable. It may incorporate various irrational elements, including prejudices absorbed from our parents, our religion, and the general culture. Why should we simply assume that our feelings are always correct? And why should we reject a plausible, rational theory of ethics such as Utilitarianism simply because it conflicts with those feelings? Perhaps it is the feelings, not the theory, that should be discarded.

In light of this, consider again McCloskey's example of the person tempted to bear false witness. McCloskey argues that it would be wrong to have a man convicted of a crime he did not commit, because it would be unjust. But wait:

such a judgment serves *that man's* interests well enough, but what of the *other* innocent people who will be hurt if the rioting and lynchings are allowed to continue? What of them? Surely we might hope that we never have to face a situation like this, for the options are all extremely distasteful. But if we *must* choose between (a) securing the conviction of one innocent person and (b) allowing the deaths of several innocent people, is it so unreasonable to think that the first option, bad as it is, is preferable to the second?

On this way of thinking, Act-Utilitarianism is a perfectly defensible doctrine and does not need to be modified. Rule-Utilitarianism, by contrast, is an unnecessarily watered-down version of the theory, which gives rules a greater importance than they merit. Act-Utilitarianism is, however, recognized to be a radical doctrine which implies that many of our ordinary moral feelings may be mistaken. In this respect, it does what good philosophy always does—it challenges us to rethink matters that we have heretofore taken for granted.

WHAT IS CORRECT AND WHAT IS INCORRECT IN UTILITARIANISM

There is a sense in which no moral philosopher can completely reject Utilitarianism. The consequences of one's actions—whether they promote happiness, or cause misery—must be admitted by all to be extremely important. John Stuart Mill once remarked that, insofar as we are benevolent, we must accept the utilitarian standard; and he was surely right. Moreover, the utilitarian emphasis on impartiality must also be a part of any defensible moral theory. The question is whether these are the *only* kinds of considerations an adequate theory must acknowledge. Aren't there *other* considerations that are also important?

If we consult what Smart calls our "common moral consciousness," it seems that there are *many* other considerations that are morally important. . . . But I believe the radical act-utilitarians are right to warn us that "common sense" cannot be trusted. Many people once felt that there is an important difference between whites and blacks, so that the interests of whites

are somehow more important. Trusting the "common sense" of their day, they might have insisted that an adequate moral theory should accommodate this "fact." Today, no one worth listening to would say such a thing. But who knows how many *other* irrational prejudices are still a part of our moral common sense? At the end of his classic study of race relations, *An American Dilemma* (1944), the Swedish sociologist Gunnar Myrdal reminds us:

There must be still other countless errors of the same sort that no living man can yet detect, because of the fog within which our type of Western culture envelops us. Cultural influences have set up the assumptions about the mind, the body, and the universe with which we begin; pose the questions we ask; influence the facts we seek; determine the interpretation we give these facts; and direct our reaction to these interpretations and conclusions.

The strength of Utilitarianism is that it firmly resists "corruption" by possibly irrational elements. By sticking to the Principle of Utility as the *only* standard for judging right and wrong, it avoids all danger of incorporating into moral theory prejudices, feelings, and "intuitions" that have no rational basis.

The warning should be heeded. "Common sense" can, indeed, mislead us. At the same time, however, there might be at least some nonutilitarian considerations that an adequate theory *should* accept, because there *is* a rational basis for them. Consider, for example, the matter of what people deserve. A person who has worked hard in her job may deserve a promotion more than someone who has loafed, and it would be unjust for the loafer to be promoted first. This is a point that we would expect any fair-minded employer to acknowledge; we would all be indignant if we were passed over for promotion in favor of someone who had not worked as hard or as well as we. Now utilitarians might agree with this, and say that it can be explained by their theory—they might argue that it promotes the general welfare to encourage hard work by rewarding it. But this does not seem to be an adequate explanation of the importance of desert. The woman who worked harder has a superior claim to the promotion, *not* because it promotes the general welfare for her to get it, but *because she has earned it*. The reason she should be promoted has to do with *her* merits. This does not appear to be the kind of consideration a utilitarian could admit.

Does this way of thinking express a mere prejudice, or does it have a rational basis? I believe it has a rational basis, although it is not one that utilitarians could accept. We ought to recognize individual desert as a reason for treating people in certain ways—for example, as a reason for promoting the woman who has worked harder—because that is the principal way we have of treating individuals as autonomous, responsible beings. If in fact people have the power to choose their own actions, in such a way that they are *responsible* for those actions and what results from them, then acknowledging their deserts is just a way of acknowledging their standing as autonomous individuals. In treating them as they deserve to be treated, we are responding to the way they have freely chosen to behave. Thus in some instances we will not treat everyone alike, because people are not just members of an undifferentiated crowd. Instead, they are individuals who, by their own choices, show themselves to deserve different kinds of responses. . . .

REVIEW QUESTIONS

1. Rachels says that classical Utilitarianism can be summed up in three propositions. What are they?
2. Explain the problem with Hedonism. How do defenders of Utilitarianism respond to this problem?
3. What are the objections about justice, rights, and promises?
4. Distinguish between Rule- and Act-Utilitarianism. How does Rule-Utilitarianism reply to the objections?
5. What is the third line of defense?

DISCUSSION QUESTIONS

1. Smart's defense of Utilitarianism is to reject common moral beliefs when they conflict with Utilitarianism. Is this acceptable to you or not? Explain your answer.
2. A utilitarian is supposed to give moral consideration to all concerned. Who must be considered? What about nonhuman animals? How about lakes and streams?
3. Rachels claims that merit should be given moral consideration independent of utility. Do you agree?

Immanuel Kant

The Categorical Imperative

Immanuel Kant (1724–1804), a German, was one of the most important philosophers of all time. He made significant contributions to all areas of philosophy. He wrote many books; the most important ones are Critique of Pure Reason, Prolegomena to All Future Metaphysics, Critique of Practical Reason, Critique of Judgment, *and* The Foundations of the Metaphysics of Morals, *from which the reading is taken.*

Kant believes that our moral duty can be formulated in one supreme rule, the Categorical Imperative, from which all our duties can be derived. Although he says that there is just one rule, he gives different versions of it, and two of them seem to be distinct. He arrives at the supreme rule or rules by considering the nature of the good will and duty.

THE GOOD WILL

It is impossible to conceive anything at all in the world, or even out of it, which can be taken as

From *The Moral Law: Kant's Groundwork of the Metaphysic of Morals*, trans. H. J. Paton (New York: Barnes & Noble, Inc., 1948).

good without qualification, except a *good will*. Intelligence, wit, judgment, and any other *talents* of the mind we may care to name, or courage, resolution, and constancy of purpose, as qualities of *temperament*, are without doubt good and desirable in many respects; but they can also be extremely bad and hurtful when the will is not good which has to make use of these gifts of nature, and which for this reason has the term *'character'* applied to its peculiar quality. It is exactly the same with *gifts of fortune*. Power, wealth, honour, even health and that complete well-being and contentment with one's state which goes by the name of *'happiness'*, produce boldness, and as a consequence often over-boldness as well, unless a good will is present by which their influence on the mind—and so too the whole principle of action—may be corrected and adjusted to universal ends; not to mention that a rational and impartial spectator can never feel approval in contemplating the uninterrupted prosperity of a being graced by no touch of a pure and good will, and that consequently a good will seems to constitute the indispensable condition of our very worthiness to be happy.

Some qualities are even helpful to this good will itself and can make its task very much easier. They have none the less no inner unconditioned worth, but rather presuppose a good will which sets a limit to the esteem in which they are rightly held and does not permit us to regard them as absolutely good. Moderation in affections and passions, self-control, and sober reflexion are not only good in many respects: they may even seem to constitute part of the *inner* worth of a person. Yet they are far from being properly described as good without qualification (however unconditionally they have been commended by the ancients). For without the principles of a good will they may become exceedingly bad; and the very coolness of a scoundrel makes him, not merely more dangerous, but also immediately more abominable in our eyes than we should have taken him to be without it.

THE GOOD WILL AND ITS RESULTS

A good will is not good because of what it effects or accomplishes—because of its fitness for attaining some proposed end: it is good through its willing alone—that is, good in itself. Considered in itself it is to be esteemed beyond comparison as far higher than anything it could ever bring about merely in order to favour some inclination or, if you like, the sum total of inclinations. Even if, by some special disfavour of destiny or by the niggardly endowment of stepmotherly nature, this will is entirely lacking in power to carry out its intentions; if by its utmost effort it still accomplishes nothing, and only good will is left (not, admittedly, as a mere wish, but as the straining of every means so far as they are in our control); even then it would still shine like a jewel for its own sake as something which has its full value in itself. Its usefulness or fruitlessness can neither add to, nor subtract from, this value. Its usefulness would be merely, as it were, the setting which enables us to handle it better in our ordinary dealings or to attract the attention of those not yet sufficiently expert, but not to commend it to experts or to determine its value. . . .

THE GOOD WILL AND DUTY

We have now to elucidate the concept of a will estimable in itself and good apart from any further end. This concept, which is already present in a sound natural understanding and requires not so much to be taught as merely to be clarified, always holds the highest place in estimating the total worth of our actions and constitutes the condition of all the rest. We will therefore take up the concept of *duty*, which includes that of a good will, exposed, however, to certain subjective limitations and obstacles. These, so far from hiding a good will or disguising it, rather bring it out by contrast and make it shine forth more brightly.

THE MOTIVE OF DUTY

I will here pass over all actions already recognized as contrary to duty, however useful they may be with a view to this or that end; for about these the question does not even arise whether they could have been done *for the sake of duty* inasmuch as they are directly opposed to it. I will also set aside actions which in fact accord with duty, yet for which men have *no immediate inclination,* but perform them because impelled to do so by some other inclination. For there it is easy to decide whether the action which accords with duty has been done *from duty* or from some purpose of self-interest. This distinction is far more difficult to perceive when the action accords with duty and the subject has in addition an *immediate* inclination to the action. For example, it certainly accords with duty that a grocer should not overcharge his inexperienced customer; and where there is much competition a sensible shopkeeper refrains from so doing and keeps to a fixed and general price for everybody so that a child can buy from him just as well as anyone else. Thus people are served *honestly;* but this is not nearly enough to justify us in believing that the shopkeeper has acted in this way from duty or from principles of fair dealing; his interests required him to do so. We cannot assume him to have in addition an immediate inclination towards his customers, leading him, as it were out of love, to give no man preference over another in the matter of price. Thus the action was done neither from duty nor from immediate inclination, but solely from purposes of self-interest.

On the other hand, to preserve one's life is a duty, and besides this every one has also an immediate inclination to do so. But on account of this the often anxious precautions taken by the greater part of mankind for this purpose have no inner worth, and the maxim of their action is without moral content. They do protect their lives *in conformity with duty,* but not *from the motive of duty.* When on the contrary, disappointments and hopeless misery have quite taken away the taste for life; when a wretched man, strong in soul and more angered at his fate than faint-hearted or cast down, longs for death and still preserves his life without loving it—not from inclination or fear but from duty; then indeed his maxim has a moral content.

To help others where one can is a duty, and besides this there are many spirits of so sympathetic a temper that, without any further motive of vanity or self-interest, they find an inner pleasure in spreading happiness around them and can take delight in the contentment of others as their own work. Yet I maintain that in such a case an action of this kind, however right and however amiable it may be, has still no genuinely moral worth. It stands on the same footing as other inclinations—for example, the inclination for honour, which if fortunate enough to hit on something beneficial and right and consequently honourable, deserves praise and encouragement, but not esteem; for its maxim lacks moral content, namely, the performance of such actions, not from inclination, but *from duty.* Suppose then that the mind of this friend of man were overclouded by sorrows of his own which extinguished all sympathy with the fate of others, but that he still had power to help those in distress, though no longer stirred by the need of others because sufficiently occupied with his own; and suppose that, when no longer moved by any inclination, he tears himself out of this deadly insensibility and does the action without any inclination for the sake of duty alone; then for the first time his action has its genuine moral worth. Still further: if nature had implanted little sympathy in this or that man's heart; if (being in other respects an honest fellow) he were cold in temperament and indifferent to the sufferings of others—perhaps because, being endowed with the special gift of patience and robust endurance in his own sufferings, he assumed the like in others or even demanded it; if such a man (who would in truth not be the worth product of nature) were not exactly fashioned by her to be a philanthropist, would he not still find in himself a source from which he might draw a worth far higher than any that a good-natured temperament can have? Assuredly he would. It is precisely in this that the worth of character begins to show—a moral worth and beyond all comparison the highest—namely, that he does good, not from inclination, but from duty. . . .

Thus the moral worth of an action does not depend on the result expected from it, and so too does not depend on any principle of action that needs to borrow its motive from this expected result. For all these results (agreeable states and even the promotion of happiness in others) could have been brought about by other causes as well, and consequently their production did not require the will of a rational being, in which, however, the highest and unconditioned good can alone be found. Therefore nothing but the *idea of the law* in itself, *which admittedly is present only in a rational being*—so far as it, and not an expected result, is the ground determining the will—can constitute that preeminent good which we call moral, a good which is already present in the person acting on this idea and has not to be awaited merely from the result.

THE CATEGORICAL IMPERATIVE

But what kind of law can this be the thought of which, even without regard to the results expected from it, has to determine the will if this is to be called good absolutely and without qualification? Since I have robbed the will of every inducement that might arise for it as a consequence of obeying any particular law, nothing is left but the conformity of actions to universal law as such, and this alone must serve the will as its principle. That is to say, I ought never to act except in such a way *that I can also will that my maxim should become a universal law*. Here bare conformity to universal law as such (without having as its base any law prescribing particular actions) is what serves the will as its principle, and must so serve it if duty is not to be everywhere an empty delusion and a chimerical concept. The ordinary reason of mankind also agrees with this completely in its practical judgements and always has the aforesaid principle before its eyes. . . .

When I conceive a *hypothetical imperative* in general, I do not know beforehand what it will contain—until its condition is given. But if I conceive a *categorical imperative,* I know at once what it contains. For since besides the law this imperative contains only the necessity that our maxim[1] should conform to this law, while the law, as we have seen, contains no condition to limit it, there remains nothing over to which the maxim has to conform except the universality of a law as such; and it is this conformity alone that the imperative properly asserts to be necessary.

There is therefore only a single categorical imperative and it is this: *'Act only on that maxim through which you can at the same time will that it should become a universal law'*.

Now if all imperatives of duty can be derived from this one imperative as their principle, then even although we leave it unsettled whether what we call duty may not be an empty concept, we shall still be able to show at least what we understand by it and what the concept means. . . .

ILLUSTRATIONS

We will now enumerate a few duties, following their customary division into duties towards self and duties towards others and into perfect and imperfect duties.[2]

1. A man feels sick of life as the result of a series of misfortunes that has mounted to the point of despair, but he is still so far in possession of his reason as to ask himself whether taking his own life may not be contrary to his duty to himself. He now applies the test 'Can the maxim of my action really become a universal law of nature?' His maxim is 'From self-love I make it my principle to shorten my life if its continuance threatens more evil than it promises pleasure'. The only further question to ask is whether this principle of self-love can become a universal law of nature. It is then seen at once that a system of nature by whose law the very same feeling whose function (*Bestimmung*) is to stimulate the furtherance of life should actually destroy life would contradict itself and consequently could not subsist as a system of nature. Hence this maxim cannot possibly hold as a universal law of nature and is therefore entirely opposed to the supreme principle of all duty.

2. Another finds himself driven to borrowing money because of need. He well knows that he will not be able to pay it back; but he sees too that he will get no loan unless he gives a firm promise to pay it back within a fixed time. He is inclined to make such a promise; but he has still enough conscience to ask 'Is it not unlawful and contrary to duty to get out of difficulties in this way?' Supposing, however, he did resolve to do so, the maxim of his action would run thus: 'Whenever I believe myself short of money, I will borrow money and promise to pay it back, though I know that this will never be done'. Now this principle of self-love or personal advantage is perhaps quite compatible

with my own entire future welfare; only there remains the question 'Is it right?' I therefore transform the demand of self-love into a universal law and frame my question thus: 'How would things stand if my maxim became a universal law?' I then see straight away that this maxim can never rank as a universal law of nature and be self-consistent, but must necessarily contradict itself. For the universality of a law that every one believing himself to be in need can make any promise he pleases with the intention not to keep it would make promising, and the very purpose of promising, itself impossible, since no one would believe he was being promised anything, but would laugh at utterances of this kind as empty shams.

3. A third finds in himself a talent whose cultivation would make him a useful man for all sorts of purposes. But he sees himself in comfortable circumstances, and he prefers to give himself up to pleasure rather than to bother about increasing and improving his fortunate natural aptitudes. Yet he asks himself further 'Does my maxim of neglecting my natural gifts, besides agreeing in itself with my tendency to indulgence, agree also with what is called duty?' He then sees that a system of nature could indeed always subsist under such a universal law, although (like the South Sea Islanders) every man should let his talents rust and should be bent on devoting his life solely to idleness, indulgence, procreation, and, in a word, to enjoyment. Only he cannot possibly *will* that this should become a universal law of nature or should be implanted in us as such a law by a natural instinct. For as a rational being he necessarily wills that all his powers should be developed, since they serve him, and are given him, for all sorts of possible ends.

4. Yet a *fourth* is himself flourishing, but he sees others who have to struggle with great hardships (and whom he could easily help); and he thinks 'What does it matter to me? Let every one be as happy as Heaven wills or as he can make himself; I won't deprive him of anything; I won't even envy him; only I have no wish to contribute anything to his well-being or to his support in distress!' Now admittedly if such an attitude were a universal law of nature, mankind could get on perfectly well—better no doubt than if everybody prates about sympathy and goodwill, and even takes pains, on occasion, to practise them, but on the other hand cheats where he can, traffics in human rights, or violates them in other ways. But although it is possible that a universal law of nature could subsist in harmony with this maxim, yet it is impossible to *will* that such a principle should hold everywhere as a law of nature. For a will which decided in this way would be in conflict with itself, since many a situation might arise in which the man needed love and sympathy from others, and in which, by such a law of nature sprung from his own will, he would rob himself of all hope of the help he wants for himself. . . .

THE FORMULA OF THE END IN ITSELF

The will is conceived as a power of determining oneself to action *in accordance with the idea of certain laws*. And such a power can be found only in rational beings. Now what serves the will as a subjective ground of its self-determination is an *end*; and this, if it is given by reason alone, must be equally valid for all rational beings. What, on the other hand, contains merely the ground of the possibility of an action whose effect is an end is called a *means*. . . .

Now I say that man, and in general every rational being, *exists* as an end in himself, *not merely as a means* for arbitrary use by this or that will: he must in all his actions, whether they are directed to himself or to other rational beings, always be viewed *at the same time as an end*. All the objects of inclination have only a conditioned value; for if there were not these inclinations and the needs grounded on them, their object would be valueless. Inclinations themselves, as sources of needs, are so far from having an absolute value to make them desirable for their own sake that it must rather be the universal wish of every rational being to be wholly free from them. Thus the value of all objects that can *be produced* by our action is always conditioned. Beings whose existence depends, not on our will, but on nature, have none the less, if they are non-rational beings, only a relative value as means and are consequently called *things*. Rational beings, on the other hand, are called *persons* because their nature already marks them out as ends in themselves—that is, as something which ought not to be used merely as a means—and consequently imposes to that extent a limit on all arbitrary treatment of them (and is an object of reverence). Persons, therefore, are not merely subjective ends whose existence as an object of our actions has a value *for us*: they are *objective ends*—that is, things whose existence is in itself an end, and indeed an end such that in its place we can put no other end to which they should serve *simply* as means; for unless this is so, nothing at all of *absolute* value would be found anywhere. But if all value were conditioned—that is, contingent—then no supreme principle could be found for reason at all.

If then there is to be a supreme practical principle and—so far as the human will is concerned—a categorical imperative, it must be such that from the idea of something which is necessarily an end for every one because it is an *end in itself* it forms an *objective* principle of the will and consequently can serve as a practical law. The ground of this principle is: *Rational nature exists as an end in itself*. This is the way in which a man necessarily conceives his own existence: it is therefore so far a *subjective* principle of human actions. But it is also the way in which every other rational being conceives his existence on the same rational ground which is valid also for me; hence it is at the same time an *objective* principle, from which, as a supreme practical ground, it must be possible to derive all laws for the will. The practical imperative will therefore be as follows: *Act in such a way that you always treat humanity, whether in your own person or in the person of any other, never simply as a means, but always at the same time as an end*. . . .

Endnotes

1. A *maxim* is a subjective principle of action and must be distinguished from an *objective principle*—namely, a practical law. The former contains a practical rule determined by reason in accordance with the conditions of the subject (often his ignorance or again his inclinations): it is thus a principle on which the subject *acts*. A law, on the other hand, is an objective principle valid for every rational being; and it is a principle on which he *ought to act*—that is, an imperative.

2. It should be noted that I reserve my division of duties entirely for a future *Metaphysic of Morals* and that my present division is therefore put forward as arbitrary (merely for the purpose of arranging my examples). Further, I understand here by a perfect duty one which allows no exception in the interests of inclination, and so I recognize among *perfect duties*, not only outer ones, but also inner. This is contrary to the accepted usage of the schools, but I do not intend to justify it here, since for my purpose it is all one whether this point is conceded or not.

REVIEW QUESTIONS

1. Explain Kant's account of the good will.
2. Distinguish between hypothetical and categorical imperatives.
3. State the first formulation of the Categorical Imperative (using the notion of a universal law) and explain how Kant uses this rule to derive some specific duties towards self and others.
4. State the second version of the Categorical Imperative (using the language of means and end), and explain it.

DISCUSSION QUESTIONS

1. Are the two different versions of the Categorical Imperative just different expressions of one basic rule, or are they two different rules? Defend your view.
2. Kant claims that an action that is not done from the motive of duty has no moral worth. Do you agree or not? If not, give some counter-examples.
3. Some commentators think that the Categorical Imperative (particularly the first formulation) can be used to justify nonmoral or immoral actions. Is this a good criticism?

Onora O'Neill

A Simplified Account
of Kant's Ethics

Onora O'Neill is Principal of Newnham College, Cambridge, England. She is the author of Acting on Principle *(1975),* Faces of Hunger *(1986), and* Constructions of Reason: Exploration of Kant's Practical Philosophy *(1989).*

   O'Neill interprets and explains the formulation of the Categorical Imperative called the Formula of the End in Itself, and then compares the Kantian and utilitarian moral theories on the value of human life.

Kant's moral theory has acquired the reputation of being forbiddingly difficult to understand and, once understood, excessively demanding in its requirements. I don't believe that this reputation has been wholly earned, and I am going to try to undermine it. . . . I shall try to reduce some of the difficulties. . . . Finally, I shall compare Kantian and utilitarian approaches and assess their strengths and weaknesses.

   The main method by which I propose to avoid some of the difficulties of Kant's moral theory is by explaining only one part of the theory. This does not seem to me to be an irresponsible approach in this case. One of the things that makes Kant's moral theory hard to understand is that he gives a number of different versions of the principle that he calls the Supreme Principle of Morality, and these different versions don't look at all like one another. They also don't look at all like the utilitarians' Greatest Happiness Principle. But the Kantian principle is supposed to play a similar role in arguments about what to do.

   Kant calls his Supreme Principle the *Categorical Imperative;* its various versions also have so-

norous names. One is called the *Formula of Universal Law;* another is the *Formula of the Kingdom of Ends.* The one on which I shall concentrate is known as the *Formula of the End in Itself.* To understand why Kant thinks that these picturesquely named principles are equivalent to one another takes quite a lot of close and detailed analysis of Kant's philosophy. I shall avoid this and concentrate on showing the implications of this version of the Categorical Imperative.

THE FORMULA OF THE END
IN ITSELF

Kant states the Formula of the End in Itself as follows:

Act in such a way that you always treat humanity, whether in your own person or in the person of any other, never simply as a means but always at the same time as an end.[1]

To understand this we need to know what it is to treat a person as a means or as an end. According to Kant, each of our acts reflects one or more *maxims.* The maxim of the act is the principle on which one sees oneself as acting. A maxim expresses a person's policy, or if he or she has no settled policy, the principle underlying the particular intention or decision on which he or she acts. Thus, a person who decides "This year I'll give 10 percent of my income to famine relief" has as a maxim the principle of tithing his or her income for famine relief. In practice, the difference between intentions and maxims is of little importance, for given any intention, we can formulate the corresponding maxim by deleting references to particular times, places, and persons. In what follows I shall take the terms 'maxim' and 'intention' as equivalent.

   Whenever we act intentionally, we have at least one maxim and can, if we reflect, state what it is. (There is of course room for self-deception here—"I'm only keeping the wolf from the door" we may claim as we wolf down

From Onora O'Neill, "A Simplified Account of Kant's Ethics," *Matters of Life and Death,* ed. Tom Regan (New York: McGraw-Hill Publishing Company, 1986).
Reprinted by permission of The McGraw-Hill Companies.

enough to keep ourselves overweight, or, more to the point, enough to feed someone else who hasn't enough food.)

When we want to work out whether an act we propose to do is right or wrong, according to Kant, we should look at our maxims and not at how much misery or happiness the act is likely to produce, and whether it does better at increasing happiness than other available acts. We just have to check that the act we have in mind will not use anyone as a mere means, and, if possible, that it will treat other persons as ends in themselves.

USING PERSONS AS MERE MEANS

To use someone as a *mere means* is to involve them in a scheme of action *to which they could not in principle consent*. Kant does not say that there is anything wrong about using someone as a means. Evidently we have to do so in any cooperative scheme of action. If I cash a check I use the teller as a means, without whom I could not lay my hands on the cash; the teller in turn uses me as a means to earn his or her living. But in this case, each party consents to her or his part in the transaction. Kant would say that though they use one another as means, they do not use one another as *mere* means. Each person assumes that the other has maxims of his or her own and is not just a thing or a prop to be manipulated.

But there are other situations where one person uses another in a way to which the other could not in principle consent. For example, one person may make a promise to another with every intention of breaking it. If the promise is accepted, then the person to whom it was given must be ignorant of what the promisor's intention (maxim) really is. If one knew that the promisor did not intend to do what he or she was promising, one would, after all, not accept or rely on the promise. It would be as though there had been no promise made. Successful false promising depends on deceiving the person to whom the promise is made about what one's real maxim is. And since the person who is deceived doesn't know that real maxim, he or she can't in principle consent to his or her part

in the proposed scheme of action. The person who is deceived is, as it were, a prop or a tool— a mere means—in the false promisor's scheme. A person who promises falsely treats the acceptor of the promise as a prop or a thing and not as a person. In Kant's view, it is this that makes false promising wrong.

One standard way of using others as mere means is by deceiving them. By getting someone involved in a business scheme or a criminal activity on false pretenses, or by giving a misleading account of what one is about, or by making a false promise or a fraudulent contract, one involves another in something to which he or she in principle cannot consent, since the scheme requires that he or she doesn't know what is going on. Another standard way of using others as mere means is by coercing them. If a rich or powerful person threatens a debtor with bankruptcy unless he or she joins in some scheme, then the creditor's intention is to coerce; and the debtor, if coerced, cannot consent to his or her part in the creditor's scheme. To make the example more specific: If a moneylender in an Indian village threatens not to renew a vital loan unless he is given the debtor's land, then he uses the debtor as a mere means. He coerces the debtor, who cannot truly consent to this "offer he can't refuse." (Of course the outward form of such transactions may look like ordinary commercial dealings, but we know very well that some offers and demands couched in that form are coercive.)

In Kant's view, acts that are done on maxims that require deception or coercion of others, and so cannot have the consent of those others (for consent precludes both deception and coercion), are wrong. When we act on such maxims, we treat others as mere means, as things rather than as ends in themselves. If we act on such maxims, our acts are not only wrong but unjust: such acts wrong the particular others who are deceived or coerced.

TREATING PERSONS AS ENDS IN THEMSELVES

Duties of justice are, in Kant's view (as in many others'), the most important of our duties.

When we fail in these duties, we have used some other or others as mere means. But there are also cases where, though we do not use others as mere means, still we fail to use them as ends in themselves in the fullest possible way. To treat someone as an end in him or herself requires in the first place that one not use him or her as mere means, that one respect each as a rational person with his or her own maxims. But beyond that, one may also seek to foster others' plans and maxims by sharing some of their ends. To act beneficently is to seek others' happiness, therefore to intend to achieve some of the things that those others aim at with their maxims. If I want to make others happy, I will adopt maxims that not merely do not manipulate them but that foster some of their plans and activities. Beneficent acts try to achieve what others want. However, we cannot seek everything that others want; their wants are too numerous and diverse, and, of course, sometimes incompatible. It follows that beneficence has to be selective.

There is then quite a sharp distinction between the requirements of justice and of beneficence in Kantian ethics. Justice requires that we act on *no* maxims that use others as mere means. Beneficence requires that we act on *some* maxims that foster others' ends, though it is a matter for judgment and discretion which of their ends we foster. Some maxims no doubt ought not to be fostered because it would be unjust to do so. Kantians are not committed to working interminably through a list of happiness-producing and misery-reducing acts; but there are some acts whose obligatoriness utilitarians may need to debate as they try to compare total outcomes of different choices, to which Kantians are stringently bound. Kantians will claim that they have done nothing wrong if none of their acts is unjust, and that their duty is complete if in addition their life plans have in the circumstances been reasonably beneficent.

In making sure that they meet all the demands of justice, Kantians do not try to compare all available acts and see which has the best effects. They consider only the proposals for action that occur to them and check that these proposals use no other as mere means. If they do not, the act is permissible; if omitting the act would use another as mere means, the act is obligatory. Kant's theory has less scope than utilitarianism. Kantians do not claim to discover whether acts whose maxims they don't know fully are just. They may be reluctant to judge others' acts or policies that cannot be regarded as the maxim of any person or institution. They cannot rank acts in order of merit. Yet, the theory offers more precision than utilitarianism when data are scarce. One can usually tell whether one's act would use others as mere means, even when its impact on human happiness is thoroughly obscure.

THE LIMITS OF KANTIAN ETHICS: INTENTIONS AND RESULTS

Kantian ethics differs from utilitarian ethics both in its scope and in the precision with which it guides action. Every action, whether of a person or of an agency, can be assessed by utilitarian methods, provided only that information is available about all the consequences of the act. The theory has unlimited scope, but owing to lack of data, often lacks precision. Kantian ethics has a more restricted scope. Since it assesses actions by looking at the maxims of agents, it can only assess intentional acts. This means that it is most at home in assessing individuals' acts; but it can be extended to assess acts of agencies that (like corporations and governments and student unions) have decision-making procedures. It can do nothing to assess patterns of action that reflect no intention or policy, hence it cannot assess the acts of groups lacking decision-making procedures, such as the student movement, the women's movement, or the consumer movement.

It may seem a great limitation of Kantian ethics that it concentrates on intentions to the neglect of results. It might seem that all conscientious Kantians have to do is to make sure that they never intend to use others as mere means, and that they sometimes intend to foster others' ends. And, as we all know, good intentions sometimes lead to bad results and correspondingly, bad intentions sometimes do no harm, or even produce good. If Hardin[2] is right, the good intentions of those who feed the starving lead to dreadful results in the long run. If some traditional arguments in favor of capitalism are right, the greed and selfishness of the profit motive have produced unparalleled prosperity for many.

But such discrepancies between intentions and results are the exception and not the rule. For we cannot just *claim* that our intentions are good and do what we will. Our intentions reflect what we expect the immediate results of our action to be. Nobody credits the "intentions" of a couple who practice neither celibacy nor contraception but still insist "we never meant to have (more) children." Conception is likely (and known to be likely) in such cases. Where people's expressed intentions ignore the normal and predictable results of what they do, we infer that (if they are not amazingly ignorant) their words do not express their true intentions. The Formula of the End in Itself applies to the intentions on which one acts—not to some prettified version that one may avow. Provided this intention—the agent's real intention—uses no other as mere means, he or she does nothing unjust. If some of his or her intentions foster others' ends, then he or she is sometimes beneficent. It is therefore possible for people to test their proposals by Kantian arguments even when they lack the comprehensive causal knowledge that utilitarianism requires. Conscientious Kantians can work out whether they will be doing wrong by some act even though it blurs the implications of the theory. If we peer through the blur, we see that the utilitarian view is that lives may indeed be sacrificed for the sake of a greater good even when the persons are not willing. There is nothing wrong with using another as a mere means provided that the end for which the person is so used is a happier result than could have been achieved any other way, taking into account the misery the means have caused. In utilitarian thought persons are not ends in themselves. Their special moral status derives from their being means to the production of happiness. Human life has therefore a high though derivative value, and one life may be taken for the sake of greater happiness in other lives, or for ending of misery in that life. Nor is there any deep difference between ending a life for the sake of others' happiness by not helping (e.g., by triaging) and

doing so by harming. Because the distinction between justice and beneficence is not sharply made within utilitarianism, it is not possible to say that triaging is a matter of not benefiting, while other interventions are a matter of injustice.

Utilitarian moral theory has then a rather paradoxical view of the value of human life. Living, conscious humans are (along with other sentient beings) necessary for the existence of everything utilitarians value. But it is not their being alive but the state of their consciousness that is of value. Hence, the best results may require certain lives to be lost—by whatever means—for the sake of the total happiness and absence of misery that can be produced.

KANT AND RESPECT FOR PERSONS

Kantians reach different conclusions about human life. Human life is valuable because humans (and conceivably other beings, e.g., angels or apes) are the bearers of rational life. Humans are able to choose and to plan. This capacity and its exercise are of such value that they ought not to be sacrificed for anything of lesser value. Therefore, no one rational or autonomous creature should be treated as mere means for the enjoyment or even the happiness of another. We may in Kant's view justifiably—even nobly—risk or sacrifice our lives for others. For in doing so we follow our own maxim and nobody uses us as mere means. But no others may use either our lives or our bodies for a scheme that they have either coerced or deceived us into joining. For in doing so they would fail to treat us as rational beings; they would use us as mere means and not as ends in ourselves.

It is conceivable that a society of Kantians, all of whom took pains to use no other as mere means, would end up with less happiness or with fewer persons alive than would some societies of complying utilitarians. For since the Kantians would be strictly bound only to justice, they might without wrongdoing be quite selective in their beneficence and fail to maximize either survival rates or happiness, or even to achieve as much of either as a strenuous group of utilitarians, who they know that their foresight is limited and that they may cause some harm or fail to cause some benefit. But they will not cause harms that they can foresee without this being reflected in their intentions.

UTILITARIANISM AND RESPECT FOR LIFE

From the differing implications that Kantian and utilitarian moral theories have for our actions towards those who do or may suffer famine, we can discover two sharply contrasting views of the value of human life. Utilitarians value happiness and the absence or reduction of misery. As a utilitarian one ought (if conscientious) to devote one's life to achieving the best possible balance of happiness over misery. If one's life plan remains in doubt, this will be because the means to this end are often unclear. But whenever the causal tendency of acts is clear, utilitarians will be able to discern the acts they should successively do in order to improve the world's balance of happiness over unhappiness.

This task is not one for the faint-hearted. First, it is dauntingly long, indeed interminable. Second, it may at times require the sacrifice of happiness, and even of lives, for the sake of a greater happiness. Such sacrifice may be morally required not only when the person whose happiness or even whose life is at stake volunteers to make the sacrifice. It may be necessary to sacrifice some lives for the sake of others. As our control over the means of ending and preserving human life has increased, analogous dilemmas have arisen in many areas for utilitarians. Should life be preserved at the cost of pain when modern medicine makes this possible? Should life be preserved without hope of consciousness? Should triage policies, because they may maximize the number of survivors, be used to determine who should be left to starve? Should population growth be fostered wherever it will increase the total of human happiness—or on some views so long as average happiness is not reduced? All these questions can be fitted into utilitarian frameworks and answered *if* we have the relevant information. And sometimes the answer will be that human happiness demands the sacrifice of lives, including the sacrifice of unwilling lives. Further, for most utilitarians, it makes no difference if the unwilling sacrifices involve acts of injustice to those whose lives are to be lost. It might, for example, prove necessary for maximal happiness that some persons have their allotted rations, or their hard-earned income, diverted for others' benefit. Or it might turn out that some generations must sacrifice comforts or liberties and even lives to rear "the fabric of felicity" for their successors. Utilitarians do not deny these possibilities, though the imprecision of our knowledge of consequences often somehow makes the right calculations. On the other hand, nobody will have been made an instrument of others' survival or happiness in the society of complying Kantians.

Endnotes

1. [See the end of the reading from Kant—Ed.]
2. [See the reading by Garrett Hardin in Chapter 5—Ed.]

REVIEW QUESTIONS

1. According to O'Neill, what is involved in using someone as a mere means? Give some examples. Why is this wrong?
2. On O'Neill's interpretation, how does one treat people as ends in themselves? Give examples.
3. Distinguish between the requirements of justice and beneficence.
4. According to O'Neill, how does Kantian ethics differ from utilitarian ethics?

DISCUSSION QUESTIONS

1. Does Kantian ethics require us to help strangers or people in other countries? Why or why not?
2. As O'Neill explains it, Kant's view is that a life is valuable because it is rational. This seems to imply that the life of a fetus or a comatose person is not valuable because it is not rational—it involves no choosing or planning. Do you agree with this?
3. Which theory is more acceptable to you, Utilitarianism or Kant's theory? Why?

W. D. Ross

What Makes Right Acts Right?

W. D. Ross (1877–1967) was a British moral philosopher and classical scholar who taught at Oxford University. He is the translator of our reading from Aristotle; his book Aristotle *(1959) explains the general features of Aristotle's ethical theory. Our reading is taken from his best-known book,* The Right and the Good *(1930).*

Ross begins by distinguishing between Hedonistic Utilitarianism (John Stuart Mill's view that the good is pleasure) and Ideal Utilitarianism (G. E. Moore's theory that other things besides pleasure are good, such as beauty). He then makes a telling objection to these theories: The reason we ought to fulfill a promise is not because this produces good consequences, but simply because it is our prima facie duty (our duty at first view). Ross' definition of prima facie duty is not very clear. Generally speaking, a prima facie duty is an actual duty that may be overridden by some other moral considerations. The basic idea is that we can have conflicts between prima facie duties where we cannot satisfy them all. For example, we may be able to help someone (a duty of beneficence) only if we break a promise. In such cases we can only make a judgment about what to do using moral intuition. Moral intuition also reveals self-evident principles about duty that are more certain than judgments about particular acts. Because Ross appeals to the apprehension of rightness by intuition, his theory is often called Intuitionism. *It is also said to be a pluralistic deontology because it recognizes different types of duty.*

The real point at issue between hedonism and utilitarianism on the one hand and their oppo-

From W. D. Ross, *The Right and the Good* (Oxford: Clarendon Press, 1930). Reprinted by permission of Oxford University Press.

nents on the other is not whether 'right' means 'productive of so and so'; for it cannot with any plausibility be maintained that it does. The point at issue is that to which we now pass, viz. whether there is any general character which makes right acts right, and if so, what it is. Among the main historical attempts to state a single characteristic of all right actions which is the foundation of their rightness are those made by egoism and utilitarianism. But I do not propose to discuss these, not because the subject is unimportant, but because it has been dealt with so often and so well already, and because there has come to be so much agreement among moral philosophers that neither of these theories is satisfactory. A much more attractive theory has been put forward by Professor Moore: that what makes actions right is that they are productive of more *good* than could have been produced by any other action open to the agent.[1]

This theory is in fact the culmination of all the attempts to base rightness on productivity of some sort of result. The first form this attempt takes is the attempt to base rightness on conduciveness to the advantage or pleasure of the agent. This theory comes to grief over the fact, which stares us in the face, that a great part of duty consists in an observance of the rights and a furtherance of the interests of others, whatever the cost to ourselves may be. Plato and others may be right in holding that a regard for the rights of others never in the long run involves a loss of happiness for the agent, that 'the just life profits a man'. But this, even if true, is irrelevant to the rightness of the act. As soon as a man does an action *because* he thinks he will promote his own interests thereby, he is acting not from a sense of its rightness but from self-interest.

To the egoistic theory hedonistic utilitarianism supplies a much-needed amendment. It points out correctly that the fact that a certain pleasure will be enjoyed by the agent is no reason why he *ought* to bring it into being rather than an equal or greater pleasure to be enjoyed by another, though, human nature being what it is, it makes it not unlikely that he *will* try to bring it into being. But hedonistic utilitarianism in its turn needs a correction. On reflection it seems clear that pleasure is not the only thing in life that we think good in itself, that for instance we think the possession of a good character, or an intelligent understanding of the world, as good or better. A great advance is made by the substitution of 'productive of the greatest good' for 'productive of the greatest pleasure'.

Not only is this theory more attractive than hedonistic utilitarianism, but its logical relation to that theory is such that the latter could not be true unless *it* were true, while it might be true though hedonistic utilitarianism were not. It is in fact one of the logical bases of hedonistic utilitarianism. For the view that what produces the maximum pleasure is right has for its bases the views (1) that what produces the maximum good is right, and (2) that pleasure is the only thing good in itself. If they were not assuming that what produces the maximum *good* is right, the utilitarians' attempt to show that pleasure is the only thing good in itself, which is in fact the point they take most pains to establish, would have been quite irrelevant to their attempt to prove that only what produces the maximum *pleasure* is right. If, therefore, it can be shown that productivity of the maximum good is not what makes all right actions right, we shall *a fortiori* have refuted hedonistic utilitarianism.

When a plain man fulfills a promise because he thinks he ought to do so, it seems clear that he does so with no thought of its total consequences, still less with any opinion that these are likely to be the best possible. He thinks in fact much more of the past than of the future. What makes him think it right to act in a certain way is the fact that he has promised to do so— that and, usually, nothing more. That his act will produce the best possible consequences is not his reason for calling it right. What lends colour to the theory we are examining, then, is not the actions (which form probably a great majority of our actions) in which some such reflection as 'I have promised' is the only reason we give ourselves for thinking a certain action

right, but the exceptional cases in which the consequences of fulfilling a promise (for instance) would be so disastrous to others that we judge it right not to do so. It must of course be admitted that such cases exist. If I have promised to meet a friend at a particular time for some trivial purpose, I should certainly think myself justified in breaking my engagement if by doing so I could prevent a serious accident or bring relief to the victims of one. And the supporters of the view we are examining hold that my thinking so is due to my thinking that I shall bring more good into existence by the one action than by the other. A different account may, however, be given of the matter, an account which will, I believe, show itself to be the true one. It may be said that besides the duty of fulfilling promises I have and recognize a duty of relieving distress,[2] and that when I think it right to do the latter at the cost of not doing the former, it is not because I think I shall produce more good thereby but because I think it the duty which is in the circumstances more of a duty. This account surely corresponds much more closely with what we really think in such a situation. If, so far as I can see, I could bring equal amounts of good into being by fulfilling my promise and by helping someone to whom I had made no promise, I should not hesitate to regard the former as my duty. Yet on the view that what is right is right because it is productive of the most good I should not so regard it.

There are two theories, each in its way simple, that offer a solution of such cases of conscience. One is the view of Kant, that there are certain duties of perfect obligation, such as those of fulfilling promises, of paying debts, of telling the truth, which admit of no exception whatever in favour of duties of imperfect obligation, such as that of relieving distress. The other is the view of, for instance, Professor Moore and Dr. Rashdall, that there is only the duty of producing good, and that all 'conflicts of duties' should be resolved by asking 'by which action will most good be produced?' But it is more important that our theory fit the facts than that it be simple, and the account we have given above corresponds (it seems to me) better than either of the simpler theories with what we really think, viz. that normally promise-keeping, for example, should come before benevolence, but that when and only when the good to be produced by the benevolent act is very great and the promise comparatively trivial, the act of benevolence becomes our duty.

In fact the theory of 'ideal utilitarianism', if I may for brevity refer so to the theory of Professor Moore, seems to simplify unduly our relations to our fellows. It says, in effect, that the only morally significant relation in which my neighbours stand to me is that of being possible beneficiaries by my action.[3] They do stand in this relation to me, and this relation is morally significant. But they may also stand to me in the relation of promisee to promiser, or creditor to debtor, of wife to husband, of child to parent, of friend to friend, of fellow countryman to fellow countryman, and the like; and each of these relations is the foundation of a *prima facie* duty, which is more or less incumbent on me according to the circumstances of the case. When I am in a situation, as perhaps I always am, in which more than one of these *prima facie* duties is incumbent on me, what I have to do is to study the situation as fully as I can until I form the considered opinion (it is never more) that in the circumstances one of them is more incumbent than any other; then I am bound to think that to do this *prima facie* duty is my duty *sans phrase* in the situation.

I suggest '*prima facie* duty' or 'conditional duty' as a brief way of referring to the characteristic (quite distinct from that of being a duty proper) which an act has, in virtue of being of a certain kind (e.g. the keeping of a promise), of being an act which would be a duty proper if it were not at the same time of another kind which is morally significant. Whether an act is a duty proper or actual duty depends on *all* the morally significant kinds it is an instance of. The phrase '*prima facie* duty' must be apologized for, since (1) it suggests that what we are speaking of is a certain kind of duty, whereas it is in fact not a duty, but something related in a special way to duty. Strictly speaking, we want not a phrase in which duty is qualified by an adjective, but a separate noun. (2) '*Prima' facie* suggests that one is speaking only of an appearance which a moral situation presents at first sight, and which may turn out to be illusory; whereas what I am speaking of is an objective fact involved in the nature of the situation, or more strictly in an element of its nature, though not, as duty proper does, arising from its *whole* nature. I can, however, think of no term which fully meets the case. . . .

There is nothing arbitrary about these *prima facie* duties. Each rests on a definite circumstance which cannot seriously be held to be without moral significance. Of *prima facie* duties I suggest, without claiming completeness or finality for it, the following division.[4]

(1) Some duties rest on previous acts of my own. These duties seem to include two kinds, (a) those resting on a promise or what may fairly be called an implicit promise, such as the implicit undertaking not to tell lies which seems to be implied in the act of entering into conversation (at any rate by civilized men), or of writing books that purport to be history and not fiction. These may be called the duties of fidelity. (b) Those resting on a previous wrongful act. These may be called the duties of reparation. (2) Some rest on previous acts of other men, i.e. services done by them to me. These may be loosely described as the duties of gratitude. (3) Some rest on the fact or possibility of a distribution of pleasure or happiness (or of the means thereto) which is not in accordance with the merit of the persons concerned; in such cases there arises a duty to upset or prevent such a distribution. These are the duties of justice. (4) Some rest on the mere fact that there are other beings in the world whose condition we can make better in respect of virtue, or of intelligence, or of pleasure. These are the duties of beneficence. (5) Some rest on the fact that we can improve our own condition in respect of virtue or of intelligence. These are the duties of self-improvement. (6) I think that we should distinguish from (4) the duties that may be summed up under the title of 'not injuring others'. No doubt to injure others is incidentally to fail to do them good; but it seems to me clear that nonmaleficence is apprehended as a duty distinct from that of beneficence, and as a duty of a more stringent character. It will be noticed that this alone among the types of duty has been stated in a negative way. An attempt might no doubt be made to state this duty, like the others, in a

positive way. It might be said that it is really the duty to prevent ourselves from acting either from an inclination to harm others or from an inclination to seek our own pleasure, in doing which we should incidentally harm them. But on reflection it seems clear that the primary duty here is the duty not to harm others, this being a duty whether or not we have an inclination that if followed would lead to our harming them; and that when we have such an inclination the primary duty not to harm others gives rise to a consequential duty to resist the inclination. The recognition of this duty of non-maleficence is the first step on the way to the recognition of the duty of beneficence; and that accounts for the prominence of the commands 'thou shalt not kill', 'thou shalt not commit adultery', 'thou shalt not steal', 'thou shalt not bear false witness', in so early a code as the Decalogue. But even when we have come to recognize the duty of beneficence, it appears to me that the duty of non-maleficence is recognized as a distinct one, and as *prima facie* more binding. We should not in general consider it justifiable to kill one person in order to keep another alive, or to steal from one in order to give alms to another.

The essential defect of the 'ideal utilitarian' theory is that it ignores, or at least does not do full justice to, the highly personal character of duty. If the only duty is to produce the maximum of good, the question who is to have the good—whether it is myself, or my benefactor, or a person to whom I have made a promise to confer that good on him, or a mere fellow man to whom I stand in no such special relation—should make no difference to my having a duty to produce that good. But we are all in fact sure that it makes a vast difference.

One or two other comments must be made on this provisional list of the divisions of duty. (1) The nomenclature is not strictly correct. For by 'fidelity' or 'gratitude' we mean, strictly, certain states of motivation; and, as I have urged, it is not our duty to have certain motives, but to do certain acts. By 'fidelity', for instance, is meant, strictly, the disposition to fulfill promises and implicit promises *because we have made them*. We have no general word to cover the actual fulfillment of promises and implicit promises *irrespective of motive*; and I use 'fidel-

ity', loosely but perhaps conveniently, to fill this gap. So too I use 'gratitude' for the returning of services, irrespective of motive. The term 'justice' is not so much confined, in ordinary usage, to a certain state of motivation, for we should often talk of a man as acting justly even when we did not think his motive was the wish to do what was just simply for the sake of doing so. Less apology is therefore needed for our use of 'justice' in this sense. And I have used the word 'beneficence' rather than 'benevolence', in order to emphasize the fact that it is our duty to do certain things, and not to do them from certain motives.

(2) If the objection be made, that this catalogue of the main types of duty is an unsystematic one resting on no logical principle, it may be replied, first, that it makes no claim to being ultimate. It is a *prima facie* classification of the duties which reflection on our moral convictions seems actually to reveal. And if these convictions are, as I would claim that they are, of the nature of knowledge, and if I have not misstated them, the list will be a list of authentic conditional duties, correct as far as it goes though not necessarily complete. The list of *goods* put forward by the rival theory is reached by exactly the same method—the only sound one in the circumstances—viz. that of direct reflection on what we really think. Loyalty to the facts is worth more than a symmetrical architectonic or a hastily reached simplicity. If further reflection discovers a perfect logical basis for this or for a better classification, so much the better.

(3) It may, again, be objected that our theory that there are these various and often conflicting types of *prima facie* duty leaves us with no principle upon which to discern what is our actual duty in particular circumstances. But this objection is not one which the rival theory is in a position to bring forward. For when we have to choose between the production of two heterogeneous goods, say knowledge and pleasure, the 'ideal utilitarian' theory can only fall back on an opinion, for which no logical basis can be offered, that one of the goods is the greater; and this is no better than a similar opinion that one of two duties is the more urgent. And again, when we consider the infinite variety of the ef-

fects of our actions in the way of pleasure, it must surely be admitted that the claim which *hedonism* sometimes makes, that it offers a readily applicable criterion of right conduct, is quite illusory.

I am unwilling, however, to content myself with an **argumentum ad hominem,** and I would contend that in principle there is no reason to anticipate that every act that is our duty is so for one and the same reason. Why should two sets of circumstances, or one set of circumstances, *not* possess different characteristics, any one of which makes a certain act our *prima facie* duty? When I ask what it is that makes me in certain cases sure that I have a *prima facie* duty to do so and so, I find that it lies in the fact that I have made a promise; when I ask the same question in another case, I find the answer lies in the fact that I have done a wrong. And if on reflection I find (as I think I do) that neither of these reasons is reducible to the other, I must not on any a *priori* ground assume that such a reduction is possible. . . .

Something should be said of the relation between our apprehension of the *prima facie* rightness of certain types of act and our mental attitude towards particular acts. It is proper to use the word 'apprehension' in the former case and not in the latter. That an act, *qua* fulfilling a promise, or *qua* effecting a just distribution of good, or *qua* returning services rendered, or *qua* promoting the good of others, or *qua* promoting the virtue or insight of the agent, is *prima facie* right, is self-evident; not in the sense that it is evident from the beginning of our lives, or as soon as we attend to the proposition for the first time, but in the sense that when we have reached sufficient mental maturity and have given sufficient attention to the proposition it is evident without any need of proof, or of evidence beyond itself. It is self-evident just as a mathematical axiom, or the validity of a form of inference, is evident. The moral order expressed in these propositions is just as much part of the fundamental nature of the universe (and, we may add, of any possible universe in which there were moral agents at all) as is the spatial or numerical structure expressed in the axioms of geometry or arithmetic. In our confidence that these propositions are true there is involved

the same trust in our reason that is involved in our confidence in mathematics; and we should have no justification for trusting it in the latter sphere and distrusting it in the former. In both cases we are dealing with propositions that cannot be proved, but that just as certainly need no proof. . . .

The general principles of duty are obviously not self-evident from the beginning of our lives. How do they come to be so? The answer is, that they come to be self-evident to us just as mathematical axioms do. We find by experience that this couple of matches and that couple make four matches, that this couple of balls on a wire and that couple make four balls: and by reflection on these and similar discoveries we come to see that it is of the nature of two and two to make four. In a precisely similar way, we see the *prima facie* rightness of an act which would be the fulfilment of a particular promise, and of another which would be the fulfilment of another promise, and when we have reached sufficient maturity to think in general terms, we apprehend *prima facie* rightness to belong to the nature of any fulfilment of promise. What comes first in time is the apprehension of the self-evident *prima facie* rightness of an individual act of a particular type. From this we come by reflection to apprehend the self-evident general principle of *prima facie* duty. . . .

In what has preceded, a good deal of use has been made of 'what we really think' about moral questions; a certain theory has been rejected because it does not agree with what we really think. It might be said that this is in principle wrong; that we should not be content to expound what our present moral consciousness tells us but should aim at a criticism of our existing moral consciousness in the light of theory. Now I do not doubt that the moral consciousness of men has in detail undergone a good deal of modification as regards the things we think right, at the hands of moral theory. But if we are told, for instance, that we should give up our view that there is a special obligatoriness attaching to the keeping of promises because it is self-evident that the only duty is to produce as much good as possible, we have to ask ourselves whether we really, when we reflect, *are* convinced that this is self-evident, and whether we really *can* get rid of our view that promise-keeping has a binding-ness independent of productiveness of maximum good. In my own experience I find that I cannot, in spite of a very genuine attempt to do so; and I venture to think that most people will find the same, and that just because they cannot lose the sense of special obligation, they cannot accept as self-evident, or even as true, the theory which would require them to do so. In fact it seems, on reflection, self-evident that a promise, simply as such, is something that *prima facie* ought to be kept, and it does *not,* on reflection, seem self-evident that production of maximum good is the only thing that makes an act obligatory. And to ask us to give up at the bidding of a theory our actual apprehension of what is right and what is wrong seems like asking people to repudiate their actual experience of beauty, at the bidding of a theory which says 'only that which satisfies such and such conditions can be beautiful'. If what I have called our actual apprehension is (as I would maintain that it is) truly an apprehension, i.e. an instance of knowledge, the request is nothing less than absurd.

I would maintain, in fact, that what we are apt to describe as 'what we think' about moral questions contains a considerable amount that we do not think but know, and that this forms the standard by reference to which the truth of any moral theory has to be tested, instead of having itself to be tested by reference to any theory. I hope that I have in what precedes indicated what in my view these elements of knowledge are that are involved in our ordinary moral consciousness.

It would be a mistake to found a natural science on 'what we really think', i.e. on what reasonably thoughtful and well-educated people think about the subjects of the science before they have studied them scientifically. For such opinions are interpretations, and often misinterpretations, of sense-experience; and the man of science must appeal from these to sense-experience itself, which furnishes his real data. In ethics no such appeal is possible. We have no more direct way of access to the facts about rightness and goodness and about what things are right or good, than by thinking about them; the moral convictions of thoughtful and well-educated people are the data of ethics just as

sense-perceptions are the data of a natural science. Just as some of the latter have to be rejected as illusory, so have some of the former; but as the latter are rejected only when they are in conflict with other more accurate sense-perceptions, the former are rejected only when they are in conflict with other convictions which stand better the test of reflection. The existing body of moral convictions of the best people is the cumulative product of the moral reflection of many generations, which has developed an extremely delicate power of appreciation of moral distinctions; and this the theorist cannot afford to treat with anything other than the greatest respect. The verdicts of the moral consciousness of the best people are the foundation on which he must build; though he must first compare them with one another and eliminate any contradictions they may contain. . . .

Endnotes

1. I take the theory which, as I have tried to show, seems to be put forward in *Ethics* rather than the earlier and less plausible theory put forward in *Principia Ethica*. . . .
2. These are not strictly speaking duties, but things that tend to be our duty, or *prima facie* duties.
3. Some will think it, apart from other considerations, a sufficient refutation of this view to point out that I also stand in that relation to myself, so that for this view the distinction of oneself from others is morally insignificant.
4. I should make it plain at this stage that I am *assuming* the correctness of some of our main convictions as to *prima facie* duties, or, more strictly, am claiming that we *know* them to be true. To me it seems as self-evident as anything could be, that to make a promise, for instance, is to create a moral claim on us in someone else. Many readers will perhaps say that they do *not* know this to be true. If so, I certainly cannot prove it to them; I can only ask them to reflect again, in the hope that they will ultimately agree that they also know it to be true. The main moral convictions of the plain man seem to me to be, not opinions which it is for philosophy to prove or disprove, but knowledge from the start; and in my own case I seem to find little difficulty in distinguishing these essential convictions from other moral convictions which I also have, which are merely fallible opinions based on an imperfect study of the working for good or evil or certain institutions or types of action.

REVIEW QUESTIONS

1. Distinguish between Egoism, Hedonistic Utilitarianism, and Ideal Utilitarianism.

2. What criticism does Ross make of Utilitarianism?
3. Distinguish between prima facie duty and actual duty or duty proper.
4. Describe the different types of duty.

2. Is his theory compatible with Kant's theory?
3. Are all the different types of duty equally compelling or are some more important than others?
4. Can you think of any general principles of duty that are really self-evident, as self-evident as axioms in mathematics?

DISCUSSION QUESTIONS

1. Has Ross refuted Utilitarianism or not?

Bernard Mayo

Virtue and Moral Theory

Bernard Mayo is a British philosopher and the author of Ethics and the Moral Life *(1958), from which the reading is taken.*

Mayo claims that Plato and Aristotle give us a theory about what to be rather than what to do, an ethics of Virtue rather than a Kantian ethics of Duty. According to Mayo, this ethics of Virtue advocates a unity of character exemplified by ideal persons, saints, and heroes.

The philosophy of moral principles, which is characteristic of Kant and the post-Kantian era, is something of which hardly a trace exists in Plato. . . . Plato says nothing about rules or principles or laws, except when he is talking politics. Instead he talks about virtues and vices, and about certain types of human character. The key word in Platonic ethics is Virtue; the key word in Kantian ethics is Duty. And modern ethics is a set of footnotes, not to Plato, but to Kant. . . .

Attention to the novelists can be a welcome correction to a tendency of philosophical ethics of the last generation or two to lose contact with

From Bernard Mayo, *Ethics and the Moral Life* (Macmillan Press Ltd., 1958), Copyright © by Bernard Mayo, 1958. Reprinted by permission of Macmillan Press Ltd.

the ordinary life of man which is just what the novelists, in their own way, are concerned with. Of course there are writers who can be called in to illustrate problems about Duty (Graham Greene is a good example). but there are more who perhaps never mention the words duty, obligation, or principle. Yet they are all concerned—Jane Austen, for instance, entirely and absolutely—with the moral qualities or defects of their heroes and heroines and other characters. This points to a radical one-sidedness in the philosophers' account of morality in terms of principles: it takes little or no account of qualities, of what people *are*. It is just here that the old-fashioned word Virtue used to have a place; and it is just here that the work of Plato and Aristotle can be instructive. Justice, for Plato, though it is closely connected with acting according to law, does not *mean* acting according to law: it is a quality of character, and a just action is one such as a just man would do. Telling the truth, for Aristotle, is not, as it was for Kant, fulfilling an obligation; again it is a quality of character, or, rather, a whole range of qualities of character, some of which may actually be defects, such as tactlessness, boastfulness, and so on—a point which can be brought out, in terms of principles, only with the greatest complexity and artificiality, but quite simply and naturally in terms of character.

If we wish to enquire about Aristotle's moral views, it is no use looking for a set of principles. Of course we can find *some* principles to which he must have subscribed—for instance, that one ought not to commit adultery. But what we find much more prominently is a set of character-traits, a list of certain types of person—the courageous man, the niggardly man, the boaster, the lavish spender, and so on. The basic moral question, for Aristotle, is not, What shall I do? but, What shall I be?

These contrasts between doing and being, negative and positive, and modern as against Greek morality were noted by John Stuart Mill; I quote from the *Essay on Liberty*:

Christian morality (so-called) has all the characters of a reaction; it is, in great part, a protest against Paganism. Its ideal is negative rather than positive, passive rather than active; Innocence rather than Nobleness; Abstinence from Evil, rather than energetic Pursuit of the Good; in its precepts (as has been well said) "Thou shalt not" predominates unduly over "Thou shalt . . ." Whatever exists of magnanimity, highmindedness, personal dignity, even the sense of honour, is derived from the purely human, not the religious part of our education, and never could have grown out of a standard of ethics in which the only worth, professedly recognized, is that of obedience.

Of course, there are connections between being and doing. It is obvious that a man cannot just *be*; he can only be what he is by doing what he does; his moral qualities are ascribed to him because of his actions, which are said to manifest those qualities. But the point is that an ethics of Being must include this obvious fact, that Being involves Doing; whereas an ethics of Doing, such as I have been examining, may easily overlook it. As I have suggested, a morality of principles is concerned only with what people do or fail to do, since that is what rules are for. And as far as this sort of ethics goes, people might well have no moral qualities at all except the possession of principles and the will (and capacity) to act accordingly.

When we speak of a moral quality such as courage, and say that a certain action was courageous, we are not merely saying something about the action. We are referring, not so much to what is done, as to the kind of person by whom we take it to have been done. We connect, by means of imputed motives and intentions, with the character of the agent as courageous. This explains, incidentally, why both Kantians and Utilitarians encounter, in their different

ways, such difficulties in dealing with motives, which their principles, on the face of it, have no room for. A Utilitarian, for example, can only praise a courageous action in some such way as this: the action is of a sort such as a person of courage is likely to perform, and courage is a quality of character the cultivation of which is likely to increase rather than diminish the sum total of human happiness. But Aristotelians have no need of such circumlocution. For them a courageous action just is one which proceeds from and manifests a certain type of character, and is praised because such a character trait is good, or better than others, or is a virtue. An evaluative criterion is sufficient: there is no need to look for an imperative criterion as well, or rather instead, according to which it is not the character which is good, but the cultivation of the character which is right. . . .

No doubt the fundamental moral question is just "What ought I to do?" And according to the philosophy of moral principles, the answer (which must be an imperative "Do this") must be derived from a conjunction of premises consisting (in the simplest case) firstly of a rule, or universal imperative, enjoining (or forbidding) all actions of a certain type in situations of a certain type, and, secondly, a statement to the effect that this is a situation of that type, falling under that rule. In practice the emphasis may be on supplying only one of these premises, the other being assumed or taken for granted: one may answer the question "What ought I to do?" either by quoting a rule which I am to adopt, or by showing that my case is legislated for by a rule which I do adopt. . . . [I]f I am in doubt whether to tell the truth about his condition to a dying man, my doubt may be resolved by showing that the case comes under a rule about the avoidance of unnecessary suffering, which I am assumed to accept. But if the case is without precedent in my moral career, my problem may be soluble only by adopting a new principle about what I am to do now and in the future about cases of this kind.

This second possibility offers a connection with moral ideas. Suppose my perplexity is not merely an unprecedented situation which I could cope with by adopting a new rule. Suppose the new rule is thoroughly inconsistent with my existing moral code. This may happen, for instance, if the moral code is one to which I only pay lip-service, if . . . its authority is not yet internalised, or if it has ceased to be so; it is ready for rejection, but its final rejection awaits a moral crisis such as we are assuming to occur. What I now need is not a rule for deciding how to act in this situation and others of its kind. I need a whole set of rules, a complete morality, new principles to live by.

Now, according to the philosophy of moral character, there is another way of answering the fundamental question "What ought I to do?" Instead of quoting a rule, we quote a quality of character, a virtue: we say "Be brave," or "Be patient" or "Be lenient." We may even say "Be a man": if I am in doubt, say, whether to take a risk, and someone says "Be a man," meaning a morally sound man, in this case a man of sufficient courage. (Compare the very different ideal invoked in "Be a gentleman." I shall not discuss whether this is a *moral* ideal.) Here, too, we have the extreme cases, where a man's moral perplexity extends not merely to a particular situation but to his whole way of living. And now the question "What ought I to do?" turns into the question "What ought I to be?"—as, indeed, it was treated in the first place. ("Be brave.") It is answered, not by quoting a rule or a set of rules, but by describing a quality of character or a type of person. And here the ethics of character gains a practical simplicity which offsets the greater logical simplicity of the ethics of principles. We do not have to give a list of characteristics or virtues, as we might list a set of principles. We can give a unity to our answer.

Of course we can in theory give a unity to our principles: this is implied by speaking of a *set* of principles. But if such a set is to be a system and not merely aggregate, the unity we are looking for is a logical one, namely the possibility that some principles are deductible from others, and ultimately from one. But the attempt to construct a deductive moral system is notoriously difficult, and in any case ill-founded. Why should we expect that all rules of conduct should be ultimately reducible to a few?

SAINTS AND HEROES

But when we are asked "What shall I be?" we can readily give a unity to our answer, though not a logical unity. It is the unity of character. A person's character is not merely a list of dispositions; it has the organic unity of something that is more than the sum of its parts. And we can say, in answer to our morally perplexed questioner, not only "Be this" and "Be that," but also "Be like So-and-So"—where So-and-So is either an ideal type of character, or else an actual person taken as representative of the ideal, as exemplar. Examples of the first are Plato's "just man" in the Republic; Aristotle's man of practical wisdom, in the *Nicomachean Ethics;* Augustine's citizen of the City of God; the good Communist; the American way of life (which is a collective expression for a type of character). Examples of the second kind, the exemplar, are Socrates, Christ, Buddha, St. Francis, the heroes of epic writers and of novelists. Indeed the idea of the Hero, as well as the idea of the Saint, are very much the expression of this attitude to morality. Heroes and saints are not merely people who did things. They are people whom we are expected, and expect ourselves, to imitate. And imitating them means not merely doing what they did; it means being like them. Their status is not in the least like that of legislators whose laws we admire; for the character of a legislator is irrelevant to our judgment about his legislation. The heroes and saints did not merely give us principles to live by (though some of them did that as well): they gave us examples to follow.

Kant, as we should expect, emphatically rejects this attitude as "fatal to morality." According to him, examples serve only to render *visible* an instance of the moral principle, and thereby to demonstrate its practical feasibility. But every exemplar, such as Christ himself, must be judged by the independent criterion of the moral law, before we are entitled to recognize him as worthy of imitation. I am not suggesting that the subordination of exemplars to principles is incorrect, but that it is one-sided and fails to do justice to a large area of moral experience.

Imitation can be more or less successful. And this suggests another defect of the ethics of principles. It has no room for ideals, except the ideal of a perfect set of principles (which, as a matter of fact, is intelligible only in terms of an ideal character or way of life), and the ideal of perfect conscientiousness (which is itself a character-trait). This results, of course, from the "black-or-white" nature of moral verdicts based on rules. There are no degrees by which we approach or recede from the attainment of a certain quality or virtue; if there were not, the word "ideal" would have no meaning. Heroes and saints are not people whom we try to be *just* like, since we know that is impossible. It is precisely because it is impossible for ordinary human beings to achieve the same qualities as the saints, and in the same degree, that we do set them apart from the rest of humanity. It is enough if we try to be a little like them. . . .

REVIEW QUESTIONS

1. Distinguish between the ethics of Duty and the ethics of Virtue. Which philosophers have which kind of ethics?
2. How does Mill characterize Christian morality?
3. What is the relation between Being and Doing on Mayo's view?
4. According to Mayo, what makes a person a saint or hero?

DISCUSSION QUESTIONS

1. Is Mill's account of Christian morality accurate?
2. Is the courage of an evil person still a virtue?
3. Is unity of character always morally good? Why or why not?

Aristotle

Happiness and Virtue

Aristotle (384–322 B.C.) made important contributions to all areas of philosophy, including the formulation of traditional logic. Along with his teacher Plato, he is regarded as one of the founders of western philosophy.

Aristotle argues that all human beings seek happiness, and that happiness is not pleasure, honor, or wealth, but an activity of the soul in accordance with virtue. Virtue is of two kinds: moral and intellectual. Moral virtue comes from training and habit, and generally is a state of character that is a mean between the vices of excess and deficiency. For example, Aristotle portrays the virtue of courage as a mean between the extremes of rashness (an excess) and cowardice (a deficiency). Intellec-

tual virtue produces the most perfect happiness and is found in the activity of reason or contemplation.

Our discussion will be adequate if it has as much clearness as the subject-matter admits of, for precision is not to be sought for alike in all discussions, any more than in all the products of the crafts. Now fine and just actions, which political science investigates, admit of much variety and fluctuation of opinion, so that they may be thought to exist only by convention, and not by nature. And goods also give rise to a similar fluctuation because they bring harm to many people; for before now men have been undone by reason of their wealth, and others by reason of their courage. We must be content, then, in speaking of such subjects and with such premises to indicate the truth roughly and in outline, and in speaking about things which are only for the most part true and with premises of the same kind to reach conclusions that are no better. In the same spirit, therefore, should each type of statement be received; for it is the mark of an educated man to look for precision in each class of things just so far as the nature of the subject admits; it is evidently equally foolish to accept probable reasoning from a

Aristotle, *Happiness and Virtue,* Books I: 3–5, 7–9, 13; II: 1, 6, 7, 9; and X: 7, 8 from *Ethica Nicomachea* trans. by W. D. Ross in *The Oxford Translation of Aristotle,* vol. 9 (Oxford: Oxford University Press, 1925). Reprinted by permission of Oxford University Press.

mathematician and to demand from a rhetorician scientific proofs.

Now each man judges well the things he knows, and of these he is a good judge. And so the man who has been educated in a subject is a good judge of that subject, and the man who has received an all-round education is a good judge in general. Hence a young man is not a proper hearer of lectures on political science; for he is inexperienced in the actions that occur in life, but its discussions start from these and are about these; and, further, since he tends to follow his passions, his study will be vain and unprofitable, because the end aimed at is not knowledge but action. And it makes no difference whether he is young in years or youthful in character; the defect does not depend on time, but on his living, and pursuing each successive object, as passion directs. For to such persons, as to the incontinent, knowledge brings no profit; but to those who desire and act in accordance with a rational principle knowledge about such matters will be of great benefit.

These remarks about the student, the sort of treatment to be expected, and the purpose of the inquiry, may be taken as our preface.

Let us resume our inquiry and state, in view of the fact that all knowledge and every pursuit aims at some good, what it is that we say political science aims at and what is the highest of all goods achievable by action. Verbally there is very general agreement; for both the general run of men and people of superior refinement say that it is happiness, and identify living well and doing well with being happy; but with regard to what happiness is they differ, and the many do not give the same account as the wise. For the former think it is some plain and obvious thing, like pleasure, wealth, or honour; they differ, however, from one another—and often even the same man identifies it with different things, with health when he is ill, with wealth when he is poor; but, conscious of their ignorance, they admire those who proclaim some great ideal that is above their comprehension. Now some thought that apart from these many goods there is another which is self-subsistent and causes the goodness of all these as well. To examine all the opinions that have been held were perhaps somewhat fruitless; enough to examine those

that are most prevalent or that seem to be arguable. . . .

Let us, however, resume our discussion from the point at which we digressed. To judge from the lives that men lead, most men, and men of the most vulgar type, seem (not without some ground) to identify the good, or happiness, with pleasure; which is the reason why they love the life of enjoyment. For there are, we may say, three prominent types of life—that just mentioned, the political, and thirdly the contemplative life. Now the mass of mankind are evidently quite slavish in their tastes, preferring a life suitable to beasts, but they get some ground for their view from the fact that many of those in high places share the tastes of Sardanapallus. A consideration of the prominent types of life shows that people of superior refinement and of active disposition identify happiness with honour; for this is, roughly speaking, the end of the political life. But it seems too superficial to be what we are looking for, since it is thought to depend on those who bestow honour rather than on him who receives it, but the good we divine to be something proper to a man and not easily taken from him. Further, men seem to pursue honour in order that they may be assured of their goodness; at least it is by men of practical wisdom that they seek to be honoured, and among those who know them, and on the ground of their virtue; clearly, then, according to them, at any rate, virtue is better. And perhaps one might even suppose this to be, rather than honour, the end of the political life. But even this appears somewhat incomplete; for possession of virtue seems actually compatible with being asleep, or with life-long inactivity, and, further, with the greatest sufferings and misfortunes; but a man who was living so no one would call happy, unless he were maintaining a thesis at all costs. But enough of this; for the subject has been sufficiently treated even in the current discussions. Third comes the contemplative life, which we shall consider later.

The life of money-making is one undertaken under compulsion, and wealth is evidently not the good we are seeking; for it is merely useful and for the sake of something else. And so one might rather take the aforenamed objects to be ends; for they are loved for themselves. But it is evident that not even these are ends; yet many arguments have been thrown away in support of them. . . .

Let us again return to the good we are seeking, and ask what it can be. It seems different in different actions and arts; it is different in medicine, in strategy, and in the other arts likewise. What then is the good of each? Surely that for whose sake everything else is done. In medicine this is health, in strategy victory, in architecture a house, in any other sphere something else, and in every action and pursuit the end; for it is for the sake of this that all men do whatever else they do. Therefore, if there is an end for all that we do, this will be the good achievable by action, and if there are more than one, these will be the goods achievable by action.

So the argument has by a different course reached the same point; but we must try to state this even more clearly. Since there are evidently more than one end, and we choose some of these (e.g. wealth, flutes, and in general instruments) for the sake of something else, clearly not all ends are final ends; but the chief good is evidently something final. Therefore, if there is only one final end, this will be what we are seeking, and if there are more than one, the most final of these will be what we are seeking. Now we call that which is in itself worthy of pursuit more final than that which is worthy of pursuit for the sake of something else, and that which is never desirable for the sake of something else more final than the things that are desirable both in themselves and for the sake of that other thing, and therefore we call final without qualification that which is always desirable in itself and never for the sake of something else.

Now such a thing happiness, above all else, is held to be; for this we choose always for itself and never for the sake of something else, but honour, pleasure, reason, and every virtue we choose indeed for themselves (for if nothing resulted from them we should still choose each of them), but we choose them also for the sake of happiness, judging that by means of them we shall be happy. Happiness, on the other hand, no one chooses for the sake of these, nor, in general, for anything other than itself. . . .

Presumably, however, to say that happiness is the chief good seems a platitude, and a clearer account of what it is is still desired. This might perhaps be given, if we could first ascertain the function of man. For just as for a fluteplayer, a sculptor, or any artist, and, in general, for all things that have a function or activity, the good and the 'well' is thought to reside in the function, so would it seem to be for man, if he has a function. Have the carpenter, then, and the tanner certain functions or activities, and has man none? Is he born without a function? Or as eye, hand, foot, and in general each of the parts evidently has a function, may one lay it down that man similarly has a function apart from all these? What then can this be? Life seems to be common even to plants, but we are seeking what is peculiar to man. Let us exclude, therefore, the life of nutrition and growth. Next there would be a life of perception, but *it* also seems to be common even to the horse, the ox, and every animal. There remains, then, an active life of the element that has a rational principle; of this, one part has such a principle in the sense of being obedient to one, the other in the sense of possessing one and exercising thought. And, as 'life of the rational element' also has two meanings, we must state that life in the sense of activity is what we mean; for this seems to be the more proper sense of the term. Now if the function of man is an activity of soul which follows or implies a rational principle, and if we say 'a so-and-so' and 'a good so-and-so' have a function which is the same in kind, e. g. a lyre-player and a good lyre-player, and so without qualification in all cases, eminence in respect of goodness being added to the name of the function (for the function of a lyre-player is to play the lyre, and that of a good lyre-player is to do so well): if this is the case, [and we state the function of man to be a certain kind of life, and this to be an activity or actions of the soul implying a rational principle, and the function of a good man to be the good and noble performance of these, and if any action is well performed when it is performed in accordance with the appropriate excellence: if this is the case,] human good turns out to be activity of soul in accordance with virtue, and if there are more than one virtue, in accordance with the best and most complete.

But we must add 'in a complete life.' For one swallow does not make a summer, nor does one day; and so too one day, or a short time, does not make a man blessed and happy. . . .

We must consider it, however, in the light not only of our conclusion and our premises, but also of what is commonly said about it; for with a true view all the data harmonize, but with a false one the facts soon clash. Now goods have been divided into three classes, and some are described as external, others as relating to soul or to body; we call those that relate to soul most properly and truly goods, and psychical actions and activities we class as relating to soul. Therefore our account must be sound, at least according to this view, which is an old one and agreed on by philosophers. It is correct also in that we identify the end with certain actions and activities; for thus it falls among goods of the soul and not among external goods. Another belief which harmonizes with our account is that the happy man lives well and does well; for we have practically defined happiness as a sort of good life and good action. The characteristics that are looked for in happiness seem also, all of them, to belong to what we have defined happiness as being. For some identify happiness with virtue, some with practical wisdom, others with a kind of philosophic wisdom, others with these, or one of these, accompanied by pleasure or not without pleasure; while others include also external prosperity. Now some of these views have been held by many men and men of old, others by a few eminent persons; and it is not probable that either of these should be entirely mistaken, but rather that they should be right in at least some one respect or even in most respects.

With those who identify happiness with virtue or some one virtue our account is in harmony; for to virtue belongs virtuous activity. But it makes, perhaps, no small difference whether we place the chief good in possession or in use, in state of mind or in activity. For the state of mind may exist without producing any good result, as in a man who is asleep or in some other way quite inactive, but the activity cannot; for one who has the activity will of necessity be acting, and acting well. And as in the Olympic Games it is not the most beautiful and the strongest that are crowned but those who compete (for it is some of these that are victorious), so those who act win, and rightly win, the noble and good things in life.

Their life is also in itself pleasant. For pleasure is a state of *soul,* and to each man that which he is said to be a lover of is pleasant; e. g. not only is a horse pleasant to the lover of horses, and a spectacle to the lover of sights, but also in the same way just acts are pleasant to the lover of justice and in general virtuous acts to the lover of virtue. Now for most men their pleasures are in conflict with one another because these are not by nature pleasant, but the lovers of what is noble find pleasant the things that are by nature pleasant; and virtuous actions are such, so that these are pleasant for such men as well as in their own nature. Their life, therefore, has no further need of pleasure as a sort of adventitious charm, but has its pleasure in itself. For, besides what we have said, the man who does not rejoice in noble actions is not even good; since no one would call a man just who did not enjoy acting justly, nor any man liberal who did not enjoy liberal actions; and similarly in all other cases. If this is so, virtuous actions must be in themselves pleasant. But they are also *good* and *noble,* and have each of these attributes in the highest degree, since the good man judges well about these attributes; his judgment is such as we have described. Happiness then is the best, noblest, and most pleasant thing in the world. . . .

Yet evidently, as we said, it needs the external goods as well; for it is impossible, or not easy, to do noble acts without the proper equipment. In many actions we use friends and riches and political power as instruments; and there are some things the lack of which takes the lustre from happiness, as good birth, goodly children, beauty; for the man who is very ugly in appearance or ill-born or solitary and childless is not very likely to be happy, and perhaps a man would be still less likely if he had thoroughly bad children or friends or had lost good children or friends by death. As we said, then, happiness seems to need this sort of prosperity in addition; for which reason some identify happiness with good fortune, though others identify it with virtue.

For this reason also the question is asked, whether happiness is to be acquired by learning or by habituation or some other sort of training, or comes in virtue of some divine providence or again by chance. Now if there is *any* gift of the gods to men, it is reasonable that happiness should be god-given, and most surely god-given of all human things inasmuch as it is the best. But this question would perhaps be more appropriate to another inquiry; happiness seems, however, even if it is not god-sent but comes as a result of virtue and some process of learning or training, to be among the most god-like things; for that which is the prize and end of virtue seems to be the best thing in the world, and something godlike and blessed.

It will also on this view be very generally shared; for all who are not maimed as regards their potentiality for virtue may win it by a certain kind of study and care. But if it is better to be happy thus than by chance, it is reasonable that the facts should be so, since everything that depends on the action of nature is by nature as good as it can be, and similarly everything that depends on art or any rational cause, and especially if it depends on the best of all causes. To entrust to chance what is greatest and most noble would be a very defective arrangement.

The answer to the question we are asking is plain also from the definition of happiness; for it has been said to be a virtuous activity of soul, of a certain kind. Of the remaining goods, some must necessarily pre-exist as conditions of happiness, and others are naturally co-operative and useful as instruments. And this will be found to agree with what we said at the outset; for we stated the end of political science to be the best end, and political science spends most of its pains on making the citizens to be of a certain character, viz. good and capable of noble acts.

It is natural, then, that we call neither ox nor horse nor any other of the animals happy; for none of them is capable of sharing in such activity. For this reason also a boy is not happy; for he is not yet capable of such acts, owing to his age; and boys who are called happy are being congratulated by reason of the hopes we have for them. For there is required, as we said, not only complete virtue but also a complete life, since many changes occur in life, and all manner of chances, and the most prosperous may fall into great misfortunes in old age, as is told of Priam in the Trojan Cycle; and one who has experienced such chances and has ended wretchedly no one calls happy. . . .

Since happiness is an activity of soul in accordance with perfect virtue, we must consider the nature of virtue; for perhaps we shall thus see better the nature of happiness. . . .

Virtue, then, being of two kinds, intellectual and moral, intellectual virtue in the main owes both its birth and its growth to teaching (for which reason it requires experience and time), while moral virtue comes about as a result of habit. . . . From this it is also plain that none of the moral virtues arises in us by nature; for nothing that exists by nature can form a habit contrary to its nature. For instance the stone which by nature moves downwards cannot be habituated to move upwards, not even if one tries to train it by throwing it up ten thousand times; nor can fire be habituated to move downwards, nor can anything else that by nature behaves in one way be trained to behave in another. Neither by nature, then, nor contrary to nature do the virtues arise in us; rather we are adapted by nature to receive them, and are made perfect by habit. . . .

We must, however, not only describe virtue as a state of character, but also say what sort of state it is. We may remark, then, that every virtue or excellence both brings into good condition the thing of which it is the excellence and makes the work of that thing be done well; e. g. the excellence of the eye makes both the eye and its work good; for it is by the excellence of the eye that we see well. Similarly the excellence of the horse makes a horse both good in itself and good at running and at carrying its rider and at awaiting the attack of the enemy. Therefore, if this is true in every case, the virtue of man also will be the state of character which makes a man good and which makes him do his own work well.

How this is to happen we have stated already, but it will be made plain also by the following consideration of the specific nature of virtue. In everything that is continuous and divisible it is possible to take more, less, or an equal amount, and that either in terms of the thing itself or relatively to us; and the equal is an intermediate between excess and defect. By the intermediate in the object I mean that which is equidistant from each of the extremes, which is one and the same for all men; by the intermediate relatively to us that which is neither too much nor too little—and this is not one, nor the same for all. For instance, if ten is many and two is few, six is the intermediate, taken in terms of the object; for it exceeds and is exceeded by an equal amount; this is intermediate according to arithmetical proportion. But the intermediate relatively to us is not to be taken so; if ten pounds are too much for a particular person to eat and two too little, it does not follow that the trainer will order six pounds; for this also is perhaps too much for the person who is to take it, or too little—too little for Milo, too much for the beginner in athletic exercises. The same is true of running and wrestling. Thus a master of any art avoids excess and defect, but seeks the intermediate and chooses this—the intermediate not in the object but relatively to us.

If it is thus, then, that every art does its work well—by looking to the intermediate and judging its works by this standard (so that we often say of good works of art that it is not possible either to take away or to add anything, implying that excess and defect destroy the goodness of the works of art, while the mean preserves it; and good artists, as we say, look to this in their work), and if, further, virtue is more exact and better than any art, as nature also is, then virtue must have the quality of aiming at the intermediate. I mean moral virtue; for it is this that is concerned with passions and actions, and in these there is excess, defect, and the intermediate. For instance, both fear and confidence and appetite and anger and pity and in general pleasure and pain may be felt both too much and too little, and in both cases not well; but to feel them at the right times, with reference to the right objects, towards the right people, with the right motive, and in the right way, is what is both intermediate and best, and this is characteristic of virtue. Similarly with regard to actions also there is excess, defect, and the intermediate. Now virtue is concerned with passions and actions, in which excess is a form of

failure, and so is defect, while the intermediate is praised and is a form of success; and being praised and being successful are both characteristics of virtue. Therefore virtue is a kind of mean, since, as we have seen, it aims at what is intermediate.

Again, it is possible to fail in many ways (for evil belongs to the class of the unlimited, as the Pythagoreans conjectured, and good to that of the limited), while to succeed is possible only in one way (for which reason also one is easy and the other difficult—to miss the mark easy, to hit it difficult); for these reasons also, then, excess and defect are characteristic of vice, and the mean of virtue;

For men are good in but one way, but bad in many.

Virtue, then, is a state of character concerned with choice, lying in a mean, i. e. the mean relative to us, this being determined by a rational principle, and by that principle by which the man of practical wisdom would determine it. Now it is a mean between two vices, that which depends on excess and that which depends on defect; and again it is a mean because the vices respectively fall short of or exceed what is right in both passions and actions, while virtue both finds and chooses that which is intermediate. Hence in respect of its substance and the definition which states its essence virtue is a mean, with regard to what is best and right an extreme.

But not every action nor every passion admits of a mean; for some have names that already imply badness, e. g. spite, shamelessness, envy, and in the case of actions adultery, theft, murder; for all of these and suchlike things imply by their names that they are themselves bad, and not the excesses or deficiencies of them. It is not possible, then, ever to be right with regard to them; one must always be wrong. Nor does goodness or badness with regard to such things depend on committing adultery with the right woman, at the right time, and in the right way, but simply to do any of them is to go wrong. It would be equally absurd, then, to expect that in unjust, cowardly, and voluptuous action there should be a mean, an excess, and a deficiency; for at that rate there would be a mean of excess and of deficiency, an excess of excess, and a deficiency of deficiency. But as there is no excess and deficiency of temperance and courage because what is intermediate is in a sense an extreme, so too of the actions we have mentioned there is no mean nor any excess and deficiency, but however they are done they are wrong; for in general there is neither a mean of excess and deficiency, nor excess and deficiency of a mean.

We must, however, not only make this general statement, but also apply it to the individual facts. For among statements about conduct those which are general apply more widely, but those which are particular are more genuine, since conduct has to do with individual cases, and our statements must harmonize with the facts in these cases. We may take these cases from our table. With regard to feelings of fear and confidence courage is the mean; of the people who exceed, he who exceeds in fearlessness has no name (many of the states have no name), while the man who exceeds in confidence is rash, and he who exceeds in fear and falls short in confidence is a coward. With regard to pleasures and pains—not all of them, and not so much with regard to the pains—the mean is temperance, the excess self-indulgence. Persons deficient with regard to the pleasures are not often found; hence such persons also have received no name. But let us call them 'insensible'.

With regard to giving and taking of money the mean is liberality, the excess and the defect prodigality and meanness. In these actions people exceed and fall short in contrary ways; the prodigal exceeds in spending and falls short in taking, while the mean man exceeds in taking and falls short in spending. (At present we are giving a mere outline or summary, and are satisfied with this; later these states will be more exactly determined.) With regard to money there are also other dispositions—a mean, magnificence (for the magnificent man differs from the liberal man; the former deals with large sums, the latter with small ones), and excess, tastelessness, and vulgarity, and a deficiency, niggardliness; these differ from the states opposed to liberality. . . .

That moral virtue is a mean, then, and in what sense it is so, and that it is a mean between

two vices, the one involving excess, the other deficiency, and that it is such because its character is to aim at what is intermediate in passions and in actions, has been sufficiently stated. Hence also it is no easy task to be good. For in everything it is no easy task to find the middle, e. g. to find the middle of a circle is not for every one but for him who knows; so, too, any one can get angry—that is easy—or give or spend money; but to do this to the right person, to the right extent, at the right time, with the right motive, and in the right way, *that* is not for every one, nor is it easy; wherefore goodness is both rare and laudable and noble. . . .

If happiness is activity in accordance with virtue, it is reasonable that it should be in accordance with the highest virtue; and this will be that of the best thing in us. Whether it be reason or something else that is this element which is thought to be our natural ruler and guide and to take thought of things noble and divine, whether it be itself also divine or only the most divine element in us, the activity of this in accordance with its proper virtue will be perfect happiness. That this activity is contemplative we have already said.

Now this would seem to be in agreement both with what we said before and with the truth. For, firstly, this activity is the best (since not only is reason the best thing in us, but the objects of reason are the best of knowable objects); and, secondly, it is the most continuous, since we can contemplate truth more continuously than we can do anything. And we think happiness has pleasure mingled with it, but the activity of philosophic wisdom is admittedly the pleasantest of virtuous activities; at all events the pursuit of it is thought to offer pleasures marvellous for their purity and their enduringness, and it is to be expected that those who know will pass their time more pleasantly than those who inquire. And the self-sufficiency that is spoken of must belong most to the contemplative activity. For while a philosopher, as well as a just man or one possessing any other virtue, needs the necessaries of life, when they are sufficiently equipped with things of that sort the just man needs people towards whom and with whom he shall act justly, and the temperate man, the brave man, and each of the others is in the same case, but the philosopher, even when by himself, can contemplate truth, and the better the wiser he is; he can perhaps do so better if he has fellow-workers, but still he is the most self-sufficient. And this activity alone would seem to be loved for its own sake; for nothing arises from it apart from the contemplating, while from practical activities we gain more or less apart from the action. And happiness is thought to depend on leisure; for we are busy that we may have leisure, and make war that we may live in peace. Now the activity of the practical virtues is exhibited in political or military affairs, but the actions concerned with these seem to be unleisurely. Warlike actions are completely so (for no one chooses to be at war, or provokes war, for the sake of being at war; any one would seem absolutely murderous if he were to make enemies of his friends in order to bring about battle and slaughter); but the action of the statesman is also unleisurely, and—apart from the political action itself—aims at despotic power and honours, or at all events happiness, for him and his fellow citizens—a happiness different from political action, and evidently sought as being different. So if among virtuous actions political and military actions are distinguished by nobility and greatness, and these are unleisurely and aim at an end and are not desirable for their own sake, but the activity of reason, which is contemplative, seems both to be superior in serious worth and to aim at no end beyond itself, and to have its pleasure proper to itself (and this augments the activity), and the self-sufficiency, leisureliness, unweariedness (so far as this is possible for man), and all the other attributes ascribed to the supremely happy man are evidently those connected with this activity, it follows that this will be the complete happiness of man, if it be allowed a complete term of life (for none of the attributes of happiness is *incomplete*).

But such a life would be too high for man; for it is not in so far as he is man that he will live so, but in so far as something divine is present in him; and by so much as this is superior to our composite nature is its activity superior to that which is the exercise of the other kind of virtue. If reason is divine, then in comparison with man, the life according to it is divine in comparison with human life. But we must not follow those who advise us, being men, to think of human things, and, being mortal, of mortal things, but must, so far as we can, make ourselves immortal, and strain every nerve to live in accordance with the best thing in us; for even if it be small in bulk, much more does it in power and worth surpass everything. This would seem, too, to be each man himself, since it is the authoritative and better part of him. It would be strange, then, if he were to choose not the life of his self but that of something else. And what we said before will apply now; that which is proper to each thing is by nature best and most pleasant for each thing; for man, therefore, the life according to reason is best and pleasantest, since reason more than anything else *is* man. This life therefore is also the happiest.

But in a secondary degree the life in accordance with the other kind of virtue is happy; for the activities in accordance with this befit our human estate. Just and brave acts, and other virtuous acts, we do in relation to each other, observing our respective duties with regard to contracts and services and all manner of actions and with regard to passions; and all of these seem to be typically human. Some of them seem even to arise from the body, and virtue of character to be in many ways bound up with the passions. Practical wisdom, too, is linked to virtue of character, and this to practical wisdom, since the principles of practical wisdom are in accordance with the moral virtues and rightness in morals is in accordance with practical wisdom. Being connected with the passions also, the moral virtues must belong to our composite nature; and the virtues of our composite nature are human; so, therefore, are the life and the happiness which correspond to these. The excellence of the reason is a thing apart; we must be content to say this much about it, for to describe it precisely is a task greater than our purpose requires. It would seem, however, also to need external equipment but little, or less than moral virtue does. Grant that both need the necessaries, and do so equally, even if the statesman's work is the more concerned with the body and things of that sort; for there will be little difference there; but in what they need for the exercise of their activities there will be much difference. The liberal man will need money for the doing of his liberal deeds, and the just man too will need it for the returning of services (for wishes are hard to discern, and even people who are not just pretend to wish to act justly); and the brave man will need power if he is to accomplish any of the acts that correspond to his virtue, and the temperate man will need opportunity; for how else is either he or any of the others to be recognized? It is debated, too, whether the will or the deed is more essential to virtue, which is assumed to involve both; it is surely clear that its perfection involves both; but for deeds many things are needed, and more, the greater and nobler the deeds are. But the man who is contemplating the truth needs no such thing, at least with a view to the exercise of his activity; indeed they are, one may say, even hindrances, at all events to his contemplation; but in so far as he is a man and lives with a number of people, he chooses to do virtuous acts; he will therefore need such aids to living a human life.

But that perfect happiness is a contemplative activity will appear from the following consideration as well. We assume the gods to be above all other beings blessed and happy; but what sort of actions must we assign to them? Acts of justice? Will not the gods seem absurd if they make contracts and return deposits, and so on? Acts of a brave man, then, confronting dangers and running risks because it is noble to do so? Or liberal acts? To whom will they give? It will be strange if they are really to have money or anything of the kind. And what would their temperate acts be? Is not such praise tasteless, since they have no bad appetites? If we were to run through them all, the circumstances of action would be found trivial and unworthy of gods. Still, every one supposes that they *live* and therefore that they are active; we cannot suppose them to sleep like Endymion. Now if you take away from a living being action, and still more production, what is left but contemplation? Therefore the activity of God, which surpasses all others in blessedness, must be contemplative; and of human activities, therefore, that which is most akin to this must be most of the nature of happiness.

This is indicated, too, by the fact that the other animals have no share in happiness, being completely deprived of such activity. For while the whole life of the gods is blessed, and that of men too in so far as some likeness of such activity belongs to them, none of the other animals is happy, since they in no way share in contemplation. Happiness extends, then, just so far as contemplation does, and those to whom contemplation more fully belongs are more truly happy, not as a mere concomitant but in virtue of the contemplation; for this is in itself precious. Happiness, therefore, must be some form of contemplation.

But, being a man, one will also need external prosperity; for our nature is not self-sufficient for the purpose of contemplation, but our body also must be healthy and must have food and other attention. Still, we must not think that the man who is to be happy will need many things or great things, merely because he cannot be supremely happy without external goods; for self-sufficiency and action do not involve excess, and we can do noble acts without ruling earth and sea; for even with moderate advantages one can act virtuously (this is manifest enough; for private persons are thought to do worthy acts no less than despots—indeed even more); and it is enough that we should have so much as that; for the life of the man who is active in accordance with virtue will be happy. . . .

REVIEW QUESTIONS

1. What is happiness according to Aristotle? How is it related to virtue? How is it related to pleasure?
2. How does Aristotle explain moral virtue? Give some examples.
3. Is it possible for everyone in our society to be happy, as Aristotle explains it? If not, who cannot be happy?

DISCUSSION QUESTIONS

1. Aristotle characterizes a life of pleasure as suitable for beasts. But what, if anything, is wrong with a life of pleasure?
2. Aristotle claims that the philosopher will be happier than anyone else. Why is this? Do you agree or not?

Joel Feinberg

The Nature and Value of Rights

Joel Feinberg is professor of philosophy at the University of Arizona. He is the author of Doing and Deserving *(1970),* Social Philosophy *(1973), and the* Moral Limits of the Criminal Law *(1984–1989) in four volumes. He is the editor of* Reason and Responsibility, *sixth edition (1985) and* Moral Concepts *(1969).*

Feinberg wants to demonstrate that rights are morally important. To do this, he imagines Nowheresville, a world like our own except that people do not have rights. As a result, people in this world cannot make moral claims when they are treated unjustly. They cannot demand or claim just treatment, and so they are deprived of self-respect and human dignity.

1

I would like to begin by conducting a thought experiment. Try to imagine Nowheresville—a world very much like our own except that no one, or hardly any one (the qualification is not important), has *rights*. If this flaw makes Nowheresville too ugly to hold very long in contemplation, we can make it as pretty as we wish in other moral respects. We can, for example, make the human beings in it as attractive and virtuous as possible without taxing our conceptions of the limits of human nature. In particular, let the virtues of moral sensibility flourish. Fill this imagined world with as much benevolence, compassion, sympathy, and pity as it will conveniently hold without strain. Now we can imagine men helping one another from compassionate motives merely, quite as much or

From Joel Feinberg, "The Nature and Value of Rights," *The Journal of Value Inquiry* 4(1970):243–257, © 1970, Martinus Nijhoff Publishers, Dordrecht, Netherlands. Reprinted by permission of Kluwer Academic Publishers.

even more than they do in our actual world from a variety of more complicated motives.

This picture, pleasant as it is in some respects, would hardly have satisfied Immanuel Kant. Benevolently motivated actions do good, Kant admitted, and therefore are better, **ceteris paribus**, than malevolently motivated actions; but no action can have supreme kind of worth—what Kant called "moral worth"—unless its whole motivating power derives from the thought that it is *required by duty*. Accordingly, let us try to make Nowheresville more appealing to Kant by introducing the idea of duty into it, and letting the sense of duty be a sufficient motive for many beneficent and honorable actions. But doesn't this bring our original thought experiment to an abortive conclusion? If duties are permitted entry into Nowheresville, are not rights necessarily smuggled in along with them?

The question is well-asked, and requires here a brief digression so that we might consider the so-called "doctrine of the logical correlativity of rights and duties." This is the doctrine that (i) all duties entail other people's rights and (ii) all rights entail other people's duties. Only the first part of the doctrine, the alleged entailment from duties to rights, need concern us here. Is this part of the doctrine correct? It should not be surprising that my answer is: "In a sense yes and in a sense no." Etymologically, the word "duty" is associated with actions that are *due* someone else, the payments of debts *to* creditors, the keeping of agreements with promises, the payment of club dues, or legal fees, or tariff levies to appropriate authorities or their representatives. In this original sense of "duty," all duties are correlated with the rights of those *to* whom the duty is owed. On the other hand, there seem to be numerous classes of duties, both of a legal and non-legal kind, that are *not* logically correlated with the rights of other persons. This seems to be a consequence of the fact that the word "duty" has come to be used for *any* action understood to be *required,* whether by the rights of others, or by law, or by higher authority, or by conscience, or whatever. When the notion of requirement is in clear focus it is likely to seem the only element in the idea of duty that is essential, and the other component notion—that a duty is something *due* someone else—drops off. Thus, in this widespread but derivative usage, "duty" tends to be used for any action we feel we *must* (for whatever reason) do. It comes, in short, to be a term of moral modality merely; and it is no wonder that the first thesis of the logical correlativity doctrine often fails.

Let us then introduce duties into Nowheresville, but only in the sense of actions that are, or believed to be, morally mandatory, but not in the older sense of actions that are due others and can be claimed by others as their right. Nowheresville now can have duties of the sort imposed by positive law. A legal duty is not something we are implored or advised to do merely; it is something the law, or an authority under the law, *requires* us to do whether we want to or not, under pain of penalty. When traffic lights turn red, however, there is no determinate person who can plausibly be said to claim our stopping as his due, so that the motorist owes it to *him* to stop, in the way a debtor owes it to his creditor to pay. In our own actual world, of course, we sometimes owe it to our *fellow motorists* to stop; but that kind of right-correlated duty does not exist in Nowheresville. There, motorists "owe" obedience to the Law, but they owe nothing to one another. When they collide, no matter who is at fault, no one is accountable to anyone else, and no one has any sound grievance or "right to complain."

When we leave legal contexts to consider moral obligations and other extra-legal duties, a greater variety of duties-without-correlative-rights present themselves. Duties of charity, for example, require us to contribute to one or another of a large number of eligible recipients, no one of whom can claim our contribution from us as his due. Charitable contributions are more like gratuitous services, favours, and gifts than like repayments of debts or reparations; and yet we do have duties to be charitable. Many persons, moreover, in our actual world believe that they are required by their own consciences to do more than that "duty" that *can* be demanded of them by their prospective beneficiaries. I have quoted elsewhere the citation from H. B. Acton of a character in a Malraux novel who "gave all

his supply of poison to his fellow prisoners to enable them by suicide to escape the burning alive which was to be their fate and his." This man, Acton adds, "probably did not think that [the others] had more of a right to the poison than he had, though he thought it his duty to give it to them." [1] I am sure that there are many actual examples, less dramatically heroic than this fictitious one, of persons who believe, rightly or wrongly, that they *must do* something (hence the word "duty") for another person in excess of what that person can appropriately demand of him (hence the absence of "right").

Now the digression is over and we can return to Nowheresville and summarize what we have put in it thus far. We now find spontaneous benevolence in somewhat larger degree than in our actual world, and also the acknowledged existence of duties of obedience, duties of charity, and duties imposed by exacting private consciences, and also, let us suppose, a degree of conscientiousness in respect to those duties somewhat in excess of what is to be found in our actual world. I doubt that Kant would be fully satisfied with Nowheresville even now that duty and respect for law and authority have been added to it; but I feel certain that he would regard their addition at least as an improvement. I will now introduce two further moral practices into Nowheresville that will make the world very little more appealing to Kant, but will make it appear more familiar to us. These are the practices connected with the notions of *personal desert* and what I call a *sovereign monopoly of rights*.

When a person is said to deserve something good from us what is meant in parts is that there would be a certain propriety in our giving that good thing to him in virtue of the kind of person he is, perhaps, or more likely, in virtue of some specific thing he has done. The propriety involved here is a much weaker kind than that which derives from our having promised him the good thing or from his having qualified for it by satisfying the well-advertised conditions of some public rule. In the latter case he could be said not merely to deserve the good thing but also to have a *right* to it, that is to be in a position to demand it as his due; and of course we will not have that sort of thing in Nowheresville. That weaker kind of propriety which is mere desert is simply a kind of *fittingness* between one party's character or action and another party's favorable response, much like that between humor and laughter, or good performance and applause.

The following seems to be the origin of the idea of deserving good or bad treatment from others: A master or lord was under no obligation to reward his servant for especially good service; still a master might naturally feel that there would be a special fittingness in giving a gratuitous reward as a grateful response to the good service (or conversely imposing a penalty for bad service). Such an act while surely fitting and proper was entirely **supererogatory**. The fitting response in turn from the rewarded servant should be gratitude. If the deserved reward had not been given him he should have had no complaint, since he only *deserved* the reward, as opposed to having a *right* to it, or a ground for claiming it as his due.

The idea of desert has evolved a good bit away from its beginnings by now, but nevertheless, it seems clearly to be one of those words J. L. Austin said "never entirely forget their pasts." [2] Today servants qualify for their wages by doing their agreed upon chores, no more and no less. If their wages are not forthcoming, their contractual rights have been violated and they can make legal claim to the money that is their due. If they do less than they agreed to do, however, their employers may "dock" them, by paying them proportionately less than the agreed upon fee. This is all a matter of right. But if the servant does a splendid job, above and beyond his minimal contractual duties, the employer is under no further obligation to reward him, for this was not agreed upon, even tacitly, in advance. The additional service was all the servant's idea and done entirely on his own. Nevertheless, the morally sensitive employer may feel that it would be exceptionally appropriate for him to respond, freely on *his* own, to the servant's meritorious service, with a reward. The employee cannot demand it as his due, but he will happily accept it, with gratitude, as a fitting response to his desert.

In our age of organized labor, even this picture is now archaic; for almost every kind of exchange of service is governed by hard bargained contracts so that even bonuses can sometimes be demanded as a matter of right, and nothing is given for nothing on either side of the bargaining table. And perhaps that is a good thing; for consider an anachronistic instance of the earlier kind of practice that survives, at least as a matter of form, in the quaint old practice of "tipping." The tip was originally conceived as a reward that has to be earned by "zealous service." It is not something to be taken for granted as a standard response to *any* service. That is to say that its payment is a *"gratuity,"* not a discharge of obligation, but something given apart from, or in addition to, anything the recipient can expect as a matter of right. That is what tipping originally meant at any rate, and tips are still referred to as "gratuities" in the tax forms. But try to explain all that to a New York cab driver! If he has *earned* his gratuity, by God, he has it coming, and there had better be sufficient acknowledgement of his desert or he'll give you a piece of his mind! I'm not generally prone to defend New York cab drivers, but they do have a point here. There is the making of a paradox in the queerly unstable concept of an "earned gratuity." One can understand how "desert" in the weak sense of "propriety" or "mere fittingness" tends to generate a stronger sense in which desert is itself the ground for a claim of right.

In Nowheresville, nevertheless, we will have only the original weak kind of desert. Indeed, it will be impossible to keep this idea out if we allow such practices as teachers grading students, judges awarding prizes, and servants serving benevolent but class-conscious masters. Nowheresville is a reasonably good world in many ways, and its teachers, judges, and masters will generally try to give students, contestants, and servants the grades, prizes, and rewards they deserve. For this the recipients will be grateful; but they will never think to complain, or even feel aggrieved, when expected responses to desert fail. The masters, judges, and teachers don't *have* to do good things, after all, for *anyone*. One should be happy that they *ever* treat us well, and not grumble over their occasional lapses. Their hoped for responses, after all, are *gratuities,* and there is no wrong in the omission of what is merely gratuitous. Such is the response of persons who have no concept of *rights,* even persons who are proud of their own deserts.[3]

Surely, one might ask, rights have to come in somewhere, if we are to have even moderately complex forms of social organization. Without rules that confer rights and impose obligations, how can we have ownership of property, bargains and deals, promises and contracts, appointments and loans, marriages and partnerships? Very well, let us introduce all of these social and economic practices into Nowheresville, but *with one big twist.* With them I should like to introduce the curious notion of a "sovereign right-monopoly." You will recall that the subjects in Hobbes's *Leviathan* had no rights whatever against their sovereign. He could do as he liked with them, even gratuitously harm them, but this gave them no valid grievance against him. The sovereign, to be sure, had a certain duty to treat his subjects well, but this duty was owed not to the subjects directly, but to God, just as we might have a duty to a person to treat his property well, but of course no duty to the property itself but only to its owner. Thus, while the sovereign was quite capable of *harming* his subjects, he could commit no wrong against them that they could complain about, since they had no prior claims against his conduct. The only party *wronged* by the sovereign's mistreatment of his subjects was God, the supreme lawmaker. Thus, in repenting cruelty to his subjects, the sovereign might say to God, as David did after killing Uriah, "to Thee only have I sinned." [4]

Even in the *Leviathan,* however, ordinary people had ordinary rights *against one another.* They played roles, occupied offices, made agreements, and signed contracts. In a genuine "sovereign right-monopoly," as I shall be using that phrase, they will do all those things too, and thus incur genuine obligations toward one another; but the obligations (here is the twist) will not be owed directly *to* promisees, creditors, parents, and the like, but rather to God alone, or to the members of some elite, or to a single sovereign under God. Hence, the rights correlative to the obligations that derive from these transactions are all owned by some "outside" authority.

As far as I know, no philosopher has ever suggested that even our role and contract obligations

(in this, our actual world) are all owed directly to a divine intermediary, but some theologians have approached such extreme moral occasionalism. I have in mind the familiar phrase in certain widely distributed religious tracts that "it takes three to marry," which suggests that marital vows are not made between bride and groom directly but between each spouse and God, so that if one breaks his vow, the other cannot rightly complain of being wronged, since only God could have claimed performance of the marital duties as his *own* due; and hence God alone had a claim-right violated by the nonperformance. If John breaks his vow to God, he might then properly repent in the words of David: "To Thee only have I sinned."

In our actual world, very few spouses conceive of their mutual obligations in this way; but their small children, at a certain stage in their moral upbringing, are likely to feel precisely this way toward *their* mutual obligations. If Billy kicks Bobby and is punished by Daddy, he may come to feel contrition for his naughtiness induced by his painful estrangement from the loved parent. He may then be happy to make amends and sincere apology to *Daddy;* but when Daddy insists that he apologize to his wronged brother, that is another story. A direct apology to Billy would be a tacit recognition of Billy's status as a right-holder against him, someone he can wrong as well as harm, and someone to whom he is directly accountable for his wrongs. This is a status Bobby will happily accord Daddy, but it would imply a respect for Billy that he does not presently feel, so he bitterly resents according it to him. On the "three-to-marry" model, the relations between each spouse and God would be like those between Bobby and Daddy; respect for the other spouse as an independent claimant would not even be necessary; and where present, of course, never sufficient.

The advocates of the "three-to-marry" model who conceive it either as a description of our actual institution of marriage or a recommendation of what marriage ought to be, may wish to escape this embarrassment by granting rights to spouses in capacities other than as promisees. They may wish to say, for example, that when John promises God that he will be faithful to Mary, a right is thus conferred not only on God as promisee but also on Mary herself as third-party beneficiary, just as when John contracts with an insurance company and names Mary as his intended beneficiary, she has a right to the accumulated funds after John's death, even though the insurance company made no promise to her. But this seems to be an unnecessarily cumbersome complication contributing nothing to our understanding of the marriage bond. The life insurance transaction is necessarily a three party relation, involving occupants of three distinct offices, no two of whom alone could do the whole job. The transaction, after all, is defined as the purchase by the customer (first office) from the vendor (second office) of protection for a beneficiary (third office) against the customer's untimely death. Marriage, on the other hand, in this our actual world, appears to be a binary relation between a husband and wife, and even though third parties such as children, neighbors, psychiatrists, and priests may sometimes be helpful and even causally necessary for the survival of the relation, they are not **logically necessary** to our *conception* of the relation, and indeed many married couples do quite well without them. Still I am not now purporting to describe our actual world, but rather trying to contrast it with a counterpart world of the imagination. In *that* world, it takes three to make almost *any* moral relation and all rights are owned by God or some sovereign under God.

There will, of course, be delegated authorities in the imaginary world, empowered to give commands to their underlings and to punish them for their disobedience. But the commands are all given in the name of the right-monopoly who in turn are the only persons to whom obligations are owed. Hence, even intermediate superiors do not have claim-rights against their subordinates but only legal *powers* to create obligations in the subordinates *to* the monopolistic right-holders, and also the legal *privilege* to impose penalties in the name of that monopoly.

2

So much for the imaginary "world without rights." If some of the moral concepts and prac-

tices I have allowed into that world do not sit well with one another, no matter. Imagine Nowheresville with all of these practices if you can, or with any harmonious subset of them, if you prefer. The important thing is not what I've let into it, but what I have kept out. The remainder of this paper will be devoted to an analysis of what precisely a world is missing when it does not contain rights and why that absence is morally important.

The most conspicuous difference, I think, between the Nowheresvillians and ourselves has something to do with the activity of *claiming*. Nowheresvillians, even when they are discriminated against invidiously, or left without the things they need, or otherwise badly treated, do not think to leap to their feet and make righteous demands against one another though they may not hesitate to resort to force and trickery to get what they want. They have no notion of rights, so they do not have a notion of what is their due; hence they do not claim before they take. The conceptual linkage between personal rights and claiming has long been noticed by legal writers and is reflected in the standard usage in which "claim-rights" are distinguished from other mere liberties, immunities, and powers, also sometimes called "rights," with which they are easily confused. When a person has a legal claim-right to X, it must be the case (i) that he is at liberty in respect to X, i.e. that he has no duty to refrain from or relinquish X, and also (ii) that his liberty is the ground of other people's *duties* to grant him X or not to interfere with him in respect to X. Thus, in the sense of claim-rights, it is true by definition that rights logically entail other people's duties. The paradigmatic examples of such rights are the creditor's right to be paid a debt by his debtor, and the landowner's right not to be interfered with by anyone in the exclusive occupancy of his land. The creditor's right against his debtor, for example, and the debtor's duty to his creditor, are precisely the same relation seen from two different vantage points, as inextricably linked as the two sides of the same coin.

And yet, this is not quite an accurate account of the matter, for it fails to do justice to the way claim-rights are somehow prior to, or more basic than, the duties with which they are necessarily correlated. If Nip has a claim-right against Tuck, it is because of this fact that Tuck has a duty to Nip. It is only because something from Tuck is *due* Nip (directional element) that there is something Tuck *must do* (modal element). This is a relation, moreover, in which Tuck is bound and Nip is free. Nip not only *has* a right, but he can choose whether or not to exercise it, whether to claim it, whether to register complaints upon its infringement, even whether to release Tuck from his duty, and forget the whole thing. If the personal claim-right is also backed up by criminal sanctions, however, Tuck may yet have a duty of obedience to the law from which no one, not even Nip, may release him. He would even have such duties if he lived in Nowheresville; but duties subject to acts of claiming, duties derivative from the contingent upon the personal rights of others, are unknown and undreamed of in Nowheresville.

Many philosophical writers have simply identified rights with claims. The dictionaries tend to define "claims," in turn as "assertions of right," a dizzying piece of circularity that led one philosopher to complain—"We go in search of rights and are directed to claims, and then back again to rights in bureaucratic futility." [5] What then is the relation between a claim and a right?

As we shall see, a right *is* a kind of claim, and a claim is "an assertion of right," so that a formal definition of either notion in terms of the other will not get us very far. Thus if a "formal definition" of the usual philosophical sort is what we are after, the game is over before it has begun, and we can say that the concept of a right is a "simple, undefinable, unanalysable primitive." Here as elsewhere in philosophy this will have the effect of making the commonplace seem unnecessarily mysterious. We would be better advised, I think, not to attempt definition of either "right" or "claim," but rather to use the idea of a claim in informal elucidation of the idea of a right. This is made possible by the fact that *claiming* is an elaborate sort of rule-governed *activity*. A claim is that which is claimed, the object of the act of claiming. . . . If we concentrate on the whole activity of claiming, which is public, familiar, and open to our observation, rather

than on its upshot alone, we may learn more about the generic nature of rights than we could ever hope to learn from a formal definition, even if one were possible. Moreover, certain facts about rights more easily, if not solely, expressible in the language of claims and claiming are essential to a full understanding not only of what rights are, but also why they are so vitally important.

Let us begin then by distinguishing between: (i) making claim to . . . , (ii) claiming that . . . , and (iii) having a claim. One sort of thing we may be doing when we claim is to *make claim to something.* This is "to petition or seek by virtue of supposed right; to demand as due." Sometimes this is done by an acknowledged right-holder when he serves notice that he now wants turned over to him that which has already been acknowledged to be his, something borrowed, say, or improperly taken from him. This is often done by turning in a chit, a receipt, an I.O.U., a check, an insurance policy, or a deed, that is, a *title* to something currently in the possession of someone else. On other occasions, making claim is making application for titles or rights themselves, as when a mining prospector stakes a claim to mineral rights, or a householder to a tract of land in the public domain, or an inventor to his patent rights. In the one kind of case, to make claim is to exercise rights one already has by presenting title; in the other kind of case it is to apply for the title itself, by showing that one has satisfied the conditions specified by a rule for the ownership of title and therefore that one can demand it as one's due.

Generally speaking, only the person who has a title or who has qualified for it, or someone speaking in his name, can make claim to something as a matter of right. It is an important fact about rights (or claims), then, that they can be claimed only by those who have them. Anyone can claim, of course, *that* this umbrella is yours, but only you or your representative can actually claim the umbrella. If Smith owes Jones five dollars, only Jones can claim the five dollars as his own, though any bystander can *claim that* it belongs to Jones. One important difference then between *making legal claim to* and *claiming that* is that the former is a legal performance with direct legal consequences whereas the latter is often a mere piece of descriptive commentary with no legal force. Legally speaking, *making claim to* can itself make things happen. This sense of "claiming," then, might well be called "the performative sense." The legal power to claim (performatively) one's right or the things to which one has a right seems to be essential to the very notion of a right. A right to which one could not make claim (i.e. not even for recognition) would be a very "imperfect" right indeed!

Claiming that one has a right (what we can call "propositional claiming" as opposed to "performative claiming") is another sort of thing one can do with language, but it is not the sort of doing that characteristically has legal consequences. To claim that one has rights is to make it in such a manner as to demand or insist that they be recognized. In this sense of "claim" many things in addition to rights can be claimed, that is, many other kinds of proposition can be asserted in the claiming way. I can claim, for example, that you, he, or she has certain rights, or that Julius Caesar once had certain rights; or I can claim that certain statements are true, or that I have certain skills, or accomplishments, or virtually anything at all. I can claim that the earth is flat. What is essential to *claiming that* is the manner of assertion. One can assert without even caring very much whether anyone is listening, but part of the point of propositional claiming is to *make sure* people listen. When I claim to others that I know something, for example, I am not merely asserting it, but rather "obtruding my putative knowledge upon their attention, demanding that it be recognized, that appropriate notice be taken of it by those concerned. . . ." [6] Not every truth is properly assertable, much less claimable, in every context. To claim that something is the case in circumstances that justify no more than calm assertion is to behave like a boor. (This kind of boorishness, I might add, is probably less common in Nowheresville.) But not to claim in the appropriate circumstances that one has a right is to be spiritless or foolish. A list of "appropriate circumstances" would include occasions when one is challenged, when one's possession is denied, or seems insufficiently acknowledged or appreciated; and of course even

in these circumstances, the claiming should be done only with an appropriate degree of vehemence.

Even if there are conceivable circumstances in which one would admit rights diffidently, there is no doubt that their characteristic use and that for which they are distinctively well suited, is to be claimed, demanded, affirmed, insisted upon. They are especially sturdy objects to "stand upon," a most useful sort of moral furniture. Having rights, of course, makes claiming possible; but it is claiming that gives rights their special moral significance. This feature of rights is connected in a way with the customary rhetoric about what it is to be a human being. Having rights enables us to "stand up like men," to look others in the eye, and to feel in some fundamental way the equal of anyone. To think of oneself as the holder of rights is not to be unduly but properly proud, to have that minimal self-respect that is necessary to be worthy of the love and esteem of others. Indeed, respect for persons (this is an intriguing idea) may simply be respect for their rights, so that there cannot be the one without the other; and what is called "human dignity" may simply be the recognizable capacity to assert claims. To respect a person then, or to think of him as possessed of human dignity, simply *is* to think of him as a potential maker of claims. Not all of this can be packed into a definition of "rights"; but these are *facts* about the possession of rights that argue well their supreme moral importance. More than anything else I am going to say, these facts explain what is wrong with Nowheresville. . . .

Endnotes

1. H. B. Acton, "Symposium of 'Rights'," *Proceedings of the Aristotelian Society,* Supplementary Volume 24 (1950): 107–108.
2. J. L. Austin, "A Plea for Excuses," *Proceedings of the Aristotelian Society,* Vol. 57 (1956–57).
3. For a fuller discussion of the concept of personal desert see my "Justice and Personal Desert," in C. J. Chapman, ed. *Nomos VI, Justice* (New York: Atherton Press, 1963), pp. 69–97.
4. II Sam. 11. Cited with approval by Thomas Hobbes in *The Leviathan,* Part II, Chapter 21.
5. H. B. Acton, *op. cit.*
6. G. J. Warnock, "Claims to Knowledge," *Proceedings of the Aristotelian Society,* Supplementary Volume 36 (1962): 21.

1. Describe Nowheresville. How is this world different from our world?
2. Explain the doctrine of the logical correlativity of rights and duties. What is Feinberg's position on this doctrine?
3. How does Feinberg explain the concept of personal desert? How would personal desert work in Nowheresville?
4. Explain the notion of a sovereign right-monopoly. How would this work in Nowheresville according to Feinberg?

5. What are claim-rights? Why does Feinberg think they are morally important?

DISCUSSION QUESTIONS

1. Does Feinberg make a convincing case for the importance of rights? Why or why not?
2. Can you give a noncircular definition of claim-right?

Ronald Dworkin

Taking Rights Seriously

Ronald Dworkin is university professor of jurisprudence, Oxford University, and professor of law, New York University. He is the author of A Matter of Principle *(1985),* Law's Empire *(1986),* A Bill of Rights for Britain *(1990), and* Taking Rights Seriously *(1978), from which our reading is taken.*

On Dworkin's view, if a people have a right to do something, then it is wrong to interfere with them. For example, if citizens have a right to free speech, then it is wrong for the government to interfere with the exercise of this right (unless this is necessary to protect other rights). This notion of rights, Dworkin believes, rests on the Kantian idea of treating people with dignity as members of the moral community, and also on the idea of political equality.

THE RIGHTS OF CITIZENS

The language of rights now dominates political debate in the United States. Does the Govern-

ment respect the moral and political rights of its citizens? Or does the Government's foreign policy, or its race policy, fly in the face of these rights? Do the minorities whose rights have been violated have the right to violate the law in return? Or does the silent majority itself have rights, including the right that those who break the law be punished? It is not surprising that these questions are now prominent. The concept of rights, and particularly the concept of rights against the Government, has its most natural use when a political society is divided, and appeals to co-operation or a common goal are pointless.

The debate does not include the issue of whether citizens have *some* moral rights against their Government. It seems accepted on all sides that they do. Conventional lawyers and politicians take it as a point of pride that our legal system recognizes, for example, individual rights of free speech, equality, and due process. They base their claim that our law deserves respect, at least in part, on that fact, for they would not claim that totalitarian systems deserve the same loyalty.

Some philosophers, of course, reject the idea that citizens have rights apart from what the law happens to give them. Bentham thought that the idea of moral rights was 'nonsense on stilts'. But that view has never been part of our orthodox political theory, and politicians of both parties appeal to the rights of the people to justify a great part of what they want to do. I shall not be concerned, in this essay, to defend the thesis that citizens have moral rights against their governments; I want instead to explore the implications of that thesis for those, including the present United States Government, who profess to accept it.

It is much in dispute, of course, what *particular* rights citizens have. Does the acknowledged right to free speech, for example, include the right to participate in nuisance demonstrations? In practice the Government will have the last word on what an individual's rights are, because its police will do what its officials and courts say. But that does not mean that the Government's view is necessarily the correct view; anyone who thinks it does must believe that men and women have only such moral rights as Government chooses to grant, which means that they have no moral rights at all.

All this is sometimes obscured in the United States by the constitutional system. The American Constitution provides a set of individual *legal* rights in the First Amendment, and in the due process, equal protection, and similar clauses. Under present legal practice the Supreme Court has the power to declare an act of Congress or of a state legislature void if the Court finds that the act offends these provisions. This practice has led some commentators to suppose that individual moral rights are fully protected by this system, but that is hardly so, nor could it be so.

The Constitution fuses legal and moral issues, by making the validity of a law depend on the answer to complex moral problems, like the problem of whether a particular statute respects the inherent equality of all men. This fusion has important consequences for the debates about civil disobedience. . . . But it leaves open two prominent questions. It does not tell us whether the Constitution, even properly interpreted, recognizes all the moral rights that citizens have, and it does not tell us whether, as many suppose, citizens would have a duty to obey the law even if it did invade their moral rights. . . .

Even if the Constitution were perfect, of course, and the majority left it alone, it would not follow that the Supreme Court could guarantee the individual rights of citizens. A Supreme Court decision is still a legal decision, and it must take into account precedent and in-stitutional considerations like relations between the Court and Congress, as well as morality. And no judicial decision is necessarily the right decision. Judges stand for different positions on controversial issues of law and morals and, as the fights over Nixon's Supreme Court nominations showed, a President is entitled to appoint judges of his own persuasion, provided that they are honest and capable.

So, though the constitutional system adds something to the protection of moral rights against the Government, it falls far short of guaranteeing these rights, or even establishing what they are. . . .

RIGHTS AND THE RIGHT TO BREAK THE LAW

. . . In most cases when we say that someone has 'right' to do something, we imply that it would be wrong to interfere with his doing it, or at least that some special grounds are needed for justifying any interference. I use this strong sense of right when I say that you have the right to spend your money gambling, if you wish, though you ought to spend it in a more worth-while way. I mean that it would be wrong for anyone to interfere with you even though you propose to spend your money in a way that I think is wrong.

There is a clear difference between saying that someone has a right to do something in this sense and saying that it is the 'right' thing for him to do, or that he does no 'wrong' in doing it. Someone may have the right to do something that is the wrong thing for him to do, as might be the case with gambling. Conversely, something may be the right thing for him to do and yet he may have no right to do it, in the sense that it would not be wrong for someone to interfere with his trying. If our army captures an enemy soldier, we might say that the right thing for him to do is to try to escape, but it would not follow that it is wrong for us to try to stop him. . . .

These distinctions enable us to see an ambiguity in the orthodox question: Does a man ever have a right to break the law? Does that question mean to ask whether he ever has a right to break the law in the strong sense, so that the Government would do wrong to stop him, by arresting and prosecuting him? Or does it mean to ask whether he ever does the right thing to break the law, so that we should all respect him even though the Government should jail him? . . .

Conservatives and liberals do agree that sometimes a man does not do the wrong thing to break a law, when his conscience so requires. They disagree, when they do, over the different issue of what the State's response should be. Both parties do think that sometimes the State should prosecute. But this is not inconsistent with the proposition that the man prosecuted did the right thing in breaking the law. . . .

I said that in the United States citizens are supposed to have certain fundamental rights against their Government, certain moral rights made into legal rights by the Constitution. If this idea is significant, and worth bragging about, then these rights must be rights in the strong sense I just described. The claim that citizens have a right to free speech must imply that it would be wrong for the Government to stop them from speaking, even when the Government believes that what they will say will cause more harm than good. The claim cannot mean, on the prisoner-of-war analogy, only that citizens do no wrong in speaking their minds, though the Government reserves the right to prevent them from doing so.

This is a crucial point, and I want to labour it. Of course a responsible government must be ready to justify anything it does, particularly when it limits the liberty of its citizens. But normally it is a sufficient justification, even for an act that limits liberty, that the act is calculated to increase what the philosophers call general utility—that it is calculated to produce more over-all benefit than harm. So, though the New York City government needs a justification for forbidding motorists to drive up Lexington Avenue, it is sufficient justification if the proper officials believe, on sound evidence, that the gain to the many will outweigh the inconvenience to the few. When individual citizens are said to have rights against the Government, however, like the right of free speech, that must mean that this sort of justification is not

enough. Otherwise the claim would not argue that individuals have special protection against the law when their rights are in play, and that is just the point of the claim.

Not all legal rights, or even Constitutional rights, represent moral rights against the Government. I now have the legal right to drive either way on Fifty-seventh Street, but the Government would do no wrong to make that street one-way if it thought it in the general interest to do so. I have a Constitutional right to vote for a congressman every two years, but the national and state governments would do no wrong if, following the amendment procedure, they made a congressman's term four years instead of two, again on the basis of a judgment that this would be for the general good.

But those Constitutional rights that we call fundamental like the right of free speech, are supposed to represent rights against the Government in the strong sense; that is the point of the boast that our legal system respects the fundamental rights of the citizen. If citizens have a moral right of free speech, then governments would do wrong to repeal the First Amendment that guarantees it, even if they were persuaded that the majority would be better off if speech were curtailed.

I must not overstate the point. Someone who claims that citizens have a right against the Government need not go so far as to say that the State is *never* justified in overriding that right. He might say, for example, that although citizens have a right to free speech, the Government may override that right when necessary to protect the rights of others, or to prevent a catastrophe, or even to obtain a clear and major public benefit (though if he acknowledged this last as a possible justification he would be treating the right in question as not among the most important or fundamental). What he cannot do is to say that the Government is justified in overriding a right on the minimal grounds that would be sufficient if no such right existed. He cannot say that the Government is entitled to act on no more than a judgment that its act is likely to produce, overall, a benefit to the community. That admission would make his claim of a right pointless, and would show him to be using some sense of 'right' other than the strong sense necessary to give his claim the political importance it is normally taken to have. . . .

I said that any society that claims to recognize rights at all must abandon the notion of a general duty to obey the law that holds in all cases. This is important, because it shows that there are no short cuts to meeting a citizen's claim to right. If a citizen argues that he has a moral right not to serve in the Army, or to protest in a way he finds effective, then an official who wants to answer him, and not simply bludgeon him into obedience, must respond to the particular point he makes, and cannot point to the draft law or a Supreme Court decision as having even special, let alone decisive, weight. Sometimes an official who considers the citizen's moral arguments in good faith will be persuaded that the citizen's claim is plausible, or even right. It does not follow, however, that he will always be persuaded or that he always should be.

I must emphasize that all these propositions concern the strong sense of right, and they therefore leave open important questions about the right thing to do. If a man believes he has the right to break the law, he must then ask whether he does the right thing to exercise that right. He must remember that reasonable men can differ about whether he has a right against the Government, and therefore the right to break the law, that he thinks he has; and therefore that reasonable men can oppose him in good faith. He must take into account the various consequences his acts will have, whether they involve violence, and such other considerations as the context makes relevant; he must not go beyond the rights he can in good faith claim, to acts that violate the rights of others. . . .

CONTROVERSIAL RIGHTS

The argument so far has been hypothetical: if a man has a particular moral right against the Government, that right survives contrary legislation or adjudication. But this does not tell us what rights he has, and it is notorious that reasonable men disagree about that. There is wide agreement on certain clearcut cases; almost everyone who believes in rights at all would admit, for example, that a man has a moral right to speak his mind in a non-provocative way on matters of political concern, and that this is an important right that the State must go to great pains to protect. But there is great controversy as to the limits of such paradigm rights; and the so-called 'anti-riot' law involved in the famous Chicago Seven trial of the last decade is a case in point.

The defendants were accused of conspiring to cross state lines with the intention of causing a riot. This charge is vague—perhaps unconstitutionally vague—but the law apparently defines as criminal emotional speeches which argue that violence is justified in order to secure political equality. Does the right of free speech protect this sort of speech? That, of course, is a legal issue, because it invokes the free-speech clause of the First Amendment of the Constitution. But it is also a moral issue, because, as I said, we must treat the First Amendment as an attempt to protect a moral right. It is part of the job of governing to 'define' moral rights through statutes and judicial decisions, that is, to declare officially the extent that moral rights will be taken to have in law. Congress faced this task in voting on the anti-riot bill, and the Supreme Court has faced it in countless cases. How should the different departments of government go about defining moral rights?

They should begin with a sense that whatever they decide might be wrong. History and their descendants may judge that they acted unjustly when they thought they were right. If they take their duty seriously, they must try to limit their mistakes, and they must therefore try to discover where the dangers of mistake lie.

They might choose one of two very different models for this purpose. The first model recommends striking a balance between the rights of the individual and the demands of society at large. If the Government *infringes* on a moral right (for example, by defining the right of free speech more narrowly than justice requires), then it has done the individual a wrong. On the other hand, if the Government *inflates* a right (by defining it more broadly than justice requires) then it cheats society of some general benefit, like safe streets, that there is no reason it should not have. So a mistake on one side is as serious as a mistake on the other. The course of government is to steer to the middle, to balance the general good and personal rights, giving to each its due. . . .

The first model, described in this way, has great plausibility, and most laymen and lawyers, I think, would respond to it warmly. The metaphor of balancing the public interest against personal claims is established in our political and judicial rhetoric, and this metaphor gives the model both familiarity and appeal. Nevertheless, the first model is a false one, certainly in the case of rights generally regarded as important, and the metaphor is the heart of its error.

The institution of rights against the Government is not a gift of God, or an ancient ritual, or a national sport. It is a complex and troublesome practice that makes the Government's job of securing the general benefit more difficult and more expensive, and it would be a frivolous and wrongful practice unless it served some point. Anyone who professes to take rights seriously, and who praises our Government for respecting them, must have some sense of what that point is. He must accept, at the minimum, one or both of two important ideas. The first is the vague but powerful idea of human dignity. This idea, associated with Kant, but defended by philosophers of different schools, supposes that there are ways of treating a man that are inconsistent with recognizing him as a full member of the human community, and holds that such treatment is profoundly unjust.

The second is the more familiar idea of political equality. This supposes that the weaker members of a political community are entitled to the same concern and respect of their government as the more powerful members have secured for themselves, so that if some men have freedom of decision whatever the effect on the general good, then all men must have the same freedom. I do not want to defend or elaborate these ideas here, but only to insist that anyone who claims that citizens have rights must accept ideas very close to these.[1]

It makes sense to say that a man has a fundamental right against the Government, in the strong sense, like free speech, if that right is necessary to protect his dignity, or his standing as equally entitled to concern and respect, or some other personal value of like consequence. It does not make sense otherwise.

So if rights make sense at all, then the invasion of a relatively important right must be a very serious matter. It means treating a man as less than a man, or as less worthy of concern than other men. The institution of rights rests on the conviction that this is a grave injustice, and that it is worth paying the incremental cost in social policy or efficiency that is necessary to prevent it. But then it must be wrong to say that inflating rights is as serious as invading them. If the Government errs on the side of the individual, then it simply pays a little more in social efficiency than it has to pay; it pays a little more, that is, of the same coin that it has already decided must be spent. But if it errs against the individual it inflicts an insult upon him that, on its own reckoning, is worth a great deal of that coin to avoid. . . .

It cannot be an argument for curtailing a right, once granted, simply that society would pay a further price for extending it. There must be something special about that further cost, or there must be some other feature of the case, that makes it sensible to say that although great social cost is warranted to protect the original right, this particular cost is not necessary. Otherwise, the Government's failure to extend the right will show that its recognition of the right in the original case is a sham, a promise that it intends to keep only until that becomes inconvenient.

How can we show that a particular cost is not worth paying without taking back the initial recognition of a right? I can think of only three sorts of grounds that can consistently be used to limit the definition of a particular right. First, the Government might show that the values protected by the original right are not really at stake in the marginal case, or are at stake only in some attenuated form. Second, it might show that if the right is defined to include the marginal case, then some competing right, in the strong sense I described earlier, would be abridged. Third, it might show that if the right were so defined, then the cost to society would not be simply incremental, but would be of a degree far beyond the cost paid to grant the original right, a degree great enough to justify whatever assault on dignity or equality might be involved. . . .

But what of the individual rights of those who will be destroyed by a riot, of the passerby who will be killed by a sniper's bullet or the shopkeeper who will be ruined by looting? To put the issue in this way, as a question of competing rights, suggests a principle that would undercut the effect of uncertainty. Shall we say that some rights to protection are so important that the Government is justified in doing all it can to maintain them? Shall we therefore say that the Government may abridge the rights of others to act when their acts might simply increase the risk, by however slight or speculative a margin, that some person's right to life or property will be violated?

Some such principle is relied on by those who oppose the Supreme Court's recent liberal rulings on police procedure. These rulings increase the chance that a guilty man will go free, and therefore marginally increase the risk that any particular member of the community will be murdered, raped, or robbed. Some critics believe that the Court's decisions must therefore be wrong.

But no society that purports to recognize a variety of rights, on the ground that a man's dignity or equality may be invaded in a variety of ways, can accept such a principle. If forcing a man to testify against himself, or forbidding him to speak, does the damage that the rights against self-incrimination and the right of free speech assume, then it would be contemptuous for the State to tell a man that he must suffer this damage against the possibility that other men's risk of loss may be marginally reduced. If rights make sense, then the degrees of their importance cannot be so different that some count not at all when others are mentioned.

Of course the Government may discriminate and may stop a man from exercising his right to speak when there is a clear and substantial risk that his speech will do great damage to the person or property of others, and no other means of preventing this are at hand, as in the case of the man shouting 'Fire!' in a theater. But we must reject the suggested principle that the Government can simply ignore rights to speak when life and property are in question. So long as the impact of speech on these other rights remains speculative and marginal, it must look elsewhere for levers to pull.

WHY TAKE RIGHTS SERIOUSLY?

I said at the beginning of this essay that I wanted to show what a government must do that professes to recognize individual rights. It must dispense with the claim that citizens never have a right to break its law, and it must not define citizens' rights so that these are cut off for supposed reasons of the general good. Any Government's harsh treatment of civil disobedience, or campaign against vocal protest, may therefore be thought to count against its sincerity.

One might well ask, however, whether it is wise to take rights all that seriously after all. America's genius, at least in her own legend, lies in not taking any abstract doctrine to its logical extreme. It may be time to ignore abstractions, and concentrate instead on giving the majority of our citizens a new sense of their Government's concern for their welfare, and of their title to rule.

That, in any event, is what former Vice-President Agnew seemed to believe. In a policy statement on the issue of 'weirdos' and social misfits, he said that the liberals' concern for individual rights was a headwind blowing in the face of the ship of state. That is a poor metaphor, but the philosophical point it expresses is very well taken. He recognized, as many liberals do not, that the majority cannot travel as fast or as far as it would like if it recognizes the rights of individuals to do what, in the majority's terms, is the wrong thing to do.

Spiro Agnew supposed that rights are divisive, and that national unity and a new respect for law may be developed by taking them more skeptically. But he is wrong. America will continue to be divided by its social and foreign policy, and if the economy grows weaker again the divisions will become more bitter. If we want our laws and our legal institutions to provide the ground rules within which these issues will be contested then these ground rules must not be the conqueror's law that the dominant class imposes on the weaker, as Marx supposed the law of a capitalist society must be. The bulk of the law—that part which defines and implements social, economic, and foreign policy—cannot be neutral. It must state, in its greatest part, the majority's view of the common good. The institution of rights is therefore crucial, because it represents the majority's promise to the minorities that their dignity and equality will be respected. When the divisions among the groups are most violent, then this gesture, if law is to work, must be most sincere.

The institution requires an act of faith on the part of the minorities, because the scope of their rights will be controversial whenever they are important, and because the officers of the majority will act on their own notions of what these rights really are. Of course these officials will disagree with many of the claims that a minority makes. That makes it all the more important that they take their decisions gravely. They must show that they understand what rights are, and they must not cheat on the full implications of the doctrine. The Government will not re-establish respect for law without giving the law some claim to respect. It cannot do that if it neglects the one feature that distinguishes law from ordered brutality. If the Government does not take rights seriously, then it does not take law seriously either.

Endnote

1. He need not consider these ideas to be axiomatic. He may, that is, have reasons for insisting that dignity or equality

are important values, and these reasons may be utilitarian. He may believe, for example, that the general good will be advanced, *in the long run,* only if we treat indignity or inequality as very great injustices, and never allow our *opinions* about the general good to justify them. I do not know of any good arguments for or against this sort of 'institutional' utilitarianism, but it is consistent with my point, because it argues that we must treat violations of dignity and equality as special moral crimes, beyond the reach of ordinary utilitarian justification.

REVIEW QUESTIONS

1. What does Dworkin mean by right in the strong sense? What rights in this sense are protected by the U.S. Constitution?
2. Distinguish between legal and moral rights. Give some examples of legal rights that are not moral rights, and moral rights that are not legal rights.
3. What are the two models of how a government might define the rights of its citizens? Which does Dworkin find more attractive?
4. According to Dworkin, what two important ideas are behind the institution of rights?

DISCUSSION QUESTIONS

1. Does a person have a right to break the law? Why or why not?
2. Are rights in the strong sense compatible with Mill's Utilitarianism? (See the footnote about Institutional Utilitarianism.)
3. Do you think that Kant would accept rights in the strong sense or not?

John Rawls

A Theory of Justice

John Rawls is professor of philosophy at Harvard University. Our reading is taken from his well-known book A Theory of Justice *(1971).*

Rawls' theory states that there are two Principles of Justice: The first principle involves equal

basic liberties, and the second principle concerns the arrangement of social and economic inequalities. According to Rawls' theory, these are the principles that free and rational persons would ac-

cept in a hypothetical original position where there is a veil of ignorance hiding from the contractors all the particular facts about themselves.

THE MAIN IDEA OF THE THEORY OF JUSTICE

My aim is to present a conception of justice which generalizes and carries to a higher level of abstraction the familiar theory of the social contract as found, say, in Locke, Rousseau, and Kant.[1] In order to do this we are not to think of the original contract as one to enter a particular society or to set up a particular form of government. Rather, the guiding idea is that the principles of justice for the basic structure of society are the object of the original agreement. They are the principles that free and rational persons concerned to further their own interests would accept in an initial position of equality as defining the fundamental terms of their association. These principles are to regulate all further agreements; they specify the kinds of social cooperation that can be entered into and the forms of government that can be established. This way of regarding the principles of justice I shall call justice as fairness.

Thus we are to imagine that those who engage in social cooperation choose together, in one joint act, the principles which are to assign basic rights and duties and to determine the division of social benefits. Men are to decide in advance how they are to regulate their claims against one another and what is to be the foundation charter of their society. Just as each person must decide by rational reflection what constitutes his good, that is, the system of ends which it is rational for him to pursue, so a group of persons must decide once and for all what is to count among them as just and unjust. The choice which rational men would make in this hypothetical situation of equal liberty, assuming for the present that this choice problem has a solution, determines the principles of justice.

In justice as fairness the original position of equality corresponds to the state of nature in the traditional theory of the social contract. This original position is not, of course, thought of as an actual historical state of affairs, much less as

a primitive condition of culture. It is understood as a purely hypothetical situation characterized so as to lead to a certain conception of justice.[2] Among the essential features of this situation is that no one knows his place in society, his class position or social status, nor does any one know his fortune in the distribution of natural assets and abilities, his intelligence, strength, and the like. I shall even assume that the parties do not know their conceptions of the good or their special psychological propensities. The principles of justice are chosen behind a veil of ignorance. This ensures that no one is advantaged or disadvantaged in the choice of principles by the outcome of natural chance or the contingency of social circumstances. Since all are similarly situated and no one is able to design principles to favor his particular condition, the principles of justice are the result of a fair agreement or bargain. For given the circumstances of the original position, the symmetry of everyone's relations to each other, this initial situation is fair between individuals as moral persons, that is, as rational beings with their own ends and capable, I shall assume, of a sense of justice. The original position is, one might say, the appropriate initial status quo, and thus the fundamental agreements reached in it are fair. This explains the propriety of the name "justice as fairness": it conveys the idea that the principles of justice are agreed to in an initial situation that is fair. The name does not mean that the concepts of justice and fairness are the same, any more than the phrase "poetry as metaphor" means that the concepts of poetry and metaphor are the same.

Justice as fairness begins, as I have said, with one of the most general of all choices which persons might make together, namely, with the choice of the first principles of a conception of justice which is to regulate all subsequent criticism and reform of institutions. Then, having chosen a conception of justice, we can suppose that they are to choose a constitution and a legislature to enact laws, and so on, all in accordance with the principles of justice initially agreed upon. Our social situation is just if it is such that by this sequence of hypothetical agreements we would have contracted into the general system of rules which defines it. Moreover, assuming that the original position does determine a set of principles (that is, that a particular conception of justice would be chosen), it will then be true that whenever social institutions satisfy these principles those engaged in them can say to one another that they are co-operating on terms to which they would agree if they were free and equal persons whose relations with respect to one another were fair. They could all view their arrangements as meeting the stipulations which they would acknowledge in an initial situation that embodies widely accepted and reasonable constraints on the choice of principles. The general recognition of this fact would provide the basis for a public acceptance of the corresponding principles of justice. No society can, of course, be a scheme of cooperation which men enter voluntarily in a literal sense; each person finds himself placed at birth in some particular position in some particular society, and the nature of this position materially affects his life prospects. Yet a society satisfying the principles of justice as fairness comes as close as a society can to being a voluntary scheme, for it meets the principles which free and equal persons would assent to under circumstances that are fair. In this sense its members are autonomous and the obligations they recognize self-imposed.

One feature of justice as fairness is to think of the parties in the initial situation as rational and mutually disinterested. This does not mean that the parties are egoists, that is, individuals with only certain kinds of interests, say in wealth, prestige, and domination. But they are conceived as not taking an interest in one another's interests. They are to presume that even their spiritual aims may be opposed, in the way that the aims of those of different religions may be opposed. Moreover, the concept of rationality must be interpreted as far as possible in the narrow sense, standard in economic theory, of taking the most effective means to given ends. I shall modify this concept to some extent . . . but one must try to avoid introducing into it any controversial ethical elements. The initial situation must be characterized by stipulations that are widely accepted.

In working out the conception of justice as fairness one main task clearly is to determine which principles of justice would be chosen in the original position. To do this we must describe this situation in some detail and formulate with care the problem of choice which it presents. . . . It may be observed, however, that once the principles of justice are thought of as arising from an original agreement in a situation of equality, it is an open question whether the principle of utility would be acknowledged. Off-hand it hardly seems likely that persons who view themselves as equals, entitled to press their claims upon one another, would agree to a principle which may require lesser life prospects for some simply for the sake of a greater sum of advantages enjoyed by others. Since each desires to protect his interests, his capacity to advance his conception of the good, no one has a reason to acquiesce in an enduring loss for himself in order to bring about a greater net balance of satisfaction. In the absence of strong and lasting benevolent impulses, a rational man would not accept a basic structure merely because it maximized the algebraic sum of advantages irrespective of its permanent effects on his own basic rights and interests. Thus it seems that the principle of utility is incompatible with the conception of social cooperation among equals for mutual advantage. It appears to be inconsistent with the idea of reciprocity implicit in the notion of a well-ordered society. Or, at any rate, so I shall argue.

I shall maintain instead that the persons in the initial situation would choose two rather different principles: the first requires equality in the assignment of basic rights and duties, while the second holds that social and economic inequalities, for example inequalities of wealth and authority, are just only if they result in compensating benefits for everyone, and in particular for the least advantaged members of society. These principles rule out justifying institutions on the grounds that the hardships of some are offset by a greater good in the aggregate. It may be expedient but it is not just that some should have less in order that others may prosper. But there is no injustice in the greater benefits earned by a few provided that the situation of persons not so fortunate is thereby improved. The intuitive idea is that since everyone's well-being depends upon a scheme of cooperation without which no one could have a satisfactory life, the division of advantages should be such as to draw forth the willing cooperation of everyone taking part in it, including those less well situated. Yet this can be expected only if reasonable terms are proposed. The two principles mentioned seem to be a fair agreement on the basis of which those better endowed, or more fortunate in their social position, neither of which we can be said to deserve, could expect the willing cooperation of others when some workable scheme is a necessary condition of the welfare of all.[3] Once we decide to look for a conception of justice that nullifies the accidents of natural endowment and the contingencies of social circumstance as counters in quest for political and economic advantage, we are led to these principles. They express the result of leaving aside those aspects of the social world that seem arbitrary from a moral point of view.

The problem of the choice of principles, however, is extremely difficult. I do not expect the answer I shall suggest to be convincing to everyone. It is, therefore, worth noting from the outset that justice as fairness, like other contract views, consists of two parts: (1) an interpretation of the initial situation and of the problem of choice posed there, and (2) a set of principles which, it is argued, would be agreed to. One may accept the first part of the theory (or some variant thereof), but not the other, and conversely. The concept of the initial contractual situation may seem reasonable although the particular principles proposed are rejected. To be sure, I want to maintain that the most appropriate conception of this situation does lead to principles of justice contrary to utilitarianism and perfectionism, and therefore that the contract doctrine provides an alternative to these views. . . .

A final remark. Justice as fairness is not a complete contract theory. For it is clear that the contractarian idea can be extended to the choice of more or less an entire ethical system, that is, to a system including principles for all the virtues and not only for justice. Now for the most part I shall consider only principles of justice and others closely related to them; I make no attempt to discuss the virtues in a systematic way. Obviously if justice as fairness succeeds reasonably well, a next step would be to study the more general view suggested by the name

"rightness as fairness." But even this wider theory fails to embrace all moral relationships, since it would seem to include only our relations with other persons and to leave out of account how we are to conduct ourselves toward animals and the rest of nature. I do not contend that the contract notion offers a way to approach these questions which are certainly of the first importance; and I shall have to put them aside. We must recognize the limited scope of justice as fairness and of the general type of view that it exemplifies. How far its conclusions must be revised once these other matters are understood cannot be decided in advance. . . .

TWO PRINCIPLES OF JUSTICE

I shall now state in a provisional form the two principles of justice that I believe would be chosen in the original position. In this section I wish to make only the most general comments, and therefore the first formulation of these principles is tentative. As we go on I shall run through several formulations and approximate step by step the final statement to be given much later. I believe that doing this allows the exposition to proceed in a natural way.

The first statement of the two principles reads as follows.

First: each person is to have an equal right to the most extensive basic liberty compatible with a similar liberty for others.
Second: social and economic inequalities are to be arranged so that they are both (a) reasonably expected to be to everyone's advantage, and (b) attached to positions and offices open to all. . . .

By way of general comment, these principles primarily apply, as I have said, to the basic structure of society. They are to govern the assignment of rights and duties and to regulate the distribution of social and economic advantages. As their formulation suggests, these principles presuppose that the social structure can be divided into two more or less distinct parts, the first principle applying to the one, the second to the other. They distinguish between those aspects of the social system that define and secure the equal liberties of citizenship and those that specify and establish social and economic inequalities. The basic liberties of citizens are, roughly speaking, political liberty (the right to vote and to be eligible for public office) together with freedom of speech and assembly; liberty of conscience and freedom of thought; freedom of the person along with the right to hold (personal) property; and freedom from arbitrary arrest and seizure as defined by the concept of the rule of law. These liberties are all required to be equal by the first principle, since citizens of a just society are to have the same basic rights.

The second principle applies, in the first approximation, to the distribution of income and wealth and to the design of organizations that make use of differences in authority and responsibility, or chains of command. While the distribution of wealth and income need not be equal, it must be to everyone's advantage, and at the same time, positions of authority and offices of command must be accessible to all. One applies the second principle by holding positions open, and then, subject to this constraint, arranges social and economic inequalities so that everyone benefits.

These principles are to be arranged in a serial order with the first principle prior to the second. This ordering means that a departure from the institutions of equal liberty required by the first principle cannot be justified by, or compensated for, by greater social and economic advantages. The distribution of wealth and income, and the hierarchies of authority, must be consistent with both the liberties of equal citizenship and equality of opportunity.

It is clear that these principles are rather specific in their content, and their acceptance rests on certain assumptions that I must eventually try to explain and justify. A theory of justice depends upon a theory of society in ways that will become evident as we proceed. For the present, it should be observed that the two principles (and this holds for all formulations) are a special case of a more general conception of justice that can be expressed as follows.

All social values—liberty and opportunity, income and wealth, and the bases of self-respect—are to be distributed equally unless an unequal distribution of any, or all, of these values is to everyone's advantage.

Injustice, then, is simply inequalities that are not to the benefit of all. Of course, this conception is extremely vague and requires interpretation.

As a first step, suppose that the basic structure of society distributes certain primary goods, that is, things that every rational man is presumed to want. These goods normally have a use whatever a person's rational plan of life. For simplicity, assume that the chief primary goods at the disposition of society are rights and liberties, powers and opportunities, income and wealth. . . . These are the social primary goods. Other primary goods such as health and vigor, intelligence and imagination, are natural goods; although their possession is influenced by the basic structure, they are not so directly under its control. Imagine, then, a hypothetical initial arrangement in which all the social primary goods are equally distributed: everyone has similar rights and duties, and income and wealth are evenly shared. This state of affairs provides a benchmark for judging improvements. If certain inequalities of wealth and organizational powers would make everyone better off than in this hypothetical starting situation, then they accord with the general conception.

Now it is possible, at least theoretically, that by giving up some of their fundamental liberties men are sufficiently compensated by the resulting social and economic gains. The general conception of justice imposes no restrictions on what sort of inequalities are permissible; it only requires that everyone's position be improved. We need not suppose anything so drastic as consenting to a condition of slavery. Imagine instead that men forego certain political rights when the economic returns are significant and their capacity to influence the course of policy by the exercise of these rights would be marginal in any case. It is this kind of exchange which the two principles as stated rule out; being arranged in serial order they do not permit exchanges between basic liberties and economic and social gains. The serial ordering of principles expresses an underlying preference among primary social goods. When this preference is rational so likewise is the choice of these principles in this order.

In developing justice as fairness I shall, for the most part, leave aside the general conception of justice and examine instead the special case of the two principles in serial order. The advantage of this procedure is that from the first the matter of priorities is recognized and an effort made to find principles to deal with it. One is led to attend throughout to the conditions under which the acknowledgment of the absolute weight of liberty with respect to social and economic advantages, as defined by the lexical order of the two principles, would be reasonable. Offhand, this ranking appears extreme and too special a case to be of much interest; but there is more justification for it than would appear at first sight. Or at any rate, so I shall maintain. . . . Furthermore, the distinction between fundamental rights and liberties and economic and social benefits marks a difference among primary social goods that one should try to exploit. It suggests an important division in the social system. Of course, the distinctions drawn and the ordering proposed are bound to be at best only approximations. There are surely circumstances in which they fail. But it is essential to depict clearly the main lines of a reasonable conception of justice; and under many conditions anyway, the two principles in serial order may serve well enough. When necessary we can fall back on the more general conception.

The fact that the two principles apply to institutions has certain consequences. Several points illustrate this. First of all, the rights and liberties referred to by these principles are those which are defined by the public rules of the basic structure. Whether men are free is determined by the rights and duties established by the major institutions of society. Liberty is a certain pattern of social forms. The first principle simply requires that certain sorts of rules, those defining basic liberties, apply to everyone equally and that they allow the most extensive liberty compatible with a like liberty for all. The only reason for circumscribing the rights defining liberty and making men's freedom less extensive than it might otherwise be is that these equal rights as institutionally defined would interfere with one another.

Another thing to bear in mind is that when principles mention persons, or require that everyone gain from an inequality, the reference is to representative persons holding the various social positions, or offices, or whatever, established by the basic structure. Thus in applying the second principle I assume that it is possible to assign an expectation of well-being to representative individuals holding these positions. This expectation indicates their life prospects as viewed from their social station. In general, the expectations of representative persons depend upon the distribution of rights and duties throughout the basic structure. When this changes, expectations change. I assume, then, that expectations are connected: by raising the prospects of the representative man in one position we presumably increase or decrease the prospects of representative men in other positions. Since it applies to institutional forms, the second principle (or rather the first part of it) refers to the expectations of representative individuals. As I shall discuss below, neither principle applies to distributions of particular goods to particular individuals who may be identified by their proper names. The situation where someone is considering how to allocate certain commodities to needy persons who are known to him is not within the scope of the principles. They are meant to regulate basic institutional arrangements. We must not assume that there is much similarity from the standpoint of justice between an administrative allotment of goods to specific persons and the appropriate design of society. Our common sense intuitions for the former may be a poor guide to the latter.

Now the second principle insists that each person benefit from permissible inequalities in the basic structure. This means that it must be reasonable for each relevant representative man defined by this structure, when he views it as a going concern, to prefer his prospects with the inequality to his prospects without it. One is not allowed to justify differences in income or organizational powers on the ground that the disadvantages of those in one position are outweighed by the greater advantages of those in another. Much less can infringements of liberty be counterbalanced in this way. Applied to the basic structure, the principle of utility would have us maximize the sum of expectations of representative men (weighted by the number of persons they represent, on the classical view);

and this would permit us to compensate for the losses of some by the gains of others. Instead, the two principles require that everyone benefit from economic and social inequalities. It is obvious, however, that there are indefinitely many ways in which all may be advantaged when the initial arrangement of equality is taken as a benchmark. How then are we to choose among these possibilities? The principles must be specified so that they yield a determinate conclusion. I now turn to this problem. . . .

Endnotes

1. As the text suggests, I shall regard Locke's *Second Treatise of Government,* Rousseau's *The Social Contract,* and Kant's ethical works beginning with *The Foundations of the Metaphysics of Morals* as definitive of the contract tradition. For all of its greatness, Hobbes's *Leviathan* raises special problems. A general historical survey is provided by J. W. Gough, *The Social Contract,* 2nd ed. (Oxford, The Clarendon Press, 1957), and Otto Gierke, *Natural Law and the Theory of Society,* trans. with an introduction by Ernest Barker (Cambridge, The University Press, 1934). A presentation of the contract view as primarily an ethical theory is to be found in G. R. Grice, *The Grounds of Moral Judgment* (Cambridge, The University Press, 1967). See also § 19, note 30. [The footnotes have been renumbered—Ed.]
2. Kant is clear that the original agreement is hypothetical. See *The Metaphysics of Morals,* pt. I (*Rechtslehre*), especially §§ 47, 52; and pt. II of the essay "Concerning the Common Saying: This May Be True in Theory but It Does Not Apply in Practice," in *Kant's Political Writings,* ed. Hans Reiss and trans. by H. B. Nisbet (Cambridge, The University Press, 1970), pp. 73–87. See Georges Vlachos, *La Pensée politique de Kant* (Paris, Presses Universitaires de France, 1962), pp. 326–335; and J. G. Mur-

phy, *Kant: The Philosophy of Right* (London, Macmillan, 1970), pp. 109–112, 133–136, for a further discussion.
3. For the formulation of this intuitive idea I am indebted to Allan Gibbard.

REVIEW QUESTIONS

1. Carefully explain Rawls' conception of the original position.
2. State and explain Rawls' first Principle of Justice.
3. State and explain the second principle. Which principle has priority such that it cannot be sacrificed?

DISCUSSION QUESTIONS

1. On the first principle, each person has an equal right to the most extensive basic liberty as long as this does not interfere with a similar liberty for others. What does this allow people to do? Does it mean, for example, that people have a right to engage in homosexual activities as long as they don't interfere with others? Can people produce and view pornography if it does not restrict anyone's freedom? Are people allowed to take drugs in the privacy of their homes?
2. Is it possible for free and rational persons in the original position to agree upon different principles than those given by Rawls? For example, why wouldn't they agree to an equal distribution of wealth and income rather than an unequal distribution? That is, why wouldn't they adopt socialism rather than capitalism? Isn't socialism just as rational as capitalism?

Annette Baier

What Do Women Want in a Moral Theory?

Annette Baier teaches philosophy at the University of Pittsburgh. She is the author of many articles on feminist theory and other topics in ethics.

Baier claims that an ethics of love best expresses women's insights and concerns, whereas male theories in ethics take obligation to be the central concern. Both theories have problems. The Ethics of Love ignores obligation, and the theories of obligation assume that parents have some kind of nat-

From Annette Baier, "What Do Women Want in a Moral Theory?" *Moral Prejudices: Essays on Ethics* (Camrbidge, MA: Harvard University Press), Copyright © 1994, 1995 by the President and Fellows of Harvard College. Reprinted by permission of Harvard University Press.

ural duty to care for their children and that loving children is a virtue. As a better alternative theory, Baier proposes a theory of appropriate or proper trust which includes both love and obligation.

When I finished reading Carol Gilligan's *In a Different Voice,* I asked myself the obvious question for a philosopher reader: what differences should one expect in the moral philosophy done by women, supposing Gilligan's sample of women to be representative and supposing her analysis of their moral attitudes and moral development to be correct? Should one expect women to want to produce moral theories, and if so, what sort of moral theories? How will any moral theories they produce differ from those produced by men?

Obviously one does not have to make this an entirely **a priori** and hypothetical question. One can look and see what sort of contributions women have made to moral philosophy: Such a look confirms, I think, Gilligan's findings. What one finds *is* a bit different in tone and approach from the standard sort of moral philosophy as done by men following in the footsteps of the great moral philosophers (all men). Generalizations are extremely rash, but when I think of Phillipa Foot's work on the moral virtues, Elizabeth Anscombe's work on intention and on modern moral philosophy, Iris Murdoch's philosophical writings, Ruth Barcan Marcus's work on moral dilemmas, the work of the radical feminist moral philosophers who are not content with orthodox Marxist lines of thought, Jenny Teichman's book on illegitimacy, Susan Wolf's articles, Claudia Card's essay on mercy, Sabina Lovibond's writings, Gabriele Taylor's work on pride, love, and on integrity, Cora Diamond's and Mary Midgeley's work on our attitude toward animals, Sissela Bok's work on lying and on secrecy, Virginia Held's work, the work of Alison Jaggar, Marilyn Frye, and many others, I seem to hear a different voice from the standard moral philosophers' voice. I hear the voice Gilligan heard, made reflective and philosophical. What women want in moral philosophy is what they are providing. And what they are providing seems to me to confirm Gilligan's theses about women. One has to be careful here, of course, for not all important contributions to moral phi-

losophy by women fall easily into the Gilligan stereotype or its philosophical extension. Nor has it been only women who have been proclaiming discontent with the standard approach in moral philosophy and trying new approaches. Michael Stocker, Alasdair MacIntyre, and Ian Hacking when he assesses the game-theoretic approach to morality, all should be given the status of honorary women, if we accept the hypothesis that there are some moral insights for whatever reason women seem to attain more easily or more reliably than men do. Still, exceptions confirm the rule, so I shall proceed undaunted by these important exceptions to my generalizations.

If Hacking is right, preoccupation with prisoners and prisoners' dilemmas is a big boys' game, and a pretty silly one too. It is, I think, significant that women have not rushed into the field of game-theoretic moral philosophy, and that those who have dared enter that male locker room have said distinctive things there. Edna Ullmann Margalit's book *The Emergence of Norms* puts **prisoner's dilemma** in its limited moral place. Supposing that at least part of the explanation for the relatively few women in this field is disinclination rather than disability, one might ask if this disinclination also extends to the construction of moral theories. For although we find out what sort of moral philosophy women want by looking to see what they have provided, if we do that for moral theory, the answer we get seems to be "none." None of the contributions to moral philosophy by women really counts as a moral theory, nor is seen as such by its author.

Is it that reflective women, when they become philosophers, want to do without moral theory, want no part in the construction of such theories? To conclude this at this early stage, when we have only a few generations of women moral philosophers to judge from, would be rash indeed. The term "theory" can be used in wider and narrower ways, and in its widest sense a moral theory is simply an internally consistent fairly comprehensive account of what morality is and when and why it merits our acceptance and support. In that wide sense, a moral theory is something it would take a skeptic, or one who believes that our intellectual vision is necessarily blurred or distorted when we let it try to take in too much, to be an antitheorist. Even if there were some truth in the latter claim, one might compatibly with it still hope to build up a coherent total account by a mosaic method, assembling a lot of smaller-scale works until one had built up a complete account—say, taking the virtues or purported virtues one by one until one had a more or less complete account. But would that sort of comprehensiveness in one's moral philosophy entitle one to call the finished work a moral theory? If it would, then many women moral philosophers today can be seen as engaged in moral theory construction. In the weakest sense of "theory," as a coherent near-comprehensive account, there are plenty of incomplete theories to be found in the works of women moral philosophers. And in *that* sense of theory, most of what are recognized as the current moral theories are also incomplete, because they do not yet purport to be really comprehensive. Wrongs to animals and wrongful destruction of our physical environment are put to one side by John Rawls, and in most "liberal" theories there are only hand waves concerning our proper attitude toward our children, toward the ill, toward our relatives, friends, and lovers.

Is comprehensiveness too much to ask of a moral theory? The paradigm examples of moral theories—those that are called by their authors "moral theories"—are distinguished not by the comprehensiveness of their internally coherent account but by the *sort* of coherence which is aimed at over a fairly broad area. Their method is not the mosaic method but the broad brush-stroke method. Moral theories, as we know them, are, to change the art form, vaults rather than walls—they are not built by assembling painstakingly made brick after brick. In *this* sense of theory—a fairly tightly systematic account of a large area of morality, with a keystone supporting all the rest—women moral philosophers have not yet, to my knowledge, produced moral theories or claimed that they have.

Leaving to one side the question of what purpose (other than good clean intellectual fun) is served by such moral theories, and supposing for the sake of argument that women can, if they wish, systematize as well as the next man and, if

need be, systematize in a mathematical fashion as well as the next mathematically minded moral philosopher, then what key concept or guiding motif might hold together the structure of a moral theory hypothetically produced by a reflective woman, Gilligan-style, who has taken up moral theorizing as a calling? What would be a suitable central question, principle, or concept to structure a moral theory which might accommodate those moral insights which women tend to have more readily than men, and to answer those moral questions which, it seems, worry women more than men? I hypothesized that the women's theory, expressive mainly of women's insights and concerns, would be an ethics of love, and this hypothesis seems to be Gilligan's too, since she has gone on from *In a Different Voice* to write about the limitations of Freud's understanding of love as women know it. But presumably women theorists will be like enough to men to want their moral theory to be acceptable to all, so acceptable both to reflective women and reflective men. Like any good theory, it will need not to ignore the partial truth of previous theories. It must therefore accommodate both the insights men have more easily than women and those women have more easily than men. It should swallow up its predecessor theories. Women moral theorists, if any, will have this very great advantage over the men whose theories theirs supplant, that they can stand on the shoulders of male moral theorists, as no man has yet been able to stand on the shoulders of any female moral theorist. There can be advantages as well as handicaps in being latecomers. So women theorists will need to connect their ethics of love with what has been the men theorists' preoccupation, namely, obligation.

The great and influential moral theorists have in the modern era taken *obligation* as the key and the problematic concept, and have asked what justifies treating a person as morally bound or obliged to do a particular thing. Since to be bound is to be unfree, by making obligation central one at the same time makes central the question of the justification of coercion, of forcing or trying to force someone to act in a particular way. The concept of obligation as justified limitation of freedom does just what one wants a good theoretical concept to do—to divide up the field (as one looks at different ways one's freedom may be limited, freedom in different spheres, different sorts and versions and levels of justification) and at the same time to hold the subfields together. There must in a theory be some generalization and some speciation or diversification, and a good rich key concept guides one both in recognizing the diversity and in recognizing the unity in it. The concept of obligation has served this function very well for the area of morality it covers, and so we have some fine theories about that area. But as Aristotelians and Christians, as well as women, know, there is a lot of morality *not* covered by that concept, a lot of very great importance even for the area where there are obligations.

This is fairly easy to see if we look at what lies behind the perceived obligation to keep promises. Unless there is some good moral reason why someone should assume the responsibility of rearing a child to be *capable* of taking promises seriously, once she understands what a promise is, the obligation to obey promises will not effectively tie her, and any force applied to punish her when she breaks promises or makes fraudulent ones will be of questionable justice. Is there an *obligation* on someone to make the child into a morally competent promisor? If so, on whom? Who has failed in his or her obligations when, say, war orphans who grew up without parental love or any other love arrive at legal adulthood very willing to be untrue to their word? Who failed in what obligation in all those less extreme cases of attempted but unsuccessful moral education? The parents who didn't produce promise-keeping offspring? Those who failed to educate the parents in how to educate their children (whoever it might be who could plausibly be thought to have the responsibility for training parents to fulfill their obligations)? The liberal version of our basic moral obligations tends to be fairly silent on who has what obligations to new members of the moral community, and it would throw most theories of the justification of obligations into some confusion if the obligation to rear one's children lovingly were added to the list of obligations. Such evidence as we have about the conditions in which children do successfully "learn" the morality of the community of which they are members suggests that we cannot substitute "conscientiously" for "lovingly" in this hypothetical extra needed obligation. But an obligation to love, in the strong sense needed, would be an embarrassment to the theorist, given most accepted versions of "ought implies can."

It is hard to make fair generalizations here, so I shall content myself with indicating how this charge I am making against the current men's moral theories, that their version of the justified list of obligations does not ensure the proper care of the young and so does nothing to ensure the stability of the morality in question over several generations, can be made against what I regard as the best of the men's recent theories, Rawls's theory of justice. One of the great strengths of Rawls's theory is the careful attention given to the question of how just institutions produce the conditions for their continued support, across generations, and in particular of how the sense of justice will arise in children, once there are minimally just institutions structuring the social world into which they are born. Rawls, more than most moral theorists, has attended to the question of the stability of his just society, given what we know about child development. But Rawls's sensitive account of the conditions for the development of that sense of justice needed for the maintenance of his version of a just society takes it for granted that there will be loving parents rearing the children in whom the sense of justice is to develop. "The parents, we may suppose, love the child, and in time the child comes to love and trust the parents." Why may we suppose this? Not because compliance with Rawls's version of our obligations and duties will ensure it. Rawl's theory, like so many other theories of obligation, in the end must take out a loan not only on the natural duty of parents to care for children (which he will have no trouble including) but on the natural *virtue* of parental love (or even a loan on the maternal instinct?). The virtue of being a *loving* parent must supplement the natural duties and obligations of justice, if the just society is to last beyond the first generation. And as Nancy Chodorow's work indicates, the loving parents must also accept a certain division of child-care responsibility if their version of the obligations and virtues of men and women is, along with their version of the division of labor accompanying that allocation of virtues, to be passed on.

Reliance on a recognized obligation to turn oneself into a good parent or else to avoid becoming a parent would be a problematic solution. Good parents tend to be the children of good parents, so this obligation would collapse into the obligation to avoid parenthood unless one expected to be a good parent. That, given available methods of contraception, may itself convert into the obligation, should one expect not to be a good parent, to sexual abstinence, or sterilization, or resolute resort to abortion when contraception fails. The conditional obligation to abort, and in effect also the conditional obligation to sterilization, falls on the women. There may be conditions in which the rational moral choice is between obligatory sexual abstinence and obligatory sterilization, but obligatory abortion, such as women in China now face, seems to me a moral monster. I do not believe that liberal moral theorists will be able to persuade reflective women that a morality that in any conditions makes abortion obligatory, as distinct from permitted or advisable or, on occasion, best, is in their own as well as their male fellows' long-term self-interest. It would be tragic if such moral questions in the end came to the question of whose best interests to sacrifice, men's or women's. I do not believe that they *do* come to this, but should they, then justice would require that, given the long history of the subordination of women's to men's interests, men's interests be sacrificed. Justice, of course, never decides these issues unless power reinforces justice, so I am not predicting any victory for women, should it ever come to a fight over obligatory abortion or over who is to face obligatory sterilization.

No liberal moral theorist, as far as I know, is advocating obligatory abortion or obligatory sterilization when necessary to prevent the conception of children whose parents do not expect to love them. My point rather is that they escape this conclusion only by avoiding the issue of what is to ensure that new members of the moral community do get the loving care they need to become morally competent persons. Liberal moral theories assume that women either will provide loving maternal care, or will persuade their mates to provide loving paternal care, or when pregnant will decide for abortion, encouraged by their freedom-loving men. These theories, in other words, exploit the culturally encouraged maternal instinct and/or the culturally encouraged docility of women. The liberal system would receive a nasty spanner in its works should women use their freedom of choice as regards abortion to choose *not* to abort, and then leave their newborn children on their fathers' doorsteps. That would test liberal morality's ability to provide for its own survival.

At this point it may be objected that every moral theory must make some assumptions about the natural psychology of those on whom obligations are imposed. Why shouldn't the liberal theory count on a continuing sufficient supply of good loving mothers, as it counts on continuing self-interest and, perhaps, on a continuing supply of pugnacious men who are able and willing to become good soldiers, without turning any of these into moral *obligations*? Why waste moral resources recognizing as obligatory or as virtuous what one can count on getting without moral pressure? If, in the moral economy, one can get enough good mothers and good warriors "for free," why not gladly exploit what nature and cultural history offer? I cannot answer this question fully here, but my argument does depend upon the assumption that a decent morality will *not* depend for its stability on forces to which it gives no moral recognition. Its account books should be open to scrutiny, and there should be no unpaid debts, no loans with no prospect of repayment. I also assume that once we are clear about these matters and about the interdependencies involved, our principles of justice will not allow us to recognize either a special obligation on every woman to initiate the killing of the fetus she has conceived, should she and her mate be, or think they will be, deficient in parental love, or a special obligation on every young man to kill those his elders have labeled enemies of his country. Both such "obligations" are prima facie suspect, and difficult to make consistent with any of the principles supposedly generating obligations in modern moral theories.

I also assume that, on reflection, we will not want to recognize as *virtues* the character traits of women and men which lead them to supply such life and death services "for free." Neither maternal servitude, nor the resoluteness needed to kill off one's children to prevent their growing up unloved, nor the easy willingness to go out and kill when ordered to do so by authorities seems to me to be a character trait a decent morality will encourage by labeling a virtue. But the liberals' morality must somehow encourage such traits if its stability depends on enough people showing them. There is, then, understandable motive for liberals' avoidance of the question of whether such qualities are or are not morally approved of, and of whether or not there is any obligation to act as one with such character traits would act.

It is symptomatic of the bad faith of liberal morality as understood by many of those who defend it that issues such as whether to fight or not to fight, to have or not to have an abortion, or to be or not to be an unpaid maternal drudge are left to individual conscience. Since there is no coherent guidance liberal morality can give on these issues, which clearly are *not* matters of moral indifference, liberal morality tells each of us, "the choice is yours," hoping that enough will choose to be self-sacrificial life providers and self-sacrificial death dealers to suit the purposes of the rest.

Rawls's theory does explicitly face the question of the moral justification of refusal to bear arms, and how a just society justly provides for its own defense. The hardships imposed on conscripted soldiers are, he says, a necessary evil, and the most that just institutions can do is to "make sure that the risks of suffering from those misfortunes are more or less evenly shared by all members of society over the course of their life, and that there is no avoidable class bias in selecting those who are called for duty." What of sex/gender bias? Or is that assumed to be unavoidable? Rawls's principles seem to me to imply that women should be conscripted, if anyone is (and I think that is right), but since he avoids the questions of justice between men and women one does not know whether he intended this implication. His suggestion that one argument in favor of a conscripted army is that it is

less likely to be an instrument of unjustified foreign adventures will become even stronger, I believe, if half the conscripts are women. Like most male moral theorists, Rawls does not discuss the morality of having children, refusing to have them, refusing to care for them, nor does he discuss how just institutions might equalize the responsibilities involved in ensuring that there be new members of society and that they become morally competent members of it, so one does not know whether he accepts a gender-based division of social service here, leaving it to the men to do the dangerous defensive destruction of life and cities, while the support of new life, and any costs going or contrived to go with that, are left to the women. I hope that is not what he meant.

I do not wish, by having myself spoken of these two traditionally gender-based allocations of responsibility (producing and caring for new human life and the destruction of the lives of those officially labeled enemies) together, to leave the impression that I see any parallel between them except that they have both been treated as gender based and that both present embarrassments for liberal moral theory. Not all allocations of responsibility are allocations of burdens, and parenthood, unlike unchosen military life, need not be seen as essentially burden bearing. Good mothers and good soldiers make contributions of [very different sorts and sort of importance] to the ongoing life of a moral community, and they should not be seen, as they sometimes are, as fair mutual substitutes, as forms of social service. Good mothers will always be needed by a moral community, in the best conditions as well as the worst; the need for good military men, though foreseeably permanent, is a sign of some failure of our morality, a failure of our effectively acted upon moral laws to be valid theorems for the conservation of men in multitudes. Nor do the burdens of soldiering have any real analogue in the case of motherhood, which today *need* not impose real costs on the mother. If there are significant costs—loss of career opportunity, improperly recompensed drudgery in the home, or health risks—this is due to bad but largely remediable social arrangements, as the failure of parents to experience any especially parental satisfactions may be also due to bad but remediable socially produced attitudes toward parental responsibility. We do not, I think, want our military men to enjoy killing the enemy and destroying their cities, and any changes we made in social customs and institutions to make such pleasures more likely would be deplorable ones. Military life in wartime should always be seen as a sacrifice, while motherhood should never need to be seen as self-sacrificial service. If it is an honor and a privilege to bear arms for one's country, as we understandably tell our military conscripts and volunteers, part of the honor is being trusted with activities that are a necessary evil, being trusted not to enjoy their evil aspects, and being trusted to see the evil as well as the necessity. Only if we contrive to make the bringing into the world of new persons as nasty a business as killing already present persons will there be any just reason to exclude young women from conscripted armies or to exclude men from equal parental responsibility.

Granted that the men's theories of obligation need supplementation, to have much chance of integrity and coherence, and that the women's hypothetical theories will want to cover obligation as well as love, then what concept brings them together? My tentative answer is—the concept of appropriate trust, oddly neglected in moral theory. This concept also nicely mediates between reason and feeling, those tired old candidates for moral authority, since to trust is neither quite to believe something about the trusted nor necessarily to feel any emotion toward them—but to have a belief-informed and action-influencing attitude. To make it plausible that the neglected concept of appropriate trust is a good one for the enlightened moral theorist to make central, I need to show, or begin to show, how it could include obligation, indeed shed light on obligations and their justification, as well as include love, the other moral concerns of Gilligan's women, and many of the topics women moral philosophers have chosen to address, mosaic fashion. I would also need to show that it could connect all of these in a way which holds out promise both of synthesis and of comprehensive moral coverage. A moral theory which looked at the conditions for proper trust of all the various sorts we show, and at

what sorts of reasons justify inviting such trust, giving it, and meeting it, would, I believe, not have to avoid turning its gaze on the conditions for the survival of the practices it endorses, so it could avoid that unpleasant choice many current liberal theories seem to have—between incoherence and bad faith. I do not pretend that we will easily agree once we raise the questions I think we should raise, but at least we may have a language adequate to the expression of both men's and women's moral viewpoints.

My trust in the concept of trust is based in part on my own attempts to restate and consider what is right and what is wrong with men's theories, especially Hume's, which I consider the best of the lot. I have found myself reconstructing his account of the artifices of justice as an account of the progressive enlargement of a climate of trust, and have found that a helpful way to see it. It has some textual basis, but it is nevertheless a reconstruction, and one I have found, immodestly, an improvement. So it is because I have tried the concept and explored its dimensions a bit—the variety of goods we may trust others not to take from us, the sort of security or insurance we have when we do, the sorts of defenses or potential defenses we lay down when we trust, the various conditions for reasonable trust of various types—that I am hopeful about its power as a theoretical, and not just an exegetical, tool. I also found myself needing to use it when I made a brief rash attempt at that women's topic, caring (invited in by a male philosopher, I should say). I am reasonably sure that trust does generalize some central moral features of the recognition of binding obligations and moral virtues and of loving, as well as of other important relations between persons such as teacher-pupil, confider-confidante, worker to co-worker in the same cause, and professional to client. Indeed, it is fairly obvious that love, the main moral phenomenon women want attended to, involves trust, so I anticipate little quarrel when I claim that, if we had a moral theory spelling out the conditions for appropriate trust and distrust, that would include a morality of love in all its varients—parental love, love of children for their parents, love of family members, love of friends, of lovers in the strict sense, of co-workers, of one's country and its figureheads, of exemplary heroines and heroes, of goddesses and gods.

Love and loyalty demand maximal trust of one sort, and maximal trustworthiness, and in investigating the conditions for maximal trust and maximal risk we must think about the ethics of love. More controversial may be my claim that the ethics of obligation will also be covered. I see it as covered because to recognize a set of obligations is to trust some group of persons to instill them, to demand that they be met, possibly to levy sanctions if they are not, and this is to trust persons with very significant coercive power over others. Less coercive but still significant power is possessed by those shaping our conception of the virtues and expecting us to display them, approving when we do, disapproving and perhaps shunning us when we do not. Such coercive and manipulative power over others requires justification, and is justified only if we have reason to trust those who have it to use it properly and to use the discretion which is always given when trust is given in a way which serves the purpose of the whole system of moral control, and not merely self-serving or morally improper purposes. Since the question of the justification of coercion becomes, at least in part, the question of the wisdom of trusting the coercers to do their job properly, the morality of obligation, in as far as it reduces to the morality of coercion, is covered by the morality of proper trust. Other forms of trust may also be involved, but trusting enforcers with the use of force is the most problematic form of trust involved.

The coercers and manipulators are, to some extent, all of us, so to ask what our obligations are and what virtues we should exhibit is to ask what it is reasonable to trust us to demand, expect, and contrive to get from one another. It becomes, in part, a question of what powers we can in reason trust ourselves to exercise properly. But self-trust is a dubious or limit case of trust, so I prefer to postpone the examination of the concept of proper self-trust at least until proper trust of others is more clearly understood. Nor do we distort matters too much if we concentrate on those cases where moral sanctions and moral pressure and moral manip-

ulation are not self-applied but applied to others, particularly by older persons to younger persons. Most moral pressuring that has any effect goes on in childhood and early youth. Moral sanctions may continue to be applied, formally and informally, to adults, but unless the criminal courts apply them it is easy enough for adults to ignore them, to brush them aside. It is not difficult to become a sensible knave, and to harden one's heart so that one is insensible to the moral condemnation of one's victims and those who sympathize with them. Only if the pressures applied in the morally formative stage have given one a heart that rebels against the thought of such ruthless independence of what others think will one see any reason *not* to ignore moral condemnation, not to treat it as mere powerless words and breath. Condemning sensible knaves is as much a waste of breath as arguing with them—all we can sensibly do is to try to protect children against their criminal influence, and ourselves against their knavery. Adding to the criminal law will not be the way to do the latter, since such moves will merely challenge sensible knaves to find new knavish exceptions and loopholes, not protect us from sensible knavery. Sensible knaves are precisely those who exploit us without breaking the law. So the whole question of when moral pressure of various sorts, formative, reformative, and punitive, ought to be brought to bear by whom is subsumed under the question of whom to trust when and with what, and for what good reasons.

In concentrating on obligations, rather than virtues, modern moral theorists have chosen to look at the cases where more trust is placed in enforcers of obligations than is placed in ordinary moral agents, the bearers of obligations. In taking, as contractarians do, contractual obligations as the model of obligations, they concentrate on a case where the very minimal trust is put in the obligated person, and considerable punitive power entrusted to the one to whom the obligation is owed (I assume here that Hume is right in saying that when we promise or contract, we formally subject ourselves to the penalty, in case of failure, of never being trusted as a promisor again). This is an interesting case of the allocation of trust of various sorts, but it surely distorts our moral vision to suppose that *all* obligations, let alone all morally pressured expectations we impose on others, conform to that abnormally coercive model. It takes very special conditions for it to be safe to trust persons to inflict penalties on other persons, conditions in which either we can trust the penalizers to have the virtues necessary to penalize wisely and fairly, or else we can rely on effective threats to keep virtuous penalizers from abusing their power—that is to say, rely on others to coerce the first coercers into proper behavior. But that reliance too will either be trust or will have to rely on threats from coercers of the coercers of coercers, and so on. Morality on this model becomes a nasty, if intellectually intriguing, game of mutual mutually corrective threats. The central question of who should deprive whom of what freedom soon becomes the question of whose anger should be dreaded by whom (the theory of obligation), supplemented perhaps by an afterthought on whose favor should be courted by whom (the theory of the virtues).

Undoubtedly some important part of morality does depend in part on a system of threats and bribes, at least for its survival in difficult conditions when normal goodwill and normally virtuous dispositions may be insufficient to motivate the conduct required for the preservation and justice of the moral network of relationships. But equally undoubtedly life will be nasty, emotionally poor, and worse than brutish (even if longer), if that is all morality is, or even if that coercive structure of morality is regarded as the backbone, rather than as an available crutch, should the main support fail. For the main support has to come from those we entrust with the job of rearing and training persons so that they can be trusted in various ways, some trusted with extraordinary coercive powers, some with public decision-making powers, all trusted as parties to promise, most trusted by some who love them and by one or more willing to become co-parents with them, most trusted by dependent children, dependent elderly relatives, sick friends, and so on. A very complex network of a great variety of sorts of trust structures our moral relationships with our fellows, and if there is a *main* support to this network it

is the trust we place in those who respond to the trust of new members of the moral community, namely, children, and prepare them for new forms of trust.

A theory which took as its central question "Who should trust whom with what, and why?" would not have to forego the intellectual fun and games previous theorists have had with the various paradoxes of morality—curbing freedom to increase freedom, curbing self-interest the better to satisfy self-interest, not aiming at happiness in order to become happier. For it is easy enough to get a paradox of trust to accompany or, if I am right, to generalize the paradoxes of freedom, self-interest, and hedonism. To trust is to make oneself or to let oneself be more vulnerable than one might have been to harm from others—to give them an opportunity to harm one, in the confidence that they will not take it, because they have no good reason to. Why would one take such a risk? For risk it always is, given the partial opaqueness to us of the reasoning and motivation of those we trust and with whom we cooperate. Our confidence may be, and quite often is, misplaced. That is what we risk when we trust. If the best reason to take such a risk is the expected gain in security which comes from a climate of trust, then in trusting we are always giving up security to get greater security, exposing our throats so that others become accustomed to not biting. A moral theory which made proper trust its central concern could have its own categorical imperative, could replace obedience to self-made laws and freely chosen restraint on freedom with security-increasing sacrifice of security, distrust in the promoters of a climate of distrust, and so on.

Such reflexive use of one's central concept, negative or affirmative, is an intellectually satisfying activity which is bound to have appeal to those system lovers who want to construct moral theories, and it may help them design their theory in an intellectually pleasing manner. But we should beware of becoming hypnotized by our slogans or of sacrificing truth to intellectual elegance. Any theory of proper trust should not *prejudge* the question of when distrust is proper. We might find more objects of proper distrust than just the contributors to a climate of reasonable distrust, just as freedom should be restricted not just to increase human freedom but to protect human life from poisoners and other killers. I suspect, however, that all the objects of reasonable distrust are more reasonably seen as falling into the category of ones who contribute to a decrease in the scope of proper trust than can all who are reasonably coerced be seen as themselves guilty of wrongful coercion. Still, even if all proper trust turns out to be for such persons and on such matters as will increase the scope or stability of a climate of reasonable trust, and all proper distrust for such persons and on such matters as increase the scope of reasonable distrust, overreliance on such nice reflexive formulae can distract us from asking all the questions about trust which need to be asked if an adequate moral theory is to be constructed around that concept. These questions should include when to *respond* to trust with *untrustworthiness*, when and when not to invite trust, as well as when to give and refuse trust. We should not assume that promiscuous trustworthiness is any more a virtue than is undiscriminating distrust. It is appropriate trustworthiness, appropriate trustingness, appropriate encouragement to trust which will be virtues, as will be judicious untrustworthiness, selective refusal to trust, discriminating discouragement of trust.

Women are particularly well placed to appreciate these last virtues, since they have sometimes needed them to get into a position even to consider becoming moral theorizers. The long exploitation and domination of women by men depended on men's trust in women and women's trustworthiness to play their allotted role and so to perpetuate their own and their daughters' servitude. However keen women now are to end the lovelessness of modern moral philosophy, they are unlikely to lose sight of the cautious virtue of appropriate distrust or of the tough virtue of the principled betrayal of the exploiters' trust.

Gilligan's girls and women saw morality as a matter of preserving valued ties to others, of preserving the conditions for that care and mutual care without which human life becomes bleak, lonely, and after a while, as the mature men in her study found, not self-affirming, however successful in achieving the egoistic goals which had been set. The boys and men saw morality as a matter of finding workable traffic rules for self-assertors, so that they not needlessly frustrate one another and so that they could, should they so choose, cooperate in more positive ways to mutual advantage. Both for the women's sometimes unchosen and valued ties with others and for the men's mutual respect as sovereigns and subjects of the same minimal moral traffic rules (and for their more voluntary and more selective associations of profiteers), trust is important. Both men and women are concerned with cooperation, and the dimensions of trust-distrust structure the different cooperative relations each emphasize. The various considerations which arise when we try to defend an answer to any question about the appropriateness of a particular form of cooperation with its distinctive form of trust or distrust, that is, when we look into the terms of all sorts of cooperation, at the terms of trust in different cases of trust, at what are fair terms and what are trust-enhancing and trust-preserving terms, are suitably many and richly interconnected. A moral theory (or family of theories) that made trust its central problem could do better justice to men's and women's moral intuitions than do the going men's theories. Even if we don't easily agree on the answer to the question of who should trust whom with what, who should accept and who should meet various sorts of trust, and why, these questions might enable us better to reason morally together than we can when the central moral questions are reduced to those of whose favor one must court and whose anger one must dread. But such programmatic claims as I am making will be tested only when women standing on the shoulders of men, or men on the shoulders of women, or some theorizing Tiresias actually works out such a theory. I am no Tiresias, and have not foresuffered all the labor pains of such a theory. I aim here only to fertilize.

REVIEW QUESTIONS

1. Baier distinguishes between different kinds of moral theory. What are they? What kind of moral theory do women give us?

2. According to Baier, why do women adopt an ethics of love?
3. What is wrong with male theories that focus on obligation? In particular, what are Baier's criticisms of Rawls' Theory of Justice?

DISCUSSION QUESTIONS

1. Do people have a duty to be good parents? Is this something that morality requires?

2. Suppose a pregnant woman hates children and will be a bad mother. Does she have an obligation to get an abortion?
3. Consider this objection to Baier: The ethics of obligation is prior to the ethics of trust because we need to see if people satisfy obligations before we can trust them. How would Baier respond?

Virginia Held

Feminism and Moral Theory

Virginia Held is professor of philosophy at the Graduate Center, City University of New York. She is the author of Rights and Goods: Justifying Social Action *(1989) and* Feminist Morality: Transforming Culture, Society, and Politics *(1993).*

Traditional moral theory, Held argues, has ignored the experience of women, particularly their experiences of birthing and mothering. She contends that an adequate moral theory must take these into account. The result is a feminist theory that places its priority on caring and trusting relationships with particular other people rather than on abstract principles and buyer-seller relationships.

The tasks of moral inquiry and moral practice are such that different moral approaches may be appropriate for different domains of human activity. I have argued in a recent book that we need a division of moral labor.[1] In *Rights and Goods*, I suggest that we ought to try to develop moral inquiries that will be as satisfactory as possible for the actual contexts in which we live

From Virginia Held, "Feminism and Moral Theory," *Women and Moral Theory*, edited by Eva Feder and Diana T. Meyers (Savage, MD: Rowman and Littlefield Publishers, 1987).

and in which our experience is located. Such a division of moral labor can be expected to yield different moral theories for different contexts of human activity, at least for the foreseeable future. In my view, the moral approaches most suitable for the courtroom are not those most suitable for political bargaining; the moral approaches suitable for economic activity are not those suitable for relations within the family, and so on. The task of achieving a unified moral field theory covering all domains is one we may do well to postpone, while we do our best to devise and to "test" various moral theories in actual contexts and in light of our actual moral experience.

What are the implications of such a view for women? Traditionally, the experience of women has been located to a large extent in the context of the family. In recent centuries, the family has been thought of as a "private" domain distinct not only from that of the "public" domain of the polis, but also from the domain of production and of the marketplace. Women (and men) certainly need to develop moral inquiries appropriate to the context of mothering and of family relations, rather than accepting the application to this context of theories developed for the marketplace or the polis. We can certainly show that the moral guidelines appropriate to mothering are different from those that now seem suitable for various other domains of activity as presently constituted. But we need to do more as well: we need to consider whether distinctively feminist moral theories, suitable for the contexts in which the experience of women has or will continue to be located, are better moral theories than those already available, and better for other domains as well.

THE EXPERIENCE OF WOMEN

We need a theory about how to count the experience of women. It is not obvious that it should count equally in the construction or validation of moral theory. To merely survey the moral views of women will not necessarily lead to better moral theories. In the Greek thought that developed into the Western philosophical tradition,[2] reason was associated with the public domain from which women were largely excluded. If the development of adequate moral theory is best based on experience in the public domain, the experience of women so far is less relevant. But that the public domain is the appropriate locus for the development of moral theory is among the tacit assumptions of existing moral theory being effectively challenged by feminist scholars. We cannot escape the need for theory in confronting these issues.

We need to take a stand on what moral experience is. As I see it, moral experience is "the experience of consciously choosing, of voluntarily accepting or rejecting, of willingly approving or disapproving, of living with these choices, and above all of acting and of living with these actions and their outcomes. . . . Action is as much a part of experience as is perception."[3] Then we need to take a stand on whether the moral experience of women is as valid a source or test of moral theory as is the experience of men, or on whether it is more valid.

Certainly, engaging in the process of moral inquiry is as open to women as it is to men, although the domains in which the process has occurred have been open to men and women in different ways. Women have had fewer occasions to experience for themselves the moral problems of governing, leading, exercising power over others (except children), and engaging in physically violent conflict. Men, on the other hand, have had fewer occasions to experience the moral problems of family life and the relations between adults and children. Although vast amounts of moral experience are open to all human beings who make the effort to become conscientious moral inquirers, the contexts in which experience is obtained may make a difference. It is essential that we avoid taking a given moral theory, such as a Kantian one, and deciding that those who fail to develop toward it are deficient, for this procedure imposes a theory on experience, rather than letting experience determine the fate of theories, moral and otherwise.

We can assert that as long as women and men experience different problems, moral theory ought to reflect the experience of women as fully as it reflects the experience of men. The insights and judgments and decisions of women as they engage in the process of moral inquiry should be presumed to be as valid as those of men. In the development of moral theory, men ought to have no privileged position to have their experience count for more. If anything, their privileged position in society should make their experience more suspect rather than more worthy of being counted, for they have good reasons to rationalize their privileged positions by moral arguments that will obscure or purport to justify these privileges.[4]

If the differences between men and women in confronting moral problems are due to biological factors that will continue to provide women and men with different experiences, the experience of women should still count for at least as much as the experience of men. There is no justification for discounting the experience of women as deficient or underdeveloped on biological grounds. Biological "moral inferiority" makes no sense.

The empirical question of whether and to what extent women think differently from men about moral problems is being investigated.[5] If, in fact, women approach moral problems in characteristic ways, these approaches should be reflected in moral theories as fully as are those of men. If the differing approaches to morality that seem to be displayed by women and by men are the result of historical conditions and not biological ones, we could assume that in nonsexist societies, the differences would disappear, and the experience of either gender might adequately substitute for the experience of the other.[6] Then feminist moral theory might be the same as moral theory of any kind. But since we can hardly imagine what a nonsexist society would be like, and surely should not wait for one before evaluating the experience of women, we can say that we need feminist moral theory to deal with the differences of which we are now aware and to contribute to the development of the nonsexist society that might make the need for a distinctively feminist moral theory obsolete. Specifically, we need feminist moral theory to deal with the regions of experience that have been central to women's experience and neglected by traditional moral theory. If the resulting moral theory would be suitable for all humans in all contexts, and thus could be thought of as a human moral theory or a universal moral theory, it would be a feminist moral theory as well if it adequately reflected the experience and standpoint of women.

That the available empirical evidence for differences between men and women with respect to morality is tentative and often based on reportage and interpretation, rather than on something more "scientific," [7] is no problem at all for the claim that we need feminist moral theory. If such differences turn out to be further substantiated, we will need theory to evaluate their implications, and we should be prepared now for this possibility (or, as many think, probability). If the differences turn out to be insignificant, we still need feminist moral theory to make the moral claim that the experience of women is of equal worth to the experience of men, and even more important, that women themselves are of equal worth as human beings. If it is true that the only differences between women and men are anatomical, it still does not follow that women are the moral equals of men. Moral equality has to be based on moral claims. Since the devaluation of women is a constant in human society as so far developed, and has been accepted by those holding a wide variety of traditional moral theories, it is apparent that feminist moral theory is needed to provide the basis for women's claims to equality.

We should never forget the horrors that have resulted from acceptance of the idea that women think differently from men, or that men are rational beings, women emotional ones. We should be constantly on guard for misuses of such ideas, as in social roles that determine that women belong in the home or in educational programs that discourage women from becoming for example, mathematicians. Yet, excessive fear of such misuses should not stifle exploration of the ways in which such claims may, in some measure, be true. As philosophers, we can be careful not to conclude that whatever tendencies exist ought to be reinforced. And if we succeed in making social scientists more alert to the naturalistic fallacy than they would otherwise be, that would be a side benefit to the development of feminist moral theory.

Mothering and Markets

When we bring women's experience fully into the domain of moral consciousness, we can see how questionable it is to imagine contractual relationships as central or fundamental to society and morality. They seem, instead, the relationships of only very particular regions of human activity.[8]

The most central and fundamental social relationship seems to be that between mother or mothering person and child. It is this relationship that creates and recreates society. It is the activity of mothering which transforms biological entities into human social beings. Mothers and mothering persons produce children and empower them with language and symbolic representations. Mothers and mothering persons thus produce and create human culture.

Despite its implausibility, the assumption is often made that human mothering is like the mothering of other animals rather than being distinctively human. In accordance with the traditional distinction between the family and the polis, and the assumption that what occurs in the public sphere of the polis is distinctively human, it is assumed that what human mothers do within the family belongs to the "natural" rather than to the "distinctively human" domain. Or, if it is recognized that the activities of human mothers do not resemble the activities of the mothers of other mammals, it is assumed that, at least, the difference is far narrower than the difference between what animals do and what humans who take part in government and industry and art do. But, in fact, mothering is among the most human of human activities.

Consider the reality. A human birth is thoroughly different from the birth of other animals, because a human mother can choose not to give birth. However extreme the alternative, even when abortion is not a possibility, a woman can choose suicide early enough in her pregnancy to consciously prevent the birth. A human mother comprehends that she brings about the birth of another human being. A human mother is then responsible, at least in an existentialist sense, for the creation of a new human life. The event is essentially different from what is possible for other animals.

Human mothering is utterly different from the mothering of animals without language. The human mother or nurturing person constructs with and for the child a human social reality. The child's understanding of language and of symbols, and of all that they create and make real, occurs in interactions between child and caretakers. Nothing seems more distinctively human than this. In comparison, government can be thought to resemble the governing of ant colonies, industrial production to be similar to the building of beaver dams, a market exchange to be like the relation between a large fish that protects and a small fish that grooms, and the conquest by force of arms that characterizes so much of human history to be like the aggression of packs of animals. But the imparting of language and the creation within and for each individual of a human social reality, and often a new human social reality, seems utterly human.

An argument is often made that art and industry and government create new human reality, while mothering merely "reproduces" human beings, their cultures, and social structures. But consider a more accurate view: in bringing up children, those who mother create new human *persons*. They change persons, the culture, and the social structures that depend on them, by creating the kinds of persons who can continue to transform themselves and their surroundings. Creating new and better persons is surely as "creative" as creating new and better objects or institutions. It is not only bodies that do not spring into being unaided and fully formed; neither do imaginations, personalities, and minds.

Perhaps morality should make room first for the human experience reflected in the social bond between mothering person and child, and for the human projects of nurturing and of growth apparent for both persons in the relationship. In comparison, the transactions of the marketplace seem peripheral; the authority of weapons and the laws they uphold, beside the point.

The relation between buyer and seller has often been taken as the model of all human interactions.[9] Most of the social contract tradition has seen this relation of contractual exchange as fundamental to law and political authority as well as to economic activity. And some contemporary moral philosophers see the contractual relation as the relation on which even morality itself should be based. The marketplace, as a model for relationships, has become so firmly entrenched in our normative theories that it is rarely questioned as a proper foundation for recommendations extending beyond he marketplace. Consequently, much moral thinking is built on the concept of rational economic man. Relationships between human beings are seen as arising, and as justified, when they serve the interests of individual rational contractors.

In the society imagined in the model based on assumptions about rational economic man, connections between people become no more than instrumental. Nancy Hartsock effectively characterizes the worldview of these assumptions, and shows how misguided it is to suppose that the relationship between buyer and seller can serve as a model for all human relations: "the paradigmatic connections between people [on this view of the social world] are instrumental or extrinsic and conflictual, and in a world populated by these isolated individuals, relations of competition and domination come to be substitutes for a more substantial and encompassing community."[10]

Whether the relationship between nurturing person (who need not be a biological mother) and child should be taken as itself paradigmatic, in place of the contractual paradigm, or whether it should be seen only as an obviously important relationship that does not fit into the contractual framework and should not be overlooked, remains to be seen. It is certainly instructive to consider it, at least tentatively, as paradigmatic. If this were done, the competition and desire for domination thought of as acceptable for rational economic man might appear as a very particular and limited human connection, suitable perhaps, if at all, only for a restricted marketplace. Such a relation of conflict and competition can be seen to be unacceptable for establishing the social trust on which public institutions must rest,[11] or for upholding the bonds on which caring, regard, friendship, or love must be based.[12]

The social map would be fundamentally altered by adoption of the point of view here suggested. Possibly, the relationship between "mother" and child would be recognized as a much more promising source of trust and concern than any other, for reasons to be explored later. In addition, social relations would be seen as dynamic rather than as fixed-point exchanges. And assumptions that human beings are equally capable of entering or not entering into the contractual relations taken to characterize social relations generally would be seen for the distortions they are. Although human mothers could do other than give birth, their choices to do so or not are usually highly constrained. And children, even human children, cannot choose at all whether to be born.

It may be that no human relationship should be thought of as paradigmatic for all the others. Relations between mothering persons and children can become oppressive for both, and relations between equals who can decide whether to enter into agreements may seem attractive in contrast. But no mapping of the social and moral landscape can possibly be satisfactory if it does not adequately take into account and provide appropriate guidance for relationships between mothering persons and children.

Between the Self and the Universal

Perhaps the most important legacy of the new insights will be the recognition that more attention must be paid to the domain *between* the self—the ego, the self-interested individual—on the one hand, and the universal—everyone, others in general—on the other hand. Ethics traditionally has dealt with these poles, trying to reconcile their conflicting claims. It has called for impartiality against the partiality of the egoistic

self, or it has defended the claims of egoism against such demands for a universal perspective.

In seeing the problems of ethics as problems of reconciling the interests of the self with what would be right or best for everyone, moral theory has neglected the intermediate region of family relations and relations of friendship, and has neglected the sympathy and concern people actually feel for particular others. As Larry Blum has shown, "contemporary moral philosophy in the Anglo-American tradition has paid little attention to [the] morally significant phenomena" of sympathy, compassion, human concern, and friendship.[13]

Standard moral philosophy has construed personal relationships as aspects of the self-interested feelings of individuals, as when a person might favor those he loves over those distant because it satisfies his own desires to do so. Or it has let those close others stand in for the universal "other," as when an analysis might be offered of how the conflict between self and others is to be resolved in something like "enlightened self-interest" or "acting out of respect for the moral law," and seeing this as what should guide us in our relations with those close, particular others with whom we interact.

Owen Flanagan and Jonathan Adler provide useful criticism of what they see as Kohlberg's "adequacy thesis"—the assumption that the more formal the moral reasoning, the better.[14] But they themselves continue to construe the tension in ethics as that between the particular self and the universal. What feminist moral theory will emphasize, in contrast, will be the domain of particular others in relations with one another.

The region of "particular others" is a distinct domain, where it can be seen that what becomes artificial and problematic are the very "self" and "all others" of standard moral theory. In the domain of particular others, the self is already closely entwined in relations with others, and the relation may be much more real, salient, and important than the interests of any individual self in isolation. But the "others" in the picture are not "all others," or "everyone," or what a universal point of view could provide. They are particular flesh and blood others for whom we have actual feelings in our insides and in our skin, not the others of rational constructs and universal principles.

Relationships can be characterized as trusting or mistrustful, mutually considerate or selfish, and so forth. Where trust and consideration are appropriate, we can find ways to foster them. But doing so will depend on aspects of what can be understood only if we look at relations between persons. To focus on either self-interested individuals or the totality of all persons is to miss the qualities of actual relations between actual human beings.

Moral theories must pay attention to the neglected realm of particular others in actual contexts. In doing so, problems of egoism vs. the universal moral point of view appear very different, and may recede to the region of background insolubility or relative unimportance. The important problems may then be seen to be how we ought to guide or maintain or reshape the relationships, both close and more distant, that we have or might have with actual human beings.

Particular others can, I think, be actual starving children in Africa with whom one feels empathy or even the anticipated children of future generations, not just those we are close to in any traditional context of family, neighbors, or friends. But particular others are still not "all rational beings" or "the greatest number."

In recognizing the component of feeling and relatedness between self and particular others, motivation is addressed as an inherent part of moral inquiry. Caring between parent and child is a good example.[15] We should not glamorize parental care. Many mothers and fathers dominate their children in harmful or inappropriate ways, or fail to care adequately for them. But when the relationship between "mother" and child is as it should be, the caretaker does not care for the child (nor the child for the caretaker) because of universal moral rules. The love and concern one feels for the child already motivate much of what one does. This is not to say that morality is irrelevant. One must still decide what one ought to do. But the process of addressing the moral questions in mothering and of trying to arrive at answers one can find acceptable involves motivated acting, not just thinking. And neither egoism nor a morality of universal rules will be of much help.

Mothering is, of course, not the only context in which the salient moral problems concern relations between particular others rather than conflicts between egoistic self and universal moral laws; all actual human contexts may be more like this than like those depicted by Hobbes or Kant. But mothering may be one of the best contexts in which to make explicit why familiar moral theories are so deficient in offering guidance for action. And the variety of contexts within mothering, with the different excellences appropriate of dealing with infants, young children, or adolescents, provide rich sources of insight for moral inquiry.

The feelings characteristic of mothering— that there are too many demands on us, that we cannot do everything that we ought to do—are highly instructive. They give rise to problems different from those of universal rule vs. self-interest. They require us to weigh the claims of one self-other relationship against the claims of other self-other relationships, to try to bring about some harmony between them, to see the issues in an actual temporal context, and to act rather than merely reflect.

For instance, we have limited resources for caring. We cannot care for everyone or do everything a caring approach suggests. We need moral guidelines for ordering our priorities. The hunger of our own children comes before the hunger of children we do not know. But the hunger of children in Africa ought to come before some of the expensive amusements we may wish to provide for our own children. These are moral problems calling to some extent for principled answers. But we have to figure out what we ought to do when actually buying groceries, cooking meals, refusing the requests of our children for the latest toy they have seen advertised, and sending money to UNICEF. The context is one of real action, not of ideal thought.

Principles and Particulars

When we take the context of mothering as central, rather than peripheral, for moral theory, we run the risk of excessively discounting other contexts. It is a commendable risk, given the enormously more prevalent one of excessively discounting mothering. But I think that the attack on principles has sometimes been carried too far by critics of traditional moral theory.

Noddings, for instance, writes that "To say, 'It is wrong to cause pain needlessly,' contributes nothing by way of knowledge and can hardly be thought likely to change the attitude or behavior of one who might ask, 'Why is it wrong?' . . . Ethical caring . . . depends not upon rule or principle" but upon the development of a self "in congruence with one's best remembrance of caring and being cared-for." [16]

We should not forget that an absence of principles can be an invitation to capriciousness. Caring may be a weak defense against arbitrary decisions, and the person cared for may find the relation more satisfactory if both persons, but especially the person caring, are guided, to some extent, by principles concerning obligations and rights. To argue that no two cases are ever alike is to invite moral chaos. Furthermore, for one person to be in a position of caretaker means that that person has the power to withhold care, to leave the other without it. The person cared for is usually in a position of vulnerability. The moral significance of this needs to be addressed along with other aspects of the caring relationship. Principles may remind a giver of care to avoid being capricious or domineering. While most of the moral problems involved in mothering contexts may deal with issues above and beyond the moral minimums that can be covered by principles concerning rights and obligations, that does not mean that these minimums can be dispensed with.

Noddings's discussion is unsatisfactory also in dealing with certain types of questions, for instance those of economic justice. Such issues cry out for relevant principles. Although caring may be needed to motivate us to act on such principles, the principles are not dispensable. Noddings questions the concern people may have for starving persons in distant countries, because she sees universal love and universal justice as masculine illusions. She refrains from judging that the rich deserve less or the poor more, because caring for individuals cannot yield such judgments. But this may amount to taking a given economic stratification as given, rather than as the appropriate object of critical scrutiny that it should be. It may lead to accepting that the rich will care for the rich and the poor for the poor, with the gap between them, however unjustifiably wide, remaining what it is. Some important moral issues seem beyond the reach of an ethic of caring, once caring leads us, perhaps through empathy, to be concerned with them.

On ethical views that renounce principles as excessively abstract, we might have few arguments to uphold the equality of women. After all, as parents can care for children recognized as weaker, less knowledgeable, less capable, and with appropriately restricted rights, so men could care for women deemed inferior in every way. On a view that ethics could satisfactorily be founded on caring alone, men could care for women considered undeserving of equal rights in all the significant areas in which women have been struggling to have their equality recognized. So an ethic of care, essential as a component of morality seems deficient if taken as an exclusive preoccupation.

That aspect of the attack on principles which seems entirely correct is the view that not all ethical problems can be solved by appeal to one or a very few simple principles. It is often argued that all more particular moral rules or principles can be derived from such underlying ones as the Categorical Imperative or the Principle of Utility, and that these can be applied to all moral problems. The call for an ethic of care may be a call, which I share, for a more pluralistic view of ethics, recognizing that we need a division of moral labor employing different moral approaches for different domains, at least for the time being.[17] Satisfactory intermediate principles for areas such as those of international affairs, or family relations, cannot be derived from simple universal principles, but must be arrived at in conjunction with experience within the domains in question.

Attention to particular others will always require that we respect the particularity of the context, and arrive at solutions to moral problems that will not give moral principles more weight than their due. But their due may remain considerable. And we will need principles concerning relationships, not only concerning the actions of individuals, as we will need evaluations of kinds of relationships, not only of the character traits of individuals.

Birth and Valuing

To a large extent, the activity of mothering is potentially open to men as well as to women. Fathers can conceivably come to be as emotionally close, or as close through caretaking, to children as are mothers. The experience of relatedness, of responsibility for the growth and empowerment of new life, and of responsiveness to particular others, ought to be incorporated into moral theory, and will have to be so incorporated for moral theory to be adequate. At present, in this domain, it is primarily the experience of women (and of children) that has not been sufficiently reflected in moral theory and that ought to be so reflected. But this is not to say that it must remain an experience available only to women. If men came to share fully and equitably in the care of all persons who need care—especially children, the sick, the old—the moral values that now arise for women in the context of caring might arise as fully for men.

There are some experiences, however, that are open only to women: menstruating, having an abortion, giving birth, suckling. We need to consider their possible significance or lack of significance for moral experience and theory. I will consider here only one kind of experience not open to men but of obviously great importance to women: the experience of giving birth or of deciding not to. Does the very experience of giving birth, or of deciding not to exercise the capacity to do so, make a significant difference for moral experience and moral theory? I think the answer must be: perhaps.

Of course birthing is a social as well as a personal or biological event. It takes place in a social context structured by attitudes and arrangements that deeply affect how women experience it: whether it will be accepted as "natural," whether it will be welcomed and celebrated, or whether it will be fraught with fear or shame. But I wish to focus briefly on the conscious awareness women can have of what they are doing in giving birth, and on the specifically personal and biological aspects of human birthing.

It is women who give birth to other persons. Women are responsible for the existence of new persons in ways far more fundamental than are men. It is not bizarre to recognize that women can, through abortion or suicide, choose not to give birth. A woman can be aware of the possibility that she can act to prevent a new person from existing, and can be aware that if this new person exists, it is because of what she has done and made possible.

In the past we have called attention to the extent to which women do not control their capacity to give birth. They are under extreme economic and social pressure to engage in intercourse, to marry, and to have children. Legal permission to undergo abortion is a recent, restricted, and threatened capacity. When the choice not to give birth requires grave risk to life, health, or well-being, or requires suicide, we should be careful not to misrepresent the situation when we speak of a woman's "choice" to become a mother, or of how she "could have done other" than have a child, or that "since she chose to become a mother, she is responsible for her child." It does not follow that because women are responsible for creating human beings, they should be held responsible by society for caring for them, either alone, primarily, or even at all. These two kinds of responsibility should not be confused, and I am speaking here only of the first. As conscious human beings, women can do other than give birth, and if they do give birth, they are responsible for the creation of other human beings. Though it may be very difficult for women to avoid giving birth, the very familiarity of the literary image of the woman who drowns herself or throws herself from a cliff rather than bear an illegitimate child should remind us that such eventualities are not altogether remote from consciousness.

Women have every reason to be justifiably angry with men who refuse to take responsibility for their share of the events of pregnancy and birth, or for the care children require. Because, for so long, we have wanted to increase the extent to which men would recognize their responsibilities for causing pregnancy, and would share in the long years of care needed to bring a child to independence, we have tended to emphasize the ways in which the responsibilities for creating a new human being are equal between women and men.[18] But in fact, men produce sperm and women produce babies, and the difference is enormous. Excellent arguments can be made that boys and men suffer "womb envy"; indeed, men lack a wondrous capacity that women possess.[19]

Of all the human capacities, it is probably the capacity to create new human beings that is most worth celebrating. We can expect that a woman will care about and feel concern for a child she has created as the child grows and develops, and that she feels responsible for having given the child life. But her concern is more than something to be expected. It is, perhaps, justifiable in certain ways unique to women.

Children are born into actual situations. A mother cannot escape ultimate responsibility for having given birth to this particular child in these particular circumstances. She can be aware that she could have avoided intercourse, or used more effective contraception, or waited to get pregnant until her circumstances were different; that she could have aborted this child and had another later; or that she could have killed herself and prevented this child from facing the suffering or hardship of this particular life. The momentousness of all these decisions about giving or not giving life can hardly fail to affect what she experiences in relation to the child.

Perhaps it might be thought that many of these issues arise in connection with infanticide, and that if one refrains from killing an infant, one is responsible for giving the infant life. Infanticide is as open to men as to women. But to kill or refrain from killing a child, once the child is capable of life with caretakers different from the person who is responsible for having given birth to the child, is a quite different matter from creating or not creating this possibility, and I am concerned in this discussion with the moral significance of giving birth.

It might also be thought that those, including the father, who refrain from killing the mother, or from forcing her to have an abortion, are also responsible for not preventing the birth of the child.[20] But unless the distinction between suicide and murder, and between having an abor-

tion and forcing a woman to have an abortion against her will, are collapsed completely, the issues would be very different. To refrain from murdering someone else is not the same as deciding not to kill oneself. And to decide not to force someone else to have an abortion is different from deciding not to have an abortion when one could. The person capable of giving birth who decides not to prevent the birth is the person responsible, in the sense of "responsible" I am discussing, for creating another human being. To create a new human being is not the same as to refrain from ending the life of a human being who already exists.

Perhaps there is a tendency to want to approve of or to justify what one has decided with respect to giving life. In deciding to give birth, perhaps a woman has a natural tendency to approve of the birth, to believe that the child ought to have been born. Perhaps this inclines her to believe whatever may follow from this: that the child is entitled to care, and that feelings of love for the child are appropriate and justified. The conscious decision to create a new human being may provide women with an inclination to value the child and to have hope for the child's future. Since, in her view, the child ought to have been born, a woman may feel that the world ought to be hospitable to the child. And if the child ought to have been born, the child ought to grow into an admirable human adult. The child's life has, and should continue to have, value that is recognized.

Consider next the phenomenon of sacrifice. In giving birth, women suffer severe pain for the sake of new life. Having suffered for the child in giving the child life, women may have a natural tendency to value what they have endured pain for. There is a tendency, often noted in connection with war, for people to feel that because sacrifices have been made, the sacrifice should have been "worth it," and if necessary, other things ought to be done so that the sacrifice "shall not have been in vain." There may be a similar tendency for those who have suffered to give birth to assure themselves that the pain was for the good reason of creating a new life that is valuable and that will be valued.

Certainly, this is not to say that there is anything good or noble about suffering, or that merely because people want to believe that what they suffered for was worthwhile, it was. A vast amount of human suffering has been in vain, and could and should have been avoided. The point is that once suffering has already occurred and the "price," if we resort to such calculations, has already been paid, it will be worse if the result is a further cost, and better if the result is a clear benefit that can make the price, when it is necessary for the result, validly "worth it."

The suffering of the mother who has given birth will more easily have been worthwhile if the child's life has value. The chance that the suffering will be outweighed by future happiness is much greater if the child is valued by the society and the family into which the child is born. If the mother's suffering yields nothing but further suffering and a being deemed to be of no value, her suffering may truly have been in vain. Anyone can have reasons to value children. But the person who has already undergone the suffering needed to create one has a special reason to recognize that the child is valuable and to want the child to be valued so that the suffering she has already borne will have been, truly, worthwhile.

These arguments can be repeated for the burdens of work and anxiety normally expended in bringing up a child. Those who have already borne these burdens have special reasons for wanting to see the grown human being for whom they have cared as valuable and valued. Traditionally, women have not only borne the burdens of childbirth, but, with little help, the much greater burdens of child rearing. Of course, the burdens of child rearing could be shared fully by men, as they have been partially shared by women other than natural mothers. Although the concerns involved in bringing up a child may greatly outweigh the suffering of childbirth itself, this does not mean that giving birth is incidental.

The decision not to have children is often influenced by a comparable tendency to value the potential child.[21] Knowing how much care the child would deserve and how highly, as a mother, she would value the child, a woman who gives up the prospect of motherhood can recognize how much she is losing. For such reasons, a woman may feel overwhelming ambivalence concerning the choice.

Consider, finally, how biology can affect our ways of valuing children. Although men and women may share a desire or an instinctive tendency to wish to reproduce, and although these feelings may be equally strong for both men and women, such feelings might affect their attitudes toward a given child very differently. In terms of biological capacity, a mother has a relatively greater stake in a child to which she has given birth. This child is about one-twentieth or one twenty-fifth of all the children she could possibly have, whereas a man could potentially have hundreds or thousands of other children. In giving birth, a woman has already contributed a large amount of energy and effort toward the production of this particular child, while a man has, biologically, contributed only a few minutes. To the extent that such biological facts may influence attitudes, the attitudes of the mother and father toward the "worth" or "value" of a particular child may be different. The father might consider the child more easily replaceable in the sense that the father's biological contribution can so easily and so painlessly be repeated on another occasion or with another woman; for the mother to repeat her biological contribution would be highly exhausting and painful. The mother, having already contributed so much more to the creation of this particular child than the father, might value the result of her effort in proportion. And her pride at what she has accomplished in giving birth can be appropriately that much greater. She has indeed "accomplished" far more than has the father.

So even if instincts or desires to reproduce oneself or one's genes, or to create another human being, are equally powerful among men and women, a given child is, from the father's biological standpoint, much more incidental and interchangeable: any child out of the potential thousands he might sire would do. For the mother, on the other hand, if this particular child does not survive and grow, her chances for biological reproduction are reduced to a much greater degree. To suggest that men may think of their children as replaceable is offensive to many men, and women. Whether such biological facts as those I have mentioned have any significant effect on parental attitudes is not known. But arguments from biological facts to social attitudes, and even to moral norms, have a very long history and are still highly popular; we should be willing to examine the sorts of unfamiliar arguments I have suggested that can be drawn from biological facts. If anatomy is destiny, men may be "naturally" more indifferent toward particular children than has been thought.

Since men, then, do not give birth, and do not experience the responsibility, the pain, and momentousness of childbirth, they lack the particular motives to value the child that may spring from this capacity and this fact. Of course, many other reasons for valuing a child are felt by both parents, by caretakers of either gender, and by those who are not parents, but the motives discussed, and others arising from giving birth, may be morally significant. The long years of child care may provide stronger motives for valuing a child than do the relatively short months of pregnancy and hours of childbirth. The decisions and sacrifices involved in bringing up a child can be more affecting than those normally experienced in giving birth to a child. So the possibility for men to acquire such motives through child care may outweigh any long-term differences in motivation between women and men. But it might yet remain that the person responsible for giving birth would continue to have a greater sense of responsibility for how the child develops, and stronger feelings of care and concern for the child.

That adoptive parents can feel as great concern for and attachment to their children as can biological parents may indicate that the biological components in valuing children are relatively modest in importance. However, to the extent that biological components are significant, they would seem to affect men and women in different ways.

MORALITY AND HUMAN TENDENCIES

So far, I have been describing possible feelings rather than attaching any moral value to them. That children are valued does not mean that they are valuable, and if mothers have a natural tendency to value their children, it does not follow that they ought to. But if feelings are taken to be relevant to moral theory, the feelings of valuing the child, like the feelings of empathy for other persons in pain, may be of moral significance.

To the extent that a moral theory takes natural male tendencies into account, it would at least be reasonable to take natural female tendencies into account. Traditional moral theories often suppose it is legitimate for individuals to maximize self-interest, or satisfy their preferences, within certain constraints based on the equal rights of others. If it can be shown that the tendency to want to pursue individual self-interest is a stronger tendency among men than among women, this would certainly be relevant to an evaluation of such theory. And if it could be shown that a tendency to value children and a desire to foster the developing capabilities of the particular others for whom we care is a stronger tendency among women than among men, this too would be relevant in evaluating moral theories.

The assertion that women have a tendency to value children is still different from the assertion that they ought to. Noddings speaks often of the "natural" caring of mothers for children.[22] I do not intend to deal here with the disputed empirical question of whether human mothers do or do not have a strong natural tendency to love their children. And I am certainly not claiming that natural mothers have greater skills or excellences in raising children than have others, including, perhaps, men. I am trying, rather, to explore possible "reasons" for mothers to value children, reasons that might be different for mothers and potential mothers than they would be for anyone else asking the question: why should we value human beings? And it does seem that certain possible reasons for valuing living human beings are present for mothers in ways that are different from what they would be for others. The reason, if it is one, that the child should be valued because I have suffered to give the child life is different from the reason, if it is one, that the child should be valued because someone unlike me suffered to give the child life. And both of these reasons are different from the reason, if it is one, that the child should be valued because the continued existence of the child satisfies a preference of a parent, or because the child is a bearer of universal rights, or has the capacity to experience pleasure.

Many moral theories, and fields dependent on them such as economics, employ the assumption that to increase the utility of individuals is a good thing to do. But if asked *why* it is a good thing to increase utility, or satisfy desire, or produce pleasure, or *why* doing so counts as a good reason for something, it is very difficult to answer. The claim is taken as a kind of starting assumption for which no *further* reason can be given. It seems to rest on a view that people seek pleasure, or that we can recognize pleasure as having intrinsic value. But if women recognize quite different assumptions as more likely to be valid, that would certainly be of importance to ethics. We might then take it as one of our starting assumptions that creating good relations of care and concern and trust between ourselves and our children, and creating social arrangements in which children will be valued and well cared for, are more important than maximizing individual utilities. And the moral theories that might be compatible with such assumptions might be very different from those with which we are familiar.

A number of feminists have independently declared their rejection of the Abraham myth.[23] We do not approve the sacrifice of children out of religious duty. Perhaps, for those capable of giving birth, reasons to value the actual life of the born will, in general, seem to be better than reasons justifying the sacrifice of such life.[24] This may reflect an accordance of priority to caring for particular others over abstract principle. From the perspectives of Rousseau, of Kant, of Hegel, and of Kohlberg, this is a deficiency of women. But from a perspective of what is needed for late twentieth century survival, it may suggest a superior morality. Only feminist moral theory can offer a satisfactory evaluation of such suggestions, because only feminist moral theory can adequately understand the alternatives to traditional moral theory that the experience of women requires.

Endnotes

1. See Virginia Held, *Rights and Goods: Justifying Social Action* (New York: Free Press, Macmillan, 1984).

2. See Genevieve Lloyd, *The Man of Reason: "Male" and "Female" in Western Philosophy* (Minneapolis: University of Minnesota Press, 1984).

3. Virginia Held, *Rights and Goods*, p. 272. See also V. Held, "The Political 'Testing' of Moral Theories," *Midwest Studies in Philosophy* 7 (1982): 343–63.

4. For discussion, see especially Nancy Hartsock, *Money, Sex, and Power* (New York: Longman, 1983), chaps. 10, 11.

5. Lawrence Kohlberg's studies of what he claimed to be developmental stages in moral reasoning suggested that girls progress less well and less far than boys through these stages. See his *The Philosophy of Moral Development* (San Francisco: Harper & Row, 1981); and L. Kohlberg and R. Kramer, "Continuities and Discontinuities in Child and Adult Moral Development," *Human Development* 12 (1969): 93–120. James R. Rest, on the other hand, claims in his study of adolescents in 1972 and 1974 that "none of the male-female differences on the Defining Issues Test . . . and on the Comprehension or Attitudes tests were significant." See his "Longitudinal Study of the Defining Issues Test of Moral Judgment: A Strategy for Analyzing Developmental Change," *Developmental Psychology* (Nov. 1975): 738–48; quotation at 741. Carol Gilligan's *In A Different Voice* (Cambridge: Harvard University Press, 1982) suggests that girls and women tend to organize their thinking about moral problems somewhat differently from boys and men; her subsequent work supports the view that whether people tend to construe moral problems in terms of rules of justice or in terms of caring relationships is at present somewhat associated with gender (Carol Gilligan, address at Conference on Women and Moral Thought, SUNY Stony Brook, March 21, 1985). Other studies have shown that females are significantly more inclined than males to cite compassion and sympathy as reasons for their moral positions; see Constance Boucher Holstein, "Irreversible, Stepwise Sequence in the Development of Moral Judgment: A Longitudinal Study of Males and Females," *Child Development* 47, no. 1 (March 1976): 51–61.

6. For suggestions on how Gilligan's stages, like Kohlberg's, might be thought to be historically and culturally, rather than more universally, based, see Linda Nicholson, "Women, Morality, and History," *Social Research* 50, no. 3 (Autumn 1983): 514–36.

7. See, e.g., Debra Nails, "Social-Scientific Sexism: Gilligan's Mismeasure of Man," *Social Research* 50, no. 3 (Autumn 1983): 643–64.

8. I have discussed this in a paper that has gone through several major revisions and changes of title, from its presentation at a conference at Loyola University on April 18, 1983, to its discussion at Dartmouth College, April 2, 1984. I will refer to it as "Non-Contractual Society: A Feminist Interpretation." See also Carole Pateman, "The Fraternal Society Contract: Some Observations on Patriarchy," paper presented at American Political Science Association meeting, Aug. 30–Sept. 2, 1984, and "The Shame of the Marriage Contract," in

Women's Views of the Political World of Men, edited by Judith Hicks Stiehm (Dobbs Ferry, N.Y.: Transnational Publishers, 1984).

9. For discussion, see especially Nancy Hartsock, *Money, Sex, and Power.*
10. Ibid., p. 39.
11. See Held, *Rights and Goods,* chap. 5.
12. Ibid., chap. 11.
13. Lawrence A. Blum, *Friendship, Altruism and Morality* (London: Routledge and Kegan Paul, 1980), p. 1.
14. Owen J. Flanagan, Jr., and Jonathan E. Alder, "Impartiality and Particularity," *Social Research* 50, no. 3 (Autumn 1983): 576–96.
15. See, e.g., Nell Noddings, *Caring: A Feminine Approach to Ethics and Moral Education* (Berkeley: University of California Press, 1984) pp. 91–94.
16. Ibid., pp. 91–94.
17. Participants in the conference on Women and Moral Theory offered the helpful term "domain relativism" for the version of this view that I defended.
18. See, e.g., Virginia Held, "The Obligations of Mothers and Fathers," repr. in *Mothering: Essays in Feminist Theory,* edited by Joyce Trebilcot (Totowa, N.J.: Rowman and Allanheld, 1984).
19. See Eva Kittay, "Womb Envy: An Explanatory Concept," in *Mothering,* edited by Joyce Trebilcot. To overcome the pernicious aspects of the "womb envy" she skillfully identifies and describes, Kittay argues that boys should be taught that their "procreative contribution is of equal significance" (p. 123). While boys should certainly be told the truth, the truth may remain that, as she states elsewhere, "there is the . . . awesome quality of creation itself—the transmutation performed by the parturient woman" (p. 99).
20. This point was made by Marcia Baron in correspondence with me.
21. In exploring the values involved in birth and mothering, we need to develop views that include women who do not give birth. As Margaret Simons writes, "we must define a feminist maternal ethic that supports a woman's right not to have children." See Margaret A. Simons, "Motherhood, Feminism and Identity," *Hypatia, Women's Studies International Forum* 7, 5 (1984): 353.
22. E.g., Noddings, *Caring,* pp. 31, 43, 49.
23. See Gilligan, *In a Different Voice,* p. 104; Held, "Non-Contractual Society: A Feminist Interpretation"; and Noddings, *Caring,* p. 43.
24. That some women enthusiastically send their sons off to war may be indicative of a greater than usual acceptance of male myths rather than evidence against this claim, since the enthusiasm seems most frequent in societies where women have the least influence in the formation of prevailing religious and other beliefs.

REVIEW QUESTIONS

1. According to Held, why should moral theory reflect the experience of women rather than just men?
2. Why is mothering the most central and fundamental social relationship in Held's view?
3. What criticism does Held make of standard moral philosophy?
4. What is the moral significance of giving birth according to Held? What sort of ethical perspective results?

DISCUSSIONS QUESTIONS

1. Held says that the activity of mothering is open to men as well as women. Do you agree or not? Is the biological fact that only women give birth relevant or not? Explain your view.
2. Exactly who is included in the category of particular others? For example, could a pet dog or cat be a particular other? Who is excluded?
3. How would Rawls or a utilitarian or a Kantian reply to Held? Do they have a good response?
4. Does feminist ethics ignore the moral experience of men? If so, how does it escape the charge of being arbitrary?

PROBLEM CASES

1. The Winner-Take-All Society. In a recent book titled *The Winner-Take-All Society* (The Free Press, 1995), Robert H. Frank and Philip J. Cook claim that the United States is becoming a winner-take-all society where a few winners (who make up about 1 percent of the population) make an enormous amount of money compared to the losers who make up the bottom 20 percent of the population. Examples of winners are Michael Jordan, John Grisham, Elle Macpherson, Diane Sawyer, and Michael Douglas; they are all superstars who are at the top of their professions. The losers are people living at or below the poverty level.

To support their claim, Frank and Cook cite numerous statistics. They say, for example, that the incomes of the top 1 percent have more than doubled in real terms between 1979 and 1989, while the bottom 20 percent have seen their incomes fall by 10 percent. They cite the fact that the pay of a typical chief executive of a large American company is 120 times that of a manufacturing worker. The average auto worker makes, say, $35,000 a year without overtime. If the executive makes 120 times that, the executive makes $4,200,000! That is indeed a big difference, and it is hard to see what justifies it. Certainly the executive does not work 120 times harder or 120 times more hours. And the company may lose money, as Chrysler Motor Company did before it was bailed out by massive government loans.

Besides having dramatic inequality, the winner-take-all society produces bad consequences for some people. One obvious consequence is that some of the people entering highly competitive professions like acting or basketball are going to end up losers. Not many people can be movie stars or play in the NBA. Another bad consequence is what Frank and Cook call the "Lake Woebegone Effect" (after the Garrison Keillor town where all the children are above average). People are attracted to highly competitive markets like basketball or acting because they overestimate their chances of success; they all think they are above average if not excellent. They are like gamblers who think they can win the lottery. But of course most of these people fail and end up losers. It would be better if not so many people entered these competitive markets, for then there would be fewer losers. Consider NBA basketball. Thousands of young men aspire to play in this league because of the huge financial rewards, but the fact is that only a handful of them, if any, will ever be superstars like Michael Jordan. These men would be better off, Frank and Cook argue, if they entered some less competitive field like auto mechanics.

Is the inequality of the winner-take-all society justified on Rawls' view? Does this inequality benefit everyone? Does everyone have an equal chance to be a winner?

What would Mill's position be on this inequality? Do the bad consequences outweigh the good consequences? Does the happiness of the winners outweigh the suffering of the losers or vice versa?

Frank and Cook propose higher taxes on the winners, despite the fact that most conservatives want to lower taxes. Are higher taxes a good idea or not?

2. *Tobacco and Marijuana.* In the United States it is legal for adults to smoke tobacco in cigars, cigarettes, and pipes. Even though the tobacco companies deny it, most doctors agree that smoking tobacco is unhealthy. Tobacco contains nicotine, a poisonous drug that is as addictive as cocaine and is associated with coronary heart disease and pe-

ripheral vascular disease. In addition, the tar in tobacco smoke damages the lung tissue and causes lung cancer. Despite these facts, smokers and the tobacco companies insist that people have a right to smoke.

Do people have a right to smoke? If so, do they have a right to smoke in public places?

Is it morally wrong to smoke? What would Mill say? How about Kant and Ross?

Is smoking a moral vice? Why or why not?

Should smoking be illegal for minors?

Even though it is legal for adults to smoke tobacco, it is illegal to smoke marijuana in the United States. When smoked, marijuana produces physical effects such as a dry mouth, mild reddening of the eyes, slight clumsiness, and increased appetite. The main psychological effects are feelings of well-being and calmness, and more vivid visual and auditory perceptions. In large doses it may cause panicky states or illusions. In rare cases, large doses may cause psychosis or loss of contact with reality. Prolonged use has been associated with apathy and loss of motivation. But all things considered, marijuana does not seem to be any more dangerous or unhealthy than tobacco, and is perhaps less so. If you agree that smoking should be legal for adults and that they have a right to smoke, then why not legalize marijuana for adults? On the other hand, if you think that marijuana should be illegal, then why shouldn't tobacco be illegal too?

3. *Breaking a Promise and Lying.* Jane Rachel has been reading about people suffering from famine in Africa and she wants to help. But what can she do? She is unemployed at the moment, having lost her job teaching an introduction to ethics course because of poor student evaluations. Students complained that she was too demanding and gave low grades. Despite the fact that she has no spare money and has a brother who needs medical care (he is dying of AIDS), Jane decides that she has a moral obligation to contribute to a famine relief fund. To do this, she asks John, one of the full-time professors of philosophy, to loan her $5,000. She tells him that she needs the money for food, rent, and drugs for her dying brother. This is not true, however. She is still getting unemployment compensation checks, and her brother has a supply of drugs. Also, she promises to pay the money back as soon as she can although she has no intention of doing so. She figures John can afford the $5,000 because he is a full professor with tenure. John feels sorry for Jane and feels guilty because he was partly responsible for her unemployment, so he gives her the money. Jane promptly gives all the

money to famine relief, and the money is used to provide food for starving children in Africa.

Jane told a lie and she is not going to keep her promise. Are these actions morally wrong? What would be the view of Ross, Kant, and Mill?

Instead of giving the money to famine relief, Jane could have given the money to her dying brother.

Given proper treatment, his life might be prolonged. Is this alternative better than giving to famine relief? What is the feminist view?

Is giving to famine relief virtuous? Why or why not?

SUGGESTED READINGS

1. *The Divine Command Theory of Ethics*, ed. Paul Helm (Oxford University Press, 1979), contains articles on the Divine Command Theory by Frankena, Rachels, Quinn, Adams, and Young. Robert M. Adams defends the theory in "A Modified Divine Command Theory of Ethical Wrongness," in *The Virtue of Faith* (Oxford University Press, 1987). Philip L. Quinn gives a sophisticated defense and explanation of the theory using deontic logic in *Divine Commands and Moral Requirements* (Clarendon Press, 1978). Kai Nielson in *Ethics Without God* (Pemberton Books, 1973) argues that ethics can exist without belief in God.

2. *Ethical Relativism*, ed. John Ladd (Wadsworth, 1973), has readings on Cultural Relativism. For a well-written critical discussion of Cultural Relativism and Subjectivism, see James Rachels, *The Elements of Moral Philosophy* (Random House, 1986), Chapters 2 and 3. Chapter 4 of this book covers the Divine Command Theory and Natural Law Theory, and Chapter 5 is on Egoism. Gilbert Harman defends a version of Relativism in *The Nature of Morality: An Introduction to Ethics* (Oxford University Press, 1977). J. L. Mackie presents a subjectivist theory in *Ethics* (Penguin Books, 1977).

3. Ayn Rand explains and defends Egoism in *The Virtue of Selfishness* (Signet, 1964). Paul W. Taylor argues that Ethical Egoism contains an inconsistency in *Principles of Ethics, An Introduction* (Wadsworth Publishing Co., 1975). Joseph Butler makes the classical attack on Egoism in *Fifteen Sermons Upon Human Nature* (London, 1729).

4. J. J. C. Smart defends Act-Utilitarianism and Bernard Williams attacks it in *Utilitarianism: For and Against*, J. J. C. Smart and Bernard Williams (Cambridge University Press, 1973). *Utilitarianism and Beyond*, ed. A. Sen and Bernard Williams (Cambridge University Press, 1973) is a collection of articles on Utilitarianism. *Ethics*, ed. Peter Singer (Oxford University Press, 1994) has a selection of classical and modern readings on Utilitarianism in the section called "Consequentialism."

5. G. E. Moore's nonhedonistic version of Utilitarianism is developed in his *Ethics* (Oxford University Press, 1912) and his *Principia Ethica* (Cambridge University Press, 1959).

6. Kant's work in ethics is difficult. A good place to begin is his *Lectures on Ethics*, trans. Louis Infield (Harper, 1963). His ethical theory is developed in *Critique of Practical Reason*, trans. Lewis White Beck (Bobbs-Merrill, 1956); *The Metaphysical Elements of Justice*, trans. John Ladd (Bobbs-Merrill, 1965); and *The Metaphysical Principles of Virtue*, trans. James Ellington (Bobbs-Merrill, 1964).

7. For commentaries on Kant's moral philosophy, see H. J. Paton, *The Categorical Imperative* (Harper, 1967) and H. B. Acton, *Kant's Moral Philosophy* (Macmillan, 1970). Onora O'Neill discusses Kantian ethics in her article "Kant After Virtue," *Inquiry* 26 (1983), pp. 387–405, and in her book written under the name Onora Nell (instead of O'Neill) *Acting on Principle: An Essay on Kantian Ethics* (Columbia University Press, 1975).

8. A clear exposition of Ross' theory of prima facie duty together with criticism can be found in "An ethic of prima facie duties," by Jonathan Dancy, in *A Companion to Ethics*, ed. Peter Singer (Blackwell, 1991). This book has useful articles on all the important moral theories and many moral problems as well.

9. W. D. Ross explains Aristotle's ethics in his *Aristotle* (Meridan Books, 1959), Chapter 7. John M. Cooper defends Aristotelian ethics in *Reason and the Human Good in Aristotle* (Harvard University Press, 1975).

10. For articles on virtue theory by classical and contemporary philosophers, see *Vice and Virtue in Everyday Life*, third edition, by Christina Sommers

and Fred Sommers (Harcourt Brace Jovanovich, 1993). James Rachels raises objections to virtue theory in *The Elements of Moral Philosophy* (McGraw-Hill, Inc., 1993). Peter Geach discusses classical virtues such as courage in *The Virtues* (Cambridge University Press, 1977).

11. *Human Rights,* ed. Ellen Paul, Fred Mill, and Jeffrey Paul (Blackwell, 1984) is a collection of articles on rights. Another anthology on rights is *Theories of Rights,* ed. Jeremy Waldron (Oxford University Press, 1984). Judith Jarvis Thomson, *The Realm of Rights* (Harvard University Press, 1990), develops a systematic theory of the nature and foundation of rights. John Locke's classical theory of God-given natural rights is found in his *Two Treatises* (1690).

12. The classical formulations of the Social Contract Theory are Thomas Hobbes' *Leviathan* (1651), John Locke's *The Second Treatise of Government* (1690), and Jean-Jacque Rousseau's *The Social Contract* (1762). These books are available in different editions.

13. Since it first appeared in 1971, Rawls' Theory of Justice has been widely discussed. One of the first books on the theory to appear was *The Liberal Theory of Justice* by Brian Barry (Oxford University Press, 1973). Another useful critical discussion is *Understanding Rawls* by Robert Paul Wolff (Princeton University Press, 1977). The journal *Ethics* devoted its entire July 1989 issue to a symposium on developments in the Rawlsian theory of justice.

14. Feminist theory has been much discussed in recent years. A big anthology which covers the application of feminist theory to current issues such as affirmative action, abortion, reproductive technology, meat-eating, militarism, and environmentalism is *Living With Contradictions,* ed. Allison M. Jaggar (WestView Press, Inc., 1994). Another recent collection of readings on feminist theory and its application to religion, art, law, and social and political philosophy is *Woman and Values,* second edition, ed. Marilyn Pearsall (Wadsworth, Inc., 1993). For a comprehensive introduction to different feminist theories, see *Feminist Thought,* ed. Rosemarie Tong (WestView Press, 1989). Another comprehensive anthology is *Feminism and Philosophy,* ed. Nancy Tuana and Rosemarie Tond (WestView Press, 1995). This book covers liberal, Marxist, radical, psychoanalytic, socialist, ecological, phenomenological, and postmodern feminist perspectives.

Chapter Two

ABORTION

Introduction

Factual Background   Abortion is the intentional termination of pregnancy resulting in the death of the fetus. Although the term "fetus" is often used to describe the prenatal organism from conception to birth, the prenatal organism is, strictly speaking, an embryo until the eighth week and a zygote when it is a fertilized egg or ovum. In the future, it may be possible to terminate pregnancy at any stage without causing the fetus to die; perhaps the fetus could be kept alive in an artificial womb or incubator. Then the decision to terminate pregnancy could be separated from the decision about the life of the fetus. Given the present state of medical technology, however, the decision to terminate pregnancy in the early stages is also a decision to kill the fetus or let it die.

Pregnancy is usually understood as beginning with conception (the fertilization of the egg by the sperm); and an abortion is said to be any artificial termination of the pregnancy from conception to birth (so a spontaneous miscarriage is not considered an abortion). But there is a dispute about when pregnancy begins. Recently some doctors have been saying that pregnancy does not really begin until the zygote becomes implanted in the lining of the uterus about a week or two after conception. From this perspective, the prevention or termination of pregnancy by means of drugs is not really an abortion, and it is not exactly contraception either. Some doctors call it postcoital contraception; but because conception may have already occurred, others say it is more accurate to call it an interception. This is some of the controversy surrounding the morning-after pill (Ovral, a birth-control pill) which is widely prescribed on college campuses. Depending on when a woman takes it, this pill prevents either fertilization or implantation. (For more details on the morning-after pill, see the Problem Cases at the end of the chapter.)

In the past, most abortions performed before the tenth week (and after implantation) were done by the medical procedure called dilation and curettage. In this procedure, the cervix is dilated and the fetus is removed from the interior lining of the uterus by scraping it with a curette, a spoonlike instrument. Now abortions are more often done by vacuum aspiration where a suction device rather than a scraping instrument is used to remove the fetus. This involves less risk of internal bleeding than scraping the lining of the uterus. In the future it seems likely that more pregnancies will be terminated by drugs such as Ovral, RU-486, or other drugs under development. Drugs are cheaper, easier, and safer than medical procedures if used early in the pregnancy.

Abortion performed by a qualified doctor is a relatively safe procedure for the mother, particularly if performed in the early stages of pregnancy. (About nine out of ten abortions are done before the twelfth week of pregnancy.) In fact, having an early abortion is roughly seven times safer than bearing a child. Abortion is also a common medical procedure. About 1.6 million abortions are performed each year in the United States; this is more than one abortion for every three babies born alive.

Legal Background   In the 1960s, most states had laws restricting abortion. All fifty states and the District of Columbia, however, allowed abortion to save the life of the mother, and Colorado and New Mexico permitted abortion to prevent serious harm to the mother. In the landmark decision of *Roe* v. *Wade* (1973), the Supreme Court overturned these abortion laws. Our first reading for the chapter is taken from this decision. In this case, the Court ruled that restrictive abortion laws, except in certain narrowly defined circumstances, are unconstitutional. This decision made abortion before viability legally available to women who could afford it and who could find a doctor willing to perform the procedure or prescribe the necessary drugs. It is not accurate to say, as critics do, that the Court has legalized "abortion on demand." In fact, the Court has allowed a number of restrictions on the abortion right, as we shall see.

The decision has been very controversial, and it has been repeatedly challenged. Opponents of the decision have proposed to amend the Constitution with the Human Life Bill, which affirms that human life begins at conception and that every human life has intrinsic worth and equal value under the Constitution. (As Blackmun notes, the Constitution says that the bearers of rights are "persons" and not "human lives.") A recent legal challenge to the decision was the case of *Webster* v. *Reproductive Health Services* (1989). In a 5–4 decision, the Court did not overturn *Roe* but allowed as constitutional certain restrictions placed on abortion by a Missouri law, namely (1) banning the use of public funds for abortion and abortion counseling, (2) banning abortions in public hospitals and clinics, and (3) forbidding public employees to assist in the performance of an abortion.

The latest challenge to *Roe* was in the case of *Planned Parenthood* v. *Casey* (1992). In a complicated and controversial decision that left people on both sides of the issue unsatisfied, the Court again reaffirmed the essential holding of *Roe* that a woman has a right to abortion. However, it permitted states to impose further restrictions on abortion provided they do not impose an undue burden on the woman. The majority of the present Supreme Court has indicated that they do not intend to reconsider the basic abortion right, but given the ongoing controversy about abortion, it seems likely that it will be revisited by the Court in the future.

The Moral Issue   We shall not concern ourselves with the legal aspects of the abortion controversy, but instead concentrate on the moral issue. For many writers, the basic moral issue is whether or not abortion is morally wrong.

In our readings, we can find three main positions on this issue: the conservative view, the liberal view, and the moderate view. The conservative view is that abortion is wrong because it is the killing of an innocent person, the fetus, and as such it amounts to murder. The representatives of this view in the readings are Noonan and Marquis. It seems more accurate to label this the conservative view rather than the pro-life view because those who hold it do not usually favor preserving all life, such as would include the lives of murderers or those engaging in an unjust war. Nor is it accurate to call it the anti-abortion view, for conservatives such as Noonan would allow abortions to save the life of the mother. Noonan mentions the cases of ectopic pregnancy and cancer in the uterus. The most common form of ectopic pregnancy (where the fetus is not in the usual position) is tubal pregnancy; in this condition the zygote does not descend to the uterus but remains lodged in the fallopian tube. The mother will die if the abortion is not performed in this situation, and there is no hope for the survival of the zygote at the present stage of medical technology. Noonan grants that abortion is not wrong in this case; Marquis simply ignores it, along with other hard cases such as pregnancy due to rape.

The second position, the liberal view, takes a view of the fetus that is dramatically opposed to that of the conservative. Instead of viewing the fetus as a person with rights, liberals adopt the Kantian view that only rational beings are persons with a moral status, and because fetuses are not rational self-conscious beings, they have no moral status. As Mary Anne Warren puts it in our readings, the fetus is no more conscious or rational than a fish. It seems to follow that abortion is morally permissible whenever the mother chooses it. This is called the liberal view rather than the pro-abortion or pro-choice view because those who hold it certainly do not recommend that all pregnant women have abortions, nor do they endorse all choices. They are in favor of women having a right to choose an abortion.

But why should a pregnant woman want an abortion? There are various answers to this question. If a woman is pregnant due to rape or incest, she may feel justified in seeking an abortion. Or a woman may want an abortion to avoid giving birth to a defective child. (See the case of "Mrs. Sherri Finkbine and Thalidomide" in the Problem Cases.) A pregnancy that interferes with a woman's career is sometimes cited as a legitimate reason. The liberal insists that abortion is permissible in all of these cases.

Liberals do not agree, however, about infanticide. Some liberals see little difference between abortion and killing newborn infants; in both cases what is killed is not a rational being with full moral status. Mary Anne Warren does not agree. When responding to the objection that her view allows infanticide, she claims that it does not follow from her view that infanticide is morally permissible in our society. She believes that adoption is a better alternative because many people in our society value the lives of infants.

The third view is the moderate one that abortion is justified in some cases, but not in others. Judith Jarvis Thomson, Jane English, L. W. Sumner, and the Supreme Court decision in *Roe* are all representatives of this position in our readings. Although moderates agree in rejecting both the conservative and liberal views, they disagree about when abortion is morally justified. Thomson and English both appeal to rights, and specifically to the woman's rights. Even assuming that the fetus is a person with rights, the woman's rights (for example, her right to life, her right to self-defense, and her right to control her own body) are strong enough to override the right to life of the fetus, at least in some cases. Both Thomson and English agree, however, that the fetus's right to life is not always overridden. In some cases, for example, where an abortion is desired merely for the sake of convenience, an abortion is not justified.

Sumner and the *Roe* decision take a different approach, a dividing-line approach. That is, they try to draw a line in the development of the fetus before which abortion is justified, and after which it is harder to justify. Sumner adopts the utilitarian view that consciousness is the dividing line; when the fetus becomes conscious or sentient (that is, capable of feeling pleasure and pain) somewhere in the second trimester, it acquires a moral standing, that is, it deserves moral consideration in its own right. Before that, abortion is unproblematic; it is morally equivalent to the decision to use contraception. In the *Roe* decision, Justice Blackmun adopts a different dividing line, namely viability. Viability occurs when the fetus is capable of surviving outside the womb. Just when this occurs is the subject of debate. Blackmun puts viability at the twenty-eighth week of pregnancy, but many doctors say it occurs at twenty-four weeks, or perhaps as early as twenty weeks. In any case, Blackmun holds that abortion is legal before viability but that after viability, the state may impose restrictions or even proscribe it except when it is necessary to save the life or health of the woman.

Both Thomson and English reject dividing-line approaches. One problem is that such an approach allows late abortions merely for the sake of convenience, say to avoid postponing a trip to Europe, and both Thomson and English agree that such an abortion would not be justified. Conservatives such as Noonan also object to lines drawn in the development of the fetus separating what is a person and a nonperson. These lines, they argue, are always arbitrary and inadequate. Consciousness is not a good place to draw the line, they say, because animals are conscious, and it is obvious (the conservative claims) that they are not persons with the same moral status as human beings. As for viability, it is a shifting point. The development of artificial incubation may make the fetus viable at any time, even shortly after conception. Furthermore, the time at which the fetus is viable varies according to circumstances such as its weight, age, and race. Opponents of dividing lines often use what are called **slippery slope arguments** to argue that a line cannot be securely drawn at any point in the development of the fetus because such a line inevitably slides down the slope of development to conception; they insist that the only place to draw the line is at conception. This argument is discussed by Thomson in the readings.

The Feminist View of Abortion The views discussed so far do not exhaust the possibilities. There remains another important view to be discussed, the feminist view. In certain critical respects, the feminist view is different from the nonfeminist ones. In the last reading for the chapter, Susan Sherwin explains some of these differences. The nonfeminist positions we have been discussing all begin with the moral status of the fetus; the moral status of the fetus must be established before the wrongness or permissibility of abortion can be determined. But on Sherwin's feminist analysis, the pregnant woman is of central concern, and not the fetus. This does not mean that the fetus has no moral status at all (as in Warren's view), or a moral status only after a certain stage of development (as in *Roe* and in Sumner's view), or a moral status more or less equal to that of the woman (as Thomson supposes), or a full moral status from the moment of conception (as Noonan believes). In contrast to all these views of the fetus as a distinct and independent individual, the feminist views the fetus as having a primary and intimate relationship with the pregnant woman, and as having a moral status dependent on the value the woman places on it. This means that it would be wrong to force a woman to terminate her pregnancy if she does not want this. Unlike the conservative view, the feminist view holds that the pregnant woman is in the best position to make the appropriate abortion decision in her circumstances, and she may decide that termination is the best course of action. In any event, there is no abstract moral rule that must be followed, including the rule that abortion is always permitted. In some circumstances it is not, and the woman who has one has made a mistake. So Sherwin's view is different from Warren's. It is perhaps closest to the position of Thomson and English; Sherwin could agree with much of what they say. But still her approach is different because she does not want to appeal to masculinist conceptions of freedom and rights such as the right to freedom and self-defense. Instead she wants women to be accepted as full moral agents with not only the right to make moral decisions about the pregnancies, but the responsibility to do so.

Philosophical Issues   How can we resolve the moral issue about the wrongness of abortion? Most writers agree that settling this issue requires solving some difficult problems in ethics. One is formulating an acceptable principle about the wrongness of killing. Such a principle is relevant not only in the abortion controversy, but also in discussions of euthanasia, capital punishment, war, and killing nonhuman animals. But as Marquis points out in his interesting and useful discussion, it is very hard to find a moral principle about killing that is not too broad or too narrow or subject to counterexamples. For example, the conservative principle that it is wrong to take a human life is too broad, since it makes it wrong to kill a human cancer-cell culture (since it is both human and living). The alternative conservative principle that it is wrong to kill a human being is too narrow; it doesn't seem to apply to the fetus in the early stages of development. The liberal principle that it is wrong to kill persons or rational beings has similar problems. Even Marquis' own principle about killing is not without difficulties. His suggested principle forbids killing someone because it inflicts on the victim the loss of a future containing valuable experiences, activities, projects, and enjoyments. The principle may be too broad because it seems to imply that killing nonhuman animals is wrong, and this is problematic in our meat-eating society. (See Chapter 9.) Perhaps it is too narrow as well, for it implies that active euthanasia is not morally wrong and this is debatable.

An alternative to this search for moral principles is to abandon it in favor of the feminist view that responsible moral agents should make their own decisions according to the circumstances and not abstract principles. But perhaps this is itself a moral principle, and in any event it is hard to see how one can make a moral decision without using moral principles at all.

As we have seen, the nonfeminist debate about abortion has often centered on the nature and status of the fetus. Is it a person or not, and how do we tell if something is a person or not? One common approach to these problems is to search for a **criterion** of personhood, that is, some feature such as human genetic coding or rationality that is both necessary and sufficient for being a person. Utilitarians like Sumner say that consciousness is the criterion for personhood or moral standing, and Kantians such as Warren hold that there are five features that constitute the criterion for being a person, namely consciousness, reasoning, self-motivated activity, the capacity to communicate, and the presence of self-concepts. Noonan thinks that human genetic coding is the criterion for personhood. Others have held that it is the immortal soul that makes one a person, and so on.

As noted above, the feminist objection to this approach is that the focus on the nature and status of the fetus leaves the pregnant woman out; she is being viewed as a mere container or flowerpot that is holding the fetus and not as a full-fledged moral agent in her own right. Jane English makes another objection. The search for a criterion of personhood is doomed from the outset because the concept of person has fuzzy borders. That is, there are borderline cases in which we cannot say whether an entity is a person or not, and the fetus constitutes just such a case.

If we cannot conclusively determine the nature and moral status of the fetus, then how can we answer the moral question about abortion? Perhaps the most straightforward answer is given by Sherwin. We should ask the pregnant woman herself and accept her answer. She should be allowed to give her own answer as a fully responsible and capable moral agent, and we should not try to impose some other answer on her. Of course, different women will give different answers, but this is what we should expect given the different circumstances of pregnant women and their unborn children.

The tactic of Thomson is to shift the focus of debate from the status of the fetus to the rights of the pregnant woman. She argues that even if the fetus is a person with a right to life, it still does not follow that abortions are never justified. The rights of the mother can justify an abortion. English adopts a similar tactic and uses it to attack both the conservative and the liberal views. Even if we assume that the fetus is a person, the mother's right of self-defense is sufficient to justify abortion in a number of cases including rape, serious harm, or great inconvenience. On the other hand, even if we assume that the fetus is not a person, it still has some rights because it is at least personlike. Therefore, we have an obligation to not kill or harm it without a good reason.

The methods of Thomson and English are open to criticism, however. Both of them rely on puzzling imaginary cases—for example, Thomson's case of the famous violinist who is plugged into another person, and English's case of the mad scientist who hypnotizes people to attack innocent passersby with knives. They ask us what we would say or think about these cases; that is, they appeal to our moral intuitions. Although intuitionists like Ross assume that such appeal will produce agreement, this is not so clear when we are talking about a difficult controversy like abortion. It seems that conservatives simply do not have the same intuitions about these cases as Thomson and English do. Another problem with appealing to intuitions is that these intuitions may merely reflect different backgrounds—for example, the different backgrounds of Thomson and Noonan. If so, then they are not an infallible guide to moral conduct.

The Supreme Court

Excerpts from
Roe v. Wade (1973)

Harry A. Blackmun was an associate justice of the United States Supreme Court. He is a graduate of Harvard Law School, and he was appointed to the Court in 1970. He retired from the Court in 1994.

Byron R. White was an associate justice of the United States Supreme Court. He was appointed in 1962 and retired from the Court in 1993. He is a graduate of Yale Law School.

In the case of Roe v. Wade, *a pregnant single woman challenged a Texas abortion law making abortion (except to save the mother's life) a crime punishable by a prison sentence of two to five years. The Court invalidated this law.*

The reading includes excerpts from the majority opinion written by Justice Blackmun (concurred in by six other justices), and from the dissenting opinion written by Justice White (concurred in by Justice William H. Rehnquist).

Justice Blackmun argues that the abortion decision is included in the right of personal privacy. But this right is not absolute. It must yield at some point to the state's legitimate interest in protecting potential life, and this interest becomes compelling at the point of viability.

Justice White in his dissenting opinion holds that the Court has no constitutional basis for its decision and that it values the convenience of the mother more than the existence and development of human life.

MAJORITY OPINION

A recent review of the common law precedents argues . . . that even post-quickening abortion was never established as a common law crime. This is of some importance because while most American courts ruled, in holding or dictum, that abortion of an unquickened fetus was not criminal under their received common law, others followed Coke in stating that abortion of a quick fetus was a "misprison," a term they translated to mean "misdemeanor." That their reliance on Coke on this aspect of the law was uncritical and, apparently in all the reported cases, dictum (due probably to the paucity of common law prosecutions for post-quickening abortion), makes it now appear doubtful that abortion was ever firmly established as a common law crime even with respect to the destruction of a quick fetus. . . .

It is thus apparent that at common law, at the time of the adoption of our Constitution, and throughout the major portion of the 19th century, abortion was viewed with less disfavor than under most American statutes currently in effect. Phrasing it another way, a woman enjoyed a substantially broader right to terminate a pregnancy than she does in most States today. At least with respect to the early stage of pregnancy, and very possibly without such a limitation, the opportunity to make this choice was present in this country well into the 19th century. Even later, the law continued for some time to treat less punitively an abortion procured in early pregnancy. . . .

Three reasons have been advanced to explain historically the enactment of criminal abortion laws in the 19th century and to justify their continued existence.

It has been argued occasionally that these laws were the product of a Victorian social concern to discourage illicit sexual conduct. Texas, however, does not advance this justification in the present case, and it appears that no court or commentator has taken the argument seriously. . . .

A second reason is concerned with abortion as a medical procedure. When most criminal abortion laws were first enacted, the procedure was a hazardous one for the woman. This was particularly true prior to the development of antisepsis. Antiseptic techniques, of course, were based on discoveries by Lister, Pasteur, and others first announced in 1867, but were not generally accepted and employed until about the turn of the century. Abortion mortality was high. Even after 1900, and perhaps until as late as the development of antibiotics in the 1940s, standard modern techniques such as dilation and curettage were not nearly so safe as they are today. Thus it has been argued that a State's real concern in enacting a criminal abortion law was to protect the pregnant woman, that is, to re-

strain her from submitting to a procedure that placed her life in serious jeopardy.

Modern medical techniques have altered this situation. Appellants and various *amici* refer to medical data indicating that abortion in early pregnancy, that is, prior to the end of first trimester, although not without its risk, is now relatively safe. Mortality rates for women undergoing early abortions, where the procedure is legal, appear to be as low as or lower than the rates for normal childbirth. Consequently, any interest of the State in protecting the woman from an inherently hazardous procedure, except when it would be equally dangerous for her to forgo it, has largely disappeared. Of course, important state interests in the area of health and medical standards do remain. The State has a legitimate interest in seeing to it that abortion, like any other medical procedure, is performed under circumstances that insure maximum safety for the patient. This interest obviously extends at least to the performing physician and his staff, to the facilities involved, to the availability of aftercare, and to adequate provision for any complication or emergency that might arise. The prevalence of high mortality rates at illegal "abortion mills" strengthens, rather than weakens, the State's interest in regulating the conditions under which abortions are performed. Moreover, the risk to the woman increases as her pregnancy continues. Thus the State retains a definite interest in protecting the woman's own health and safety when an abortion is performed at a late stage of pregnancy.

The third reason is the State's interest—some phrase it in terms of duty—in protecting prenatal life. Some of the argument for this justification rests on the theory that a new human life is present from the moment of conception. . . .

Parties challenging state abortion laws have sharply disputed in some courts the contention that a purpose of these laws, when enacted, was to protect prenatal life. Pointing to the absence of legislative history to support the contention, they claim that most state laws were designed solely to protect the woman. Because medical advances have lessened this concern, at least with respect to abortion in early pregnancy, they argue that with respect to such abortions the laws can no longer be justified by any state interest. There is some scholarly support for this view of original purpose. The few state courts called upon to interpret their laws in the late 19th and early 20th centuries did focus on the State's interest in protecting the woman's health rather than in preserving embryo and fetus. . . .

The Constitution does not explicitly mention any right of privacy. In a line of decisions, however, going back perhaps as far as *Union Pacific R. Co.* v. *Botsford,* 141 U.S. 250, 251 (1891), the Court has recognized that a right of personal privacy, or a guarantee of certain areas or zones of privacy, does exist under the Constitution. In varying contexts the Court or individual Justices have indeed found at least the roots of that right in the First Amendment, . . . in the Fourth and Fifth Amendments . . . in the penumbras of the Bill of Rights . . . in the Ninth Amendment . . . or in the concept of liberty guaranteed by the first section of the Fourteenth Amendment. . . . These decisions make it clear that only personal rights that can be deemed "fundamental" or "implicit in the concept of ordered liberty," . . .are included in this guarantee of personal privacy. They also make it clear that the right has some extension to activities relating to marriage, . . . procreation, . . . contraception, . . . family relationships, . . . and child rearing and education. . . .

This right of privacy, whether it be founded in the Fourteenth Amendment's concept of personal liberty and restrictions upon state action, as we feel it is or, as the District Court determined, in the Ninth Amendment's reservation of rights to the people, is broad enough to encompass a woman's decision whether or not to terminate her pregnancy. . . .

. . . Appellants and some *amici* argue that the woman's right is absolute and that she is entitled to terminate her pregnancy at whatever time, in whatever way, and for whatever reason she alone chooses. With this we do not agree. Appellants' arguments that Texas either has no valid interest at all in regulating the abortion decision, or no interest strong enough to support any limitation upon the woman's sole determination, is unpersuasive. The Court's decisions recognizing a right of privacy also acknowledge that some state regulation in areas protected by that right is appropriate. As noted above, a state may properly assert important interests in safeguarding health, in maintaining medical standards, and in protecting potential life. At some point in pregnancy, these respective interests become sufficiently compelling to sustain regulation of the factors that govern the abortion decision. The privacy right involved, therefore, cannot be said to be absolute. . . .

We therefore conclude that the right of personal privacy includes the abortion decision, but that this right is not unqualified and must be considered against important state interests in regulation.

We note that those federal and state courts that have recently considered abortion law challenges have reached the same conclusion. . . .

Although the results are divided, most of these courts have agreed that the right of privacy, however based, is broad enough to cover the abortion decision; that the right, nonetheless, is not absolute and is subject to some limitations; and that at some point the state interests as to protection of health, medical standards, and prenatal life, become dominant. We agree with this approach.

The appellee and certain *amici* argue that the fetus is a "person" within the language and meaning of the Fourteenth Amendment. In support of this they outline at length and in detail the well-known facts of fetal development. If this suggestion of personhood is established, the appellant's case, of course, collapses, for the fetus' right to life is then guaranteed specifically by the Amendment. The appellant conceded as much on reargument. On the other hand, the appellee conceded on reargument that no case could be cited that holds that a fetus is a person within the meaning of the Fourteenth Amendment.

All this, together with our observation, supra, that throughout the major portion of the 19th century prevailing legal abortion practices were far freer than they are today, persuades us that the word "person," as used in the Fourteenth Amendment, does not include the unborn. . . . Indeed, our decision in *United States* v. *Vuitch,* 402 U.S. 62 (1971), inferentially is to the same effect, for we there would not have indulged in statutory interpretation favorable to abortion in specified circumstances if the necessary consequence was the termination of life entitled to Fourteenth Amendment protection.

. . . As we have intimated above, it is reasonable and appropriate for a State to decide that at some point in time another interest, that of health of the mother or that of potential human life, becomes significantly involved. The woman's privacy is no longer sole and any right of privacy she possesses must be measured accordingly.

. . . We need not resolve the difficult question of when life begins. When those trained in the respective disciplines of medicine, philosophy, and theology are unable to arrive at any consensus, the judiciary, at this point in the development of man's knowledge, is not in a position to speculate as to the answer.

It should be sufficient to note briefly the wide divergence of thinking on this most sensitive and difficult question. There has always been strong support for the view that life does not begin until live birth. This was the belief of the Stoics. It appears to be the predominant, though not the unanimous, attitude of the Jewish faith. It may be taken to represent also the position of a large segment of the Protestant community, insofar as that can be ascertained; organized groups that have taken a formal position on the abortion issue have generally regarded abortion as a matter for the conscience of the individual and her family. As we have noted, the common law found greater significance in quickening. Physicians and their scientific colleagues have regarded that event with less interest and have tended to focus either upon conception or upon live birth or upon the interim point at which the fetus becomes "viable," that is, potentially able to live outside the mother's womb, albeit with artificial aid. Viability is usually placed at about seven months (28 weeks) but may occur earlier, even at 24 weeks. . . .

In areas other than criminal abortion the law has been reluctant to endorse any theory that life, as we recognize it, begins before live birth or to accord legal rights to the unborn except in narrowly defined situations and except when the rights are contingent upon live birth. . . . In short, the unborn have never been recognized in the law as persons in the whole sense.

In view of all this, we do not agree that, by adopting one theory of life, Texas may override the rights of the pregnant woman that are at stake. We repeat, however, that the State does have an important and legitimate interest in preserving and protecting the health of the pregnant woman, whether she be a resident of the State or a nonresident who seeks medical consultation and treatment there, and that it has still *another* important and legitimate interest in protecting the potentiality of human life. These interests are separate and distinct. Each grows in substantiality as the woman approaches term and, at a point during pregnancy, each becomes "compelling."

With respect to the State's important and legitimate interest in the health of the mother, the "compelling" point, in the light of present medical knowledge, is at approximately the end of the first trimester. This is so because of the now established medical fact . . . that until the end of the first trimester mortality in abortion is less than mortality in normal childbirth. It follows that, from and after this point, a State may regulate the abortion procedure to the extent that the regulation reasonably relates to the preservation and protection of maternal health. Examples of permissible state regulation in this area are requirements as to the qualifications of the person who is to perform the abortion; as to the licensure of that person; as to the facility in which the procedure is to be performed, that is, whether it must be a hospital or may be a clinic or some other place of less-than-hospital status; as to the licensing of the facility; and the like.

This means, on the other hand, that, for the period of pregnancy prior to this "compelling" point, the attending physician, in consultation with his patient, is free to determine, without regulation by the State, that in his medical judgment the patient's pregnancy should be terminated. If that decision is reached, the judgment may be effectuated by an abortion free of interference by the State.

With respect to the State's important and legitimate interest in potential life, the "compelling" point is at viability. . . . State regulation protective of fetal life after viability thus has both logical and biological justifications. If the State is interested in protecting fetal life after viability, it may go so far as to proscribe abortion during that period except when it is necessary to preserve the life or health of the mother. . . .

To summarize and repeat:

1. A state criminal abortion statute of the current Texas type, that excepts from criminality only a *life-saving* procedure on behalf of the mother, without regard to pregnancy stage and without recognition of the other interests involved, is violative of the Due Process Clause of the Fourteenth Amendment.

   (a) For the stage prior to approximately the end of the first trimester, the abortion decision and its effectuation must be left to the medical judgment of the pregnant woman's attending physician.

   (b) For the stage subsequent to approximately the end of the first trimester, the State, in promoting its interest in the health of the mother, may, if it chooses, regulate the abortion procedure in ways that are reasonably related to maternal health.

   (c) For the stage subsequent to viability the State, in promoting its interest in the potentiality of human life, may, if it chooses, regulate, and even proscribe, abortion except where it is necessary, in appropriate medical judgment, for the preservation of the life or health of the mother.

2. The State may define the term "physician," as it has been employed in the preceding numbered paragraphs of this Part XI of this opinion, to mean only a physician currently licensed by the State, and may proscribe any abortion by a person who is not a physician as so defined.

   . . . The decision leaves the State free to place increasing restrictions on abortion as the period of pregnancy lengthens, so long as those restrictions are tailored to the recognized state interests. The decision vindicates the right of the physician to administer medical treatment according to his professional judgment up to the points where important state interests provide compelling justifications for intervention. Up to those points the abortion decision in all its aspects is inherently, and primarily, a medical decision, and basic responsibility for it must rest with the physician. If an individual practitioner abuses the privilege of exercising proper medical judgment, the usual remedies, judicial and intraprofessional, are available. . . .

DISSENT

At the heart of the controversy in these cases are those recurring pregnancies that pose no danger whatsoever to the life or health of the mother but are nevertheless unwanted for any one or more of a variety of reasons—convenience, family planning, economics, dislike of children, the embarrassment of illegitimacy, etc. The common claim before us is that for any one of such reasons, or for no reason at all, and without asserting or claiming any threat to life or health, any woman is entitled to an abortion at her request if she is able to find a medical advisor willing to undertake the procedure.

The Court for the most part sustains this position: During the period prior to the time the fetus becomes viable, the Constitution of the United States values the convenience, whim or caprice of the putative mother more than the life or potential life of the fetus; the Constitution, therefore, guarantees the right to an abortion as against any state law or policy seeking to protect the fetus from an abortion not prompted by more compelling reasons of the mother.

With all due respect, I dissent. I find nothing in the language or history of the Constitution to support the Court's judgment. . . . As an exercise of raw judicial power, the Court perhaps has authority to do what it does today; but in my view its judgment is an improvident and extravagant exercise of the power of judicial review which the Constitution extends to this Court.

The Court apparently values the convenience of the pregnant mother more than the continued existence and development of the life or potential life which she carries. . . .

It is my view, therefore, that the Texas statute is not constitutionally infirm because it denies abortions to those who seek to serve only their convenience rather than to protect their life or health. . . .

REVIEW QUESTIONS

1. Justice Blackmun discusses three reasons for the enactment of criminal abortion laws. Why doesn't he accept these reasons?
2. Where does the Constitution guarantee a right of privacy according to Justice Blackmun?
3. Is the fetus a person in the legal sense according to Justice Blackmun?
4. According to Justice Blackmun, when is the *compelling* point in the state's interest in the health of the mother?
5. When, according to Justice Blackmun, is the *compelling* point in the state's interest in potential life?
6. Explain Justice Blackmun's conclusions.

7. What are Justice White's objections?

DISCUSSION QUESTIONS

1. What is the right to privacy? Try to define it.
2. What do you think is properly included in the right to privacy, and what is properly excluded?
3. Do you think that the fetus has any legal rights or any moral rights? Defend your view.
4. Justice White complains that Justice Blackmun's opinion allows a woman to get an abortion "without asserting or claiming any threat to life or health" provided she is able to find a doctor willing to undertake the procedure. Do you think that women should be allowed to get such abortions? Explain your answer. Do you believe that doctors have any obligation to perform such abortions? Why or why not?

John T. Noonan, Jr.

An Almost Absolute Value in History

John T. Noonan, Jr., is professor of law at the University of California, Berkeley. His books include Contraception: A History of Its Treatment by the Catholic Theologians and Canonists *(1965), (1970), and* Persons and Masks of the Law *(1976).*

Noonan begins with the question, How do you determine the humanity of a being? The answer he defends is what he says is the view of traditional Christian theology, namely that you are human if you are conceived by human parents. This view is compared to other alleged criteria of hu-

manity such as viability, experience, feelings of adults, sensations of adults, and social visibility. Each of these is rejected as inadequate and arbitrary. In his defense of the traditional view, Noonan does not appeal to the medieval theory of ensoulment, that is, the theory that the soul enters the body at conception. Instead, he rests his case on the fact that at conception the fetus (or strictly speaking, the zygote) receives the full genetic code of a human being. He assumes that anything with human genetic coding is a human being with rights equal to those of other humans. It follows that the fetus is a human being with rights from the moment of conception. Once this has been granted, we can see that abortion is morally wrong except in rare cases where it is necessary to save the mother's life.

The most fundamental question involved in the long history of thought on abortion is: How do you determine the humanity of a being? To phrase the question that way is to put in comprehensive humanistic terms what the theologians either dealt with as an explicitly theological question under the heading of "ensoulment" or dealt with implicitly in their treatment of abortion. The Christian position as it originated did not depend on a narrow theological or philosophical concept. It had no relation to theories of infant baptism.[1] It appealed to no special **theory of instantaneous ensoulment**. It took the world's view on ensoulment as that view changed from Aristotle to Zacchia. There was, indeed, theological influence affecting the theory of ensoulment finally adopted, and, of course, ensoulment itself was a theological concept, so that the position was always explained in theological terms. But the theological notion of ensoulment could easily be translated into humanistic language by substituting "human" for "rational soul"; the problem of knowing when a man is a man is common to theology and humanism.

If one steps outside the specific categories used by the theologians, the answer they gave can be analyzed as a refusal to discriminate among human beings on the basis of their varying potentialities. Once conceived, the being was recognized as man because he had man's potential. The criterion for humanity, thus, was simple and all-embracing: if you are conceived by human parents, you are human.

The strength of this position may be tested by a review of some of the other distinctions offered in the contemporary controversy over legalizing abortion. Perhaps the most popular distinction is in terms of viability. Before an age of so many months, the fetus is not viable, that is, it cannot be removed from the mother's womb and live apart from her. To that extent, the life of the fetus is absolutely dependent on the life of the mother. This dependence is made the basis of denying recognition to its humanity.

There are difficulties with this distinction. One is that the perfection of artificial incubation may make the fetus viable at any time: it may be removed and artificially sustained. Experiments with animals already show that such a procedure is possible. This hypothetical extreme case relates to an actual difficulty: there is considerable elasticity to the idea of viability. Mere length of life is not an exact measure. The viability of the fetus depends on the extent of its anatomical and functional development. The weight and length of the fetus are better guides

to the state of its development than age, but weight and length vary. Moreover, different racial groups have different ages at which their fetuses are viable. Some evidence, for example, suggests that Negro fetuses mature more quickly than white fetuses. If viability is the norm, the standard would vary with race and with many individual circumstances.

The most important objection to this approach is that dependence is not ended by viability. The fetus is still absolutely dependent on someone's care in order to continue existence; indeed a child of one or three or even five years of age is absolutely dependent on another's care for existence; uncared for, the older fetus or the younger child will die as surely as the early fetus detached from the mother. The unsubstantial lessening in dependence at viability does not seem to signify any special acquisition of humanity.

A second distinction has been attempted in terms of experience. A being who has had experience, has lived and suffered, who possesses memories, is more human than one who has not. Humanity depends on formation by experience. The fetus is thus "unformed" in the most basic human sense.

This distinction is not serviceable for the embryo which is already experiencing and reacting. The embryo is responsive to touch after eight weeks and at least at that point is experiencing. At an earlier stage the zygote is certainly alive and responding to its environment. The distinction may also be challenged by the rare case where aphasia has erased adult memory: has it erased humanity? More fundamentally, this distinction leaves even the older fetus or the younger child to be treated as an unformed inhuman thing. Finally, it is not clear why experience as such confers humanity. It could be argued that certain central experiences such as loving or learning are necessary to make a man human. But then human beings who have failed to love or to learn might be excluded from the class called man.

A third distinction is made by appeal to the sentiments of adults. If a fetus dies, the grief of the parents is not the grief they would have for a living child. The fetus is an unnamed "it" till birth, and is not perceived as personality until at least the fourth month of existence when movements in the womb manifest a vigorous presence demanding joyful recognition by the parents.

Yet feeling is notoriously an unsure guide to the humanity of others. Many groups of humans have had difficulty in feeling that persons of another tongue, color, religion, sex, are as human as they. Apart from reactions to alien groups, we mourn the loss of a ten-year-old boy more than the loss of his one-day-old brother or his 90-year-old grandfather. The difference felt and the grief expressed vary with the potentialities extinguished, or the experience wiped out; they do not seem to point to any substantial difference in the humanity of baby, boy, or grandfather.

Distinctions are also made in terms of sensation by the parents. They embryo is felt within the womb only after about the fourth month. The embryo is seen only at birth. What can be neither seen nor felt is different from what is tangible. If the fetus cannot be seen or touched at all, it cannot be perceived as man.

Yet experience shows that sight is even more untrustworthy than feeling in determining humanity. By sight, color became an appropriate index for saying who was a man, and the evil of racial discrimination was given foundation. Nor can touch provide the test; a being confined by sickness, "out of touch" with others, does not thereby seem to lose his humanity. To the extent that touch still has appeal as a criterion, it appears to be a survival of the old English idea of "quickening"—a possible mistranslation of the Latin *animatus* used in the canon law. To that extent touch as a criterion seems to be dependent on the Aristotelian notion of ensoulment, and to fall when this notion is discarded.

Finally, a distinction is sought in social visibility. The fetus is not socially perceived as human. It cannot communicate with others. Thus, both subjectively and objectively, it is not a member of society. As moral rules are rules for the behavior of members of society to each other, they cannot be made for behavior toward what is not yet a member. Excluded from the society of men, the fetus is excluded from the humanity of men.[2]

By force of the argument from the consequences, this distinction is to be rejected. It is

more subtle than that founded on an appeal to physical sensation, but it is equally dangerous in its implications. If humanity depends on social recognition, individuals or whole groups may be dehumanized by being denied any status in their society. Such a fate is fictionally portrayed in *1984* and has actually been the lot of many men in many socieites. In the Roman empire, for example, condemnation to slavery meant the practical denial of most human rights; in the Chinese Communist world, landlords have been classified as enemies of the people and so treated as nonpersons by the state. Humanity does not depend on social recognition, though often the failure of society to recognize the prisoner, the alien, the heterodox as human has led to the destruction of human beings. Anyone conceived by a man and a woman is human. Recognition of this condition by society follows a real event in the objective order, however imperfect and halting the recognition. Any attempt to limit humanity to exclude some group runs the risk of furnishing authority and precedent for excluding other groups in the name of the consciousness or perception of the controlling group in the society.

A philosopher may reject the appeal to the humanity of the fetus because he views "humanity" as a secular view of the soul and because he doubts the existence of anything real and objective which can be identified as humanity. One answer to such a philosopher is to ask how he reasons about moral questions without supposing that there is a sense in which he and the others of whom he speaks are human. Whatever group is taken as the society which determines who may be killed is thereby taken as human. A second answer is to ask if he does not believe that there is a right and wrong way of deciding moral questions. If there is such a difference, experience may be appealed to: to decide who is human on the basis of the sentiment of a given society has led to consequences which rational men would characterize as monstrous.

The rejection of the attempted distinctions based on viability and visibility, experience and feeling, may be buttressed by the following considerations: Moral judgments often rest on distinctions, but if the distinctions are not to appear arbitrary *fiat,* they should relate to some real difference in probabilities. There is a kind of continuity in all life, but the earlier stages of the elements of human life possess tiny probabilities of development. Consider, for example, the spermatozoa in any normal ejaculate: There are about 200,000,000 in any single ejaculate, of which one has a chance of developing into a zygote. Consider the oocytes which may become ova: there are 100,000 to 1,000,000 oocytes in a female infant, of which a maximum of 390 are ovulated. But once spermatozoon and ovum meet and the conceptus is formed, such studies as have been made show that roughly in only 20 percent of the cases will spontaneous abortion occur. In other words, the chances are about 4 out of 5 that this new being will develop. At this stage in the life of the being there is a sharp shift in probabilities, an immense jump in potentialities. To make a distinction between the rights of spermatozoa and the rights of the fertilized ovum is to respond to an enormous shift in possibilities. For about twenty days after conception the egg may split to form twins or combine with another egg to form a chimera, but the probability of either event happening is very small.

It may be asked, What does a change in biological probabilities have to do with establishing humanity? The argument from probabilities is not aimed at establishing humanity but at establishing an objective discontinuity which may be taken into account in moral discourse. As life itself is a matter of probabilities, as most moral reasoning is an estimate of probabilities, so it seems in accord with the structure of reality and the nature of moral thought to found a moral judgment on the change in probabilities at conception. The appeal to probabilities is the most commonsensical of arguments; to a greater or smaller degree all of us base our actions on probabilities, and in morals, as in law, prudence and negligence are often measured by the account one has taken of the probabilities. If the chance is 200,000,000 to 1 that the movement in the bushes into which you shoot is a man's, I doubt if many persons would hold you careless in shooting; but if the chances are 4 out of 5 that the movement is a human being's, few

would acquit you of blame. Would the argument be different if only one out of ten children conceived came to term? Of course this argument would be different. This argument is an appeal to probabilities that actually exist, not to any and all states of affairs which may be imagined.

The probabilities as they do exist do not show the humanity of the embryo in the sense of a demonstration in logic any more than the probabilities of the movement in the bush being a man demonstrate beyond all doubt that the being is a man. The appeal is a "buttressing" consideration, showing the plausibility of the standard adopted. The argument focuses on the decisional factor in any moral judgment and assumes that part of the business of a moralist is drawing lines. One evidence of the nonarbitrary character of the line drawn is the difference of probabilities on either side of it. If a spermatozoon is destroyed, one destroys a being which had a chance of far less than 1 in 200 million of developing into a reasoning being, possessed of the genetic code, a heart and other organs, and capable of pain. If a fetus is destroyed, one destroys a being already possessed of the genetic code, organs, and sensitivity to pain, and one which had an 80 percent chance of developing further into a baby outside the womb who, in time, would reason.

The positive argument for conception as the decisive moment of humanization is that at conception the new being receives the genetic code. It is this genetic information which determines his characteristics, which is the biological carrier of the possibility of human wisdom, which makes him a self-evolving being. A being with a human genetic code is man.

This review of current controversy over the humanity of the fetus emphasizes what a fundamental question the theologicans resolved in asserting the inviolability of the fetus. To regard the fetus as possessed of equal rights with other humans was not, however, to decide every case where abortion might be employed. It did decide the case where the argument was that the fetus should be aborted for its own good. To say a being was human was to say it had a destiny to decide for itself which could not be taken from it by another man's decision. But human beings with equal rights often come in conflict with each other, and some decision must be made as to whose claims are to prevail. Cases of conflict involving the fetus are different only in two respects: the total inability of the fetus to speak for itself and the fact that the right of the fetus regularly at stake is the right to life itself.

The approach taken by the theologians to these conflicts was articulated in terms of "direct" and "indirect." Again, to look at what they were doing from outside their categories, they may be said to have been drawing lines or "balancing values." "Direct" and "indirect" are spatial metaphors; "line-drawing" is another. "To weigh" or "to balance" values is a metaphor of a more complicated mathematical sort hinting at the process which goes on in moral judgments. All the metaphors suggest that, in the moral judgments made, comparisons were necessary, that no value completely controlled. The principle of double effect was no doctrine fallen from heaven, but a method of analysis appropriate where two relative values were being compared. In Catholic moral theology, as it developed, life even of the innocent was not taken as an absolute. Judgments on acts affecting life issued from a process of weighing. In the weighing, the fetus was always given a value greater than zero, always a value separate and independent from its parents. This valuation was crucial and fundamental in all Christian thought on the subject and marked it off from any approach which considered that only the parents' interests needed to be considered.

Even with the fetus weighed as human, one interest could be weighed as equal or superior: that of the mother in her own life. The casuists between 1450 and 1895 were willing to weigh this interest as superior. Since 1895, that interest was given decisive weight only in the two special cases of the cancerous uterus and the ectopic pregnancy. In both of these cases the fetus itself had little chance of survival even if the abortion were not performed. As the balance was once struck in favor of the mother whenever her life was endangered, it could be so struck again. The balance reached between 1895 and 1930 attempted prudentially and pastorally

to forestall a multitude of exceptions for interests less than life.

The perception of the humanity of the fetus and the weighing of fetal rights against other human rights constituted the work of the moral analysts. But what spirit animated their abstract judgments? For the Christian community it was the injunction of Scripture to love your neighbor as yourself. The fetus as human was a neighbor; his life had parity with one's own. The commandment gave life to what otherwise would have been only rational calculation.

The commandment could be put in humanistic as well as theological terms: Do not injure your fellow man without reason. In these terms, once the humanity of the fetus is perceived, abortion is never right except in self-defense. When life must be taken to save life, reason alone cannot say that a mother must prefer a child's life to her own. With this exception, now of great rarity, abortion violates the rational humanist tenet of the equality of human lives.

For Christians the commandment to love had received a special imprint in that the exemplar proposed of love was the love of the Lord for his disciples. In the light given by this example, self-sacrifice carried to the point of death seemed in the extreme situations not without meaning. In the less extreme cases, preference for one's own interests to the life of another seemed to express cruelty or selfishness irreconcilable with the demands of love.

Endnotes

1. According to Glanville Williams (*The Sanctity of Human Life supra* n. 169, at 193), "The historical reason for the Catholic objection to abortion is the same as for the Christian Church's historical opposition to infanticide: the horror of bringing about the death of an unbaptized child." This statement is made without any citation of evidence. As has been seen, desire to administer baptism could, in the Middle Ages, even be urged as a reason for procuring an abortion. It is highly regrettable that the American Law Institute was apparently misled by Williams' account and repeated after him the same baseless statement. See American Law Institute, *Model Penal Code: Tentative Draft No. 9* (1959), p. 148, n. 12.

2. . . . Thomas Aquinas gave an analogous reason against baptizing a fetus in the womb: "As long as it exists in the womb of the mother, it cannot be subject to the operation of the ministers of the Church as it is not known to men" (*In sententias Petri Lombardi* 4.6 1.1.2).

1. According to Noonan, what is the simple Christian criterion for humanity?
2. Noonan discusses five different distinctions (starting with viability) used by defenders of abortion. Explain Noonan's critique of these distinctions.
3. State and explain Noonan's argument from probabilities.
4. What is Noonan's positive argument for saying that conception is "the decisive moment of humanization"?
5. In Noonan's view, why does the fetus have rights equal to those of other human beings?
6. According to Noonan, how do Christian theologians resolve conflicts of rights such as that between the mother's right to life and the fetus' right to life?
7. According to the traditional view defended by Noonan, in which cases do the fetus's right to life outweigh the mother's right to life?

1. Consider the following objection to Noonan's claim that "a being with a human genetic code is a man." A human cell also is a being with a human genetic code, but obviously it is not a man in the sense of being a human being; therefore, Noonan's claim is false. How could Noonan respond to this objection?
2. Is it possible for a nonhuman being, for example an angel or an intelligent alien being, to have rights equal to those of human beings? Defend your answer.
3. Noonan admits that abortion can be justified by appealing to the right of self-defense. Does this right justify an abortion in a case of rape? Why or why not?

Judith Jarvis Thomson

A Defense of Abortion

Judith Jarvis Thomson is professor of philosophy at Massachusetts Institute of Technology and author of Rights, Restitution, and Risk *(1986),* Acts and Other Events *(1977), and* The Realm of Rights *(1990).*

Thomson assumes, just for the sake of argument, that the fetus is a person from the moment of conception. It does not follow, she argues, that the fetus's right to life always outweighs the mother's rights. Using a series of imaginary examples (such as being plugged into a famous violinist), she tries to convince us that the mother's rights, for example, her right to control her own body, are strong enough to justify abortion in cases of

rape, threat to her life, or when she has taken reasonable precautions not to get pregnant. Abortion is not justified in all cases, however. The moral requirement to be a Minimally Decent Samaritan (as she puts it) makes abortion wrong if it is done just for the sake of convenience. To use her example, it would be wrong for a woman in her seventh month of pregnancy to get an abortion just to avoid the nuisance of postponing a trip abroad.

Most opposition to abortion relies on the premise that the fetus is a human being, a person, from the moment of conception. The premise is argued for, but, as I think, not well. Take, for example, the most common argument. We are asked to notice that the development of a human being from conception through birth into childhood is continuous; then it is said that to draw a line, to choose a point in this development and say "before this point the thing is not a person, after this point it is a person" is to make an arbitrary choice, a choice for which in the nature of things no good reason can be given. It is concluded that the fetus is, or anyway that we had better say it is, a person from

Thomson, Judith Jarvis; "A Defense of Abortion," *Philosophy of Public Affairs,* vol. 1, no. 1. Copyright © 1971 by Princeton University Press. Reprinted by permission of Princeton University Press.

the moment of conception. But this conclusion does not follow. Similar things might be said about the development of an acorn into an oak tree, and it does not follow that acorns are oak trees, or that we had better say they are. Arguments of this form are sometimes called "slippery slope arguments"—the phrase is perhaps self-explanatory—and it is dismaying that opponents of abortion rely on them so heavily and uncritically.

I am inclined to agree, however, that the prospects for "drawing a line" in the development of the fetus look dim. I am inclined to think also that we shall probably have to agree that the fetus has already become a human person well before birth. Indeed, it comes as a surprise when one first learns how early in its life it begins to acquire human characteristics. By the tenth week, for example, it already has a face, arms and legs, fingers and toes; it has internal organs, and brain activity is detectable.[1] On the other hand, I think that the premise is false, that the fetus is not a person from the moment of conception. A newly fertilized ovum, a newly implanted clump of cells, is no more a person than an acorn is an oak tree. But I shall not discuss any of this. For it seems to me to be of great interest to ask what happens if, for the sake of argument, we allow the premise. How, precisely, are we supposed to get from there to the conclusion that abortion is morally impermissible? Opponents of abortion commonly spend most of their time establishing that the fetus is a person, and hardly any time explaining the step from there to the impermissibility of abortion. Perhaps they think the step too simple and obvious to require much comment. Or perhaps instead they are simply being economical in argument. Many of those who defend abortion rely on the premise that the fetus is not a person, but only a bit of tissue that will become a person at birth; and why pay out more arguments than you have to? Whatever the explanation, I suggest that the step they take is neither easy nor obvious, that it calls for closer examination than it is commonly given, and that when we do give it this closer examination we shall feel inclined to reject it.

I propose, then, that we grant that the fetus is a person from the moment of conception.

How does the argument go from here? Something like this, I take it. Every person has a right to life. So the fetus has a right to life. No doubt the mother has a right to decide what shall happen in and to her body; everyone would grant that. But surely a person's right to life is stronger and more stringent than the mother's right to decide what happens in and to her body, and so outweighs it. So the fetus may not be killed; an abortion may not be performed.

It sounds plausible. But now let me ask you to imagine this. You wake up in the morning and find yourself back to back in bed with an unconscious violinist. A famous unconscious violinist. He has been found to have a fatal kidney ailment, and the Society of Music Lovers has canvassed all the available medical records and found that you alone have the right blood type to help. They have therefore kidnapped you, and last night the violinist's circulatory system was plugged into yours, so that your kidneys can be used to extract poisons from his blood as well as your own. The director of the hospital now tells you, "Look, we're sorry the Society of Music Lovers did this to you—we would never have permitted it if we had known. But still, they did it, and the violinist now is plugged into you. To unplug you would be to kill him. But never mind, it's only for nine months. By then he will have recovered from his ailment, and can safely be unplugged from you." Is it morally incumbent on you to accede to this situation? No doubt it would be very nice of you if you did, a great kindness. But do you *have* to accede to it? What if it were not nine months, but nine years? Or longer still? What if the director of the hospital says, "Tough luck, I agree, but you've now got to stay in bed, with the violinist plugged into you, for the rest of your life. Because remember this. All persons have a right to life, and violinists are persons. Granted you have a right to decide what happens in and to your body, but a person's right to life outweighs your right to decide what happens in and to your body. So you cannot ever be unplugged from him." I imagine you would regard this as outrageous, which suggests that something really is wrong with that plausible-sounding argument I mentioned a moment ago.

In this case, of course, you were kidnapped; you didn't volunteer for the operation that plugged the violinist into your kidneys. Can those who oppose abortion on the ground I mentioned make an exception for a pregnancy due to rape? Certainly. They can say that persons have a right to life only if they didn't come into existence because of rape; or they can say that all persons have a right to life, but that some have less of a right to life than others, in particular, that those who came into existence because of rape have less. But these statements have a rather unpleasant sound. Surely the question of whether you have a right to life at all, or how much of it you have, shouldn't turn on the question of whether or not you are the product of a rape. And in fact the people who oppose abortion on the ground I mentioned do not make this distinction, and hence do not make an exception in case of rape.

Nor do they make an exception for a case in which the mother has to spend the nine months of her pregnancy in bed. They would agree that would be a great pity, and hard on the mother; but all the same, all persons have a right to life, the fetus is a person, and so on. I suspect, in fact, that they would not make an exception for a case in which, miraculously enough, the pregnancy went on for nine years, or even the rest of the mother's life.

Some won't even make an exception for a case in which continuation of the pregnancy is likely to shorten the mother's life; they regard abortion as impermissible even to save the mother's life. Such cases are nowadays very rare, and many opponents of abortion do not accept this extreme view. All the same, it is a good place to begin; a number of points of interest come out in respect to it.

1. Let us call the view that abortion is impermissible even to save the mother's life "the extreme view." I want to suggest first that it does not issue from the argument I mentioned earlier without the addition of some fairly powerful premises. Suppose a woman has become pregnant, and now learns that she has a cardiac condition such that she will die if she carries the baby to term. What may be done for her? The fetus, being a person, has a right to life, but as the mother is a person too, so has she a right

to life. Presumably they have an equal right to life. How is it supposed to come out that an abortion may not be performed? If mother and child have an equal right to life, shouldn't we perhaps flip a coin? Or should we add to the mother's right to life her right to decide what happens in and to her body, which everybody seems to be ready to grant—the sum of her rights now outweighing the fetus' right to life?

The most familiar argument here is the following. We are told that performing the abortion would be directly killing[2] the child, whereas doing nothing would not be killing the mother, but only letting her die. Moreover, in killing the child, one would be killing an innocent person, for the child has committed no crime, and is not aiming at his mother's death. And then there are a variety of ways in which this might be continued: (1) But as directly killing an innocent person is always and absolutely impermissible, an abortion may not be performed. Or (2) as directly killing an innocent person is murder, and murder is always and absolutely impermissible, an abortion may not be performed.[3] Or (3) as one's duty to refrain from directly killing an innocent person is more stringent than one's duty to keep a person from dying, an abortion may not be performed. Or (4) if one's only options are directly killing an innocent person or letting a person die, one must prefer letting the person die, and thus an abortion may not be performed.[4]

Some people seem to have thought that these are not further premises which must be added if the conclusion is to be reached, but that they follow from the very fact that an innocent person has a right to life.[5] But this seems to me to be a mistake, and perhaps the simplest way to show this is to bring out that while we must certainly grant that innocent persons have a right to life, the theses in (1) through (4) are all false. Take (2), for example. If directly killing an innocent person is murder, and thus is impermissible, then the mother's directly killing the innocent person inside her is murder, and thus is impermissible. But it cannot seriously be thought to be murder if the mother performs an abortion on herself to save her life. It cannot seriously be said that she *must* refrain, that she *must* sit passively by and wait for her death. Let us look again at the case of you and the violinist. There you are, in bed with the violinist, and the director of the hospital says to you, "It's all most distressing, and I deeply sympathize, but you see this is putting an additional strain on your kidneys, and you'll be dead within the month. But you *have* to stay where you are all the same. Because unplugging you would be directly killing an innocent violinist, and that's murder, and that's impermissible." If anything in the world is true, it is that you do not commit murder, you do not do what is impermissible, if you reach around to your back and unplug yourself from that violinist to save your life.

The main focus of attention in writings on abortion has been on what a third party may or may not do in answer to a request from a woman for an abortion. This is in a way understandable. Things being as they are, there isn't much a woman can safely do to abort herself. So the question asked is what a third party may do, and what the mother may do, if it is mentioned at all, is deduced, almost as an afterthought, from what it is concluded that third parties may do. But it seems to me that to treat the matter in this way is to refuse to grant to the mother that very status of person which is so firmly insisted on for the fetus. For we cannot simply read off what a person may do from what a third party may do. Suppose you find yourself trapped in a tiny house with a growing child. I mean a very tiny house, and a rapidly growing child—you are already up against the wall of the house and in a few minutes you'll be crushed to death. The child on the other hand won't be crushed to death; if nothing is done to stop him from growing he'll be hurt, but in the end he'll simply burst open the house and walk out a free man. Now I could well understand it if a bystander were to say, "There's nothing we can do for you. We cannot choose between your life and his, we cannot be the ones to decide who is to live, we cannot intervene." But it cannot be concluded that you too can do nothing, that you cannot attack it to save your life. However innocent the child may be, you do not have to wait passively while it crushes you to death. Perhaps a pregnant woman is vaguely felt to have the status of house, to which we don't allow the right of self-

defense. But if the woman houses the child, it should be remembered that she is a person who houses it.

I should perhaps stop to say explicitly that I am not claiming that people have a right to do anything whatever to save their lives. I think, rather, that there are drastic limits to the right of self-defense. If someone threatens you with death unless you torture someone else to death, I think you have not the right, even to save your life, to do so. But the case under consideration here is very different. In our case there are only two people involved, one whose life is threatened, and one who threatens it. Both are innocent: the one who is threatened is not threatened because of any fault, the one who threatens does not threaten because of any fault. For this reason we may feel that we bystanders cannot intervene. But the person threatened can.

In sum, a woman surely can defend her life against the threat to it posed by the unborn child, even if doing so involves its death. And this shows not merely that the theses in (1) through (4) are false; it shows also that the extreme view of abortion is false, and so we need not canvass any other possible ways of arriving at it from the argument I mentioned at the outset.

2. The extreme view could of course be weakened to say that while abortion is permissible to save the mother's life, it may not be performed by a third party, but only by the mother herself. But this cannot be right either. For what we have to keep in mind is that the mother and the unborn child are not like two tenants in a small house which has, by an unfortunate mistake, been rented to both: the mother *owns* the house. The fact that she does adds to the offensiveness of deducing that the mother can do nothing from the supposition that third parties can do nothing. But it does more than this: it casts a bright light on the supposition that third parties can do nothing. Certainly it lets us see that a third party who says "I cannot choose between you" is fooling himself if he thinks this is impartiality. If Jones has found and fastened on a certain coat, which he needs to keep him from freezing, but which Smith also needs to keep him from freezing, then it is not impartiality that says "I cannot choose between you" when

Smith owns the coat. Women have said again and again "This body is *my* body!" and they have reason to feel angry, reason to feel that it has been like shouting into the wind. Smith, after all, is hardly likely to bless us if we say to him, "Of course it's your coat, anybody would grant that it is. But no one may choose between you and Jones who is to have it." . . .

3. Where the mother's life is not at stake, the argument I mentioned at the outset seems to have a much stronger pull. "Everyone has a right to life, so the unborn person has a right to life." And isn't the child's right to life weightier than anything other than the mother's own right to life, which she might put forward as ground for an abortion?

This argument treats the right to life as if it were unproblematic. It is not, and this seems to me to be precisely the source of the mistake.

For we should now, at long last, ask what it comes to, to have a right to life. In some views having a right to life includes having a right to be given at least the bare minimum one needs for continued life. But suppose that what in fact *is* the bare minimum a man needs for continued life is something he has no right at all to be given? If I am sick unto death, and the only thing that will save my life is the touch of Henry Fonda's cool hand on my fevered brow, then all the same, I have no right to be given the touch of Henry Fonda's cool hand on my fevered brow. It would be frightfully nice of him to fly in from the West Coast to provide it. It would be less nice, though no doubt well meant, if my friends flew out to the West Coast and carried Henry Fonda back with them. But I have no right at all against anybody that he should do this for me. Or again, to return to the story I told earlier, the fact that for continued life that violinist needs the continued use of your kidneys does not establish that he has a right to be given the continued use of your kidneys. He certainly has no right against you that *you* should give him continued use of your kidneys. For nobody has any right to use your kidneys unless you give him such a right; and nobody has the right against you that you shall give him this right—if you do allow him to go on using your kidneys, this is a kindness on your part, and not something he can claim from you as his

due. Nor has he any right against anybody else that *they* should give him continued use of your kidneys. Certainly he had no right against the Society of Music Lovers that they should plug him into you in the first place. And if you now start to unplug yourself, having learned that you will otherwise have to spend nine years in bed with him, there is nobody in the world who must try to prevent you, in order to see to it that he is given something he has a right to be given.

Some people are rather stricter about the right to life. In their view, it does not include the right to be given anything, but amounts to, and only to, the right not to be killed by anybody. But here a related difficulty arises. If everybody is to refrain from killing that violinist, then everybody must refrain from doing a great many different sorts of things. Everybody must refrain from slitting his throat, everybody must refrain from shooting him—and everybody must refrain from unplugging you from him. But does he have a right against everybody that they shall refrain from unplugging you from him? To refrain from doing this is to allow him to continue to use your kidneys. It could be argued that he has a right against us that *we* shall allow him to continue to use your kidneys. That is, while he had no right against us that we should give him the use of your kidneys, it might be argued that he anyway has a right against us that we shall not now intervene and deprive him of the use of your kidneys. I shall come back to third-party interventions later. But certainly the violinist has no right against you that *you* shall allow him to continue to use your kidneys. As I said, if you do allow him to use them, it is a kindness on your part, and not something you owe him.

The difficulty I point to here is not peculiar to the right to life. It reappears in connection with all the other natural rights; and it is something which an adequate account of rights must deal with. For present purposes it is enough just to draw attention to it. But I would stress that I am not arguing that people do not have a right to life—quite to the contrary, it seems to me that the primary control we must place on the acceptability of an account of rights is that it should turn out in that account to be a truth that all persons have a right to life. I am arguing only that having a right to life does not guarantee having either a right to be given the use of or a right to be allowed continued use of another person's body—even if one needs it for life itself. So the right to life will not serve the opponents of abortion in the very simple and clear way in which they seem to have thought it would.

4. There is another way to bring out the difficulty. In the most ordinary sort of case, to deprive someone of what he has a right to is to treat him unjustly. Suppose a boy and his small brother are jointly given a box of chocolates for Christmas. If the older boy takes the box and refuses to give his brother any of the chocolates, he is unjust to him, for the brother has been given a right to half of them. But suppose that, having learned that otherwise it means nine years in bed with that violinist, you unplug yourself from him. You surely are not being unjust to him, for you gave him no right to use your kidneys, and no one else can have given him any such right. But we have to notice that in unplugging yourself, you are killing him; and violinists, like everybody else, have a right to life, and thus in the view we were considering just now, the right not to be killed. So here you do what he supposedly has a right you shall not do, but you do not act unjustly to him in doing it.

The emendation which may be made at this point is this: the right to life consists not in the right not to be killed, but rather in the right not to be killed unjustly. This runs a risk of circularity, but never mind: it would enable us to square the fact that the violinist has a right to life with the fact that you do not act unjustly toward him in unplugging yourself, thereby killing him. For if you do not kill him unjustly, you do not violate his right to life, and so it is no wonder you do him no injustice.

But if this emendation is accepted, the gap in the argument against abortion stares us plainly in the face: it is by no means enough to show that the fetus is a person, and to remind us that all persons have a right to life—we need to be shown also that killing the fetus violates its right to life, i.e., that abortion is unjust killing. And is it?

I suppose we may take it as a datum that in a case of pregnancy due to rape the mother has not given the unborn person a right to the use of her body for food and shelter. Indeed, in what pregnancy could it be supposed that the mother has given the unborn person such a right? It is not as if there were unborn persons drifting about the world, to whom a woman who wants a child says "I invite you in."

But it might be argued that there are other ways one can have acquired a right to the use of another person's body than by having been invited to use it by that person. Suppose a woman voluntarily indulges in intercourse, knowing of the chance it will issue in pregnancy, and then she does become pregnant; is she not in part responsible for the presence, in fact the very existence, of the unborn person inside her? No doubt she did not invite it in. But doesn't her partial responsibility for its being there itself give it a right to the use of her body? [6] If so, then her aborting it would be more like the boy's taking away the chocolate, and less like your unplugging yourself from the violinist—doing so would be depriving it of what it does have a right to, and thus would be doing it an injustice.

And then, too, it might be asked whether or not she can kill it even to save her own life: If she voluntarily called it into existence, how can she now kill it, even in self-defense?

The first thing to be said about this is that it is something new. Opponents of abortion have been so concerned to make out the independence of the fetus, in order to establish that it has a right to life, just as its mother does, that they have tended to overlook the possible support they might gain from making out that the fetus is *dependent* on the mother, in order to establish that she has a special kind of responsibility for it, a responsibility that gives it rights against her which are not possessed by any independent person—such as an ailing violinist who is a stranger to her.

On the other hand, this argument would give the unborn person a right to its mother's body only if her pregnancy resulted from a voluntary act, undertaken in full knowledge of the chance a pregnancy might result from it. It would leave out entirely the unborn person whose existence is due to rape. Pending the availability of some further argument, then, we would be left with the conclusion that unborn persons whose existence is due to rape have no right to the use of their mothers' bodies, and thus that aborting them is not depriving them of anything they have a right to and hence is not unjust killing.

And we should also notice that it is not at all plain that this argument really does go even as far as it purports to. For there are cases and cases, and the details make a difference. If the room is stuffy, and I therefore open a window to air it, and a burglar climbs in, it would be absurd to say, "Ah, now he can stay, she's given him a right to the use of her house—for she is partially responsible for his presence there, having voluntarily done what enabled him to get in, in full knowledge that there are such things as burglars, and that burglars burgle." It would be still more absurd to say this if I had had bars installed outside my windows, precisely to prevent burglars from getting in, and a burglar got in only because of a defect in the bars. It remains equally absurd if we imagine it is not a burglar who climbs in, but an innocent person who blunders or falls in. Again, suppose it were like this: people-seeds drift about in the air like pollen, and if you open your windows, one may drift in and take root in your carpets or upholstery. You don't want children, so you fix up your windows with fine mesh screens, the very best you can buy. As can happen, however, and on very, very rare occasions does happen, one of the screens is defective; and a seed drifts in and takes root. Does the person-plant who now develops have a right to the use of your house? Surely not—despite the fact that you voluntarily opened your windows, you knowingly kept carpets and upholstered furniture, and you knew that screens were sometimes defective. Someone may argue that you are responsible for its rooting, that it does have a right to your house, because after all you could have lived out your life with bare floors and furniture, or with sealed windows and doors. But this won't do—for by the same token anyone can avoid a pregnancy due to rape by having a hysterectomy, or anyway by never leaving home without a (reliable!) army.

It seems to me that the argument we are looking at can establish at most that there are some cases in which the unborn person has a right to the use of its mother's body, and therefore some cases in which abortion is unjust killing. There is room for much discussion and argument as to precisely which, if any. But I think we should sidestep this issue and leave it open, for at any rate the argument certainly does not establish that all abortion is unjust killing.

5. There is room for yet another argument here, however. We surely must all grant that there may be cases in which it would be morally indecent to detach a person from your body at the cost of his life. Suppose you learn that what the violinist needs is not nine years of your life, but only one hour; all you need do to save his life is to spend one hour in that bed with him. Suppose also that letting him use your kidneys for that one hour would not affect your health in the slightest. Admittedly you were kidnapped. Admittedly you did not give anyone permission to plug him into you. Nevertheless it seems to me plain you ought to allow him to use your kidneys for that hour—it would be indecent to refuse.

Again, suppose pregnancy lasted only an hour, and constituted no threat to life or health. And suppose that a woman becomes pregnant as a result of rape. Admittedly she did not voluntarily do anything to bring about the existence of a child. Admittedly she did nothing at all which would give the unborn person a right to the use of her body. All the same it might well be said, as in the newly amended violinist story, that she ought to allow it to remain for that hour—that it would be indecent of her to refuse.

Now some people are inclined to use the term "right" in such a way that it follows from the fact that you ought to allow a person to use your body for the hour he needs, that he has a right to use your body for the hour he needs, even though he has not been given that right by any person or act. They may say that it follows also that if you refuse, you act unjustly toward him. This use of the term is perhaps so common that it cannot be called wrong; nevertheless it seems to me to be an unfortunate loosening of what we would do better to keep a tight rein on. Suppose that box of chocolates I mentioned earlier had not been given to both boys jointly, but was given only to the older boy. There he sits, stolidly eating his way through the box, his small brother watching enviously. Here we are likely to say "You ought not to be so mean. You ought to give your brother some of those chocolates." My own view is that it just does not follow from the truth of this that the brother has any right to any of the chocolates. If the boy refuses to give his brother any, he is greedy, stingy, callous—but not unjust. I suppose that the people I have in mind will say it does follow that the brother has a right to some of the chocolates, and thus that the boy does act unjustly if he refuses to give his brother any. But the effect of saying this is to obscure what we should keep distinct, namely the difference between the boy's refusal in this case and the boy's refusal in the earlier case, in which the box was given to both boys jointly, and in which the small brother thus had what was from any point of view clear title to half.

A further objection to so using the term "right" that from the fact that A ought to do a thing for B, it follows that B has a right against A that A do it for him, is that it is going to make the question of whether or not a man has a right to a thing turn on how easy it is to provide him with it; and this seems not merely unfortunate, but morally unacceptable. Take the case of Henry Fonda again. I said earlier that I had no right to the touch of his cool hand on my fevered brow, even though I needed it to save my life. I said it would be frightfully nice of him to fly in from the West Coast to provide me with it, but that I had no right against him that he should do so. But suppose he isn't on the West Coast. Suppose he has only to walk across the room, place a hand briefly on my brow—and lo, my life is saved. Then surely he ought to do it, it would be indecent to refuse. Is it to be said "Ah, well, it follows that in this case she has a right to the touch of his hand on her brow, and so it would be an injustice in him to refuse"? So that I have a right to it when it is easy for him to provide it, though no right when it's hard? It's rather a shocking idea that anyone's rights should fade away and disappear as it gets harder and harder to accord them to him.

So my own view is that even though you ought to let the violinist use your kidneys for the one hour he needs, we should not conclude that he has a right to do so—we should say that if you refuse, you are, like the boy who owns all the chocolates and will give none away, self-centered and callous, indecent in fact, but not unjust. And similarly, that even supposing a case in which a woman pregnant due to rape ought to allow the unborn person to use her body for the hour he needs, we should not conclude that he has a right to do so; we should conclude that she is self-centered, callous, indecent, but not unjust if she refuses. The complaints are no less grave; they are just different. However, there is no need to insist on this point. If anyone does wish to deduce "he has a right" from "you ought," then all the same he must surely grant that there are cases in which it is not morally required of you that you allow that violinist to use your kidneys, and in which he does not have a right to use them, and in which you do not do him an injustice if you refuse. And so also for mother and unborn child. Except in such cases as the unborn person has a right to demand it—and we were leaving open the possibility that there may be such cases—nobody is morally *required* to make large sacrifices, of health, of all other interests and concerns, of all other duties and commitments, for nine years, or even for nine months, in order to keep another person alive. . . .

6. My argument will be found unsatisfactory on two counts by many of those who want to regard abortion as morally permissible. First, while I do argue that abortion is not impermissible, I do not argue that it is always permissible. There may well be cases in which carrying the child to term requires only Minimally Decent Samaritanism of the mother, and this is a standard we must not fall below. I am inclined to think it a merit of my account precisely that it does *not* give a general yes or a general no. It allows for and supports our sense that, for example, a sick and desperately frightened fourteen-year-old schoolgirl, pregnant due to rape, may *of course* choose abortion, and that any law which rules this out is an insane law. And it also allows for and supports our sense that in other cases resort to abortion is even positively indecent. It would be indecent in the woman to request an abortion, and indecent in a doctor to perform it, if she is in her seventh

month, and wants the abortion just to avoid the nuisance of postponing a trip abroad. The very fact that the arguments I have been drawing attention to treat all cases of abortion, or even all cases of abortion in which the mother's life is not at stake, as morally on a par ought to have made them suspect at the outset.

Secondly, while I am arguing for the permissibility of abortion in some cases, I am not arguing for the right to secure the death of the unborn child. It is easy to confuse these two things in that up to a certain point in the life of the fetus it is not able to survive outside the mother's body; hence removing it from her body guarantees its death. But they are importantly different. I have argued that you are not morally required to spend nine months in bed, sustaining the life of that violinist; but to say this is by no means to say that if, when you unplug yourself, there is a miracle and he survives, you then have a right to turn around and slit his throat. You may detach yourself even if this costs him his life; you have no right to be guaranteed his death, by some other means, if unplugging yourself does not kill him. There are some people who will feel dissatisfied by this feature of my argument. A woman may be utterly devastated by the thought of a child, a bit of herself, put out for adoption and never seen or heard of again. She may therefore want not merely that the child be detached from her, but more, that it die. Some opponents of abortion are inclined to regard this as beneath contempt—thereby showing insensitivity to what is surely a powerful source of despair. All the same, I agree that the desire for the child's death is not one which anybody may gratify, should it turn out to be possible to detach the child alive.

At this place, however, it should be remembered that we have only been pretending throughout that the fetus is a human being from the moment of conception. A very early abortion is surely not the killing of a person, and so is not dealt with by anything I have said here.

Endnotes

1. Daniel Callahan, *Abortion: Law, Choice and Morality* (New York, 1970), p. 373. This book gives a fascinating survey of the available information on abortion. The Jewish tradition is surveyed in David M. Feldman, *Birth Control in Jewish Law* (New York, 1968), Part 5, the Catholic tradition in John T. Noonan, Jr., "An Almost Absolute Value in History," in *The Morality of Abortion,* ed. John T. Noonan, Jr. (Cambridge, Mass., 1970).

2. The term "direct" in the arguments I refer to is a technical one. Roughly, what is meant by "direct killing" is either killing as an end in itself, or killing as a means to some end, for example, the end of saving someone else's life. See note 5, below, for an example of its use.

3. Cf. *Encyclical Letter of Pope Pius XI on Christian Marriage,* St. Paul Editions (Boston, n.d.), p. 32; "however much we may pity the mother whose health and even life is gravely imperiled in the performance of the duty allotted to her by nature, nevertheless what could ever be a sufficient reason for excusing in any way the direct murder of the innocent? This is precisely what we are dealing with here." Noonan (*The Morality of Abortion*, p. 43) reads this as follows: "What cause can ever avail to excuse in any way the direct killing of the innocent? For it is a question of that."

4. The thesis in (4) is in an interesting way weaker than those in (1), (2), and (3): they rule out abortion even in cases in which both mother *and* child will die if the abortion is not performed. By contrast, one who held the view expressed in (4) could consistently say that one needn't prefer letting two persons die to killing one.

5. Cf. the following passage from Pius XII, *Address to the Italian Catholic Society of Midwives:* "The baby in the maternal breast has the right to life immediately from God. Hence there is no man, no human authority, no science, no medical, eugenic, social, economic or moral 'indication' which can establish or grant a valid juridical ground for a direct deliberate disposition of an innocent human life, that is, a disposition which looks to its destruction either as an end or as a means to another end perhaps in itself not illicit. The baby, still not born, is a man in the same degree and for the same reason as the mother" (quoted in Noonan, *The Morality of Abortion,* p. 45).

6. The need for a discussion of this argument was brought home to me by members of the Society for Ethical and Legal Philosophy, to whom this paper was originally presented.

REVIEW QUESTIONS

1. What are "slippery slope arguments," and why does Thomson reject them?

2. Explain the example about the famous violinist.

3. What is the "extreme view," and what argument is used to defend it? How does Thomson attack this argument?

4. What is the point of the example about the tiny house and the growing child?

5. Why do women say, "This body is *my* body"? Do they say this?
6. Explain the example about "Henry Fonda's cool hand on my fevered brow."
7. What is the point of the example about people-seeds taking root in the carpet?
8. What are Thomson's conclusions? When is abortion justified and when is it not justified?

DISCUSSION QUESTIONS

1. Is the case of the famous violinist really analogous to a case of pregnancy due to rape?

2. What are the limits to the right to self-defense? Do these limits apply to abortion in cases of rape?
3. What obligations do we have towards people who have a right to life? Do we have an obligation, for example, to take care of them and feed them?
4. Does a woman who is accidentally pregnant have a right to get an abortion?

Mary Anne Warren

On the Moral and Legal Status of Abortion

Mary Anne Warren teaches at San Francisco State University. She is the author of several articles, including "Do Potential People Have Moral Rights?" and "Secondary Sexism and Quota Hiring." She is also the author of Gendercide: The Implications of Sex Selection *(1985).*

The first part of Warren's article is a response to Thomson. She argues that even though Thomson's argument from analogy is probably conclusive in showing that abortion is justified in the case of pregnancy due to rape, it does not show that abortion is permissible in numerous other cases where pregnancy is not due to rape and is not life threatening. Warren feels that more argument is needed to show the permissibility of abortion in those cases.

In the second part of the article, Warren presents her case for the liberal view that abortion can be justified in any case. Her argument de-

From Mary Anne Warren, "On the Moral and Legal Status of Abortion," *The Monist*, vol. 57, no. 1 (January 1973), p. 43–51. Reprinted with permission from *The Monist* and Dr. Mary Anne Warren, San Francisco State University.

pends on a distinction between two senses of the word human. *The first sense is a genetic sense where something is human if it is a member of the biological species* Homo sapiens; *the second is a moral sense where something is human if it is a member of the moral community. She claims that conservatives like Noonan confuse these two senses of human. They fallaciously argue from the fact that fetuses are genetically human to the conclusion that they are morally human, that is, persons with a right to life. But an analysis of the concept of person shows that fetuses are unlike persons in too many areas to have a significant right to life. There are five features central to personhood—consciousness, reasoning, self-motivated activity, the capacity to communicate, and self-awareness. The fetus lacks all of these features in the early stages of development and continues to lack most of them in the later stages. Furthermore, the fetus' potential for becoming a person does not provide us with a good reason for ascribing to it a significant right to life. The rights of a merely potential person, even assuming it has rights, would always be outweighed by the rights of an actual person, in this case, the mother. The mother's right to have an abortion, then, is absolute; it can never be outweighed by the rights of the fetus.*

In the postscript, Warren replies to the objection that her view would justify infanticide. She admits that infants do not have a significant right to life in her view, but she claims that it does not follow that infanticide is permissible for two reasons. First, there may be people willing to adopt the unwanted child and in that case it would be wrong to kill it. Second, many people in our country value infants and would prefer that they be preserved, even if foster parents are not available.

We will be concerned with both the moral status of abortion, which for our purposes we may define as the act which a woman performs in voluntarily terminating, or allowing another person to terminate, her pregnancy, and the legal status which is appropriate for this act. I will argue that, while it is not possible to produce a satisfactory defense of a woman's right to obtain an abortion without showing that a fetus is not a human being, in the morally relevant sense of that term, we ought not to conclude that the difficulties involved in determining whether or not a fetus is human make it impossible to produce any satisfactory solution to the problem of the moral status of abortion. For it is possible to show that, on the basis of intuitions which we may expect even the opponents of abortion to share, a fetus is not a person, and hence not the sort of entity to which it is proper to ascribe full moral rights.

Of course, while some philosophers would deny the possibility of any such proof,[1] others will deny that there is any need for it, since the moral permissibility of abortion appears to them to be too obvious to require proof. But the inadequacy of this attitude should be evident from the fact that both the friends and the foes of abortion consider their position to be morally self-evident. Because pro-abortionists have never adequately come to grips with the conceptual issues surrounding abortion, most if not all, of the arguments which they advance in opposition to laws restricting access to abortion fail to refute or even weaken the traditional antiabortion argument, i.e., that a fetus is a human being, and therefore abortion is murder.

These arguments are typically one of two sorts. Either they point to the terrible side effects of the restrictive laws, e.g., the deaths due to illegal abortions, and the fact that it is poor women who suffer the most as a result of these laws, or else they state that to deny a woman access to abortion is to deprive her of her right to control her own body. Unfortunately, however, the fact that restricting access to abortion has tragic side effects does not, in itself, show that the restrictions are unjustified, since murder is wrong regardless of the consequences of prohibiting it; and the appeal to the right to control one's body, which is generally construed as a property right, is at best a rather feeble argument for the permissibility of abortion. Mere ownership does not give me the right to kill innocent people whom I find on my property, and indeed I am apt to be held responsible if such people injure themselves while on my property. It is equally unclear that I have any moral right to expel an innocent person from my property when I know that doing so will result in his death.

Furthermore, it is probably inappropriate to describe a woman's body as her property, since it seems natural to hold that a person is something distinct from her property, but not from her body. Even those who would object to the identification of a person with his body, or with the conjunction of his body and his mind, must admit that it would be very odd to describe, say, breaking a leg, as damaging one's property, and much more appropriate to describe it as injuring one*self*. Thus it is probably a mistake to argue that the right to obtain an abortion is in any way derived from the right to own and regulate property.

But however we wish to construe the right to abortion, we cannot hope to convince those who consider abortion a form of murder of the existence of any such right unless we are able to produce a clear and convincing refutation of the traditional antiabortion argument, and this has not, to my knowledge, been done. With respect to the two most vital issues which that argument involves, i.e., the humanity of the fetus and its implication for the moral status of abortion, confusion has prevailed on both sides of the dispute.

Thus, both pro-abortionists and antiabortionists have tended to abstract the question of whether abortion is wrong to that of whether it is wrong to destroy a fetus, just as though the rights of another person were not necessarily involved. This mistaken abstraction has led to the almost universal assumption that if a fetus is a human being, with a right to life, then it follows immediately that abortion is wrong (except perhaps when necessary to save the woman's life), and that it ought to be prohibited. It has also been generally assumed that unless the question about the status of the fetus is answered, the moral status of abortion cannot possibly be determined.

Two recent papers, one by B. A. Brody,[2] and one by Judith Thomson,[3] have attempted to settle the question of whether abortion ought to be prohibited apart from the question of whether or not the fetus is human. Brody examines the possibility that the following two statements are compatible: (1) that abortion is the taking of innocent human life, and therefore wrong; and (2) that nevertheless it ought not to be prohibited by law, at least under the present circumstances.[4] Not surprisingly, Brody finds it impossible to reconcile these two statements, since, as he rightly argues, none of the unfortunate side effects of the prohibition of abortion is bad enough to justify legalizing the *wrongful* taking of human life. He is mistaken, however, in concluding that the incompatibility of (1) and (2), in itself, shows that "the legal problem about abortion cannot be resolved independently of the status of the fetus problem. . . ."

What Brody fails to realize is that (1) embodies the questionable assumption that if a fetus is a human being, then of course abortion is morally wrong, and that an attack on *this* assumption is more promising, as a way of reconciling the humanity of the fetus with the claim that laws prohibiting abortion are unjustified, than is an attack on the assumption that if abortion is the wrongful killing of innocent human beings then it ought to be prohibited. He thus overlooks the possibility that a fetus may have a right to life and abortion still be morally permissible, in that the right of a woman to terminate an unwanted pregnancy might override the right of the fetus to be kept alive. The immorality of abortion is no more demonstrated by the humanity of the fetus, in itself, than the immorality of killing in self-defense is demonstrated by the fact that the assailant is a human being. Neither is it demonstrated by the *innocence* of the fetus, since

there may be situations in which the killing of innocent human beings is justified.

It is perhaps not surprising that Brody fails to spot this assumption, since it has been accepted with little or no argument by nearly everyone who has written on the morality of abortion. John Noonan is correct in saying that "the fundamental question in the long history of abortion is, How do you determine the humanity of a being?"[5] He summarizes his own antiabortion argument, which is a version of the official position of the Catholic Church, as follows:

. . . it is wrong to kill humans, however poor, weak, defenseless, and lacking in opportunity to develop their potential they may be. It is therefore morally wrong to kill Biafrans. Similarly, it is morally wrong to kill embryos.[6]

Noonan bases his claim that fetuses are human upon what he calls the theologians' criterion of humanity: that whoever is conceived of human beings is human. But although he argues at length for the appropriateness of this criterion, he never questions the assumption that if a fetus is human then abortion is wrong for exactly the same reason that murder is wrong.

Judith Thomson is, in fact, the only writer I am aware of who has seriously questioned this assumption; she has argued that, even if we grant the antiabortionist his claim that a fetus is a human being, with the same right to life as any other human being, we can still demonstrate that, in at least some and perhaps most cases, a woman is under no moral obligation to complete an unwanted pregnancy.[7] Her argument is worth examining, since if it holds up it may enable us to establish the moral permissibility of abortion without becoming involved in problems about what entitles an entity to be considered human, and accorded full moral rights. To be able to do this would be a great gain in the power and simplicity of the pro-abortion position, since, although I will argue that these problems can be solved at least as decisively as can any other moral problem, we should certainly be pleased to be able to avoid having to solve them as part of the justification of abortion.

On the other hand, even if Thomson's argument does not hold up, her insight, i.e., that it requires *argument* to show that if fetuses are human then abortion is properly classified as murder, is an extremely valuable one. The assumption she attacks is particularly invidious, for it amounts to the decision that it is appropriate, in deciding the moral status of abortion, to leave the rights of the pregnant woman out of consideration entirely, except possibly when her life is threatened. Obviously, this will not do; determining what moral rights, if any, a fetus possesses is only the first step in determining the moral status of abortion. Step two, which is at least equally essential, is finding a just solution to the conflict between whatever rights the fetus may have, and the rights of the woman who is unwillingly pregnant. While the historical error has been to pay far too little attention to the second step, Ms. Thomson's suggestion is that if we look at the second step first we may find that a woman has a right to obtain an abortion *regardless* of what rights the fetus has.

Our own inquiry will also have two stages. In Section I, we will consider whether or not it is possible to establish that abortion is morally permissible even on the assumption that a fetus is an entity with a full-fledged right to life. I will argue that in fact this cannot be established, at least not with the conclusiveness which is essential to our hopes of convincing those who are skeptical about the morality of abortion, and that we therefore cannot avoid dealing with the question of whether or not a fetus really does have the same right to life as a (more fully developed) human being.

In Section II, I will propose an answer to this question, namely, that a fetus cannot be considered a member of the moral community, the set of beings with full and equal moral rights, for the simple reason that it is not a person, and that it is personhood, and not genetic humanity, i.e., humanity as defined by Noonan, which is the basis for membership in this community. I will argue that a fetus, whatever its stage of development, satisfies none of the basic criteria of personhood, and is not even enough *like* a person to be accorded even some of the same rights on the basis of this resemblance. Nor, as we will see, is a fetus's *potential* personhood a threat to the morality of abortion, since, whatever the

rights of potential people may be, they are invariably overridden in any conflict with the moral rights of actual people.

I

We turn now to Professor Thomson's case for the claim that even if a fetus has full moral rights, abortion is still morally permissible, at least sometimes, and for some reasons other than to save the woman's life. Her argument is based upon a clever, but I think faulty, analogy. She asks us to picture ourselves waking up one day, in bed with a famous violinist. Imagine that you have been kidnapped, and your bloodstream hooked up to that of the violinist, who happens to have an ailment which will certainly kill him unless he is permitted to share your kidneys for a period of nine months. No one else can save him, since you alone have the right type of blood. He will be unconscious all that time, and you will have to stay in bed with him, but after the nine months are over he may be unplugged, completely cured, that is provided that you have cooperated.

Now then, she continues, what are your obligations in this situation? The antiabortionist, if he is consistent, will have to say that you are obligated to stay in bed with the violinist: for all people have a right to life, and violinists are people, and therefore it would be murder for you to disconnect yourself from him and let him die. . . . But this is outrageous, and so there must be something wrong with the same argument when it is applied to abortion. It would certainly be commendable of you to agree to save the violinist, but it is absurd to suggest that your refusal to do so would be murder. His right to life does not obligate you to do whatever is required to keep him alive; nor does it justify anyone else in forcing you to do so. A law which required you to stay in bed with the violinist would clearly be an unjust law, since it is no proper function of the law to force unwilling people to make huge sacrifices for the sake of other people toward whom they have no such prior obligation.

Thomson concludes that, if this analogy is an apt one, then we can grant the antiabortionist his claim that a fetus is a human being, and still hold that it is at least sometimes the case that a pregnant woman has the right to refuse to be a Good Samaritan towards the fetus, i.e., to obtain an abortion. For there is a great gap between the claim that *x* has a right to life, and the claim that *y* is obligated to do whatever is necessary to keep *x* alive, let alone that he ought to be forced to do so. It is *y*'s duty to keep *x* alive only if he has somehow contracted a *special* obligation to do so; and a woman who is unwillingly pregnant, e.g., who was raped, has done nothing which obligates her to make the enormous sacrifice which is necessary to preserve the conceptus.

This argument is initially quite plausible, and in the extreme case of pregnancy due to rape it is probably conclusive. Difficulties arise, however, when we try to specify more exactly the range of cases in which abortion is clearly justifiable even on the assumption that the fetus is human. Professor Thomson considers it a virtue of her argument that it does not enable us to conclude that abortion is *always* permissible. It would, she says, be "indecent" for a woman in her seventh month to obtain an abortion just to avoid having to postpone a trip to Europe. On the other hand, her argument enables us to see that "a sick and desperately frightened [. . .] schoolgirl pregnant due to rape may *of course* choose abortion, and that any law which rules this out is an insane law." . . . So far, so good; but what are we to say about the woman who becomes pregnant not through rape but as a result of her own carelessness, or because of contraceptive failure, or who gets pregnant intentionally and then changes her mind about wanting a child? With respect to such cases, the violinist analogy is of much less use to the defender of the woman's right to obtain an abortion.

Indeed, the choice of a pregnancy due to rape, as an example of a case in which abortion is permissible even if a fetus is considered a human being, is extremely significant; for it is only in the case of pregnancy due to rape that the woman's situation is adequately analogous to the violinist case for our intuitions about the latter to transfer convincingly. The crucial difference between a pregnancy due to rape and the *normal* case of an unwanted pregnancy is

that in the normal case we cannot claim that the woman is in no way responsible for her predicament; she could have remained chaste, or taken her pills more faithfully, or abstained on dangerous days, and so on. If, on the other hand, you are kidnapped by strangers, and hooked up to a strange violinist, then you are free of any shred of responsibility for the situation, on the basis of which it could be argued that you are obligated to keep the violinist alive. Only when her pregnancy is due to rape is a woman clearly just as nonresponsible.[8]

Consequently, there is room for the antiabortionist to argue that in the normal case of unwanted pregnancy a woman has, by her own actions, assumed responsibility for the fetus. For if *x* behaves in a way which he could have avoided, and which he knows involves, let us say, a 1 percent chance of bringing into existence a human being, with a right to life, and does so knowing that if this should happen then that human being will perish unless *x* does certain things to keep him alive, then it is by no means clear that when it does happen *x* is free of any obligation to what he knew in advance would be required to keep that human being alive.

The plausibility of such an argument is enough to show that the Thomson analogy can provide a clear and persuasive defense of a woman's right to obtain an abortion only with respect to those cases in which the woman is in no way responsible for her pregnancy, e.g., where it is due to rape. In all other cases, we would almost certainly conclude that it was necessary to look carefully at the particular circumstances in order to determine the extent of the woman's responsibility, and hence the extent of her obligation. This is an extremely unsatisfactory outcome, from the viewpoint of the opponents of restrictive abortion laws, most of whom are convinced that a woman has a right to obtain an abortion regardless of how and why she got pregnant.

Of course a supporter of the violinist analogy might point out that it is absurd to suggest that forgetting her pill one day might be sufficient to obligate a woman to complete an unwanted pregnancy. And indeed it *is* absurd to suggest this. As we will see, the moral right to obtain an abortion is not in the least dependent upon the extent to which the woman is responsible for her pregnancy. But unfortunately, once we allow the assumption that a fetus has full moral rights, we cannot avoid taking this absurd suggestion seriously. Perhaps we can make this point more clear by altering the violinist story just enough to make it more analogous to a normal unwanted pregnancy and less to a pregnancy due to rape, and then seeing whether it is still obvious that you are not obligated to stay in bed with the fellow.

Suppose, then, that violinists are peculiarily prone to the sort of illness the only cure for which is the use of someone else's blood-stream for nine months, and that because of this there has been formed a society of music lovers who agree that whenever a violinist is stricken they will draw lots and the loser will, by some means, be made the one and only person capable of saving him. Now then, would you be obligated to cooperate in curing the violinist if you had voluntarily joined this society, knowing the possible consequences, and then your name had been drawn and you had been kidnapped? Admittedly, you did not promise ahead of time that you would, but you did deliberately place yourself in a position in which it might happen that a human life would be lost if you did not. Surely this is at least a prima facie reason for supposing that you have an obligation to stay in bed with the violinist. Suppose that you had gotten your name drawn deliberately; surely *that* would be quite a strong reason for thinking that you had such an obligation.

It might be suggested that there is one important disanalogy between the modified violinist case and the case of an unwanted pregnancy, which makes the woman's responsibility significantly less, namely, the fact that the fetus *comes into existence* as the result of the woman's actions. This fact might give her a right to refuse to keep it alive, whereas she would not have had this right had it existed previously, independently, and then as a result of her actions become dependent upon her for its survival.

My own intuition, however, is that x has no more right to bring into existence, either deliberately or as a foreseeable result of actions he could have avoided, a being with full moral rights (y), and then refuse to do what he knew beforehand would be required to keep that being alive, than he has to enter into an agreement with an existing person, whereby he may be called upon to save that person's life, and then refuse to do so when so called upon. Thus, x's responsibility for y's existence does not seem to lessen his obligation to keep y alive, if he is also responsible for y's being in a situation in which only he can save him.

Whether or not this intuition is entirely correct, it brings us back once again to the conclusion that once we allow the assumption that a fetus has full moral rights it becomes an extremely complex and difficult question whether and when abortion is justifiable. Thus the Thomson analogy cannot help us produce a clear and persuasive proof of the moral permissibility of abortion. Nor will the opponents of the restrictive laws thank us for anything less; for their conviction (for the most part) is that abortion is obviously *not* a morally serious and extremely unfortunate, even though sometimes justified act, comparable to killing in self-defense or to letting the violinist die, but rather is closer to being a morally neutral act, like cutting one's hair.

The basis of this conviction, I believe, is the realization that a fetus is not a person, and thus does not have a full-fledged right to life. Perhaps the reason why this claim has been so inadequately defended is that it seems self-evident to those who accept it. And so it is, insofar as it follows from what I take to be perfectly obvious claims about the nature of personhood, and about the proper grounds for ascribing moral rights, claims which ought, indeed, to be obvious to both the friends and foes of abortion. Nevertheless, it is worth examining these claims, and showing how they demonstrate the moral innocuousness of abortion, since this apparently has not been adequately done before.

II

The question which we must answer in order to produce a satisfactory solution to the problem of the moral status of abortion is this: How are we to define the moral community, the set of beings with full and equal moral rights, such that we can decide whether a human fetus is a member of this community or not? What sort of entity, exactly, has the inalienable rights to life, liberty, and the pursuit of happiness? Jefferson attributed these rights to all *men,* and it may or may not be fair to suggest that he intended to attribute them *only* to men. Perhaps he ought to have attributed them to all human beings. If so, then we arrive, first, at Noonan's problem of defining what makes a being human, and, second, at the equally vital question which Noonan does not consider, namely, What reason is there for identifying the moral community with the set of all human beings, in whatever way we have chosen to define that term?

On the Definition of "Human"

One reason why this vital second question is so frequently overlooked in the debate over the moral status of abortion is that the term "human" has two distinct, but not often distinguished, senses. This fact results in a slide of meaning, which serves to conceal the fallaciousness of the traditional argument that since (1) it is wrong to kill innocent human beings, and (2) fetuses are innocent human beings, then (3) it is wrong to kill fetuses. For if "human" is used in the same sense in both (1) and (2) then, which ever of the two senses is meant, one of these premises is question-begging. And if it is used in two different senses then of course the conclusion doesn't follow.

Thus, (1) is a self-evident moral truth,[9] and avoids begging the question about abortion, only if "human being" is used to mean something like "a full-fledged member of the moral community." (It may or may not also be meant to refer exclusively to members of the species *Homo sapiens.*) We may call this the *moral* sense of "human." It is not to be confused with what we will call the *genetic* sense, i.e., the sense in which *any* member of the species is a human being, and no member of any other species could be. If (1) is acceptable only if the moral sense is intended, (2) is non-question-begging only if what is intended is the genetic sense.

In "Deciding Who Is Human," Noonan argues for the classification of fetuses with human beings by pointing to the presence of the full ge-

netic code, and the potential capacity for rational thought. . . . It is clear that what he needs to show, for his version of the traditional argument to be valid, is that fetuses are human in the moral sense, the sense in which it is analytically true that all human beings have full moral rights. But, in the absence of any argument showing that whatever is genetically human is also morally human, and he gives none, nothing more than genetic humanity can be demonstrated by the presence of the human genetic code. And, as we will see, the *potential* capacity for rational thought can at most show that an entity has the potential for *becoming* human in the moral sense.

Defining the Moral Community

Can it be established that genetic humanity is sufficient for moral humanity? I think that there are very good reasons for not defining the moral community in this way. I would like to suggest an alternative way of defining the moral community, which I will argue for only to the extent of explaining why it is, or should be, self-evident. The suggestion is simply that the moral community consists of all and only *people,* rather than all and only human beings;[10] and probably the best way of demonstrating its self-evidence is by considering the concept of personhood, to see what sorts of entity are and are not persons, and what the decision that a being is or is not a person implies about its moral rights.

What characteristics entitle an entity to be considered a person? This is obviously not the place to attempt a complete analysis of the concept of personhood, but we do not need such a full adequate analysis just to determine whether and why a fetus is or isn't a person. All we need is a rough and approximate list of the most basic criteria of personhood, and some idea of which, or how many, of these an entity must satisfy in order to properly be considered a person.

In searching for such criteria, it is useful to look beyond the set of people with whom we are acquainted, and ask how we would decide whether a totally alien being was a person or not. (For we have no right to assume that genetic humanity is necessary for personhood.)

Imagine a space traveler who lands on an unknown planet and encounters a race of beings utterly unlike any he has ever seen or heard of. If he wants to be sure of behaving morally toward these beings, he has to somehow decide whether they are people, and hence have full moral rights, or whether they are the sort of thing which he need not feel guilty about treating as, for example, a source of food.

How should he go about making this decision? If he has some anthropological background, he might look for such things as religion, art, and the manufacturing of tools, weapons, or shelters, since these factors have been used to distinguish our human from our prehuman ancestors, in what seems to be closer to the moral than the genetic sense of "human." And no doubt he would be right to consider the presence of such factors as good evidence that the alien beings were people, and morally human. It would, however, be overly anthropocentric of him to take the absence of these things as adequate evidence that they were not, since we can imagine people who have progressed beyond, or evolved without ever developing, these cultural characteristics.

I suggest that the traits which are most central to the concept of personhood, or humanity in the moral sense, are, very roughly, the following:

1. consciousness (of objects and events external and/or internal to the being), and in particular the capacity to feel pain;
2. reasoning (the *developed* capacity to solve new and relatively complex problems);
3. self-motivated activity (activity which is relatively independent of either genetic or direct external control);
4. the capacity to communicate, by whatever means, messages of an indefinite variety of types, that is, not just with an indefinite number of possible contents, but on indefinitely many possible topics;
5. the presence of self-concepts, and self-awareness, either individual or racial, or both.

Admittedly, there are apt to be a great many problems involved in formulating precise definitions of these criteria, let alone in developing universally valid behavioral criteria for deciding when they apply. But I will assume that both we and our explorer know approximately what (1)–(5) mean, and that he is also able to determine whether or not they apply. How, then, should he use his findings to decide whether or not the alien beings are people? We needn't suppose that an entity must have *all* of these attributes to be properly considered a person; (1) and (2) alone may well be sufficient for personhood, and quite probably (1)–(3) are sufficient. Neither do we need to insist that any one of these criteria is *necessary* for personhood, although once again (1) and (2) look like fairly good candidates for **necessary conditions**, as does (3), if "activity" is construed so as to include the activity of reasoning.

All we need to claim, to demonstrate that a fetus is not a person, is that any being which satisfies *none* of (1)–(5) is certainly not a person. I consider this claim to be so obvious that I think anyone who denied it, and claimed that a being which satisfied none of (1)–(5) was a person all the same, would thereby demonstrate that he had no notion at all of what a person is—perhaps because he had confused the concept of a person with that of genetic humanity. If the opponents of abortion were to deny the appropriateness of these five criteria, I do not know what further arguments would convince them. We would probably have to admit that our conceptual schemes were indeed irreconcilably different, and that our dispute could not be settled objectively.

I do not expect this to happen, however, since I think that the concept of a person is one which is very nearly universal (to people), and that it is common to both proabortionists and antiabortionists, even though neither group has fully realized the relevance of this concept to the resolution of their dispute. Furthermore, I think that on reflection even the antiabortionists ought to agree not only that (1)–(5) are central to the concept of personhood, but also that it is a part of this concept that all and only people have full moral rights. The concept of a person is in part a moral concept; once we have admitted that x is a person we have recognized, even if we have not agreed to respect, x's right to be treated as a member of the moral community. It is true that the claim that x is a *hu-*

man being is more commonly voiced as part of an appeal to treat *x* decently than is the claim that *x* is a person, but this is either because "human being" is here used in the sense which implies personhood, or because the genetic and moral senses of "human" have been confused.

Now if (1)–(5) are indeed the primary criteria of personhood, then it is clear that genetic humanity is neither necessary nor sufficient for establishing that an entity is a person. Some human beings are not people, and there may well be people who are not human beings. A man or woman whose consciousness has been permanently obliterated but who remains alive is a human being which is no longer a person; defective human beings, with no appreciable mental capacity, are not and presumably never will be people; and a fetus is a human being which is not yet a person, and which therefore cannot coherently be said to have full moral rights. Citizens of the next century should be prepared to recognize highly advanced, self-aware robots or computers, should such be developed, and intelligent inhabitants of other worlds, should such be found, as people in the fullest sense, and to respect their moral rights. But to ascribe full moral rights to an entity which is not a person is as absurd as to ascribe moral obligations and responsibilities to such an entity.

Fetal Development and the Right to Life

Two problems arise in the application of these suggestions for the definition of the moral community to the determination of the precise moral status of a human fetus. Given that the paradigm example of a person is a normal adult human being, then (1) How like this paradigm, in particular how far advanced since conception, does a human being need to be before it begins to have a right to life by virtue, not of being fully a person as of yet, but of being *like* a person? and (2) To what extent, if any, does the fact that a fetus has the *potential* for becoming a person endow it with some of the same rights? Each of these questions requires some comment.

In answering the first question, we need not attempt a detailed consideration of the moral rights of organisms which are not developed enough, aware enough, intelligent enough, etc., to be considered people, but which resemble people in some respects. It does seem reasonable to suggest that the more like a person, in the relevant respects, a being is, the stronger is the case for regarding it as having a right to life, and indeed the stronger its right to life is. Thus we ought to take seriously the suggestion that, insofar as "the human individual develops biologically in a continuous fashion . . . the rights of a human person might develop in the same way." [11] But we must keep in mind that the attributes which are relevant in determining whether or not an entity is enough like a person to be regarded as having some of the same moral rights are no different from those which are relevant to determining whether or not it is fully a person—i.e., are no different from (1)–(5)—and that being genetically human, or having recognizably human facial and other physical features, or detectable brain activity, or the capacity to survive outside the uterus, are simply not among these relevant attributes.

Thus it is clear that even though a seven- or eight-month fetus has features which make it apt to arouse in us almost the same powerful protective instinct as is commonly aroused by a small infant, nevertheless it is not significantly more personlike than is a very small embryo. It is *somewhat* more personlike; it can apparently feel and respond to pain, and it may even have a rudimentary form of consciousness, insofar as its brain is quite active. Nevertheless, it seems safe to say that it is not fully conscious, in the way that an infant of a few months is, and that it cannot reason, or communicate messages of indefinitely many sorts, does not engage in self-motivated activity, and has no self-awareness. Thus, in the *relevant* respects, a fetus, even a fully developed one, is considerably less personlike than is the average fish. And I think that a rational person must conclude that if the right to life of a fetus is to be based upon its resemblance to a person, then it cannot be said to have any more right to life than, let us say, a newborn guppy (which also seems to be capable of feeling pain), and that a right of that magnitude could never override a woman's right to obtain an abortion, at any stage of her pregnancy.

There may, of course, be other arguments in favor of placing legal limits upon the stage of pregnancy in which an abortion may be performed. Given the relative safety of the new techniques of artificially inducing labor during the third trimester, the danger to the woman's life or health is no longer such an argument. Neither is the fact that people tend to respond to the thought of abortion in the later stages of pregnancy with emotional repulsion, since mere emotional responses cannot take the place of moral reasoning in determining what ought to be permitted. Nor, finally, is the frequently heard argument that legalizing abortion, especially late in the pregnancy, may erode the level of respect for human life, leading, perhaps, to an increase in unjustified euthanasia and other crimes. For this threat, if it is a threat, can be better met by educating people to the kinds of moral distinctions which we are making here than by limiting access to abortion (which limitation may, in its disregard for the rights of women, be just as damaging to the level of respect for human rights).

Thus, since the fact that even a fully developed fetus is not person-like enough to have any significant right to life on the basis of its person-likeness shows that no legal restrictions upon the stage of pregnancy in which an abortion may be performed can be justified on the grounds that we should protect the rights of the older fetus; and since there is no other apparent justification for such restrictions, we may conclude that they are entirely unjustified. Whether or not it would be *indecent* (whatever that means) for a woman in her seventh month to obtain an abortion just to avoid having to postpone a trip to Europe, it would not, in itself, be *immoral*, and therefore it ought to be permitted.

Potential Personhood and the Right to Life

We have seen that a fetus does not resemble a person in any way which can support the claim that it has even some of the same rights. But what about its *potential*, the fact that if nurtured and allowed to develop naturally it will very probably become a person? Doesn't that alone give it at least some right to life? It is hard to deny that the fact that an entity is a potential person is a strong prima facie reason for not destroying it; but we need not conclude from this that a potential person has a right to life, by virtue of that potential. It may be that our feeling that it is better, other things being equal, not to destroy a potential person is better explained by the fact that potential people are still (felt to be) an invaluable resource, not to be lightly squandered. Surely, if every speck of dust were a potential person, we would be much less apt to conclude that every potential person has a right to become actual.

Still, we do not need to insist that a potential person has no right to life whatever. There may well be something immoral, and not just imprudent, about wantonly destroying potential people, when doing so isn't necessary to protect anyone's rights. But even if a potential person does have some prima facie right to life, such a right could not possibly outweigh the right of a woman to obtain an abortion, since the rights of any actual person invariably outweigh those of any potential person, whenever the two conflict. Since this may not be immediately obvious in the case of a human fetus, let us look at another case.

Suppose that our space explorer falls into the hands of an alien culture, whose scientists decide to create a few hundred thousand or more human beings, by breaking his body into its component cells, and using these to create fully developed human beings, with, of course, his genetic code. We may imagine that each of these newly created men will have all of the original man's abilities, skills, knowledge, and so on, and also have an individual self-concept, in short that each of them will be a bona fide (though hardly unique) person. Imagine that the whole project will take only seconds, and that its chances of success are extremely high, and that our explorer knows all of this, and also knows that these people will be treated fairly. I maintain that in such a situation he would have every right to escape if he could, and thus to deprive all of these potential people of their potential lives; for his right to life outweighs all of theirs together, in spite of the fact that they are all genetically human, all innocent, and all have a very high probability of becoming people very soon, if only he refrains from acting.

Indeed, I think he would have a right to escape even if it were not his life which the alien scientists planned to take, but only a year of his freedom, or, indeed, only a day. Nor would he be obligated to stay if he had gotten captured (thus bringing all these people-potentials into existence) because of his own carelessness, or even if he had done so deliberately, knowing the consequences. Regardless of how he got captured, he is not morally obligated to remain in captivity for *any* period of time for the sake of permitting any number of potential people to come into actuality, so great is the margin by which one actual person's right to liberty outweighs whatever right to life even a hundred thousand potential people have. And it seems reasonable to conclude that the rights of a woman will outweigh by a similar margin whatever right to life a fetus may have by virtue of its potential personhood.

Thus, neither a fetus's resemblance to a person, nor its potential for becoming a person provides any basis whatever for the claim that it has any significant right to life. Consequently, a woman's right to protect her health, happiness, freedom, and even her life,[12] by terminating an unwanted pregnancy, will always override whatever right to life it may be appropriate to ascribe to a fetus, even a fully developed one. And thus, in the absence of any overwhelming social need for every possible child, the laws which restrict the right to obtain an abortion, or limit the period of pregnancy during which an abortion may be performed, are a wholly unjustified violation of a woman's most basic moral and constitutional rights.[13]

POSTSCRIPT ON INFANTICIDE

Since the publication of this article, many people have written to point out that my argument appears to justify not only abortion, but infanticide as well. For a new-born infant is not significantly more person-like than an advanced fetus, and consequently it would seem that if the destruction of the latter is permissible so too must be that of the former. Inasmuch as most people, regardless of how they feel about the morality of abortion, consider infanticide a form of murder, this might appear to represent a serious flaw in my argument.

Now, if I am right in holding that it is only people who have a full-fledged right to life, and who can be murdered, and if the criteria of personhood are as I have described them, then it obviously follows that killing a newborn infant isn't murder. It does *not* follow, however, that infanticide is permissible, for two reasons. In the first place, it would be wrong, at least in this country and in this period of history, and other things being equal, to kill a new-born infant, because even if its parents do not want it and would not suffer from its destruction, there are other people who would like to have it, and would, in all probability, be deprived of a great deal of pleasure by its destruction. Thus, infanticide is wrong for reasons analogous to those which make it wrong to wantonly destroy natural resources, or great works of art.

Secondly, most people, at least in this country, value infants, and would much prefer that they be preserved, even if foster parents are not immediately available. Most of us would rather be taxed to support orphanages than allow unwanted infants to be destroyed. So long as there are people who want an infant preserved, and who are willing and able to provide the means of caring for it, under reasonably humane conditions, it is, *ceteris paribus*, wrong to destroy it.

But, it might be replied, if this argument shows that infanticide is wrong, at least at this time and in this country, doesn't it also show that abortion is wrong? After all, many people value fetuses, are disturbed by their destruction, and would much prefer that they be preserved, even at some cost to themselves. Furthermore, as a potential source of pleasure to some foster family, a fetus is just as valuable as an infant. There is, however, a crucial difference between the two cases: so long as the fetus is unborn, its preservation, contrary to the wishes of the pregnant woman, violates her rights to freedom, happiness, and self-determination. Her rights override the rights of those who would like the fetus preserved, just as if someone's life or limb is threatened by a wild animal, his right to protect himself by destroying the animal overrides the rights of those who would prefer that the animal not be harmed.

The minute the infant is born, however, its preservation no longer violates any of its mother's rights, even if she wants it destroyed, because she is free to put it up for adoption. Consequently, while the moment of birth does not mark any sharp discontinuity in the degree to which an infant possesses the right to life, it does mark the end of its mother's right to determine its fate. Indeed, if abortion could be performed without killing the fetus, she would never possess the right to have the fetus destroyed, for the same reasons that she has no right to have an infant destroyed.

On the other hand, it follows from my argument that when an unwanted or defective infant is born into a society which cannot afford and/or is not willing to care for it, then its destruction is permissible. This conclusion will, no doubt, strike many people as heartless and immoral; but remember that the very existence of people who feel this way, and who are willing and able to provide care for unwanted infants, is reason enough to conclude that they should be preserved.

Endnotes

1. For example, Roger Wertheimer, who in "Understanding the Abortion Argument" (*Philosophy and Public Affairs,* 1, No. 1 [Fall 1971], 67–95), argues that the problem of the moral status of abortion is insoluble, in that the dispute over the status of the fetus is not a question of fact at all, but only a question of how one responds to the facts.
2. B. A. Brody, "Abortion and the Law," *The Journal of Philosophy,* 68, No. 12 (June 17, 1971), 357–69.
3. Judith Thomson, "A Defense of Abortion," *Philosophy and Public Affairs,* 1, No. 1 (Fall 1971), 47–66.
4. I have abbreviated these statements somewhat, but not in a way which affects the argument.
5. John Noonan, "Abortion and the Catholic Church: A Summary History," *Natural Law Forum,* 12 (1967), 125.
6. John Noonan, "Deciding Who Is Human," *Natural Law Forum,* 13 (1968), 134.
7. "A Defense of Abortion."
8. We may safely ignore the fact that she might have avoided getting raped, e.g., by carrying a gun, since by similar means you might likewise have avoided getting kidnapped, and in neither case does the victim's failure to take all possible precautions against a highly unlikely event (as opposed to reasonable precautions against a rather likely event) mean that he is morally responsible for what happens.

9. Of course, the principle that it is (always) wrong to kill innocent human beings is in need of many modifications, e.g., that it may be permissible to do so to save a greater number of other innocent human beings, but we may safely ignore these complications here.
10. From here on, we will use "human" to mean genetically human, since the moral sense seems closely connected to, and perhaps derived from, the assumption that genetic humanity is sufficient for membership in the moral community.
11. Thomas L. Hayes, "A Biological View," *Commonweal,* 85 (March 17, 1967), 667–78; quoted by Daniel Callahan, in *Abortion, Law, Choice, and Morality* (London: Macmillan & Co., 1970).
12. That is, insofar as the death rate, for the woman, is higher for childbirth than for early abortion.
13. My thanks to the following people, who were kind enough to read and criticize an earlier version of this paper: Herbert Gold, Gene Glass, Anne Lauterbach, Judith Thomson, Mary Mothersill, and Timothy Binkley.

REVIEW QUESTIONS

1. What is the traditional anti-abortion argument according to Warren?
2. According to Warren, why are the two typical pro-abortion arguments inadequate?
3. What difficulties does Warren raise in Thomson's argument?
4. Warren claims that the word *human* has two different senses, a *genetic sense* and a *moral sense*. Explain the distinction between the two.
5. Why does Warren think that it is obvious that a fetus is not a person, and why does she expect anti-abortionists to agree with her?
6. Warren admits that she has two problems when it comes to applying her account of personhood to human fetuses. What are these two problems, and how does Warren solve them?
7. How does Warren reply to the objection that her position justifies infanticide as well as abortion?

DISCUSSION QUESTIONS

1. Warren asserts that neither defective humans with little mental capacity nor permanently comatose humans are persons with moral rights. Do you agree? Why or why not?
2. Warren also claims that there can be nonhuman persons, for example, self-aware robots and alien beings from other planets. Is this possible? Explain your answer.

3. Warren says that an infant of a few months is less personlike than the average fish. Is this true?
4. Warren says, in opposition to Thomson, that a woman in her seventh month of pregnancy ought to be permitted to have an abortion just to avoid postponing a trip to Europe. Do yo agree with this judgment? Defend your answer.

Don Marquis

Why Abortion Is Immoral

Don Marquis is professor of philosophy at the University of Kansas.

Marquis argues that abortion is seriously immoral, except in some rare or hard cases, because it deprives the fetus of a future having valuable experiences, activities, projects, and enjoyments; this is the same reason why killing an innocent adult human being is wrong.

The view that abortion is, with rare exceptions, seriously immoral has received little support in the recent philosophical literature. No doubt most philosophers affiliated with secular institutions of higher education believe that the anti-abortion position is either a symptom of irrational religious dogma or a conclusion generated by seriously confused philosophical argument. The purpose of this essay is to undermine this general belief. This essay sets out an argument that purports to show, as well as any argument in ethics can show, that abortion is, except possibly in rare cases, seriously immoral, that it is in the same moral category as killing an innocent adult human being.

The argument is based on a major assumption. Many of the most insightful and careful writers on the ethics of abortion—such as Joel Feinberg, Michael Tooley, Mary Anne Warren,

From Don Marquis, "Why Abortion Is Immoral," *The Journal of Philosophy* LXXXVI, 4 (April 1989): 183–202; selections 183–194, 201–2. Reprinted by permission of the author and *The Journal of Philosophy*.

H. Tristram Engelhardt, Jr., L. W. Sumner, John T. Noonan, Jr., and Philip Devine[1]—believe that whether or not abortion is morally permissible stands or falls on whether or not a fetus is the sort of being whose life it is seriously wrong to end. The argument of this essay will assume, but not argue, that they are correct.

Also, this essay will neglect issues of great importance to a complete ethics of abortion. Some anti-abortionists will allow that certain abortions, such as abortion before implantation or abortion when the life of a woman is threatened by a pregnancy or abortion after rape, may be morally permissible. This essay will not explore the casuistry of these hard cases. The purpose of this essay is to develop a general argument for the claim that the overwhelming majority of deliberate abortions are seriously immoral.

I

A sketch of standard anti-abortion and pro-choice arguments exhibits how those arguments possess certain symmetries that explain why partisans of those positions are so convinced of the correctness of their own positions, why they are not successful in convincing their opponents, and why, to others, this issue seems to be unresolvable. An analysis of the nature of this standoff suggests a strategy for surmounting it.

Consider the way a typical anti-abortionist argues. She will argue or assert that life is present from the moment of conception or that fetuses look like babies or that fetuses possess a characteristic such as a genetic code that is both necessary and sufficient for being human. Anti-abortionists seem to believe that (1) the truth of all of these claims is quite obvious, and

(2) establishing any of these claims is sufficient to show that abortion is morally akin to murder.

A standard pro-choice strategy exhibits similarities. The pro-choicer will argue or assert that fetuses are not persons or that fetuses are not rational agents or that fetuses are not social beings. Pro-choicers seem to believe that (1) the truth of any of these claims is quite obvious, and (2) establishing any of these claims is sufficient to show that an abortion is not a wrongful killing.

In fact, both the pro-choice and the anti-abortion claims do seem to be true, although the "it looks like a baby" claim is more difficult to establish the earlier the pregnancy. We seem to have a standoff. How can it be resolved?

As everyone who has taken a bit of logic knows, if any of these arguments concerning abortion is a good argument, it requires not only some claim characterizing fetuses, but also some general moral principle that ties a characteristic of fetuses to having or not having the right to life or to some other moral characteristic that will generate the obligation or the lack of obligation not to end the life of a fetus. Accordingly, the arguments of the anti-abortionist and the pro-choicer need a bit of filling in to be regarded as adequate.

Note what each partisan will say. The anti-abortionist will claim that her position is supported by such generally accepted moral principles as "It is always prima facie seriously wrong to take a human life" or "It is always prima facie seriously wrong to end the life of a baby." Since these are generally accepted moral principles, her position is certainly not obviously wrong. The pro-choicer will claim that her position is supported by such plausible moral principles as "Being a person is what gives an individual intrinsic moral worth" or "It is only seriously prima facie wrong to take the life of a member of the human community." Since these are generally accepted moral principles, the pro-choice position is certainly not obviously wrong. Unfortunately, we have again arrived at a standoff.

Now, how might one deal with this standoff? The standard approach is to try to show how the moral principles of one's opponent lose their plausibility under analysis. It is easy to see how this is possible. On the one hand, the anti-abortionist will defend a moral principle concerning the wrongness of killing which tends to be broad in scope in order that even fetuses at an early stage of pregnancy will fall under it. The problem with broad principles is that they often embrace too much. In this particular instance, the principle "It is always prima facie wrong to take a human life" seems to entail that it is wrong to end the existence of a living human cancer-cell culture, on the grounds that the culture is both living and human. Therefore, it seems that the anti-abortionist's favored principle is too broad.

On the other hand, the pro-choicer wants to find a moral principle concerning the wrongness of killing which tends to be narrow in scope in order that fetuses will *not* fall under it. The problem with narrow principles is that they often do not embrace enough. Hence, the needed principles such as "It is prima facie seriously wrong to kill only persons" or "It is prima facie wrong to kill only rational agents" do not explain why it is wrong to kill infants or young children or the severely retarded or even perhaps the severely mentally ill. Therefore, we seem again to have a standoff. The anti-abortionist charges, not unreasonably, that pro-choice principles concerning killing are too narrow to be acceptable; the pro-choicer charges, not unreasonably, that anti-abortionist principles concerning killing are too broad to be acceptable.

Attempts by both sides to patch up the difficulties in their positions run into further difficulties. The anti-abortionist will try to remove the problem in her position by reformulating her principle concerning killing in terms of human beings. Now we end up with: "It is always prima facie seriously wrong to end the life of a human being." This principle has the advantage of avoiding the problem of the human cancer-cell culture counterexample. But this advantage is purchased at a high price. For although it is clear that a fetus is both human and alive, it is not at all clear that a fetus is a human *being*. There is at least something to be said for the view that something becomes a human being only after a process of development, and that therefore first trimester fetuses and perhaps all fetuses are not yet human beings. Hence, the anti-abortionist, by this move, has merely exchanged one problem for another.[2]

The pro-choicer fares no better. She may attempt to find reasons why killing infants, young children, and the severely retarded is wrong which are independent of her major principle that is supposed to explain the wrongness of taking human life, but which will not also make abortion immoral. This is no easy task. Appeals to social utility will seem satisfactory only to those who resolve not to think of the enormous difficulties with a utilitarian account of the wrongness of killing and the significant social costs of preserving the lives of the unproductive.[3] A pro-choice strategy that extends the definition of 'person' to infants or even to young children seems just as arbitrary as an anti-abortion strategy that extends the definition of 'human being' to fetuses. Again, we find symmetries in the two positions and we arrive at a standoff.

There are even further problems that reflect symmetries in the two positions. In addition to counterexample problems, or the arbitrary application problems that can be exchanged for them, the standard anti-abortionist principle "It is prima facie seriously wrong to kill a human being," or one of its variants, can be objected to on the grounds of ambiguity. If 'human being' is taken to be a *biological* category, then the anti-abortionist is left with the problem of explaining why a merely biological category should make a moral difference. Why, it is asked, is it any more reasonable to base a moral conclusion on the number of chromosomes in one's cells than on the color of one's skin?[4] If 'human being', on the other hand, is taken to be a *moral* category, then the claim that a fetus is a human being cannot be taken to be a premise in the anti-abortion argument, for it is precisely what needs to be established. Hence, either the anti-abortionist's main category is a morally irrelevant, merely biological category, or it is of no use to the anti-abortionist in establishing (noncircularly, of course) that abortion is wrong.

Although this problem with the anti-abortionist position is often noticed, it is less often noticed that the pro-choice position suffers from an analogous problem. The principle "Only

persons have the right to life" also suffers from an ambiguity. The term 'person' is typically defined in terms of psychological characteristics, although there will certainly be disagreement concerning which characteristics are most important. Supposing that this matter can be settled, the pro-choicer is left with the problem of explaining why *psychological* characteristics should make a *moral* difference. If the pro-choicer should attempt to deal with this problem by claiming that an explanation is not necessary, that in fact we do treat such a cluster of psychological properties as having moral significance, the sharp-witted anti-abortionist should have a ready response. We do treat being both living and human as having moral significance. If it is legitimate for the pro-choicer to demand that the anti-abortionist provide an explanation of the connection between the biological character of being a human being and the wrongness of being killed (even though people accept this connection), then it is legitimate for the anti-abortionist to demand that the pro-choicer provide an explanation of the connection between psychological criteria for being a person and the wrongness of being killed (even though that connection is accepted).[5]

Feinberg has attempted to meet this objection (he calls psychological personhood "commonsense personhood"):

The characteristics that confer commonsense personhood are not arbitrary bases for rights and duties, such as race, sex or species membership; rather they are traits that make sense out of rights and duties and without which those moral attributes would have no point or function. It is because people are conscious; have a sense of their personal identities; have plans, goals, and projects; experience emotions; are liable to pains, anxieties, and frustrations; can reason and bargain, and so on—it is because of these attributes that people have values and interests, desires and expectations of their own, including a stake in their own futures, and a personal well-being of a sort we cannot ascribe to unconscious or nonrational beings. Because of their developed capacities they can assume duties and responsibilities and can have and make claims on one another. Only because of their sense of self, their life plans, their value hierarchies, and their stakes in their own futures can they be ascribed fundamental rights. There is nothing arbitrary about these linkages (*op. cit.*, p. 270).

The plausible aspects of this attempt should not be taken to obscure its implausible features. There is a great deal to be said for the view that being a psychological person under some description is a necessary condition for having duties. One cannot have a duty unless one is capable of behaving morally, and a being's capability of behaving morally will require having a certain psychology. It is far from obvious, however, that having rights entails consciousness or rationality, as Feinberg suggests. We speak of the rights of the severely retarded or the severely mentally ill, yet some of these persons are not rational. We speak of the rights of the temporarily unconscious. The New Jersey Supreme Court based their decision in the Quinlan case on Karen Ann Quinlan's right to privacy, and she was known to be permanently unconscious at that time. Hence, Feinberg's claim that having rights entails being conscious is, on its face, obviously false.

Of course it might not make sense to attribute rights to a being that would never in its natural history have certain psychological traits. This modest connection between psychological personhood and moral personhood will create a place for Karen Ann Quinlan and the temporarily unconscious. But then it makes a place for fetuses also. Hence, it does not serve Feinberg's pro-choice purposes. Accordingly, it seems that the pro-choicer will have as much difficulty bridging the gap between psychological personhood and personhood in the moral sense as the anti-abortionist has bridging the gap between being a biological human being and being a human being in the moral sense.

Furthermore, the pro-choicer cannot any more escape her problem by making person a purely moral category than the anti-abortionist could escape by the analogous move. For if person is a moral category, then the pro-choicer is left without the resources for establishing (noncircularly, of course) the claim that a fetus is not a person, which is an essential premise in her argument. Again, we have both symmetry and a standoff between pro-choice and anti-abortion views.

Passions in the abortion debate run high. There are both plausibilities and difficulties with the standard positions. Accordingly, it is

hardly surprising that partisans of either side embrace with fervor the moral generalizations that support the conclusions they preanalytically favor, and reject with disdain the moral generalizations of their opponents as being subject to inescapable difficulties. It is easy to believe that the counterexamples to one's own moral principles are merely temporary difficulties that will dissolve in the wake of further philosophical research, and that the counterexamples to the principles of one's opponents are as straightforward as the contradiction between *A* and *O* propositions in traditional logic. This might suggest to an impartial observer (if there are any) that the abortion issue is unresolvable.

There is a way out of this apparent dialectical quandry. The moral generalizations of both sides are not quite correct. The generalizations hold for the most part, for the usual cases. This suggests that they are all *accidental* generalizations, that the moral claims made by those on both sides of the dispute do not touch on the *essence* of the matter.

This use of the distinction between essence and accident is not meant to invoke obscure metaphysical categories. Rather, it is intended to reflect the rather atheoretical nature of the abortion discussion. If the generalization a partisan in the abortion dispute adopts were derived from the reason why ending the life of a human being is wrong, then there could not be exceptions to that generalization unless some special case obtains in which there are even more powerful countervailing reasons. Such generalizations would not be merely accidental generalizations; they would point to, or be based upon, the essence of the wrongness of killing, what it is that makes killing wrong. All this suggests that a necessary condition of resolving the abortion controversy is a more theoretical account of the wrongness of killing. After all, if we merely believe, but do not understand, why killing adult human beings such as ourselves is wrong, how could we conceivably show that abortion is either immoral or permissible?

II

In order to develop such an account, we can start from the following unproblematic assumption concerning our own case: it is wrong to kill *us*. Why is it wrong? Some answers can be easily eliminated. It might be said that what makes killing us wrong is that a killing brutalizes the one who kills. But the brutalization consists of being inured to the performance of an act that is hideously immoral; hence, the brutalization does not explain the immorality. It might be said that what makes killing us wrong is the great loss others would experience due to our absence. Although such hubris is understandable, such an explanation does not account for the wrongness of killing hermits, or those whose lives are relatively independent and whose friends find it easy to make new friends.

A more obvious answer is better. What primarily makes killing wrong is neither its effect on the murderer nor its effect on the victim's friends and relatives, but its effect on the victim. The loss of one's life is one of the greatest losses one can suffer. The loss of one's life deprives one of all the experiences, activities, projects, and enjoyments that would otherwise have constituted one's future. Therefore, killing someone is wrong, primarily because the killing inflicts (one of) the greatest possible losses on the victim. To describe this as the loss of life can be misleading, however. The change in my biological state does not by itself make killing me wrong. The effect of the loss of my biological life is the loss to me of all those activities, projects, experiences, and enjoyments which would otherwise have constituted my future personal life. These activities, projects, experiences, and enjoyments are either valuable for their own sakes or are means to something else that is valuable for its own sake. Some parts of my future are not valued by me now, but will come to be valued by me as I grow older and as my values and capacities change. When I am killed, I am deprived both of what I now value which would have been part of my future personal life, but also what I would come to value. Therefore, when I die, I am deprived of all of the value of my future. Inflicting this loss on me is ultimately what makes killing me wrong. This being the case, it would seem that what makes killing *any* adult human being prima facie seriously wrong is the loss of his or her future.[6]

How should this rudimentary theory of the wrongness of killing be evaluated? It cannot be faulted for deriving an 'ought' from an 'is' for it does not. The analysis assumes that killing me (or you, reader) is prima facie seriously wrong. The point of the analysis is to establish which natural property ultimately explains the wrongness of the killing, given that it is wrong. A natural property will ultimately explain the wrongness of killing, only if (1) the explanation fits without intuitions about the matter and (2) there is no other natural property that provides the basis for a better explanation of the wrongness of killing. This analysis rests on the intuition that what makes killing a particular human or animal wrong is what it does to that particular human or animal. What makes killing wrong is some natural effect or other of the killing. Some would deny this. For instance, a divine-command theorist in ethics would deny it. Surely this denial is, however, one of those features of divine-command theory which renders it so implausible.

The claim that what makes killing wrong is the loss of the victim's future is directly supported by two considerations. In the first place, this theory explains why we regard killing as one of the worst of crimes. Killing is especially wrong, because it deprives the victim of more than perhaps any other crime. In the second place, people with AIDS or cancer who know they are dying believe, of course, that dying is a very bad thing for them. They believe that the loss of a future to them that they would otherwise have experienced is what makes their premature death a very bad thing for them. A better theory of the wrongness of killing would require a different natural property associated with killing which better fits with the attitudes of the dying. What could it be?

The view that what makes killing wrong is the loss to the victim of the value of the victim's future gains additional support when some of its implications are examined. In the first place, it is incompatible with the view that it is wrong to kill only beings who are biologically human. It is possible that there exists a different species from another planet whose members have a future like ours. Since having a future like that is what makes killing someone wrong, this theory entails that it would be wrong to kill members of such a species. Hence, this theory is opposed to the claim that only life that is biologically human has great moral worth, a claim which many anti-abortionists have seemed to adopt. This opposition, which this theory has in common with parenthood theories, seems to be a merit of the theory.

In the second place, the claim that the loss of one's future is the wrong-making feature of one's being killed entails the possibility that the futures of some actual nonhuman mammals on our own planet are sufficiently like ours that it is seriously wrong to kill them also. Whether some animals do have the same right to life as human beings depends on adding to the account of the wrongness of killing some additional account of just what it is about my future or the futures of other adult human beings which makes it wrong to kill us. No such additional account will be offered in this essay. Undoubtedly, the provision of such an account would be a very difficult matter. Undoubtedly, any such account would be quite controversial. Hence, it surely should not reflect badly on this sketch of an elementary theory of the wrongness of killing that it is indeterminate with respect to some very difficult issues regarding animal rights.

In the third place, the claim that the loss of one's future is the wrong-making feature of one's being killed does not entail, as sanctity of human life theories do, that active euthanasia is wrong. Persons who are severely and incurably ill, who face a future of pain and despair, and who wish to die will not have suffered a loss if they are killed. It is, strictly speaking, the value of a human's future which makes killing wrong in this theory. This being so, killing does not necessarily wrong some persons who are sick and dying. Of course, there may be other reasons for a prohibition of active euthanasia, but that is another matter. Sanctity of human life theories seem to hold that active euthanasia is seriously wrong even in an individual case where there seems to be good reason for it independently of public policy considerations. This consequence is most implausible, and it is a plus for the claim that the loss of a future of value is what makes killing wrong that it does not share this consequence.

In the fourth place, the account of wrongness of killing defended in this essay does straightforwardly entail that it is prima facie seriously wrong to kill children and infants, for we do presume that they have futures of value. Since we do believe that it is wrong to kill defenseless little babies, it is important that a theory of the wrongness of killing easily account for this. Personhood theories of the wrongness of killing, on the other hand, cannot straightforwardly account for the wrongness of killing infants and young children.[7] Hence, such theories must add special ad hoc accounts of the wrongness of killing the young. The plausibility of such ad hoc theories seems to be a function of how desperately one wants such theories to work. The claim that the primary wrong-making feature of a killing is the loss to the victim of the value of its future accounts for the wrongness of killing young children and infants directly; it makes the wrongness of such acts as obvious as we actually think it is. This is a further merit of this theory. Accordingly, it seems that this value of a future-like-ours theory of the wrongness of killing shares strengths of both sanctity of life and personhood accounts while avoiding weaknesses of both. In addition, it meshes with a central intuition concerning what makes killing wrong.

The claim that the primary wrong-making feature of a killing is the loss to the victim of the values of its future has obvious consequences for the ethics of abortion. The future of a standard fetus includes a set of experiences, projects, activities, and such which are identical with the futures of adult human beings and are identical with the futures of young children. Since the reason that is sufficient to explain why it is wrong to kill human beings after the time of birth is a reason that also applies to fetuses, it follows that abortion is prima facie seriously morally wrong.

This argument does not rely on the invalid inference that, since it is wrong to kill persons, it is wrong to kill potential persons also. The category that is morally central to this analysis is the category of having a valuable future like ours; it is not the category of personhood. The argument to the conclusion that abortion is prima facie seriously morally wrong proceeded independently of the notion of person or potential person or any equivalent. Someone may wish to start with this analysis in terms of the value of a human future, conclude that abortion is, except perhaps in rare circumstances, seriously morally wrong, infer that fetuses have the right to life, and then call fetuses "persons" as a result of their having the right to life. Clearly, in this case, the category of person is being used to state the *conclusion* of the analysis rather than to generate the *argument* of the analysis.

The structure of this anti-abortion argument can be both illuminated and defended by comparing it to what appears to be the best argument for the wrongness of the wanton infliction of pain on animals. This latter argument is based on the assumption that it is prima facie wrong to inflict pain on me (or you, reader). What is the natural property associated with the infliction of pain which makes such infliction wrong? The obvious answer seems to be that the infliction of pain causes suffering and that suffering is a misfortune. The suffering caused by the infliction of pain is what makes the wanton infliction of pain on me wrong. The wanton infliction of pain on other adult humans causes suffering. The wanton infliction of pain on animals causes suffering. Since causing suffering is what makes wanton infliction of pain wrong and since the wanton infliction of pain on animals causes suffering, it follows that the wanton infliction of pain on animals is wrong.

This argument for the wrongness of the wanton infliction of pain on animals shares a number of structural features with the argument for the serious prima facie wrongness of abortion. Both arguments start with an obvious assumption concerning what it is wrong to do to me (or you, reader). Both then look for the characteristic or the consequence of the wrong action which makes the action wrong. Both recognize that the wrong-making feature of these immoral actions is a property of actions sometimes directed at individuals other than postnatal human beings. If the structure of the argument for the wrongness of the wanton infliction of pain on animals is sound, then the structure of the argument for the prima facie serious wrongness of abortion is also sound, for the structure of the two arguments is the same.

The structure common to both is the key to the explanation of how the wrongness of abortion can be demonstrated without recourse to the category of person. In neither argument is that category crucial.

This defense of an argument for the wrongness of abortion in terms of a structurally similar argument for the wrongness of the wanton infliction of pain on animals succeeds only if the account regarding animals is the correct account. Is it? In the first place, it seems plausible. In the second place, its major competition is Kant's account. Kant believed that we do not have direct duties to animals at all, because they are not persons. Hence, Kant had to explain and justify the wrongness of inflicting pain on animals on the grounds that "he who is hard in his dealings with animals becomes hard also in his dealing with men."[8] The problem with Kant's account is that there seems to be no reason for accepting this latter claim unless Kant's account is rejected. If the alternative to Kant's account is accepted, then it is easy to understand why someone who is indifferent to inflicting pain on animals is also indifferent to inflicting pain on humans, for one is indifferent to what makes inflicting pain wrong in both cases. But, if Kant's account is accepted, there is no intelligible reason why one who is hard in his dealings with animals (or crabgrass or stones) should also be hard in his dealings with men. After all, men are persons: animals are no more person than crabgrass or stones. Persons are Kant's crucial moral category. Why, in short, should a Kantian accept the basic claim in Kant's argument?

Hence, Kant's argument for the wrongness of inflicting pain on animals rests on a claim that, in a world of Kantian moral agents, is demonstrably false. Therefore, the alternative analysis, being more plausible anyway, should be accepted. Since this alternative analysis has the same structure as the anti-abortion argument being defended here, we have further support for the argument for the immorality of abortion being defended in this essay.

Of course, this value of a future-like-ours argument, if sound, shows only that abortion is prima facie wrong, not that it is wrong in any and all circumstances. Since the loss of the future to a standard fetus, if killed, is, however, at least as great a loss as the loss of the future to a standard adult human being who is killed, abortion, like ordinary killing, could be justified only by the most compelling reasons. The loss of one's life is almost the greatest misfortune that can happen to one. Presumably abortion could be justified in some circumstances, only if the loss consequent on failing to abort would be at least as great. Accordingly, morally permissible abortions will be rare indeed unless, perhaps, they occur so early in pregnancy that a fetus is not yet definitely an individual. Hence, this argument should be taken as showing that abortion is presumptively very seriously wrong, where the presumption is very strong—as strong as the presumption that killing another adult human being is wrong. . . .

In this essay, it has been argued that the correct ethic of the wrongness of killing can be extended to fetal life and used to show that there is a strong presumption that any abortion is morally impermissible. If the ethic of killing adopted here entails, however, that contraception is also seriously immoral, then there would appear to be a difficulty with the analysis of this essay.

But this analysis does not entail that contraception is wrong. Of course, contraception prevents the actualization of a possible future of value. Hence, it follows from the claim that futures of value should be maximized that contraception is prima facie immoral. This obligation to maximize does not exist, however; furthermore, nothing in the ethics of killing in this paper entails that it does. The ethics of killing in this essay would entail that contraception is wrong only if something were denied a human future of value by contraception. Nothing at all is denied such a future by contraception, however.

Candidates for a subject of harm by contraception fall into four categories: (1) some sperm or other, (2) some ovum or other, (3) a sperm and an ovum separately, and (4) a sperm and an ovum together. Assigning the harm to some sperm is utterly arbitrary, for no reason can be given for making a sperm the subject of harm rather than an ovum. Assigning the harm to some ovum is utterly arbitrary, for no reason

can be given for making an ovum the subject of harm rather than a sperm. One might attempt to avoid these problems by insisting that contraception deprives both the sperm and the ovum separately of a valuable future like ours. On this alternative, too many futures are lost. Contraception was supposed to be wrong, because it deprived us of one future of value, not two. One might attempt to avoid this problem by holding that contraception deprives the combination of sperm and ovum of a valuable future like ours. But here the definite article misleads. At the time of contraception, there are hundreds of millions of sperm, one (released) ovum and millions of possible combinations of all of these. There is no actual combination at all. Is the subject of the loss to be a merely possible combination? Which one? This alternative does not yield an actual subject of harm either. Accordingly, the immorality of contraception is not entailed by the loss of a future-like-ours argument simply because there is no nonarbitrarily identifiable subject of the loss in the case of contraception.

The purpose of this essay has been to set out an argument for the serious presumptive wrongness of abortion subject to the assumption that the moral permissibility of abortion stands or falls on the moral status of the fetus. Since a fetus possesses a property, the possession of which in adult human beings is sufficient to make killing an adult human being wrong, abortion is wrong. This way of dealing with the problem of abortion seems superior to other approaches to the ethics of abortion, because it rests on an ethics of killing which is close to self-evident, because the crucial morally relevant property clearly applies to fetuses, and because the argument avoids the usual equivocations on 'human life', 'human being', or 'person'. The argument rests neither on religious claims or on Papal dogma. It is not subject to the objection of "speciesism." Its soundness is compatible with the moral permissibility of euthanasia and contraception. It deals with our intuitions concerning young children.

Finally, this analysis can be viewed as resolving a standard problem—indeed, *the* standard problem—concerning the ethics of abortion. Clearly, it is wrong to kill adult human beings.

Clearly, it is not wrong to end the life of some arbitrarily chosen single human cell. Fetuses seem to be like arbitrarily chosen human cells in some respects and like adult humans in other respects. The problem of the ethics of abortion is the problem of determining the fetal property that settles this moral controversy. The thesis of this essay is that the problem of the ethics of abortion, so understood, is solvable.

Endnotes

1. Feinberg, "Abortion," in *Matters of Life and Death: New Introductory Essays in Moral Philosophy*, Tom Regan, ed. (New York: Random House, 1986), pp. 256–293; Tooley, "Abortion and Infanticide," *Philosophy and Public Affairs*, II, 1 (1972):37–65, Tooley, *Abortion and Infanticide* (New York: Oxford, 1984); Warren, "On the Moral and Legal Status of Abortion," *The Monist*, LVII, 1 (1973):43–61; Engelhardt, "The Ontology of Abortion," *Ethics*, LXXXIV, 3 (1974):217–234; Sumner, *Abortion and Moral Theory* (Princeton: University Press, 1981); Noonan, "An Almost Absolute Value in History," in *The Morality of Abortion: Legal and Historical Perspectives*, Noonan, ed. (Cambridge: Harvard, 1970); and Devine, *The Ethics of Homocide* (Ithaca: Cornell, 1978).
2. For interesting discussions of this issue, see Warren Quinn, "Abortion: Identity and Loss," *Philosophy and Public Affairs*, XIII, 1 (1984):24–54; and Lawrence C. Becker, "Human Being: The Boundaries of the Concept," *Philosophy and Public Affairs*, IV, 4 (1975): 334–359.
3. For example, see my "Ethics and The Elderly: Some Problems," in Stuart Spicker, Kathleen Woodward, and David Van Tassel, eds., *Aging and the Elderly: Humanistic Perspectives in Gerontology* (Atlantic Highlands, NJ: Humanities, 1978), pp. 341–355.
4. See Warren, *op. cit.*, and Tooley, "Abortion and Infanticide."
5. This seems to be the fatal flaw in Warren's treatment of this issue.
6. I have been most influenced on this matter by Jonathan Glover, *Causing Death and Saving Lives* (New York: Penguin, 1977), ch. 3; and Robert Young, "What Is So Wrong with Killing People?" *Philosophy*, LIV, 210 (1979):515–528.
7. Feinberg, Tooley, Warren, and Englehardt have all dealt with this problem.
8. "Duties to Animals and Spirits," in *Lectures on Ethics*, Louis Infeld, trans. (New York: Harper, 1963), p. 239.

REVIEW QUESTIONS

1. According to Marquis, what similar problems confront both the standard anti-abortion and pro-choice positions (as he calls them)?
2. Why is killing wrong according to Marquis?
3. Why is abortion wrong? State and explain Marquis' argument.
4. What is Marquis' position on active euthanasia?

DISCUSSION QUESTIONS

1. Marquis allows that there may be rare or hard cases in which abortion is not wrong. What are these cases? Do you agree that abortion is not wrong in these cases?
2. Does Marquis' moral principle about killing imply that killing nonhuman animals is wrong? Is such killing wrong?
3. Is killing a severely defective fetus wrong according to Marquis' moral principle? Do you think it is wrong?
4. Does Marquis convince you that his position does not imply that contraception is wrong?

Jane English

Abortion and the Concept of a Person

Jane English (1947–1978) taught at the University of North Carolina, Chapel Hill, and published several articles in ethics. She was the editor of Sex Equality *(1977).*

English argues that one of the central issues in the abortion debate, whether the fetus is a person or not, cannot be conclusively settled because of the nature of the concept of a person. This concept is said to be a cluster concept because it cannot be defined in terms of necessary and sufficient conditions. Given this lack of defining features,

Reprinted with the permission of the editors from *Canadian Journal of Philosophy*, vol. V, no. 2 (October 1975), pp. 233–243.

we cannot say whether a fetus is a person or not; it remains in a conceptually fuzzy borderline area.

English argues that regardless of whether or not the fetus is a person we must accept the moderate view that abortion is justified in some cases and not in others. Even if the fetus is a person, as the conservatives hold, it does not follow that abortion is never morally permissible. For the self-defense model not only justifies abortion to save the mother's life, but also justifies abortion to avoid serious harm or injury. On the other hand, the liberal view that the fetus is not a person does not warrant abortion on demand because we still have a duty to not harm or kill nonpersons that are sufficiently personlike. This duty makes late abortions for the sake of convenience (such as the woman who does not want to postpone a trip to Europe) morally wrong.

The abortion debate rages on. Yet the two most popular positions seem to be clearly mistaken. Conservatives maintain that a human life begins at conception and that therefore abortion must be wrong because it is murder. But not all killings of humans are murders. Most notably, self-defense may justify even the killing of an innocent person.

Liberals, on the other hand, are just as mistaken in their argument that since a fetus does not become a person until birth, a woman may do whatever she pleases in and to her own body. First, you cannot do as you please with your own body if it affects other people adversely.[1] Second, if a fetus is not a person, that does not imply that you can do to it anything you wish. Animals, for example, are not persons, yet to kill or torture them for no reason at all is wrong.

At the center of the storm has been the issue of just when it is between ovulation and adulthood that a person appears on the scene. Conservatives draw the line at conception, liberals at birth. In this paper I first examine our concept of a person and conclude that no single criterion can capture the concept of a person and no sharp line can be drawn. Next I argue that if a fetus is a person, abortion is still justifiable in many cases; and if a fetus is not a person, killing it is still wrong in many cases.

To a large extent, these two solutions are in agreement. I conclude that our concept of a person cannot and need not bear the weight that the abortion controversy has thrust upon it.

I

The several factions in the abortion argument have drawn battle lines around various proposed criteria for determining what is and what is not a person. For example, Mary Anne Warren[2] lists five features (capacities for reasoning, self-awareness, complex communication, etc.) as her criteria for personhood and argues for the permissibility of abortion because a fetus falls outside this concept. Baruch Brody[3] uses brain waves. Michael Tooley[4] picks having-a-concept-of-self as his criterion and concludes that infanticide and abortion are justifiable, while the killing of adult animals is not. On the other side, Paul Ramsey[5] claims a certain gene structure is the defining characteristic. John Noonan[6] prefers conceived-of-humans and presents counterexamples to various other candidate criteria. For instance, he argues against viability as the criterion because the newborn and infirm would then be nonpersons, since they cannot live without the aid of others. He rejects any criterion that calls upon the sorts of sentiments a being can evoke in adults on the grounds that this would allow us to exclude other races as nonpersons if we could just view them sufficiently unsentimentally.

These approaches are typical: foes of abortion propose **sufficient conditions** for personhood which fetuses satisfy, while friends of abortion counter with necessary conditions for personhood which fetuses lack. But these both presuppose that the concept of a person can be captured in a strait jacket of necessary and/or sufficient conditions.[7] Rather, 'person' is a cluster of features, of which rationality, having a self concept and being conceived of humans are only part.

What is typical of persons? Within our concept of a person we include, first, certain biological factors: descended from humans, having a certain genetic makeup, having a head, hands, arms, eyes, capable of locomotion, breathing, eating, sleeping. There are psychological factors: sentience, perception, having a concept of self and of one's own interests and desires, the ability to use tools, the ability to use language or symbol systems, the ability to joke, to be angry, to doubt. There are rationality factors: the ability to reason and draw conclusions, the ability to generalize and to learn from past experience, the ability to sacrifice present interests for greater gains in the future. There are social factors: the ability to work in groups and respond to peer pressures, the ability to recognize and consider as valuable the interests of others, seeing oneself as one among "other minds," the ability to sympathize, encourage, love, the ability to evoke from others the responses of sympathy, encouragement, love, the ability to work with others for mutual advantage. Then there are legal factors: being subject to the law and protected by it, having the ability to sue and enter contracts, being counted in the census, having a name and citizenship, the ability to own property, inherit, and so forth.

Now the point is not that this list is incomplete, or that you can find counterinstances to each of its points. People typically exhibit rationality, for instance, but someone who was irrational would not thereby fail to qualify as a person. On the other hand, something could exhibit the majority of these features and still fail to be a person, as an advanced robot might. There is no single core of necessary and sufficient features which we can draw upon with the assurance that they constitute what really makes a person; there are only features that are more or less typical.

This is not to say that no necessary or sufficient conditions can be given. Being alive is a necessary condition for being a person, and being a U.S. Senator is sufficient. But rather than falling inside a sufficient condition or outside a necessary one, a fetus lies in the penumbra region where our concept of a person is not so simple. For this reason I think a conclusive answer to the question whether a fetus is a person is unattainable.

Here we might note a family of simple fallacies that proceed by stating a necessary condition for personhood and showing that a fetus has that characteristic. This is a form of the **fallacy of affirming the consequent**. For example, some have mistakenly reasoned from the premise that a fetus is human (after all, it is a human fetus rather than, say, a canine fetus), to the conclusion that it is a human. Adding an **equivocation** on 'being', we get the fallacious argument that since a fetus is something both living and human, it is a human being.

Nonetheless, it does seem clear that a fetus has very few of the above family of characteristics, whereas a newborn baby exhibits a much larger proportion of them—and a two-year-old has even more. Note that one traditional anti-abortion argument has centered on pointing out the many ways in which a fetus resembles a baby. They emphasize its development ("It already has ten fingers . . .") without mentioning its dissimilarities to adults (it still has gills and a tail). They also try to evoke the sort of sympathy on our part that we only feel toward other persons ("Never to laugh . . . or feel the sunshine?"). This all seems to be a relevant way to argue, since its purpose is to persuade us that a fetus satisfies so many of the important features on the list that it ought to be treated as a person. Also note that a fetus near the time of birth satisfies many more of these factors than a fetus in the early months of development. This could provide reason for making distinctions among the different stages of pregnancy, as the U.S. Supreme Court has done.[8]

Historically, the time at which a person has been said to come into existence has varied widely. Muslims date personhood from fourteen days after conception. Some medievals followed Aristotle in placing ensoulment at forty days after conception for a male fetus and eighty days for a female fetus.[9] In European common law since the Seventeenth Century, abortion was considered the killing of a person only after quickening, the time when a pregnant woman first feels the fetus move on its own. Nor is this variety of opinions surprising. Biologically, a human being develops gradually. We shouldn't expect there to be any specific time or sharp dividing point when a person appears on the scene.

For these reasons I believe our concept of a person is not sharp or decisive enough to bear the weight of a solution to the abortion controversy. To use it to solve that problem is to clarify *obscurum per obscurius*.

II

Next let us consider what follows if a fetus is a person after all. Judith Jarvis Thomson's landmark article, "A Defense of Abortion," [10] correctly points out that some additional argumentation is needed at this point in the conservative argument to bridge the gap between the premise that a fetus is an innocent person and the conclusion that killing it is always wrong. To arrive at this conclusion, we would need the additional premise that killing an innocent person is always wrong. But killing an innocent person is sometimes permissible, most notably in self-defense. Some examples may help draw out our intuitions or ordinary judgments about self-defense.

Suppose a mad scientist, for instance, hypnotized innocent people to jump out of the bushes and attack innocent passers-by with knives. If you are so attacked, we agree you have a right to kill the attacker in self-defense, if killing him is the only way to protect your life or to save yourself from serious injury. It does not seem to matter here that the attacker is not malicious but himself an innocent pawn, for your killing of him is not done in a spirit of retribution but only in self-defense.

How severe an injury may you inflict in self-defense? In part this depends upon the severity of the injury to be avoided: you may not shoot someone merely to avoid having your clothes torn. This might lead one to the mistaken conclusion that the defense may only equal the threatened injury in severity; that to avoid death you may kill, but to avoid a black eye you may only inflict a black eye or the equivalent. Rather, our laws and customs seem to say that you may create an injury somewhat, but not enormously, greater than the injury to be avoided. To fend off an attack whose outcome would be as serious as rape, a severe beating or the loss of a finger, you may shoot; to avoid having your clothes torn, you may blacken an eye.

Aside from this, the injury you may inflict should only be the minimum necessary to deter or incapacitate the attacker. Even if you know he intends to kill you, you are not justified in shooting him if you could equally well save yourself by the simple expedient of running away. Self-defense is for the purpose of avoiding harms rather than equalizing harms.

Some cases of pregnancy present a parallel situation. Though the fetus is itself innocent, it may pose a threat to the pregnant woman's well-being, life prospects or health, mental or physical. If the pregnancy prevents a slight threat to her interests, it seems self-defense cannot justify abortion. But if the threat is on a par with a serious beating or the loss of a finger, she may kill the fetus that poses such a threat, even if it is an innocent person. If a lesser harm to the fetus could have the same defensive effect, killing it would not be justified. It is unfortunate that the only way to free the woman from the pregnancy entails the death of the fetus (except in very late stages of pregnancy). Thus a self-defense model supports Thomson's point that the woman has a right only to be freed from the fetus, not a right to demand its death. [11]

The self-defense model is most helpful when we take the pregnant woman's point of view. In the pre-Thomson literature, abortion is often framed as a question for a third party: do you, a doctor, have a right to choose between the life of the woman and that of the fetus? Some have claimed that if you were a passer-by who witnessed a struggle between the innocent hypnotized attacker and his equally innocent victim, you would have no reason to kill either in defense of the other. They have concluded that the self-defense model implies that a woman may attempt to abort herself, but that a doctor should not assist her. I think the position of the third party is somewhat more complex. We do feel some inclination to intervene on behalf of the victim rather than the attacker, other things equal. But if both parties are innocent, other factors come into consideration. You would rush to the aid of your husband whether he was attacker or attackee. If a hypnotized famous violinist were attacking a skid row bum, we would try to save the individual who is of more value to society. These considerations would tend to support abortion in some cases.

But suppose you are a frail senior citizen who wishes to avoid being knifed by one of these innocent hypnotics, so you have hired a bodyguard to accompany you. If you are attacked, it is clear we believe that the bodyguard, acting as your agent, has a right to kill the attacker to save you from a serious beating. Your rights of self-defense are transferred to your agent. I suggest that we should similarly view the doctor as the pregnant woman's agent in carrying out a defense she is physically incapable of accomplishing herself.

Thanks to modern technology, the cases are rare in which a pregnancy poses as clear a threat to a woman's bodily health as an attacker brandishing a switchblade. How does self-defense fare when more subtle, complex and long-range harms are involved?

To consider a somewhat fanciful example, suppose you are a highly trained surgeon when you are kidnapped by the hypnotic attacker. He says he does not intend to harm you but to take you back to the mad scientist who, it turns out, plans to hypnotize you to have a permanent mental block against all your knowledge of medicine. This would automatically destroy your career which would in turn have a serious adverse impact on your family, your personal relationships and your happiness. It seems to me that if the only way you can avoid this outcome is to shoot the innocent attacker, you are justified in so doing. You are defending yourself from a drastic injury to your life prospects. I think it is no exaggeration to claim that unwanted pregnancies (most obviously among teenagers) often have such adverse life-long consequences as the surgeon's loss of livelihood.

Several parallels arise between various views on abortion and the self-defense model. Let's suppose further that these hypnotized attackers only operate at night, so that it is well known that they can be avoided completely by the considerable inconvenience of never leaving your house after dark. One view is that since you could stay home at night, therefore if you go out and are selected by one of these hypnotized people, you have no right to defend yourself. This parallels the view that abstinence is the only acceptable way to avoid pregnancy. Others might hold that you ought to take along some defense such as mace which will deter the hyponotized person without killing him, but that if this defense fails, you are obliged to submit to the resulting injury, no matter how severe it is. This parallels the view that contraception is all right but abortion is always wrong, even in cases of contraceptive failure.

A third view is that you may kill the hypnotized person only if he will actually kill you, but not if he will only injure you. This is like the position that abortion is permissible only if it is required to save a woman's life. Finally we have the view that it is all right to kill the attacker, even if only to avoid a very slight inconvenience to yourself and even if you knowingly walked down the very street where all these incidents have been taking place without taking along any mace or protective escort. If we assume that a fetus is a person, this is the analogue of the view that abortion is always justifiable, "on demand."

The self-defense model allows us to see an important difference that exists between abortion and infanticide, even if a fetus is a person from conception. Many have argued that the only way to justify abortion without justifying infanticide would be to find some characteristic of personhood that is acquired at birth. Michael Tooley, for one, claims infanticide is justifiable because the really significant characteristics of person are acquired some time after birth. But all such approaches look to characteristics of the developing human and ignore the relation between the fetus and the woman. What if, after birth, the presence of an infant or the need to support it posed a grave threat to the woman's sanity or life prospects? She could escape this threat by the simple expedient of running away. So a solution that does not entail the death of the infant is available. Before birth, such solutions are not available because of the biological dependence of the fetus on the woman. Birth is the crucial point not because of any characteristics the fetus gains, but because after birth the woman can defend herself by a means less drastic than killing the infant. Hence self-defense can be used to justify abortion without necessarily thereby justifying infanticide.

III

On the other hand, supposing a fetus is not after all a person, would abortion always be morally permissible? Some opponents of abortion seem worried that if a fetus is not a full-fledged person, then we are justified in treating it in any way at all. However, this does not follow. Non-persons do get some consideration in our moral code, though of course they do not have the same rights as persons have (and in general they do not have moral responsibilities), and though their interests may be overridden by the interests of persons. Still, we cannot just treat them in any way at all.

Treatment of animals is a case in point. It is wrong to torture dogs for fun or to kill wild birds for no reason at all. It is wrong Period, even though dogs and birds do not have the same rights persons do. However, few people think it is wrong to use dogs as experimental animals, causing them considerable suffering in some cases, provided that the resulting research will probably bring discoveries of great benefit to people. And most of us think it all right to kill birds for food or to protect our crops. People's rights are different from the consideration we give to animals, then, for it is wrong to experiment on people, even if others might later benefit a great deal as a result of their suffering. You might volunteer to be a subject, but this would be supererogatory; you certainly have a right to refuse to be a medical guinea pig.

But how do we decide what you may or may not do to nonpersons? This is a difficult problem, one for which I believe no adequate account exists. You do not want to say, for instance, that torturing dogs is all right whenever the sum of its effects on people is good—when it doesn't warp the sensibilities of the torturer so much that he mistreats people. If that were the case, it would be all right to torture dogs if you did it in private, or if the torturer lived on a desert island or died soon afterward, so that his actions had no effect on people. This is an inadequate account, because whatever moral consideration animals get, it has to be indefeasible, too. It will have to be a general proscription of certain actions, not merely a weighing of the impact on people on a case-by-case basis.

Rather, we need to distinguish two levels on which consequences of actions can be taken into account in moral reasoning. The traditional objections to Utilitarianism focus on the fact that it operates solely on the first level, taking all the consequences into account in particular cases only. This Utilitarianism is open to "desert island" and "lifeboat" counterexamples because these cases are rigged to make the consequences of actions severely limited.

Rawls' theory could be described as a teleological sort of theory, but with teleology operating on a higher level.[12] In choosing the principles to regulate society from the original position, his hypothetical choosers make their decision on the basis of the total consequences of various systems. Furthermore, they are constrained to choose a general set of rules which people can readily learn and apply. An ethical theory must operate by generating a set of sympathies and attitudes toward others which reinforces the functioning of that set of moral principles. Our prohibition against killing people operates by means of certain moral sentiments including sympathy, compassion and guilt. But if these attitudes are to form a coherent set, they carry us further: we tend to perform supererogatory actions, and we tend to feel similar compassion toward person-like nonpersons.

It is crucial that psychological facts play a role here. Our psychological constitution makes it the case that for our ethical theory to work, it must prohibit certain treatment of nonpersons which are significantly person-like. If our moral rules allowed people to treat some person-like nonpersons in ways we do not want people to be treated, this would undermine the system of sympathies and attitudes that makes the ethical system work. For this reason, we would choose in the original position to make mistreatment of some sorts of animals wrong in general (not just wrong in the cases with public impact), even though animals are not themselves parties in the original position. Thus it makes sense that it is those animals whose appearance and behavior are most like those of people that get the most consideration in our moral scheme.

It is because of "coherence of attitudes," I think, that the similarity of a fetus to a baby is very significant. A fetus one week before birth is so much like a newborn baby in our psychological space that we cannot allow any cavalier treatment of the former while expecting full sympathy and nurturative support for the latter. Thus, I think that anti-abortion forces are indeed giving their strongest arguments when they point to the similarities between a fetus and a baby, and when they try to evoke our emotional attachment to and sympathy for the fetus. An early horror story from New York about nurses who were expected to alternate between caring for six-week premature infants and disposing of viable 24-week aborted fetuses is just that—a horror story. These beings are so much alike that no one can be asked to draw a distinction and treat them so very differently.

Remember, however, that in the early weeks after conception, a fetus is very much unlike a person. It is hard to develop these feelings for a set of genes which doesn't yet have a head, hands, beating heart, response to touch or the ability to move by itself. Thus it seems to me that the alleged "slippery slope" between conception and birth is not so very slippery. In the early stages of pregnancy, abortion can hardly be compared to murder for psychological reasons, but in the latest stages it is psychologically akin to murder.

Another source of similarity is the bodily continuity between fetus and adult. Bodies play a surprisingly central role in our attitudes toward persons. One has only to think of the philosophical literature on how far physical identity suffices for personal identity or Wittgenstein's remark that the best picture of the human soul is the human body. Even after death, when all agree the body is no longer a person, we still observe elaborate customs of respect for the human body; like people who torture dogs, necrophiliacs are not to be trusted with people.[13] So it is appropriate that we show respect to a fetus as the body continuous with the body of a person. This is a degree of resemblance to persons that animals cannot rival.

Michael Tooley also utilizes a parallel with animals. He claims that it is always permissible to drown newborn kittens and draws conclusions about infanticide.[14] But it is only permissible to drown kittens when their survival would cause some hardship. Perhaps it would be a burden to feed and house six more cats or to find other homes for them. The alternative of letting them starve produces even more suffering than the drowning. Since the kittens get their rights second-hand, so to speak, via the need for coherence in our attitudes, their interests are often overridden by the interests of full-fledged persons. But if their survival would be no inconvenience to people at all, then it is wrong to drown them, contra Tooley.

Tooley's conclusions about abortion are wrong for the same reason. Even if a fetus is not a person, abortion is not always permissible, because of the resemblance of a fetus to a person. I agree with Thomson that it would be wrong for a woman who is seven months pregnant to have an abortion just to avoid having to postpone a trip to Europe. In the early months of pregnancy when the fetus hardly resembles a baby at all, then, abortion is permissible whenever it is in the interests of the pregnant woman or her family. The reasons would only need to outweigh the pain and inconvenience of the abortion itself. In the middle months, when the fetus comes to resemble a person, abortion would be justifiable only when the continuation of the pregnancy or the birth of the child would cause harms—physical, psychological, economic or social—to the woman. In the late months of pregnancy, even on our current assumption that a fetus is not a person, abortion seems to be wrong except to save a woman from significant injury or death.

The Supreme Court has recognized similar gradations in the alleged slippery slope stretching between conception and birth. To this point, the present paper has been a discussion of the moral status of abortion only, not its legal status. In view of the great physical, financial and sometimes psychological costs of abortion, perhaps the legal arrangement most compatible with the proposed moral solution would be the absence of restrictions, that is, so-called abortion "on demand."

So I conclude, first, that application of our concept of a person will not suffice to settle the abortion issue. After all, the biological development of a human being is gradual. Second, whether a fetus is a person or not, abortion is justifiable early in pregnancy to avoid modest harms and seldom justifiable late in pregnancy except to avoid significant injury or death.[15]

Endnotes

1. We also have paternalistic laws which keep us from harming our own bodies even when no one else is affected. Ironically, anti-abortion laws were originally designed to protect pregnant women from a dangerous but tempting procedure.
2. Mary Anne Warren, "On the Moral and Legal Status of Abortion," *Monist* 57 (1973).
3. Baruch Brody, "Fetal Humanity and the Theory of Essentialism," in Robert Baker and Frederick Elliston (eds.), *Philosophy and Sex* (Buffalo, N.Y., 1975).
4. Michael Tooley, "Abortion and Infanticide," *Philosophy and Public Affairs* 2 (1972).
5. Paul Ramsey, "The Morality of Abortion," in James Rachels, ed., *Moral Problems* (New York, 1971).
6. John Noonan, "Abortion and the Catholic Church: A Summary History," *Natural Law Forum* 12 (1967), pp. 125–131.
7. Wittgenstein has argued against the possibility of so capturing the concept of a game, *Philosophical Investigations* (New York, 1958), § 66–71.
8. Not because the fetus is partly a person and so has some of the rights of persons, but rather because of the rights of person-like non-persons. This I discuss in part III below.
9. Aristotle himself was concerned, however, with the different question of when the soul takes form. For historical data, see Jimmye Kimmey, "How the Abortion Laws Happened," *Ms* 1 (April, 1973), pp. 48ff, and John Noonan, *loc. cit.*
10. J. J. Thomson, "A Defense of Abortion," *Philosophy and Public Affairs* 1 (1971).
11. *Ibid.* [p. 187].
12. John Rawls, *A Theory of Justice* (Cambridge, Mass., 1971), § 3–4.
13. On the other hand, if they can be trusted with people, then our moral customs are mistaken. It all depends on the facts of psychology.
14. *Op. cit.*, pp. 40, 60–61.
15. I am deeply indebted to Larry Crocker and Arthur Kuflik for their constructive comments.

REVIEW QUESTIONS

1. What is wrong with the conservative view according to English?
2. What two objections does she make to the liberal argument?
3. According to English, why do the various attempts to find the necessary and/or sufficient conditions for personhood all fail?
4. Explain English's own account of the concept of person including the biological, psychological, rationality, social, and legal factors.
5. According to English, in what cases does the self-defense model justify abortion, as distinguished from merely extracting the fetus and keeping it alive?
6. English discusses four different views of abortion and self-defense. Distinguish between these four different views.
7. According to English, why isn't abortion always morally permissible even if the fetus is not a person?

DISCUSSION QUESTIONS

1. Is English's analysis of the concept of person correct? To find out, try to state necessary and sufficient conditions for being a person.
2. English never commits herself to one of the four views on abortion and self-defense. Which of these do you think is the most plausible? Why?
3. English asserts that it is wrong—period—to kill wild birds for no reason at all. Do you agree? Why or why not?

L. W. Sumner

Abortion: A Moderate View

L. W. Sumner is professor of philosophy at the University of Toronto. He is the author of Abor- tion and Moral Theory *(1981) and* The Moral Foundation of Rights *(1987).*

After discussing and rejecting both the liberal and conservative views of abortion, Sumner proposes a moderate view. On this moderate view, the

From L. W. Sumner, "Abortion," *Health Care Ethics*, ed. Donald VanDeVeer and Tom Regan, pp. 162–181. © 1987 by Temple University Press. Reprinted with permission.

fetus acquires a moral standing when it becomes sentient, that is, capable of feeling pleasure and pain. This occurs somewhere in the second trimester and provides an important dividing line or "threshold," as he calls it, in the development of the fetus. Before this threshold, abortions are morally unproblematic; they are the moral equivalent to the decision to employ contraception. But after this threshold, when the fetus is sentient, abortions become morally equivalent to the decision to commit infanticide. Nevertheless, abortions after the threshold can still be justified for therapeutic and eugenic reasons.

Among the assortment of moral problems that have come to be known as biomedical ethics none has received as much attention from philosophers as abortion. Philosophical inquiry into the moral status of abortion is virtually as old as philosophy itself and has a continuous history of more than two millennia in the main religious traditions of the West. The upsurge of interest in the problem among secular philosophers is more recent, coinciding roughly with the public debate of the past fifteen years or so in most of the Western democracies over the shape of an acceptable abortion policy. Despite both the quantity and the quality of this philosophical work, however, abortion remains one of the most intractable moral issues of our time.

Its resistance to a generally agreed settlement stems primarily from its unique combination of two ingredients, each of which is perplexing in its own right. Abortion, in the sense in which it is controversial, is the intentional termination of pregnancy for its own sake—that is, regardless of the consequences for the fetus. Pregnancy, in turn, is a peculiar sort of relationship between a woman and a peculiar sort of being. It is a peculiar sort of relationship because the fetus is temporarily lodged within and physically connected to the body of its mother, on whom it is directly dependent for life support. The closest approximation elsewhere in our experience to this dependency is that of a parasite upon its host. But the host-parasite relationship typically differs in some material respects from pregnancy and is therefore only an imperfect analogue to it.

The fetus is a peculiar sort of being because it is a human individual during the earliest stage in its life history. Although there are some difficult and puzzling questions to be asked about when the life history of such an individual may properly be said to begin, we will assume for convenience that this occurs at conception. It will also be convenient, though somewhat inaccurate, to use the term 'fetus' to refer indiscriminately to all gestational stages from fertilized ovum through blastocyst and embryo to fetus proper. A (human) fetus, then, is a human individual during that period temporally bounded in one direction by conception and in the other (at the latest) by birth. The closest approximations elsewhere in our experience to this sort of being are the gametes (sperm and ovum) that precede it before conception and the infant that succeeds it after birth. But both gametes and infant differ in material respects from a fetus and are also only imperfect analogues to it.

Abortion is morally perplexing because it terminates this peculiar relationship and causes the death of this peculiar being. It thus occupies an ambiguous position between two other practices—contraception and infanticide—of whose moral status we are more certain. Contraception cannot be practiced after conception, while infanticide cannot be practiced before birth. Since an abortion can be performed only between conception and birth, contraception and infanticide are its immediate temporal neighbors. Although both of these practices have occasioned their own controversies, there is a much broader concensus concerning their moral status than there is concerning abortion. Thus, most of us are likely to believe that, barring special circumstances, infanticide is morally serious and requires some special justification while contraception is morally innocuous and requires no such justification. One way of clarifying the moral status of abortion, therefore, is to locate it on this contraception-infanticide continuum, thus telling us whether it is in relevant respects more like the former or the latter.

Of the two ingredients whose combination renders abortion morally perplexing, the peculiar nature of the fetus is the more troublesome. Clarifying the moral status of abortion thus requires above all clarifying the moral status of the fetus. Contraception is less perplexing in virtue of the fact that it operates not on any temporal stage of a human being but only on the materials out of which such a being might be formed. An infanticide is less perplexing in virtue of the fact that it operates on a later temporal stage of a human being, of whose moral status we are more certain. Deciding whether abortion is in relevant respects more like contraception or infanticide therefore requires above all deciding whether a fetus is in relevant respects more like a pair of gametes or an infant. The moral category in which we choose to locate abortion will be largely determined by the moral category in which we choose to locate the fetus. Let us say that a being has *moral standing* if it merits moral consideration in its own right and not just in virtue of its relations with other beings. To have moral standing is to be more than a mere thing or item of property. What, more precisely, moral standing consists of can be given different interpretations; thus, it might be the possession of some set of basic moral rights, or the requirement that one be treated as an end and not merely as a means, or the inclusion of one's interest in a calculus of social welfare. However it is interpreted, whether a being is accorded moral standing must make a great difference in the way in which we take that being into account in our moral thinking. Whether a fetus is accorded moral standing must therefore make a great difference in the way in which we think about abortion. An account of the moral status of abortion must be supported by an account of the moral status of the fetus.

There is also a political question concerning abortion to which we need an answer. Every society must decide how, if at all, it will regulate the practice of abortion. Broadly speaking, three different types of abortion policy are available.[1] A permissive policy allows abortion whenever it has been agreed upon between a woman and a qualified practitioner, while a restrictive policy prohibits it altogether. A moderate policy occupies a middle ground between the other two, imposing either (or both) of two constraints on the practice of abortion: a time limit (which stipulates *when* an abortion may be performed) and recognized grounds (which stipulate *why* an abortion may be performed). A view of abor-

tion should tell us which type of abortion policy a society ought to adopt, and if a moderate policy is favored then it should also tell us where to locate the time limit and/or which grounds to recognize. There will clearly be an intimate relation between the determination of the moral status of abortion and the defense of an abortion policy. If abortion is as morally innocuous as contraception, then that seems a good reason for favoring a permissive policy, while if it is as morally serious as infanticide, then that seems a good reason for favoring a restrictive policy.

A complete view of abortion, one that answers the main moral questions posed by the practice of abortion, is an ordered compound of three elements: an account of the moral status of the fetus, which grounds an account of the moral status of abortion, which in turn grounds a defense of an abortion policy. It is not enough, however, that a view of abortion be complete— it must also be well grounded. If we explore what is required to support an account of the moral status of the fetus, we will discover what it means for a view of abortion to be well grounded. The main requirement at this level is a *criterion of moral standing* that will specify the (natural) characteristic(s) whose possession is both necessary and sufficient for the possession of moral standing. A criterion of moral standing will therefore have the following form: all and only beings with characteristic C have moral standing. (Characteristic C may be a single property or a conjunction or disjunction of such properties.) A criterion of moral standing thus determines, both exhaustively and exclusively, the membership of the class of beings with such standing. Such a criterion will define the proper scope of our moral concern, telling us for all moral contexts which beings must be accorded moral consideration in their own right. Thus it will determine, among other things, the moral status of inanimate natural objects, artifacts, nonhuman animals, body parts, superintelligent computers, androids, and extraterrestrials. It will also determine the moral status of (human) fetuses. An account of the moral status of the fetus is well grounded when it is derivable from an independently plausible criterion of moral standing. The independent plausibility of such a criterion is partly established by following out its implications for moral contexts other than abortion. But a criterion or moral standing can also be given a deeper justification by being grounded in a moral theory. The function of a moral theory is to identify those features of the world to which we should be morally sensitive and to guide that sensitivity. By providing us with a picture of the content and structure of morality, a moral theory will tell us, among other things, which beings merit moral consideration in their own right and what form this consideration should take. It will thereby generate and support a criterion of moral standing, thus serving as the last line of defense for a view of abortion.

THE ESTABLISHED VIEWS

We are seeking a view of abortion that is both complete and well grounded. These requirements are not easily satisfied. They key elements remain an account of the moral status of the fetus and a supporting criterion of moral standing. Our search will be facilitated if we begin by examining the main contenders. The abortion debate in most of the Western democracies has been dominated by two positions that are so well entrenched that they may be called the established views. The liberal view supports what is popularly known as the "pro-choice" position on abortion.[2] At its heart is the contention that the fetus at every stage of pregnancy has no moral standing. From this premise it follows that although abortion kills the fetus it does not wrong it, since a being with no moral standing cannot be wronged. Abortion at all stages of pregnancy lacks a victim; circumstantial differences aside, it is the moral equivalent of contraception. The decision to seek an abortion, therefore, can properly be left to a woman's discretion. There is as little justification for legal regulation of abortion as there is for such regulation of contraception. The only defensible abortion policy is a permissive policy. The conservative view, however, supports what is popularly known as the "pro-life" position on abortion. At its heart is the contention that the fetus at every stage of pregnancy has full moral standing—the same status as an adult human being. From this premise it follows that because abortion kills the fetus it also wrongs it. Abortion at all stages of pregnancy has a victim; circumstantial differences aside, it is the moral equivalent of infanticide (and of other forms of homicide as well). The decision to seek an abortion, therefore, cannot properly be left to a woman's discretion. There is as much justification for legal regulation of abortion as there is for such regulation of infanticide. The only defensible abortion policy is a restrictive policy.

Before exploring these views separately, we should note an important feature that they share. On the substantive issue that is at the heart of the matter, liberals and conservatives occupy positions that are logical contraries, the latter holding that all fetuses have standing and the former that none do. Although contrary positions cannot both be true, they can both be false. From a logical point of view, it is open to someone to hold that some fetuses have standing while others do not. Thus while the established views occupy the opposite extremes along the spectrum of possible positions on this issue, there is a logical space between them. This logical space reflects the fact that each of the established views offers a *uniform* account of the moral status of the fetus—each, that is, holds that all fetuses have the same status, regardless of any respects in which they might differ. The most obvious respect in which fetuses can differ is in their gestational age and thus their level of development. During the normal course of pregnancy, a fetus gradually evolves from a tiny one-celled organism into a medium-sized and highly complex organism consisting of some six million differentiated cells. Both of the established views are committed to holding that all of the beings at all stages of this transition have precisely the same moral status. The gestational age of the fetus at the time of abortion is thus morally irrelevant on both views. So also is the reason for the abortion. This is irrelevant on the liberal view because no reason is necessary to justify abortion at any stage of pregnancy and equally irrelevant on the conservative view because no reason is sufficient to do so. The established views, therefore, despite their differences, agree on two very important matters: the moral irrelevance of both when and why an abortion is performed.

This agreement places the established views at odds with both common practice and common opinion in most of the Western democracies. A moderate abortion policy regulates abortion either by imposing a time limit or by stipulating recognized grounds (or both). The abortion policies of virtually all of the Western democracies (and many other countries as well) now contain one or both of these constraints. But neither of the established views can provide any support for a moderate policy. Further, in countries with moderate policies there generally exists a broad public consensus supporting such policies. Opinion polls typically disclose majority agreement on the relevance both of the timing of an abortion and of the grounds for it. On the question of timing there is widespread agreement that early abortions are less problematic than late ones. Abortion may be induced within the first two weeks following conception by an intrauterine device or a "morning after" pill, both of which will prevent the implantation of a blastocyst. Most people seem to find nothing objectionable in the use of these abortifacients. At the opposite extreme, abortion may be induced during the sixth month of pregnancy (or even later) by saline injection or hysterotomy. Most people seem to have some qualms about the use of these techniques at such an advanced stage of pregnancy. On the question of grounds there is widespread agreement that some grounds are less problematic than others. The grounds commonly cited for abortion may be conveniently divided into four categories: therapeutic (risk to the life or health of the mother), eugenic (risk of fetal deformity), humanitarian (pregnancy resulting from the commission of some crime, such as rape or incest), and socioeconomic (e.g., poverty, desertion, family size). Popular support for abortion on therapeutic grounds tends to be virtually unanimous (especially when the risk is particularly serious), but this unanimity gradually diminishes as we move through the other categories until opinion is about evenly divided concerning socioeconomic grounds. Whatever the detailed breakdown of opinion on these issues, there is a widely shared conviction that it does matter both when and why an abortion is performed. Since these are the very factors whose relevance is denied by both of the established views, there is a serious gap between those views and current public opinion.

The existence of this gap is not in itself a reason for rejecting either of the established views. The majority may simply be mistaken on these issues, and the dominance of moderate policies may reflect nothing more than the fact that they are attractive political compromises when the public debate has been polarized by the established views. Neither political practice nor public opinion can provide a justification for a moderate view of abortion or a moderate abortion policy. But the gap does provide us with a motive for exploring the logical space between the established views a little more carefully.

The Liberal View

Meanwhile, however, it is time for a closer examination of the established views. We have identified the accounts they offer of the moral standing of the fetus. Such an account is well grounded when it is derivable from an independently plausible criterion of moral standing. We will focus attention, therefore, on the criteria that could serve as underpinnings of the established views. The liberal view requires some criterion that will deny moral standing to fetuses at all stages of pregnancy. Obviously no characteristic will serve that is acquired sometime during the normal course of fetal development. One characteristic that would certainly suffice is that of *having been born*. This characteristic cannot (logically) belong to any fetus, and it also serves to distinguish fetuses as a class from all later stages of human beings. Building this characteristic into a criterion of moral standing would thus enable the liberal to distinguish abortion, even late abortion, from infanticide, and thus to condone the former while condemning the latter.

But it is pretty clear that no acceptable criterion of moral standing can be constructed in this fashion; it is simply an ad hoc device designed to yield a liberal view of abortion while avoiding an equally liberal view of infanticide. Nor does it seem to be supportable by some more plausible criterion. Its effect is to mark birth as a crucial moral watershed, separating beings that lack moral standing (gametes, fetuses) from beings that possess it (infants, children, adults). But birth is merely the process whereby the fetus ceases to be housed within and physically connected to the body of its mother. It is difficult to see how we could justify denying moral standing to a being simply because it is housed within or physically connected to the body of another. Neither of these characteristics appears to be relevant to the question of whether we must accord the being some degree of moral consideration in its own right. Furthermore, birth is an abrupt discontinuity in the normal course of human reproduction. It seems unlikely on the face of it that moral standing could be acquired so suddenly (i.e., that killing a full-term fetus moments before birth could be morally inconsequential while killing a neonate moments after birth could constitute homicide). But if this is so, then birth cannot be a crucial moral watershed, and being born cannot be a necessary condition of having moral standing.

This way of supporting a liberal view is arbitrary and shallow. Liberals need a more plausible criterion of moral standing that will nonetheless deny standing to all fetuses. It is apparent that any such criterion will need to set a fairly high standard, one that is beyond the reach of any fetus, however highly developed. Liberals who have sought such a standard have tended to favor such capacities as self-consciousness and rationality.[3] Each of these capacities is complex and each is also open to differing interpretations. In order to avoid needless controversy, we will assume that the core of self-consciousness is the capacity to recognize oneself as the "I" who is the unifying subject of all of one's states of consciousness. Such a capacity appears to require, at least in rudimentary form, the ability to distinguish oneself from the contents of one's states of consciousness, and the ability to conceive of oneself as enduring through time. We will further assume that the core of rationality is the capacity to represent to oneself objects or states of affairs that are spatially or temporally distant. Such a capacity appears to require, at least in rudimentary form, the ability to remember the past and

to anticipate the future, the ability to manipulate symbols, and the ability to take **propositional attitudes** toward the world. On these accounts, self-consciousness and rationality are intimately connected and partially overlapping. If some other accounts are preferred, they may be substituted for these without affecting the course of the argument.

The best defense of a liberal view of abortion grounds it in either a self-consciousness or a rationality criterion of moral standing. Such a criterion is not arbitrary or ad hoc, since it could be appealed to in any moral context in order to distinguish between beings that have moral standing and beings that do not. And it will readily yield the result the liberal is seeking for abortion, since even the most highly developed fetus is neither self-conscious nor rational. But such a high standard generates its own difficulties. Some of these will arise in contexts other than abortion. Thus, for instance, some mentally handicapped adults may have difficulty meeting this standard and may therefore be denied moral standing by it. But the problem that is more pertinent to our inquiry concerns newborn infants. If a full-term fetus is neither self-conscious nor rational, so also a newborn infant is neither self-conscious nor rational. But then the liberal view of abortion has become also a liberal view of infanticide.

It certainly appears that liberals will have the greatest difficulty in defending a moral boundary between abortion and infanticide. In all morally relevant respects, a full-term fetus and a newborn infant appear to be identical. A liberal will therefore find it difficult or impossible to support the common conviction of the moral seriousness of infanticide. This may not in itself constitute a decisive reason for rejecting the liberal view. Even if both fetuses and neonates lack moral standing, infanticide may be more difficult to justify than abortion. At least some of the reasons for seeking an abortion cannot apply to infanticide: an infant cannot pose a physical threat to the life or health of its mother and if rearing it would be burdensome, there is the alternative of adoption. Furthermore, when the same reason can apply in both contexts—as in the case of a severe abnormality—it is not obvious that infanticide is morally indefensible.

Finally, it is also open to the liberal simply to bite the bullet and challenge the common conviction of the moral seriousness of infanticide as a taboo for which there is no rational justification. Abandoning the taboo would in that case be a small price to pay for an otherwise plausible view of abortion.

However, the liberal's difficulties concerning infanticide are not so easily dealt with. Both self-consciousness and rationality are sophisticated bundles of abilities; they may, for instance, be beyond the reach of all nonhuman animals. They are therefore likely to be lacked not only by newborn infants but also by all infants, and perhaps as well by young children. We would need a much fuller account of these capacities in order to be able to locate the stage in the normal course of human development when they are acquired. But it seems very likely that such a high standard will deny moral standing to all infants and at least some children. This result is more troubling than the denial of moral standing to neonates. It means that killing an infant or a young child cannot be a wrong *to that infant or child*. It may, of course, be a wrong to others who are thereby deprived of an object of affection, but the deprivation—and therefore the wrong—would be the same in principle as if some valued item of property were destroyed. We ordinarily assume that what is wrong with homicide is not primarily the injury that it incidentally does to third parties but the injury that it necessarily does to the victim. There seems no good reason for altering this assessment if the victim is an infant or a young child. If a view of abortion yields the result that the killing of such a victim is really a property offense, then we are entitled to conclude that it has somehow gone seriously wrong.

The Conservative View

When we turn to the conservative view, most of the difficulties that we encounter are counterparts of those that confront the liberal. This discovery should not surprise us, since these difficulties are caused by the adoption of a uniform account of the moral status of the fetus, a feature that is common to both established views. The conservative requires a criterion of moral standing that will confer such standing upon fetuses at all stages of pregnancy. Obviously no characteristic will serve that is acquired sometime during the normal course of fetal development. One characteristic that would certainly suffice is that of *having been conceived*. This characteristic must logically belong to all fetuses, and it also serves to distinguish all temporal stages of human beings from the genetic materials out of which they are formed. Building this characteristic into a criterion of moral standing would thus enable the conservative to distinguish abortion, even early abortion, from contraception, and thus to condemn the former while condoning the latter.

But it is fairly clear that no acceptable criterion of moral standing can be constructed in this fashion; it is simply an **ad hoc device** designed to yield a conservative view of abortion while avoiding an equally conservative view of contraception. Nor does it seem to be supportable by some more plausible criterion. Its effect is to mark conception as a crucial moral watershed, separating beings that lack moral standing (gametes) from beings that possess it (fetuses, infants, children, adults). But conception is merely the process whereby two haploid cells unite to form a diploid cell. It is difficult to see how we could justify conferring moral standing on a being simply because it possesses a complete set of paired chromosomes. This characteristic does not appear to be relevant to the question of whether we must accord the being some degree of moral consideration in its own right. Furthermore, conception is an abrupt discontinuity in the normal course of human reproduction. It seems unlikely on the face of it that moral standing could be acquired so suddenly (i.e., that killing a pair of gametes moments before conception could be morally inconsequential while killing a fertilized ovum moments after conception could constitute homicide). But if this is so, then conception cannot be a crucial moral watershed, and being conceived cannot be a necessary condition of having moral standing.

This way of supporting a conservative view is also arbitrary and shallow. However, conservatives might have something slightly different in mind. Let us continue to assume that conception marks the beginning of the life history of a human individual. Then conservatives can confer moral standing on all human fetuses (and all infants, children, and adults as well) while denying it to all gametes simply by adopting *being a human individual or belonging to the human species* as their criterion of moral standing.[4] Doing so will, by implication, mark conception as a crucial moral watershed. Furthermore, a humanity condition is implicit in both the liberal's birth criterion and the conservative's conception criterion, since liberals mean to confer moral standing upon all (and only) human beings who have been born and conservatives mean to confer such standing upon all (and only) human beings who have been conceived. A birth or a conception criterion that lacked this condition would distribute moral standing in a rather profligate manner. Nevertheless, a humanity criterion of moral standing is also arbitrary and shallow. Whatever our views on the complex issue of the moral status of nonhuman animals, it cannot be true that they lack moral standing simply because they are not human. Membership in some favored species has no more moral relevance than membership in some favored race or nation. If it is true that all and only human beings have moral standing, this must be because of some further, and morally relevant, property that is both common and peculiar to them.

Thus, conservatives need a more plausible criterion of moral standing that will nonetheless confer such standing upon all fetuses. But here we encounter a curiosity, for conservatives have tended to favor a high standard—such as self-consciousness or rationality—since they are not eager to accord moral standing to nonhuman animals.[5] As we have seen, however, a high standard appears to yield the liberal view of abortion, and of infanticide as well. Since both these results are abhorrent to conservatives, there is considerable tension between their favored criterion of moral standing on the one hand and their view of abortion on the other.

At least two strategies are available for resolving this tension. The first of them rests on the notion of a paradigm member of a species (or **natural kind**).[6] The basic idea is that if the paradigm member of a particular species displays the characteristic—self-consciousness or rationality—that entails possession of moral standing, then all members of that species have such standing whether or not they display that characteristic. Assuming that the paradigm member of our species is an adult of normal faculties, and assuming further that such an adult is both self-conscious and rational, then these facts are sufficient to accord all human beings moral standing—including fetuses, infants, children, the severely handicapped, and so on. This strategy solves the conservative's problem at one blow, but at the cost of apparent inconsistency. The conservative's reason for favoring a high standard is to deny moral standing to those beings (such as nonhuman animals) who fall below that standard. Yet the paradigm-member strategy ends by according moral standing to large numbers of beings, including fetuses, who fall below that standard. Therefore, the strategy seems rather arbitrary. It is, to be sure, less arbitrary than the humanity criterion that it resembles since it will confer moral standing upon all members of any species whose paradigm member is self-conscious or rational. If there are any such species, then some nonhuman beings will have moral standing; if not, then the two criteria will define precisely the same class of beings with moral standing. The difference between them is that the paradigm-member strategy employs as its characteristic the more general *belonging to some species whose paradigm member is rational* in place of the more particular *belonging to the human species*. But it still treats a being's species membership as sufficient for its possession of moral standing.

The second strategy available to the conservative rests on the notion of potentiality.[7] The basic idea is that any being has moral standing who is *either actually or potentially* self-conscious or rational. The added potentiality condition is intended to confer moral standing on fetuses, infants, and children and marks a distinctive break with a liberal criterion of moral standing. The second strategy defines the same class of beings with moral standing as the first—except for one range of cases. Let us assume that a being has the potential for self-consciousness or rationality if that being will in the normal course of its development either come to display these capacities itself or be transformed into a being that displays these capacities. The potentiality strategy will then confer moral standing upon normal but immature members of the species, but not upon sufficiently abnormal ones. It will therefore, like the liberal's criterion, deny moral standing to some handicapped fetuses, infants, children, and adults. This result is an embarrassment for conservatives, who would clearly prefer to distribute moral standing to all members of the species. But the embarrassment appears to be unavoidable if conservatives wish to employ a standard high enough to deny standing to members of other species.

Like the paradigm-member strategy, the potentiality strategy has an air of arbitrariness about it. Recall again that the point of a high standard is to deny moral standing to those beings that fail to meet the standard. A being that is actually self-conscious or rational clearly meets the standard, but a being that is only potentially self-conscious or rational does not yet meet the standard. Conservatives wish to accord these latter beings moral standing in advance of meeting the standard on the ground that they will come to meet it later in the course of their normal development. But there is an obvious, and seemingly more consistent, alternative available: we may say that beings with potential self-consciousness or rationality have potential moral standing. They will come to have moral standing if and when they pass the threshold of self-consciousness or rationality, but they do not have it in advance of passing that threshold. This line of thought, which seems the more straightforward, leads however directly back to the liberal criterion of moral standing and the liberal view of abortion.

If the potentiality strategy is not arbitrary, it is easy to see how it will generate a conservative view of both abortion and infanticide. The conservative therefore has no problem supporting the common conviction of the moral seriousness of infanticide. But a problem does arise at the other temporal boundary of pregnancy. Conception, as we have seen, is the union of two haploid cells to form a diploid cell. If a newly fertilized ovum contains the potential for a self-conscious or rational being, then it appears that the pair of gametes that united to form it must also have contained that potential (otherwise where did it come from?). If every fertilized ovum has moral standing, then it must also be true that every unfertilized ovum and every spermatozoon—or perhaps every pair consisting of one ovum and one sperm—also has moral standing. Artificial means of contraception prevent gametes from realizing their potential, just as abortion prevents a fetus from realizing its potential. But then the conservative view of abortion has become also a conservative view of contraception.

It certainly does appear that conservatives will have the greatest difficulty in defending a moral boundary between abortion and contraception. In all morally relevant respects, a newly fertilized ovum and a pair of gametes appear to be identical. A conservative will therefore find it difficult or impossible to support the common conviction of the moral innocuousness of contraception. This may not in itself constitute a decisive reason for rejecting the conservative view. Conservatives too may choose to bite the bullet—some clearly choose to do so and reject contraception as well. But this time there can be no doubt of the practical costs of the awkward result. Such conservatives appear to be committed to the view that the use of artificial means of contraception is the moral equivalent of homicide. To be consistent, therefore, they must advocate a restrictive contraception policy as well as a restrictive abortion policy. But the consequences of such a policy for women's sexuality, as well as for the problem of overpopulation, are unthinkable.

A Moderate View

We can now catalogue the defects of the established views. The common source of these defects lies in their uniform accounts of the moral status of the fetus. These accounts yield three different sorts of awkward implications. First, they require that all abortions be accorded the same moral status regardless of the stage of pregnancy at which they are performed. Thus, liberals must hold that late abortions are as morally innocuous as early ones, and conservatives must hold that early abortions are as morally serious as late ones. Neither view is able to support the common conviction that late abortions are more serious than early ones. Second, these accounts require that all abortions be accorded the same moral status regardless of the reason for which they are performed. Thus, liberals must hold that all abortions are equally innocuous whatever their grounds, and conservatives must hold that all abortions are equally serious whatever their grounds. Neither view is able to support the common conviction that some grounds justify abortion more readily than others. Third, these accounts require that contraception, abortion, and infanticide all be accorded the same moral status. Thus, liberals must hold that all three practices are equally innocuous, while conservatives must hold that they are all equally serious. Neither view is able to support the common conviction that infanticide is more serious than abortion, which is in turn more serious than contraception. . . .

Our critique of the established views has equipped us with specifications for the design of a moderate alternative to them. The fundamental flaw of the established views was their adoption of a uniform account of the moral status of the fetus. A moderate view of abortion must therefore be built on a *differential* account of the moral status of the fetus, awarding moral standing to some fetuses and withholding it from others. The further defects of the established views impose three constraints on the shape of such a differential account. It must explain the moral relevance of the gestational age of the fetus at the time of abortion and thus must correlate moral status with level of fetal development. It must also explain the moral relevance, at least at some stages of pregnancy, of the reason for which an abortion is performed. And finally it must preserve the distinction between the moral innocuousness of contraception and the moral seriousness of infanticide. When we combine these specifications, we obtain the rough outline of a moderate view. Such a view will identify the stage of pregnancy during which the fetus gains moral standing. Before that threshold, abortion will be as morally innocuous as contraception and no grounds will be needed to justify it. After the threshold, abortion will be as morally serious as infanticide and

some special grounds will be needed to justify it (if it can be justified at this stage at all).

A moderate view is well grounded when it is derivable from an independently plausible criterion of moral standing. It is not difficult to construct a criterion that will yield a threshold somewhere during pregnancy.[8] Let us say that a being is sentient when it has the capacity to experience pleasure and pain and thus the capacity for enjoyment and suffering. Beings that are self-conscious or rational are generally (though perhaps not necessarily) also sentient, but many sentient beings lack both self-consciousness and rationality. A sentience criterion of moral standing thus sets a lower standard than that shared by the established views. Such a criterion will accord moral standing to the mentally handicapped regardless of impairments of their cognitive capacities. It will also accord moral standing to many, perhaps most, nonhuman animals.

The plausibility of a sentience criterion would be partially established by tracing out its implications for moral contexts other than abortion. But it would be considerably enhanced if such a criterion could also be given a deeper grounding. Such a grounding can be supplied by what seems a reasonable conception of the nature of morality. The moral point of view is just one among many evaluative points of view. It appears to be distinguished from the others in two respects: its special concern for the interest, welfare, or well-being of creatures and its requirement of impartiality. Adopting the moral point of view requires in one way or another according equal consideration to the interests of all beings. If this is so, then a being's having an interest to be considered is both necessary and sufficient for its having moral standing. While the notion of interest or welfare is far from transparent, its irreducible core appears to be the capacity for enjoyment and suffering: all and only beings with this capacity have an interest or welfare that the moral point of view requires us to respect. But then it follows easily that sentience is both necessary and sufficient for moral standing. . . .

When we apply a sentience criterion to the course of human development, it yields the result that the threshold of moral standing is the stage during which the capacity to experience pleasure and pain is first acquired. This capacity is clearly possessed by a newborn infant (and a full-term fetus) and is clearly not possessed by a pair of gametes (or a newly fertilized ovum). It is therefore acquired during the normal course of gestation. But when? A definite answer awaits a better understanding than we now possess of the development of the fetal nervous system and thus of fetal consciousness. We can, however, venture a provisional answer. It is standard practice to divide the normal course of gestation into three trimesters of thirteen weeks each. It is likely that a fetus is unable to feel pleasure or pain at the beginning of the second trimester and likely that it is able to do so at the end of that trimester. If this is so, then the threshold of sentience, and thus also the threshold of moral standing, occurs sometime during the second trimester.

We can now fill in our earlier sketch of a moderate view of abortion. A fetus acquires moral standing when it acquires sentience, that is to say at some stage in the second trimester of pregnancy. Before that threshold, when the fetus lacks moral standing, the decision to seek an abortion is morally equivalent to the decision to employ contraception; the effect in both cases is to prevent the existence of a being with moral standing. Such decisions are morally innocuous and should be left to the discretion of the parties involved. Thus, the liberal view of abortion, and a permissive abortion policy, are appropriate for early (prethreshold) abortions. After the threshold, when the fetus has moral standing, the decision to seek an abortion is morally equivalent to the decision to commit infanticide; the effect in both cases is to terminate the existence of a being with moral standing. Such decisions are morally serious and should not be left to the discretion of the parties involved (the fetus is now one of the parties involved).

It should follow that the conservative view of abortion and a restrictive abortion policy are appropriate for late (post-threshold) abortions. But this does not follow. Conservatives hold that abortion, because it is homicide, is unjustified on any grounds. This absolute position is indefensible even for post-threshold fetuses

with moral standing. Of the four categories of grounds for abortion, neither humanitarian nor socioeconomic grounds will apply to post-threshold abortions, since a permissive policy for the period before the threshold will afford women the opportunity to decide freely whether they wish to continue their pregnancies. Therapeutic grounds will however apply, since serious risks to maternal life or health may materialize after the threshold. If they do, there is no justification for refusing an abortion. A pregnant woman is providing life support for another being that is housed within her body. If continuing to provide that life support will place her own life or health at serious risk, then she cannot justifiably be compelled to do so, even though the fetus has moral standing and will die if deprived of that life support. Seeking an abortion in such circumstances is a legitimate act of self-preservation.[9]

A moderate abortion policy must therefore include a therapeutic ground for post-threshold abortions. It must also include a eugenic ground. Given current technology, some tests for fetal abnormalities can be carried out only in the second trimester. In many cases, therefore, serious abnormalities will be detected only after the fetus has passed the threshold. Circumstantial differences aside, the status of a severely deformed post-threshold fetus is the same as the status of a severely deformed newborn infant. The moral issues concerning the treatment of such newborns are themselves complex, but there appears to be a good case for selective infanticide in some cases. If so, then there is an even better case for late abortion on eugenic grounds, since here we must also reckon in the terrible burden of carrying to term a child that a woman knows to be deformed.

A moderate abortion policy will therefore contain the following ingredients: a time limit that separates early from late abortions, a permissive policy for early abortions, and a policy for late abortions that incorporates both therapeutic and eugenic grounds. This blueprint leaves many smaller questions of design to be settled. The grounds for late abortions must be specified more carefully by determining what is to count as a serious risk to maternal life or health and what is to count as a serious fetal abnormality. While no general formulation of a policy can settle these matters in detail, guidelines can and should be applied. A policy should also specify the procedure that is to be followed in deciding when a particular case has met these guidelines.

But most of all, a moderate policy must impose a defensible time limit. As we saw earlier, from the moral point of view there can be no question of a sharp breakpoint. Fetal development unfolds gradually and cumulatively, and sentience like all other capacities is acquired slowly and by degrees. Thus we have clear cases of presentient fetuses in the first trimester and clear cases of sentient fetuses in the third trimester. But we also have unclear cases, encompassing many (perhaps most) second-trimester fetuses. From the moral point of view, we can say only that in these cases the moral status of the fetus, and thus the moral status of abortion, is indeterminate. This sort of moral indeterminacy occurs also at later stages of human development, for instance when we are attempting to fix the age of consent or of competence to drink or drive. We do not pretend in these latter cases that the capacity in question is acquired overnight on one's sixteenth or eighteenth birthday, and yet for legal purposes we must draw a sharp and determinate line. Any such line will be somewhat arbitrary, but it is enough if it is drawn within the appropriate threshold stage. So also in the case of a time limit for abortion, it is sufficient if the line for legal purposes is located within the appropriate threshold stage. A time limit anywhere in the second trimester is therefore defensible, at least until we acquire the kind of information about fetal development that will enable us to narrow the threshold stage and thus to locate the time limit with more accuracy. . . .

Endnotes

1. These categories are adapted from Daniel Callahan, *Abortion: Law, Choice and Morality* (New York: Macmillan, 1970).
2. The terms 'liberal' and 'conservative,' as used in the chapter generally, refer respectively to those who think abortion permissible and those who believe it impermissible. Thus, 'liberal' here is not synonymous with 'political liberal' and 'conservative' is not synonymous with 'political conservative.'

3. A self-consciousness criterion is defended in Michael Tooley, *Abortion and Infanticide* (Oxford: Oxford University Press, 1983). A more complex criterion including both self-consciousness and rationality is defended in Mary Anne Warren, "On the Moral and Legal Status of Abortion," in *Contemporary Issues in Bioethics*, ed. Tom L. Beauchamp and LeRoy Walters. Second ed. (Belmont, Calif.: Wadsworth, 1982).
4. A humanity criterion is defended in John T. Noonan, Jr., "An Almost Absolute Value in History," in *The Morality of Abortion: Legal and Historical Perspectives*, ed. Noonan (Cambridge, Mass.: Harvard University Press, 1970).
5. A rationality criterion is defended in Alan Donegan, *The Theory of Morality* (Chicago: University of Chicago Press, 1977), 82–83, 170–71.
6. Different versions of this strategy may be found in Donegan, *The Theory of Morality*, and Philip E. Devine, *The Ethics of Homicide* (Ithaca, N.Y.: Cornell University Press, 1978), 51–55.
7. This strategy is employed in Devine, *The Ethics of Homicide*, 94–100.
8. The sentience criterion is defended in my *Abortion and Moral Theory* (Princeton, N.J.: Princeton University Press, 1981), 128–46.
9. This position is defended in Judith Jarvis Thomson, "A Defense of Abortion," in *The Rights and Wrongs of Abortion*, ed. Marshall Cohen et al. (Princeton, N.J.: Princeton University Press, 1974); for contrary views, see John Finnis, "The Rights and Wrongs of Abortion," in *The Rights and Wrongs of Abortion*, and Baruch Brody, *Abortion and the Sanctity of Human Life: A Philosophical View* (Cambridge, Mass.: MIT Press, 1975), Chapters 1 and 2.

REVIEW QUESTIONS

1. What is the liberal view according to Sumner? Why doesn't he accept it?
2. What is the conservative view, and what is wrong with it?
3. Explain Sumner's moderate view. Why is it supposed to be better than the other views?

DISCUSSION QUESTIONS

1. Has Sumner refuted the views of both liberals and conservatives? How might they reply?
2. Is a sentient fetus a person with a full moral status? If so, are sentient animals persons with a full moral status too?
3. Does a nonsentient fetus really have no moral status so that killing it is the moral equivalent of contraception?

Susan Sherwin

Abortion Through a Feminist Ethics Lens

Susan Sherwin is professor of philosophy and women's studies at Dalhousie University in Canada. She is the author of No Longer Patient: Feminist Ethics and Health Care *(1992) and a coeditor of* Moral Problems in Medicine, *second edition (1983).*

Sherwin gives a feminist analysis of abortion. On this feminist view, the pregnant woman is a subject of principal concern, and she is in the best position to make an appropriate decision about abortion. This freedom to choose is essential for sexual and reproductive freedom; without it, women will continue to be oppressed by men. As for the fetus, it is not a distinct individual, nor is it something without value. Rather it has a status dependent on its relationship with the woman who sustains it; and this status is secondary to that of the woman, who should be treated as a responsible moral agent.

Abortion has long been a central issue in the arena of applied ethics, but the distinctive analysis of feminist ethics is generally overlooked in most philosophic discussions. Authors and readers commonly presume a familiarity with the feminist position and equate it with liberal defences of women's right to choose abortion, but, in fact, feminist ethics yields a different analysis of the moral questions surrounding abortion than that usually offered by the more familiar liberal defenders of abortion rights. Most feminists can agree with some of the conclusions that arise from certain non-feminist arguments on abortion, but they often disagree about the way the issues are formulated and the sorts of reasons that are invoked in the mainstream literature.

From Susan Sherwin, "Abortion Through a Feminist Ethics Lens," *Dialogue* 30 (1991): 327–42. Reprinted with permission.

Among the many differences found between feminist and non-feminist arguments about abortion, is the fact that most non-feminist discussions of abortion consider the questions of the moral or legal permissibility of abortion in isolation from other questions, ignoring (and thereby obscuring) relevant connections to other social practices that oppress women. They are generally grounded in masculinist conceptions of freedom (e.g., privacy, individual choice, individuals' property rights in their own bodies) that do not meet the needs, interests, and intuitions of many of the women concerned. In contrast, feminists seek to couch their arguments in moral concepts that support their general campaign of overcoming injustice in all its dimensions, including those inherent in moral theory itself.[1] There is even disagreement about how best to understand the moral question at issue: non-feminist arguments focus exclusively on the morality and/or legality of performing abortions, whereas feminists insist that other questions, including ones about accessibility and delivery of abortion services, must also be addressed.

Although feminists welcome the support of non-feminists in pursuing policies that will grant women control over abortion decisions, they generally envision very different sorts of policies for this purpose than those considered by non-feminist sympathizers. . . . Here, I propose one conception of the shape such an analysis should take.

The most obvious difference between feminist and non-feminist approaches to abortion can be seen in the relative attention each gives to the interests and experiences of women in its analysis. Feminists consider it self-evident that the pregnant woman is a subject of principal concern in abortion decisions. In most non-feminist accounts, however, not only is she not perceived as central, she is rendered virtually invisible. Non-feminist theorists, whether they support or oppose women's right to choose abortion, focus almost all their attention on the moral status of the developing embryo or the fetus.

In pursuing a distinctively feminist ethics, it is appropriate to begin with a look at the role of abortion in women's lives. Clearly, the need for abortion can be very intense; women have pursued abortions under appalling and dangerous conditions, across widely diverse cultures and historical periods. No one denies that if abortion is not made legal, safe, and accessible, women will seek out illegal and life-threatening abortions to terminate pregnancies they cannot accept. Anti-abortion activists seem willing to accept this price, but feminists judge the inevitable loss of women's lives associated with restrictive abortion policies to be a matter of fundamental concern.

Although anti-abortion campaigners imagine that women often make frivolous and irresponsible decisions about abortion, feminists recognize that women have abortions for a wide variety of reasons. . . .

Whatever the reason, most feminists believe that a pregnant woman is in the best position to judge whether abortion is the appropriate response to her circumstances. Since she is usually the only one able to weigh all the relevant factors, most feminists reject attempts to offer any general abstract rules for determining when abortion is morally justified. Women's personal deliberations about abortion include contextually defined considerations reflecting her commitment to the needs and interests of everyone concerned—including herself, the fetus she carries, other members of her household, etc. Because there is no single formula available for balancing these complex factors through all possible cases, it is vital that feminists insist on protecting each woman's right to come to her own conclusions. Abortion decisions are, by their very nature, dependent on specific features of each woman's experience; theoretically dispassionate philosophers and other moralists should not expect to set the agenda for these considerations in any universal way. Women must be acknowledged as full moral agents with the responsibility for making moral decisions about their own pregnancies.[2] Although I think that it is possible for a woman to make a mistake in her moral judgment on this matter (i.e., it is possible that a woman may come to believe that she was wrong about her decision to continue or terminate a pregnancy), the intimate nature of this sort of decision makes it unlikely that

anyone else is in a position to arrive at a more reliable conclusion; it is, therefore, improper to grant others the authority to interfere in women's decisions to seek abortions.

Feminist analysis regards the effects of unwanted pregnancies on the lives of women individually and collectively as a central element in the moral evaluation of abortion. Even without patriarchy, bearing a child would be a very important event in a woman's life. It involves significant physical, emotional, social, and (usually) economic changes for her. The ability to exert control over the incidence, timing, and frequency of childbearing is often tied to her ability to control most other things she values. Since we live in a patriarchal society, it is especially important to ensure that women have the authority to control their own reproduction.[3] Despite the diversity of opinion among feminists on most other matters, virtually all feminists seem to agree that women must gain full control over their own reproductive lives if they are to free themselves from male dominance.[4] Many perceive the commitment of the political right wing to opposing abortion as part of a general strategy to reassert patriarchal control over women in the face of significant feminist influence (Petchesky 1980, p. 112).

Women's freedom to choose abortion is also linked with their ability to control their own sexuality. Women's subordinate status often prevents them from refusing men sexual access to their bodies. If women cannot end the unwanted pregnancies that result from male sexual dominance, their sexual vulnerability to particular men can increase, because caring for an(other) infant involves greater financial needs and reduced economic opportunities for women.[5] As a result, pregnancy often forces women to become dependent on men. Since a woman's dependence on a man is assumed to entail that she will remain sexually loyal to him, restriction of abortion serves to channel women's sexuality and further perpetuates the cycle of oppression.

In contrast to most non-feminist accounts, feminist analyses of abortion direct attention to the question of how women get pregnant. Those who reject abortion seem to believe that women can avoid unwanted pregnancies by avoiding sexual intercourse. Such views show little appreciation for the power of sexual politics in a culture that oppresses women. Existing patterns of sexual dominance mean that women often have little control over their sexual lives. They may be subject to rape by strangers, or by their husbands, boyfriends, colleagues, employers, customers, fathers, brothers, uncles, and dates. Often, the sexual coercion is not even recognized as such by the participants, but is the price of continued "good will"—popularity, economic survival, peace, or simple acceptance. Few women have not found themselves in circumstances where they do not feel free to refuse a man's demands for intercourse, either because he is holding a gun to her head or because he threatens to be emotionally hurt if she refuses (or both). Women are socialized to be compliant and accommodating, sensitive to the feelings of others, and frightened of physical power; men are socialized to take advantage of every opportunity to engage in sexual intercourse and to use sex to express dominance and power. Under such circumstances, it is difficult to argue that women could simply "choose" to avoid heterosexual activity if they wish to avoid pregnancy. Catherine MacKinnon neatly sums it up: "the logic by which women are supposed to consent to sex [is]: preclude the alternatives, then call the remaining option 'her choice'" (MacKinnon 1989, p. 192). . . .

From a feminist perspective, a central moral feature of pregnancy is that it takes place in *women's bodies* and has profound effects on *women's* lives. Gender-neutral accounts of pregnancy are not available; pregnancy is explicitly a condition associated with the female body.[6] Because the need for abortion is experienced only by women, policies about abortion affect women uniquely. Thus, it is important to consider how proposed policies on abortion fit into general patterns of oppression for women. Unlike non-feminist accounts, feminist ethics demands that the effects on the oppression of women be a principal consideration when evaluating abortion policies.

THE FETUS

In contrast, most non-feminist analysts believe that the moral acceptability of abortion turns on the question of the moral status of the fetus. Even those who support women's right to choose abortion tend to accept the central premise of the anti-abortion proponents that abortion can only be tolerated if it can be proved that the fetus is lacking some criterion of full personhood.[7] Opponents of abortion have structured the debate so that it is necessary to define the status of the fetus as either valued the same as other humans (and hence entitled not to be killed) or as lacking in all value. Rather than challenging the logic of this formulation, many defenders of abortion have concentrated on showing that the fetus is indeed without significant value (Tooley 1972, Warren 1973); others, such as Wayne Sumner (1981), offer a more subtle account that reflects the gradual development of fetuses whereby there is some specific criterion that determines the degree of protection to be afforded them which is lacking in the early stages of pregnancy but present in the later stages. Thus, the debate often rages between abortion opponents who describe the fetus as an "innocent," vulnerable, morally important, separate being whose life is threatened and who must be protected at all costs, and abortion supporters who try to establish some sort of deficiency inherent to fetuses which removes them from the scope of the moral community.

The woman on whom the fetus depends for survival is considered as secondary (if she is considered at all) in these debates. The actual experiences and responsibilities of real women are not perceived as morally relevant (unless they, too, can be proved innocent by establishing that their pregnancies are a result of rape or incest). It is a common assumption of both defenders and opponents of women's right to choose abortion that many women will be irresponsible in their choices. The important question, though, is whether fetuses have the sort of status that justifies interfering in women's choices at all. In some contexts, women's role in gestation is literally reduced to that of "fetal containers"; the individual women disappear or are perceived simply as mechanical life-support systems.[8] . . .

Within anti-abortion arguments, fetuses are identified as individuals; in our culture which views the (abstract) individual as sacred, fetuses *qua* individuals should be honoured and preserved. Extraordinary claims are made to try to establish the individuality and moral agency of fetuses. At the same time, the women who carry these fetal individuals are viewed as passive hosts whose only significant role is to refrain from aborting or harming their fetuses. Since it is widely believed that the woman does not actually have to *do* anything to protect the life of the fetus, pregnancy is often considered (abstractly) to be a tolerable burden to protect the life of an individual so like us.[9]

Medicine has played its part in supporting these sorts of attitudes. Fetal medicine is a rapidly expanding specialty, and it is commonplace in professional medical journals to find references to pregnant women as "fetal environments." Fetal surgeons now have at their disposal a repertory of sophisticated technology that can save the lives of dangerously ill fetuses; in light of such heroic successes, it is perhaps understandable that women have disappeared from their view. These specialists see fetuses as their patients, not the women who nurture them. Doctors perceive themselves as the *active* agents in saving fetal lives and, hence, believe that they are the ones in direct relationship with the fetuses they treat.

Perhaps even more distressing than the tendency to ignore the woman's agency altogether and view her as a purely passive participant in the medically controlled events of pregnancy and childbirth is the growing practice of viewing women as genuine threats to the well-being of the fetus. Increasingly, women are viewed as irresponsible or hostile towards their fetuses, and the relationship between them is characterized as adversarial (Overall 1987, p. 60). Concern for the well-being of the fetus is taken as license for doctors to intervene to ensure that women comply with medical "advice." Courts are called upon to enforce the doctors' orders when moral pressure alone proves inadequate, and women are being coerced into undergoing unwanted Caesarean deliveries and technologically monitored hospital births. Some states have begun to imprison women for endangering their fetuses through drug abuse and other socially unacceptable behaviours. An Austra-

lian state recently introduced a bill that makes women liable to criminal prosecution "if they are found to have smoked during pregnancy, eaten unhealthful foods, or taken any other action which can be shown to have adversely affected the development of the fetus" (Warren 1989, p. 60).

In other words, physicians have joined with anti-abortionist activists in fostering a cultural acceptance of the view that fetuses are distinct individuals, who are physically, ontologically, and socially separate from the women whose bodies they inhabit, and who have their own distinct interests. In this picture, pregnant women are either ignored altogether or are viewed as deficient in some crucial respect and hence subject to coercion for the sake of their fetuses. In the former case, the interests of the women concerned are assumed to be identical with those of the fetus; in the latter, the women's interests are irrelevant because they are perceived as immoral, unimportant, or unnatural. Focus on the fetus as an independent entity has led to presumptions which deny pregnant women their roles as active, independent, moral agents with a primary interest in what becomes of the fetuses they carry. Emphasis on the fetus's status has led to an assumed license to interfere with women's reproductive freedom.

A Feminist View of the Fetus

Because the public debate has been set up as a competition between the rights of women and those of fetuses, feminists have often felt pushed to reject claims of fetal value in order to protect women's claims. Yet, as Addelson (1987) has argued, viewing abortion in this way "tears [it] out of the context of women's lives" (p. 107). There are other accounts of fetal value that are more plausible and less oppressive to women.

On a feminist account, fetal development is examined in the context in which it occurs, within women's bodies rather than in the imagined isolation implicit in many theoretical accounts. Fetuses develop in specific pregnancies which occur in the lives of particular women. They are not individuals housed in generic female wombs, nor are they full persons at risk only because they are small and subject to the whims of women. Their very existence is relational, developing as they do within particular women's bodies, and their principal relationship is to the women who carry them.

On this view, fetuses are morally significant, but their status is relational rather than absolute. Unlike other human beings, fetuses do not have any independent existence; their existence is uniquely tied to the support of a specific other. Most non-feminist commentators have ignored the relational dimension of fetal development and have presumed that the moral status of fetuses could be resolved solely in terms of abstract metaphysical criteria of personhood. They imagine that there is some set of properties (such as genetic heritage, moral agency, self-consciousness, language use, or self-determination) which will entitle all who possess them to be granted the moral status of persons (Warren 1973, Tooley 1972). They seek some particular feature by which we can neatly divide the world into the dichotomy of moral persons (who are to be valued and protected) and others (who are not entitled to the same group privileges); it follows that it is a merely empirical question whether or not fetuses possess the relevant properties.

But this vision misinterprets what is involved in personhood and what it is that is especially valued about persons. Personhood is a social category, not an isolated state. Persons are members of a community; they develop as concrete, discrete, and specific individuals. To be a morally significant category, personhood must involve personality as well as biological integrity.[10] It is not sufficient to consider persons simply as Kantian atoms of rationality; persons are all embodied, conscious beings with particular social histories. Annette Baier (1985) has developed a concept of persons as "second persons" which helps explain the sort of social dimension that seems fundamental to any moral notion of personhood:

A person, perhaps, is best seen as one who was long enough dependent upon other persons to acquire the essential arts of personhood. Persons essentially are *second* persons, who grow up with other persons. . . . The fact that a person has a life *history*, and that a people collectively have a history depends upon the humbler fact that each person has a childhood in which a cultural heritage is transmitted, ready for adolescent rejection and adult discriminating selection and contribution. Persons come after and before other persons. (P. 84–85; her emphasis.)

Persons, in other words, are members of a social community which shapes and values them, and personhood is a relational concept that must be defined in terms of interactions and relationships with others.

A fetus is a unique sort of being in that it cannot form relationships freely with others, nor can others readily form relationships with it. A fetus has a primary and particularly intimate relationship with the woman in whose womb it develops; any other relationship it may have is indirect, and must be mediated through the pregnant woman. The relationship that exists between a woman and her fetus is clearly asymmetrical, since she is the only party to the relationship who is capable of making a decision about whether the interaction should continue and since the fetus is wholly dependent on the woman who sustains it while she is quite capable of surviving without it.

However much some might prefer it to be otherwise, no one else can do anything to support or harm a fetus without doing something to the woman who nurtures it. Because of this inexorable biological reality, she bears a unique responsibility and privilege in determining her fetus's place in the social scheme of things. Clearly, many pregnancies occur to women who place very high value on the lives of the particular fetuses they carry, and choose to see their pregnancies through to term despite the possible risks and costs involved; hence, it would be wrong of anyone to force such a woman to terminate her pregnancy under these circumstances. Other women, or some of these same women at other times, value other things more highly (e.g., their freedom, their health, or previous responsibilities which conflict with those generated by the pregnancies), and choose not to continue their pregnancies. The value that women ascribe to individual fetuses varies dramatically from case to case, and may well change over the course of any particular pregnancy. There is no absolute value that attaches to fetuses apart from their relational status determined in the context of their particular development. . . .

FEMINIST POLITICS AND ABORTION

Feminist ethics directs us to look at abortion in the context of other issues of power and not to limit discussion to the standard questions about its moral and legal acceptability. Because coerced pregnancy has repercussions for women's oppressed status generally, it is important to ensure that abortion not only be made legal but that adequate services be made accessible to all women who seek them. This means that within Canada, where medically approved abortion is technically recognized as legal (at least for the moment), we must protest the fact that it is not made available to many of the women who have the greatest need for abortions: vast geographical areas offer no abortion services at all, but unless the women of those regions can afford to travel to urban clinics, they have no meaningful right to abortion. Because women depend on access to abortion in their pursuit of social equality, it is a matter of moral as well as political responsibility that provincial health plans should cover the cost of transport and service in the abortion facilities women choose. Ethical study of abortion involves understanding and critiquing the economic, age, and social barriers that currently restrict access to medically acceptable abortion services.[11]

Moreover, it is also important that abortion services be provided in an atmosphere that fosters women's health and well-being; hence, the care offered should be in a context that is supportive of the choices women make. Abortions should be seen as part of women's overall reproductive health and could be inclined within centres that deal with all matters of reproductive health in an open, patient-centered manner where effective counselling is offered for a wide range of reproductive decisions.[12] Providers need to recognize that abortion is a legitimate option so that services will be delivered with respect and concern for the physical, psychological, and emotional effects on a patient. All too frequently, hospital-based abortions are pro-vided by practitioners who are uneasy about their role and treat the women involved with hostility and resentment. Increasingly, many anti-abortion activists have personalized their attacks and focussed their attention on harassing the women who enter and leave abortion clinics. Surely requiring a woman to pass a guantlet of hostile protestors on her way to and from an abortion is not conducive to effective health care. Ethical exploration of abortion raises questions about how women are treated when they seek abortions,[13] achieving legal permission for women to dispose of their fetuses if they are determined enough to manage the struggle should not be accepted as the sole moral consideration. . . .

Feminists support abortion on demand because they know that women must have control over their reproduction. For the same reason, they actively oppose forced abortion and coerced sterilization, practices that are sometimes inflicted on the most powerless women, especially those in the Third World. Feminist ethics demands that access to voluntary, safe, effective birth control be part of any abortion discussion, so that women have access to other means of avoiding pregnancy.[14]

Feminist analysis addresses the context as well as the practice of abortion decisions. Thus, feminists also object to the conditions which lead women to abort wanted fetuses because there are not adequate financial and social supports available to care for a child. Because feminist accounts value fetuses that are wanted by the women who carry them, they oppose practices which force women to abort because of poverty or intimidation. Yet, the sorts of social changes necessary if we are to free women from having abortions out of economic necessity are vast; they include changes not only in legal and health-care policy, but also in housing, child care, employment, etc. (Petchesky 1980, p. 112). Nonetheless, feminist ethics defines reproductive freedom as the condition under which women are able to make truly voluntary choices about their reproductive lives, and these many dimensions are implicit in the ideal.

Clearly, feminists are not "pro-abortion," for they are concerned to ensure the safety of each pregnancy to the greatest degree possible; wanted fetuses should not be harmed or lost. Therefore, adequate pre- and postnatal care and nutrition are also important elements of any feminist position on reproductive freedom. Where anti-abortionists direct their energies to trying to prevent women from obtaining abortions, feminists seek to protect the health of wanted fetuses. They recognize that far more could be done to protect and care for fetuses if the state directed its resources at supporting women who continue their pregnancies, rather than draining away resources in order to police women who find that they must interrupt their pregnancies. Caring for the women who carry fetuses is not only a more legitimate policy than is regulating them; it is probably also more effective at ensuring the health and well-being of more fetuses.

Feminist ethics also explores how abortion policies fit within the politics of sexual domination. Most feminists are sensitive to the fact that many men support women's right to abortion out of the belief that women will be more willing sexual partners if they believe that they can readily terminate an unwanted pregnancy. Some men coerce their partners into obtaining abortions the women may not want.[15] Feminists understand that many women oppose abortion for this very reason, being unwilling to support a practice that increases women's sexual vulnerability (Luker 1984, p. 209–15). Thus, it is important that feminists develop a coherent analysis of reproductive freedom that includes sexual freedom (as women choose to define it). That requires an analysis of sexual freedom that includes women's right to refuse sex; such a right can only be assured if women have equal power to men and are not subject to domination by virtue of their sex.[16]

In sum, then, feminist ethics demands that moral discussions of abortion be more broadly defined than they have been in most philosophic discussions. Only by reflecting on the meaning of ethical pronouncements on actual women's lives and the connections between judgments on abortion and the conditions of domination and subordination can we come to an adequate understanding of the moral status of abortion in our society. As Rosalind Petchesky (1980) argues, feminist discussion of abortion "must be moved beyond the framework of a 'woman's right to choose' and connected to a much broader revolutionary movement that addresses all of the conditions of women's liberation" (p. 113).

Endnotes

Earlier versions of this paper were read to the Department of Philosophy, Dalhousie University and to the Canadian Society for Women in Philosophy in Kingston. I am very grateful for the comments received from colleagues in both forums; particular thanks go to Lorraine Code, David Braybrooke, Richmond Campbell, Sandra Taylor, Terry Tomkow and Kadri Vihvelin for their patience and advice.

1. For some idea of the ways in which traditional moral theory oppresses women, see Morgan (1987) and Hoagland (1988).

2. Critics continue to want to structure the debate around the *possibility* of women making frivolous abortion decisions and hence want feminists to agree to setting boundaries on acceptable grounds for choosing abortion. Feminists ought to resist this injunction, though. There is no practical way of drawing a line fairly in the abstract; cases that may appear "frivolous" at a distance, often turn out to be substantive when the details are revealed, i.e., frivolity is in the eyes of the beholder. There is no evidence to suggest that women actually make the sorts of choices worried critics hypothesize about: e.g., a woman eight months pregnant who chooses to abort because she wants to take a trip or gets in "a tiff" with her partner. These sorts of fantasies, on which demands to distinguish between legitimate and illegitimate personal reasons for choosing abortion chiefly rest, reflect on offensive conception of women as irresponsible; they ought not to be perpetuated. Women, seeking moral guidance in their own deliberations about choosing abortion, do not find such hypothetical discussions of much use.

3. In her monumental historical analysis of the early roots of Western patriarchy, Gerda Lerner (1986) determined that patriarchy began in the period from 3100 to 600 B.C. when men appropriated women's sexual and reproductive capacity; the earliest states entrenched patriarchy by institutionalizing the sexual and procreative subordination of women to men.

4. There are some women who claim to be feminists against choice in abortion. See, for instance, Callahan (1987), though few spell out their full feminist program. For reasons I develop in this paper, I do not think this is a consistent position.

5. There is a lot the state could do to ameliorate this condition. If it provided women with adequate financial support, removed the inequities in the labour market, and provided affordable and reliable childcare, pregnancy need not so often lead to a woman's dependence on a particular man. The fact that it does not do so is evidence of the state's complicity in maintaining women's subordinate position with respect to men.

6. See Zillah Eisenstein (1988) for a comprehensive theory of the role of the pregnant body as the central element in the cultural subordination of women.
7. Thomson (1971) is a notable exception to this trend.
8. This seems reminiscent of Aristotle's view of women as "flower pots" where men implant the seed with all the important genetic information and the movement necessary for development and women's job is that of passive gestation, like the flower pot. For exploration of the flower pot picture of pregnancy, see Whitbeck (1973) and Lange (1983).
9. The definition of pregnancy as a purely passive activity reaches its ghoulish conclusion in the increasing acceptability of sustaining brain-dead women on life support systems to continue their functions as incubators until the fetus can be safely delivered. For a discussion of this new trend, see Murphy (1989).
10. This apt phrasing is taken from Petchesky (1984), p. 342.
11. Some feminists suggest we seek recognition of the legitimacy of non-medical abortion services. This would reduce costs and increase access dramatically, with no apparent increase in risk, provided that services were offered by trained, responsible practitioners concerned with the well-being of their clients. It would also allow the possibility of increasing women's control over abortion. See, for example, McDonnell (1984), chap. 8.
12. For a useful model of such a centre, see Van Wagner and Lee (1989).
13. See CARAL/Halifax (1990) for women's stories about their experiences with hospitals and free-standing abortion clinics.
14. Therefore, the Soviet model, where women have access to multiple abortions but where there is no other birth control available, must also be opposed.
15. See CARAL/Halifax (1990), p. 20–21, for examples of this sort of abuse.
16. It also requires that discussions of reproductive and sexual freedom not be confined to "the language of control and sexuality characteristic of a technology of sex" (Diamond and Quinby 1988, p. 197), for such language is alienating and constrains women's experiences of their own sexuality.

References

Addelson, Kathryn Pyne. 1987. "Moral Passages." In *Women and Moral Theory*. Edited by Eva Feder Kittay and Diana T. Meyers. Totowa, NJ: Rowman & Littlefield.

Baier, Annette. 1985. *Postures of the Mind. Essays on Mind and Morals*. Minneapolis: University of Minnesota Press.

Callahan, Sidney. 1987. "A Pro-life Feminist Makes Her Case." *Utne Reader* (March/April): 104–14.

CARAL/Halifax. 1990. *Telling Our Stories: Abortion Stories from Nova Scotia*. Halifax: CARAL/Halifax (Canadian Abortion Rights Action League).

Diamond, Irene, and Lee Quinby. 1988. "American Feminism and the Language of Control." In *Feminism & Foucault: Reflections on Resistance*. Edited by Irene Diamond and Lee Quinby. Boston: Northeastern University Press.

Eisenstein, Zillah R. 1988. *The Female Body and the Law*. Berkeley: University of California Press.

Hoagland, Sara Lucia. 1988. *Lesbian Ethics: Toward New Value*. Palo Alto, CA: Institute of Lesbian Studies.

Lange, Lynda. 1983. "Woman is Not a Rational Animal: On Aristotle's Biology of Reproduction." In *Discovering Reality: Feminist Perspectives on Epistemology, Metaphysics, Methodology, and Philosophy of Science*. Edited by Sandra Harding and Merill B. Hintickka. Dordrecht, Holland: D. Reidel.

Lerner, Gerda. 1986. *The Creation of Patriarchy*. New York: Oxford.

Luker, Kristin. 1984. *Abortion and the Politics of Motherhood*. Berkeley: University of California Press.

MacKinnon, Catherine. 1989. *Toward a Feminist Theory of the State*. Cambridge, MA: Harvard University Press.

McDonnell, Kathleen. 1984. *Not an Easy Choice: A Feminist Re-examines Abortion*. Toronto: The Women's Press.

Morgan, Kathryn Pauly. 1987. "Women and Moral Madness." In *Science, Morality and Feminist Theory*. Edited by Marsha Hanen and Kai Nielsen. *Canadian Journal of Philosophy*, Supplemental Volume 13: 201–26.

Murphy, Julien S. 1989. "Should Pregnancies Be Sustained in Brain-dead Women?: A Philosophical Discussion of Postmortem Pregnancy." In *Healing Technology: Feminist Perspectives*. Edited by Kathryn Srother Ratcliff et al. Ann Arbor: The University of Michigan Press.

Overall, Christine. 1987. *Ethics and Human Reproduction: A Feminist Analysis*. Winchester, MA: Allen & Unwin.

Petchesky, Rosalind Pollack. 1980. "Reproductive Freedom: Beyond 'A Woman's Right to Choose.'" In *Women: Sex and Sexuality*. Edited by Catharine R. Stimpson and Ethel Spector Person. Chicago: University of Chicago Press.

Sumner, L. W. 1981. *Abortion and Moral Theory*. Princeton: Princeton University Press.

Thomson, Judith Jarvis. 1971. "A Defense of Abortion." *Philosophy and Public Affairs,* 1: 47–66.

Tooley, Michael. 1972. "Abortion and Infanticide." *Philosophy and Public Affairs*, 2, 1 (Fall): 37–65.

Van Wagner, Vicki, and Bob Lee. 1989. "Principles into Practice: An Activist Vision of Feminist Reproductive Health Care." In *The Future of Human Reproduction*. Edited by Christine Overall. Toronto: The Women's Press.

Warren, Mary Anne. 1973. "On the Moral and Legal Status of Abortion." *The Monist*, 57: 43–61.

———. 1989. "The Moral Significance of Birth." *Hypatia*, 4, 2 (Summer): 46–65.

Whitbeck, Carolyn. 1973. "Theories of Sex Difference." *The Philosophical Forum*, 5, 1–2 (Fall/Winter 1973–74): 54–80.

REVIEW QUESTIONS

1. According to Sherwin, what are the differences between the feminist and the nonfeminist approaches to abortion?
2. Why does Sherwin think that women have no control over their sexual lives?

3. How does medicine view pregnant women according to Sherwin?
4. What is Sherwin's view of the fetus?
5. What are the political implications of Sherwin's feminist analysis of abortion?

2. Is the pregnant woman really in the best position to judge whether she should or should not have an abortion, as Sherwin says?
3. Are feminists such as Sherwin pro-abortion? Are they pro-choice?

DISCUSSION QUESTIONS

1. Do you agree that it is "self-evident that the pregnant woman is a subject of principal concern in abortion decisions"?

PROBLEM CASES

1. The Rapper. KC Juice is the twenty-year-old lead rapper in a hip-hop group called In Your Face. When she isn't performing, she loves to party. She smokes, drinks, takes drugs, and if she is in the mood, she has sex with whoever is looking good. Since KC looks pretty good herself, she has no trouble connecting with partners. Sometimes she uses contraceptives and sometimes she doesn't, particularly when she is wasted on drugs. But she has been lucky—no AIDS, diseases, or other problems so far. Despite her destructive lifestyle, she is fabulously successful. Three of her albums have gone platinum, and she has lots of heavy gold jewelry, three new luxury cars, several Harleys, two beach houses, and millions of dollars in the bank.

During the week of recording sessions for her fourth album, she discovers she is pregnant (she is already in the second month). The father is unknown. This is not a good time for her to be pregnant because after the release of the album, she has a nationwide tour scheduled. If she cancels, she will lose a million dollars or more, and the group will be unhappy and might even find a new lead singer. Besides, she thinks that motherhood is no fun; it will interfere with her partying and make her less attractive. As for being a parent, forget it. So without making a big deal out of it, she has a quick abortion and then gets back to business.

Does KC have a right to get an abortion? Did she do the right thing? Explain and defend your answers.

2. The Morning-After Pill. (Discussed in "The Morning-After Pill," by Jan Hoffman in *The New York Times Magazine,* January 10, 1993.) Depending on when a woman takes it, the morning-after pill prevents either fertilization (occurring up to eighteen hours after intercourse) or implantation of the fertilized egg in the lining of the uterus (occurring about a week or two after conception). Because pregnancy tests do not register positive until a day or two after implantation, a woman who takes the pill after intercourse will not know if she has prevented conception or implantation.

The drug most often used as a morning-after pill is Ovral. It is also used as a birth-control pill, and it was approved as such by the FDA (the Federal Food and Drug Administration) in 1968. Other lower-dose pills that can be used as morning-after pills are Lo/Ovral, Nordette, Levlen, Triphasil, and Tri Levlen. All these pills combine estrogen and progestin. They affect a woman's hormones in such a way that the egg cannot be fertilized; or if it is, it cannot become implanted in the lining of the uterus. Instead the egg is sloughed off during menstruation.

The morning-after pill can be effectively taken up to seventy-two hours after intercourse, and it reduces the likelihood of pregnancy to below eight percent. (On her most fertile day, a woman's chance of becoming pregnant is at most about twenty-five percent.) Although it certainly reduces the chances of becoming pregnant, it is not completely effective because it does not prevent tubal pregnancies. The side effects of the morning-after pill include temporary nausea and breast tenderness, and it is not recommended for women who should not take oral contraceptives.

According to the *Times* article, the morning-after pill is widely prescribed on college campuses, and it has been part of standard care for rape victims for more than a decade. Planned Parenthood affiliates have been offering it for about three years. Use of birth-control pills as morning-after pills has not received the approval of the FDA, largely because no drug company has sought approval, and without FDA approval they cannot be dispensed in federally supported Title X clinics which serve poor women.

Doctors estimate that by making the morning-after pill widely available, the number of unwanted pregnancies could be reduced by 1.7 million annually and the number of abortions could be reduced by 800,000 annually. Currently there are about 3.5 million unwanted pregnancies per year in the United States and about 1.6 million abortions.

The morning-after pill raises several interesting questions:

Is preventing implantation an abortion, contraception, interception, or what?

Is the zygote or fertilized egg a person with rights before it becomes implanted?

The IUD (interuterine device) also prevents fertilization or implantation. Does using it amount to getting an abortion?

In the one or two weeks before implantation, many fertilized eggs are naturally sloughed off, and women don't usually think of this as miscarriage. So why should a woman think of preventing implantation as an abortion?

3. Mrs. Sherri Finkbine and Thalidomide. In 1962, Mrs. Sherri Finkbine, the mother of four normal children, became pregnant. During the pregnancy, Mrs. Finkbine had trouble sleeping, so without consulting her physician, she took some tranquilizers containing the drug thalidomide which her husband had brought back from a trip to Europe. In Europe, the sedative was widely used.

Later Mrs. Finkbine read that a number of severely deformed children had been born in Europe. These children's limbs failed to develop or developed in malformed ways; some were born blind and deaf or had seriously defective internal organs. The birth defects were traced to the use in pregnancy of a widely used tranquilizer whose active ingredient was thalidomide, the very tranquilizer that she had taken.

Mrs. Finkbine went to her physician, and he confirmed her fears. The tranquilizer did contain thalidomide, and she had a very good chance of delivering a seriously deformed baby. The physician recommended an abortion. Mrs. Finkbine then presented her case to the three-member medical board of Phoenix, and they granted approval for the abortion.

In her concern for other women who might have taken thalidomide, Mrs. Finkbine told her story to a local newspaper. The story made the front page, and it wasn't long before reporters had discovered and published Mrs. Finkbine's identity. She became the object of an intense anti-abortion campaign, and she was condemned as a murderer by the Vatican newspaper.

As a result of the controversy, the medical board decided that their approval for an abortion would not survive a court test because the Arizona statute at that time allowed abortion only to save the mother's life. So the board withdrew their approval.

Eventually Mrs. Finkbine found it necessary to get an abortion in Sweden. After the abortion, Mrs. Finkbine asked if the fetus was a boy or a girl. The doctor could not say because the fetus was too badly deformed.

Do you think that Mrs. Finkbine acted wrongly in having an abortion? Explain your answer.

Do you think that the government has a right to prohibit abortions in such cases? Why or why not?

SUGGESTED READINGS

1. Alison M. Jaggar, *Living With Contradictions* (WestView Press, 1994), Part IV, A, has eleven articles on abortion by feminists including Catherine A. MacKinnon and Alison Jaggar.

2. Rosalind Pollack Petchesky, "Fetal Images: The Power of Visual Culture in the Politics of Reproduction," in *Theorizing Feminism,* ed. Anne C. Herrmann and Abigail J. Stewart (WestView Press, 1994), gives a feminist analysis of videos such as *The Silent Scream* that are used to persuade people in the abortion debate.

3. *Feminist Philosophies,* ed. Janet A. Kourany, James P. Sterba, and Rosemarie Tong (Prentice-Hall, 1992), has four feminist articles on abortion and reproduction, including "Abortion: Is a Woman a Person?" by Ellen Willis. Willis claims that the conservative views the woman as a womb, and not as a person.

4. Angela Davis, *Women, Race, and Class* (Random House, 1981), Chapter 12, discusses the abortion rights movement in the context of race, class, and the women's liberation movement.

5. Brenda Timmins, "What about Us?" in *Gender Basics,* ed. Anne Minas (Wadsworth Publishing Co., 1993), argues that because of the difficulties in caring for handicapped children, women should have unrestricted access to abortion.

6. Alan Zaitchik, "Viability and the Morality of Abortion," *Philosophy & Public Affairs,* 10:1 (1981), pp. 18–24, defends the view that viability is a morally significant dividing line.

7. Tristram H. Engelhardt, Jr., "The Ontology of Abortion," *Ethics* 84 (April 1974), pp. 217–234, maintains that the fetus is not a person until the later stages of infancy, but after viability it can be treated as if it were a person.

8. Baruch Brody, "On the Humanity of the Fetus," in *Abortion: Pro and Con,* ed. Robert L. Perkins (Schenkman, 1974), takes a dividing-line approach to the humanity of the fetus and suggests that the most sensible place to draw the line is when fetal brain waves can be detected, at about the eighth week of development. This anthology has several other useful articles on abortion.

9. Peter Singer, *Practical Ethics,* second edition (Cambridge University Press, 1993), Chapter 6, presents a utilitarian view of abortion. The version of Utilitarianism that Singer accepts is called Preference Utilitarianism.

10. Fred Feldman, *Confrontations with the Reaper* (Oxford University Press, 1992), Chapter 12, defends a utilitarian theory called Justicized Act Utilitarianism which entails that abortion is morally right in cases of rape, a severely deformed fetus, and possibly in other cases where the universal justice level is maximized.

11. Sissela Bok, "Ethical Problems of Abortion," *Hastings Center Studies* 2 (January 1974), pp. 33–52, rejects attempts to define "humanity" and suggests that various reasons for not getting an abortion become stronger as the fetus develops.

12. Daniel Callahan, *Abortion, Law, Choice and Morality* (Macmillan, 1970), defends the moderate view that the fetus has what he calls a "partial moral status."

13. Philip E. Devine, *The Ethics of Homicide* (Cornell University Press, 1978), Chapter 11, discusses killing fetuses and the comatose.

14. Joel Feinberg and Barbara Baum Levenbook, "Abortion," in *Matters of Life and Death,* third edition, ed. Tom Regan (Random House, 1993), provide a sophisticated discussion of various issues connected to abortion, including the status of the fetus. Feinberg and Levenbook end up with a more or less moderate position, but in a postscript on the law they decide that a legal ban on abortion may be justified even if abortion is not generally morally wrong.

15. R. M. Hare, "Abortion and the Golden Rule," *Philosophy & Public Affairs* 4 (Spring 1975), pp. 201–22, attacks those who appeal to intuition, such as Thomson, and uses the Golden Rule as a basic ethical principle to defend a moderate view of abortion.

16. Germain Grisez, *Abortion: The Myths, the Realities, and the Arguments* (Corpus Books, 1970), defends a conservative view on abortion in Chapter VI.

17. Susan Nicholson, *Abortion and the Roman Catholic Church* (Religious Ethics, 1974), explains the position of the Catholic Church on abortion.

18. Michael Tooley, "Abortion and Infanticide," *Philosophy & Public Affairs,* 2 (Fall 1972), pp. 47–66, presents a classic defense of the extreme liberal view that neither a fetus nor a newborn infant has a serious right to continued existence and that both abortion and infanticide are morally acceptable. Tooley also has a book titled *Abortion and Infanticide* (Oxford University Press, 1983) in which he develops his position.

19. *The Rights and Wrongs of Abortion,* ed. Marshall Cohen, Thomas Nagel, and Thomas Scanlon (Princeton University Press, 1974), has five articles on abortion including two by Judith Jarvis Thomson.

20. *The Problem of Abortion,* ed. Joel Feinberg (Wadsworth, 1984), is an excellent anthology with a wide range of articles representing different points of view.

Chapter Three

SUICIDE AND EUTHANASIA

Introduction

Suicide is the taking of one's own life, and euthanasia is killing someone for the sake of mercy to relieve great suffering. But when a doctor helps an injured or ill person commit suicide, as Dr. Jack Kervorkian does, it seems that there is little difference between assisted suicide and euthanasia. This point is made by Singer in the readings. Gay-Williams and Dyck go further. Their view is that suicide and euthanasia both involve intentionally causing the death of a person and that both are morally wrong.

The distinction between suicide and euthanasia, then, may be fuzzy or even nonexistent in some cases. To clarify matters, it is customary to distinguish between different types of euthanasia. *Voluntary euthanasia* is mercy killing with the consent of the terminally ill or suffering person. This is the type of euthanasia that includes suicide, at least in the view of Gay-Williams and Dyck. For example, a patient suffering from very painful and terminal cancer may ask to be killed with a fatal injection of morphine. Or the patient may turn a switch that triggers the fatal injection as in one of Dr. Kevorkian's suicide devices. (See the second Problem Case.) *Nonvoluntary euthanasia*, by contrast, is mercy killing without the consent of the person who is ill or suffering— although the consent of others such as parents or relatives can be obtained. This type of euthanasia does not include suicide. Writers who discuss nonvoluntary euthanasia usually have in mind the killing of those how are unable to give consent, for example a comatose person such as Karen Quinlan or a defective infant. Obviously, such a person cannot commit suicide. There is another possibility, however, and that is the mercy killing of a person who is able to give consent but is not asked. If the person killed does not wish to die, it might be more accurate to call this *involuntary euthanasia*. This is not discussed in the readings, but it may be safely assumed that all of the authors in this book would consider it to be wrong.

A further distinction is often made between active and passive euthanasia, or between killing and letting a patient die for the sake of mercy. Just how this distinction should be drawn and whether the distinction should be made at all are matters of debate. As Rachels explains it in the reading, active euthanasia is taking a direct action designed to kill the patient, such as giving the patient a lethal injection of morphine. Passive euthanasia, by contrast, is allowing the patient to die by withholding treatment—not performing life-saving surgery on a defective infant, for example.

Rachels believes that this distinction has no moral significance and that using it leads to confused moral thinking. Gay-Williams also objects to the distinction, but for a different reason. He believes that the phrase "passive euthanasia" is misleading and mistaken. In his view, what is called passive euthanasia is not really euthanasia at all because it is not intentional killing. Either the killing is an unintended consequence, a side effect of the real intention—the elimination of suffering—or the cause of death is the person's injuries or disease, not the failure to receive treatment.

Dyck makes the distinction in a different way. In his terminology, the important moral distinction is between intentionally causing death and merely permitting death. Deliberately causing one's death, whether by action or inaction, is wrong. But if a patient chooses to forego medical interventions that will prolong life, this is not wrong in Dyck's view. It does not involve a rejection of life, but rather a decision about how one is to spend the remainder of life.

The positions of Gay-Williams and Dyck both focus on intentions, whereas Rachels is concerned with consequences. Although Gay-Williams and Dyck do not discuss it, it is worth noting that both seem to accept a traditional view about intentions called the **Doctrine of Double Effect**. According to this doctrine, as long as the intended consequence of an act is good, a bad foreseen consequence (such as death) can be morally allowed provided it is not intended and prevents a greater evil (such as great suffering). To use Gay-Williams' example, suppose that a doctor gives a terminal cancer patient an overdose of morphine, that is, an amount sufficient to kill the patient. If the doctor intends only to reduce or eliminate the patient's pain, and not to kill the patient, and if the death of the patient is not as bad as the patient's suffering, then according to the Doctrine of Double Effect, the doctor's action is not wrong, even though the doctor foresees that the patient will die from the overdose.

The Moral Issue   The moral issue is whether suicide and euthanasia are wrong. The issue is complicated by the fact that writers do not agree on the meaning of the term "euthanasia," as we have seen. It seems accurate enough to say that the traditional conservative view is that active euthanasia and suicide are wrong (unless God commands it—this exception is mentioned by Brandt). The representatives of the conservative view in our readings are St. Thomas Aquinas, Gay-Williams, Dyck, and the statement of the American Medical Association (AMA) discussed by Rachels and Steinbock. St. Thomas argues that suicide is wrong because it is contrary to **natural law** and charity, harms the community, and destroys God's gift to us. The basic idea of natural law is that there are prescriptive moral laws that can be derived from human nature using reasoning. Gay-Williams is influenced by this idea when he argues that euthanasia is unnatural. Also he seems to be following St. Thomas when he argues that euthanasia is contrary to self-interest, produces bad effects on others, and violates the nature and dignity of humans. Dyck has a different reason for condemning suicide and euthanasia: People who cause their death repudiate the meaningfulness and worth of life; they lack the courage to be—the acceptance of life as having worth no matter what it brings.

The AMA position is different from that of Gay-Williams and Dyck. According to Steinbock, the AMA statement on euthanasia does not rest on any distinction between active and passive euthanasia, as Rachels says. Both are wrong if they involve the "intentional termination of life of one human being by another." The AMA statement does depend on a distinction between ordinary and extraordinary means, however, because it allows the cessation of extraordinary means of treatment. But this is based on the patient's right to refuse treatment and does not assume any right to die.

The liberal view on euthanasia and suicide, as distinguished from what we are calling the traditional conservative view, is that active euthanasia and suicide are morally right in some cases. The representatives of this position in the readings are Rachels, Singer, and Brandt (in two readings). Rachels argues that in some cases active euthanasia is preferable to passive euthanasia because it reduces suffering. If there is a choice between a quick and painless death and prolonged suffering, and no other alternative, then Rachels would prefer a quick and painless death. Singer appeals to the principle of respect for autonomy. This principle tells us to allow rational agents to live their lives according to their own decisions, and if they choose to die, they should be allowed to do so and even should be assisted in carrying out their decision. In Brandt's first reading on suicide, he argues that suicide is both rational and morally right when a patient is suffering from a painful and terminal illness. In the second reading by Brandt, he uses similar arguments to justify the active termination of defective newborn infants.

Philosophical Issues   As far as voluntary euthanasia and suicide are concerned, one basic issue is whether or not persons who are rational and fully informed should be free to decide to die and then to bring about that decision by themselves or with others' help. Singer argues that active voluntary euthanasia is morally permissible, even in those cases where it is basically the same as assisted suicide. Brandt agrees that suicide in such a case is rational and morally permissible. Gay-

Williams and Dyck do not agree. Gay-Williams argues that a person who chooses to die, whether by suicide or by active euthanasia, is acting contrary to nature and contrary to self-interest. Dyck claims that such a person has repudiated the meaningfulness and worth of his or her life and lacks the Jewish-Christian virtue of the courage to live no matter what life brings.

Another important issue, as we have seen, is whether or not there is a morally significant difference between killing and letting a patient die, or between active and passive euthanasia, or between intentionally causing death and merely permitting death. There is also controversy about the Doctrine of Double Effect. Critics doubt that a clear distinction can be made between the two effects, the intended one and the unintended but foreseen one. If a doctor intends to reduce the patient's suffering, but also knows that she is giving a patient a lethal dose of morphine, does it make sense to say that she doesn't also intend to kill the patient? Furthermore, critics worry that the doctrine can be used to defend wicked actions. If a religious leader kills her followers with the intention of sending them to heaven, does this good intention make the killing allowable? Defenders of the doctrine insist that a clear distinction between the two effects in question can be made, in some important cases anyway, and that it does not allow any evil or wicked action, but only those that prevent an even greater evil.

Another matter of controversy is the distinction between ordinary and extraordinary means of prolonging life. This distinction is found in the AMA statement. Rachels thinks that the cessation of extraordinary means of treatment amounts to passive euthanasia because it is the intentional termination of life. Steinbock does not agree. In some cases, at least, the decision to stop treatment is based on the right of the patient to make decisions about treatment and does not necessarily involve any decision to die. Perhaps the reason for stopping extraordinary treatment is to save money or to avoid treatment that causes more discomfort than the disease.

Another important issue is how to make life-or-death decisions. One standard answer, given by Rachels and Brandt, is to appeal to the quality of a person's life: If a person will have a bad life, then his or her life should be ended; but if a person will have a good life, then his or her life should be continued. But how do we distinguish between good and bad lives? That is a classical problem in ethics that resists easy solution. One answer given by Dyck is that all lives are worthwhile, no matter how much suffering they contain. Another answer is that we ask ourselves if we would want to live the life in question. But it seems unlikely that everyone will agree about which lives are or are not worth living. Dyck would say that every life is worth living, whereas Rachels and Brandt would say that lives filled with suffering, and with little or no happiness, are not worth living. Brandt's suggestion is that we use a "happiness criterion." A life is good or worth living if over the whole lifetime there are more moments of happiness than moments of unhappiness. But is happiness the only thing to be considered? What about other things like knowledge and achievement? Perhaps an unhappy life could still be good because of achievements or knowledge, or just because life is good in itself.

St. Thomas Aquinas

Suicide Is Unnatural and Immoral

St. Thomas Aquinas (1225–1274), a member of the Dominican Order, was one of the greatest medieval philosophers. As an Angelic Doctor of the Roman Catholic Church, his teachings have a position of special authority, but this does not mean that all Catholic thinkers agree with him on every point of doctrine.

St. Thomas employs the scholastic style of presenting objections to his own position and then replying to each objection in turn. After stating five arguments for the moral permissibility of suicide, St. Thomas presents three arguments against suicide and then replies to each of the first five arguments. (St. Thomas refers to Artistotle as the Philosopher, and to Aristotle's Nichomachean Ethics as Ethic.)

We proceed thus to the Fifth Article:

Objection 1. It would seem lawful for a man to kill himself. For murder is a sin in so far as it is contrary to justice. But no man can do an injustice to himself, as is proved in *Ethic.* v. 11. Therefore no man sins by killing himself.

Obj. 2. Further, It is lawful, for one who exercises public authority, to kill evildoers. Now he who exercises public authority is sometimes an evildoer. Therefore he may lawfully kill himself.

Obj. 3. Further, It is lawful for a man to suffer spontaneously a lesser danger that he may avoid a greater. Thus it is lawful for a man to cut off a decayed limb even from himself, that he may save his whole body. Now sometimes a man, by killing himself, avoids a greater evil, for an example an unhappy life, or the shame of sin. Therefore a man may kill himself.

Obj. 4. Further, Sampson killed himself, as related in Judges xvi, and yet he is numbered among the saints (Heb. xi). Therefore it is lawful for a man to kill himself.

Obj. 5. Further, It is related (2 Mach. xiv. 42) that a certain Razias killed himself, *choosing to die nobly rather than to fall into the hands of the wicked, and to suffer abuses unbecoming his noble birth.* Now nothing that is done nobly and bravely is unlawful. Therefore suicide is not unlawful.

On the contrary, Augustine says (*De Civ. Dei* i. 20): *Hence it follows that the words "Thou shalt not kill" refer to the killing of a man; not another man; therefore, not even thyself. For he who kills himself, kills nothing else than a man.*

From *Summa Theologica*, vol. II (New York: Benziger Brothers, 1925), part II, question 64, A5.

I answer that, It is altogether unlawful to kill oneself, for three reasons. First, because everything naturally loves itself, the result being that everything naturally keeps itself in being, and resists corruption so far as it can. Wherefore suicide is contrary to the inclination of nature and to charity, whereby every man should love himself. Hence suicide is always a mortal sin, as being contrary to the natural law and to charity.

Secondly, because every part, as such, belongs to the whole. Now every man is part of the community, and so, as such, he belongs to the community. Hence by killing himself he injures the community, as the Philosopher declares (*Ethic.* v. ii).

Thirdly, because life is God's gift to man, and is subject to His power, Who kills and makes to live. Hence whoever takes his own life sins against God, even as he who kills another's slave sins against that slave's master, and as he who usurps himself judgment of a matter not entrusted to him. For it belongs to God alone to pronounce sentence of death and life, according to Duet. xxxii. 39, *I will kill and I will make to live.*

Reply Obj. 1. Murder is a sin, not only because it is contrary to justice, but also because it is opposed to charity, which a man should have towards himself; in this respect suicide is a sin in relation to oneself. In relation to the community and to God, it is sinful, by reason also to its opposition to justice.

Reply Obj. 2. One who exercises public authority may lawfully put to death an evildoer, since he can pass judgment on him. But no man is judge of himself. Wherefore it is not lawful for one who exercises public authority to put himself to death for any sin whatever, although he may lawfully commit himself to the judgment of others.

Reply Obj. 3. Man is made master of himself through his **free will**: wherefore he can lawfully dispose of himself as to those matters which pertain to this life, which is ruled by man's free will. But the passage from this life to another and happier one is subject not to man's free will but to the power of God. Hence it is not lawful for a man to take his own life that he may pass to a happier life, nor that he may escape any unhappiness whatsoever to the present life, be-

cause the ultimate and most fearsome evil of this life is death, as the Philosopher states (*Ethic.* iii. 6). Therefore to bring death upon oneself in order to escape the other afflictions of this life is to adopt a greater evil in order to avoid a lesser. In like manner it is unlawful to take one's own life on account of one's having committed a sin, both because by so doing one does oneself a very great injury, by depriving oneself of the time needful for repentance, and because it is not lawful to slay an evildoer except by the sentence of the public authority. Again it is unlawful for a woman to kill herself lest she be violated, because she ought not to commit on herself the very great sin of suicide to avoid the lesser sin of another. For she commits no sin in being violated by force, provided she does not consent, since *without consent of the mind there is no stain on the body,* as the Blessed Lucy declared. Now it is evident that fornication and adultery are less grievous sins than taking a man's, especially one's own, life, since the latter is most grievous, because one injures oneself, to whom one owes the greatest love. Moreover it is most dangerous since no time is left wherein to expiate it by repentance. Again it is not lawful for anyone to take his own life for fear he should consent to sin, because *evil must not be done that good may come* (Rom. iii. 8) or that evil maybe avoided, especially if the evil be of small account and an uncertain event, for it is uncertain whether one will at some future time consent to a sin, since God is able to deliver man from sin under any temptation whatever.

Reply Obj. 4. As Augustine says (*De Civ. Dei* i. 21), *not even Samson is to be excused that he crushed himself together with his enemies under the ruins of the house, except the Holy Ghost, Who had wrought many wonders through him, had secretly commanded him to do this.* He assigns the same reason in the case of certain holy women who at the time of persecution took their own lives and who are commemorated by the Church.

Reply Obj. 5. It belongs to fortitude that a man does not shrink from being slain by another, for the sake of the good of virtue and that he may avoid sin. But that a man take his own life in order to avoid penal evils has indeed an appearance of fortitude (for which reason some

... have killed themselves, thinking to act from fortitude), yet it is not true fortitude, but rather a weakness of soul unable to bear penal evils, as the Philosopher (*Ethic.* iii. 7) and Augustine (*De Civ. Dei* i. 22, 23) declare.

REVIEW QUESTIONS

1. State and explain the five arguments for the lawfulness of suicide, and St. Thomas' replies.

2. What are St. Thomas' arguments against suicide?

DISCUSSION QUESTION

1. Does St. Thomas convince you that suicide is wrong? Why or why not?

Richard B. Brandt

On the Morality and Rationality of Suicide

Richard B. Brandt is professor emeritus of philosophy at the University of Michigan. He is the author of Ethical Theory *(1959),* A Theory of the Good and the Right *(1979), and* Morality, Utilitarianism, and Rights *(1992).*

Brandt discusses three questions about suicide: Is it morally blameworthy? Is it objectively wrong? and Is it rational? He finds that in some cases, for example, where a person is suffering from a painful terminal illness, suicide is not blameworthy, not wrong, and not irrational.

From the point of view of contemporary philosophy, suicide raises the following distinct questions: whether a person who commits suicide (assuming that there is suicide if and only if there is intentional termination of one's own life) is morally blameworthy, reprehensible, sinful in all circumstances; whether suicide is objectively right or wrong, and in what circumstances it is right or wrong, from a moral point of view; and whether, or in which circumstances, suicide is

From *A Handbook for the Study of Suicide* edited by Seymour Perlin. Copyright © 1975 by Oxford University Press, Inc. Reprinted by permission.

the best or the rational thing to do from the point of view of the agent's personal welfare.

THE MORAL BLAMEWORTHINESS OF SUICIDE

In former times the question of whether suicide is sinful was of great interest because the answer to it was considered relevant to how the agent would spend eternity. At present the practical issue is not as great, although a normal funeral service may be denied a person judged to have committed suicide sinfully. The chief practical issue now seems to be that persons may disapprove of a decedent for having committed suicide, and his friends or relatives may wish to defend his memory against moral charges.

The question of whether an act of suicide was sinful or morally blameworthy is not apt to arise unless it is already believed that the agent morally ought not to have done it: for instance, if he really had very poor reason for doing so, and his act foreseeably had catastrophic consequences for his wife and children. But, even if a given suicide is morally wrong, it does not follow that it is morally reprehensible. For, while asserting that a given act of suicide was wrong, we may still think that the act was hardly morally blameworthy or sinful if, say, the agent was in a state of great emotional turmoil at the time. We might then say that, although what he did was wrong, his action is *excusable*, just as in the criminal law it may be decided that, although a person broke the law, he should not be punished because he was *not responsible,* that is, was temporarily insane, did what he did inadvertently, and so on.

The foregoing remarks assume that to be morally blameworthy (or sinful) on account of an act is one thing, and for the act to be wrong is another. But, if we say this, what after all does it *mean* to say that a person is morally blameworthy on account of an action? We cannot say there is agreement among philosophers on this matter, but I suggest the following account as being safe from serious objection: "X is morally blameworthy on account of an action A" may be taken to mean "X and A, and X would not have done A had not his character been in some respect below standard; and in view of this it is fitting or justified for X to have some disapproving attitudes including remorse toward himself, and for some other persons Y to have some disapproving attitudes toward X and to express them in behavior." Traditional thought would include God as one of the "other persons" who might have and express disapproving attitudes.

In case the foregoing definition does not seem obviously correct, it is worthwhile pointing out that it is usually thought that an agent is not blameworthy or sinful for an action unless it is a *reflection on him;* the definition brings this fact out and makes clear why.

If someone charges that a suicide was sinful, we may now properly ask, "What defect of character did it show?" Some writers have claimed that suicide is blameworthy because it is *cowardly,* and since being cowardly is generally conceded to be a defect of character, if an act of suicide is admitted to be both objectively wrong and also cowardly, the claim to blameworthiness might be warranted in terms of the above definition. Of course, many people would hesitate to call taking one's own life a cowardly act, and there will certainly be controversy about which acts are cowardly and which are not. But at least we can see part of what has to be done to make a change of blameworthiness valid.

The most interesting question is the general one: which types of suicide in general are ones that, even if objectively wrong (in a sense to be explained below) are not sinful or blameworthy? Or, in other words, when is a suicide *morally excused* even if it is objectively wrong? We can at least identify some types that are morally excusable.

1. Suppose I *think* I am morally bound to commit suicide because I have a terminal illness and continued medical care will ruin my family financially. Suppose, however, that I am mistaken in this belief, and that suicide in such circumstances is not right. But surely I am not morally blameworthy; for I may be doing, out of a sense of duty to my family, what I would personally prefer not to do and is hard for me to do. What defect of character might my action show? Suicide from a genuine sense of duty is not blameworthy, even when the moral conviction in question is mistaken.

2. Suppose that I commit suicide when I am temporarily of unsound mind, either in the sense of the M'Naghten rule that I do not know that what I am doing is wrong, or of the Durham rule that, owing to a mental defect, I am substantially unable to do what is right. Surely, any suicide in an unsound state of mind is morally excused.

3. Suppose I commit suicide when I could not be said to be temporarily of unsound mind, but simply because I am not myself. For instance, I may be in an extremely depressed mood. Now a person may be in a very depressed mood, and commit suicide on account of being in that mood, when there is nothing the matter with his character—or, in other words, his character is not in any relevant way below standard. What are other examples of being "not myself," or emotional states that might be responsible for a person's committing suicide, and that might render the suicide excusable even if wrong? Being frightened; being distraught; being in almost any highly emotional frame of mind (anger, frustration, disappointment in love); perhaps just being terribly fatigued.

So there are at least three types of suicide which can be morally excused even if they are objectively wrong. The main point is this: Mr. X may commit suicide and it may be conceded that he ought not to have done so, but it is another step to show that he is sinful, or morally blameworthy, for having done so. To make out that further point, it must be shown that his act is attributable to some substandard trait of character. So, Mrs. *X* after the suicide can concede that her husband ought not to have done what he did, but she can also point out that it is no reflection on his character. The distinction, unfortunately, is often overlooked. St. Thomas Aquinas, who recognizes the distinction in other places, seems blind to it in his discussion of suicide.

THE MORAL REASONS FOR AND AGAINST SUICIDE

Persons who say suicide is morally wrong must be asked which of two positions they are affirming: Are they saying that *every* act of suicide is wrong, *everything considered;* or are they merely saying that there is always *some* moral obligation—doubtless of serious weight—not to commit suicide, so that very often suicide is wrong, although it is possible that there are *countervailing considerations* which in particular situations make it right or even a moral duty? It is quite evident that the first position is absurd; only the second has a chance of being defensible.

In order to make clear what is wrong with the first view, we may begin with an example. Suppose an army pilot's single-seater plane goes out of control over a heavily populated area; he has the choice of staying in the plane and bringing it down where it will do little damage but at the cost of certain death for himself, and of bailing out and letting the plane fall where it will, very possibly killing a good many civilians. Suppose he chooses to do the former, and so, by our definition, commits suicide. Does anyone want to say that his action is morally wrong? Even Immanuel Kant, who opposed suicide in all circumstances, apparently would not wish to say that it is; he would, in fact, judge that this act is not one of suicide, for he says, "It is no suicide to risk one's life against one's enemies, and even to sacrifice it, in order to preserve one's duties toward oneself." [1] St. Thomas Aquinas, in his discussion of suicide, may seem to take the position that such an act would be wrong, for he says, "It is altogether unlawful to kill oneself," admitting as an exception only the case of being under special command of God. But I believe St. Thomas would, in fact, have concluded that the act is right because the basic intention of the pilot was to save the lives of civilians, and whether an act is right or wrong is a matter of basic intention. [2]

In general, we have to admit that there are things with some moral obligation to avoid which, on account of other morally relevant considerations, it is sometimes right or even morally obligatory to do. There may be some obligation to tell the truth on every occasion, but surely in many cases the consequences of telling the truth would be so dire that one is obligated to lie. The same goes for promises. There is some moral obligation to do what one has promised (with a few exceptions); but, if one can keep a trivial promise only at serious cost to another person (i.e., keep an appointment only by failing to give aid to someone injured in an accident), it is surely obligatory to break the promise.

The most that the moral critic of suicide could hold, then, is that there is *some* moral obligation not to do what one knows will cause one's death; but he surely cannot deny that circumstances exist in which there are obligations to do things which, in fact, will result in one's death. If so, then in principle it would be possible to argue, for instance, that in order to meet my obligation to my family, it might be right for me to take my own life as the only way to avoid catastrophic hospital expenses in a terminal illness. Possibly the main point that critics of suicide on moral grounds would wish to make is that it is never right to take one's own life *for reasons of one's own personal welfare,* of any kind whatsoever. Some of the arguments used to support the immorality of suicide, however, are so framed that if they were supportable at all, they would prove that suicide is *never* moral.

One well-known type of argument against suicide may be classified as *theological.* St. Augustine and others urged that the Sixth Commandment ("Thou shalt not kill.") prohibits suicide, and that we are bound to obey a divine commandment. To this reasoning one might first reply that it is arbitrary exegesis of the

Sixth Commandment to assert that it was intended to prohibit suicide. The second reply is that if there is not some consideration which shows on the merits of the case that suicide is morally wrong, God had no business prohibiting it. It is true that some will object to this point, and I must refer them elsewhere for my detailed comments on the divine-will theory of morality.[3]

Another theological argument with wide support was accepted by John Locke, who wrote: ". . . Men being all the workmanship of one omnipotent and infinitely wise Maker; all the servants of one sovereign Master, sent into the world by His order and about His business; they are His property, whose workmanship they are made to last during His, not one another's pleasure. . . . Every one . . . is bound to preserve himself, and not to quit his state on wilfully. . . ."[4] And Kant: "We have been placed in this world under certain conditions and for specific purposes. But a suicide opposes the purpose of his Creator; he arrives in the other world as one who has deserted his post; he must be looked upon as a rebel against God. So long as we remember the truth that it is God's intention to preserve life, we are bound to regulate our activities in conformity with it. This duty is upon us until the time comes when God expressly commands us to leave this life. Human beings are sentinels on earth and may not leave their posts until relieved by another beneficent hand."[5] Unfortunately, however, even if we grant that it is the duty of human beings to do what God commands or intends them to do, more argument is required to show that God does *not* permit human beings to quit this life when their own personal welfare would be maximized by so doing. How does one draw the requisite inference about the intentions of God? The difficulties and contradictions in arguments to reach such a conclusion are discussed at length and perspicaciously by David Hume in his essay "On Suicide," and in view of the unlikelihood that readers will need to be persuaded about these, I shall merely refer those interested to that essay."[6]

A second group of arguments may be classed as arguments *from natural law*. St. Thomas says:

"It is altogether unlawful to kill oneself, for three reasons. First, because everything naturally loves itself, the result being that everything naturally keeps itself in being, and resists corruptions so far as it can. Wherefore suicide is contrary to the inclination of nature and to charity, whereby every man should love himself. Hence suicide is always a mortal sin, as being contrary to the natural law and to charity."[7] Here St. Thomas ignores two obvious points. First, it is not obvious why a human being is morally bound to do what he or she has some inclination to do. (St. Thomas did not criticize chastity.) Second, while it is true that most human beings do feel a strong urge to live, the human being who commits suicide obviously feels a stronger inclination to do something else. It is natural for a human being to dislike, and to take steps to avoid, say, great pain, as it is to cling to life.

A somewhat similar argument by Immanuel Kant may seem better. In a famous passage Kant writes that the maxim of a person who commits suicide is "From self-love I make it my principle to shorten my life if its continuance threatens more evil than it promises pleasure. The only further question to ask is whether this principle of self-love can become a universal law of nature. It is then seen at once that a system of nature by whose law the very same feeling whose function is to stimulate the furtherance of life should actually destroy life would contradict itself and consequently could not subsist as a system of nature. Hence this maxim cannot possibly hold as a universal law of nature and is therefore entirely opposed to the supreme principle of all duty."[8] What Kant finds contradictory is that the motive of self-love (interest in one's own long-range welfare) should sometimes lead one to struggle to preserve one's life, but at other times to end it. But where is the contradiction? One's circumstances change, and, if the argument of the following section in this chapter is correct, one sometimes maximizes one's own long-range welfare by trying to stay alive, but at other times by bringing about one's demise.

A third group of arguments, a form of which goes back at least to Aristotle, has a more modern and convincing ring. These are arguments to show that, in one way or another, a suicide necessarily does harm to other persons, or to society at large. Aristotle says that the suicide treats the *state* unjustly.[9] Partly following Aristotle, St. Thomas says: "Every man is part of the community, and so, as such, he belongs to the community. Hence by killing himself he injures the community." [10] Blackstone held that a suicide is an offense against the king "who hath an interest in the preservation of all his subjects," perhaps following Judge Brown in 1563, who argued that suicide cost the king a subject—"he being the head has lost one of his mystical members." [11] The premise of such arguments is, as Hume pointed out, obviously mistaken in many instances. It is true that Freud would perhaps have injured society had he, instead of finishing his last book, committed suicide to escape the pain of throat cancer. But surely there have been many suicides whose demise was not a noticeable loss to society; an honest man could only say that in some instances society was better off without them.

It need not be denied that suicide is often injurious to other persons, especially the family of a suicide. Clearly it sometimes is. But, we should notice what this fact establishes. Suppose we admit, as generally would be done, that there is some obligation not to perform any action which will probably or certainly be injurious to other people, the strength of the obligation being dependent on various factors, notably the seriousness of the expected injury. Then there is *some* obligation not to commit suicide, when that act would probably or certainly be injurious to other people. But, as we have already seen, many cases of *some* obligation to do something nevertheless are *not* cases of duty to do that thing, *everything considered.* So it could sometimes be morally justified to commit suicide, even if the act will harm someone. Must a man with terminal illness undergo excruciating pain because his death will cause his wife sorrow—when she will be caused sorrow a month later anyway, when he is dead of natural causes? Moreover, to repeat, the fact that an individual has some obligation not to commit suicide when that act will probably injure other persons does not imply that, every-

thing considered, it is wrong for him to do it, namely, that in all circumstances suicide *as such* is something there is some obligation to avoid.

Is there any sound argument, convincing to the modern mind, to establish that there is (or is not) *some moral obligation* to avoid suicide *as such,* an obligation, of course, which might be overridden by other obligations in some or many cases? (Captain Oates may have had a moral obligation not to commit suicide as such, but his obligation not to stand in the way of his comrades' getting to safety might have been so strong that, everything considered, he was justified in leaving the polar camp and allowing himself to freeze to death.)

To present all the arguments necessary to answer this question convincingly would take a great deal of space. I shall, therefore, simply state one answer to it which seems plausible to some contemporary philosophers. Suppose it could be shown that it would maximize the long-run welfare of everybody affected if people were taught that there is a moral obligation to avoid suicide—so that people would be motivated to avoid suicide just because they thought it wrong (would have anticipatory guilt feelings at the very idea), and so that other people would be inclined to disapprove of persons who commit suicide unless there were some excuse (such as those mentioned in the first section). One might ask: how could it maximize utility to mold the conceptual and motivational structure of persons in this way? To which the answer might be: feeling in this way might make persons who are impulsively inclined to commit suicide in a bad mood, or a fit of anger or jealousy, take more time to deliberate; hence, some suicides that have bad effects generally might be prevented. In other words, it might be a good thing in its effects for people to feel about suicide in the way they feel about breach of promise or injuring others, just as it might be a good thing for people to feel a moral obligation not to smoke, or to wear seat belts. However, it might be that negative moral feelings about suicide as such would stand in the way of action by those persons whose welfare really is best served by suicide and whose suicide is the best thing for everybody concerned.

When a Decision to Commit Suicide Is Rational from the Person's Point of View

The person who is contemplating suicide is obviously making a choice between future world-courses; the world-course that includes his demise, say, an hour from now, and several possible ones that contain his demise at a later point. One cannot have precise knowledge about many features of the latter group of world-courses, but it is certain that they will all end with death some (possibly short) finite time from now.

Why do I say the choice is between *world-courses* and not just a choice between future life-courses of the prospective suicide, the one shorter than the other? The reason is that one's suicide has some impact on the world (and one's continued life has some impact on the world), and that conditions in the rest of the world will often make a difference in one's evaluation of the possibilities. One *is* interested in things in the world other than just oneself and one's own happiness.

The basic question a person must answer, in order to determine which world-course is best or rational for him to choose, is which he *would* choose under conditions of optimal use of information, when *all* of his desires are taken into account. It is not just a question of what we prefer *now*, with some clarification of all the possibilities being considered. Our preferences change, and the preferences of tomorrow (assuming we can know something about them) are just as legitimately taken into account in deciding what to do now as the preferences of today. Since any reason that can be given today for weighting heavily today's preference can be given tomorrow for weighting heavily tomorrow's preference, the preferences of any time-stretch have a rational claim to an equal vote. Now the importance of that fact is this: we often know quite well that our desires, aversions, and preferences may change after a short while. When a person is in a state of despair—perhaps brought about by a rejection in love or discharge from a long held position—nothing but the thing he cannot have seems desirable; everything else is turned to ashes. Yet we know

quite well that the passage of time is likely to reverse all this; replacements may be found or other types of things that are available to use may begin to look attractive. So, if we were to act on the preferences of today alone, when the emotion of despair seems more than we can stand, we might find death preferable to life; but if we allow for the preferences of the weeks and years ahead, when many goals will be enjoyable and attractive, we might find life much preferable to death. So, if a choice of what is best is to be determined by what we want not only now but later (and later desires on an equal basis with the present ones)—as it should be—then what is the best or preferable world-course will often be quite different from what it would be if the choice, or what is best for one, were fixed by one's desires and preferences now.

Of course, if one commits suicide there are no future desires or aversions that may be compared with present ones and that should be allowed an equal vote in deciding what is best. In that respect the course of action that results in death is different from any other course of action we may undertake. I do not wish to suggest the rosy possibility that it is often or always reasonable to believe that next week "I shall be more interested in living than I am today, if today I take a dim view of continued existence." On the contrary, when a person is seriously ill, for instance, he may have no reason to think that the preference-order will be reversed—it may be that tomorrow he will prefer death to life more strongly.

The argument is often used that one can never be *certain* what is going to happen, and hence one is never rationally justified in doing anything as drastic as committing suicide. But we always have to live by probabilities and make our estimates as best we can. As soon as it is clear beyond reasonable doubt not only that death is now preferable to life, but also that it will be every day from now until the end, the rational thing is to act promptly.

Let us not pursue the question of whether it is rational for a person with a painful terminal illness to commit suicide; it is. However, the issue seldom arises, and few terminally ill patients do commit suicide. With such patients matters usually get worse slowly so that no particular time seems to call for action. They are often so heavily sedated that it is impossible for the mental processes of decision leading to action to occur; or else they are incapacitated in a hospital and the very physical possibility of ending their lives is not available. Let us leave this grim topic and turn to a practically more important problem: whether it is rational for persons to commit suicide for some reason other than painful terminal physical illness. Most persons who commit suicide do so, apparently, because they face a nonphysical problem that depresses them beyond their ability to bear.

Among the problems that have been regarded as good and sufficient reasons for ending life, we find (in addition to serious illness) the following: some event that has made a person feel ashamed or lose his prestige and status; reduction from affluence to poverty; the loss of a limb or of physical beauty; the loss of sexual capacity; some event that makes it seem impossible to achieve things by which one sets store; loss of a loved one; disappointment in love; the infirmities of increasing age. It is not to be denied that such things can be serious blows to a person's prospects of happiness.

Whatever the nature of an individual's problem, there are various plain errors to be avoided—errors to which a person is especially prone when he is depressed—in deciding whether, everything considered, he prefers a world-course containing his early demise to one in which his life continues to its natural terminus. Let us forget for a moment the relevance to the decision of preferences that he may have tomorrow, and concentrate on some errors that may infect his preference as of today, and for which correction or allowance must be made.

In the first place, depression, like any severe emotional experience, tends to primitivize one's intellectual processes. It restricts the range of one's survey of the possibilities. One thing that a rational person would do is compare the world-course containing his suicide with his *best* alternative. But his best alternative is precisely a possibility he may overlook if, in a depressed mood, he thinks only of how badly off he is and cannot imagine any way of improving his situation. If a person is disappointed in love, it is possible to adopt a vigorous plan of action

that carries a good chance of acquainting him with someone he likes at least as well; and if old age prevents a person from continuing the tennis game with his favorite partner, it is possible to learn some other game that provides the joys of competition without the physical demands.

Depression has another insidious influence on one's planning: it seriously affects one's judgment about probabilities. A person disappointed in love is very likely to take a dim view of himself, his prospects, and his attractiveness; he thinks that because he has been rejected by one person he will probably be rejected by anyone who looks desirable to him. In a less gloomy frame of mind he would make different estimates. Part of the reason for such gloomy probability estimates is that depression tends to repress one's memory of evidence that supports a nongloomy prediction. Thus, a rejected lover tends to forget any cases in which he has elicited enthusiastic response from ladies in relation to whom he has been the one who has done the rejecting. Thus his pessimistic self-image is based upon a highly selected, and pessimistically selected, set of data. Even when he is reminded of the data, moreover, he is apt to resist an optimistic inference.

Another kind of distortion of the look of future prospects is not a result of depression, but is quite normal. Events distant in the future feel small, just as objects distant in space look small. Their prospect does not have the effect on motivational processes that it would have if it were of an event in the immediate future. Psychologists call this the "goal-gradient" phenomenon; a rat, for instance, will run faster toward a perceived food box than a distant unseen one. In the case of a person who has suffered some misfortune, and whose situation now is an unpleasant one, this reduction of the motivational influence of events distant in time has the effect that present unpleasant states weigh far more heavily than probable future pleasant ones in any choice of world-courses.

If we are trying to determine whether we now prefer, or shall later prefer, the outcome of the world-course to that of another (and this is leaving aside the questions of the weight of the votes of preferences at a later date), we must take into account these and other infirmities of our "sensing" machinery. Since knowing that the machinery is out of order will not tell us what results it would give if it were working, the best recourse might be to refrain from making any decision in a stressful frame of mind. If decisions have to be made, one must recall past reactions, in a normal frame of mind, to outcomes like those under assessment. But many suicides seem to occur in moments of despair. What should be clear from the above is that a moment of despair, if one is seriously contemplating suicide, ought to be a moment of reassessment of one's goals and values, a reassessment which the individual must realize is very difficult to make objectively, because of the very quality of his depressed frame of mind.

A decision to commit suicide may in certain circumstances be a rational one. But a person who wants to act rationally must take into account the various possible "errors" and make appropriate rectification of his initial evaluations.

Endnotes

1. Immanuel Kant, *Lectures on Ethics* (New York: Harper Torchbook, 1963), p. 150.

2. See St. Thomas Aquinas, *Summa Theologica,* Second Part of the Second Part, Q. 64, Art. 5. In Article 7, he says: "Nothing hinders one act from having two effects, only one of which is intended, while the other is beside the intention. Now moral acts take their species according to what is intended, and not according to what is beside the intention, since this is accidental as explained above" (Q. 43, Art. 3: I–II, Q. 1, Art. 3, as 3). Mr. Norman St. John-Stevas, the most articulate contemporary defender of the Catholic view, writes as follows: "Christian thought allows certain exceptions to its general condemnation of suicide. That covered by a particular divine inspiration has already been noted. Another exception arises where suicide is the method imposed by the State for the execution of a just death penalty. A third exception is *altruistic* suicide, of which the best known example is Captain Oates. Such suicides are justified by involving the principles of double effect. The act from which death results must be good or at least morally indifferent; some other good effect must result: The death must not be directly intended or the real means to the good effect: and a grave reason must exist for adopting the course of action" [*Life, Death and the Law* (Bloomington, Ind.: Indiana University Press, 1961), pp. 250–51]. Presumably the Catholic doctrine is intended to allow suicide when this is required for meeting strong moral obligations; whether it can do so consistently depends partly on the interpretation given to "real means to the good effect." Readers interested in pursuing further the Catholic doctrine of double effect and its implications for our problem should read Philippa Foot, "The Problem of Abortion and the Doctrine of Double Effect," *The Oxford Review*, 5 (Trinity 1967), 5–15.

3. R. B. Brandt, *Ethical Theory* (Englewood Cliffs, N.J.: Prentice-Hall, Inc., 1959), pp. 61–82.

4. John Locke, *The Second Treatise on Civil Government,* Chap. 2.

5. Kant, *Lectures on Ethics*, p. 154.

6. This essay appears in collections of Hume's works.

7. For an argument similar to Kant's, see also St. Thomas Aquinas, *Summa Theologica*, II, II, Q. 64, Art. 5.

8. Immanuel Kant, *The Fundamental Principles of the Metaphysic of Morals,* trans. H. J. Paton (London: The Hutchinson Group, 1948), Chap. 2.

9. Aristotle, *Nicomachaean Ethics*, Bk. 5, Chap. 10, p. 1138a.

10. St. Thomas Aquinas, *Summa Theologica*, II, II, Q. 64, Art. 5.

11. Sir William Blackstone, *Commentaries*, 4:189, Brown in *Hales* v. *Petit.* I Plow. 253, 75 E.R. 387 (C.B. 1563). Both cited by Norman St. John-Stevas, *Life, Death and the Law*, p. 235.

REVIEW QUESTIONS

1. What reasons does Brandt give for saying that suicide is not morally blameworthy?

2. When is suicide permissible according to Brandt?

3. How does he reply to theological arguments, the argument from natural law, and the arguments claiming that suicide necessarily harms others?

4. When is suicide rational in Brandt's view? When is it irrational?

DISCUSSION QUESTIONS

1. Do you agree with Brandt that it is rational for a person with a painful terminal illness to commit suicide? Why or why not?

2. Is it morally right for a person to commit suicide to save the lives of others? If so, is this morally required, that is, a duty?

J. Gay-Williams

The Wrongfulness of Euthanasia

J. Gay-Williams has requested that no biographical information be provided.

Gay-Williams defines "euthanasia" as intentionally taking the life of a presumably hopeless person. Suicide can count as euthanasia, but not "passive euthanasia" because the latter does not involve intentional killing. Three main arguments are presented to show that euthanasia is wrong: the argument from nature, the argument from self-interest, and the argument from practical effects.

My impression is that euthanasia—the idea, if not the practice—is slowly gaining acceptance within our society. Cynics might attribute this to an increasing tendency to devalue human life, but I do not believe this is the major factor. The acceptance is much more likely to be the result of unthinking sympathy and benevolence. Well-publicized, tragic stories like that of Karen Quinlan elicit from us deep feelings of compassion. We think to ourselves, "She and her family would be better off if she were dead." It is an easy step from this very human response to the view that if someone (and others) would be better off dead, then it must be all right to kill that person.[1] Although I respect the compassion that leads to this conclusion, I believe the conclusion is wrong. I want to show that euthanasia is wrong. It is inherently wrong, but it is also wrong judged from the standpoints of self-interest and of practical effects.

Before presenting my arguments to support this claim, it would be well to define "euthana-sia." An essential aspect of euthanasia is that it involves taking a human life, either one's own or that of another. Also, the person whose life is taken must be someone who is believed to be suffering from some disease or injury from which recovery cannot reasonably be expected. Finally, the action must be deliberate and intentional. Thus, euthanasia is intentionally taking the life of a presumably hopeless person. Whether the life is one's own or that of another, the taking of it is still euthanasia.

It is important to be clear about the deliberate and intentional aspect of the killing. If a hopeless person is given an injection of the wrong drug by mistake and this causes his death, this is wrongful killing but not euthanasia. The killing cannot be the result of accident. Furthermore, if the person is given an injection of a drug that is believed to be necessary to treat his disease or better his condition and the person dies as a result, then this is neither wrongful killing nor euthanasia. The intention was to make the patient well, not kill him. Similarly, when a patient's condition is such that it is not reasonable to hope that any medical procedures or treatments will save his life, a failure to implement the procedures or treatments is not euthanasia. If the person dies, this will be as a result of his injuries or disease and not because of his failure to receive treatment.

The failure to continue treatment after it has been realized that the patient has little chance of benefiting from it has been characterized by some as "passive euthanasia." This phrase is misleading and mistaken.[2] In such cases, the person involved is not killed (the first essential aspect of euthanasia), nor is the death of the person intended by the withholding of additional treatment (the third essential aspect of euthanasia). The aim may be to spare the person additional and unjustifiable pain, to save him from the indignities of hopeless manipulations, and to avoid increasing the financial and emotional burden on his family. When I buy a pencil it is so that I can use it to write, not to contribute to an increase in the gross national product. This may be the unintended consequence of my action, but it is not the aim of my action. So it is with failing to continue the treatment of a dying person. I intend his death no more than I intend to reduce the GNP by not using medical supplies. His is an unintended dying, and so-called "passive euthanasia" is not euthanasia at all.

THE ARGUMENT FROM NATURE

Every human being has a natural inclination to continue living. Our reflexes and responses fit us to fight attackers, flee wild animals, and dodge out of the way of trucks. In our daily lives we exercise the caution and care necessary to protect ourselves. Our bodies are similarly structured for survival right down to the molecular level. When we are cut, our capillaries seal shut, our blood clots, and fibrinogen is produced to start the process of healing the wound. When we are invaded by bacteria, antibodies are produced to fight against the alien organisms, and their remains are swept out of the body by special cells designed for clean-up work.

Euthanasia does violence to this natural goal of survival. It is literally acting against nature because all the processes of nature are bent towards the end of bodily survival. Euthanasia defeats these subtle mechanisms in a way that, in a particular case, disease and injury might not.

It is possible, but not necessary, to make an appeal to revealed religion in this connection.[3] Man as trustee of his body acts against God, its rightful possessor, when he takes his own life. He also violates the commandment to hold life sacred and never to take it without just and compelling cause. But since this appeal will persuade only those who are prepared to accept that religion has access to revealed truths, I shall not employ this line of argument.

It is enough, I believe, to recognize that the organization of the human body and our patterns of behavioral responses make the continuation of life a natural goal. By reason alone, then, we can recognize that euthanasia sets us against our own nature.[4] Furthermore, in doing so, euthanasia does violence to our dignity. Our dignity comes from seeking our ends. When one of our goals is survival, and actions are taken that eliminate that goal, then our natural dignity suffers. Unlike animals, we are conscious through reason of our nature and our ends. Euthanasia involves acting as if this dual nature—inclination towards survival and awareness of this as an end—did not exist. Thus, euthanasia denies our basic human character and requires that we regard ourselves or others as something less than fully human.

THE ARGUMENT FROM SELF-INTEREST

The above arguments are, I believe, sufficient to show that euthanasia is inherently wrong. But there are reasons for considering it wrong when judged by standards other than reason. Because death is final and irreversible, euthanasia contains within it the possibility that we will work against our own interest if we practice it or allow it to be practiced on us.

Contemporary medicine has high standards of excellence and a proven record of accomplishment, but it does not possess perfect and complete knowledge. A mistaken diagnosis is possible, and so is a mistaken prognosis. Consequently, we may believe that we are dying of a disease when, as a matter of fact, we may not be. We may think that we have no hope of recovery when, as a matter of fact, our chances are quite good. In such circumstances, if euthanasia were permitted, we would die needlessly. Death is final and the chance of error too great to approve the practice of euthanasia.

Also, there is always the possibility that an experimental procedure or a hitherto untried technique will pull us through. We should at least keep this option open, but euthanasia closes it off. Furthermore, spontaneous remission does occur in many cases. For no apparent reason, a patient simply recovers when those all around him, including his physicians, expected him to die. Euthanasia would just guarantee their expectations and leave no room for the "miraculous" recoveries that frequently occur.

Finally, knowing that we can take our life at any time (or ask another to take it) might well incline us to give up too easily. The will to live is strong in all of us, but it can be weakened by pain and suffering and feelings of hopelessness.

If during a bad time we allow ourselves to be killed, we never have a chance to reconsider. Recovery from a serious illness requires that we fight for it, and anything that weakens our determination by suggesting that there is an easy way out is ultimately against our own interest. Also, we may be inclined towards euthanasia because of our concern for others. If we see our sickness and suffering as an emotional and financial burden on our family, we may feel that to leave our life is to make their lives easier.[5] The very presence of the possibility of euthanasia may keep us from surviving when we might.

THE ARGUMENT FROM PRACTICAL EFFECTS

Doctors and nurses are, for the most part, totally committed to saving lives. A life lost is, for them, almost a personal failure, an insult to their skills and knowledge. Euthanasia as a practice might well alter this. It could have a corrupting influence so that in any case that is severe doctors and nurses might not try hard enough to save the patient. They might decide that the patient would simply be "better off dead" and take the steps necessary to make that come about. This attitude could then carry over to their dealings with patients less seriously ill. The result would be an overall decline in the quality of medical care.

Finally, euthanasia as a policy is a slippery slope. A person apparently hopelessly ill may be allowed to take his own life. Then he may be permitted to deputize others to do it for him should he no longer be able to act. The judgment of others then becomes the ruling factor. Already at this point euthanasia is not personal and voluntary, for others are acting "on behalf of" the patient as they see fit. This may well incline them to act on behalf of other patients who have not authorized them to exercise their judgment. It is only a short step, then, from voluntary euthanasia (self-inflicted or authorized), to directed euthanasia administered to a patient who has given no authorization, to involuntary euthanasia conducted as part of a social policy.[6] Recently many psychiatrists and sociologists

have argued that we define as "mental illness" those forms of behavior that we disapprove of.[7] This gives us license then to lock up those who display the behavior. The category of the "hopelessly ill" provides the possibility of even worse abuse. Embedded in a social policy, it would give society or its representatives the authority to eliminate all those who might be considered too "ill" to function normally any longer. The dangers of euthanasia are too great to all to run the risk of approving it in any form. The first slippery step may well lead to a serious and harmful fall.

I hope that I have succeeded in showing why the benevolence that inclines us to give approval of euthanasia is misplaced. Euthanasia is inherently wrong because it violates the nature and dignity of human beings. But even those who are not convinced by this must be persuaded that the potential personal and social dangers inherent in euthanasia are sufficient to forbid our approving it either as a personal practice or as a public policy.

Suffering is surely a terrible thing, and we have a clear duty to comfort those in need and to ease their suffering when we can. But suffering is also a natural part of life with values for the individual and for others that we should not overlook. We may legitimately seek for others and for ourselves an easeful death, as Arthur Dyck has pointed out.[8] Euthanasia, however, is not just an easeful death. It is a wrongful death. Euthanasia is not just dying. It is killing.

Endnotes

1. For a sophisticated defense of this position see Philippa Foot, "Euthanasia," *Philosophy and Public Affairs* 6 (1977): 85–112. Foot does not endorse the radical conclusion that euthanasia, voluntary and involuntary, is always right.
2. James Rachels rejects the distinction between active and passive euthanasia as morally irrelevant in his "Active and Passive Euthanasia," *New England Journal of Medicine,* 292: 78–80. But see the criticism by Foot, pp. 100–103.
3. For a defense of this view see J. V. Sullivan, "The Immorality of Euthanasia," in *Beneficent Euthanasia,* ed. Marvin Kohl (Buffalo, NY: Prometheus Books, 1975), pp. 34–44.
4. This point is made by Ray V. McIntyre in "Voluntary Euthanasia: The Ultimate Perversion," *Medical Counterpoint* 2: 26–29.
5. See McIntyre, p. 28.

6. See Sullivan, "Immorality of Euthanasia," pp. 34–44, for a fuller argument in support of this view.
7. See, for example, Thomas S. Szasz, *The Myth of Mental Illness*, rev. ed. (New York: Harper & Row, 1974).
8. Arthur Dyck, "Beneficent Euthanasia and Benemortasia," Kohl, op. cit., pp. 117–129.

REVIEW QUESTIONS

1. How does Gay-Williams define euthanasia?
2. Why does he object to the phrase "passive euthanasia"?
3. Explain the three arguments he uses to show that euthanasia is wrong.

DISCUSSION QUESTIONS

1. Is Gay-Williams' definition of euthanasia acceptable? Defend your view.
2. Are his arguments sound or not?

James Rachels

Active and Passive Euthanasia

For biographical information on Rachels, see his reading in Chapter 1.

Here Rachels attacks the distinction between active and passive euthanasia, and the doctrine apparently accepted by the American Medical Association that taking direct action to kill a patient (active euthanasia) is wrong, but withholding treatment and allowing a patient to die (passive euthanasia) is allowable. Rachels makes three criticisms of this doctrine. First, it results in unnecessary suffering for patients who die slowly and painfully rather than quickly and painlessly. Second, the doctrine leads to moral decisions based on irrelevant considerations. Third, the distinction between killing and letting die assumed by the doctrine is of no moral significance.

The distinction between active and passive euthanasia is thought to be crucial for medical ethics. The idea is that it is permissible, at least in some cases, to withhold treatment and allow a patient to die, but it is never permissible to take any direct action designed to kill the pa-

From James Rachels, "Active and Passive Euthanasia," *The New England Journal of Medicine*, vol. 292, no. 2 (9 January 1975): 79–80.

tient. This doctrine seems to be accepted by most doctors, and it is endorsed in a statement adopted by the House of Delegates of the American Medical Association on December 4, 1973:

The intentional termination of the life of one human being by another—mercy killing—is contrary to that for which the medical profession stands and is contrary to the policy of the American Medical Association. The cessation of the employment of extraordinary means to prolong the life of the body when there is irrefutable evidence that biological death is imminent is the decision of the patient and/or his immediate family. The advice and judgment of the physician should be freely available to the patient and/or his immediate family.

However, a strong case can be made against this doctrine. In what follows I will set out some of the relevant arguments, and urge doctors to reconsider their views on this matter.

To begin with a familiar type of situation, a patient who is dying of incurable cancer of the throat is in terrible pain, which can no longer be satisfactorily alleviated. He is certain to die within a few days, even if present treatment is continued, but he does not want to go on living for those days since the pain is unbearable. So he asks the doctor for an end to it, and his family joins in the request.

Suppose the doctor agrees to withhold treatment, as the conventional doctrine says he may. The justification for his doing so is that the patient is in terrible agony, and since he is going to die anyway, it would be wrong to prolong his suffering needlessly. But now notice this. If one simply withholds treatment, it may take the patient longer to die, and so he may suffer more than he would if more direct action were taken and a lethal injection given. This fact provides strong reason for thinking that, once the initial decision not to prolong his agony has been made, active euthanasia is actually preferable to passive euthanasia, rather than the reverse. To say otherwise is to endorse the option that leads to more suffering rather than less, and is contrary to the humanitarian impulse that prompts the decision not to prolong his life in the first place.

Part of my point is that the process of being "allowed to die" can be relatively slow and painful, whereas being given a lethal injection is relatively quick and painless. Let me give a different sort of example. In the United States about one in 600 babies is born with Down's syndrome. Most of these babies are otherwise healthy—that is, with only the usual pediatric care, they will proceed to an otherwise normal infancy. Some, however, are born with congenital defects such as intestinal obstructions that require operations if they are to live. Sometimes, the parents and the doctor will decide not to operate, and let the infant die. Anthony Shaw describes what happens then:

... When surgery is denied [the doctor] must try to keep the infant from suffering while natural forces sap the baby's life away. As a surgeon whose natural inclination is to use the scalpel to fight off death, standing by and watching a salvageable baby die is the most emotionally exhausting experience I know. It is easy at a conference, in a theoretical discussion, to decide that such infants should be allowed to die. It is altogether different to stand by in the nursery and watch as dehydration and infection wither a tiny being over hours and days. This is a terrible ordeal for me and the hospital staff—much more so than for the parents who never set foot in the nursery.[1]

I can understand why some people are opposed to all euthanasia, and insist that such infants must be allowed to live. I think I can also understand why other people favor destroying these babies quickly and painlessly. But why should anyone favor letting "dehydration and infection wither a tiny being over hours and days"? The doctrine that says that a baby may

be allowed to dehydrate and wither, but may not be given an injection that would end its life without suffering, seems so patently cruel as to require no further refutation. The strong language is not intended to offend, but only to put the point in the clearest possible way.

My second argument is that the conventional doctrine leads to decisions concerning life and death made on irrelevant grounds.

Consider again the case of the infants with Down's syndrome who need operations for congenital defects unrelated to the syndrome to live. Sometimes, there is no operation, and the baby dies, but when there is no such defect, the baby lives on. Now, an operation such as that to remove an intestinal obstruction is not prohibitively difficult. The reason why such operations are not performed in these cases is, clearly, that the child has Down's syndrome and the parents and doctor judge that because of that fact it is better for the child to die.

But notice that this situation is absurd, no matter what view one takes of the lives and potentials of such babies. If the life of such an infant is worth preserving, what does it matter if it needs a simple operation? Or, if one thinks it better that such a baby should not live on, what difference does it make that it happens to have an unobstructed intestinal tract? In either case, the matter of life and death is being decided on irrelevant grounds. It is the Down's syndrome, and not the intestines, that is the issue. The matter should be decided, if at all, on that basis, and not be allowed to depend on the essentially irrelevant question of whether the intestinal tract is blocked.

What makes this situation possible, of course, is the idea that when there is an intestinal blockage, one can "let the baby die," but when there is no such defect there is nothing that can be done, for one must not "kill" it. The fact that this idea leads to such results as deciding life or death on irrelevant grounds is another good reason why the doctrine should be rejected.

One reason why so many people think that there is an important moral difference between active and passive euthanasia is that they think killing someone is morally worse than letting someone die. But is it? Is killing, in itself, worse than letting die? To investigate this issue, two cases may be considered that are exactly alike except that one involves killing whereas the other involves letting someone die. Then, it can be asked whether this difference makes any difference to the moral assessments. It is important that the cases be exactly alike, except for this one difference, since otherwise one cannot be confident that it is this difference and not some other that accounts for any variation in the assessments of the two cases. So, let us consider this pair of cases:

In the first, Smith stands to gain a large inheritance if anything should happen to his six-year-old cousin. One evening while the child is taking his bath, Smith sneaks into the bathroom and drowns the child, and then arranges things so that it will look like an accident.

In the second, Jones also stands to gain if anything should happen to his six-year-old cousin. Like Smith, Jones sneaks in planning to drown the child in his bath. However, just as he enters the bathroom Jones sees the child slip and hit his head, and fall face down in the water. Jones is delighted; he stands by, ready to push the child's head back under if it is necessary, but it is not necessary. With only a little thrashing about, the child drowns all by himself, "accidentally," as Jones watches and does nothing.

Now Smith killed the child, whereas Jones "merely" let the child die. That is the only difference between them. Did either man behave better, from a moral point of view? If the difference between killing and letting die were in itself a morally important matter, one should say that Jones's behavior was less reprehensible than Smith's. But does one really want to say that? I think not. In the first place, both men acted from the same motive, personal gain, and both had exactly the same end in view when they acted. It may be inferred from Smith's conduct that he is a bad man, although that judgment may be withdrawn or modified if certain further facts are learned about him—for example, that he is mentally deranged. But would not the very same thing be inferred about Jones from his conduct? And would not the same further considerations also be relevant to any modification of this judgment? Moreover, suppose Jones pleaded, in his own defense, "After all, I didn't do anything except just stand there and watch the child drown. I didn't kill him; I only let him die." Again, if letting die were in itself less bad than killing, this defense should have at least some weight. But it does not. Such a "defense" can only be regarded as a grotesque perversion of moral reasoning. Morally speaking, it is no defense at all.

Now, it may be pointed out, quite properly, that the cases of euthanasia with which doctors are concerned are not like this at all. They do not involve personal gain or the destruction of normal healthy children. Doctors are concerned only with cases in which the patient's life is of no further use to him, or in which the patient's life has become or will soon become a terrible burden. However, the point is the same in these cases: the bare difference between killing and letting die does not, in itself, make a moral difference. If a doctor lets a patient die, for humane reasons, he is in the same moral position as if he had given the patient a lethal injection for humane reasons. If his decision was wrong—if, for example, the patient's illness was in fact curable—the decision would be equally regrettable no matter which method was used to carry it out. And if the doctor's decision was the right one, the method used is not in itself important.

The AMA policy statement isolates the crucial issue very well; the crucial issue is "the intentional termination of the life of one human being by another." But after identifying this issue, and forbidding "mercy killing," the statement goes on to deny that the cessation of treatment is the intentional termination of a life. This is where the mistake comes in, for what is the cessation of treatment, in these circumstances, if it is not "the intentional termination of the life of one human being by another"? Of course it is exactly that, and if it were not, there would be no point to it.

Many people will find this judgment hard to accept. One reason, I think, is that it is very easy to conflate the question of whether killing is, in itself, worse than letting die, with the very different question of whether most actual cases of killing are more reprehensible than most actual cases of letting die. Most actual cases of killing are clearly terrible (think, for example, of all the murders reported in the newspapers), and one hears of such cases every day. On the other hand, one hardly ever hears of a case of letting die, except for the actions of doctors who are motivated by humanitarian reasons. So one learns to think of killing in a much worse light than of letting die. But this does not mean that there is something about killing that makes it in itself worse than letting die, for it is not the bare difference between killing and letting die that makes the difference in these cases. Rather, the other factors—the murderer's motive of personal gain, for example, contrasted with the doctor's humanitarian motivation—account for different reactions to the different cases.

I have argued that killing is not in itself any worse than letting die; if my contention is right, it follows that active euthanasia is not any worse than passive euthanasia. What arguments can be given on the other side? The most common, I believe, is the following:

The important difference between active and passive euthanasia is that, in passive euthanasia, the doctor does not do anything to bring about the patient's death. The doctor does nothing, and the patient dies of whatever ills already afflict him. In active euthanasia, however, the doctor does something to bring about the patient's death: he kills him. The doctor who gives the patient with cancer a lethal injection has himself caused his patient's death; whereas if he merely ceases treatment, the cancer is the cause of the death.

A number of points need to be made here. The first is that it is not exactly correct to say that in passive euthanasia the doctor does nothing, for he does do one thing that is very important: he lets the patient die. "Letting someone die" is certainly different, in some respects, from other types of action—mainly in that it is a kind of action that one may perform by way of not performing certain other actions. For example, one may let a patient die by way of not giving medication, just as one may insult someone by way of not shaking his hand. But for any purpose of moral assessment, it is a type of action nonetheless. The decision to let a patient die is subject to moral appraisal in the same way that a decision to kill him would be subject to moral appraisal: it may be assessed as wise or unwise, compassionate or sadistic, right or wrong. If a

doctor deliberately let a patient die who was suffering from a routinely curable illness, the doctor would certainly be to blame for what he had done, just as he would be to blame if he had needlessly killed the patient. Charges against him would then be appropriate. If so, it would be no defense at all for him to insist that he didn't "do anything." He would have done something very serious indeed, for he let his patient die.

Fixing the cause of death may be very important from a legal point of view, for it may determine whether criminal charges are brought against the doctor. But I do not think that this notion can be used to show a moral difference between active and passive euthanasia. The reason why it is considered bad to be the cause of someone's death is that death is regarded as a great evil—and so it is. However, if it has been decided that euthanasia—even passive euthanasia—is desirable in a given case, it has also been decided that in this instance death is no greater an evil than the patient's continued existence. And if this is true, the usual reason for not wanting to be the cause of someone's death simply does not apply.

Finally, doctors may think that all of this is only of academic interest—the sort of thing that philosophers may worry about but that has no practical bearing on their own work. After all, doctors must be concerned about the legal consequences of what they do, and active euthanasia is clearly forbidden by the law. But even so, doctors should also be concerned with the fact that the law is forcing upon them a moral doctrine that may well be indefensible, and has a considerable effect on their practices. Of course, most doctors are not now in the position of being coerced in this matter, for they do not regard themselves as merely going along with what the law requires. Rather in statements such as the AMA policy statement that I have quoted, they are endorsing this doctrine as a central point of medical ethics. In that statement, active euthanasia is condemned not merely as illegal but as "contrary to that for which the medical profession stands," whereas passive euthanasia is approved. However, the preceding considerations suggest that there is really no moral difference between the two, considered in themselves (there may be important moral differences in some case in their *consequences*, but, as I pointed out, these differences may make active euthanasia, and not passive euthanasia, the morally preferable option). So, whereas doctors may have to discriminate between active and passive euthanasia to satisfy the law, they should not do any more than that. In particular, they should not give the distinction any added authority and weight by writing it into official statements of medical ethics.

Endnote

1. A. Shaw, "Doctor, Do We Have a Choice?" *The New York Times Magazine,* January 30, 1972, p. 54.

REVIEW QUESTIONS

1. According to Rachels, what is the distinction between active and passive euthanasia?

2. Why does Rachels think that being allowed to die is worse in some cases than a lethal injection?
3. What is Rachels' second argument against the conventional doctrine?
4. According to Rachels, why isn't killing worse than letting die?

DISCUSSION QUESTIONS

1. The AMA statement quoted by Rachels does not use the terminology of active and passive euthanasia. Furthermore, so-called passive euthanasia could be the intentional termination of life rejected by the AMA. Does the AMA really accept this distinction? Why or why not?
2. Is the distinction between killing and letting die morally relevant? What do you think?
3. Should the law be changed to allow active euthanasia or not? Defend your view.

Bonnie Steinbock

The Intentional Termination of Life

Bonnie Steinbock is professor of philosophy at the State University of New York at Albany. She is the editor of Killing and Letting Die *(1980) and the author of* Life Before Birth *(1992).*

Steinbock defends the AMA statement on euthanasia from the attack made by Rachels. She argues that the AMA statement does not make the distinction between active and passive euthanasia that Rachels attacks. According to Steinbock, the AMA statement instead rejects both active and passive euthanasia, but does permit the cessation

Reprinted with permission from *Ethics in Science and Medicine* (now *Social Science and Medicine*), vol. 6, no. 1, pp. 59–64, Bonnie Steinbock, "The Intentional Termination of Life," 1979, Elsevier Science Ltd., Oxford, England.

of extraordinary means of treatment. This is not the same as passive euthanasia. Cessation of extraordinary means can be done to respect the patient's right to refuse treatment or because continued treatment is painful; neither reason is the same as letting the patient die. She grants, however, that in some cases the cessation of extraordinary means does amount to letting the patient die and that in some cases a quick and painless death may be preferable to letting a patient die slowly.

According to James Rachels[1] a common mistake in medical ethics is the belief that there is a moral difference between active and passive euthanasia. This is a mistake, [he] argues, because the rationale underlying the distinction between active and passive euthanasia is the idea that there is a significant moral difference between intentionally killing and letting die. . . . Whether the belief that there is a significant moral difference (between intentionally killing and intentionally letting die) is mistaken is not my concern here. For it is far from clear that this distinction *is* the basis of the doctrine of the

American Medical Association which Rachels attacks. And if the killing/letting die distinction is not the basis of the AMA doctrine, then arguments showing that the distinction has no moral force do not, in themselves, reveal in the doctrine's adherents either "confused thinking" or "a moral point of view unrelated to the interests of individuals." Indeed, as we examine the AMA doctrine, I think it will become clear that it appeals to and makes use of a number of overlapping distinctions, which may have moral significance in particular cases, such as the distinction between intending and foreseeing, or between ordinary and extraordinary care. Let us then turn to the statement, from the House of Delegates of the American Medical Association, which Rachels cites:

The intentional termination of the life of one human being by another—mercy-killing—is contrary to that for which the medical profession stands and is contrary to the policy of the American Medical Association. The cessation of the employment of extraordinary means to prolong the life of the body when there is irrefutable evidence that biological death is imminent is the decision of the patient and/or his immediate family. The advice and judgment of the physician should be freely available to the patient and/or his immediate family.[2]

Rachels attacks this statement because he believes that it contains a moral distinction between active and passive euthanasia. . . .

I intend to show that the AMA statement does not imply support of the active/passive euthanasia distinction. In forbidding the intentional termination of life, the statement rejects both active and passive euthanasia. It does allow for ". . . the cessation of the employment of extraordinary means . . ." to prolong life. The mistake Rachels makes is in identifying the cessation of life-prolonging treatment with passive euthanasia, or intentionally letting die. If it were right to equate the two, then the AMA statement would be self-contradictory, for it would begin by condemning, and end by allowing, the intentional termination of life. But if the cessation of life-prolonging treatment is not always or necessarily passive euthanasia, then there is no confusion and no contradiction.

Why does Rachels think that the cessation of life-prolonging treatment is the intentional termination of life? He says:

The AMA policy statement isolates the crucial issue very well: the crucial issue is "the intentional termination of the life of one human being by another." But after identifying this issue, and forbidding "mercy-killing," the statement goes on to deny that the cessation of treatment is the intentional termination of a life. That is where the mistake comes in, for what is the cessation of treatment, in these circumstances, if it is not "the intentional termination of the life of one human being by another"? Of course it is exactly that, and if it were not, there would be no point to it.[3]

However, there *can* be a point (to the cessation of life-prolonging treatment) other than an endeavor to bring about the patient's death, and so the blanket identification of cessation of treatment with the intentional termination of a life is inaccurate. There are at least two situations in which the termination of life-prolonging treatment cannot be identified with the intentional termination of the life of one human being by another.

The first situation concerns the patient's right to refuse treatment. Rachels gives the example of a patient dying of an incurable disease, accompanied by unrelievable pain, who wants to end the treatment which cannot cure him but can only prolong his miserable existence. Why, they ask, may a doctor accede to the patient's request to stop treatment, but not provide a patient in a similar situation with a lethal dose? The answer lies in the patient's right to refuse treatment. In general, a competent adult has the right to refuse treatment, even where such treatment is necessary to prolong life. Indeed, the right to refuse treatment has been upheld even when the patient's reason for refusing treatment is generally agreed to be inadequate.[4] This right can be overridden (if, for example, the patient has dependent children) but, in general, no one may legally compel you to undergo treatment to which you have not consented. "Historically, surgical intrusion has always been considered a technical battery upon the person and one to be excused or justified by consent of the patient or justified by necessity created by the circumstances of the moment. . . ." [5]

At this point, it might be objected that if one has the right to refuse life-prolonging treatment, then consistency demands that one have the right to decide to end his life, and to obtain help in doing so. The idea is that the right to refuse treatment somehow implies a right to voluntary euthanasia, and we need to see why someone might think this. The right to refuse treatment has been considered by legal writers as an example of the right to privacy or, better, the right to bodily self-determination. You have the right to decide what happens to your own body, and the right to refuse treatment is an instance of that more general right. But if you have the right to determine what happens to your body, then should you not have the right to choose to end your life, and even a right to get help in doing so?

However, it is important to see that the right to refuse treatment is not the same as, nor does it entail, a right to voluntary euthanasia, even if both can be derived from the right to bodily self-determination. The right to refuse treatment is not itself a "right to die"; that one may choose to exercise this right even at the risk of death, or even *in order to die,* is irrelevant. The purpose of the right to refuse medical treatment is not to give persons a right to decide whether to live or die, but to protect them from the unwanted interferences of others. Perhaps we ought to interpret the right to bodily self-determination more broadly so as to include a right to die: but this would be a substantial extension of our present understanding of the right to bodily self-determination, and not a consequence of it. Should we recognize a right to voluntary euthanasia, we would have to agree that people have the right not merely to be left alone, but also the right to be killed. I leave to one side that substantive moral issue. My claim is simply that there can be a reason for terminating life-prolonging treatment other than "to bring about the patient's death."

The second case in which termination of treatment cannot be identified with intentional termination of life is where continued treatment has little chance of improving the patient's condition and brings greater discomfort than relief.

The question here is what treatment is appropriate to the particular case. A cancer specialist describes it in this way:

My general rule is to administer therapy as long as a patient responds well and has the potential for a reasonably good quality of life. But when all feasible therapies have been administered and a patient shows signs of rapid deterioration, the continuation of therapy can cause more discomfort than the cancer. From that time I recommend surgery, radiotherapy, or chemotherapy only as a means of relieving pain. But if a patient's condition should once again stabilize after the withdrawal of active therapy and if it should appear that he could still gain some good time, I would immediately reinstitute active therapy. The decision to cease anticancer treatment is never irrevocable, and often the desire to live will push a patient to try for another remission, or even a few more days of life.[6]

The decision here to cease anticancer treatment cannot be construed as a decision that the patient die, or as the intentional termination of life. It is a decision to provide the most appropriate treatment for that patient at that time. Rachels suggests that the point of the cessation of treatment is the intentional termination of life. But here the point of discontinuing treatment is not to bring about the patient's death, but to avoid treatment that will cause more discomfort than the cancer and has little hope of benefiting the patient. Treatment that meets this description is often called "extraordinary." [7] The concept is flexible, and what might be considered "extraordinary" in one situation might be ordinary in another. The use of a respirator to sustain a patient through a severe bout with a respiratory disease would be considered ordinary; its use to sustain the life of a severely brain damaged person in an irreversible coma would be considered extraordinary.

Contrasted with extraordinary treatment is ordinary treatment, the care a doctor would normally be expected to provide. Failure to provide ordinary care constitutes neglect, and can even be construed as the intentional infliction of harm, where there is a legal obligation to provide care. The importance of ordinary/extraordinary care distinction lies partly in its connection to the doctor's intention. The withholding of extraordinary care should be seen as a decision not to inflict painful treatment on a patient without reasonable hope of success. The withholding of ordinary care, by contrast, must be seen as neglect. Thus, one doctor says, "We have to draw a distinction between ordinary and extraordinary means. We never withdraw what's needed to make a baby comfortable, we would never withdraw the care a parent would provide. We never kill a baby. . . . But we may decide certain heroic intervention is not worthwhile." [8]

We should keep in mind the ordinary/extraordinary care distinction when considering an example given by Rachels to show the irrationality of the active/passive distinction with regard to infanticide. The example is this: a child is born with Down's syndrome and also has an intestinal obstruction which requires corrective surgery. If the surgery is not performed, the infant will starve to death, since it cannot take food orally. This may take days or even weeks, as dehydration and infection set in. Commenting on this situation, Rachels says:

I can understand why some people are opposed to all euthanasia, and insist that such infants must be allowed to live. I think I can also understand why other people favor destroying these babies quickly and painlessly. But why should anyone favor letting "dehydration and infection wither a tiny being over hours and days"? The doctrine that says that a baby may be allowed to dehydrate and wither, but may not be given an injection that would end its life without suffering, seems so patently cruel as to require no further refutation.[9]

Such a doctrine perhaps does not need further refutation; but this is not the AMA doctrine. For the AMA statement criticized by Rachels allows only for the cessation of extraordinary means to prolong life when death is imminent. Neither of these conditions is satisfied in this example. Death is not imminent in this situation, any more than it would be if a normal child had an attack of appendicitis. Neither the corrective surgery to remove the intestinal obstruction, nor the intravenous feeding required to keep the infant alive until such surgery is performed, can be regarded as extraordinary means, for neither is particularly expensive, nor does either place

an overwhelming burden on the patient or others. (The continued existence of the child might be thought to place an overwhelming burden on its parents, but that has nothing to do with the characterization of the means to prolong its life as extraordinary. If it had, then *feeding* a severely defective child who required a great deal of care could be regarded as extraordinary.) The chances of success if the operation is undertaken are quite good, though there is always a risk in operating on infants. Though the Down's syndrome will not be alleviated, the child will proceed to an otherwise normal infancy.

It cannot be argued that the treatment is withheld for the infant's sake, unless one is prepared to argue that all mentally retarded babies are better off dead. This is particularly implausible in the case of Down's syndrome babies who generally do not suffer and are capable of giving and receiving love, of learning and playing, to varying degrees.

In a film on this subject entitled, "Who Should Survive?", a doctor defended a decision not to operate, saying that since the parents did not consent to the operation, the doctors' hands were tied. As we have seen, surgical intrusion requires consent, and in the case of infants, consent would normally come from the parents. But, as their legal guardians, parents are required to provide medical care for their children, and failure to do so can constitute criminal neglect or even homicide. In general, courts have been understandably reluctant to recognize a parental right to terminate life-prolonging treatment.[10] Although prosecution is unlikely, physicians who comply with invalid instructions from the parents and permit the infant's death could be liable for aiding and abetting, failure to report child neglect, or even homicide. So it is not true that, in this situation, doctors are legally bound to do as the parents wish.

To sum up, I think that Rachels is right to regard the decision not to operate in the Down's syndrome example as the intentional termination of life. But there is no reason to believe that either the law or the AMA would regard it otherwise. Certainly the decision to withhold treatment is not justified by the AMA statement. That such infants have been allowed to die cannot be denied; but this, I think, is the result of doctors misunderstanding the law and the AMA position.

Withholding treatment in this case is the intentional termination of life because the infant is deliberately allowed to die; that is the point of not operating. But there are other cases in which that is not the point. If the point is to avoid inflicting painful treatment on a patient with little or no reasonable hope of success, this is not the intentional termination of life. The permissibility of such withholding of treatment, then, would have no implications for the permissibility of euthanasia, active or passive.

The decision whether or not to operate, or to institute vigorous treatment, is particularly agonizing in the case of children born with spina bifida, an opening in the base of the spine usually accompanied by hydrocephalus and mental retardation. If left unoperated, these children usually die of meningitis or kidney failure within the first few years of life. Even if they survive, all affected children face a lifetime of illness, operations and varying degrees of disability. The policy used to be to save as many as possible, but the trend now is toward selective treatment, based on the physician's estimate of the chances of success. If operating is not likely to improve significantly the child's condition, parents and doctors may agree not to operate. This is not the intentional termination of life, for again the purpose is not the termination of the child's life but the avoidance of painful and pointless treatment. Thus, the fact that withholding treatment is justified does not imply that killing the child would be equally justified.

Throughout the discussion, I have claimed that intentionally ceasing life-prolonging treatment is not the intentional termination of life unless the doctor has, as his or her purpose in stopping treatment, the patient's death.

It may be objected that I have incorrectly characterized the conditions for the intentional termination of life. Perhaps it is enough that the doctor intentionally ceases treatment, foreseeing that the patient will die; perhaps the reason for ceasing treatment is irrelevant to its characterization as the intentional termination of life. I find this suggestion implausible, but am willing to consider arguments for it. Rachels has provided no such arguments: indeed, he apparently shares

my view about the intentional termination of life. For when he claims that the cessation of life-prolonging treatment is the intentional termination of life, his reason for making the claim is that "if it were not, there would be no point to it." Rachels believes that the point of ceasing treatment, "in these cases," is to bring about the patient's death. If that were not the point, he suggests, why would the doctor cease treatment? I have shown, however, that there can be a point to ceasing treatment which is not the death of the patient. In showing this, I have refuted Rachels' reason for identifying the cessation of life-prolonging treatment with the intentional termination of life, and thus his argument against the AMA doctrine.

Here someone might say: Even if the withholding of treatment is not the intentional termination of life, does that make a difference, morally speaking? If life-prolonging treatment may be withheld, for the sake of the child, may not an easy death be provided, for the sake of the child, as well? The unoperated child with spina bifida may take months or even years to die. Distressed by the spectacle of children "lying around waiting to die," one doctor has written, "It is time that society and medicine stopped perpetuating the fiction that withholding treatment is ethically different from terminating a life. It is time that society began to discuss mechanisms by which we can alleviate the pain and suffering for those individuals whom we cannot help." [11]

I do not deny that there may be cases in which death is in the best interests of the patient. In such cases, a quick and painless death may be the best thing. However, I do not think that, once active or vigorous treatment is stopped, a quick death is always preferable to a lingering one. We must be cautious about attributing to defective children *our* distress at seeing them linger. Waiting for them to die may be tough on parents, doctors and nurses—it isn't necessarily tough on the child. The decision not to operate need not mean a decision to neglect, and it may be possible to make the remaining months of the child's life comfortable, pleasant and filled with love. If this alternative is possible, surely it is more decent and humane than killing the child. In such a situation, withholding treatment, foreseeing the child's death, is not ethically equivalent to killing the child, and we cannot move from the permissibility of the former to that of the latter. I am worried that there will be a tendency to do precisely that if active euthanasia is regarded as morally equivalent to the withholding of life-prolonging treatment.

Conclusion

The AMA statement does not make the distinction Rachels wishes to attack, i.e. that between active and passive euthanasia. Instead, the statement draws a distinction between the intentional termination of life, on the one hand, and the cessation of the employment of extraordinary means to prolong life, on the other. Nothing said by Rachels shows that this distinction is confused. It may be that doctors have misinterpreted the AMA statement, and that this had led, for example, to decisions to allow defective infants slowly to starve to death. I quite agree with Rachels that the decisions to which they allude were cruel and made on irrelevant grounds. Certainly it is worth pointing out that allowing someone to die can be the intentional termination of life, and that it can be just as bad as, or worse than, killing someone. However, the withholding of life-prolonging treatment is not necessarily the intentional termination of life, so that if it is permissible to withhold life-prolonging treatment, it does not follow that, other things being equal, it is permissible to kill. Furthermore, most of the time, other things are not equal. In many of the cases in which it would be right to cease treatment, I do not think that it would also be right to kill.

Endnotes

1. James Rachels. Active and passive euthanasia. *New Engl.J.Med.*, 292, 78–80, 1975.
2. Rachels, p. 78.
3. Rachels, pp. 79–80.
4. For example, *In re Yetter*, 62 Pa. D. & C. 2d 619, C.P., Northampton County Ct., 1974.
5. David W. Meyers, Legal aspects of voluntary euthanasia, *Dilemmas of Euthanasia* (Edited by John Behnke and Sissela Bok), p. 56. Anchor Books, New York, 1975.
6. Ernest H. Rosenbaum, Md., *Living with Cancer,* p. 27. Praeger, New York, 1975.
7. Cf. H. Tristram Engelhardt, Jr., Ethical issues in aiding the death of young children, *Beneficent Euthanasia* (Edited by Marvin Kohl), Prometheus Books, Buffalo, N.Y. 1975.
8. B. D. Colen, *Karen Ann Quinlan: Living and Dying in the Age of Eternal Life,* p. 115. Nash, 1976.
9. Rachels, p. 79.
10. Cf. Norman L. Cantor, Law and the termination of an incompetent patient's life-preserving care. *Dilemmas of Euthanasia op. cit.,* pp. 69–105.
11. John Freeman, Is there a right to die—quickly?, *J. Pediat.* 80. p. 905.

Review Questions

1. According to Steinbock, what mistake does Rachels make in his interpretation of the AMA statement?
2. How does Steinbock understand the right to refuse treatment?
3. How does Steinbock distinguish between extraordinary and ordinary treatment?
4. What is Steinbock's view of the case of the child with Down's syndrome, and how does her view differ from that of Rachels?
5. What is Steinbock's view of the treatment of children with spina bifida?
6. Why does Steinbock think that she has refuted Rachels' attack against the AMA statement?
7. Explain Steinbock's conclusion.

Discussion Questions

1. In what cases can the right to refuse medical treatment be overriden and why?
2. Steinbock grants that in some cases "a quick and painless death may be the best thing." Can you think of any such cases? Why is death "the best thing" in such cases?

Peter Singer

Justifying Voluntary Euthanasia

Peter Singer is professor of philosophy, co-director of the Institute of Ethics and Public Affairs, and deputy director of the Center for Human Bioethics at Monash University, Melbourne. He is the author and editor of many books. His best-known book is Animal Liberation *(1975), which started the Animal Liberation movement. Our reading is taken from his* Practical Ethics, *second edition (1993).*

Singer argues that voluntary euthanasia and assisted suicide are morally justified in cases where a patient is suffering from an incurable and painful or very distressing condition. In such cases, Utilitarianism, the theory of rights, and respect for autonomy all provide reasons for allowing voluntary euthanasia or assisted suicide.

VOLUNTARY EUTHANASIA

Most of the groups currently campaigning for changes in the law to allow euthanasia are campaigning for voluntary euthanasia—that is, euthanasia carried out at the request of the person killed.

Sometimes voluntary euthanasia is scarcely distinguishable from assisted suicide. In *Jean's Way*, Derek Humphry has told how his wife Jean, when dying of cancer, asked him to provide her with the means to end her life swiftly and without pain. They had seen the situation coming and discussed it beforehand. Derek obtained some tablets and gave them to Jean, who took them and died soon afterwards.

Dr. Jack Kevorkian, a Michigan pathologist, went one step further when he built a 'suicide machine' to help terminally ill people commit suicide. His machine consisted of a metal pole with three different bottles attached to a tube of the kind used to provide an intravenous drip. The doctor inserts the tube in the patient's vein, but at this stage only a harmless saline solution can pass through it. The patient may then flip a switch, which will allow a coma-inducing drug to come through the tube; this is automatically followed by a lethal drug contained in the third bottle. Dr. Kevorkian announced that he was prepared to make the machine available to any terminally ill patient who wished to use it. (Assisting suicide is not against the law in Michigan.) In June 1990, Janet Adkins, who was suffering from Alzheimer's disease, but still competent to make the decision to end her life, contacted Dr. Kevorkian and told him of her wish to die, rather than go through the slow and progressive deterioration that the disease involves. Dr. Kevorkian was in attendance while she made use of his machine, and then reported Janet Adkin's death to the police. He was subsequently charged with murder, but the judge refused to allow the charge to proceed to trial, on the grounds that Janet Adkins had caused her own death. The following year Dr. Kevorkian made his device available to two other people, who used it in order to end their lives.[1]

In other cases, people wanting to die may be unable to kill themselves. In 1973 George Zygmaniak was injured in a motorcycle accident near his home in New Jersey. He was taken to hospital, where he was found to be totally paralysed from the neck down. He was also in considerable pain. He told his doctor and his brother, Lester, that he did not want to live in this condition. He begged them both to kill him. Lester questioned the doctor and the hospital staff about George's prospects of recovery: he was told that they were nil. He then smuggled a gun into the hospital, and said to his brother: 'I am here to end your pain, George. Is it all right with you?' George, who was not unable to speak because of an operation to assist his breathing, nodded affirmatively. Lester shot him through the temple.

The Zygmaniak case appears to be a clear instance of voluntary euthanasia, although without some of the procedural safeguards that advocates of the legalisation of voluntary euthanasia propose. For instance, medical opinions about the patient's prospects of recovery were obtained only in an informal manner. Nor was there a careful attempt to establish, before independent witnesses, that George's desire for death was of a fixed and rational kind, based on the best available information about his situation. The killing was not carried out by a doctor. An injection would have been less distressing to others than shooting. But these choices were not open to Lester Zygmaniak, for the law in New Jersey, as in most other places, regards mercy killing as murder, and if he had made his plans known, he would not have been able to carry them out.

Euthanasia can be voluntary even if a person is not able, as Jean Humphry, Janet Adkins, and George Zygmaniak were able, to indicate the wish to die right up to the moment the tablets are swallowed, the switch thrown, or the trigger pulled. A person may, while in good health, make a written request for euthanasia if, through accident or illness, she should come to be incapable of making or expressing a decision to die, in pain, or without the use of her mental faculties, and there is no reasonable hope of recovery. In killing a person who has made such a request, who has re-affirmed it from time to time, and who is now in one of the states described, one could truly claim to be acting with her consent.

There is now one country in which doctors can openly help their patients to die in a peaceful and dignified way. In the Netherlands, a series of court cases during the 1980s upheld a doctor's right to assist a patient to die, even if that assistance amounted to giving the patient a lethal injection. Doctors in the Netherlands who comply with certain guidelines (which will be described later in this chapter) can now quite openly carry out euthanasia and can report this on the death certificate without fear of prosecution. It has been estimated that about 2,300 deaths each year result from euthanasia carried out in this way. . . .

JUSTIFYING VOLUNTARY EUTHANASIA

Under existing laws in most countries, people suffering unrelievable pain or distress from an incurable illness who beg their doctors to end their lives are asking their doctors to risk a murder charge. Although juries are extremely reluctant to convict in cases of this kind the law is clear that neither the request, nor the degree of suffering, nor the incurable condition of the person killed, is a defence to a charge of murder. Advocates of voluntary euthanasia propose that this law be changed so that a doctor could legally act on a patient's desire to die without further suffering. Doctors have been able to do this quite openly in the Netherlands, as a result of a series of court decisions during the 1980s, as long as they comply with certain conditions. In Germany, doctors may provide a patient with the means to end her life, but they may not administer the substance to her.

The case for voluntary euthanasia has some common ground with the case for non-voluntary euthanasia, in that death is a benefit for the one killed. The two kinds of euthanasia differ, however, in that voluntary euthanasia involves the killing of a person, a rational and self-conscious being and not a merely conscious being. (To be strictly accurate it must be said that this is not always so, because although only rational and self-conscious beings can consent to their own deaths, they may not be rational and self-conscious at the time euthanasia is contemplated—the doctor may, for instance, be acting on a prior written request for euthanasia if, through accident or illness, one's rational faculties should be irretrievably lost. For simplicity we shall, henceforth, disregard this complication.)

We have seen that it is possible to justify ending the life of a human being who lacks the capacity to consent. We must now ask in what way the ethical issues are different when the being is capable of consenting, and does in fact consent.

Let us return to the general principles about killing. . . . I [have] argued . . . that killing a self-conscious being is a more serious matter than killing a merely conscious being. I gave four distinct grounds on which this could be argued:

1. The classical utilitarian claim that since self-conscious beings are capable of fearing their own death, killing them has worse effects on others.
2. The preference utilitarian calculation that counts the thwarting of the victim's desire to go on living as an important reason against killing.
3. A theory of rights according to which to have a right one must have the ability to desire that to which one has a right, so that to have a right to life one must be able to desire one's own continued existence.
4. Respect for the autonomous decisions of rational agents.

Now suppose we have a situation in which a person suffering from a painful and incurable disease wishes to die. If the individual were not a person—not rational or self-conscious—euthanasia would, as I have said, be justifiable. Do any of the four grounds for holding that it is normally worse to kill a person provide reasons against killing when the individual is a person who wants to die?

The classical utilitarian objection does not apply to killing that takes place only with the genuine consent of the person killed. That people are killed under these conditions would have no tendency to spread fear or insecurity, since we have no cause to be fearful of being killed with our own genuine consent. If we do not wish to be killed, we simply do not consent. In fact, the argument from fear points in favour of voluntary euthanasia, for if voluntary euthanasia is not permitted we may, with good cause, be fearful that our deaths will be unnecessarily drawn out and distressing. In the Netherlands, a nationwide study commissioned by the government found that 'Many patients want an assurance that their doctor will assist them to die should suffering become unbearable.' Often,

having received this assurance, no persistent request for euthanasia eventuated. The availability of euthanasia brought comfort without euthanasia having to be provided.

Preference utilitarianism also points in favour of, not against, voluntary euthanasia. Just as preference utilitarianism must count a desire to go on living as a reason against killing, so it must count a desire to die as a reason for killing.

Next, according to the theory of rights we have considered, it is an essential feature of a right that one can waive one's rights if one so chooses. I may have a right to privacy; but I can, if I wish, film every detail of my daily life and invite the neighbours to my home movies. Neighbours sufficiently intrigued to accept my invitation could do so without violating my right to privacy, since the right has on this occasion been waived. Similarly, to say that I have a right to life is not to say that it would be wrong for my doctor to end my life, if she does so at my request. In making this request I waive my right to life.

Lastly, the principle of respect for autonomy tells us to allow rational agents to live their own lives according to their own autonomous decisions, free from coercion or interference; but if rational agents should autonomously chose to die, then respect for autonomy will lead us to assist them to do as they choose.

So, although there are reasons for thinking that killing a self-conscious being is normally worse than killing any other kind of being, in the special case of voluntary euthanasia most of these reasons count for euthanasia rather than against. Surprising as this result might at first seem, it really does no more than reflect the fact that what is special about self-conscious beings is that they can know that they exist over time and will, unless they die, continue to exist. Normally this continued existence is fervently desired; when the foreseeable continued existence is dreaded rather than desired however, the desire to die may take the place of the normal desire to live, reversing the reasons against killing based on the desire to live. Thus the case for voluntary euthanasia is arguably much stronger than the case for non-voluntary euthanasia.

Some opponents of the legalisation of voluntary euthanasia might concede that all this follows, if we have a genuinely free and rational decision to die: but, they add, we can never be sure that a request to be killed is the result of a free and rational decision. Will not the sick and elderly be pressured by their relatives to end their lives quickly? Will it not be possible to commit outright murder by pretending that a person has requested euthanasia? And even if there is no pressure of falsification, can anyone who is ill, suffering pain, and very probably in a drugged and confused state of mind, make a rational decision about whether to live or die?

These questions raise technical difficulties for the legalisation of voluntary euthanasia, rather than objections to the underlying ethical principles; but they are serious difficulties nonetheless. The guidelines developed by the courts in the Netherlands have sought to meet them by proposing that euthanasia is acceptable only if

- It is carried out by a physician.
- The patient has explicitly requested euthanasia in a manner that leaves no doubt of the patient's desire to die.
- The patient's decision is well-informed, free, and durable.
- The patient has an irreversible condition causing protracted physical or mental suffering that the patient finds unbearable.
- There is no reasonable alternative (reasonable from the patient's point of view) to alleviate the patient's suffering.
- The doctor has consulted another independent professional who agrees with his or her judgment.

Euthanasia in these circumstances is strongly supported by the Royal Dutch Medical Association, and by the general public in the Netherlands. The guidelines make murder in the guise of euthanasia rather far-fetched, and there is no evidence of an increase in the murder rate in the Netherlands.

It is often said, in debates about euthanasia, that doctors can be mistaken. In rare instances patients diagnosed by two competent doctors as suffering from an incurable condition have survived and enjoyed years of good health. Possibly the legalisation of voluntary euthanasia would, over the years, mean the deaths of a few people who would otherwise have recovered from their immediate illness and lived for some extra years. This is not, however, the knockdown argument against euthanasia that some imagine it to be. Against a very small number of unnecessary deaths that might occur if euthanasia is legalised we must place the very large amount of pain and distress that will be suffered if euthanasia is not legalised, by patients who really are terminally ill. Longer life is not such a supreme good that it outweighs all other considerations. (If it were, there would be many more effective ways of saving life—such as a ban on smoking, or a reduction of speed limits to 40 kilometres per hour—than prohibiting voluntary euthanasia.) The possibility that two doctors may make a mistake means that the person who opts for euthanasia is deciding on the balance of probabilities and giving up a very slight chance of survival in order to avoid suffering that will almost certainly end in death. This may be a perfectly rational choice. Probability is the guide of life, and of death, too. Against this, some will reply that improved care for the terminally ill has eliminated pain and made voluntary euthanasia unnecessary. Elisabeth Kübler-Ross, whose *On Death and Dying* is perhaps the best-known book on care for the dying, has claimed that none of her patients request euthanasia. Given personal attention and the right medication, she says, people come to accept their deaths and die peacefully without pain.

Kübler-Ross may be right. It may be possible, now, to eliminate pain. In almost all cases, it may even be possible to do it in a way that leaves patients in possession of their rational faculties and free from vomiting, nausea, or other distressing side-effects. Unfortunately only a minority of dying patients now receive this kind of care. Nor is physical pain the only problem. There can also be other distressing conditions, like bones so fragile they fracture at sudden movements, uncontrollable nausea and vomiting, slow starvation due to a cancerous growth, inability to control one's bowels or bladder, difficulty in breathing, and so on.

Dr. Timothy Quill, a doctor from Rochester, New York, has described how he prescribed barbiturate sleeping pills for 'Diane', a patient with a severe form of leukaemia, knowing that she wanted the tablets in order to be able to end her life. Dr. Quill had known Diane for many years, and admired her courage in dealing with previous serious illnesses. In an article in the *New England Journal of Medicine,* Dr. Quill wrote:

It was extraordinarily important to Diane to maintain control of herself and her own dignity during the time remaining to her. When this was no longer possible, she clearly wanted to die. As a former director of a hospice program, I know how to use pain medicines to keep patients comfortable and lessen suffering. I explained the philosophy of comfort care, which I strongly believe in. Although Diane understood and appreciated this, she had known of people lingering in what was called relative comfort, and she wanted no part of it. When the time came, she wanted to take her life in the least painful way possible. Knowing of her desire for independence and her decision to stay in control, I thought this request made perfect sense. . . . In our discussion it became clear that preoccupation with her fear of a lingering death would interfere with Diane's getting the most out of the time she had left until she found a safe way to ensure her death.

Not all dying patients who wish to die are fortunate enough to have a doctor like Timothy Quill. Betty Rollin has described, in her moving book *Last Wish,* how her mother developed ovarian cancer that spread to other parts of her body. One morning her mother said to her:

I've had a wonderful life, but now it's over, or it should be. I'm not afraid to die, but I am afraid of this illness, what it's doing to me. . . . There's never any relief from it now. Nothing but nausea and this pain. . . . There won't be any more chemotherapy. There's no treatment anymore. So what happens to me now? I know what happens. I'll die slowly. . . . I don't want that. . . . Who does it benefit if I die slowly? If it benefits my children I'd be willing. But it's not going to do you any good. . . . There's no point in a slow death, none. I've never liked doing things with no point. I've got to end this.

Betty Rollin found it very difficult to help her mother to carry out her desire: 'Physician after physician turned down our pleas for help (How many pills? What kind?).' After her book about her mother's death was published, she received hundreds of letters, many from people, or close relatives of people, who had tried to die, failed, and suffered even more. Many of these people were denied help from doctors, because although suicide is legal in most jurisdictions, assisted suicide is not.

Perhaps one day it will be possible to treat all terminally ill and incurable patients in such a way that no one requests euthanasia and the subject becomes a non-issue; but this is now just a utopian ideal, and no reason at all to deny euthanasia to those who must live and die in far less comfortable conditions. It is, in any case, highly paternalistic to tell dying patients that they are now so well looked after that they need not be offered the option of euthanasia. It would be more in keeping with respect for individual freedom and autonomy to legalise euthanasia and let patients decide whether their situation is bearable.

Do these arguments for voluntary euthanasia perhaps give too much weight to individual freedom and autonomy? After all, we do not allow people free choices on matters like, for instance, the taking of heroin. This is a restriction of freedom but, in the view of many, one that can be justified on paternalistic grounds. If preventing people from becoming heroin addicts is justifiable paternalism, why isn't preventing people from having themselves killed?

The question is a reasonable one, because respect for individual freedom can be carried too far. John Stuart Mill thought that the state should never interfere with the individual except to prevent harm to others. The individual's own good, Mill thought, is not a proper reason for state intervention. But Mill may have had too high an opinion of the rationality of a human being. It may occasionally be right to prevent people from making choices that are obviously not rationally based and that we can be sure they will later regret. The prohibition of voluntary euthanasia cannot be justified on paternalistic grounds, however, for voluntary euthanasia is an act for which good reasons exist. Voluntary euthanasia occurs only when, to the best of medical knowledge, a person is suffering from an incurable and painful or extremely distressing condition. In these circumstances one cannot say that to choose to die quickly is obviously irrational. The strength of the case for voluntary euthanasia lies in this combination of respect for the preferences, or autonomy, of those who decide for euthanasia; and the clear rational basis of the decision itself. . . .

Endnote

1. Dr. Kevorkian was again charged with murder, and with providing a prohibited substance, in connection with the latter two cases, but was once more discharged.

REVIEW QUESTIONS

1. Distinguish between the cases of Janet Adkins and George Zygmaniak.
2. What are the four grounds for holding that killing a person is wrong? According to Singer, how do these grounds support voluntary euthanasia and assisted suicide?
3. What difficulties does Singer discuss? How does he reply?

DISCUSSION QUESTIONS

1. Singer accepts the guidelines for voluntary euthanasia developed by the courts in the Netherlands. Are these acceptable? Why or why not?
2. Did Janet Adkins do anything wrong? How about Lester Zygmaniak?
3. Should the law be changed to allow voluntary euthanasia or assisted suicide for terminally ill patients?

Arthur J. Dyck

An Alternative to the Ethic of Euthanasia

Arthur J. Dyck is the Mary B. Saltonstall Professor of Population Ethics at the Harvard School of Public Health and a faculty member of the Harvard Divinity School.

Dyck attacks the ethic of euthanasia and defends an ethic of benemortasia that does not allow a person to cause his or her own death by suicide or assisted suicide, but only to refuse medical interventions that prolong dying.

The arguments for euthanasia focus upon two humane and significant concerns: compassion for those who are painfully and terminally ill; and concern for the human dignity associated with freedom of choice. Compassion and freedom are values that sustain and enhance the common good. The question here, however, is

From Arthur J. Dyck, "An Alternative to the Ethic of Euthanasia," *To Live and to Let Die,* ed. R. H. Williams (New York: Springer-Verlag, 1973), pp. 98–112. Reprinted by permission of the author and publisher.

how these values affect our behavior toward the dying.

The argument for compassion usually occurs in the form of attacking the inhumanity of keeping dying people alive when they are in great pain or when they have lost almost all of their usual functions, particularly when they have lost the ability or will to communicate with others. . . . The argument for compassion is supplemented by an argument for greater freedom for a patient to choose how and when he or she will die. For one thing, the patient should not be subjected to medical treatment to which that patient does not consent. Those who argue for voluntary euthanasia extend this notion by arguing that the choice to withhold techniques that would prolong life is a choice to shorten life. Hence, if one can choose to shorten one's life, why cannot one ask a physician by a simple and direct act of intervention to put an end to one's life? Here it is often argued that physicians already curtail life by means of pain-killing drugs, which in the doses administered, will hasten death. Why should not the law recognize and sanction a simple and direct hastening of death, should the patient wish it?

How do the proponents of euthanasia view the general prohibition against killing? First of all, they maintain that we are dealing here with people who will surely die regardless of the intervention of medicine. They advocate the termination of suffering and the lawful foreshortening of the dying process. Secondly, although the patient is committing suicide, and the physician is an accomplice in such a suicide, both acts are morally justifiable to cut short the suffering of one who is dying.

It is important to be very clear about the precise moral reasoning by which advocates of voluntary euthanasia justify suicide and assisting a suicide. They make no moral distinction between those instances when a patient or a physician chooses to have life shortened by failing to accept or use life-prolonging techniques and those instances when a patient or a physician shortens life by employing a death-dealing chemical or instrument. They make no moral distinction between a drug given to kill pain, which also shortens life, and a substance given precisely to shorten life and for no other reason. Presumably these distinctions are not honored, because regardless of the stratagem employed—regardless of whether one is permitting to die or killing directly—the result is the same, the patient's life is shortened. Hence, it is maintained that, if you can justify one kind of act that shortens the life of the dying, you can justify any act that shortens the life of the dying when this act is seen to be willed by the one who is dying. Moral reasoning of this sort is strictly utilitarian; it focuses solely on the consequences of acts, not on their intent. . . .

Because of this loss of a merely descriptive term for a happy death, it is necessary to invent a term for a happy or good death—namely, benemortasia. The familiar derivatives for this new term are *bene* (good) and *mors* (death). . . . An ethic of benemortasia does not stand in opposition to the values of compassion and human freedom. It differs, however, from the ethic of euthanasia in its understanding of how these values are best realized. In particular, certain constraints upon human freedom are recognized and emphasized as enabling human beings to increase compassion and freedom rather than diminish them. . . .

Our ethic of benemortasia acknowledges the freedom of patients who are incurably ill to refuse interventions that prolong dying and the freedom of physicians to honor such wishes.

However, these actions are not acts of suicide and assisting in suicide. In our ethic of benemortasia, suicide and assisting in suicide are unjustifiable acts of killing. Unlike the ethic of those who would legalize voluntary euthanasia, our ethic makes a moral distinction between acts that permit death and acts that cause death. . . . From the point of view of the dying person, when could his or her decisions be called a deliberate act to end life, the act we usually designate as suicide? Only, it seems to me, when the dying person commits an act that has the immediate intent of ending life and has no other purpose. That act may be to use, or ask the physician to use, a chemical or an instrument that has no other immediate effect than to end the dying person's life. If, for the sake of relieving pain, a dying person chooses drugs administered in potent doses, the intent of this act is not to shorten life, even though it has that effect. It is a choice as to how to live while dying. Similarly, if a patient chooses to forego medical interventions that would have the effect of prolonging his or her life without in any way promising release from death, this also is a choice as to what is the most meaningful way to spend the remainder of life, however short that may be. The choice to use drugs to relieve pain and the choice not to use medical measures that cannot promise a cure for one's dying are no different in principle from the choices we make throughout our lives as to how much we will rest, how hard we will work, how little and how much medical intervention we will seek or tolerate, and the like. For society or physicians to map out life styles for individuals with respect to such decisions is surely beyond anything that we find in Stoic, Jewish, or Christian ethics. Such intervention in the liberty of individuals is far beyond what is required in any society whose rules are intended to constrain people against harming others.

But human freedom should not be extended to include the taking of one's own life. Causing one's own death cannot generally be justified, even when one is dying. To see why this is so, we have to consider how causing one's death does violence to one's self and harms others.

The person who causes his or her own death repudiates the meaningfulness and worth of his or her own life. To decide to initiate an act that has as its primary purpose to end one's life is to decide that that life has no worth to anyone, especially to oneself. It is an act that ends all choices regarding what one's life and whatever is left of it is to symbolize.

Suicide is the ultimately effective way of shutting out all other people from one's life. Psychologists have observed how hostility for others can be expressed through taking one's own life. People who might want access to the dying one to make restitution, offer reparation, bestow last kindnesses, or clarify misunderstandings are cut off by such an act. Every kind of potentially and actually meaningful contact and relation among persons is irrevocably severed except by means of memories and whatever life beyond death may offer. Certainly for those who are left behind by death, there can remain many years of suffering occasioned by that death. The sequence of dying an inevitable death can be much better accepted than the decision on the part of a dying one that he or she has no worth to anyone. An act that presupposes that final declaration leaves tragic overtones for anyone who participated in even the smallest way in that person's dying.

But the problem is even greater. If in principle a person can take his or her own life whenever he or she no longer finds it meaningful, there is nothing in principle that prevents anyone from taking his or her life, no matter what the circumstances. For if the decision hinges on whether one regards his or her own life as meaningful, anyone can regard his or her own life as meaningless even under circumstances that would appear to be most fortunate and opportune for an abundant life.

What about those who would commit suicide or request euthanasia in order to cease being a "burden" on those who are providing care for them? If it is a choice to accept death by refusing non-curative care that prolongs dying, the freedom to embrace death or give one's life in this way is honored by our ethic of benemortasia. What is rejected is the freedom to cause death whether by suicide or by assisting in one.

How a person dies has a definite meaning for those to whom that person is related. In the first year of bereavement, the rate of death among bereaved relatives of those who die in hospitals is twice that of bereaved relatives of those who die at home; sudden deaths away from hospital and home increase the death rate of the bereaved even more.

The courage to be, as expressed in Christian and Jewish thought, is more than the overcoming of the fear of death, although it includes that Stoic dimension. It is the courage to accept one's own life as having worth no matter what life may bring, including the threat of death, because that life remains meaningful and is regarded as worthy by God, regardless of what that life may be like. . . . The courage to be as a part recognizes that one is not merely one's own, that one's life is a gift bestowed and protected by the human community and by the ultimate forces that make up the cycle of birth and death. In the cycle of birth and death, there may be suffering, as there is joy, but suffering does not render a life meaningless or worthless. Suffering people need the support of others; suffering people should not be encouraged to commit suicide by their community, or that community ceases to be a community.

This consideration brings us to a further difficulty with voluntary euthanasia and its legalization. Not only does euthanasia involve suicide, but also, if legalized, it sanctions assistance in suicide by physicians. Legislation like the Voluntary Euthanasia Act of 1969 makes it a duty of the medical profession to take someone else's life for him. Here the principle not to kill is even further eroded and violated by giving the physician the power and the encouragement to decide that someone else's life is no longer worth living. The whole notion that a physician can engage in euthanasia implies acceptance of the principle that another person's life is no longer meaningful enough to sustain, a principle that does not afford protection for the lives of any of the most defenseless, voiceless, or otherwise dependent members of a community. Everyone in a community is potentially a victim of such a principle, particularly among members of racial minorities, the very young, and the very old.

Those who would argue that these consequences of a policy of voluntary euthanasia cannot be predicted fail to see two things: that we have already had an opportunity to observe what happens when the principle that sanctions euthanasia is accepted by a society; and that regardless of what the consequences may be of such acts, the acts themselves are wrong in principle.

With respect to the first point, Leo Alexander's (1949) very careful analysis of medical practices and attitudes of German physicians before and during the reign of Nazism in Germany should serve as a definite warning against the consequences of making euthanasia a public policy. He notes that the outlook of German physicians that led to their cooperation in what became a policy of mass murders,

started with the acceptance of that attitude, basic in the euthanasia movement, that there is such a thing as life not worthy to be lived. This attitude in its early stages concerned itself merely with the severely and chronically sick. Gradually the sphere of those to be included in this category was enlarged to include the socially unproductive, the racially unwanted, and finally all non-Germans. But it is important to realize that the infinitely small wedged-in lever from which this entire trend of mind received its impetus was the attitude toward the nonrehabilitable sick.

Those who reject out of hand any comparison of what happened in Nazi Germany with what we can expect here in the United States should consider current examples of medical practice in this nation. The treatment of mongoloids is a case in point. Now that the notion is gaining acceptance that a fetus diagnosed in the womb as mongoloid can, at the discretion of a couple or the pregnant woman, be justifiably aborted, instances of infanticide in hospitals are being reported. At Johns Hopkins Hospital, for example, an allegedly mongoloid infant whose parents would not permit an operation that is generally successful in securing normal physical health and development, was ordered to have "nothing by mouth," condemning that infant to a death that took 15 days. . . .

Someone may argue that the mongoloid was permitted to die, not killed. But this is faulty reasoning. In the case of an infant whose future life and happiness could be reasonably assured through surgery, we are not dealing with someone who is dying and with intervention that has no curative effect. The fact that some physicians refer to this as a case of permitting to die is an ominous portent of the dangers inherent in accepting the principle that a physician or another party can decide for a patient that his or her life is not worth living. Equally ominous is the assumption that this principle, once accepted, can easily be limited to cases of patients for whom no curative intervention is known to exist. . . .

The hesitation to commit suicide and the ambivalence of the dying about their worth should give one pause before one signs a declaration that empowers a physician to decide that at some point one can no longer be trusted as competent to judge whether or not one wants to die. Physicians are also frail humans, and mistaken diagnoses, research interests, and sometimes errors of judgment that stem from a desire for organs, are part of the practice of medicine.

Comatose patients pose special problems for an ethic of benemortasia as they do for the advocates of voluntary euthanasia. Where patients are judged to be irreversibly comatose and where sustained efforts have been made to restore such persons to consciousness, no clear case can be made for permitting to die, even though it seems merciful to do so. It seems that the best we can do is to develop some rough social and medical consensus about a reasonable length of time for keeping "alive" a person's organ systems after "brain death" has been decided. Because of the pressures to do research and to transplant organs, it may also be necessary to employ special patient advocates who are not physicians and nurses. These patient advocates, trained in medical ethics, would function as ombudsmen.

In summary, even if the practice of euthanasia were to be confined to those who voluntarily request an end to their lives, no physician could in good conscience participate in such an act. To decide directly to cause the death of a patient is to abandon a cardinal principle of medical practice—namely, to do no harm to one's patient. The relief of suffering, which is surely a time-honored role for the physician, does not extend to an act that presupposes that the life of a patient who is suffering is not worthy to be lived. As we have argued, not even the patient who is dying can justifiably and unilaterally universalize the principle by which a dying life would be declared to be worthless.

Richard B. Brandt

Defective Newborns and the Morality of Termination

For biographical information on Brandt, see the second reading in this chapter.

Brandt argues that it is morally right to actively or passively terminate the life of a defective newborn if its life is bad according to a "happiness criterion." Consent is irrelevant; the infant cannot give consent, and it will be indifferent to continued life. But the cost of caring for the infant is relevant to the decision to terminate in addition to the quality of the prospective life.

The *legal* rights of a fetus are very different from those of a newborn. The fetus may be aborted, legally, for any reason or no reason up to twenty-four or twenty-eight weeks (U.S. Supreme Court, *Roe* v. *Wade*). But, at least in theory, immediately after birth an infant has all the legal rights of the adult, including the right to life.

From *Infanticide and the Value of Life*, ed. by Marvin Kohl (Prometheus Books, 1978). Reprinted with permission.

The topic of this paper, however, is to identify the moral rights of the newborn, specifically whether *defective* newborns have a right to life. But it is simpler to talk, not about "rights to life," but about when or whether it is *morally right* either actively or passively (by withdrawal of life-supportive measures) to terminate defective newborns. It is also better because the conception of a right involves the notion of a sphere of autonomy—something is to be done or omitted, but only if the subject of the rights wants or consents—and this fact is apt to be confusing or oversimplifying. Surely what we want to know is whether termination is morally right or wrong, and nothing can turn on the **semantics** of the concept of a "right." [1]

What does one have to do in order to support some answers to these questions? One thing we can do is ask—and I think myself that the answer to this question is definitive for our purposes—whether rational or fully informed persons would, in view of the total consequences, support a moral code for a society in which they expected to live, with one or another, provision on this matter. (I believe a fully rational person will at least normally have some degree of benevolence, or positive interest in the welfare or happiness of others; I shall not attempt to specify how much.) Since, however, I do not expect that everyone else will agree that answering this question would show what is morally right, I shall, for their benefit, also argue that certain moral principles on this matter are coherent with strong moral convictions of reflective people; or, to use Rawls's terminology, that a certain principle on the matter would belong to a system of moral principles in "reflective equilibrium."

Historically, many writers, including Pope Pius XI in *Casti Connubii* (1930), have affirmed an absolute prohibition against killing anyone who is neither guilty of a capital crime nor an unjust assailant threatening one's life (self-defense), except in case of "extreme necessity." Presumably the prohibition is intended to include withholding of food or liquid from a newborn, although strictly speaking this is only *failing* to do something, not actually *doing* something to bring about a death. (Would writers in this tradition demand, on moral grounds, that complicated and expensive surgery be undertaken to save a life? Such surgery is going beyond normal care, and in some cases beyond what earlier writers even conceived.) However the intentions of these writers may be, we should observe that historically their moral condemnation of all killing (except for the cases mentioned) derives from the Biblical injunction, "Thou shalt not kill," which, as it stands and without interpretation, may be taken to forbid suicide, killing of animals, perhaps even plants, and hence cannot be taken seriously.

Presumably a moral code that is coherent with our intuitions and that rational persons would support for their society would include some prohibition of killing, but it is another matter to identify the exact class to which such a prohibition is to apply. For one thing, I would doubt that killing one's self would be included—although one might be forbidden to kill one's self if that would work severe hardship on others, or conflict with the discharge of one's other moral obligations. And, possibly, defective newborns would *not* be included in the class. Further, a decision has to be made whether the prohibition of killing is *absolute* or only *prima facie*, meaning by "prima facie" that the duty not to kill might be outweighed by some other duty (or right) stronger in the circumstances, which could be fulfilled only by killing. In case this distinction is made, we would have to decide whether defective newborns fall within the scope of even a prima facie moral prohibition

against killing. I shall, however, not attempt to make this fine distinction here, and shall simply inquire whether, everything considered, defective newborns—or some identifiable group of them—are excluded from the moral prohibition against killing.

THE PROSPECTIVE QUALITY OF LIFE OF DEFECTIVE NEWBORNS

Suppose that killing a defective newborn, or allowing it to die, would not be an *injury*, but would rather be doing the infant a favor. In that case we should feel intuitively less opposed to termination of newborns, and presumably rational persons would be less inclined to support a moral code with a prohibition against such action. In that case we would feel rather as we do about a person's preventing a suicide attempt from being successful, in order that the person be elaborately tortured to death at a later stage. It is no favor to the prospective suicide to save his life; similarly, if the prospective life of defective newborns is bad we are doing them a favor to let them die.

It may be said that we have no way of knowing what the conscious experiences of defective children are like, and that we have no competence in any case to decide when or what kind of life is bad or not worth living. Further, it may be said that predictions about a defective newborn's prospects for the future are precarious, in view of possible further advances of medicine. It does seem, however, that here, as everywhere, the rational person will follow the evidence about the present or future facts. But there is a question how to decide whether a life is bad or not worth living.

In the case of *some* defective newborns, it seems clear that their prospective life is bad. Suppose, as sometimes happens, a child is hydrocephalic with an extremely low I.Q., is blind and deaf, has no control over its body, can only lie on its back all day and have all its needs taken care of by others, and even cries out with pain when it is touched or lifted. Infants born with spina bifida—and these number over two per one thousand births—are normally not quite so badly off, but are often nearly so.

But what criterion are we using if we say that such a life is bad? One criterion might be called a "happiness" criterion. If a person *likes* a moment of experience while he is having it, his life is so far good; if a person *dislikes* a moment of experience while he is having it, his life is so far bad. Based on such reactions, we might construct a "happiness curve" for a person, going up above the indifference axis when a moment of experience is liked—and how far above depending on how strongly it is liked—and dipping down below the line when a moment is disliked. Then this criterion would say that a life is worth living if there is a net balance of positive area under the curve over a lifetime, and that it is bad if there is a net balance of negative area. One might adopt some different criterion: for instance, one might say that a life is worth living if a person would *want* to live it over again given that, at the end, he could remember the whole of it with perfect vividness in some kind of grand intuitive awareness. Such a response to this hypothetical holistic intuition, however, would likely be affected by the state of the person's drives or moods at the time, and the conception strikes me as unconvincing, compared with the moment-by-moment reaction to what is going on. Let us, for the sake of the argument, adopt the happiness criterion.[2]

Is the prospective life of the seriously defective newborn, like the one described above, bad or good according to this criterion? One thing seems clear: that it is *less* good than is the prospective life of a normal infant. But is it bad?

We have to do some extrapolating from what we know. For instance, such a child will presumably suffer from severe sensory deprivation; he is simply not getting interesting stimuli. On the basis of laboratory data, it is plausible to think the child's experience is at best boring or uncomfortable. If the child's experience is painful, of course, its moments are, so far, on the negative side. One must suppose that such a child hardly suffers from disappointment, since it will not learn to expect anything exciting, beyond being fed and fondled, and these events will be regularly forthcoming. One might expect such a child to suffer from isolation and loneliness, but insofar as this is true, the object of

dislike probably should be classified as just sensory deprivation; dislike of loneliness seems to depend on the deprivation of past pleasures of human company. There are also some positive enjoyments: of eating, drinking, elimination, seeing the nurse coming with food, and so on. But the brief enjoyments can hardly balance the long stretches of boredom, discomfort, or even pain. On the whole, the lives of such children are bad according to the happiness criterion.

Naturally we cannot generalize about the cases of all "defective" newborns; there are all sorts of defects, and the cases I have described are about the worst. A child with spina bifida may, if he survives the numerous operations, I suppose, adjust to the frustration of immobility; he may become accustomed to the embarrassments of no bladder or bowel control; he may have some intellectual enjoyments like playing chess; he will suffer from observing what others have but he cannot, such as sexual satisfactions, in addition to the pain of repeated surgery. How does it all balance out? Surely not as very good, but perhaps above the indifference level.

It may fairly be said, I think, that the lives of some defective newborns are destined to be bad on the whole, and it would be a favor to them if their lives were terminated. Contrariwise, the prospective lives of many defective newborns are modestly pleasant, and it would be some injury to them to be terminated, albeit the lives they will live are ones some of us would prefer not to live at all.

CONSENT

Let us now make a second suggestion, not this time that termination of a defective newborn would be doing him a favor, but this time that he *consents* to termination, in the sense of expressing a rational deliberated preference for this. In that case I suggest that intuitively we would be *more* favorably inclined to judge that it is right to let the defective die, and I suggest also that for that case rational persons would be more ready to support a moral code permitting termination. Notice that we think that if an ill person has signified what we think a rational and deliberated desire to die, we are morally better justified in withdrawing life-supporting measures than we otherwise would be.

The newborn, however, is incapable of expressing his preference (giving consent) at all, much less expressing a rational deliberated preference. There could in theory be court-appointed guardians or proxies, presumably disinterested parties, authorized to give such consent on his behalf, but even so this would not be *his* consent.

Nevertheless, there is a fact about the mental life of the newborn (defective or not) such that, if he could understand the fact, it seems he would not object—even rationally or after deliberation, if that were possible—to his life being terminated, or to his parents substituting another child in his place. This suggestion may seem absurd, but let us see. The explanation runs along the lines of an argument I once used to support the morality of abortion. I quote the paragraph in which this argument was introduced.[3]

Suppose I were seriously ill, and were told that, for a sizeable fee, an operation to save "my life" could be performed, of the following sort: my brain would be removed to another body which could provide a normal life, but the unfortunate result would be that my memory and learned abilities would be wholly erased, and that the forming of memory brain traces must begin again from scratch, as in a newborn baby. Now, how large a fee would I be willing to pay for this operation, when the alternative is my peaceful demise? My own answer would be: None at all. I would take no interest in the continued existence of "myself" in that sense, and I would rather add the sizeable fee to the inheritance of my children. . . . I cannot see the point of forfeiting my children's inheritance in order to start off a person who is brand new except that he happens to enjoy the benefit of having my present brain, without the memory traces. It appears that some continuity of memory is a necessary condition for personal identity in an important sense.

My argument was that the position of a fetus, at the end of the first trimester, is essentially the same as that of the person contemplating this operation: he will consider that the baby born after six months will not be *he* in any *important* and *motivating* sense (there will be no continuity of memory, and, indeed, maybe nothing to have been remembered), and the later existence of this baby, in a sense bodily continuous with his present body, would be a matter of indifference to him. So, I argued, nothing is being done to the fetus that he would object to having done if he understood the situation.

What do I think is necessary in order for the continuation of my body with its conscious experiences to be worthwhile? One thing is that it is able to remember the events I can now remember; another is that it takes some interest in the projects I am now planning and remembers them as my projects; another is that it recognizes my friends and has warm feelings for them, and so on. Reflection on these states of a future continuation of my body with its experiences is what makes the idea motivating. But such motivating reflection for a newborn is impossible: he has no memories that he wants recalled later; he has no plans to execute; he has no warm feelings for other persons. He has simply not had the length of life necessary for these to come about. Not only that: the conception of these things cannot be motivating because the concept of some state of affairs being motivating requires roughly a past experience in which similar states of affairs were satisfying, and he has not lived long enough for the requisite conditioning to have taken place. (The most one could say is that the image of warm milk in his mouth is attractive; he might answer affirmatively if it could be put to him whether he would be aversive to the idea of no more warm milk.) So we can say not merely that the newborn does not want the continuation of himself as a subject of experiences (he has not the conceptual framework for this), he does not want *anything* that his own survival would promote. It is like the case of the operation: there is nothing I want that the survival of my brain with no memory would promote. Give the newborn as much *conceptual* framework as you like; the *wants* are not there, which could give significance to the continuance of his life.

The newborn, then, is bound to be *indifferent* to the idea of a continuation of the stream of his experiences, even if he clearly has the idea of that. It seems we can know this about him.

The truth of all this is still not for it to be the case that the newborn, defective or not, gives *consent* to, or expresses a preference for, the termination of his life. *Consent* is a performance, normally linguistic, but always requiring some conventional *sign*. A newborn, who has not yet learned how to signalize consent, cannot give consent. And it may be thought that this difference makes all the difference.

In order to see what difference it does make in this case, we should ask what makes adult consent morally important. Why is it that we think euthanasia can be practiced on an adult only if he gives his consent, at least his implied consent (e.g., by previous statements)? There seem to be two reasons. The first is that a person is more likely to be concerned with his own welfare, and to take steps to secure it, than are others, even his good friends. Giving an individual control over his own life, and not permitting others to take control except when he consents, is normally to promote his welfare. An individual may, of course, behave stupidly or shortsightedly, but we think that on the whole a person's welfare is best secured if decisions about it are in his hands; and it is best for society in the normal case (not for criminals, etc.) if persons' own lives are well-served. The second reason is the feeling of security a person can have if he knows the major decisions about himself are in his own hands. When they are not, a person can easily, and in some cases very reasonably, suppose that other persons may well be able to do something to him that he would very much like them not to do. He does not have to worry about that if he knows they cannot do it without his consent.

Are things different with the newborn? At least he, like the fetus, is not yet able to suffer from insecurity; he cannot worry about what others may do to him. So the second reason for requiring consent cannot have any importance in his case. His situation is thus very unlike that of the senile adult, for an adult can worry about what others may do to him if they judge him senile. And this worry can well cast a shadow over a lot of life. But how about the first reason? Here matters are more complex. In the case of children, we think their own lives are better cared for if certain decisions are in the hands of others; the child may not want to visit the dentist, but the parents know that his best interests are served by going, and they make him go. The

same for compulsory school attendance. And the same for the newborn. But there is another point: that society has an interest, at certain crucial points, that may not be served by doing just exactly what is for the lifelong interest of the newborn. There are huge costs that are relevant, in the case of the defective newborn. I shall go into that problem in a moment. It seems, then, that in the case of the newborn, *consent* cannot have the moral importance that it has in the case of adults.

On the other hand, then, the newborn will not *care* whether his life is terminated, even if he understands his situation perfectly; and, on the other hand, consent does not have the moral importance in his case that it has for adults. So, while it seems true that we would feel better about permitting termination of defective newborns if only they could give rational and deliberated consent and gave it, nevertheless when we bear the foregoing two points in mind, the absence of consent does not seem morally crucial in their case. We can understand why rational persons deciding which moral code to support for their society would not make the giving of consent a necessary condition for feeling free to terminate an infant's life when such action was morally indicated by the other features of the situation.

REPLACEMENT IN ORDER TO GET A BETTER LIFE

Let us now think of an example owing to Derek Parfit. Suppose a woman wants a child, but is told that if she conceives a child now it will be defective, whereas if she waits three months she will produce a normal child. Obviously we think it would be wrong for the mother not to delay. (If she delays, the child she will have is not the *same* child as the one she would have had if she had not delayed, but it will have a better life.) This is the sole reason why we think she should delay and have the later-born child.

Suppose, however, a woman conceives but discovers only three months later that the fetus will become a defective child, but that she can have a normal child if she has an abortion and tries again. Now this time there is still the same reason for having the abortion that there formerly was for the delay: that she will produce a child with a better life. Ought she not then to have the abortion? If the child's life is bad, he could well complain that he had been injured by deliberately being brought to term. Would he complain if he were aborted, in favor of the later normal child? Not if the argument of the preceding section is correct.

But now suppose the woman does not discover until after she gives birth, that the child is severely defective, but that she could conceive again and have a normal child. Are things really different, in the first few days? One might think that a benevolent person would want, in each of these cases, the substitution of a normal child for the defective one, of the better life for the worse one.

THE COST AND ITS RELEVANCE

It is agreed that the burden of care for a defective infant, say one born with spina bifida, is huge. The cost of surgery alone for an infant with spina bifida has been estimated to be around $275,000.[4] In many places this cost must be met by the family of the child, and there is the additional cost of care in an institution, if the child's condition does not permit care at home—and a very modest estimate of the monthly cost at present is $1,100. To meet even the surgical costs, not to mention monthly payments for continuing care, the lives of members of the family must be at a most spartan level for many years. The psychological effects of this, and equally, if not more so, of care provided at home, are far-reaching; they are apt to destroy the marriage and to cause psychological problems for the siblings. There is the on-going anxiety, the regular visits, the continuing presence of a caretaker if the child is in the home. In one way or another the continued existence of the child is apt to reduce dramatically the quality of life of the family as a whole.

It can be and has been argued that such costs, while real, are irrelevant to the moral problem of what should be done.[5] It is obvious, however, that rational persons, when deciding which moral code to support, would take these human

costs into account. As indeed they should: the parents and siblings are also human beings with lives to live, and any sacrifices a given law or moral system might call on them to make must be taken into account in deciding between laws and moral codes. Everyone will feel sympathy for a helpless newborn; but everyone should also think, equally vividly, of all the others who will suffer and just how they will suffer—and, of course, as indicated above, of just what kind of life the defective newborn will have in any case. There is a choice here between allowing a newborn to die (possibly a favor to it, and in any case not a serious loss), and imposing a very heavy burden on the family for many years to come.

Philosophers who think the cost to others is irrelevant to what should be done should reflect that we do not accept the general principle that lives should be saved at no matter what cost. For instance, ships are deliberately built with only a certain margin of safety; they could be built so that they would hardly sink in any storm, but to do so would be economically unfeasible. We do not think we should require a standard of safety for automobiles that goes beyond a certain point of expense and inconvenience; we are prepared to risk a few extra deaths. And how about the lives we are willing to lose in war, in order to assure a certain kind of economic order or democracy or free speech? Surely there is a point at which the loss of a life (or the abbreviation of a life) and the cost to others become comparable. Is it obvious that the continuation of a marginal kind of life for a child takes moral precedence over providing a college education for one or more of his siblings? Some comparisons will be hard to make, but continuing even a marginally pleasant life hardly has absolute priority.

DRAWING LINES

There are two questions that must be answered in any complete account of what is the morally right thing to do about defective newborns.

The first is: If a decision to terminate is made, how soon must it be made? Obviously it could not be postponed to the age of five, or of three, or even a year and a half. At those ages, all the reasons for insisting on consent are already cogent. And at those ages, the child will already care what happens to him. But ten days is tolerable. Doubtless advances in medicine will permit detection of serious prospective defects early in pregnancy, and this issue of how many days will not arise.

Second, the argument from the quality of the prospective life of the defective newborn requires that we decide which defects are so serious that the kind of life the defective child can have gives it no serious claim as compared with the social costs. This issue must be thought through, and some guidelines established, but I shall not attempt this here.

One might argue that, if the newborn cannot rationally care whether its life ends or not, the parents are free to dispose of a child irrespective of whether he is defective, if they simply do not want it. To this there are two replies. First, in practice there are others who want a child if the parents do not, and they can put it up for adoption. But second, the parents are *injuring* a child if they prevent it from having the good life it could have had. We do not in general accept the argument that a person is free to injure another, for no reason, even if he has that person's consent. In view of these facts, we may expect that rational, benevolent persons deciding which moral code to support would select one that required respect for the life of a normal child, but would permit the termination of the life of a seriously defective child.

ACTIVE AND PASSIVE PROCEDURES

There is a final question: that of a choice between withdrawal of life-supporting measures (such as feeding), and the active, painless taking of life. It seems obvious, however, that once the basic decision is made that an infant is not to receive the treatment necessary to sustain life beyond a few days, it is mere stupid cruelty to allow it to waste away gradually in a hospital bed—for the child to suffer, and for everyone involved also to suffer in watching the child suffer. If death is the outcome decided upon, it is far kinder for it to come quickly and painlessly.

Endnotes

1. Here I disagree with Michael Tooley, "Abortion and Infanticide," *Philosophy and Public Affairs* 2 (1972): 37–65, especially pp. 44–49.

2. Professor P. Foot has made interesting remarks on when a life is worth living. See her "Euthanasia," *Philosophy and Public Affairs,* 6 (1977): 85–112, especially pp. 95–96. She suggests that a good life must "contain a minimum of basic goods," although not necessarily a favorable balance of good over evil elements. When does she think this minimum fails? For one thing, in extreme senility or severe brain damage. She also cites as examples of conditions for minimum goods that "a man is not driven to work far beyond his capacity; that he has the support of a family or community; that he can more or less satisfy his hunger; that he has hopes for the future; that he can lie down to rest at night." Overwhelming pain or nausea, or crippling depression, she says, also can make life not worth living. All of these, of course, except for cases of senility and brain damage, are factors fixing whether stretches of living are highly unpleasant.

   If a person thinks that life is not good unless it realizes certain human potentialities, he will think life can be bad even if liked—and so far sets a higher standard than the happiness criterion. But Foot and such writers may say that even when life is not pleasant on balance, it can still be good if human potentialities are being realized or these basic minimal conditions are met; and in that sense they set a lower standard.

3. Richard B. Brandt, "The Morality of Abortion," in an earlier form in *The Monist* 56 (1972): 504–526, and in revised form in R. L. Perkins, ed., *Abortion: Pro and Con* (Cambridge, MA: Schenkman Publishing Co., 1974).

4. See A. M. Shaw and I. A. Shaw, in S. Gorovitz, et al., *Moral Problems in Medicine* (Englewood Cliffs, NJ: Prentice-Hall, Inc., 1976), pp. 335–341.

5. See, for instance, Philippa Foot; "Euthanasia," especially pp. 109–111. She writes: "So it is not for their sake but to avoid trouble to others that they are allowed to die. When brought out into the open this seems unacceptable; at least we do not easily accept the principle that adults who need special care should be counted too burdensome to be kept alive." I would think that "to avoid trouble to others" is hardly the terminology to describe the havoc that is apt to be produced. I agree that adults should not be allowed to die, or actively killed, without their consent, possibly except when they cannot give consent but are in great pain; but the reasons that justify different behavior in the two situations have appeared in the section, "Consent."

REVIEW QUESTIONS

1. According to Brandt, how should one answer questions about moral rightness?
2. According to Brandt, why can't the Biblical injunction "Thou shalt not kill" be taken seriously?

3. Explain Brandt's happiness criterion.
4. In Brandt's view, in what cases would the life of a defective infant be bad?
5. Why would a newborn be indifferent to continued life according to Brandt?
6. In Brandt's view, why is it better to replace a defective child with a normal one?
7. According to Brandt, why is active euthanasia better than passive euthanasia in some cases?

DISCUSSION QUESTIONS

1. Is Brandt's happiness criterion acceptable? Defend your view.
2. Is the cost of caring for a defective infant morally relevant? Defend your position.
3. Do you agree that in some cases active euthanasia is better than passive euthanasia? Why or why not?

PROBLEM CASES

1. Cruzan v. Director, Missouri Department of Health (*United States Supreme Court. 110 S. Ct. 2841* [*1990*]). In this case, the U.S. Supreme Court ruled on a petition to terminate the artificial nutrition and hydration of Nancy Cruzan, a twenty-five-year-old woman existing in a persistent vegetative state following an automobile accident.

On the night of January 11, 1983, Cruzan rolled her car over while driving down Elm Road in Jasper County, Missouri. She was found lying in a ditch. She was not breathing, and her heart was not beating. Paramedics were able to restore her breathing and heartbeat, but she remained unconscious. She remained in a coma for about three weeks. To keep her alive, surgeons implanted a gastrostomy feeding and hydration tube; she remained in a persistent vegetative state—a condition in which a person exhibits motor reflexes but no sign of consciousness or cognitive function.

After it became clear that Cruzan had practically no chance of recovery, her parents asked the doctors to terminate the artificial feeding and hydration. The doctors and the parents agreed that this would cause Cruzan's death. The doctors refused to do this without a court order. The parents petitioned a court and received authorization to terminate treatment. But the Supreme Court of Missouri reversed the decision of the trial court and ruled that treatment could not be terminated without "clear and convincing evidence" that termination is what Cruzan would have wanted.

The case went to the U.S. Supreme Court, and it upheld the judgment of the Missouri Supreme Court that termination of treatment was unconstitutional in this case. The decision was five to four, and the majority opinion was written by Justice William H. Rehnquist. In his opinion, Rehnquist granted that a competent person has a right to refuse lifesaving nutrition and hydration. But he ruled that in the case of an incompetent person such as Nancy Cruzan, it is constitutional for Missouri to require that feeding and hydration be terminated only if there is clear and convincing evidence that this is what Cruzan would have wanted. Because such evidence was not provided, the decision to deny the request for termination was upheld.

In later developments, the parents presented new evidence to show that Cruzan would have chosen termination of treatment, and the feeding and hydration were stopped. Nancy Cruzan finally died in December of 1990, seven years after the accident.

This case raises several troubling questions:

1. What would be the AMA position in this case? Are artificial feeding and hydration ordinary or extraordinary means of prolonging life? If they are ordinary means, then is cessation of treatment not allowed? If they are extraordinary means, then is cessation of treatment allowed? Is the AMA position defensible in this case?
2. Is termination of treatment in this case active or passive euthanasia? Is it an act that causes Cruzan's death, or does it just allow her to die from natural causes? Does it cause death or permit death?
3. Suppose that there were no "clear and convincing evidence" that termination of treatment is what Cruzan would have wanted. Does this mean that termination is wrong in this case? On the other hand, suppose that there were such evidence. Does this mean that termination is not wrong?

2. *Dr. Jack Kevorkian.* Dr. Kevorkian is a retired Michigan pathologist who has become famous for assisting suicides. In recent years, he has helped many people commit suicide.

Kevorkian's standard method of assisted suicide is to provide patients with one of several suicide devices he has made. Some inject a lethal drug and others allow the patient to breathe a lethal gas. The lethal drug device allows the patient to push a button or switch forcing a lethal drug (potassium chloride for example) through a tube and into a vein in the arm producing a quick and relatively painless death.

Perhaps the most famous case involved Janet Adkins, a woman suffering from Alzheimer's disease who killed herself by lethal injection using one of Kevorkian's suicide devices. The next day, Kevorkian appeared on practically every talk show and news program in the country. Although Adkins was not terminally ill in the usual sense of the term, a Michigan judge did not prosecute Kevorkian for murder because the state had no laws against assisted suicide. There is a court injunction forbidding Kevorkian to use his devices, but he has continued to use them.

Is Dr. Kevorkian doing something wrong? If so, what? And why is it wrong?

Should there be a law against assisted suicide? How should the law read?

3. *The Case of Baby Jane Doe.* In October 1983, Baby Jane Doe (as the infant was called by the court to protect her anonymity) was born with spina bifida and a host of other congenital defects. According to the doctors consulted by the parents, the child would be severely mentally retarded, bedridden, and suffer considerable pain. After consultations with doctors and religious counselors, Mr. and Mrs. A (as the parents were called in the court documents) decided not to consent to lifesaving surgery.

At this point, a right-to-life activist lawyer tried to legally force lifesaving surgery in the Baby Doe case, but two New York appeals courts and a state children's agency decided not to override the parent's right to make a decision in the case. Then the U.S. Justice Department intervened in the case. It sued to obtain records from the University Hospital in Stony Brook, New York, to determine if the hospital had violated a federal law that forbids discrimination against the handicapped. Dr. C. Everett Koop, the U.S. surgeon general, appeared on television to express the view that the government has the moral obligation to intercede on behalf of such infants in order to protect their right to life.

Two weeks later, Federal District Judge Leonard Wexler threw out the Justice Department's unusual suit. Wexler found no discrimination. The hospital had been willing to do the surgery but had failed to do so because the parents refused to consent to the surgery. Wexler found the parents' decision to be a reasonable one in view of the circumstances.

The day after the ruling, the Justice Department appealed. On January 9, 1984, federal regulations were issued preventing federally funded hospitals from withholding treatment in such cases.

Do parents have a right to make life-or-death decisions for their defective children? Why or why not?

Do you agree with Dr. Koop that the government has a moral obligation to save the lives of such infants, even when their parents do not wish it? Explain your position.

If the government forces us to save the lives of defective infants like Baby Doe, then should it assume the responsibility for the cost of surgery, intensive care, and so on? If so, then how much money should be spent on this program? If not, then who is going to pay the bills?

Suggested Readings

1. Albert Camus, *The Myth of Sisyphus*, trans. J. O'Brien (Vintage Books, 1955), argues that we should not commit suicide even if life seems meaningless or without value.

2. *Suicide: The Philosophical Issues*, ed. Margaret Pabst Battin and David J. Mayo (St. Martin's Press, 1980), has a useful collection of articles on suicide.

3. Derek Humphry, *Final Exit* (The Hemlock Society, 1991), gives advice on how to commit suicide or get assistance from a doctor. Also covered are other practical matters like living wills, autopsies, letters of instruction, and so on.

4. Tristram H. Englehardt, Jr., "Ethical Issues in Aiding the Death of Young Children," in *Beneficient Euthanasia,* ed. Marvin Kohl (Prometheus Books, 1975), claims that adult euthanasia can be justified by the appeal to freedom but that children do not have the right to choose to die because they are not persons in the strict sense. Child euthanasia is justified when parents decide that the child has little chance of a full human life and a great chance of suffering.

5. Philippa Foot, "Euthanasia," *Philosophy and Public Affairs* 6 (Winter 1977), pp. 85–112, defines

euthanasia as producing death (by act or omission) that is good for the one who dies, and she distinguishes between active, passive, voluntary, and nonvoluntary euthanasia. She finds that nonvoluntary active euthanasia is never justified, but she allows that the other types can be justified in some cases.

6. Philippa Foot, "The Problem of Abortion and the Doctrine of Double Effect," *Oxford Review,* no. 5, 1973, gives a classic discussion of the Doctrine of Double Effect.

7. Jonathan Glover, *Causing Death and Saving Lives* (Penguin Books, 1977), applies Utilitarianism to the problem of euthanasia and to other problems of killing such as abortion and capital punishment.

8. *Infanticide and the Value of Life,* ed. Marvin Kohl (Prometheus Books, 1978), is an anthology that concentrates on the morality of euthanasia for severely defective newborns.

9. *Beneficent Euthanasia,* ed. Marvin Kohl (Prometheus Books, 1975), is an anthology with a number of articles on various aspects of euthanasia.

10. *Killing and Letting Die,* ed. Bonnie Steinbock (Prentice-Hall, 1980), is a collection of readings that focus on the controversial killing and letting die distinction.

11. Tom L. Beauchamp, "A Reply to Rachels on Active and Passive Euthanasia," in *Ethical Issues in Death and Dying,* ed. Tom L. Beauchamp and Seymour Perlin (Prentice-Hall, 1978), defends the moral significance of the distinction between active and passive euthanasia and appeals to Rule-Utilitarianism to support the conclusion that active euthanasia is wrong.

12. Thomas D. Sullivan, "Active and Passive Euthanasia: An Impertinent Distinction?" *Human Life Review* III (Summer 1977), pp. 40–46, argues that Rachels' distinction between active and passive euthanasia is impertinent and irrelevant. Rachels' reply to Sullivan is entitled "More Impertinent Distinctions," in *Biomedical Ethics,* ed. T. A. Mappes and J. S. Zembaty (McGraw-Hill, 1981).

13. John Ladd, "Positive and Negative Euthanasia," in *Ethical Issues Relating to Life and Death,* ed. John Ladd (Oxford University Press, 1979), prefers to talk about positive and negative euthanasia rather than active and passive euthanasia. He argues that no clear distinction can be made between killing and letting a patient die but that they are not morally equivalent either. His own position is called a contextual position; it is the view that the distinction always depends on the context.

14. James Rachels, "Euthanasia," in *Matters of Life and Death,* third edition, ed. Tom Regan (Random House, 1993), relates the history of euthanasia, discusses the arguments for and against active euthanasia, and concludes with a proposal on how to legalize active euthanasia.

15. James Rachels, *The End of Life: Euthanasia and Morality* (Oxford University Press, 1986), develops his liberal view of euthanasia and defends it from criticism.

16. Robert Young, "Voluntary and Nonvoluntary Euthanasia," *The Monist* 59 (April 1976), pp. 264–82, reviews a number of arguments used to show that voluntary active euthanasia is not justified and concludes that none of them is successful.

17. John A. Robertson, "Involuntary Euthanasia of Defective Newborns," *Stanford Law Review* 27 (Jan. 1975), pp. 213–61, argues that the utilitarian defense of euthanasia for defective newborns does not succeed in showing that it is justified.

18. Robert F. Weir, *Selective Nontreatment of Handicapped Newborns: Moral Dilemmas in Neonatal Medicine* (Oxford University Press, 1984), discusses moral issues relating to the care and treatment of defective or handicapped newborns.

19. "Cruzan: Clear and Convincing?" *Hastings Center Report* 20 (Sept./Oct. 1990), has six articles discussing the Cruzan case.

20. Donald Van DeVeer, "Wither Baby Doe?" in *Matters of Life and Death,* second edition, ed. Tom Regan (Random House, 1986), examines various moral issues raised by the Baby Doe case.

Chapter Four

CAPITAL PUNISHMENT

Introduction

Legal Background   The Eighth Amendment to the Constitution of the United States prohibits cruel and unusual punishment. For example, the medieval punishment of cutting off the hands of thieves seems to be cruel and unusual. Is the death penalty another example of cruel and unusual punishment, and thus unconstitutional? This is a matter of debate. In the case of *Furman* v. *Georgia* (1972), the Supreme Court ruled (by a five-to-four majority) that the death penalty was unconstitutional because it was being administered in an arbitrary and capricious manner. Juries were allowed to inflict the death sentence without any explicit guidelines or standards, and the result was that blacks were much more likely to receive the death penalty than whites.

After the *Furman* decision, states wishing to retain the death penalty reacted in two ways. One was to correct the arbitrary discretion of juries by making the death penalty mandatory for certain crimes. But in *Woodson* v. *North Carolina* (1976), the Court ruled (again by a mere five-to-four majority) that mandatory death sentences were unconstitutional.

The second attempt to counter the objection raised in *Furman* was to provide standards for juries. Georgia specified in its law ten statutory aggravating circumstances, one of which the jury had to find beyond a reasonable doubt in order to render a death sentence. This second approach proved to be successful. In *Gregg* v. *Georgia* (1976), the first reading for the chapter, the majority ruled, with Justice Marshall and Justice Brennan dissenting, that the death penalty is not unconstitutional for the crime of murder, provided there are

227

safeguards against any arbitrary or capricious imposition by juries.

But why isn't the death penalty cruel and unusual? In their majority opinion, Justices Stewart, Powell, and Stevens answered this important question. First, they gave an explanation of the concept of cruel and unusual. In their view, a punishment is cruel and unusual if it either fails to accord with evolving standards of decency or fails to accord with the dignity of humans that is the basic concept underlying the Eighth Amendment. This second stipulation rules out excessive punishment that involves unnecessary pain or is disproportionate to the crime. They argued that the death penalty does not satisfy either of these stipulations. It is acceptable to the majority of people, since thirty-five states have statutes providing for the death penalty, and it is not excessive because it achieves two important social purposes, retribution and deterrence.

Retribution   To fully understand the appeal to retribution, it is necessary to examine the theory on which it is based, namely **Retributivism**. The classical formulation of this theory is given by Immanuel Kant in the second reading. According to Kant, the only justification for punishing a person is guilt. If a person is guilty of a crime, then justice requires that he or she be punished; and if a person is not guilty, then no punishment is justified. In other words, guilt is both a necessary and a sufficient condition for justified punishment. Furthermore, Kant's view is that punishment must fit the crime (or be proportionate to the crime) according to the biblical principle of retaliation (*lex talionis*) that says, "eye for eye, tooth for tooth, life for life." Now what punishment fits the crime of murder using this principle? Kant insists that death, and only death, is the proper punishment for murder; no other punishment will satisfy the requirements of legal justice.

Various objections have been made to the retributive view. In the third reading for the chapter, Glover claims that it is open to the objection that it leads to what he considers to be pointless suffering, that is, suffering without any real benefits, either to the person punished or to other people. But the retributivist such as Kant or van den Haag (in the fourth reading) can reply that punishment does provide an important benefit, namely that justice is served by giving the criminal the punishment he or she deserves. If punishment is not given, then people will not be held accountable for their actions nor will they realize the consequences of their deeds.

In the last reading for the chapter, Bedau objects to the principle of *lex talionis*. He thinks that this principle can be interpreted loosely or literally. If it is taken loosely to mean that punishments should be graded to fit the crime, then Bedau has no objection to it. On this interpretation, the principle does not justify the death penalty because in Bedau's view there is an alternative punishment that fits the crime of murder, namely life imprisonment. If the principle is taken literally, however, then according to Bedau, it is not a sound principle for punishment. For one thing, it would require us to execute all murderers, even those who have killed in self-defense or for the sake of mercy, and presumably this is not acceptable. Furthermore, it would seem to justify punishments that are indeed cruel and unusual such as torturing those who have tortured or raping those who have raped.

But Retributivism can be defended against the charge that it justifies cruel and unusual punishment. The retributivist can admit that there are limits to the severity of the punishment, limits that rule out torture and rape. The criminal must be treated with the respect due to a member of the community (as Kant would say). But Kant and van den Haag both think that the death penalty is compatible with respectful treatment. They think that the death penalty actually treats criminals with humanity and dignity because it affirms their rationality and accountability for actions.

Deterrence   The principle of deterrence is an appeal to the social benefits of punishment. Defenders of the death penalty claim that its particular social benefits are deterrence and prevention. It deters other potential criminals from killing, and it prevents the criminal who is executed from committing further crimes. No doubt an executed criminal can commit no more crimes; but does the death penalty actually deter other potential criminals? This is a factual question that is much debated.

Without going into the details, the Supreme Court justices note that statistical attempts to prove that the death penalty is a deterrent have been inconclusive. However, the justices think that the death penalty is undoubtedly a significant deterrent for some potential murderers, for example, those who carefully contemplate their actions. Unfortunately, the justices cite no empirical evidence to support this claim. It seems to rest on their intuitions, and criminals may not have the same intuitions.

Bedau claims that there is little or no evidence that the death penalty is a better deterrent to murder than imprisonment. In fact the evidence seems to show that both punishments are equally effective or ineffective as deterrents to murder. In short, Bedau does not think that appealing to facts about deterrence is going to settle the issue.

Van den Haag agrees that evidence for saying that the death penalty is a better deterrent than alternative punishments is inconclusive. In any event, he thinks that deterrence is not decisive for either side: Abolitionists will not change their minds even if it is shown that capital punishment is a deterrent, and retentionists will not give up even if it is shown to fail as a deterrent. Nevertheless, van den Haag goes on to use a subtle argument, called the best-bet argument by Glover, to conclude that we should still use the death penalty rather than alternative punishments because it might save innocent victims whose lives are more valuable than those of the murderers who are executed. Both Glover and Bedau discuss this argument and attempt to refute it.

Glover's own view about deterrence, as distinguished from that of the others in the chapter, is that if capital punishment has not been proven to be a substantial deterrent, then there is a strong presumption against it because of its special evils and bad side effects.

The Supreme Court

Gregg v. Georgia (1976)

Potter Stewart, Lewis F. Powell, Jr., and John Paul Stevens are associate justices of the United States Supreme Court. Justice Stewart, a graduate of Yale Law School, was appointed to the Court in 1958. Justice Powell, LL.M. (Harvard), was appointed in 1971. Justice Stevens graduated from Northwestern University School of Law and was appointed to the Court in 1975. Thurgood Marshall, associate justice of the United States Supreme Court, was appointed in 1967; he was the first black person ever to be appointed. (He is now deceased.)

The main issue before the Court in the case of Gregg v. Georgia (1976) was whether or not the death penalty violates the Eighth Amendment

prohibition of cruel and unusual punishment. The majority of the Court, with Justice Marshall and Justice Brennan dissenting, held that the death penalty does not violate the Eighth Amendment because it is in accord with contemporary standards of decency. It serves both a deterrent and retributive purpose, and in the case of the Georgia law being reviewed, it is no longer arbitrarily applied.

In his dissenting opinion, Justice Marshall objects that the death sentence is excessive because a less severe penalty—life imprisonment—would accomplish the legitimate purposes of punishment. In reply to the claim that the death sentence is necessary for deterrence, Marshall asserts that the available evidence shows that this is not the case. As for the appeal to retribution, Marshall argues that the purely retributive justification for the death penalty is not consistent with human dignity.

The issue in this case is whether the imposition of the sentence of death for the crime of murder under the law of Georgia violates the Eighth and Fourteenth Amendments.

I

The petitioner, Troy Gregg, was charged with committing armed robbery and murder. In accordance with Georgia procedure in capital cases, the trial was in two stages, a guilt stage and a sentencing stage. . . .

. . . The jury found the petitioner guilty of two counts of murder.

At the penalty stage, which took place before the same jury, . . . the trial judge instructed the jury that it could recommend either a death sentence or a life prison sentence on each count. . . . The jury returned verdicts of death on each count.

The Supreme Court of Georgia affirmed the convictions and the imposition of the death sentences for murder. . . . The death sentences imposed for armed robbery, however, were vacated on the grounds that the death penalty had rarely been imposed in Georgia for that offense. . . .

II

. . . The Georgia statute, as amended after our decision in *Furman* v. *Georgia* (1972), retains the death penalty for six categories of crime: murder, kidnapping for ransom or where the victim is harmed, armed robbery, rape, treason, and aircraft hijacking. . . .

III

We address initially the basic contention that the punishment of death for the crime of murder is, under all circumstances, "cruel and unusual" in violation of the Eighth and Fourteenth Amendments of the Constitution. In Part IV of this opinion, we will consider the sentence of death imposed under the Georgia statutes at issue in this case.

The Court on a number of occasions has both assumed and asserted the constitutionality of capital punishment. In several cases that assumption provided a necessary foundation for the decision, as the Court was asked to decide whether a particular method of carrying out a capital sentence would be allowed to stand under the Eighth Amendment. But until *Furman* v. *Georgia* (1972), the Court never confronted squarely the fundamental claim that the punishment of death always, regardless of the enormity of the offense or the procedure followed in imposing the sentence, is cruel and unusual punishment in violation of the Constitution. Although this issue was presented and addressed in *Furman,* it was not resolved by the Court. Four Justices would have held that capital punishment is not unconstitutional *per se;* two Justices would have reached the opposite conclusion; and three Justices, while agreeing that the statutes then before the Court were invalid as applied, left open the question whether such punishment may ever be imposed. We now hold that the punishment of death does not invariably violate the Constitution.

A

The history of the prohibition of "cruel and unusual" punishment already has been reviewed at length. The phrase first appeared in the English Bill of Rights of 1689, which was drafted by Parliament at the accession of William and Mary. The English version appears to have been directed against punishments unauthorized by statute and beyond the jurisdiction of the sentencing court, as well as those disproportionate to the offense involved. The American draftsmen, who adopted the English phrasing in drafting the Eighth Amendment, were primarily concerned, however, with proscribing "tortures" and other "barbarous" methods of punishment.

In the earliest cases raising Eighth Amendment claims, the Court focused on particular methods of execution to determine whether they were too cruel to pass constitutional muster. The constitutionality of the sentence of death itself was not at issue, and the criterion used to evaluate the mode of execution was its similarity to "torture" and other "barbarous" methods. . . .

But the Court has not confined the prohibition embodied in the Eighth Amendment to "barbarous" methods that were generally outlawed in the 18th century. Instead, the Amendment has been interpreted in a flexible and dynamic manner. The Court early recognized that "a principle to be vital must be capable of wider application than the mischief which gave it birth." Thus the clause forbidding "cruel and unusual" punishments "is not fastened to the obsolete but may acquire meaning as public opinion becomes enlightened by a humane justice." . . .

It is clear from the foregoing precedents that the Eighth Amendment has not been regarded as a static concept. As Mr. Chief Justice Warren said, in an oftquoted phrase, "[t]he Amendment must draw its meaning from the evolving standards of decency that mark the progress of a maturing society." Thus, an assessment of contemporary values concerning the infliction of a challenged sanction is relevant to the application of the Eighth Amendment. As we develop below more fully, this assessment does not call for a subjective judgment. It requires, rather, that we look to objective indicia that reflect the public attitude toward a given sanction.

But our cases also make clear that public perceptions of standards of decency with respect to criminal sanctions are not conclusive. A penalty also must accord with "the dignity of man," which is the "basic concept underlying the Eighth Amendment." This means, at least, that the punishment not be "excessive." When a form of punishment in the abstract (in this case, whether capital punishment may ever be imposed as a sanction for murder) rather than in the particular (the propriety of death as a penalty to be applied to a specific defendant for a specific crime) is under consideration, the inquiry into "excessiveness" has two aspects. First, the punishment must not involve the unnecessary and wanton infliction of pain. Second, the punishment must not be grossly out of proportion to the severity of the crime.

B

Of course, the requirements of the Eighth Amendment must be applied with an awareness of the limited role to be played by the courts. This does not mean that judges have no role to play, for the Eighth Amendment is a restraint upon the exercise of legislative power. . . .

But, while we have an obligation to ensure that constitutional bounds are not over-reached, we may not act as judges as we might as legislators. . . .

Therefore, in assessing a punishment selected by a democratically elected legislature against the constitutional measure, we presume its validity. We may not require the legislature to select the least severe penalty possible so long as the penalty selected is not cruelly inhumane or disproportionate to the crime involved. And a heavy burden rests on those who would attack the judgment of the representatives of the people.

This is true in part because the constitutional test is intertwined with an assessment of contemporary standards and the legislative judgment weighs heavily in ascertaining such standards. "[I]n a democratic society legislatures, not courts, are constituted to respond to the will and consequently the moral values of the people."

The deference we owe to the decisions of the state legislatures under our federal system is enhanced where the specification of punishments is concerned, for "these are peculiarly questions of legislative policy." Caution is necessary lest this Court become, "under the aegis of the Cruel and Unusual Punishment Clause, the ultimate arbiter of the standards of criminal responsibility . . . throughout the country." A decision that a given punishment is impermissible under the Eighth Amendment cannot be reversed short of a constitutional amendment. The ability of the people to express their preference through the normal democratic processes, as well as through ballot referenda, is shut off. Revisions cannot be made in the light of further experience.

C

In the discussion to this point we have sought to identify the principles and considerations that guide a court in addressing an Eighth Amendment claim. We now consider specifically whether the sentence of death for the crime of murder is a *per se* violation of the Eighth and Fourteenth Amendments to the Constitution. We note first that history and precedent strongly support a negative answer to this question.

The imposition of the death penalty for the crime of murder has a long history of acceptance both in the United States and in England. . . .

It is apparent from the text of the Constitution itself that the existence of capital punishment was accepted by the Framers. At the time the Eighth Amendment was ratified, capital punishment was a common sanction in every State. Indeed, the First Congress of the United States enacted legislation providing death as the penalty for specified crimes. . . .

For nearly two centuries, this Court, repeatedly and often expressly, has recognized that capital punishment is not invalid *per se*. . . .

Four years ago, the petitioners in *Furman* and its companion cases predicated their argument primarily upon the asserted proposition that standards of decency had evolved to the point where capital punishment no longer could be tolerated. The petitioners in those cases said, in effect, that the evolutionary process had come to an end, and that standards of decency required that the Eighth Amendment be construed finally as prohibiting capital punishment for any crime regardless of its depravity and impact on society. This view was accepted by two Justices. Three other Justices were unwilling to go so far; focusing on the procedures by which convicted defendants were selected for the death penalty rather than on the actual punishment inflicted, they joined in the conclusion that the statutes before the Court were constitutionally invalid.

The petitioners in the capital cases before the Court today renew the "standards of decency" argument, but developments during the four years since *Furman* have undercut substantially the assumptions upon which their argument rested. Despite the continuing debate, dating back to the nineteenth century, over the morality and utility of capital punishment, it is now evident that a large proportion of American society continues to regard it as an appropriate and necessary criminal sanction.

The most marked indication of society's endorsement of the death penalty for murder is the legislative response to *Furman*. The legislatures of at least thirty-five States have enacted new statutes that provide for the death penalty for at least some crimes that result in the death of another person. And the Congress of the United States, in 1974, enacted a statute providing the death penalty for aircraft piracy that results in death. These recently adopted statutes have attempted to address the concerns expressed by the Court in *Furman* primarily (i) by specifying the factors to be weighed and the procedures to be followed in deciding when to impose a capital sentence, or (ii) by making the death penalty mandatory for specified crimes. But all of the post-*Furman* statutes make clear that capital punishment itself has not been rejected by the elected representatives of the people. . . .

The jury also is a significant and reliable objective index of contemporary values because it is so directly involved. The Court has said that "one of the most important functions any jury can perform in making . . . a selection [between life imprisonment and death for a defendant convicted in a capital case] is to maintain a link between contemporary community values and the penal system." It may be true that evolving standards have influenced juries in recent decades to be more discriminating in imposing the sentence of death. But the relative infrequency of jury verdicts imposing death sentence does not indicate rejection of capital punishment *per se*. Rather, the reluctance of juries in many cases to impose the sentence may well reflect the humane feeling that this most irrevocable of sanctions should be reserved for a small number of extreme cases. Indeed, the actions of juries in many states since *Furman* are fully compatible with the legislative judgments, reflected in the new statutes, as to the continued utility and necessity of capital punishment in appropriate cases. At the close of 1974 at least 254 persons had been sentenced to death since *Furman,* and by the end of March 1976, more than 460 persons were subject to death sentences.

As we have seen, however, the Eighth Amendment demands more than that a challenged punishment be acceptable to contemporary society. The Court also must ask whether it comports with the basic concept of human dignity at the core of the amendment. Although we cannot "invalidate a category of penalties because we deem less severe penalties adequate to serve the ends of penology," the sanction imposed cannot be so totally without penological justification that it results in the gratuitous infliction of suffering.

The death penalty is said to serve two principal social purposes: retribution and deterrence of capital crimes by prospective offenders.[1]

In part, capital punishment is an expression of society's moral outrage at particularly offensive conduct. This function may be unappealing to many, but it is essential in an ordered society that asks its citizens to rely on legal processes rather than self-help to vindicate their wrongs.

The instinct for retribution is part of the nature of man, and channeling that instinct in the administration of criminal justice serves an important purpose in promoting the stability of a society governed by law. When people begin to believe that organized society is unwilling or unable to impose upon criminal offenders the punishment they "deserve," then there are sown the seeds of anarchy—of self-help, vigilante justice, and lynch law. *Furman* v. *Georgia* (Stewart, J., concurring).

Retribution is no longer the dominant objective of the criminal law, but neither is it a forbidden objective nor one inconsistent with our respect for the dignity of men. Indeed, the decision that capital punishment may be the appropriate sanction in extreme cases is an expression of the community's belief that certain crimes are themselves so grievous an affront to humanity that the only adequate response may be the penalty of death.

Statistical attempts to evaluate the worth of the death penalty as a deterrent to crimes of potential offenders have occasioned a great deal of debate. The results simply have been inconclusive. . . .

Although some of the studies suggest that the death penalty may not function as a significantly greater deterrent than lesser penalties, there is no convincing empirical evidence either supporting or refuting this view. We may nevertheless assume safely that there are murderers, such as those who act in passion, for whom the threat of death has little or no deterrent effect. But for many others, the death penalty undoubtedly is a significant deterrent. There are carefully contemplated murders, such as murder for hire, where the possible penalty of death may well enter into the cold calculus that precedes the decision to act. And there are some categories of murder, such as murder by a life prisoner, where other sanctions may not be adequate.

The value of capital punishment as a deterrent of crime is a complex factual issue the resolution of which properly rests with the legislatures, which can evaluate the results of statistical studies in terms of their own local conditions and with a flexibility of approach that is not available to the courts. Indeed, many of the post-*Furman* statutes reflect just such a responsible effort to define those crimes and those criminals for which capital punishment is most probably an effective deterrent.

In sum, we cannot say that the judgment of the Georgia Legislature that capital punishment may be necessary in some cases is clearly wrong. Considerations of federalism, as well as respect for the ability of a legislature to evaluate, in terms of its particular State, the moral consensus concerning the death penalty and its social utility as a sanction, require us to conclude, in the absence of more convincing evidence, that the infliction of death as a punishment for murder is not without justification and thus is not constitutionally severe.

Finally, we must consider whether the punishment of death is disproportionate in relation to the crime for which it is imposed. There is no question that death as a punishment is unique in its severity and irrevocability. When a defendant's life is at stake, the Court has been particularly sensitive to insure that every safeguard is observed. But we are concerned here only with the imposition of capital punishment for the crime of murder, and when a life has been taken deliberately by the offender,[2] we cannot say that the punishment is invariably disproportionate to the crime. It is an extreme sanction, suitable to the most extreme of crimes.

We hold that the death penalty is not a form of punishment that may never be imposed, regardless of the circumstances of the offense, regardless of the character of the offender, and regardless of the procedure followed in reaching the decision to impose it.

IV

We now consider whether Georgia may impose the death penalty on the petitioner in this case.

A

While *Furman* did not hold that the infliction of the death penalty *per se* violates the Constitution's ban on cruel and unusual punishments, it did recognize that the penalty of death is different in kind from any other punishment imposed under our system of criminal justice. Because of the uniqueness of the death penalty, *Furman* held that it could not be imposed under sentencing procedures that created a substantial risk that it would be inflicted in an arbitrary and capricious manner. . . .

Furman mandates that where discretion is afforded a sentencing body on a matter so grave as the determination of whether a human life should be taken or spared, that discretion must be suitably directed and limited so as to minimize the risk of wholly arbitrary and capricious action.

It is certainly not a novel proposition that discretion in the area of sentencing be exercised in an informed manner. We have long recognized that "[f]or the determination of sentences, justice generally requires . . . that there be taken into account the circumstances of the offense together with the character and propensities of the offender." . . .

Jury sentencing has been considered desirable in capital cases in order "to maintain a link between contemporary community values and the penal system—a link without which the determination of punishment could hardly reflect 'the evolving standards of decency that mark the progress of a maturing society.'" But it creates special problems. Much of the information that is relevant to the sentencing decision may have no relevance to the question of guilt, or may even be extremely prejudicial to a fair determination of that question. This problem, however, is scarcely insurmountable. Those who have studied the question suggest that a bifurcated procedure—one in which the question of sentence is not considered until the determination of guilt has been made—is the best answer. . . . When a human life is at stake and when the jury must have information prejudicial to the question of guilt but relevant to the question of penalty in order to impose a rational sentence, a bifurcated system is more likely to ensure elimination of the constitutional deficiencies identified in *Furman*.

But the provision of relevant information under fair procedural rules is not alone sufficient to guarantee that the information will be properly used in the imposition of punishment, especially if sentencing is performed by a jury. Since the members of a jury will have had little, if any, previous experience in sentencing, they are unlikely to be skilled in dealing with the information they are given. To the extent that this problem is inherent in jury sentencing, it may not be totally correctable. It seems clear, however, that the problem will be alleviated if the jury is given guidance regarding the factors about the crime and the defendant that the State, representing organized society, deems particularly relevant to the sentencing decision. . . .

While some have suggested that standards to guide a capital jury's sentencing deliberations are impossible to formulate, the fact is that such standards have been developed. When the drafters of the Model Penal Code faced this problem, they concluded "that it is within the realm of possibility to point to the main circumstances of aggravation and of mitigation that should be weighed *and weighed against each other* when they are presented in a concrete case."[3] While such standards are by necessity somewhat general, they do provide guidance to the sentencing authority and thereby reduce the likelihood that it will impose a sentence that fairly can be called capricious or arbitrary. Where the sentencing authority is required to specify the factors it relied upon in reaching its decision, the further safeguard of meaningful appellate review is available to ensure that death sentences are not imposed capriciously or in a freakish manner.

In summary, the concerns expressed in *Furman* that the penalty of death not be imposed in an arbitrary or capricious manner can be met by a carefully drafted statute that ensures that the sentencing authority is given adequate information and guidance. As a general proposition these concerns are best met by a system that provides for a bifurcated proceeding at which the sentencing authority is apprised of the information relevant to the imposition of sentence and provided with standards to guide its use of the information.

We do not intend to suggest that only the above-described procedures would be permissible under *Furman* or that any sentencing system constructed along these general lines would inevitably satisfy the concerns of *Furman,* for each distinct system must be examined on an individual basis. Rather, we have embarked upon this general exposition to make clear that it is possible to construct capital-sentencing systems capable of meeting *Furman*'s constitutional concerns.

B

We now turn to consideration of the constitutionality of Georgia's capital-sentencing procedures. In the wake of *Furman,* Georgia amended its capital punishment statute, but chose not to narrow the scope of its murder provisions. Thus, now as before *Furman,* in Georgia "[a] person commits murder when he unlawfully and with malice aforethought, either express or implied, causes the death of another human being." All persons convicted of murder "shall be punished by death or by imprisonment for life."

Georgia did act, however, to narrow the class of murderers subject to capital punishment by specifying ten statutory aggravating circumstances, one of which must be found by the jury to exist beyond a reasonable doubt before a death sentence can ever be imposed. In addition, the jury is authorized to consider any other appropriate aggravating or mitigating circumstances. The jury is not required to find any mitigating circumstance in order to make a recommendation of mercy that is binding on the trial court, but it must find a *statutory* aggravating circumstance before recommending a sentence of death.

These procedures require the jury to consider the circumstances of the crime and the criminal before it recommends sentence. No longer can

a Georgia jury do as Furman's jury did: reach a finding of the defendant's guilt and then, without guidance or direction, decide whether he should live or die. Instead, the jury's attention is directed to the specific circumstances of the crime: Was it committed in the course of another capital felony? Was it committed for money? Was it committed on a peace officer or judicial officer? Was it committed in a particularly heinous way or in a manner that endangered the lives of many persons? In addition, the jury's attention is focused on the characteristics of the person who committed the crime: Does he have a record of prior convictions for capital offenses? Are there any special facts about this defendant that mitigate against imposing capital punishment (*e.g.,* his youth, the extent of his cooperation with the police, his emotional state at the time of the crime)? As a result, while some jury discretion still exists, "the discretion to be exercised is controlled by clear and objective standards so as to produce nondiscriminatory application."

As an important additional safeguard against arbitrariness and caprice, the Georgia statutory scheme provides for automatic appeal of all death sentences to the State's Supreme Court. That court is required by statute to review each sentence of death and determine whether it was imposed under the influence of passion or prejudice, whether the evidence supports the jury's finding of statutory aggravating circumstance, and whether the sentence is disproportionate compared to those sentences imposed in similar cases.

In short, Georgia's new sentencing procedures require as a prerequisite to the imposition of the death penalty, specific jury findings as to the circumstances of the crime or the character of the defendant. Moreover, to guard further against a situation comparable to that presented in *Furman,* the Supreme Court of Georgia compares each death sentence with the sentences imposed on similarly situated defendants to ensure that the sentence of death in a particular case is not disproportionate. On their face these procedures seem to satisfy the concerns of *Furman.* No longer should there be "no meaningful basis for distinguishing the few cases in which [the death penalty] is imposed from the many cases in which it is not." . . .

V

The basic concern of *Furman* centered on those defendants who were being condemned to death capriciously and arbitrarily. Under the procedures before the Court in that case, sentencing authorities were not directed to give attention to the nature or circumstances of the crime committed or to the character or record of the defendant. Left unguided, juries imposed the death sentence in a way that could only be called freakish. The new Georgia sentencing procedures, by contrast, focus the jury's attention on the particularized nature of the crime and the particularized characteristics of the individual defendant. While the jury is permitted to consider any aggravating or mitigating circumstances, it must find and identify at least one statutory aggravating factor before it may impose a penalty of death. In this way the jury's discretion is channeled. No longer can a jury wantonly and freakishly impose the death sentence; it is always circumscribed by the legislative guidelines. In addition, the review function of the Supreme Court of Georgia affords additional assurance that the concerns that prompted our decision in *Furman* are not present to any significant degree in the Georgia procedure applied here.

For the reasons expressed in this opinion, we hold that the statutory system under which Gregg was sentenced to death does not violate the Constitution. Accordingly, the judgment of the Georgia Supreme Court is affirmed.

DISSENTING OPINION

In *Furman* v. *Georgia* (1972) (concurring opinion), I set forth at some length my views on the basic issue presented to the Court in [this case]. The death penalty, I concluded, is a cruel and unusual punishment prohibited by the Eighth and Fourteenth Amendments. That continues to be my view.

I have no intention of retracing the "long and tedious journey" that led to my conclusion in *Furman*. My sole purposes here are to consider the suggestion that my conclusion in *Furman* has been undercut by developments since then,

and briefly to evaluate the basis for my Brethren's holding that the extinction of life is a permissible form of punishment under the Cruel and Unusual Punishments Clause.

In *Furman,* I concluded that the death penalty is constitutionally invalid for two reasons. First, the death penalty is excessive. And second, the American people, fully informed as to the purposes of the death penalty and its liabilities, would in my view reject it as morally unacceptable.

Since the decision in *Furman,* the legislatures of thirty-five States have enacted new statutes authorizing the imposition of the death sentence for certain crimes, and Congress has enacted a law providing the death penalty for air piracy resulting in death. I would be less than candid if I did not acknowledge that these developments have a significant bearing on a realistic assessment of the moral acceptability of the death penalty to the American people. But if the constitutionality of the death penalty turns, as I have urged, on the opinion of an *informed* citizenry, then even the enactment of new death statutes cannot be viewed as conclusive. In *Furman,* I observed that the American people are largely unaware of the information critical to a judgment on the morality of the death penalty, and concluded that if they were better informed they would consider it shocking, unjust, and unacceptable. A recent study, conducted after the enactment of the post-*Furman* statutes, has confirmed that the American people know little about the death penalty, and that the opinions of an informed public would differ significantly from those of a public unaware of the consequences and effects of the death penalty.

Even assuming, however, that the post-*Furman* enactment of statutes authorizing the death penalty renders the prediction of the views of an informed citizenry an uncertain basis for a constitutional decision, the enactment of those statutes has no bearing whatsoever on the conclusion that the death penalty is unconstitutional because it is excessive. An excessive penalty is invalid under the Cruel and Unusual Punishments Clause "even though popular sentiment may favor" it. The inquiry here, then, is simply whether the death penalty is necessary to accomplish the legitimate legislative purposes in punishment, or whether a less severe penalty—life imprisonment—would do as well.

The two purposes that sustain the death penalty as nonexcessive in the Court's view are general deterrence and retribution. In *Furman,* I canvassed the relevant data on the deterrent effect of capital punishment. The state of knowledge at that point, after literally centuries of debate, was summarized as follows by a United Nations Committee:

It is generally agreed between the retentionists and abolitionists, whatever their opinions about the validity of comparative studies of deterrence, that the data which now exist show no correlation between the existence of capital punishment and lower rates of capital crime.

The available evidence, I concluded in *Furman,* was convincing that "capital punishment is not necessary as a deterrent to crime in our society." . . .

The evidence I reviewed in *Furman* remains convincing, in my view, that "capital punishment is not necessary as a deterrent to crime in our society." The justification for the death penalty must be found elsewhere.

The other principal purpose said to be served by the death penalty is retribution. The notion that retribution can serve as a moral justification for the sanction of death finds credence in the opinion of my Brothers Stewart, Powell, and Stevens. . . . It is this notion that I find to be the most disturbing aspect of today's unfortunate [decision].

The concept of retribution is a multifaceted one, and any discussion of its role in the criminal law must be undertaken with caution. On one level, it can be said that the notion of retribution or reprobation is the basis of our insistence that only those who have broken the law be punished, and in this sense the notion is quite obviously central to a just system of criminal sanctions. But our recognition that retribution plays a crucial role in determining who may be punished by no means requires approval of retribution as a general justification for punishment. It is the question whether retribution can provide a moral justification for punishment—in particular, capital punishment—that we must consider.

My Brothers Stewart, Powell, and Stevens offer the following explanation of the retributive justification for capital punishments:

The instinct for retribution is part of the nature of man, and channeling that instinct in the administration of criminal justice serves an important purpose in promoting the stability of a society governed by law. When people begin to believe that organized society is unwilling or unable to impose upon criminal offenders the punishment they "deserve," then there are sown the seeds of anarchy—of self-help, vigilante justice, and lynch law.

This statement is wholly inadequate to justify the death penalty. As my Brother Brennan stated in *Furman,* "[t]here is no evidence whatever that utilization of imprisonment rather than death encourages private blood feuds and other disorders." It simply defies belief to suggest that the death penalty is necessary to prevent the American people from taking the law into their own hands.

In a related vein, it may be suggested that the expression of moral outrage through the imposition of the death penalty serves to reinforce basic moral values—that it marks some crimes as particularly offensive and therefore to be avoided. The argument is akin to a deterrence argument, but differs in that it contemplates the individual's shrinking from antisocial conduct, not because he fears punishment, but because he has been told in the strongest possible way that the conduct is wrong. This contention, like the previous one, provides no support for the death penalty. It is inconceivable that any individual concerned about conforming his conduct to what society says is "right" would fail to realize that murder is "wrong" if the penalty were simply life imprisonment.

The foregoing contentions—that society's expression of moral outrage through the imposition of the death penalty preempts the citizenry from taking the law into its own hands and reinforces moral values—are not retributive in the purest sense. They are essentially utilitarian in that they portray the death penalty as valuable because of its beneficial results. These justifications for the death penalty are inadequate because the penalty is, quite clearly I think, not necessary to the accomplishment of those results.

There remains for consideration, however, what might be termed the purely retributive justification for the death penalty—that the death penalty is appropriate, not because of its beneficial effect on society, but because the taking of the murderer's life is itself morally good. Some of the language of the opinion of my Brothers Stewart, Powell, and Stevens . . . appears positively to embrace this notion of retribution for its own sake as a justification for capital punishment. They state:

[T]he decision that capital punishment may be the appropriate sanction in extreme cases is an expression of the community's belief that certain crimes are themselves so grievous an affront to humanity that the only adequate response may be the penalty of death.

They then quote with approval from Lord Justice Denning's remarks before the British Royal Commission on Capital Punishment:

The truth is that some crimes are so outrageous that society insists on adequate punishment, because the wrong-doer deserves it, irrespective of whether it is a deterrent or not.

Of course, it may be that these statements are intended as no more than observations as to the popular demands that it is thought must be responded to in order to prevent anarchy. But the implication of the statements appears to me to be quite different—namely, that society's judgment that the murderer "deserves" death must be respected not simply because the preservation of order requires it, but because it is appropriate that society make the judgment and carry it out. It is the latter notion, in particular, that I consider to be fundamentally at odds with the Eighth Amendment. The mere fact that the community demands the murderer's life in return for the evil he has done cannot sustain the death penalty, for as Justices Stewart, Powell, and Stevens remind us, "the Eighth Amendment demands more than that a challenged punishment be acceptable to contemporary society." To be sustained under the Eighth Amendment, the death penalty must "compor[t] with the basic concept of human dignity at the core of the Amendment"; the objective in imposing it must be "[consistent] with our respect for the dignity of [other] men." Under these standards, the taking of life "because the wrongdoer deserves it" surely must fail, for such a punishment has as its very basis the total denial of the wrongdoer's dignity and worth.

The death penalty, unnecessary to promote the goal of deterrence or to further any legitimate notion of retribution, is an excessive penalty forbidden by the Eighth and Fourteenth Amendments. I respectfully dissent from the Court's judgment upholding the [sentence] of death imposed upon the [petitioner in this case].

Endnotes

1. Another purpose that has been discussed is the incapacitation of dangerous criminals and the consequent prevention of crimes that they may otherwise commit in the future.
2. We do not address here the question whether the taking of the criminal's life is a proportionate sanction where no victim has been deprived of life—for example, when capital punishment is imposed for rape, kidnapping, or armed robbery that does not result in the death of any human being.
3. The Model Penal Code proposes the following standards:
"(3) Aggravating Circumstances.
"(a) The murder was committed by a convict under sentence of imprisonment.
"(b) The defendant was previously convicted of another murder or of a felony involving the use or threat of violence to the person.
"(c) At the time the murder was committed the defendant also committed another murder.
"(d) The defendant knowingly created a great risk of death to many persons.
"(e) The murder was committed while the defendant was engaged or was an accomplice in the commission of, or an attempt to commit, or flight after committing or attempting to commit robbery, rape or deviate sexual intercourse by force or threat of force, arson, burglary or kidnapping.
"(f) The murder was committed for the purpose of avoiding or preventing a lawful arrest or effecting an escape from lawful custody.

"(g) The murder was committed for pecuniary gain.

"(h) The murder was especially heinous, atrocious or cruel, manifesting exceptional depravity.

"(4) Mitigating Circumstances.

"(a) The defendant has no significant history of prior criminal activity.

"(b) The murder was committed while the defendant was under the influence of extreme mental or emotional disturbance.

"(c) The victim was a participant in the defendant's homicide conduct or consented to the homicidal act.

"(d) The murder was committed under circumstances which the defendant believed to provide a moral justification or extenuation for his conduct.

"(e) The defendant was an accomplice in a murder committed by another person and his participation in the homicide act was relatively minor.

"(f) The defendant acted under duress or under the domination of another person.

"(g) At the time of the murder, the capacity of the defendant to appreciate the criminality [wrongfulness] of his conduct or to conform his conduct to the requirements of law was impaired as a result of mental disease or defect or intoxication.

"(h) The youth of the defendant at the time of the crime." ALI Model Penal Code §210.6 (Proposed Official Draft 1962).

REVIEW QUESTIONS

1. How did the justices rule in *Furman* v. *Georgia* (1972), and by contrast, how do they rule in this case?

2. According to the justices, what is the basic concept underlying the Eighth Amendment?

3. According to the justices, in what two ways may a punishment be excessive?

4. According to the justices, why doesn't the death penalty violate contemporary standards of decency?

5. The justices say that the death penalty serves two principal social purposes. What are they, and how are they supposed to work?

6. What safeguards against the arbitrary and capricious application of the death sentence are suggested by the justices?

7. Explain Justice Marshall's objections and his criticisms of the majority opinion.

DISCUSSION QUESTIONS

1. The Georgia statute retains the death penalty for six crimes, including rape, armed robbery, and treason. Do you agree that persons guilty of these crimes should receive the death sentence? Explain your view.

2. Try to give a precise definition of the phrase "cruel and unusual." Can you do it?

3. How could it be conclusively proven that the death penalty deters potential criminals better than life imprisonment?

4. Should the instinct for retribution be satisfied? Defend your answer.

Immanuel Kant

The Retributive Theory of Punishment

For biographical information on Kant, see his reading in Chapter 1.

In Kant's Retributive Theory of punishment, punishment is not justified by any good results, but

---

Immanuel Kant, *The Philosophy of Law*, Part II, trans. W. Hastie (1887).

simply by the criminal's guilt. Criminals must pay for their crimes; otherwise an injustice has occurred. Furthermore, the punishment must fit the crime. Kant asserts that the only punishment that is appropriate for the crime of murder is the death of the murderer. As he puts it, "Whoever has committed a murder must die."

Judicial or juridical punishment (*poena forensis*) is to be distinguished from natural punishment (*poena naturalis*), in which crime as vice punishes itself, and does not as such come within the cognizance of the legislator. Juridical punishment can never be administered merely as a means for promoting another good, either with regard to the criminal himself or to civil society, but must in all cases be imposed only because the individual on whom it is inflicted *has committed a crime.* For one man ought never to be dealt with merely as a means subservient to the purpose of another, nor be mixed up with the subjects of real right. Against such treatment his inborn personality has a right to protect him, even although he may be condemned to lose his civil personality. He must first be found guilty and *punishable,* before there can be any thought of drawing from his punishment any benefit for himself or his fellow-citizens. The penal law is a categorical imperative; and woe to him who creeps through the serpent-windings of utilitarianism to discover some advantage that may discharge him from the justice of punishment, or even from the due measure of it, according to the pharisaic maxim: 'It is better that *one* man should die than that the whole people should perish.' For if justice and righteousness perish, human life would no longer have any value in the world. What, then, is to be said of such a proposal as to keep a criminal alive who has been condemned to death, on his being given to understand that if he agreed to certain dangerous experiments being performed upon him, he would be allowed to survive if he came happily through them? It is argued that physicians might thus obtain new information that would be of value to the commonweal. But a court of justice would repudiate with scorn any proposal of this kind if made to it by the medical faculty; for justice would cease to be justice, if it were bartered away for any consideration whatever.

But what is the mode and measure of punishment which public justice takes as its principle and standard? It is just the principle of equality, by which the pointer of the scale of justice is made to incline no more to the one side than the other. It may be rendered by saying that the undeserved evil which any one commits on another, is to be regarded as perpetrated on himself. Hence it may be said: 'If you slander another, you slander yourself; if you steal from another, you steal from yourself; if you strike another, you strike yourself; if you kill another, you kill yourself.' This is the right of retaliation (*jus talionis*); and properly understood, it is the only principle which in regulating a public

court, as distinguished from mere private judgment, can definitely assign both the quality and the quantity of a just penalty. All other standards are wavering and uncertain; and on account of other considerations involved in them, they contain no principle comformable to the sentence of pure and strict justice. It may appear, however, that difference of social status would not admit the application of the principle of retaliation, which is that of 'like with like.' But although the application may not in all cases be possible according to the letter, yet as regards the effect it may always be attained in practice, by due regard being given to the disposition and sentiment of the parties in the higher social sphere. Thus a pecuniary penalty on account of a verbal injury, may have no direct proportion to the injustice of slander; for one who is wealthy may be able to indulge himself in this offense for his own gratification. Yet the attack committed on the honor of the party aggrieved may have its equivalent in the pain inflicted upon the pride of the aggressor, especially if he is condemned by the judgment of the court, not only to retract and apologize, but to submit to some meaner ordeal, as kissing the hand of the injured person. In like manner, if a man of the highest rank has violently assaulted an innocent citizen of the lower orders, he may be condemned not only to apologize but to undergo a solitary and painful imprisonment, whereby, in addition to the discomfort endured, the vanity of the offender would be painfully affected, and the very shame of his position would constitute an adequate retaliation after the principle of like with like. But how then would we render the statement: 'If you *steal* from another, you steal from yourself'? In this way, that whoever steals anything makes the property of all insecure; he therefore robs himself of all security in property, according to the right of retaliation. Such a one has nothing, and can acquire nothing, but he has the will to live; and this is only possible by others supporting him. But as the state should not do this gratuitously, he must for this purpose yield his powers to the state to be used in penal labour; and thus he falls for a time, or it may be for life, into a condition of slavery. But whoever has committed murder, must *die.* There is, in this case, no juridical substitute or surrogate, that can be given or taken for the satisfaction of justice. There is no *likeness* or proportion between life, however painful, and death; and therefore there is no equality between the crime of murder and the retaliation of it but what is judicially accomplished by the execution of the criminal. His death, however, must be kept free from all maltreatment that would make the humanity suffering in his person loathsome or abominable. Even if a civil society resolved to dissolve itself with the consent of all its members—as might be supposed in the case of a people inhabiting an island resolving to separate and scatter themselves throughout the whole world—the last murderer lying in the prison ought to be executed before the resolution was carried out. This ought to be done in order that everyone may realize the desert of his deeds, and that blood-guiltiness may not remain upon the people; for otherwise they might all be regarded as participators in the murder as a public violation of justice.

The equalization of punishment with crime, is therefore only possible by the cognition of the judge extending even to the penalty of death, according to the right of retaliation.

REVIEW QUESTIONS

1. According to Kant, who deserves judicial punishment?
2. Why does Kant reject the maxim "It is better that *one* man should die than that the whole people should perish"?
3. How does Kant explain the principle of retaliation?

DISCUSSION QUESTIONS

1. Does Kant have any good reason to reject the "serpent-windings of utilitarianism"?
2. Is death always a just punishment for murder? Can you think of any exceptions?

Jonathan Glover

Execution and Assassination

Johnathan Glover is a fellow and tutor in philosophy at New College, Oxford, and has written Responsibility *(1970),* Causing Death and Saving Lives *(1977), and* What Sort of People Should There Be? *(1984).*

Glover begins with a discussion of Kant's Retributive Theory and the absolutist rejection of capital punishment. He finds both of these to be unacceptable from a utilitarian point of view. The

utilitarian approach is that the death penalty is justified if the number of lives saved exceeds the number of executions. But due to the bad side effects of execution on the person executed and on others, as well as other undesirable features, the death penalty is not justified unless it has a substantial deterrent effect. After considering arguments for this deterrent effect, Glover concludes that the case for capital punishment as a substantial deterrent fails.

The Penal Law is a Categorical Imperative; and woe to him who creeps through the serpent-windings of Utilitarianism to discover some advantage that may discharge him from the Justice of Punishment, or even from the due measure of it. . . . For if Justice and Righteousness perish, human life would no longer have any value in the world. . . . Whoever has committed murder must die.

Immanuel Kant, *The Philosophy of Law*

It is curious, but till that moment I had never realized what it means to destroy a healthy, conscious man. When I saw the prisoner step aside to avoid the puddle

I saw the mystery, the unspeakable wrongness, of cutting a life short when it is in full tide. This man was not dying, he was alive just as we are alive. All the organs of his body were working—bowels digesting food, skin renewing itself, nails growing, tissues forming—all toiling away in solemn foolery. His nails would still be growing when he stood on the drop, when he was falling through the air with a tenth of a second to live. His eyes saw the yellow gravel and the gray walls, and his brain still remembered, foresaw, reasoned, even about puddles. He and we were a party of men walking together, seeing, hearing, feeling, understanding the same world; and in two minutes, with a sudden snap, one of us would be gone—one mind less, one world less.
George Orwell, "A Hanging," *Adelphi*, 1931

The debate about capital punishment for murder is, emotionally at least, dominated by two absolutist views. On the retributive view, the murderer must be given the punishment he deserves, which is death. On the other view, analogous to pacifism about war, there is in principle no possibility of justifying capital punishment; in execution there is only "the unspeakable wrongness of cutting a life short when it is in full tide." Supporters of these two approaches agree only in rejecting the serpent-windings of utilitarianism.

Let us look first at the retributive view. According to retributivism in its purest form, the aim of punishment is quite independent of any beneficial social consequences it may have. To quote Kant again:

Even if a Civil Society resolved to dissolve itself with the consent of all its members—as might be supposed in the case of a people inhabiting an island resolving to separate and scatter themselves throughout the whole world—the last Murderer lying in the prison ought to be executed before the resolution was carried out. This ought to be done in order that everyone may realize the desert of his deeds, and that blood-guiltiness may not remain upon the people; for otherwise they might all be regarded as participants in the murder as a public violation of justice.

This view of punishment, according to which it has a value independent of its contribution to reducing the crime rate, is open to the objection that acting on it leads to what many consider to be pointless suffering. To impose suffering or deprivation on someone, or to take his life, is something that those of us who are not retributivists think needs very strong justification in terms of benefits, either to the person concerned or to other people. The retributivist has to say either that the claims of justice can make it right to harm someone where no one benefits, or else to cite the curiously **metaphysical** "benefits" of justice being done, such as Kant's concern that we should have "blood-guiltiness" removed. I have no way of refuting these positions, as they seem to involve no clear intellectual mistake. I do not expect to win the agreement of those who hold them, and I am simply presupposing the other view, that there is already enough misery in the world, and that adding to it requires a justification in terms of nonmetaphysical benefits to people.

This is not to rule out retributive moral principles perhaps playing a limiting role in a general theory of punishment. There is a lot to be said for the retributive restrictions that *only* those who deserve punishment should receive it and that they should never get more punishment than they deserve. (The case for this, which at least partly rests on utilitarian considerations, has been powerfully argued by H. L. A. Hart.[1]) But the approach to be adopted here rules out using retributive considerations to justify any punishment not already justifiable in terms of social benefits. In particular it rules out the argument that capital punishment can be justified, whether or not it reduces the crime rate, because the criminal deserves it.

This approach also has the effect of casting doubt on another way of defending capital punishment, which was forthrightly expressed by Lord Denning: "The ultimate justification of any punishment is not that it is a deterrent, but that it is the emphatic denunciation by the community of a crime: and from this point of view, there are some murders which, in the present state of public opinion, demand the most emphatic denunciation of all, namely the death penalty." [2] The question here is whether the point of the denunciation is to reduce the murder rate, in which case this turns out after all to be a utilitarian justification, or whether denunciation is an end in itself. If it is an end in itself, it starts to look like the retributive view in disguise, and should be rejected for the same reasons.

If we reject retribution for its own sake as a justification for capital punishment we are left with two alternative general approaches to the question. One is an absolute rejection in principle of any possibility of capital punishment being justified, in the spirit of Orwell's remarks. The other is the rather more messy approach, broadly utilitarian in character, of weighing up likely social costs and benefits.

THE ABSOLUTIONIST REJECTION OF CAPITAL PUNISHMENT

To some people, it is impossible to justify the act of killing a fellow human being. They are absolute pacifists about war and are likely to think of capital punishment as "judicial murder." They will sympathize with Beccaria's question: "Is it not absurd that the laws which detest and punish homicide, in order to prevent murder, publicly commit murder themselves?"

The test of whether an opponent of capital punishment adopts this absolutionist position is whether he would still oppose it if it could be shown to save many more lives than it cost, if, say, every execution deterred a dozen potential murderers. The absolutist, unlike the utilitarian opponent of the death penalty, would be unmoved by any such evidence. This question brings out the links between the absolutionist position and the **acts and omissions doctrine.** For those of us who reject the acts and omissions doctrine, the deaths we fail to prevent have to be given weight, as well as the deaths we cause by execution. So those of us who do not accept the acts and omissions doctrine cannot be absolutist opponents of capital punishment.

There is a variant on the absolutist position that at first sight seems not to presuppose the acts and omissions doctrine. On this view, while saving a potential murder victim is in itself as important as not killing a murderer, there is something so cruel about the kind of death involved in capital punishment that this rules out the possibility of its being justified. Those of us who reject the acts and omissions doctrine have to allow that sometimes there can be side effects associated with an act of killing, but not with failure to save a life, which can be sufficiently

bad to make a substantial moral difference between the two. When this view is taken of the cruelty of the death penalty, it is not usually the actual method of execution that is objected to, though this can seem important, as in the case where international pressure on General Franco led him to substitute shooting for the garrote. What seems peculiarly cruel and horrible about capital punishment is that the condemned man has the period of waiting, knowing how and when he is to be killed. Many of us would rather die suddenly then linger for weeks or months knowing we were fatally ill, and the condemned man's position is several degrees worse than that of the person given a few months to live by doctors. He has the additional horror of knowing exactly when he will die, and of knowing that his death will be in a ritualized killing by other people, symbolizing his ultimate rejection by the members of his community. The whole of his life may seem to have a different and horrible meaning when he sees it leading up to this end.

For reasons of this kind, capital punishment can plausibly be claimed to fall under the United States Constitution's ban on "cruel and unusual punishments," so long as the word unusual is not interpreted too strictly. The same reasons make the death penalty a plausible candidate for falling under a rather similar ethical ban, which has been expressed by H. L. A. Hart: "There are many different ways in which we think it morally incumbent on us to *qualify* or *limit* the pursuit of the utilitarian goal by methods of punishment. Some punishments are ruled out as too barbarous to use *whatever their social utility*" [3] (final italics mine). Because of the extreme cruelty of capital punishment, many of us would, if forced to make a choice between two horrors, prefer to be suddenly murdered than be sentenced to death and executed. This is what makes it seem reasonable to say that the absolutist rejection of the death penalty need not rest on the acts and omissions doctrine.

But this appearance is illusory. The special awfulness of capital punishment may make an execution even more undesirable than a murder (though many would disagree on the grounds that this is outweighed by the desirability that the guilty rather than the innocent should die).

Even if we accept that an execution is worse than an average murder, it does not follow from this that capital punishment is too barbarous to use *whatever its social utility*. For supposing a single execution deterred many murders? Or suppose that some of the murders deterred would themselves have been as cruel as an execution? When we think of the suffering imposed in a famous kidnapping case, where the mother received her son's ear through the post, we may feel uncertain even that capital punishment is more cruel than some "lesser" crimes than murder. The view that some kinds of suffering are too great to impose, whatever their social utility, rules out the possibility of justifying them, however much more suffering they would prevent. And this does presuppose the acts and omissions of us even from this version of absolutism.

A UTILITARIAN APPROACH

It is often supposed that the utilitarian alternative to absolutism is simply one of adopting an unqualified maximizing policy. On such a view, the death penalty would be justified if, and only if, it was reasonable to think the number of lives saved exceeded the number of executions. (The question of what to do where the numbers exactly balance presupposes a fineness of measurement that is unattainable in these matters.) On any utilitarian view, numbers of lives saved must be a very important consideration. But there are various special features that justify the substantial qualification of a maximizing policy.

The special horror of the period of waiting for execution may not justify the absolutist rejection of the death penalty, but it is a powerful reason for thinking that an execution may normally cause more misery than a murder, and so for thinking that, if capital punishment is to be justified, it must do better than break even when lives saved through deterrence are compared with lives taken by the executioner.

This view is reinforced when we think of some of the other side effects of the death penalty. It must be appalling to be told that your husband, wife, or child has been murdered, but this is surely less bad than the experience of

waiting a month or two for your husband, wife, or child to be executed. And those who think that the suffering of the murderer himself matters less than that of an innocent victim will perhaps not be prepared to extend this view to the suffering of the murderer's parents, wife, and children.

There is also the possibility of mistakenly executing an innocent man, something which it is very probable happened in the case of Timothy Evans. The German Federal Ministry of Justice is quoted in the Council of Europe's report on *The Death Penalty in European Countries* as saying that in the hundred years to 1953, there were twenty-seven death sentences "now established or presumed" to be miscarriages of justice. This point is often used as an argument against capital punishment, but what is often not noticed is that its force must depend on the special horrors of execution as compared with other forms of death, including being murdered. For the victim of murder is innocent too, and he also has no form of redress. It is only the (surely correct) assumption that an innocent man faces something much worse in execution than in murder that gives this argument its claim to prominence in this debate. For, otherwise, the rare cases of innocent men being executed would be completely overshadowed by the numbers of innocent men being murdered. (Unless, of course, the acts and omissions doctrine is again at work here, for execution is something that we, as a community, *do* while a higher murder rate is something, we at most *allow*.)

The death penalty also has harmful effects on people other than the condemned man and his family. For most normal people, to be professionally involved with executions, whether as judge, prison warden, chaplain, or executioner, must be highly disturbing. Arthur Koestler quotes the case of the executioner Ellis, who attempted suicide a few weeks after he executed a sick woman "whose insides fell out before she vanished through the trap." [4] (Though the chances must be very small of the experience of Mr. Pierrepoint, who describes in his autobiography how he had to execute a friend with whom he often sang duets in a pub.[5]) And there are wider effects on society at large. When there is capital punishment, we are all involved in the horrible business of a long-premeditated killing, and most of us will to some degree share in the emotional response George Orwell had so strongly when he had to be present. It cannot be good for children at school to know that there is an execution at the prison down the road. And there is another bad effect, drily stated in the *Report of the Royal Commission on Capital Punishment:* "No doubt the ambition that prompts an average of five applications a week for the post of hangman, and the craving that draws a crowd to the prison where a notorious murderer is being executed, reveal psychological qualities that no state would wish to foster in its citizens."

Capital punishment is also likely to operate erratically. Some murderers are likely to go free because the death penalty makes juries less likely to convict. (Charles Dickens, in a newspaper article quoted in the 1868 Commons debate, gave the example of a forgery case, where a jury found a £10 note to be worth thirty-nine shillings, in order to save the forger's life.) There are also great problems in operating a reprieve system without arbitrariness, say, in deciding whether being pregnant or having a young baby should qualify a woman for a reprieve.

Finally, there is the drawback that the retention or reintroduction of capital punishment contributes to a tradition of cruel and horrible punishment that we might hope would wither away. Nowadays we never think of disemboweling people or chopping off their hands as a punishment. Even if these punishments would be especially effective in deterring some very serious crimes, they are not regarded as a real possibility. To many of us, it seems that the utilitarian benefits from this situation outweigh the loss of any deterrent power they might have if reintroduced for some repulsive crime like kidnapping. And the longer we leave capital punishment in abeyance, the more its use will seem as out of the question as the no more cruel punishment of mutilation. (At this point, I come near to Hart's view that some punishments are too barbarous to use whatever their social utility. The difference is that I think that arguments for and against a punishment should be based on social utility, but that a wide-spread view that some things are unthinkable is itself of great social utility.)

For these reasons, a properly thought-out utilitarianism does not enjoin an unqualified policy of seeking the minimum loss of life, as the no trade-off view does. Capital punishment has its own special cruelties and horrors, which change the whole position. In order to be justified, it must be shown, with good evidence, that it has a deterrent effect not obtainable by less awful means, and one that is quite substantial rather than marginal.

DETERRENCE AND MURDER

The arguments over whether capital punishment deters murder more effectively than less drastic methods are of two kinds: statistical and intuitive. The statistical arguments are based on various kinds of comparisons of murder rates. Rates are compared before and after abolition in a country, and where possible, further comparisons are made with rates after reintroduction of capital punishment. Rates are compared in neighboring countries, or neighboring states of the U.S., with and without the death penalty. I am not a statistician and have no special competence to discuss the issue, but will merely purvey the received opinion of those who have looked into the matter. Those who have studied the figures are agreed that there is no striking correlation between the absence of capital punishment and any alteration in the curve of the murder rate. Having agreed on this point they then fall into two schools. On one view, we can conclude that capital punishment is not a greater deterrent to murder than the prison sentences that are substituted for it. On the other, more cautious, view, we can only conclude that we do not know that capital punishment is a deterrent. I shall not attempt to choose between these interpretations. For, given that capital punishment is justified only where there is good evidence that it is a substantial deterrent, either interpretation fails to support the case for it.

If the statistical evidence were conclusive that capital punishment did not deter more than milder punishments, this would leave no room for any further discussion. But, since the statistical evidence may be inconclusive, many people feel there is room left for intuitive arguments. Some of these deserve examination. The intuitive case was forcefully stated in 1864 by Sir James Fitzjames Stephen: [6]

No other punishment deters men so effectually from committing crimes as the punishment of death. This is one of those propositions which it is difficult to prove, simply because they are in themselves more obvious than any proof can make them. It is possible to display ingenuity in arguing against it, but that is all. The whole experience of mankind is in the other direction. The threat of instant death is the one to which resort has always been made when there was an absolute necessity for producing some result. . . . No one goes to certain inevitable death except by compulsion. Put the matter the other way. Was there ever yet a criminal who, when sentenced to death and brought out to die, would refuse the offer of a commutation of his sentence for the severest secondary punishment? Surely not. Why is this? It can only be because "All that a man has will he give for his life." In any secondary punishment, however terrible, there is hope; but death is death; its terrors cannot be described more forcibly.

These claims turn out when scrutinized to be much more speculative and doubtful than they at first sight appear.

The first doubt arises when Stephen talks of "certain inevitable death." The Royal Commission, in their *Report,* after quoting the passage from Stephen above, quote figures to show that, in the fifty years from 1900 to 1949, there was in England and Wales one execution for every twelve murders known to the police. In Scotland in the same period there was less than one execution for every twenty-five murders known to the police. Supporters of Stephen's view could supplement their case by advocating more death sentences and fewer reprieves, or by optimistic speculations about better police detection or greater willingness of juries to convict. But the reality of capital punishment as it was in these countries, unmodified by such recommendations and speculations, was not one where the potential murderer faced certain, inevitable death. This may incline us to modify Stephen's estimate of its deterrent effect, unless

we buttress his view with the further speculation that a fair number of potential murderers falsely believed that what they would face was certain, inevitable death.

The second doubt concerns Stephen's talk of "the threat of instant death." The reality again does not quite fit this. By the time the police conclude their investigation, the case is brought to trial, and verdict and sentence are followed by appeal, petition for reprieve, and then execution, many months have probably elapsed, and when this time factor is added to the low probability of the murderers being executed, the picture looks very different. For we often have a time bias, being less affected by threats of future catastrophes than by threats of instant ones. The certainty of immediate death is one thing; it is another thing merely to increase one's chances of death in the future. Unless this were so, no one would smoke or take on such high-risk jobs as diving in the North Sea.

There is another doubt when Stephen very plausibly says that virtually all criminals would prefer life imprisonment to execution. The difficulty is over whether this entitles us to conclude that it is therefore a more effective deterrent. For there is the possibility that, compared with the long term of imprisonment that is the alternative, capital punishment is what may appropriately be called an "overkill." It may be that, for those who will be deterred by threat of punishment, a long prison sentence is sufficient deterrent. I am not suggesting that this is so, but simply that it is an open question whether a worse alternative here generates any additional deterrent effect. The answer is *not* intuitively obvious.

Stephen's case rests on the speculative psychological assumptions that capital punishment is not an overkill compared with a prison sentence, and that its additional deterrent effect is not obliterated by time bias, nor by the low probability of execution, nor by a combination of these factors. Or else it must be assumed that, where the additional deterrent effect would be obliterated by the low probability of death, either on its own or in combination with time bias, the potential murderer thinks the probability is higher than it is. Some of these assumptions may be true, but, when they are brought out into the open, it is by no means obvious that the required combination of them can be relied upon.

Supporters of the death penalty also sometimes use what David A. Conway, in his valuable discussion of this issue, calls "the best-bet argument." [7] On this view, since there is no certainty whether or not capital punishment reduces the number of murders, either decision about it involves gambling with lives. It is suggested that it is better to gamble with the lives of murderers than with the lives of their innocent potential victims. This presupposes the attitude, rejected here, that a murder is a greater evil than the execution of a murderer. But, since this attitude probably has overwhelmingly widespread support, it is worth noting that, even if it is accepted, the best-bet argument is unconvincing. This is because, as Conway has pointed out, it overlooks the fact that we are not choosing between the chance of a murderer dying and the chance of a victim dying. In leaving the death penalty, we are opting for the certainty of the murderer dying that we hope will give us a chance of a potential victim being saved. This would look like a good bet only if we thought an execution substantially preferable to a murder and either the statistical evidence or the intuitive arguments made the effectiveness of the death penalty as a deterrent look reasonably likely.

Since the statistical studies do not give any clear indication that capital punishment makes any difference to the number of murders committed, the only chance of its supporters discharging the heavy burden of justification would be if the intuitive arguments were extremely powerful. We might then feel justified in supposing that other factors distorted the murder rate, masking the substantial deterrent effect of capital punishment. The intuitive arguments, presented as the merest platitudes, turn out to be speculative and unobvious. I conclude that the case for capital punishment as a substantial deterrent fails.

DETERRENCE AND POLITICAL CRIMES BY OPPOSITION GROUPS

It is sometimes suggested that the death penalty may be an effective deterrent in the case of a special class of "political" crimes. The "ordinary" murder (killing one's wife in a moment of rage, shooting a policeman in panic after a robbery, killing someone in a brawl) may not be particularly sensitive to different degrees of punishment. But some killings for political purposes have a degree of preparation and thought that may allow the severity of the penalty to affect the calculation. Two different kinds of killing come to mind here. There are killings as part of a political campaign, ranging from assassination through terrorist activities up to full-scale guerrilla war. And then there are policies carried out by repressive governments, varying from "liquidation" of individual opponents with or without "trial" to policies of wholesale extermination, sometimes, but not always, in wartime.

Let us look first at killings by groups opposed to governments. Would the various sectarian terrorist groups in Ireland stop their killings if those involved were executed? Would independence movements in countries like Algeria or Kenya have confined themselves to nonviolent means if more executions had taken place? Could the Nazis have deterred the French resistance by more executions? Could the Americans have deterred guerrilla war in Vietnam by more executions?

To ask these questions is to realize both the variety of different political situations in which the question of deterrent killing arises, and also to be reminded, if it is necessary, that moral right is not always on the side of the authorities trying to do the deterring. But let us, for the sake of argument, assume a decent government is trying to deal with terrorists or guerrillas whose cause has nothing to be said for it. People have always gone to war knowing they risk their lives, and those prepared to fight in a guerrilla war seem scarcely likely to change their mind because of the marginal extra risk of capital punishment if they are arrested. If the case is to be made, it must apply to lower levels of violence than full-scale guerrilla war.

Given the death penalty's drawbacks, is there any reason to think it would be sufficiently effective in deterring a campaign of terrorist violence to be justified? The evidence is again inconclusive. In many countries there have been terrorist campaigns where the authorities have responded with executions without stopping the campaign. It is always open to someone to say that the level of terrorist activity might have been even higher but for the executions, but it is hard to see why this should be likely. Those who do the shooting or the planting of bombs are not usually the leaders and can be easily replaced by others willing to risk their lives. Danger to life does not deter people from fighting in wars, and a terrorist gunman may be just as committed to his cause as a soldier. And executions create martyrs, which helps the terrorist cause. They may even raise the level of violence by leading to reprisals.

But it may be that a sufficiently ruthless policy of executions would be effective enough to overcome these drawbacks. It has been claimed that the policy of the Irish government in 1922-3 is an instance of this. David R. Bates describes it as follows: [8]

In the turbulent period following the establishment of the Irish Free State, military courts with power to inflict the death penalty were set up to enable the Irregulars (opposing the Treaty) to be crushed. These powers were first used on 17 November 1922, when four young men were arrested in Dublin and, on being found to be armed, were executed. Shortly afterwards the Englishman, Erskine Childers, captured while carrying a revolver, was also executed. On 7 December two Deputies were shot (one fatally) by the Irregulars. The Minister for Defense, with the agreement of the Cabinet, selected four Irregular leaders who had been in prison since the fall of the Four Courts on 29 June. They were wakened, told to prepare themselves, and were executed by firing squad at dawn. During a six-month period, almost twice as many Irregular prisoners were executed as had been executed by the British from 1916 to 1921. At the end of April 1923, the Irregulars sought a cease fire to discuss terms. The Free State Government refused. In May 1924, the Irregulars conceded military defeat.

This is an impressive case, and it may be that this degree of ruthlessness by the government involved fewer deaths than would have taken place during a prolonged terrorist campaign. But against this must be set some doubts. What would have happened if the terrorists had been as ruthless in reprisal as the government, per-haps announcing that for every man executed there would be two murders? Is it clear that after a period of such counter-retaliation it would have been the Irregulars rather than the government who climbed down? Does not any net saving of lives by the government's ruthless policy depend on the terrorists refraining from counter-retaliation, and can this be relied on in other cases? And is there not something dangerous in the precedent set when a government has prisoners executed without their having been convicted and sentenced for a capital offense? And, in this case, is it even clear that the defeat of the Irregulars ended once and for all the violence associated with the issues they were campaigning about? I raise these questions, not to claim that the government policy was clearly wrong, but to show how even a case like this is ambiguous in the weight it lends to the argument for using the death penalty against terrorism.

I do not think that the chance of a net saving of lives will in general outweigh the combination of the general drawbacks of capital punishment combined with the danger of its merely leading to a higher level of violence in a terrorist situation. But this is a matter of judgment rather than proof, and I admit that it *may* be that the opposite view had better results than mine would have had in 1922.

DETERRENCE AND POLITICAL CRIMES BY THE AUTHORITIES

The other category of political crimes that sometimes seems so special as to justify the death penalty is atrocities committed by governments or their agents. The executions of leading Nazis after the Nuremberg trials and the execution of Eichmann after his trial in Jerusalem come to mind. The justification usually advanced for these executions is retributive, and it is hard to imagine any more deserving candidates for the death penalty. But, for those of us who do not consider retribution an acceptable aim of punishment, the question must be whether executing them made their kind of activity less likely to happen again in the future. For, if not, we have no answer to the question asked by Victor Gollancz at the time of the

Eichmann trial: why should we think we improve the world by turning six million deaths into six million and one?

The chances of people who design or carry out governmental policies of murder being tried and sentenced must often be very small. Sometimes this happens as the result of revolution or defeat in war, but those in power stand a fairly good chance of being killed under these circumstances anyway, and the additional hazard of capital punishment may not have much deterrent effect. As with "ordinary" murderers, the hope of not being caught reduces the punishment's terrors. Some of those who murdered for Hitler were executed; their opposite numbers under Stalin paid no penalty. The torturers who worked for the Greek colonels were brought to trial, but those now at work in Chile, Brazil, and South Africa have every expectation of not being punished.

When considering isolated cases of governmental murder (perhaps the assassination of a troublesome foreign leader by a country's intelligence agency, or the single killing of a political opponent) there seems no reason to think capital punishment more of a deterrent than it is of "ordinary" nonpolitical murder. If anything, it is likely to be less of a deterrent because of the reduced chance of a murder charge ever being brought. So there seems no case for treating these crimes as other than ordinary murders. But when considering large-scale atrocities, on the scale of those of Hitler or Stalin, or even on the scale of Lyndon Johnson in Vietnam or General Gowon in Nigeria, a version of the best-bet argument comes into play. There are two possible advantages to the death penalty here. One is simply that of totally eliminating the chance of the same mass murderer occupying a position of leadership again. Suppose Hitler had been captured at the end of the Second World War and the question of executing him had arisen. If he had not been executed, it is overwhelmingly probable that he would have spent the rest of his life in Spandau prison, writing his memoirs and giving increasingly senile lectures on world history to visiting journalists. But there would always be the very slight risk of an escape and return to power in the style of Napoleon. This slight risk is removed by execution. The other advantage of the death penalty is the chance, which we have seen to be probably very slight, of deterring repetition of such policies by other leaders.

The best-bet argument in these cases can be used by someone who accepts that the dangers of a defeated leader returning to power are very small and that the chances of execution deterring future leaders from similar policies are also very small. The argument is simply that, where the prevention of such enormous atrocities is in question, even an extremely small probability of prevention is valuable. Consider a case in which numbers and probabilities are parallel, but in which act and omission are reversed. Suppose someone in the hospital can have his life saved only by the making of some organism that has previously been banned. The reason for the ban is that there is a danger, but only a very faint one, of the organism getting out of control. If it does this, the death rate will run into millions. Let us suppose that our intuitive estimate of the unquantifiable risk here is the same as our intuitive estimate of the unquantifiable reduction of risk caused by executing the murdering leader. Those who would rather let the hospital patient die than breach the ban on the dangerous organism must either rely on the acts and omissions doctrine, or else rely on some difference of side effects, if they are not prepared to support executing the murdering politician or official.

Part of the difficulty in interpreting comparisons of this sort arises from the fact that we are dealing with probabilities that cannot be measured. And, even if they could be measured, most of us are unclear what sacrifices are worth making for the reduction of some risk that is already very small. But if we make the highly artificial assumption that the alterations in probability of risk are the same in the medical case as in the executions case, the dilemma remains. Let us suppose that the risk is one that we would not take in the medical case to save a single life. Those of us who do not accept the acts and omissions doctrine must then either find some difference of side effects or else support the execution.

Side effects do go some way towards separating the two cases. For, to breach the ban on producing the organism, even if it does no harm itself, contributes by example to a less strict observance of that ban (and possibly others) in cases in which the risk may be much greater. In the case of the Nazi leaders, such bad side effects as exist follow from execution rather than from saving their lives. These side effects include the contribution made to a climate of opinion where the death penalty seems more acceptable in other contexts, and the precedent that may encourage politicians to have their overthrown rivals, at home or abroad, executed. This last effect could be mitigated by more effort than was made at Nuremberg to remove the impression of the defeated being tried by the victors. It would be possible to set up a court of a genuinely international kind, independent of governmental pressure, to which prosecutions for a large-scale murder could be brought. But the general effect on the public consciousness of having capital punishment as a series of possibility would remain. I am uncertain how to weigh this against the small chance of helping to avert a great evil. For this reason my own views on this question are undecided.

Endnotes

1. H. L. A. Hart, "Prolegomenon to the Principles of Punishment," *Proceedings of the Aristotelian Society,* . 1959–60.
2. Quoted in the *Report of the Royal Commission on Capital Punishment,* 1953.
3. H. L. A. Hart, "Murder and the Principles of Punishment," *Northwestern Law Review,* 1958.
4. Arthur Koestler, *Reflections on Hanging,* London, 1956.
5. Albert Pierrepoint, *Executioner: Pierrepoint,* London, 1974.
6. James Fitzjames Stephen, "Capital Punishments," *Fraser's Magazine,* 1864.
7. David A. Conway, "Capital Punishment and Deterrence," *Philosophy and Public Affairs,* 1974.

8. Professor David R. Bates, Letter to *The Times,* 14 October 1975.

REVIEW QUESTIONS

1. Why doesn't Glover accept Kant's view of capital punishment?
2. What is the other view that Glover is presupposing?
3. Why doesn't Glover accept the absolutist rejection of capital punishment?
4. Why does Glover think that capital punishment can plausibly be claimed to be a "cruel and unusual punishment"?
5. According to Glover, in what cases can capital punishment be justified even if it is cruel?
6. State the maximizing policy and the considerations that Glover introduces to qualify it.
7. According to Glover, how can capital punishment be justified?
8. Glover discusses three arguments (beginning with the statistical argument) that are used to defend capital punishment. What are these arguments, and why doesn't Glover accept them?
9. What is Glover's position on capital punishment for political crimes?

DISCUSSION QUESTIONS

1. "Whoever has committed murder must *die.*" Do you agree with this statement? Explain your view.
2. Is the death penalty a cruel and unusual punishment? Explain your answer.
3. Glover concludes that the case for capital punishment as a substantial deterrent fails. Do you agree? Defend your position.
4. Can you think of any cases in which capital punishment would be justified? What are they?

Ernest van den Haag

The Ultimate Punishment: A Defense

Ernest van den Haag is professor of jurisprudence and public policy at Fordham University. He is the author of The Fabric of Society (1957), Political Violence and Civil Disobedience (1973), and Punishing Criminals: Concerning a Very Old and Painful Question (1975).

Van den Haag replies to various objections to capital punishment, including Glover's objection (in the preceding reading) that capital punishment is not justified because it has not been shown to be a deterrent. In replying to this objection, van den Haag uses a version of the best-bet argument discussed by Glover; also he claims that deterrence is not a decisive consideration for either abolitionists or retentionists. The other objections answered by van den Haag include the following: Capital punishment is discriminatory; innocents are executed; it is too costly; it is an excessive punishment; it violates the right to life; and it is inconsistent with human dignity.

In an average year about 20,000 homicides occur in the United States. Fewer than 300 convicted murderers are sentenced to death. But because no more than thirty murderers have been executed in any recent year, most convicts sentenced to death are likely to die of old age.[1] Nonetheless, the death penalty looms large in discussions: it raises important moral questions independent of the number of executions.

The death penalty is our harshest punishment.[2] It is irrevocable: it ends the existence of those punished, instead of temporarily imprisoning them. Further, although not intended to

cause physical pain, execution is the only corporal punishment still applied to adults.[3] These singular characteristics contribute to the perennial, impassioned controversy about capital punishment.

I. DISTRIBUTION

Consideration of the justice, morality, or usefulness of capital punishment is often conflated with objections to its alleged discriminatory or capricious distribution among the guilty. Wrongly so. If capital punishment is immoral in se, no distribution among the guilty could make it moral. If capital punishment is moral, no distribution would make it immoral. Improper distribution cannot affect the quality of what is distributed, be it punishments or rewards. Discriminatory or capricious distribution thus could not justify abolition of the death penalty. Further, maldistribution inheres no more in capital punishment than in any other punishment.

Maldistribution between the guilty and the innocent is, by definition, unjust. But the injustice does not lie in the nature of the punishment. Because of the finality of the death penalty, the most grievous maldistribution occurs when it is imposed upon the innocent. However, the frequent allegations of discrimination and capriciousness refer to maldistribution among the guilty and not to the punishment of the innocent.

Maldistribution of any punishment among those who deserve it is irrelevant to its justice or morality. Even if poor or black convicts guilty of capital offenses suffer capital punishment, and other convicts usually guilty of the same crimes do not, a more equal distribution, however desirable, would merely be more equal. It would not be more just to the convicts under sentence of death.

Punishments are imposed on persons, not on racial or economic groups. Guilt is personal. The only relevant question is: does the person to be executed deserve the punishment? Whether or not others who deserved the same punishment, whatever their economic or racial group, have avoided execution is irrelevant. If they have, the guilt of the executed convicts would not be diminished, nor would their punishment be less deserved. To put the issue starkly, if the death penalty were imposed on guilty blacks, but not on guilty whites, or, if it were imposed by a lottery among the guilty, this irrationally discriminatory or capricious distribution would neither make the penalty unjust, nor cause anyone to be unjustly punished, despite the undue impunity bestowed on others.[4]

Equality, in short, seems morally less important than justice. And justice is independent of distributional inequalities. The ideal of equal justice demands that justice be equally distributed, not that it be replaced by equality. Justice requires that as many of the guilty as possible be punished, regardless of whether others have avoided punishment. To let these others escape the deserved punishment does not do justice to them, or to society. But it is not unjust to those who could not escape.

These moral considerations are not meant to deny that irrational discrimination, or capriciousness, would be inconsistent with constitutional requirements. But I am satisfied that the Supreme Court has in fact provided for adherence to the constitutional requirement of equality as much as is possible. Some inequality is indeed unavoidable as a practical matter in any system.[5] But, *ultra posse nemo obligatur*. (Nobody is bound beyond ability.)

Recent data reveal little direct racial discrimination in the sentencing of those arrested and convicted of murder.[6] The abrogation of the death penalty for rape has eliminated a major source of racial discrimination. Concededly, some discrimination based on the race of murder victims may exist; yet, this discrimination affects criminal victimizers in an unexpected way. Murderers of whites are thought more likely to be executed than murderers of blacks. Black victims, then, are less fully vindicated than white ones. However, because most black murderers kill blacks, black murderers are spared the death penalty more often than are white murderers. They fare better than most white murderers.[7] The motivation behind unequal distribution of the death penalty may well

have been to discriminate against blacks, but the result has favored them. Maldistribution is thus a straw man for empirical as well as analytical reasons.

II. MISCARRIAGES OF JUSTICE

In a recent survey Professors Hugo Adam Bedau and Michael Radelet found that 7000 persons were executed in the United States between 1900 and 1985 and that 25 were innocent of capital crimes.[8] Among the innocents they list Sacco and Vanzetti as well as Ethel and Julius Rosenberg. Although their data may be questionable, I do not doubt that, over a long enough period, miscarriages of justice will occur even in capital cases.

Despite precautions, nearly all human activities, such as trucking, lighting, or construction, cost the lives of some innocent bystanders. We do not give up those activities, because the advantages, moral or material, outweigh the unintended losses. Analogously, for those who think the death penalty just, miscarriages of justice are offset by the moral benefits and the usefulness of doing justice. For those who think the death penalty unjust even when it does not miscarry, miscarriages can hardly be decisive.

III. DETERRENCE

Despite much recent work, there has been no conclusive statistical demonstration that the death penalty is a better deterrent than are alternative punishments.[9] However, deterrence is less than decisive for either side. Most abolitionists acknowledge that they would continue to favor abolition even if the death penalty were shown to deter more murders than alternatives could deter.[10] Abolitionists appear to value the life of a convicted murderer or, at least, his non-execution, more highly than they value the lives of the innocent victims who might be spared by deterring prospective murderers.

Deterrence is not altogether decisive for me either. I would favor retention of the death penalty as retribution even if it were shown that the threat of execution could not deter prospective murderers not already deterred by the threat of imprisonment.[11] Still, I believe the death penalty, because of its finality, is more feared than imprisonment, and deters some prospective murderers not deterred by the threat of imprisonment. Sparing the lives of even a few prospective victims by deterring their murderers is more important than preserving the lives of convicted murderers because of the possibility, or even the probability, that executing them would not deter others. Whereas the lives of the victims who might be saved are valuable, that of the murderer has only negative value, because of his crime. Surely the criminal law is meant to protect the lives of potential victims in preference to those of actual murderers.

Murder rates are determined by many factors; neither the severity nor the probability of the threatened sanction is always decisive. However, for the long run, I share the view of Sir James Fitzjames Stephen: "Some men, probably, abstain from murder because they fear that if they committed murder they would be hanged. Hundreds of thousands abstain from it because they regard it with horror. One great reason why they regard it with horror is that murderers are hanged." [12] Penal sanctions are useful in the long run for the formation of the internal restraints so necessary to control crime. The severity and finality of the death penalty is appropriate to the seriousness and the finality of murder.[13]

IV. INCIDENTAL ISSUES: COST, RELATIVE SUFFERING, BRUTALIZATION

Many nondecisive issues are associated with capital punishment. Some believe that the monetary cost of appealing a capital sentence is excessive.[14] Yet most comparisons of the cost of life imprisonment with the cost of execution, apart from their dubious relevance, are flawed at least by the implied assumption that life prisoners will generate no judicial costs during their imprisonment. At any rate, the actual monetary costs are trumped by the importance of doing justice.

Others insist that a person sentenced to death suffers more than his victim suffered, and that

this (excess) suffering is undue according to the *lex talionis* (rule of retaliation).[15] We cannot know whether the murderer on death row suffers more than his victim suffered; however, unlike the murderer, the victim deserved none of the suffering inflicted. Further, the limitations of the *lex talionis* were meant to restrain private vengeance, not the social retribution that has taken its place. Punishment—regardless of the motivation—is not intended to revenge, offset, or compensate for the victim's suffering or to be measured by it. Punishment is to vindicate the law and the social order undermined by the crime. This is why a kidnapper's penal confinement is not limited to the period for which he imprisoned his victim; nor is a burglar's confinement meant merely to offset the suffering or the harm he caused his victim; nor is it meant only to offset the advantage he gained.[16]

Another argument heard at least since Beccaria is that, by killing a murderer, we encourage, endorse, or legitimize unlawful killing. Yet, although all punishments are meant to be unpleasant, it is seldom argued that they legitimize the unlawful imposition of identical unpleasantness. Imprisonment is not thought to legitimize kidnapping; neither are fines thought to legitimize robbery. The difference between murder and execution, or between kidnapping and imprisonment, is that the first is unlawful and undeserved, the second a lawful and deserved punishment for an unlawful act. The physical similarities of the punishment to the crime are irrelevant. The relevant difference is not physical, but social.[17]

V. JUSTICE, EXCESS, DEGRADATION

We threaten punishments in order to deter crime. We impose them not only to make the threats credible but also as retribution (justice) for the crimes that were not deterred. Threats and punishments are necessary to deter and deterrence is a sufficient practical justification for them. Retribution is an independent moral justification.[18] Although penalties can be unwise, repulsive, or inappropriate, and those punished can be pitiable, in a sense the infliction of legal punishment on a guilty person cannot be unjust.

By committing the crime, the criminal volunteered to assume the risk of receiving a legal punishment that he could have avoided by not committing the crime. The punishment he suffers is the punishment he voluntarily risked suffering and, therefore, it is no more unjust to him than any other event for which one knowingly volunteers to assume the risk. Thus, the death penalty cannot be unjust to the guilty criminal.[19]

There remain, however, two moral objections. The penalty may be regarded as always excessive as retribution and always morally degrading. To regard the death penalty as always excessive, one must believe that no crime—no matter how heinous—could possibly justify capital punishment. Such a belief can be neither corroborated nor refuted; it is an article of faith.

Alternatively, or concurrently, one may believe that everybody, the murderer no less than the victim, has an imprescriptible (natural?) right to life. The law therefore should not deprive anyone of life. I share Jeremy Bentham's view that any such "natural and imprescriptible rights" are "nonsense upon stilts."[20]

Justice Brennan has insisted that the death penalty is "uncivilized," "inhuman," inconsistent with "human dignity" and with "the sanctity of life,"[21] that it "treats members of the human race as nonhumans, as objects to be toyed with and discarded,"[22] that it is "uniquely degrading to human dignity"[23] and "by its very nature, [involves] a denial of the executed person's humanity."[24] Justice Brennan does not say why he thinks execution "uncivilized." Hitherto most civilizations have had the death penalty, although it has been discarded in Western Europe, where it is currently unfashionable probably because of its abuse by totalitarian regimes.

By "degrading," Justice Brennan seems to mean that execution degrades the executed convicts. Yet philosophers, such as Immanuel Kant and G. W. F. Hegel have insisted that, when deserved, execution, far from degrading the executed convict, affirms his humanity by affirming his rationality and his responsibility for his actions. They thought that execution, when deserved, is required for the sake of the convict's dignity. (Does not life imprisonment violate human dignity more than executions, by keeping alive a prisoner deprived of all autonomy?)[25]

Common sense indicates that it cannot be death—our common fate—that is inhuman. Therefore, Justice Brennan must mean that death degrades when it comes not as a natural or accidental event, but as a deliberate social imposition. The murderer learns through his punishment that his fellow men have found him unworthy of living; that because he has murdered, he is being expelled from the community of the living. The degradation is self-inflicted. By murdering, the murderer has so dehumanized himself that he cannot remain among the living. The social recognition of self-degradation is the punitive essence of execution. To believe, as Justice Brennan appears to, that the degradation is inflicted by the execution reverses the direction of causality.

Execution of those who have committed heinous murders may deter only one murder per year. If it does, it seems quite warranted. It is also the only fitting retribution for murder I can think of.

Endnotes

1. Death row as a semipermanent residence is cruel, because convicts are denied the normal amenities of prison life. Thus, unless death row residents are integrated into the prison population, the continuing accumulation of convicts on death row should lead us to accelerate either the rate of execution or the rate of commutations. I find little objection to integration.

2. Some writers, for example, Cesare Bonesana, Marchese di Beccaria, have thought that life imprisonment is more severe. See C. Beccaria, *Dei Delitti c Delle Pene* 62–70 (1764). More recently, Jacques Barzum has expressed this view. See Barzun, *In Favor of Capital Punishment,* in *The Death Penalty of America* 154. (H. Bedau ed. 1964). However, the overwhelming majority of both abolitionists and of convicts under death sentence prefer life imprisonment to execution.

3. For a discussion of the sources of opposition to corporal punishment, see E. van den Haag, *Punishing Criminals* 196–206 (1975).

4. Justice Douglas, concurring in Furman v. Georgia, 408 U.S. 238 (1972), wrote that "a law which . . . reaches that [discriminatory] result in practice has no more sanctity than a law which in terms provides the same." *Id.* at 256 (Douglas, J., concurring). Indeed, a law legislating this result "in terms" would be inconsistent with the "equal protection of the laws" provided by the fourteenth amendment, as would the discriminatory result reached in practice. But that result could be changed by changing the distributional practice. Thus, Justice Douglas notwithstanding, a discriminatory result does not make the death penalty unconstitutional,

unless the penalty ineluctably must produce that result to an unconstitutional degree.

5. The ideal of equality, unlike the ideal of retributive justice (which can be approximated separately in each instance), is clearly unattainable unless all guilty persons are apprehended, and thereafter tried, convicted and sentenced by the same court, at the same time. Unequal justice is the best we can do; it is still better than the injustice, equal or unequal, which occurs if, for the sake of equality, we deliberately allow some who could be punished to escape.

6. See Bureau of Justice Statistics, U.S. Dept. of Justice, Bulletin No. NCJ-98, 399, *Capital Punishment 1984*, at 9 (1985); Johnson, *The Executioner's Bias, Nat'l Rev.*, Nov. 15, 1985, at 44.

7. It barely need be said that any discrimination *against* (for example, black murderers of whites) must also be discrimination *for* (for example, black murderers of blacks).

8. Bedau & Radelet, *Miscarriages of Justice in Potentially Capital Cases* (1st draft, Oct. 1985) (on file at Harvard Law School Library).

9. For a sample of conflicting views on the subject, see Baldus & Cole, *A Comparison of the Work of Thorsten Sellin and Isaac Ehrlich on the Deterrent Effect of Capital Punishment,* 85 *Yale L. J.* 170 (1975); Bowers & Pierce, *Deterrence or Brutilization: What Is the Effect of Executions?,* 26 *Crime & Delinq.* 453 (1980); Bowers & Pierce, *The Illustration of Deterrence in Isaac Ehrlich's Research on Capital Punishment,* 85 *Yale L. J.* 187 (1975); Ehrlich, *Fear of Deterrence: A Critical Evaluation of the "Report of the Panel on Research on Deterrent and Incapacitative Effects,"* 6 *J. Legal Stud.* 293 (1977); Ehrlich, *The Deterrent Effect of Capital Punishment: A Question of Life and Death,* 65 *Am. Econ. Rev.* 397, 415–16 (1975); Ehrlich & Gibbons, *On the Measurement of the Deterrent Effect of Capital Punishment and the Theory of Deterrence,* 6 *J. Legal Stud.* 35 (1977).

10. For most abolitionists, the discrimination argument . . . is similarly nondecisive: they would favor abolition even if there could be no racial discrimination.

11. If executions were shown to increase the murder rate in the long run, I would favor abolition. Sparing the innocent victims who would be spared, *ex hypothesi,* by the nonexecution of murderers would be more important to me than the execution, however just, of murderers. But although there is a lively discussion of the subject, no serious evidence exists to support the hypothesis that executions produce a higher murder rate. *Cf.,* Phillips, *The Deterrent Effect of Capital Punishment: New Evidence on an Old Controversy,* 86 *Am. J. Soc.* 139 (1980) (arguing that murder rates drop immediately after executions of criminals).

12. H. Gross, *A Theory of Criminal Justice* 489 (1979) (attributing this passage to Sir James Fitzjames Stephen).

13. Weems v. United States, 217 U.S. 349 (1910), suggests that penalties be proportionate to the seriousness of the crime—a common theme of the criminal law. Murder, therefore, demands more than life imprisonment, if, as I believe, it is a more serious crime than other crimes

punished by life imprisonment. In modern times, our sensibility requires that the range of punishments be narrower than the range of crimes—but not so narrow as to exclude the death penalty.

14. *Cf.* Kaplan, *Administering Capital Punishment,* 36 *U. Fla. L. Rev.* 177, 178, 190–91 (1984) (noting the high cost of appealing a capital sentence).

15. For an example of this view, see A. Camus, *Reflections on the Guillotine* 24–30 (1959). On the limitations allegedly imposed by the *lex talionis,* see Reiman, *Justice, Civilization, and the Death Penalty: Answering van den Haag,* 14 *Phil. & Pub. Aff.* 115, 119–34 (1985).

16. Thus restitution (a civil liability) cannot satisfy the punitive purpose of penal sanctions, whether the purpose be retributive or deterrent.

17. Some abolitionists challenge: if the death penalty is just and serves as a deterrent, why not televise executions? The answer is simple. The death even of a murderer, however well-deserved, should not serve as public entertainment. It so served in earlier centuries. But in this respect our sensibility has changed for the better, I believe. Further, television unavoidably would trivialize executions, wedged in, as they would be, between game shows, situation comedies, and the like. Finally, because televised executions would focus on the physical aspects of the punishment, rather than the nature of the crime and the suffering of the victim, a televised execution would present the murderer as the victim of the state. Far from communicating the moral significance of the execution, television would shift the focus to the pitiable fear of the murderer. We no longer place in cages those sentenced to imprisonment to expose them to public view. Why should we so expose those sentenced to execution?

18. See van den Haag, *Punishment as a Device for Controlling the Crime Rate,* 33 *Rutgers L. Rev.* 706, 719 (1981) (explaining why the desire for retribution, although independent, would have to be satisfied even if deterrence were the only purpose of punishment).

19. An explicit threat of punitive action is necessary to the justification of any legal punishment: *nulla poena sine lege* (no punishment without [preexisting] law). To be sufficiently justified, the threat must in turn have a rational and legitimate purpose. "Your money or your life" does not qualify; nor does the threat of an unjust law; nor, finally, does a threat that is altogether disproportionate to the importance of its purpose. In short, preannouncement legitimizes the threatened punishment only if the threat is warranted. But this leaves a very wide range of justified threats. Furthermore, the punished person is aware of the penalty for his punishment. His victim, however, did not volunteer to risk anything. The question whether any self-inflicted injury—such as a legal punishment—ever can be unjust to a person who knowingly risked it is a matter that requires more analysis than is possible here.

20. *The Works of Jeremy Bentham* 105 (J. Bowring ed. 1972). However, I would be more polite about prescriptible natural rights, which Bentham described as

"simple nonsense." *Id.* (It does not matter whether natural rights are called "moral" or "human" rights as they currently are by most writers.)

21. *The Death Penalty in America* 256–63 (H. Bedau ed., 3d ed. 1982) quoting Furman v. Georgia, 408 U.S. 238, 286, 305 (1972) (Brennan, J., concurring).
22. *Id.* at 272–73; see also Gregg v. Georgia, 428 U.S. 153, 230 (1976) (Brennan, J., dissenting).
23. Furman v. Georgia, 408 U.S. 238, 291 (1972) (Brennan, J., concurring).
24. *Id.* at 290.
25. *See* Barzun, *supra* [endnote 2].

REVIEW QUESTIONS

1. How does van den Haag reply to the objection that capital punishment is discriminatory?
2. What is his response to the claim that innocent people are mistakenly executed?
3. According to van den Haag, why does the mere possibility of deterrence support the use of the death penalty?

4. How does he reply to the objections about cost, excessive suffering, legitimizing killing, the right to life, and human dignity?

DISCUSSION QUESTIONS

1. Is the death penalty a more severe punishment than life imprisonment without the possibility of parole?
2. Van den Haag admits that the death penalty has been used to discriminate against blacks. Is this a reason to abolish the death penalty? If not, what should be done about this racism?
3. Is talk about natural rights such as the right to life just "nonsense on stilts"?
4. Is van den Haag's "best-bet argument" about deterrence sound? (You may want to review Glover's criticisms in the preceding reading; also Bedau attacks the argument in the next reading.)

Hugo Adam Bedau

How to Argue about the Death Penalty

Hugo Adam Bedau is Justin B. Fletcher Professor of Philosophy at Tufts University and the author of The Courts, the Constitution, and Capital Punishment *(1977). He is the editor of* The Death Penalty in America *(third edition, 1982) and the coeditor of* Capital Punishment in the United States *(1976). He is a past president of the American League to Abolish Capital Punishment.*

Bedau agrees with van den Haag that factual considerations do not settle the issue about capital punishment. Instead he thinks that we must see if it satisfies important social goals and moral principles. He states five social goals relevant to the death penalty and maintains that none of them justifies it. Then he lists six relevant moral principles; he argues that appealing to them doesn't provide any justification for capital punishment either. He concludes that the preponderance of reasons favors the abolition of the death penalty.

From Hugo Adam Bedau, "How to Argue about the Death Penalty," *Israel Law Review* 25, nos. 3–4 (Summer–Autumn 1991): 466–480. Reprinted by permission of the author and publisher.

I

Argument over the death penalty—especially in the United States during the past generation—has been concentrated in large part on trying to answer various disputed *questions of fact*. Among them two have been salient: Is the death penalty a better deterrent to crime (especially murder) than the alternative of imprisonment? Is the death penalty administered in a discriminatory way, and, in particular, are black or other nonwhite offenders (or offenders whose victims are white) more likely to be tried, convicted, sentenced to death, and executed than whites (or offenders whose victims are nonwhite)? Other questions of fact have also been explored, including these two: What is the risk that an innocent person could actually be executed for a crime he did not commit? What is the risk that a person convicted of a capital felony but not executed will commit another capital felony?

Varying degrees of effort have been expended in trying to answer these questions. Although I think the current answers are capable of further refinement, I also think anyone who studies the evidence today must conclude that the best current answers to these four questions are as follows. (1) There is little or no evidence that the death penalty is a better deterrent to murder than is imprisonment; on the contrary, most evidence shows that these two punishments are about equally (in)effective as deterrents to murder. Furthermore, as long as the death penalty continues to be used relatively rarely, there is no prospect of gaining more decisive evidence on the question.[1] (2) There is evidence that the death penalty has been and continues to be administered, whether intentionally or not, in a manner that produces arbitrary and racially discriminatory results in death sentencing. At the very least, this is true in those jurisdictions where the question has been investigated in recent years.[2] (3) It is impossible to calculate the risk that an innocent person will be executed, but the risk is not zero, as the record of convicted, sentenced, and executed innocents shows.[3] (4) Recidivism data show that some murderers have killed after a conviction and prison sentence for murder; so there is a risk that others will do so as well.[4]

Let us assume that my summary of the results of research on these four questions is correct, and that further research will not significantly change these answers. The first thing to notice is that even if everyone agreed on these answers, this would not by itself settle the dispute over whether to keep, expand, reduce, or abolish the death penalty. Knowing these **empirical truths** about the administration and effects of the death penalty in our society does not entail knowing whether one should support its retention or abolition. This would still be true even if we knew with finality the answers to *all* the factual questions that can be asked about it.

There are two reasons for this. The facts as they currently stand and as seen from the abo-

litionist perspective do not point strongly and overwhelmingly to the futility of the death penalty or to the harm it does, at least as long as it continues to be used only in the limited and restricted form of the past decade: confirmed to the crime of murder, with trial courts empowered to exercise "guided discretion" in sentencing, with defense counsel able to introduce anything as mitigating evidence, and with automatic review of both conviction and sentence by some appellate court.[5] Nor do the facts show that the alternative of life imprisonment is on balance a noticeably superior punishment. For example, the evidence of racial discrimination in the administration of the death penalty, while incontestable, may be no worse than the racial discrimination that occurs where lesser crimes and punishments are concerned. No one who has studied the data thinks that the administration of justice for murder approaches the level of racial discrimination reached a generation ago in the South by the administration of justice for rape.[6] Besides, it is always possible to argue that such discrimination is diminishing, or will diminish over time, and that, in any case, since the fault does not lie in the capital statutes themselves— they are color-blind on their face—the remedy does not lie in repealing them.

But the marginal impact of the empirical evidence is not the major factor in explaining why settling disputes over matters of fact does not and cannot settle the larger controversy over the death penalty itself. As a matter of sheer logic, it is not possible to deduce a policy conclusion (such as the desirability of abolishing the death penalty) from any set of factual premises, however general and well supported. Any argument intended to recommend continuing or reforming current policy on the death penalty must include among its premises one or more **normative propositions.** Unless disputants over the death penalty can agree about these normative propositions, their agreement on the general facts will never suffice to resolve their dispute.

II

Accordingly, the course of wisdom for those interested in arguing about the death penalty is to focus attention on the normative propositions crucial to the dispute, in the hope that some headway may be made in narrowing disagreement over their number, content, and weight.

If this is to be done effectively, the context of these norms in general political ideology needs to be fixed. Suffice it to say here that I proceed from within the context of liberal pluralistic constitutional democracy and the conception of punishment appropriate therein.[7]

Logically prior to the idea of punishment is the idea of a crime. What counts as a criminal harm depends in part on our conception of persons as bearers of rights deserving respect and protection. In this setting, liability to punishment and its actual infliction serve the complex function of reinforcing compliance with a set of laws deemed necessary to protect the fundamental equal rights of all members of society. The normative propositions relevant to the death penalty controversy are interwoven with the basic purposes and principles of liberal society, including the recognition and protection of individual rights to life and liberty, and to security of person and property.

These norms can be divided into two groups: those that express relevant and desirable *social goals* or *purposes,* and those that express relevant and respectable *moral principles.* Punishment is thus a practice or institution defined through various policies—such as the death penalty for murder—and intended to be the means or instrument whereby certain social goals are achieved within the constraints imposed by acknowledged moral principles.[8]

Reduction of crime, or at least prevention of an increase in crime, is an example of such a goal. This goal influences the choice of punishments because of their impact (hypothesized or verified) on the crime rate. No one, except for purists of a retributive stripe, would dissent from the view that this goal is relevant to the death penalty controversy. Because of its relevance, there is continuing interest in the outcome of research on the differential deterrent efficacy of death versus imprisonment. The only questions normally in dispute are what that research shows (I have summarized it above) and how important this goal is (some regard it as decisive).

Similarly, that no one should be convicted and sentenced to death without a fair trial (i.e., in violation of "due process of law") is a principle of law and morality generally respected. Its general acceptance explains the considerable reformation in the laws governing the death penalty in the United States that have been introduced since 1972 by the Supreme Court.[9] The Court argued that capital trials and death sentencing were in practice unfair (in constitutional jargon, they were in violation of the Eighth and Fourteenth Amendments, which bar "cruel and unusual punishments" and require "equal protection of the laws," respectively). State legislatures and thoughtful observers agreed. Here again the only questions concern how important it is to comply with this principle (some regard it as decisive) and the extent to which the death penalty currently violates it (I have remarked on this point above, too).

The chief use of a moral principle in the present setting is to constrain the methods used in pursuit of policy (as when respect for "due process" rules out curbstone justice as a tactic in crime fighting). However, identifying the relevant goals, acknowledging the force of the relevant principles, and agreeing on the relevant general facts will still not suffice to resolve the dispute. The relative importance of achieving a given goal and the relative weight of a given principle remain to be settled, and disagreement over these matters is likely to show up in disagreement over the justification of the death penalty itself.

If this is a correct sketch of the structural character of debate and disagreement over the death penalty, then (as I noted earlier) the best hope for progress may lie in looking more carefully at the nonfactual normative ingredients so far isolated in the dispute. Ideally, we would identify and evaluate the policy goals relevant to punishment generally, as well as the moral principles that constrain the structure and content of the penalty schedule. We would also settle the proper relative weights to attach to these goals and constraints, if not in general, then at least for their application in the present context. Then, with whatever relevant general facts are at our disposal, we would be in a position to draw the appropriate inferences and resolve the entire dispute, confident that we have examined and duly weighed everything that reason and morality can bring to bear on the problem.

As an abstract matter, therefore, the question is whether the set of relevant policies and principles, taken in conjunction with the relevant facts, favors reduction (even complete abolition) of the death penalty, or whether it favors retention (or even extension) of the death penalty. Lurking in the background, of course, is the troubling possibility that the relevant norms and facts underdetermine the resolution of the dispute. But let us not worry about sharks on dry land, not yet.

III

Where choice of punishments is concerned, the relevant social goals, I suggest, are few. Two in particular generally commend themselves:

(G1) Punishment should contribute to the reduction of crime; accordingly, the punishment for a crime should not be so idle a threat or so slight a deprivation that it has no deterrent or incapacitative effects; and it certainly should not contribute to an increase in crime.

(G2) Punishments should be "economical"—they should not waste valuable social resources in futile or unnecessarily costly endeavors.

The instrumental character of these purposes and goals is evident. They reflect the fact that society does not institute and maintain the practice of punishment for its own sake, as though it were a good in itself. Rather, punishment is and is seen to be a means to an end or ends. The justification of a society's punitive policies and practices must therefore involve two steps: first, it must be shown that these ends are desirable; second, it must be shown that the practice of punishment is the best means to these ends. What is true of the justification of punishment generally is true a fortiori of justifying the death penalty.

Endorsement of these two policy goals tends to encourage support for the death penalty. Opponents of capital punishment need not reject these goals, however, and its defenders cannot

argue that accepting these goals vindicates their preferred policy. Traditionally, it is true, the death penalty has often been supported on the ground that it provides the best social defense and is extremely cheap to administer. But since the time of Beccaria and Bentham, these empirical claims have been challenged,[10] and rightly so. If support for the death penalty today in a country such as the United States rests on the high priority placed on these goals, then there is much (some would say compelling) evidence to undermine this support. The most that can be said solely by reference to these goals is that recognition of their importance can always be counted on to kindle interest in capital punishment, and to that extent put its opponents on the defensive.

Whether punishment is intended to serve only the two goals so far identified is disputable. An argument can be made that there are two or three further goals:

(G3) Punishment should rectify the harm and injustice caused by crime.

(G4) Punishment should serve as a recognized channel for the release of public indignation and anger at the offender.

(G5) Punishment should make convicted offenders into better persons rather than leave them as they are or make them worse.

Obviously, anyone who accepts the fifth goal must reject the death penalty. I shall not try here to argue the merits of this goal, either in itself or relative to the other goals of punishment. Whatever its merits, this goal is less widely sought than the others, and for that reason alone is less useful in trying to develop rational agreement over the death penalty. Its persuasive power for those not already persuaded against the death penalty on other grounds is likely to be slight to zero. Although I am unwilling to strike it from the list of goals that punishment in general is and should be practiced to achieve, it would be unreasonable to stress its pre-eminence in the present context.

The proposed third goal is open to the objection that rectification of injustice is not really a goal of punishment, even if it is a desirable goal in other settings. (Indeed, it is widely believed that rectification is not a goal of punishment but of noncriminal tort judgments.) But even if it is a goal of punishment generally, it seems irrelevant to the death penalty controversy, because neither death nor imprisonment (as practiced in the United States) rectifies anything. Nonetheless, this goal may be indirectly important for the death penalty controversy. To the extent that one believes punishments ought to serve this goal, and that there is no possible way to rectify the crime of murder, one may come to believe that the fourth goal is of even greater importance than would otherwise be the case. Indeed, striving to achieve this fourth goal and embracing the death penalty as a consequence is quite parallel to striving to achieve the fifth goal and consequently embracing its abolition.

Does this fourth goal have a greater claim on our support than I have allowed is true of the fifth goal, so obviously incompatible with it? Many would say that it does. Some[11] would even argue that it is this goal, not any of the others, that is the paramount purpose of punishment under law. Whatever else punishment does, its threat and infliction are to be seen as the expression of social indignation at deliberate harm to the innocent. Preserving a socially acceptable vehicle for the expression of anger at offenders is absolutely crucial to the health of a just society.

There are in principle three ways to respond to this claim insofar as it is part of an argument for capital punishment. One is to reject it out of hand as a false proposition from start to finish. A second is to concede that the goal of providing a visible and acceptable channel for the emotion of anger is legitimate, but to argue that this goal could at best justify the death penalty only in a very small number of cases (the occasional Adolf Eichmann, for example), since otherwise its importance would be vastly exaggerated. A third response is to concede both the legitimacy and the relative importance of this goal, but to point out that its pursuit, like that of all other goals, is nonetheless constrained by moral principles (yet to be examined), and that once these principles are properly employed, the death penalty ceases to be a permissible method of achieving this goal. I think both the second and third ob-

jections are sound, and a few further words here about each are appropriate.

First of all, anger is not the same as resentment or indignation, since the latter feeling or emotion can be aroused only through the perceived violation of some moral principle, whereas the former does not have this constraint. But whether the feeling aroused by a horrible murder is really only anger rather than indignation is just the question whether the principles of morality have been violated or not. Knowing that the accused offender has no legal excuse or justification for his criminal conduct is not enough to warrant the inference that he and his conduct are appropriate objects of our unqualified moral hostility. More about the context of the offense and its causation must be supplied; it may well be that in ordinary criminal cases one rarely or never knows enough to reach such a condemnatory judgment with confidence. Even were this not so, one has no reason to suppose that justified anger at offenders is of overriding importance, and that all countervailing considerations must yield to its preeminence. For one thing, the righteous anger needed for that role is simply not available in a pluralistic secular society. Even if it were, we have been assured from biblical times that it passes all too easily into self-righteous and hypocritical repression by some sinners or others.

Quite apart from such objections, there is a certain anomaly, even irony, in the defense of the death penalty by appeal to this goal. On the one hand, we are told of the importance of a publicly recognized ritual for extermination of convicted murderers as a necessary vent for otherwise unchanneled disruptive public emotions. On the other hand, our society scrupulously rejects time-honored methods of execution that truly do express hatred and anger at offenders: beheading, crucifixion, dismemberment, and even hanging and the electric chair are disappearing. Execution by lethal injection, increasingly the popular option, hardly seems appropriate as the outlet of choice for such allegedly volatile energies! And is it not ironic that this technique, invented to facilitate life-saving surgery, now turns out to be the preferred channel for the expression of moral indignation?

IV

If the purposes or goals of punishment lend a utilitarian quality to the practice of punishment, the moral principles relevant to the death penalty operate as deontological constraints on their pursuit. Stating all and only the principles relevant to the death penalty controversy is not easy, and the list that follows is no more than the latest approximation to the task. . . .[12] With some overlap here and there, these principles are six:

(P1) No one should deliberately and intentionally take another's life where there is a feasible alternative.

(P2) The more severe a penalty is, the more important it is that it be imposed only on those who truly deserve it.

(P3) The more severe a penalty is, the weightier the justification required to warrant its imposition on anyone.

(P4) Whatever the criminal offense, the accused and convicted offender does not forfeit all his rights and dignity as a person. Accordingly, there is an upper limit to the severity—cruelty, destructiveness, finality—of permissible punishments, regardless of the offense.

(P5) Fairness requires that punishments should be graded in their severity according to the gravity of the offense.

(P6) If human lives are to be risked, the risk should fall more heavily on wrong-doers (the guilty) than on others (the innocent).

I cannot argue here for all these principles, but they really need no argument from me. Each is recognized implicitly or explicitly in our practice; each can be seen to constrain our conduct as individuals and as officers in democratic institutions. Outright repudiation or cynical disregard of any of these principles would disqualify one from engaging in serious discourse and debate over punishment in a liberal society. All can be seen as corollaries or theorems of the general proposition that life, limb, and security of person—of all persons—are of paramount value. Thus, only minimal interference (in the jargon of the law, "the least restrictive

(means") is warranted with anyone's life, limb, and security in order to protect the rights of others.

How do these principles direct or advise us in regard to the permissibility or desirability of the death penalty? The first thing to note is that evidently none directly rules it out. I know of no moral principle that is both sufficiently rigid and sufficiently well established for us to point to it and say: "The practice of capital punishment is flatly contradictory to the requirements of this moral principle." (Of course, we could invent a principle that would have this consequence, but that is hardly to the point.) This should not be surprising; few if any of the critics or the defenders of the death penalty have supposed otherwise. Second, several of these principles do reflect the heavy burden that properly falls on anyone who advocates that certain human beings be deliberately killed by others, when those to be killed are not at the time a danger to anyone. For example, whereas the first principle may permit lethal force in self-defense, it directly counsels against the death penalty in *all* cases without exception. The second and third principles emphasize the importance of "due process" and "equal protection" as the finality and incompensability of punishments increase. The fourth principle draws attention to the nature and value of persons, even those convicted of terrible crimes. It reminds us that even if crimes know no upper limit in their wantonness, cruelty, destructiveness, and horror, punishments under law in a civilized society cannot imitate crimes in this regard. Punishment does operate under limits, and these limits are not arbitrary.

The final two principles, however, seem to be exceptions to the generalization that the principles as a group tend to favor punishments other than death. The fifth principle seems to entail that if murder is the gravest crime, then it should receive the severest punishment. This does not, of course, *require* a society to invoke the death penalty for murder—unless one accepts *lex talionis* ("a life for a life, an eye for an eye") in a singularly literal-minded manner. Since *lex talionis* is not a sound principle on which to construct the penalty schedule generally, appealing to this interpretation of the fifth principle here simply begs the question. Nevertheless, the principle that punishments should be graded to fit the crime does encourage consideration of the death penalty, especially if it seems that there is no other way to punish murder with the utmost permissible severity.

Of rather more interest is the sixth principle. Some[13] make it the cornerstone of their defense of the death penalty. They argue that it is better to execute all convicted murderers, lest on a future occasion any of them murder again, than it is to execute none of them, thereby averting the risk of executing any who may be innocent. A policy of complete abolition—at least in the United States today—would result in thousands of convicted killers (only a few of whom are innocent) being held behind bars for life. This cohort would constitute a permanent risk to the safety of many millions of innocent citizens. The sole gain to counterbalance this risk is the guarantee that no lives (innocent or guilty) will be lost through legal executions. The practice of executions thus protects far more innocent citizens than the same practice puts in jeopardy.

This argument is far less conclusive than it may at first seem. Even if we grant it full weight, it is simply unreasonable to use it (or any other argument) as a way of dismissing the relevance of principles that counsel a different result, or as a tactic to imply the subordinate importance of those other principles. If used in this manner, the sixth principle would be thoroughly transformed. It has become a disguised version of the first policy goal (viz., Reduce crime!) and in effect would elevate that goal to pre-eminence over every competing and constraining consideration. The argument also fosters the illusion that we can in fact reasonably estimate, if not actually calculate, the number of lives risked by a policy of abolition as opposed to a policy of capital punishment. This is false; we do not and cannot reasonably hope to know what the risk is of convicting the innocent,[14] even if we could estimate the risk of recidivist murder. We therefore cannot really compare the two risks with any precision. Finally, the argument gains whatever strength it appears to have by tacitly ignoring the following dilemma. If the policy of killing the convicted in order to reduce risk to the innocent is to achieve maximum effect, then death must be the *mandatory* penalty for everyone convicted of murder (never mind other crimes). But such a policy cannot really be carried out. It flies in the face of two centuries of political reality, which demonstrates the impossibility of enforcing truly mandatory death penalties for murder and other crimes against the person. The only realistic policy alternative is some version of a *discretionary* death penalty. However, every version of this policy actually tried has proved vulnerable to criticism on grounds of inequity in its administration, as critic after critic has shown. Meanwhile, history tells us that our society is unable to avoid all risk of recidivist murder.[15]

The upshot is that we today run both the risk of executing the innocent and the risk of recidivist murder, even though it is necessary to run only one of these risks.

V

What has our examination of the relevant goals and principles shown about the possibility of resolving the death penalty controversy on rational grounds? First, the death penalty is primarily a means to one or more ends or goals, but it is not the only (and arguably not the best) means to them. Second, several principles of relevance to sound punitive policy in general favor (although they do not demand) abolition of the death penalty. Third, there is no goal or principle that constitutes a conclusive reason favoring either side in the dispute. Unless, of course, some one goal or principle is interpreted or weighted in such a manner (cf. the fifth goal, or the fifth principle). But in that case, one side or the other will refuse to accept it. Finally, the several goals and principles of punishment that have been identified have no obvious rank order or relative weighting. As they stand, these goals and principles do indeed underdetermine the policy dispute over capital punishment. Perhaps such a ranking could be provided by some comprehensive socioethical theory. But the failure of every known such theory to secure general acceptance so far does not bode well for prompt and rational resolution of the controversy along these lines.

Despite the absence of any conclusive reasons or decisive ranking of principles, we may take refuge[16] in the thought . . . that a preponderance of reasons does favor one side rather than the other. Such a preponderance emerges, however, only when the relevant goals and principles of punishment are seen in a certain light, or from a particular angle of vision. Perhaps this amounts to one rather than another weighting of goals and principles but without conscious reliance upon any manifest theory. In any case, I shall mention three such considerations that are important in my assessment of the moral objections to the death penalty.

The first and by far the most important concerns the role and function of power in the hands of government. It is in general preferable, *ceteris paribus*, that such power over individuals should shrink rather than expand. Where such power must be used, then let it be devoted to constructive rather than destructive purposes, thus enhancing the autonomy and liberty of those directly affected. But the death penalty contradicts this concern; it is government power used in a dramatically destructive manner upon individuals in the absence of any compelling social necessity. No wonder it is the ultimate symbol of such power.

Another consideration that shapes my interpretation of the goals and principles of evaluation is an orientation to the *future* rather than to the past. We cannot do anything for the dead victims of crime. (How many of those who oppose the death penalty would continue to do so if, *mirabile dictu,* executing the murderer brought the victim back to life?) But we can—or at least we can try to—do something for the living: we can protect the innocent, prevent illegitimate violence, and help those in despair over their own victimization. None of these constructive tasks involves punishing anyone for expressive, vindictive, or retributive reasons. The more we stress these factors in our choice of punishments, the more we orient our punitive policies toward the past—toward trying to use government power over the lives of a few as a socially approved instrument of moral bookkeeping.

Finally, the death penalty projects a false and misleading picture of man and society. Its professed message for those who support it is this: justice requires killing the convicted murderer. So we focus on the death that all murderers supposedly deserve and overlook our inability to give a rational account of why so few actually get it. Hence, the lesson taught by the practice of capital punishment is really quite different. Far from being a symbol of justice, it is a symbol of brutality and stupidity. Perhaps if we lived in a world of autonomous Kantian moral agents, where all the criminals freely expressed their rational will in the intention to kill others without their consent or desert, then death for the convicted murderer might be just (as even Karl Marx was inclined to think[17]). But a closer look at the convicts who actually are on our death rows shows that these killers are a far cry from the rational agents of Kant's metaphysical imagination. We fool ourselves if we think a system of ideal retributive justice designed for such persons is the appropriate model for the penal system in our society.

Have I implicitly conceded that argument over the death penalty is irrational? If I am right that the death penalty controversy does not really turn on controversial social goals or controversial moral principles, any more than it does on disputed general facts, but instead turns on how all three are to be balanced or weighed, does it follow that reason alone cannot resolve the controversy, because reason alone cannot determine which weighting or balancing is the correct one? Or can reason resolve this problem, perhaps by appeal to further theory, theory that would deepen our appreciation of what truly underlies a commitment to liberal institutions and a belief in the possibilities for autonomy of all persons?[18] I think it can—but this is the right place to end the present investigation because we have reached the launching platform for another one.

Endnotes

1. Lawrence R. Klein et al., "The Deterrent Effects of Capital Punishment: An Assessment of the Estimates," in Alfred Blumstein et al., eds., *Deterrence and Incapacitation: Estimating the Effects of Criminal Sanctions on Crime Rates* (Washington, D.C., National Academy of Sciences, 1978) 336–60.
2. David C. Baldus, George C. Woodworth, and Charles A. Pulaski, Jr., *Equal Justice and the Death Penalty: A*

Legal and Empirical Analysis (Boston, Northeastern U.P., 1990).

3. H. A. Bedau and Michael L. Radelet, "Miscarriages of Justice in Potentially Capital Cases" (1987) 40 Stan. L. R. 21–180.

4. H. A. Bedau, ed., *The Death Penalty in America* (New York, Oxford U. P., 3rd ed., 1982) 173–80.

5. *Gregg v. Georgia,* 428 U.S. 153 (1976); *Proffitt v. Florida,* 428 U.S. 242 (1976); *Jurek v. Texas,* 428 U.S. 262 (1976).

6. Marvin E. Wolfgang and Marc Riedel, "Rape, Racial Discrimination, and the Death Penalty," in H. A. Bedau and Chester M. Pierce, eds., *Capital Punishment in the United States* (New York, AMS Press, 1976) 99–121.

7. See, e.g., John Rawls, *A Theory of Justice* (Cambridge, Mass., Harvard U. P., 1971) and H. L. A. Hart, *Punishment and Responsibility: Essays in the Philosophy of Law* (New York, Oxford U.P., 1968).

8. *Cf.* Ronald Dworkin, *Taking Rights Seriously* (Cambridge, Mass., Harvard U. P., 1977) 22–23, 169–71.

9. *Furman v. Georgia,* 408 U.S. 238 (1972).

10. See H. A. Bedau, "Bentham's Utilitarian Critique of the Death Penalty" (1983) 74 J. Crim. L. & Criminology 1033–66, reprinted in H. A. Bedau, *Death is Different: Studies in the Morality, Law, and Politics of Capital Punishment* (Boston, Northeastern U. P., 1987) 64–91.

11. Walter Berns, *For Capital Punishment: Crime and the Morality of the Death Penalty* (New York, Basic Books, 1979).

12. H. A. Bedau, "Capital Punishment," in Tom Regan, ed., *Matters of Life and Death* (New York, Random House, 1980) 159–60; reprinted in Bedau, *Death is Different,* supra n. 10, at 24.

13. Ernest van den Haag, "The Ultimate Punishment: A Defense" (1986) 99 Harv. L. R. 1662–69, at 1665 ff.

14. See Bedau and Radelet, *supra* n. 3, at 78–81, 83–85.

15. Vivian Berger, "Justice Delayed or Justice Denied?—A Comment on Recent Proposals to Reform Habeas Corpus" (1990) 90 Colum. L. R. 1665–1714; Anthony G. Amsterdam, "The Supreme Court and Capital Punishment" (1987) 14 Human Rights 1, at 14–18; Ronald J. Tabak, "The Death of Fairness: The Arbitrary and Capricious Imposition of the Death Penalty in the 1980s" (1986) 14 N.Y.U.R.L. & Soc. Change 797–848; H. A. Bedau, "*Gregg* v. *Georgia* and the 'New' Death Penalty"

(1985) 4 Crim. Justice Ethics 2, at 3–17; Robert Weisberg, "Deregulating Death" in S. Ct. R. 1983 (1984) 305–95; and Baldus et al., *supra* n. 2.

16. Bedau, *Death is Different, supra* n. 10, at 45.

17. Karl Marx, "Capital Punishment" (1853), reprinted in Lewis Feuer, ed., *Basic Writings on Politics and Philosophy: Karl Marx and Frederick Engels* (New York, Doubleday Anchor, 1959) 485–86.

18. Bedau, *Death is Different, supra* n. 10, at 123–28.

REVIEW QUESTIONS

1. What are the four disputed questions of fact which Bedau answers? How does he answer them?
2. According to Bedau, why don't these answers, even if assumed to be correct, settle the issue about capital punishment?
3. What are the five social goals relevant to punishment? Why don't they justify the death penalty according to Bedau?
4. What are the six moral principles relevant to punishment? Why don't they justify capital punishment?
5. What considerations lead Bedau to favor abolition of the death penalty?

DISCUSSION QUESTIONS

1. Are factual questions irrelevant to the issue about the death penalty? Why or why not?
2. Does Bedau refute van den Haag's best-bet argument?
3. The fifth moral principle says that punishments should be graded in their severity according to the gravity of the offense. The crime of first-degree murder is one of the worst offenses. So why shouldn't it receive the most severe punishment, namely the death penalty?

PROBLEM CASES

1. Paul Jennings Hill. (Reported by Tom Kuntz in *The New York Times,* September 24, 1995.) Paul Jennings Hill is a forty-one-year-old Presbyterian minister. He is also a murderer, condemned to die in Florida's electric chair for the shotgun slayings of an abortion doctor, Dr. John Bayard Britton, and a security escort, James H. Barrett. He shot and

killed both men outside a Pensacola, Florida, abortion clinic in July 1995.

On the morning of July 29, 1995, Hill waited outside the abortion clinic. Dr. Britton arrived in a pickup truck with his wife and Mr. Barrett, a seventy-four-year-old retired Air Force officer. Mr. Barrett was driving, Dr. Britton was next to him, and Mrs. Britton was sitting in the jumpseat in back. All were unarmed. Hill opened fire with his new .12-gauge semiautomatic shotgun, bought two days before the killings. He fired three shots at the driver's side of the truck, reloaded, and fired four more shots, killing Mr. Barrett and Dr. Britton. June Barrett was wounded in her left arm but was not killed.

Hill says he believes in the death penalty, but he maintains that it is not justified in his case. He argues that the homicides were justified because he was defending innocent lives. He compares his action to that of police who kill people to prevent other people from being killed. His argument goes more or less as follows: Abortion is the murder of innocent unborn people. God wants us to save the lives of innocent people, and killing guilty abortion doctors (who are comparable to Nazis in Hill's view) is a way of saving innocent lives. Saving innocent lives in accord with God's will is morally right. So killing guilty abortion doctors is morally right.

Does Hill deserve the death penalty? If not, then what punishment, if any, is justified in this case?

Several pro-life murderers of abortion doctors have been sentenced to death recently, some of them before the Hill murders, but it seems that this had no deterrent effect on Hill. On the contrary, he says he welcomes death. He believes that his death would make him a martyr who died to save innocent lives. If the death penalty does not work as deterrent, and in fact encourages people to commit murders, then is it still justified?

2. *The Case of Paul Crump.* (See Ronald Bailey, "Facing Death: A New Life Perhaps Too Late," *Life*, July 27, 1962, pp. 28–29.) In the early 1950s, Paul Crump was convicted of a vicious murder, sentenced to death, and put in an Illinois prison. At his trial, he was said to be full of hatred, "animalistic and belligerent," and a danger to society. Yet under the influence of Warden Jack Johnson and his prison reforms, Crump became rehabilitated. Even though he had only a ninth-grade education, he took courses in reading and writing. Soon he was reading poetry, fiction, and philosophy, and writing stories, articles, and poems which were published in small magazines. He wrote an autobiographical novel, *Burn, Killer, Burn.* Eventually, he began to help his fellow prisoners and was put in charge of caring for the sick and disabled in the convalescent section of the jail hospital. All this did not happen overnight, but took a period of seven years. At the end of this time, Warden Johnson claimed that Crump was "completely rehabilitated," and on August 1, 1962, Illinois Governor Otto Ker-

ner commuted Crump's death sentence to 199 years with the possibility of parole.

Do you think that Governor Kerner made the right decision or not? Explain your answer.

Would it have been morally right to free Crump? Why or why not?

Would it have been morally justifiable to execute Crump despite his rehabilitation? What do you think?

3. *The Sacco-Vanzetti Case.* On April 15, 1920, a paymaster for a shoe company in South Braintree, Massachusetts, and his guard were shot and killed by two men who escaped with more than $15,000. Witnesses thought the two men were Italians, and Nicola Sacco and Bartolomeo Vanzetti were arrested. Both men were anarchists and had evaded the army draft. Upon their arrest, they made false statements. Both carried firearms; but neither had a criminal record, nor was there any evidence that they had the money. In July 1921, they were found guilty and sentenced to death. The conduct of the trial by Judge Webster Thayer was criticized, and indeed much of the evidence against them was later discredited. The court denied their appeal for a new trial, and Governor Alvan T. Fuller, after postponing the execution, allowed them to be executed on August 22, 1927. Many regarded them as innocent, prompting worldwide sympathy demonstrations. The case has been the subject of many books, most of which agree that Vanzetti was innocent, but that Sacco may have been guilty. The gun found on Sacco was tested with modern ballistics equipment in 1961, and these tests seem to show that the gun had been used to kill the guard.

Was it morally right to execute these two men? Why or why not?

4. *William Alvin Smith.* (Reported in *Time*, July 19, 1989.) William Alvin Smith robbed and killed the owner of a grocery store in rural Georgia when he was twenty years old. Smith turned himself in to the police and signed a confession. A local jury condemned Smith to death in the electric chair, but in July 1989, a federal judge ordered a new sentencing hearing for Smith on the grounds that he lacked the ability to understand the significance of waiving his rights to remain silent and to have an attorney present. Smith has the mental capacity of a ten-year-old.

Does he deserve the death sentence?

It is estimated that about 30 percent of the 2,200 convicts on death row are mentally retarded or mentally impaired. Should they be executed?

SUGGESTED READINGS

1. Anthony G. Amsterdam, "Race and the Death Penalty," *Criminal Justice Ethics*, vol. 7, no. 1 (Winter/Spring 1988), pp. 82–86, argues that the Supreme Court ruling in *McCleskey* allowing the discriminatory practice of imposing the death sentence on African-American males in Georgia amounts to a license to discriminate against people of color.

2. Anthony G. Amsterdam, "Capital Punishment," *Stanford Magazine* (Fall/Winter 1977), pp. 422–47, argues that capital punishment is wrong because it is intentionally killing a person, it results in killing innocent people, and it is unfairly applied.

3. Hugo Adam Bedau, "Capital Punishment," in *Matters of Life and Death,* third edition, ed. Tom Regan (Random House, 1993), argues that neither the appeal to retribution nor the appeal to deterrence justifies the death penalty as opposed to the alternative punishment of life imprisonment.

4. The anthology *The Death Penalty in America,* third edition, ed. Hugo Adam Bedau (Oxford, 1982), provides a number of useful articles on factual data relevant to the death penalty, and articles both for and against the death penalty.

5. Raoul Berger, *Death Penalties* (Harvard University Press, 1982), argues that the death penalty is not unconstitutional.

6. Tom Sorell, *Moral Theory and Capital Punishment* (Blackwell, 1988), defends the death penalty.

7. In *The Death Penalty: A Debate,* by Ernest van den Haag and John P. Conrad (Plenum Press, 1983), van den Haag is in favor of retaining the death penalty and Conrad wants to abolish it.

8. Charles L. Black, Jr., *Capital Punishment: The Inevitability of Caprice and Mistake* (Norton, 1981), argues that mistakes cannot be eliminated from the imposition of the death penalty and for that reason it ought to be abolished.

9. Walter Berns, *For Capital Punishment* (Basic Books, 1979), presents a retributivist justification for capital punishment.

10. Albert Camus, *Reflections on the Guillotine: An Essay on Capital Punishment,* translated by Richard Howard (Fridjof-Karla Press, 1959), expresses his opposition to the death penalty.

11. The anthology *Philosophical Perspectives on Punishment,* ed. Gertrude Ezorsky (University of New York Press, 1972), covers capital punishment and general philosophical questions about punishment.

12. Robert S. Gerstein, "Capital Punishment—'Cruel and Unusual?' A Retributivist Response," *Ethics* 85 (January 1975), pp. 75–79, defends retributivism against the complaint that it is mere vengeance. Gerstein says that retributivism is the view that punishment restores the balance of advantages to a just community and that, as such, it treats the offender with the respect due a member of a just community.

13. Steven Goldberg, "On Capital Punishment," *Ethics* 85 (October 1974), pp. 67–74, examines the factual issue of whether or not the death penalty is a uniquely effective deterrent. A revised version entitled "Does Capital Punishment Deter?" appears in *Today's Moral Problems,* second edition, ed. Richard A. Wasserstrom (Macmillan, 1979).

14. Sidney Hook, "The Death Sentence," in *The Death Penalty in America,* ed. Hugo Adam Bedau (Doubleday, 1967), supports the retention of the death penalty in two cases: (1) defendants convicted of murder who choose death rather than life imprisonment, and (2) those who have been sentenced to prison for murder and then murder again while in prison. Since the publication of this essay, Professor Hook advises that he is now prepared to extend the scope of discretionary death sentences in cases of multiple and aggravated capital crimes.

15. Robert Johnson, "This Man Has Expired. Witness to an Execution," *Commonweal* (January 13, 1989), pp. 9–13, gives a detailed and graphic description of an electric-chair execution as well as the events before and after the event.

16. Thomas Long, "Capital Punishment—'Cruel and Unusual'?" *Ethics* 83 (April 1973), pp. 214–23, discusses various arguments for the view that capital punishment is cruel and unusual.

17. *Punishment and Rehabilitation,* second edition, ed. Jeffrie B. Murphy (Wadsworth, 1985), is an anthology that covers various philosophical aspects of punishment including capital punishment.

18. Stephen Nathanson, *An Eye for an Eye? The Morality of Punishing by Death* (Rowman & Littlefield, 1987), discusses issues surrounding the death penalty and develops a case for abolishing it.

19. Welsh S. White, *The Death Penalty in the Nineties* (University of Michigan Press, 1991), examines the way the death penalty has been administered in the current decade.

Chapter Five

HUNGER AND WELFARE

Introduction

There are millions of needy people in the world today. In the first reading for the chapter, Peter Singer claims that there are 400 million people who suffer from malnutrition, including 180 million children, and that fourteen million children under the age of five die every year from malnutrition and infections. These people live in what Robert McNamara called "absolute poverty"; this is, according to McNamara, "a condition of life so characterized by malnutrition, illiteracy, disease, squalid surroundings, high infant mortality, and low life expectancy as to be beneath human decency." Most of these people live in countries on the subcontinent (India, Pakistan, and Bangladesh) and in poor nations of the Caribbean, Latin America, Southeast Asia, and Africa. What should be done to help them? This is the world hunger problem.

Not all of the needy people live in poor countries; some of them live in rich countries such as the United States. According to recent reports, the United States has about thirty million people living below the poverty level, and the number is increasing. The Coalition for the Homeless estimates that there are more than six million homeless people in the United States. What should be done about these needy people? This is the welfare problem.

Before turning to these two related problems, we should briefly discuss two factual issues: (1) Can rich countries provide welfare for their needy citizens? (2) Is it possible to feed all the hungry people in the world?

The first question is easily answered: No doubt some poor countries cannot provide welfare for all their citizens; that is one reason why we have the problem of world hunger. But rich countries like the United States can and do provide welfare for some of their needy citizens—for example, disabled persons and unemployed mothers with small children. No doubt they could provide welfare for all their needy citizens if this was considered as important as national defense. The main issue about welfare is not whether it is actually possible in rich countries—obviously it is. Rather, the moral issue is whether needy citizens in rich countries have a right to welfare and the governments a corresponding duty to provide it.

The second factual question is not so easy to answer. Is it even possible to feed all the hungry people in the world? To determine the amount of aid actually required to do this, we need to know how many people need food, what their nutritional requirements are, how distribution can be made, what population growth will be, and other facts relevant to the problem. If there are two billion hungry people to be fed, as the Overseas Development Council claims, then the task is difficult but perhaps not impossible. Statistics on world grain production show that the world's farmers produce enough grain to provide every human being with 3,600 calories a day—more than enough for healthy men or women. Given some international cooperation, everyone could be fed, at least in principle. Furthermore, even more food could be produced by using available land. According to the Worldwatch Institute, less than 60 percent of the world's farmland is under cultivation, and in almost every country where there is widespread hunger and environmental destruction, much of the best agricultural land is used to raise export crops or livestock. These countries could produce more food by growing grain instead of raising livestock and growing export crops.

But if enough food is produced to feed everyone, then why do people go hungry and starve? The standard answer given by Singer is that the rich nations consume more than their fair share of the food. Specifically, Singer says that people in the poor countries consume, on average, 180 kilos of grain a year, while greedy North Americans average around 900 kilos. The reason that the rich countries con-sume so much is that they feed most of their grain to animals and then eat the animals' flesh or their milk and eggs. If the wasteful rich countries stopped giving grain to animals and fed people instead, then there would be plenty of food to end world hunger. According to Singer, this shows that the problem is one of distribution rather than production.

The World Hunger Problem Let us assume that it is at least theoretically possible to feed all of the world's hungry people. Is there any moral obligation to do this? Do rich nations have any moral obligation to help needy people in poor countries?

One view of the problem, expressed by Philipa Foot (in her article "Euthanasia," cited in the Suggested Readings for Chapter 2) and others who distinguish between killing and letting die, is that we are morally required to not kill people, but not morally required to prevent people from suffering and dying from lack of food. Sometimes this is put as an Acts and Omissions Doctrine: Acts of killing innocent people are wrong, but omissions that result in death, for example, failing to feed starving people, are not wrong. To be sure, it is a good thing to help starving and needy people. However, this is optional and above and beyond the call of duty; it is not required by morality.

Singer does not accept this view. In the first place, like Rachels in Chapter 2, he believes that there is no intrinsic difference between killing and allowing to die (although he grants that there may be what he calls extrinsic differences). Second, he formulates a plausible argument for saying that people in rich countries are morally obligated to help needy people provided they can do this without sacrificing anything of comparable moral significance. Singer thinks that people in rich countries living in "absolute affluence" (as he puts it) waste their money on luxuries such as stylish clothes, expensive dinners, and second cars—things which do not, in Singer's view, have a moral significance comparable to the suffering of the needy. So instead of spending their money on luxuries, rich people living in absolute affluence have a moral obligation to give at least some of their extra money to charities to help needy people.

Garrett Hardin does not agree. He objects to welfare-style transfers from rich nations to poor ones. In his view, nations are lifeboats with limited carrying capacity; they cannot afford to feed poor nations. Besides, aid to poor nations just makes matters worse; the result is a vicious cycle of overpopulation, starvation, more aid, and so on until there is ecological disaster. The implication is that we should let people in poor nations die.

Robert N. Van Wyk objects to the utilitarian approach used by both Singer and Hardin. Singer expands the area of our moral duty to the point of eliminating the moral supererogatory and fails to take seriously the bad long-term consequences of keeping everybody alive. Hardin's use of metaphor is inappropriate; rich countries are more like luxury liners than lifeboats. Even most poor countries have the resources to feed their people if the resources were only used for that purpose. Instead of a utilitarian approach, Van Wyk suggests a Kantian ethic to solve the problem of world hunger. From Kant's principle of respect for persons, we can derive a duty of reparation to poor countries for past harms committed against them by rich countries and a duty of the affluent to do their fair share to help those who are needy.

The Welfare Problem Even if we agree that rich nations should not help people in poor nations, there remains the question of what to do about the poor people in the rich nations themselves. The most conservative view, expressed by John Hospers in the readings, is Libertarianism; this is the view that needy people in rich nations have no right to welfare and the government has no obligation to satisfy their basic needs. The view is called Libertarianism because it is based on a basic principle of liberty, the principle that individuals have a right to act as they choose unless their action interferes with a similar right of others to act as they choose. This right of freedom is a right of noninterference: It requires others to not interfere in your life, but it does not involve any right to help from others, or

any welfare right. An implication of this is that the only function of the government is to protect people from interference; the government has no business taking money from the rich in order to feed the poor. But what happens to the needy then? Hospers does not believe that they will suffer and die. Rather he thinks that most will be gainfully employed instead of subsisting on welfare and that the remainder will be supported by their families or by voluntary charity.

At the other end of the political spectrum is the Radical Egalitarianism explained and defended by Kai Nielsen in the readings. According to this liberal view, everyone in an affluent society has an equal right to have his or her basic needs met by the government. Any surplus income and wealth remaining after basic needs are met is to be divided so that each person will get an equal share. The necessary burdens of society, that is, the work needed to keep the society going and to produce well-being, are also to be equally shared, subject to the ability to contribute. Perhaps the most famous statement of this view, quoted with approval by Nielsen, is Marx's slogan: "From each according to his ability, to each according to his needs."

Trudy Govier objects to both of these views in the reading. She calls the libertarian view the "individualist position" because it emphasizes the freedom of the individual. She thinks that disaster would result if all nonoptional government welfare programs were simply terminated, as the libertarian or individualist recommends. People would die and suffer tremendously. She does not believe that we can assume that people's needs would be met by voluntary charities. Furthermore, she thinks there might be violence as crowds of needy people attack the rich.

Govier does not discuss Radical Egalitarianism. She accepts the view that everyone in an affluent society has a right to welfare benefits; she thinks that this view, the Permissive Position as she calls it, satisfies the demands of both justice and utility. But she rejects the view that the right to welfare benefits ought to be conditional on the willingness to work (she calls this the Puritan Position). Thus she accepts only one of the principles of Radical Egalitarianism, the principle that everyone in an affluent society has an equal right to have his or her basic needs met and not the principle that everyone should share equally the burdens of society, that is, the work necessary to keep the society going. Her objection to the work requirement is that it has bad consequences. To be enforced, it requires a complicated, wasteful, and cumbersome bureaucracy, and it has undesirable effects on those who are forced to work.

The views that Govier discusses are not just theoretical. One can accurately say that the United States follows a puritan type of welfare system. Indeed the political tide in the United States seems to be going toward more work requirements for welfare recipients. One such proposal is Workfare, as explained by Peter Germanis in the readings. Canada, where both Nielsen and Govier live, has a more permissive system. Which system works best, the puritan or the permissive system? The answer is debatable, but when it comes to medical care, there is evidence that the Canadian system is more efficient. Consider some statistics cited in *The New York Times* (September 24, 1989).

The United States spends about 12 percent of its gross national product on health care, while ignoring thirty-one million Americans with no health insurance. By contrast, Canada spends less than 9 percent of its GNP providing health care for all of its citizens. In the Canadian system, the government is responsible for practically all health care expenses, paying hospitals at a negotiated rate and doctors according to a binding fee schedule.

In the last reading for the chapter, Nancy Fraser presents still another view of welfare, the feminist perspective. In her analysis, Fraser concentrates on the United States' social welfare system, and she uncovers some very disturbing facts. Most of the welfare recipients and employees are women. Programs like Aid to Families with Dependent Children keep mothers poor and on welfare. The system assumes that women should be caregivers and domestic workers. It treats women as dependent clients rather than bearers of rights. Finally, important political issues about the interpretation of people's needs and social roles are reduced to mere legal, administrative, and/or therapeutic matters.

Peter Singer

Rich and Poor

From Peter Singer, "Rich and Poor," *Practical Ethics*, 2nd ed., pp. 218–246. © Cambridge University Press 1993. Reprinted with the permission of the author and Cambridge University Press.

For biographical information on Singer, see his reading in Chapter 3.

After discussing some relevant facts about poverty and wealth in the world, and the moral implications of these facts, Singer presents a powerful argument for holding that people who enjoy absolute wealth have a moral obligation to help those who suffer in absolute poverty. Then he answers objections about taking care of our own, property rights, government responsibility, and setting too high a standard.

SOME FACTS ABOUT POVERTY

. . . Consider these facts: by the most cautious estimates, 400 million people lack the calories, protein, vitamins and minerals needed to sustain their bodies and minds in a healthy state. Millions are constantly hungry; others suffer from deficiency diseases and from infections they would be able to resist on a better diet. Children are the worst affected. According to one study, 14 million children under five die every year from the combined effects of malnutrition and infection. In some districts half the children born can be expected to die before their fifth birthday.

Nor is lack of food the only hardship of the poor. To give a broader picture, Robert McNamara, when president of the World Bank, suggested the term 'absolute poverty'. The poverty we are familiar with in industrialised nations is relative poverty—meaning that some citizens are poor, relative to the wealth enjoyed by their neighbours. People living in relative poverty in Australia might be quite comfortably off by comparison with pensioners in Britain, and British pensioners are not poor in comparison with the poverty that exists in Mali or Ethiopia. Absolute poverty, on the other hand, is poverty by any standard. In McNamara's words:

Poverty at the absolute level . . . is life at the very margin of existence. The absolute poor are severely deprived human beings struggling to survive in a set of squalid and degraded circumstances almost beyond the power of our sophisticated imaginations and privileged circumstances to conceive.

Compared to those fortunate enough to live in developed countries, individuals in the poorest nations have:

An infant mortality rate eight times higher

A life expectancy one-third lower

An adult literacy rate 60 per cent less

A nutritional level, for one out of every two in the population, below acceptable standards;

And for millions of infants, less protein than is sufficient to permit optimum development of the brain.

McNamara has summed up absolute poverty as 'a condition of life so characterised by malnutrition, illiteracy, disease, squalid surroundings, high infant mortality and low life expectancy as to be beneath any reasonable definition of human decency'.

Absolute poverty is, as McNamara has said, responsible for the loss of countless lives, especially among infants and young children. When absolute poverty does not cause death, it still causes misery of a kind not often seen in the affluent nations. Malnutrition in young children stunts both physical and mental devel-

opment. According to the United Nations Development Programme, 180 million children under the age of five suffer from serious malnutrition. Millions of people on poor diets suffer from deficiency diseases, like goitre, or blindness caused by a lack of vitamin A. The food value of what the poor eat is further reduced by parasites such as hookworm and ringworm, which are endemic in conditions of poor sanitation and health education.

Death and disease apart, absolute poverty remains a miserable condition of life, with inadequate food, shelter, clothing, sanitation, health services and education. The Worldwatch Institute estimates that as many as 1.2 billion people—or 23 per cent of the world's population—live in absolute poverty. For the purposes of this estimate, absolute poverty is defined as "the lack of sufficient income in cash or kind to meet the most basic biological needs for food, clothing, and shelter." Absolute poverty is probably the principal cause of human misery today.

SOME FACTS ABOUT WEALTH

This is the background situation, the situation that prevails on our planet all the time. It does not make headlines. People died from malnutrition and related diseases yesterday, and more will die tomorrow. The occasional droughts, cyclones, earthquakes, and floods that take the lives of tens of thousands in one place and at one time are more newsworthy. They add greatly to the total amount of human suffering; but it is wrong to assume that when there are no major calamities reported, all is well.

The problem is not that the world cannot produce enough to feed and shelter its people. People in the poor countries consume, on average, 180 kilos of grain a year, while North Americans average around 900 kilos. The difference is caused by the fact that in the rich countries we feed most of our grain to animals, converting it into meat, milk, and eggs. Because this is a highly inefficient process, people in rich countries are responsible for the consumption of far more food than those in poor countries who eat few animal products. If we stopped feeding animals on grains and soybeans, the amount of food saved would—if distributed to those who need it—be more than enough to end hunger throughout the world.

These facts about animal food do not mean that we can easily solve the world food problem by cutting down on animal products, but they show that the problem is essentially one of distribution rather than production. The world does produce enough food. Moreover, the poorer nations themselves could produce far more if they made more use of improved agricultural techniques.

So why are people hungry? Poor people cannot afford to buy grain grown by farmers in the richer nations. Poor farmers cannot afford to buy improved seeds, or fertilisers, or the machinery needed for drilling wells and pumping water. Only by transferring some of the wealth of the rich nations to the poor can the situation be changed.

That this wealth exists is clear. Against the picture of absolute poverty that McNamara has painted, one might pose a picture of 'absolute affluence'. Those who are absolutely affluent are not necessarily affluent by comparison with their neighbours, but they are affluent by any reasonable definition of human needs. This means that they have more income than they need to provide themselves adequately with all the basic necessities of life. After buying (either directly or through their taxes) food, shelter, clothing, basic health services, and education, the absolutely affluent are still able to spend money on luxuries. The absolutely affluent choose their food for the pleasures of the palate, not to stop hunger; they buy new clothes to look good, not to keep warm; they move to a new house to be in a better neighbourhood or have a playroom for the children, not to keep out the rain; and after all this there is still money to spend on stereo systems, video-cameras, and overseas holidays.

At this stage I am making no ethical judgments about absolute affluence, merely pointing out that it exists. Its defining characteristic is a significant amount of income above the level necessary to provide for the basic human needs of oneself and one's dependents. By this standard, the majority of citizens of Western Europe, North America, Japan, Australia, New Zealand, and the oil-rich Middle Eastern states are all absolutely affluent. To quote McNamara once more:

The average citizen of a developed country enjoys wealth beyond the wildest dreams of the one billion people in countries with per capita incomes under $200. These, therefore, are the countries—and individuals—who have wealth that they could, without threatening their own basic welfare, transfer to the absolutely poor.

At present, very little is being transferred. Only Sweden, the Netherlands, Norway, and some of the oil-exporting Arab states have reached the modest target, set by the United Nations, of 0.7 per cent of gross national products (GNP). Britain gives 0.31 per cent of its GNP in official development assistance and a small additional amount in unofficial aid from voluntary organisations. The total comes to about £2 per month per person, and compares with 5.5 per cent of GNP spent on alcohol, and 3 per cent on tobacco. Other, even wealthier nations, give little more: Germany gives 0.41 per cent and Japan 0.32 per cent. The United States gives a mere 0.15 per cent of its GNP.

THE MORAL EQUIVALENT OF MURDER?

If these are the facts, we cannot avoid concluding that by not giving more than we do, people in rich countries are allowing those in poor countries to suffer from absolute poverty, with consequent malnutrition, ill health, and death. This is not a conclusion that applies only to governments. It applies to each absolutely affluent individual, for each of us has the opportunity to do something about the situation; for instance, to give our time or money to voluntary organisations like Oxfam, Care, War on Want, Freedom from Hunger, Community Aid Abroad, and so on. If, then, allowing someone to die is not intrinsically different from killing someone, it would seem that we are all murderers.

Is this verdict too harsh? Many will reject it as self-evidently absurd. They would sooner take it as showing that allowing to die cannot be equivalent to killing than as showing that living in an affluent style without contributing to an overseas aid agency is ethically equivalent to going over to Ethiopia and shooting a few peasants. And no doubt, put as bluntly as that, the verdict is too harsh.

There are several significant differences between spending money on luxuries instead of using it to save lives, and deliberately shooting people.

First, the motivation will normally be different. Those who deliberately shoot others go out of their way to kill; they presumably want their victims dead, from malice, sadism, or some equally unpleasant motive. A person who buys a new stereo system presumably wants to enhance her enjoyment of music—not in itself a terrible thing. At worst, spending money on luxuries instead of giving it away indicates selfishness and indifference to the sufferings of others, characteristics that may be undesirable but are not comparable with actual malice or similar motives.

Second, it is not difficult for most of us to act in accordance with a rule against killing people: it is, on the other hand, very difficult to obey a rule that commands us to save all the lives we can. To live a comfortable, or even luxurious life it is not necessary to kill anyone; but it is necessary to allow some to die whom we might have saved, for the money that we need to live comfortably could have been given away. Thus the duty to avoid killing is much easier to discharge completely than the duty to save. Saving every life we could would mean cutting our standard of living down to the bare essentials needed to keep us alive.[1] To discharge this duty completely would require a degree of moral heroism utterly different from that required by mere avoidance of killing.

A third difference is the greater certainty of the outcome of shooting when compared with not giving aid. If I point a loaded gun at someone at close range and pull the trigger, it is virtually certain that the person will be killed; whereas the money that I could give might be spent on a project that turns out to be unsuccessful and helps no one.

Fourth, when people are shot there are identifiable individuals who have been harmed. We can point to them and to their grieving families. When I buy my stereo system, I cannot know who my money would have saved if I had given it away. In a time of famine I may see dead bodies and grieving families on television reports, and I might not doubt that my money would have saved some of them; even then it is impossible to point to a body and say that had I not bought the stereo, that person would have survived.

Fifth, it might be said that the plight of the hungry is not my doing, and so I cannot be held responsible for it. The starving would have been starving if I had never existed. If I kill, however, I am responsible for my victims' deaths, for those people would not have died if I had not killed them. . . .

To explain our conventional ethical attitudes is not to justify them. Do the five differences not only explain, but also justify, our attitudes? Let us consider them one by one:

1. Take the lack of an identifiable victim first. Suppose that I am a travelling salesperson, selling tinned food, and I learn that a batch of tins contains a contaminant, the known effect of which, when consumed, is to double the risk that the consumer will die from stomach cancer. Suppose I continue to sell the tins. My decision may have no identifiable victims. Some of those who eat the food will die from cancer. The proportion of consumers dying in this way will be twice that of the community at large, but who among the consumers died because they ate what I sold, and who would have contracted the disease anyway? It is impossible to tell; but surely this impossibility makes my decision no less reprehensible than it would have been had the contaminant had more readily detectable, though equally fatal, effects.

2. The lack of certainty that by giving money I could save a life does reduce the wrongness of not giving, by comparison with deliberate killing; but it is insufficient to show that not giving is acceptable conduct. The motorist who speeds through pedestrian crossings, heedless of anyone who might be on them, is not a murderer. She may never actually hit a pedestrian; yet what she does is very wrong indeed.

3. The notion of responsibility for acts rather than omissions is more puzzling. On the one

hand, we feel ourselves to be under a greater obligation to help those whose misfortunes we have caused. (It is for this reason that advocates of overseas aid often argue that Western nations have created the poverty of third world nations, through forms of economic exploitation that go back to the colonial system.) On the other hand, any consequentialist would insist that we are responsible for all the consequences of our actions, and if a consequence of my spending money on a luxury item is that someone dies, I am responsible for that death. It is true that the person would have died even if I had never existed, but what is the relevance of that? The fact is that I do exist, and the consequentialist will say that our responsibilities derive from the world as it is, not as it might have been.

One way of making sense of the non-consequentialist view of responsibility is by basing it on a theory of rights of the kind proposed by John Locke or, more recently, Robert Nozick. If everyone has a right to life, and this right is a right *against* others who might threaten my life, but not a right to assistance from others when my life is in danger, then we can understand the feeling that we are responsible for acting to kill but not for omitting to save. The former violates the rights of others, the latter does not.

Should we accept such a theory of rights? If we build up our theory of rights by imagining, as Locke and Nozick do, individuals living independently from each other in a 'state of nature', it may seem natural to adopt a conception of rights in which as long as each leaves the other alone, no rights are violated. I might, on this view, quite properly have maintained my independent existence if I had wished to do so. So if I do not make you any worse off than you would have been if I had had nothing at all to do with you, how can I have violated your rights? But why start from such an unhistorical, abstract and ultimately inexplicable idea as an independent individual? Our ancestors were—like other primates—social beings long before they were human beings, and could not have developed the abilities and capacities of human beings if they had not been social beings first. In any case, we are not, now, isolated individuals. So why should we assume that rights must be restricted to rights against interference? We

might, instead, adopt the view that taking rights to life seriously is incompatible with standing by and watching people die when one could easily save them.

4. What of the difference in motivation? That a person does not positively wish for the death of another lessens the severity of the blame she deserves; but not by as much as our present attitudes to giving aid suggest. The behaviour of the speeding motorist is again comparable, for such motorists usually have no desire at all to kill anyone. They merely enjoy speeding and are indifferent to the consequences. Despite their lack of malice, those who kill with cars deserve not only blame but also severe punishment.

5. Finally, the fact that to avoid killing people is normally not difficult, whereas to save all one possibly could save is heroic, must make an important difference to our attitude to failure to do what the respective principles demand. Not to kill is a minimum standard of acceptable conduct we can require of everyone; to save all one possibly could is not something that can realistically be required, especially not in societies accustomed to giving as little as ours do. Given the generally accepted standards, people who give, say, $1,000 a year to an overseas aid organisation are more aptly praised for above average generosity than blamed for giving less than they might. The appropriateness of praise and blame is, however, a separate issue from the rightness or wrongness of actions. The former evaluates the agent: the latter evaluates the action. Perhaps many people who give $1,000 really ought to give at least $5,000, but to blame them for not giving more could be counterproductive. It might make them feel that what is required is too demanding, and if one is going to be blamed anyway, one might as well not give anything at all.

(That an ethic that put saving all one possibly can on the same footing as not killing would be an ethic for saints or heroes should not lead us to assume that the alternative must be an ethic that makes it obligatory not to kill, but puts us under no obligation to save anyone. There are positions in between these extremes, as we shall soon see.)

Here is a summary of the five differences that normally exist between killing and allowing to die, in the context of absolute poverty and overseas aid. The lack of an identifiable victim is of no moral significance, though it may play an important role in explaining our attitudes. The idea that we are directly responsible for those we kill, but not for those we do not help, depends on a questionable notion of responsibility and may need to be based on a controversial theory of rights. Differences in certainty and motivation are ethically significant, and show that not aiding the poor is not to be condemned as murdering them; it could, however, be on a par with killing someone as a result of reckless driving, which is serious enough. Finally the difficulty of completely discharging the duty of saving all one possibly can makes it inappropriate to blame those who fall short of this target as we blame those who kill; but this does not show that the act itself is less serious. Nor does it indicate anything about those who, far from saving all they possibly can, make no effort to save anyone.

These conclusions suggest a new approach. Instead of attempting to deal with the contrast between affluence and poverty by comparing not saving with deliberate killing, let us consider afresh whether we have an obligation to assist those whose lives are in danger, and if so, how this obligation applies to the present world situation.

THE OBLIGATION TO ASSIST

The Argument for an Obligation to Assist

The path from the library at my university to the humanities lecture theatre passes a shallow ornamental pond. Suppose that on my way to give a lecture I notice that a small child has fallen in and is in danger of drowning. Would anyone deny that I ought to wade in and pull the child out? This will mean getting my clothes muddy and either cancelling my lecture or delaying it until I can find something dry to change into; but compared with the avoidable death of a child this is insignificant.

A plausible principle that would support the judgment that I ought to pull the child out is this: if it is in our power to prevent something

very bad from happening, without thereby sacrificing anything of comparable moral significance, we ought to do it. This principle seems uncontroversial. It will obviously win the assent of **consequentialists**; but non-consequentialists should accept it too, because the injunction to prevent what is bad applies only when nothing comparably significant is at stake. Thus the principle cannot lead to the kinds of actions of which non-consequentialists strongly disapprove—serious violations of individual rights, injustice, broken promises, and so on. If non-consequentialists regard any of these as comparable in moral significance to the bad thing that is to be prevented, they will automatically regard the principle as not applying in those cases in which the bad thing can only be prevented by violating rights, doing injustice, breaking promises, or whatever else is at stake. Most non-consequentialists hold that we ought to prevent what is bad and promote what is good. Their dispute with consequentialists lies in their insistence that this is not the sole ultimate ethical principle: that it is an ethical principle is not denied by any plausible ethical theory.

Nevertheless the uncontroversial appearance of the principle that we ought to prevent what is bad when we can do so without sacrificing anything of comparable moral significance is deceptive. If it were taken seriously and acted upon, our lives and our world would be fundamentally changed. For the principle applies, not just to rare situations in which one can save a child from a pond, but to the everyday situation in which we can assist those living in absolute poverty. In saying this I assume that absolute poverty, with its hunger and malnutrition, lack of shelter, illiteracy, disease, high infant mortality, and low life expectancy, is a bad thing. And I assume that it is within the power of the affluent to reduce absolute poverty, without sacrificing anything of comparable moral significance. If these two assumptions and the principle we have been discussing are correct, we have an obligation to help those in absolute poverty that is no less strong than our obligation to rescue a drowning child from a pond. Not to help would be wrong, whether or not it is intrinsically equivalent to killing. Helping is not, as conventionally thought, a charitable act that it is praiseworthy to do, but not wrong to omit; it is something that everyone ought to do.

This is the argument for an obligation to assist. Set out more formally, it would look like this.

First premise: If we can prevent something bad without sacrificing anything of comparable significance, we ought to do it.

Second premise: Absolute poverty is bad.

Third premise: There is some absolute poverty we can prevent without sacrificing anything of comparable moral significance.

Conclusion: We ought to prevent some absolute poverty.

The first premise is the substantive moral premise on which the argument rests, and I have tried to show that it can be accepted by people who hold a variety of ethical positions.

The second premise is unlikely to be challenged. Absolute poverty is, as McNamara put it, 'beneath any reasonable definition of human decency' and it would be hard to find a plausible ethical view that did not regard it as a bad thing.

The third premise is more controversial, even though it is cautiously framed. It claims only that some absolute poverty can be prevented without the sacrifice of anything of comparable moral significance. It thus avoids the objection that any aid I can give is just 'drops in the ocean' for the point is not whether my personal contribution will make any noticeable impression on world poverty as a whole (of course it won't) but whether it will prevent some poverty. This is all the argument needs to sustain its conclusion, since the second premise says that any absolute poverty is bad, and not merely the total amount of absolute poverty. If without sacrificing anything of comparable moral significance we can provide just one family with the means to raise itself out of absolute poverty, the third premise is vindicated.

I have left the notion of moral significance unexamined in order to show that the argument does not depend on any specific values or ethical principles. I think the third premise is true for most people living in industrialised nations, on any defensible view of what is morally significant. Our affluence means that we have income

we can dispose of without giving up the basic necessities of life, and we can use this income to reduce absolute poverty. Just how much we will think ourselves obliged to give up will depend on what we consider to be of comparable moral significance to the poverty we could prevent: stylish clothes, expensive dinners, a sophisticated stereo system, overseas holidays, a (second?) car, a larger house, private schools for our children, and so on. For a utilitarian, none of these is likely to be of comparable significance to the reduction of absolute poverty; and those who are not utilitarians surely must, if they subscribe to the **principle of universalisability**, accept that at least some of these things are of far less moral significance than the absolute poverty that could be prevented by the money they cost. So the third premise seems to be true on any plausible ethical view—although the precise amount of absolute poverty that can be prevented before anything of moral significance is sacrificed will vary according to the ethical view one accepts.

Objections to the Argument

Taking Care of Our Own Anyone who has worked to increase overseas aid will have come across the argument that we should look after those near us, our families, and then the poor in our own country, before we think about poverty in distant places.

No doubt we do instinctively prefer to help those who are close to us. Few could stand by and watch a child drown; many can ignore a famine in Africa. But the question is not what we usually do, but what we ought to do, and it is difficult to see any sound moral justification for the view that distance, or community membership, makes a crucial difference to our obligations.

Consider, for instance, racial affinities. Should people of European origin help poor Europeans before helping poor Africans? Most of us would reject such a suggestion out of hand, and our discussion of the **principle of equal consideration of interests** . . . [shows] why we should reject it: people's need for food has nothing to do with their race, and if Africans need food more than Europeans, it would be a violation of the principle of equal consideration to give preference to Europeans.

The same point applies to citizenship or nationhood. Every affluent nation has some relatively poor citizens, but absolute poverty is limited largely to the poor nations. Those living on the streets of Calcutta, or in the drought-prone Sahel region of Africa, are experiencing poverty unknown in the West. Under these circumstances it would be wrong to decide that only those fortunate enough to be citizens of our own community will share our abundance.

We feel obligations of kinship more strongly than those of citizenship. Which parents could give away their last bowl of rice if their own children were starving? To do so would seem unnatural, contrary to our nature as biologically evolved beings—although whether it would be wrong is another question altogether. In any case, we are not faced with that situation, but with one in which our own children are well-fed, well-clothed, well-educated, and would now like new bikes, a stereo set, or their own car. In these circumstances any special obligations we might have to our children have been fulfilled, and the needs of strangers make a stronger claim upon us.

The element of truth in the view that we should first take care of our own, lies in the advantage of a recognised system of responsibilities. When families and local communities look after their own poorer members, ties of affection and personal relationships achieve ends that would otherwise require a large, impersonal bureaucracy. Hence it would be absurd to propose that from now on we all regard ourselves as equally responsible for the welfare of everyone in the world; but the argument for an obligation to assist does not propose that. It applies only when some are in absolute poverty, and others can help without sacrificing anything of comparable moral significance. To allow one's own kin to sink into absolute poverty would be to sacrifice something of comparable significance; and before that point had been reached, the breakdown of the system of family and community responsibility would be a factor to weigh the balance in favour of a small degree of preference for family and community. This small degree of preference is, however, decisively outweighed by existing discrepancies in wealth and property.

Property Rights   Do people have a right to private property, a right that contradicts the view that they are under an obligation to give some of their wealth away to those in absolute poverty? According to some theories of rights (for instance, Robert Nozick's), provided one has acquired one's property without the use of unjust means like force and fraud, one may be entitled to enormous wealth while others starve. This individualistic conception of rights is in contrast to other views, like the early Christian doctrine to be found in the works of Thomas Aquinas, which holds that since property exists for the satisfaction of human needs, 'whatever a man has in superabundance is owed, of natural right, to the poor for their sustenance'. A socialist would also, of course, see wealth as belonging to the community rather than the individual, while utilitarians, whether socialist or not, would be prepared to override property rights to prevent great evils.

Does the argument for an obligation to assist others therefore presuppose one of these other theories of property rights, and not an individualistic theory like Nozick's? Not necessarily. A theory of property rights can insist on our *right* to retain wealth without pronouncing on whether the rich *ought* to give to the poor. Nozick, for example, rejects the use of compulsory means like taxation to redistribute income, but suggests that we can achieve the ends we deem morally desirable by voluntary means. So Nozick would reject the claim that rich people have an 'obligation' to give to the poor, in so far as this implies that the poor have a right to our aid, but might accept that giving is something we ought to do and failing to give, though within one's rights, is wrong—for there is more to an ethical life than respecting the rights of others.

The argument for an obligation to assist can survive, with only minor modifications, even if we accept an individualistic theory of property rights. In any case, however, I do not think we should accept such a theory. It leaves too much to chance to be an acceptable ethical view. For instance, those whose forefathers happened to inhabit some sandy wastes around the Persian Gulf are now fabulously wealthy, because oil lay under those sands; while those whose forefathers settled on better land south of the Sahara live in absolute poverty, because of drought and bad harvests. Can this distribution be acceptable from an impartial point of view? If we imagine ourselves about to begin life as a citizen of either Bahrein or Chad—but we do not know which—would we accept the principle that citizens of Bahrein are under no obligation to assist people living in Chad?

Population and the Ethics of Triage Perhaps the most serious objection to the argument that we have an obligation to assist is that since the major cause of absolute poverty is overpopulation, helping those now in poverty will only ensure that yet more people are born to live in poverty in the future.

In its most extreme form, this objection is taken to show that we should adopt a policy of 'triage'. The term comes from medical policies adopted in wartime. With too few doctors to cope with all the casualties, the wounded were divided into three categories: those who would probably survive without medical assistance, those who might survive if they received assistance, but otherwise probably would not, and those who even with medical assistance probably would not survive. Only those in the middle category were given medical assistance. The idea, of course, was to use limited medical resources as effectively as possible. For those in the first category, medical treatment was not strictly necessary; for those in the third category, it was likely to be useless. It has been suggested that we should apply the same policies to countries, according to their prospects of becoming self-sustaining. We would not aid countries that even without our help will soon be able to feed their populations. We would not aid countries that, even with our help, will not be able to limit their population to a level they can feed. We would aid those countries where our help might make the difference between success and failure in bringing food and population into balance.

Advocates of this theory are understandably reluctant to give a complete list of the countries they would place into the 'hopeless' category; Bangladesh has been cited as an example, and so have some of the countries of the Sahel region of Africa. Adopting the policy of triage

would, then, mean cutting off assistance to these countries and allowing famine, disease, and natural disasters to reduce the population of those countries to the level at which they can provide adequately for all.

In support of this view Garrett Hardin has offered a metaphor: we in the rich nations are like the occupants of a crowded lifeboat adrift in a sea full of drowning people. If we try to save the drowning by bringing them aboard, our boat will be overloaded and we shall all drown. Since it is better that some survive than none, we should leave the others to drown. In the world today, according to Hardin, 'lifeboat ethics' apply. The rich should leave the poor to starve, for otherwise the poor will drag the rich down with them.

Against this view, some writers have argued that overpopulation is a myth. The world produces ample food to feed its population, and could, according to some estimates, feed ten times as many. People are hungry not because there are too many but because of inequitable land distribution, the manipulation of third world economies by the developed nations, wastage of food in the West, and so on.

Putting aside the controversial issue of the extent to which food production might one day be increased, it is true, as we have already seen, that the world now produces enough to feed its inhabitants—the amount lost by being fed to animals itself being enough to meet existing grain shortages. Nevertheless population growth cannot be ignored. Bangladesh could, with land reform and using better techniques, feed its present population of 115 million; but by the year 2000, according to United Nations Population Division estimates, its population will be 150 million. The enormous effort that will have to go into feeding an extra 35 million people, all added to the population within a decade, means that Bangladesh must develop at full speed to stay where it is. Other low-income countries are in similar situations. By the end of the century, Ethiopia's population is expected to rise from 49 to 66 million; Somalia's from 7 to 9 million, India's from 853 to 1041 million, Zaire's from 35 to 49 million.[2]

What will happen if the world population continues to grow? It cannot do so indefinitely.

It will be checked by a decline in birth rates or a rise in death rates. Those who advocate triage are proposing that we allow the population growth of some countries to be checked by a rise in death rates—that is, by increased malnutrition, and related diseases; by widespread famines; by increased infant mortality; and by epidemics of infectious diseases.

The consequences of triage on this scale are so horrible that we are inclined to reject it without further argument. How could we sit by our television sets, watching millions starve while we do nothing? Would not that be the end of all notions of human equality and respect for human life? . . . Don't people have a right to our assistance, irrespective of the consequences?

Anyone whose initial reaction to triage was not one of repugnance would be an unpleasant sort of person. Yet initial reactions based on strong feelings are not always reliable guides. Advocates of triage are rightly concerned with the long-term consequences of our actions. They say that helping the poor and starving now merely ensures more poor and starving in the future. When our capacity to help is finally unable to cope—as one day it must be—the suffering will be greater than it would be if we stopped helping now. If this is correct, there is nothing we can do to prevent absolute starvation and poverty, in the long run, and so we have no obligation to assist. Nor does it seem reasonable to hold that under these circumstances people have a right to our assistance. If we do accept such a right, irrespective of the consequences, we are saying that, in Hardin's metaphor, we should continue to haul the drowning into our lifeboat until the boat sinks and we all drown.

If triage is to be rejected it must be tackled on its own ground, within the framework of consequentialist ethics. Here it is vulnerable. Any consequentialist ethics must take probability of outcome into account. A course of action that will certainly produce some benefit is to be preferred to an alternative course that may lead to a slightly larger benefit, but is equally likely to result in no benefit at all. Only if the greater magnitude of the uncertain benefit outweighs its uncertainty should we choose it. Better one certain unit of benefit than a 10 per cent chance of five units; but better a 50 per cent chance of three units than a single certain unit. The same principle applies when we are trying to avoid evils.

The policy of triage involves a certain, very great evil: population control by famine and disease. Tens of millions would die slowly. Hundreds of millions would continue to live in absolute poverty, at the very margin of existence. Against this prospect, advocates of the policy place a possible evil that is greater still: the same process of famine and disease, taking place in, say, fifty years' time, when the world's population may be three times its present level, and the number who will die from famine, or struggle on in absolute poverty, will be that much greater. The question is: how probable is this forecast that continued assistance now will lead to greater disasters in the future?

Forecasts of population growth are notoriously fallible, and theories about the factors that affect it remain speculative. One theory, at least as plausible as any other, is that countries pass through a 'demographic transition' as their standard of living rises. When people are very poor and have no access to modern medicine their fertility is high, but population is kept in check by high death rates. The introduction of sanitation, modern medical techniques, and other improvements reduces the death rate, but initially has little effect on the birth rate. Then population grows rapidly. Some poor countries, especially in sub-Saharan Africa, are now in this phase. If standards of living continue to rise, however, couples begin to realise that to have the same number of children surviving to maturity as in the past, they do not need to give birth to as many children as their parents did. The need for children to provide economic support in old age diminishes. Improved education and the emancipation and employment of women also reduce the birth-rate, and so population growth begins to level off. Most rich nations have reached this stage, and their populations are growing only very slowly, if at all.

If this theory is right, there is an alternative to the disasters accepted as inevitable by supporters of triage. We can assist poor countries to raise the living standards of the poorest members of their population. We can encourage the governments of these countries to enact land reform measures, improve education, and liberate women from a purely child-bearing role. We can also help other countries to make contraception and sterilisation widely available. There is a fair chance that these measures will hasten the onset of the demographic transition and bring population growth down to a manageable level. According to United Nations estimates, in 1965 the average woman in the third world gave birth to six children, and only 8 per cent were using some form of contraception; by 1991 the average number of children had dropped to just below four, and more than half the women in the third world were taking contraceptive measures. Notable successes in encouraging the use of contraception had occurred in Thailand, Indonesia, Mexico, Colombia, Brazil, and Bangladesh. This achievement reflected a relatively low expenditure in developing countries—considering the size and significance of the problem—of $3 billion annually, with only 20 per cent of this sum coming from developed nations. So expenditure in this area seems likely to be highly cost-effective. Success cannot be guaranteed; but the evidence suggests that we can reduce population growth by improving economic security and education, and making contraceptives more widely available. This prospect makes triage ethically unacceptable. We cannot allow millions to die from starvation and disease when there is a reasonable probability that population can be brought under control without such horrors.

Population growth is therefore not a reason against giving overseas aid, although it should make us think about the kind of aid to give. Instead of food handouts, it may be better to give aid that leads to a slowing of population growth. This may mean agricultural assistance for the rural poor, or assistance with education, or the provision of contraceptive services. Whatever kind of aid proves most effective in specific circumstances, the obligation to assist is not reduced.

One awkward question remains. What should we do about a poor and already overpopulated country that, for religious or nationalistic reasons, restricts the use of contraceptives and refuses to slow its population growth? Should we

nevertheless offer development assistance? Or should we make our offer conditional on effective steps being taken to reduce the birth-rate? To the latter course, some would object that putting conditions on aid is an attempt to impose our own ideas on independent sovereign nations. So it is—but is this imposition unjustifiable? If the argument for an obligation to assist is sound, we have an obligation to reduce absolute poverty; but we have no obligation to make sacrifices that, to the best of our knowledge, have no prospect of reducing poverty in the long run. Hence we have no obligation to assist countries whose governments have policies that will make our aid ineffective. This could be very harsh on poor citizens of these countries—for they may have no say in the government's policies—but we will help more people in the long run by using our resources where they are most effective. (The same principles may apply, incidentally, to countries that refuse to take other steps that could make assistance effective—like refusing to reform systems of land holding that impose intolerable burdens on poor tenant farmers.)

Leaving It to the Government We often hear that overseas aid should be a government responsibility, not left to privately run charities. Giving privately, it is said, allows the government to escape its responsibilities.

Since increasing government aid is the surest way of making a significant increase to the total amount of aid given, I would agree that the governments of affluent nations should give much more genuine, no-strings-attached, aid than they give now. Less than one-sixth of one per cent of GNP is a scandalously small amount for a nation as wealthy as the United States to give. Even the official UN target of 0.7 per cent seems much less than affluent nations can and should give—though it is a target few have reached. But is this a reason against each of us giving what we can privately, through voluntary agencies? To believe that it is seems to assume that the more people there are who give through voluntary agencies, the less likely it is that the government will do its part. Is this plausible? The opposite view—that if no one gives voluntarily the government will assume that its citizens are not in favour of overseas aid, and will cut its programme accordingly—is more reasonable. In any case, unless there is a definite probability that by refusing to give we would be helping to bring about an increase in government assistance, refusing to give privately is wrong for the same reason that triage is wrong: it is a refusal to prevent a definite evil for the sake of a very uncertain gain. The onus of showing how a refusal to give privately will make the government give more is on those who refuse to give.

This is not to say that giving privately is enough. Certainly we should campaign for entirely new standards for both public and private overseas aid. We should also work for fairer trading arrangements between rich and poor countries, and less domination of the economies of poor countries by multinational corporations more concerned about producing profits for shareholders back home than food for the local poor. Perhaps it is more important to be politically active in the interests of the poor than to give to them oneself—but why not do both? Unfortunately, many use the view that overseas aid is the government's responsibility as a reason against giving, but not as a reason for being politically active.

Too High a Standard? The final objection to the argument for an obligation to assist is that it sets a standard so high that none but a saint could attain it. This objection comes in at least three versions. The first maintains that, human nature being what it is, we cannot achieve so high a standard, and since it is absurd to say that we ought to do what we cannot do, we must reject the claim that we ought to give so much. The second version asserts that even if we could achieve so high a standard, to do so would be undesirable. The third version of the objection is that to set so high a standard is undesirable because it will be perceived as too difficult to reach, and will discourage many from even attempting to do so.

Those who put forward the first version of the objection are often influenced by the fact that we have evolved from a natural process in which those with a high degree of concern for their own interests, or the interests of their offspring and kin, can be expected to leave more descendants in future generations, and eventually to completely replace any who are entirely altruistic. Thus the biologist Garrett Hardin has argued, in support of his 'lifeboat ethics', that **altruism** can only exist 'on a small scale, over the short term, and within small, intimate groups'; while Richard Dawkins has written, in his provocative book *The Selfish Gene:* 'Much as we might wish to believe otherwise, universal love and the welfare of the species as a whole are concepts which simply do not make evolutionary sense.' I have already noted, in discussing the objection that we should first take care of our own, the very strong tendency for partiality in human beings. We naturally have a stronger desire to further our own interests, and those of our close kin, than we have to further the interests of strangers. What this means is that we would be foolish to expect widespread conformity to a standard that demands impartial concern, and for that reason it would scarcely be appropriate or feasible to condemn all those who fail to reach such a standard. Yet to act impartially, though it might be very difficult, is not impossible. The commonly quoted assertion that 'ought' implies 'can' is a reason for rejecting such moral judgments as 'You ought to have saved all the people from the sinking ship', when in fact if you had taken one more person into the lifeboat, it would have sunk and you would not have saved any. In that situation, it is absurd to say that you ought to have done what you could not possibly do. When we have money to spend on luxuries and others are starving, however, it is clear that we can all give much more than we do give, and we can therefore all come closer to the impartial standard proposed in this chapter. Nor is there, as we approach closer to this standard, any barrier beyond which we cannot go. For that reason there is no basis for saying that the impartial standard is mistaken because 'ought' implies 'can' and we cannot be impartial.

The second version of the objection has been put by several philosophers during the past decade, among them Susan Wolf in a forceful article entitled 'Moral Saints'. Wolf argues that if we all took the kind of moral stance defended in this chapter, we would have to do without a great deal that makes life interesting: opera, gourmet cooking, elegant clothes, and professional sport, for a start. The kind of life we come to see as ethically required of us would be a single-minded pursuit of the overall good, lacking that broad diversity of interests and activities that, on a less demanding view, can be part of our ideal of a good life for a human being. To this, however, one can respond that while the rich and varied life that Wolf upholds as an ideal may be the most desirable form of life for a human being in a world of plenty, it is wrong to assume that it remains a good life in a world in which buying luxuries for oneself means accepting the continued avoidable suffering of others. A doctor faced with hundreds of injured victims of a train crash can scarcely think it defensible to treat fifty of them and then go to the opera, on the grounds that going to the opera is part of a well-rounded human life. The life-or-death needs of others must take priority. Perhaps we are like the doctor in that we live in a time when we all have an opportunity to help to mitigate a disaster.

Associated with this second version of the objection is the claim that an impartial ethic of the kind advocated here makes it impossible to have serious personal relationships based on love and friendship; these relationships are, of their nature, partial. We put the interests of our loved ones, our family, and our friends ahead of those of strangers; if we did not do so, would these relationships survive? I have already indicated, in the response I gave when considering the objection that we should first take care of our own, that there is a place, within an impartially grounded moral framework, for recognising some degree of partiality for kin, and the same can be said for other close personal relationships. Clearly, for most people, personal relationships are among the necessities of a flourishing life, and to give them up would be to sacrifice something of great moral significance. Hence no such sacrifice is required by the principle for which I am here arguing.

The third version of the objection asks: might it not be counterproductive to demand that people give up so much? Might not people say: 'As I can't do what is morally required anyway, I won't bother to give at all.' If, however, we were to set a more realistic standard, people might

make a genuine effort to reach it. Thus setting a lower standard might actually result in more aid being given.

It is important to get the status of this third version of the objection clear. Its accuracy as a prediction of human behaviour is quite compatible with the argument that we are obliged to give to the point at which by giving more we sacrifice something of comparable moral significance. What would follow from the objection is that public advocacy of this standard of giving is undesirable. It would mean that in order to do the maximum to reduce absolute poverty, we should advocate a standard lower than the amount we think people really ought to give. Of course we ourselves—those of us who accept the original argument, with its higher standard—would know that we ought to do more than we publicly propose people ought to do, and we might actually give more than we urge others to give. There is no inconsistency here, since in both our private and our public behaviour we are trying to do what will most reduce absolute poverty.

For a consequentialist, this apparent conflict between public and private morality is always a possibility, and not in itself an indication that the underlying principle is wrong. The consequences of a principle are one thing, the consequences of publicly advocating it another. A variant of this idea is already acknowledged by the distinction between the intuitive and critical levels of morality, of which I have made use in previous chapters. If we think of principles that are suitable for the intuitive level of morality as those that should be generally advocated, these are the principles that, when advocated, will give rise to the best consequences. Where overseas aid is concerned, those will be the principles that lead to the largest amount being given by the affluent to the poor.

Is it true that the standard set by our argument is so high as to be counterproductive? There is not much evidence to go by, but discussions of the argument, with students and others have led me to think it might be. Yet, the conventionally accepted standard—a few coins in a collection tin when one is waved under your nose—is obviously far too low. What level should we advocate? Any figure will be arbitrary, but there may be something to be said for a round percentage of one's income like, say, 10 per cent—more than a token donation, yet not so high as to be beyond all but saints. (This figure has the additional advantage of being reminiscent of the ancient tithe, or tenth, that was traditionally given to the church, whose responsibilities included care of the poor in one's local community. Perhaps the idea can be revived and applied to the global community.) Some families, of course, will find 10 per cent a considerable strain on their finances. Others may be able to give more without difficulty. No figure should be advocated as a rigid minimum or maximum; but it seems safe to advocate that those earning average or above average incomes in affluent societies, unless they have an unusually large number of dependents or other special needs, ought to give a tenth of their income to reducing absolute poverty. By any reasonable ethical standards this is the minimum we ought to do, and we do wrong if we do less.

Endnotes

1. Strictly, we would need to cut down to the minimum level compatible with earning the income which, after providing for our needs, left us most to give away. Thus if my present position earns me, say, $40,000 a year, but requires me to spend $5,000 a year on dressing respectably and maintaining a car, I cannot save more people by giving away the car and clothes if that will mean taking a job that, although it does not involve me in these expenses, earns me only $20,000.
2. Ominously, in the twelve years that have passed between editions of this book, the signs are that the situation is becoming even worse than was then predicted.

In 1979 Bangladesh had a population of 80 million and it was predicted that by 2000 its population would reach 146 million; Ethiopia's was only 29 million, and was predicted to reach 54 million; and India's was 620 million and predicted to reach 958 million.

REVIEW QUESTIONS

1. What are absolute poverty and absolute wealth according to Singer?
2. What reasons does Singer consider for saying that spending money on luxuries is not morally equivalent to murdering people?
3. Why does Singer think that these reasons do not justify spending money on luxuries instead of on poverty relief?
4. State and explain the argument for an obligation to assist (as Singer calls it).
5. What are the objections to the argument that Singer discusses?

DISCUSSION QUESTIONS

1. What does the right to life imply? Does it require us to save lives, as Singer says, or merely to not take innocent lives?
2. Is Singer's argument for an obligation to assist sound? Explain your answer.
3. Is it true, as Singer seems to hold, that luxuries such as stereo systems and stylish clothes have little or no moral significance?
4. Does Singer give satisfactory answers to the various objections?

Garrett Hardin

Living on a Lifeboat

Garrett Hardin is professor emeritus of biology at the University of California at Santa Barbara. He is the author of many books, including The Limits of Altruism: An Ecologist's View of Survival *(1977) and* Naked Emperors *(1983).*

Hardin uses the metaphor of a lifeboat to argue that rich nations such as the United States do not have a moral obligation to help poor nations. In fact, he claims, aid in the form of food makes matters worse; it results in more population growth, and eventually the ruin of natural resources such as oceans.

Susanne Langer (1942) has shown that it is probably impossible to approach an unsolved problem save through the door of metaphor. Later, attempting to meet the demands of rigor, we may achieve some success in cleansing theory of metaphor, though our success is limited if we are unable to avoid using common language, which is shot through and through with fossil metaphors. (I count no less than five in the preceding two sentences.)

Since metaphorical thinking is inescapable it is pointless merely to weep about our human limitations. We must learn to live with them, to understand them, and to control them. "All of us," said George Eliot in *Middlemarch*, "get our thoughts entangled in metaphors, and act fatally on the strength of them." To avoid unconscious suicide we are well advised to pit one metaphor against another. From the interplay of competitive metaphors, thoroughly developed, we may come closer to metaphor-free solutions to our problems.

No generation has viewed the problem of the survival of the human species as seriously as we have. Inevitably, we have entered this world of concern through the door of metaphor. Environmentalists have emphasized the image of the earth as a spaceship—Spaceship Earth. Kenneth Boulding (1966) is the principal architect of this metaphor. It is time, he says, that we replace the wasteful "cowboy economy" of the past with the frugal "spaceship economy" required for continued survival in the limited world we now see ours to be. The metaphor is notably useful in justifying pollution-control measures.

Unfortunately, the image of a spaceship is also used to promote measures that are suicidal. One of these is a generous immigration policy, which is only a particular instance of a class of policies that are in error because they lead to the tragedy of the commons (Hardin 1968). These suicidal policies are attractive because they mesh with what we unthinkingly take to be the ideals of "the best people." What is missing in the idealistic view is an insistence that rights and responsibilities must go together. The "generous" attitude of all too many people results in asserting inalienable rights while ignoring or denying matching responsibilities.

For the metaphor of a spaceship to be correct the aggregate of people on board would have to be under unitary sovereign control (Ophuls 1974). A true ship always has a captain. It is conceivable that a ship could be run by a committee. But it could not possibly survive if its course were determined by bickering tribes that claimed rights without responsibilities.

What about Spaceship Earth? It certainly has no captain, and no executive committee. The United Nations is a toothless tiger, because the signatories of its charter wanted it that way. The spaceship metaphor is used only to justify spaceship demands on common resources without acknowledging corresponding spaceship responsibilities.

An understandable fear of decisive action leads people to embrace "incrementalism"—moving toward reform by tiny stages. As we shall see, this strategy is counterproductive in the area discussed here if it means accepting rights before responsibilities. Where human survival is at stake, the acceptance of responsibilities is a precondition to the acceptance of rights, if the two cannot be introduced simultaneously.

LIFEBOAT ETHICS

Before taking up certain substantive issues let us look at an alternative metaphor, that of a lifeboat. In developing some relevant examples the following numerical values are assumed. Approximately two-thirds of the world is desperately poor, and only one-third is comparatively rich. The people in poor countries have an average per capita GNP (Gross National Product) of about $200 per year; the rich, of about $3,000. (For the United States it is nearly $5,000 per year.) Metaphorically, each rich nation amounts to a lifeboat full of comparatively rich people. The poor of the world are in other, much more crowded lifeboats. Continuously, so to speak, the poor fall out of their lifeboats and swim for a while in the water outside, hoping to be admitted to a rich lifeboat, or in some other way to benefit from the "goodies" on board. What should the passengers on a rich lifeboat do? This is the central problem of "the ethics of a lifeboat."

First we must acknowledge that each lifeboat is effectively limited in capacity. The land of every nation has a limited carrying capacity. The exact limit is a matter for argument, but the energy crunch is convincing more people every day that we have already exceeded the carrying capacity of the land. We have been living on "capital"—stored petroleum and coal—and soon we must live on income alone.

Let us look at only one lifeboat—ours. The ethical problem is the same for all, and is as follows. Here we sit, say fifty people in a lifeboat. To be generous, let us assume our boat has a capacity of ten more, making sixty. (This, however, is to violate the engineering principle of the "safety factor." A new plant disease or a bad change in the weather may decimate our population if we don't preserve some excess capacity as a safety factor.)

The fifty of us in the lifeboat see 100 others swimming in the water outside, asking for admission to the boat, or for handouts. How shall we respond to their calls? There are several possibilities.

One. We may be tempted to try to live by the Christian ideal of being "our brother's keeper," or by the Marxian ideal (Marx 1875) of "from each according to his abilities, to each according to his needs." Since the needs of all are the same, we take all the needy into our boat, making a total of 150 in a boat with a capacity of sixty. The boat is swamped, and everyone drowns. Complete justice, complete catastrophe.

Two. Since the boat has an unused excess capacity of ten, we admit just ten more to it. This has the disadvantage of getting rid of the safety factor, for which action we will sooner or later pay dearly. Moreover, *which* ten do we let in? "First come, first served"? The best ten? The neediest ten? How do we *discriminate*? And what do we say to the ninety who are excluded?

Three. Admit no more to the boat and preserve the small safety factor. Survival of the people in the lifeboat is then possible (though we shall have to be on our guard against boarding parties).

The last solution is abhorrent to many people. It is unjust, they say. Let us grant that it is.

"I feel guilty about my good luck," say some. The reply to this is simple: *Get out and yield your place to others.* Such a selfless action might satisfy the conscience of those who are addicted to guilt but it would not change the ethics of the lifeboat. The needy person to whom a guilt-addict yields his place will not himself feel guilty about his sudden good luck. (If he did he would not climb aboard.) The net result of conscience-stricken people relinquishing their unjustly held positions is the elimination of their kind of conscience from the lifeboat. The lifeboat, as it were, purifies itself of guilt. The ethics of the lifeboat persist, unchanged by such momentary aberrations.

This then is the basic metaphor within which we must work out our solutions. Let us enrich the image step by step with substantive additions from the real world.

REPRODUCTION

The harsh characteristics of lifeboat ethics are heightened by reproduction, particularly by reproductive differences. The people inside the lifeboats of the wealthy nations are doubling in numbers every eighty-seven years; those outside are doubling every thirty-five years, on the average. And the relative difference in prosperity is becoming greater.

Let us, for a while, think primarily of the U.S. lifeboat. As of 1973 the United States had a population of 210 million people, who were increasing by 0.8% per year, that is, doubling in number every eighty-seven years.

Although the citizens of rich nations are outnumbered two to one by the poor, let us imagine an equal number of poor people outside our lifeboat—a mere 210 million poor people reproducing at a quite different rate. If we imagine these to be the combined populations of Columbia, Venezuela, Ecuador, Morocco, Thailand, Pakistan, and the Philippines, the average rate of increase of the people "outside" is 3.3% per year. The doubling time of this population is twenty-one years.

Suppose that all these countries, and the United States, agreed to live by the Marxian ideal, "to each according to his needs," the ideal of most Christians as well. Needs, of course, are determined by population size, which is affected by reproduction. Every nation regards its rate of reproduction as a sovereign right. If our lifeboat were big enough in the beginning it might be possible to live *for a while* by Christian-Marxian ideals. *Might.*

Initially, in the model given, the ratio of non-Americans to Americans would be one to one. But consider what the ratio would be eighty-seven years later. By this time Americans would have doubled to a population of 420 million. The other group (doubling every twenty-one years) would now have swollen to 3,540 million. Each American would have more than eight people to share with. How could the lifeboat possibly keep afloat?

All this involves extrapolation of current trends into the future, and is consequently suspect. Trends may change. Granted: but the change will not necessarily be favorable. If—as seems likely—the rate of population increase falls faster in the ethnic group presently inside the lifeboat than it does among those now outside, the future will turn out to be even worse than mathematics predicts, and sharing will be even more suicidal.

RUIN IN THE COMMONS

The fundamental error of the sharing ethics is that it leads to the tragedy of the commons. Under a system of private property the man (or group of men) who own property recognize their responsibility to care for it, for if they don't they will eventually suffer. A farmer, for instance, if he is intelligent, will allow no more cattle in a pasture than its carrying capacity justifies. If he overloads the pasture, weeds take over, erosion sets in, and the owner loses in the long run.

But if a pasture is run as a common open to all, the right of each to use it is not matched by an operational responsibility to take care of it. It is no use asking independent herdsmen in a commons to act responsibly, for they dare not. The considerate herdsman who refrains from overloading the commons suffers more

than a selfish one who says his needs are greater. (As Leo Durocher says, "Nice guys finish last.") Christian-Marxian idealism is counterproductive. That it *sounds* nice is no excuse. With distribution systems, as with individual morality, good intentions are no substitute for good performance.

A social system is stable only if it is insensitive to errors. To the Christian-Marxian idealist a selfish person is a sort of "error." Prosperity in the system of the commons cannot survive errors. If *everyone* would only restrain himself, all would be well; but it takes *only one less than everyone* to ruin a system of voluntary restraint. In a crowded world of less than perfect human beings—and we will never know any other—mutual ruin is inevitable in the commons. This is the core of the tragedy of the commons.

One of the major tasks of education today is to create such an awareness of the dangers of the commons that people will be able to recognize its many varieties, however disguised. There is pollution of the air and water because these media are treated as commons. Further growth of population and growth in the per capita conversion of natural resources into pollutants require that the system of the commons be modified or abandoned in the disposal of "externalities."

The fish populations of the oceans are exploited as commons, and ruin lies ahead. No technological invention can prevent this fate; in fact, all improvements in the art of fishing merely hasten the day of complete ruin. Only the replacement of the system of the commons with a responsible system can save oceanic fisheries.

The management of western range lands, though nominally rational, is in fact (under the steady pressure of cattle ranchers) often merely a government-sanctioned system of the commons, drifting toward ultimate ruin for both the rangelands and the residential enterprisers.

WORLD FOOD BANKS

In the international arena we have recently heard a proposal to create a new commons, namely an international depository of food reserves to which nations will contribute according to their abilities, and from which nations may draw according to their needs. Nobel laureate Norman Borlaug has lent the prestige of his name to this proposal.

A world food bank appeals powerfully to our humanitarian impulses. We remember John Donne's celebrated line, "Any man's death diminishes me." But before we rush out to see for whom the bell tolls let us recognize where the greatest political push for international granaries comes from, lest we be disillusioned later. Our experience with Public Law 480 clearly reveals the answer. This was the law that moved billions of dollars worth of U.S. grain to food-short, population-long countries during the past two decades. When P.L. 480 first came into being, a headline in the business magazine *Forbes* (Paddock and Paddock 1970) revealed the power behind it: "Feeding the World's Hungry Millions: How it will mean billions for U.S. business."

And indeed it did. In the years 1960 to 1970 a total of $7.9 billion was spent on the "Food for Peace" program, as P.L. 480 was called. During the years 1948 to 1970 an additional $49.9 billion were extracted from American taxpayers to pay for other economic aid programs, some of which went for food and food-producing machinery. (This figure does *not* include military aid.) That P.L. 480 was a giveaway program was concealed. Recipient countries went through the motions of paying for P.L. 480 food—with IOUs. In December 1973 the charade was brought to an end as far as India was concerned when the United States "forgave" India's $3.2 billion debt (Anonymous 1974). Public announcement of the cancellation of the debt was delayed for two months; one wonders why.

"Famine—1974!" (Paddock and Paddock 1970) is one of the few publications that points out the commercial roots of this humanitarian attempt. Though all U.S. taxpayers lost by P.L. 480, special interest groups gained handsomely. Farmers benefited because they were not asked to contribute the grain—it was bought from them by the taxpayers. Besides the direct benefit there was the indirect effect of increasing demand and thus raising prices of farm products generally. The manufacturers of farm machinery, fertilizers, and pesticides benefited by the farmers' extra efforts to grow more food. Grain elevators profited from storing the grain for varying lengths of time. Railroads made money hauling it to port, and shipping lines by carrying it overseas. Moreover, once the machinery for P.L. 480 was established an immense bureaucracy had a vested interest in its continuance regardless of its merits.

Very little was ever heard of these selfish interests when P.L. 480 was defended in public. The emphasis was always on its humanitarian effects. The combination of multiple and relatively silent selfish interests with highly vocal humanitarian apologists constitutes a powerful lobby for extracting money from taxpayers. Foreign aid has become a habit that can apparently survive in the absence of any known justification. A news commentator in a weekly magazine (Lansner 1974), after exhaustively going over all the conventional arguments for foreign aid— self-interest, social justice, political advantage, and charity—and concluding that none of the known arguments really held water, concluded: "So the search continues for some logically compelling reasons for giving aid. . . ." In other words, *Act now, justify later*—if ever. (Apparently a quarter of a century is too short a time to find the justification for expending several billion dollars yearly.)

The search for a rational justification can be short-circuited by interjecting the word "emergency." Borlaug uses this word. We need to look sharply at it. What is an "emergency"? It is surely something like an accident, which is correctly defined as *an event that is certain to happen, though with a low frequency* (Hardin 1972a). A well-run organization prepares for everything that is certain, including accidents and emergencies. It budgets for them. It saves for them. It expects them—and mature decision-makers do not waste time complaining about accidents when they occur.

What happens if some organizations budget for emergencies and others do not? If each organization is solely responsible for its own well-being, poorly managed ones will suffer. But they should be able to learn from experience. They have a chance to mend their ways and learn to budget for infrequent but certain emergencies.

The weather, for instance, always varies and periodic crop failures are certain. A wise and competent government saves out of the production of the good years in anticipation of bad years that are sure to come. This is not a new idea. The Bible tells us that Joseph taught this policy to Pharaoh in Egypt more than 2,000 years ago. Yet it is literally true that the vast majority of the governments of the world today have no such policy. They lack either the wisdom or the competence, or both. Far more difficult than the transfer of wealth from one country to another is the transfer of wisdom between sovereign powers or between generations.

"But it isn't their fault! How can we blame the poor people who are caught in an emergency? Why must we punish them?" The concepts of blame and punishment are irrelevant. The question is, what are the operational consequences of establishing a world food bank? If it is open to every country every time a need develops, slovenly rulers will not be motivated to take Joseph's advice. Why should they? Others will bail them out whenever they are in trouble.

Some countries will make deposits in the world food bank and others will withdraw from it; there will be almost no overlap. Calling such a depository-transfer unit a "bank" is stretching the metaphor of *bank* beyond its elastic limits. The proposers, of course, never call attention to the metaphorical nature of the word they use.

THE RATCHET EFFECT

An "international food bank" is really, then, not a true bank but a disguised one-way transfer device for moving wealth from rich countries to poor. In the absence of such a bank, in a world inhabited by individually responsible sovereign nations, the population of each nation would repeatedly go through a cycle of the sort shown in Exhibit A. P_2 is greater than P_1, either in absolute numbers or because a deterioration of the food supply has removed the safety factor and produced a dangerously low ratio of resources to population. P_2 may be said to represent a state of overpopulation, which becomes obvious

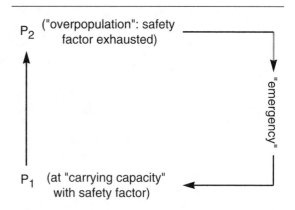

Exhibit A. The population cycle of a nation that has no effective conscious population control, and which receives no aid from the outside. P_2 is greater than P_1.

upon the appearance of an "accident," e.g., a crop failure. If the "emergency" is not met by outside help, the population drops back to the "normal" level—the "carrying capacity" of the environment—or even below. In the absence of population control by a sovereign, sooner or later the population grows to P_2 again and the cycle repeats. The long-term population curve (Hardin 1966) is an irregularity fluctuating one, equilibrating more or less about the carrying capacity.

A demographic cycle of this sort obviously involves great suffering in the restrictive phase, but such a cycle is normal to any independent country with inadequate population control. The third century theologian Tertullian (Hardin 1969a) expressed what must have been the recognition of many wise men when he wrote: "The scourges of pestilence, famine, wars, and earthquakes have come to be regarded as a blessing to overcrowded nations, since they serve to prune away the luxuriant growth of the human race."

Only under a strong and farsighted sovereign—which theoretically could be the people themselves, democratically organized—can a population equilibrate at some set point below the carrying capacity, thus avoiding the pains normally caused by periodic and unavoidable disasters. For this happy state to be achieved it is necessary that those in power be able to contemplate with equanimity the "waste" of surplus food in times of bountiful harvests. It is essential that those in power resist the temptation to convert extra food into extra babies. On the public relations level it is necessary that the phrase "surplus food" be replaced by "safety factor."

But wise sovereigns seem not to exist in the poor world today. The most anguishing problems are created by poor countries that are governed by rulers insufficiently wise and powerful. If such countries can draw on a world food bank in times of "emergency," the population *cycle* of Exhibit A will be replaced by the population *escalator* of Exhibit B. The input of food from a food bank acts as the pawl of a ratchet, preventing the population from retracting its steps to a lower level. Reproduction pushes the population upward, inputs from the world bank prevent its moving downward. Population size escalates, as does the absolute magnitude of "accidents" and "emergencies." The process is brought to an end only by the total collapse of the whole system, producing a catastrophe of scarcely imaginable proportions.

Such are the implications of the well-meant sharing of food in a world of irresponsible reproduction.

I think we need a new word for systems like this. The adjective "melioristic" is applied to systems that produce continual improvement; the English word is derived from the Latin *meliorare*, to become or make better. Parallel with this it would be useful to bring in the word *pejoristic* (from the Latin *pejorare*, to become or make worse). This word can be applied to those systems that by their very nature, can be relied upon to make matters worse. A world food bank coupled with sovereign state irresponsibility in reproduction is an example of a pejoristic system.

This pejoristic system creates an unacknowledged commons. People have more motivation to draw from than to add to the common store. The

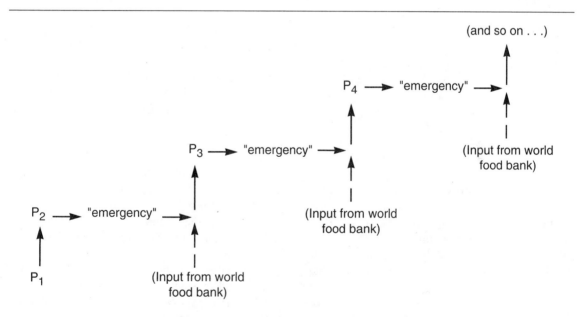

Exhibit B. The population escalator. Note that input from a world food bank acts like the pawl of a ratchet, preventing the normal population cycle shown in Exhibit A from being completed. P_{n+1} is greater than P_n, and the absolute magnitude of the "emergencies" escalates. Ultimately the entire system crashes. The crash is not shown, and few can imagine it.

license to make such withdrawals diminishes whatever motivation poor countries might otherwise have to control their populations. Under the guidance of this ratchet, wealth can be steadily moved in one direction only, from the slowly-breeding rich to the rapidly-breeding poor, the process finally coming to a halt only when all countries are equally and miserably poor.

All this is terribly obvious once we are acutely aware of the persuasiveness and danger of the commons. But many people still lack this awareness and the euphoria of the "benign demographic transition" (Hardin 1973) interferes with the realistic appraisal of pejoristic mechanisms. As concerns public policy, the deductions drawn from the benign demographic transition are these:

1. If the per capital GNP rises the birth rate will fall; hence, the rate of population increase will fall, ultimately producing ZPG (Zero Population Growth).
2. The long-term trend all over the world (including the poor countries) is of a rising per capita GNP (for which no limit is seen).
3. Therefore, all political interference in population matters is unnecessary; all we need to do is foster economic "development"—*note the metaphor*—and population problems will solve themselves.

Those who believe in the benign demographic transition dismiss the pejoristic mechanism of Exhibit B in the belief that each input of food from the world outside fosters development within a poor country thus resulting in a drop in the rate of population increase. Foreign aid has proceeded on this assumption for more than two decades. Unfortunately it has produced no indubitable instance of the asserted effect. It has, however, produced a library of excuses. The air is filled with plaintive calls for more massive foreign aid appropriations so that the hypothetical melioristic process can get started. The doctrine of demographic laissez-faire implicit in the hypothesis of the benign demographic transition is immensely attractive. Unfortunately there is more evidence against the melioristic system than there is for it (Davis 1963). On the histor-

ical side there are many counter-examples. The rise in per capita GNP in France and Ireland during the past century has been accompanied by a rise in population growth. In the twenty years following the Second World War the same positive correlation was noted almost everywhere in the world. Never in world history before 1950 did the worldwide population growth reach one percent per annum. Now the average population growth is over two percent and shows no signs of slackening.

On the theoretical side, the denial of the pejoristic scheme of Exhibit B probably springs from the hidden acceptance of the "cowboy economy" that Boulding castigated. Those who recognize the limitations of a spaceship, if they are unable to achieve population control at a safe and comfortable level, accept the necessity of the corrective feedback of the population cycle shown in Exhibit A. No one who knew in his bones that he was living on a true spaceship would countenance political support of the population escalator shown in Exhibit B.

ECO-DESTRUCTION VIA THE GREEN REVOLUTION

The demoralizing effect of charity on the recipient has long been known. "Give a man a fish and he will eat for a day; teach him how to fish and he will eat for the rest of his days." So runs an ancient Chinese proverb. Acting on this advice the Rockefeller and Ford Foundations have financed a multipronged program for improving agriculture in the hungry nations. The result, known as the "Green Revolution," has been quite remarkable. "Miracle wheat" and "miracle rice" are splendid technological achievements in the realm of plant genetics.

Whether or not the Green Revolution can increase food production is doubtful (Harris 1972, Paddock 1970, Wilkes 1972), but in any event not particularly important. What is missing in this great and well-meaning humanitarian effort is a firm grasp of fundamentals. Considering the importance of the Rockefeller Foundation in this effort it is ironic that the late Alan Gregg, a much-respected vice-president of the Foundation, strongly expressed his doubts of the wisdom of all attempts to increase food production some two decades ago. (This was before Borlaug's work—supported by Rockefeller—had resulted in the development of "miracle wheat.") Gregg (1955) likened the growth and spreading of humanity over the surface of the earth to the metastasis of cancer in the human body, wryly remarking that "Cancerous growths demand food; but, as far as I know, they have never been cured by getting it."

"Man does not live by bread alone"—the scriptural statement has a rich meaning even in the material realm. Every human being born constitutes a draft on all aspects of the environment—food, air, water, unspoiled scenery, occasional and optional solitude, beaches, contact with wild animals, fishing, hunting—the list is long and incompletely known. Food can, perhaps, be significantly increased, but what about clean beaches, unspoiled forests, and solitude? If we satisfy the need for food in a growing population we necessarily decrease the supply of other goods, and thereby increase the difficulty of equitably allocating scarce goods (Hardin 1969b, 1972b).

The present population of India is 600 million, and it is increasing by fifteen million per year. The environmental load of this population is already great. The forests of India are only a small fraction of what they were three centuries ago. Soil erosion, floods, and the psychological costs of crowding are serious. Every one of the net fifteen million lives added each year stresses the Indian environment more severely. *Every life saved this year in a poor country diminishes the quality of life for subsequent generations.*

Observant critics have shown how much harm we wealthy nations have already done to poor nations through our well-intentioned but misguided attempts to help them (Paddock and Paddock 1973). Particularly reprehensible is our failure to carry out post-audits of these attempts (Farver and Milton 1972). Thus have we shielded our tender consciences from knowledge of the harm we have done. Must we Americans continue to fail to monitor the consequences of our external "do-gooding"? If, for instance, we thoughtlessly make it possible for the present 600 million Indians to swell to 1,200 million by the year 2001—as their present growth rate promises—will posterity in India thank *us* for facilitating an even greater destruction of *their* environment? Are good intentions ever a sufficient excuse for bad consequences?

IMMIGRATION CREATES A COMMONS

I come now to the final example of a commons in action, one for which the public is least prepared for rational discussion. The topic is at present enveloped by a great silence that reminds me of a comment made by Sherlock Holmes in A. Conan Doyle's story, "Silver Blaze." Inspector Gregory had asked, "Is there any point to which you wish to draw my attention?" To this Holmes responded:

"To the curious incident of the dog in the night-time."
"The dog did nothing in the night-time," said the Inspector.
"That was the curious incident," remarked Sherlock Holmes.

By asking himself what would repress the normal barking instinct of a watch dog Holmes realized that it must be the dog's recognition of his master as the criminal trespasser. In a similar way we should ask ourselves what repression keeps us from discussing something as important as immigration?

It cannot be that immigration is numerically of no consequence. Our government acknowledges a *net* inflow of 400,000 a year. Hard data are understandably lacking on the extent of illegal entries, but a not implausible figure is 600,000 per year (Buchanan 1973). The natural increase of the resident population is now about 1.7 million per year. This means that the yearly gain from immigration is at least nineteen percent, and may be thirty-seven percent, of the total increase. It is quite conceivable that educational campaigns like that of Zero Population Growth, Inc., coupled with adverse social and economic factors—inflation, housing shortage, depression, and loss of confidence in national leaders—may lower the fertility of American women to a point at which all of the yearly increase in population would be accounted for by immigration. Should we not at least ask if that is what we want? How curious it is that we so seldom discuss immigration these days!

Curious, but understandable—as one finds out the moment he publicly questions the wisdom of the status quo in immigration. He who does so is promptly charged with *isolationism, bigotry, prejudice, ethnocentrism, chauvinism,* and *selfishness.* These are hard accusations to bear. It is pleasanter to talk about other matters, leaving immigration policy to wallow in the crosscurrents of special interests that take no account of the good of the whole—*or of the interests of posterity.*

We Americans have a bad conscience because of things we said in the past about immigrants. Two generations ago the popular press was rife with references to *Dagos, Wops, Pollacks, Japs, Chinks,* and *Krauts*—all pejorative terms that failed to acknowledge our indebtedness to Goya, Leonardo, Copernicus, Hiroshige, Confuscius, and Bach. Because the implied inferiority of foreigners was *then* the justification for keeping them out, it is *now* thoughtlessly assumed that restrictive policies can only be based on the assumption of immigrant inferiority. *This is not so.*

Existing immigration laws exclude idiots and known criminals; future laws will almost certainly continue this policy. But should we also consider the quality of the average immigrant, as compared with the quality of the average resident? Perhaps we should, perhaps we shouldn't. (What is "quality" anyway?) But the quality issue is not our concern here.

From this point on, *it will be assumed that immigrants and native-born citizens are of exactly equal quality,* however quality may be defined. The focus is only on quantity. The conclusions reached depend on nothing else, so all charges of ethnocentrism are irrelevant.

World food banks move food to the people, thus facilitating the exhaustion of the environment of the poor. By contrast, unrestricted immigration moves people to the food, thus speeding up the destruction of the environment in rich countries. Why poor people should want to make this transfer is no mystery, but why should rich hosts encourage it? This transfer, like the reverse one, is supported by both selfish interests and humanitarian impulses.

The principal selfish interest in unimpeded immigration is easy to identify: it is the interest of the employers of cheap labor, particularly that needed for degrading jobs. We have been deceived about the forces of history by the lines of Emma Lazarus inscribed on the Statute of Liberty:

Give me your tired, your poor,
Your huddled masses yearning to breath free,
The wretched refuse of your teeming shore,
Send these, the homeless, tempest-tossed to me:
  I lift my lamp beside the golden door.

The image is one of an infinitely generous earth-mother, passively opening her arms to hordes of immigrants who come here on their own initiative. Such an image may have been adequate for the early days of colonization, but by the time these lines were written (1886) the force for immigration was largely manufactured inside our own borders by factory and mine owners who sought cheap labor not to be found among laborers already here. One group of foreigners after another was thus enticed into the United States to work at wretched jobs for wretched wages.

At present, it is largely the Mexicans who are being so exploited. It is particularly to the advantage of certain employers that there be many illegal immigrants. Illegal immigrant workers dare not complain about their working conditions for fear of being repatriated. Their presence reduces the bargaining power of all Mexican-American laborers. Cesar Chavez has repeatedly pleaded with congressional committees to close the doors to more Mexicans so that those here can negotiate effectively for higher wages and decent working conditions. Chavez understands the ethics of a lifeboat.

The interests of the employers of cheap labor are well served by the silence of the intelligentsia of the country. WASPS—White Anglo-Saxon Protestants—are particularly reluctant to call for a closing of the doors to immigration for fear of being called ethnocentric bigots. It was, therefore, an occasion of pure delight for this particular WASP to be present at a meeting when the points he would like to have made were made better by a non-WASP speaking to other non-WASPS. It was in Hawaii, and most of the people in the room were second-level Hawaiian officials of Japanese ancestry. All Hawaiians are keenly aware of the limits of their environment, and the speaker had asked how it might be practically and constitutionally possible to close the doors to more immigrants to the islands. (To Hawaiians, immigrants from the other forty-nine states are as much of a threat as those from other nations. There is only so much room in the islands, and the islanders know it. Sophistical arguments that imply otherwise do not impress them.)

Yet the Japanese-Americans of Hawaii have active ties with the land of their origin. This point was raised by a Japanese-American member of the audience who asked the Japanese-American speaker: "But how can we shut the doors now? We have many friends and relations in Japan that we'd like to bring to Hawaii some day so that they can enjoy this beautiful land."

The speaker smiled sympathetically and responded slowly, "Yes, but we have children now and someday we'll have grandchildren. We can bring more people here from Japan only by giving away some of the land that we hope to pass on to our grandchildren some day. What right do we have to do that?"

To be generous with one's own possessions is one thing; to be generous with posterity's is quite another. This, I think, is the point that must be gotten across to those who would, from a commendable love of **distributive justice**, institute a ruinous system of the commons, either in the form of a world food bank or that of unrestricted immigration. Since every speaker is a member of some ethnic group it is always possible to charge him with ethnocentrism. But even after purging an argument of ethnocentrism the rejection of the commons is still valid and necessary if we are to save at least some parts of the world from environmental ruin. Is it not desirable that at least some of the grandchildren of people now living should have a decent place in which to live?

THE ASYMMETRY OF DOOR-SHUTTING

We must now answer this telling point: "How can you justify slamming the door once you're inside? You say that immigrants should be kept out. But aren't we all immigrants, or the descendants of immigrants? Since we refuse to leave, must we not, as a matter of justice and symmetry, admit all others?"

It is literally true that we Americans of non-Indian ancestry are the descendants of thieves. Should we not, then, "give back" the land to the Indians, that is, give it to the now-living Americans of Indian ancestry? As an exercise in pure logic I see no way to reject this proposal. Yet I am unwilling to live by it, and I know no one who is. Our reluctance to embrace pure justice may spring from pure selfishness. On the other hand, it may arise from an unspoken recognition of consequences that have not yet been clearly spelled out.

Suppose, becoming intoxicated with pure justice, we "Anglos" should decide to turn our land over to the Indians. Since all our other wealth has also been derived from the land, we would have to give that to the Indians, too. Then what would we non-Indians do? Where would we go? There is no open land in the world on which men without capital can make their living (and not much unoccupied land on which men with capital can either). Where would 209 million putatively justice-loving, non-Indian Americans go? Most of them—in the persons of their ancestors—came from Europe, but they wouldn't be welcomed back there. Anyway, Europeans have no better title to their land than we to ours. They also would have to give up their homes. (But to whom? And where would *they* go?)

Clearly, the concept of pure justice produces an **infinite regress**. The law long ago invented statutes of limitations to justify the rejection of pure justice, in the interest of preventing massive disorder. The law zealously defends property rights—but only *recent* property rights. It is as though the physical principle of exponential decay applies to property rights. Drawing a line in time may be unjust, but any other action is practically worse.

We are all the descendants of thieves, and the world's resources are inequitably distributed, but we must begin the journey to tomorrow from the point where we are today. We cannot remake the past. We cannot, without violent disorder and suffering, give land and resources back to the "original" owners—who are dead anyway.

We cannot safely divide the wealth equitably among all present peoples, so long as people reproduce at different rates, because to do so would guarantee that our grandchildren—everyone's grandchildren—would have only a ruined world to inhabit.

MUST EXCLUSION BE ABSOLUTE?

To show the logical structure of the immigration problem I have ignored many factors that would enter into real decisions made in a real world. No matter how convincing the logic may be, it is probable that we would want, from time to time, to admit a few people from the outside to our lifeboat. Political refugees in particular are likely to cause us to make exceptions: We remember the Jewish refugees from Germany after 1933, and the Hungarian refugees after 1956. Moreover, the interests of national defense, broadly conceived, could justify admitting many men and women of unusual talents, whether refugees or not. (This raises the quality issue, which is not the subject of this essay.)

Such exceptions threaten to create runaway population growth inside the lifeboat, i.e., the receiving country. However, the threat can be neutralized by a population policy that includes immigration. An effective policy is one of flexible control.

Suppose, for example, that the nation has achieved a stable condition of ZPG, which (say) permits 1.5 million births yearly. We must suppose that an acceptable system of allocating birth-rights to potential parents is in effect. Now suppose that an inhumane regime in some other part of the world creates a horde of refugees, and that there is a wide-spread desire to admit some to our country. At the same time, we do not want to sabotage our population control system. Clearly, the rational path to pursue is the following. If we decide to admit 100,000 refugees this year we should compensate for this by reducing the allocation of birth-rights in the following year by a similar amount, that is, downward to a total of 1.4 million. In that way we could achieve both humanitarian and pop-

ulation control goals. (And the refugees would have to accept the population controls of the society that admits them. It is not inconceivable that they might be given proportionately fewer rights than the native population.)

In a democracy, the admission of immigrants should properly be voted on. But by whom? It is not obvious. The usual rule of a democracy is votes for all. But it can be questioned whether a universal franchise is the most just one in a case of this sort. Whatever benefits there are in the admission of immigrants presumably accrue to everyone. But the costs would be seen as falling most heavily on potential parents, some of whom would have to postpone or forego having their (next) child because of the influx of immigrants. The double question *Who benefits? Who pays?* suggests that a restriction of the usual democratic franchise would be appropriate and just in this case. Would our particular quasi-democratic form of government be flexible enough to institute such a novelty? If not, the majority might, out of humanitarian motives, impose an unacceptable burden (the foregoing of parenthood) on a minority, thus producing political instability.

Plainly many new problems will arise when we consciously face the immigration question and seek rational answers. No workable answers can be found if we ignore population problems. And—if the argument of this essay is correct—so long as there is no true world government to control reproduction everywhere it is impossible to survive in dignity if we are to be guided by spaceship ethics. Without a world government that is sovereign in reproductive matters mankind lives, in fact, on a number of sovereign lifeboats. For the foreseeable future survival demands that we govern our actions by the ethics of a lifeboat. Posterity will be ill served if we do not.

References

Anonymous. 1974. *Wall Street Journal* 19 Feb.
Borlaug, N. 1973. Civilization's future: a call for international granaries. *Bull. At. Sci.* 29: 7–15.
Boulding, K. 1966. The economists of the coming Spaceship Earth. *In* H. Jarrett, ed. Environmental Quality in a Growing Economy. Baltimore: Johns Hopkins Press.
Buchanan, W. 1973. Immigration statistics. *Equilibrium* 1(3): 16–19.

Davis, K. 1963. Population. *Sci. Amer.* 209(3): 62–71.

Farvar, M. T., and J. P. Milton. 1972. The Careless Technology. Garden City, NY: Natural History Press.

Gregg, A. 1955. A medical aspect of the population problem. *Science* 121:681–682.

Hardin, G. 1966. Chap. 9 *in* Biology: Its Principles and Implications, 2nd ed. San Francisco: Freeman.

————. 1968. The tragedy of the commons. *Science* 162: 1243–1248.

————. 1969a. Page 18 *in* Population, Evolution, and Birth Control, 2nd ed. San Francisco: Freeman.

————. 1969b. The economics of wilderness. *Nat. Hist.* 78(6): 20–27.

————. 1972a. Pages 81–82 *in* Exploring New Ethics for Survival: The Voyage of the Spaceship *Beagle.* New York: Viking. ————. 1972b. Preserving quality on Spaceship Earth. *In* J. B. Trefethen, ed. Transactions of the Thirty-Seventh North American Wildlife and Natural Resources Conference. Wildlife Management Institute, Washington, D.C.

————. 1973. Chap. 23 *in* Stalking the Wild Taboo. Los Altos, CA: Kaufmann.

Harris, M. 1972. How green the revolution. *Nat. Hist.* 81(3):28–30.

Langer, S. K. 1942. Philosophy in a New Key. Cambridge, MA: Harvard University Press.

Lansner, K. 1974. Should foreign aid begin at home? *Newsweek,* 11 Feb., p. 32.

Marx, K. 1875. Critique of the Gotha program. Page 388 *in* R. C. Tucker, ed. The Marx-Engels Reader. New York: Norton, 1972.

Ophuls, W. 1974. The scarcity society. *Harpers* 248 (1487): 47–52.

Paddock, W. C. 1970. How green is the green revolution? *BioScience* 20: 897–902.

Paddock, W., and E. Paddock. 1973. We Don't Know How. Ames, IA: Iowa State University Press.

Paddock, W., and P. Paddock. 1967. Famine—1975! Boston: Little, Brown.

Wilkes, H. G. 1972. The green revolution. *Environment* 14(8): 32–39.

REVIEW QUESTIONS

1. What is wrong with the spaceship metaphor according to Hardin?
2. Explain Hardin's lifeboat metaphor.
3. According to Hardin, why can't we live by the Christian or the Marxian ideal?
4. Explain what Hardin calls the tragedy of the commons. How is this supposed to apply to rich and poor nations?
5. Explain the ratchet effect and a pejoristic system.
6. Why isn't benign demographic transition possible according to Hardin?
7. Why doesn't Hardin think that the Green Revolution will solve the problem of world hunger?
8. Explain Hardin's opposition to present immigration policies.

DISCUSSION QUESTIONS

1. Are there any respects in which the United States is not a lifeboat?
2. Is there any solution to the problem of overpopulation in poor countries that does not involve letting people die? What is it?
3. Is there any way to avoid the tragedy of the commons that does not involve private ownership? Explain.
4. Is there any way to avoid the ratchet effect? Explain.
5. Should we allow more people to immigrate into the United States? Why or why not?

Robert N. Van Wyk

Perspectives on World Hunger and the Extent of Our Positive Duties

Robert N. Van Wyk is associate professor of philosophy at the University of Pittsburgh.

Van Wyk attacks both Singer's and Hardin's utilitarian approach to the problem of world hunger and suggests an alternative Kantian ethic. In the Kantian view, individuals have a strict duty to give a fair share and a duty of reparation to needy people in other countries because of past harms

From Robert N. Van Wyk, "Perspectives on World Hunger and the Extent of Our Positive Duties," *Public Affairs Quarterly,* vol. 2 (April 1988): 75–90. Reprinted with permission.

done to them in violation of the duty not to harm others.

I. INTRODUCTION TO THE ISSUE

A moral problem that faces institutions—especially governments, as well as individuals, is the question of the extent of the duty to prevent harm to other people, and/or benefit them. This is not an academic problem but one that stares us in the face through the eyes of starving and malnourished people, and in particular, children. . . .

II. UTILITARIAN/CONSEQUENTIALIST APPROACHES

A. The Views of Peter Singer and Garrett Hardin

According to some moral theories the very fact of widespread hunger imposes a duty on each person to do whatever he or she is capable of doing to accomplish whatever is necessary to see to it that all people have enough to eat. Peter Singer, a utilitarian, writes:

> I begin with the assumption that suffering and death from lack of food, shelter, and medical care are bad. . . . My next point is this: if it is in our power to prevent something bad from happening without thereby sacrificing anything of comparable moral importance, we ought, morally, to do it.[1]

Does this mean that governments of prosperous countries ought to call upon their citizens to sacrifice enough of the luxuries of life to pay taxes that will be used to see to it that everyone in the world has the basic necessities of life? Suppose that governments do not do this. Suppose I give a considerable amount of famine relief but the need remains great because many others have not given. Is this case parallel to the following one to which Singer compares it? I have saved the life of one drowning person. There is still another person who needs to be saved. Other people could have saved the sec-

ond person while I was saving the first but no one did. Even though I have saved one, and even though other people have failed in their duty to try to save the other, it would seem reasonable to claim that I have a duty to try to do so. Would I similarly have a duty to keep on giving more to aid the hungry regardless of the personal sacrifice involved? Many objections raised against giving sacrificially have to do with whether certain kinds of assistance really do much good. But such objections do not really affect the question of how much one should sacrifice to help others, but only have to do with the best way of using what is given (for example, for food assistance, development assistance, family planning, encouraging political change, supporting education, and so on). But if we reach the conclusion that we have a duty to do all we can, just as in the case of the drowning people, we are faced with the problem that James Fishkin has written about, of being overwhelmed with obligations in a way that expands the area of moral duty to the point of obliterating both the area of the morally indifferent and the area of the morally supererogatory.[2]

There are, however, other considerations. What are the long range consequences of keeping people alive? "Neo-malthusians" and "crisis environmentalists" argue that population growth is outstripping food production and also leading both to the depletion of the world's natural resources and the pollution of the environment, so that the more people who are saved the more misery there will be in the long run. Garrett Hardin compares rich nations to lifeboats and the poor of the world to drowning people trying to get into the lifeboats. To allow them in would be to risk sinking the lifeboats and so to risk bringing disaster on everyone. The high rate of population growth among the poor nations insures that even if there is enough room at the moment, eventually the lifeboats will be swamped.[3] The lifeboat ethic is an application of what Hardin calls the logic of the commons. If a pasture is held as common property each herdsman is tempted to overgraze it for the sake of short-term profits. Even the individual who wants to preserve the land for the future has no reason to stop as long as there are others who will continue to overgraze it. Similarly, if we regard the food production of the world as a "commons" to which everyone is entitled we undermine any incentive among the poor of the world to increase production and limit population growth. The increasing population will continually reduce the amount available for each individual while at the same time increasing pollution and putting other strains on the environment.[4] So Hardin writes that "for posterity's sake we should never send food to any population that is beyond the realistic carrying capacity of its land."[5] This view that certain countries should be left to have "massive diebacks of population,"[6] while others should perhaps be helped, has been called "triage."

B. Questions about These Approaches

One way of responding to Hardin's argument is to raise questions about the choice of metaphors and their applicability.[7] Why speak of lifeboats rather than of luxury liners? Why should the Asian or African people be compared to the "sheep" who are the greatest threat to the commons when the average American uses up thirty times the amount of the earth's resources as does the average Asian or African, and when the developed nations import more protein from the developing nations than they export to them? How are the lifeboat metaphors applicable when apart from special famine conditions almost every country in the world has the resources necessary to feed its people if they were used primarily for that purpose?

The focus here, however, will be on moral theory. In spite of their very different conclusions, Singer and Hardin both presuppose a utilitarian position that says that what we ought to do depends completely on the anticipated consequences of our choices. A defender of Singer might say that all Hardin's observations do is to impose on all people a duty to redouble their efforts to find and support solutions that avoid both short range hunger and long range disaster. But that answer only increases the problem of overload that Fishkin is concerned with.

III. HUNGER, RESPECT FOR PERSONS AND NEGATIVE DUTIES

Many philosophers, especially those emphasizing the stringency of negative duties, subscribe to Kant's principle of respect for persons, whether or not they are supporters of Kant's moral philosophy taken as a whole. Robert Nozick uses the principle of respect for persons to defend absolute duties to do no harm while at the same time denying the existence of any duties to benefit others.[8] Kant himself, however, maintained that we have **imperfect duties** to help others. One might still claim that government may not collect taxes for the sake of aiding others, since one ought not to force people (taxpayers) to fulfill imperfect duties when doing so violates the **perfect duty** to respect the right of citizens to use their resources as they themselves choose to do so. Kant himself did not reach such a conclusion,[9] but Nozick does, arguing that since "individuals are ends and not merely means, they may not be sacrificed, or used for the achieving of other ends without their consent."[10]

Nozick's views can be attacked at many points. Even if they were correct, however, it would not follow that governments would have no right to tax citizens to aid people in distress. This is because individuals, corporations (to which individuals are related as stockholders and employees), and governments would still have duties not to harm, and thus also duties to take corrective action in response to past harms. So wealthy countries and their citizens could still have many responsibilities of compensatory justice with respect to the world's poor. Some countries face poverty because their economies are heavily dependent on a single export material or crop (for example, copper in Chile), the prices of which are subject to great fluctuations. If the original situation, or the subsequent fluctuations, were brought about by policies of wealthy nations or their corporations, then suffering does not just happen but is caused by the actions of people in developed nations. If corporations can strangle economies of developing nations and choose to do so if they do not get special tax advantages, or unfairly advantageous contracts, then poverty and hunger are harms caused by the decisions of the wealthy. If, furthermore, government officials are bribed to keep taxes down, as was done in Honduras by the banana companies, then poverty is directly caused by human actions. If a developed nation overthrows the government of a poor nation which tries to correct some past injustice (as was done when the C.I.A. helped overthrow the democratically elected government of Guatamala in 1954 in order to protect the interests of the United Fruit Company), then poverty is a harm caused by human actions. The decisions of the Soviet Union to import large amounts of grain from the United States during the Nixon administration led to a dramatic and unexpected rise in the price of grain on the world market, which in turn caused hunger. Americans' use of energy at twice the rate of Western Europeans must raise energy prices for the poor. Dramatic price increases by oil exporting nations no doubt meant that people went without petroleum-based fertilizers, or energy to transport food or pump water for irrigation, and so led to additional people dying of hunger. When petroleum prices fall the poverty of people in some oil-exporting countries is aggravated because of the difficulty their governments have financing their debts—debts which were acquired partially due to the encouragement of the banks in the wealthy countries.

What duties do the wealthy countries have to the poor and hungry of the world? The first duty is not to harm them. While seldom are the hungry intentionally killed, they are often killed in the same way that someone is killed by a reckless driver who just does not take into consideration what his actions might do to other vulnerable human beings, and there is no doubt that reckless drivers are to be held accountable for what they do. In some cases it may be morally justifiable to endanger the lives of people in order to work toward some desirable goal, as it may be morally justifiable to risk people's lives in order to rush a critically ill person to the hospital. But a person who is speeding for good reason, or who benefits from that speeding, is not thereby relieved of responsibility for someone who is thereby injured, for otherwise the

endangered or harmed would be treated only as means to the ends of others. Similarly, those who make or benefit from economic and political decisions are not relieved of responsibility for those who are thereby harmed or endangered. So even if we were to accept the view that no individual or government has any duty to aid those in distress simply because they are in distress, there would still be a few people of more than adequate means in the real world who would not have an obligation to aid those in need. As Onora Nell writes:

Only if we knew that we were not part of any system of activities causing unjustifiable deaths could we have no duties to support policies which seek to avoid such deaths. Modern economic causal chains are so complex that it is likely that only those who are economically isolated and self-sufficient could know that they are part of no such system of activities.[11]

With respect to compensating those who have been harmed we do not have to be part of the causal chain that causes harm in order to have an obligation to those who still bear the effects of past harm. If A stole B's money yesterday and gave the money to C today, C obviously has a duty to return it. While in some cases mentioned above decisions were made by companies, individuals and governments still were beneficiaries of such decisions through lower prices and increased tax revenue. Furthermore, it would not make any difference if A stole B's money before C was born. Consider the following case:

Bengal (today's Bangladesh and the West Bengal state of India), the first territory the British conquered in Asia, was a prosperous province with highly developed centers of manufacturing and trade, and an economy as advanced as any prior to the industrial revolution. The British reduced Bengal to poverty through plunder, heavy land taxes and trade restrictions that barred competitive Indian goods from England, but gave British goods free entry into India. India's late Prime Minister Nehru commented bitterly, "Bengal can take pride in the fact that she helped greatly in giving birth to the Industrial Revolution in England."[12]

Those who benefited from the Industrial Revolution in England, including those alive today, would still have duties to aid Bengal, just as those who inherited a fortune partially based on stolen money have a duty to return what was stolen, with interest, even though they themselves are in no way guilty of the theft. So it is with most citizens of the industrialized West with respect to the poor of some parts of the world. However, in the light of the complexity of both the causal chains of harm and the causal chains of benefit, we are again faced with a great deal of uncertainty as to the allocation of responsibility for correcting for past injustices.[13]

IV. HUNGER, POSITIVE DUTIES, AND THE IDEA OF A FAIR SHARE

So there is no doubt that a Kantian ethic would include duties of reparation for harms done to people in the past and that this would be a basis of obligations to aid many of the underdeveloped countries in the world today, even though it would be difficult to specify the extent of obligation. But is there a duty to help those in severe need even if the causes of the need are not due to any past injustice or are unknown, as may also be true about parts of the world today? Kant does not always treat duties to aid others as fully binding, but whether or not, as one Kantian argues, "it is impermissible not to promote the well-being of others,"[14] it can be argued that it is impermissible not to relieve others in distress and provide them with the basic necessities of life, for this is to fail to treat them as having any value as ends in themselves. To put it another way, failing to help is to violate subsistence rights, and, as Henry Shue argues, whatever sorts of reasons can be given in favor of regarding human beings as having security rights can also be given in favor of regarding them as having subsistence rights.[15] Or, to put it another way, it is to fail to take into account the vulnerability of the world's poor toward the affluent (taken collectively), and it is the vulnerability of people to others (individually or collectively) that is the foundation of most (or all) of both our **positive and negative duties** to others.[16]

To what extent do individuals and nations have a duty to relieve those in distress? Is there a middle way between Singer and Nozick? Perhaps the following line of reasoning would provide a guideline. An estimate can be made of what resources would be needed to feed the hungry, bring about political and economic change, promote development, limit population growth, and to do whatever is necessary to see that all people have a minimally decent standard of living (or that their basic rights are met). Some formula based on ability to help could determine what a fair share would be for each citizen of a developed country to contribute to the needs of those in distress in that country and to that country's share of helping the people of other nations. To the extent that nations adopt this procedure and make it part of their tax structure a person could fulfill the duty of doing her share by paying her taxes. The ideal would be for nations to do this so that the responsibilities would be carried out and the burden would be distributed fairly. To the extent that nations have not done this (and it is unlikely that any have) what duties do citizens have to contribute through private or religious agencies? Henry Shue correctly observes that "How much sacrifice can reasonably be expected from one person for the sake of another, even for the sake of honoring the other's rights, is one of the most fundamental questions in morality."[17] Nozick, as we have seen, answers with "None." Many answer with "Some" without going on to give a more precise answer. In the absence of adequate government action each individual could still make some sort of estimate of what a fair share would be and give that amount (or what remains of that amount after taking into consideration that part of her taxes that are used for appropriate purposes) through private or religious agencies. I am claiming that it is a strict duty or duty of perfect obligation for an individual to give at least her fair share, according to some plausible formula, toward seeing that all human beings are treated as ends in themselves, which involves seeing that they have the basic necessities of life in so far as that can depend on the actions of others. This conclusion can also be supported by a generalization argument. If everyone contributed at least a fair share the subsistence rights of human beings would cease to be violated (since that would be one of the criteria for deciding on a fair share). There is a problem about the applicability of generalization arguments where the efforts of one individual accomplish nothing if most other people do not also do their fair share. (It is, for example, probably pointless to be the only person who refrains from taking a short cut across the grass; the grass will not grow.) In such cases the failure of some to fulfill their duties may relieve others of theirs. The duty to contribute to the cause of combatting hunger, however, is not of this sort, since one individual's contributions still accomplish some good whether or not other people are giving their fair share.

On the other hand there is the problem of whether the failure of some people to fulfill their duties increases the duties of others. If many are not giving a fair share, does the individual who is already giving a fair share have a duty to give more? The example of the two drowning people suggests that the individual who has done his fair share does have a duty to do more. But there is a major difference between the two cases. Saving people from drowning, in so far as the chances of losing one's own life are not great, is something that takes a minimal amount of time out of the rescuer's life and does not threaten his ability to live a life of pursuing goals he sets for himself. A similar duty to keep on giving of one's resources, even after one has done his fair share, would threaten to eclipse everything else a person might choose to do with his life, for example, develop his talents, raise a family, send his children to college, and so on, so that that person would become nothing but a means to meeting the needs of others. The idea of a strict duty to do at least one's fair share seems to avoid the problem of overload (unless the total need is overwhelming) and draws a line at a plausible point somewhere between doing nothing and sacrificing one's whole life to the cause of relieving the distress of others. This approach does make one's duty to those in need agent-specific, since one's duty does depend on one's past history, on what sacrifices one has already made, but it is not clear to me why this is a defect. Of course a person might choose to make the rescuing of those in distress her special vocation, and it may be noble for her to do so, but to claim that if the needs of others are great enough she has a duty to surrender any choice about the direction of her own life is to claim that a person has a duty to be purely the means to meeting the needs of others, and so in fact a duty to love others not as oneself, but instead of oneself. On the other hand, not to recognize a duty to give a fair share is to indicate that one believes either that it is not important that the needs of those in distress should be met (perhaps because they do not have subsistence rights) or that others should do more than their fair share.[18] It might be said that the first is at least a sin against compassion (if not also against justice) and the second is a sin against fairness or justice. In either case one is treating the ends and purposes of others as having less validity than one's own, or, from another point of view, one is not loving others as oneself.

V. CONSIDERATIONS BEYOND A FAIR SHARE

If redistribution of wealth were in fact the major need of the most vulnerable in the world, and if in fact government foreign aid programs could be modified so that they could be trusted to meet that need, then, in agreement with Shue and Goodin, I would claim that for the sake of fairness both to those in need and those willing to help, it would be better if everyone did his or her fair share and it would be legitimate to coerce people through the tax system to do so.[19] In the absence of such taxation and in the absence of any official calculation of such a share, individuals generally do not have the information on which to assess their own fair share, and if they did they would probably tend to underestimate it. What most people tend to think of as their fair share depends much less on any informed calculation than on what they think their neighbors, fellow citizens, or fellow church members, are contributing,[20] consoling themselves with the thought that it cannot really be their duty to do more than others. But since most people who do something probably tend to think that they are doing more with respect to their resources than others, the idea of a duty to do a fair share is in danger of succumbing to a downward pressure to require less and less. If the vulnerable are to be protected, then perhaps doing one's fair share to meet their needs is not the only duty. Rather there must also be a duty to put upward pressure on the prevailing idea of a fair share. This can be done only by those who do considerably more than what is perceived of as a fair share, and often more than an actual fair share. This is embodied in Christian ethics in the ideal of being a light to witness to a higher and more demanding way of life and in the ideal of being the salt of the earth that preserves it from decay, perhaps primarily the decay brought about by downward pressure on prevailing standards. Probably a secular counterpart to these ideals would be accepted by others.

There are doubts about whether redistribution of wealth is the major need, as opposed to various changes in policies, including trade policies. There are also grave doubts concerning the degree to which government aid in the past has really benefited the most vulnerable and about its prospects of doing so in the future. That raises the possibility that the major duty individuals have is that of exerting pressure on government to make sure that policies do protect the vulnerable. (In American society people are not quick to recognize this as a moral duty. Churches have much more success in getting their members to contribute to "One Great Hour of Sharing" and "Hunger Fund" offerings than they do in getting them to write letters to their Senators and Congressmen about hunger issues.) Donald Regan writes that our duty is "to cooperate with whoever else is cooperating, in the production of the best consequences possible given the behaviour of non-cooperators." [21] There is an organization, Bread for the World, which analyzes policy, supports legislation on hunger issues, and conducts coordinated letter-writing drives through its members and its affiliated churches. Those who would write letters to their representatives in conjunction with such an effort would be acting in accordance with Regan's principle. But the principle does not say how much time, effort, and money an individual has a duty to devote to cooperating with others to bring it about that governments act in ways that protect the vulnerable. [22] Giving one's fair share to help those in need accomplishes some good whether or not others are cooperating by doing their share. In the matter of influencing legislation an insufficient number of people doing their fair share (with respect to all who might participate in the effort) may accomplish nothing. Does the failure of enough others to do their fair share release one from one's duty to work for change (as it may release one from the duty not to walk on the grass)? If so, the vulnerable are left without protection. Or does such a failure impose a duty on others to do as much as possible (as in the case of saving drowning people), so that we could again be faced with the problem of overload? In this case, however, one sort of fair share is so minimal there is no problem in doing much more. If an individual wrote at least one letter a year to her Senators and Congressman on one piece of legislation critical to meeting the needs of the hungry in the world, that individual would on this matter be doing perhaps 50 times a fair share, in that letters from two percent of the electorate would be regarded by those legislators as an overwhelming mandate on the issue. But an individual could write many such letters a year, and encourage others to do likewise, without sacrificing anything significant. Perhaps there is no precise answer to the question of just how much more money or effort than prevailing standards require one "ought" to devote to the cause here being considered, since this may be a matter of living up to an ideal rather than fulfilling a perfect duty to a specific individual, or a perfect duty of doing a fair share. Even in the absence of any way of determining what a fair share might be one can attempt to live by this ideal by doing significantly more than the society as a whole generally thinks is required.

Furthermore, may not some people have an agent-specific duty to do more than a fair share (perhaps much more) about some specific matter because of their peculiar awareness of the problem, knowledge of what needs to be done, and sensitivity to it? Religious people might say that all people have a duty to ask themselves whether they may have been "called" to a special vocation of taking on this cause, with the assurance that some people are called to this vocation and all people are called to some such vocation(s). In addition, a religious ethic generally emphasizes the faithfulness of one's witness more than the extent of one's accomplishments, and so may succeed in sustaining an individual's effort to bring about change when the prospects of succeeding seem slight. Perhaps some would argue for secular equivalents to these emphases.

VI. POSTSCRIPT: ADDITIONAL KANTIAN REFLECTIONS ON DUTIES OF OTHERS

There are still a number of things to be taken into consideration. Kant says that a person should "not push the expenditure of his means in beneficence . . . to the point where he would finally need the beneficence of others." [23] That could be regarded as treating others as a means to one's own end of trying to achieve some kind of sainthood. Secondly, help should not be given in a manner or to an extent that reduces the ability of the person (or group) that is helped to be self-reliant and self-determining. It is doubtful whether the wealthy have ever given too much help to the poor, but they have sometimes (perhaps frequently) given in a manner which made the recipients more dependent in the long run, for example, in a way that reduced the incentives of local farmers to increase production. Thirdly, according to Kant, every effort must be made to "carefully avoid any appearance of intending to obligate the other person, lest he (the giver) not render a true benefit, inasmuch as by his act he expresses that he wants to lay an obligation upon the receiver." [24] Presumably nations such as the United States can and do give aid for ulterior purposes, such as to get rid of agricultural surpluses, help farm prices, gain political influence, or to stimulate markets and/or a favorable climate of investment for U.S. companies, but then citizens of these nations ought not congratulate themselves on their generosity (as Americans often do). Such acts are not acts of beneficence and from Kant's point of view they have no moral worth since they are not done for the sake of duty, nor are they done from other motives that might be regarded as being other than morally neutral.

Fourthly, there are conditions under which it could be argued that a wealthy country has the right to refuse to give aid, other than emergency disaster aid, if it is not something that is owed as reparations. Suppose that achieving the goal of advancing the self-sufficiency and self-determination of a nation depends in part on the receiving nation's own effort to make necessary changes such as redistributing land, bringing population growth under control, and so on. It could be argued that if the receiving nation fails to make a good-faith effort to bring about these changes, and if it then asks for additional aid, the developed country may legitimately claim that it is being used, and its people are being used, solely as means to the ends of the underdeveloped country or its people. The major problem with using this line of argument is that the people who are facing hunger may have little to say about the decisions of their government. That problem, however, does not prevent the aid-giving country from legitimately making demands for reform in advance, from doing what it can to see to it that they are carried out, and from threatening sanctions other than those that would increase the deprivation of hungry people. [25] Perhaps it has seldom, if ever, happened that a developed nation has given enough non-military aid to an underdeveloped nation to be in a position to dictate what steps the receiving nation should take to improve the ability of its people to be self-sufficient; or perhaps it has been in the interest of the political strategy, military effort, or business investment of the developed nations not to demand that specific remedial steps be taken on the part of the receiving country; but it would seem to be legitimate to make such demands.

Endnotes

1. Peter Singer, "Famine, Affluence, and Morality," *Philosophy and Public Affairs,* vol. 1 (1972), p. 231.
2. James Fishkin, *The Limits of Obligation* (New Haven: Yale University Press, 1982), especially chapters 1–7, 9 and 18.
3. Garrett Hardin, "Lifeboat Ethics: "The Case Against Helping the Poor," *Psychology Today,* vol. 8 (1974), pp. 38–43, 123–126.

4. Garrett Hardin, "The Tragedy of the Commons," *Science*, vol. 102 (1968), pp. 1243–1248.
5. Garrett Hardin, "Carrying Capacity as an Ethical Concept," in George R. Lucas and Thomas W. Ogletree (eds.), *Lifeboat Ethics: The Moral Dilemmas of World Hunger* (New York: Harper and Row, 1976), p. 131.
6. Part of the title of an article by Garrett Hardin, "Another Face of Bioethics: The Case for Massive 'Diebacks' of Population," *Modern Medicine*, vol. 65 (March 1, 1975).
7. Paul Verghese, "Muddled Metaphors," in Lucas and Ogletree, *op. cit.*, p. 152.
8. Robert Nozick, *Anarchy, State and Utopia* (New York: Basic Books, Inc., 1974), pp. 30–35.
9. Immanuel Kant, *The Metaphysical Elements of Justice* (Part 1 of the *Metaphysics of Morals*), tr. by John Ladd (Indianapolis: Bobbs-Merrill Co., 1965), p. 93 (326).
10. Nozick, *op. cit.*, p. 31.
11. Onora Nell, "Lifeboat Earth," *Philosophy and Public Affairs*, vol. 4 (1975), p. 286.
12. Arthur Simon, *Bread for the World* (New York: Paulist Press, 1975), p. 41.
13. For some of these problems see Goodin, *Protecting the Vulnerable* (Chicago: University of Chicago Press, 1986), pp. 159–160.
14. Alan Donagan, *Theory of Morality* (Chicago: University of Chicago Press, 1977), p. 85.
15. Henry Shue, *Basic Rights* (Princeton: Princeton University Press, 1980), Chapters 1 & 2.
16. This is the thesis of Goodin's book (*op. cit.*) with which I am in general agreement.
17. Shue, *op. cit.*, p. 114.
18. See also Goodin, *op. cit.*, p. 165.
19. *Ibid.*, p. 164; Shue, *op. cit.*, p. 118.
20. See Singer, "Famine, Affluence, and Morality," *op. cit.*, p. 30.
21. Donald Regan, *Utilitarianism and Cooperation* (Oxford: Clarendon Press, 1980), p. 124; also cited by Goodin as expressing his own view (*op. cit.*, p. 164).
22. For some suggestions concerning such ways, see Frances Moore Lappé and Joseph Collins, *World Hunger: 10 Myths* (San Francisco: Institute for Food and Development Policy, 4th ed., 1982), pp. 49–50.
23. *Metaphysical Principles of Virtue, op. cit.*, p. 118 (454).
24. *Ibid.* (453).
25. See Shue, *Basic Rights*, Part III, "Policy Implications," *op. cit.*, pp. 155–174.

REVIEW QUESTIONS

1. What criticisms does Van Wyk make of Singer and Hardin?
2. How does a Kantian ethic view obligations to others according to Van Wyk?
3. What is Van Wyk's proposal for helping the hungry?

DISCUSSION QUESTIONS

1. Is Van Wyk's proposal for aid acceptable?
2. Do individuals have a strict duty to help others or is this optional? If there is such a strict duty, just what does it require us to do?

John Hospers

What Libertarianism Is

John Hospers is professor of philosophy at the University of Southern California. He is the author of Human Conduct: Problems of Ethics *(1972),* Libertarianism: A Political Philosophy for Tomorrow *(1971), and* Understanding the Arts *(1982). He was the Libertarian party's candidate*

From John Hospers, "What Libertarianism Is," *The Libertarian Alternative,* ed. Tibor R. Machan (Chicago: Nelson-Hall Co., 1974), pp. 3–20. Reprinted with permission.

for president of the United States in a past presidential election.

Hospers begins with several different statements of the libertarian thesis which says that every person is the owner of his or her life. This basic thesis entails a right to liberty and a right to act as you choose, unless your action infringes on the equal liberty of others to act as they choose. Hospers also recognizes a right to life and a right to property. These rights are interpreted negatively. That is, they imply only that no one, including the government, has a right to interfere with a person's liberty, life, or property; they do not require any positive actions. Since these rights are violated by an initial use of force, the only proper rule of government is to prevent this use of force and to retaliate against those who do initiate the use of force. All other possible roles of government, including protecting individuals from themselves or requiring people to help each other, are emphatically rejected by Hospers.

The political philosophy that is called libertarianism (from the Latin *libertas*, liberty) is the doctrine that every person is the owner of his own life, and that no one is the owner of anyone else's life; and that consequently every human being has the right to act in accordance with his own choices, unless those actions infringe on the equal liberty of other human beings to act in accordance with their choices.

There are several other ways of stating the same libertarian thesis:

1. *No one is anyone else's master, and no one is anyone else's slave.* Since I am the one to decide how my life is to be conducted just as you decide about yours, I have no right (even if I had the power) to make you my slave and be your master, nor have you the right to become the master by enslaving me. Slavery is *forced* servitude, and since no one owns the life of anyone else, no one has the right to enslave another. Political theories past and present have traditionally been concerned with who should be the master (usually the king, the dictator, or government bureaucracy) and who should be the slaves, and what the extent of the slavery should be. Libertarianism holds that no one has the right to use force to enslave the life of another, or any portion or aspect of that life.

2. *Other men's lives are not yours to dispose of.* I enjoy seeing operas; but operas are expensive to produce. Opera-lovers often say, "The state (or the city, etc.) should subsidize opera, so that we can all see it. Also it would be for people's betterment, cultural benefit, etc." But what they are advocating is nothing more or less than legalized plunder. They can't pay for the productions themselves, and yet they want to see opera, which involves a large number of people and their labor; so what they are saying in effect is, "Get the money through legalized force. Take a little bit more out of every worker's paycheck every week to pay for the operas we want to see." But I have no right to take by force from the workers' pockets to pay for what I want.

Perhaps it would be better if he *did* go to see opera—then I should try to convince him to go voluntarily. But to take the money from him forcibly, because in my opinion it would be good for *him,* is still seizure of his earnings, which is plunder.

Besides, if I have the right to force him to help pay for my pet projects, hasn't he equally the right to force me to help pay for his? Perhaps he in turn wants the government to subsidize rock-and-roll, or his new car, or a house in the country. If I have the right to milk him, why hasn't he the right to milk me? If I can be a moral cannibal, why can't he too?

We should beware of the inventors of utopias. They would remake the world according to their vision—with the lives and fruits of the labor of *other* human beings. Is it someone's utopian vision that others should build pyramids to beautify the landscape? Very well, then other men should provide the labor; and if he is in a position of political power, and he can't get men to do it voluntarily, then he must *compel* them to "cooperate"—i.e. he must enslave them.

A hundred men might gain great pleasure from beating up or killing just one insignificant human being; but other men's lives are not theirs to dispose of. "In order to achieve the worthy goals of the next five-year-plan, we must forcibly collectivize the peasants . . ."; but other men's lives are not theirs to dispose of. Do you want to occupy, rent-free, the mansion that another man has worked for twenty years to buy? But other men's lives are not yours to dispose of. Do you want operas so badly that everyone is forced to work harder to pay for their subsidization through taxes? But other men's lives are not yours to dispose of. Do you want to have free medical care at the expense of other people, whether they wish to provide it or not? But this would require them to work longer for you whether they want to or not, and other men's lives are not yours to dispose of. . . .

3. *No human being should be a nonvoluntary mortgage on the life of another.* I cannot claim your life, your work, or the products of your effort as mine. The fruit of one man's labor should not be fair game for every freeloader who comes along and demands it as his own. The

orchard that has been carefully grown, nurtured, and harvested by its owner should not be ripe for the plucking for any bypasser who has a yen for the ripe fruit. The wealth that some men have produced should not be fair game for looting by government, to be used for whatever purposes its representatives determine, no matter what their motives in so doing may be. The theft of your money by a robber is not justified by the fact that he used it to help his injured mother.

It will already be evident that libertarian doctrine is embedded in a view of the rights of man. Each human being has the right to live his life as he chooses, compatibly with the equal right of all other human beings to live their lives as they choose.

All man's rights are implicit in the above statement. Each man has the right to life: any attempt by others to take it away from him, or even to injure him, violates this right, through the use of coercion against him. Each man has the right to liberty: to conduct his life in accordance with the alternatives open to him without coercive action by others. And every man has the right to property: to work to sustain his life (and the lives of whichever others he chooses to sustain, such as his family) and to retain the fruits of his labor.

People often defend the rights of life and liberty but denigrate property rights, and yet the right to property is as basic as the other two: indeed, without property rights no other rights are possible. Depriving you of property is depriving you of the means by which you live. . . .

I have no right to decide how *you* should spend your time or your money. I can make that decision for myself, but not for you, my neighbor. I may deplore your choice of life-style, and I may talk with you about it provided you are willing to listen to me. But I have no right to use force to change it. Nor have I the right to decide how you should spend the money you have earned. I may appeal to you to give it to the Red Cross, and you may prefer to go to prize-fights. But that is your decision, and however much I may chafe about it I do not have the right to interfere forcibly with it, for example by robbing you in order to use the money

in accordance with *my* choices. (If I have the right to rob you, have you also the right to rob me?)

When I claim a right, I carve out a niche, as it were, in my life, saying in effect, "This activity I must be able to perform without interference from others. For you and everyone else, this is off limits." And so I put up a "no trespassing" sign, which marks off the area of my right. Each individual's right is his "no trespassing" sign in relation to me and others. I may not encroach upon his domain any more than he upon mine, without my consent. Every right entails a duty, true—but the duty is only that of *forbearance*— that is, of *refraining* from violating the other person's right. If you have a right to life, I have no right to take your life; if you have a right to the products of your labor (property), I have no right to take it from you without your consent. The nonviolation of these rights will not guarantee you protection against natural catastrophes such as floods and earthquakes, but it will protect you against the aggressive activities *of other men*. And rights, after all, have to do with one's relations to other human beings, not with one's relations to physical nature.

Nor were these rights created by government; governments—some governments, obviously not all—*recognize* and *protect* the rights that individuals already have. Governments regularly forbid homicide and theft; and, at a more advanced stage, protect individuals against such things as libel and breach of contract. . . .

The *right to property* is the most misunderstood and unappreciated of human rights, and it is one most constantly violated by governments. "Property" of course does not mean only real estate; it includes anything you can call your own—your clothing, your car, your jewelry, your books and papers.

The right of property is not the right to just *take* it from others, for this would interfere with *their* property rights. It is rather the right to work for it, to obtain non-coercively, the money or services which you can present in voluntary exchange.

The right to property is consistently underplayed by intellectuals today, sometimes even frowned upon, as if we should feel guilty for upholding such a right in view of all the poverty in the world. But the right to property is absolutely basic. It is your hedge against the future. It is your assurance that what you have worked to earn will still be there and be yours, when you wish or need to use it, especially when you are too old to work any longer.

Government has always been the chief enemy of the right to property. The officials of government, wishing to increase their power, and finding an increase of wealth an effective way to bring this about seize some or all of what a person has earned—and since government has a monopoly of physical force within the geographical area of the nation, it has the power (but not the right) to do this. When this happens, of course, every citizen of that country is insecure: he knows that no matter how hard he works the government can swoop down on him at any time and confiscate his earnings and possessions. A person sees his life savings wiped out in a moment when the tax-collectors descend to deprive him of the fruits of his work; or, an industry which has been fifty years in the making and cost millions of dollars and millions of hours of time and planning, is nationalized overnight. Or the government, via inflation, cheapens the currency, so that hard-won dollars aren't worth anything any more. The effect of such actions, of course, is that people lose hope and incentive; if no matter how hard they work the government agents can take it all away, why bother to work at all, for more than today's needs? Depriving people of property is *depriving them of the means by which they live*—the freedom of the individual citizen to do what he wishes with his own life and to plan for the future. Indeed only if property rights are respected is there any point to planning for the future and working to achieve one's goals. *Property rights are what makes long-range planning possible*—the kind of planning which is a distinctively human endeavor, as opposed to the day-by-day activity of the lion who hunts, who depends on the supply of game tomorrow but has no real insurance against starvation in a day or a week. Without the right to property, the right to life itself amounts to little: how can you sustain your life if you cannot plan ahead? and how can you plan ahead if the fruits of your labor can at any moment be confiscated by government? . . .

Indeed, the right to property may well be considered second only to the right to life. Even the freedom of speech is limited by considerations of property. If a person visiting in your home behaves in a way undesired by you, you have every right to evict him; he can scream or agitate elsewhere if he wishes, but not in your home without your consent. Does a person have a right to shout obscenities in a cathedral? No, for the owners of the cathedral (presumably the Church) have not allowed others on their property for that purpose; one may go there to worship or to visit, but not just for any purpose one wishes. Their property right is prior to your or my wish to scream or expectorate or write graffiti on their building. Or, to take the stock example, does a person have a right to shout "Fire!" falsely in a crowded theater? No, for the theater owner has permitted others to enter and use his property only for a specific purpose, that of seeing a film or watching a stage show. If a person heckles or otherwise disturbs other members of the audience, he can be thrown out. (In fact, he can be removed for any reason the owner chooses, provided his admission money is returned.) And if he shouts "Fire!" when there is no fire, he may be endangering other lives by causing a panic or stampede. The right to free speech doesn't give one the right to say anything anywhere; it is circumscribed by property rights.

Again, some people seem to assume that the right to free speech (including written speech) means that they can go to a newspaper publisher and demand that he print in his newspaper some propaganda or policy statement for their political party (or other group). But of course they have no right to the use of his newspaper. Ownership of the newspaper is the product of his labor, and he has a right to put into his newspaper whatever he wants, for whatever reason. If he excludes material which many readers would like to have in, perhaps they can find it in another newspaper or persuade him to print it himself (if there are enough of them, they will usually do just that). Perhaps they can even cause his newspaper to fail. But as long as he owns it, he has the right to put in it what he wishes; what would a property right be if he could not do this? They have no right to place their material in his newspaper without his consent—not for free, nor even for a fee. Perhaps other newspapers will include it, or perhaps they can start their own newspaper (in which case they have a right to put in it what they like). If not, an option open to them would be to mimeograph and distribute some handbills.

In exactly the same way, no one has a right to "free television time" unless the owner of the television station consents to give it; it is his station, he has the property rights over it, and it is for him to decide how to dispose of his time. He may not decide wisely, but it is his right to decide as he wishes. If he makes enough unwise decisions, and courts enough unpopularity with the viewing public or the sponsors, he may have to go out of business; but as he is free to make his own decisions, so is he free to face their consequences. (If the government owns the television station, then government officials will make the decisions, and there is no guarantee of *their* superior wisdom. The difference is that when "the government" owns the station, you are forced to help pay for its upkeep through your taxes, whether the bureaucrat in charge decides to give you television time or not.)

"But why have *individual* property rights? Why not have lands and houses owned by everybody together?" Yes, this involves no violation of individual rights, as long as everybody consents to this arrangement and no one is forced to join it. The parties to it may enjoy the communal living enough (at least for a time) to overcome certain inevitable problems: that some will work and some not, that some will achieve more in an hour than others can do in a day, and still they will all get the same income. The few who do the most will in the end consider themselves "workhorses" who do the work of two or three or twelve, while the others will be "freeloaders" on the efforts of these few. But as long as they can get out of the arrangement if they no longer like it, no violation of rights is involved. They got in voluntarily, and they can get out voluntarily; no one has used force.

"But why not say that everybody owns everything? That we *all* own everything there is?"

To some this may have a pleasant ring—but let us try to analyze what it means. If everybody owns everything, then everyone has an equal right to go everywhere, do what he pleases, take what he likes, destroy if he wishes, grow crops or burn them, trample them under, and so on. Consider what it would be like in practice. Suppose you have saved money to buy a house for yourself and your family. Now suppose that the principle, "everybody owns everything," becomes adopted. Well then, why shouldn't every itinerant hippie just come in and take over, sleeping in your beds and eating in your kitchen and not bothering to replace the food supply or clean up the mess? After all, it belongs to all of us, doesn't it? So we have just as much right to it as you, the buyer, have. What happens if we *all* want to sleep in the bedroom and there's not room for all of us? Is it the strongest who wins?

What would be the result? Since no one would be responsible for anything, the property would soon be destroyed, the food used up, the facilities nonfunctional. Beginning as a house that *one* family could use, it would end up as a house that *no one* could use. And if the principle continued to be adopted, no one would build houses any more—or anything else. What for? They would only be occupied and used by others, without remuneration.

Suppose two men are cast ashore on an island, and they agree that each will cultivate half of it. The first man is industrious and grows crops and builds a shelter, making the most of the situation with which he is confronted. The second man, perhaps thinking that the warm days will last forever, lies in the sun, picks coconuts while they last, and does a minimum of work to sustain himself. At the time of harvest, the second man has nothing to harvest, nor does he assist the first man in his labors. But later when there is a dearth of food on the island, the second man comes to the first man and demands half of the harvest as his right. But of course he has no right to the product of the first man's labors. The first man may freely choose to give part of his harvest to the second out of charity rather than see him starve; but that is just what it is—charity, not the second man's right.

How can any of man's rights be violated? Ultimately, only by the use of force. I can make suggestions to you, I can reason with you, entreat you (if you are willing to listen), but I cannot *force* you without violating your rights; only by forcing you do I cut the cord between your free decisions and your actions. Voluntary relations between individuals involve no deprivation of rights, but murder, assault, and rape do, because in doing these things I make you the unwilling victim of my actions. A man's beating his wife involves no violation of rights if she *wanted* to be beaten. *Force is behavior that requires the unwilling involvement of other persons.*

Thus the use of force need not involve the use of physical violence. If I trespass on your property or dump garbage on it, I am violating your property rights, as indeed I am when I steal your watch; although this is not force in the sense of violence, it *is* a case of your being an unwilling victim of my action. Similarly, if you shout at me so that I cannot be heard when I try to speak, or blow a siren in my ear, or start a factory next door which pollutes my land, you are again violating my rights (to free speech, to property); I am, again, an unwilling victim of your actions. Similarly, if you steal a manuscript of mine and publish it as your own, you are confiscating a piece of my property and thus violating my right to keep what is the product of my labor. Of course, if I give you the manuscript with permission to sign your name to it and keep the proceeds, no violation of rights is involved—any more than if I give you permission to dump garbage on my yard.

According to libertarianism, the role of government should be limited to the retaliatory use of force against those who have initiated its use. It should not enter into any other areas, such as religion, social organization, and economics.

GOVERNMENT

Government is the most dangerous institution known to man. Throughout history it has violated the rights of men more than any individual or group of individuals could do: it has killed people, enslaved them, sent them to forced labor and concentration camps, and regularly robbed and pillaged them of the fruits of their expended labor. Unlike individual criminals, government has the power to arrest and try; unlike individual criminals, it can surround and encompass a person totally, dominating every aspect of one's life, so that one has no recourse from it but to leave the country (and in totalitarian nations even that is prohibited). Government throughout history has a much sorrier record than any individual, even that of a ruthless mass murderer. The signs we see on bumper stickers are chillingly accurate: "Beware: the Government Is Armed and Dangerous."

The only proper role of government, according to libertarians, is that of the protector of the citizen against agression by other individuals. The government, of course, should never initiate aggression; its proper role is as the embodiment of the *retaliatory* use of force against anyone who initiates its use.

If each individual had constantly to defend himself against possible aggressors, he would have to spend a considerable portion of his life in target practice, karate exercises, and other means of self-defenses, and even so he would probably be helpless against groups of individuals who might try to kill, maim, or rob him. He would have little time for cultivating those qualities which are essential to civilized life, nor would improvements in science, medicine, and the arts be likely to occur. The function of government is to take this responsibility off his shoulders: the government undertakes to defend him against aggressors and to punish them if they attack him. When the government is effective in doing this, it enables the citizen to go about his business unmolested and without constant fear for his life. To do this, of course, government must have physical power—the police, to protect the citizen from aggression within its borders, and the armed forces, to protect him from aggressors outside. Beyond that, the government should not intrude upon his life, either to run his business, or adjust his daily activities, or prescribe his personal moral code.

Government, then, undertakes to be the individual's protector; but historically governments have gone far beyond this function. Since they already have the physical power, they have not hesitated to use it for purposes far beyond that which was entrusted to them in the first place. Undertaking initially to protect its citizens against aggression, it has often itself become an aggressor—a far greater aggressor, indeed, than the criminals against whom it was supposed to protect its citizens. Governments have done what no private citizen can do: arrest and imprison individuals without a trial and send them to slave labor camps. Government must have power in order to be effective—and yet the very means by which alone it can be effective make it vulnerable to the abuse of power, leading to managing the lives of individuals and even inflicting terror upon them.

What then should be the function of government? In a word, the *protection of human rights*.

1. *The right to life:* libertarians support all such legislation as will protect human beings against the use of force by others, for example, laws against killing, attempted killing, maiming, beating, and all kinds of physical violence.
2. *The right to liberty:* there should be no laws compromising in any way freedom of speech, of the press, and of peaceable assembly. There should be no censorship of ideas, books, films, or of anything else by government.
3. *The right to property:* libertarians support legislation that protects the property rights of individuals against confiscation, nationalization, eminent domain, robbery, trespass, fraud and misrepresentation, patent and copyright, libel and slander.

Someone has violently assaulted you. Should he be legally liable? Of course. He has violated one of your rights. He has knowingly injured you, and since he has initiated aggression against you he should be made to expiate.

Someone has negligently left his bicycle on the sidewalk where you trip over it in the dark and injure yourself. He didn't do it intentionally; he didn't mean you any harm. Should he be legally liable? Of course; he has, however unwittingly, injured you, and since the injury is caused by him and you are the victim, he should pay.

Someone across the street is unemployed. Should you be taxed extra to pay for his expenses? Not at all. You have not injured him, you are not responsible for the fact that he is unemployed (unless you are a senator or bureaucrat who agitated for further curtailing of business, which legislation passed, with the result that your neighbor was laid off by the curtailed business). You may voluntarily wish to help him out, or better still, try to get him a job to put him on his feet again; but since you have initiated no aggressive act against him, and neither purposely nor accidentally injured him in any way, you should not be legally penalized for the fact of his unemployment. (Actually, it is just such penalties that increase unemployment.)

One man, A, works hard for years and finally earns a high salary as a professional man. A second man, B, prefers not to work at all, and to spend wastefully what money he has (through inheritance), so that after a year or two he has nothing left. At the end of this time he has a long siege of illness and lots of medical bills to pay. He demands that the bills be paid by the government—that is, by the taxpayers of the land, including Mr. A.

But of course B has no such right. He chose to lead his life in a certain way—that was his voluntary decision. One consequence of that choice is that he must depend on charity in case of later need. Mr. A chose not to live that way. (And if everyone lived like Mr. B, on whom would he depend in case of later need?) Each has a right to live in the way he pleases, but each must live with the consequences of his own decision (which, as always, fall primarily on himself). He cannot, in time of need, claim A's beneficence as his right. . . .

Laws may be classified into three types: (1) laws protecting individuals against themselves, such as laws against fornication and other sexual behavior, alcohol, and drugs; (2) laws protecting individuals against aggressions by other individuals, such as laws against murder, robbery, and fraud; (3) laws requiring people to help one another; for example, all laws which rob Peter to pay Paul, such as welfare.

Libertarians reject the first class of laws totally. Behavior which harms no one else is strictly the individual's own affair. Thus, there should be no laws against becoming intoxicated, since whether or not to become intoxicated is the individual's own decision; but there should be laws against driving while intoxicated, since the drunken driver is a threat to every other motorist on the highway (drunken driving falls into type 2). Similarly, there should be no laws against drugs (except the prohibition of sale of drugs to minors) as long as the taking of these drugs poses no threat to anyone else. Drug addiction is a psychological problem to which no present solution exists. Most of the social harm caused by addicts, other than to themselves, is the result of thefts which they perform in order to continue their habit—and then the *legal* crime is the theft, not the addiction. The actual cost of heroin is about ten cents a shot; if it were legalized, the enormous traffic in illegal sale and purchase of it would stop, as well as the accompanying proselytization to get new addicts (to make more money for the pusher) and the thefts performed by addicts who often require eighty dollars a day just to keep up the habit. Addiction would not stop, but the crimes would: it is estimated that 75 percent of the burglaries in New York City today are performed by addicts, and all these crimes could be wiped out at one stroke through the legalization of drugs. (Only when the taking of drugs could be shown to constitute a threat to *others,* should it be prohibited by law. It is only laws protecting people against *themselves* that libertarians oppose.)

Laws should be limited to the second class only: aggression by individuals against other individuals. These are laws whose function is to protect human beings against encroachment by others; and this, as we have seen, is (according to libertarianism) the sole function of government.

Libertarians also reject the third class of laws totally: no one should be forced by law to help others, not even to tell them the time of day if requested, and certainly not to give them a portion of one's weekly paycheck. Governments, in the guise of humanitarianism, have given to some by taking from others (charging a "handling fee" in the process, which, because of the government's waste and inefficiency, sometimes is several hundred percent). And in so doing they have decreased incentive, violated the rights of individuals, and lowered the standard of living of almost everyone.

All such laws constitute what libertarians call *moral cannibalism.* A cannibal in the physical sense is a person who lives off the flesh of other human beings. A *moral* cannibal is one who believes he has a right to live off the "spirit" of other human beings—who believes that he has a moral claim on the productive capacity, time, and effort expended by others.

It has become fashionable to claim virtually everything that one needs or desires as one's *right.* Thus, many people claim that they have a right to a job, the right to free medical care, to free food and clothing, to a decent home, and so on. Now if one asks, apart from any specific context, whether it would be desirable if everyone had these things, one might well say yes. But there is a gimmick attached to each of them: *At whose expense?* Jobs, medical care, education, and so on, don't grow on trees. These are goods and services *produced only by men.* Who, then, is to provide them, and under what conditions?

If you have a right to a job, who is to supply it? Must an employer supply it even if he doesn't want to hire you? What if you are unemployable, or incurably lazy? (If you say "the government must supply it," does that mean that a job must be created for you which no employer needs done, and that you must be kept in it regardless of how much or little you work?) If the employer is forced to supply it at his expense even if he doesn't need you, then isn't *he* being enslaved to that extent? What ever happened to *his* right to conduct his life and his affairs in accordance with his choices?

If you have a right to free medical care, then, since medical care doesn't exist in nature as wild apples do, some people will have to supply it to you for free: that is, they will have to spend their time and money and energy taking care of you whether they want to or not. What ever happened to *their* right to conduct their lives as they see fit? Or do you have a right to violate theirs? Can there be a right to violate rights?

All those who demand this or that as a "free service" are consciously or unconsciously evading the fact that there is in reality no such thing as free services. All man-made goods and services are the result of human expenditure of time and effort. There is no such thing as "something for nothing" in this world. If you demand something free, you are demanding that other men give their time and effort to you without compensation. If they voluntarily choose to do this, there is no problem; but if you demand that they be *forced* to do it, you are interfering with their right not to do it if they so choose. "Swimming in this pool ought to be free!" says the indignant passerby. What he means is that others should build a pool, others should provide the materials, and still others should run it and keep it in functioning order, so that *he* can use it without fee. But what right has he to the expenditure of *their* time and effort? To expect something "for free" is to expect it *to be paid for by others* whether they choose to or not.

Many questions, particularly about economic matters, will be generated by the libertarian account of human rights and the role of government. Should government have no role in assisting the needy, in providing social security, in legislating minimum wages, in fixing prices and putting a ceiling on rents, in curbing monopolies, in erecting tariffs, in guaranteeing jobs, in managing the money supply? To these and all similar questions the libertarian answers with an unequivocal no.

"But then you'd let people go hungry!" comes the rejoinder. This, the libertarian insists, is precisely what would not happen; with the restrictions removed, the economy would flourish as never before. With the controls taken off business, existing enterprises would expand and new ones would spring into existence satisfying more and more consumer needs; millions more people would be gainfully employed instead of subsisting on welfare, and all kinds of research and production, released from the stranglehold of government, would proliferate, fulfilling man's needs and desires as never before. It has always been so whenever government has permitted men to be free traders on a free market. But *why* this is so, and how the free market is the best solution to all problems relating to the material aspect of man's life, is another and far longer story. . . .

REVIEW QUESTIONS

1. How does Hospers explain Libertarianism?
2. According to Hospers, why is the government the chief enemy of the right to property?
3. What is the only proper role of government according to Hospers?
4. Which type of laws do libertarians accept? Which laws do they reject and why?
5. How does Hospers propose to deal with needy people?

DISCUSSION QUESTIONS

1. Is the right to property just as important as the right to life?
2. Hospers claims that human rights can be violated only by the use of force. Is this true? Explain your answer.
3. Hospers rejects all laws that protect individuals from themselves, for example, laws prohibiting prostitution and drugs. Should all such laws be abolished or not?
4. Hospers is totally opposed to any welfare laws. Should all these laws be eliminated? What would be the result?

Kai Nielsen

Radical Egalitarianism

Kai Nielsen is emeritus professor of philosophy at the University of Calgary. He is the author of Marxism and the Moral Point of View *(1985) and* Ethics without God *(1990).*

Nielsen explains and defends Radical Egalitarianism, the view that everyone in an affluent society has an equal right to have his or her basic needs met and that everyone also has an obligation to share equally the necessary burdens of society.

From Kai Nielsen, "Radical Egalitarianism," *Equality and Liberty,* pp. 283–292, 302–306, 309. Copyright © 1985 by Rowman and Allanheld Publishers. Reprinted by permission of Rowman and Littlefield Publishers.

I

I have talked of equality as a right and of equality as a goal. And I have taken, as the principal thing, to be able to state what goal we are seeking when we say equality is a goal. When we are in a position actually to achieve that goal, then that same equality becomes a right. The goal we are seeking is an equality of basic condition for everyone. Let me say a bit what this is: everyone, as far as possible, should have equal life prospects, short of genetic engineering and the like and the rooting out any form of the family and the undermining of our basic freedoms. There should, where this is possible, be an equality of access to equal resources over each person's life as a whole, though this should be qualified by people's varying needs. Where psychiatrists are in short supply only people who are in need of psychiatric help should have equal access to such help. This equal access to resources should be such that it stands as a barrier to their being the sort of differences between people that allow some to be in a position to control and to exploit others; such equal access to resources should also stand as a barrier to one adult person having power over other adult persons that does not rest on the revokable consent on the part of the persons over whom he comes to have power. Where, because of some remaining scarcity in a society of considerable productive abundance, we cannot reasonably distribute resources equally, we should first, where considerations of desert are not at issue, distribute according to stringency of need, second according to the strength of unmanipulated preferences and third, and finally, by lottery. We should, in trying to attain equality of condition, aim at a condition of autonomy (the fuller and the more rational the better) for everyone and at a condition where everyone alike, to the fullest extent possible, has his or her needs and wants satisfied. The limitations on the satisfaction of people's wants should be only where that satisfaction is incompatible with everyone getting the same treatment. Where we have conflicting wants, such as where two persons want to marry the same person, the fair thing to do will vary with the circumstances. In the marriage case, freedom of choice is obviously the fair thing. But generally, what should be aimed at is having everyone have their wants satisfied as far as possible. To achieve equality of condition would be, as well, to achieve a condition where the necessary burdens of the society are equally shared, where to do so is reasonable, and where each person has an equal voice in deciding what these burdens shall be. Moreover, everyone, as much as possible, should be in a position—and should be equally in that position—to control his own life. The goals of egalitarianism are to achieve such equalities.

Minimally, classlessness is something we should all aim at if we are egalitarians. It is necessary for the stable achievement of equalities of the type discussed in the previous paragraph. Beyond that, we should also aim at a statusless society, though not at an undifferentiated society or a society which does not recognize merit. . . . It is only in such a classless, statusless society that the ideals of equality (the conception of equality as a very general goal to be achieved) can be realized. In aiming for a statusless society, we are aiming for a society which, while remaining a society of material abundance, is a society in which there are to be no extensive differences in life prospects between people because some have far greater income, power, authority or prestige than others. This is the *via negativia* of the egalitarian way. The *via positiva* is to produce social conditions, where there is generally material abundance, where well-being and satisfaction are not only maximized (the utilitarian thing) but, as well, a society where this condition, as far as it is achievable, is sought equally for all (the egalitarian thing). This is the underlying conception of the egalitarian commitment to equality of condition.

II

Robert Nozick asks "How do we decide how much equality is enough?"[1] In the preceding section we gestured in the direction of an answer. I should now like to be somewhat more explicit. Too much equality, as we have been at pains to point out, would be to treat everyone identically, completely ignoring their differing needs. Various forms of "barracks equality" approximating that would also be too much. Too little equality would be to limit equality of condition, as did the old egalitarianism, to achieving equal legal and political rights, equal civil liberties, to equality of opportunity and to a redistribution of gross disparities in wealth sufficient to keep social peace, the rationale for the latter being that such gross inequalities if allowed to stand would threaten social stability. This Hobbesist stance indicates that the old egalitarianism proceeds in a very pragmatic manner. Against the old egalitarianism I would argue that we must at least aim at an equality of whole life prospects, where that is not read simply as the right to compete for scarce positions of advantage, but where there is to be brought into being the kind of equality of condition that would provide everyone equally, as far as possible, with the resources and the social conditions to satisfy their needs as fully as possible compatible with everyone else doing likewise. (Note that between people these needs will be partly the same but will still often be importantly different as well.) Ideally, as a kind of ideal limit for a society of wondrous abundance, a radical egalitarianism would go beyond that to a similar thing for wants. We should, that is, provide all people equally, as far as possible, with the resources and social conditions to satisfy their wants, as fully as possible compatible with everyone else doing likewise. (I recognize that there is a slide between wants and needs. As the wealth of a society increases and its structure changes, things that started out as wants tend to become needs, e.g., someone in the Falkland Islands might merely reasonably want an auto while someone in Los Angeles might not only want it but need it as well. But this does not collapse the distinction between wants and needs. There are things in any society people need, if they are to survive at all in anything like a commodious condition, whether they want them or not, e.g., they need food, shelter, security, companionship and the like. An egalitarian starts with basic needs, or at least with what are taken in the cultural environment in which a given person lives to be basic needs, and moves out to other needs and finally to wants as the productive power of the society increases.)

I qualified my above formulations with "as far as possible" and with "as fully as possible compatible with everyone else doing likewise." These are essential qualifications. Where, as in societies that we know, there are scarcities, even rather minimal scarcities, not everyone can have the resources or at least all the resources necessary to have their needs satisfied. Here we must first ensure that, again as far as possible, their basic needs are all satisfied and then we move on to other needs and finally to wants. But sometimes, to understate it, even in very affluent societies, everyone's needs cannot be met, or at least they cannot be equally met. In such circumstances we have to make some hard choices. I am thinking of a situation where there are not enough dialysis machines to go around so that everyone who needs one can have one. What then should we do? The thing to aim at, to try as far as possible to approximate, if only as a heuristic ideal, is the full and equal meeting of needs and wants of everyone. It is when we have that much equality that we have enough equality. But, of course, "ought implies can," and where we can't achieve it we can't achieve it. But where we reasonably can, we ought to do it. It is something that fairness requires.

The "reasonably can" is also an essential modification: we need situations of sufficient abundance so that we do not, in going for such an equality of condition, simply spread the misery around or spread very Spartan conditions around. Before we can rightly aim for the equality of condition I mentioned, we must first have the productive capacity and resource conditions to support the institutional means that would make possible the equal satisfaction of basic needs and the equal satisfaction of other needs and wants as well.

Such achievements will often not be possible; perhaps they will never be fully possible, for, no doubt, the physically handicapped will always be with us. Consider, for example, situations where our scarcities are such that we cannot, without causing considerable misery, create the institutions and mechanisms that would work to satisfy all needs, even all basic needs. Suppose we have the technology in place to develop all sorts of complicated life-sustaining machines all of which would predictably provide people with a quality of life that they, viewing the matter clearly, would rationally choose if they were simply choosing for themselves. But suppose, if we put such technologies in place, we will then not have the wherewithal to provide basic health care in outlying regions in the country or adequate educational services in such places. We should not, under those circumstances, put those technologies in place. But we should also recognize that where it becomes possible to put these technologies in place without sacrificing other more pressing needs, we should do so. The underlying egalitarian rationale is evident enough: produce the conditions for the most extensive satisfaction of needs for everyone. Where A's need and B's need are equally important (equally stringent) but cannot both be satisfied, satisfy A's need rather than B's if the satisfaction of A's need would be more fecund for the satisfaction of the needs of others than B's, or less undermining of the satisfaction of the needs of others than B's. (I do not mean to say that that is our only criterion of choice but it is the criterion most relevant for us here.) We should seek the satisfaction of the greatest compossible set of needs where the conditions for compossibility are (a) that everyone's needs be considered, (b) that everyone's needs be *equally* considered and where two sets of needs cannot both be satisfied, the more stringent set of needs shall first be satisfied. (Do not say we have no working criteria for what they are. If you need food to keep you from starvation or debilitating malnutrition and I need a vacation to relax after a spate of hard work, your need is plainly more stringent than mine. There would, of course, be all sorts of disputable cases, but there are also a host of perfectly determinate cases indicating that we have working criteria.) The underlying rationale is to seek compossible sets of needs so that we approach as far as possible as great a satisfaction of needs as possible for everyone.

This might, it could be said, produce a situation in which very few people got those things that they needed the most, or at least wanted the most. Remember Nozick with his need for the resources of Widner Library in an annex to his house. People, some might argue, with expensive tastes and extravagent needs, say a need for really good wine, would never, with a stress

on such compossibilia, get things they are really keen about.[2] Is that the kind of world we would reflectively want? Well, *if* their not getting them is the price we have to pay for everyone having their basic needs met, then it is a price we ought to pay. I am very fond of very good wines as well as fresh ripe mangos, but if the price of my having them is that people starve or suffer malnutrition in the Sahel, or indeed anywhere else, then plainly fairness, if not just plain human decency, requires that I forego them.

In talking about how much equality is enough, I have so far talked of the benefits that equality is meant to provide. But egalitarians also speak of an equal sharing of the necessary burdens of the society as well. Fairness requires a sharing of the burdens, and for a radical egalitarian this comes to an equal sharing of the burdens where people are equally capable of sharing them. Translated into the concrete this does *not* mean that a child or an old man or a pregnant woman are to be required to work in the mines or that they be required to collect garbage, but it would involve something like requiring every able bodied person, say from nineteen to twenty, to take his or her turn at a fair portion of the necessary unpleasant jobs in the world. In that way we all, where we are able to do it, would share equally in these burdens—in doing the things that none of us want to do but that we, if we are at all reasonable, recognize the necessity of having done. (There are all kinds of variations and complications concerning this—what do we do with the youthful wonder at the violin? But, that notwithstanding, the general idea is clear enough.) And, where we think this is reasonably feasible, it squares with our considered judgments about fairness.

I have given you, in effect appealing to my considered judgments but considered judgments I do not think are at all eccentric, a picture of what I would take to be enough equality, too little equality and not enough equality. But how can we know that my proportions are right? I do not think we can avoid or should indeed try to avoid an appeal to considered judgments here. But working with them there are some arguments we can appeal, to get them in wide reflective equilibrium. Suppose we go back to the formal principle of justice, namely that we must treat like cases alike. Because it does not tell us *what* are like cases, we cannot derive substantive criteria from it. But it may, indirectly, be of some help here. We all, if we are not utterly zany, want a life in which our needs are satisfied and in which we can live as we wish and do what we want to do. Though we differ in many ways, in our abilities, capacities for pleasure, determination to keep on with a job, we do not differ about wanting our needs satisfied or being able to live as we wish. Thus, *ceteris paribus,* where questions of desert, entitlement and the like do not enter, it is only fair that all of us should have our needs equally considered and that we should, again *ceteris paribus,* all be able to do as we wish in a way that is compatible with others doing likewise. From the formal principle of justice and a few key facts about us, we can get to the claim that *ceteris paribus* we should go for this much equality. But this is the core content of a radical egalitarianism.

However, how do we know that *ceteris is paribus* here? What about our entitlements and deserts? Suppose I have built my house with my own hands, from materials I have purchased and on land that I have purchased and that I have lived in it for years and have carefully cared for it. The house is mine and I am entitled to keep it even if by dividing the house into two apartments greater and more equal satisfaction of need would obtain for everyone. Justice requires that such an entitlement be respected here. (Again, there is an implicit *ceteris paribus* clause. In extreme situations, say after a war with housing in extremely short supply, that entitlement could be rightly overridden.)

There is a response on the egalitarian's part similar to a response utilitarianism made to criticisms of a similar logical type made of utilitarians by pluralistic deontologists. One of the things that people in fact need, or at least reflectively firmly want, is to have such entitlements respected. Where they are routinely overridden to satisfy other needs or wants, we would *not* in fact have a society in which the needs of everyone are being maximally met. To the reply, but what if more needs for everyone were met by ignoring or overriding such entitlements, the radical egalitarian should respond

that that is, given the way we are, a thoroughly hypothetical situation and that theories of morality cannot be expected to give guidance for all logically possible worlds but only for worlds which are reasonably like what our actual world is or plausibly could come to be. Setting this argument aside for the moment, even if it did turn out that the need satisfaction linked with having other things—things that involved the overriding of those entitlements—was sufficient to make it the case that more need satisfaction all around for *everyone* would be achieved by overriding those entitlements, then, for reasonable people who clearly saw that, these entitlements would not have the weight presently given to them. They either would not have the importance presently attached to them or the need for the additional living space would be so great that their being overridden would seem, everything considered, the lesser of two evils (as in the example of the postwar housing situation).

There are without doubt genuine entitlements and a theory of justice must take them seriously, but they are not absolute. If the need is great enough we can see the merit in overriding them, just as in law as well as morality the right of eminent domain is recognized. Finally, while I have talked of entitlements here, parallel arguments will go through for desert.

III

I want now to relate this articulation of . . . equality . . . to my radically egalitarian principles of justice. My articulation of justice is a certain spelling out of the slogan proclaimed by Marx "From each according to his ability, to each according to his needs." The egalitarian conception of society argues for the desirability of bringing into existence a world, once the springs of social wealth flow freely, in which everyone's needs are as fully satisfied as possible and in which everyone gives according to his ability. Which means, among other things, that everyone, according to his ability, shares the burdens of society. There is an equal giving and equal responsibility here according to ability. It is here, with respect to giving according to ability and with respect to receiving according to need, that a complex equality of result, i.e., equality of condition, is being advocated by the radical egalitarian. What it comes to is this: each of us, where each is to count for one and none to count for more than one, is to give according to ability and receive according to need.

My radical egalitarian principles of justice read as follows:

1. Each person is to have an equal right to the most extensive total system of equal basic liberties and opportunities (including equal opportunities for meaningful work, for self-determination and political and economic participation) compatible with a similar treatment of all. (This principle gives expression to a commitment to attain and/or sustain equal moral autonomy and equal self-respect.)

2. After provisions are made for common social (community) values, for capital overhead to preserve the society's productive capacity, allowances made for differing unmanipulated needs and preferences, and due weight is given to the just entitlements of individuals, the income and wealth (the common stock of means) is to be so divided that each person will have a right to an equal share. The necessary burdens requisite to enhance human well-being are also to be equally shared, subject, of course, to limitations by differing abilities and differing situations. (Here I refer to different natural environments and the like and not to class position and the like.)

Here we are talking about equality as a right rather than about equality as a goal as has previously been the subject matter of equality in this chapter. These principles of egalitarianism spell out rights people have and duties they have under *conditions of very considerable productive abundance*. We have a right to certain basic liberties and opportunities and we have, subject to certain limitations spelled out in the second principle, a right to an equal share of the income and wealth in the world. We also have a duty, again subject to the qualifications mentioned in the principle, to do our equal share in shouldering the burdens necessary to protect us from ills and to enhance our well-being.

What is the relation between these rights and the ideal of equality of condition discussed earlier? That is a goal for which we can struggle now to bring about conditions which will some day make its achievement possible, while these rights only become rights when the goal is actually achievable. We have no such rights in slave, feudal or capitalist societies or such duties in those societies. In that important way they are not natural rights for they depend on certain social conditions and certain social structures (socialist ones) to be realizable. What we can say is that it is always desirable that socio-economic conditions come into being which would make it possible to achieve the goal of equality of condition so that these rights and duties I speak of could obtain. But that is a far cry from saying we have such rights and duties now.

It is a corollary of this, if these radical egalitarian principles of justice are correct, that capitalist societies (even capitalist welfare state societies such as Sweden) and statist societies such as the Soviet Union or the People's Republic of China cannot be just societies or at least they must be societies, structured as they are, which are defective in justice. (This is not to say that some of these societies are not juster than others. Sweden is juster than South Africa, Canada than the United States and Cuba and Nicaragua than Honduras and Guatemala.) But none of these statist or capitalist societies can satisfy these radical egalitarian principles of justice, for equal liberty, equal opportunity, equal wealth or equal sharing of burdens are not at all possible in societies having their social structure. So we do not have such rights now but we can take it as a goal that we bring such a society into being with a commitment to an equality of condition in which we would have these rights and duties. Here we require first the massive development of productive power.

The connection between equality as a goal and equality as a right spelled out in these principles of justice is this. The equality of condition appealed to in equality as a goal would, if it were actually to obtain, have to contain the rights and duties enunciated in those principles.

There could be no equal life prospects between all people or anything approximating an equal satisfaction of needs if there were not in place something like the system of equal basic liberties referred to in the first principle. Furthermore, without the rough equality of wealth referred to in the second principle, there would be disparities in power and self-direction in society which would render impossible an equality of life prospects or the social conditions required for an equal satisfaction of needs. And plainly, without a roughly equal sharing of burdens, there cannot be a situation where everyone has equal life prospects or has the chance equally to satisfy his needs. The principles of radical egalitarian justice are implicated in its conception of an ideally adequate equality of condition.

IV

The principles of radical egalitarian justice I have articulated are meant to apply globally and not just to particular societies. But it is certainly fair to say that not a few would worry that such principles of radical egalitarian justice, if applied globally, would force the people in wealthier sections of the world to a kind of financial hari-kari. There are millions of desperately impoverished people. Indeed millions are starving or malnourished and things are not getting any better. People in the affluent societies cannot but worry about whether they face a bottomless pit. Many believe that meeting, even in the most minimal way, the needs of the impoverished is going to put an incredible burden on people—people of all classes—in the affluent societies. Indeed it will, if acted on non-evasively, bring about their impoverishment, and this is just too much to ask. Radical egalitarianism is forgetting Rawls' admonitions about "the strains of commitment"—the recognition that in any rational account of what is required of us, we must at least give a minimal healthy self-interest its due. We must construct our moral philosophy for human beings and not for saints. Human nature is less fixed than conservatives are wont to assume, but it is not so elastic that we can reasonably expect people to impoverish themselves

to make the massive transfers between North and South—the industrialized world and the Third World—required to begin to approach a situation where even Rawls' principles would be in place on a global level, to say nothing of my radical egalitarian principles of justice.[3]

The first thing to say in response to this is that my radical egalitarian principles are meant actually to guide practice, to directly determine what we are to do, only in a world of extensive abundance where, as Marx put it, the springs of social wealth flow freely. If such a world cannot be attained with the undermining of capitalism and the full putting into place, stabilizing, and developing of socialist relations of production, then such radical egalitarian principles can only remain as heuristic ideals against which to measure the distance of our travel in the direction of what would be a perfectly just society.

Aside from a small capitalist class, along with those elites most directly and profitably beholden to it (together a group constituting not more than 5 percent of the world's population), there would, in taking my radical egalitarian principles as heuristic guides, be no impoverishment of people in the affluent societies, if we moved in a radically more egalitarian way to start to achieve a global fairness. There would be massive transfers of wealth between North and South, but this could be done in stages so that, for the people in the affluent societies (capitalist elites apart), there need be no undermining of the quality of their lives. Even what were once capitalist elites would not be impoverished or reduced to some kind of bleak life though they would, the incidental Spartan types aside, find their life styles altered. But their health and general well-being, including their opportunities to do significant and innovative work, would, if anything, be enhanced. And while some of the sources of their enjoyment would be a thing of the past, there would still be a considerable range of enjoyments available to them sufficient to afford anyone a rich life that could be lived with verve and zest.

A fraction of what the United States spends on defense spending would take care of immediate problems of starvation and malnutrition for most of the world. For longer range problems such as bringing conditions of life in the Third World more in line with conditions of life in Sweden and Switzerland, what is necessary is the dismantling of the capitalist system and the creation of a socio-economic system with an underlying rationale directing it toward producing for needs—everyone's needs. With this altered productive mode, the irrationalities and waste of capitalist production would be cut. There would be no more built-in obsolescence, no more merely cosmetic changes in consumer durables, no more fashion roulette, no more useless products and the like. Moreover, the enormous expenditures that go into the war industry would be a thing of the past. There would be great transfers from North to South, but it would be from the North's capitalist fat and not from things people in the North really need. (There would, in other words, be no self-pauperization of people in the capitalist world.) . . .

V

It has been repeatedly argued that equality undermines liberty. Some would say that a society in which principles like my radical egalitarian principles were adopted, or even the liberal egalitarian principles of Rawls or Dworkin were adopted, would not be a free society. My arguments have been just the reverse. I have argued that it is only in an egalitarian society that full and extensive liberty is possible.

Perhaps the egalitarian and the anti-egalitarian are arguing at cross purposes? What we need to recognize, it has been argued, is that we have two kinds of rights both of which are important to freedom but to rather different freedoms and which are freedoms which not infrequently conflict.[4] We have rights to *fair terms of cooperation* but we also have rights to *non-interference*. If a right of either kind is overridden our freedom is diminished. The reason why it might be thought that the egalitarian and the anti-egalitarian may be arguing at cross purposes is that the egalitarian is pointing to the fact that rights to fair terms of cooperation and their associated liberties require equality while the anti-egalitarian is pointing to the fact that rights to non-interference and their associated liberties conflict with equality. They focus on different liberties.

What I have said above may not be crystal clear, so let me explain. People have a right to fair terms of cooperation. In political terms this comes to the equal right of all to effective participation in government and, in more broadly social terms, for a society of economic wealth, it means people having a right to a roughly equal distribution of the benefits and burdens of the basic social arrangements that affect their lives and for them to stand in such relations to each other such that no one has the power to dominate the life of another. By contrast, rights to non-interference come to the equal right of all to be left alone by the government and more broadly to live in a society in which people have a right peacefully to pursue their interests without interference.

The conflict between equality and liberty comes down to, very essentially, the conflicts we get in modern societies between rights to fair terms of cooperation and rights to noninterference. As Joseph Schumpeter saw and J. S. Mill before him, one could have a thoroughly democratic society (at least in conventional terms) in which rights to non-interference might still be extensively violated. A central anti-egalitarian claim is that we cannot have an egalitarian society in which the very precious liberties that go with the rights to non-interference would not be violated.

Socialism and egalitarianism plainly protect rights to fair terms of cooperation. Without the social (collective) ownership and control of the means of production, involving with this, in the initial stages of socialism at least, a workers' state, economic power will be concentrated in the hands of a few who will in turn, as a result, dominate effective participation in government. Some right-wing libertarians blind themselves to that reality, but it is about as evident as can be. Only an utter turning away from the facts of social life could lead to any doubts about this at all. But then this means that in a workers' state, if some people have capitalistic impulses, that they would have their rights peacefully to pursue their own interests interfered with. They might wish to invest, retain and bequeath in economic domains. In a workers' state these capitalist acts in many circumstances would have to be forbidden, but that would be a violation of an individual's right to non-interference and the fact, if it was a fact, that we by democratic vote, even with vast majorities, had made such capitalist acts illegal would still not make any difference because individuals' rights to non-interference would still be violated.

We are indeed driven, by egalitarian impulses, of a perfectly understandable sort, to accept interference with laissez-faire capitalism to protect non-subordination and non-domination of people by protecting the egalitarian right to fair terms of cooperation and the enhanced liberty that that brings. Still, as things stand, this leads inevitably to violations of the right to non-interference and this brings with it a diminution of liberty. There will be people with capitalist impulses and they will be interfered with. It is no good denying, it will be said, that egalitarianism and particularly socialism will lead to interference with very precious individual liberties, namely with our right peacefully to pursue our interests without interference.[5]

The proper response to this, as should be apparent from what I have argued throughout, is that to live in any society at all, capitalist, socialist or whatever, is to live in a world in which there will be some restriction or other on our rights peacefully to pursue our interests without interference. I can't lecture in Albanian or even in French in a standard philosophy class at the University of Calgary, I can't jog naked on most beaches, borrow a book from your library without your permission, fish in your trout pond without your permission, take your dog for a walk without your say so and the like. At least some of these things have been thought to be things which I might peacefully pursue in my own interests. Stopping me from doing them is plainly interfering with my peaceful pursuit of my own interests. And indeed it is an infringement on liberty, an interference with my doing what I may want to do.

However, for at least many of these activities, and particularly the ones having to do with property, even right-wing libertarians think that such interference is perfectly justified. But, justified or not, they still plainly constitute a restriction on our individual freedom. However, what we must also recognize is that there will always be some such restrictions on freedom in any society whatsoever, just in virtue of the fact that a normless society, without the restrictions that having norms imply, is a contradiction in terms.[6] Many restrictions are hardly felt as restrictions, as in the attitudes of many people toward seat-belt legislation, but they are, all the same, plainly restrictions on our liberty. It is just that they are thought to be unproblematically justified.

To the question would a socialism with a radical egalitarianism restrict some liberties, including some liberties rooted in rights to non-interference, the answer is that it indeed would; but so would laissez-faire capitalism, aristocratic conceptions of justice, liberal conceptions or any social formations at all, with their associated conceptions of justice. The relevant question is which of these restrictions are justified.

The restrictions on liberty proffered by radical egalitarianism and socialism, I have argued, are justified for they, of the various alternatives, give us both the most extensive and the most abundant system of liberty possible in modern conditions with their thorough protection of the right to fair terms of cooperation. Radical egalitarianism will also, and this is central for us, protect our civil liberties and these liberties are, of course, our most basic liberties. These are the liberties which are the most vital for us to protect. What it will not do is to protect our unrestricted liberties to invest, retain and bequeath in the economic realm and it will not protect our unrestricted freedom to buy and sell. There is, however, no good reason to think that these restrictions are restrictions of anything like a basic liberty. Moreover, we are justified in restricting our freedom to buy and sell if such restrictions strengthen, rather than weaken, our total system of liberty. This is in this way justified, for only by such market restrictions can the rights of the vast majority of people to effective participation in government and an equal role in the control of their social lives be protected. I say this because if we let the market run free in this way, power will pass into the hands of a few who will control the lives of the many and determine the fundamental design of the society. The actual liberties that are curtailed in a radically egalitarian social order are inessential liberties whose restriction in contemporary circumstances enhances human well-being and indeed makes for a firmer entrenchment of basic liberties and for their greater extension globally. That is to say, we here restrict some liberty in order to attain more liberty and a more equally distributed pattern of liberty. More people will be able to do what they want and have a greater control over their own lives than in a capitalist world order with its at least implicit inegalitarian commitments.

However, some might say I still have not faced the most central objection to radical egalitarianism, namely its **statism.** (I would prefer to say its putative statism.) The picture is this. The egalitarian state must be in the redistribution business. It has to make, or make sure there is made, an equal relative contribution to the welfare of every citizen. But this in effect means that the socialist state or, for that matter, the welfare state, will be deeply interventionist in our personal lives. It will be in the business, as one right-winger emotively put it, of cutting one person down to size in order to bring about that person's equality with another person who was in a previously disadvantageous position.[7] That is said to be morally objectionable and it would indeed be deeply morally objectionable in many circumstances. But it isn't in the circumstances in which the radical egalitarian presses for redistribution. (I am not speaking of what might be mere equalizing upwards.) The circumstances are these: Capitalist A gets his productive property confiscated so that he could no longer dominate and control the lives of proletarians B, C, D, E, F, and G. But what is wrong with it where this "cutting down to size"—in reality the confiscation of productive property or the taxation of the capitalist—involves no violation of A's civil liberties or the harming of his actual well-being (health, ability to work, to cultivate the arts, to have fruitful personal relations, to live in comfort and the like) and where B, C, D, E, F, and G will have their freedom and their well-being thoroughly enhanced if such confiscation or taxation occurs? Far from being morally objectionable, it is precisely the sort of state of affairs that people ought to favor. It certainly protects more liberties and more significant liberties than it undermines.

There is another familiar anti-egalitarian argument designed to establish the liberty-undermining qualities of egalitarianism. It is an argument we have touched upon in discussing meritocracy. It turns on the fact that in any society there will be both talents and handicaps. Where they exist, what do we want to do about maintaining equal distribution? Egalitarians, radical or otherwise, certainly do not want to penalize people for talent. That being so, then surely people should be allowed to retain the benefits of superior talent. But this in some circumstances will lead to significant inequalities in resources and in the meeting of needs. To sustain equality there will have to be an ongoing redistribution in the direction of the less talented and less fortunate. But this redistribution from the more to the less talented does plainly penalize the talented for their talent. That, it will be said, is something which is both unfair and an undermining of liberty.

The following, it has been argued, makes the above evident enough.[8] If people have talents they will tend to want to use them. And if they use them they are very likely to come out ahead. Must not egalitarians say they ought not to be able to come out ahead no matter how well they use their talents and no matter how considerable these talents are? But that is intolerably restrictive and unfair.

The answer to the above anti-egalitarian argument is implicit in a number of things I have already said. But here let me confront this familiar argument directly. Part of the answer comes out in probing some of the ambiguities of "coming out ahead." Note, incidentally, that (1) not all reflective, morally sensitive people will be so concerned with that, and (2) that being very concerned with that is a mentality that capitalism inculcates. Be that as it may, to turn to the ambiguities, note that some take "coming out ahead" principally to mean "being paid well for the use of those talents" where "being paid well" is being paid sufficiently well so that it creates inequalities sufficient to disturb the preferred egalitarian patterns. (Without that, being paid well would give one no relative advantage.) But, as we have seen, "coming out ahead" need not take that form at all. Talents can be recognized and acknowledged in many ways. First, in just the respect and admiration of a fine employment of talents that would naturally come from people seeing them so displayed where these people were not twisted by envy; second, by having, because of these talents, interesting and secure work that their talents fit them for and they merit in virtue of those talents. Moreover, having more money is not going to matter much—for familiar marginal utility reasons—where what in capitalist societies would be called the welfare floors are already very high, this being made feasible by the great productive wealth of the society. Recall that in such a society of abundance everyone will be well off and secure. In such a society people are not going to be very concerned about being a little better off than someone else. The talented are in no way, in such a situation, robbed to help the untalented and handicapped or penalized for their talents. They are only prevented from amassing wealth (most particularly productive wealth), which would enable them to dominate the untalented and the handicapped and to control the social life of the world of which they are both a part. . . .

I think that the moral authority for abstract egalitarianism, for the belief that the interests of everyone matter and matter equally, comes from its being the case that it is *required by the moral point of view*.[9] What I am predicting is that a person who has a good understanding of what morality is, has a good knowledge of the facts, is not ideologically mystified, takes an impartial point of view, and has an attitude of impartial caring, would, if not conceptually confused, come to accept the abstract egalitarian thesis. I see no way of arguing someone into such an egalitarianism who does not in this general way have a love of humankind.[10] A hard-hearted Hobbesist is not reachable here. But given that a person has that love of humankind—that impartial and impersonal caring—together with the other qualities mentioned above, then, I predict, that that person would be an egalitarian at least to the extent of accepting the abstract egalitarian thesis. What I am claiming is that if these conditions were to obtain (if they ceased to be just counterfactuals), then there would be a consensus among moral agents about accepting the abstract egalitarian thesis. . . .

Endnotes

1. See the debate between Robert Nozick, Daniel Bell and James Tobin, "If Inequality Is Inevitable What Can Be Done About It?" *The New York Times,* January 3, 1982, p. E5. The exchange between Bell and Nozick reveals the differences between the old egalitarianism and right-wing libertarianism. It is not only that the right and left clash but sometimes right clashes with right.
2. Amartya Sen, "Equality of What?" *The Tanner Lectures on Human Values,* vol. 1 (1980), ed. Sterling M. McMurrin (Cambridge, England: Cambridge University Press, 1980), pp. 198–220.
3. Henry Shue, "The Burdens of Justice," *The Journal of Philosophy* 80, no. 10 (October 1983): 600–601; 606–608.
4. Richard W. Miller, "Marx and Morality," in *Marxism,* eds. J. R. Pennock and J. W. Chapman. Nomos 26 (New York: New York University Press, 1983), pp. 9–11.
5. Ibid., p. 10.
6. This has been argued from both the liberal center and the left. Ralf Dahrendorf, *Essays in the Theory of Society* (Stanford, Cal.: Stanford University Press, 1968), pp. 151–178; and G. A. Cohen, "Capitalism, Freedom and the Proletariat" in *The Idea of Freedom: Essays in Honour of Isaiah Berlin,* ed. Alan Ryan (Oxford: Oxford University Press, 1979).
7. The graphic language should be duly noted. Jan Narveson, "On Dworkinian Equality," *Social Philosophy and Policy* 1, no. 1 (autumn 1983): 4.
8. Ibid., p. 1–24.
9. Some will argue that there is no such thing as a moral point of view. My differences with him about the question of whether the amoralist can be argued into morality not withstanding, I think Kurt Baier, in a series of articles written subsequent to his *The Moral Point of View,* has clearly shown that there is something reasonably determinate that can, without ethnocentrism, be called "the moral point of view."
10. Richard Norman has impressively argued that this is an essential background assumption of the moral point of view. Richard Norman, "Critical Notice of Rodger Beehler's *Moral Life,*" *Canadian Journal of Philosophy* 11, no. 1 (March 1981): 157–183.

REVIEW QUESTIONS

1. What sort of equality does Nielsen want for everyone?
2. According to Nielsen, what are basic needs, as distinguished from wants?
3. Nielsen says that fairness requires sharing of burdens. What does this mean?
4. What are Nielsen's radical egalitarian principles of justice?
5. How does Nielsen respond to the objection that equality undermines liberty?

6. What answer does Nielsen give to the objections that Radical Egalitarianism requires statism (centralized government control of the economy) and that it fails to reward merit and superior talent?

DISCUSSION QUESTIONS

1. Would Radical Egalitarianism put an intolerable burden on the rich people in affluent societies?

2. Nielsen suggests that every able-bodied person be required to take a turn at the necessary and unpleasant jobs. Is this a good idea?
3. Nielsen claims that a capitalist society such as the United States cannot be a just society. Is this true?
4. How would Hospers respond to Nielsen? Which view is better, Hosper's or Nielsen's?

Trudy Govier

The Right to Eat and the Duty to Work

Trudy Govier has taught philosophy at Trent University in Ontario. She is the author of God, the Devil, and the Perfect Pizza *(1989) and* A Practical Study of Argument *(1991).*

Govier discusses three different positions on the welfare question: Do needy people in an affluent society have a legal right to welfare benefits? First, there is the individualist position (called Libertarianism by Hospers) that no one has a legal right to welfare benefits, not even in an affluent society. Second, there is the permissive position that in an affluent society, everyone has an unconditional legal right to welfare benefits. Third, there is the puritan position that everyone has a legal right to welfare, but this right ought to be conditional on one's willingness to work. After evaluating these three positions in terms of their social consequences (the "teleological appraisal") and social justice, Govier concludes that the permissive position is superior.

Although the topic of welfare is not one with which philosophers have often concerned them-

selves, it is a topic which gives rise to many complex and fascinating questions—some in the area of political philosophy, some in the area of ethics, and some of a more practical kind. The variety of issues related to the subject of welfare makes it particularly necessary to be clear just which issue one is examining in a discussion of welfare. In a recent book on the subject, Nicholas Rescher asks:

In what respects and to what extent is society, working through the instrumentality of the state, responsible for the welfare of its members? What demands for the promotion of his welfare can an individual reasonably make upon his society? These are questions to which no answer can be given in terms of some *a priori* approach with reference to universal ultimates. Whatever answer can appropriately be given will depend, in the final analysis, on what the society decides it should be.[1]

Rescher raises this question only to avoid it. His response to his own question is that a society has all and only those responsibilities for its members that it thinks it has. Although this claim is trivially true as regards legal responsibilities, it is inadequate from a moral perspective. If one imagines the case of an affluent society which leaves the blind, the disabled, and the needy to die of starvation, the incompleteness of Rescher's account becomes obvious. In this imagined case one is naturally led to raise the question as to whether those in power ought to supply those in need with the necessities of life. Though the needy have no legal right to

From Trudy Govier, "The Right to Eat and the Duty to Work," *Philosophy of the Social Sciences*, vol. 5 (1975), pp. 125–143. Reprinted with permission of the author and *Philosophy of the Social Sciences*.

welfare benefits of any kind, one might very well say that they ought to have such a right. It is this claim which I propose to discuss here.[2]

I shall approach this issue by examining three positions which may be adopted in response to it. These are:

1. *The Individualist Position:* Even in an affluent society, one ought not to have any legal right to state-supplied welfare benefits.
2. *The Permissive Position:* In a society with sufficient resources, one ought to have an unconditional legal right to receive state-supplied welfare benefits. (That is, one's right to receive such benefits ought not to depend on one's behavior, it should be guaranteed.)
3. *The Puritan Position:* In a society with sufficient resources one ought to have a legal right to state-supplied welfare benefits; this right ought to be conditional, however, on one's willingness to work.

But before we examine these positions, some preliminary clarification must be attempted. . . .

Welfare systems are state-supported systems which supply benefits, usually in the form of cash income, to those who are in need. Welfare systems thus exist in the sort of social context where there is some private ownership of property. If no one owned anything individually (except possibly his own body), and all goods were considered to be the joint property of everyone, then this type of welfare system could not exist. A state might take on the responsibility for the welfare of its citizens, but it could not meet this responsibility by distributing a level of cash income which such citizens would spend to purchase the goods essential for life. The welfare systems which exist in the western world do exist against the background of extensive private ownership of property. It is in this context that I propose to discuss moral questions about having a right to welfare benefits. By setting out my questions in this way, I do not intend to endorse the institution of private property, but only to discuss questions which many people find real and difficult in the context of the social organization which they actually do experience. The present analysis of welfare is intended to apply to societies which (a) have the institution

of private property, if not for means of production, at least for some basic good; and (b) possess sufficient resources so that it is at least possible for every member of the society to be supplied with the necessities of life.

THE INDIVIDUALIST VIEW

It might be maintained that a person in need has no legitimate moral claim on those around him and that the hypothetical inattentive society which left its blind citizens to beg or starve cannot rightly be censured for doing so. This view, which is dramatically at odds with most of contemporary social thinking, lives on in the writings of Ayn Rand and her followers.[3] The Individualist sets a high value on uncoerced personal choice. He sees each person as a responsible agent who is able to make his own decisions and to plan his own life. He insists that with the freedom to make decisions goes responsibility for the consequences of those decisions. A person has every right, for example, to spend ten years of his life studying Sanskrit— but, if as a result of this choice, he is unemployable, he ought not to expect others to labour on his behalf. No one has a proper claim on the labour of another, or on the income ensuing from that labour, unless he can repay the labourer in a way acceptable to that labourer himself. Government welfare schemes provide benefits from funds gained largely by taxing earned income. One cannot "opt out" of such schemes. To the Individualist, this means that a person is forced to work part of his time for others.

Suppose that a man works forty hours and earns two hundred dollars. Under modern-day taxation, it may well be that he can spend only two-thirds of that money the way he chooses. The rest is taken by government and goes to support programmes which the working individual may not himself endorse. The beneficiaries of such programmes—those beneficiaries who do not work themselves—are as though they have slaves working for them. Backed by the force which government authorities can command, they are able to exist on the earnings of others. Those who support them do not do so voluntarily, out of charity; they do so on government command.

Someone across the street is unemployed. Should you be taxed extra to pay for his expenses? Not at all. You have not injured him, you are not responsible for the fact that he is unemployed (unless you are a senator or bureaucrat who agitated for further curtailing of business which legislation passed, with the result that your neighbor was laid off by the curtailed business). You may voluntarily wish to help him out, or better still, try to get him a job to put him on his feet again; but since you have initiated no aggressive act against him, and neither purposefully nor accidentally injured him in any way, you should not be legally penalized for the fact of his unemployment.[4]

The Individualist need not lack concern for those in need. He may give generously to charity; he might give more generously still, if his whole income were his to use, as he would like it to be. He may also believe, that, as a matter of empirical fact, existing government programmes do not actually help the poor. They support a cumbersome bureaucracy and they use financial resources which, if untaxed, might be used by those with initiative to pursue job-creating endeavors. The thrust of the Individualist's position is that each person owns his own body and his own labour; thus each person is taken to have a virtually unconditional right to the income which that labour can earn him in a free market place.[5] For anyone to pre-empt part of a worker's earnings without the worker's voluntary consent is tantamount to robbery. And the fact that the government is the intermediary through which this deed is committed does not change its moral status one iota.

On an Individualist's view, those in need should be cared for by charities or through other schemes to which contributions are voluntary. Many people may wish to insure themselves against unforeseen calamities and they should be free to do so. But there is no justification for non-optional government schemes financed by taxpayers' money. . . .

THE PERMISSIVE VIEW

Directly contrary to the Individualist view of welfare is what I have termed the Permissive view. According to this view, in a society which has sufficient resources so that everyone could be supplied with the necessities of life, every individual ought to be given the legal right to social security, and this right ought not to be conditional in any way upon an individual's behavior. *Ex hypothesi* the society which we are discussing has sufficient goods to provide everyone with food, clothing, shelter and other necessities. Someone who does without these basic goods is scarcely living at all, and a society which takes no steps to change this state of affairs implies by its inaction that the life of such a person is without value. It does not execute him; but it may allow him to die. It does not put him in prison; but it may leave him with a life of lower quality than that of some prison inmates. A society which can rectify these circumstances and does not can justly be accused of imposing upon the needy either death or lifelong deprivation. And those characteristics which make a person needy—whether they be illness, old age, insanity, feeblemindedness, inability to find paid work, or even poor moral character—are insufficient to make him deserve the fate to which an inactive society would in effect condemn him. One would not be executed for inability or failure to find paid work; neither should one be allowed to die for this misfortune or failing.

A person who cannot or does not find his own means of social security does not therefore forfeit his status as a human being. If other human beings, with physical, mental and moral qualities different from his, are regarded as having the right to life and to the means of life, then so too should he be regarded. A society which does not accept the responsibility for supplying such a person with the basic necessities of life is, in effect, endorsing a difference between its members which is without moral justification. . . .

The adoption of a Permissive view of welfare would have significant practical implications. If there were a legal right, unconditional upon behaviour, to a specified level of state-supplied benefits, then state investigation of the prospective welfare recipient could be kept to a minimum. Why he is in need, whether he can work, whether he is willing to work, and what he does while receiving welfare benefits are on this view quite irrelevant to his right to receive those benefits. A welfare recipient is a person who claims from his society that to which he is legally entitled under a morally based welfare scheme. The fact that he makes this claim licenses no special state or societal interference with his behaviour. If the Permissive view of welfare were widely believed, then there would be no social stigma attached to being on welfare. There is such a stigma, and many long-term welfare recipients are considerably demoralized by their dependent status.[6] These facts suggest that the Permissive view of welfare is not widely held in our society.

THE PURITAN VIEW

This view of welfare rather naturally emerges when we consider that no one can have a right to something without someone else's, or some group of other persons', having responsibilities correlative to this right. In the case in which the right in question is a legal right to social security, the correlative responsibilities may be rather extensive. They have been deemed responsibilities of "the state." The state will require resources and funds to meet these responsibilities, and these do not emerge from the sky miraculously, or zip into existence as a consequence of virtually effortless acts of will. They are taken by the state from its citizens, often in the form of taxation on earned income. The funds given to the welfare recipient and many of the goods which he purchases with these funds are produced by other members of society, many of whom give a considerable portion of their time and their energy to this end. If a state has the moral responsibility to ensure the social security of its citizens then all the citizens of that state have the responsibility to provide state agencies with the means to carry out their duties. This responsibility, in our present contingent circumstances, seems to generate an obligation to *work*.

A person who works helps to produce the goods which all use in daily living and, when paid, contributes through taxation to government endeavours. The person who does not work, even though able to work, does not make his contribution to social efforts towards obtaining the means of life. He is not entitled to a share of the goods produced by others if he chooses not to take part in their labours. Unless he can show that there is a moral justification for his not making the sacrifice of time and energy which others make, he has no legitimate claim to welfare benefits. If he is disabled or unable to obtain work, he cannot work; hence he has no need to justify his failure to work. But if he does choose not to work, he would have to justify his choice by saying "others should sacrifice their time and energy for me; I have no need to sacrifice time and energy for them." This principle, a version of what Rawls refers to as a **free-rider's principle**, simply will not stand up to criticism.[7] To deliberately avoid working and benefit from the labours of others is morally indefensible.

Within a welfare system erected on these principles, the right to welfare is conditional upon one's satisfactorily accounting for his failure to obtain the necessities of life by his own efforts. Someone who is severely disabled mentally or physically, or who for some other reason cannot work, is morally entitled to receive welfare benefits. Someone who chooses not to work is not. The Puritan view of welfare is a kind of compromise between the Individualist view and the Permissive view. . . .

The Puritan view of welfare, based as it is on the inter-relation between welfare and work, provides a rationale for two connected principles which those establishing welfare schemes in Canada and in the United States seem to endorse. First of all, those on welfare should never receive a higher income than the working poor. Secondly, a welfare scheme should, in some way or other, incorporate incentives to work. These principles, which presuppose that it is better to work than not to work, emerge rather naturally from the contingency which is at the basis of the Puritan view: the goods essential for social security are products of the labour of some members of society. If we wish to have a continued supply of such goods, we must encourage those who work to produce them. . . .

APPRAISAL OF POLICIES: SOCIAL CONSEQUENCES AND SOCIAL JUSTICE

In approaching the appraisal of prospective welfare policies under these two aspects I am, of course, making some assumptions about the moral appraisal of suggested social policies. Although these cannot possibly be justified here, it may be helpful to articulate them, at least in a rough way.

Appraisal of social policies is in part teleological. To the extent that a policy, P, increases the total human welfare more than does an alternate policy, P', P is a better social policy than P'. Or, if P leaves the total human welfare as it is, while P' diminishes it, then to that extent, P is a better social policy than P'. Even this skeletal formulation of the teleological aspect of appraisal reveals why appraisal cannot be entirely teleological. We consider total consequences—effects upon the total of "human well-being in a society." But this total is a summation of consequences on different individuals. It includes no judgements as to how far we allow one individual's well-being to decrease while another's increases, under the same policy. Judgements relating to the latter problems are judgements about social justice.

In appraising social policies we have to weigh up considerations of total well-being against considerations of justice. Just how this is to be done, precisely, I would not pretend to know. However, the absence of precise methods does not mean that we should relinquish attempts at appraisal: some problems are already with us, and thought which is necessarily tentative and imprecise is still preferable to no thought at all.

CONSEQUENCES OF WELFARE SCHEMES

First, let us consider the consequences of the non-scheme advocated by the Individualist. He would have to abolish all non-optional government programmes which have as their goal the improvement of anyone's personal welfare. This rejection extends to health schemes, pension plans and education, as well as to welfare and unemployment insurance. So following the Individualist would lead to very sweeping changes.

The Individualist will claim (as do Hospers and Ayn Rand) that on the whole his non-scheme will bring beneficial consequences. He will admit, as he must, that there are people who would suffer tremendously if welfare and other social security

programmes were simply terminated. Some would even die as a result. We cannot assume that spontaneously developing charities would cover every case of dire need. Nevertheless the Individualist wants to point to benefits which would accrue to businessmen and to working people and their families if taxation were drastically cut. It is his claim that consumption would rise, hence production would rise, job opportunities would be extended, and there would be an economic boom, if people could only spend all their earned income as they wished. This boom would benefit both rich and poor.

There are significant omissions which are necessary in order to render the Individualist's optimism plausible. Either workers and businessmen would have insurance of various kinds, or they would be insecure in their prosperity. If they did have insurance to cover health problems, old age and possible job loss, then they would pay for it; hence they would not be spending their whole earned income on consumer goods. Those who run the insurance schemes could, of course, put this money back into the economy—but government schemes already do this. The economic boom under Individualism would not be as loud as originally expected. Furthermore the goal of increased consumption–increased productivity must be questioned from an ecological viewpoint: many necessary materials are available only in limited quantities.

Finally, a word about charity. It is not to be expected that those who are at the mercy of charities will benefit from this state, either materially or psychologically. Those who prosper will be able to choose between giving a great deal to charity and suffering from the very real insecurity and guilt which would accompany the existence of starvation and grim poverty outside their padlocked doors. It is to be hoped that they would opt for the first alternative. But, if they did, this might be every bit as expensive for them as government-supported benefit schemes are now. If they did not give generously to charity, violence might result. However one looks at it, the consequences of Individualism are unlikely to be good.

Welfare schemes operating in Canada today are almost without exception based upon the principles of the Puritan view. To see the consequences of that type of welfare scheme we have only to look at the results of our own welfare programmes. Taxation to support such schemes is high, though not so intolerably so as to have led to widescale resentment among taxpayers. Canadian welfare programmes are attended by complicated and often cumbersome bureaucracy, some of which results for the interlocking of municipal, provincial and federal governments in the administration and financing of welfare programmes. The cost of the programmes is no doubt increased by this bureaucracy; not all the tax money directed to welfare programmes goes to those in need. Puritan welfare schemes do not result in social catastrophe or in significant business stagnation—this much we know, because we already live with such schemes. Their adverse consequences, if any, are felt primarily not by society generally nor by businessmen and the working segment of the public, but rather by recipients of welfare.

Both the Special Senate Committee Report on Poverty and the Real Poverty Report criticize our present system of welfare for its demoralization of recipients, who often must deal with several levels of government and are vulnerable to arbitrary interference on the part of administering officials. Welfare officials have the power to check on welfare recipients and cut off or limit their benefits under a large number of circumstances. The dangers to welfare recipients in terms of anxiety, threats to privacy and loss of dignity are obvious. According to the Senate Report, the single aspect shared by all Canada's welfare system is "a record of failure and insufficiency, of bureaucratic rigidities that often result in the degradation, humiliation and alienation of recipients." [8] The writers of this report cite many instances of humiliation, leaving the impression that these are too easily found to be "incidental aberrations." [9] Concern that a welfare recipient either be unable to work or be willing to work (if unemployed) can easily turn into concern about how he spends the income supplied him, what his plans for the future are, where he lives, how many children he has. And the rationale underlying the Puritan scheme makes the degradation of welfare recipients a natural consequence of welfare institutions.

Work is valued and only he who works is thought to contribute to society. Welfare recipients are regarded as parasites and spongers—so when they are treated as such, this is only what we should have expected. Being on welfare in a society which thinks and acts in this fashion can be psychologically debilitating. Welfare recipients who are demoralized by their downgraded status and relative lack of personal freedom can be expected to be made less capable of self-sufficiency. To the extent that this is so, welfare systems erected on Puritan principles may defeat their own purposes.

In fairness, it must be noted here that bureaucratic checks and controls are not a feature only of Puritan welfare systems. To a limited extent, Permissive systems would have to incorporate them too. Within those systems, welfare benefits would be given only to those whose income was inadequate to meet basic needs. However, there would be no checks on "willingness to work," and there would be no need for welfare workers to evaluate the merits of the daily activities of recipients. If a Permissive guaranteed income system were administered through income tax returns, everyone receiving the basic income and those not needing it paying it back in taxes, then the special status of welfare recipients would fade. They would no longer be singled out as a special group within the population. It is to be expected that living solely on government-supplied benefits would be psychologically easier in that type of situation.

Thus it can be argued that for the recipients of welfare, a Permissive scheme has more advantages that a Puritan one. This is not a very surprising conclusion. The Puritan scheme is relatively disadvantageous to recipients, and Puritans would acknowledge this point; they will argue that the overall consequences of Permissive schemes are negative in that these schemes benefit some at too great a cost to others. (Remember, we are not yet concerned with the *justice* of welfare policies, but solely with their consequences as regards *total* human well-being within the society in question.) The concern which most people have regarding the Permissive scheme relates to its costs and its dangers to the "work ethic." It is commonly thought that people work only because they have to work to survive in a tolerable style. If a guaranteed income scheme were adopted by the government, this incentive to work would disappear. No one would be faced with the choice between a nasty and boring job and starvation. Who would do the nasty and boring jobs then? Many of them are not eliminable and they have to be done somehow, by someone. Puritans fear that a great many people—even some with relatively pleasant jobs—might simply cease to work if they could receive non-stigmatized government money to live on. If this were to happen, the permissive society would simply grind to a halt.

In addressing these anxieties about the consequences of Permissive welfare schemes, we must recall that welfare benefits are set to ensure only that those who do not work have a bearable existence, with an income sufficient for basic needs, and that they have this income regardless of why they fail to work. Welfare benefits will not finance luxury living for a family of five! If jobs are adequately paid so that workers receive more than the minimum welfare income in an earned salary, then there will still be a financial incentive to take jobs. What guaranteed income schemes will do is to raise the salary floor. This change will benefit the many non-unionized workers in service and clerical occupations.

Furthermore it is unlikely that people work solely due to (i) the desire for money and the things it can buy and (ii) belief in the Puritan work ethic. There are many other reasons for working, some of which would persist in a society which had adopted a Permissive welfare system. Most people are happier when their time is structured in some way, when they are active outside their own homes, when they feel themselves part of an endeavour whose purposes transcend their particular egoistic ones. Women often choose to work outside the home for these reasons as much as for financial ones. With these and other factors operating I cannot see that the adoption of a Permissive welfare scheme would be followed by a level of slothfulness which would jeopardize human well-being.

Another worry about the Permissive scheme concerns cost. It is difficult to comment on this in a general way, since it would vary so much from case to case. Of Canada at the present it has been said that a guaranteed income scheme administered through income tax would cost less than social security payments administered through the present bureaucracies. It is thought that this saving would result from a drastic cut in administrative costs. The matter of the work ethic is also relevant to the question of costs. Within a Puritan framework it is very important to have a high level of employment and there is a tendency to resist any reorganization which results in there being fewer jobs available. Some of these proposed reorganizations would save money; strictly speaking we should count the cost of keeping jobs which are objectively unnecessary as part of the cost of Puritanism regarding welfare.

In summary, we can appraise Individualism, Puritanism and Permissivism with respect to their anticipated consequences, as follows: Individualism is unacceptable; Puritanism is tolerable, but has some undesirable consequences for welfare recipients; Permissivism appears to be the winner. Worries about bad effects which Permissive welfare schemes might have due to high costs and (alleged) reduced work-incentives appear to be without solid basis.

SOCIAL JUSTICE UNDER PROPOSED WELFARE SCHEMES

We must now try to consider the merits of Individualism, Puritanism and Permissivism with regard to their impact on the distribution of the goods necessary for well-being. [Robert] Nozick has argued against the whole conception of a distributive justice on the grounds that it presupposes that goods are like manna from heaven: we simply get them and then have a problem—to whom to give them. According to Nozick we know where things come from and we do not have the problem of to whom to give them. There is not really a problem of distributive justice, for there is no central distributor giving out manna from heaven! It is necessary to counter Nozick on this point since his reaction to the (purported) problems of distributive justice would undercut much of what follows.[10]

There is a level at which Nozick's point is obviously valid. If A discovers a cure for cancer, then it is A and not B or C who is responsible for this discovery. On Nozick's view this is taken to imply that A should reap any monetary profits which are forthcoming; other people will benefit from the cure itself. Now although it cannot be doubted that A is a bright and hard-working person, neither can it be denied that A and his circumstances are the product of many co-operative endeavours: schools and laboratories, for instance. Because this is so, I find Nozick's claim that "we know where things come from" unconvincing at a deeper level. Since achievements like A's presuppose extensive social co-operation, it is morally permissible to regard even the monetary profits accruing from them as shareable by the "owner" and society at large.

Laws support existing income levels in many ways. Governments specify taxation so as to further determine net income. Property ownership is a legal matter. In all these ways people's incomes and possibilities for obtaining income are affected by deliberate state action. It is always possible to raise questions about the moral desirability of actual conventional arrangements. Should university professors earn less than lawyers? More than waitresses? Why? Why not? Anyone who gives an account of distributive justice is trying to specify principles which will make it possible to answer questions such as these, and nothing in Nozick's argument suffices to show that the questions are meaningless or unimportant.

Any human distribution of anything is unjust insofar as differences exist for no good reason. If goods did come like manna from heaven and the Central Distributor gave A ten times more than B, we should want to know why. The skewed distribution might be deemed a just one if A's needs were objectively ten times greater than B's, or if B refused to accept more than his small portion of goods. But if no reason at all could be given for it, or if only an irrelevant reason could be given (e.g., A is blue-eyed and B is not), then it is an unjust distribution. All the views we have expounded concerning welfare permit differences in income level. Some philosophers would say that such differences are never just, although they may be necessary, for historical or utilitarian reasons. Whether or

not this is so, it is admittedly very difficult to say just what would constitute a good reason for giving A a higher income than B. Level of need, degree of responsibility, amount of training, unpleasantness of work—all these have been proposed and all have some plausibility. We do not need to tackle all this larger problem in order to consider justice under proposed welfare systems. For we can deal here solely with the question of whether everyone should receive a floor level of income; decisions on this matter are independent of decisions on overall equality or principles of variation among incomes above the floor. The Permissivist contends that all should receive at least the floor income; the Individualist and the Puritan deny this. All would claim justice for their side.

The Individualist attempts to justify extreme variations in income, with some people below the level where they can fulfill their basic needs, with reference to the fact of people's actual accomplishments. This approach to the question is open to the same objections as those which have already been raised against Nozick's non-manna-from-heaven argument, and I shall not repeat them here. Let us move on to the Puritan account. It is because goods emerge from human efforts that the Puritan advances his view of welfare. He stresses the unfairness of a system which would permit some people to take advantage of others. A Permissive welfare system would do this, as it makes no attempt to distinguish between those who choose not to work and those who cannot work. No one should be able to take advantage of another under the auspices of a government institution. The Puritan scheme seeks to eliminate this possibility, and for that reason, Puritans would allege, it is a more just scheme than the Permissive one.

Permissivists can best reply to this contention by acknowledging that any instance of free-riding would be an instance where those working were done an injustice, but by showing that any justice which the Puritan preserves by eliminating free-riding is outweighed by *injustice* perpetrated elsewhere. Consider the children of the Puritan's free-riders. They will suffer greatly for the "sins" of their parents. Within the institution of the family, the Puritan cannot suitably hurt the guilty without cruelly depriving the innocent. There is a sense, too, in which Puritanism does injustice to the many people on welfare who are not free-riders. It perpetuates the opinion that they are non-contributors to society and this doctrine, which is over-simplified if not downright false, has a harmful effect upon welfare recipients.

Social justice is not simply a matter of the distribution of goods, or the income with which goods are to be purchased. It is also a matter of the protection of rights. Western societies claim to give their citizens equal rights in political and legal contexts; they also claim to endorse the larger conception of a right to life. Now it is possible to interpret these rights in a limited and formalistic way, so that the duties correlative to them are minimal. On the limited, or negative, interpretation, to say that A has a right to life is simply to say that others have a duty not to interfere with A's attempts to keep himself alive. This interpretation of the right to life is compatible with Individualism as well as with Puritanism. But it is an inadequate interpretation of the right to life and of other rights. A right to vote is meaningless if one is starving and unable to get to the polls; a right to equality before the law is meaningless if one cannot afford to hire a lawyer. And so on.

Even a Permissive welfare scheme will go only a very small way towards protecting people's rights. It will amount to a meaningful acknowledgment of a right to life, by ensuring income adequate to purchase food, clothing and shelter—at the very least. These minimum necessities are presupposed by all other rights a society may endorse in that their possession is a precondition of being able to exercise these other rights. Because it protects the rights of all within a society better than do Puritanism and Individualism, the Permissive view can rightly claim superiority over the others with regard to justice.

Endnotes

1. Nicholas Rescher, *Welfare: Social Issues in Philosophical Perspective,* p. 114.
2. One might wish to discuss moral questions concerning welfare in the context of **natural rights** doctrines. Indeed, Article 22 of the United Nations Declaration of Human Rights states, "Everyone, as a member of society, has the right to social security and is entitled, through a national effort and international cooperation and in accordance with the organization and resources of each State, to the economic, social, and cultural rights indispensable for his dignity and the free development of his personality." I make no attempt to defend the right to welfare as a natural right. Granting that rights imply responsibilities or duties and that "ought" implies "can," it would only be intelligible to regard the right to social security as a natural right if all states were able to ensure the minimum well-being of their citizens. This is not the case. And a natural right is one which is by definition supposed to belong to all human beings simply in virtue of their status as human beings. The analysis given here in the Permissive view is compatible with the claim that all human beings have a *prima facie* natural right to social security. It is not, however, compatible with the claim that all human beings have a natural right to social security if this right is regarded as one which is so absolute as to be inviolable under any and all conditions.
3. See, for example, Ayn Rand's *Atlas Shrugged, The Virtue of Selfishness,* and *Capitalism: the Unknown Ideal.*
4. John Hospers, *Libertarianism: A Political Philosophy for Tomorrow,* p. 67.
5. I say virtually unconditional, because an Individualist such as John Hospers sees a legitimate moral role for government in preventing the use of force by some citizens against others. Since this is the case, I presume that he would also regard as legitimate such taxation as was necessary to support this function. Presumably that taxation would be seen as consented to by all, on the grounds that all "really want" government protection.
6. Ian Adams, William Cameron, Brian Hill, and Peter Penz, *The Real Poverty Report,* pp. 167–187.
7. See *A Theory of Justice,* pp. 124, 136. Rawls defines the free-rider as one who relies on the principle "everyone is to act justly except for myself, if I choose not to," and says that his position is a version of egoism which is eliminated as a morally acceptable principle by formal constraints. This conclusion regarding the tenability of egoism is one which I accept and which is taken for granted in the present context.
8. *Senate Report on Poverty,* p. 73.
9. The Hamilton Public Welfare Department takes automobile license plates from recipients, making them available again only to those whose needs meet with the Department's approval (*Real Poverty Report,* p. 186). The *Globe and Mail* for 12 January 1974 reported that welfare recipients in the city of Toronto are to be subjected to computerized budgeting. In the summer of 1973, the two young daughters of an Alabama man on welfare were sterilized against their own wishes and without their parents' informed consent. (See *Time,* 23 July 1973.)
10. Robert Nozick, "Distributive Justice," *Philosophy and Public Affairs,* Fall 1973.

REVIEW QUESTIONS

1. Distinguish between the individualist view, the permissive view, and the puritan view (as Govier explains them).

2. State the free-rider principle. Why does Govier reject it?
3. Compare the consequences of the three views as Govier describes them.
4. What is Govier's conclusion with respect to the consequences of the three positions?
5. What is Govier's objection to the individualist's view with respect to justice?
6. How does Govier characterize social justice?
7. Which of the three positions is superior according to Govier and why?

DISCUSSION QUESTIONS

1. Does everyone in a rich society such as the United States have a right to welfare? Explain your answer.

2. Does everyone in a society who is able to work have a right to work? Why or why not?
3. Is a person who is able to work but who chooses not to work entitled to welfare? What is your position on this free-rider problem?
4. Some women with dependent children receive more money from welfare than they could make working at low-paying jobs. This gives them an incentive not to work. Is this acceptable? What is your view?
5. Is a guaranteed income administered through the income tax a good idea? What do you think of Govier's suggestion?

Peter G. Germanis

Workfare: Breaking the Poverty Cycle

Peter G. Germanis is a policy analyst at the Heritage Foundation in Washington, D.C., and the coauthor of Understanding Reaganomics *(1982).*

Germanis defends the view that those receiving welfare benefits who are able-bodied and have school-age children should be required to work.

Expenditures on welfare programs have been rising at an alarming rate over the last two decades. A principal cause of this enormous expansion is the work disincentive created by continual benefit liberalizations. Rather than paving the way for a higher standard of living, however, many of these government programs have tended to foster permanent dependency on welfare by providing benefits of greater value than the income an individual could earn by

From Peter G. Germanis, "Workfare: Breaking the Poverty Cycle," *Backgrounder*, no. 195 (9 July 1982): 144–160. Reprinted by permission of The Heritage Foundation.

working. In effect, the American welfare system allows an able-bodied individual to ask himself: "Will I be better off if I work or if I allow myself and my family to become dependent upon the work of other individuals?" A system permitting this question to be posed is a system desperately in need of review and reform.

STILL ON THE DOLE

Encouraging welfare recipients to become self-supporting is supposed to be a major objective of many government programs. Most of these programs provide recipients cash incentives to work their way off the dole. In many cases, however, the result has been that individuals with relatively high incomes continue to receive welfare benefits. . . . Moreover, although these programs may be designed to aid the poor, in the long run they may actually lower their living standard by discouraging them from entering the labor market where they could acquire the job skills that eventually could lift many from poverty's depths.

There is an alternative to the self-defeating, degrading system of the dole which long has characterized the U.S. welfare system. This alternative is widely known as Community Work

Experience Programs (CWEP), or more commonly as "workfare," in which employable recipients of public assistance—primarily able-bodied males and mothers of school age children—must perform some public service without pay in return for their welfare benefits. . . . As such, workfare reflects the American work ethic. Its objective is to promote financial independence by giving people greater incentives to seek out unsubsidized employment. This work requirement is crucial for successful welfare reform because it is the most effective way to offset the work disincentives now created by the welfare system. . . . Several existing job search programs already are cost-effective.

Example: Oregon's Coordinated Job Placement Program. About 10 percent of the applicant pool was kept off the rolls in fiscal 1981 because the applicants had found employment. Oregon's AFDC caseload has declined by 25 percent since the job search program began in August 1980, despite a 40 percent rise in the unemployment rate.

Example: In Kent County, Michigan, the job search demonstration program for unemployed parents cut the caseload by 60 percent. Of that, one-third found jobs before collecting benefits and the remainder either withdrew their applications or were dropped from consideration for refusing to participate.

The program thus tends to discourage those unwilling to work from viewing welfare as an alternative. Other states and localities also report that job search is an effective tool in placing welfare recipients in jobs, even in areas plagued by high unemployment. . . .

BENEFITS OF WORKFARE

There are several inherent advantages to the *quid pro quo* concept of workfare.

I. The community receives something in exchange for its assistance. All communities surely have work that needs doing but has been ignored because of budgetary constraints. Admittedly, workfare participants' contributions may be small, but since the welfare grants would be paid whether or not work is performed, the community's gain nevertheless is real. Among the jobs created by workfare in some of the optional CWEP programs are maintenance, custodial, day care and library services and assistance to police and emergency medical personnel. Existing workers are not displaced since workfare project tasks would not otherwise have been performed. . . .

II. Participants in the program may find that their attractiveness to potential employers has been enhanced through their exposure to a working environment. Even if the jobs provided give little in the way of training, they introduce work disciplines. Such informal training encourages development of crucial work habits—punctuality, dependability and good working relations with fellow workers. The work experience also gives participants a chance to gain the kind of references, such as a letter of recommendation, which will help them in future job searches. The workfare experience thus may very well enhance the value of participants as productive members of the workforce and ease their transition into unsubsidized employment.

III. A workfare program may reduce welfare costs by deterring some persons who should be self-supporting from remaining on the dole. Though not intended as a primary objective, workfare has "deterrent effect" that eliminates welfare recipients who either refuse to participate or have another source of employment which prevents them from doing so. Establishing a work requirement would give employable recipients an incentive to seek other, more attractive means of support when they realize that their benefits no longer are free. Workfare has proved an effective means of sizeably reducing the fraud and abuse so prevalent in our current system by encouraging the departure of undeserving recipients, thereby reducing the burden on the taxpayer and making more money available for those in genuine need. . . .

One of the most efficiently administered workfare programs is in Cincinnati, which has been part of the General Relief welfare program for over 40 years. Most of the work has little skill content, with heavy emphasis placed on having the participants put in their time. The program appears to have been cost-effective. Notes one evaluation:

There is a very high initial attrition rate, when people realize they have to work for their benefits. It is sometimes necessary to assign 200 people to get 50 to show up at the work site. The average no show rate may run as high as 60–75 percent. . . . although the deterrent effect and the reduction in the caseload is not an explicit objective, it is an obvious reality.

Although no formal cost/benefit assessments have been made, the amount of GR grant money saved from case closings and the deterrent effect, appear to be far more than the costs of administering the program. On that score alone the program has won general support and agency endorsement. . . .

A second workfare program, and one which very likely will receive a great deal of attention because it is part of the AFDC program, is the Utah Work Experience and Training Program (WEAT). For many years, Utah was the only state with a statewide mandatory work program that included AFDC recipients, although it exempted mothers with children under the age of six. Utah's WEAT program, established in 1974, requires employable recipients to work three days a week and to participate in job search for two days. This approach assures work-site sponsors a stable work schedule. A twelve-week limit on workfare participation ensures that workfare participants do not become permanently dependent on workfare in place of regular employment.

Of those assigned to projects, 27 percent were removed because they failed to perform. Usher West, who heads the Utah program, acknowledges that "WEAT had a general housecleaning effect." In addition, the program also helped many of those assigned work by enhancing their employability. The *Wall Street Journal* reported:

One of those who benefited is Dennis Wickert, a 42-year-old Marine Corps veteran with a ninth-grade education. A combination of inadequate training and absences caused by problems with bad gums, plus relentless bill collectors, bounced him from the last of several service-station jobs and back onto AFDC several years ago, Mr. Wickert recalls. Indeed, he was feeling like a loser, until the WEAT program assigned him to a neighborhood maintenance crew working out of a local community-action office.

After that "I could walk up to my neighbor and say I earn my welfare money, it's honest," he says with conviction. Mr. Wickert's performance persuaded his employer to hire him as a crew chief. Today he is off AFDC, earning $800 a month plus some extra cash from odd hauling jobs done with his own truck. . . .

Although not all experiences in workfare have met expectations, it does appear that a properly administered program could reduce significantly burgeoning welfare costs while helping many of the poor overcome the "poverty wall" created by America's current welfare and tax systems.

It is quite possible that the recent immigrants to this country who speak no English are better off than many of the poor because the newcomers do not know how to take advantage of the welfare programs. Social analyst Tom Bethell has characterized their plight: "The newcomers are compelled to take those demeaning jobs at the bottom, but they soon work their way up, as immigrants always have in the past, and eventually rise above those on the isolated welfare platform." The purpose of workfare is not to put the poor to work on workfare projects, but to get them into the productive and rewarding labor force by improving the incentives for serious job search.

REVIEW QUESTIONS

1. Why don't the current U.S. welfare programs work according to Germanis?
2. What is the alternative? Why does Germanis think that this alternative is better?

DISCUSSION QUESTIONS

1. What sort of work would be required for those on welfare? If it is just menial work, then it would lead to a minimum-wage job. But does such a job end the need for welfare?
2. What would happen to the children of those who are unwilling to work? Do we have any duty to save them?

Nancy Fraser

Women, Welfare, and the Politics of Need Interpretation

Nancy Fraser teaches political science at the New School for Social Research. The reading is taken from her book Unruly Practices: Power, Discourse, and Gender in Contemporary Social Theory *(1989).*

Fraser gives a feminist analysis of the U.S. social-welfare system. She claims the system reflects patriarchal gender norms that relegate women to the role of caregiver and unpaid domestic worker while assigning men the role of breadwinner. The system also defines women as dependent clients and men as rights-bearing beneficiaries. Thus, political issues about the interpretation of people's needs have been translated into legal, administrative, and/or therapeutic matters.

What some writers are calling "the coming welfare wars" will be largely wars about, even against, women. Because women comprise the overwhelming majority of social-welfare program recipients and employees, women and women's needs will be the principal stakes in the battles over social spending likely to dominate national politics in the coming period. Moreover, the welfare wars will not be limited to the tenure of Reagan or even of Reaganism. On the contrary, they will be protracted wars both in time and in space. What James O'Connor (1973) theorized nearly fifteen years ago as "the fiscal crisis of the state" is a long-term, structural phenomenon of international proportions. Not just the U.S., but every late-capitalist

welfare state in Western Europe and North America is facing some version of it. And the fiscal crisis of the welfare state coincides everywhere with a second long-term, structural tendency: the feminization of poverty. This is Diana Pearce's (1979) term for the rapidly increasing proportion of women in the adult poverty population, an increase tied to, *inter alia,* the rise in "female-headed households." In the U.S., this trend is so pronounced and so steep that analysts project that, should it continue, the poverty population will consist entirely of women and their children before the year 2000 (Ehrenreich and Piven 1984).

This conjunction of the fiscal crisis of the state and the feminization of poverty suggests that struggles around social-welfare will and should become increasingly focal for feminists. But such struggles raise a great many problems. Some of these, like the following, can be thought of as structural: On the one hand, increasing numbers of women depend directly for their livelihoods on social-welfare programs; and many others benefit indirectly, since the existence of even a minimal and inadequate "safety net" increases the leverage of women who are economically dependent on individual men. Thus, feminists have no choice but to oppose social-welfare cuts. On the other hand, economists like Pearce (1979), Nancy Barrett (1984) and Steven Erie, Martin Rein, and Barbara Wiget (1983) have shown that programs like Aid to Families with Dependent Children actually institutionalize the feminization of poverty. The benefits they provide are system-conforming ones which reinforce rather than challenge basic structural inequalities. Thus, feminists cannot simply support existing social-welfare programs. To use the suggestive but ultimately too simple terms popularized by Carol Brown (1981): If to eliminate or to reduce welfare is to bolster "private patriarchy," then simply to defend it is to consolidate "public patriarchy." [1]

Feminists also face a second set of problems in the coming welfare wars. These problems, seemingly more ideological and less structural than the first set, arise from the typical way in which issues get framed as a result of the institutional dynamics of the political system.[2] Typically, social-welfare issues are posed as follows: Shall the state undertake to satisfy the social needs of a given constituency and to what degree? Now, this way of framing issues permits only a relatively small number of answers; and it tends to cast debates in quantitative terms. More importantly, it takes for granted the definition of the needs in question, as if that were self-evident and beyond dispute. It therefore occludes the fact that the interpretation of people's needs is itself a political stake, indeed sometimes *the* political stake. Clearly, this way of framing issues poses obstacles for feminist politics, since at the heart of such politics lie questions like, what do various groups of women really need, and whose interpretations of women's needs should be authoritative. Only in terms of a discourse oriented to the *politics of need interpretation*[3] can feminists meaningfully intervene in the coming welfare wars. But this requires a challenge to the dominant policy framework.

Both sets of problems, the structural and the ideological, are extremely important and difficult. In what follows, I shall not offer solutions to either of them. Rather, I want to attempt the much more modest and preliminary task of exploring how they might be thought about in relation to one another. Specifically, I want to propose a framework for inquiry which can shed light on both of them simultaneously.

Consider that, in order to address the structural problem, it will be necessary to clarify the phenomenon of "public patriarchy." One type of inquiry which is useful here is the familiar sort of economic analysis alluded to earlier, analysis which shows, for example, that "workfare" programs function to subsidize employers of low-wage, "women's work" in the service sector and thus to reproduce the sex-segmented, dual-labor market. Now, important as such inquiry is, it does not tell the whole story, since it leaves out of focus the discursive or ideological dimension of social-welfare programs. By the discursive or ideological dimension, I do not mean anything distinct from or epiphenomenal with respect to welfare practices; I mean, rather, the tacit norms and implicit assumptions which are constitutive of those practices. To get at this dimension requires a meaning-oriented sort of inquiry, one

which considers welfare programs as, among other things, institutionalized patterns of interpretation.[4] Such inquiry would make explicit the social meanings embedded within welfare programs, meanings which tend otherwise simply to go without saying.

In spelling out such meanings, the inquiry I am proposing could do two things simultaneously. First, it could tell us something important about the structure of the U.S. welfare system, since it might identify some underlying norms and assumptions which lend a measure of coherence to diverse programs and practices. Second, it could illuminate what I called "the politics of need interpretation," since it could expose the processes by which welfare practices construct women and women's needs according to certain specific and in principle contestable interpretations, even as they lend those interpretations an aura of facticity which discourages contestation. Thus, this inquiry could shed light on both the structural and ideological problems identified earlier.

The principal aim of this paper is to provide an account of this sort for the present U.S. social-welfare system. The account is intended to help clarify some key structural aspects of male dominance in welfare-capitalist societies. At the same time, it is meant to point the way to a broader, discourse-oriented focus which can address political conflicts over the interpretation of women's needs.

The paper proceeds from some relatively "hard," uncontroversial facts about the U.S. social-welfare system (section I) through a series of increasingly interpreted accounts of the system (sections II and III). These culminate (in section IV) in a highly theorized characterization of the welfare system as a "juridical-administrative-therapeutic state apparatus" (JAT). Finally (in section V), the paper situates that apparatus as one actor among others in a larger and highly contested political field of discourse about needs which also includes the feminist movement.

I

Long before the emergence of welfare states, governments have defined legally secured arenas of social action. In so doing, they have at the same time codified corresponding patterns of agency or social roles. Thus, early modern states defined an economic arena and the corresponding role of an economic person capable of entering into contracts. More or less at the same time, they codified the "private sphere" of the household and the role of household head with dependents. Somewhat later, governments were led to secure a sphere of political participation and the corresponding role of citizen with (limited) political rights. In each of these cases, the original and paradigmatic subject of the newly codified social role was male. Only secondarily and much later was it conceded that women, too, could occupy these subject-positions, without however entirely dispelling the association with masculinity.

Matters are different, however, with the contemporary welfare state. When this type of government defined a new arena of activity—call it "the social"—and a new social role, the welfare client, it included women among its original and paradigmatic subjects. Today, in fact, women have become the principal subjects of the welfare state. On the one hand, they comprise the overwhelming majority both of program recipients and of paid social service workers. On the other hand, they are the wives, mothers and daughters whose unpaid activities and obligations are redefined as the welfare state increasingly oversees forms of caregiving. Since this beneficiary-social worker-caregiver nexus of roles is constitutive of the social-welfare arena, one might even call the latter as feminized terrain.

A brief statistical overview confirms women's greater involvement with and dependence on the U.S. social-welfare system. Consider first women's greater dependence as program clients and beneficiaries. In each of the major "means-tested" programs in the U.S., women and the children for whom they are responsible now comprise the overwhelming majority of clients. For example, more than 81% of households receiving Aid to Families with Dependent Children (AFDC) are headed by women; more than 60% of families receiving food stamps or Medicaid are headed by women; and 70% of all households in publicly owned or subsidized housing are headed by women (Erie, Rein, Wiget 1983; Nelson 1984). High as they are,

these figures actually underestimate the representation of women. As Barbara Nelson (1984) notes, in the androcentric reporting system, households counted as male-headed by definition contain no healthy adult men. But healthy adult women live in most households counted as male-headed. Such women may directly or indirectly receive benefits going to "male-headed" households, but they are invisible in the statistics, even though they usually do the work of securing and maintaining program eligibility.

Women also predominate in the major U.S. "age-tested" programs. For example, 61.6% of all adult beneficiaries of Social Security are women; and 64% of those covered by Medicare are women (Erie, Rein, Wiget 1983; Nelson 1984). In sum, because women as a group are significantly poorer than men—indeed they now comprise nearly two-thirds of all U.S. adults below the official poverty line—and because women tend to live longer than men, women depend more on the social-welfare system as clients and beneficiaries.

But this is not the whole story. Women also depend more on the social-welfare system as paid human service workers—a category of employment which includes education and health, as well as social work and services administration. In 1980, 70% of the 17.3 million paid jobs in this sector in the U.S. were held by women. This accounts for one-third of U.S. women's total paid employment and a full 80% of all professional jobs held by women. The figures for women of color are even higher than this average, since 37% of their total paid employment and 82.4% of their professional employment is in this sector (Erie, Rein, Wiget 1983). It is a distinctive feature of the U.S. social-welfare system, as opposed to, say, the British and Scandinavian systems, that only 3% of these jobs are in the form of direct federal government employment. The rest are in state and local government, in the "private non-profit" sector and in the "private" sector. But the more decentralized and privatized character of the U.S. system does not make paid welfare workers any less vulnerable in the face of federal program cuts. On the contrary, the level of federal social-welfare spending affects the level of human service employment in *all* sectors. State and local government jobs depend on federal and federally financed state and local government contracts; and private profit and non-profit jobs depend on federally financed transfer payments to the individuals and households for the purchase of services like health care in the market (Erie, Rein, Wiget 1983). Thus, reductions in social spending mean the loss of jobs for women. Moreover, as Barbara Ehrenreich and Frances Fox Piven (1984) note, this loss is not compensated when spending is shifted to the military, since only 0.5% of the entire female paid workforce is employed in work on military contracts. In fact, one study they cite estimates that with each one billion dollar increase in military spending, 9,500 jobs are lost to women.

Finally, women are subjects of and to the social-welfare system in their traditional capacity as unpaid caregivers. It is well known that the sexual division of labor assigns women primary responsibility for the care of those who cannot care for themselves. (I leave aside women's traditional obligations to provide personal services to adult males—husbands, fathers, grown sons, lovers—who can very well care for themselves.) Such responsibility includes child care, of course, but also care for sick and/or elderly relatives, often parents. For example, a 1975 British study cited by Hilary Land (1978) found that three times as many elderly people live with married daughters as with married sons, and that those without a close female relative were more likely to be institutionalized, irrespective of degree of infirmity. As unpaid caregivers, then, women are more directly affected than men by the level and character of government social services for children, the sick and the elderly.

As clients, paid human service workers and unpaid caregivers, then, women are the principal subjects of the social-welfare system. It is as if this branch of the state were in effect a "Bureau of Women's Affairs."

II

Of course, the welfare system does not deal with women on women's terms. On the contrary, it has its own characteristic ways of interpreting women's needs and positioning women as subjects. In order to understand these, we need to examine how gender norms and meanings are reflected in the structure of the U.S. social-welfare system.

This issue is quite complicated. On the one hand, nearly all U.S. social-welfare programs are officially gender neutral. Yet the system as a whole is a dual or two-tiered one; and it has an unmistakable gender subtext.[5] There is one set of programs oriented to *individuals* and tied to participation in the paid workforce, for example, unemployment insurance and Social Security. These programs are designed to supplement and compensate for the primary market in paid labor power. There is a second set of programs oriented to *households* and tied to combined household income, for example, AFDC, food stamps and Medicaid. These programs are designed to compensate for what are considered to be family failures, generally the absence of a male breadwinner.

What integrates the two sets of programs is a common core of assumptions, underlying both, concerning the sexual division of labor, domestic and non-domestic. It is assumed that families do or should contain one primary breadwinner who is male and one unpaid domestic worker (homemaker and mother) who is female. It is further assumed that when a woman undertakes paid work outside the home this is or should be in order to supplement the male breadwinner's wage and so it neither does nor ought override her primary housewifely and maternal responsibilities. It is assumed, in other words, that society is divided into two separate spheres of home and outside work and that these are women's and men's spheres respectively.[6]

These assumptions are increasingly counterfactual. At present, fewer than 15% of U.S. families conform to the normative ideal of a domicile shared by a husband who is the sole breadwinner, a wife who is a full-time homemaker and their offspring.

Nonetheless, the separate spheres norms determine the structure of the social-welfare system. They determine that it contain a primary labor market-related subsystem and a family or household-related subsystem. Moreover, they determine that these subsystems be gender-linked, that the labor market-related system be implicitly "masculine" and the family-related system be implicitly "feminine." Consequently, the normative, ideal-typical recipient of primary labor market-oriented programs is a (white) male, while the normative, ideal-typical client of household-based programs is a female.

This gender subtext of the U.S. welfare system is confirmed when we take a second look at participation figures. Consider again the figures just cited for the "feminine" or family-based programs, which I earlier referred to as "means-tested" programs: more than 81% of households receiving AFDC are female-headed, as are more than 70% of those receiving housing assistance and more than 60% of those receiving Medicaid and food stamps. Now recall that these figures do not compare female vs. male individuals, but rather female vs. male-headed *households*. They therefore confirm four things: 1) these programs have a distinctive administrative identity in that their recipients are not individualized but *familialized*; 2) they serve what are considered to be defective families, overwhelmingly families without a male breadwinner; 3) the ideal-typical (adult) client is female; and 4) she makes her claim for benefits on the basis of her status as an unpaid domestic worker, a homemaker and mother, not as a paid worker based in the labor market.

Now contrast this with the case of a typical labor market-based and thus "masculine" program, namely, unemployment insurance. Here the percentage of female claimants drops to 38%, a figure which contrasts female vs. male *individuals*, as opposed to households. As Diana Pearce (1979) notes, this drop reflects at least two different circumstances. First, and most straightforwardly, it reflects women's lower rate of participation in the paid workforce. Second, it reflects the fact that many women wage-workers are not eligible to participate in this program, for example, paid household service workers, part-time workers, pregnant workers and workers in the "irregular economy" such as prostitutes, baby-sitters and home typists. The exclusion of these predominantly female wage-workers testifies to the existence of a gender segmented labor market, divided into "primary" and "secondary" employment. It reflects the more general assumption that women's earnings are "merely supplementary," not on a par with those of the primary (male) breadwinner. Altogether, then, the figures tell us four things about programs like unemployment insurance: 1) they are administered in a way which *individualizes* rather than familializes recipients; 2) they are designed to compensate primary labor market effects, such as the temporary displacement of a primary breadwinner; 3) the ideal-typical recipient is male; and 4) he makes his claim on the basis of his identity as a paid worker, not as an unpaid domestic worker or parent. . . .

III

So far, we have established the dualistic structure of the U.S. social-welfare system and the gender subtext of the dualism. Now, we can better tease out the system's implicit norms and tacit assumptions by examining its mode of operation. To see how welfare programs interpret women's needs, we should consider what benefits consist in. To see how programs position women as subjects, we should examine administrative practices. In general, we shall see that the "masculine" and "feminine" subsystems are not only separate but also unequal.

Consider that the "masculine" social-welfare programs are social insurance schemes. They include unemployment insurance, Social Security (retirement insurance), Medicare (age-tested health insurance) and Supplemental Social Security Insurance (disability insurance for those with paid work records). These programs are contributory; wage-workers and their employers pay into trust funds. They are administered on a national basis and benefit levels are uniform across the country. Though bureaucratically organized and administered, they require less, and less demeaning effort on the part of beneficiaries in qualifying and maintaining eligibility than do "feminine" programs. They are far less subject to intrusive controls and in most cases lack the dimension of surveillance. They also tend to require less of beneficiaries in the way of benefit-collection efforts, with the notable exception of unemployment insurance.

In sum, "masculine" social insurance schemes position recipients primarily as *rights-bearers*. The beneficiaries of these programs are in the main not stigmatized. Neither administrative practice nor popular discourse constitutes them as "on the dole." They are constituted rather as receiving what they deserve, what they, in "partnership" with their employers, have already paid in for, what they, therefore, have a *right* to. Moreover, these beneficiaries are also positioned as *purchasing consumers*. They receive cash as opposed to "in kind" benefits and so are positioned as having "the liberty to strike the best bargain they can in purchasing services of their choice on the open market." In sum, these beneficiaries are what C. B. MacPherson (1964) calls "possessive individuals." Proprietors of their own persons who have freely contracted to sell their labor-power, they become participants in social insurance schemes and, thence, paying consumers of human services. They therefore qualify as *social citizens* in virtually the fullest sense that term can acquire within the framework of a male-dominated capitalist society.

All this stands in stark contrast to the "feminine" sector of the U.S. social-welfare system. This sector consists in relief programs, such as AFDC, food stamps, Medicaid and public housing assistance. These programs are not contributory, but are financed out of general tax revenues, usually with one-third of the funds coming from the federal government and two-thirds coming from the states. They are not administered nationally but rather by the states. As a result, benefit levels vary dramatically, though they are everywhere inadequate, deliberately pegged below the official poverty line. The relief programs are notorious for the varieties of administrative humiliation they inflict upon clients. They require considerable work in qualifying and maintaining eligibility; and they have a heavy component of surveillance.

These programs do not in any meaningful sense position their subjects as rights-bearers. Far from being considered as having a right to what they receive, recipients are defined as "beneficiaries of governmental largesse" or "clients of public charity." [7] In the androcentric-administrative framework, "welfare mothers" are considered not to work and so are sometimes required, that is to say coerced, to work off their benefits via "workfare." They thus become inmates of what Diana Pearce (1979) calls a "workhouse without walls." Indeed, the only sense in which the category of rights is relevant to these clients' situation is the somewhat dubious one according to which they are entitled to treatment governed by the standards of formal-bureaucratic procedural rationality. But if that right is construed as protection from administrative caprice, then even it is widely and routinely disregarded. Moreover, recipients of public relief are generally not positioned as purchasing consumers. A significant portion of their benefits is "in kind" and what cash they get comes already carved up and ear-marked for specific, administratively designated purposes. These recipients are therefore essentially *clients*, a subject-position which carries far less power and dignity in capitalist societies than does the alternative position of purchaser. In these societies, to be a client in the sense relevant to relief recipients is to be an abject dependent. Indeed, this sense of the term carries connotations of a fall from autonomy, as when we speak, for example, of "the client-states of empires or superpowers." As clients, then, recipients of relief are *the negatives of possessive individuals.* Largely excluded from the market, both as workers and as consumers, claiming benefits not as individuals but as members of "failed" families, these recipients are effectively denied the trappings of social-citizenship as the latter are defined within male-dominated capitalist societies.[8]

Clearly, this system creates a double-bind for women raising children without a male breadwinner. By failing to offer them day care, job training, a job that pays a "family wage" or some combination of these, it constructs them exclusively as mothers. As a consequence, it interprets their needs as maternal needs and their sphere of activity as that of "the family." Now, according to the ideology of separate spheres, this should be an honorific social identity. Yet the system does not honor these women. On the contrary, instead of providing them with a guaranteed income equivalent to a family wage as a matter of right, it stigmatizes, humiliates and harasses them. In effect, it decrees that these women must be, yet cannot be, normative mothers.

Moreover, the way in which the U.S. social-welfare system interprets "maternity" and "the family" is race- and culture-specific. The bias is made plain by Carol Stack's (1974) study, *All Our Kin*. Stack analyzes domestic arrangements of very poor Black welfare recipients in a midwestern city. Where ideologues see "the disorganization of *the* [sic] black family," she finds complex, highly organized kinship structures. These include kin-based networks of resource pooling and exchange which enable those in direct poverty to survive economically and communally. The networks organize delayed exchanges or "gifts," in Mauss' (1967) sense, of prepared meals, food stamps, cooking, shopping, groceries, furniture, sleeping space, cash (including wages and AFDC allowances), transportation, clothing, child care, even children. They span several physically distinct households and so transcend the principal administrative category which organizes relief programs. It is significant that Stack took great pains to conceal the identities of her subjects, even going so far as to disguise the identity of their city. The reason, though unstated, is obvious: these people would lose their benefits if program administrators learned that they did not utilize them within the confines and boundaries of a "household."

We can summarize the separate and unequal character of the two-tiered, gender-linked, race- and culture-biased U.S. social-welfare system in the following formulae: Participants in the "masculine" subsystem are positioned as *rights-bearing beneficiaries and purchasing consumers of services*. Participants in the "feminine" subsystem, on the other hand, are positioned as *dependent clients*.

IV

Clearly, the identities and needs which the social-welfare system fashions for its recipients are *interpreted* identities and needs. Moreover, they are highly political interpretations which are in principle subject to dispute. Yet these needs and identities are not always recognized as interpretations. Too often, they simply go without saying and are rendered immune from analysis and critique.

Doubtless one reason for this "reification effect" is the depth at which gender meanings and norms are embedded in our general culture. But there may also be another reason more specific to the welfare system.

Let me suggest yet another way of analyzing the U.S. social-welfare system, this time as a "juridical-administrative-therapeutic state apparatus" (JAT).[9] The point is to emphasize a distinctive style of operation. *Qua* JAT, the welfare system works by linking together a series of juridical, administrative and therapeutic procedures. As a consequence, it tends to translate political issues concerning the interpretation of people's needs into legal, administrative and/or therapeutic matters. Thus, the system executes political policy in a way which appears nonpolitical and tends to be depoliticizing.

Consider that, at an abstract level, the subject-positions constructed for beneficiaries of *both* the "masculine" and the "feminine" components of the system can be analyzed as combinations of three distinct elements. The first element is a *juridical* one which positions recipients vis-a-vis the legal system by according or denying them various *rights*. Thus, the subject of the "masculine" subsystem has a right to benefits and is protected from some legally sanctioned forms of administrative caprice, while the subject of the "feminine" subsystem largely lacks rights.

This juridical element is then linked with a second one, an *administrative* element. For in order to qualify to receive benefits, subjects must assume the stance of petitioners with respect to an administrative body; they must petition a bureaucratic institution empowered to decide their claims on the basis of administratively defined criteria. In the "masculine" subsystem, for example, claimants must prove their "cases" meet administratively defined criteria of entitlement; in the "feminine" subsystem, on the other hand, they must prove conformity to administratively defined criteria of need. The enormous qualitative differences between the two sets of procedures notwithstanding, both are variations on the same administrative moment. Both require claimants to translate their experienced situations and life-problems into administerable needs, to present the former as bonafide instances of specified generalized states of affairs which could in principle befall anyone (Habermas 1981).

If and when they qualify, social-welfare claimants get positioned either as purchasing consumers or dependent clients. In either case, their needs are redefined as correlates of bureaucratically administered satisfactions. This means they are quantified, rendered as equivalents of a sum of money (Habermas 1981). Thus, in the "feminine" subsystem, clients are positioned passively to receive monetarily measured, predefined and prepackaged services; in the "masculine" subsystem, on the other hand, they receive a specified, predetermined amount of cash.

In both subsystems, then, people's needs are subject to a sort of rewriting operation. Experienced situations and life-problems are translated into administerable needs. And since the latter are not necessarily isomorphic to the former, the possibility of a gap between them arises. This possibility is especially likely in the "feminine" subsystem. For there, as we saw, clients are constructed as deviant and service provision has the character of normalization— albeit normalization designed more to stigmatize than to "reform."

Here, then is the opening for the third, *therapeutic* moment of the JAT's *modus operandi*. Especially in the "feminine" subsystem, service provision often includes an implicit or explicit therapeutic or quasi-therapeutic dimension. In AFDC, for example, social workers concern themselves with the "mental health" aspects of their clients' lives, often construing these in terms of "character problems." More explicitly and less moralistically, municipal programs for poor, unmarried, pregnant teenage women include not only pre-natal care, mothering instruction and tutoring or schooling, but also counseling sessions with psychiatric social workers. As observed by Prudence Rains (1971), such sessions are intended to bring girls to acknowledge what are considered to be their true, deep, latent, emotional problems on the assumption that this will enable them to avoid future pregnancies. Ludicrous as this sounds, it is only an extreme example of a more pervasive phenomenon, namely, the tendency of especially "feminine" social-welfare programs to construct gender-political and political-

economic issues as individual, psychological problems. In fact, some therapeutic or quasi-therapeutic welfare services can be regarded as second-order services. In any case, the therapeutic dimension of the U.S. social-welfare encourages clients to close gaps between their culturally shaped lived experience and their administratively defined situation by bringing the former into line with the latter.

Clearly, this analysis of the U.S. welfare system as a "juridical-administrative-therapeutic state apparatus" lets us see both subsystems more critically. It suggests that the problem is not only that women are disempowered by the *denial* of social citizenship in the "feminine" subsystem, although they are. It is also that women and men are disempowered by the *realization* of an androcentric, possessive individualist form of social citizenship in the "masculine" subsystem. In *both* subsystems, including the "masculine" one, the JAT positions its subjects in ways which do not empower them. It individualizes them as "cases" and so militates against collective identification. It imposes monological, administrative definitions of situation and need and so preempts dialogically achieved self-definition and self-determination. It positions its subjects as passive client or consumer recipients and not as active co-participants involved in shaping their life-conditions. Lastly, it construes experienced discontent with these arrangements as material for adjustment-oriented, usually sexist therapy and not as material for empowering processes of consciousness-raising.

All told, then, the form of social citizenship constructed even in the *best* part of the U.S. social-welfare system is a degraded and depoliticized one. It is a form of passive citizenship in which the state preempts the power to define and satisfy people's needs.

This form of passive citizenship arises in part as a result of the JAT's distinctive style of operation. The JAT treats the interpretation of people's needs as pregiven and unproblematic, while itself redefining them as amenable to system-conforming satisfactions. Thus, the JAT shifts attention away from the question: Who interprets social needs and how? It tends to substitute the *juridicial, administrative and therapeutic management of need satisfaction* for the *politics of need interpretation*. That is, it tends to substitute *monological, administrative processes of need definition* for *dialogical, participatory processes of need interpretation*.[10]. . .

Endnotes

1. I believe that Brown's terms are too simple on two counts. First, for reasons elaborated by Gayle Rubin (1975), I prefer not to use 'patriarchy' as a generic term for male dominance but rather as the destination of a specific historical social formation. Second, Brown's public/private contrast oversimplifies the structure of both laissez-faire and welfare capitalism, since it posits two major societal zones where there are actually four (family, official-economy, state, and sphere of public political discourse) and conflates two distinct public-private divisions. (For a discussion of this second problem, see Fraser 1985b.) These problems notwithstanding, it remains the case that Brown's terms are immensely suggestive and that we currently have no better terminology. Thus, in what follows I occasionally use 'public patriarchy' for want of an alternative.

2. For an analysis of the dynamics whereby late-capitalist political systems tend to select certain types of interests while excluding others, see Claus Offe (1972, 1974, 1980). For a feminist application of Offe's approach, see Drude Dahlerup (1984).

3. This phrase owes its inspiration to Jürgen Habermas (1975).

4. I owe this phrase to Thomas McCarthy (personal communication).

5. I owe the phrase 'gender subtext' to Dorothy Smith (1984). A number of writers have noticed the two-tiered character of the U.S. social-welfare system. Andrew Hacker (1985) correlates the dualism with class but not with gender. Diana Pearce (1979) and Erie, Rein and Wiget (1983) correlate the dualism with gender and with the dual labor market, itself gender-correlated. Barbara Nelson (1984) correlates the dualism with gender, the dual labor market and the sexual division of paid *and unpaid* labor. My account owes a great deal to all of these writers, especially Barbara Nelson.

6. Hilary Land (1978) identifies similar assumptions at work in the British social-welfare system. My formulation of them is much indebted to her.

7. I owe these formulations to Virginia Held (personal communication).

8. It should be noted that I am here taking issue with the view of some left theorists that "decommodification" in the form of in kind social-welfare benefits represents an emancipatory or progressive development. In the context of a two-tiered welfare system like the one described here, this assumption is clearly false, since in kind benefits are qualitatively and quantitatively inferior to the corresponding commodities and since they function to stigmatize those who receive them.

9. This term echoes Louis Althusser's (1984) term, "ideological state apparatus." Certainly, the U.S. social-welfare system as described in the present section of this paper counts as an "ISA" in Althusser's sense. However, I prefer the term "juridical-administrative-therapeutic state apparatus" as more concrete and descriptive of the specific ways in which welfare programs produce and reproduce ideology. In general, then, a JAT can be understood as a subclass of an ISA. On the other hand, Althusserian-like terminology aside, readers will find that the account in this section owes more to Michael Foucault (1979) and Jürgen Habermas (1981) than to Althusser. Of course, neither Habermas nor Foucault is sensitive to the gendered character of social-welfare programs. For a critique of Habermas in this respect, see Fraser (1985b). For my views about Foucault, see Fraser (1981, 1983 and 1985a).

10. These formulations owe much to Jürgen Habermas (1975, 1981). . . .

References

Althusser, Louis. 1984. Ideology and ideological state apparatuses: Notes towards an investigation. In *Essays on ideology,* ed. Althusser. London: Verso.

Arendt, Hannah. 1958. *The human condition.* Chicago and London: The University of Chicago Press.

Barrett, Nancy S. 1984. Mothers, fathers, and children: From private to public patriarchy. In *Women and revolution,* ed. Lydia Sargent. Boston: South End Press.

Dahlerup, Drude. 1984. Overcoming the barriers: An approach to the study of how women's issues are kept from the political agenda. In *Women's views of the political world of men,* ed. Judith H. Stiehm. Dobbs Ferry, NY: Transnational Publishers.

Ehrenreich, Barbara and Frances Fox Piven. 1984. The feminization of poverty. *Dissent,* Spring: 162–170.

Erie, Steven P., Martin Rein, and Barbara Wiget. 1983. Women and the Reagan revolution: Thermidor for the social welfare economy. In *Families, politics, and public policies: A feminist dialogue on women and the state,* ed. Irene Diamond. New York and London.: Longman.

Foucault, Michel. 1979. *Discipline and punish: The birth of the prison.* Trans. Alan Sheridan. New York: Vintage.

Fraser, Nancy. 1981. Foucault on modern power: Empirical insights and normative confusions. *Praxis International* 1:272–87.

————. 1983. Foucault's body-language: A post-humanist political rhetoric? *Salmagundi* 61:55–70.

————. 1985a. Michel Foucault: A "Young Conservative"? *Ethics,* vol. 96, no. 1 (October, 1985).

————. 1985b. The case of Habermas and gender. *New German Critique* 35:97–131.

Habermas, Jürgen. 1975. *Legitimation crisis.* Boston: Beacon.

————. 1981. *Theorie des kommunikativen Handelns,* Band II, *Zur Kritik der funktionalistischen Vernunft.* Frankfurt am Main: Suhrkamp Verlag.

Hacker, Andrew. 1985. 'Welfare': The future of an illusion. *New York Review of Books* February 28:37–43.

Land, Hilary. 1978. Who cares for the family? *Journal of Social Policy* 7:257–284.

MacPherson, C. B. 1964. *The political theory of possessive individualism: Hobbs to Locke.* New York and London: Oxford University Press.

Mauss, Marcel. 1967. *The gift: Forms and functions of exchange in archaic societies.* Trans. Ian Cunnison. New York and London: W. W. Norton & Company.

Nelson, Barbara J. 1984. Women's poverty and women's citizenship: Some political consequences of economic marginality. *Signs: Journal of Women in Culture and Society* 10:209–231.

O'Connor, James. 1973. *The fiscal crisis of the state.* New York: St. Martin's Press.

Offe, Claus. 1972. Political authority and class structure: An analysis of late capitalist societies. *International Journal of Sociology* 2:73–108.

—————. 1974. Structural problems of the capitalist state: Class rule and the political system. On the selectiveness of political institutions. In *German Political Studies*, ed., Klaus von Beyme. London: Sage Publications.

—————. 1980. The separation of form and content in liberal democratic politics. *Studies in Political Economy* 3:5–16.

Pearce, Diana. 1979. Women, work, and welfare: The feminization of poverty. In *Working Women and Families*, ed. Karen Wolk Feinstein. Beverly Hills, CA: Sage Publications.

Rains, Prudence Mors. 1971. *Becoming an unwed mother: A sociological account.* Chicago: Aldine Atherton, Inc.

Rubin, Gayle. 1975. The traffic in women: Notes on the "Political Economy" of sex. In *Towards an Anthropology of Women*, ed. Rayna R. Reiter. New York: Monthly Review Press.

Skocpol, Theda. 1980. Political response to capitalist crisis: Neo-Marxist theories of the state and the case of the New Deal. *Politics and Society* 10:155–201.

Smith, Dorothy. 1984. The gender subtext of power. Unpublished manuscript.

Stack, Carol B. 1974. *All our kin: Strategies for survival in a black community.* New York, Evanston, San Francisco, London: Harper & Row.

REVIEW QUESTIONS

1. In Fraser's analysis, why are women the principal subjects and workers in the welfare system?
2. How do welfare programs interpret women and their needs? How are men treated?
3. Explain Fraser's interpretation of the U.S. welfare system as a judicial-administrative-therapeutic state apparatus.

DISCUSSION QUESTIONS

1. Why shouldn't men be breadwinners and women wives and mothers? What is wrong with these gender roles?
2. Do women have real needs that are different from the ones constructed in a male-dominated capitalistic society? If so, what are they?

PROBLEM CASES

1. Periodic Famines and Somalia. (This topic is discussed by Sylvia Nassar in an article in The *New York Times,* January 17, 1993.) The view of Thomas Malthus and his followers (see the Suggested Readings), like Hardin's in the readings, is that famines are caused by food shortages which are in turn caused by drought or other natural disasters. There is a long history of periodic famines which seems to bear this out: Potato famines in Ireland in 1846–51, China's famine in 1928 after a drought, Ethiopia's famine in 1973 after a drought, Bangladesh's famine in 1974 after floods, and the ongoing problems in sub-Saharan Africa (including Ethiopia, Sudan, and Somalia) after a prolonged drought in the area.

The view that famines and food shortages are caused by natural disasters has been challenged by Amartya Sen and others (see the Suggested Readings). Sen argues that world food production has kept ahead of population growth and that famines are not caused by drought, flood, or other natural disasters. Typically a country that has people dying of starvation has enough food to go around. The problem is that the starving people cannot get the food because of high prices, unemployment, distribution problems, civil war, or other human factors.

Consider the recent and continuing starvation of hundreds of thousands of people in Somalia and Sudan. The United States and other countries have contributed a massive amount of aid, probably enough aid to prevent starvation, but the relief efforts have been frustrated by the continuing fighting between various rival political factions. Many foreign-aid workers have been killed in the fighting. The United States led a military intervention in Somalia in December 1992, but the coalition force failed to ensure peace. Bandits continued to rob or extort money from relief groups, and rioting and clan fighting continued to interrupt food deliveries. The situation seems to be even worse in Sudan where there is enough food to feed the people, but difficulties in delivering it to remote villages.

The pessimistic view of Sen is that military intervention will not solve the problems of countries like Somalia and Sudan. The only lasting solution is a stable democratic government that protects the poor and lets farmers grow.

Do you agree with Sen? If so, how can we bring about stable democratic governments in countries like Somalia and Sudan?

2. *The Boarder Baby Scandal.* (As reported by Andrew Stein, president of the New York City Council in *The New York Times,* January 17, 1987.) New York City is the most prosperous city in the world with a twenty-one-billion-dollar budget and immense private and community wealth. Yet it has a very serious problem—abandoned and homeless children. At the end of 1986, the city officially counted 11,000 such children and babies living in municipal shelters, decrepit welfare hotels, and hospitals. Many have been living this way for years. They are known as boarder babies because their parents abandoned them in hospitals. Due to a lack of certified foster parents or couples willing to adopt them, they are likely to remain there. Others have been removed from their homes for their own protection; reports of child abuse and neglect (including a 250-percent increase in cases of drug-addicted babies) have risen so dramatically that welfare offices are overwhelmed with children, often keeping them overnight in the offices or placing them illegally in group foster homes.

What, if anything, should be done about these babies and children? Explain your recommendations carefully.

3. *Paul G. Allen.* (Reported by Timothy Egan in *The New York Times,* October 29, 1995.) With a net worth of $6.5 billion, Paul G. Allen is one of the richest men in the world. How did he make so much money? In 1975 he started Microsoft with his grade-school friend Bill Gates. Microsoft is now the world's largest software company and has been very profitable. Allen's critics say that Bill Gates is responsible for the success of the company, and not Allen. These critics complain that Allen's vast fortune is a fluke, and result of hitching up with the superstar Bill Gates. Allen left Microsoft in 1983 after a cancer scare. He was diagnosed as having

Hodgkin's disease, but radiation therapy cured him. Since 1983 Allen has invested in various computer companies such as Medio and Skypix but has not been very successful. Meanwhile the value of his Microsoft stock (he owns 55.7-million shares) just keeps going up.

Allen lives alone on a six-acre waterfront compound in Mercer Island, an exclusive enclave for the very wealthy near Seattle. Allen's compound has a twenty-seat theater, video screens in most rooms, a swimming pool, a waterfall, and, most impressive of all, a skylit, regulation-size basketball court. Allen is the owner of the Trailblazers, a professional basketball team, and sometimes he has private games for his entertainment between his own team and the Seattle Supersonics. When bored with basketball, he can use his private jet to go to tropical islands or sail on his 150-foot yacht. He is also interested in the late Jimi Hendrix (a Seattle native), and he has spent $60 million for a Jimi Hendrix Museum to be called the Experience Music Project (named after the Hendrix sex-and-drug song "Are You Experienced?"). He paid $50,000 for a broken Stratocaster once played by Hendrix and has acquired 10,000 more Hendrix artifacts to be displayed in the museum. Allen plays the guitar himself in a rock band called the Threads and can play "Purple Haze," a famous Hendrix number.

Allen has given away money for a library to be named after his father and for a park in downtown Seattle, but so far he has shown no interest in giving money to the needy. Does he have any moral obligation to give money to needy people?

Suppose Allen develops an interest in baseball similar to his interest in basketball. He buys a professional baseball team, say the Atlanta Braves, moves them to Seattle, and provides them with his own private full-size baseball field so that he can privately watch games between his team and other professional teams brought in for the occasion. The price tag for this entertainment is more than $100 million. Is there anything wrong with this? After all, Allen can certainly afford it.

Bill Gates has about twice as much Microsoft stock as Allen and is worth twice as much as Allen. In other words, Gates is worth about $12 billion. Gates is often portrayed as predatory and ruthless; no doubt these qualities have helped make him one of the most successful businessmen of all time. Gates is keeping his money, at least for the present. Does he have any obligation to contribute to the needy?

1. Contract With America: The Bold Plan by Rep. Newt Gingrich, Rep. Dick Armey and the House Republicans to Change the Nation, ed. Ed Gillespie and Bob Schellhas (Random House, 1994). The proposal for welfare reform in the contract is to "end welfare as we know it" by introducing limits to benefits and work requirements.

2. Charles Murray, *Losing Ground: American Social Policy, 1950–1980* (Basic Books, 1984), advocates an elimination of all federal welfare, except unemployment insurance, for working-age persons.

3. Peter Marin, "Helping and Hating the Homeless," *Harper's Magazine* (January 1987), argues that those who are involuntarily homeless such as the mentally or physically ill should receive welfare benefits and that those who choose to be homeless should at least be given a place to exist.

4. John Arthur, "Rights and Duty to Bring Aid," in *World Hunger and Moral Obligation,* ed. William Aiken and Hugh LaFollette (Prentice-Hall, 1977), attacks Singer's view that we have a moral obligation to provide aid to those suffering from lack of food and medical care.

5. Thomas Malthus, *Essay on the Principle of Population as It Affects the Future Improvement of Society* (London, 1798), gives the classic statement of the influential view that human populations naturally increase beyond adequate food supply and are naturally checked by periodic famines.

6. Famine, ed. G. A. Harrisson (Oxford University Press, 1988), is a collection of articles on famines and their causes.

7. Onora O'Neill, "Lifeboat Earth," *Philosophy and Public Affairs,* vol. 4, no. 3 (Spring 1975), assumes that people on the lifeboat Earth have a right not to be killed and a corollary duty not to kill others. It follows from this, she argues, that we ought to adopt policies to prevent others from dying of starvation.

8. Onora O'Neill, *Faces of Hunger: An Essay on Poverty, Development and Justice* (George Allen and Unwin, 1986), develops her views on the duty to aid needy people.

9. Onora O'Neill, "Ending World Hunger," in *Matters of Life and Death,* third edition, ed. Tom Regan (Random House, 1993), discusses and compares utilitarian and Kantian approaches to hunger and famine.

10. Nick Eberstadt, "Myths of the Food Crisis," *The New York Review of Books* (February 19, 1976), pp. 32–37, argues that the cause of starvation today is not overpopulation but inequalities in food distribution.

11. Milton Friedman, *Capitalism and Freedom* (University of Chicago Press, 1962), espouses a principle of distribution of income according to what one produces or what one's instruments produce.

12. Michael Harrington, *Socialism* (Saturday Review Press, 1970), presents a version of socialism that is different from both communism and the welfare state.

13. Frances Moore Lappe, *World Hunger: Twelve Myths* (Grove Press, 1986). This is an informed look at various aspects of the problem of world hunger by a liberal who thinks that people in rich countries should change their diet.

14. Diet for a Small Planet by Frances Moore Lappe (Ballantine Books, 1975) is a classic vegetarian book that gives facts and figures about how eating meat wastes resources and explains how to get adequate protein without eating meat. Recipes are included.

15. William M. Murdoch and Allen Oaten, "Population and Food: Metaphors and the Reality," *Bioscience* (September 9, 1975), pp. 561–67, attack Hardin's lifeboat ethics; they argue that factors other than food supply affect population growth.

16. Robert Nozick, *Anarchy, State, and Utopia* (Basic Books, 1974), defends a libertarian conception of justice.

17. James Rachels, "Killing and Starving to Death," *Philosophy* 54, no. 208 (April 1979), pp. 159–71, argues that our duty not to let people die of starvation is just as strong as our duty not to kill them.

18. Amartya Sen, *Poverty and Famines* (Oxford University Press, 1981), argues that famines are not caused by natural disasters such as droughts and floods but by human problems including unemployment, high prices, civil unrest, and war.

19. Henry Shue, *Basic Rights* (Princeton University Press, 1980), defends the view that everyone has a right to subsistence and that this economic right is as important as political rights such as the right to liberty.

20. Charles B. Shuman, "Food Aid and the Free Market," in *Food Policy,* ed. Peter G. Brown and Henry Shue (The Free Press, 1977), pp. 145–63. In opposition to Shue, Shuman advocates a free-market approach to the problem of hunger and starvation.

21. Julian L. Simon, *The Ultimate Resource* (Princeton University Press, 1981), argues for a position directly opposed to Hardin.

22. James P. Sterba, "Human Rights: A Social Contract Perspective," *American Catholic Philosophical Association Proceedings,* vol. 55 (1981), pp. 268–75, develops a conception of human rights based on Rawls' social contract theory. In Sterba's view, the right to life has priority over the right to property.

Chapter Six

DISCRIMINATION AND AFFIRMATIVE ACTION

Introduction

Facts about Discrimination   In the last century women were denied many of the legal rights they have today. They could not vote, own property, enter into contracts, serve on juries, or be doctors or lawyers. In addition to this sexual discrimination (or "gender" discrimination), there was blatant racial discrimination. African-Americans were not allowed to vote in some states, even after slavery was abolished by the Thirteenth Amendment in 1865. Also, African-Americans were excluded from union membership, they were denied access to nonmenial jobs, they could not marry whites, they had to sit in designated places on buses and in restaurants, and they received an inferior education.

In the late 1960s and early 1970s, two laws were passed that benefited women and minorities to some extent. The Equal Pay Act of 1963 asserted that men and women have to be given equal pay for substantially equal work by companies engaged in production for commerce. Title VII of the Civil Rights Act of 1964 prohibited discrimination in employment on the basis of race, color, religion, sex, or national origin by private employers, employment agencies, and unions with fifteen or more employees. Also it prohibited the sex (or "gender") segregation of jobs, and it required that there be a Bona Fide Occupational Qualification to allow preference for a specific group for certain jobs, such as wet nurse or male clothing model.

Despite these antidiscrimination laws, sexual and racial discrimination continued, although perhaps not quite as blatantly as before the laws were enacted. Consider some of the state laws that discriminate against women. There are laws that permit women to be imprisoned for three years for habitual drunkenness, whereas for men the penalty for the same offense is thirty days; there are laws that excuse all women from jury duty, laws that permit the withholding of credit from married women on the grounds that they are financially dependent on their husbands, laws that permit the plea of passion killing for wronged husbands but not wronged wives, laws that give the husband the right of action in divorce cases of adultery but not the wife, and so on. Why not eliminate all these sexist laws at one sweep? That is the goal of the ERA, or Equal Rights Amendment, which simply states that "equality of rights under the law shall not be denied or abridged by the United States or by any state on account of sex." This amendment was proposed by Alice Paul in 1923, three years after the Nineteenth Amendment which gave women the right to vote. The amendment was approved by Congress in 1971, but it was not ratified by three-fourths of the state legislatures. It is now dead, apparently a victim of sexism.

The evidence for discrimination against women and minorities in employment and admission is enormous and difficult to summarize. Nevertheless, it seems clear that women and minorities remain at a disadvantage. Let us review some statistics. (1) At all occupational levels, women make less money than men, even for the same work, despite the Equal Pay Act of 1963. In 1986, the median weekly income of male workers was $419; the comparable figure for women was $290. This is only a slight improvement over the figures in 1955, when women's earnings were 64 percent of men's. More recently, women have made some gains. According to the Economic Policy Institute in Washington, D.C., in the first half of 1993 women's wages reached 78 percent of men's, a "historic high," but hardly proving that there is no longer a problem of unequal pay. (2) The latest census statistics available indicate that the most desirable occupations (management and administration,

professions, and technical jobs) are dominated by whites, whereas the less desirable jobs (service and farm work) are dominated by African-Americans, Hispanics, and other ethnic minorities. Women predominate in the lowest-paying jobs: librarians, nurses, elementary school teachers, sales clerks, secretaries, bank tellers, and waitresses. At the same time, men dominate in the highest-paying jobs: lawyers, doctors, U.S. senators, and so on. (3) In the well-known AT&T case, that enormous company signed a settlement giving tens of millions of dollars to women and minority workers, thus admitting to massive discrimination against women and minorities. (4) Female college teachers with identical credentials in terms of publications and experience are promoted at almost exactly one-half the rate of their male counterparts. There is more evidence, but why go on? It seems clear that there is still racial and sexual discrimination in employment and pay.

Why Is Discrimination Wrong? Discrimination on the basis of sex or race is not always wrong. It does not seem to matter much that rest rooms are segregated by sex, and it does not seem unjust to make a movie about African-American people in Harlem with only African-American actors. On the other hand, it does seem unfair to not hire a qualified person as a lawyer just because she is a woman, or to not admit a qualified student to medical school just because he is white. What is it about racial and sexual discrimination that makes them wrong? As Peter Singer points out in the first reading for the chapter, the standard view is that sexual and racial discrimination are wrong when race and sex or gender are irrelevant to whether a person should be given a job, the vote, higher education, or some other benefit. Qualifications are relevant to getting these benefits, but not race or sex. If women or minorities are not allowed to vote just because of their sex or race, then this is wrong because sex and race are irrelevant to voting. But sex is relevant when it comes to maternity leave, and race may be relevant when one is making a movie about African-American people and their culture.

But as Singer shows in the reading, there are problems with the standard view. One difficulty is that it forbids us to take race or sex into account in employment and admission to school, because in most cases race or sex is irrelevant. But as we shall see in the readings, defenders of affirmative-action programs that involve preferential treatment do want to take race or sex into account when it comes to employment and admission to school. Furthermore, the standard view allows sexual or racial discrimination when sex or race is relevant to the treatment in question, and this seems to allow objectionable racial or sexual discrimination. For example, landlords may refuse to rent apartments to African-American people because the white tenants will move out. Even though this racial discrimination is in the landlord's self-interest, and thus not arbitrary, it does not seem to be morally justified. Or consider women in combat. It may be true that, on the average, women are not as strong and aggressive as men, and thus they are not as good in fighting as men. So sex does seem relevant when it comes to choosing people for combat duty. Does this mean that sexual discrimination is justified in this case? Again, some people want to deny this, but the reason can't be that sex is irrelevant to the treatment in question.

Because of objections like these, Singer rejects the standard view that discrimination is wrong because it is arbitrary. In his view it is wrong when it violates a basic moral principle—the principle of equal consideration of interests. This principle says that we ought to give equal consideration to everyone's interests. This principle not only shows why racism and sexism are wrong (they violate the principle); it also shows what is wrong with our treatment of animals. (See the reading by Singer in Chapter 8.) To see how it works, let us apply the principle to the two problematic cases mentioned in the preceding paragraph. Suppose we have qualified women and men who have an equal interest in combat duty; they want to do this because it is easier to get a promotion in the army if one does combat duty. According to Singer's principle of equality, we must give equal consideration to the

interests of both the men and the women; we are not justified in choosing the men and rejecting the women. Or suppose we have both an African-American family and a white family that want to rent an apartment. Because their interest in renting is equal, we must give them equal consideration, and we cannot refuse the African-American family just because of its race.

How Can Unjust Discrimination Be Corrected?

If it is a fact that people have been wrongfully discriminated against in the past and continue to be discriminated against in the present, then what should we do about it? Is there any way to correct this injustice? Two sorts of solutions have been proposed. Backward-looking solutions to the problem of unjust discrimination seek to compensate groups or individuals who have been unfairly discriminated against in the past. For example, in the readings, Mary Anne Warren adopts this approach to counteract primary and secondary sexist hiring practices which have unfairly discriminated against women. She argues that preferential treatment of women in the form of numerical quotas for hiring and promotion is justified to compensate women for past and ongoing sexism. This sort of solution also is defended by Bernard Boxill in the readings. He argues that preferential treatment of African-Americans is justified as compensation for past wrongful and harmful discrimination.

Forward-looking solutions try to realize a future society free of discrimination, or at least with reduced discrimination. For example, we might try to produce a colorblind society where race and sex are no more significant than eye color is in our society. In the reading, T. Alexander Aleinikoff criticizes this strategy of strong colorblindness. He argues that it is impossible to eliminate race-consciousness and that pretending to do so just reinforces racial oppression and domination instead of eliminating them. Instead of color-blindness, we should have color-consciousness. Instead of antidiscrimination, we ought to seek racial justice, and this requires race discrimination laws, including affirmative action.

Affirmative Action   As amended by the Equal Employment Opportunity Act of 1972, the Civil Rights Act of 1964 requires businesses that have substantial dealings with the federal government to undertake so-called affirmative-action programs that are supposed to correct imbalances in employment that exist as a result of past discrimination. The programs that have been the focus of most debate are often called preferential treatment programs by those who favor them, or reverse discrimination by those who oppose them. Two sorts of preferential treatment programs are at issue. The first type involves quotas or specific numerical goals; a school or employer will specify some set number or proportion of women or minority applicants who must be accepted or hired. The second type involves no quota or numerical goal but requires that women or minorities be given preferential treatment over white men who are equally or even better qualified.

The first type of program has resulted in some landmark lawsuits. One of these, *University of California* v. *Bakke* (1978), went to the Supreme Court and is described in more detail in the Problem Cases. In this case the Court ruled that the Medical School of the University of California at Davis acted illegally in using a specific quota approach and in refusing to admit Alan Bakke while admitting less-qualified minority students. Another famous case is *De-Funis* v. *Odegaard* (1973). In this case, Marco DeFunis, a nonminority applicant, was denied admission to the University of Washington Law School's class of 1971. He filed a suit claiming that he had been treated unfairly insofar as he had been denied admission on the basis of race. Preferential treatment that year was accorded to African-Americans, Native Americans, Chicanos, and Filipinos. Thirty-seven of these minority applicants were accepted, and eighteen actually enrolled. The Law School admission test scores and projected grade-point averages of almost all these minority students were lower than those of some of the rejected non-minority students. The Supreme Court of the state of Washington ruled against DeFunis. The Court argued that racial classifications are not

unconstitutional, that their use is acceptable if there is a compelling state interest, and that the shortage of minority attorneys constituted a compelling state interest. The case was appealed to the United States Supreme Court, but the Supreme Court did not hand down a ruling. DeFunis had been attending law school while the case was being appealed, and the case was declared moot.

The unequal treatment given Bakke and DeFunis is called reverse discrimination, usually by those who oppose it. In our readings, Barry R. Gross makes at least four objections to reverse discrimination. First, the procedures for identifying those who have suffered from discrimination are flawed. We cannot assume that a group is discriminated against just because they are underrepresented in certain jobs. Second, reverse discrimination is undesirable because it has bad effects (for example, incompetent people are hired). Third, reverse discrimination does not fit the standard legal models of compensation. Fourth, reverse discrimination is unjust discrimination, and the fact that it is directed against white males does not make it less unjust.

In the next reading, Bernard Boxill replies to the first and last objections made by Gross. Boxill thinks that the evidence that African-Americans have suffered from discrimination is found in the fact that they are underrepresented in all attractive jobs, and not just in some of them. Also, he denies that reverse discrimination is unfair to whites. In his view, whites deserve to be discriminated against because they have benefited from the past discrimination of others, for example, in unfair educational opportunities. African-Americans deserve compensation for this discrimination, while whites who have benefited from it should pay by being discriminated against.

Shelby Steele develops the objection that affirmative action has bad results; ironically, it is bad for the very ones it is supposed to benefit, namely African-Americans. It hinders the advance of African-Americans by enlarging their self-doubt and fostering the cultural myth of African-American inferiority; it replaces overt discrimination with a more subtle discrimination; and it creates a glass ceiling at the point where competence overrules color.

In the last reading, T. Alexander Aleinikoff defends race-conscious programs such as affirmative action. He thinks that the good effects outweigh the bad effects and that the burden of proof is on those who claim, as Steele does, that affirmative action programs contribute to racism rather than reduce it.

Peter Singer

Is Racial Discrimination Arbitrary?

For biographical information on Singer, see his reading in Chapter 3.

Singer uses the term racial discrimination *in a morally neutral, descriptive sense to refer to discrimination based on race. He claims that such discrimination is not always wrong, and when it is wrong, it is not wrong because it is arbitrary. In Singer's view, racial discrimination is wrong when it violates the basic moral principle of equal consideration of interests. As Singer formulates it, this principle says that we should give equal weight in our moral considerations to the like interests of all those affected by our actions.*

INTRODUCTION

There is nowadays wide agreement that racism is wrong. To describe a policy, law, movement or nation as 'racist' is to condemn it. It may be thought that since we all agree that racism is wrong, it is unnecessary to speculate on exactly what it is and why it is wrong. This indifference to moral fundamentals could, however, prove dangerous. For one thing, the fact that most

From Peter Singer, "Is Racial Discrimination Arbitrary?" *Philosophia*. Reprinted from *Philosophia* 8: 2–3 (1978) by permission of the author, Peter Singer, and the editor of *Philosophia*, Asa Kasher.

people agree today that racism is wrong does not mean that this attitude will always be so widely shared. Even if we had no fears for the future, though, we need to have some understanding of what it is about racism that is wrong if we are to handle satisfactorily all the problems that we face today. For instance, there is the contentious issue of 'reverse discrimination' or discrimination in favor of members of oppressed minority groups. It must be granted that a university which admits members of minority groups who do not achieve the minimum standard that others must reach in order to be admitted is discriminating on racial lines. Is such discrimination therefore wrong?

Or, to take another issue, the efforts of Arab nations to have the United Nations declare Zionism a form of racism provoked an extremely hostile reaction in nations friendly to Israel, particularly the United States, but it led to virtually no discussion of whether Zionism is a form of racism. Yet the charge is not altogether without plausibility, for if Jews are a race, then Zionism promotes the idea of a state dominated by one race, and this has practical consequences in, for instance, Israel's immigration laws. Again, to consider whether this makes Zionism a form of racism we need to understand what it is that makes a policy racist and wrong.

First it is necessary to get our terms clear. 'Racism' is, as I have said, a word which now has an inescapable evaluative force, although it also has some descriptive content. Words with these dual functions can be confusing if their use is not specified. People sometimes try to argue: 'X is a case of racial discrimination, therefore X is racist; racism is wrong, therefore X is wrong'. This argument may depend on an equivocation in the meaning of 'racist', the term being used first in a morally neutral, descriptive sense, and secondly in its evaluative sense.

To avoid this kind of confusion, I shall accept the usual evaluative force of the term 'racist' and reserve it for practices that are judged to be wrong. Thus we cannot pronounce a policy, law etc. 'racist' unless we have decided that it is wrong. 'Racial discrimination' on the other hand I shall use in a descriptive, and morally neutral sense, so that to say that a policy or law discriminates racially is simply to point to the fact of discrimination based on race, leaving open the question of whether it can be justified. With this terminology it becomes possible to ask whether a given form of racial discrimination is racist; this is another way of asking whether it is justifiable.[1]

If we ask those who regard racial discrimination as wrong to say why it is wrong, it is commonly said that it is wrong to pick on race as a reason for treating one person differently from others, because race is irrelevant to whether a person should be given a job, the vote, higher education, or any benefits or burdens of this sort. The irrelevance of race, it is said, makes it quite arbitrary to give these things to people of one race while withholding them from those of another race. I shall refer to this account of what is wrong with racial discrimination as the 'standard objection' to racial discrimination.

A sophisticated theory of justice can be invoked in support of this standard objection to racial discrimination. Justice requires, as Aristotle so plausibly said, that equals be treated equally and unequals be treated unequally. To this we must add the obvious proviso that the equalities or inequalities should be relevant to the treatment in question. Now when we consider things like employment, it becomes clear that the relevant inequalities between candidates for a vacant position are inequalities in their ability to carry out the duties of the position and, perhaps, inequalities in the extent to which they will benefit through being offered the position. Race does not seem to be relevant at all. Similarly with the vote, capacity for rational choice between candidates or policies might be held a relevant characteristic, but race should not be; and so on for other goods. It is

hard to think of anything for which race in itself is a relevant characteristic, and hence to use race as a basis for discrimination is arbitrarily to single out an irrelevant factor, no doubt because of a bias or prejudice against those of a different race.[2]

As we shall see, this account of why racial discrimination is wrong is inadequate because there are many situations in which, from at least one point of view, the racial factor is by no means irrelevant, and therefore it can be denied that racial discrimination in these situations is arbitrary.

One type of situation in which race must be admitted to be relevant to the purposes of the person discriminating need not delay us at this stage; this is the situation in which those purposes themselves favor a particular race. Thus if the purpose of Hitler and the other Nazi leaders was, among other things, to produce a world in which there were no Jews, it was certainly not irrelevant to their purposes that those rounded up and murdered by the S.S. were Jews rather than so-called 'Aryans'. But the fundamental wrongness of the aims of the Nazis makes the 'relevance' of race to those aims totally inefficacious so far as justifying Nazi racial discrimination is concerned. While their type of racial discrimination may not have been arbitrary discrimination in the usual sense, it was no less wrong for that. *Why* it was wrong is something that I hope will become clearer later in this article. Meanwhile I shall look at some less cataclysmic forms of racial discrimination, for too much contemporary discussion of racial discrimination has focussed on the most blatant instances: Nazi Germany, South Africa, and the American 'Deep South' during the period of legally enforced racial segregation.[3] These forms of racism are not the type that face us now in our own societies (unless we live in South Africa) and to discuss racial discrimination in terms of these examples today is to present an over-simplified picture of the problem of racial discrimination. By looking at some of the reasons for racial discrimination that might actually be offered today in countries all over the world I hope to show that the real situation is usually much more complex than consideration of the more blatant instances of racial discrimination would lead us to believe.

EXAMPLES

I shall start by describing an example of racial discrimination which may at first glance seem to be an allowable exception to a general rule that racial discrimination is arbitrary and therefore wrong; and I shall then suggest that this case has parallels with other cases we may not be so willing to allow as exceptions.

Case 1

A film director is making a film about the lives of blacks living in New York's Harlem. He advertises for black actors. A white actor turns up, but the director refuses to allow him to audition, saying that the film is about blacks and there are no roles for whites. The actor replies that, with the appropriate wig and make-up, he can look just like a black; moreover he can imitate the mannerisms, gestures, and speech of Harlem blacks. Nevertheless the director refuses to consider him for the role, because it is essential to the director's conception of the film that the black experience be authentically portrayed, and however good a white actor might be, the director would not be satisfied with the authenticity of the portrayal.

The film director is discriminating along racial lines, yet he cannot be said to be discriminating arbitrarily. His discrimination is apt for his purpose. Moreover his purpose is a legitimate one. So the standard objection to racial discrimination cannot be made in this instance.

Racial discrimination may be acceptable in an area like casting for films or the theatre, when the race of a character in the film or play is important, because this is one of the seemingly few areas in which a person's race is directly relevant to his capacity to perform a given task. As such, it may be thought, these areas can easily be distinguished from other areas of employment, as well as from areas like housing, education, the right to vote, and so on, where race has no relevance at all. Unfortunately there are many other situations in which race is not as totally irrelevant as this view assumes.

Case 2

The owner of a cake shop with a largely white and racially prejudiced clientele wishes to hire an assistant. The owner has no prejudice against blacks himself, but is reluctant to employ one, for fear that his customers will go elsewhere. If his fears are well-founded (and this is not impossible) then the race of a candidate for the position is, again, relevant to the purpose of the employer, which in this case is to maintain the profitability of his business.

What can we say about this case? We cannot deny the connection between race and the owner's purposes, and so we must recognize that the owner's discrimination is not arbitrary, and does not necessarily indicate a bias or prejudice on his part. Nor can we say that the owner's purpose is an illegitimate one, for making a profit from the sale of cakes is not generally regarded as wrong, at least if the amount of profit made is modest.

We can, of course, look at other aspects of the matter. We can object to the racial discrimination shown by customers who will search out shops staffed by whites only—such people do discriminate arbitrarily, for race is irrelevant to the quality of the goods and the proficiency of service in a shop—but is this not simply a fact that the shop owner must live with, however much he may wish he could change it? We might argue that by pandering to the prejudices of his customers, the owner is allowing those prejudices to continue unchallenged; whereas if he and other shopkeepers took no notice of them, people would eventually become used to mixing with those of another race, and prejudices would be eroded. Yet it is surely too much to ask an individual shop owner to risk his livelihood in a lone and probably vain effort to break down prejudice. Few of the most dedicated opponents of racism do as much. If there were national legislation which distributed the burden more evenly, by a general prohibition of discrimination on racial grounds (with some recognized exceptions for cases like casting for a film or play) the situation would be different. Then we could reasonably ask every shop owner to play his part. Whether there should be such legislation is a different question from whether the shop owner may be blamed for discriminating in the absence of legislation. I shall discuss the issue of legislation shortly, after we consider a different kind of racial discrimination that, again, is not arbitrary.

Case 3

A landlord discriminates against blacks in letting the accommodation he owns. Let us say that he is not so rigid as never to let an apartment to a black, but if a black person and a white person appear to be equally suitable as tenants, with equally good references and so on, the landlord invariably prefers the white. He defends his policy along the following lines:

If more than a very small proportion of my tenants get behind in their rent and then disappear without paying the arrears, I will be out of business. Over the years, I have found that more blacks do this than whites. I admit that there are many honest blacks (some of my best tenants have been black) and many dishonest whites, but, for some reason I do not claim to understand, the odds on a white tenant defaulting are longer than on a black doing so, even when their references and other credentials appear equally good. In this business you can't run a full-scale probe of every prospective tenant—and if I tried I would be abused for invading privacy—so you have to go by the average rather than the individual. That is why blacks have to have better indications of reliability than whites before I will let to them.

Now the landlord's impression of a higher rate of default among blacks than among comparable whites may itself be the result of prejudice on his part. Perhaps in most cases when landlords say this kind of thing, there is no real factual basis to their allegations. People have grown up with racial stereotypes, and these stereotypes are reinforced by a tendency to notice occurrences which conform to the stereotype and to disregard those which conflict with it. So if unreliability is part of the stereotype of blacks held by many whites, they may take more notice of blacks who abscond without paying the rent than of blacks who are reliable tenants; and conversely they will take less notice of absconding whites and more of those whites who conform to their ideas of normal white behaviour.

If it is prejudice that is responsible for the landlord's views about black and white tenants, and there is no factual basis for his claims, then the problem becomes one of eliminating this prejudice and getting the landlord to see his mistake. This is by no means an easy task, but

it is not a task for philosophers, and it does not concern us here, for we are interested in attempts to justify racial discrimination, and an attempted justification based on an inaccurate description of a situation can be rejected without raising the deeper issue of justification.

On the other hand, the landlord's impression of a higher rate of default among black tenants *could* be entirely accurate. (It might be explicable in terms of the different cultural and economic circumstances in which blacks are brought up.) Whether or not we think this likely, we need to ask what its implications would be for the justifiability of the racial discrimination exercised by the landlord. To refuse even to consider this question would be to rest all one's objections to the landlord's practice on the falsity of his claims, and thereby to fail to examine the possibility that the landlord's practice could be open to objection even if his impressions on tenant reliability are accurate.

If the landlord's impressions were accurate, we would have to concede, once again, that racial discrimination in this situation is not arbitrary; that it is, instead, relevant to the purposes of the landlord. We must also admit that these purposes—making a living from letting property that one owns—are not themselves objectionable, provided the rents are reasonable, and so on. Nor can we, this time, locate the origin of the problem in the prejudices of others, except insofar as the problem has its origin in the prejudices of those responsible for the conditions of deprivation in which many of the present generation of blacks grew up—but it is too late to do anything to alter those prejudices anyway, since they belong to previous generations.

We have now looked at three examples of racial discrimination, and can begin to examine the parallels and differences between them. Many people, as I have already said, would make no objection to the discriminatory hiring practice of the film director in the first of these cases. But we can now see that if we try to justify the actions of the film director in this case on the grounds that his purpose is a legitimate one and the discrimination he uses is relevant for his purpose, we will have to accept the actions of the cake-shop owner and the landlord as well. I suspect that many of those ready to accept the discriminatory practice in the first case will be much more reluctant about the other two cases. But what morally significant difference is there between them?

It might be suggested that the difference between them lies in the nature of what blacks are being deprived of, and their title to it. The argument would run like this: No-one has a right to be selected to act in a film; the director must have absolute discretion to hire whomsoever he wishes to hire. After all, no-one can force the director to make the film at all, and if he didn't make it, no-one would be hired to play in it; if he does decide to make it, therefore, he must be allowed to make it on his own terms. Moreover, since so few people ever get the chance to appear in a film, it would be absurd to hold that the director violates someone's rights by not giving him something which most people will never have anyway. On the other hand, people do have a right to employment, and to housing. To discriminate against blacks in an ordinary employment situation, or in the letting of accommodation, threatens their basic rights and therefore should not be tolerated.

Plausible as it appears, this way of distinguishing the first case from the other two will not do. Consider the first and second cases: almost everything that we have said about the film director applies to the cake-shop owner as well. No-one can force the cake-shop owner to keep his shop open, and if he didn't, no one would be hired to work in it. If in the film director's case this was a reason for allowing him to make the film on his own terms, it must be a reason for allowing the shop owner to run his shop on his own terms. In fact, such reasoning, which would allow unlimited discrimination in restaurants, hotels and shops, is invalid. There are plenty of examples where we would not agree that the fact that someone did not have to make an offer or provide an opportunity at all means that if he does do it he must be allowed to make the offer or provide the opportunity on his own terms. The United States Civil Rights Act of 1965 certainly does not recognize this line of argument, for it prohibits those offering food and lodgings to the public from excluding customers on racial grounds. We may, as a society, decide that we shall not allow people to make certain offers, if the way in which the offers are made will cause hardship or offense to others. In so doing we are balancing people's freedom to do as they please against the harm this may do to others, and coming down on the side of preventing harm rather than enlarging freedom. This is a perfectly defensible position, if the harm is sufficiently serious and the restriction of freedom not grave.[4]

Nor does it seem possible to distinguish the first and second cases by the claim that since so few people ever get the chance to appear in a film, no-one's rights are violated if they are not given something that most people will never have anyway. For if the number of jobs in cake shops was small, and the demand for such jobs high, it would also be true that few people would ever have the chance to work in a cake shop. It would be odd if such an increase in competition for the job justified an otherwise unjustifiable policy of hiring whites only. Moreover, this argument would allow a film director to discriminate on racial lines even if race was irrelevant to the roles he was casting; and that is quite a different situation from the one we have been discussing.

The best way to distinguish the situations of the film director and the shop owner is by reference to the nature of the employment offered, and to the reasons why racial discrimination in these cases is not arbitrary. In casting for a film about blacks, the race of the actor auditioning is intrinsically significant, independently of the attitudes of those connected with the film. In the case of hiring a shop assistant, race is relevant only because of the attitudes of those connected (as customers) with the shop; it has nothing to do with the selling of cakes in itself, but only with the selling of cakes to racially prejudiced customers. This means that in the case of the shop assistant we could eliminate the relevance of race if we could eliminate the prejudices of the customers; by contrast there is no way in which we could eliminate the relevance of the race of an actor auditioning for a role in a film about blacks, without altering the nature of the film. Moreover, in the case of the shop owner racial discrimination probably serves to perpetuate the very prejudices that make such discrimination relevant and (from the point of view of the owner seeking to maintain his profits) necessary. Thus people who can buy all their cakes and other necessities in shops staffed only by whites will never come into the kind of contact with comparable blacks which might break down their aversion to being served by blacks; whereas if shop owners were to hire more blacks, their customers would no doubt become used to it and in time might wonder why they ever opposed the idea. (Compare the change of attitudes toward racial integration in the American South since the 1956 United States Supreme Court decision against segregated schools and subsequent measures against segregation were put into effect.[5])

Hence if we are opposed to arbitrary discrimination we have reason to take steps against racial discrimination in situations like Case 2, because such discrimination, while not itself arbitrary, both feeds on and gives support to discrimination by others which is arbitrary. In prohibiting it we would, admittedly, be preventing the employer from discriminating in a way that is relevant to his purposes; but if the causal hypothesis suggested in the previous paragraph is correct, this situation would only be temporary, and after some time the circumstances inducing the employer to discriminate racially would have been eliminated.

The case of the landlord presents a more difficult problem. If the facts he alleges are true his non-arbitrary reasons for discrimination against blacks are real enough. They do not depend on present arbitrary discrimination by others, and they may persist beyond an interval in which there is no discrimination. Whatever the roots of hypothetical racial differences in reliability as tenants might be, they would probably go too deep to be eradicated solely by a short period in which there was no racial discrimination.

We should recognize, then, that if the facts are as alleged, to legislate against the landlord's racially discriminatory practice is to impose a long-term disadvantage upon him. At the very least, he will have to take greater care in ascertaining the suitability of prospective tenants. Perhaps he will turn to data-collecting agencies for assistance, thus contributing to the growth of institutions that are threats, potential or actual, to our privacy. Perhaps, if these methods

are unavailable or unavailing, the landlord will have to take greater losses than he otherwise would have, and perhaps this will lead to increased rents or even to a reduction in the amount of rentable housing available.

None of this forces us to conclude that we should not legislate against the landlord's racial discrimination. There are good reasons why we should seek to eliminate racial discrimination even when such discrimination is neither arbitrary in itself, nor relevant only because of the arbitrary prejudices of others. These reasons may be so important as to make the disadvantage imposed on the landlord comparatively insignificant.

An obvious point that can be made against the landlord is that he is judging people, at least in part, as members of a race rather than as individuals. The landlord does not deny that some black prospective tenants he turns away would make better tenants than some white prospective tenants he accepts. Some highly eligible black prospective tenants are refused accommodation simply because they are black. If the landlord assessed every prospective tenant as an individual this would not happen.

A similar point is often made in the debate over alleged differences between blacks and whites in America in whatever is measured by IQ tests. Even if, as Jensen and others have suggested, there is a small inherited difference in IQ between blacks and whites, it is clear that this difference shows up only when we compare averages, and not when we compare individuals. Even if we accept the controversial estimates that the average IQ of American blacks is 15 points lower than the average IQ of American whites, there is still a tremendous amount of overlap between the IQs of blacks and whites, with many whites scoring lower than the majority of blacks. Hence the difference in averages between the races would be of limited significance. For any purpose for which IQ mattered—like entrance into higher levels of education—it would still be essential to consider each applicant individually, rather than as a member of a certain race.

There are plenty of reasons why in situations like admitting people to higher education or providing them with employment or other benefits we should regard people as individuals and not as members of some larger group. For one thing we will be able to make a selection better suited for our own purposes, for selecting or discarding whole groups of people will generally result in, at best, a crude approximation to the results we hope to achieve. This is certainly true in an area like education. On the other hand it must be admitted that in some situations a crude approximation is all that can be achieved anyway. The landlord claims that his situation is one of these, and that as he cannot reliably tell which individuals will make suitable tenants, he is justified in resorting to so crude a means of selection as race. Here we need to turn our attention from the landlord to the prospective black tenant.

To be judged merely as a member of a group when it is one's individual qualities on which the verdict should be given is to be treated as less than the unique individual that we see ourselves as. Even where our individual qualities would merit less than we receive as a member of a group—if we are promoted over better-qualified people because we went to the 'right' private school—the benefit is usually less welcome than it would be if it had been merited by our own attributes. Of course in this case qualms are easily stilled by the fact that a benefit has been received, never mind how. In the contrary case, however, when something of value has been lost, the sense of loss will be compounded by the feeling that one was not assessed on one's own merits, but merely as a member of a group.

To this general preference for individual as against group assessment must be added a consideration arising from the nature of the group. To be denied a benefit because one was, say, a member of the Communist Party would be unjust and a violation of basic principles of political liberty, but if one has chosen to join the Communist Party, then one is, after all, being assessed for what one has done, and one can choose between living with the consequences of continued party membership or leaving the party.[6] Race, of course, is not something that one chooses to adopt or that one can ever choose to give up. The person who is denied advantages because of his race is totally unable to alter this particular circumstance of his existence and so may feel with added sharpness that his life is clouded, not merely because he is not being judged as an individual, but because of something over which he has no control at all. This makes racial discrimination peculiarly invidious.

So we have the viewpoint of the victim of racial discrimination to offset against the landlord's argument in favor, and it seems that the victim has more at stake and hence should be given preference, even if the landlord's reason for discriminating is non-arbitrary and hence is in a sense legitimate. The case against racial discrimination becomes stronger still when we consider the long-term social effects of discrimination.

When members of a racial minority are overwhelmingly among the poorest members of a society, living in a deprived area, holding jobs low in pay and status, or no jobs at all, and less well educated than the average member of the community, racial discrimination serves to perpetuate a divided society in which race becomes a badge of a much broader inferiority. It is the association of race with economic status and educational disadvantages which in turn gives rise to the situation in which there could be a coloring of truth to the claim that race is a relevant ground for discriminating between prospective tenants, applicants for employment, and so on. Thus there is, in the end, a parallel between the situation of the landlord and the cake-shop owner, for both, by their discrimination, contribute to the maintenance of the grounds for claiming that this discrimination is non-arbitrary. Hence prohibition of such discrimination can be justified as breaking this circle of deprivation and discrimination. The difference between the situations, as I have already said, is that in the case of the cake-shop owner it is only a prejudice against contact with blacks that needs to be broken down, and experience has shown that such prejudices do evaporate in a relatively short period of time. In the case of the landlord, however, it is the whole social and economic position of blacks that needs to be changed, and while overcoming discrimination would be an essential part of this process it may not be sufficient. That is why, if the facts are as the landlord alleges them to be, prohibition of racial discrimination is likely to impose more of a long-term disadvantage on the landlord than on the shop owner—a disadvantage which is, however, outweighed by the costs of continuing the circle of racial discrimination and deprivation for those discriminated against; and the costs of greater social inequality and racial divisiveness for the community as a whole.

A BASIC PRINCIPLE

If our discussion of the three examples has been sound, opposition to racial discrimination cannot rely on the standard objection that racial discrimination is arbitrary because race is irrelevant to employment, housing, and other things that matter. While this very often will be true, it will not always be true. The issue is more complicated than that appealing formula suggests, and has to do with the effect of racial discrimination on its victims, and on society as a whole. Behind all this, however, there is a more basic moral principle, and at this more basic level the irrelevance of race and the arbitrariness of racial discrimination reappear and help to explain why racism is wrong. This basic moral principle is the principle of equal consideration of interests.

The principle of equal consideration of interests is easy to state, though difficult to apply. Bentham's famous 'each to count for one and none for more than one' is one way of putting it, though not free from ambiguity; Sidgwick's formulation is more precise, if less memorable: 'The good of any one individual is of no more importance, from the point of view (if I may say so) of the Universe, than the good of any other.' [7] Perhaps the best way of explaining the effect of the principle is to follow C. I. Lewis's suggestion that we imagine ourselves living, one after the other, the lives of everyone affected by our actions; in this way we would experience all of their experiences as our own.[8] R. M. Hare's insistence that moral judgments must be universalizable comes to much the same thing, as he has pointed out.[9] The essence of the principle of equal consideration of interests is that we give equal weight in our moral deliberations to the like interests of all those affected by our actions. This means that if only X and Y would be affected by a possible act, and if X stands to lose more than Y stands to gain (for instance, X will lose his job and find it difficult to get another, whereas Y will merely get a small promotion) then it is better not to do the act. We cannot, if we accept the principle of equal consideration of interests, say that doing the act is better, despite the facts described, because we are more concerned about Y than we are about X. What the principle is really saying is that an interest is an interest, whoever's interest it may be.

We can make this more concrete by considering a particular interest, say the interest we have in the relief of pain. Then the principle says that the ultimate moral reason for relieving pain is simply the undesirability of pain as such, and not the undesirability of X's pain, which might be different from the undesirability of Y's pain. Of course, X's pain might be more undesirable than Y's pain because it is more painful, and then the principle of equal consideration would give greater weight to the relief of X's pain. Again, even where the pains are equal, other factors might be relevant, especially if others are affected. If there has been an earthquake we might give priority to the relief of a doctor's pain so that he can treat other victims. But the doctor's pain itself counts only once, and with no added weighting. The principle of equal consideration of interests acts like a pair of scales, weighing interests impartially. True scales favor the side where the interest is stronger, or where several interests combine to outweigh a smaller number of similar interests; but they take no account of whose interests they are weighing.

It is important to understand that the principle of equal consideration of interests is, to adopt Sidgwick's suggestive phrase, a 'point of view of the universe' principle. The phrase is, of course, a metaphor. It is not intended to suggest that the universe as a whole is alive, or conscious, or capable of having a point of view; but we can, without getting involved in any pantheist suppositions, imagine how matters would be judged by a being who was able to take in all of the universe, viewing all that was going on with an impartial benevolence.[10]

It is from this universal point of view that race is irrelevant to the consideration of interests; for all that counts are the interests themselves. To give less consideration to a specified amount of pain because that pain was experienced by a black would be to make an arbitrary distinction. Why pick on race? Why not on whether a person was born in a leap year? Or whether there is more than one vowel in his surname? All these characteristics are equally irrelevant to the undesirability of pain from the universal point of view. Hence the principle of equal consideration of interests shows straightforwardly why the most blatant forms of racism, like that of the Nazis, are wrong. For the Nazis were concerned only for the welfare of members of the 'Aryan' race, and the sufferings of Jews, Gypsies and Slavs were of no concern to them.

That the principle of equal consideration of interests is a 'point of view of the universe' principle allows us to account for the fact that it is a principle upon which it seems virtually impossible to act. Who of us can live as if our own welfare and that of our family and friends were of no more concern to us than the welfare of anonymous individuals in far away countries, of whom we know no more than the fact of their existence? Only a saint or a robot could live in this way; but this does not mean that only a saint or a robot can live in accordance with the principle of equal consideration of interests, for a principle which is valid from a universal point of view may yield subordinate principles to be acted upon by those who have limited resources and are involved in a particular segment of the world, rather than looking down upon the whole from a position of impartiality.

So subordinate principles giving members of families responsibility for the welfare of others in the family, or giving national governments responsibility for the welfare of their citizens, will be derivable from the principle of equal consideration, *if* everyone's interests are best promoted by such arrangements; and this is likely to be the case if, first, people are more knowledgeable about the interests of those close to them and more inclined to work to see that these interests are catered for, and, second, if the distribution of resources between families and between nations is not so unequally distrib-

uted that some families or nations are simply unable to provide for themselves the means to satisfying interests that could be satisfied with ease by other families or nations. In the world as it is presently constituted the first condition seems to hold, but not the second. For that reason I do not think that the subordinate principles mentioned correctly set out our present moral responsibilities, though they could do so if resources were more evenly distributed. Until then, we ought to strive to be more saint-like.[11]

Subordinate principles based on race, giving each race responsibility for the welfare of other members of that race are, I think, considerably less likely to be derivable from the principle of equal consideration than subordinate principles based on family or membership of a nation. For where they are not living together as a nation, races tend to be widely scattered; thee is usually little knowledge of the circumstances of other members of one's race in different parts of the world, and there is nobody with the capacity to look after all members of a race as a national government can look after the interests of its citizens. There is, admittedly, often a degree of sentiment connecting members of a race, however widely they are separated. The contributions of American Jews to the support of members of their race in Israel is a well-known example of this, and there are many others. But the intermingling of races still makes it very doubtful that interests could be generally promoted by dividing responsibilities along racial lines.

The fundamental principle of equal consideration of interests, then, pays no regard to the race of those whose interests are under consideration; nor can we plausibly derive from the basic principle a subordinate principle enjoining us to consider the interests of members of our own race before we consider the interests of others; yet it cannot be said that the principle rules out racial discrimination in all circumstances. For the principle is an abstract one, and can only be applied in a concrete situation, in which the facts of the situation will be relevant. For instance, I have heard it said that somewhere in ancient Hindu writings members of the Brahmin or priestly caste are claimed to be so much more sensitive than members of the lower castes that their pleasures and pains are twenty times as intense as those of lesser human beings. We would, of course, do well to be suspicious of such a claim, particularly as the author of the document would no doubt have been a Brahmin himself. But let us assume that we somehow discovered that this extraordinary difference in sensitivity did in fact exist; it would follow that Brahmins have a greater interest in having access to a source of pleasure, and in avoiding a source of pain, than others. It would be as if when a Brahmin scratches his finger he feels a pain similar to that which others feel when they dislocate their shoulder. Then, consistently with the principle of equal consideration of interests, if a Brahmin and an ordinary person have both scratched their fingers, and we have only enough soothing ointment to cover one scratch, we should favor the Brahmin—just as, in the case of two normal people, if one had scratched a finger while the other had dislocated a shoulder we should favor the person with the more painful injury.

Needless to say, the example is a fanciful one, and intended to show only how, within the confines of the principle of equal consideration of interests, factual differences could be relevant to racial discrimination. In the absence of any real evidence of racial differences in sensitivity to pleasure and pain, the example has no practical relevance. Other differences between races—if they were differences between all members of races, and not differences which showed up only when averages were taken—could also justify forms of discrimination which ran parallel to the boundary of race. Examples would be substantial differences in intelligence, educability or the capacity to be self-governing. Strictly, if there were such differences then discrimination based on them would not be *racial* discrimination but rather discrimination on the ground of differences which happened to coincide with racial differences. But perhaps this is hairsplitting, since it would certainly be popularly known as racial discrimination. The kind of discrimination that such differences would justify would be only that to which these differences were relevant. For instance, a respectable argument for benevolent colonialism could be mounted if it really were true that certain races

were so incapable of self-government as to be obviously better off on the whole when ruled by people of a different race. I hasten to add that the historical record gives no support to such a hypothesis, but rather suggests the contrary. Again, this fictional example shows only that, given peculiar enough factual assumptions, any acceptable principle of equality can lead to racial discrimination.

On the other hand, the principle of equal consideration of interests does underpin the decisions we reached when considering the three more realistic examples of racial discrimination in the preceding section of this article. Although the principle is too general to allow the derivation of straightforward and indisputable conclusions from it in complex situations, it does seem that an impartial consideration of the interests of all involved would, for reasons already discussed, rule out discrimination by the shop owner and the landlord, though allowing that of the film director. Hence it is the arbitrariness of racial discrimination at the level of the principle of equal consideration of interests, rather than at the level of the particular decision of the person discriminating, that governs whether a given act of racial discrimination is justifiable.

This conclusion may be applied to other controversial cases. It suggests, for instance, that the problem of 'reverse discrimination' or 'compensatory discrimination' which arises when a university or employer gives preference to members of minority groups should be discussed by asking not whether racial discrimination is always and intrinsically wrong, but whether the proposal is, on balance, in the interests of all those affected by it. This is a difficult question, and not one that can be answered generally for all types of reverse discrimination. For instance, if white communities have a far better doctor-patient ratio than black communities because very few blacks are admitted to medical school and white doctors tend to work in white communities, there is a strong case for admitting some black candidates to medical school ahead of whites who are better qualified by the standard entry procedures, provided, of course, that the blacks admitted are not so poorly qualified as to be unable to become competent doctors. The case for separate and easier entry would be less strong in an area where there is no equivalent community need, for instance, in philosophy. Here much would depend on whether black students who would not otherwise have been admitted were able to make up ground and do as well as whites with higher ratings on standard entry procedures. If so, easier entry for blacks could be justified in terms of the conventional goal of admitting those students most likely to succeed in their course; taking into account a student's race would merely be a way of correcting for the failure of standard tests to allow for the disadvantages that face blacks in competing with whites on such tests. If, on the other hand, blacks admitted under easier entry in a field like philosophy did not do as well as the whites they displaced could have been expected to do, discrimination in their favor would be much harder to justify.

Immigration policy, too, is an area in which the principle of equal consideration of interests suggests the kinds of facts we should look for, instead of giving a definite answer. The relevant questions are the extent to which an immigrant will be benefited by admission, and the extent to which the admitting nation will be benefited. Race certainly does not provide an answer to the first of these questions. A country which chooses to give only those of a certain race the benefit of permanent residence fails to give equal consideration to those not of the favored race who may have a greater interest in leaving their present country than others who are accepted because of their race. While this kind of racial discrimination would in itself be unjustifiable, it has been defended on the grounds that the alternative would be disastrous for citizens of the admitting nation, and ultimately for those admitted too. An extreme version of this kind of defense is the line taken by the British politician Enoch Powell, who prophesied 'rivers of blood' if black immigration was not stopped and blacks who had already arrived were not encouraged to go back to where they had come from.[12] Here again, the facts are relevant. If Powell's claims had been soundly based, if it really were impossible for blacks and whites to live together without widespread bloodshed, then continued immigration would have been in the interests of neither blacks nor whites, and

stopping immigration could not have been condemned as racist—though the epithet could have been applied to those Britons who were so hostile to blacks as to produce the situation Powell predicted. Despite occasional racial disturbances in Britain, however, there is no sign that Powell's predictions will come true. While a sudden influx of large numbers of immigrants of a different racial (or ethnic) group may cause problems, it is clear that people of different races can live together without serious strife. This being so, there is no justification for immigration policies that impose blanket prohibitions on people of a different race from that of the residents of the country. The most that can be defended in terms of the principle of equal consideration of interests is a quota system that leads to a gradual adjustment in the racial composition of a society.[13]

Endnotes

1. In popular usage, even the term 'discrimination' is often used to suggest that the practice referred to is wrong; this is, of course, an abuse of language, for to discriminate is merely to distinguish, or differentiate, and we could hardly get along without doing that.

2. For a brief and clear statement on this idea of justice, see H. L. A. Hart, *The Concept of Law* (Clarendon Press, Oxford, 1961) pp. 156–8; see also Joel Feinberg, *Social Philosophy* (Prentice-Hall, Englewood Cliffs, N.J., 1973) ch. 7.

3. See, for instance, R. M. Hare, *Freedom and Reason* (Clarendon Press, Oxford, 1963) chs. 9, 11; Richard Wasserstrom, 'Rights, Human Rights, and Racial Discrimination', *Journal of Philosophy*, vol. 61 (1964) and reprinted in James Rachels, ed., *Moral Problems* (Harper and Row, New York, 1975).

4. See Feinberg, *op. cit.*, p. 78.

5. "In most southern communities . . . the adjustment to public desegregation following the enactment of the 1964 Civil Rights Act was amazing." Lewis M. Killian, *White Southerners* (New York: Random House, 1970). Similar comments have been made by many other observers; for a more recent report, see *Time*, September 27, 1976, especially the favorable comments of Northern blacks who have recently moved to the South (p. 44). That contact with those of another race helps to reduce racial prejudice had been demonstrated as early as 1949, when a study of U.S. soldiers showed that the more contact white soldiers had with black troops, the more favorable were their attitudes to integration. See Samuel Stouffer, *et al.*, *The American Soldier: Adjustment During Army Life* (Princeton: Princeton University Press, 1949) p. 594. This finding was supported by a later study, 'Project Clear', reported by Charles Moskos, Jr., 'Racial Integration in the

Armed Forces', *American Journal of Sociology,* vol. 72 (1966) pp. 132–48.

6. The situation is different if it is because of a past rather than a present political connection that one is subjected to disadvantages. Perhaps this is why the hounding of ex-communists in the McCarthy era was a particularly shameful episode in American history.

7. Henry Sidgwick, *The Methods of Ethics* (Macmillan, London, 7th Edition, 1907), p. 382.

8. C. I. Lewis, *Analysis of Knowledge and Valuation* (La Salle, 1946), p. 547; I owe this reference to R. M. Hare.

9. See Hare, 'Rules of War and Moral Reasoning', *Philosophy and Public Affairs,* vol. 1 (1972).

10. See the discussion of the Ideal Observer theory in Roderick Firth, 'Ethical Absolutism and the Ideal Observer'. *Philosophy and Phenomenological Research,* vol. XII (1952) and the further discussion in the same journal by Richard Brandt, vol. XV (1955).

11. For a general discussion of this issue, see Sidgwick, *op. cit.* pp. 432–3; for considerations relevant to the present distribution of resources, see my 'Famine, Affluence and Morality'. *Philosophy and Public Affairs,* vol. I (1972) and reprinted in James Rachels (ed.) *Understanding Moral Philosophy* (Dickenson, Encino, Calif., 1976) and Paula and Karsten Struhl (eds.) *Philosophy Now* (Random House, New York, 2nd Edition, 1975).

12. *The Times* (London) April 21, 1968.

13. I am grateful to Robert Young for comments and criticism on this paper.

REVIEW QUESTIONS

1. Distinguish between the evaluative and descriptive senses of a term. How does Singer use the terms *racist* and *racial discrimination*?

2. What is the standard objection to racial discrimination according to Singer? Why doesn't he accept this objection?

3. State and explain the principle of equal consideration of interests accepted by Singer.

4. When is racial discrimination wrong according to Singer? Give examples.

5. What is Singer's view of reverse discrimination?

6. What is his position on immigration policies?

DISCUSSION QUESTIONS

1. Can sexual discrimination be treated in the same way as Singer treats racial discrimination? Why or why not?

2. Can you think of any objections to the principle of equal consideration of interests? What are they?

3. Should we apply the principle of equal consideration of interests to children, nonhuman animals, other species, and the natural environment? What is your view? (In Chapter 8, we find Singer applying this principle to nonhuman animals.)

4. Singer is willing to allow reverse discrimination in some cases—for example, admitting a black candidate to medical school ahead of whites who are better qualified. Is such reverse discrimination acceptable?

Mary Anne Warren

Secondary Sexism and Quota Hiring

For biographical information on Mary Anne Warren, see her reading in Chapter 2.

Warren begins by distinguishing between primary and secondary sexism. Primary sexism is simply unfair discrimination on the basis of sex. Secondary sexism involves the use of sex-correlated criteria which are not valid measures

of merit. One such criterion is: Does the candidate have an uninterrupted work record? This criterion discriminates against women who have interrupted their careers to have and raise children. To counteract primary and secondary sexist hiring practices which have put women at a disadvantage, Warren favors mandatory hiring quotas of a

From Warren, Mary Anne; "Secondary Sexism and Quota Hiring," *Philosophy and Public Affairs,* vol. 6, no. 3 (Spring 1977), pp. 240–261. Copyright © 1977 by Princeton University Press. Reprinted by permission of Princeton University Press. [Some of the footnotes have been renumbered—Ed.]

minimum sort based on the proportion of women among qualified and available candidates. Even though employers may have to use weak discrimination in favor of women to meet these quotas, Warren does not think that this is especially unfair to men. She feels that men have benefited in the past and will benefit in the future from sexist discrimination against women.

I want to call attention to a pervasive form of discrimination against women, one which helps to explain the continuing male monopoly of desirable jobs in the universities, as elsewhere. Discrimination of this sort is difficult to eliminate or even, in some cases, to recognize, because (1) it is not explicitly based on sex, and (2) it typically *appears* to be justified on the basis of plausible moral or practical considerations. The recognition of this form of discrimination gives rise to a new argument for the use of numerical goals or quotas in the hiring of women for college and university teaching and administrative positions.

I shall argue that because of these de facto discriminatory hiring practices, minimum numerical quotas for the hiring and promotion of women are necessary, not (just) to compensate women for past discrimination or its results, or to provide women with role models, but to counteract this *ongoing* discrimination and thus make the competition for such jobs more nearly fair. Indeed, given the problems inherent in the compensatory justice and role-model arguments for reverse discrimination, this may well be the soundest argument for the use of such quotas.

I. PRIMARY AND SECONDARY SEXISM

Most of us try not to be sexists; that is, we try not to discriminate unfairly in our actions or attitudes toward either women or men. But it is not a simple matter to determine just which actions or attitudes discriminate unfairly, and a sincere effort to avoid unfair discrimination is often not enough. This is true of both of the forms of sexism that I wish to distinguish.

In its primary sense, "sexism" means *unfair discrimination on the basis of sex*. The unfairness

may be unintentional; but the cause or reason for the discrimination must be the sex of the victim, not merely some factor such as size or strength that happens to be correlated with sex. Primary sexism may be due to dislike, distrust, or contempt for women, or, in less typical cases, for men or hermaphrodites. Or it may be due to sincerely held but objectively unjustified beliefs about women's properties or capacities. It may also be due to beliefs about the properties women *tend* to have, which are objectively justified but inappropriately applied to a particular case, in which the woman discriminated against does not have those properties.

For instance, if members of a philosophy department vote against hiring or promoting a woman logician because they dislike women (logicians), or because they think that women cannot excel in logic, or because they know that most women do not so excel and wrongly conclude that this one does not, then they are guilty of primary sexism. This much, I think, is noncontroversial.

But what should we say if they vote to hire or promote a man rather than a woman because he has a wife and children to support, while she has a husband who is (capable of) supporting her? Or because they believe that the woman has childcare responsibilities which will limit the time she can spend on the job? What if they hire a woman at a lower rank and salary than is standard for a man with comparable qualifications, for one of the above reasons? These actions are not sexist in the primary sense because there is no discrimination on the basis of sex itself. The criteria used *can* at least be applied in a sex-neutral manner. For instance, it might be asserted that if the woman candidate had had a spouse and children who depended upon her for support, this would have counted in her favor just as much as it would in the case of a man.

Of course, appeals to such intrinsically sex-neutral criteria may, in some cases, be mere rationalizations of what is actually done from primary sexist motives. In reality, the criteria cited may not be applied in a sex-neutral manner. But let us assume for the sake of argument that the application of these criteria *is* sex-neutral, not merely a smoke screen for primary sexism. On this assumption, the use of such criteria discriminates against women only because of certain contingent features of this society, such as the persistence of the traditional division of labor in marriage and childrearing.[1]

Many people see nothing morally objectionable in the use of such intrinsically sex-neutral yet de facto discriminatory criteria. For not only may employers who use such criteria be free of primary sexism, but their actions may appear to be justified on both moral and pragmatic grounds. It might, for instance, be quite clear that a department will really do more to alleviate economic hardship by hiring or promoting a man with dependents rather than a woman with none, or that a particular woman's domestic responsibilities will indeed limit the time she can spend on the job. And it might seem perfectly appropriate for employers to take account of such factors.

Nevertheless, I shall argue that the use of such considerations is unfair. It is an example of secondary sexism, which I define as comprising all those actions, attitudes and policies which, while not using sex itself as a reason for discrimination, do involve sex-correlated factors or criteria and do result in an unfair impact upon (certain) women. In the case of university hiring policies, secondary sexism consists in the use of sex-correlated selection criteria which are not valid measures of academic merit, with the result that women tend to be passed over in favor of men who are not, in fact, better qualified. I call sexism of this sort *secondary,* not because it is any less widespread or harmful than primary sexism, but because (1) it is, in this way, indirect or covert, and (2) it is typically parasitic upon primary sexism, in that the injustices it perpetuates—for example, those apparent from the male monopoly of desirable jobs in the universities—are usually due in the first instance to primary sexism.

Two points need to be made with respect to this definition. First, it is worth noting that, although in the cases we will be considering the correlations between sex and the apparently independent but de facto discriminatory criteria are largely due to past and present injustices against women, this need not always be the case. The discriminatory impact of excluding

pregnancy-related disabilities from coverage by employee health insurance policies, for example, probably makes this an instance of secondary sexism. Yet it is certainly not (human) injustice which is responsible for the fact that it is only women who become pregnant. The fact that the correlation is due to biology rather than prior injustice does not show that the exclusion is not sexist. Neither does the fact that pregnancy is often undertaken voluntarily. If such insurance programs fail to serve the needs of women employees as well as they serve those of men, then they can escape the charge of sexism only if—as seems unlikely—it can be shown that they cannot possibly be altered to include disabilities related to pregnancy without ceasing to serve their mutually agreed upon purposes, and/or producing an even greater injustice.

This brings us to the second point. It must be stressed that on the above definition the use of valid criteria of merit in hiring to university positions is not an instance of secondary sexism. Some might argue that merit criteria discriminate unfairly against women, because it is harder for women to earn the advanced degrees, to write the publications, and to obtain the professional experience that are the major traditional measures of academic merit. But it would be a mistake to suppose that merit criteria as such are therefore sexist. They are sexist only to the extent that they understate women's actual capacity to perform well in university positions; and to that extent, they are invalid as criteria of merit. To the extent that they are valid, that is, the most reliable available measurements of capacities which are indeed crucial for the performance of the job, they are not unjust, even though they may result in more men than women being hired.

If this seems less than obvious, the following analogy may help. It is surely not unjust to award first prize in a discus throwing contest to the contestant who actually makes the best throw (provided, of course, that none of the contestants have been unfairly prevented from performing up to their capacity on this particular occasion), even if some of the contestants have in the past been wrongly prevented from developing their skill to the fullest, say by sexist discrimination in school athletic programs.

Such contestants may be entitled to other relevant forms of compensation, for example, special free training programs to help them make up for lost time, but they are not entitled to win this particular contest. For the very *raison d'être* of an athletic contest dictates that prizes go to the best performers, not those who perhaps *could* have been the best, had past conditions been ideally fair.

So too, a university's central reasons for being dictate that positions within it be filled by candidates who are as well qualified as can be found. Choosing less qualified candidates deprives students of the best available instruction, colleagues of a more intellectually productive environment, and—in the case of state-funded universities—the public of the most efficient use of its resources.[2] To appoint inferior candidates defeats the primary purposes of the university, and is therefore wrong-headed, however laudable its motivations. It is also, as we shall see, a weapon of social change which is apt to backfire against those in whose interest it is advocated. . . .

II. SECONDARY SEXISM IN UNIVERSITY HIRING

Consider the following policies, which not infrequently influence hiring, retention, and promotion decisions in American colleges and universities:

1. Antinepotism rules, proscribing the employment of spouses of current employees.
2. Giving preference to candidates who (are thought to) have the greater financial need, where the latter is estimated by whether someone has, on the one hand, financial dependents, or, on the other hand, a spouse capable of providing financial support.
3. The "last hired-first fired" principle, used in determining who shall be fired or not rehired as a result of staffing cutbacks.
4. Refusing promotions, tenure, retention seniority, or pro-rata pay to persons employed less than full time, where some are so employed on a relatively long-term basis and where there is no evidence that such persons

are (all) less well qualified than full time employees.
5. Hiring at a rank and salary determined primarily by previous rank and salary rather than by more direct evidence of a candidate's competence, for example, degrees, publications, and student and peer evaluations.
6. Counting as a negative factor the fact that a candidate has or is thought to have, or to be more likely to have, childcare or other domestic responsibilities which may limit the time s/he can spend on the job.
7. Giving preference to candidates with more or less uninterrupted work records over those whose working careers have been interrupted (for example, by raising children) in the absence of more direct evidence of a present difference in competence.
8. Not hiring, especially to administrative or supervisory positions, persons thought apt to encounter disrespect or lack of cooperation from peers or subordinates, without regard for whether this presumed lack of respect may be itself unjustified, for example, as the result of primary sexism.
9. Discriminating against candidates on the grounds of probable mobility due to the mobility of a spouse, present or possible.

Each of these practices is an example of secondary sexism, in that while the criterion applied does not mention sex, its use nevertheless tends to result in the hiring and promotion of men in preference to women who are not otherwise demonstrably less well qualified. I suggest that in seeking to explain the continuing underrepresentation of women in desirable jobs in the universities, we need to look only toward primary sexist attitudes within those institutions, and certainly not toward any intrinsic lack of merit on the part of women candidates,[3] but toward covertly, and often unintentionally, discriminatory practices such as these.

Of course, none of these practices operates to the detriment of women in every case; but each operates against women much more often than against men, and the cumulative effect is enormous. No doubt some of them are more widespread than others and some (for example, the use of antinepotism rules) are already declining in response to pressures to remove barriers to the employment of women. Others, such as policies 3 and 4, are still fairly standard and have barely begun to be seriously challenged in most places. Some are publicly acknowledged and may have been written into law or administrative policy, for example, policies 1, 3, 4, and 5. Others are more apt to be private policies on the part of individual employers, to which they may not readily admit or of which they may not even be fully aware, for example, policies 2, 6, 7, and 8. It is obviously much more difficult to demonstrate the prevalence of practices of the latter sort. Nevertheless, I am certain that all of these practices occur, and I strongly suspect that none is uncommon, even now.

This list almost certainly does not include all of the secondary sexist practices which influence university hiring. But these examples are typical, and an examination of certain of their features will shed light on the way in which secondary sexism operates in the academic world and on the reasons why it is morally objectionable.

In each of these examples, a principle is used in choosing between candidates that in practice acts to discriminate against women who may even be better qualified intrinsically than their successful rivals, on any reliable and acceptable measure of merit.[4] Nevertheless, the practice may *seem* to be justified. Nepotism rules, for instance, act to exclude women far more often than men, since women are more apt to seek employment in academic and/or geographical areas in which their husbands are already employed than vice versa. Yet nepotism rules may appear to be necessary to ensure fairness to those candidates and appointees, both male and female, who are *not* spouses of current employees and who, it could be argued, would otherwise be unfairly disadvantaged. Similarly, giving jobs or promotions to those judged to have the greatest financial need may seem to be simple humanitarianism, and the seniority system may seem to be the only practical way of providing job security to *any* portion of the faculty. For policies 5 through 9, it could be argued that, although the criteria used are not entirely reliable, they may still have *some* use in predicting job performance.

Thus each practice, though discriminatory in its results, may be defended by reference to principles which are not intrinsically sex-biased. In the context of an otherwise sexually egalitarian society, these practices would probably not result in de facto discrimination against either sex. In such a society, for instance, men would not hold a huge majority of desirable jobs, and women would be under no more social or financial pressure than men to live where their spouses work rather than where they themselves work; thus they would not be hurt by nepotism rules any more often, on the average, than men.[5] The average earning power of men and women would be roughly equal, and no one could assume that women, any more than men, ought to be supported by their spouses, if possible. Thus the fact that a woman has an employed spouse would not be thought to reduce her need for a job any more—or less—than in the case of a man. We could proceed down the list; in a genuinely nonsexist society, few or none of the conditions would exist which cause these practices to have a discriminatory impact upon women.

Of course, there may be other reasons for rejecting these practices, besides their discriminatory impact upon women. Nepotism rules might be unfair to married persons of both sexes, even in a context in which they were not *especially* unfair to women. My point is simply that these practices would not be instances of sexism in a society which was otherwise free of sexism and its results. Hence, those who believe that the test of the justice of a practice is whether or not it would unfairly disadvantage any group or individual *in the context of an otherwise just society* will see no sexual injustice whatever in these practices.

But surely the moral status of a practice, as it operates in a certain context, must be determined at least in part by its actual consequences, in that context. The fact is that each of these practices acts to help preserve the male monopoly of desirable jobs, in spite of the availability of women who are just as well qualified on any defensible measure of merit. This may or may not suffice to show that these practices are morally objectionable. It certainly shows that they are inconsistent with the "straight merit" principle, that is, that jobs should go to those best qualified for them on the more reliable measures of merit. Hence, it is ironic that attempts to counteract such de facto discriminatory practices are often interpreted as attacks on the "straight merit" principle.

III. WHY SECONDARY SEXISM IS UNFAIR

Two additional points need to be stressed in order to show just why these practices are unfair. In the first place, the contingent social circumstances which explain the discriminatory impact of these practices are themselves morally objectionable, and/or due to morally objectionable practices. It is largely because men *are* more able to make good salaries, and because married women are still expected to remain financially dependent upon their husbands, if possible, that the fact that a woman has an employed husband can be seen as evidence that she doesn't "need" a job. It is because a disproportionate number of women must, because of family obligations and the geographical limitations these impose, accept part-time employment even when they would prefer full time, that the denial of tenure, promotion and pro-rata pay to part-time faculty has a discriminatory impact upon women. That women accept such obligations and limitations may seem to be their own free choice; but, of course, that choice is heavily conditioned by financial pressures—for example, the fact that the husband can usually make more money—and by sexually stereotyped social expectations.

Thus, the effect of these policies is to compound and magnify prior social injustices against women. When a woman is passed over on such grounds, it is rather as if an athlete who had without her knowledge been administered a drug to hamper her performance were to be disqualified from the competition for failing the blood-sample test. In such circumstances, the very least that justice demands is that the unfairly imposed handicap not be used as a rationale for the imposition of further handicaps. If the unfair handicaps that society imposes upon women cause them to be passed over by employers because of a lack of straight merit, that

is one thing, and it is unfortunate, but it is not obvious that it involves unfairness on the part of the employers. But if those handicaps are used as an excuse for excluding them from the competition regardless of their merit, as all too often happens, this is quite another thing, and it is patently unfair.

In the second place, practices such as these often tend to perpetuate the very (unjust) circumstances which underlie their discriminatory impact, thus creating a vicious circle. Consider the case of a woman who is passed over for a job or promotion because of her childcare responsibilities. Given a (better) job, she might be able to afford day care, or to hire someone to help her at home, or even to persuade her husband to assume more of the responsibilities. Denying her a job because of her domestic responsibilities may make it almost impossible for her to do anything to lessen those responsibilities. Similarly, denying her a job because she has a husband who supports her may force him to continue supporting her and her to continue to accept that support.

Both of these points may be illustrated by turning to a somewhat different sort of example. J. R. Lucas has argued that there are cases in which women may justifiably be discriminated against on grounds irrelevant to their merit. He claims, for example, that it is "not so evidently wrong to frustrate Miss Amazon's hopes of a military career in the Grenadier Guards on the grounds not that she would make a bad soldier, but that she would be a disturbing influence in the mess room." [6]

But this is a paradigm case of secondary, and perhaps also primary, sexism; it is also quite analogous to practice 8. To exclude women from certain jobs or certain branches of the military on the grounds that certain third parties are not apt to accept them, when that nonacceptance is itself unreasonable and perhaps based on sexual bigotry, is to compound the injustice of that bigotry. If it is inappropriate for soldiers to be disturbed or to make a disturbance because there are women in the mess room, then it is wrong to appeal to those soldiers' attitudes as grounds for denying women the opportunities available to comparably qualified men. It is also to help ensure the perpetuation of those attitudes, by preventing male soldiers from having an opportunity to make the sorts of observations which might lead to their eventually accepting women as comrades.

Thus, these practices are morally objectionable because they compound and perpetuate prior injustices against women, penalizing them for socially imposed disadvantages which cannot be reliably shown to detract from their actual present capacities. We may conclude that the hiring process will never be fair to women, nor will it be based on merit alone, so long as such practices persist on a wide scale. But it remains to be seen whether numerical hiring quotas for women are a morally acceptable means of counteracting the effects of sexist hiring practices.

IV. WEAK QUOTAS

I shall discuss the case for mandatory hiring quotas of a certain very minimal sort: those based on the proportion of women, not in the population as a whole, but among qualified and available candidates in each academic field. Such a "weak" quota system would require that in each institution, and ideally within each department and each faculty and administrative rank and salary, women be hired and promoted at least in accordance with this proportion. If, for instance, a tenured or tenure-track position became available in a given department on an average of every other year, and if women were twenty percent of the qualified and available candidates in the field, then such a quota system would require that the department hire a woman to such a position at least once in ten years.[7]

Needless to say, this is not a formula for rapid change in the sexual composition of the universities. Suppose that the above department has twenty members, all male and all or almost all tenured, that it does not grow, and that it perhaps shrinks somewhat. Under these not atypical circumstances, it could easily take over forty years for the number of women in the department to become proportional to the number of qualified women available, even if the quota is

strictly adhered to, and the proportion of qualified women does not increase in the meantime. Consequently, some would agree that such a quota system would be inadequate.[8]

Furthermore, it *could* be argued that if the job competition were actually based on merit, women would be hired and promoted at a *higher* rate than such a weak quota system would require, since the greater obstacles still encountered by women on the way to obtaining qualifications ensure that only very able women make it.[9] Or, it might be argued that women should be hired and promoted in more than such proportional numbers, in order to compensate for past discrimination or to provide other women with role models. Indeed, some existing affirmative action plans, so I am told, already require that women be hired in more than proportional numbers. Nevertheless, I will not defend quotas higher than these minimal ones. For, as will be argued in Section VIII, higher quotas at least give the appearance of being unfair to male candidates, and it is not clear that either the compensatory justice or the role-model argument is sufficient to dispel that appearance.

V. QUOTAS OR GOALS?

Before turning to the case of such minimal hiring quotas, we need to comment on the "quotas vs. goals" controversy. Those who oppose the use of numerical guidelines in the hiring of women or racial minorities usually refer to such guidelines as *quotas,* while their defenders usually insist that they are not quotas but *goals.* What is at issue here? Those who use the term "quotas" pejoratively tend to assume that the numerical standards will be set so high or enforced so rigidly that strong reverse discrimination—that is, the deliberate hiring of demonstrably less well qualified candidates—will be necessary to implement them.[10] The term "goal," on the other hand, suggests that this will not be the case, and that good faith efforts to comply with the standards by means short of strong reverse discrimination will be acceptable.[11]

But whatever one calls such minimum numerical standards, and whether or not one suspects that strong reverse discrimination has in fact occurred in the name of affirmative action, it should be clear that it is not *necessary* for the implementation of a quota system such as I have described. Neither, for that matter, is weak reverse discrimination—that is, the deliberate hiring of women in preference to equally but not better qualified men.[12] For if hiring decisions are solely based on reliable measures of merit and wholly uncorrupted by primary or secondary sexist policies, then qualified women would *automatically* be hired and promoted at least in proportion to their numbers, except, of course, in statistically abnormal cases.[13] Consequently, reverse discrimination will *appear* to be necessary to meet proportional quotas only where the hiring process continues to be influenced by sexist practices—primary or secondary, public or private.

In effect, the implementation of a minimum quota system would place a price upon the continued use of sexist practices. Employers would be forced to choose between eliminating sexist practices, thus making it possible for quotas to be met without discriminating for or against anyone on the basis of sex, and practicing reverse discrimination on an ad hoc basis in order to meet quotas without eliminating sexist practices. Ideally, perhaps, they would all choose the first course, in which case the quota system would serve only to promote an ongoing check upon, and demonstration of, the nonsexist nature of the hiring process.

In reality, however, not all secondary sexist practices can be immediately eliminated. Some forms of secondary sexism have probably not yet been recognized, and given the nature of the interests involved it is likely that new forms will tend to spring up to replace those which have been discredited. More seriously, perhaps, some secondary sexist policies, such as the seniority system, cannot be eliminated without an apparent breach of contract (or of faith) with present employees. Others—for example, hiring on the basis of need—may survive because they are judged, rightly or wrongly, to be on the whole the lesser evil. A quota system, however, would require that the impact of such secondary sexist practices be counterbalanced by preferential treatment of women in other instances. Fur-

thermore, it would hasten the elimination of all sexist policies by making it in the interest of all employees, men as well as women, that this be done, since until it is done both will run the risk of suffering from (sexist or reverse) discrimination. Certainly their elimination would be more probable than it is at present, when it is primarily women who have a reason based on self-interest for opposing them, yet primarily men who hold the power to eliminate or preserve them.

The most crucial point, however, is that under such a quota system, even if (some) employers do use weak discrimination in favor of women to meet their quota, this will not render the job competition especially unfair to men. For, as I will argue, unfairness would result only if the average male candidate's chances of success were reduced to below what they would be in an ongoing, just society, one in which men and women had complete equality of opportunity and the competition was based on merit alone; and I will argue that the use of weak reverse discrimination to meet proportional hiring quotas will not have this effect.

VI. QUOTAS AND FAIRNESS

Now one way to support this claim would be to argue that in an ongoing, just society women would constitute a far higher proportion of the qualified candidates in most academic fields and that therefore the average male candidate's chances would, other things being equal, automatically be reduced considerably from what they are now. Unfortunately, however, the premise of this argument is overly speculative. It is possible that in a fully egalitarian society women would still tend to avoid certain academic fields and to prefer others, much as they do now, or even that they would fail to (attempt to) enter the academic profession as a whole in much greater numbers than at present.

But whatever the proportion of male and female candidates may be, it must at least be the case that in a just society the chances of success enjoyed by male candidates must be no greater, on the average, and no less than those enjoyed by comparably qualified women. Individual differences in achievement, due to luck or to differences in ability, are probably inevitable; but overall differences in the opportunities accorded to comparably qualified men and women, due to discrimination, would not be tolerated.

The question, then is: Would the use of weak discrimination in favor of women, to a degree just sufficient to offset continuing sexist discrimination against women and thus to meet minimum quotas, result in lowering the average chances of male candidates to below those of comparably qualified women? The answer, surely, is that it would not, since by hypothesis men would be passed over, in order to fill a quota, in favor of women no better qualified only as often as women continue to be passed over, because of primary or secondary sexism, in favor of men no better qualified.

In this situation, individual departures from the "straight merit" principle might be no less frequent than at present; indeed, their frequency might even be doubled. But since it would no longer be predominantly women who were repeatedly disadvantaged by those departures, the overall fairness of the competition would be improved. The average long-term chances of success of *both* men and women candidates would more closely approximate those they would enjoy in an ongoing just society. If individual men's careers are temporarily set back because of weak reverse discrimination, the odds are good that these same men will have benefited in the past and/or will benefit in the future—not necessarily in the job competition, but in *some* ways—from sexist discrimination against women. Conversely, if individual women receive apparently unearned bonuses, it is highly likely that these same women will have suffered in the past and/or will suffer in the future from primary or secondary sexist attitudes. Yet, the primary purpose of a minimum quota system would not be to compensate the victims of discrimination or to penalize its beneficiaries, but rather to increase the overall fairness of the situation—to make it possible for the first time for women to enjoy the same opportunity to obtain desirable jobs in the universities as enjoyed by men with comparable qualifications.

It is obvious that a quota system implemented by weak reverse discrimination is not the ideal long-term solution to the problem of sexist discrimination in academic hiring. But it would be a great improvement over the present situation, in which the rate of unemployment among women Ph.D.'s who are actively seeking employment is still far higher than among men with Ph.D.'s, and in which women's starting salaries and chances of promotion are still considerably lower than those of men.[14] Strong reverse discrimination is clearly the least desirable method of implementing quotas. Not only is it unfair to the men who are passed over, and to their potential students and colleagues, to hire demonstrably less well qualified women, but it is very apt to reinforce primary sexist attitudes on the part of all concerned, since it appears to presuppose that women cannot measure up on their merits. But to presume that proportional hiring quotas could not be met without strong reverse discrimination is also to make that discredited assumption. If, as all available evidence indicates, women in the academic world are on the average just as hard-working, productive, and meritorious as their male colleagues, then there can be no objection to hiring and promoting them at least in accordance with their numbers, and doing so will increase rather than decrease the extent to which success is based upon merit.

VII. ARE QUOTAS NECESSARY?

I have argued that minimum proportional quotas such as I have described would not make the job competition (especially) unfair to men. But it might still be doubted that quotas are necessary to make the competition fair to women. Why not simply attack sexist practices wherever they exist and then let the chips fall as they may? Alan Goldman argues that quotas are not necessary, since, he says, other measures—for example, "active recruitment of minority candidates, the advertisement and application of nondiscriminatory hiring criteria . . . and the enforcement of these provisions by a neutral government agency"[15] would suffice to guarantee equal treatment for women. Goldman claims that if women candidates are as well qualified as men then, given these other measures, they will automatically be hired at least in proportion to their numbers. Indeed, he suggests that the only basis for doubting this claim is "an invidious suspicion of the real inferiority of women . . . even those with Ph.D.'s" [16] That discrimination against women might continue to occur in spite of such affirmative measures short of quotas, he regards as "an untested empirical hypothesis without much *prima facie* plausibility." [17]

In a similar vein, George Sher has argued that blacks, but not women, are entitled to reverse discrimination in hiring, since the former but not the latter have suffered from a poverty syndrome which has denied them the opportunity to obtain the qualifications necessary to compete on an equal basis with white men. [18] He views reverse discrimination—and presumably hiring quotas—as primarily a way of compensating those who suffer from present competitive disadvantages due to past discrimination, and claims that since women are not disadvantaged with respect to (the opportunity to obtain) qualifications, they are not entitled to reverse discrimination.

What both Goldman and Sher overlook, of course, is that women suffer from competitive disadvantages quite apart from any lack of qualifications. Even if primary sexism were to vanish utterly from the minds of all employers, secondary sexist practices such as those we have considered would in all likelihood suffice to perpetuate the male monopoly of desirable jobs well beyond our lifetimes. Such practices cannot be expected to vanish quickly or spontaneously; to insist that affirmative action measures stop short of the use of quotas is to invite their continuation and proliferation.

VIII. THE COMPENSATORY JUSTICE AND ROLE-MODEL ARGUMENTS

Most of the philosophers who have recently defended the use of goals or quotas in the hiring of women and/or minority group members have assumed that this will necessarily involve at least weak and perhaps strong reverse discrimination, but have argued that it is nevertheless justified as a way of compensating individuals or groups for past injustices or for present disadvantages stemming from past injustices. [19] Others have argued that reverse discrimination is justified not (just) as a form of compensatory justice, but as a means of bringing about certain future goods—for example, raising the status of downtrodden groups, [20] or providing young women and blacks with role models and thus breaking the grip of self-fulfilling expectations which cause them to fail. [21]

If one is intent upon arguing for a policy which would give blacks or women "advantages in employment . . . greater than these same blacks or women would receive in an ongoing just society," [22] then perhaps it is necessary to appeal to compensatory justice or to the role model or to other utilitarian arguments to justify the *prima facie* unfairness to white males which such a policy involves. But there is no need to use these arguments in justifying a weak quota system such as the one described here, and indeed, it is somewhat misleading to do so. For, as we have seen, such a system would not lower the average male candidate's overall chances of success to below what they would be if the selection were based on merit alone. It would simply raise women's chances, and lower men's, to a closer approximation of what they would be in an ongoing just society, in which the "straight merit" principle prevailed. This being the case, the fact that quotas may serve to compensate some women for past or present wrongs, or to provide others with role models, must be seen as a fortuitous side effect of their use and not their primary reasons for being. The primary reason for weak quotas is simply to increase the present fairness of the competition.

Furthermore, there are problems with the compensatory justice and role-model arguments which make their use hazardous. It is not clear that either suffices to justify any use of reverse discrimination beyond what may in practice (appear to) be necessary to implement weak quotas. For, granted that society as a whole has some obligation to provide compensation to the victims of past discrimination, and assuming that at least some women candidates for university positions are suitable beneficiaries of such compensation, it is by no means clear that male candidates should be forced to bear most of the burden for providing that compensation. It would be plausible to argue on the basis of compensatory justice for, say, tax-supported *extra* positions for women, since then the burden would be distributed relatively equitably. But compensatory justice provides no case for placing an extra, and seemingly punitive, burden on male candidates, who are no more responsible for past and present discrimination against women than the rest of us.

Similarly, however badly women may need role models, it is not clear that male candidates should be disproportionately penalized in order to provide them. It can be argued on the basis of simple fairness that male candidates' chances should not be allowed to remain *above* what they would be in a just society; but to justify reducing them to *below* that point requires a stronger argument than simply appealing to compensatory justice or the need for role models.

Nor does it help to argue that the real source of the injustice to male candidates, if and when preferential hiring of women results in lowering the former's chances to below what they would be in a just society, is not the preferential hiring policy itself, but something else. Thomas Nagel, for instance, argues that reverse discrimination is not seriously unjust, even if it means that it is harder for white men to get certain sorts of jobs than it is for women and blacks who are no better qualified, since, he suggests, the real source of the injustice is the entire system of providing differential rewards on the basis of differential abilities.[23] And Marlene Fried argues that the root of the injustice is not preferential hiring, but the failure of those with the power to do so to expand job opportunities so that blacks and women could be hired in increasing numbers without hiring fewer men.[24]

Unfortunately, we cannot, on the one hand, reject secondary sexist practices because of their contingent and perhaps unintended discriminatory effects, and, on the other hand, accept extenuations such as these for a policy which would, in practice, discriminate unfairly against (white) men. These other sources of injustice are real enough; but this does not alter the fact that if reverse discrimination were practiced to the extent that certain men's chances of success were reduced to below those enjoyed, on the average, by comparably qualified women, then it would at least give every appearance of being unfair to those men. After all, the primary insight necessary for recognizing the injustice of secondary sexist policies is that a policy must be judged, at least in part, by its consequences in practice, regardless of whether or not these consequences are a stated or intended part of the policy. If a given policy results in serious and extensive injustice, then it is no excuse that this injustice has its roots in deeper social injustices which are not themselves easily amenable to change, at least not if there is any feasible way of altering the policy so as to lessen the resulting injustice.

I think we may conclude that while proportional quotas for the hiring of women are justified both on the basis of the merit principle and as a way of improving the overall fairness of the competition, it is considerably more difficult to justify the use of higher quotas. The distinction between such weak quotas and higher quotas is crucial, since although higher quotas have in practice rarely been implemented, the apparent injustice implied by what are typically *assumed* to be higher quotas has generated a backlash which threatens to undermine affirmative action entirely. If quotas are abandoned, or if they are nominally adopted but never enforced, then employers will be free to continue using secondary and even primary sexist hiring criteria, and it is probable that none of us will see the day when women enjoy job opportunities commensurate with their abilities and qualifications.

Endnotes

1. I mean, of course, the tradition that the proper husband earns (most of) the family's income, while the proper wife does (most of) the housekeeping and childrearing.
2. It might be argued that the hiring process ought not to be based on merit alone, because there are cases in which being a woman, or being black, might itself be a crucial job qualification. As Michael Martin points

out, this might well be the case in hiring for, say, a job teaching history in a previously all white-male department which badly needs to provide its students with a more balanced perspective. See "Pedagogical Arguments for Preferential Hiring and Tenuring of Women Teachers in the University," *The Philosophical Forum* 5, no. 2: 325–333. I think it is preferable, however, to describe such cases, not as instances requiring a departure from the merit principle, but as instances in which sex or race itself, or rather certain interests and abilities that are correlated with sex or race, constitutes a legitimate qualification for a certain job, and hence a measure of merit, vis-à-vis that job.

3. With respect to one such measure, books and articles published, married women Ph.D.'s published as much or slightly more than men, and unmarried women only slightly less. See "The Woman Ph.D.: A Recent Profile," by R. J. Simon, S. M. Clark, and K. Galway, in *Social Problems* 15, no. 2 (Fall 1967): 231.

4. I am assuming that whether a candidate is married to a current employee, or has dependents, or a spouse capable of supporting her, whether she is employed on a part-time or a full-time basis, her previous rank and salary, the continuity of her work record, and so on, are not in themselves reliable and acceptable measures of merit. As noted in example 5, more direct and pertinent measures of merit can be obtained. Such measures as degrees, publications, and peer and student evaluations have the moral as well as pragmatic advantage of being based on the candidate's actual past performance, rather than on unreliable and often biased conjectures of various sorts. Furthermore, even if there is or were *some* correlation (it would surely not be a *reliable* one) between certain secondary sexist criteria and job performance, it could still be argued that employers are not morally entitled to use such criteria, because of the unfair consequences of doing so. As Mary Vetterling has observed, there might well be some correlation between having "a healthy and active sex life" and "the patience and good humor required of a good teacher"; yet employers are surely not entitled to take into account the quality of a person's sex life in making hiring and promotion decisions. "Some Common Sense Notes on Preferential Hiring," *The Philosophical Forum* 5, no. 2: 321.

5. Unless, perhaps a significant average age difference between wives and husbands continued to exist.

6. J. R. Lucas, "Because You Are a Woman," *Moral Problems,* ed. James Rachels (New York: Harper & Row, 1975), p. 139.

7. In practice problems of statistical significance will probably require that quotas be enforced on an institution-wide basis rather than an inflexible department-by-department basis. Individual departments, especially if they are small and if the proportion of qualified women in the field is low, may fail to meet hiring quotas, not because of primary or secondary sexism, but because the best qualified candidates happen in fact to be men. But if no real discrimination against women is occurring, then such statistical deviations should be canceled out on the institutional level, by deviations in the opposite direction.

8. See Virginia Held, "Reasonable Progress and Self-Respect," *The Monist* 57, no. 1: 19.

9. Gertrude Ezorsky cites in support of this point a study by L. R. Harmon for over 20,000 Ph.D.'s, which showed that "Women . . . Ph.D.'s are superior to their male counterparts on all measures derived from high school records, in all . . . specializations." *High School Ability Patterns: A Backward Look from the Doctorate,* Scientific Manpower [*sic*] Report No. 6, 1965, pp. 27–28; cited by Ezorsky in "The Fight Over University Women," *The New York Review of Books* 21, no. 8 (16 May 1974): 32.

10. See, for instance, Paul Seaburg, "HEW and the Universities," *Commentary* 53, no. 2 (February 1972): 38–44.

11. In practice, strong reverse discrimination is specifically prohibited by HEW affirmative action guidelines, and good faith efforts to implement affirmative action programs without resorting to strong reverse discrimination have been accepted as adequate. Nevertheless, though I would not wish to see *these* features of affirmative action policies changed, I prefer the term "quota" for what I am proposing, because this term suggests a standard which will be enforced, in one way or another, while the term "goal" suggests—and affirmative action is in great danger of becoming—a mere expression of good intentions, compliance with which is virtually unenforceable.

12. The distinction between strong and weak reverse discrimination is explored by Michael Bayles in "Compensatory Reverse Discrimination in Hiring," *Social Theory and Practice* 2, no. 3: 303–304, and by Vetterling, "Common Sense Notes," pp. 320–323.

13. This conclusion can be avoided only by assuming either that qualified women would not want better jobs if these were available, or that they are somehow less meritorious than comparably qualified men. The first assumption is absurd, since women who do not want desirable jobs are not apt to take the trouble to become qualified for them; and the second assumption is amply refuted by empirical data. See, for instance, the studies cited in fn. 9.

14. Elizabeth Scott tells me that her survey of 1974–1976 figures reveals that, in spite of affirmative action policies, unemployment among women Ph.D.'s who are actively seeking work is about twice as high as among men Ph.D.'s and that the starting salaries of women Ph.D.'s average $1,200 to $1,500 lower than those of men.

15. Alan H. Goldman, "Affirmative Action," *Philosophy & Public Affairs* 5, no. 2 (Winter 1976): 185.

16. Goldman, p. 186.

17. Goldman, p. 185.

18. George Sher, "Justifying Reverse Discrimination in Employment," *Philosophy & Public Affairs* 4, no. 2 (Winter 1975): 168.

19. See Bayles and Sher, respectively.

20. Irving Thalberg, "Reverse Discrimination and the Future," *The Philosophical Forum* 5, no. 2: 307.

21. See Marlene Gerber Fried, "In Defense of Preferential Hiring," *The Philosophical Forum* 5, no. 2: 316.
22. Charles King, "A Problem Concerning Discrimination," *Reason Papers*, no. 2 (Fall 1975), p. 92.
23. Thomas Nagel, "Equal Treatment and Compensatory Justice," *Philosophy & Public Affairs* 2, no. 4 (Summer 1973): 348–363, especially p. 353.
24. Fried, p. 318.

REVIEW QUESTIONS

1. According to Warren, what is primary sexism?
2. What is secondary sexism, as it is explained by Warren?
3. Why does Warren think that secondary sexism is unfair?
4. What is the weak quota system recommended by Warren?
5. How does Warren characterize the quota vs. goals controversy?

6. According to Warren why is the use of weak reverse discrimination to meet proportional hiring quotas not unfair?
7. Why does Warren think that quotas are necessary to make competition for jobs fair for women?
8. What are the compensatory justice and role-model arguments?
9. Why doesn't Warren accept these arguments?

DISCUSSION QUESTIONS

1. Is the sort of weak reverse discrimination advocated by Warren unfair to men? Explain your position.
2. Are the use of hiring quotas really necessary as Warren says? What do you think?

Barry R. Gross

Is Turn About Fair Play?

Barry R. Gross (1936–1995) taught philosophy at The City University of New York.

Gross makes several objections to reverse discrimination. One problem is that the methods used to identify victims of past discrimination are flawed; these victims cannot be identified, for example, just by looking for underrepresentation in certain jobs. Another problem is that reverse discrimination produces bad effects, such as hiring incompetent people, making those who get preferential treatment feel inferior, and encouraging discrimination in other circumstances. It cannot be justified by appealing to the usual models of com-

pensation, reparation, or restitution. Finally, it is unfair to the victims of reverse discrimination.*

The balance of argument weighs against reverse discrimination for four interrelated sets of reasons. First, the procedures designed to isolate the discriminated are flawed. Second, the practice has undesirable and dangerous consequences. Third, it fails to fit any of the models of compensation or reparations. Fourth, it falls unjustly upon both those it favors and those it disfavors. I conclude that if to eliminate discrimination against the members of one group we find ourselves discriminating against another, we have gone too far.

Sociologically, groups are simply not represented in various jobs and at various levels in percentages closely approximating their percentage of the population. When universities in general and medical schools in particular discriminated heavily against them, Jews were represented in the medical profession in far greater percentages than their percentage of the population. At the same time, they were represented in far lower percentages in banking, finance,

From Barry R. Gross, "Is Turn About Fair Play?" *Journal of Critical Analysis* 5, no. 4 (January/April 1975). Reprinted with permission.

construction, and engineering than their percentage in the population, especially the population of New York City. A similar analysis by crudely drawn group traits—Jews, Roman Catholics, WASP, Irish, and so forth—of almost any trade, business or profession would yield similar results.

But the argument from population percentages may be meant not as an analysis of what is the case, but as an analysis of what ought to be the case. A proponent might put it this way: It is true that groups are not usually represented in the work force by their percentage in the population at large, but minority C has been systematically excluded from the good places. Therefore, in order to make sure that they get some of them, we should now systematically include them in the good places, and a clear way of doing it is by their percentage in the population. Or we might conclude instead: therefore, in order to make up for past exclusion, they should be included in the good places as reparation, and an easy way to do it is by their percentage in the population.

If the definition of a minority discriminated against is ipso facto their representation in certain jobs in percentages less than their percentage in the general population, then one has to remark that the reasoning is circular. For we are trying to prove: (1) that minority C is discriminated against.

We use as a premise (3) that minority C is underrepresented in good jobs. Since (1) does not follow from (3) (mere underrepresentation not being even prima facie evidence of discrimination), it is necessary to insert (2) that their underrepresentation is due to discrimination. But this completes the circle.

A critic might reply that we know perfectly well what is meant. The groups discriminated against are blacks, Puerto Ricans, Mexican-Americans, American Indians, and women. He is correct, though his answer does not tell us *how to find out* who is discriminated against. This critic, for example, left out Jews and Orientals. If he should reply that Jews and Orientals do well enough, we point out that the question was not "Who fails to do well?" but rather, "Who is discriminated against?" This argument shows that the mechanisms for identifying the victims of discrimination and for remedying it are seriously deficient.

Even if we allow that the percentage of the group in the work force versus its percentage in the population is the criterion of discrimination, who is discriminated against will vary depending upon how we divide the groups. We may discover that Republicans are discriminated against by our literary or intellectual journals—*New York Review, Dissent, Commentary*. We may also discover that wealthy Boston residents are discriminated against by the Los Angeles Dodgers, that women are discriminated against by the Army, and that idiots (we hope) are discriminated against by universities.

What employment or profession a person chooses depends upon a number of variables—background, wealth, parents' employment, schooling, intelligence, drive, ambition, skill, and not least, luck. Moreover, the analysis will differ depending upon what group identification or stratification you choose. None seems to have priority over the others. Every person can be typed according to many of these classifications. It seems, therefore, that the relevant analysis cannot even be made, much less justified.

In addition, some proponents of the population-percentage argument seem to hold: (4) From the contingent fact that members of the group C were discriminated against, it follows necessarily that they are underrepresented in the good positions. They then go on to assert (5) if members of group C were not discriminated against they would not be underrepresented, or (6) if they are underrepresented, then they are discriminated against.

But clearly (4) is itself a contingent, not a necessary truth. Clearly also neither (5) nor (6) follows from it, (5) being the fallacy of denying the antecedent and (6) the fallacy of affirming the consequent. Last, neither (5) nor (6) is necessarily true. The members of a group might simply lack interest in certain jobs (for example, Italians in the public school system are in short supply). Could one argue that, even though neither (4), (5), nor (6) is *necessarily* true, the mere fact of underrepresentation in certain occupations does provide evidence of discrimination? The answer is no—no more than the fact of "overrepresentation" in certain occupations is evidence of favoritism.

At most, underrepresentation can be used to support the contention of discrimination when there is *other* evidence as well.

FAIR PLAY: OUGHT WE TO DISCRIMINATE IN REVERSE?

There are at least three difficulties with reverse discrimination: first, it is inconsistent; second, it licenses discrimination; third, it is unfair.

If we believe the principle that equal opportunity is a right of everyone, then if members of group C are excluded from enjoying certain opportunities merely because they are members of group C, their right is being abrogated. They are entitled to this right, but so is everybody else, even those persons who presently deny it to them. If both are made to enjoy equal opportunity, then both are enjoying their right. To give either oppressors or oppressed more than equal opportunity is equally to deny the rights of one or the other in violation of the principle of equal opportunity.

Proponents of reverse discrimination seem to be caught on the horns of a dilemma: either discrimination is illegitimate or it is not. If it is illegitimate, then it ought not to be practiced against anyone. If it is not, then there exists no reason for *now* favoring blacks, Puerto Ricans, Chicanos, Indians, women, and so forth over whites.

Two strategies present themselves. Either we can analyze one disjunct with a view to showing that distinctions can be made which require compensation or reparations in the form of reverse discrimination to be made to wronged individuals or groups; or we can try to soften one of the disjuncts so as to make a case for exceptions in favor of the wronged. The first appeals both to our reason and our sense of justice. The second appeals to our emotions. I shall argue that neither strategy works.

Now reverse discrimination can take several forms, but I think that what many of its proponents have in mind is a strong form of compensation—a form which requires us to discriminate against non-C members and favor C members even if less qualified. One may well wonder whether there is not a little retribution hidden in this form of compensation.

THE "SOFTENED" GENERAL PRINCIPLE

The argument of construing reverse discrimination as compensation or reparation has a great appeal which can be brought out by contrasting it with another approach. One might agree that as a general rule reverse discrimination is illegitimate but that it need not be seen as universally illegitimate. In particular, in the case where people have been so heavily discriminated against as to make it impossible for them now to gain a good life, there is no possibility of their having a fair chance, no possibility of their starting out on anything like equal terms, then and only then is it legitimate to discriminate in their favor and hence against anyone else.

Against this "softened" general principle I shall urge two sorts of objections which I call respectively "practical" and "pragmatic." Against the reparations type of argument, I shall urge first that there is some reason to think the conditions for exacting and accepting them are lacking, and second that, owing to the peculiar nature of the reparations to be exacted (reverse discrimination), the very exaction of them is unreasonable and unfair to both parties—exactors and exactees.

I mention briefly two sorts of practical objections to the "softened" general principle. First, it is simply the case that when discrimination is made in favor of someone regardless of his qualifications, there is the greatest possible danger that the person getting the position will not be competent to fill it. Second, when a person is placed in a position because of discrimination in his favor, he may come to feel himself inferior. This may easily lead to the permanent conferral of inferior status on the group, an inferiority which is all the stronger because self-induced. Its psychological effects should not be underestimated.

The pragmatic objection to the "softened" general principle is much stronger. Discrimination in any form is invidious. Once licensed, its licenses rebound upon its perpetrators as well as others. Principles tend to be generalized without consideration of restrictions or the circumstances to which they were intended to apply. Students of the Nazi movement will have noticed that in licensing the discrimination, isolation, persecution, and "final solution" of the Jews, the Nazis (foreign and German) licensed their own. (Hitler's plans for extermination included political groups, for example, the Rohm faction of the SA, as well as other racial groups, for example, Slavs and Balts who fought on the German side.) It is necessary to be quite careful what principles one adopts. In view of the long and bloody history of discrimination, one ought to be very chary of sanctioning it.

COMPENSATION, REPARATIONS, AND RESTITUTION

Because it escapes most of these objections, the reparations argument becomes very attractive. What is more obvious than the principle that people ought to be compensated for monetary loss, pain and suffering inflicted by others acting either as agents of government or as individuals? From the negligence suit to reparations for war damage, the principle is comfortable, familiar, and best of all, legal. For victims of broken sidewalks, open wells, ignored stop signs, the conditions under which damages are awarded are quite clear. (1) There is specific injury, specific victim, specific time and place. (2) A specific individual or set of individuals must be found responsible either (a) by actually having done the injury, or (b) by failing to act in such a way (for example, repairing the sidewalk, sealing the well) so as to remove a particular potential source of injury on their property. (3) A reasonable assessment of the monetary value of the claim can be made. In such cases no moral blame is attached to the person forced to pay compensation.

But reparations are somewhat less clear. How much does Germany owe France for causing (losing?) World War I? Can we say that *Germany* caused the war? Can we say that Germany *caused* the war? Germany did pay, at least in part, based upon rough calculations of the cost of the Allied armies, including pensions, the loss of allied GNP, indemnities for death and for the destruction of property.

Besides the ability to calculate the indemnities, reparations between countries require at least three other conditions to be met: (1) Responsibility for the events must be able to be assigned and accepted. (2) There must be governments or government-like agencies between which the transfer of goods and services and money takes place. (3) There must be a *modus agendi* worked out. The transfer of vast amounts of goods, money, and services is immensely complicated. In the end Germany could refuse to pay and the Allies to accept large parts of the reparations. Part of the Allied refusal is instructive. Britain, for example, simply could not absorb the payments without extreme economic dislocation.

The meaning of *reparations* was extended to cover payments to Israel and payments to individuals both in and out of Germany who suffered losses through the actions of the Third Reich. The payments to Israel, which did not exist during the war, were to reimburse that state, as the representative of the Jewish people, for the expenses incurred by Jewish organizations during the war in resettling persons uprooted by persecutions and made victims of "unspeakable Nazi crimes."

German payments to individuals were called *Wiedergutmachung* (restitution). *Wiedergutmachung* was awarded not merely for damages or injuries but in order to restore a person to his former position in life. It was calculated on a precise basis. You could be indemnified for: (1) loss of property; (2) loss of income; (3) loss of family; (4) length and type of imprisonment; (5) what you would have earned based upon a reasonable calculation, if you were young and had not yet begun a career. To qualify for indemnities, one had to produce, respectively, proof of ownership and value of property, a calculation of the difference between what one earned as a refugee and would have earned, proof of loss of family, proof of imprisonment.

INAPPLICABILITY OF THESE PARADIGMS

Can reverse discrimination be construed to fit any of these paradigms? Can favoring blacks, Chicanos, Indians, women, and so forth over whites or males be seen as compensation, reparations, or restitution? The answer is no for two general reasons and for several which are specific to the various paradigms. The general reasons are, first, that responsibility for discrimination past and present and for its deleterious consequences is neither clearly assigned nor accepted. Some seem to think that the mere fact of its existence makes all whites (or males in the case of antifeminism) responsible. But I do not know an analysis of responsibility which bears out this claim. Second, there is a great difficulty, if not an impossibility, in assigning a monetary value to the damage done and the compensation allegedly owed—that is to say, reverse discrimination.

If we turn to the negligence paradigm, all the conditions seem to fail. *Specific* injury is lacking, *specific* individual responsibility is lacking, and there is no way to assess the monetary value of the "loss." Indeed, in the case of reverse discrimination it is not monetary value which is claimed but preferential treatment. Under the large-scale reparations paradigm two conditions beyond responsibility are lacking. There are no governments or government-like agencies between which the transfer could take place, and there is no *modus agendi* for the transfer to take place.

Where the transfer is to be of preferential treatment, it is unclear how it is even to be begun. So we come to the third paradigm: individual restitution. This is much closer, for it deals with compensating individual victims of persecution. Again, however, it fails to provide a model, first, because reverse discrimination cannot be looked at in monetary terms, and second, even if it could, the restitution is designed to bring a person back to where he was before the deprivation. In the case of the minorities in question, there can be no question of restoring them to former positions or property. Precisely, the point of the reparation is to pay them for what they, because of immoral social practices, never had in the first place.

But doesn't Condition 5 under *Wiedergutmachung* seem ready-made for the purpose here? Does it not require calculation of what the person would have earned had his life not been blighted? If A was a doctor, lawyer, office manager, beginning a career, or even a mere student, you could get a rough estimate of what he might earn based upon his family position, the average earnings for that occupation, and so forth. But suppose A is young, uneducated, unskilled, unemployed, from a broken home; what might he have been had circumstances been different? Anything. And that is the tragedy. But how can you calculate his earnings on that basis, and how can you translate them into reverse discrimination?

JUSTICE

Finally, if we ignore all that has been said and simply go ahead and discriminate in reverse, calling it reparation, it remains to ask whether it would be either reasonable or just. I think the answer is no. It is possible to hold that in some set of cases, other things being equal, compensation is required and yet to argue either that since other things are not equal compensation is not required, or that even if some compensation is required it ought not to take the form of reverse discrimination. Certainly, from the fact that some form of compensation or reparation must be made it does not follow that any *specific* form of compensation is in order. If X is discriminated against in awarding professorships because he is a member of C group, it scarcely follows that if compensation is in order it *must* take the form of his being discriminated in favor of for another professorship, at least not without adopting the principle of "an eye for an eye" (and only an *eye* for an eye?). Consider X being turned down for an apartment because he is a C member. Must compensation consist just in his being offered another ahead of anybody else? Even if he has one already? To go from the relatively innocuous principle that where *possible* we ought to compensate for damages, to sanction reverse discrimination as the proper or preferred form of redress, requires us to go beyond mere compensation to some principle very much like "let the punishment mirror the crime." But here the person "punished," the person from whom the compensation is exacted, is often not the "criminal." Nor will it help to say that the person deprived of a job or advancement by reverse discrimination is not really being punished or deprived, since the job did not belong to him in the first place. Of course it didn't; nor did it belong to the successful candidate. What belonged to both is equal consideration, and that is what one of them is being deprived of.

There is an element of injustice or unfairness in all reparations. The money derived from taxes paid by all citizens is used for reparations regardless of whether they were responsible for, did nothing about, opposed, or actually fought the policies or government in question. Yet we say that this is the only way it can be done, that the element of unfairness is not great, and that on the whole it is better that this relatively painless way of appropriating money from Jones, who is innocent, be used than that the victims of persecution or crime go uncompensated. But the consequences of reverse discrimination are quite different, especially when it is based upon group membership rather than individual desert. It is possible and is sometimes the case that though most C members are discriminated against, Y is a C member who has met with no discrimination at all. Under the principle that all C members should be discriminated in favor of, we would offer "compensation" to Y. But what are we compensating him for? By hypothesis he was no victim of discrimination. Do we compensate him for what happened to others? Do we pay Jones for what we buy from Smith? We seem to be compensating him for being a C member, but why? Do we secretly hold C members inferior? Some claim that society as a whole must bear the burden of reparation. But then reverse discrimination will hardly do the trick. It does not exact redress from the government, or even from all white (responsible?) citizens

equally, but falls solely against those who apply for admissions, or jobs *for which blacks or other minorities are applying at the same time.* By the same token, it does not compensate or "reparate" all minority persons equally but merely those applying for admission, jobs, promotions, and so forth. Those whose positions are secure would not be made to pay, and those who do not apply for anything would not be paid. A white person who fought for civil rights for blacks may be passed over for promotion or displaced, a victim of reverse discrimination, while a Ku Klux Klan man at the top of the job ladder pays nothing. This would be a laughably flawed system if it were not seriously advocated by responsible people, and partly implemented by the government. Surely, it violates the principles of both compensatory and distributive justice.

REVIEW QUESTIONS

1. Why does Gross think that the mechanisms for identifying victims of past discrimination are seriously flawed?
2. What bad consequences are produced by reverse discrimination according to Gross?
3. What is the "softened" general principle of discrimination? What objections does Gross make to this principle?
4. What is the reparations argument? Why doesn't it justify reverse discrimination according to Gross?
5. Why does Gross think that reverse discrimination is unjust or unfair?

DISCUSSION QUESTIONS

1. Does the need for compensation or reparation for past discrimination justify preferential treatment in the present? Why or why not?
2. Gross claims that reverse discrimination has bad effects. But in the next reading, Boxill claims that it has good effects. All things considered, do the bad effects outweigh the good effects, or vice versa?

Bernard R. Boxill

Blacks and Social Justice

Professor Bernard R. Boxill is professor of philosophy at the University of North Carolina at Chapel Hill.

Boxill distinguishes between backward-looking and forward-looking arguments for preferential treatment of minorities in hiring and admission. Most of the reading is concerned with the backward-looking argument that blacks deserve compensation in the form of preferential treatment in hiring and admission because they have been wronged and harmed by racial discrimination. After explaining his version of the argument, Boxill replies to a number of objections including the one made by Gross in the previous reading that underrepresentation in jobs is not evidence for discrimination. At the end of the reading, Boxill briefly explains and defends the forward-looking argument that preferential treatment is justified because it produces greater equality or increases social utility.

LIBERALS INTO FORMER LIBERALS

As Michael Kinsley has observed in *Harper's,* "No single development of the past fifteen years has turned more liberals into former liberals than affirmative action." [1] This metamorphosis, if it is not merely an unmasking, is ostensibly due to the belief that affirmative action perverts the just goal of civil rights. That goal, protest the disillusioned liberals, is to guarantee that persons be treated as individuals and judged on their merits; but affirmative action, they complain, guarantees that individuals are treated as

From Bernard R. Boxill, *Blacks and Social Justice,* rev. ed., pp. 147–72. Copyright 1984, 1992 by Roman and Littlefield Publishers. Reprinted by permission. [Some of the footnotes have been renumbered—Ed.]

mere members of racial groups, and their merits disparaged and ignored.

These liberals are not appeased by Allan Bakke's victory in the Supreme Court in 1978. For although the court ruled that Bakke was wrongly denied admission to the medical school at the University of California at Davis, it allowed that race could be used as a factor in considering applicants. As *Time* announced on its cover: "What Bakke Means. Race: Yes. Quotas: No."

As with busing, the arguments for preferential treatment fell into two classes, backward-looking and forward-looking. Backward-looking arguments justify preferential treatment considered as compensation for past and present wrongs done to blacks and their effects. Forward-looking arguments justify preferential treatment considered as a means to present or future goods, particularly equality. Both the assumptions and the aims of these two kinds of argument must be carefully distinguished.

Backward-looking arguments assume that blacks have been, or are being, wronged. Forward-looking arguments assume that blacks are generally inferior to whites in status, education, and income. Backward-looking arguments aim at compensating blacks. Forward-looking arguments aim at improving the status, education, and income of blacks.

THE BACKWARD-LOOKING ARGUMENT

The fundamental backward-looking argument is simply stated: Black people have been and are being harmed by racists attitudes and practices. Those wronged deserve compensation. Therefore, black people deserve compensation. Preferential treatment is an appropriate form of compensation for black people. Therefore black people deserve preferential treatment.

Criticism of this argument falls into two main classes: on the one hand, critics charge that the claims to compensation of the black beneficiaries of preferential treatment are unfounded or vacuously satisfied; on the other hand, they charge that these claims are outweighed by other considerations.

The most common version of the first type always uttered by the critic with an air of having played a trump, is that, since those members of groups that have been discriminated against who benefit from preferential hiring must be minimally qualified, they are not the members of the group who deserve compensation. The philosopher Alan Goldman, for example, argues this way: "Since hiring within the preferred group still depends upon relative qualifications and hence upon past opportunities for acquiring qualifications, there is in fact a reverse ratio established between past discriminations and present benefits, so that those who most benefit from the program, those who actually get jobs, are those who least deserve to." [2] But surely a conclusion that preferential hiring is unjustified based on the argument above is a non sequitur. Let us grant that qualified blacks are less deserving of compensation than unqualified blacks, that those who most deserve compensation should be compensated first, and finally that preferential hiring is a form of compensation. How does it follow that preferential hiring of qualified blacks is unjustified? Surely the assumption that unqualified blacks are more deserving of compensation than qualified blacks does not require us to conclude that qualified blacks deserve no compensation. Because I have lost only one leg, I may be less deserving of compensation than another who has lost two legs, but it does not follow that I deserve no compensation at all.

Even Thomas Nagel, one of the country's leading philosophers and a strong defender of preferential treatment on the basis of the forward-looking argument, resorts to this criticism of the backward-looking argument. Thus he labels a "bad" argument, one that maintains that the "beneficiaries of affirmative action deserve it as compensation for past discrimination," because, he says, "no effort is made to give preference to those who have suffered most from discrimination." [3] Indeed, Nagel makes exactly the same point as Goldman: Because the blacks who benefit from preferential treatment are qualified, "they are not necessarily, or even probably the ones who especially deserve it.

Women or blacks who don't have the qualifications even to be considered are likely to have been handicapped more by the effects of discrimination than those who receive preference." [4] But for the reasons given, this criticism is bogus. Furthermore, since Nagel defends preferential treatment on forward-looking, egalitarian grounds, this puts him into deeper trouble than it does those who reject preferential treatment altogether.

For, if preferential treatment makes no effort to give preference to those who have suffered most, neither does it make an effort to give preference to those who are most unequal to whites. In other words, if the qualified have suffered least, they are also least unequal, and it seems a bad strategy, if one is aiming for equality, to prefer them. Nagel could object that preferring the qualified is a good egalitarian strategy because it will lead indirectly to equality. But a variant of the idea is open to the advocate of the backward-looking argument. He could argue that preferential treatment of the qualified also helps to compensate the unqualified insofar as it shows them that if one is qualified, being black is no longer a bar to promotion.

One claim which would make this objection to compensating qualified blacks stick, and which the critics appear not to have made, is that compensation can be made to only one section of a group—either the qualified or the unqualified—but not to both. If this were true, and if the unqualified are most deserving of compensation, then a case could be mounted for claiming that, under the circumstances, a policy of preferential hiring should not be instituted because it takes from those who are most deserving of compensation (the unqualified) to give to those who are less deserving (the qualified). But if the critics are making this assumption, they have not stated it.

But perhaps the critics mean that qualified blacks are not simply less deserving of compensation than unqualified blacks, but that they deserve no compensation at all, precisely because they are qualified.

Why should this be so? I am not questioning the possibility that, on practical grounds, we may be unable to compensate the qualified members of a group generally discriminated against. I am questioning the assumption that, just because a person has overcome his injury, he no longer has a right to compensation. If I am swindled and through time and effort retrieve my money, shouldn't I be compensated for my time and effort? And if I have plenty of money and hire a good lawyer, shouldn't I also claim from my swindlers the money I paid the lawyer?

But in their eagerness to demolish the case for preferential treatment the critics have become extraordinarily careless, and *have* moved from the claim that qualified blacks are the least harmed and wronged blacks to the unsubstantiated claim that qualified blacks are not harmed or wronged at all. Thus Goldman first made the claim in his essay, "Reparations to Individuals or Groups" that in preferential hiring of qualified minority candidates, there is "an inverse ratio established between past discrimination and present benefits." But then, almost immediately, he makes the very much stronger claim—which does not at all proceed logically from the first—that preferential hiring "singles out for benefits within a generally unjustly treated minority just that minority that has not been unjustly treated." [5] And he makes a similar error in his book, *Justice and Reverse Discrimination*. First he says that "those who are not most qualified will tend to be those who have been discriminated against least," then follows this observation with the assertion that blacks "who have altogether escaped harm from previous injustice . . . will be the ones benefitting from preference." [6] These transitions from one argument to another and others like them, embody several confusions. Most obviously, there is the submerged conflation of those least harmed or wronged, slightly harmed or wronged, and not at all harmed or wronged. Less obviously, the distinction between being harmed, and being wronged or treated unjustly, is not taken seriously enough.

The argument I am proposing in support of preferential treatment should be distinguished from another argument which, I admit, has a certain superficial attractiveness. My argument is that qualified blacks deserve compensation for discrimination because even they have been wronged and probably harmed by it, and that preferential treatment is appropriate compensation for them because it suits their objectives and abilities. The other, superficially attractive, argument is that qualified blacks deserve compensation because they are probably the very blacks who would, in the absence of discrimination, have qualified without preferential treatment. But only a moment's reflection is needed to see that this argument is flawed. As James S. Fishkin points out in *Justice, Equal Opportunity and the Family,* "There is no reason to believe that those blacks who are presently 'best prepared' offer even a remote approximation to those blacks 'who in the absence of discrimination probably would have qualfied.' " [7]

But this eminently sound observation does not imply that the "best prepared" are not wronged or harmed by discrimination. That is an altogether distinct claim. The best prepared need not be the ones who would have qualified in the absence of discrimination, but they may nevertheless be disadvantaged by discrimination. Thus, I reject Fishkin's concomitant, completely unsupported, claim that, "it is far from clear that the more advantaged members of a racial minority generally are worse off than they would otherwise have been, were it not for discrimination practiced against their forebears in previous generations." [8] This assumes that discrimination does not generally disadvantage those who are discriminated against, and that is an outrageous and gratuitous conclusion.

But suppose I am wrong and many blacks have in fact escaped the effects of discrimination? This is the fundamental objection to preferential treatment, for, if so many blacks have escaped discrimination and its effects that it results in "compensation" being given large numbers of people who did not deserve it, then it would be unfair. However, even if some blacks escape discrimination altogether, it must be admitted that there is a pervasive prejudice against blacks as a group and a tendency to discriminate against them. Consequently, if . . . the realistic threat of transgression is itself transgression, even those who escape discrimination are wronged and possibly harmed by the discrimination against other blacks. This leads us to the argument proposed by Judith Jarvis Thomson that "even those who were not themselves down-graded for being black or female have suffered the consequences of the down-grading of other blacks and women: lack of self-confidence and lack of self-respect." [9] Goldman has taken this argument as the basis for belief in the concept of a kind of "indirect," "vicarious" wrong. Thus he objects that we should reserve "vicarious compensation"—and what he means by this I do not know—"to those who suffer psychologically or vicariously from injustice toward others, and that we should draw the line [past which compensation is no longer called for] at indirect psychological pressures." [10] But his objection misses the point about the harmfulness of discrimination.

Consider, for example, how Goldman illustrates his point: "A traumatized witness," he writes, "does not suffer the harm of the real victim. Similarly, a Jewish millionaire in Scarsdale, no matter how much he suffered vicariously or psychologically from hearing of the German concentration camps, is not owed the reparations due a former inmate." [11] But Goldman fails to distinguish two kinds of witness to injustice. There is the witness who identifies with the victim, and there is the witness who the transgressors identify with the victim. The first suffers vicariously. The second may not suffer vicariously. However, it does not follow that the latter does not suffer at all. He certainly might suffer at the realization that he too was under sentence and could be next. Therefore there are two completely different kinds of suffering that a witness to the persecution of others might endure. The first stems from sympathy for the victims; it is vicarious and could be called indirect. The second stems from the witness's self-interested realization that he may [be] under sentence too and could be the next to be harmed. But, though this suffering may be "psychological," it is not vicarious, and there is nothing indirect about it. The example of the Scarsdale Jew—the stipulation that he is a millionaire is irrelevant—obscures this. Safely ensconced in Scarsdale, any Jew, millionaire or not, was safe from Hitler. Goldman's example insinuates that the Jew who was not himself victimized could feel only vicarious suffering. To make the argument more balanced, I suggest pondering the plight of a Jewish multimillionaire in Berlin.

Failure to distinguish these two kinds of suffering is responsible for the idea that vicarious suffering is relevant to a consideration of the undermining of self-confidence and self-respect to which Judith Jarvis Thomson was presumably referring. For while the realization that, like the actual victim, the witness to discrimination is also under sentence and could be next, has everything to do with the undermining of his self-confidence and self-respect, vicarious suffering has nothing to do with it. Consequently, the vicarious suffering of middle-class blacks for lower-class blacks, if it exists to any appreciable degree, is completely irrelevant to the question of what undermines their self-confidence and self-respect. What does is the uncertainty and ambiguity of their own lives.

But the red herring of vicarious suffering is misleading in yet another way: It suggests that the undermining of self-confidence and self-respect is a consequence of "injustice toward others." Of course, one's vicarious suffering is no indication of injustice to oneself. Though a white person may suffer vicariously at the thought of discrimination against lower-class blacks, the injustice is to them and not to him. However, when black people feel threatened and insulted when other black people are discriminated against because of their color, the injustice is both to those actually discriminated against and to those who are spared. Because the blacks discriminated against are discriminated against because they are black, all black people receive a warning that they too may experience the same treatment. They are wronged, and liable to be wrongfully harmed, in two ways. First, they are wronged because the realistic threat under which they live transgresses their right to equal security. Second, they are wronged by the judgmental injustice that assumes that because they are black they deserve less consideration than others. Justice Thurgood Marshall's comment in *Bakke* is apropos: "It is unnecessary in twentieth century America to have individual Negroes demonstrate that they have been victims of racial discrimination. [It] has been so pervasive that none, regardless of wealth or position, has managed to escape its impact." [12]

To sum up to this point: The criticism of the backward-looking argument for preferential treatment under consideration is unsound in one of its forms, and irrelevant in the other. Insofar as it assumes that many blacks have escaped wrongful harm as a result of discrimination it is unsound. Even if some blacks have escaped harm this would not be sufficient to make preferential treatment unjustified, because the overwhelming majority it benefited would deserve compensation. Insofar as the criticism assumes the black preferred are less wronged or harmed than other blacks it is irrelevant. The backward-looking argument does not exclude compensating unqualified blacks, or deny that they are more deserving of compensation. Neither does it say that qualified blacks must be compensated first. It asserts only that blacks deserve compensation for the wrongful harms of discrimination. Thus, it is unaffected by the claim that qualified blacks may be the least wronged and harmed of blacks. The fact that qualified blacks are wrongfully harmed at all, and that preferential treatment is appropriate compensation, is sufficient justification for it.

Now, I have admitted that it is a weak argument which tries to justify preferential treatment of qualified blacks applying for desirable places and positions on the grounds that, had there been no discrimination, these blacks would probably have qualified for such places and positions without preferential treatment. The key assumption in this argument is simply not plausible. But if we assume that compensation is owed to blacks as a group, then a stronger version of that argument can be advanced, which goes as follows: Blacks as a group have been wronged, and are disadvantaged, by slavery and discrimination. Consequently, blacks as a group deserve compensation. Furthermore, had it not been for slavery and discrimination, blacks as a group would be more nearly equal in income, education, and well-being to other groups who did not suffer from slavery or the extent and kind of discrimination from which blacks have suffered. Consequently, assuming that compensating a group for wrongful disadvantages requires bringing it to the condition it would have been in had it not been wrongfully disadvantaged, compensating blacks as a group requires making them, as a group, more nearly equal to those other groups. But if

blacks as a group were more nearly equal in income, education, and well-being to such groups, some blacks would then fill desirable positions. Accordingly, compensating blacks as a group requires putting some blacks in desirable positions. However, only the blacks who are now most qualified can, fittingly, be placed in desirable positions. Hence, even if those blacks are *not* the very ones who would have filled such places and positions had there been no slavery and discrimination, compensating blacks as a group may specifically require preferential treatment of qualified blacks.

Many objections can be raised to this argument. Perhaps the most obvious is that its concept of compensation differs from the conception of compensation used in the argument that blacks, as individuals, deserve compensation. In that argument, I did not contend that compensating blacks requires placing them in positions they would have occupied had there been no slavery and discrimination. I contended that blacks deserve compensation because they are wronged by discrimination, and that places in universities and professional schools are appropriate compensation for qualified blacks because of their interests and objectives. However, in outlining the group compensation argument I am saying that compensating blacks as a group requires placing them in positions they would have occupied had there been no slavery and discrimination. Is this inconsistent? I think I can demonstrate that it isn't.

I endorse the view that, ideally, compensating either individuals or groups for wrongs requires placing them in positions they would have occupied had they not been wronged. The problem is that this ideal conception of compensation cannot be applied in the case of compensation for individual blacks for the wrongs of slavery and discrimination. To place a wronged individual in a position he would have occupied had he not been wronged depends on an estimate of how much the wrong has detracted from his assets, which in turn depends on an estimate of his assets. For an individual's assets—his capacities, abilities, goals, interests, and enjoyments—determine in large part the position he will come to occupy if he is not wronged. For example, if thugs break the basketball player Dr. J's legs, he will receive more compensation than I would if they broke my legs, because it is known that his legs are a greater asset to him than are my legs to me. Similarly, some years ago the newspapers reported that a certain screen star had insured her legs with Lloyd's of London for several million pounds. Whether or not the story was true, it seemed good sense to many people because they thought the star's legs were such an enormous asset that it would take several million pounds to compensate her for them if they were flawed or lost. It should now be clear why the ideal conception of compensation cannot be used to support an argument in favor of compensating black individuals for the wrongs of slavery and discrimination. In most cases, it simply makes no sense to even try to estimate what any black individual's assets might have been before he was wronged by slavery and discrimination. For, from the very start of their lives—while they are yet in the womb—and of their parents' lives, and of the lives of their ancestors, all the way back to the first black slaves born in the New World, blacks have been wronged by slavery and discrimination. Yet the fact remains that because they have been wronged they deserve compensation. Accordingly, under the circumstances the ideal conception of compensation must be discarded. By way of compensating blacks all that can practically be done is to adopt my proposal and award them some benefit—such as preferential treatment—appropriate to their interests and objectives.

The argument for group compensation does not run into this sort of difficulty. We can form some estimate of the assets blacks as a group had before slavery and discrimination. Consequently, we can apply the ideal conception of compensation, and reasonably propose to place blacks as a group in the position they would have occupied had there been no slavery and discrimination.

It may be objected, however, that placing blacks in the position they would have occupied had there been no slavery and discrimination would not make blacks equal or nearly equal to other groups because blacks are inferior to other groups, especially white groups, in native talent. But this objection begs the question. The claim that blacks are inferior to whites in native talent is an inference based largely on the fact that the average black I.Q. is lower than the average white I.Q. But that inference is highly controversial. Another, possibly sounder inference, is that black I.Q.s have been lowered as a result of slavery and discrimination. If this assumption is sound, and if I.Q.s are as important for determining people's lives as they are said to be, then blacks' lower average I.Q., far from supporting the case against compensation, very [much] supports the case for it.

A somewhat less radical objection is that the estimate we can form of the assets of blacks as a group before slavery and discrimination suggests that even without slavery and discrimination they would not have been nearly equal to other groups. Thomas Sowell, for example, suggests this. ". . . the wide diversity among American ethnic groups," he argues, "precludes any assumptions that any group—especially from a non-urban, non-industrial background—would earn the national average in income." [13] But this is not only a weak argument in itself, it is also inconsistent with many other points Sowell himself has stressed as important and decisive in relation to the issue of discrimination.

It is a weak argument, first, because some groups from a "non-urban, non-industrial background," for example, the Irish Catholics, earn *above* the national average income. [14] If Irish Catholics can, why not blacks? Sowell's assertion that such groups tend to earn considerably less than the national average income may be true if we look only at relatively recent immigrants such as the Puerto Ricans. But blacks have been in America for three hundred years. It is invidious to assume that, unlike other groups from non-urban, non-industrial backgrounds, they would not have bettered themselves had it not been for slavery and its aftermath. Finally, although blacks originally came from a non-urban, non-industrial background, it does not follow that they lacked economically valuable assets. . . . Sowell's master, Booker T. Washington, [boasted] that the policy of importing black slaves proved that blacks had economically valuable skills, and given the importance Sowell attributes to motives of economic self-interest, he is in no position to confound Washington's argument. Given that blacks did have economically valuable skills, surely, in the absence of slavery and discrimination, they would have realized their assets, parlayed their earnings in order to further improve their skills, and, with three hundred years in which to do it, would today be as urbanized and industrialized as anybody else.

Sowell's argument that because of their non-urban, non-industrial origins, blacks, even if there had been no slavery, would be unlikely to be earning near the national average income, is also inconsistent with certain other theories he holds dear. Recall, for example, his view that middle-class blacks are almost always descended from blacks who were freed before emancipation, a view which he uses in support of the theory that progress is an "intergenerational race." . . . If this view and theory are correct, it is difficult to advance any reason why most blacks would not be earning much nearer the national average income if there had been no slavery and discrimination. And there is an even more striking inconsistency in Sowell's argument. The fact he most prizes in support of his contention that it is American blacks' culture, not racial discrimination, which holds them back, is that West Indian blacks, who are physically indistinguishable from American blacks, earn just a little less than white Americans. But the West Indies hardly constitute an industrialized region of the world. Consequently, the fact that a group has a non-industrialized background cannot be the basis of an argument that they are unlikely to earn near the national average income. And so it is with much of Sowell's reasoning. He says one thing to support one point, and the opposite to support another point, and never notices anything amiss.

But what if Sowell is right, and "culture—not discrimination—decides who gets ahead." [15] Assuming that a group's culture is what determines the jobs and positions its members are interested in, certain philosophers seem to agree with him. Thus, Barry Gross implies that blacks may simply not be interested in desirable positions, and argues that black under-representation in desirable positions is no clear indication of discrimination: "The members of a group might simply lack interest in certain jobs (for example, Italians in the public school system are in short supply)." [16] But this analogy fails, though Gross does not appear to notice it, when applied to the case of blacks. For it isn't as if blacks are under-represented in the public school system, or in law, or in banking, or in the professions. They are under-represented in all of these fields. Consequently, though Gross may be right and that sociologically, certain groups are simply not represented in various jobs and at various levels in percentages closely approximating their percentage of the population, he fails to see that the case of blacks presents a matter of an altogether different order. Lack of interest—presumably culturally determined—in this or in that area may explain away the under-representation of a cultural group in one or two specific areas. However, unless we assume that some cultural groups have no interest in *any* of the traditional professional areas, we cannot explain a group's under-representation in all desirable positions by citing cultural differences.

The deeper and more serious implication of the claim that blacks are disadvantaged by their culture, not by discrimination, is that blacks, because of their culture, lack the discipline necessary for becoming qualified for desirable positions. But whether or not this is true, it cannot weigh against the argument for group compensation for blacks. For even if the traits which inhibit the success of blacks—supposedly a lack of appropriate work habits and discipline—are cultural traits it does not follow that they are not the result of wrongful harm. In order to survive and retain their sanity and equilibrium in impossibly unjust situations, people may have to resort to patterns of behavior, and consequently may develop habits or traits, which are debilitating and unproductive in a more humane environment. I see no reason why these cultural traits—which may be deeply ingrained and extremely difficult to eradicate—should not be classed as unjust injuries. This being the case, we have discovered another inconsistency in Sowell's argument. The cultural characteristics he blames for holding back blacks he considers to be the result of slavery and its aftermath. The "legacy of slavery," he declares, is "foot-dragging, work avoiding patterns," "duplicity and theft," and a "tragic hostility to menial jobs." Consequently, if it is blacks' culture which holds them back, then blacks deserve compensation for the culture which slavery imposed on them. Yet Sowell affirms the premise and denies the conclusion.

It is admittedly unusual to think of cultural traits as wrongful harms because we think of culture as, in an important sense, self-imposed. This is true of most cultures in the traditional sense of ethnic and national cultures. Such cultures come with built-in philosophical self-justifications. In the sense that participants in them therefore have elaborate resources with which to justify themselves, they may be viewed as self-imposed. Consequently, though such cultures may encourage development of traits which inhibit advancement in modern society, it would be philosophically hazardous to call such traits wrongful harms. At most, they might be considered self-imposed harms. But not all cultures are self-imposed, and certain cultures contain no mechanism of philosophical self-justification and self-definition. Thus, in describing what he calls the "culture of poverty," Oscar Lewis notes that though it is a genuine culture in the traditional anthropological sense, in that it provides human beings with a "design for living," it "does not provide much support . . . poverty of culture is one of the crucial traits of the culture of poverty." [17] Consequently, if we assume that the cultural legacy of slavery is of this nature and is harmful, inasmuch as it tends to block self-development, self-realization, and autonomy, as well as undermine self-respect and self-esteem, it follows that blacks have been wrongfully harmed, and therefore, according to the terms of the backward-looking argument, deserve compensation.

Moreover, there are other grounds on which the claim that blacks constitute a cultural group is not notably advantageous for the critics of preferential treatment. For, if it is true, it confounds the objection of some critics that blacks do not comprise a group in the sense required by the group compensation argument. For example, Goldman objects to treating blacks as a legitimate group eligible for compensatory treatment because they "do not qualify as genuine groups or social organizations in the sense in which sociologists generally use these terms."

He goes on to point out that in genuine groups there is "actual interaction among members, each of whom occupies a certain position or plays a certain role in the group reciprocal to other roles, roles being reciprocal when their performances are mutually dependent." [18] But by that very account cultural groups do qualify as genuine groups. There is "actual interaction" among the members of a cultural group. That interaction is, of course, not specifically economic or political. Members of a cultural group do not, for example, necessarily buy from each other or employ each other or rule each other. Still, they do interact and that interaction is just as important as economic or political interaction.

Members of a cultural group share basic values and ideals—that is what we mean by culture—and they interact intellectually by exchanging ideas about these values and ideals; by clarifying, criticizing, and extending them; and by severing and drawing connections between them. In this way they come better to understand themselves. All prosperous and progressive peoples engage in this bustling process of self-clarification. W. E. B. Dubois thought that it was a condition of progress, and it was the basis of his theory of "the talented tenth." If a group is to progress, he argued, it must pay special attention to the cultural education of its talented tenth. If we make "technical skill the object of education," he observed, "we may possess artisans but not, in nature, men." [19] Other writers, Booker T. Washington particularly, have believed that cultural activity is the reward of progress. [20] In either case, it is obviously a great good. If, then, it is argued that blacks are underrepresented in positions of wealth and prestige because of culturally-induced differences, then they have been wronged as a group, and preferential hiring of qualified blacks is justified as a way of compensating the group. For, it needs no argument to show that the intellectually most active and advanced of a cultural group play a crucial role in the process of self-clarification. If, then, as seems likely, they will be among those qualified, and preferential hiring will give them the opportunity to play this crucial role, then preferential hiring is a way of compensating the group.

I am not, myself, altogether comfortable with the claim that blacks are a cultural group, or that they interact enough, and are sufficiently interdependent, to support the group compensation argument. These claims ultimately depend on empirical investigation, and even if the contention I made earlier is correct, and all blacks, whatever their class, are wronged, and have good reason to feel threatened by racial discrimination, the often cited disparity between the black middle, and the black under class still undermines the force of the group compensation argument. That point conceded, I must however reject certain other criticisms of the group compensation argument. For example, according to Fishkin the objection to compensating present-day blacks for slavery and past discrimination . . .—that were it not for these injustices, these individuals would not exist— can also be offered when the argument for compensating blacks is reformulated to rest on the premise that blacks deserve compensation as a group. For, says Fishkin, just as it is impossible to return black individuals to the positions they would have held had there been no slavery and discrimination, because without these injustices present-day blacks would not exist, so also it is impossible to return the black group to the position it would have held had there been no slavery and discrimination, because had it not been for these injustices the group would not have the kind of inter-dependence among its members required by the group compensation argument. In support of this Fishkin reasons as follows: "had injustices to blacks not been committed, it is arguable that we might have a society in which race functioned the way eye-color does now. In a racially neutral society, blacks would not constitute a social group or natural class. Their status, identity, and welfare would not be tied to their group membership." [21] But if Fishkin's thesis is "arguable," it is, at best, barely so. Its gratuitous premise is that racial persecution is the only factor which binds blacks together as a social group. The slaves did not all share an identical culture and language, but their cultures and languages certainly had a family resemblance which, together with their common African origins, could well have op-

erated to bind them together. Indeed, without slavery these factors would have operated more strongly than they did with slavery, since, as is well known, slave masters did their very best to destroy the slaves' cultures, languages, and traditions. Why does Fishkin write as if he believes blacks are different from other people? Many European minorities, without the benefit of slavery, manage to retain their identities. Why suppose that blacks would be so anxious to lose theirs? And, if Fishkin's observations are in any way correct, is it not likely that this is because of the very persecution which has served to bind them together in another way? . . .

. . . it has seemed to many critics that preferential treatment, insofar as it involves preferential admissions and hiring, is unfair to young white males. For example, according to Robert K. Fullinwider, a research associate at the Center for Philosophy and Public Policy at the University of Maryland, the compensation argument for preferential treatment confuses the sound compensation principle—"he who wrongs another shall pay for the wrong"—with the "suspect" principle—"he who benefits from a wrong shall pay for the wrong." [22] To clinch the point, Fullinwider asks us to consider the following ingenious example: A neighbor pays a construction company to pave his driveway, but someone maliciously directs the workmen to pave Fullinwider's driveway instead. Fullinwider admits that his neighbor has been "wronged and damaged" and that he himself has "benefited from the wrong." However, since he is not responsible for the wrong, he denies that he is "morally required to compensate" his neighbor by "paying" him for it.

This example makes us see that not all cases where compensation may be due are straightforward, though one kind of case clearly is. If John steals Jeff's bicycle and "gives" it to me, however innocent I may be, I have no right to it and must return it to Jeff as soon as I discover the theft. Given that this example is unproblematic, in what way does it differ from Fullinwider's, which is problematic?

One difference is that, whereas I can simply hand over Jeff's bicycle to him, Fullinwider cannot simply hand over the pavement in his driveway. It will be objected that the proposal was not that Fullinwider should hand over the pavement, but that he should pay his neighbor for it. But this is a different case. I did not say that I had a duty to pay Jeff for his bicycle. I said that I had a duty to return the bicycle to Jeff. If Jeff told me to keep the bicycle but pay him for it, I do not admit that I would have a duty to do so. I could object fairly that when I accepted the bicycle I did not believe that I would have to pay for it, and if I had thought that I would have to, I might have not accepted it. Paying for the bicycle now would impose on me, because I might have preferred to spend my money in a different way and, being innocent of any wrongdoing, I see no reason why I should be penalized. The point is that though the beneficiary of an injustice has no right to his advantage, if he is innocent of the injustice, he does not deserve to be penalized. Thus, where compensation is concerned, the obligations of the innocent beneficiary of injustice and of the person responsible for the injustice are quite different. Though the former has no right to his benefits, the process of compensation cannot impose any losses on him over and above the loss of his unfair benefits. If compensation is impossible without such loss, it is unjustified. On the other hand, in the case of the person responsible for injustice, even if compensation requires him to give up more than he has unfairly gained, it is still justified.

But, though Fullinwider's example is cogent as far as it goes, it is irrelevant as an argument against preferential hiring. It is cogent as far as it goes because, as the above analysis shows, requiring young white males to pay women and minorities for all the unfair advantages they have enjoyed would indeed be unfair. The advantages cannot, as in my example of the bicycle, simply be transferred from their hands into those of the preferred group. Compensation of this kind would impose on young white males time and effort over and above the cost of the unfair advantages they are required to return. They could justly protest that they are being penalized, because they might not have accepted the advantages had they known what they would cost them—now they are "out" both the advantages and their time and effort. But preferential hiring does not require young white males to pay, at an additional cost to themselves, the price of their advantages. It proposes instead to compensate the injured with goods no one has yet established a right to and therefore in a way that imposes no unfair losses on anyone. And these goods are, of course, jobs.

It may be objected that, although a white male applicant may not have established a right to this or that job, he has a right to fair competition for it, and preferential hiring violates that right. But, on the contrary, by refusing to allow him to get the job because of an unfair advantage, preferential hiring makes the competition fairer. The white male applicant can still complain, of course, that, had he known that preferential hiring would be instituted, he would not have accepted his advantages in the first place. Since, if he knew that preferential hiring would be instituted, he would necessarily also have known that his advantages were unfair, his complaint would amount to his saying that, had he known his advantages were unfair, he would not have accepted them. But then, if he is concerned with fairness, and if preferential hiring makes the competition fairer, he should have no objections to it. Or to state the proposition somewhat less contentiously, preferential hiring imposes no unfair losses on him.

Thus, a fairer application of Fullinwider's example about the driveway to the case of preferential hiring would be as follows: Suppose an "improve-your-neighborhood group" offered a valuable prize for the best driveway on the block. Would Fullinwider be justified in insisting that he deserves to get the prize over his neighbor who has, at further cost to himself, built another somewhat inferior driveway?

To sum up my discussion of forms of the backward-looking argument for preferential treatment, while I have insisted that all, or nearly all, blacks are victims of racial injustice, I have conceded that it has handicapped some blacks more than others, and that other kinds of injustice have handicapped some whites more than racial injustice has handicapped blacks. Consequently, although the backward-looking argument is the bedrock of the case for preferential treatment, to complete that case we must look forward.

THE FORWARD-LOOKING ARGUMENT

Whereas the backward-looking argument tried to justify preferential treatment as compensation for past wrongful harms, the forward-looking argument tries to justify preferential treatment on the grounds that it may secure greater equality or increase total social utility. Moreover, the fact that blacks were slaves and the victims of discrimination is irrelevant to the forward-looking argument, which its proponents imply, would not lose force even if blacks had never been slaves and never discriminated against. All that is relevant to the argument is that blacks are often poor, generally less than equal to whites in education, influence, and income, and preferentially treating them will alleviate their poverty, reduce their inequality, and generally increase total utility.

The forward-looking argument has one very clear advantage over the backward-looking argument. As we have seen, a persistent criticism of the backward-looking argument is that, although some blacks deserve no compensation for discrimination because they have not been harmed by discrimination, they are precisely the ones benefiting from preferential treatment. I have tried to rebut this criticism, but this is unnecessary if the forward-looking argument is adopted. For that argument does not require the assumption that the beneficiaries of preferential treatment have been harmed by discrimination, or even that they have been harmed at all. Indeed, it does not require that they be less than equal to whites, and is consistent with their being relatively privileged. For it endorses a strategy of increasing the incomes and education even of blacks superior in those respects to most whites if, however indirectly, this will, in the long run, effectively increase blacks' equality and increase total social utility.

Now whether or not preferential treatment has such consequences is in the end an empirical question, but some critics, as I will show,

insist on concocting specious a priori arguments to show that preferential treatment necessarily causes a loss in social utility.

Thus it has been argued that since, by definition, preferential treatment awards positions to the less qualified over the more qualified, and since the more qualified perform more efficiently than the less qualified, therefore preferential treatment causes a loss of utility. But suppose that less qualified blacks are admitted to medical school in preference to more qualified whites, and suppose the resulting black doctors practice in poor black neighborhoods treating serious illnesses, while if the whites they were preferred to had been admitted they would have practiced in affluent white neighborhoods, treating minor illnesses. In that sort of case, it is not at all necessarily true that preferential treatment causes a loss in utility. Some authors try to avoid the force of this argument by switching the basis of their criticism from the fact that preferential treatment may reward the less qualified to the false assertion that preferential treatment may reward the "unqualified." Thus, Goldman reminds us that "all will suffer when unqualified persons occupy many positions." [23] This is criticism of a straw man.

It has also been claimed that the forward-looking argument that preferential treatment increases utility is open to a serious philosophical objection. Thus philosopher George Sher writes that the utilitarian, or forward-looking, defence of preferential treatment is "vulnerable" to the "simple but serious" objection that "if it is acceptable to discriminate in favor of minorities and women when doing so maximises utility then it is hard to see why it should not also be acceptable to discriminate against minorities and women when that policy maximises welfare." [24] And against Thomas Nagel who argues that racial discrimination, unlike reverse discrimination, "has no social advantages . . . and attaches a sense of reduced worth to a feature with which people are born," [25] Sher makes a similar objection. He says that Nagel gives us no reason to believe that "there could never be alternative circumstances in which racial, ethnic, or sexual discrimination had social advantages which did outweigh the sense of reduced worth it produced," and maintains that Nagel still has not shown us that such discrimination is illegitimate under "any circumstances at all." [26]

The serious utilitarian is likely to dismiss Sher's criticisms with the same impatience with which he dismisses the stock criticism that utilitarianism allows slavery. As R. M. Hare notes, it is the "strength" of the utilitarian doctrine that "the utilitarian cannot reason a priori that whatever the facts about the world and human nature, slavery is wrong. He has to show it is wrong by showing, through a study of history and other factual observation, that slavery does have the effects (namely the production of misery) that make it wrong." [27] In particular, he is not undone by the arguments of the intuitionist who thinks up "fantastic" examples which show slavery to be right according to the principles of utilitarianism, because these show only that the intuitionist has "lost contact with the actual world." [28] Much the same thing can be said about Sher's notion that there are circumstances in which racial discrimination would be legitimate according to utilitarian principles.

Finally, consider the way Sher deals with Dworkin's defence of preferential treatment. As we have seen, Dworkin's view is that if a policy is to be based on pure utilitarianism, which counts each person as equal, then it must consider only how personal preferences are affected. It cannot consider how external preferences are affected, and if it does, it fails to treat people with equal respect and concern. Dworkin's distinction between personal and external preferences may or may not be sound. I have offered emendations to the argument on which he bases it in my discussion of busing. But Sher accepts Dworkin's distinction because he thinks that even if he does, Dworkin's argument fails. "Neither, despite his bare assertion to the contrary has Dworkin produced any reason to suppose that such [racial] discrimination could never maximize the satisfaction of purely personal preferences," he writes.[29] But Sher seems to be confused by the ambiguous nature of the expression "racial discrimination."

If discrimination is taken to mean policies based on weighing the external preferences of whites that blacks be given less, then Sher has simply misunderstood Dworkin. Dworkin does not simply say that we must maximize the satisfaction of personal preferences. He also says that we must not give any weight to external preferences. Consequently, if we grant that Dworkin is right in his theory that racial discrimination gives weight to external preferences, then, contrary to what Sher says, that theory does not permit racial discrimination even if racial discrimination did maximize the satisfaction of personal preferences.

On the other hand, "racial discrimination" may, especially if one is careless, be taken to mean policies based on something like "reverse discrimination," which does not weigh external preferences. In that case, just as reverse discrimination can prefer blacks to whites, racial discrimination can prefer whites to blacks. Now, understood in this sense, racial discrimination may, of course, maximize the satisfaction of personal preferences without weighing external preferences, and certainly Dworkin's theory does not exclude it. But, what Sher seems to overlook is that such racial discrimination, not based on weighing external preferences, would be free of the insult of racial discrimination as we now know it.

Sher also attacks the argument that preferential treatment is justified because it conduces to equality. He allows that preferential treatment may reduce inequality between the races but points out that it does not reduce inequalities between individuals. "To practise reverse discrimination," he says, is ". . . merely to rearrange the inequalities of distribution which now prevail." [30] "What the defender [of reverse discrimination] needs to show," Sher declares, "is that it is consistent to denounce whichever inequalities follow racial, ethnic or sexual lines, while at the same time not denouncing those other inequalities which reverse discrimination inevitably perpetuates." [31]

There is a well-recognized ambiguity in the term "equality" that it is relevant to consider here. "Equality" may mean equality of opportunity, or equality of result, or equality of wealth. By his championship of direct redistribution of wealth, Sher assumes that the notion of equality advanced by the forward-looking argument is equality of wealth. In this way he saves himself the trouble of considering the argument for reverse discrimination that maintains that, although it sins against a present equality of opportunity, promotes a future equality of opportunity by providing blacks with their own successful "role models."

Sher's critique is made even weaker by the fact that he concedes to Nagel his point that racial inequalities are especially wrong because they are apt to "lead to further inequalities of self-respect." [32] He thinks he can safely concede this because even if he does the egalitarian defense of reverse discrimination fails decisively. "At best," he writes, this concession allows only that racial "inequalities would have first claim on our attention if we were forced to choose among inequalities—which as we have seen, there is no reason to think we are. It does not show, and no further argument *could* show, that any consistent egalitarian could ignore the import of the other inequalities altogether." [33]

But on what grounds has Sher managed to conclude that the advocates of reverse discrimination, presumably consistent egalitarians, "ignore the import of the other inequalities altogether"? By what bizarre train of reasoning does it follow from the fact that the advocate of reverse discrimination thinks racial inequalities particularly harmful, that he must therefore "ignore the import of the other inequalities altogether"? And granting that other inequalities have a claim on our attention, how does it follow, as Sher says, that a policy of reverse discrimination is "dubious"? Even if, *contra* our assumption, racial inequalities are *not* more harmful than others, since we are *not* forced to choose among inequalities, why can't we attack all inequalities at once, racial inequalities through reverse discrimination, and other inequalities through other policies?

The only argument against this would be that the other policies might make reverse discrimination superfluous. But there are obvious weaknesses in it. Stigmas are not likely to be erased just because *incomes* are equalized. Apart from the extraordinary difficulties of equalizing incomes in a capitalist context—if this is possible at all—stigmas are likely to remain attached to members of groups because of the menial work many of them do, however equal their incomes. Preferential treatment is aimed at removing such stigmas.

. . . I have used more space in rebutting criticisms than in arguing positively for conclusions. This is because the main arguments for affirmative action are straightforward, and yet philosophers persist in concocting ever more desperately ingenious objections to it. Not that I believe that any one of the various backward- and forward-looking arguments is by itself sufficient to justify affirmative action. Affirmative action is justified by the combined force of these arguments and by the way they complement and support each other. The weaknesses in some are made up by the strengths of others. For example, the weakness in the case for compensation on an individual basis is made up for by the case for compensation on a group basis, and the weaknesses of both these cases are strengthened by considerations stemming from the forward-looking argument. A society which tries to be just tries to compensate the victims of its injustice, and when these victims are easily identified, either as individuals or as a group less than equal to others, the case for treating them preferentially is overwhelming.

Endnotes

1. Michael Kinsley, "Equal Lack of Opportunity," *Harper's*, June 1983, 8.
2. Alan Goldman, "Reparations to Individuals or Groups," in *Reverse Discrimination,* ed. Barry Gross (New York: Prometheus Books, 1977), 322.
3. Thomas Nagel, "A Defense of Affirmative Action," *Report from the Center for Philosophy and Public Policy* 1, no. 4 (Fall 1981): 7.
4. Ibid.
5. Goldman, "Reparations to Individuals," 322, 323.
6. Goldman, *Justice and Reverse Discrimination* (Princeton: Princeton University Press, 1978), 90, 91.
7. James S. Fishkin, *Justice, Equal Opportunity and the Family* (New Haven: Yale University Press, 1983), 92.
8. Ibid., 97.
9. Judith Jarvis Thomson, "Preferential Hiring," in *Equality and Preferential Treatment*, 36.
10. Alan Goldman, "Reverse Discrimination and the Future: A Reply to Irving Thalberg," *The Philosophical Forum* 6, nos. 2–3 (Winter–Spring 1974–75): 324.
11. Alan Goldman, "Affirmative Action," in *Equality and Preferential Treatment*, 206.
12. 438 U.S. 265 (1978).
13. Thomas Sowell, *Markets and Minorities* (Oxford: Basil Blackwell, 1981), 110.

14. See the table in Christopher Jencks, "Discrimination and Thomas Sowell," *New York Review of Books*, 3 Mar. 1983, 34.
15. Thomas Sowell, "Culture—Not Discrimination—Decides Who Gets Ahead," *U.S. News and World Report*, 12 Oct. 1981, 74.
16. Barry Gross, "Is Turn About Fair Play?" *Journal of Critical Analysis* 5, no. 4 (January/April 1975), 381.
17. Oscar Lewis, "The Culture of Poverty," *Scientific American* 215, no. 4 (Oct. 1966): 25.
18. Alan Goldman, "Limits to the Justification of Reverse Discrimination," *Social Theory and Practice* 3, no. 3 (1975): 292.
19. Dubois makes this point about the talented tenth of every group. See Dubois, "The Talented Tenth," in *Negro Social and Political Thought 1850–1920, Representative Texts*, ed. Howard Brotz (New York: Basic Books, 1966), 518.
20. See, for example, his "address delivered at Hampton Institute" in *Negro Social and Political Thought 1850–1920, Representative Texts*, ed. Howard Brotz (New York: Basic Books, 1966), 372.
21. Fishkin, *Justice, Equal Opportunity and the Family*, 117.
22. Robert Fullinwider, "Preferential Hiring and Compensation," *Social Theory and Practice* 3 (Spring 1975): 316, 317.
23. Goldman, *Justice and Reverse Discrimination*, 29.
24. George Sher, "Reverse Discrimination, the Future and the Past," *Ethics* (Oct. 1979): 83.
25. Ibid.
26. Ibid.
27. R. M. Hare, "What Is Wrong with Slavery?" *Philosophy and Public Affairs* 8, no. 2 (Winter 1979): 118.
28. Ibid.
29. Sher, "Reverse Discrimination," 84.
30. Ibid., 85.
31. Ibid., 86.
32. Ibid., 85.
33. Ibid., 86.

REVIEW QUESTIONS

1. What is the fundamental backward-looking argument for affirmative action? What is the standard objection, and how does Boxill reply to it?
2. What is Boxill's own argument for preferential treatment?
3. Boxill discusses several different objections to his argument. What are these objections, and how does he respond to them?
4. How does Boxill answer the common objection that preferential treatment of minorities and women is unfair to young white males?
5. What is the forward-looking argument for preferential treatment?

DISCUSSION QUESTIONS

1. Boxill says that no blacks have escaped from harmful discrimination. Is this true? What about professional basketball players such as Michael Jordan? Have they been wronged and harmed by racial discrimination, and do they deserve compensation?
2. Is preferential treatment of blacks and women unfair to young white males? Why or why not?

Shelby Steele

Affirmative Action: The Price of Preference

Professor Shelby Steele teaches at San Jose State University and is the author of The Content of Character *(1990), from which our reading is taken.*

Steele maintains that affirmative action is the product of white guilt and black power and that it is supposed to compensate blacks for past injustice, but does not do so. Worse still, it has numerous bad effects on the blacks it is supposed to help. It enlarges their self-doubt, continues the myth of black inferiority, encourages blacks to rely on victimization as a source of power, produces subtle discrimination, and results in a glass ceiling when considerations of competence come into play. Instead of affirmative action, blacks need education

From Shelby Steele, *The Content of Our Character* (St. Martin's Press, Inc., 175 Fifth Avenue, New York, NY 10010), Chapter 7, pp. 111–25. Copyright © 1990 by Shelby Steele. Reprinted by permission of the author and St. Martin's Press, Incorporated.

and economic development, and the eradication of racial discrimination.

In a few short years, when my two children will be applying to college, the affirmative action policies by which most universities offer black students some form of preferential treatment will present me with a dilemma. I am a middle-class black, a college professor, far from wealthy, but also well-removed from the kind of deprivation that would qualify my children for the label "disadvantaged." Both of them have endured racial insensitivity from whites. They have been called names, have suffered slights, and have experienced firsthand the peculiar malevolence that racism brings out in people. Yet, they have never experienced racial discrimination, have never been stopped by their race on any path they have chosen to follow. Still, their society now tells them that if they will only designate themselves as black on their college applications, they will likely do better in the college lottery than if they conceal this fact. I think there is something of a Faustian bargain in this.

Of course, many blacks and a considerable number of whites would say that I was sanctimoniously making affirmative action into a test of character. They would say that this small preference is the meagerest recompense for centuries of unrelieved oppression. And to these arguments other very obvious facts must be added. In America, many marginally competent or flatly incompetent whites are hired everyday—some because their white skin suits the conscious or unconscious racial preference of their employer. The white children of alumni are often grandfathered into elite universities in what can only be seen as a residual benefit of historic white privilege. Worse, white incompetence is always an individual matter, while for blacks it is often confirmation of ugly stereotypes. The Peter Principle was not conceived with only blacks in mind. Given that unfairness cuts both ways, doesn't it only balance the scales of history that my children now receive a slight preference over whites? Doesn't this repay, in a small way, the systematic denial under which their grandfather lived out his days?

So, in theory, affirmative action certainly has all the moral symmetry that fairness requires—

the injustice of historical and even contemporary white advantage is offset with black advantage; preference replaces prejudice, inclusion answers exclusion. It is reformist and corrective, even repentent and redemptive. And I would never sneer at these good intentions. Born in the late forties in Chicago, I started my education (a charitable term in this case) in a segregated school and suffered all the indignities that come to blacks in a segregated society. My father, born in the South, only made it to the third grade before the white man's fields took permanent priority over his formal education. And though he educated himself into an advanced reader with an almost professorial authority, he could only drive a truck for a living and never earned more than ninety dollars a week in his entire life. So yes, it is crucial to my sense of citizenship, to my ability to identify with the spirit and the interests of America, to know that this country, however imperfectly, recognizes its past sins and wishes to correct them.

Yet good intentions, because of the opportunity for innocence they offer us, are very seductive and can blind us to the effects they generate when implemented. In our society, affirmative action is, among other things, a testament to white goodwill and to black power, and in the midst of these heavy investments, its effects can be hard to see. But after twenty years of implementation, I think affirmative action has shown itself to be more bad than good and that blacks—whom I will focus on in this essay—now stand to lose more from it than they gain.

In talking with affirmative action administrators and with blacks and whites in general, it is clear that supporters of affirmative action focus on its good intentions while detractors emphasize its negative effects. Proponents talk about "diversity" and "pluralism"; opponents speak of "reverse discrimination," the unfairness of quotas and set-asides. It was virtually impossible to find people outside either camp. The closest I came was a white male manager at a large computer company who said, "I think it amounts to reverse discrimination, but I'll put up with a little of that for a little more diversity." I'll live with a little of the effect to gain a little of the intention, he seemed to be saying. But this only makes him a halfhearted supporter of affirmative action. I think many people who don't really like affirmative action support it to one degree or another anyway.

I believe they do this because of what happened to white and black Americans in the crucible of the sixties when whites were confronted with their racial guilt and blacks tasted their first real power. In this stormy time white absolution and black power coalesced into virtual mandates for society. Affirmative action became a meeting ground for these mandates in the law, and in the late sixties and early seventies it underwent a remarkable escalation of its mission from simple anti-discrimination enforcement to social engineering by means of quotas, goals, timetables, set-asides and other forms of preferential treatment.

Legally, this was achieved through a series of executive orders and EEOC guidelines that allowed racial imbalances in the workplace to stand as proof of racial discrimination. Once it could be assumed that discrimination explained racial imbalances, it became easy to justify group remedies to presumed discrimination, rather than the normal case-by-case redress for proven discrimination. Preferential treatment through quotas, goals, and so on is designed to correct imbalances based on the assumption that they always indicate discrimination. This expansion of what constitutes discrimination allowed affirmative action to escalate into the business of social engineering in the name of anti-discrimination, to push society toward statistically proportionate racial representation, without any obligation of proving actual discrimination.

What accounted for this shift, I believe, was the white mandate to achieve a new racial innocence and the black mandate to gain power. Even though blacks had made great advances during the sixties without quotas, these mandates, which came to a head in the very late sixties, could no longer be satisfied by anything less than racial preferences. I don't think these mandates in themselves were wrong, since whites clearly needed to do better by blacks and blacks needed more real power in society. But, as they came together in affirmative action, their effect was to distort our understanding of racial discrimination in a way that allowed us to offer the remediation of preference on the basis of mere color rather than actual injury. By making black the color of preference, these mandates have reburdened society with the very marriage of color and preference (in reverse) that we set out to eradicate. The old sin is reaffirmed in a new guise.

But the essential problem with this form of affirmative action is the way it leaps over the hard business of developing a formerly oppressed people to the point where they can achieve proportionate representation on their own (given equal opportunity) and goes straight for the proportionate representation. This may satisfy some whites of their innocence and some blacks of their power, but it does very little to truly uplift blacks.

A white female affirmative action officer at an Ivy League university told me what many supporters of affirmative action now say: "We're after diversity. We ideally want a student body where racial and ethnic groups are represented according to their population in society." When affirmative action escalated into social engineering, diversity became a golden word. It grants whites an egalitarian fairness (innocence) and blacks an entitlement to proportionate representation (power). *Diversity* is a term that applies democratic principles to races and cultures rather than to citizens, despite the fact that there is nothing to indicate that real diversity is the same thing as proportionate representation. Too often the result of this on campuses (for example) has been a democracy of colors rather than of people, an artificial diversity that gives the appearance of an educational parity between black and white students that has not yet been achieved in reality. Here again, racial preferences allow society to leapfrog over the difficult problem of developing blacks to parity with whites and into a cosmetic diversity that covers the blemish of disparity—a full six years after admission, only about 26 percent of black students graduate from college.

Racial representation is not the same thing as racial development, yet affirmative action fosters a confusion of these very different needs. Representation can be manufactured; development is always hard-earned. However, it is the music of innocence and power that we hear in affirmative action that causes us to cling to it and to its distracting emphasis on representation. The fact is that after twenty years of racial preferences, the gap between white and black median income is greater than it was in the seventies. None of this is to say that blacks don't need policies that ensure our right to equal opportunity, but what we need more is the development that will let us take advantage of society's efforts to include us.

I think that one of the most troubling effects of racial preferences for blacks is a kind of demoralization, or put another way, an enlargement of self-doubt. Under affirmative action the quality that earns us preferential treatment is an implied inferiority. However this inferiority is explained—and it is easily enough explained by the myriad deprivations that grew out of our oppression—it is still inferiority. There are explanations, and then there is the fact. And the fact must be borne by the individual as a condition apart from the explanation, apart even from the fact that others like himself also bear this condition. In integrated situations where blacks must compete with whites who may be better prepared, these explanations may quickly wear thin and expose the individual to racial as well as personal self-doubt.

All of this is compounded by the cultural myth of black inferiority that blacks have always lived with. What this means in practical terms is that when blacks deliver themselves into integrated situations, they encounter a nasty little reflex in whites, a mindless, atavistic reflex that responds to the color black with alarm. Attributions may follow this alarm if the white cares to indulge them, and if they do, they will most likely be negative—one such attribution is intellectual ineptness. I think this reflex and the attributions that may follow it embarrass most whites today, therefore, it is usually quickly repressed. Nevertheless, on an equally atavistic level, the black will be aware of the reflex his color triggers and will feel a stab of horror at seeing himself reflected in this way. He, too, will do a quick repression, but a lifetime of such stabbings is what constitutes his inner realm of racial doubt.

The effects of this may be a subject for another essay. The point here is that the implication of inferiority that racial preferences engender in both the white and black mind expands rather than contracts this doubt. Even when the black sees no implication of inferiority in racial preferences, he knows that whites do, so that—consciously or unconsciously—the result is virtually the same. The effect of preferential treatment—the lowering of normal standards to increase black representation—puts blacks at war with an expanded realm of debilitating doubt, so that the doubt itself becomes an unrecognized preoccupation that undermines their ability to perform, especially in integrated situations. On largely white campuses, blacks are five times more likely to drop out than whites. Preferential treatment, no matter how it is justified in the light of day, subjects blacks to a midnight of self-doubt, and so often transforms their advantage into a revolving door.

Another liability of affirmative action comes from the fact that it indirectly encourages blacks to exploit their own past victimization as a source of power and privilege. Victimization, like implied inferiority, is what justifies preference, so that to receive the benefits of preferential treatment one must, to some extent, become invested in the view of one's self as a victim. In this way, affirmative action nurtures a victim-focused identity in blacks. The obvious irony here is that we become inadvertently invested in the very condition we are trying to overcome. Racial preferences send us the message that there is more power in our past suffering than our present achievements—none of which could bring us a *preference* over others.

When power itself grows out of suffering, then blacks are encouraged to expand the boundaries of what qualifies as racial oppression, a situation that can lead us to paint our victimization in vivid colors, even as we receive the benefits of preference. The same corporations and institutions that give us preference are also seen as our oppressors. At Stanford University minority students—some of whom enjoy as much as $15,000 a year in financial aid—recently took over the president's office demanding, among other things, more financial aid. The power to be found in victimization, like any power, is intoxicating and can lend itself to the creation of a new class of super-victims who can feel the pea of victimization under twenty mattresses. Preferential treatment rewards us for being underdogs rather than for moving beyond that status—a misplacement of incentives that, along with its deepening of our doubt, is more a yoke than a spur.

But, I think, one of the worst prices that blacks pay for preference has to do with an illusion. I saw this illusion at work recently in the mother of a middle-class black student who was going off to his first semester of college. "They owe us this, so don't think for a minute that you don't belong there." This is the logic by which many blacks, and some whites, justify affirmative action—it is something "owed," a form of reparation. But this logic overlooks a much harder and less digestible reality, that it is impossible to repay blacks living today for the historic suffering of the race. If all blacks were given a million dollars tomorrow morning it would not amount to a dime on the dollar of three centuries of oppression, nor would it obviate the residues of that oppression that we still carry today. The concept of historical reparation grows out of man's need to impose a degree of justice on the world that simply does not exist. Suffering can be endured and overcome, it cannot be repaid. Blacks cannot be repaid for the injustice done to the race, but we can be corrupted by society's guilty gestures of repayment.

Affirmative action is such a gesture. It tells us that racial preferences can do for us what we cannot do for ourselves. The corruption here is in the hidden incentive *not* to do what we believe preferences will do. This is an incentive to be reliant on others just as we are struggling for self-reliance. And it keeps alive the illusion that we can find some deliverance in repayment. The hardest thing for any sufferer to accept is that his suffering excuses him from very little and never has enough currency to restore him. To think otherwise is to prolong the suffering.

Several blacks I spoke with said they were still in favor of affirmative action because of the "subtle" discrimination blacks were subject to once on the job. One photojournalist said, "They have ways of ignoring you." A black female television producer said, "You can't file a lawsuit when your boss doesn't invite you to the insider meetings without ruining your career. So we still need

affirmative action." Others mentioned the infamous "glass ceiling" through which blacks can see the top positions of authority but never reach them. But I don't think racial preferences are a protection against this subtle discrimination; I think they contribute to it.

In any workplace, racial preferences will always create two-tiered populations composed of preferreds and unpreferreds. This division makes automatic a perception of enhanced competence for the unpreferreds and of questionable competence for the preferreds—the former earned his way, even though others were given preference, while the latter made it by color as much as by competence. Racial preferences implicitly mark whites with an exaggerated superiority just as they mark blacks with an exaggerated inferiority. They not only reinforce America's oldest racial myth but, for blacks, they have the effect of stigmatizing the already stigmatized.

I think that much of the "subtle" discrimination that blacks talk about is often (not always) discrimination against the stigma of questionable competence that affirmative action delivers to blacks. In this sense, preferences scapegoat the very people they seek to help. And it may be that at a certain level employers impose a glass ceiling, but this may not be against the race so much as against the race's reputation for having advanced by color as much as by competence. Affirmative action makes a glass ceiling virtually necessary as a protection against the corruptions of preferential treatment. This ceiling is the point at which corporations shift the emphasis from color to competency and stop playing the affirmative action game. Here preference backfires for blacks and becomes a taint that holds them back. Of course, one could argue that this taint, which is, after all, in the minds of whites, becomes nothing more than an excuse to discriminate against blacks. And certainly the result is the same in either case—blacks don't get past the glass ceiling. But this argument does not get around the fact that racial preferences now taint this color with a new theme of suspicion that makes it even more vulnerable to the impulse in others to discriminate. In this crucial yet gray area of perceived competence, preferences make whites look better than they are and blacks worse, while doing nothing whatever to stop the very real discrimination that blacks may encounter. I don't wish to justify the glass ceiling here, but only to suggest the very subtle ways that affirmative action revives rather than extinguishes the old rationalizations for racial discrimination.

In education, a revolving door; in employment, a glass ceiling.

I believe affirmative action is problematic in our society because it tries to function like a social program. Rather than ask it to ensure equal opportunity we have demanded that it create parity between the races. But preferential treatment does not teach skills, or educate, or instill motivation. It only passes out entitlement by color, a situation that in my profession has created an unrealistically high demand for black professors. The social engineer's assumption is that this high demand will inspire more blacks to earn Ph.D.'s and join the profession. In fact, the number of blacks earning Ph.D.'s has declined in recent years. A Ph.D. must be developed from preschool on. He requires family and community support. He must acquire an entire system of values that enables him to work hard while delaying gratification. There are social programs, I believe, that can (and should) help blacks *develop* in all these areas, but entitlement by color is not a social program; it is a dubious reward for being black.

It now seems clear that the Supreme Court, in a series of recent decisions, is moving away from racial preferences. It has disallowed preferences except in instances of "identified discrimination," eroded the precedent that statistical racial imbalances are *prima facie* evidence of discrimination, and in effect granted white males the right to challenge consent degrees that use preference to achieve racial balances in the workplace. One civil rights leader said, "Night has fallen on civil rights." But I am not so sure. The effect of these decisions is to protect the constitutional rights of everyone rather than take rights away from blacks. What they do take away from blacks is the special entitlement to more rights than others that preferences always grant. Night has fallen on racial preferences, not on the fundamental rights of black Americans. The reason for this shift, I believe, is that the white mandate for absolution from past racial sins has weakened considerably during the eighties. Whites are now less willing to endure unfairness to themselves in order to grant special entitlements to blacks, even when these entitlements are justified in the name of past suffering. Yet the black mandate for more power in society has remained unchanged. And I think part of the anxiety that many blacks feel over these decisions has to do with the loss of black power they may signal. We had won a certain specialness and now we are losing it.

But the power we've lost by these decisions is really only the power that grows out of our victimization—the power to claim special entitlements under the law because of past oppression. This is not a very substantial or reliable power, and it is important that we know this so we can focus more exclusively on the kind of development that will bring enduring power. There is talk now that Congress will pass new legislation to compensate for these new limits on affirmative action. If this happens, I hope that their focus will be on development and anti-discrimination rather than entitlement, on achieving racial parity rather than jerry-building racial diversity.

I would also like to see affirmative action go back to its original purpose of enforcing equal opportunity—a purpose that in itself disallows racial preferences. We cannot be sure that the discriminatory impulse in America has yet been shamed into extinction, and I belive affirmative action can make its greatest contribution by providing a rigorous vigilance in this area. It can guard constitutional rather than racial rights, and help institutions evolve standards of merit and selection that are appropriate to the institution's needs yet as free of racial bias as possible (again, with the understanding that racial imbalances are not always an indication of racial bias). One of the most important things affirmative action can do is to define exactly what racial discrimination is and how it might manifest itself within a specific institution. The impulse to discriminate is subtle and cannot be ferreted out unless its many guises are made clear to people. Along with this there should be monitoring of institutions and heavy sanctions brought to bear when actual discrimination is found. This is the sort of affirmative action that America owes to blacks and to itself. It goes after the evil of discrimination itself, while preferences only sidestep the evil and grant entitlement to its *presumed* victims.

But if not preferences, then what? I think we need social policies that are committed to two goals: the educational and economic development of disadvantaged people, regardless of race, and the eradication from our society—through close monitoring and severe sanctions—of racial, ethnic, or gender discrimination. Preferences will not deliver us to either of these goals, since they tend to benefit those who are not disadvantaged—middle-class white women and middle-class blacks—and attack one form of discrimination with another. Preferences are inexpensive and carry the glamour of good intentions—change the numbers and the good deed is done. To be against them is to be unkind. But I think the unkindest cut is to bestow on children like my own an undeserved advantage while neglecting the development of those disadvantaged children on the East Side of my city who will likely never be in a position to benefit from a preference. Give my children fairness; give disadvantaged children a better shot at development—better elementary and secondary schools, job training, safer neighborhoods, better financial assistance for college, and so on. Fewer blacks go to college today than ten years ago; more black males of college age are in prison or under the control of the criminal justice system than in college. This despite racial preferences.

The mandates of black power and white absolution out of which preferences emerged were not wrong in themselves. What was wrong was that both races focused more on the goals of these mandates than on the means to the goals. Blacks can have no real power without taking responsibility for their own educational and economic development. Whites can have no racial innocence without earning it by eradicating discrimination and helping the disadvantaged to develop. Because we ignored the means, the goals have not been reached, and the real work remains to be done.

REVIEW QUESTIONS

1. How does Steele explain the development of affirmative-action programs?
2. Why does Steele think that affirmative action doesn't "truly uplift blacks"?
3. Steele claims that affirmative action has various bad effects on blacks. What are these bad effects?
4. What social programs does Steele recommend instead of affirmative action?

DISCUSSION QUESTIONS

1. What does Steele have in mind when he talks about "racial development"? What produces this?
2. All things considered, does affirmative action have more bad effects than good effects, or vice versa?
3. Steele claims that "blacks cannot be repaid for the injustice done to the race." Is this true?

T. Alexander Aleinikoff

A Case for Race-Consciousness

T. Alexander Aleinikoff is a professor at the University of Michigan School of Law.

Aleinikoff attacks colorblindness as a social ideal and defends its opposite, race-consciousness. He distinguishes between a strong and a weak version of colorblindness. The strong version makes

From T. Alexander Aleinikoff, "A Case for Race-Consciousness." This article originally appeared at *91 Columbia Law Review* 1060 (1991). Reprinted by permission. [Some of the footnotes have been renumbered—Ed.]

race just as irrelevant as eye color. Aleinikoff claims that this is impossible and undesirable. The weak version allows some recognition of race, but not when it comes to the distribution of resources or opportunities. This is not acceptable either, Aleinikoff argues, because it does not overcome white domination and thus it does not provide for racial justice. Racial justice requires race-conscious laws and programs like affirmative action.

I want, in this article, to consider and critique "colorblindness.". . .

Specifically, I will argue that we are not currently a colorblind society, and that race has a deep social significance that continues to disadvantage blacks and other Americans of color. While the legal strategy of colorblindness achieved great victories in the past, it has now become an impediment in the struggle to end racial inequality. At the base of racial injustice is a set of assumptions—a way of understanding the world—that so characterizes blacks as to make persistent inequality seem largely untroubling. A remedial regime predicated on colorblindness will have little influence at this deep level of social and legal consciousness because it cannot adequately challenge white attitudes or recognize a role for black self-definition. In the pages ahead I will explain and justify this somewhat paradoxical claim that a norm of colorblindness supports racial domination. I will conclude that in order to make progress in ending racial oppression and racism, our political and moral discourse must move from colorblindness to color-consciousness, from antidiscrimination to racial justice.

I. COLORBLINDNESS AND RACE-CONSCIOUSNESS: CLARIFYING THE CATEGORIES

. . . In the colorblind world, race is an arbitrary factor—one upon which it is doubly unfair to allocate benefits and impose burdens: one's race is neither voluntarily assumed nor capable of change. For nearly all purposes, it is maintained, the race of a person tells us nothing about an individual's capabilities and certainly nothing

about her moral worth. Race-consciousness, from this perspective, is disfavored because it assigns a value to what should be a meaningless variable. To categorize on the basis of race is to miss the individual.

Adhering to a strategy of colorblindness does not make race a prohibited classification. Violations of the colorblind principle cannot be recognized and remedied without "noticing" the race of the harmed individual or racial group. But, to be true to the model, race-conscious measures must be limited to identified instances of past discrimination.

The debate over colorblindness and race-consciousness has usually appeared in the cases and literature discussing programs that give preferences in employment or other opportunities to nonwhites. In now familiar terms, advocates of colorblindness characterize affirmative action programs as unjustifiably altering meritocratic standards and requiring a distribution of social goods that reflect the proportionate representation of minority groups in the population as a whole.

The presuppositions of supports of affirmative action may be closer to those of their opponents than is usually recognized. Many advocate "goals" of rough proportional representation upon the claim that since race is, or ought to be, an irrelevant factor in the distribution of the good in question, deviation from proportionate shares is the result either of present discrimination or the continuing effects of past discrimination. That is, the justification for affirmative action programs is usually stated in terms of remedying past and present violations of the colorblind principle. What separates most of the participants in the debate is not so much the goal of colorblindness, but rather differing views about the cause of current inequality and of the efficacy of race-blind or race-conscious remedies in reaching a colorblind future.[1]

In this article, I will use the term "race-consciousness" to apply to more than just "affirmative action" programs intended to help bring about a colorblind world or remedy past discrimination. There are many other situations in which race qua race might be seen as relevant to the pursuit of a legitimate and important governmental goal. These include: ensuring the presence of persons of color on juries; taking race into account in allocating radio and television licenses; seeking nonwhites to fill positions in social service agencies that deal largely with minority populations; requiring voting rules and districts that improve the chances of electing minority representatives; fostering integration by adopting race-based school assignment plans and housing programs; taking measures to integrate police forces; adding the works of minority authors to the "literary canon" taught to college students; and giving weight to the race of applicants for teaching positions in higher education. In each of these situations, the race-consciousness of the program may be justified in other than remedial (and colorblind) terms.

II. THE DIFFERENCE THAT RACE MAKES

We live in a world of racial inequality. In almost every important category, blacks as a group are worse off than whites. Compared to whites, blacks have higher rates of unemployment, lower family incomes, lower life expectancy, higher rates of infant mortality, higher rates of crime victimization, and higher rates of teenage pregnancies and single-parent households. Blacks are less likely to go to college, and those who matriculate are less likely to graduate. Blacks are underrepresented in the professions, in the academy, and in the national government.[2]

Of course there has been progress. Comparing the situation of blacks half a century ago to their situation today shows a difference that is startling, and even encouraging, although the last decade evidences a slowing progress and some backsliding. But when the comparison is made between whites and blacks today, it is impossible to ignore the deep and widening difference that race makes.[3]

To say that race makes a difference means more than simply identifying material disadvantages facing people of color in contemporary America. It also recognizes that race may have an influence on how members of society understand their worlds and each other, and how such understandings may serve to perpetuate

racial inequalities in our society. The next two sections pursue these psychological and cultural claims.

A. Race and Cognition

Race matters. Race is among the first things that one notices about another individual. To be born black is to know an unchangeable fact about oneself that matters every day. "[I]n my life," wrote W. E. B. Du Bois in his autobiography *Dusk of Dawn*, "the chief fact has been race—not so much scientific race, as that deep conviction of myriads of men that congenital differences among the main masses of human beings absolutely condition the individual destiny of every member of a group."[4] To be born white is to be free from confronting one's race on a daily, personal, interaction-by-interaction basis. Being white, it has been said, means not having to think about it. Understandably, white people have a hard time recognizing this difference.[5] Most blacks have to overcome, when meeting whites, a set of assumptions older than this nation about one's abilities, one's marriageability, one's sexual desires, and one's morality. Most whites, when they are being honest with themselves, know that these racial understandings are part of their consciousness.

Race matters with respect to the people we choose to spend time with or marry, the neighborhoods in which we choose to live, the houses of worship we join, our choice of schools for our children, the people for whom we vote, and the people we allow the state to execute. We make guesses about the race of telephone callers we do not know and about persons accused of crimes. While not every decision we make necessarily has a racial component, when race is present it almost invariably influences our judgments. We are intensely—even if subconsciously—race-conscious.

It is common to speak of racial attitudes as being based on "stereotypes"—an incorrect or unthinking generalization applied indiscriminately to individuals simply on the basis of group membership. From this perspective, stereotypes can be overcome by supplying more information about an individual or the group to which that individual belongs.

But this explanation fails to recognize race-consciousness as an entrenched structure of thought that affects how we organize and process information. Social science research suggests that stereotypes serve as powerful heuristics, supplying explanations for events even when evidence supporting nonstereotypical explanations exists, and leading us to interpret situations and actions differently when the race of the actors varies. It is often more likely that our mental schema will influence how we understand new information than it is that the new information will alter our mental schema.

A troubling example can be found in *Larry P. by Lucile P. v. Riles,*[6] a case challenging the use of IQ tests that disproportionately assigned black children to special classes for the "educable mentally retarded." In discussing the expert testimony presented on the adequacy of the tests, the court of appeals observed:

> Since the 1920's it has been generally known that black persons perform less well than white persons on the standardized intelligence tests. IQ tests had been standardized so that they yielded no bias because of sex. For example, when sample tests yielded different scores for boys and girls, the testing experts assumed such differences were unacceptable and modified the tests so that the curve in the standardization sample for boys and girls was identical. No such modification on racial grounds has ever been tried by the testing companies.[7]

The testing companies received two sets of data and chose to act on just one. Their assumptions made one set of data "surprising" and the other "expected" or "natural."

Because cognitive racial categories predispose us to select information that conforms to existing categories and to process information in such a way that it will fit into those categories, they are self-justifying and self-reinforcing. And because we adopt racial categories more through a process of cultural absorption than rational construction, we are likely to be unaware of the role that the categories play in the way we perceive the world. . . .

This deeply imbedded race-consciousness has a distressing effect on discourse between the races. In many ways, whites and blacks talk past each other. The stories that African-Americans tell about America—stories of racism and exclusion, brutality and mendacity—simply do not ring true to the white mind. Whites have not been trained to hear it, and to credit such accounts would be to ask whites to give up too much of what they "know" about the world. It would also argue in favor of social programs and an alteration in power relations that would fundamentally change the status quo. White versions of substantial progress on racial attitudes are also likely to ring hollow for many blacks. One might see an equality of missed communication here. But there is actually a great inequality because it is the white version that becomes the "official story" in the dominant culture.

B. The Power of Definition

In our society, race has not been a benign mode of classification. The designation of one's race has had a double function, both defining social categories and assigning characteristics to members of those categories. The predominant power of social and cultural definition has, from the start, been exercised by and for whites.

The theme of invisibility that permeates black literature portrays white erasure of black attempts at self-definition. Listen to Audre Lorde:

> . . . I can recall without counting
> eyes
> cancelling me out
> like an unpleasant appointment
> postage due
> stamped in yellow red purple
> any color
> except Black[8]

Blacks are "invisible" not in the sense that whites do not see them; they are "invisible" in the sense that whites see primarily what a white dominant culture has trained them to see. In a curious yet powerful way, whites create and reflect a cultural understanding of blackness that requires little contribution from blacks. The dominant and dominating story excludes or ignores black representations of blackness not out of vindictiveness or animus but because the black stories simply do not register. Robert Berkhofer's description of the process by which whites understand American Indians applies here: "preconception became conception and conception became fact." [9]. . . .

Continued white ignorance of blacks and lack of contact in daily life makes white understandings of race difficult to alter.[10] Whites are only dimly aware of how blacks live or what it means to be black in America. Despite attempts to bring African-American history into the classroom, most whites do not understand the role of black slavery in the economic development of the United States, nor are they familiar with major trends in black political and social thought, or even the contributions of Frederick Douglass, W. E. B. Du Bois, and Malcolm X. Absence of knowledge is compounded by physical and social segregation. Blacks and whites rarely get to know each other in neighborhoods, schools, or churches; and interracial friendships remain surprisingly rare. As a result, most of what a white person in American knows about blacks is likely to have been learned from white family, friends, or the white-dominated media.

That the white-created image of African-Americans should remain largely unchallenged by black conceptions is troubling not only because the white version reflects stereotypes, myths, and half-truths, but also because of the role the white definition plays in explaining the historical treatment and current condition of blacks. Given strong incentives to absolve whites and blame blacks for existing social and economic inequalities, the white story about blacks has never been flattering. As Kimberle Crenshaw has powerfully argued, when the white image of blacks is combined with other American stories—such as equality of opportunity—it becomes "difficult for whites to see the Black situation as illegitimate or unnecessary." It works this way:

Believing both that Blacks are inferior and that the economy impartially rewards the superior over the inferior, whites see that most Blacks are indeed worse off than whites are, which reinforces their sense that the market is operating "fairly and impartially"; those who should logically be on the bottom are on the bottom. This strengthening of whites' belief in the system in turn reinforces their beliefs that Blacks are *indeed* inferior. After all, equal opportunity *is* the rule, and the market *is* an impartial judge; if Blacks are on the bottom, it must reflect their relative inferiority.[11]

In sum, racial inequality has many faces. Social and economic statistics paint a clear and distressing picture of the differences among racial groups. Yet other inequalities are less obvious, based on nearly inaccessible and usually unchallenged assumptions that hide power and explain away domination. The next section examines alternative legal responses to this complex web of inequalities based on race. . . .

III. From Colorblindness to Race-Consciousness

Colorblindness may seem to be a sensible strategy in a world in which race has unjustly mattered for so long. Yet the claim that colorblindness today is the most efficacious route to colorblindness tomorrow has always been controversial. Justice Blackmun's paradoxical aphorism in *Bakke* reflects the usual counterclaim: "In order to get beyond racism, we must first take account of race. There is no other way. And in order to treat some persons equally, we must treat them differently." [12]. . .

The claim I wish to press here is different from Blackmun's familiar stance in the affirmative action debate. I will argue in this section that a legal norm of colorblindness will not end race-consciousness; rather, it will simply make the unfortunate aspects and consequences of race-consciousness less accessible and thus less alterable. Furthermore, colorblind strategies are likely to deny or fail to appreciate the contribution that race-consciousness can make in creating new cultural narratives that would support serious efforts aimed at achieving racial justice.

Before these claims can be made, however, two varieties of colorblindness should be distinguished. The first, which I will call "strong colorblindness," argues that race should truly be an irrelevant, virtually unnoticed, human characteristic. Richard Wasserstrom has described this "assimilationist ideal";

> [A] nonracist society would be one in which the race of an individual would be the functional equivalent of the eye color of individuals in our society today. In our society no basic political rights and obligations are determined on the basis of eye color. No important institutional benefits and burdens are connected with eye color. Indeed, except for the mildest sort of aesthetic preferences, a person would be thought odd who even made private, social decisions by taking eye color into account.[13]

The second type, "weak colorblindness," would not outlaw all recognition of race, but would condemn the use of race as a basis for the distribution of scarce resources or opportunities and the imposition of burdens. Under "weak colorblindness," race might function like ethnicity: an attribute that could have significance for group members, and one that society as a whole could recognize, but not one upon which legal distinctions could be based. Furthermore, individuals would be able to choose how important a role race would play in their associations and identifications, but their race would not be used by others to limit their opportunities or define their identities. Thus, college courses on "African-American literature" might well be permissible under a weak colorblindness regime, but such a regime would not tolerate allocating places in the class based on race or allowing race to be used as a factor in the choice of an instructor. In the sections that follow, I will argue that strong colorblindness is impossible and undesirable, and that weak colorblindness—although perhaps able to be implemented as a legal strategy—is an inadequate response to current manifestations of racial inequality.

A. Masking Race-Consciousness

It is apparently important, as a matter of widespread cultural practice, for whites to assert that they are strongly colorblind, in the sense that they do not notice or act on the basis of race. One can see this at work in such statements as: "I judge each person as an individual." Of course, it cannot be that whites do not notice the race of others. Perhaps what is being said is

that the speaker does not begin her evaluation with any preconceived notions. But this too is difficult to believe, given the deep and implicit ways in which our minds are color-coded. To be truly colorblind in this way, as David Strauss has shown, requires color-consciousness: one must notice race in order to tell oneself not to trigger the usual mental processes that take race into account.

The denial of race-consciousness occasioned by the desire to be strongly colorblind is described in a recent study of a desegregated junior high school by psychologist Janet Schofield. She reports that teachers, apparently concerned that acknowledging racial awareness would be viewed as a sign of prejudice, claimed not to notice the race of their students. In pursuit of colorblindness, teachers rarely used the words "white" or "black," and avoided racial topics and identifications in class.[14]

This act of denial is troubling not only because it distorts reality, but also because it will make less accessible the ways in which color-consciousness influences our understanding of the world and of others. Strong colorblindness will perpetuate the white image of blacks by rendering irrelevant the kind of race-based discussion and data necessary for a serious critique of white definitions. Schofield's study documents how teachers' desires to act in a colorblind fashion harmed the educational experience by ignoring or denying race when it would have been appropriate to notice it:

> [One] teacher included George Washington Carver on a list of great Americans from which students could pick individuals to learn about but specifically decided not to mention he was black for fear of raising racial issues. In the best of all worlds, there would be no need to make such mention, because children would have no preconceptions that famous people are generally white. However, in a school where one white child was surprised to learn from a member of our research team that Martin Luther King was black, not white[!], it would seem reasonable to argue that highlighting the accomplishments of black Americans and making sure that students do not assume famous figures are white is a reasonable practice.[15]

Certainly such conduct creates possibilities for serious miscommunication. There is significant evidence of cultural differences between whites and blacks. . . . When white teachers, unaware of such differences, ask questions in a way that conforms to white middle-class practice, they unwittingly disadvantage black school children.

But the problem runs deeper than the level of miscommunication. Whites believe that they can act in a colorblind fashion merely by acting as they always have. Colorblindness puts the burden on blacks to change; to receive "equal" treatment, they must be seen by whites as "white." [16] Hence, the "compliment" that some whites pay to blacks: "I don't think of you as black." Colorblindness is, in essence, not the absence of color, but rather monochromatism: whites can be colorblind when there is only one race—when blacks become white.

B. Local Knowledge: Race-Consciousness as Cultural Critique

Strong colorblindness, I have argued, is unlikely to produce the result it promises—a world in which race does not matter. In this section, I want to make the case for race-consciousness more direct by focusing on the benefits of race-consciousness in undermining and shifting deep cultural assumptions and ultimately, perhaps, making progress in overcoming racism. In presenting these claims, I hope also to undermine the case for weak colorblindness. To be effective, strategies for attacking racism may well demand affirmative race-conscious governmental policies. Clifford Geertz, in a collection of his essays entitled *Local Knowledge,* has stated that:

To see ourselves as others see us can be eye-opening. To see others as sharing a nature with ourselves is the merest decency. But it is from the far more difficult achievement of seeing ourselves amongst others, as a local example of the forms human life has locally taken, a case among cases, a world among worlds, that the largeness of mind, without which objectivity is self-congratulation and tolerance a sham, comes.[17]

Colorblindness operates at Geertz's level of "merest decency." It begins and ends with the observation that there is something, under the skin, common to all human beings. . . . But Geertz clearly seeks more than this; he would reorient the usual hierarchical relationship between dominant and subordinate cultures by rotating the axis through its center point, making the vertical horizontal. This shift requires two related transformations: the first is to appreciate the contingency, the nonuniversalism of one's own culture—to view it as an example of "local knowledge"; the second is to recognize and credit the "local knowledges" of other groups. Of course, these two efforts are related. By valorizing the dominated, one is likely to cast doubts on the dominant group's characterizations or definition of the dominated group, which, in turn, tells us something new about the dominant group as well.

My claim outlined in the pages that follow is that race-consciousness can aid in these cultural transformations. . . .

Rotating the axis helps us to be open to other accounts and perspectives, and in doing so it reminds us of the fictional or constructed nature of "local knowledges"—including our own. Once white Americans shed the false assumption that "they know all they need to know" about African-Americans, they will begin to learn as much about themselves as about others.

1. Understanding Domination

The American Negro has the great advantage of having never believed that collection of myths to which white Americans cling. . . .[18]

James Baldwin

"[T]he quickest way to bring the reason of the world face to face [with white racism]," Du Bois wrote, "is to listen to the complaint of those human beings today who are suffering most from white attitudes, from white habits, from the conscious and unconscious wrongs which white folk are today inflicting on their victims." [19] . . .

The claim here is limited, but important. One need not believe that subordinated groups hold world views thoroughly differentiated from the dominant culture in order to give credit to the claim that the views of subordinated groups on the extent and nature of subordination are likely to differ from those of majority groups. This is so for a number of reasons.

Dominant groups may have neither the inclination nor the ability to be fully aware of their domination. Dominant groups generally do not consider themselves to be oppressive, particularly in a society in which tolerance for diversity is valued, and they can provide descriptions of themselves and the disadvantaged that explain inequality as either justified or natural. To the extent that these descriptions effectively absolve dominant groups of responsibility for inequality, and therefore from bearing any of the costs of ameliorating inequality, there is little motivation for the dominant culture to question them.

Furthermore, the dominant culture's conceptions of the dominated are often not explicit. They are likely to be rooted, as Du Bois notes, in "long followed habits, customs, and folkways; [in] subconscious trains of reasoning and unconscious nervous reflexes."[20] These assumptions and mental structures, as noted above, may well have a significant influence on conduct and attitudes, yet they are rarely subjected to careful scrutiny because they seem so natural, so much a part of us.

Finally, since dominant groups are not the direct victims of their acts toward dominated groups, they may underestimate the burdens suffered by the dominated groups. This problem is compounded if dominant and dominated groups inhabit separate geographical and social spaces, so that the extent and harms of domination remain largely hidden from the dominant groups. . . .

2. *Recognizing the Dominated* Finally, recognizing race validates the lives and experiences of those who have been burdened because of their race. White racism has made "blackness" a relevant category in our society. Yet color-blindness seeks to deny the continued social significance of the category, to tell blacks that they are no different from whites, even though blacks as blacks are persistently made to feel that difference. Color-consciousness allows for recognition of the distinct and difficult difference that race has made; it facilitates white awareness of

the efforts of African-Americans to describe and examine that difference. This is not simply the telling of a story of oppression. Color-consciousness makes blacks subjects and not objects, undermining the durability of white definitions of "blackness." It permits recognition of the strength and adaptive power of a black community able to survive slavery and oppression; and it acknowledges the contributions of black culture—not simply as windows on "the race question" but as distinct (if varied) voices and traditions, worthy of study in their own right. . . .

C. Weak Colorblindness and Its Costs

It is common for advocates of affirmative action to point out that a legal strategy dedicated to "equality of opportunity" is likely to replicate deeply imbedded inequalities. The familiar metaphor is of a race between two runners, one of whom starts many yards back from the starting line, or is encumbered by ankle weights. Color-conscious policies are said to remove the advantage that has for several centuries been granted to whites. The simplicity of this argument should not disguise its soundness or moral power. Unfortunately, however, affirmative action programs based on the objective of overcoming past societal discrimination are deemed to run afoul of the Court's model of weak colorblindness.[21] To the extent race-conscious policies help ameliorate material disadvantage due to societal discrimination, the negative injunction of weak colorblindness imposes heavy costs.

Beyond this familiar terrain in the affirmative action debate, there are other advantages to race-conscious programs that also call into question the adequacy of weak colorblindness. As Justice Stevens has noted, there are a number of situations in which it seems eminently reasonable for government decision makers to take race into account.[22] For example:

in a city with a recent history of racial unrest, the superintendent of policy might reasonably conclude that an integrated police force could develop a better relationship with the community and thereby do a more effective job of maintaining law and order than a force composed only of white officers.[23]

Similar claims could be made about integrated civil service and school administrations. That situations exist that could benefit from race-conscious policies should hardly be surprising, given the prominent role that race has played in allocating benefits and burdens throughout American history. Indeed, Justice Powell's famous "diversity" argument in *Bakke*[24] implicitly acknowledges the reasonableness of some manner of color-conscious decision making in a world in which race has mattered and continues to matter. To the extent that weak colorblindness makes these forms of race-consciousness problematic, it is simply nearsighted social policy. . . .

Universities need more than African-American literature classes; they need a diversity of students in all literature classes, and not simply to show white students that students of color can perform as well as white students, but also to help all students become more self-conscious of the underlying assumptions with which they approach the world. To be sure, there are risks. Given the power of imbedded ways of thinking, new information may simply be "processed" in accordance with pre-existing views; or, white students may make the error of assuming that comments by black students express "the" black perspective. But to students and faculty open to a Geertzian moment, the intellectual rewards are enormous.

D. An Objection to Race-Consciousness

. . . [An] objection . . . that figures prominently in the attack on affirmative action is that race-consciousness is self-defeating to the extent that it reinforces rather than undermines racism. Affirmative action, it is argued, may have this effect because it inevitably creates the impression of a lowering of standards in order to benefit minorities. Furthermore, as Shelby Steele argues, the "implication of inferiority in racial preferences" has a demoralizing effect on blacks, contributing to "an enlargement of self doubt."[25]

One response is that we ought to run this claim by those who have been the victims of racism. Despite assertions by whites that race-conscious programs "stigmatize" beneficiaries, blacks remain overwhelmingly in favor of affirmative action.[26] Would we not expect blacks to be the first to recognize such harms and therefore to oppose affirmative action if it produced serious stigmatic injury? It might be argued, however, that individual blacks are willing to participate in affirmative action programs because of the direct benefits they receive, yet those blacks who are not beneficiaries suffer the stigmatic harm without the compensating gains. But, again, one would expect that if this were the case, then blacks as a class would oppose affirmative action since the vast majority of blacks are not beneficiaries of affirmative action. Furthermore, Randall Kennedy provides a convincing argument that affirmative action, on balance, is more likely to reduce stigma than to impose it:

It is unrealistic to think . . . that affirmative action causes most white disparagement of the abilities of blacks. Such disparagement, buttressed for decades by the rigid exclusion of blacks from educational and employment opportunities, is precisely what engendered the explosive crisis to which affirmative action is a response. . . . In the end, the uncertain extent to which affirmative action diminishes the accomplishments of blacks must be balanced against the stigmatization that occurs when blacks are virtually absent from important institutions in the society.[27]

Confident measures of the costs and benefits of affirmative action do not exist. Given the material gains afforded minorities by race-conscious programs and the fact that these gains are likely, as Kennedy notes, to counteract "conventional stereotypes about the place of the Negro,"[28] I would put the burden of proof on those who claim that affirmative action contributes more to racism than it diminishes racism. Significantly, the case for race-consciousness suggested here would affect the evaluation of the costs and benefits because it would count as one of the benefits—as colorblindness cannot—the gains to white society of increased association with minorities and greater awareness of nondominant cultures. . . .

IV. FROM ANTIDISCRIMINATION TO RACIAL JUSTICE

Discussion about the appropriateness of race-conscious measures is but the doctrinal manifestation of a broader debate regarding the animating principle of race discrimination law. The strategy of colorblindness follows from an understanding of discrimination law that views the use of racial classifications as morally and politically objectionable. In contrast, support for broad race-conscious policies is usually imbedded in a description of race discrimination law as aimed at ending the second-class citizenship of African-Americans and other subordinated minorities. . . .

Starting fresh, it appears obvious that an antidiscrimination model that sees the use of racial classifications as the central problem to be addressed ill fits this society's current racial situation. There is no symmetry in either the use of racial classifications or the experiences of different racial groups. To see the problem of race discrimination as the problem of using racial criteria is to wrench legal theory out of social reality.[29] . . .

The choice among race discrimination law principles is, in the deepest sense, moral and political. Arrayed on the side of the antidiscrimination-as-colorblindness model is the knowledge of the terrible wrongs that color-consciousness has wrought in our history, the ending of legal segregation effectuated by colorblindness, an ideology of individualism that stresses evaluation and rewards based on individual effort and personal characteristics over which a person has control, and the antagonisms that race-based preferences may breed. These, of course, are not trivial arguments, which suggests why colorblindness has had such significant appeal.

But the claim that race should be ignored would be far more persuasive if the difference that race had made in the past had been overcome. What cannot be denied—even if it is often ignored—is that blacks, as a class, have never attained economic or social equality with whites. Reconstruction ended long before it achieved its (some would say limited) set of goals. The "Second Reconstruction" of the 1960s wiped away some of the additional legal insults added by the race hysteria of the late nineteenth century, but it did little to fundamentally alter the material well-being of blacks. The narrowing of the economic gap between blacks and whites that occurred in the 1950s and 1960s—due primarily to the overall growth in the economy—stalled by the middle of the 1970s and did not improve during the Reagan years. A prodigious study sponsored by the National Academy of Sciences has recently concluded that the United States faces "an unfinished agenda: many black Americans remain separated from the mainstream of national life under conditions of great inequality.". . .

There are strong reasons for continuing the struggle to fulfill the initial goals of race discrimination law. Whether phrased as "anti-caste," "anti-group disadvantage," or "anti-subjugation," the task remains where it began: the ending of second class status of an historically oppressed group and the achieving of racial justice.

There are two interrelated aspects to this agenda for race discrimination law. The first supports programs that would produce material improvements in the lives of black people: programs promoting jobs, medical care, and decent housing. Such programs, it should be noted, need not be race-based. A "racial justice" perspective need not entail explicitly race-conscious policies. It seems clear, however, that a racial justice perspective is friendly to race-conscious policies directed at overcoming the effects of past and present societal discrimination. . . . Set-aside programs . . . are modest examples of the kind of state intervention that is needed.

The second aspect of a racial justice perspective is an attack on the set of beliefs that makes existing inequalities untroubling. What must be addressed is not just old-fashioned racism, but also the deeply ingrained mental structures that categorize and define race to the disadvantage of blacks and other nonwhite groups. As suggested above, altering the image of blacks in the white mind requires paying attention to, and crediting, black voices, and to refashioning institutions in ways that will allow those voices to be heard. Here race-conscious programs may be crucial. . . .

V. CONCLUSION: TOWARD AN INCLUSIVE AMERICAN STORY

In the current political and social climate, a call for color-consciousness poses real risks. For several centuries of American history, noticing race provided the basis for a caste system that institutionalized second-class status for people of color. It was precisely this oppressive use of race that colorblindness sought to overcome. Furthermore, central to white opposition to affirmative action is the belief that blacks have attained equality of opportunity, and therefore any assistance directed to minorities qua minorities affords them an undeserved benefit and an unfair advantage. . . .[30]

[But] race-neutral strategies simply postpone our society's inevitable rendezvous with its history of racism. Constant liminal and subliminal messages of the difference that race makes take their toll—no matter what justificatory rhetoric enshrouds official governmental action—and will ultimately breed a powerful claim of enough-is-enough. Such a call can take the form of a national commitment to end racial injustice, or it can take the form of "by any means necessary" in the minds and hands of the victims of discrimination who know that colorblindness is a descriptive lie and a normative mistake.

Race-conscious programs alone will not end racism. At best, they represent a small step toward changing social relations and structures of thought and perception. What is needed is direct, self-conscious scrutiny of the way we think and of the assumptions about race that each of us holds and upon which we act. Attention to black constructions of reality can provide a counterbalance to the white construction of blacks in the white mind. . . .

Racial equality will not be attainable until American myths include blacks as full members and equal partners in society. A new set of stories is needed to provide the impetus for self and social reexamination, and to provide the foundation upon which support for race-conscious measures can be based. For example, we might develop an historical narrative not about those who *chose* America, but rather about those who *built* America. This account would be about slaves and free blacks in the South in the nineteenth century and blacks in the twentieth century who migrated to work in Northern factories; about women who worked in the factories and (unnoticed and uncompensated) in the home; and about Chinese laborers who built the railroads, Mexican workers who harvested the crops, and European immigrants who built the great cities of the East. Such a narrative would acknowledge the deep and lasting contributions of African-Americans and other groups usually marginalized in the traditional account and would focus attention on the injustice of continued inequalities founded on racial oppression.

Blacks as blacks have had a unique history in this country. It is a history that whites and blacks confront every day and will continue to confront into the indefinite future. In pretending to ignore race, this society denies itself the self-knowledge that is demanded for eradicating racism and achieving racial justice.

Endnotes

1. See *Regents of the Univ. of Cal.* v. *Bakke*, 438 U.S. 265, 407 (1978) (Blackmun, J., dissenting). ("In order to get beyond racism, we must first take account of race. There is no other way.")
2. See *A Common Destiny: Blacks & American Society* 3–32 (G. Jaynes & R. Williams, Jr. eds. 1989). . . .
3. For data to support the assertions in the preceding two paragraphs, see id. at 122–23, 278, 280–81, 293, 295, 302–03, 399, 416–17, 465, 524, 530.
4. W. E. B. Du Bois, *Dusk of Dawn* 139 (1940).
5. Much as men have a difficult time understanding the routine and ever-present fears that women have for their physical safety.
6. 793 F. 2d 969 (9th Cir. 1984).
7. Id. at 975–76; see generally S. Gould, *The Mismeasure of Man* (1981).
8. A. Lorde, "To the Poet Who Happens to Be Black and the Black Poet Who Happens to Be a Woman," in *Our Dead Behind Us* 6–7 (1986).
9. R. Berkhofer, *The White Man's Indian* 71 (1978).
10. This is not to say that simply putting white and black folks together will end discrimination. As social science studies have suggested, such contacts may actually increase prejudice unless the contact occurs under particular conditions—such as when there are

superordinate goals or institutional support in the form of superordinate norms and sanctions. For a review of the "contact" literature, see Amir, "The Role of Intergroup Contact in Change of Prejudice and Ethnic Relations," in *Towards the Elimination of Racism* 245, 245–308 (P. A. Katz ed. 1976).

11. Crenshaw, ["Race, Reform, and Retrenchment," 101 *Harv. L. Rev.* 1331], at 1380 (footnote omitted).

12. *Regents of Univ. of Cal.* v. *Bakke*, 438 U.S. 265, 407 (1978) (Blackmun, J., dissenting).

13. R. Wasserstrom, *Philosophy and Social Issues* 24 (1980). . . .

14. Schofield, "Causes and Consequences of the Colorblind Perspective," in *Prejudice, Discrimination, and Racism* (J. Dovidio & S. Gaertner eds., 1986) at 231.

15. Id. at 249.

16. James Baldwin commented on the "tone of warm congratulation with which so many [white] liberals address their Negro equals. It is the Negro, of course, who is presumed to have become equal—an achievement that not only proves the comforting fact that perseverance has no color but also overwhelmingly corroborates the white man's sense of his own value." J. Baldwin, *The Fire Next Time* 127 (1962).

17. C. Geertz, *Local Knowledge: Further Essays in Interpretive Anthropology* 16 (1983).

18. J. Baldwin, supra [note 16], at 136.

19. W. E. B. Du Bois, supra [note 4], at 172.

20. W. E. B. Du Bois, supra [note 4], at 172. . . .

21. See, e.g., *City of Richmond* v. *J. A. Croson Co.*, 109 S. Ct. 706, 720–23 (1989); *Wygant* v. *Jackson Bd. of Educ.*, 476 U.S. 267, 277–78, 293–94 (1986). . . .

22. See *Wygant*, 476 U.S. at 314–15 (Stevens, J., dissenting). . . . (analysis of *Wygant* reveals that a forward-looking justification for affirmative action would be more effective than treating it as a remedy for past wrongs).

23. *Wygant*, 476 U.S. at 314 (Stevens, J., dissenting).

24. *Regents of Univ. of Cal.* v. *Bakke*, 438 U.S. 265, 315–19 (1978).

25. S. Steele, *The Content of Our Character* 116–17 (1990).

26. D. Kinder & L. Sanders, "Pluralistic Foundations of American Opinion on Race," 9 & n.6 (August 1987) (unpublished paper) (on file with *Columbia Law Review*).

27. Kennedy, "Persuasion and Distrust: A Comment on the Affirmative Action Debate," 99 *Harv. L. Rev.* 1327, 1331 (1986) (footnotes omitted).

28. Id.

29. To its advocates, colorblindness remains an instrumental strategy for achieving racial justice. I do not mean to imply that supporters of colorblindness have no regard for the real-world consequences of their theoretical positions.

30. See J. Kluegel & E. Smith, "Whites' Beliefs about Black Opportunity," 47 *Am. Soc. Rev.* 518, 523 (1982).

REVIEW QUESTIONS

1. What does Aleinikoff mean by race-consciousness? Why does he think that race and race-consciousness are important in our society?
2. What is the strategy of colorblindness? Distinguish between the strong and the weak versions of colorblindness.
3. What are Aleinikoff's objections to strong colorblindness?
4. What is wrong with weak colorblindness?
5. How does Aleinikoff reply to Steele?
6. What is required for racial equality according to Aleinikoff?

DISCUSSION QUESTIONS

1. Does race-consciousness help eliminate racism or does it sustain it?
2. Is colorblindness really impossible to achieve and undesirable? Aren't there any situations where colorblindness might be more appropriate than race-consciousness? For example, shouldn't grading in school be colorblind?
3. Has Aleinikoff given an adequate response to Steele?
4. Which produces the best consequences for society, colorblindness or race-consciousness?

PROBLEM CASES

1. The University of California v. Bakke
(1978). In the years 1973 and 1974, Allan Bakke, a white male, applied for admission to the Medical School of the University of California at Davis. In both years, his application was rejected even though other applicants who had lower grade-point averages and lower Medical College Admissions Test scores were admitted under a special program.

After the second rejection in 1974, Bakke filed a lawsuit in the Superior Court of California. He alleged that the special program that admitted less-qualified minority students operated to exclude him from the school on the basis of race, in violation of his rights under Title VI of the Civil Rights Act of 1964 and the Equal Protection Clause of the Fourteenth Amendment. The trial court found that the special program operated as an unconstitutional racial quota because minority applicants were rated only against one another and sixteen places in the class of one hundred were reserved for them. But the court refused to order Bakke's admission. Bakke appealed, and the case went to the Supreme Court of the United States. The justices of the Supreme Court were divided four to four on the issues in the case, with Justice Powell providing the decisive vote. Justice Powell sided with Chief Justice Warren Burger and three other justices in holding that the admissions program was unconstitutional and that Bakke must be admitted to the school. But Justice Powell also sided with the other four justices in holding that colleges and universities can consider race as a factor in the admissions process.

Are quotas based on race or ethnic status unjust? What is your view?

Is it acceptable to consider race or sex as a factor in admissions? Why or why not?

2. *A Case of Academic Hiring.* Suppose that the philosophy department of a state university has a tenure-track opening. The position is advertised and there are numerous applications, including one from a woman. It is not possible to determine the race of the applicants from the documents provided, and the department does not have the resources to interview the candidates. One of the male applicants has really outstanding credentials—a Ph.D. degree from Harvard with a dissertation on justice written under the direction of John Rawls (the dissertation is being published as a book by Harvard University Press), several articles published in leading journals, evidence of being an excellent teacher, and very flattering letters of recommendation. By comparison, the woman's credentials are good, but not really outstanding. She does not yet have a Ph.D. degree, although she says that her dissertation on feminism is almost done, and she has not published any articles. However, she does possess evidence of being a good teacher, and she has positive letters of recommendation.

Should the department hire the apparently less-qualified woman or not? Why or why not?

Suppose that it is discovered that one of the candidates is a black man; this fact is mentioned in one of the letters of recommendation. This man's credentials seem to be roughly equal to those of the woman. Should he be hired rather than the woman? What choice should be made in this case?

Suppose that the woman's credentials seem roughly equal to that of the leading man, that is, she has a Ph.D. degree from a good school, has publications and good letters of recommendation,

and so on. Should the department hire her rather than the man? What do you think?

3. *Women in Combat Jets.* The current policy of the air force is that women are not allowed to fly jets in actual combat (although they are allowed to fly combat jets in training). But suppose that a qualified woman pilot demands to fly one of these jets in combat. She has logged many hours of flight time; she holds the rank of major; she is in excellent physical condition; she is unmarried and has no children; and she is a black belt in karate. Are there any good reasons for refusing to let her fly? What are they?

4. *Selling a House.* Suppose that Bob and Mary Smith have been trying to sell their three-bedroom house for two years. The house is only five years old, and it is located in a pleasant middle-class neighborhood of Denver. The house has been appraised at $200,000, and the Smiths started out asking that much money for the house. But they have come down in price several times, and now they are asking for only $150,000. They feel that they cannot really go any lower in price because they have a $100,000 mortgage on the house, and they have spent at least $50,000 on various improvements. One day their real estate agent calls and says he has qualified buyers who are willing to pay $150,000 for the house. The only problem is that the buyers, Ralph and Sara Jones, are black. The real estate agent advises the Smiths to turn the offer down. He points out that the house is in an all-white neighborhood and that if they sell to blacks, the property values in the area will go down dramatically. He has seen this happen in east Denver where houses that once sold for $500,000 are now selling for $50,000. Also, the real estate agent claims that the neighbors will be very angry if the Smiths sell their house to black people. On the other hand, the Smiths have a legal right to sell their house to qualified buyers, and the Joneses are definitely qualified. Ralph Jones is a successful lawyer, and his wife Sara is a grade-school teacher. They have three children, and they would be delighted to have the house.

Should the Smiths sell their house to the Joneses or not? Explain your position.

5. *The Equal Rights Amendment.* The proposed Equal Rights Amendment reads as follows:

"Section 1. Equality of rights under the law shall not be denied or abridged by the United States or by any state on account of sex.

"Section 2. The Congress shall have the power to enforce, by appropriate legislation, the provisions of this article.

"Section 3. This amendment shall take effect two years after the date of ratification."

This amendment was originally proposed by Alice Paul in 1923, just three years after women in the United States received the right to vote. It was approved by Congress in 1971, but it has not been ratified by the required three-fourths of the state legislatures and is now dead unless Congress revives it.

Should this amendment be ratified or not? Defend your position.

SUGGESTED READINGS

1. Thomas Sowell, *Civil Rights: Rhetoric or Reality* (William Morrow, 1984), argues that we should strive for equal opportunity without regard to race or sex. Sowell rejects affirmative action because it helps those who need it the least.

2. William Julius Wilson, *The Truly Disadvantaged: The Inner City, the Underclass, and Public Policy* (University of Chicago Press, 1987), claims that affirmative action ignores the real victims of discrimination, the truly disadvantaged, and instead benefits well-educated middle-class blacks who have no need for it.

3. Edward Tivan, *The Moral Imagination* (Simon & Schuster, 1995), Chapter 5, discusses the history of affirmative action and gives an emotional defense of it, arguing that whites must help blacks to avoid a race war.

4. Gertrude Ezorsky, *Racism and Justice: The Case for Affirmative Action* (Cornell University Press, 1991), maintains that preferential treatment of blacks (including those in the middle or upper class) is just compensation for past discrimination and enslavement.

5. Robert Nozick, *Anarchy, State, and Utopia* (Basic Books, 1974), defends the libertarian view that employers have the right to hire people who will do the best job without government interference.

6. Charles Murray, "Affirmative Racism," *New Republic* (December 31, 1984), argues that preferential treatment for blacks amounts to a new kind of racism that assumes that blacks are less competent than whites and thus continues the racism it is supposed to eliminate.

7. *Equality and Preferential Treatment,* ed. Marshall Cohen, Thomas Nagel, and Thomas Scanlon (Princeton University Press, 1971), is a collection of articles which includes Nagel's well-known defense of preferential treatment titled "Equal Treatment and Compensatory Discrimination." Also included is Ronald Dworkin's article on two important legal decisions, one dealing with a 1945 policy that denied an African-American man admission to law school, and the other on a 1971 policy that denied a white male (DeFunis) admission to law school.

8. Ronald Dworkin, "Why Bakke Has No Case," *The New York Review of Books* (November 19, 1977), argues that Bakke's rights were not violated by the University of California at Davis policy of having a quota of sixteen places out of a class of one hundred reserved for minority students. Soon after this article was published, the Supreme Court ruled five to four that the quota system at Davis was unconstitutional. (See the Problem Cases.)

9. Cornel West, "Beyond Affirmative Action: Equality and Identity," in *Race Matters* (Beacon, 1993), argues that without affirmative action, discrimination would return with a vengeance.

10. Stephen Carter, *Reflections of an Affirmative Action Baby* (Basic Books, 1991), maintains that preferential treatment has become an embarrassment and an insult to competent blacks; they would rather be hired on their merits and not because of skin color.

11. Tom Beauchamp, "The Justification of Reverse Discrimination," in *Social Justice and Preferential Treatment,* ed. William T. Blackstone and Robert Heslep (University of Georgia Press, 1976), argues that reverse discrimination in hiring is justified in order to eliminate present discriminatory practices.

12. Bernard R. Boxill, "The Morality of Preferential Hiring," *Philosophy & Public Affairs* 7, no. 3 (Spring 1978), pp. 246–68, replies to two objections to preferential hiring, that it benefits those who do not deserve compensation and that it is unfair to young white men.

13. Bernard R. Boxill, "Sexual Blindness and Sexual Equality," *Social Theory and Practice* 6, no. 3

(Fall 1980), pp. 281–98, attacks Wasserstrom's assimilationist ideal that a good and just society would be sex- and color-blind; his main objection is that this ideal has unacceptable costs.

14. Lisa Newton, "Reverse Discrimination as Unjustified," *Ethics* 83, 1973, pp. 308–12. Newton contends that reverse discrimination is just as unjust as ordinary discrimination and, as such, it undermines the moral ideal of equality.

15. William T. Blackstone, "Reverse Discrimination and Compensatory Justice," *Social Theory and Practice* 3, no. 3 (Spring 1975), pp. 253–88, argues that the bad effects of reverse discrimination outweigh the good effects, even for the women and minorities that it is supposed to help, and that therefore it is morally improper.

16. *Reverse Discrimination,* ed. Barry Gross (Prometheus Books, 1977), is an anthology which includes articles by Sidney Hook, Lisa Newton, Bernard Boxill, and Alan Goldman.

17. George Sher, "Justifying Reverse Discrimination in Employment," *Philosophy & Public Affairs* 4, no. 2 (Winter 1975), pp. 159–70, argues that a case can be made for reverse discrimination when it is compensation for lost ability to compete on equal terms due to inadequate education or other factors.

18. George Sher, "Reverse Discrimination, the Future, and the Past," *Ethics* 90 (October 1979), pp. 81–87, raises difficulties for both forward-looking and backward-looking defenses of preferential treatment.

19. Judith Jarvis Thomson, "Preferential Hiring," *Philosophy & Public Affairs* 2, no. 4 (Summer 1973), pp. 364–84, defends preferential hiring of women and minorities by universities in cases where their qualifications are equal to those of other applicants.

20. Richard Wasserstrom, "Racism and Sexism," *Today's Moral Problems,* third edition, ed. R. A. Wasserstrom (Macmillan, 1985), pp. 1–29. After describing the social reality of racism and sexism, Wasserstrom proposes a forward-looking solution— the assimilationist ideal where race and sex are no more important than eye color.

21. Steven Goldberg, *The Inevitability of Patriarchy* (William Morrow, 1973), defends the sexist view that the male hormone testosterone makes men more aggressive than women, making it impossible for women to successfully compete against men for high-status positions.

22. Joyce Trebilcot, "Sex Roles: The Argument from Nature," *Ethics* 85, no. 3 (April 1975), pp. 249–55, critically examines three arguments used to support sexism, including Goldberg's argument that psychological differences between the sexes make sex roles and male dominance inevitable.

23. Charles Murray, *The Bell Curve* (Simon & Schuster, 1994), considers the controversial evidence that blacks are inferior in intelligence to whites and the implications this has for social policy and programs.

Chapter Seven

CORPORATE RESPONSIBILITY

Introduction

Corporations engage in a variety of practices that seem to be morally questionable: polluting the environment with toxic chemical wastes, producing unsafe or lethal products, discriminating against women and minorities, bribing government officials, lying and deceiving in advertising, buying and selling companies to plunder their assets, giving executives excessive salaries and retirement benefits, and laying off thousands of employees to increase profits. Specific examples are not hard to find. There was the deadly chemical accident in Bhopal, India, that killed or severely injured thousands of people. The Rocky Flats plant in Colorado contaminated ground water and air with toxic and radioactive wastes from its production of plutonium triggers for nuclear weapons, and then denied any knowledge of its actions and refused to accept any responsibility. There was the enormous oil spill from the Exxon ship *Valdez*. Executives at Beech Nut tried to pass off flavored water as apple juice. Executives of cigarette companies continue to insist that nicotine is not addictive and that cigarette smoking is not harmful, despite overwhelming evidence to the contrary, and even in view of internal memos admitting that nicotine is addictive. Ivan Boesky and a ring of traders made huge profits by illegally trading on insider information, and after serving token jail sentences, Ivan and his friends are back in business as "advisers." Takeovers and buyouts during the 1980s ruined several airline companies, while executives and investment bankers made indecent profits. The list goes on and on; in fact according to *Time* (July 3, 1989), two-thirds of the *Fortune* 500 companies have been convicted of crimes.

Our readings begin with a detailed look at a case of pollution by a large corporation, the Hooker Chemical Company, the tenth largest chemical company in the United States, with thirty plants in eleven countries. Critics claim that this company has been one of the worst polluters in the country. It has dumped kepone (a known carcinogen) into the James River in Virginia and allowed mirex (another carcinogen) to run into Lake Ontario from improperly stored barrels. It has released a variety of dangerous gases (chlorine, phosphorous, mercury, and so on) into the air outside the company's Niagara Falls plant. From 1942 to 1953, it dumped more than 21,000 tons of toxic chemical wastes into an abandoned canal digging called Love Canal. This site was sold, and an elementary school and a tract of houses were built adjacent to it. But the site eventually leaked its toxic chemicals into houses, causing a number of health problems: liver damage, miscarriages, birth defects, cancer, epilepsy, suicide, and rectal bleeding, to name a few.

A Philosophical Problem   Critics of Hooker Chemical assume that this company has a moral responsibility to avoid immoral actions such as polluting the environment. But do corporations have moral responsibilities over and above the responsibility to make money? Should they adopt a moral point of view where they are concerned with the welfare of others, or should they act only in their own self-interest by pursuing profits? The latter view is accepted by Milton Friedman in the second reading. He believes that the only responsibility of business is to increase its profits by open and free competition without deception or fraud. Friedman attacks what he calls the "doctrine of social responsibility," the view that business has other social responsibilities besides making money, for example, the duty to reduce pollution or eliminate racial and gender discrimination. To begin with, Friedman points out that only persons have responsibilities, and because business as a whole and corporations are not persons, they cannot be said to have responsibilities. Of course business executives are persons who

have responsibilities, but their responsibility is to make money for the stockholders and not to spend the money of the stockholders without their consent. If business executives do this in the pursuit of some socially responsible goal such as reducing pollution, then they are in effect imposing taxes on the stockholders and the consumers, and this is taxation without representation. Furthermore, the doctrine of social responsibility has bad consequences: Executives who follow it will be fired, and wage restraints justified by it will produce strikes and worker revolts. Finally, Friedman denounces the doctrine of social responsibility as a fundamentally subversive doctrine that is incompatible with the ideal of a free society.

Friedman's position has been attacked on a number of points. For example, Friedman contends that corporations cannot meaningfully be said to be persons who have responsibilities. But is this true? Ordinarily a person is an agent who makes decisions and acts and is held morally responsible for these decisions and acts. But corporations are legally persons who make decisions and act, so why not hold them morally responsible too?

Christopher D. Stone criticizes some of Friedman's other points. The promissory argument (as Stone calls it in the reading) claims that the management of a corporation has promised the shareholders that it will maximize profits, so if it does not do this, management has broken its promise. Stone objects that management has made no such promise and that, even if it did, the promise is only to existent shareholders and anyway a promise can always be overridden by more important moral concerns. The agency argument is another argument used by Friedman. According to this argument, the management is the agent of the individuals who own the corporation and as such it has a duty to maximize profits. In reply, Stone points out that management often does not act like such an agent. Management not only ignores the wishes of the shareholders, it also actively opposes them in some cases.

Stone does not try to refute the so-called polestar argument, the argument that a corporation's single-minded pursuit of profits is a means of charting a straight course for what is best for society. This argument seems to be a utilitarian one: The greatest good for the greatest number can be achieved only if corporations act solely in the pursuit of profits and ignore moral concerns. But is it really true that a selfish society in which everyone pursues his or her own self-interest will turn out to be better than a moral society in which people are regulated by moral concerns? This seems very doubtful.

In the last two readings for the chapter, Norman E. Bowie and Thomas Donaldson use social contract theory to determine the moral obligations of business corporations. In Bowie's version, the social contract is between corporations and society as a whole. In return for the permission to do business, society imposes certain obligations and duties on corporations. Corporations should accept these duties and obligations because it is in their self-interest to do so; if they don't act responsibly, then society will cancel the tacit contract to do business. Further, Bowie thinks that cor-

porations have a social responsibility to help solve social problems because they helped create them and because they have the resources to resolve them.

Donaldson presents a different version of the social contract. Instead of a contract between corporations and society as a whole, the hypothetical contract he imagines is between corporations and individuals in society. Individuals benefit from corporations both as consumers and as employees, and these benefits justify the existence of corporations. If a corporation fails to provide these benefits, say by manufacturing a dangerous product or by abusing employees, then it has failed to live up to the contract, and it deserves moral condemnation. Furthermore corporations have drawbacks: Corporations pollute and deplete natural resources; they can misuse their political power; they can harm workers; and so on. These drawbacks, the social contract, and the minimum standards of justice all set limits on what corporations can be allowed to do.

*Tom L. Beauchamp
& Martha W. Elliott*

Hooker Chemical and Love Canal

Tom L. Beauchamp is a member of the philosophy department at Georgetown University. He is the author of Philosophical Ethics *and coauthor of* Hume and the Problem of Causation, Medical Ethics, *and* Principles of Biomedical Ethics.

Martha W. Elliott was a member of Beauchamp's research staff.

In the 1940s, Hooker Chemical dumped toxic chemical wastes at the Love Canal site, resulting

in pollution of the site and health concerns for nearby residents. Hooker Chemical also was involved in other cases of pollution. The authors describe the efforts of the EPA to solve the problem of dangerous waste disposal. They discuss Hooker Chemical's defense and the resolution of claims against its parent company, Occidental Petroleum. Finally, they describe the resettlement of the Love Canal community.

THE HISTORY OF LOVE CANAL

Love Canal is named for William T. Love, a businessman and visionary who in the late nineteenth century attempted to create a model industrial city near Niagara Falls. Love proposed to build a canal that would facilitate the generation and transmission of hydroelectric power from the falls to the city's industries. The combination of an economic recession that made financing difficult and the development of cheaper methods of transmitting electricity destroyed Love's vision, and the partially dug canal in what is now the southeast corner of the city of Niagara Falls remains the project's sole tangible legacy.

However, the area still attracted industrial development because it provided easy access to transportation, cheap electricity, and abundant water for industrial processes. Several chemical companies joined other corporations in taking advantage of the region's natural resources. The Hooker Electrochemical Company, now absorbed into the Occidental Chemical Corporation, built its first plant in the area in 1905. An Occidental Petroleum Corporation subsidiary since 1968, Hooker manufactures plastics, pesticides, chlorine, caustic soda, fertilizers, and a variety of other chemical products. With over 3,000 employees, Hooker remains one of the region's largest employers and a Niagara Falls area economic force.[1]

In the early 1940s Love Canal's abandoned section—for many years a summer swimming hole—became a dump for barrels of waste materials produced by the various area chemical companies. Hooker received state permission in 1942 to use the site for chemical dumping. It is estimated, although no accurate records were kept, that between the early dumping period and 1953, when this tract of land was sold, these corporations deposited approximately 21,000 tons of different kinds of chemical wastes, some extremely toxic, in the old canal. The companies stored the chemicals in drums, and considered the site ideal for chemical dumping. Located in an undeveloped, largely unpopulated area, the canal featured highly impermeable clay walls that retained liquid chemical materials with virtually no penetration. Research indicated that the canal's walls permitted water penetration at the rate of a third of an inch over a 25-year period.

In 1953 Hooker closed the dump and covered it with an impermeable clay top. The Niagara Falls School Board then acquired the land encompassing and surrounding the dump for $1.00.[2] Hooker advised against the acquisition and warned the school board of the toxic wastes. However, the board persisted and started con-

demnation proceedings to acquire land in the area. The city subsequently built an elementary school and a tract of houses adjacent to the site. The constructors removed thousands of cubic yards of top soil. The construction apparently damaged the integrity of the clay covering. Water from rain and heavy snows then seeped through the covering and entered the chemical-filled, clay-lined basin. The basin eventually overflowed into the houses, and the unfortunate residents were treated to the noxious smell and unwholesome sight of chemicals seeping into their basements and surfacing to the ground.

In 1978 evidence of toxic chemicals was found in the living area of several homes, and the state health commissioner ordered an investigation which brought a number of health hazards to light. Several adults showed incipient liver damage; young women in certain areas experienced three times the normal incidence of miscarriage; and the area had three-and-one-half times the normal incidence of birth defects. The investigation also uncovered epilepsy, suicide, rectal bleeding, hyperactivity, and a variety of other ills—all at above normal rates of occurrence.

Upon review of these findings, the health commissioner recommended that the elementary school be temporarily closed and that pregnant women and children under the age of two be temporarily evacuated. Shortly thereafter the governor of New York announced that the state would purchase the 235 houses nearest the canal and would assist in the relocation of dispossessed families. President Carter declared Love Canal a disaster area, qualifying the affected families for federal assistance.[3] However, families in the adjacent ring of houses did not receive federal assistance, although they believed that the canal chemicals endangered their health. Early studies tended to confirm this view, but in mid-July 1982 the Environmental Protection Agency (EPA) released a study that concluded there was "no evidence that Love Canal has contributed to environmental contamination" in the outer ring of 400 homes. This report focused on health hazards and did not address documented symptoms of stress. For example, the divorce rate among remaining families soared as wives and children fled the area, while husbands tried to hold onto their houses and jobs.[4]

Since the investigation first began, more than 100 different chemicals, some of them mutagens, teratogens, and carcinogens, have been identified. A number of investigations are continuing to resolve unanswered questions, including the long-range effects of chemical exposure. Cancer, for instance, often does not develop for 20 to 25 years after exposure to the cancer-producing agent. Chromosomal damage may appear only in subsequent generations.

For years many unanswered questions persisted about how to clean up the pollution and who should be held responsible for it. Answers to these questions did not come, in many cases, until twenty years after residents of Love Canal first found out about the condition of their yards and homes.

CRITICISMS OF HOOKER

The Hooker Chemical company figures prominently in many of these questions and answers. In 1977 the city of Niagara Falls employed an engineering consulting firm to study Love Canal and make cleanup recommendations. Hooker supplied technical assistance, information, and personnel. The cost of a second study was shared equally by Hooker, the city, and the school board that had originally purchased the land from Hooker. Hooker also offered to pay one-third of the estimated $850,000 cost of clean-up.[5]

In 1980 Hooker faced over $2 billion in lawsuits stemming from its activities at Love Canal and other locations. Thirteen hundred private suits had been filed by mid-1982. The additional complaints and suits stemmed from past and current activities in other states as well as from additional New York sites. In addition, in 1976 Virginia employees of Life Sciences who had been exposed to Kepone, a highly toxic chemical known to cause trembling and sterility in humans filed suits totaling more than $100 million. The suits named Hooker as a supplier of some of the raw materials used in the Virginia manufacturing process. (The par-

ties ultimately settled the suit out of court.) In 1977 Hooker was ordered to pay $176,000 for discharging HCCPD, a chemical used in the manufacture of Kepone and Mirex, which had caused cancer in laboratory animals, into Michigan's White Lake. In 1979 that state's officials sued Hooker for a $200 million cleanup due to air, water, and land pollution around its White Lake plant.[6]

While Hooker was defending its actions in Virginia and Michigan, the state of California investigated the company and ultimately brought suit on charges that Hooker's Occidental Chemical plant at Lathrop, California, had for years violated state law by dumping toxic pesticides, thereby polluting nearby ground water. Hooker officials denied the charges, but a series of memos written by Robert Edson, Occidental's environmental engineer at Lathrop, suggested that the company knew of the hazard as early as 1975 but chose to ignore it until pressured by the state investigation. In April 1975 Edson wrote, "Our laboratory records indicate that we are slowly contaminating all wells in our area, and two of our own wells are contaminated to the point of being toxic to animals and humans." A year later he wrote, "To date, we have been discharging waste water . . . containing about five tons of pesticide per year to the ground. . . . I believe we have fooled around long enough and already overpressed our luck." Another year later, Edson reiterated his charges and added that "if anyone should complain, we could be the party named in an action by the Water Quality Control Board. . . . Do we correct the situation before we have a problem or do we hold off until action is taken against us?"[7]

Other complaints about Hooker stemmed from the same area of Love Canal. In 1976 the New York Department of Environmental Conservation banned consumption of seven species of fish taken from Lake Ontario, claiming that they were contaminated with chemicals, including Mirex. The Department alleged that Hooker's Niagara Falls plant had discharged the Mirex. A Hooker-sponsored study of Lake Ontario fish disputed this allegation of Mirex contamination. Although this study has not been accepted by the state, the ban has, for the most part, been lifted.

Hooker's Hyde Park chemical waste dump, located in the Niagara Falls area, has also been a source of continuing concern and dispute to residents and government officials. In 1972 the manager of a plant adjacent to the dump complained to Hooker about "an extremely dangerous condition affecting our plant and employees . . . our midnight shift workers has [sic] complained of coughing and sore throats from the obnoxious and corrosive permeating fumes from the disposal site." [8] The dangerous condition was not adequately rectified, and in 1979 Hooker's Hyde Park landfill became the subject of a nearly $26 million lawsuit filed by the town of Niagara Falls. New York State also filed a suit for more than $200 million for alleged damages at the Hyde Park site.

In 1980 the EPA filed four additional suits against Hooker for $124.5 million in remedial work. The EPA explained that the actions against Hooker involved: (1) litigation under "imminent hazard" provisions of existing EPA laws, and (2) the creation of programs, financed by government and industry, to clean up hazardous waste sites. EPA Administrator Barbara Blum described the imminent hazard litigation as follows: "This program seeks to halt dangerous disposal practices and to force privately-funded cleanup. This approach gets results, of course, only where a responsible party can be identified and has adequate financial resources to carry some or all of the cleanup costs." [9]

Blum also detailed the specific statutes the EPA was acting under and discussed the EPA's collaboration with the Justice Department in enforcing the statutes:

Sections of the Resource Conservation and Recovery Act, Safe Drinking Water Act, Toxic Substances Control Act, Clean Water Act, and Clean Air Act all authorize EPA to ask the court for injunctive relief in situations which pose threats to public health or the environment. Section 309 of the Clean Water Act levies a penalty of up to $10,000 a day for unpermitted discharges to navigable waters (a leaking dump can be considered a discharge). . . .

People are frightened by Love Canal and by the emergence of threatening hazardous waste sites in their local communities. They are demanding action—and they are getting it. [10]

The EPA has estimated that only 10 percent of all hazardous wastes are disposed of in strict compliance with federal regulations. According to Thomas H. Maugh II, "nearly 50 percent is disposed of by lagooning in unlined surface impoundments, 30 percent in nonsecure landfills, and about 10 percent by dumping into sewers, spreading on roads, injection into deep wells, and incineration under uncontrolled conditions." [11] Maugh argues that "legal dump sites gone awry" are a lesser problem than the growing problem of illegally dumped wastes in unsecured dump sites, often in the middle of cities. [12] In October 1981 the EPA announced that "there are at least twenty-nine toxic waste disposal sites around the country as dangerous or more so than Love Canal." [13]

HOOKER'S DEFENSE AGAINST THE CHARGES

Hooker Chemical believes that its role and position have been misunderstood. Although the company neither denies using the canal as a chemical dump nor denies that the dump has created a serious problem, company officials contend that (1) the company's efforts to prevent first the public and then the private development of the canal area are generally unrecognized; (2) the company has been an industry leader in safety; (3) Hooker is being unfairly singled out for waste disposal practices that were then almost universal throughout the chemical industry; and (4) a certain level of risk is an inevitable hazard in an industrial society.

Hooker has marshaled data to support these contentions. In the first place, Hooker believes that its efforts to warn the school board and city against interfering with the waste disposal area have gone unappreciated. When the Niagara Falls School Board expressed an interest in selling a portion of the Love Canal tract to a developer, Hooker representatives argued against the plan in a public meeting and later reiterated to the board its warnings of possible hazards. When the school board persisted in its plans and began to obtain adjacent parcels of land through condemnation proceedings, Hooker, in the school board's deed, again referred to the property's past use and stipulated that all future risks and liabilities be passed to the school board. One part of the deed stipulated that:

Prior to the delivery of this instrument of conveyance, the grantee herein has been advised by the grantor that the premises above described have been filled, in whole or in part, to the present grade level thereof with waste products resulting from the manufacturing of chemicals by the grantor at its plant in the City of Niagara Falls, New York, and the grantee assumes all risk and liability incident to the use thereof. It is, therefore, understood and agreed that, as a part of the consideration for this conveyance and as a condition thereof, no claim, suit, action or demand of any nature whatsoever shall ever be made by the grantee, its successors or assigns, against the grantor, its successors or assigns, for injury to a person or persons, including the death resulting therefrom, or loss of or damage to property caused by, in connection with or by reason of the presence of said industrial wastes.[14]

When the school board later sold part of the land to a private developer who planned to build houses, Hooker officials protested the sale both verbally and in writing. Executives contend that the company has been unjustly blamed for others' imprudence. Hooker also claims that it has no legal responsibility for the Love Canal problem and that it has more than met its social and moral obligations in time and money spent on the cleanup effort. Through its Love Canal experiences, Hooker environmental health and safety specialists have developed knowledge and skills that have enabled the company to take a leadership role in problems of underground pollution.

Hooker officials also argue that their past practices satisfied and even exceeded the then-operative industry standards for waste disposal. During the 1942 to 1953 period, when Hooker filled Love Canal with barrels of chemical wastes, neither the industries involved nor the health and regulatory professions recognized the long-term environmental and personal hazards of these industrial "leftovers." Storing the chemical wastes in a clay canal at the time represented an improvement on common methods of disposal in unlined and unsecured landfills.

The company's defense of its behavior in the Love Canal situation parallels in some respects the reaction of certain Love Canal residents. They directed the major thrust of their antagonism not toward Hooker Chemical, but toward the New York State Health Department, which had failed to provide open access to the results of state-conducted health studies and experienced unexplained delays in admitting that a health problem existed. The health department attempted to discourage and actively thwarted independent researchers whose reports indicated more widespread risks to the community's health than the department was willing to admit or was prepared to pay to rectify. Given these premises, residents have concluded that the health department, not Hooker Chemical, failed to meet its obligations to the community.[15]

Hooker supports the common industry position that society will have to learn to accept a certain level of risk in order to enjoy the products of industrial society. Environmental hazards are one form of industrial "trade-off." Industrialists cite such persons as Margery W. Shaw, an independent scientist who reviewed a chromosomal study of Love Canal residents. She points out that the level of acceptable risk is a more general societal problem:

In our democratic society, perhaps we will decide that 500,000 deaths per year is an acceptable price for toxic chemicals in our environment, just as we have decided that 50,000 traffic deaths per year is an acceptable price for automobile travel. On the other hand, we may say that 5,000 deaths per year is an unacceptable price for toxic chemicals.[16]

THE CONTINUING CONTROVERSY OVER HOOKER AND THE CANAL CLEANUP

Over the years, Hooker has been among the most heavily criticized corporations for its environmental policies. Ralph Nader attacked Hooker as a "callous corporation" leaving toxic "cesspools." An ABC news documentary harshly criticized the company, focusing on the increased incidence of disease at Love Canal. Nonetheless, Hooker has won a number of defenders. A *Fortune* magazine editorial defended the corporation for having explicitly conformed to government waste disposal standards, for resisting the canal area construction, and for being the victim of exaggerated and irresponsible reports about the regional incidence of disease.[17] A *Discover* magazine editorial laid the blame for the Love Canal on the school board (but argued that Hooker did act irresponsibly in waste dumpage at a number of other sites).[18] The 1982 EPA study blunted some federal efforts and some lawsuits.

In 1983 the U.S. Center for Disease Control (CDC) conducted a study of Love Canal residents. The CDC examined 44 residents and compared them to a control group chosen from Niagara Falls residents living at least one mile from the evacuated area. The CDC concluded that residents of Love Canal do not show increased incidence of cancer or reproductive abnormalities when compared to residents of other Niagara Falls neighborhoods. CDC critics claim the study was too small to be conclusive. Health officials and state legislators called for more conclusive information.[19]

Amidst the controversy, Niagara Falls city officials had a list of more than 100 families from the Love Canal neighborhood that were waiting for housing.[20] Many people eagerly awaited the final word on Love Canal's conditions. Although the 1982 EPA study contended that adjacent neighborhoods met safety requirements, New York state health officials reported that they found dioxin (one of the world's most toxic chemicals) at levels eight times higher than the lethal dose.[21] The U.S. Office of Technology Assessment undertook an evaluation of all available evidence, but its report shed no additional light on the conditions at Love Canal. It stated that "with available information it is possible either that unsafe levels of toxic contamination exist or that they do not exist."[22]

Voles (field mice common to the Love Canal area) were the subject of another 1983 study. The mice were ideal for the study because they are sedentary, rarely moving appreciable distances. The number of voles found living in the canal area was less than in the control area. (The study placed the control area one mile from the canal area.) Mice living near the canal evidenced liver damage. Life expectancies varied significantly. Any vole in the canal area that reached an age of 30 days could only be expected to live an additional 54 days. A similar vole in the control area would be expected to live 100 days past the 30-day mark. The life expectancy thus was cut in half for those mice living near the canal.[23]

Another study of live birth weights of children born to Love Canal women has also provided cause for concern. Children born to women who lived near chemical swales had significantly lower birth weights in the years 1940–1978 than the state average. A swale is a natural low area along water drainage pathways where chemicals might collect. Several drainage pathways pass through the Love Canal region. Researchers found that 12.1 percent of the children born to women who had lived near one of the swales showed lower than average birth weights as compared to a 6.9 percent average for the state of New York (excluding New York City).[24]

Citizens and health officials have mobilized in an attempt to force the cleanup of Love Canal and keep area inhabitants informed of new findings and projects. Local citizens have grown weary of the problems and want the area cleaned up as soon as possible. Progress has been made, but efforts continue late into the 1990s. The complex cleanup project began in the spring of 1987 with the dredging of three local creeks. The site, which had remained covered with plastic sheeting and earth, was uncovered. Officials began to dredge dioxin-contaminated mud and tainted sediment from the creeks. The creeks were dewatered, and waste was removed. The EPA and the State Department of Environmental Conservation stored the wastes in a temporary landfill and storage facility near the site.

Citizens opposed the storage, fearing that it would delay possible rehabilitation of the area. They charged the EPA with negligence and undue delay. In October 1987 the EPA announced plans to complete the cleanup. The EPA planned to incinerate the stored wastes at an expected cost of $26 to $31 million. The incineration process, although costly, is considered a permanent solution. Buried wastes or other disposal methods, such as deep well injection, are considered hazardous.[25] A Technical Review Committee (TRC) oversees testing of Love Canal air and soil samples and will compare its findings to those from other neighborhoods. The TRC also develops criteria for making final Love Canal resettlement decisions. Under the TRC plan, parts of Love Canal will be converted to a reforested park.[26]

In February 1988 a new court decision altered the circumstance of legal liability for Love Canal. Federal Judge John Curtin of the U.S. District Court for the Western District of New York ruled that Occidental Petroleum Corporation's chemicals unit is responsible for the costs of cleaning up Love Canal—costs estimated at $250 million. This decision was made under the 1980 Superfund Act, the federal program to clean up the nation's most polluted environments.[27] Curtin found Occidental "at least partially responsible" for the initially inadequate storage and for leakage that has occurred over the years. Occidental argued in the case that the city of Niagara Falls was solely responsible for release of the toxic wastes because city officials ignored warnings about the site and then disrupted its hydrology. But Judge Curtin rejected this "third-party defense" because Hooker Chemical had brought the wastes to the site.[28] New York State Attorney General Robert Abrams said the judge's opinion constitutes "a tremendous victory for the state and federal governments and a resounding defeat for Occidental's strenuous and expensive public-relations campaign to shift the entire blame for Love Canal to the city of Niagara Falls, the board of education, the state of New York, and even the people who were forced to abandon their homes." [29]

In 1992 Occidental again tried to claim that the federal government was partially at fault. The company attempted to prove that the Army had dumped toxic wastes at Love Canal and then destroyed the relevant records. Although the Justice Department has denied such claims, Occidental insists that the Army dumped approximately 4,000 tons of chemicals at Love Canal.

The 1988 case that found Occidental the sole party responsible for the cleanup of Love Canal did not come to closure until June 21, 1994, after the settlement of various countersuits. On March 17, 1994, the federal court decided not to hold Occidental responsible for punitive damages. The *New York Times,* quoting Judge Curtin who was still presiding over the case, said "that while Occidental was negligent 'on a number of occasions,' the state failed to prove that the company acted with 'reckless or wanton disregard of safety or rights,' the standard he said was necessary to assess punitive damages." [30] This decision does not affect the previous 1988 ruling. In June 1994, after the long-awaited out-of-court decision, Occidental agreed to pay New York state $98 million for damages and expenditures and to take full responsibility for cleanup work. The state estimates that the cleanup charges will run around $22 million, but Occidental put the value at only $8 million. Whatever the precise figure, G. Oliver Koppel, the state attorney general, said, "the settlement was by far the largest in state history." [31] Occidental views the June decision as a vindication of its actions at Love Canal, because the company was cleared of wrongdoing. The chairman of the Chemical Manufacturers Association argued further that the decision sets a precedent that chemical companies cannot be held responsible for waste disposal practices that were appropriate at the time: "You cannot judge people or a company based on today's standards or knowledge for actions taken 40 to 60 years ago," he said.[32]

The effects of the Love Canal decision extend beyond the realms of New York state and the Occidental Chemical Company. Love Canal has become an example of how slow and costly cleanup of Superfund sites has become. Because of the attention raised by Love Canal, the Clinton administration proposed in 1994 an overhaul of the 14-year-old program. The focus was to redefine the criterion of a "clean" site so that government programs would not recognize or permit different standards of cleanliness. Love Canal suggests to many that a flexible standard is problematic because, over the course of many years, property can change hands and be used for a variety of purposes, each falling under a different standard of "clean." For this reason, the Clinton administration has insisted on implementing a definition of cleanliness that can apply to all waste sites.[33]

THE CURRENT SITUATION

In May 1990, Environmental Protection Agency Chief William K. Reilly announced that the government had opened the Love Canal neighborhoods for resettlement. After a 12-year, $250-million cleanup, the EPA concluded that four of the area's seven districts were habitable. The other three could be converted to park land and industrial areas.[34] Sixty of the area's 2,500 original residents remained through the years of turmoil. On August 15, 1990, the planning director of the Love Canal Area Revitalization Agency, James Carr, placed 236 houses on sale, at 20 percent below market value. Armed with a list of more than 200 eager potential Love Canal home buyers, Carr predicted that the area would quickly regain residents.

He was right. In 1992 the Federal Housing Administration started offering mortgages when banks declined involvement. This allowed 100 eager buyers to afford new homes. Success in sales allowed the houses' discount to be reduced to approximately 15 percent below market value. Kenneth Denman, the sole sales agent for the Love Canal Area Revitalization Agency, said that "no sooner were the words 'Love Canal' back in the news than the sales office for [the agency was] jamming up like a Tokyo subway." [35] Given the enormous government cleanup and protection programs, Love Canal's environmental dangers appear to have been eradicated, though many observers remain skeptical. Carr maintained that "a child runs far, far greater health risks if his parents smoke or drink than he does living in Love Canal." [36]

Love Canal, now changed in name to Black Creek Village, has a state-of-the-art containment system, with two three-foot-thick caps over the dumpsite. The authorities razed the roughly 240 houses nearest the site and enclosed the entire area within a chain-link fence. Home buyers ready to reinhabit Love Canal have put their faith in the cleanup process, despite environmentalists' continuing fears, which spring from inconclusive studies and uncertain conditions. One environmentalist, National Resources Defense Council attorney Rebecca Todd, commented, "Love Canal is a ticking time bomb." [37] Lois Gibbs, who in 1970 led the evacuation of residents from Love Canal and in 1994 was the director of the Citizens' Clearinghouse for Hazardous Waste in Washington, has never stopped opposing resale of homes in the area. Gibbs argues that the attempt to move people back into Love Canal is "a matter of the state trying to cover up Love Canal and pretend that it didn't exist, pretend like it was not a threat." [38]

The state and federal governments continue to assure new and potential residents that the area is habitable. Reports of tests run on neighborhood soil, air, and houses concluded that "this section of Niagara Falls was no more polluted or toxic than other parts of the city." [39] Skeptics wonder why, if health concerns were the major reason to evacuate in the first place, no one has done follow-up tests of former residents' health 15 years later.[40]

Despite the court cases, lawsuits, and cleanup responsibilities, uncertainty remains regarding safety and health risks, as well as the correct explanation of disease. As one former Love Canal resident puts it, "We'll still have the same question: Is it because I live in Love Canal? Or is it not? because those questions have never been addressed." [41]

Endnotes

1. John F. Steiner, "Love Can Be Dangerous to Your Health," in George A. Steiner and John F. Steiner, *Casebook for Business, Government and Society*, 2d ed. (New York: Random House, 1980), pp. 108–9.
2. Sam Borenkind, "Environmental Laws: How Far-Reaching?" *NPN—National Petroleum News* (March 1991), p. 60.
3. Thomas H. Maugh II, "Toxic Waste Disposal a Gnawing Problem," *Science* 204 (May 1979), p. 820.
4. Constance Holden, "Love Canal Residents Under Stress," *Science* 208 (June 13, 1980), pp. 1242–44; and Sandra Sugawara, "Some Love Canal Areas Safe, A New EPA Study Concludes," *Washington Post*, July 15, 1982, Sec. A, pp. 1, 9. See also Beverly Paigen in note 15 on the earlier data.
5. Steiner, "Love Can Be Dangerous," p. 112.
6. Michael H. Brown, "Love Canal, U.S.A.," *New York Times Magazine* (January 21, 1979), p. 23, *passim*, and Gary Whitney, "Hooker Chemical and Plastics" (HBS Case Services, Harvard Business School, 1979), p. 3.

7. "The Hooker Memos," in Robert J. Baum, ed., *Ethical Problems in Engineering,* 2d ed. (Troy, N.Y.: Center for the Study of the Human Dimensions of Science and Technology, Rensselaer Polytechnic Institute, 1980), Vol. 2, p. 38, and "An Occidental Unit Knowingly Polluted California Water, House Panel Charges," *Wall Street Journal,* June 20, 1979, p. 14.

8. Whitney, "Hooker Chemical and Plastics."

9. Ibid.

10. Ibid., p. 8.

11. Maugh, "Toxic Waste Disposal," pp. 819–21.

12. Ibid.

13. Joanne Omong, "EPA Names 115 Toxic Waste Dump Sites for Cleanup," *Washington Post,* October 24, 1981, p. 4.

14. Steiner, "Love Can Be Dangerous," p. 110.

15. Beverly Paigen, "Controversy at Love Canal," *Hastings Center Report* 12 (June 1982), pp. 29–37.

16. Margery W. Shaw, "Love Canal Chromosome Study," *Science* 209 (August 15, 1980), p. 752.

17. *Fortune* (July 27, 1981), pp. 30–31.

18. *Discover* 2, no. 4 (April 1981), p. 8.

19. "CDC Finds No Excess Illness at Love Canal," *Science* 220 (June 17, 1983), p. 1254.

20. "Love Canal: Still a Battleground," *U.S. News and World Report* 93 (July 26, 1982), p. 6.

21. Ibid.

22. "Hazards in Love Canal Monitoring," *Science News* 124 (July 9, 1983), p. 29.

23. John J. Christian, "Love Canal's Unhealthy Voles," *Natural History* 92 (October 1983), pp. 8–14.

24. Nicholas J. Vianna and Adele K. Polan, "Incidence of Low Birth Weights among Love Canal Residents," *Science* 226 (December 7, 1983), pp. 1217–19.

25. "EPA Will Burn Sediment to Clean Love Canal Area," *Wall Street Journal,* October 27, 1987, p. 72.

26. Carolyn Kuma, "Resampling Could Delay Canal Revitalization Effort," *Niagara Gazette,* November 8, 1986, p. 1.

27. "Milestone in the Love Canal Case," *Los Angeles Times,* July 5, 1994, p. 4B.

28. *U.S.A. v. Hooker Chemicals,* U.S. District Court, Western District of New York, CIV-79-990c (February 23, 1988).

29. Roy J. Harris, Jr., "Occidental Unit is Ruled Liable in Waste Case," *Wall Street Journal,* February 24, 1988, p. 2; and Michael Weisskopf, "Company Ruled Liable for Love Canal Costs," *Washington Post,* February 24, 1988, p. A10.

30. "Ex-owner of Toxic Site Wins Ruling on Damages," *New York Times,* March 18, 1994, p. 5B.

31. Matthew Wald, "Out-of-Court Settlement Reached Over Love Canal," *New York Times,* June 22, 1994, p. B5.

32. "Ex-owner of Toxic Site Wins Ruling on Damages," *New York Times,* March 18, 1994, p. 5B.

33. "Milestone in the Love Canal Case," *Los Angeles Times,* July 5, 1994, p. 4B.

34. Anne Underwood, "The Return to Love Canal: Would You Live There?" *Newsweek* (July 30, 1990), p. 25.

35. Evelyn Nieves, "Loving Love Canal Once More," *New York Times,* July 12, 1994, p. 4B.

36. Ibid.

37. Ibid.

38. Vince Winkel, "Critics Decry Sale of Homes in Love Canal," *Christian Science Monitor,* November 29, 1994, p. 10.

39. Ibid.

40. Ibid.

41. Ibid.

REVIEW QUESTIONS

1. Describe the use of Love Canal as a site for chemical waste dumping by Hooker Chemical before 1953.

2. Why did the Love Canal site overflow with toxic chemicals? What effect did this have on the residents?

3. What did the government, the residents, and Hooker Chemical do about the pollution?

4. How did Hooker Chemical defend itself against the charge that it acted irresponsibly?

5. Why did Hooker Chemical claim that it did more than meet its social and moral obligations?

6. Whom do some residents blame?

DISCUSSION QUESTIONS

1. Do you agree with the 1994 decision that found Occidental the sole party responsible for the cleanup of Love Canal? Do you think that the decision was, as Occidental claims, "a vindication" of Occidental's actions?

2. Is 500,000 deaths per year an acceptable price to pay for toxic chemicals in our environment, just as 50,000 traffic deaths per year is an acceptable price to pay for automobile travel?

Milton Friedman

The Social Responsibility of Business Is to Increase Its Profits

Milton Friedman is professor of economics at the University of Chicago and the author of Capitalism and Freedom *(1962).*

Friedman defends the conservative view that the only responsibility of business is to increase its profits by open and free competition without deception or fraud. He attacks the view that business has any other social responsibilities, such as eliminating discrimination or reducing pollution. He calls this view the doctrine of social responsibility. *Friedman thinks that the business executive who follows such doctrine will end up spending the money of the stockholders or the customers without their consent—in effect imposing taxes and spending tax money independent of the wishes of the public. He believes that this is wrong; it amounts to taxation without representation. Furthermore, the doctrine of social responsibility has bad consequences: Business executives who try to follow it will be fired, and wage restraints justified by it will produce wildcat strikes and worker revolts. Finally, Friedman condemns the doctrine of social responsibility as a fundamentally subversive doctrine that is incompatible with the ideal of a free society because if it were applied to every human activity, the result would be total conformity to general social interests and no freedom at all.*

When I hear businessmen speak eloquently about the "social responsibilities of business in a free-enterprise system," I am reminded of the wonderful line about the Frenchman who discovered at the age of 70 that he had been speak-

ing prose all his life. The businessmen believe that they are defending free enterprise when they declaim that business is not concerned "merely" with profit but also with promoting desirable "social" ends; that business has a "social conscience" and takes seriously its responsibilities for providing employment, eliminating discrimination, avoiding pollution and whatever else may be the catchwords of the contemporary crop of reformers. In fact they are—or would be if they or anyone else took them seriously—preaching pure and unadulterated socialism. Businessmen who talk this way are unwitting puppets of the intellectual forces that have been undermining the basis of a free society these past decades.

The discussion of the "social responsibilities of business" are notable for their analytical looseness and lack of rigor. What does it mean to say that "business" has responsibilities? Only people can have responsibilities. A corporation is an artificial person and in this sense may have artificial responsibilities, but "business" as a whole cannot be said to have responsibilities, even in this vague sense. The first step toward clarity to examining the doctrine of the social responsibility of business is to ask precisely what it implies for whom.

Presumably, the individuals who are to be responsible are businessmen, which means individual proprietors or corporate executives. Most of the discussion of social responsibility is directed at corporations, so in what follows I shall mostly neglect the individual proprietors and speak of corporate executives.

In a free-enterprise, private-property system, a corporate executive is an employee of the owners of the business. He has direct responsibility to his employers. That responsibility is to conduct the business in accordance with their desires, which generally will be to make as much money as possible while conforming to the basic rules of the society, both those embodied in law and those embodied in ethical custom. Of course, in some cases his employers may have a different objective. A group of persons might establish a corporation for an eleemosynary purpose—for example, a hospital or a school. The manager of such a corporation will not have money profit as his objectives but the rendering of certain services.

In either case, the key point is that, in his capacity as a corporate executive, the manager is the agent of the individuals who own the corporation or establish the eleemosynary institution, and his primary responsibility is to them.

Needless to say, this does not mean that it is easy to judge how well he is performing his task. But at least the criterion of performance is straightforward, and the persons among whom a voluntary contractual arrangement exists are clearly defined.

Of course, the corporate executive is also a person in his own right. As a person, he may have many other responsibilities that he recognizes or assumes voluntarily—to his family, his conscience, his feelings of charity, his church, his clubs, his city, his country. He may feel impelled by these responsibilities to devote part of his income to causes he regards as worthy, to refuse to work for particular corporations, even to leave his job, for example, to join his country's armed forces. If we wish, we may refer to some of these responsibilities as "social responsibilities." But in these respects he is acting as a principal, not an agent; he is spending his own money or time or energy, not the money of his employers or the time or energy he has contracted to devote to their purposes. If these are "social responsibilities," they are the social responsibilities of individuals, not of business.

What does it mean to say that the corporate executive has a "social responsibility" in his capacity as businessman? If this statement is not pure rhetoric, it must mean that he is to act in some way that is not in the interest of his employers. For example, that he is to refrain from increasing the price of the product in order to contribute to the social objective of preventing inflation, even though a price increase would be in the best interests of the corporation. Or that he is to make expenditures on reducing pollution beyond the amount that is in the best interests of the corporation or that is required by law in order to contribute to the social objective of improving the environment. Or that, at the expense of corporate profits, he is to hire "hard-core" unemployed instead of better qualified available workmen to contribute to the social objective of reducing poverty.

In each of these cases, the corporate executive would be spending someone else's money for a general social interest. Insofar as his actions in accord with his "social responsibility" reduce returns to stockholders, he is spending their money. Insofar as his actions raise the price to customers, he is spending the customers' money. Insofar as his actions lower the wages of some employees, he is spending their money.

The stockholders or the customers or the employees could separately spend their own money on the particular action if they wished to do so. The executive is exercising a distinct "social responsibility," rather than serving as an agent of the stockholders or the customers or the employees, only if he spends the money in a different way than they would have spent it.

But if he does this, he is in effect imposing taxes, on the one hand, and deciding how the tax proceeds shall be spent, on the other.

This process raises political questions on two levels: principle and consequences. On the level of political principle, the imposition of taxes and the expenditure of tax proceeds are governmental functions. We have established elaborate constitutional, parliamentary and judicial provisions to control these functions, to assure that taxes are imposed so far as possible in accordance with the preferences and desires of the public—after all, "taxation without representation" was one of the battle cries of the American Revolution. We have a system of checks and balances to separate the legislative function of imposing taxes and enacting expenditures from the executive function of collecting taxes and administering expenditure programs and from the judicial function of mediating disputes and interpreting the law.

Here the businessman—self-selected or appointed directly or indirectly by stockholders—is to be simultaneously legislator, executive and jurist. He is to decide whom to tax by how much and for what purpose, and he is to spend the proceeds—all this guided only by general exhortations from on high to restrain inflation, improve the environment, fight poverty and so on and on.

The whole justification for permitting the corporate executive to be selected by the stockholders is that the executive is an agent serving the interests of his principal. This justification disappears when the corporate executive imposes taxes and spends the proceeds for "social" purposes. He becomes in effect a public employee, a civil servant, even though he remains in name an employee of a private enterprise. On grounds of political principle, it is intolerable that such civil servants—insofar as their actions in the name of social responsibility are real and not just window-dressing—should be selected as they are now. If they are to be civil servants, then they must be elected through a political process. If they are to impose taxes and make expenditures to foster "social" objectives, then political machinery must be set up to make the assessment of taxes and to determine through a political process the objectives to be served.

This is the basic reason why the doctrine of "social responsibility" involves the acceptance of the socialist view that political mechanisms, not market mechanisms, are the appropriate way to determine the allocation of scarce resources to alternative uses.

On the grounds of consequences, can the corporate executive in fact discharge his alleged "social responsibilities"? On the one hand, suppose he could get away with spending the stockholders' or customers' or employees' money. How is he to know how to spend it? He is told that he must contribute to fighting inflation. How is he to know what action of his will contribute to that end? He is presumably an expert in running his company—in producing a product or selling it or financing it. But nothing about his selection makes him an expert on inflation. Will his holding down the price of his product reduce inflationary pressure? Or, by leaving more spending power in the hands of his customers, simply divert it elsewhere? Or, by forcing him to produce less because of the lower price, will it simply contribute to shortages? Even if he could answer these questions, how much cost is he justified in imposing on his stockholders, customers, and employees for this social purpose? What is his appropriate share and what is the appropriate share of others?

And, whether he wants to or not, can he get away with spending his stockholders', customers' or employees' money? Will not the stockholders fire him? (Either the present ones or those who take over when his actions in the name of social responsibility have reduced the corporation's profits and the price of its stock.) His customers and his employees can desert him for other producers and employers less scrupulous in exercising their social responsibilities.

This facet of "social responsibility" doctrine is brought into sharp relief when the doctrine is used to justify wage restraint by trade unions. The conflict of interest is naked and clear when union officials are asked to subordinate the interest of their members to some more general purpose. If the union officials try to enforce wage restraint, the consequence is likely to be wildcat strikes, rank-and-file revolts and the emergence of strong competitors for their jobs. We thus have the ironic phenomenon that union leaders—at least in the U.S.—have objected to Government interference with the market far more consistently and courageously than have business leaders.

The difficulty of exercising "social responsibility" illustrates, of course, the great virtue of private competitive enterprise—it forces people to be responsible for their own actions and makes it difficult for them to "exploit" other people for either selfish or unselfish purposes. They can do good—but only at their own expense.

Many a reader who has followed the argument this far may be tempted to remonstrate that it is all well and good to speak of Government's having the responsibility to impose taxes and determine expenditures for such "social" purposes as controlling pollution or training the hard-core unemployed, but that the problems are too urgent to wait on the slow course of political processes, that the exercise of social responsibility by businessmen is a quicker and surer way to solve pressing current problems.

Aside from the question of fact—I share Adam Smith's skepticism about the benefits that can be expected from "those who affected to trade for the public good"—this argument must be rejected on grounds of principle. What it amounts to is an assertion that those who favor the taxes and expenditures in question have failed to persuade a majority of their fellow citizens to be of like mind and that they are seeking to attain by undemocratic procedures what they cannot attain by democratic procedures. In a free society, it is hard for "evil" people to do "evil," especially since one man's good is another's evil.

I have, for simplicity, concentrated on the special case of the corporate executive, except only for the brief digression on trade unions. But precisely the same argument applies to the newer phenomenon of calling upon stockholders to require corporations to exercise social responsibility (the recent G.M. crusade for example). In most of these cases, what is in effect involved is some stockholders trying to get other stockholders (or customers or employees) to contribute against their will to "social" causes favored by the activists. Insofar as they succeed, they are again imposing taxes and spending the proceeds.

The situation of the individual proprietor is somewhat different. If he acts to reduce the returns of his enterprise in order to exercise his "social responsibility," he is spending his own money, not someone else's. If he wishes to spend his money on such purposes, that is his right, and I cannot see that there is any objection to his doing so. In the process, he, too, may impose costs on employees and customers. However, because he is far less likely than a large corporation or union to have monopolistic power, any such side effects will tend to be minor.

Of course, in practice the doctrine of social responsibility is frequently a cloak for actions that are justified on other grounds rather than a reason for those actions.

To illustrate, it may well be in the long-run interest of a corporation that is a major employer in a small community to devote resources to providing amenities to that community or to improving its government. That may make it easier to attract desirable employees, it may reduce the wage bill or lessen losses from pilferage and sabotage or have other worthwhile effects. Or it may be that, given the laws about the deductibility of corporate charitable contributions, the stockholders can contribute more to charities they favor by having the corporation make the gift than

by doing it themselves, since they can in that way contribute an amount that would otherwise have been paid as corporate taxes.

In each of these—and many similar—cases, there is a strong temptation to rationalize these actions as an exercise of "social responsibility." In the present climate of opinion, with its widespread aversion to "capitalism," "profits," and "soulless corporation" and so on, this is one way for a corporation to generate goodwill as a by-product of expenditures that are entirely justified in its own self-interest.

It would be inconsistent of me to call on corporate executives to refrain from this hypocritical window-dressing because it harms the foundations of a free society. That would be to call on them to exercise a "social responsibility"! If our institutions, and the attitudes of the public make it in their self-interest to cloak their actions in this way, I cannot summon much indignation to denounce them. At the same time, I can express admiration for those individual proprietors or owners of closely held corporations or stockholders of more broadly held corporations who disdain such tactics as approaching fraud.

Whether blameworthy or not, the use of the cloak of social responsibility, and the nonsense spoken in its name by influential and prestigious businessmen, does clearly harm the foundations of a free society. I have been impressed time and again by the schizophrenic character of many businessmen. They are capable of being extremely farsighted and clear-headed in matters that are internal to their businesses. They are incredibly short-sighted and muddle-headed in matters that are outside their businesses but affect the possible survival of business in general. This short-sightedness is strikingly exemplified in the calls from many businessmen for wage and price guidelines or controls or income policies. There is nothing that could do more in a brief period to destroy a market system and replace it by a centrally controlled system than effective governmental control of prices and wages.

The short-sightedness is also exemplified in speeches by businessmen on social responsibility. This may gain them kudos in the short run. But it helps to strengthen the already too prevalent view that the pursuit of profits is wicked and immoral and must be curbed and controlled by external forces. Once this view is adopted, the external forces that curb the market will not be the social consciences, however highly developed, of the pontificating executives; it will be the iron fist of Government bureaucrats. Here, as with price and wage controls, businessmen seem to me to reveal a suicidal impulse.

The political principle that underlies the market mechanism is unanimity. In an ideal free market resting on private property, no individual can coerce any other, all cooperation is voluntary, all parties to such cooperation benefit or they need not participate. There are no values, no "social" responsibilities in any sense other than the shared values and responsibilities of individuals. Society is a collection of individuals and of the various groups they voluntarily form.

The political principle that underlies the political mechanism is conformity. The individual must serve a more general social interest—whether that be determined by a church or a dictator or a majority. The individual may have a vote and say in what is to be done, but if he is overruled, he must conform. It is appropriate for some to require others to contribute to a general social purpose whether they wish to or not.

Unfortunately, unanimity is not always feasible. There are some respects in which conformity appears unavoidable, so I do not see how one can avoid the use of the political mechanism altogether.

But the doctrine of "social responsibility" taken seriously would extend the scope of the political mechanism to every human activity. It does not differ in philosophy from the most explicitly collectivist doctrine. It differs only by professing to believe that collectivist ends can be attained without collectivist means. That is why, in my book *Capitalism and Freedom,* I have called it a "fundamentally subversive doctrine"

in a free society, and have said that in such a society, "there is one and only one social responsibility of business—to use its resources and engage in activities designed to increase its profits so long as it stays within the rules of the game, which is to say, engages in open and free competition without deception or fraud."

REVIEW QUESTIONS

1. According to Friedman, why doesn't it make sense to say that business itself has responsibilities?
2. In Friedman's view, who in business does have responsibilities, and what are they?
3. Explain Friedman's account of the corporate executive who acts out of social responsibility.
4. Why does Friedman think that a corporate executive should direct his or her actions by other considerations than social responsibility?
5. According to Friedman, why does the doctrine of social responsibility involve socialism?
6. How does Friedman reply to the objection that social activities such as pollution control should be left to the government?
7. Why does Friedman find the doctrine of social responsibility to be a fundamentally subversive doctrine?
8. What is the one and only social responsibility of business according to Friedman?

DISCUSSION QUESTIONS

1. Can a business have responsibilities? Why or why not?
2. Is it possible for a business executive to follow the doctrine of social responsibility and not end up spending the money of consumers or stockholders? How?
3. If business ignores social problems such as discrimination in hiring and pay, pollution, unemployment, and so on, then how can these problems be solved? What is your view?

Christopher D. Stone

Why Shouldn't Corporations Be Socially Responsible?

Christopher D. Stone is professor of law at the University of Southern California. He is the author of Should Trees Have Standing? *(1974),* Where the Law Ends: The Social Control of Corporate Behavior *(1975), and* Earth and Other Ethics: The Case for Moral Pluralism *(1987).*

Stone attacks four arguments used by conservatives such as Milton Friedman to defend the view that corporations have no responsibilities other than maximizing profits. The four arguments are the promissory argument, the agency argument, the role argument, and the polestar argument. He finds the first three to be defective; they rest on false assumptions and are inconclusive. Stone says that the fourth argument, the so-called polestar argument, makes a number of assumptions and that the arguments based on these assumptions have a germ of validity. Their essential failure is in not pursuing the alternatives to controlling corporations by market forces and by law. Such alternatives should be pursued because corporations need additional constraints.

The opposition to corporate social responsibility comprises at least four related though separable positions. I would like to challenge the fundamental assumption that underlies all four of them. Each assumes in its own degree that the managers of the corporation are to be steered almost wholly by profit, rather than by what they think proper for society on the whole. Why should this be so? So far as ordinary morals are concerned, we often expect human beings to act

in a fashion that is calculated to benefit others, rather than themselves, and commend them for it. Why should the matter be different with corporations?

THE PROMISSORY ARGUMENT

The most widespread but least persuasive arguments advanced by the "antiresponsibility" forces take the form of a moral claim based upon the corporation's supposed obligations to its shareholders. In its baldest and least tenable form, it is presented as though management's obligation rested upon the keeping of a promise—that the management of the corporation "promised" the shareholders that it would maximize the shareholders' profits. But this simply isn't so.

Consider for contrast the case where a widow left a large fortune goes to a broker, asking him to invest and manage her money so as to maximize her return. The broker, let us suppose, accepts the money and the conditions. In such a case, there would be no disagreement that the broker had made a promise to the widow, and if he invested her money in some venture that struck his fancy for any reason other than that it would increase her fortune, we would be inclined to advance a moral (as well, perhaps, as a legal) claim against him. Generally, at least, we believe in the keeping of promises; the broker, we should say, had violated a promissory obligation to the widow.

But that simple model is hardly the one that obtains between the management of major corporations and their shareholders. Few if any American shareholders ever put their money into a corporation upon the express promise of management that the company would be operated so as to maximize their returns. Indeed, few American shareholders ever put their money directly *into* a corporation at all. Most of the shares outstanding today were issued years ago and found their way to the current shareholders only circuitously. In almost all cases, the current shareholder gave his money to some prior shareholder, who, in turn, had gotten it from B, who, in turn, had gotten it from A, and so on back to the purchaser of the original issue, who, many years before, had bought the shares through an underwriting syndicate. In the course of these transactions, one of the basic elements that exists in the broker case is missing: The manager of the corporation, unlike the broker, was never even offered a chance to refuse the shareholder's "terms" (if they were that) to maximize the shareholder's profits.

There are two other observations to be made about the moral argument based on a supposed promise running from the management to the shareholders. First, even if we do infer from all the circumstances a "promise" running from the management to the shareholders, but not one, or not one of comparable weight running elsewhere (to the company's employees, customers, neighbors, etc.), we ought to keep in mind that as a moral matter (which is what we are discussing here) sometimes it is deemed morally justified to break promises (even to break the law) in the furtherance of other social interests of higher concern. Promises can advance moral arguments, by way of creating presumptions, but few of us believe that promises, per se, can end them. My promise to appear in class on time would not ordinarily justify me from refusing to give aid to a drowning man. In other words, even if management *had* made an express promise to its shareholders to "maximize your profits," (a) I am not persuaded that the ordinary person would interpret it to mean "maximize *in every way you can possibly get away with,* even if that means polluting the environment, ignoring or breaking the law"; and (b) I am not persuaded that, even if it were interpreted as so blanket a promise, most people would not suppose it ought—morally—to be broken in some cases.

Finally, even if, in the face of all these considerations, one still believes that there is an overriding, unbreakable promise of some sort running from management to the shareholders, I do not think that it can be construed to be any stronger than one running to *existent* shareholders, arising from *their* expectations as measured by the price *they* paid. That is to say, there is nothing in the argument from promises that would wed us to a regime in which management

was bound to maximize the income of shareholders. The argument might go so far as to support compensation for existent shareholders if the society chose to announce that henceforth management would have other specified obligations, thereby driving the price of shares to a lower adjustment level. All future shareholders would take with "warning" of, and a price that discounted for, the new "risks" of shareholding (i.e., the "risks" that management might put corporate resources to *pro bonum* ends).

THE AGENCY ARGUMENT

Related to the promissory argument but requiring less stretching of the facts is an argument from agency principles. Rather than trying to infer a promise by management to the shareholders, this argument is based on the idea that the shareholders designated the management their agents. This is the position advanced by Milton Friedman in his *New York Times* article. "The key point," he says, "is that . . . the manager is the agent of the individuals who own the corporation. . . ."[1]

Friedman, unfortunately, is wrong both as to the state of the law (the directors are *not* mere agents of the shareholders)[2] and on his assumption as to the facts of corporate life (surely it is closer to the truth that in major corporations the shareholders are *not,* in any meaningful sense, selecting the directors; management is more often using its control over the proxy machinery to designate who the directors shall be, rather than the other way around).

What Friedman's argument comes down to is that for some reason the directors ought morally to consider themselves more the agents for the shareholders than for the customers, creditors, the state, or the corporation's immediate neighbors. But why? And to what extent? Throwing in terms like "principal" and "agent" begs the fundamental questions.

What is more, the "agency" argument is not only morally inconclusive, it is embarrassingly at odds with the way in which supposed "agents" actually behave. If the managers truly considered themselves the agents of the shareholders, as agents they would be expected to show an interest in determining how their principals wanted them to act—and to act accordingly. In the controversy over Dow's production of napalm, for example, one would expect, on this model, that Dow's management would have been glad to have the napalm question put to the shareholders at a shareholders' meeting. In fact, like most major companies faced with shareholder requests to include "social action" measures on proxy statements, it fought the proposal tooth and claw.[3] It is a peculiar agency where the "agents" will go to such lengths (even spending tens of thousands of dollars of their "principals'" money in legal fees) to resist the determination of what their "principals" want.

THE ROLE ARGUMENT

An argument so closely related to the argument from promises and agency that it does not demand extensive additional remarks is a contention based upon supposed considerations of *role*. Sometimes in moral discourse, as well as in law, we assign obligations to people on the basis of their having assumed some role or status, independent of any specific verbal promise they made. Such obligations are assumed to run from a captain to a seaman (and vice versa), from a doctor to a patient, or from a parent to a child. The antiresponsibility forces are on somewhat stronger grounds resting their position on this basis, because the model more nearly accords with the facts—that is, management never actually promised the shareholders that they would maximize the shareholders' investment, nor did the shareholders designate the directors their agents for this express purpose. The directors and top management are, as lawyers would say, fiduciaries. But what does this leave us? So far as the directors are fiduciaries of the shareholders in a legal sense, of course they are subject to the legal limits on fiduciaries—that is to say, they cannot engage in self-dealing, "waste" of corporate assets, and the like. But I do not understand any proresponsibility advocate to be demanding such corporate largesse as would expose the officers to legal liability; what we are talking about are expenditures on, for example, pollution control,

above the amount the company is required to pay by law, but less than an amount so extravagant as to constitute a violation of these legal fiduciary duties. (Surely no court in America today would enjoin a corporation from spending more to reduce pollution than the law requires.) What is there about assuming the role of corporate officer that makes it immoral for a manager to involve a corporation in these expenditures? A father, one would think, would have stronger obligations to his children by virtue of his status than a corporate manager to the corporation's shareholders. Yet few would regard it as a compelling moral argument if a father were to distort facts about his child on a scholarship application form on the grounds that he had obligations to advance his child's career; nor would we consider it a strong moral argument if a father were to leave unsightly refuse piled on his lawn, spilling over into the street, on the plea that he had obligations to give every moment of his attention to his children, and was thus too busy to cart his refuse away.

Like the other supposed moral arguments, the one from role suffers from the problem that the strongest moral obligations one can discover have at most only prima facie force, and it is not apparent why those obligations should predominate over some contrary social obligations that could be advanced.

Then too, when one begins comparing and weighing the various moral obligations, those running back to the shareholder seem fairly weak by comparison to the claims of others. For one thing, there is the consideration of alternatives. If the shareholder is dissatisfied with the direction the corporation is taking, he can sell out, and if he does so quickly enough, his losses may be slight. On the other hand, as Ted Jacobs observes, "those most vitally affected by corporate decisions—people who work in the plants, buy the products, and consume the effluents—cannot remove themselves from the structure with a phone call."[4]

THE "POLESTAR" ARGUMENT

It seems to me that the strongest moral argument corporate executives can advance for looking solely to profits is not one that is based on a supposed express, or even implied promise to the shareholder. Rather, it is one that says, if the managers act in such fashion as to maximize profits—if they act *as though* they had promised the shareholders they would do so—then it will be best for all of us. This argument might be called the polestar argument, for its appeal to the interests of the shareholders is not justified on supposed obligations to the shareholders per se, but as a means of charting a straight course toward what is best for the society as a whole.

Underlying the polestar argument are a number of assumptions—some express and some implied. There is, I suspect, an implicit **positivism** among its supporters—a feeling (whether its proponents own up to it or not) that moral judgments are peculiar, arbitrary, or vague—perhaps even "meaningless" in the philosophic sense of not being amenable to rational discussion. To those who take this position, profits (or sales, or price-earnings ratios) at least provide some solid, tangible standard by which participants in the organization can measure their successes and failures, with some efficiency, in the narrow sense, resulting for the entire group. Sometimes the polestar position is based upon a related view—not that the moral issues that underlie social choices are meaningless, but that resolving them calls for special expertise. "I don't know any investment adviser whom I would care to act in my behalf in any matter except turning a profit. . . . The value of these specialists . . . lies in their limitations; they ought not allow themselves to see so much of the world that they become distracted." [5] A slightly modified point emphasizes not that the executives lack moral or social expertise per se, but that they lack the social authority to make policy choices. Thus, Friedman objects that if a corporate director took "social purposes" into account, he would become "in effect a public employee, a civil servant. . . . On grounds of political principle, it is intolerable that such civil servants . . . should be selected as they are now." [6]

I do not want to get too deeply involved in each of these arguments. That the moral judgments underlying policy choices are vague, I do not doubt—although I am tempted to observe that when you get right down to it, a wide range of actions taken by businessmen every day, supposedly based on solid calculations of "profit," are probably as rooted in hunches and intuition as judgments of ethics. I do not disagree either that, ideally, we prefer those who have control over our lives to be politically accountable; although here, too, if we were to pursue the matter in detail we would want to inspect both the premise of this argument, that corporate managers are not *presently* custodians of discretionary power over us anyway, and also its logical implications: Friedman's point that "if they are to be civil servants, then they must be selected through a political process" [7] is not, as Friedman regards it, a *reductio ad absurdum*—not, at any rate, to Ralph Nader and others who want publicly elected directors.

The reason for not pursuing these counterarguments at length is that, whatever reservations one might have, we can agree that there is a germ of validity to what the "antis" are saying. But their essential failure is in not pursuing the alternatives. Certainly, *to the extent* that the forces of the market and the law can keep the corporation within desirable bounds, it may be better to trust them than to have corporate managers implementing their own vague and various notions of what is best for the rest of us. But are the "antis" blind to the fact that there are circumstances in which the law—and the forces of the market—are simply not competent to keep the corporation under control? The shortcomings of these traditional restraints on corporate conduct are critical to understand, not merely for the defects they point up in the "antis" position. More important, identifying where the traditional forces are inadequate is the first step in the design of new and alternative measures of corporate control.

Endnotes

1. *New York Times*, September 12, 1962, sect. 6, p. 33, col. 2.
2. See, for example, *Automatic Self-Cleansing Filter Syndicate Co. Ltd.* v. *Cunninghame* (1906) 2 Ch. 34.
3. "Dow Shalt Not Kill," in S. Prakash Sethi, *Up Against the Corporate Wall* (Englewood Cliffs, N.J.: Prentice-Hall, 1971), pp. 236–266, and the opinion of Judge Tamm in *Medical Committee for Human Rights* v. *S.E.C.*, 432 F.2d 659 (D.C.Cir.1970), and the dissent of Mr. Justice

Douglas in the same case in the U.S. Supreme Court, 404 U.S. 403, 407–411 (1972).

4. Theodore J. Jacobs, "Pollution, Consumerism, Accountability," *Center Magazine* 5, 1 (January–February 1971): 47.
5. Walter Goodman, "Stocks Without Sin," *Harper's,* August 1971, p. 66.
6. *New York Times,* September 12, 1962, sec. 6, p. 122, col. 3.
7. Ibid., p. 122, cols. 3–4.

REVIEW QUESTIONS

1. How does Stone attack the promissory argument?
2. What is wrong with Friedman's agency argument according to Stone?

3. How does Stone reply to the role argument?
4. State and explain the so-called polestar argument.
5. What assumptions does Stone find underlying this argument?
6. What is Stone's appraisal of the polestar argument and the assumptions underlying it?

DISCUSSION QUESTIONS

1. Has Stone given a decisive refutation of Friedman's position? Why or why not?
2. Stone admits that there is a germ of validity in what his opposition is saying. What is this germ of validity? Can you clarify this?

Norman E. Bowie

Changing the Rules

Norman E. Bowie occupies the Elmer L. Andersen Chair in Corporate Responsibility, Curtis L. Carlson School of Management, University of Minnesota, Twin Cities.

Bowie suggests that a social contract is the basis for the moral responsibilities of business corporations. Even though society has been changing the rules of the contract by giving corporations more social responsibilities, corporations should accept the revised contract for three reasons: It is in their self-interest, they have contributed to social problems, and they have the resources to deal with social problems. In return they have the right to participate in redrafting the contract, and they have the right to ask other contributors to social problems to contribute to their solution.

From Norman E. Bowie, "Changing the Rules," *Ethical Theory and Business,* ed. T. Beauchamp and N. Bowie (Englewood Cliffs, N.J.: Prentice-Hall, 1983), pp. 147–150. © 1978 by Norman E. Bowie. Reprinted by permission of the author.

It is not merely the introductory philosophy students who ask, "Why be moral?" An examination of much of the contemporary literature in business ethics indicates that the "why be moral" question is very much on the mind of business persons as well.

One possibility for providing an answer to the "why be moral" question is to indicate the contractual basis on which business rests. The operation of a business, particularly when the business is a corporation, is not a matter of right. Rather the individuals enter into a contract with society. In turn for the permission to do business, the society places certain obligations and duties on the business. The corporation is created by society for a specific purpose or purposes. Robert A. Dahl has put the point this way:

Today it is absurd to regard the corporation simply as an enterprise established for the sole purpose of allowing profit making. We the citizens give them special rights, powers, and privileges, protection, and benefits on the understanding that their activities will fulfill purposes. Corporations exist only as they continue to benefit us. . . . Every corporation should be thought of as a social enterprise whose existence and decisions can be justified only insofar as they serve public or social purposes.[1]

Actually not only does Dahl's quotation indicate that the relation between business and society is contractual, but Dahl spells out the nature of that contract. The corporation must not only benefit those who create it, it must benefit those who permit it (namely society as a whole).

In many discussions of business ethics no one defines terms like "moral" or "corporate responsibility." This inadequacy can be corrected by adopting the perspective of the contract analysis. The morality of business or corporate responsibility is determined by the terms of the contract with society. The corporation has those obligations which the society imposes on it in its charter of incorporation. In accepting its charter, the corporation accepts those moral constraints. Failure to be moral is a violation of the principle of fairness. The corporation which violates the moral rules contained in or implied by its charter is in the position of agreeing to the rules and then violating them. It is in the position of one who makes a promise and then breaks it. Such unfairness is often considered a paradigm case of injustice and immorality. The corporation which finds itself in the position of breaking the agreements it has made is in a particularly vulnerable position, since the corporate enterprise depends for its survival on the integrity of contractual relations. Understanding business as a contractual relation between the corporation and the society as a whole provides a preliminary answer to our "why be moral" question. The corporation should be moral because it has agreed to be. However, what a corporation's moral obligations are is contained in the contract itself.

Although this analysis does provide the framework for showing that certain corporate activities are immoral and provides a moral *reason* for indicating why a corporation should not engage in them, many complicated questions remain to be answered.

The first focuses on the content of the contract. Many corporate executives could accept the contract analysis as outlined thus far and argue that current demands on corporations to be more socially responsible are themselves violations of the contract. After all, corporate charters do not contain an open-ended moral requirement that the corporation promote the public interest.

Rather, corporations are founded primarily to promote the financial interests of the investors (the stockholders). Society had believed that by furthering the interests of the stockholders, society as a whole benefited. Now society has changed its mind, and frustrated corporation executives rightly argue that it is the corporate responsibility zealots and not the corporate executives who are changing the terms of the contract.

In several respects the corporate response is appropriate. Society is changing the rules of the game and it is appropriate to ask why corporations should acquiesce in these unilateral changes. Before considering these issues, however, I should like to point out one respect in which the corporate officials' charge that the rules are being changed is incorrect. In addition to the obligations spelled out in the contract itself, there are certain moral requirements, moral background conditions, if you will, which are assumed. Certain moral rules are rules that are required if contracts are to be made at all. These moral requirements are as obligatory as the obligations spelled out in the contract itself. After all, when I agree to pay my bills in order to get a Master Charge card, I do not also sign a meta-agreement that I keep my agreements. The whole market exchange mechanism rests on conditions of trust which can be embodied in moral principles. What is shocking about some of the current corporate scandals—bribery, falsification of records, theft, and corporate espionage—is that these acts violate the conditions for making contracts and market exchanges, conditions which are at the very heart of the free enterprise system. Such violations cannot be excused by saying that they do not appear in the contract. Such excuses are almost as absurd as someone defending the murder of a creditor by saying: I only promised to pay him back; I didn't promise not to murder him. Hence we can conclude that a company has moral obligations in the contract it makes with society and it has obligations to those moral rules which make contracts possible. Its agreement in the former is explicit; its agreement in the latter, implicit. Violation of either is a violation of fairness—a failure to keep one's promises.

We can now return to the charge that it is society which is changing the terms of the contract. Fortunately, not all the charges of immorality and irresponsibility leveled at corporations are directed at violations of contractual morality. Corporations are charged with neglecting to solve such social problems as pollution, racism, sexism, and urban blight. They are charged with sins of omission. At this point the corporation can argue that they have no obligation to resolve all of society's problems. Such a broad-based moral obligation is not a part of their contract with society. That corporations do not have such general contractual obligations is conceded by most experts in the field.

We now face a more complicated form of the "why be moral" question. Why should the corporation agree to a rewriting of its contract with society—a rewriting which will impose greatly expanded social responsibilities on it?

One answer is prudential. It is in the interests of the corporation to do so. This idea has been expressed in the form of a law called the Iron Law of Responsibility: In the long run those who do not use power in a manner which society considers socially responsible will tend to lose it.[2] If society demands a rewriting of the contract, society has the *power* to rewrite it unilaterally. However, can we go beyond prudence to offer any moral reasons for business to revise its agreements? I believe there are several.

One might be called the principle of contribution: If one contributes to a social harm, then one has a proportional obligation to contribute to its alleviation. Since business clearly does contribute to social problems, it has at least some obligation to correct them. In saying that business has some responsibility, I do not wish to imply that it has the only responsibility. Government, labor, and all of us as consumers contribute our part to the problems and hence have some responsibility to work toward solutions. It is neither fair nor prudent to expect one segment of society to shoulder the entire burden. Hence only a *contribution* is required.

Another moral reason for business to accept a new contract might be based on the notion of power. Those constituents of society which have the most in the way of resources should contribute the most to resolving social ills. Since business is either the most powerful force or second only to the federal government, its superior resources impose special obligations upon it. There is an analogy here to arguments made on behalf of progressive taxation.

If the moral arguments are sound, there are moral reasons as well as a very strong prudential reason for corporations to revise their contractual relations with society. However, the corporation can reciprocally require certain agreements on the part of society. First, since a contract should be mutually acceptable, the contract cannot be rewritten unilaterally. Representatives from the corporate sector have a right to participate in the redrafting. Second, grounds of consistency require that other contributors to society's problems also contribute to their solution and that the requirements for the more powerful constituencies be stronger. So long as these conditions are met, corporations should agree to a revised contract and our original fairness arguments can be used to show why individual corporations should follow it.

Endnotes

1. Robert A. Dahl, "A Prelude to Corporate Reform." In *Corporate Social Policy*, ed. Robert L. Heilbroner and Paul London (Reading, Mass.: Addison-Wesley Publishing Company, 1975), pp. 18–19.
2. Keith Davis and Robert L. Blomstrom, *Business and Society: Environment and Responsibility*, 3rd ed. (New York: McGraw-Hill Book Company, 1975), p. 50.

REVIEW QUESTIONS

1. Why should business corporations be socially responsible according to Bowie?
2. What rights do corporations have in Bowie's view?

DISCUSSION QUESTIONS

1. Bowie claims that business clearly does contribute to social problems. Give some examples.
2. Bowie argues that corporations should be socially responsible because it is in their self-interest to do so. Is this true? Why or why not?
3. Does Friedman have a good reply to Bowie? What is it?

Thomas Donaldson

Constructing a Social Contract for Business

Professor Thomas J. Donaldson teaches philosophy at Georgetown University. He is a coeditor of Case Studies in Business Ethics *(1990) and* Ethical Issues in Business, *third edition (1988), and the author of* Corporations and Morality, *from which our reading is taken.*

Donaldson wants to construct a social contract for corporations that gives the moral foundation for their existence. The contract is between individuals in society and production corporations and not, as in Bowie's reading, between corporations and society as a whole. As Donaldson envisions it, the hypothetical contract spells out the benefits that corporations produce for both consumers and employees, benefits that justify the existence of corporations. But there are limits to what corporations can do, limits set by the interests of consumers and employees and by certain minimum standards of justice.

In a speech to the Harvard Business School in 1969, Henry Ford II stated:

The terms of the contract between industry and society are changing . . . Now we are being asked to serve a wider range of human values and to accept an obligation to members of the public with whom we have no commercial transactions.

The "contract" to which Henry Ford referred concerns a corporation's *indirect* obligations. It represents not a set of formally specified obligations, but a set of binding, abstract ones. A social contract for business, if one exists, is not a typewritten contract in the real world, but a metaphysical abstraction not unlike the "social contract" between citizens and government that philosophers have traditionally discussed. Such a contract would have concrete significance, for it would help to interpret the nature of a corporation's indirect obligations—ones which are notoriously slippery.

The aim of this essay is to discover a corporation's indirect obligations by attempting to clarify the meaning of business's so-called "social contract." The task is challenging. Although people speak frequently of such a contract, few have attempted to specify its meaning.

A good starting point is the so-called "social contract" that philosophers have spoken of between society and the state. This political contract has usually been viewed as a theoretical means for justifying the existence of the state. Philosophers have asked, "Why should people let a government exist at all?" in other words, "Why should people prefer to have a government control much of their actions—to impose taxes, raise armies, and punish criminals—instead of having no government at all?" They never doubted for a moment the need for a state, but they believed raising such questions would clarify not only the justification for the state's existence, but also the reciprocal obligations between the state and its citizens. If a government began to abuse its citizenry, to trample on its rights or to diminish social welfare, then according to such philosophers it had broken the tenets of the social contract and could be overthrown. Such a theory in the hands of the seventeenth-century English philosopher John Locke, provided much of the theoretical support for the American Revolution and design of the Declaration of Independence and the U.S. Constitution.

The political social contract provides a clue for understanding the contract for business. If the political contract serves as a justification for the existence of the state, then the business contract by parity of reasoning should serve as the justification for the existence of the corporation.

Thus, crucial questions are: Why should corporations exist at all? What is the fundamental justification of their activities? How can we measure their performance and say when they have achieved their fundamental purpose? Consider a case involving General Motors and the production of automobiles. The automobiles that General Motors produced during the 1950s and 1960s all had noncollapsible steering wheels (called by Ralph Nader "ram-rodding" steering wheels), and evidence indicated that they contributed to hundreds of thousands of highway deaths. But General Motors and other auto manufacturers kept them on the cars anyway, claiming the added expense of collapsible steering wheels would reduce car sales and profits. Their claim may well have been true. However, by refusing to install safer steering wheels, had they failed to achieve a fundamental corporate mission? Had they violated a tenet of an implied social contract between them and society? Or had they just attended to business—although in a way which had unfortunate consequences for society? To answer these questions, we must first know what justifies General Motors' existence.

It is reasonable to look for a fundamental purpose, or set of purposes, that justifies corporate existence. Doing so makes conceptual sense, despite the fact one would never look for what justifies, say, human existence. Corporations, unlike humans, are artifacts, which is to say *we* create them. We *choose* to create corporations and we might choose either not to create them or to create different entities. Corporations thus are like political states in their need for justification.

One might attempt to justify corporate existence by appealing to corporate productivity: to the automobiles, irons, tools, clothing, and medical equipment corporations create. Because society demands such items, it seemingly also requires the corporations that produce them. Adam Smith, the eighteenth-century Scottish philosopher, emphasizes productivity when he justifies a set of economic practices through their contribution to the wealth of nations. But although productivity is surely a crucial piece in the puzzle of corporate justification, it fails to provide a full solution. To say that an organization produces wealth for society is not sufficient to justify it from a moral perspective, since morality encompasses the entire range of human welfare. To say something produces wealth

is to say something morally good about it—assuming that wealth is counted as a human good—but it fails to tell us what else the thing does, or how its process of creation affects society. Consider the example of a nuclear power reactor. To say that a nuclear reactor generates electricity is to say something good about it, but it fails to consider the reactor in the context of the possibility of melt-downs, the storage of nuclear waste, the costs of alternative production, and so forth. (This is true even if we suppose that ultimately nuclear reactors are fully justified.) The logic of the problem of corporate justification is similar. To achieve a complete moral picture of a corporation's existence, we must consider not only its capacity to produce wealth, but the full range of its effects upon society.

Before we attempt to spell out the terms of the social contract, a prior issue must be settled; namely, *who* are the parties to the contract? So far we have spoken of a contract between society and business, but the concepts of "business" and "society" are vague. Let us stipulate that "business" refers to *productive organizations,* i.e., ones where people cooperate to produce at least one specific product or service. Productive organizations would include corporations (of the productive sort), but would also include government owned businesses, large business partnerships, and productive firms in socialist countries.

By attempting to find the moral underpinnings of all productive organizations, we will indirectly be searching for the moral underpinnings of corporations, since virtually all corporations are productive organizations. Once the moral underpinnings of productive organizations are known, it will be possible to answer from a moral perspective the question: Why does Exxon exist? Or, speaking more precisely, it will be possible to answer this question when Exxon is considered *as a member of the class of productive organizations.*

The term "society" is similarly vague. It might refer to the aggregate of individuals who make up society, or to something over and above the sum of those individuals. For clarity, let us stipulate that the contract is between productive organizations and *individual members of society,* not between productive organizations and some supra-individual, social entity.

The simplest way of understanding the social contract is in the form: "We (the members of society) agree to do X, and you (the contracting organizations) agree to do Y." Applying this form to General Motors (or any productive organization) means that the task of a social contract argument is to specify X, where X refers to the obligations of society to productive organizations, and to specify Y, where Y refers to the obligations of productive organizations to society.

It is relatively easy in this context to specify X, because what productive organizations need from society is:

1. Recognition as a single agent, especially in the eyes of the law.
2. The authority: (a) to own or use land and natural resources, and (b) to hire employees.

It may appear presumptuous to assume that productive organizations must be warranted by society. Can one not argue that any organization has a *right* to exist and operate? That they have this right *apart* from the wishes of society? When asking such questions, one must distinguish between claims about rights of mere organizations and claims about rights of organizations with special powers, such as productive organizations. A case can be made for the unbridled right of the Elks Club, whose members unite in fraternal activities, to exist and operate (assuming it does not discriminate against minorities or women); but the same cannot be said for Du Pont Corporation, which not only must draw on existing stores of mineral resources, but must find dumping sites to store toxic chemical by-products. Even granted that people have an inalienable right to form and operate organizations, and even granted that this right exists apart from the discretion of society, the productive organization requires special status under the law and the opportunity to use society's resources: two issues in which every member of society may be said to have a vested interest.

Conditions 1 and 2 are obviously linked to each other. In order for a productive organization to use land and hire employees (conditions

of 2), it must have the authority to perform those acts as if it were an individual agent (the condition of 1). The philosophical impact of 1 should not be exaggerated. To say that productive organizations must have the authority to act as individual agents is not necessarily to affirm that they are abstract, invisible persons. Rather it is a means of stating the everyday fact that productive organizations must, for a variety of purposes, be treated as individual entities. For example, a corporation must be able to hire new employees, to sign contracts, and to negotiate purchases without getting the O.K. from *all* its employees and stockholders.

Defining the Y side of the contract is as difficult as defining the X side is easy. It is obvious that productive organizations must be allowed to exist and act. But it is not obvious precisely why societies should allow them to exist, that is, what specific benefits society should hope to gain from the bargain. What specific functions should society expect from productive organizations? What obligations should it impose? Only one assumption can be made readily: that the members of society should demand at a minimum that the benefits from authorizing the existence of productive organizations outweigh the detriments of doing so. This is nothing other than the expectation of all voluntary agreements: that no party should be asked to conclude a contract which places him or her in a position worse than before.

To specify society's terms for the social contract, let us return to a traditional device in social contract theory, the device of imagining society *without* the institution that is being analyzed. In short, let us consider society without productive organizations, in a "state of nature." Instead of the traditional state of nature where people live without government, we shall consider a state where people live without *productive organizations*. To avoid confusing this state with the traditional ones, let us call it the "state of individual production." Thus, the strategy involves:

1. Characterizing conditions in a state of individual production (without productive organizations).

2. Indicating how certain problems are remedied by the introduction of productive organizations.
3. Using the reasons generated in the second step as a basis for specifying a social contract between society and its productive organizations.

The details must be spelled out. How are we to imagine the state of individual production? What people occupy it? Are they selfish? Charitable? How do they labor?

At a minimum the people in the state of individual production should be imagined as having "economic interests," i.e., as being people for whom it is desirable to have some things or services produced by human labor. Under such a definition almost any human would qualify, except perhaps ascetics or persons who prefer death to life. Thus, the people envisioned by the present strategy are ordinary, economically interested persons who have not yet organized themselves, or been organized, into productive organizations.

Should they be imagined as purely egoistic, wanting only to satisfy their own selfish interests, or as purely benevolent, wanting only to satisfy the interest of others? In the real world both characterizations are extreme—ordinary people are neither devils nor saints—and thus is suggested the strategy of assuming the same about people in the state of individual production. Let us adopt this strategy; if the contract has application to ordinary people, it will help to keep ordinary people in mind.[1]

To imagine a state of individual production, i.e., without productive organizations, is to imagine a society in which individuals produce and work alone. It is to imagine society without factories, banks, hospitals, restaurants, or railroads, since all these organizations, as well as many others, count as productive organizations, that is, they are organizations in which people cooperate to produce at least one specific product or service. (For our purposes, noneconomic factors such as family structure, religious attitudes, and educational interests shall be disregarded.) Now in such a state we may imagine any level of technology we wish. The only crucial fact is that people produce *individually*.

THE TERMS OF THE CONTRACT

Two principal classes of people stand to benefit or be harmed by the introduction of productive organizations: (1) people who consume the organizations' products, i.e., consumers; and (2) people who work in such organizations, i.e., employees. The two classes are broadly defined and not mutually exclusive. "Consumer" refers to anyone who is economically interested; hence virtually anyone qualifies as a consumer. "Employee" refers to anyone who contributes labor to the productive process of a productive organization, including managers, laborers, part-time support personnel, and (in corporations) members of the board of directors.

Consumers

From the standpoint of our hypothetical consumers, productive organizations promise to *enhance the satisfaction of economic interests*. That is to say, people could hope for the introduction of productive organizations to better satisfy their interests for shelter, food, entertainment, transportation, health care, and clothing. The prima facie benefits for consumers include:

1. *Improving efficiency* through:
   a. Maximizing advantages of specialization.
   b. Improving decision-making resources.
   c. Increasing the capacity to use or acquire expensive technology and resources.
2. *Stabilizing levels of output and channels of distribution.*
3. *Increasing liability resources.*

Each benefit needs explanation.

The first benefit, improving efficiency, is the special excellence of productive organizations. Productive organizations tend to generate products that are equal or better in quality and price, with lower expenditures of human labor, than is possible in the state of individual production. Let us examine a few of the reasons for this remarkable capacity.

1A. Maximizing the advantages of specialization. Adam Smith's well-known thought-experiment in the *Wealth of Nations* provides ready evidence for the truth that two can often be more efficient than one. He showed that in the production of pins, one person working alone could account for a mere handful of pins, whereas in a system of first-order specialization—where one cuts the wire, another points the wire, and so on—the proportionate share of pins per worker increases dramatically. The same is true today. To produce clocks, erasers, and antibiotics efficiently, an enormous degree of cooperative specialization is required: the mere existence of products like the Space Shuttle owes itself to such specialization. Economists agree that many products are further subject to *economies of scale;* that is, their efficient production is dependent not only upon cooperative specialization, but on a certain level of it. Because of this factor, a company like American Motors may be too small to compete successfully with General Motors in the production of automobiles.

1B. Improving decision-making resources. Productive organizations share with individual persons the tendency to err in decision-making. Despite this, such organizations have decision-making advantages. First, they can utilize the ongoing talents of people with different backgrounds. Thus, a decision by Westinghouse, Inc., to manufacture a new appliance may call on the knowledge of chemists, accountants, engineers, and marketing specialists. One person could never possess such knowledge.

Second, they can increase information storage. In the same way a person can collect and remember information on a small scale, organizations do so on a large scale. Productive organizations can have superhuman memories: some corporations have libraries larger than those in universities.

1C. Increasing the capacity to use and acquire expensive technology and resources. This advantage is nearly self-evident. All other things being equal, two or more people will have greater financial resources than one; hence productive organizations can make capital expenditures on a larger scale than single individuals. Often the use of large, expensive equipment is important not only for increasing production,

but for generating higher quality production, since expensive equipment is frequently necessary to improve productive efficiency.

2. Stabilizing levels of output and channels of distribution. The imaginary inhabitants of our state of individual production stand to benefit by the merging of individual craftsmen into organizations which are relatively stable, and whose level of output and pattern of distribution are relatively constant. Individual craftsmen are subject to illness, psychological problems, and the need for rest. For example, to rely on an individual mail carrier for the delivery of one's mail is riskier than depending on a large postal organization. Individuals must sleep, eat, and rest, but a large postal organization never sleeps, never eats—it even grows larger at Christmas.

3. Increasing liability resources. Under this heading are grouped the benefits that consumers reap because organizations, in contrast to individuals, have "deep pockets." In short, they are better able to compensate injured consumers. In the late 1970's Ford Motor Company was forced by the courts to compensate victims of the Ford Pinto's exploding gas tank. Because of design defects, the Pinto's tank was prone to ignite when hit from behind. The money paid by Ford to victims (and relatives of victims) was astounding; it ran into the millions of dollars. Although few productive organizations are as large as Ford, it remains true that organizations are better able to back their products with financial resources than individuals.

Employees

These, then, are the prima facie benefits from introducing productive organizations for consumers. But productive organizations should also be viewed from the standpoint of their effects on people as workers, that is, from the standpoint of their effects upon individual laborers and craftsmen in the state of individual production who opt to work for productive organizations.

It is not difficult to discover certain prima facie benefits, such as the following:

1. Increasing income potential (and the capacity for social contributions).
2. Diffusing personal liability.
3. Adjusting personal income allocation.

1. Increasing income potential and capacity for social contributions. This benefit follows immediately from the earlier fact that second-order-cooperative specialization increases productive efficiency. The person, like Smith's hypothetical pin maker, who joins others in the production of pins is able to make many times more pins than he would alone. This increase also represents an increase in his chance to receive a higher income.

2. Diffusing personal liability. A second prima facie benefit from the standpoint of workers lies in the capacity of an organization to diffuse liability, or in short, to insure the individual against the risk of massive compensation demands. A worker in the state of individual production who sells faulty, dangerous products is morally liable for the damages her product causes. But the extent of this liability can exceed her capacity to pay. Therefore she stands to gain by working with others in a productive organization, for it then becomes the productive organization, not she, who assumes ultimate liability.

3. Adjusting personal income allocation. The increased resources of the productive organization allow the worker to participate in an income-allocation scheme which is detached from the vicissitudes of his capacity to produce, and which is more closely tied to his actual needs. The vicissitudes of the worker's capacity include occasional illness, disabling accidents, and a tendency to lose speed and strength as he ages. Yet his needs persist and sometimes even increase in the face of these vicissitudes. The employee can work harder when he is healthy; but he needs as much money, and sometimes more, when he is ill. The worker may not be able to produce more when he is 50 than when he was 20, but if he marries and has a family his need for income may be greater at 50. When the worker joins a productive organization, the organization can allocate personal income according to a scheme more equitable for him and everyone else.

These prima facie benefits to the worker may be added to the prima facie consumer benefits discussed earlier. Together they constitute a set of reasons which rational people living in a state of individual production might use to justify the introduction of productive organizations. Indeed, if some such set of prima facie benefits did *not* exist, then people would be foolish to introduce such organizations; there would be nothing to gain.

It now becomes possible in light of this analysis to begin the task of specifying the general character of a hypothetical social contract. From the standpoint of society, the goal of a productive organization may be said to be *to enhance the welfare of society through a satisfaction of consumer and worker interests.* In turn, each of the prima facie benefits that we have discussed can be construed as specific terms of the social contract.

Minimizing Drawbacks

An obvious question arises. If people in the state of individual production must agree upon the terms of the social contract, and if these terms directly relate to the task of enhancing society's welfare, then why stop with maximizing prima facie benefits? Why not also minimize prima facie drawbacks? John Locke employed a similar strategy in structuring his political social contract; he not only specified the positive goals of government, but, recognizing government's tendency to abuse privilege, also saw fit to specify certain pitfalls that government must avoid. Are there prima facie drawbacks from introducing productive organizations as well?

Our imaginary consumer stands to benefit because productive organizations, along with the technology they encourage, improve productivity and put more shoes, clothing, electricity, and automobiles on the market. But there is an unwanted consequence of which twentieth-century consumers are painfully aware: increased production tends to deplete natural resources while increasing pollution. More shoes, clothing, electricity, and automobiles require more leather, cotton, coal, and iron. The world has a finite supply. Moreover, the amazing machines so well adapted to productive organizations—the gas engines, the coal furnaces, and the nuclear reactors—all generate by-products which render the environment less fit for human life.

The problem of the increased pollution and depletion of natural resources is more obvious than a second problem, namely the diffusion of individual moral responsibility which sometimes occurs in productive organizations. In the state of individual production, consumers buy their goods from the individual craftsman who stands behind his product, or at least if he does not, the consumers know where to find him. When the cobbler sells a pair of shoes to John Doe and the shoes fall apart, he must confront Doe face to face. Contrast this situation with that of productive organizations, in which workers never see the consumer. To the employee, the consumer is faceless, and the employee's level of psychic accountability tends to lower along with a rise in consumer anonymity. The employee is responsible for his behavior, but to his superior, not to the customer; and his superior sometimes is more apathetic than he. In extreme instances the employee may participate in a form of rebellion unknown to the independent craftsman: "industrial sabotage," where workers retaliate against management by intentionally damaging products.

While speaking of potential drawbacks of productive organizations, one must also acknowledge that the political power of productive organizations is sometimes used to enhance individual interests. Such power sometimes is used to secure favors from government which damage both consumer interests and the interests of the general public. Organizations can receive favors which bolster monopoly power and aggravate inefficiency, as when the railroads in the United States in the late nineteenth century used government grants and privileges to develop a stranglehold on public transportation. Organizations can also use power to divert government expenditures from consumer items to items that actually harm the consumers' interests. In Germany prior to World Wars I and II, for example, large munitions manufacturers used their political influence to increase taxation, and thus decrease consumers' buying

power, for massive purchases of cannons, tanks, fighter planes, and warships. Undeniably, from the overall standpoint of the German public, these purchases were disastrous.

From the perspective of consumers these problems represent potential drawbacks often associated with the introduction of productive organizations. But drawbacks also exist for employees.

Workers in the state of individual production possess a few obvious advantages. For one, they are close to the product and able to take pride in their own creations and the fact that their hands were responsible for the lamp, the soap, or the shirt being sold. But workers in productive organizations are typically removed from the product. They can be, in the words of Marx, "alienated" in a way that blocks their very capacity for self-realization. During World War II the U.S. aircraft manufacturers discovered that alienation was hampering production. Production was shown to increase when the draftsmen, riveters, and sheetmetal workers were taken to *see* the finished product they had worked on— the airplane itself.

In addition to possible alienation and loss of pride, the worker may also suffer from losing control over the design of the product and of his or her work structure. Whereas the individual craftsman can structure her hours and conditions to suit herself, the organizational worker must suit the needs of the overall organization. A man or woman working on an assembly line is powerless to improve the design of the product, and equally powerless to change the design of the work process. The look of the product, the speed of the conveyor belt, and even the number of steps to perform the task all have been determined by others, who are frequently strangers to the worker. Seldom even does the worker have control over safety arrangements or levels of in-plant pollutants.

The increased capacity of productive organizations (over individuals) to use large, expensive technology and massive resources reveals on the other side a decreased capacity of the workers to control their lives. They must adapt to the machines. If a machine operates most efficiently at a certain pace, then the worker must, like the spool boys of the nineteenth-century cotton industry, hurry to meet that pace. In such cases it is as if the machine were controlling the person instead of the person controlling the machine. Similarly, the increased efficiency which results from specialization reveals, on its reverse, the monotony of the simple task repeated thousands of times. The man who knocked the struts into place on the wheels of Henry Ford's Model T was far more efficient than the old craftsman who built a carriage from the bottom up. But the Ford worker knocked struts in place on wheels every minute of every working day.

These prima facie *drawbacks* may be seen as reasons for *not* introducing productive organizations. Unless the prima facie benefits discussed earlier outweigh these prima facie drawbacks, no contract will be concluded because rational people will not choose a lesser over a greater good. And if the benefits outweigh the drawbacks, it follows that in order maximally to enhance welfare, productive organizations should both pursue positive goals and minimize negative ones. Thus, using our discussion as a basis for this list of negative goals, we have:

From the standpoint of *consumers,* productive organizations should minimize:

1. Pollution and the depletion of natural resources.
2. The destruction of personal accountability.
3. The misuse of political power.

From the standpoint of *workers* productive organizations should minimize:

1. Worker alienation.
2. Lack of worker control over work conditions.
3. Monotony and dehumanization of the worker.

The social contract sketched out requires, then, that productive organizations maximize goods and minimize evils relative to consumer and worker welfare. But how, from a moral point of view, should the inevitable trade-offs be made between maximizing and minimizing, and between consumer interests and worker interests? For example, a corporate decision may impair worker interests while at the same time

enhancing consumer interests. Consider the age-old trade-off between higher salaries and lower consumer prices. If coffee workers are paid higher salaries, then coffee drinkers pay higher prices. Conversely, if doctors are paid lower salaries, then the patients pay lower prices. These trade-offs are common not only in the area of salaries, but in many others as well.

How would the rational inhabitants of our state of individual production answer this question? Because the contract specifies that the function of productive organizations is to enhance the welfare of society, our inhabitants might choose a utilitarian standard for making trade-offs, that is, a standard that would specify that organizational policies or action should aim for *the greatest good for the greatest number.* On the other hand, they might prefer a nonutilitarian, or deontological standard, which would specify that *organizational action should accord with general policies or rules which could be universalized for all productive organizations* (i.e., which society would want all productive organizations to adopt).

Whatever the standard—and it must be acknowledged that determining the standard is difficult—two things seem certain. First, society does acknowledge that trade-offs often must be made. Society could not reasonably expect productive organizations to maximize worker interests come what may, say by adopting the policy of paying workers the absolute maximum possible at a given time, for to do so would grossly neglect consumers. If General Motors expended every bit of its resources on employees, the result for society would be catastrophic. Similarly, the consumer must not receive all the attention. Such a policy would result in poor working conditions, low salaries, and frustrated workers (no matter how satisfied employees might be in their life as consumers).

Because trade-offs must be made, it remains logically possible that people in the state of individual production would choose to introduce productive organizations and to establish the social contract, even when they expected either worker interests or consumer interests to be less satisfied than in the state of nature—so long as *overall* welfare were enhanced. In other words, the inhabitants might believe that, on balance, people as workers stand to lose from the introduction of productive organizations, and that potential alienation, loss of control, and other drawbacks make the overall condition of the worker worse than before. But if the benefits to people as consumers fully *overshadowed* these drawbacks, we should still expect the contract to be enacted.

There is a caveat which has application to the overall contract. People would make a trade-off of the kind just discussed only on the condition that it did not violate certain minimum standards of justice, however these are specified. For example, they would refuse to enact the contract if they knew that the existence of productive organizations would systematically reduce a given class of people to an inhuman existence, subsistence poverty, or enslavement. Although the contract might allow productive organizations to undertake actions requiring welfare trade-offs, it would prohibit organizational acts of injustice. It might allow productive organizations to institute layoffs under certain conditions, say, to block skyrocketing production costs; here, worker welfare would be diminished while consumer welfare would be enhanced. But it is another matter when companies commit gross injustices in the process—for example, if they lie to workers, telling them that no layoffs are planned merely to keep them on the job until the last minute. Similarly, it is another matter when organizations follow discriminatory hiring policies, refusing to hire blacks or women, in the name of "consumer advantage." These are clear injustices of the kind that society would want to prohibit as a condition of the social contract. We may infer, then, that a tenet of the social contract will be that productive organizations are to remain within the bounds of the general canons of justice.

Determining what justice requires is a notoriously difficult task. The writings of Plato, Aristotle, and more recently, John Rawls, have shed considerable light on this subject, but unfortunately we must forgo a general discussion of justice here. At a minimum, however, the application of the concept of justice to productive organizations implies *that productive organizations avoid deception or fraud, that they show respect for their workers as human beings, and that they avoid any practice that systematically worsens the situation of a given group in society.* Despite the loud controversy over what justice means, most theorists would agree that justice means at least this much for productive organizations.

Our sketch of a hypothetical social contract is now complete. By utilizing the concept of rational people existing in a state of individual production, we have indicated the terms of a contract which they would require for the introduction of productive organizations. The questions asked in the beginning were: Why should corporations exist at all? What is the fundamental justification for their activities? How can we measure their performance, to say when they have performed poorly or well? A social contract helps to answer these questions. Corporations considered as productive organizations exist to enhance the welfare of society through the satisfaction of consumer and worker interests, in a way which relies on exploiting corporations' special advantages and minimizing disadvantages. This is the *moral foundation* of the corporation when considered as a productive organization.

It is well to notice that the social contract does not specify additional obligations or rights which *corporations* have in contrast to *productive organizations* in general. The social contract justifies corporations as *productive organizations*, not as *corporations*. Presumably, then, further reasons remain to be discovered for society's establishing a certain type of productive organization, such as the corporation—with limited liability, stockholder ownership, and its other characteristics. The important task of discovering those reasons, however, must wait for another occasion. Our development of the social contract has fallen short of a full moral comprehension of corporations, but it has secured a solid footing in an equally important area: comprehending the moral underpinnings of productive organizations.

We have seen that the productive organization cannot be viewed as an isolated moral entity unconstrained by the demands of society, for its very reason for existing lies with its capacity to satisfy certain social interests. Productive organizations, whether U.S. corporations or not, are subject to moral evaluations which transcend the boundaries of the political systems that contain them. When an organization, in the United States or elsewhere, manufactures a product that is inherently dangerous, or when it pushes its employees beyond reasonable limits, it deserves moral condemnation: the organization has failed to live up to a hypothetical contract—a contract between itself and society.

When Henry Ford II referred to the social contract, he left the term "social contract" undefined. This essay has attempted to sharpen the focus of what such a contract might mean, and thereby clarify the content of a corporation's social obligations. The social contract expresses the underlying conviction that corporations exist to serve more than themselves. This conviction emerges in the speeches of businesspeople as well as in the writings of philosophers. It is the conviction expressed by the inventor of the Model T, the grandfather of Henry Ford II, when he said: "For a long time people believed that the only purpose of industry is to make a profit. They were wrong. Its purpose is to serve the general welfare." [2]

Endnotes

1. Some social contract theorists, e.g., Thomas Hobbes and John Rawls, have adopted a different approach, preferring to emphasize people's self-interested tendencies in the state of nature. This view has some definite advantages, since one can say "Even self-interested people will agree to such and such a principle," and, in turn, one's argument gains a persuasive edge. Rawls does not literally assume that people are egoists, but he does assume that they wish to maximize their possession of primary goods. But in the present instance, no compelling reasons exist for representing people to be worse than they are, and one good reason does exist for representing them to be as they are: the presence of even ordinary (i.e., non-self-interested) motives can help clarify the conditions of the social contract.

2. Quoted in David Ewing, *Freedom Inside the Organization* (New York: McGraw-Hill, 1977), p. 65.

REVIEW QUESTIONS

1. What does Donaldson mean by a social contract? Who are the parties to the contract, and what is it supposed to do for corporations?
2. How do we discover the terms of the contract according to Donaldson?
3. What are the terms of the contract for consumers and employees?
4. What are the drawbacks for consumers and workers?
5. In Donaldson's view, what are the limits to what a corporation is morally allowed to do?

DISCUSSION QUESTIONS

1. Donaldson says nothing about the profits of corporations. Has he missed something? What would Friedman say?
2. As Donaldson describes it, there seem to be conflicts between the interests of consumers and employees of a corporation. Are there such conflicts, and if so, how can they be resolved?

PROBLEM CASES

1. Rockwell's Management of the Rocky Flats Plant. (*The New York Times* covered this case extensively on September 20, 22, 23, and October 7, 1989). Rockwell International Corporation is a major defense contractor based in California. It managed the Rocky Flats nuclear weapons plant near Boulder, Colorado, for many years. The plant made plutonium triggers for nuclear weapons under contract with the Department of Energy, and it generated a massive amount of radioactive waste products. According to *The New York Times,* it dumped some of these toxic wastes into a pond that empties into a drinking water reservoir and surreptitiously operated a hazardous waste incinerator, releasing radioactive toxic materials into the air. It stored more than 29,000 gallons of toxic chemicals in two large tanks and hundreds of barrels, even though this was illegal. In addition, the plant had a very poor safety record. During Rockwell's management of the plant, there were at least eight serious accidents involving radioactive plutonium and thirteen deaths attributed to radiation poisoning. In some of these accidents, large amounts of plutonium were released into the air, enough to create the danger of an accidental nuclear reaction.

This plant is now closed, and experts are trying to figure out how to deal with the enormous amount of toxic waste. The Energy Department has identified the plant as the most dangerous in the nuclear weapons industry because it threatens both

Denver and Boulder. The company denies charges of polluting, endangering the public, and causing illness and death to employees by exposing them to radiation. It admits to storing radioactive chemical wastes illegally, but it claims that there is no legal disposal method of these chemical wastes which are laced with radiation.

What should be done about the pollution, illness, and death resulting from Rockwell's irresponsible management of this plant? Why not make Rockwell clean it up and compensate the victims? Why not put the executives of Rockwell responsible for the management of this plant on trial? If they are found guilty of polluting and causing injury, death, and disease to workers and those living nearby, then put them in jail.

2. Rose Cipollone. (This case is discussed in *Applying Ethics,* fourth edition, Jeffrey Olen and Vincent Barry, eds. [Wadsworth, Inc., 1992], pp. 461–2.) Rose Cipollone smoked cigarettes most of her life and died of lung cancer in 1984, at age 58. When doctors removed part of her cancerous right lung in 1981, they told her to stop smoking. But she could not quit; she was addicted. After they removed the rest of her right lung a year later, she finally quit smoking and sued the Liggett Group, the makers of the cigarettes she smoked—Chesterfields and L&Ms. The lawsuit charged that the company knew of the causal link between cancer and smoking in the early 1940s (memos and reports by tobacco executives were cited) but that the company conspired with other tobacco companies to conceal this evidence from the public. Liggett even published advertisements claiming that Chesterfields were safe ("Play safe—smoke Chesterfield") and that L&M filtered cigarettes were approved by doctors. (Even today tobacco companies insist that there is no conclusive evidence that smoking causes cancer, even though hundreds of thousands of smokers die of cancer every year.)

The Liggett Group spent $75 million on its defense and was found not guilty of conspiring with other tobacco companies to hide the dangers of cigarette smoking. The jury did find that the company was guilty of falsely claiming its products were safe, and it awarded $400,000 to Rose's husband in 1988, four years after her death.

There is substantial medical evidence that cigarette smoking causes cancer. Do tobacco companies have any obligation to warn smokers of this danger?

Cigarettes are now sold with a warning from the surgeon general. Does this warning absolve the tobacco companies of all responsibility for their product?

The Food and Drug Administration says that nicotine is an addictive drug in the same chemical family as cocaine and that as such it should be illegal. According to *The Wall Street Journal* (December 12, 1995), the nation's largest tobacco company, Philip Morris USA, agrees that cigarettes are essentially a delivery system for nicotine; this view is found in a company memorandum about developing a new cigarette without tar, the substance linked to cancer. If nicotine is an addictive drug like cocaine, then shouldn't it be illegal? Why not require tobacco companies to remove this addictive drug from their products?

3. Polygraph tests. Companies faced with thefts and dishonest employees have resorted to using polygraph tests, or lie detector tests, to screen employees. For example, the Adolph Coors Brewery in Golden, Colorado, uses these tests to screen job applicants. There are at least two reasons for doing this. First, the tests are a fast and economical way to check information provided by the job applicant. This is necessary because lying on job applications is common. Second, the tests identify dishonest people who might steal from the company or cheat in various ways. Stealing by employees is a common problem, and so is not working during work hours.

Critics of polygraph tests claim that they are not accurate. A report by Psychology Professor David T. Lykken ("Three Big Lies About the Polygraph," *USA Today,* February 17, 1983) says that in three studies of the accuracy of polygraphs used on actual criminal suspects, the accuracies obtained by the qualified operators were 63 percent, 39 percent, and 55 percent. How can the polygraph test be beaten? Lykken suggests that the easiest way to fool the machine is to "augment" your response to the control questions by some form of covert stimulation, for example, by biting your tongue. Because the polygraph is an instrument that records physiological changes that occur in a person when answering a question, such as an increase in heart beat or a rise in blood pressure, it can be fooled if the person produces these changes with every answer, whether true or false.

Another complaint about these polygraph tests is that they infringe on privacy, particularly if personal questions about beliefs and behavior are asked.

All things considered, do companies have a right to use polygraph tests on prospective or working employees? Do employees have a right to refuse testing?

4. Golden Parachute Payments. A large payment that an executive receives when leaving a company is called a golden parachute payment. Often it is a huge amount of money taken from the company's assets or from stock manipulations. For example, Steve Rothmeier took home $10 million when Northwest Airlines was bought. After six months on the job, Philip Smith received $5.4 million when Grand Metropolitan bought Pillsbury. Nobert Berg, former deputy chairman of Control Data, quit with a retirement bonus of $4.7 million. The latest examples involve the Sony Corporation: Peter Guber recently left the company with $40 million and a $200 million deal with Sony to back him in a new company. Michael Schulhof was fired as chairman of U.S. operations after losing $2.7 billion in 1994 in misadventures in the movie business; his reward for losing so much money was a severance package worth more than $40 million.

Are these golden parachute payments justified? Why give executives huge payments for losing money?

SUGGESTED READINGS

1. William H. Shaw, *Business Ethics* (Wadsworth Publishing Co., 1991). This is a comprehensive textbook covering moral theory, the nature of capitalism, corporations, the workplace, employees, consumers, and various problem cases.

2. *Contemporary Issues in Business Ethics,* second edition, ed. Joseph R. DesJardins and John McCall (Wadsworth Publishing Co., 1990), has articles on product liability, advertising, consumer regulation, and other issues.

3. *Moral Rights in the Workplace,* ed. Gertrude Ezorsky (State University of New York Press, 1987), contains articles on occupational health and safety, employee privacy, unions, and related topics.

4. Saul W. Gellerman, "Why 'Good' Managers Make Bad Ethical Choices," *Harvard Business Review* 64 (July–August 1986), explains how business executives try to rationalize their immoral behavior.

5. J. Patrick Wright, *On a Clear Day You Can See General Motors* (Avon Books, 1979). J. Patrick Wright is a ghostwriter for John DeLorean, the executive at General Motors who started his own DeLorean Corporation and produced the exotic DeLorean car. The book gives an insider's account of fraud, lying, false advertising, stock manipulations, and other immoral actions at one of the world's biggest corporations.

6. *Case Studies in Business Ethics,* second edition, ed. Thomas Donaldson and A. R. Gini (Prentice-Hall, 1990), describes many fascinating and shocking cases of unethical conduct in business, including the production of the Ford Pinto, the Dalkon Shield, and Laetrile; leveraged buyouts; insider stock trading; and defense contract scandals.

7. *Ethical Issues in Business,* third edition, ed. Thomas Donaldson and Patricia H. Werhane (Prentice-Hall, 1988), is a collection of readings, including articles on the profit motive, business and employee rights and obligations, business responsibility and liability with respect to the consumer, and environmental issues.

8. Tom L. Beauchamp, *Case Studies in Business, Society, and Ethics* (Prentice-Hall, 1983). This is another collection of interesting cases. Some examples are "The DC-10's Defective Doors," "Procter & Gamble's Rely Tampons," and "Dow Chemical Company and Napalm-B."

9. *Ethics in the World of Business,* ed. David Braybrooke (Rowman & Allanheld, 1983), is an anthology with twenty-three chapters covering a wide variety of topics including sexual harassment, the right to be promoted or retained, unionization, advertising, the arms business, sales tactics, and consumer concerns.

10. Robert L. Arrington, "Advertising and Behavior Control," *Journal of Business Ethics* 1 (1982), pp. 3–12, discusses questionable advertising techniques such as puffery, indirect information, and subliminal suggestion. He finds that advertising can control behavior, produce compulsive behavior, and create irrational desires.

11. Albert Carr, "Is Business Bluffing Ethical?" *Harvard Business Review* (January–February 1968), pp. 143–53, defends the use of deception in business as an essential part of the legal pursuit of profits.

12. Milton Friedman, *Capitalism and Freedom* (University of Chicago Press, 1981), explains his views about free markets, capitalism, and freedom from interference.

13. John K. Galbraith, *The New Industrial State,* fourth edition (Houghton Mifflin, 1985), critiques conservative economists such as Friedman and offers his own views on economics and modern society.

14. John Hospers, *Libertarianism* (Nash Publishing Co., 1971), defends the libertarian view that people should be free to pursue profits in a free market system and that taxation is a violation of a person's rights.

15. Alan H. Goldman, "Business Ethics: Profits, Utilities, and Moral Rights," *Philosophy & Public Affairs* 9, no. 3 (Spring 1980), pp. 260–86, argues that business executives ought to follow the same moral principles as everyone else; they cannot defend their actions by claiming that the legal pursuit of profits is a moral end in itself.

16. Kenneth E. Goodpaster and John B. Matthews, Jr., "Can a Corporation Have a Conscience?" *Harvard Business Review* (January–February 1982), 132–43, argue that there is an analogy between the individual and the corporation such that corporations can be just as morally responsible as individuals.

17. *Business Ethics,* ed. W. Michael Hoffman and Jennifer Mills Moore (McGraw-Hill, 1984), is an anthology covering topics such as the nature of the corporation, employee rights and duties, hiring practices, government regulation, deception, bribery, and anticompetitive behavior.

18. Alex C. Michalos, "Advertising: Its Logic, Ethics, and Economics," in *Informal Logic: The First International Symposium,* ed. J. A. Blair and R. H. Johnson (Edgepress, 1980), discusses various types of deception in advertising.

19. *Just Business,* ed. Tom Regan (Random House, 1984), is a collection of original essays on questions in business ethics; it includes articles on preferential hiring, advertising, corporate responsibility, and individual rights in business.

20. *Business Ethics,* ed. Milton Snoeyenbos, Robert Almeder, and James Humber (Prometheus Books, 1983), has readings on business and social responsibility, employee obligations and rights, trade secrets and patents, business and the consumer, and multinational corporations.

21. *Ethics in the Workplace,* ed. Robert A. Larmer (West Publishing Co., 1996), is a collection of readings on a number of general and specific moral issues relating to business. There are eighteen chapters, including chapters on sexual harassment, safety in the workplace, insider trading, intellectual property, bribes, advertising, collective bargaining, and whistleblowing.

Chapter Eight

ANIMALS AND
THE ENVIRONMENT

Introduction

Humans cause a great deal of animal suffering. Consider this example of animal experimentation taken from Peter Singer's book *Animal Liberation*. At the Lovelace Foundation in New Mexico, experimenters forced sixty-four beagles to inhale radioactive strontium 90. Twenty-five of the dogs died; initially most of them were feverish and enemic, suffering from hemorrhages and bloody diarrhea. One of the deaths occurred during an epileptic seizure, and another resulted from a brain hemorrhage. In a similar experiment, beagles were injected with enough strontium 90 to produce early death in 50 percent of the group. Are experiments such as these really necessary? It was already known that strontium 90 was unhealthy and that the dogs would suffer and die. Furthermore, these experiments did not save any human lives or have any important benefits for humans. So why were they done?

Another common human practice that produces considerable animal suffering is factory farming. Take the treatment of veal calves, for example. To make their flesh pale and tender, these calves are given special treatment. They are put in narrow stalls and tethered with a chain so that they cannot turn around, lie down comfortably, or groom themselves. They are fed a totally liquid diet to promote rapid weight gain. This diet is deficient in iron, and, as a result, the calves lick the sides of the stall, which are impregnated with urine containing iron. They are given no water because thirsty animals eat more than ones that drink water. Is this morally justified? Should we do this to animals just because we enjoy eating their flesh?

Speciesism   In the first reading for the chapter, Peter Singer introduces the term "speciesism." As he defines it, speciesism is "a prejudice or attitude of bias toward the interests of members of one's own species and against those of members of other species." Singer goes on to argue that speciesism is analogous to racism and sexism. It is unjust to discriminate against blacks because of their color or against women because of their sex. Their interests, for example, their interest in voting, have to be considered equally to those of whites and men. Similarly, it is unjust to discriminate against nonhuman animals because of their species. Their interests, and particularly their interest in not suffering, have to be considered too.

But how do we go about reducing animal suffering? Does this mean that we should become vegetarians and eat no meat? Singer thinks so, but of course this is very controversial in our meat-eating society. In Singer's view, we should stop eating meat to eliminate factory farming or at least to protest against it; we should not treat animals as means to our end (to use Kant's phrase).

Singer's position is attacked by Bonnie Steinbock in our readings. Steinbock thinks that Singer's view has counterintuitive results. It implies, for example, that it is unfair to feed starving children before feeding starving rats. But it seems intuitively obvious that the interests of humans are more important than those of animals. Why is this? According to Steinbock, humans have a higher moral status than animals because humans have certain morally relevant capacities that animals do not have— for example, the capacity to be morally responsible for actions, to have altruistic or moral reasons, and to desire self-respect.

Tom Regan takes a different position on the moral status of nonhuman animals. He agrees with Singer that our treatment of animals is wrong and that speciesism is unjust, but to show this he does not want to appeal to any form of Utilitarianism. Utilitarianism is not an acceptable moral theory, he argues, because it treats persons and animals as worthless receptacles for valuable pleasure and because it allows immoral actions if they happen to bring about the best balance of total satisfaction for all those affected by the action. Instead of Utilitarianism, Regan defends a rights view. On this view, animals have rights based on their inherent value as experiencing subjects of life, and our treatment of animals is wrong because it violates their rights.

Mary Anne Warren rejects Regan's strong animal rights position which gives animals the same basic moral rights as humans. She complains that Regan's notion of inherent value is a mysterious non-natural property that is not adequately explained. As a result, it fails to produce any clear distinction between those who have rights and those who don't. She calls her own alternative view a weak animal rights theory. On this theory, animals have rights, but they are weaker than human rights. Still these weak animal rights require us not to make animals suffer and not to kill them without a good reason.

Like Singer and Regan, Jordan Curnutt believes that we are morally required to be vegetarians, but the reason for this, he claims, is not to be found in either Utilitarianism or rights theory. His criticism of Utilitarianism is different from that of Regan. The problem is that Utilitarianism can be used to defend meat eating by claiming that it maximizes utility; it does this by producing human satisfactions, both from eating meat and from producing jobs and profits for those in the meat industry. As for Regan's rights view, it is vulnerable to damaging criticisms. Besides the criticisms made by Warren, there are problems in explaining what rights are, who has them, and how conflicts between rights are to be settled. Instead of appealing to utility or rights, Curnutt argues that animal eating is wrong, all things considered, because it requires harmful killing of animals that is prima facie morally wrong and is not overridden by other moral considerations such as human health or satisfaction.

Sentientism   All of the writers discussed so far (except Steinbock) seem to assume that only conscious or sentient beings can have rights or deserve moral consideration. Trees and other natural objects are not conscious, so, in their view, they cannot have rights or deserve moral consideration. But isn't this another kind of prejudice? They have escaped one prejudice, speciesism, only to embrace another, namely sentientism. Why not say that nonsentient things such as forests have rights too?

This is the approach of Christopher D. Stone in the reading. Stone argues that to protect and preserve the environment, we should extend legal rights to trees, forests, rivers, and other natural objects. Even though this may seem absurd at first, Stone maintains that natural objects should have the same legal status as other things that cannot speak for themselves such as infants, estates, corporations, or universities. Lawyers could act as friends of natural objects and protect their interests. This would make it easier to preserve the natural environment, and it would result in a different perspective on nature—where nature is not just something to be used.

Anthropocentrism   The view rejected by Stone is sometimes called anthropocentrism; this is the view that the natural environment has value only as a means of producing human benefits. Although he does not use the term, William F. Baxter seems to adopt and defend anthropocentrism in the reading. He claims that the natural environment (including penguins) counts only as a means of producing various human benefits; it is not an end in itself and has no value apart from humans.

Holism   William Godfrey-Smith rejects the anthropocentric view that the environment has only instrumental value for humans. He thinks

that instrumental justifications for environmental conservation—saving the wilderness because it is a cathedral, a laboratory, a silo, or a gymnasium—all fail to provide a satisfactory rationale. Not only are there conflicts between the activities that can be justified, there is also the feeling that the wilderness has more than instrumental value, that it has intrinsic value as an end in itself apart from any use. Instead of sentientism or an anthropocentric view, Godfrey-Smith suggests that we adopt a holistic concept of nature where we think of humans and nature together forming a moral community and where we must engage in cooperative (not exploitive) behavior for the sake of the health of the whole community. This means that we should have empathy for nature and not think of ourselves as separate from it or superior to it.

Ecofeminism   Karen J. Warren agrees that we should not think of ourselves as superior to nonhuman nature. Thinking this way, in terms of superior vs. inferior, is part of what she calls the logic of domination. This involves locating both women and nonhuman nature in an oppressive conceptual framework having "up-down" thinking which puts higher value, status, or prestige on what is "up" rather than "down." Both women and nonhuman nature are put in the "down" category, and this continues their domination and oppression. As Warren explains it, ecological feminism (or ecofeminism) seeks to develop an environmental ethic that reveals such logical connections (and historical, symbolic, and theoretical connections) between the domination of women and the domination of nonhuman nature and seeks to end this twin and interconnected domination.

Peter Singer

All Animals Are Equal

For biographical information on Singer, see his reading in Chapter 3.

Singer defines speciesism as a prejudice towards the interests of members of one's own species and against those of members of other species. He argues that speciesism is analogous to racism and sexism. If it is unjust to discriminate against women and blacks by not considering their interests, it is also unfair to ignore the interests of animals, particularly their interest in not suffering.

"Animal Liberation" may sound more like a parody of other liberation movements than a serious objective. The idea of "The Rights of Animals" actually was once used to parody the case for women's rights. When Mary Wollstonecraft, a forerunner of today's feminists, published her *Vindication of the Rights of Women* in 1792, her views were widely regarded as absurd, and before long an anonymous publication appeared entitled *A Vindication of the Rights of Brutes*. The author of this satirical work (now known to have been Thomas Taylor, a distinguished Cambridge philosopher) tried to refute Mary Wollstonecraft's arguments by showing that they could be carried one stage further. If the argument for equality was sound when applied to women, why should it not be applied to dogs, cats, and horses? The reasoning seemed to hold for these "brutes" too, yet to hold that brutes had rights was manifestly absurd; therefore the reasoning by which this conclusion had been reached must be unsound, and if unsound when applied to brutes, it must also be unsound when applied to women, since the very same arguments had been used in each case.

In order to explain the basis of the case for the equality of animals, it will be helpful to start with an examination of the case for the equality of women. Let us assume that we wish to defend the case for women's rights against the attack by Thomas Taylor. How should we reply?

One way in which we might reply is by saying that the case for equality between men and women cannot validly be extended to nonhuman animals. Women have a right to vote, for instance, because they are just as capable of making rational decisions about the future as men are; dogs, on the other hand, are incapable of understanding the significance of voting, so they cannot have the right to vote. There are many other obvious ways in which men and women resemble each other closely, while humans and animals differ greatly. So, it might be said, men and women are similar beings and should have similar rights, while humans and nonhumans are different and should not have equal rights.

The reasoning behind this reply to Taylor's analogy is correct up to a point, but it does not go far enough. There *are* important differences between humans and other animals, and these differences must give rise to *some* differences in the rights that each have. Recognizing this obvious fact, however, is no barrier to the case for extending the basic principle of equality to nonhuman animals. The differences that exist between men and women are equally undeniable, and the supporters of Women's Liberation are aware that these differences may give rise to different rights. Many feminists hold that women have the right to an abortion on request. It does not follow that since these same feminists are campaigning for equality between men and women they must support the right of men to have abortions too. Since a man cannot have an abortion, it is meaningless to talk of his right to have one. Since a dog can't vote, it is meaningless to talk of its right to vote. There is no reason why either Women's Liberation or Animal Liberation should get involved in such nonsense. The extension of the basic principle of equality from one group to another does not imply that we must treat both groups in exactly the same way, or grant exactly the same rights to both groups. Whether we should do so will depend on the nature of the members of the two groups. The basic principle of equality does not require equal or identical *treatment*; it requires equal *consideration*. Equal consideration for different beings may lead to different treatment and different rights.

So there is a different way of replying to Taylor's attempt to parody the case for women's rights, a way that does not deny the obvious differences between humans and nonhumans but goes more deeply into the question of equality and concludes by finding nothing absurd in the idea that the basic principle of equality applies to so-called brutes. At this point such a conclusion may appear odd; but if we examine more deeply the basis on which our opposition to discrimination on grounds of race or sex ultimately rests, we will see that we would be on shaky ground if we were to demand equality for blacks, women, and other groups of oppressed humans while denying equal consideration to nonhumans. To make this clear we need to see first, exactly why racism and sexism are wrong.

When we say that all human beings, whatever their race, creed, or sex, are equal, what is it that we are asserting? Those who wish to defend hierarchical, inegalitarian societies have often pointed out that by whatever test we choose it simply is not true that all humans are equal. Like it or not we must face the fact that humans come in different shapes and sizes; they come with different moral capacities, different intellectual abilities, different amounts of benevolent feeling and sensitivity to the needs of others, different abilities to communicate effectively, and different capacities to experience pleasure and pain. In short, if the demand for equality were based on the actual equality of all human beings, we would have to stop demanding equality.

Still, one might cling to the view that the demand for equality among human beings is based on the actual equality of the different races and sexes. Although, it may be said, humans differ as individuals there are no differences between the races and sexes *as such*. From the mere fact that a person is black or a woman we cannot infer anything about that person's intellectual or moral capacities. This, it may be said, is why racism and sexism are wrong. The white racist claims that whites are superior to blacks, but this is false—although there are differences among individuals, some blacks are superior to some whites in all of the capacities and abilities that could conceivably be relevant. The opponent of sexism would say the same: a person's sex is no guide to his or her abilities, and this is why it is unjustifiable to discriminate on the basis of sex.

The existence of individual variations that cut across the lines of race or sex, however, provides us with no defense at all against a more sophisticated opponent of equality, one who proposes that, say, the interests of all those with IQ scores below 100 be given less consideration than the interests of those with ratings over 100. Perhaps those scoring below the mark, would, in this society, be made the slaves of those scoring higher. Would a hierarchical society of this sort really be so much better than one based on race or sex? I think not. But if we tie the moral principle of equality to the factual equality of the different races or sexes, taken as a whole, our opposition to racism and sexism does not provide us with any basis for objecting to this kind of inegalitarianism.

There is a second important reason why we ought not to base our opposition to racism and sexism on any kind of actual equality, even the limited kind that asserts that variations in capacities and abilities are spread evenly between the different races and sexes: we can have no absolute guarantee that these capacities and abilities really are distributed evenly, without regard to race or sex, among human beings. So far as actual abilities are concerned there do seem to be certain measurable differences between both races and sexes. These differences do not, of course, appear in each case, but only when averages are taken. More important still, we do not yet know how much of these differences is really due to the different genetic endowments of the different races and sexes, and how much is due to poor schools, poor housing, and other factors that are the result of past and continuing discrimination. Perhaps all the important differences will eventually prove to be environmental rather than genetic. Anyone opposed to racism and sexism will certainly hope that this will be so, for it will make the task of ending discrimination a lot easier; nevertheless it would be dangerous to rest the case against racism and sexism on the belief that all significant differences are environmental in origin. The opponent of, say, racism who takes this line will be unable to avoid conceding that *if* differences in ability do after all prove to have some genetic connection with race, racism would in some way be defensible.

Fortunately there is no need to pin the case for equality to one particular outcome of a scientific investigation. The appropriate response to those who claim to have found evidence of genetically based differences in ability between the races or sexes is not to stick to the belief that the genetic explanation must be wrong, whatever evidence to the contrary may turn up: instead we should make it quite clear that the claim to equality does not depend on intelligence, moral capacity, physical strength, or similar matters of fact. Equality is a moral idea, not an assertion of fact. There is no logically compelling reason for assuming that a factual difference in ability between two people justifies any difference in the amount of consideration we give to their needs and interests. *The principle of the equality of human beings is not a description of an alleged actual equality among humans; it is a prescription of how we should treat humans.*

Jeremy Bentham, the founder of the reforming utilitarian school of moral philosophy, incorporated the essential basis of moral equality into his system of ethics by means of the formula: "Each to count for one and none for more than one." In other words, the interests of every being affected by an action are to be taken into account and given the same weight as the like interests of any other being. A later utilitarian, Henry Sidgwick, put the point in this way: "The good of any one individual is of no more importance, from the point of view (if I may say so) of the Universe, than the good of any other." More recently the leading figures in contemporary moral philosophy have shown a great

deal of agreement in specifying as a fundamental presupposition of their moral theories some similar requirement that operates so as to give everyone's interests equal consideration—although these writers generally cannot agree on how this requirement is best formulated.[1]

It is an implication of this principle of equality that our concern for others and our readiness to consider their interests ought not to depend on what they are like or on what abilities they may possess. Precisely what this concern or consideration requires us to do may vary according to the characteristics of those affected by what we do: concern for the well-being of a child growing up in America would require that we teach him to read; concern for the well-being of a pig may require no more than that we leave him alone with other pigs in a place where there is adequate food and room to run freely. But the basic element—the taking into account of the interests of the being, whatever those interests may be—must, according to the principle of equality, be extended to all beings, black or white, masculine or feminine, human or nonhuman.

Thomas Jefferson, who was responsible for writing the principle of the equality of men into the American Declaration of Independence, saw this point. It led him to oppose slavery even though he was unable to free himself fully from his slaveholding background. He wrote in a letter to the author of a book that emphasized the notable intellectual achievements of Negroes in order to refute the then common view that they had limited intellectual capacities:

Be assured that no person living wishes more sincerely than I do, to see a complete refutation of the doubts I have myself entertained and expressed on the grade of understanding allotted to them by nature, and to find that they are on a par with ourselves . . . but whatever be their degree of talent it is no measure of their rights. Because Sir Isaac Newton was superior to others in understanding, he was not therefore lord of the property or person of others.[2]

Similarly when in the 1850s the call for women's rights was raised in the United States a remarkable black feminist named Sojourner Truth made the same point in more robust terms at a feminist convention:

. . . they talk about this thing in the head; what do they call it? ["Intellect," whispered someone near by.] That's it. What's that got to do with women's rights or Negroes' rights? If my cup won't hold but a pint and yours holds a quart, wouldn't you be mean not to let me have my little half-measure full?[3]

It is on this basis that the case against racism and the case against sexism must both ultimately rest; and it is in accordance with this principle that the attitude that we may call "speciesism," by analogy with racism, must also be condemned. Speciesism—the word is not an attractive one, but I can think of no better term—is a prejudice or attitude of bias toward the interests of members of one's own species and against those of members of other species. It should be obvious that the fundamental objections to racism and sexism made by Thomas Jefferson and Sojourner Truth apply equally to speciesism. If possessing a higher degree of intelligence does not entitle one human to use another for his own ends, how can it entitle humans to exploit nonhumans for the same purpose?[4]

Many philosophers and other writers have proposed the principle of equal consideration of interests, in some form or other, as a basic moral principle, but not many of them have recognized that this principle applies to members of other species as well as to our own. Jeremy Bentham was one of the few who did realize this. In a forward-looking passage written at a time when black slaves had been freed by the French but the British dominions were still being treated in the way we now treat animals, Bentham wrote:

The day may come when the rest of the animal creation may acquire those rights which never could have been withholden from them but by the hand of tyranny. The French have already discovered that the blackness of the skin is no reason why a human being should be abandoned without redress to the caprice of a tormentor. It may one day come to be recognized that the number of the legs, the villosity of the skin, or the termination of the os sacrum are reasons equally insufficient for abandoning a sensitive being to the same fate. What else is it that should trace the insuperable line? Is it the faculty of reason, or perhaps the faculty of discourse? But a full-grown horse or dog is beyond comparison a more rational, as well as a more conversable animal, than an infant of day or a week or even a month old. But suppose they were otherwise, what would it avail? The question is not, Can they reason? nor Can they talk? but, Can they suffer?[5]

In this passage Bentham points to the capacity for suffering as the vital characteristic that gives a being the right to equal consideration. The capacity for suffering—or more strictly, for suffering and/or enjoyment or happiness—is not just another characteristic like the capacity for language or higher mathematics. Bentham is not saying that those who try to mark "the insuperable line" that determines whether the interests of a being should be considered happen to have chosen the wrong characteristic. By saying that we must consider the interests of all beings with the capacity for suffering or enjoyment Bentham does not arbitrarily exclude from consideration any interests at all—as those who draw the line with reference to the possession of reason or language do. The capacity for suffering and enjoyment is a *prerequisite for having interests at all,* a condition that must be satisfied before we can speak of interests in a meaningful way. It would be nonsense to say that it was not in the interests of a stone to be kicked along the road by a schoolboy. A stone does not have interests because it cannot suffer. Nothing that we can do to it could possibly make any difference to its welfare. A mouse, on the other hand, does have an interest in not being kicked along the road, because it will suffer if it is.

If a being suffers there can be no moral justification for refusing to take that suffering into consideration. No matter what the nature of the being, the principle of equality requires that its suffering be counted equally with the like suffering—insofar as rough comparisons can be made—of any other being. If a being is not capable of suffering, or of experiencing enjoyment or happiness, there is nothing to be taken into account. So the limit of sentience (using the term as a convenient if not strictly accurate shorthand for the capacity to suffer and/or experience enjoyment) is the only defensible boundary of concern for the interests of others. To mark this boundary by some other characteristic like intelligence or rationality would be to mark it in an arbitrary manner. Why not choose some other characteristic, like skin color?

The racist violates the principle of equality by giving greater weight to the interests of members of his own race when there is a clash between their interests and the interests of those of another race. The sexist violates the principle of equality by favoring the interests of his own sex. Similarly the speciesist allows the interests of his own species to override the greater interests of members of other species. The pattern is identical in each case.

Most human beings are speciesists. Ordinary human beings—not a few exceptionally cruel or heartless humans, but the overwhelming majority of humans—take an active part in, acquiesce in, and allow their taxes to pay for practices that require the sacrifice of the most important interests of members of other species in order to promote the most trivial interests of our own species. . . .

Animals can feel pain. As we saw earlier, there can be no moral justification for regarding the pain (or pleasure) that animals feel as less important than the same amount of pain (or pleasure) felt by humans. But what exactly does this mean, in practical terms? To prevent misunderstanding I shall spell out what I mean a little more fully.

If I give a horse a hard slap across its rump with my open hand, the horse may start, but it presumably feels little pain. Its skin is thick enough to protect it against a mere slap. If I slap a baby in the same way, however, the baby will cry and presumably does feel pain, for its skin is more sensitive. So it is worse to slap a baby than a horse, if both slaps are administered with equal force. But there must be some kind of blow—I don't know exactly what it would be, but perhaps a blow with a heavy stick—that would cause the horse as much pain as we cause a baby by slapping it with our hand. That is what I mean by "the same amount of pain" and if we consider it wrong to inflict that much pain on a baby for no good reason then we must, unless we are speciesists, consider it equally wrong to inflict the same amount of pain on a horse for no good reason.

There are other differences between humans and animals that cause other complications. Normal adult human beings have mental capacities that will, in certain circumstances, lead them to suffer more than animals would in the same circumstances. If, for instance, we decided to perform extremely painful or lethal scientific experiments on normal adult humans, kidnapped at random from public parks for this purpose, every adult who entered a park would become fearful that he would be kidnapped. The resultant terror would be a form of suffering additional to the pain of the experiment. The same experiments performed on nonhuman animals would cause less suffering since the animals would not have the anticipatory dread of being kidnapped and experimented upon. This does not mean, of course, that it would be right to perform the experiment on animals, but only that there is a reason, which is *not* speciesist, for preferring to use animals rather than normal adult humans, if the experiment is to be done at all. It should be noted, however, that this same argument gives us a reason for preferring to use human infants—orphans perhaps—or retarded humans for experiments, rather than adults, since infants and retarded humans would also have no idea of what was going to happen to them. So far as this argument is concerned nonhuman animals and infants and retarded humans are in the same category; and if we use this argument to justify experiments on nonhuman animals we have to ask ourselves whether we are also prepared to allow experiments on humans, on what basis can we do it, other than a barefaced—and morally indefensible—preference for members of our own species?

There are many areas in which the superior mental powers of normal adult humans make a difference: anticipation, more detailed memory, greater knowledge of what is happening, and so on. Yet these differences do not all point to greater suffering on the part of the normal human being. Sometimes an animal may suffer more because of his more limited understanding. If, for instance, we are taking prisoners in wartime we can explain to them that while they must submit to capture, search, and confinement they will not otherwise be harmed and will be set free at the conclusion of hostilities. If we capture a wild animal, however, we cannot explain that we are not threatening its life. A wild animal cannot distinguish an attempt to overpower and confine from an attempt to kill; the one causes as much terror as the other.

It may be objected that comparisons of the sufferings of different species are impossible to make, and that for this reason when the interests of animals and humans clash the principle of equality gives no guidance. It is probably true that comparisons of suffering between members of different species cannot be made precisely, but precision is not essential. Even if we were to prevent the infliction of suffering on animals only when it is quite certain that the interests of humans will not be affected to anything like the extent that animals are affected, we would be forced to make radical changes in our treatment of animals that would involve our diet, the farming methods we use, experimental procedures in many fields of science, our approach to wildlife and to hunting, trapping and the wearing of furs, and areas of entertainment like circuses, rodeos, and zoos. As a result, a vast amount of suffering would be avoided.

So far I have said a lot about the infliction of suffering on animals, but nothing about killing them. This omission has been deliberate. The application of the principle of equality to the infliction of suffering is, in theory at least, fairly straightforward. Pain and suffering are bad and should be prevented or minimized, irrespective of the race, sex, or species of the being that suffers. How bad a pain is depends on how intense it is and how long it lasts, but pains of the same intensity and duration are equally bad, whether felt by humans or animals.

The wrongness of killing a being is more complicated. I have kept, and shall continue to keep, the question of killing in the background because in the present state of human tyranny over other species the more simple, straightforward principle of equal consideration of pain or pleasure is a sufficient basis for identifying and protesting against all the major abuses of animals that humans practice. Nevertheless, it is necessary to say something about killing.

Just as most humans are speciesists in their readiness to cause pain to animals when they would not cause a similar pain to humans for the same reason, so most humans are speciesists in their readiness to kill other animals when they would not kill humans. We need to proceed more cautiously here, however, because people hold widely differing views about when it is legitimate to kill humans, as the continuing debates over abortion and euthanasia attest. Nor have moral philosophers been able to agree on exactly what it is that makes it wrong to kill humans, and under what circumstances killing a human being may be justifiable.

Let us consider first the view that it is always wrong to take an innocent human life. We may call this the "sanctity of life" view. People who take this view oppose abortion and euthanasia. They do not usually, however, oppose the killing of nonhumans—so perhaps it would be more accurate to describe this view as the "sanctity of *human* life" view.

The belief that human life, and only human life, is sacrosanct is a form of speciesism. To see this, consider the following example.

Assume that, as sometimes happens, an infant has been born with massive and irreparable brain damage. The damage is so severe that the infant can never be any more than a "human vegetable," unable to talk, recognize other people, act independently of others, or develop a sense of self-awareness. The parents of the infant, realizing that they cannot hope for any improvement in their child's condition and being in any case unwilling to spend, or ask the state to spend, the thousands of dollars that would be needed annually for proper care of the infant, ask the doctor to kill the infant painlessly.

Should the doctor do what the parents ask? Legally, he should not, and in this respect the law reflects the sanctity of life view. The life of every human being is sacred. Yet people who would say this about the infant do not object to the killing of nonhuman animals. How can they justify their different judgments? Adult chimpanzees, dogs, pigs, and many other species far surpass the brain-damaged infant in their ability to relate to others, act independently, be self-aware, and any other capacity that could reasonably be said to give value to life. With the most intensive care possible, there are retarded infants who can never achieve the intelligence level of a dog. Nor can we appeal to the concern of the infant's parents, since they themselves, in this imaginary example (and in some actual cases), do not want the infant kept alive.

The only thing that distinguishes the infant from the animal, in the eyes of those who claim it has a "right to life," is that it is, biologically, a member of the species Homo Sapiens, whereas chimpanzees, dogs, and pigs are not. But to use *this* difference as the basis for granting a right to life to the infant and not to the other animals is, of course, pure speciesism.[6] It is exactly the kind of arbitrary difference that the most crude and overt kind of racist uses in attempting to justify racial discrimination.

This does not mean that to avoid speciesism we must hold that it is as wrong to kill a dog as it is to kill a normal human being. The only position that is irredeemably speciesist is the one that tries to make the boundary of the right to life run exactly parallel to the boundary of our own species. Those who hold the sanctity of life view do this because while distinguishing sharply between humans and other animals they allow no distinctions to be made within our own species, objecting to the killing of the severely retarded and the hopelessly senile as strongly as they object to the killing of normal adults.

To avoid speciesism we must allow that beings that are similar in all relevant respects have a similar right to life—and mere membership in our own biological species cannot be a morally relevant criterion for this right. Within these limits we could still hold that, for instance, it is worse to kill a normal adult human, with a capacity for self-awareness, and the ability to plan for the future and have meaningful relations with others, than it is to kill a mouse, which presumably does not share all of these characteristics; or we might appeal to the close family and other personal ties that humans have but mice do not have to the same degree; or we might think that it is the consequences for other humans, who will be put in fear of their own lives, that makes the crucial difference; or we

might think it is some combination of these factors, or other factors altogether.

Whatever criteria we choose, however, we will have to admit that they do not follow precisely the boundary of our own species. We may legitimately hold that there are some features of certain beings which make their lives more valuable than those of other beings; but there will surely be some nonhuman animals whose lives, by any standards, are more valuable than the lives of some humans. A chimpanzee, dog, or pig, for instance, will have a higher degree of self-awareness and a greater capacity for meaningful relations with others than a severely retarded infant or someone in a state of advanced senility. So if we base the right to life on these characteristics we must grant these animals a right to life as good as, or better than, such retarded or senile humans.

Now this argument cuts both ways. It could be taken as showing that chimpanzees, dogs, and pigs, along with some other species, have a right to life and we commit a grave moral offense whenever we kill them, even when they are old and suffering and our intention is to put them out of their misery. Alternatively one could take the argument as showing that the severely retarded and hopelessly senile have no right to life and may be killed for quite trivial reasons, as we now kill animals.

Since the focus here is on ethical questions concerning animals and not on the morality of euthanasia I shall not attempt to settle this issue finally. I think it is reasonably clear, though, that while both of the positions just described avoid speciesism, neither is entirely satisfactory. What we need is some middle position that would avoid speciesism but would not make the lives of the retarded and senile as cheap as the lives of pigs and dogs now are, nor make the lives of pigs and dogs so sacrosanct that we think it wrong to put them out of hopeless misery. What we must do is bring nonhuman animals within our sphere of moral concern and cease to treat their lives as expendable for whatever trivial purposes we may have. At the same time, once we realize that the fact that a being is a member of our own species is not in itself enough to make it always wrong to kill that being, we may come to reconsider our policy of preserving human lives at all costs, even when there is no prospect of a meaningful life or of existence without terrible pain.

I conclude, then, that a rejection of species-ism does not imply that all lives are of equal worth. While self-awareness, intelligence, the capacity for meaningful relations with others, and so on are not relevant to the question of inflicting pain—since pain is pain, whatever other capacities, beyond the capacity to feel pain, the being may have—these capacities may be relevant to the question of taking life. It is not arbitrary to hold that the life of a self-aware being, capable of abstract thought, of planning for the future, of complex acts of communication, and so on, is more valuable than the life of a being without these capacities. To see the difference between the issues of inflicting pain and taking life, consider how we would choose within our own species. If we had to choose to save the life of a normal human or a mentally defective human, we would probably choose to save the life of the normal human; but if we had to choose between preventing pain in the normal human or the mental defective—imagine that both have received painful but superficial injuries, and we only have enough painkiller for one of them—it is not nearly so clear how we ought to choose. The same is true when we consider other species. The evil of pain is, in itself, unaffected by the other characteristics of the being that feels the pain; the value of life is affected by these other characteristics.

Normally this will mean that if we have to choose between the life of a human being and the life of another animal we should choose to save the life of the human, but there may be special cases in which the reverse holds true, because the human being in question does not have the capacities of a normal human being. So this view is not speciesist, although it may appear to be at first glance. The preference, in normal cases, for saving a human life over the life of an animal when a choice *has* to be made is a preference based on the characteristics that normal humans have, and not on the mere fact that they are members of our own species. This is why when we consider members of our own

species who lack the characteristics of normal humans we can no longer say that their lives are always to be preferred to those of other animals. In general, the question of when it is wrong to kill (painlessly) an animal is one to which we need give no precise answer. As long as we remember that we should give the same respect to the lives of animals as we give to the lives of those humans at a similar mental level, we shall not go far wrong.

In any case, the conclusions that are argued for here flow from the principle of minimizing suffering alone. The idea that it is also wrong to kill animals painlessly gives some of these conclusions additional support that is welcome, but strictly unnecessary. Interestingly enough, this is true even of the conclusion that we ought to become vegetarians, a conclusion that in the popular mind is generally based on some kind of absolute prohibition on killing.

Endnotes

1. For Bentham's moral philosophy, see his *Introduction to the Principles of Morals and Legislation,* and for Sidgwick's see *The Methods of Ethics* (the passage quoted is from the seventh edition, p. 382). As examples of leading contemporary moral philosophers who incorporate a requirement of equal consideration of interests, see R. M. Hare, *Freedom and Reason* (New York, Oxford University Press, 1963) and John Rawls, *A Theory of Justice* (Cambridge: Harvard University Press, Belknap Press, 1972). For a brief account of the essential agreement on this issue between these and other positions, see R. M. Hare, "Rules of War and Moral Reasoning," *Philosophy and Public Affairs* 1 (1972).
2. Letter to Henri Gregoire, February 25, 1809.
3. Reminiscences by Francis D. Gage, from Susan B. Anthony, *The History of Woman Suffrage,* vol. 1; the passage is to be found in the extract in Leslie Tanner, ed., *Voices from Women's Liberation* (New York: Signet, 1970).
4. I owe the term "speciesism" to Richard Ryder.
5. *Introduction to the Principles of Morals and Legislation,* chapter 17.
6. I am here putting aside religious views, for example the doctrine that all and only humans have immortal souls, or are made in the image of God. Historically these views have been very important, and no doubt are partly responsible for the idea that human life has a special sanctity. Logically, however, these religious views are unsatisfactory, since a reasoned explanation of why it should be that all humans and no nonhumans have immortal souls is not offered. This belief too, therefore, comes under suspicion as a form of speciesism. In any case, defenders of the "sanctity of life" view are generally reluctant to base their position on purely religious

doctrines, since these doctrines are no longer as widely accepted as they once were.

REVIEW QUESTIONS

1. Explain the principle of equality that Singer adopts.
2. How does Singer define speciesism?
3. What is the sanctity of life view? Why does Singer reject this view?

DISCUSSION QUESTIONS

1. Is speciesism analogous to racism and sexism? Why, or why not?
2. Is there anything wrong with killing animals painlessly? Defend your view.
3. Do human interests outweigh animal interests? Explain your position.

Bonnie Steinbock

Speciesism and the Idea of Equality

For biographical information on Steinbock, see her reading in Chapter 3.

Steinbock presents a defense of speciesism, the practice of weighing human interests more heavily than those of animals. While she agrees with Singer that nonhuman pain and suffering deserve some moral consideration, she denies that this consideration should be equal to that given to humans. She claims that humans have morally relevant capacities that nonhuman animals do not have, and this entitles humans to greater moral consideration. These capacities include the ability to be morally responsible, to reciprocate in ways that animals cannot, and to desire self-respect.

Most of us believe that we are entitled to treat members of other species in ways which would be considered wrong if inflicted on members of our own species. We kill them for food, keep them confined, use them in painful experiments. The moral philosopher has to ask what relevant difference justifies this difference in

From Bonnie Steinbock, "Speciesism and the Idea of Equality," *Philosophy* 53, no. 204 (April 1978): 247–256. Copyright 1978 © Cambridge University Press. Reprinted with the permission of the author and Cambridge University Press.

treatment. A look at this question will lead us to re-examine the distinctions which we have assumed make a moral difference.

It has been suggested by Peter Singer[1] that our current attitudes are 'speciesist', a word intended to make one think of 'racist' or 'sexist'. The idea is that membership in a species is in itself not relevant to moral treatment, and that much of our behaviour and attitudes towards non-human animals is based simply on this irrelevant fact.

There is, however, an important difference between racism or sexism and 'speciesism'. We do not subject animals to different moral treatment simply because they have fur and feathers, but because they are in fact different from human beings in ways that could be morally relevant. It is false that women are incapable of being benefited by education, and therefore that claim cannot serve to justify preventing them from attending school. But this is not false of cows and dogs, even chimpanzees. Intelligence is thought to be a morally relevant capacity because of its relation to the capacity for moral responsibility.

What is Singer's response? He agrees that non-human animals lack certain capacities that human animals possess, and that this may justify different *treatment*. But it does not justify giving less consideration to their needs and interests. According to Singer, the moral mistake which the racist or sexist makes is not essentially the factual error of thinking that blacks or women are inferior to white men. For even if there were no factual error, even if it were true that blacks and women are less intelligent and responsible than whites and men, this would not justify giving less consideration to their needs and interests. It is important to note that the term 'speciesism' is in one way like, and in another way unlike, the terms 'racism' and 'sexism'. What the term 'speciesism' has in common with these terms is the reference to focusing on a characteristic which is, in itself, irrelevant to moral treatment. And it is worth reminding us of this. But Singer's real aim is to bring us to a new understanding of the idea of equality. The question is, on what do claims to equality rest? The demand for *human* equality is a demand that the interests of all human beings be considered equally, unless there is a moral justification for not doing so. But why should the interests of all human beings be considered equally? In order to answer this question, we have to give some sense to the phrase, 'All-men (human beings) are created equal'. Human beings are manifestly *not* equal, differing greatly in intelligence, virtue and capacities. In virtue of what can the claim to equality be made?

It is Singer's contention that claims to equality do not rest on factual equality. Not only do human beings differ in their capacities, but it might even turn out that intelligence, the capacity for virtue, etc., are not distributed evenly among the races and sexes:

The appropriate response to those who claim to have found evidence of genetically based differences in ability between the races or sexes is not to stick to the belief that the genetic explanation must be wrong, whatever evidence to the contrary may turn up; instead we should make it quite clear that the claim to equality does not depend on intelligence, moral capacity, physical strength, or similar matters of fact. Equality is a moral ideal, not a simple assertion of fact. There is no logically compelling reason for assuming that a factual difference in ability between two people justifies any difference in the amount of consideration we give to satisfying their needs and interests. The principle of equality of human beings is not a description of an alleged actual equality among humans: it is a prescription of how we should treat humans.[2]

In so far as the subject is human equality, Singer's view is supported by other philoso-phers. Bernard Williams, for example, is concerned to show that demands for equality cannot rest on factual equality among people, for no such equality exists.[3] The only respect in which all men are equal, according to Williams, is that they are all equally men. This seems to be a platitude, but Williams denies that it is trivial. Membership in the species *homo sapiens* in itself has no special moral significance, but rather the fact that all men are human serves as a *reminder* that being human involves the possession of characteristics that are morally relevant. But on what characteristics does Williams focus? Aside from the desire for self-respect (which I will discuss later), Williams is not concerned with uniquely human capacities. Rather, he focuses on the capacity to feel pain and the capacity to feel affection. It is in virtue of these capacities, it seems, that the idea of equality is to be justified.

Apparently Richard Wasserstrom has the same idea as he sets out the racist's 'logical and moral mistakes' in 'Rights, Human Rights and Racial Discrimination'.[4] The racist fails to acknowledge that the black person is as capable of suffering as the white person. According to Wasserstrom, the reason why a person is said to have a right not to be made to suffer acute physical pain is that we all do in fact value freedom from such pain. Therefore, if anyone has a right to be free from suffering acute physical pain, *everyone* has this right, for there is no possible basis of discrimination. Wasserstrom says, 'For, if all persons do have equal capacities of these sorts and if the existence of these capacities is the reason for ascribing these rights to anyone, then all persons ought to have the right to claim equality of treatment in respect to the possession and exercise of these rights'.[5] The basis of equality, for Wasserstrom as for Williams, lies not in some uniquely human capacity, but rather in the fact that all human beings are alike in their capacity to suffer. Writers on equality have focused on this capacity, I think, because it functions as some sort of lowest common denominator, so that whatever the other capacities of a human being, he is entitled to equal consideration because, like everyone else, he is capable of suffering.

If the capacity to suffer is the reason for ascribing a right to freedom from acute pain, or a right to well being, then it certainly looks as though these rights must be extended to animals as well. This is the conclusion Singer arrives at. The demand for human equality rests on the equal capacity of all human beings to suffer and to enjoy well being. But if this is the basis of the demand for equality, then this demand must include all beings which have an equal capacity to suffer and enjoy well being. That is why Singer places at the basis of the demand for equality, not intelligence or reason, but sentience. And equality will mean, not equality of treatment, but 'equal consideration of interests'. The equal consideration of interests will often mean quite different treatment, depending on the nature of the entity being considered. (It would be as absurd to talk of a dog's right to vote, Singer says, as to talk of a man's right to have an abortion.)

It might be thought that the issue of equality depends on a discussion of rights. According to this line of thought, animals do not merit equal consideration of interests because, unlike human beings, they do not, or cannot, have rights. But I am not going to discuss rights, important as the issue is. The fact that an entity does not have rights does not necessarily imply that its interests are going to count for less than the interests of entities which are right-bearers. According to the view of rights held by H. L. A. Hart and S. I. Benn, infants do not have rights, nor do the mentally defective, nor do the insane, in so far as they all lack certain minimal conceptual capabilities for having rights.[6] Yet it certainly does not seem that either Hart or Benn would agree that *therefore* their interests are to be counted for less, or that it is morally permissible to treat them in ways in which it would not be permissible to treat right-bearers. It seems to mean only that we must give different sorts of reasons for our obligations to take into consideration the interests of those who do not have rights.

We have reasons concerning the treatment of other people which are clearly independent of the notion of rights. We would say that it is wrong to punch someone because doing that infringes his rights. But we could also say that it is wrong because doing that hurts him, and that is, ordinarily, enough of a reason not to do it. Now this particular reason extends not only to

human beings, but to all sentient creatures. One has a *prima facie* reason not to pull the cat's tail (whether or not the cat has rights) because it hurts the cat. And this is the only thing, normally, which is relevant in this case. The fact that the cat is not a 'rational being', that it is not capable of moral responsibility, that it cannot make free choices or shape its life—all of these differences from us have nothing to do with the justifiability of pulling its tail. Does this show that rationality and the rest of it are irrelevant to moral treatment?

I hope to show that this is not the case. But first I want to point out that the issue is not one of cruelty to animals. We all agree that cruelty is wrong, whether perpetrated on a moral or non-moral, rational or non-rational agent. Cruelty is defined as the infliction of unnecessary pain or suffering. What is to count as necessary or unnecessary is determined, in part, by the nature of the end pursued. Torturing an animal is cruel, because although the pain is logically necessary for the action to be torture, the end (deriving enjoyment from seeing the animal suffer) is monstrous. Allowing animals to suffer from neglect or for the sake of large profits may also be thought to be unnecessary and therefore cruel. But there may be some ends, which are very good (such as the advancement of medical knowledge), which can be accomplished by subjecting animals to pain in experiments. Although most people would agree that the pain inflicted on animals used in medical research ought to be kept to a minimum, they would consider pain that cannot be eliminated 'necessary' and therefore not cruel. It would probably not be so regarded if the subjects were non-voluntary human beings. Necessity, then, is defined in terms of human benefit, but this is just what is being called into question. The topic of cruelty to animals, while important from a practical viewpoint, because much of our present treatment of animals involves the infliction of suffering for no good reason, is not very interesting philosophically. What is philosophically interesting is whether we are justified in having different standards of necessity for human suffering and for animal suffering.

Singer says, quite rightly I think, 'If a being suffers, there can be no moral justification for refusing to take that suffering into consideration'.[7] But he thinks that the principle of equality requires that, no matter what the nature of the being, its suffering be counted equally with the like suffering of any other being. In other words sentience does not simply provide us with reasons for acting; it is the *only* relevant consideration for equal consideration of interests. It is this view that I wish to challenge.

I want to challenge it partly because it has such counter-intuitive results. It means, for example, that feeding starving children before feeding starving dogs is just like a Catholic charity's feeding hungry Catholics before feeding hungry non-Catholics. It is simply a matter of taking care of one's own, something which is usually morally permissible. But whereas we would admire the Catholic agency which did not discriminate, but fed all children, first come, first served, we would feel quite differently about someone who had this policy for dogs and children. Nor is this, it seems to me, simply a matter of a sentimental preference for our own species. I might feel much more love for my dog than for a strange child—and yet I might feel morally obliged to feed the child before I fed my dog. If I gave in to the feelings of love and fed my dog and let the child go hungry, I would probably feel guilty. This is not to say that we can simply rely on such feelings. Huck Finn felt guilty at helping Jim escape, which he viewed as stealing from a woman who had never done him any harm. But while the existence of such feelings does not settle the morality of an issue, it is not clear to me that they can be explained away. In any event, their existence can serve as a motivation for trying to find a rational justification for considering human interests above non-human ones.

However, it does seem to me that this *requires* a justification. Until now, common sense (and academic philosophy) have seen no such need. Benn says, 'No one claims equal consideration for all mammals—human beings count, mice do not, though it would not be easy to say *why* not. . . . Although we hesitate to inflict unnecessary pain on sentient creatures, such as mice or dogs, we are quite sure that we do not need to show good reasons for putting human interests before theirs'.[8]

I think we do have to justify counting our interests more heavily than those of animals. But how? Singer is right, I think, to point out that it will not do to refer vaguely to the greater value of human life, to human worth and dignity:

Faced with a situation in which they see a need for some basis for the moral gulf that is commonly thought to separate humans and animals, but can find no concrete difference that will do this without undermining the equality of humans, philosophers tend to waffle. They resort to high-sounding phrases like 'the intrinsic dignity of the human individual'. They talk of 'the intrinsic worth of all men' as if men had some worth that other beings do not have or they say that human beings, and only human beings, are 'ends in themselves', while 'everything other than a person can only have value for a person'. . . . Why should we not attribute 'intrinsic dignity' or 'intrinsic worth' to ourselves? Why should we not say that we are the only things in the universe that have intrinsic value? Our fellow human beings are unlikely to reject the accolades we so generously bestow upon them and those to whom we deny the honour are unable to object.[9]

Singer is right to be sceptical of terms like 'intrinsic dignity' and 'intrinsic worth'. These phrases are no substitute for a moral argument. But they may point to one. In trying to understand what is meant by these phrases, we may find a difference or differences between human beings and non-human animals that will justify different treatment while not undermining claims for human equality. While we are not compelled to discriminate among people because of different capacities, if we can find a significant difference in capacities between human and non-human animals, this could serve to justify regarding human interests as primary. It is not arbitrary or smug, I think, to maintain that human beings have a different moral status from members of other species because of certain capacities which are characteristic of being human. We may not all be equal in these capacities, but all human beings possess them to some measure, and non-human animals do not. For example, human beings are normally held to be responsible for what they do. In recognizing that someone is responsible for his or her actions, you accord that person a respect which is reserved for those possessed of moral autonomy, or capable of achieving such autonomy. Secondly, human beings can be expected to reciprocate in a way that non-human animals cannot. Non-human animals cannot be motivated by altruistic or moral reasons; they cannot treat you fairly or unfairly. This does not rule out the possibility of an animal being motivated by sympathy or pity. It does rule out altruistic motivation in the sense of motivation due to the recognition that the needs and interests of others provide one with certain reasons for acting.[10] Human beings are capable of altruistic motivation in this sense. We are sometimes motivated simply by the recognition that someone else is in pain, and that pain is a bad thing, no matter who suffers it. It is this sort of reason that I claim cannot motivate an animal or any entity not possessed of fairly abstract concepts. (If some non-human animals do possess the requisite concepts—perhaps chimpanzees who have learned a language—they might well be capable of altruistic motivation.) This means that our moral dealings with animals are necessarily much more limited than our dealings with other human beings. If rats invade our houses, carrying disease and biting our children, we cannot reason with them, hoping to persuade them of the injustice they do us. We can only attempt to get rid of them. And it is this that makes it reasonable for us to accord them a separate and not equal moral status, even though their capacity to suffer provides us with some reason to kill them painlessly, if this can be done without too much sacrifice of human interests. Thirdly, as Williams points out, there is the 'desire for self-respect': 'a certain human desire to be identified with what one is doing, to be able to realize purposes of one's own, and not to be the instrument of another's will unless one has willingly accepted such a role'.[11] Some animals may have some form of this desire, and to the extent that they do, we ought to consider their interest in freedom and self-determination. (Such considerations might affect our attitudes toward zoos and circuses.) But the desire for self-respect *per se* requires the intellectual capacities of human beings, and this desire provides us with special reasons not to treat human beings

in certain ways. It is an affront to the dignity of a human being to be a slave (even if a well-treated one); this cannot be true for a horse or a cow. To point this out is of course only to say that the justification for the treatment of an entity will depend on the sort of entity in question. In our treatment of other entities, we must consider the desire for autonomy, dignity and respect, but only where such a desire exists. Recognition of different desires and interests will often require different treatment, a point Singer himself makes.

But is the issue simply one of different desires and interests justifying and requiring different treatment? I would like to make a stronger claim, namely, that certain capacities, which seem to be unique to human beings, entitle their possessors to a privileged position in the moral community. Both rats and human beings dislike pain, and so we have a *prima facie* reason not to inflict pain on either. But if we can free human beings from crippling diseases, pain and death through experimentation which involves making animals suffer, and if this is the only way to achieve such results, then I think that such experimentation is justified because human lives are more valuable than animal lives. And this is because of certain capacities and abilities that normal human beings have which animals apparently do not, and which human beings cannot exercise if they are devastated by pain or disease.

My point is not that the lack of the sorts of capacities I have been discussing gives us a justification for treating animals just as we like, but rather that it is these differences between human beings and non-human animals which provide a rational basis for different moral treatment and consideration. Singer focuses on sentience alone as the basis of equality, but we can justify the belief that human beings have a moral worth that non-human animals do not, in virtue of specific capacities, and without resorting to 'highsounding phrases'.

Singer thinks that intelligence, the capacity for moral responsibility, for virtue, etc., are irrelevant to equality, because we would not accept a hierarchy based on intelligence any more than one based on race. We do not think that those with greater capacities ought to have their interests weighed more heavily than those with lesser capacities, and this, he thinks, shows that differences in such capacities are irrelevant to equality. But it does not show this at all. Kevin Donaghy argues (rightly, I think) that what entitles us human beings to a privileged position in the moral community is a certain minimal level of intelligence, which is a prerequisite for morally relevant capacities.[12] The fact that we would reject a hierarchical society based on degree of intelligence does not show that a minimal level of intelligence cannot be used as a cut-off point, justifying giving greater consideration to the interests of those entities which meet this standard.

Interestingly enough, Singer concedes the rationality of valuing the lives of normal human beings over the lives of non-human animals.[13] We are not required to value equally the life of a normal human being and the life of an animal, he thinks, but only their suffering. But I doubt that the value of an entity's life can be separated from the value of its suffering in this way. If we value the lives of human beings more than the lives of animals, this is because we value certain capacities that human beings have and animals do not. But freedom from suffering is, in general, a minimal condition for exercising these capacities, for living a fully human life. So, valuing human life more involves regarding human interests as counting for more. That is why we regard human suffering as more deplorable than comparable animal suffering.

But there is one point of Singer's which I have not yet met. Some human beings (if only a very few) are less intelligent than some non-human animals. Some have less capacity for moral choice and responsibility. What status in the moral community are these members of our species to occupy? Are their interests to be considered equally with ours? Is experimenting on them permissible where such experiments are painful or injurious, but somehow necessary for human well being? If it is certain of our capacities which entitle us to a privileged position, it looks as if those lacking those capacities are not entitled to a privileged position. To think it is justifiable to experiment on an adult chimpanzee but not on a severely mentally incapacitated human being seems to be focusing on member-

ship in a species where that has no moral relevance. (It is being 'speciesist' in a perfectly reasonable use of the word.) How are we to meet this challenge?

Donaghy is untroubled by this objection. He says that it is fully in accord with his intuitions, that he regards the killing of a normally intelligent human being as far more serious than the killing of a person so severely limited that he lacked the intellectual capacities of an adult pig. But this parry really misses the point. The question is whether Donaghy thinks that the killing of a human being so severely limited that he lacked the intellectual capacities of an adult pig would be less serious than the killing of that pig. If superior intelligence is what justifies privileged status in the moral community, then the pig who is smarter than a human being ought to have superior moral status. And I doubt that this is fully in accord with Donaghy's intuitions.

I doubt that anyone will be able to come up with a concrete and morally relevant difference that would justify, say, using a chimpanzee in an experiment rather than a human being with less capacity for reasoning, moral responsibility, etc. Should we then experiment on the severely retarded? Utilitarian considerations aside (the difficulty of comparing intelligence between species, for example), we feel a special obligation to care for the handicapped members of our own species, who cannot survive in this world without such care. Non-human animals manage very well, despite their 'lower intelligence' and lesser capacities; most of them do not require special care from us. This does not, of course, justify experimenting on them. However, to subject to experimentation those people who depend on us seems even worse than subjecting members of other species to it. In addition, when we consider the severely retarded, we think, 'That could be me'. It makes sense to think that one might have been born retarded, but not to think that one might have been born a monkey. And so, although one can imagine oneself in the monkey's place, one feels a closer identification with the severely retarded human being. Here we are getting away from such things as 'morally relevant differences' and are talking about something much more difficult to articulate, namely, the role of feeling and sentiment in moral thinking. We would be *horrified* by the use of the retarded in medical research. But what are we to make of this horror? Has it moral significance or is it 'mere' sentiment, of no more importance than the sentiment of whites against blacks? It is terribly difficult to know how to evaluate such feelings.[14] I am not going to say more about this, because I think that the treatment of severely incapacitated human beings does not pose an insurmountable objection to the privileged status principle. I am willing to admit that my horror at the thought of experiments being performed on severely mentally incapacitated human beings in cases in which I would find it justifiable and prefer able to perform the same experiments on non-human animals (capable of similar suffering) may not be a moral emotion. But it is certainly not wrong of us to extend special care to members of our own species, motivated by feelings of sympathy, protectiveness, etc. If this is speciesism, it is stripped of its tone of moral condemnation. It is not racist to provide special care to members of your own race; it is racist to fall below your moral obligation to a person because of his or her race. I have been arguing that we are morally obliged to consider the interests of all sentient creatures, but not to consider those interests equally with human interests. Nevertheless, even this recognition will mean some radical changes in our attitude toward and treatment of other species.[15]

Endnotes

1. Peter Singer, *Animal Liberation* (A New York Review Book, 1975).
2. Singer, 5.
3. Bernard Williams, 'The Idea of Equality', *Philosophy, Politics and Society* (Second Series), Laslett and Runciman (eds.) (Blackwell, 1962), 110–113, reprinted in *Moral Concepts,* Feinberg (ed.) (Oxford, 1970), 153–171.
4. Richard Wasserstrom, 'Rights, Human Rights, and Racial Discrimination', *Journal of Philosophy* 61, No. 20 (1964), reprinted in *Human Rights,* A. I. Melden (ed.) (Wadsworth, 1970), 96–110.
5. Ibid., 106.
6. H. L. A. Hart, 'Are There Any Natural Rights?', *Philosophical Review* 64 (1955), and S. I. Benn, 'Abortion, Infanticide, and Respect for Persons', *The Problem of Abortion,* Feinberg (ed.) (Wadsworth, 1973), 92–104.
7. Singer, 9.
8. Benn 'Equality, Moral and Social', *The Encyclopedia of Philosophy* 3, 40.
9. Singer, 266–267.
10. This conception of altruistic motivation comes from Thomas Nagel's *The Possibility of Altruism* (Oxford, 1970).
11. Williams, op. cit., 157.
12. Kevin Donaghy, 'Singer on Speciesism', *Philosophic Exchange* (Summer 1974).
13. Singer, 22.
14. We run into the same problem when discussing abortion. Of what significance are our feelings toward the unborn when discussing its status? Is it relevant or irrelevant that it looks like a human being?
15. I would like to acknowledge the help of, and offer thanks to, Professor Richard Arneson of the University of California, San Diego; Professor Sidney Gendin of Eastern Michigan University; and Professor Peter Singer of Monash University, all of whom read and commented on earlier drafts of this paper.

REVIEW QUESTIONS

1. According to Steinbock, what is the important difference between racism or sexism and speciesism?
2. What is the basis for equality according to Singer, Williams, Wasserstrom, and Steinbock?
3. Steinbock claims that Singer's view has counterintuitive results. What are they?
4. According to Steinbock, why are we justified in counting human interests more heavily than those of animals?

DISCUSSION QUESTIONS

1. Steinbock maintains that we should give greater moral consideration to severely mentally incapacitated humans than to animals that may have a greater mental capacity. Does she give good reasons for this? How would Singer reply?
2. Do Steinbock's criticisms of Singer also apply to Regan? Explain your answer.
3. Suppose that alien beings settle on the earth. They are superior to humans in intelligence, moral virtue, desire for self-respect, and so on. What is their moral status? Are they equal to humans? Do they have a higher moral status, just as humans have a higher moral status than animals? What would Steinbock say? What do you think?

Tom Regan

The Case for Animal Rights

Tom Regan is professor of philosophy at North Carolina State University. He has written numerous books and articles, and he has edited several textbooks. His recent books on the subject of animal rights include All That Dwell Therein: Essays on Animal Rights and Environmental Ethics *(1982) and* The Case for Animal Rights *(1984). Also, he is a coeditor of* Animal Rights and Human Obligation, *second edition (1989).*

Regan defends the view that animals have rights based on their inherent value as experiencing subjects of a life. He attacks other views including indirect-duty views, the cruelty-kindness view (as he calls it), and even Singer's Utilitarianism. Although he agrees with Singer that our treatment of animals is wrong and that speciesism is unjust, he denies that it is wrong because of animal suffering. Instead he thinks that our treatment of animals is wrong because we violate the rights of animals.

I regard myself as an advocate of animal rights—as a part of the animal rights movement. That movement, as I conceive it, is committed to a number of goals, including:

the total abolition of the use of animals in science;

the total dissolution of commercial animal agriculture;

the total elimination of commercial and sport hunting and trapping.

There are, I know, people who profess to believe in animal rights but do not avow these goals.

From Tom Regan, "The Case for Animal Rights," *In Defense of Animals,* ed. Peter Singer (New York: Perennial Library, 1986; originally published by Blackwell, 1985). Reprinted by permission of Blackwell Publishers.

Factory farming, they say, is wrong—it violates animals' rights—but traditional animal agriculture is all right. Toxicity tests of cosmetics on animals violates their rights, but important medical research—cancer research, for example—does not. The clubbing of baby seals is abhorrent, but not the harvesting of adult seals. I used to think I understood this reasoning. Not any more. You don't change unjust institutions by tidying them up.

What's wrong—fundamentally wrong—with the way animals are treated isn't the details that vary from case to case. It's the whole system. The forlornness of the veal calf is pathetic, heart wrenching; the pulsing pain of the chimp with electrodes planted deep in her brain is repulsive; the slow, tortuous death of the racoon caught in the leg-hold trap is agonizing. But what is wrong isn't the pain, isn't the suffering, isn't the deprivation. These compound what's wrong. Sometimes—often—they make it much, much worse. But they are not the fundamental wrong.

The fundamental wrong is the system that allows us to view animals as *our resources,* here for *us*—to be eaten, or surgically manipulated, or exploited for sport or money. Once we accept this view of animals—as our resources—the rest is as predictable as it is regrettable. Why worry about their loneliness, their pain, their death? Since animals exist for us, to benefit us in one way or another, what harms them really doesn't matter—or matters only if it starts to bother us, makes us feel a trifle uneasy when we eat our veal escalope, for example. So, yes, let us get veal calves out of solitary confinement, give them more space, a little straw, a few companions. But let us keep our veal escalope.

But a little straw, more space and a few companions won't eliminate—won't even touch—the basic wrong that attaches to our viewing and treating these animals as our resources. A veal calf killed to be eaten after living in close confinement is viewed and treated in this way: but so, too, is another who is raised (as they say) 'more humanely'. To right the wrong of our treatment of farm animals requires more than making rearing methods 'more humane'; it requires the total dissolution of commercial animal agriculture.

How we do this, whether we do it or, as in the case of animals in science, whether and how we abolish their use—these are to a large extent political questions. People must change their beliefs before they change their habits. Enough people, especially those elected to public office, must believe in change—must want it—before we will have laws that protect the rights of animals. This process of change is very complicated, very demanding, very exhausting, calling for the efforts of many hands in education, publicity, political organization and activity, down to the licking of envelopes and stamps. As a trained and practising philosopher, the sort of contribution I can make is limited but, I like to think, important. The currency of philosophy is ideas—their meaning and rational foundation—not the nuts and bolts of the legislative process, say, or the mechanics of community organization. That's what I have been exploring over the past ten years or so in my essays and talks and, most recently, in my book, *The Case for Animal Rights*. I believe the major conclusions I reach in the book are true because they are supported by the weight of the best arguments. I believe the idea of animal rights has reason, not just emotion, on its side.

In the space I have at my disposal here I can only sketch, in the barest outline, some of the main features of the book. Its main themes—and we should not be surprised by this—involve asking and answering deep, foundational moral questions about what morality is, how it should be understood and what is the best moral theory, all considered. I hope I can convey something of the shape I think this theory takes. The attempt to do this will be (to use a word a friendly critic once used to describe my work) cerebral, perhaps too cerebral. But this is misleading. My feelings about how animals are sometimes treated run just as deep and just as strong as those of my more volatile compatriots. Philosophers do—to use the jargon of the day—have a right side to their brains. If it's the left side we contribute (or mainly should), that's because what talents we have reside there.

How to proceed? We begin by asking how the moral status of animals has been understood by thinkers who deny that animals have rights. Then we test the mettle of their ideas by seeing how well they stand up under the heat of fair criticism. If we start our thinking in this way, we soon find that some people believe that we have no duties directly to animals, that we owe nothing to them, that we can do nothing that wrongs them. Rather, we can do wrong acts that involve animals, and so we have duties regarding them, though none to them. Such views may be called indirect duty views. By way of illustration: suppose your neighbour kicks your dog. Then your neighbour has done something wrong. But not to your dog. The wrong that has been done is a wrong to you. After all, it is wrong to upset people, and your neighbour's kicking your dog upsets you. So you are the one who is wronged, not your dog. Or again: by kicking your dog your neighbour damages your property. And since it is wrong to damage another person's property, your neighbour has done something wrong—to you, of course, not to your dog. Your neighbour no more wrongs your dog than your car would be wronged if the windshield were smashed. Your neighbour's duties involving your dog are indirect duties to you. More generally, all of our duties regarding animals are indirect duties to one another—to humanity.

How could someone try to justify such a view? Someone might say that your dog doesn't feel anything and so isn't hurt by your neighbour's kick, doesn't care about the pain since none is felt, is as unaware of anything as is your windshield. Someone might say this, but no rational person will, since, among other considerations, such a view will commit anyone who holds it to the position that no human being feels pain either—that human beings don't care about what happens to them. A second possibility is that though both humans and your dog are hurt when kicked, it is only human pain that matters. But, again, no rational person can believe this. Pain is pain wherever it occurs. If your neighbour's causing you pain is wrong because of the pain that is caused, we cannot rationally ignore or dismiss the moral relevance of the pain that your dog feels.

Philosophers who hold indirect duty views—and many still do—have come to understand that they must avoid the two defects just noted: that is, both the view that animals don't feel anything as well as the idea that only human pain can be morally relevant. Among such thinkers the sort of view now favoured is one or other form of what is called *contractarianism*.

Here, very crudely, is the root idea: morality consists of a set of rules that individuals voluntarily agree to abide by, as we do when we sign a contract (hence the name contractarianism). Those who understand and accept the terms of the contract are covered directly; they have rights created and recognized by, and protected in, the contract. And these contractors can also have protection spelled out for others who, though they lack the ability to understand morality and so cannot sign the contract themselves, are loved or cherished by those who can. Thus young children, for example, are unable to sign contracts and lack rights. But they are protected by the contract none the less because of the sentimental interests of others, most notably their parents. So we have, then, duties involving these children, duties regarding them, but no duties to them. Our duties in their case are indirect duties to other human beings, usually their parents.

As for animals, since they cannot understand contracts, they obviously cannot sign; and since they cannot sign, they have no rights. Like children, however, some animals are the objects of the sentimental interest of others. You, for example, love your dog or cat. So those animals that enough people care about (companion animals, whales, baby seals, the American bald eagle), though they lack rights themselves, will be protected because of the sentimental interests of people. I have, then, according to contractarianism, no duty directly to your dog or any other animal, not even the duty not to cause them pain or suffering; my duty not to hurt them is a duty I have to those people who care about what happens to them. As for other animals, where no or little sentimental interest is present—in the case of farm animals, for example, or laboratory rats—what duties we have grow weaker and weaker, perhaps to vanishing point. The pain and death they endure, though real, are not wrong if no one cares about them.

When it comes to the moral status of animals, contractarianism could be a hard view to refute if it were an adequate theoretical approach to the moral status of human beings. It is not adequate in this latter respect, however, which makes the question of its adequacy in the former case, regarding animals, utterly moot. For consider: morality, according to the (crude) contractarian position before us, consists of rules that people agree to abide by. What people? Well, enough to make a difference—enough, that is, *collectively* to have the power to enforce the rules that are drawn up in the contract. That is very well and good for the signatories but not so good for anyone who is not asked to sign. And there is nothing in contractarianism of the sort we are discussing that guarantees or requires that everyone will have a chance to participate equally in framing the rules of morality. The result is that this approach to ethics could sanction the most blatant forms of social, economic, moral and political injustice, ranging from a repressive caste system to systematic racial or sexual discrimination. Might, according to this theory, does make right. Let those who are the victims of injustice suffer as they will. It matters not so long as no one else—no contractor, or too few of them—cares about it. Such a theory takes one's moral breath away . . . as if, for example, there would be nothing wrong with apartheid in South Africa if few white South Africans were upset by it. A theory with so little to recommend it at the level of the ethics of our treatment of our fellow humans cannot have anything more to recommend it when it comes to the ethics of how we treat our fellow animals.

The version of contractarianism just examined is, as I have noted, a crude variety, and in fairness to those of a contractarian persuasion it must be noted that much more refined, subtle and ingenious varieties are possible. For example, John Rawls, in his *A Theory of Justice,* sets forth a version of contractarianism that forces contractors to ignore the accidental features of being a human being—for example, whether one is white or black, male or female, a genius or of modest intellect. Only by ignoring such features, Rawls believes, can we ensure that the principles of justice that contractors would agree upon are not based on bias or prejudice. Despite the improvement a view such as Rawls's represents over the cruder forms of contractarianism, it remains deficient: it systematically denies that we have direct duties to those human beings who do not have a sense of justice—young children, for instance, and many mentally retarded humans. And yet it seems reasonably certain that, were we to torture a young child or a retarded elder, we would be doing something that wronged him or her, not something that would be wrong if (and only if) other humans with a sense of justice were upset. And since this is true in the case of these humans, we cannot rationally deny the same in the case of animals.

Indirect duty views, then, including the best among them, fail to command our rational assent. Whatever ethical theory we should accept rationally, therefore, it must at least recognize that we have some duties directly to animals, just as we have some duties directly to each other. The next two theories I'll sketch attempt to meet this requirement.

The first I call the cruelty-kindness view. Simply stated, this says that we have a direct duty to be kind to animals and a direct duty not to be cruel to them. Despite the familiar, reassuring ring of these ideas, I do not believe that this view offers an adequate theory. To make this clearer, consider kindness. A kind person acts from a certain kind of motive—compassion or concern, for example. And that is a virtue. But there is no guarantee that a kind act is a right act. If I am a generous racist, for example, I will be inclined to act kindly towards members of my own race, favouring their interests above those of others. My kindness would be real and, so far as it goes, good. But I trust it is too obvious to require argument that my kind acts may not be above moral reproach—may, in fact, be positively wrong because rooted in injustice. So kindness, notwithstanding its status as a virtue to be encouraged, simply will not carry the weight of a theory of right action.

Cruelty fares no better. People or their acts are cruel if they display either a lack of sympathy for or, worse, the presence of enjoyment in another's suffering. Cruelty in all its guises is a bad thing, a tragic human failing. But just as

a person's being motivated by kindness does not guarantee that he or she does what is right, so the absence of cruelty does not ensure that he or she avoids doing what is wrong. Many people who perform abortions, for example, are not cruel, sadistic people. But that fact alone does not settle the terribly difficult question of the morality of abortion. The case is no different when we examine the ethics of our treatment of animals. So, yes, let us be for kindness and against cruelty. But let us not suppose that being for the one and against the other answers questions about moral right and wrong.

Some people think that the theory we are looking for is utilitarianism. A utilitarian accepts two moral principles. The first is that of equality: everyone's interests count, and similar interests must be counted as having similar weight or importance. White or black, American or Iranian, human or animal—everyone's pain or frustration matter, and matter just as much as the equivalent pain or frustration of anyone else. The second principle a utilitarian accepts is that of utility: do the act that will bring about the best balance between satisfaction and frustration for everyone affected by the outcome.

As a utilitarian, then, here is how I am to approach the task of deciding what I morally ought to do: I must ask who will be affected if I choose to do one thing rather than another, how much each individual will be affected, and where the best results are most likely to lie—which option, in other words, is most likely to bring about the best results, the best balance between satisfaction and frustration. That option, whatever it may be, is the one I ought to choose. That is where my moral duty lies.

The great appeal of utilitarianism rests with its uncompromising *egalitarianism*: everyone's interests count and count as much as the like interests of everyone else. The kind of odious discrimination that some forms of contractarianism can justify—discrimination based on race or sex, for example—seems disallowed in principle by utilitarianism, as is speciesism, systematic discrimination based on species membership.

The equality we find in utilitarianism, however, is not the sort an advocate of animal or human rights should have in mind. Utilitarianism has no room for the equal moral rights of different individuals because it has no room for their equal inherent value or worth. What has value for the utilitarian is the satisfaction of an individual's interests, not the individual whose interests they are. A universe in which you satisfy your desire for water, food and warmth is, other things being equal, better than a universe in which these desires are frustrated. And the same is true in the case of an animal with similar desires. But neither you nor the animal have any value in your own right. Only your feelings do.

Here is an analogy to help make the philosophical point clearer: a cup contains different liquids, sometimes sweet, sometimes bitter, sometimes a mix of the two. What has value are the liquids: the sweeter the better, the bitterer the worse. The cup, the container, has no value. It is what goes into it, not what they go into, that has value. For the utilitarian you and I are like the cup; we have no value as individuals and thus no equal value. What has value is what goes into us, what we serve as receptacles for; our feelings of satisfaction have positive value, our feelings of frustration negative value.

Serious problems arise for utilitarianism when we remind ourselves that it enjoins us to bring about the best consequences. What does this mean? It doesn't mean the best consequences for me alone, or for my family or friends, or any other person taken individually. No, what we must do is, roughly, as follows: we must add up (somehow!) the separate satisfactions and frustrations of everyone likely to be affected by our choice, the satisfactions in one column, the frustrations in the other. We must total each column for each of the options before us. That is what it means to say the theory is aggregative. And then we must choose that option which is most likely to bring about the best balance of totalled satisfactions over totalled frustrations. Whatever act would lead to this outcome is the one we ought morally to perform—it is where our moral duty lies. And that act quite clearly might not be the same one that would bring about the best results for me personally, or for my family or friends, or for a lab animal. The best aggregated consequences for everyone concerned are not necessarily the best for each individual.

That utilitarianism is an aggregative theory— different individuals' satisfactions or frustrations are added, or summed, or totalled—is the key objection to this theory. My Aunt Bea is old, inactive, a cranky, sour person, though not physically ill. She prefers to go on living. She is also rather rich. I could make a fortune if I could get my hands on her money, money she intends to give me in any event, after she dies, but which she refuses to give me now. In order to avoid a huge tax bite, I plan to donate a handsome sum of my profits to a local children's hospital. Many, many children will benefit from my generosity, and much joy will be brought to their parents, relatives and friends. If I don't get the money rather soon, all these ambitions will come to naught. The once-in-a-lifetime opportunity to make a real killing will be gone. Why, then, not kill my Aunt Bea? Oh, of course I *might* get caught. But I'm no fool and, besides, her doctor can be counted on to co-operate (he has an eye for the same investment and I happen to know a good deal about his shady past). The deed can be done . . . professionally, shall we say. There is *very* little chance of getting caught. And as for my conscience being guilt-ridden, I am a resourceful sort of fellow and will take more than sufficient comfort—as I lie on the beach at Acapulco—in contemplating the joy and health I have brought to so many others.

Suppose Aunt Bea is killed and the rest of the story comes out as told. Would I have done anything wrong? Anything immoral? One would have thought that I had. Not according to utilitarianism. Since what I have done has brought about the best balance between totalled satisfaction and frustration for all those affected by the outcome, my action is not wrong. Indeed, in killing Aunt Bea the physician and I did what duty required.

This same kind of argument can be repeated in all sorts of cases, illustrating, time after time, how the utilitarian's position leads to results that impartial people find morally callous. It *is* wrong to kill my Aunt Bea in the name of bringing about the best results for others. A good end does not justify an evil means. Any adequate moral theory will have to explain why this is so. Utilitarianism fails in this respect and so cannot be the theory we seek.

What to do? Where to begin anew? The place to begin, I think, is with the utilitarian's view of the value of the individual—or, rather, lack of value. In its place, suppose we consider that you and I, for example, do have value as individuals—what we'll call *inherent value*. To say we have such value is to say that we are something more than, something different from, mere receptacles. Moreover, to ensure that we do not pave the way for such injustices as slavery or sexual discrimination, we must believe that all who have inherent value have it equally, regardless of their sex, race, religion, birthplace and so on. Similarly to be discarded as irrelevant are one's talents or skills, ingellective and wealth, personality or pathology, whether one is loved and admired or despised and loathed. The genius and the retarded child, the prince and the pauper, the brain surgeon and the fruit vendor, Mother Teresa and the most unscrupulous used-car salesman—all have inherent value, all possess it equally, and all have an equal right to be treated with respect, to be treated in ways that do not reduce them to the status of things, as if they existed as resources for others. My value as an individual is independent of my usefulness to you. Yours is not dependent on your usefulness to me. For either of us to treat the other in ways that fail to show respect for the other's independent value is to act immorally, to violate the individual's rights.

Some of the rational virtues of this view—what I call the rights view—should be evident. Unlike (crude) contractarianism, for example, the rights view *in principle* denies the moral tolerability of any and all forms of racial, sexual and social discrimination; and unlike utilitarianism, this view *in principle* denies that we can justify good results by using evil means that violate an individual's rights—denies, for example, that it could be moral to kill my Aunt Bea to harvest beneficial consequences for others. That would be to sanction the disrespectful treatment of the individual in the name of the social good, something the rights view will not—categorically will not—ever allow.

The rights view, I believe, is rationally the most satisfactory moral theory. It surpasses all other theories in the degree to which it illuminates and explains the foundation of our duties to one another—the domain of human morality. On this score it has the best reasons, the best arguments, on its side. Of course, if it were possible to show that only human beings are included within its scope, then a person like myself, who believes in animal rights, would be obliged to look elsewhere.

But attempts to limit its scope to humans only can be shown to be rationally defective. Animals, it is true, lack many of the abilities humans possess. They can't read, do higher mathematics, build a bookcase or make *baba ghanoush*. Neither can many human beings, however, and yet we don't (and shouldn't) say that they (these humans) therefore have less inherent value, less of a right to be treated with respect, than do others. It is the *similarities* between those human beings who most clearly, most non-controversially have such value (the people reading this, for example), not our differences, that matter most. And the really crucial, the basic similarity is simply this: we are each of us the experiencing subject of a life, a conscious creature having an individual welfare that has importance to us whatever our usefulness to others. We want and prefer things, believe and feel things, recall and expect things. And all these dimensions of our life, including our pleasure and pain, our enjoyment and suffering, our satisfaction and frustration, our continued existence or our untimely death—all make a difference to the quality of our life as lived, as experienced, by us as individuals. As the same is true of those animals that concern us (the ones that are eaten and trapped, for example), they too must be viewed as the experiencing subjects of a life, with inherent value of their own.

Some there are who resist the idea that animals have inherent value. 'Only humans have such value,' they profess. How might this narrow view be defended? Shall we say that only humans have the requisite intelligence, or autonomy, or reason? But there are many, many humans who fail to meet these standards and yet are reasonably viewed as having value above and beyond their usefulness to others. Shall we claim that only humans belong to the right species, the species *Homo sapiens*? But this is blatant speciesism. Will it be said, then, that all—

and only—humans have immmortal souls? Then our opponents have their work cut out for them. I am myself not ill-disposed to the proposition that there are immortal souls. Personally, I profoundly hope I have one. But I would not want to rest my position on a controversial ethical issue on the even more controversial question about who or what has an immortal soul. That is to dig one's hole deeper, not to climb out. Rationally, it is better to resolve moral issues without making more controversial assumptions than are needed. The question of who has inherent value is such a question, one that is resolved more rationally without the introduction of the idea of immortal souls than by its use.

Well, perhaps some will say that animals have some inherent value, only less than we have. Once again, however, attempts to defend this view can be shown to lack rational justification. What could be the basis of our having more inherent value than animals? Their lack of reason, or autonomy, or intellect? Only if we are willing to make the same judgment in the case of humans who are similarly deficient. But it is not true that such humans—the retarded child, for example, or the mentally deranged—have less inherent value than you or I. Neither, then, can we rationally sustain the view that animals like them in being the experiencing subjects of a life have less inherent value. *All* who have inherent value have it *equally*, whether they be human animals or not.

Inherent value, then, belongs equally to those who are the experiencing subjects of a life. Whether it belongs to others—to rocks and rivers, trees and glaciers, for example—we do not know and may never know. But neither do we need to know, if we are to make the case for animal rights. We do not need to know, for example, how many people are eligible to vote in the next presidential election before we can know whether I am. Similarly, we do not need to know how many individuals have inherent value before we can know that some do. When it comes to the case for animal rights, then, what we need to know is whether the animals that, in our culture, are routinely eaten, hunted and used in our laboratories, for example, are like us in being subjects of a life. And we do

know this. We do know that many—literally, billions and billions—of these animals are the subjects of a life in the sense explained and so have inherent value if we do. And since, in order to arrive at the best theory of our duties to one another, we must recognize our equal inherent value as individuals, reason—not sentiment, not emotion—reason compels us to recognize the equal inherent value of these anaimls and, with this, their equal right to be treated with respect.

That, *very* roughly, is the shape and feel of the case for animal rights. Most of the details of the supporting argument are missing. They are to be found in the book to which I alluded earlier. Here, the details go begging, and I must, in closing, limit myself to four final points.

The first is how the theory that underlies the case for animal rights shows that the animal rights movement is a part of, not antagonistic to, the human rights movement. The theory that rationally grounds the rights of animals also grounds the rights of humans. Thus those involved in the animal rights movement are partners in the struggle to secure respect for human rights—the rights of women, for example, or minorities, or workers. The animal rights movement is cut from the same moral cloth as these.

Second, having set out the broad outlines of the rights view, I can now say why its implications for farming and science, among other fields, are both clear and uncompromising. In the case of the use of animals in science, the rights view is categorically abolitionist. Lab animals are not our tasters; we are not their kings. Because these animals are treated routinely, systematically as if their value were reducible to their usefulness to others, they are routinely, systematically treated with a lack of respect, and thus are their rights routinely, systematically violated. This is just as true when they are used in trivial, duplicative, unnecessary or unwise research as it is when they are used in studies that hold out real promise of human benefits. We can't justify harming or killing a human being (my Aunt Bea, for example) just for these sorts of reasons. Neither can we do so even in the case of so lowly a creature as a laboratory rat. It is not just refinement or reduction that is called for, not just larger, cleaner cages, not just more generous use of anaesthetic or the elimination of multiple surgery, not just tidying up the system. It is complete replacement. The best we can do when it comes to using animals in science is—not to use them. That is where our duty lies, according to the rights view.

As for commercial animal agriculture, the rights view takes a similar abolitionist position. The fundamental moral wrong here is not that animals are kept in stressful close confinement or in isolation, or that their pain and suffering, their needs and preferences are ignored or discounted. All these *are* wrong, of course, but they are not the fundamental wrong. They are symptoms and effects of the deeper, systematic wrong that allows these animals to be viewed and treated as lacking independent value, as resources for us—as, indeed, a renewable resource. Giving farm animals more space, more natural environments, more companions does not right the fundamental wrong, any more than giving lab animals more anaesthesia or bigger, cleaner cages would right the fundamental wrong in their case. Nothing less than the total dissolution of commerical animal agriculture will do this, just as, for similar reasons I won't develop at length here, morality requires nothing less than the total elimination of hunting and trapping for commercial and sporting ends. The rights view's implications, then, as I have said, are clear and uncompromising.

My last two points are about philosophy, my profession. It is, most obviously, no substitute for political action. The words I have written here and in other places by themselves don't change a thing. It is what we do with the thoughts that the words express—our acts, our deeds—that changes things. All that philosophy can do, and all I have attempted, is to offer a vision of what our deeds should aim at. And the why. But not the how.

Finally, I am reminded of my thoughtful critic, the one I mentioned earlier, who chastised me for being too cerebral. Well, cerebral I have been: indirect duty views, utilitarianism, contractarianism—hardly the stuff deep passions are made of. I am also reminded, however, of the image another friend once set before me—the image of the ballerina as expressive of disciplined passion. Long hours of sweat and toil, of loneliness and practice, of doubt and fatigue: those are the discipline of her craft. But the passion is there too, the fierce drive to excel, to speak through her body, to do it right, to pierce our minds. That is the image of philosophy I would leave with you, not 'too cerebral' but *disciplined passion*. Of the discipline enough has been seen. As for the passion: there are times, and these not infrequent, when tears come to my eyes when I see, or read, or hear of the wretched plight of animals in the hands of humans. Their pain, their suffering, their loneliness, their innocence, their death. Anger. Rage. Pity. Sorrow. Disgust. The whole creation groans under the weight of the evil we humans visit upon these mute, powerless creatures. It *is* our hearts, not just our heads, that call for an end to it all, that demand of us that we overcome, for them, the habits and forces behind their systematic oppression. All great movements, it is written, go through three stages: ridicule, discussion, adoption. It is the realization of this third stage, adoption, that requires both our passion and our discipline, our hearts and our heads. The fate of animals is in our hands. God grant we are equal to the task.

REVIEW QUESTIONS

1. According to Regan, what is the fundamental wrong in our treatment of animals?
2. What are indirect-duty views, and why does Regan reject them?
3. What is the cruelty-kindness view? Why isn't it acceptable according to Regan?
4. What are Regan's objections to Utilitarianism?
5. Explain Regan's rights view.
6. What are the implications of Regan's view for science and commercial animal agriculture?

DISCUSSION QUESTIONS

1. How would Singer reply to Regan's criticisms of his Utilitarianism?
2. What exactly is inherent value and who has it? Do fish and insects have it? How about comatose humans?

Mary Anne Warren

Difficulties with the Strong Animal Rights Position

For biographical information on Warren, see her reading in Chapter 2.

Warren explains and then attacks Regan's strong animal rights position, the view that non-human animals have the same basic moral rights as humans. She makes two criticisms of Regan's position: It rests on an obscure concept of inherent value, and it fails to draw a sharp line between living things which have inherent value and moral rights and other living things which don't have such value or rights. Warren concludes with a defense of the weak animal rights position—that animal rights are weaker than human rights because humans are rational and animals are not.

Tom Regan has produced what is perhaps the definitive defense of the view that the basic moral rights of at least some non-human animals are in no way inferior to our own. In *The Case for Animal Rights,* he argues that all normal mammals over a year of age have the same basic moral rights.[1] Non-human mammals have essentially the same right not to be harmed or killed as we do. I shall call this "the strong animal rights position," although it is weaker than the claims made by some animal liberationists in that it ascribes rights to only some sentient animals.[2]

I will argue that Regan's case for the strong animal rights position is unpersuasive and that this position entails consequences which a reasonable person cannot accept. I do not deny that

From Mary Anne Warren, "Difficulties with the Strong Animal Rights Position," *Between the Species* 2, no. 4 (Fall 1987): 433–441. Reprinted by permission of the author.

some non-human animals have moral rights; indeed, I would extend the scope of the rights claim to include all sentient animals, that is, all those capable of having experiences, including experiences of pleasure or satisfaction and pain, suffering, or frustration.[3] However, I do not think that the moral rights of most non-human animals are identical in strength to those of persons.[4] The rights of most non-human animals may be overridden in circumstances which would not justify overriding the rights of persons. There are, for instance, compelling realities which sometimes require that we kill animals for reasons which could not justify the killing of persons. I will call this view "the weak animal rights" position, even though it ascribes rights to a wider range of animals than does the strong animal rights position.

I will begin by summarizing Regan's case for the strong animal rights position and noting two problems with it. Next, I will explore some consequences of the strong animal rights position which I think are unacceptable. Finally, I will outline the case for the weak animal rights position.

REGAN'S CASE

Regan's argument moves through three stages. First, he argues that normal, mature mammals are not only sentient but have other mental capacities as well. These include the capacities for emotion, memory, belief, desire, the use of general concepts, intentional action, a sense of the future, and some degree of self-awareness. Creatures with such capacities are said to be subjects-of-a-life. They are not only alive in the biological sense but have a psychological identity over time and an existence which can go better or worse for them. Thus, they can be harmed or benefited. These are plausible claims, and well defended. One of the strongest parts of the book is the rebuttal of philosophers, such as R. G. Frey, who object to the application of such mentalistic terms to creatures that do not use a human-style language.[5] The second and third stages of the argument are more problematic.

In the second stage, Regan argues that subjects-of-a-life have inherent value. His concept of inherent value grows out of his opposition to utilitarianism. Utilitarian moral theory, he says, treats individuals as "mere receptacles" for morally significant value, in that harm to one individual may be justified by the production of a greater net benefit to other individuals. In opposition to this, he holds that subjects-of-a-life have a value independent of both the value they may place upon their lives or experiences and the value others may place upon them.

Inherent value, Regan argues, does not come in degrees. To hold that some individuals have more inherent value than others is to adopt a "perfectionist" theory, i.e., one which assigns different moral worth to individuals according to how well they are thought to exemplify some virtue(s), such as intelligence or moral autonomy. Perfectionist theories have been used, at least since the time of Aristotle, to rationalize such injustices as slavery and male domination, as well as the unrestrained exploitation of animals. Regan argues that if we reject these injustices, then we must also reject perfectionism and conclude that all subjects-of-a-life have equal inherent value. Moral agents have no more inherent value than moral patients, i.e., subjects-of-a-life who are not morally responsible for their actions.

In the third phase of the argument, Regan uses the thesis of equal inherent value to derive strong moral rights for all subjects-of-a-life. This thesis underlies the Respect Principle, which forbids us to treat beings who have inherent value as mere receptacles, i.e., mere means to the production of the greatest overall good. This principle, in turn, underlies the Harm Principle, which says that we have a direct *prima facie* duty not to harm beings who have inherent value. Together, these principles give rise to moral rights. Rights are defined as valid claims, claims to certain goods and against certain beings, i.e., moral agents. Moral rights generate duties not only to refrain from inflicting harm upon beings with inherent value but also to come to their aid when they are threatened by other moral agents. Rights are not absolute but may be overridden in certain circumstances. Just what these circumstances are we will con-

sider later. But first, let's look at some difficulties in the theory as thus far presented.

THE MYSTERY OF INHERENT VALUE

Inherent value is a key concept in Regan's theory. It is the bridge between the plausible claim that all normal, mature mammals—human or otherwise—are subjects-of-a-life and the more debatable claim that they all have basic moral rights of the same strength. But it is a highly obscure concept, and its obscurity makes it ill-suited to play this crucial role.

Inherent value is defined almost entirely in negative terms. It is not dependent upon the value which either the inherently valuable individual or anyone else may place upon that individual's life or experiences. It is not (necessarily) a function of sentience or any other mental capacity, because, Regan says, some entities which are not sentient (e.g., trees, rivers, or rocks) may, nevertheless, have inherent value (p. 246). It cannot attach to anything other than an individual; species, eco-systems, and the like cannot have inherent value.

These are some of the things which inherent value is not. But what is it? Unfortunately, we are not told. Inherent value appears as a mysterious non-natural property which we must take on faith. Regan says that it is a *postulate* that subjects-of-a-life have inherent value, a postulate justified by the fact that it avoids certain absurdities which he thinks follow from a purely utilitarian theory (p. 247). But why is the postulate that *subjects-of-a-life* have inherent value? If the inherent value of a being is completely independent of the value that it or anyone else places upon its experiences, then why does the fact that it has certain sorts of experiences constitute evidence that it has inherent value? If the reason is that subjects-of-a-life have an existence which can go better or worse for them, then why isn't the appropriate conclusion that all sentient beings have inherent value, since they would all seem to meet that condition? Sentient but mentally unsophisticated beings may have a less extensive range of possible satisfactions and frustrations, but why should it follow that they have—or may have—no inherent value at all?

In the absence of a positive account of inherent value, it is also difficult to grasp the connection between being inherently valuable and having moral rights. Intuitively, it seems that value is one thing, and rights are another. It does not seem incoherent to say that some things (e.g., mountains, rivers, redwood trees) are inherently valuable and yet are not the sorts of things which can have moral rights. Nor does it seem incoherent to ascribe inherent value to some things which are not individuals, e.g., plant or animal species, though it may well be incoherent to ascribe moral rights to such things.

In short, the concept of inherent value seems to create at least as many problems as it solves. If inherent value is based on some natural property, then why not try to identify that property and explain its moral significance, without appealing to inherent value? And if it is not based on any natural property, then why should we believe in it? That it may enable us to avoid some of the problems faced by the utilitarian is not a sufficient reason, if it creates other problems which are just as serious.

IS THERE A SHARP LINE?

Perhaps the most serious problems are those that arise when we try to apply the strong animal rights position to animals other than normal, mature mammals. Regan's theory requires us to divide all living things into two categories: those which have the same inherent value and the same basic moral rights that we do, and those which have no inherent value and presumably no moral rights. But wherever we try to draw the line, such a sharp division is implausible.

It would surely be arbitrary to draw such a sharp line between normal, mature mammals and all other living things. Some birds (e.g., crows, magpies, parrots, mynahs) appear to be just as mentally sophisticated as most mammals and thus are equally strong candidates for inclusion under the subject-of-a-life criterion. Regan is not in fact advocating that we draw the line here. His claim is only that normal mature mammals are clear cases, while other cases are

less clear. Yet, on his theory, there must be such a sharp line *somewhere,* since there are no degrees of inherent value. But why should we believe that there is a sharp line between creatures that are subjects-of-a-life and creatures that are not? Isn't it more likely that "subjecthood" comes in degrees, that some creatures have only a little self-awareness, and only a little capacity to anticipate the future, while some have a little more, and some a good deal more?

Should we, for instance, regard fish, amphibians, and reptiles as subjects-of-a-life? A simple yes-or-no answer seems inadequate. On the one hand, some of their behavior is difficult to explain without the assumption that they have sensations, beliefs, desires, emotions, and memories; on the other hand, they do not seem to exhibit very much self-awareness or very much conscious anticipation of future events. Do they have enough mental sophistication to count as subjects-of-a-life? Exactly how much is enough?

It is still more unclear what we should say about insects, spiders, octopi, and other invertebrate animals which have brains and sensory organs but whose minds (if they have minds) are even more alien to us than those of fish or reptiles. Such creatures are probably sentient. Some people doubt that they can feel pain, since they lack certain neurological structures which are crucial to the processing of pain impulses in vertebrate animals. But this argument is inconclusive, since their nervous systems might process pain in ways different from ours. When injured, they sometimes act as if they are in pain. On evolutionary grounds, it seems unlikely that highly mobile creatures with complex sensory systems would not have developed a capacity for pain (and pleasure), since such a capacity has obvious survival value. It must, however, be admitted that we do not *know* whether spiders can feel pain (or something very like it), let alone whether they have emotions, memories, beliefs, desires, self-awareness, or a sense of the future.

Even more mysterious are the mental capacities (if any) of mobile microfauna. The brisk and efficient way that paramecia move about in their incessant search for food *might* indicate some kind of sentience, in spite of their lack of eyes, ears, brains, and other organs associated with sentience in more complex organisms. It is conceivable—though not very probable—that they, too, are subjects-of-a-life.

The existence of a few unclear cases need not pose a serious problem for a moral theory, but in this case, the unclear cases constitute most of those with which an adequate theory of animal rights would need to deal. The subject-of-a-life criterion can provide us with little or no moral guidance in our interactions with the vast majority of animals. That might be acceptable if it could be supplemented with additional principles which would provide such guidance. However, the radical dualism of the theory precludes supplementing it in this way. We are forced to say that either a spider has the same right to life as you and I do, or it has no right to life whatever—and that only the gods know which of these alternatives is true.

Regan's suggestion for dealing with such unclear cases is to apply the "benefit of the doubt" principle. That is, when dealing with beings that may or may not be subjects-of-a-life, we should act as if they are.[6] But if we try to apply this principle to the entire range of doubtful cases, we will find ourselves with moral obligations which we cannot possibly fulfill. In many climates, it is virtually impossible to live without swatting mosquitoes and exterminating cockroaches, and not all of us can afford to hire someone to sweep the path before we walk, in order to make sure that we do not step on ants. Thus, we are still faced with the daunting task of drawing a sharp line somewhere on the continuum of life forms—this time, a line demarcating the limits of the benefit of the doubt principle.

The weak animal rights theory provides a more plausible way of dealing with this range of cases, in that it allows the rights of animals of different kinds to vary in strength. . . .

WHY ARE ANIMAL RIGHTS WEAKER THAN HUMAN RIGHTS?

How can we justify regarding the rights of persons as generally stronger than those of sentient beings which are not persons? There are a plethora of bad justifications, based on religious premises or false or unprovable claims about the differences between human and non-human nature. But there is one difference which has a clear moral relevance: people are at least sometimes capable of being moved to action or inaction by the force of reasoned argument. Rationality rests upon other mental capacities, notably those which Regan cites as criteria for being a subject-of-a-life. We share these capacities with many other animals. But it is not just because we are subjects-of-a-life that we are both able and morally compelled to recognize one another as beings with equal basic moral rights. It is also because we are able to "listen to reason" in order to settle our conflicts and cooperate in shared projects. This capacity, unlike the others, may require something like a human language.

Why is rationality morally relevant? It does not make us "better" than other animals or more "perfect." It does not even automatically make us more intelligent. (Bad reasoning reduces our effective intelligence rather than increasing it.) But it is morally relevant insofar as it provides greater possibilities for cooperation and for the nonviolent resolution of problems. It also makes us more dangerous than non-rational beings can ever be. Because we are potentially more dangerous and less predictable than wolves, we need an articulated system of morality to regulate our conduct. Any human morality, to be workable in the long run, must recognize the equal moral status of all persons, whether through the postulate of equal basic moral rights or in some other way. The recognition of the moral equality of other persons is the price we must each pay for their recognition of our moral equality. Without this mutual recognition of moral equality, human society can exist only in a state of chronic and bitter conflict. The war between the sexes will persist so long as there is sexism and male domination; racial conflict will never be eliminated so long as there are racist laws and practices. But, to the extent that we achieve a mutual recognition of equality, we can hope to live together, perhaps as peacefully as wolves, achieving (in part) through explicit moral principles what they do not seem to need explicit moral principles to achieve.

Why not extend this recognition of moral equality to other creatures, even though they cannot do the same for us? The answer is that we cannot. Because we cannot reason with most non-human animals, we cannot always solve the problems which they may cause without harming them—although we are always obligated to try. We cannot negotiate a treaty with the feral cats and foxes, requiring them to stop preying on endangered native species in return for suitable concessions on our part.

If rats invade our houses . . . we cannot reason with them, hoping to persuade them of the injustice they do us. We can only attempt to get rid of them.[7]

Aristotle was not wrong in claiming that the capacity to alter one's behavior on the basis of reasoned argument is relevant to the full moral status which he accorded to free men. Of course, he was wrong in his other premise, that women and slaves by their nature cannot reason well enough to function as autonomous moral agents. Had that premise been true, so would his conclusion that women and slaves are not quite the moral equals of free men. In the case of most non-human animals, the corresponding premise is true. If, on the other hand, there are animals with whom we can (learn to) reason, then we are obligated to do this and to regard them as our moral equals.

Thus, to distinguish between the rights of persons and those of most other animals on the grounds that only people can alter their behavior on the basis of reasoned argument does not commit us to a perfectionist theory of the sort Aristotle endorsed. There is no excuse for refusing to recognize the moral equality of some people on the grounds that we don't regard them as quite as rational as we are, since it is perfectly clear that most people can reason well enough to determine how to act so as to respect the basic rights of others (if they choose to), and that is enough for moral equality.

But what about people who are clearly not rational? It is often argued that sophisticated mental capacities such as rationality cannot be essential for the possession of equal basic moral rights, since nearly everyone agrees that human infants and mentally incompetent persons have such rights, even though they may lack those sophisticated mental capacities. But this argument is inconclusive, because there are powerful practical and emotional reasons for protecting non-rational human beings, reasons which are absent in the case of most non-human animals. Infancy and mental incompetence are human conditions which all of us either have experienced or are likely to experience at some time. We also protect babies and mentally incompetent people because we care for them. We don't normally care for animals in the same way, and when we do—e.g., in the case of much-loved pets—we may regard them as having special rights by virtue of their relationship to us. We protect them not only for their sake but also for our own, lest we be hurt by harm done to them. Regan holds that such "side-effects" are irrelevant to moral rights, and perhaps they are. But in ordinary usage, there is no sharp line between moral rights and those moral protections which are not rights. The extension of strong moral protections to infants and the mentally impaired in no way proves that non-human animals have the same basic moral rights as people.

WHY SPEAK OF "ANIMAL RIGHTS" AT ALL?

If, as I have argued, reality precludes our treating all animals as our moral equals, then why should we still ascribe rights to them? Everyone agrees that animals are entitled to some protection against human abuse, but why speak of animal *rights* if we are not prepared to accept most animals as our moral equals? The weak animal rights position may seem an unstable compromise between the bold claim that animals have the same basic moral rights that we do and the more common view that animals have no rights at all.

It is probably impossible to either prove or disprove the thesis that animals have moral rights by producing an analysis of the concept of a moral right and checking to see if some or all animals satisfy the conditions for having rights. The concept of a moral right is complex, and it is not clear which of its strands are essential. Paradigm rights holders, i.e., mature and mentally competent persons, are *both* rational and morally autonomous beings and sentient subjects-of-a-life. Opponents of animal rights claim that rationality and moral autonomy are essential for the possession of rights, while defenders of animal rights claim that they are not. The ordinary concept of a moral right is probably not precise enough to enable us to determine who is right on purely definitional grounds.

If logical analysis will not answer the question of whether animals have moral rights, practical considerations may, nevertheless, incline us to say that they do. The most plausible alternative to the view that animals have moral rights is that, while they do not have *rights,* we are, nevertheless, obligated not to be cruel to them. Regan argues persuasively that the injunction to avoid being cruel to animals is inadequate to express our obligations towards animals, because it focuses on the mental states of those who cause animal suffering, rather than on the harm done to the animals themselves (p. 158). Cruelty is inflicting pain or suffering and either taking pleasure in that pain or suffering or being more or less indifferent to it. Thus, to express the demand for the decent treatment of animals in terms of the rejection of cruelty is to invite the too easy response that those who subject animals to suffering are not being cruel because they regret the suffering they cause but sincerely believe that what they do is justified. The injunction to avoid cruelty is also inadequate in that it does not preclude the killing of animals—for any reason, however trivial—so long as it is done relatively painlessly.

The inadequacy of the anti-cruelty view provides one practical reason for speaking of animal rights. Another practical reason is that this is an age in which nearly all significant moral claims tend to be expressed in terms of rights. Thus, the denial that animals have rights, however carefully qualified, is likely to be taken to mean that we may do whatever we like to them, provided that we do not violate any human rights. In such a context, speaking of the rights of animals may be the only way to persuade many people to take seriously protests against the abuse of animals.

Why not extend this line of argument and speak of the rights of trees, mountains, oceans, or anything else which we may wish to see protected from destruction? Some environmentalists have not hesitated to speak in this way, and, given the importance of protecting such elements of the natural world, they cannot be blamed for using this rhetorical device. But, I would argue that moral rights can meaningfully be ascribed only to entities which have some capacity for sentience. This is because moral rights are protections designed to protect rights holders from harms or to provide them with benefits which matter *to them.* Only beings capable of sentience can be harmed or benefited in ways which matter to them, for only such beings can like or dislike what happens to them or prefer some conditions to others. Thus, sentient animals, unlike mountains, rivers, or species, are at least logically possible candidates for moral rights. This fact, together with the need to end current abuses of animals—e.g., in scientific research . . .—provides a plausible case for speaking of animal rights.

Conclusion

I have argued that Regan's case for ascribing strong moral rights to all normal, mature mammals is unpersuasive because (1) it rests upon the obscure concept of inherent value, which is defined only in negative terms, and (2) it seems to preclude any plausible answer to questions about the moral status of the vast majority of sentient animals. . . .

The weak animal rights theory asserts that (1) any creature whose natural mode of life includes the pursuit of certain satisfactions has the right not to be forced to exist without the opportunity to pursue those satisfactions; (2) that any creature which is capable of pain, suffering, or frustration has the right that such experiences not be deliberately inflicted upon it without some compelling reason; and (3) that no sentient being should be killed without good reason. However, moral rights are not an all-or-nothing affair. The strength of the reasons required to override the rights of a non-human organism varies, depending upon—among other things—the probability that it is sentient and (if it is clearly sentient) its probable degree of mental sophistication. . . .

Endnotes

1. Tom Regan, *The Case for Animal Rights* (Berkeley: University of California Press, 1983). All page references are to this edition.
2. For instance, Peter Singer, although he does not like to speak of rights, includes all sentient beings under the protection of his basic utilitarian principle of equal respect for like interests. (Animal Liberation [New York: Avon Books, 1975], p. 3.)
3. The capacity for sentience, like all of the mental capacities mentioned in what follows, is a disposition. Dispositions do not disappear whenever they are not currently manifested. Thus, sleeping or temporarily unconscious persons or non-human animals are still sentient in the relevant sense (i.e., still capable of sentience), so long as they still have the neurological mechanisms necessary for the occurrence of experiences.
4. It is possible, perhaps probable that some non-human animals—such as cetaceans and anthropoid apes—should be regarded as persons. If so, then the weak animal rights position holds that these animals have the same basic moral rights as human persons.
5. See R. G. Frey, *Interests and Rights: The Case Against Animals* (Oxford: Oxford University Press, 1980).
6. See, for instance, p. 319, where Regan appeals to the benefit of the doubt principle when dealing with infanticide and late-term abortion.
7. Bonnie Steinbock, "Speciesism and the Idea of Equality," *Philosophy* 53 (1978):253.

REVIEW QUESTIONS

1. Distinguish between what Warren calls the strong animal rights position and the weak animal rights position.
2. What problems does Warren find in Regan's case for the strong animal rights position?
3. Explain Warren's defense of the weak animal rights position.

DISCUSSION QUESTIONS

1. Has Warren refuted Regan's strong animal rights position? Does he have an adequate reply?
2. In Warren's view, rationality is essential for having equal basic moral rights. But infants and mentally incompetent humans are not rational; therefore, they do not have moral rights. Does Warren have an acceptable reply to this argument?

Jordan Curnutt

Reconsidering Vegetarianism

Jordan Curnutt is assistant professor of philosophy at St. Cloud State University in Minnesota. He is the author of several articles on ethics, and he is a practicing vegetarian.

After discussing the problems with Singer's Utilitarianism and Regan's rights view, Curnutt states and explains his new argument for vegetarianism. The argument tries to show that animal eating is morally wrong all things considered, or ultima facie wrong, as distinguished from being merely prima facie wrong.

From Jordan Curnutt, "Reconsidering Vegetarianism." Used by permission of the author. [This article is previously unpublished—Ed.]

The major philosophical approaches to vegetarianism that have been most rigorously pursued over the last 20 years have produced a stalemate: utilitarianism and rights-based theories have not proved fruitful for resolving the relevant problems, nor have they yielded much agreement. I would like to present an alternative to these traditional approaches. This alternative avoids the difficulties that result in the stalemate, successfully eludes subsequent objections, and justifies a moral requirement to refrain from eating animals. I will first explain why the old arguments have not been helpful. The remainder of the paper is devoted to the explanation and defense of a new argument for vegetarianism, one which does not depend on calculations of utility, or any particular conception of rights, but on a certain understanding of the concept of harm.

Old Arguments for Vegetarianism

Peter Singer has been the leading utilitarian defender of vegetarianism for over 20 years.[1] He has often cited the vast amounts of pain and suffering experienced by domesticated animals "down on the factory farm" as they await and inevitably succumb to their fate as food for human consumption.[2] A utilitarian is required to produce that state of affairs in which aggregations of certain positive and negative mental states exceed (or at least equal) such aggregations of any alternative state of affairs. Singer has argued that factory farming woefully fails to meet this standard. Vegetarianism is morally obligatory simply because it maximizes utility, precisely what utilitarians say we are supposed to do. Animal-eating promotes disutility, precisely what we are supposed to avoid.

But several philosophers have argued that utilitarianism is a perilous ally for the vegetarian. One major problem is that the end of animal-eating produces disutilities which must be accounted for in the utilitarian ledger. When that is done, animal-eating may not emerge as morally wrong after all. For example, R. G. Frey has claimed that the demise of the meat industry and its satellites which would attend a wholesale conversion to vegetarianism would be catastrophic to human welfare, and so could not be given a utilitarian justification because of it.[3] Frey lists fourteen different ways in which rampant vegetarianism would deleteriously affect human affairs, mainly in the form of economic losses for those employed in the industry. In the face of this, his utilitarian calculation yields the result that we are permitted to eat animals at will, but we must strive to reduce the amount of suffering that they experience.[4]

Not only does vegetarianism produce disutilities, but animal-eating can actually maximize utility: utilitarianism may *require* animal-eating.

Roger Crisp contends that utilitarianism leads to what he calls the "Compromise Requirement view."[5] According to Crisp, "non-intensively-reared animals lead worthwhile lives" and humans derive gustatory pleasure, satisfaction, or some other positive mental state from eating them. Vegetarianism would put an end to these two sources of utility. Thus, given the requirement to maximize utility, raising and eating animals in these circumstances becomes a utilitarian obligation.[6]

These philosophers, among others, have pinpointed why the utilitarian case for vegetarianism is a shaky one. Like any other utilitarian calculation, the issue here is an empirical and hence contingent one: vegetarianism is at the mercy of such capricious factors as the number of humans who eat meat relative to the number of animals eaten, and the negative and positive mental states attendant on a wide variety of animal husbandry situations and human living conditions. Moreover, this theory requires summing and comparing the positive and negative mental states of *billions* of individuals of several different species.[7] That prospect makes it difficult to escape the conclusion that the problem has become an intractable one. The lesson to be learned is that a successful argument for vegetarianism must be independent of any current or possible method of livestock rearing and must appeal to factors that are fairly clear and manageable.

The leading contender to utilitarian theory has been the rights-based perspective of Tom Regan. His dedication to defending animals in general and vegetarianism in particular nearly matches Singer's in duration and production.[8] In brief, Regan's position is that mammals of at least one year old are "subjects-of-a-life": they are conscious beings with a wide variety of mental states, such as preferences, beliefs, sensations, a sense of self and of the future. These features identify animals as rightsholders and possessors of "inherent" value. One implication of this view is that killing animals for food, whether or not this is done painlessly and independently of the quality of the animals' lives, is a violation of their right to respectful treatment, since it uses them as a means to our own ends. Hence, vegetarianism is morally required.

Regan is one of many philosophers who advocate the view that nonpersons in general or animals in particular (or both) qualify as moral rightsholders.[9] These philosophers identify rightsholders according to their possession of certain affective capacities, such as interests or desires, and a number of them argue that animals do have these capacities. On the other hand, many other philosophers prefer cognitive criteria, confining rightsholders to beings with certain more advanced mental capacities—rationality and autonomy are the favorites—and explicitly or by implication disqualifying animals from this category.[10]

The Case for Animal Rights represents the *opus classicus* of the deontological approach to animal issues. Through over 400 pages of dense and tightly argued text, Regan has canvassed the philosophical problems of human-animal relationships more thoroughly than anyone has ever done. Even so, his view has been subjected to some quite damaging criticisms, ranging from concern over the mysterious and controversial nature of "inherent value" to charges of inconsistency and implausibility when the rights of humans and those of animals come into conflict.[11] This fact, along with the formidable arguments marshaled by those who champion cognitive requirements for rightsholding, suggest that basing a case for vegetarianism upon the foundation of moral rights is an onerous task. The major problem is that the topic is exceedingly complex. A study of rights must address such daunting questions as: What are rights? Are they real independently existing entities (natural rights) or human inventions (political, legal) or both? What is needed to qualify as a rightsholder? Exactly what rights are held by whom and why? How are conflicts among rights settled?

Thus we have a very complicated theoretical endeavor marked by profound differences, yielding an area of philosophical debate that is highly unsettled. This tells us that a new argument for vegetarianism should traverse a relatively uncontroversial theoretical region that is fairly stable and fixed.

A New Argument for Vegetarianism (NEW)

1. Causing harm is *prima facie* morally wrong.
2. Killing animals causes them harm.
3. Therefore, killing animals is *prima facie* morally wrong.
4. Extensive animal-eating requires the killing of animals.
5. Therefore, animal-eating is *prima facie* morally wrong.
6. The wrongness of animal eating is not overridden.
7. Therefore, animal eating is *ultima facie* morally wrong.

Premise 1 is an assumption: harming is wrong, not because it violates some right or because it fails to maximize utility, but simply because it is wrong. As *"prima facie,"* however, the wrongness may be overridden in certain cases. I discuss premise 6 in the last section of the paper, and there I argue that the wrongness of the harm that eating animals causes them is not overridden, that it is "all things considered" or *ultima facie* wrong.

The term "extensive" in premise 4 indicates that the target of NEW is the industrialized practice of killing billions of animals as food for hundreds of millions of people. NEW allows small-scale subsistence hunting, and eating animals that died due to accidents, natural causes, or other sources that do not involve the deliberate actions of moral agents.

The term "animal" used here and throughout this paper refers to any vertebrate species. For reasons that I will make clear, NEW is more tentative with regard to invertebrate species. NEW is concerned with the harm caused by the killing and eating of animals, so it does not prohibit uses of animals that do not directly result in their deaths, in particular, those characteristic of the egg and dairy industries: the argument claims that "ovo-lacto vegetarianism" is morally required.

Killing and Harm

The claim that killing animals causes them harm might seem too obvious to warrant much discussion. However, its importance here is to more clearly distance NEW from other defenses of vegetarianism. As we will see, killing is harmful—and therefore morally wrong—whether or not any rights are violated, and independently of the failure to maximize utility.

Joel Feinberg's analysis of harm is especially useful here. To harm a being is to do something that adversely affects that individual's *interests*. According to Feinberg, harming amounts to "the thwarting, setting back, or defeating of an interest." [12] Interests are not univocal. Some interests are more important than others depending on their function in maintaining the basic well-being or welfare of the individual concerned. The most critical and essential interests that anyone can have are what Feinberg calls "welfare interests":

In this category are the interests in the continuance for a foreseeable interval of one's life, the interests in one's own physical health and vigor, and integrity and normal functioning of one's body, the absence of absorbing pain and suffering . . . , emotional stability, the absence of groundless anxieties and resentments, the capacity to engage normally in social intercourse . . . , a tolerable social and physical environment, and a certain amount of freedom from interference and coercion. [13]

Welfare interests are "the very most important interests . . . cry[ing] out for protection" not only because they are definitive of basic well-being, but also because their realization is necessary before one can satisfy virtually any other interest or do much of anything with one's life. We cannot achieve our (ulterior) interests in a career or personal relationships or material goods if we are unhealthy, in chronic pain, emotionally unstable, living in an intolerable social and physical environment, and are constantly interfered with and coerced by others. Feinberg concludes that when welfare interests are defeated a very serious harm indeed has been done to the possessor of those interests. [14]

What does it take to have an interest? Feinberg points out that there is a close connection between interests and desires: if A does in fact have an interest in x, we would typically not deny that A wants x. [15] However, we do speak of x *being in* A's interest, whether A wants x or not; this seems to be especially so when we are considering the welfare interests described above. We believe that normally an individual's life, physical and mental health, and personal freedom are in his or her interest even if these things are not wanted by that individual. This suggests to Feinberg that interests of this kind obtain independently of and are not derived from desires. [16]

We have here all that is needed to defend the claim that killing an animal causes it harm and is therefore morally wrong. Moreover, killing is perhaps the most serious sort of harm that can be inflicted upon an animal by a moral agent; that is so not only because of the defeat of an animal's welfare interests—in life, health, and bodily integrity—but also because these are likely the only kind of interests animals have. One understanding of such interests appeals to the desire the animal has to live in a healthy, normal state of well-being. We see this desire exhibited in animal behavior: fleeing from predators and enemies, seeking cover from severe weather, tending to injuries (such as they can), struggling to extricate themselves from potentially fatal situations, and exhibiting palpable fear in the face of threats to their lives. On Feinberg's analysis, another understanding of welfare interests makes no appeal to any such desire. This implies that killing defeats welfare interests independently of whether or not animals have a desire for life and well-being. They have an interest in this which is defeated when agents cause their deaths.

We can now see the advantages of NEW over the old arguments for vegetarianism. NEW is not contingent upon any current or possible methods of raising animals for humans to eat: no matter how it is done, animal-eating means the defeat of their welfare interests. NEW does not employ any theoretical contructs that are unsettled and divisive: the analysis of harm in terms of interests and desires that are exhibited by certain behaviors is widely accepted and intuitively appealing. NEW does not introduce any indeterminacy or unweildy ratiocination into the discussion: the desires and interests of animals, and the wrongness of defeating them, are plainly evident for all those who would simply look and see.

We can also now understand a further aspect of the vegetarianism required by NEW. Killing a creature with certain desires defeats its welfare interests, and is therefore harmful, but not all living things have such desires and interests. The judgment that some being has the requisite mental states must be formed on the basis of behavior and physiological evidence. Since invertebrates and plants either do not exhibit the appropriate behavior or they do not possess the appropriate physiological equipment (or both), consuming them is permitted. Although I do not hold that "interestless" forms of life have no moral status whatever, I cannot here develop the notion of degrees of moral value or consider what else besides interests would qualify an entity for a moral status. It will have to suffice to say that beings with certain mental states are of greater moral worth than those without them, from the moral point of view it is better (ceteris paribus) to kill and eat a plant than an animal. Moreover, much vegetable matter can be eaten without killing anything: most vegetarian fare consists of the fruits and flowers of plants that are not killed or are harvested at the end of annual life cycles.

THE MORAL WRONGNESS OF EATING ANIMALS

At this point in the defense of NEW, we have firmly established the following:

1. Causing harm is *prima facie* morally wrong.
2. Killing animals causes them harm.
3. Therefore, killing animals is *prima facie* morally wrong.

We have seen why killing animals harms them. We understand why this is one of the worst harms an animal can undergo, which indicates that this is a very serious (though *prima facie*) wrong when perpetrated by a moral agent. And we have seen why NEW represents a significant improvement over traditional approaches. The next step is to link the wrongness of killing animals with the wrongness of eating them, thus establishing:

3. Therefore, killing animals is *prima facie* morally wrong.
4. Animal-eating requires the killing of animals.
5. Therefore, animal-eating is *prima facie* morally wrong.

Many might regard this next step as especially problematic. All that has been shown so far is that moral agents who kill animals are engaged in actions that are *prima facie* wrong; how can it follow from this that different actions, done by different agents, are also *prima facie* wrong? After all, very few of those who consume animal flesh have personally killed the animals they eat. Those who actually do the killing—slaughterhouse workers—act impermissibly, while those who merely eat the body parts of dead animals supplied by those workers do not. How could the wrongness of one set of agents and actions *transfer* to an entirely different set?

One response would point out that purchasing and consuming the products of "factory farming" contributes to a morally abhorrent practice and thus perpetuates future wrongdoing. So although it is the killing that constitutes what is wrong with the practice of animal-eating, and conceding that very few animal-eaters actually kill what they eat, this contribution to and perpetuation of the killing should prompt us to act *as if* eating the animals is itself wrong.[17]

Hud Hudson has shown that this response does not work. It rests on the empirical claim that an individual's refraining from eating animals will make some difference. But as a matter of economic fact, my refraining from eating animals will not affect the meat industry in the least. The loss of my financial contribution will not spare a single animal from harm and would not produce the slightest setback to the business; I will be preventing no future wrongdoing whatever by becoming a vegetarian.[18]

Hudson's solution to the problem is to widen our perspective from the individual vegetarian to groups of individuals, attributing "collective responsibility" for the harm caused to the animals eaten. This looks like a more promising approach since it is precisely the fecklessness of individual action to prevent future wrongdoing that undermined the initial response to this objection. Hudson writes:

[I]f enough nonvegetarian consumers of factory farmed products can be identified as the members of some loosely structured group which could prevent harms . . . by devising a decision-making procedure through which they would collectively cease purchasing and consuming such products, then the failure to prevent those harms through the collective inaction of that group is something for which the members are morally responsible. . . . [T]he thrust of the argument is that in this case, certain individuals, by virtue of their membership in a loosely structured group, are at least partially morally responsible for not collectively preventing certain harms . . . , even though none of the individuals could have prevented the harm by acting independently.[19]

Unfortunately, this response will not work either. Say I am a member of "some loosely structured group which could prevent harms . . . by devising a decision-making procedure through which they would collectively cease purchasing and consuming" animal flesh. On Hudson's view, this means that I am "at least partially morally responsible" for the wrongs perpetrated by factory farming. Yet this is so despite the fact that these are harms I can do nothing about. It is a strange theory which burdens one with a responsibility which it is virtually impossible to fulfill. But the situation is even worse than this. Say I decide to become a vegetarian, so I stop purchasing and eating animal flesh. On Hudson's view I am even so *still* partially responsible for the harm, because it is still necessary for collective action to occur if the wrongdoing is to be stopped or at least severely curtailed, and this will not happen as a result of my individual action. Hudson however claims that this is not the case, that acting individually in this manner will "eliminate [my] share of the responsibility resulting from the wrongful, collective inaction" of my group.[20] But why? According to Hudson's theory, the reason why I have some degree of responsibility in the first place has *nothing* to do with any actions I take or fail to take; it is precisely the ineffectual nature of my abstinence from animal flesh that gave rise to the objection and it is my membership in a group that could prevent wrongdoing through a coordinated effort that leads to the ascription of responsibility. My refusal to eat animals changes none of this.

What has gone awry here is the concession that we must find some way to think of animal-eating *as if* it were wrong, because in actuality it is not itself wrong; the killing is the wrong, not the eating of what has been killed by others. This led to the construction of the rather bizarre theory of responsibility outlined above. We must not make this concession. Animal-eating is itself wrong, but this is not due to any "transference" of wrongness from the act of killing to the act of purchasing and eating animal flesh. The purchasing and consuming are two parts of the same wrong.

To see this, consider this modification of the objection that concerns us now:

This is a lovely lamp. You say its base is made from the bones and its shade from the skin of Jews killed in concentration camps? Well, so what? I didn't kill them. Of course what the Nazis did was wrong, a very great moral evil. But my not buying the lamp is obviously not going to bring any of them back. Nor will it prevent any future harm: this sort of thing doesn't even occur any more, so there is no future wrongdoing to prevent even if my refusal to buy were effective in this way, which of course it wouldn't be. So what's wrong with buying and using the lamp?

What makes eating animals wrong has nothing to do with collective responsibility or any impact an individual might or might not have on the meat industry. We do not need to find some way to understand this activity that will allow it to be construed "as if" it were wrong (but really isn't). Animal-eating is wrong for much the same reason why purchasing and using the products of a concentration camp or those of slave labor generally is wrong; it is wrong for the same reason why buying stolen property or accepting any of the ill-gotten gains of another is wrong: a person who eats animals, or buys and uses lamps from Auschwitz or cotton clothing from the antebellum south, or a hot stereo from a hoodlum is profiting from, benefiting from a morally nefarious practice. Doing so, and especially doing so when morally innocuous alternatives are readily available, not only indicates support for and the endorsement of moral evil, it is to participate in that evil. It is an act of complicity, partaking in condemnable exploitation, reaping personal advantages at a significant cost to others. This is so whether or not an individual's abstinence from the practice has any effect whatever on its perpetuation. It strikes me as quite uncontroversial to say that one who concurs and cooperates with wrongdoing, who garners benefits through the defeat of the basic welfare interests of others, is himself doing something that is seriously morally wrong.

OVERRIDING THE MORAL WRONGNESS OF EATING ANIMALS

The final step in the defense of NEW is to support premise 6: the *prima facie* wrongness of animal-eating is not overridden; from this it will follow that animal-eating is *ultima facie* morally wrong (the conclusion 7). There are at least four grounds for overriding this wrong: (1) traditional-cultural; (2) esthetic; (3) convenience; (4) nutrition. Do any of these supply an overriding reason that would morally justify the very serious harm that killing animals for food causes them?

(1) People eat animals because they have been raised on that diet, as have their parents and grandparents and on back through the generations. Animal-eating is a social practice that is deeply embedded into modern culture. But then slavery, the oppression of women, and institutionalized racism also once had this status, but few if any suppose that this status is what makes practices morally right or wrong. Slavery, for example, is wrong because it requires the persistent exploitation, coercion, and degradation of innocent people, not because it happens to be extinct in our society. The fact that a practice has the weight of tradition on its side and a prominent place in a given culture does not in itself carry any moral weight.[21]

(2) Animal flesh is regarded by most people as esthetically pleasing. Animal body parts are prepared for consumption in hundreds of different ways, employing many cooking techniques, spices, and accompaniments. Yet the esthetic attractions of other practices are regarded as irrelevant to their moral appraisal. Heliogabalus had masses of people gathered in fields, only to be mercilessly slaughtered solely

for the pleasing effect he found in the sight of red blood on green grass.[22] Or consider "snuff films," whose "plot" is centered around the filming of an actual murder of a person apparently chosen at random. Certainly such cinema is to be condemned in the strongest possible terms, even if it were directed by Orson Wells or Martin Scorcese and starred Dustin Hoffman or Meryl Streep. Yet one has only to enter the nearest slaughterhouse with a video camera on any given day of the week to produce a movie every bit as horrific as the most polished "snuff film."

(3) The convenience of animal-eating is largely a function of the other two factors. The pervasiveness of the desire to eat animals and its prominence within a variety of social functions naturally provokes free market economies to supply meat relatively cheaply and easily. Again, this says nothing about the moral permissibility of animal-eating. It is often quite inconvenient and very difficult to keep a promise or discharge a parental duty or make a sacrifice for a stranger—or a friend; it is often quite convenient and very easy to conceal the truth or pocket merchandise without paying or take advantage of powerless persons. Few of us believe that convenience and ease have much of anything to do with whether these actions are morally right or wrong. Why should it be any different when it comes to killing animals for food?

It might be said that the difference is that human interests in convenience, in tradition, and esthetic pleasure override animal interests in life and well-being, that the defeat of an *animal* welfare interest is not a serious moral problem. But what is it about humans that gives these non-basic interests a moral priority over the most basic and important interests an animal can have? Certainly the non-basic interests of some humans do not have a moral priority over the welfare interests of other humans. So in order to sustain the objection, some feature must be identified that is unique to our species. But, first, any such proposed feature (rationality, language, self-consciousness) would not be uniquely absent in animal species; no one would seriously contend that a taste for human baby flesh morally overrides anything, nor would anyone claim that the defeat of a child's welfare interest was not a serious moral wrong. The second problem is explaining why the proposed feature makes such an enormous moral difference, a gap so vast that it means utmost respect and consideration for humans but allows killing animals out of habit and pleasure. What could plausibly account for that?

(4) Nutrition. Most recent debate about vegetarianism has focused on the question of the adequacy of a meatless diet for human nutrition. This could provide the best reason for overriding the wrongness of killing animals. Let us assume as a fundamental principle that no moral agent can be required to destroy his or her own health and basic welfare for the sake of others; therefore, a diet having this consequence is not morally justified. Does vegetarianism seriously endanger an individual's health and well-being?

Kathryn Paxton George has argued that a vegetarian diet would make large numbers of humans worse off than they would otherwise be if they ate animals. She lists seven groups of people for whom such abstinence posses a significant risk to personal health.[23] Evelyn Pluhar has disputed many of George's findings, especially those regarding the benefits of iron and the threat of osteoporosis. Supported by numerous nutrition studies, she argues that vitamin and mineral supplementation, as well as the utilization of appropriate plant sources, will alleviate any deficiencies; furthermore, Pluhar contends that the correlation between consuming animal products and meeting certain health requirements is a dubious one.[24] George responded that Pluhar had either misinterpreted or willfully ignored certain facts of the studies she had herself cited.[25] The exchange continues; a journal has devoted an entire issue to their disagreement.[26]

Fortunately, we need not enter this debate; George's target is what she calls "strict vegetarianism," the vegan diet totally devoid of any animal product. Both George and Pluhar admit that eggs and dairy products, which are allowed by NEW, would fulfill all or most of the required protein, vitamin, and mineral intake. I am not aware of any humans who, as a matter of basic welfare, must consume animal flesh in addition to eggs and dairy products, but if there are any such people, NEW would allow them to eat animals: we are under no moral requirement to significantly harm ourselves so that others, human or nonhuman, may benefit.

On the other hand, Jack Weir has maintained that

worldwide ovolactovegetarianism would produce problems of unimaginable scope.... The animls would probably suffer horribly.... Ecological stress, increased agricultural monism, and immense pain for many of the animals [would result].... Feeding the unproductive [animals] would consume valuable resources in a poorly diversified agricultural system overburdened by producing enough milk and eggs for the huge population of ovolactovegetarians.[27]

Weir's concerns are misguided. He assumes that this universal conversion would occasion drastic and ecologically destructive changes in the current scale of egg and dairy production. But this is very unlikely. The U.S. alone already produces far more eggs and dairy products than are actually consumed by Americans or sold overseas.[28] In that case, pervasive ovolactovegetarianism either encourages the status quo or is consistent with Weir's own advocacy of a return to the small family farm; this is his alternative to factory farming and one that would (presumably) yield a comparable production.[29] I assume the set of "unproductive" animals would be dominated by males; since they are still needed to bring more of the productive animals (females) into existence, and since there are already far fewer of them than there are females, they would hardly be the useless drain on resources that Weir apparently takes them to be. Nor is there any reason to think that these animals would necessarily lead miserable, painful lives, and Weir does not provide such a reason.

I conclude that none of (1)–(4) serve as a sufficiently compelling reason to override the wrongness of harming the animals eaten. If there are any individuals who must eat animal flesh (rather than just eggs and dairy products) in order to avoid a pronounced deterioration of their health, they are not prohibited from doing so by NEW. This possible case notwithstanding, the eating of animal flesh is *ultima facie* morally wrong.

Endnotes

1. In many works, but most notably *Animal Liberation,* Avon, 1st Edition, 1975, 2nd Edition, 1990.

2. For example, *Animal Liberation,* chapter 3. See also *Animal Factories,* Harmony Books, Revised Edition, 1990, co-authored with Jim Mason.

3. *Rights, Killing, and Suffering,* Basil Blackwell, 1983.

4. Frey: 197–202.

5. "Utilitarianism and Vegetarianism," *International Journal of Applied Philosophy* 4 (1988): 41–49.

6. Crisp: 44. However, utility is not maximized by eating the products of factory farming. Crisp argues, against Frey, that utilitarian considerations do not permit us to eat "intensively-reared" animals. But Frey asserts that "millions upon millions" of animals are not intensively-reared anyway (pp. 33–34).

7. About 120 million cows, pigs, and sheep and about 5.5 billion birds (mostly chickens) are killed annually in this country alone (Jim Mason and Peter Singer, *Animal Factories,* op. cit., p. 96). Global figures are unknown. There are about 10 million vegetarians in the U.S., which leaves over 230 million animal-eaters.

8. Principally in a series of papers beginning with "The Moral Basis of Vegetarianism," *Canadian Journal of Philosophy* 5 (1975): 181–214, and culminating in *The Case for Animal Rights,* University of California Press, 1983.

9. For example: Joel Feinberg, "The Rights of Animals and Unborn Generations," *Philosophy & Environmental Crisis,* William T. Blackstone, ed., University of Georgia, 1974: 43–68 and "Human Duties and Animal Rights," *On the Fifth Day,* R. Morris and M. Fox, eds., Acropolis Books, 1978: 45–69; James Rachels, "Do Animals Have A Right to Liberty?" *Animal Rights and Human Obligations,* T. Regan & P. Singer, eds., Prentice Hall, 1976: 205–223; Stephen R. L. Clark, "The Rights of Wild Things," *Inquiry* 22 (1979): 171–178; Robert Elliot, "Moral Autonomy, Self-Determination and Animal Rights," *The Monist* 70 (1987): 83–97; Bernard Rollin, *Animal Rights and Human Morality,* Prometheus Books, Revised Edition, 1990.

10. For example: H. J. McCloskey, "Moral Rights and Animals," *Inquiry* 22 (1979): 23–54; Jan Narveson, "Animal Rights," *Canadian Journal of Philosophy* 7 (1977): 161–178 and "Animal Rights Revisited," *Ethics and Animals,* H. Miller and W. Williams, eds., Humana Press, 1983; Richard A. Watson, "Self-Consciousness and the Rights of Nonhuman Animals," *Environmental Ethics* 1 (1979): 99–129; Philip Montague, "Two Concepts of Rights," *Philosophy and Public Affairs* 9 (1980): 372–384; Tibor Machan, "Do Animals Have Rights?" *Public Affairs Quarterly* 5 (1991): 163–173.

11. For example: Paul Taylor, "Inherent Value and Moral Rights" and Jan Narveson, "On a Case for Animal Rights" both in *The Monist* 70 (1987): 15–49; David Ost, "The Case Against Animal Rights," *The Southern Journal of Philosophy* 24 (1986): 365–373; Mary Anne Warren, "Difficulties with the Strong Animal Rights Position," *Between the Species* 2 (1987): 163–173; and J.

Baird Callicott, "Review of Tom Regan, *The Case For Animal Rights*" reprint in *In Defense of the Land Ethic,* State University of New York Press, 1989: 39–47.

12. *Harm to Others,* Oxford University Press, 1984:33.

13. Feinberg: 37. Welfare interests are contrasted with "ulterior interests" which presuppose but also require as a necessary condition that certain welfare interests are satisfied. Feinberg lists raising a family, building a dream house, advancing a social cause, and others as examples of ulterior interests.

14. Feinberg: 37.

15. Feinberg: 38.

16. Feinberg: 42.

17. See Tom Regan in "The Moral Basis of Vegetarianism" (reprint in *All That Dwell Therein,* University of California Press, 1982: 24). He says that the consumer of animal flesh is "causally implicated" in the continuance of a morally impermissible activity. As far as I know, he has not taken up this issue in any of his subsequent work on vegetarianism.

18. "Collective Responsibility and Moral Vegetarianism," *Journal of Social Philosophy* 24 (1993): 94.

19. Hudson: 97.

20. Hudson: 99.

21. A point forcefully made by means of a macabre device in the classic short story by Shirley Jackson, "The Lottery."

22. As reported by R. M. Hare in *Freedom and Reason,* Clarendon Press, 1963: 161.

23. "So Animal a Human . . . , or the Moral Relevance of Being An Omnivore," *Journal of Agricultural Ethics* 3 (1990): 172–186. Her list (pp. 175–178) includes children, pregnant and lactating women, the elderly, the poor, and the "undereducated."

24. "Who Can Be Morally Obligated to Be a Vegetarian?" *Journal of Agricultural and Environmental Ethics* 5 (1992): 189–215.

25. "The Use and Abuse of Scientific Studies," *Journal of Agricultural and Environmental Ethics* 5 (1992): 217–233.

26. *Journal of Agricultural and Environmental Ethics* 7 (1994).

27. "Unnecessary Pain, Nutrition, and Vegetarianism," *Between the Species* 7 (1991): 18–19.

28. In 1991, U.S. farmers produced about 154 billion pounds of milk and dairy products, but only 135.6 billion pounds were consumed. In the same year, hens laid almost 5,800 million dozen eggs; 4,900 million dozen were consumed and 862 million dozen were either exported or used for hatching. This still leaves a surplus of about 456 million eggs. See *Statistical Abstract of the United States: 1993,* U.S. Bureau of the Census, Washington D.C., 1993: 142, 675–676.

29. Weir: 22.

Review Questions

1. According to Curnutt, why is the utilitarian case for vegetarianism a shaky one?

2. Why doesn't Regan's rights view provide an adequate defense of vegetarianism in Curnutt's view?
3. State and explain Curnutt's new argument for vegetarianism. What sort of vegetarianism is being advocated?
4. What is Hudson's view? Why doesn't Curnutt accept it?
5. Why isn't the *prima facie* wrongness of animal-eating overridden by other moral considerations according to Curnutt?

Discussion Questions

1. Curnutt argues that the *prima facie* wrongness of animal-eating is not overridden by cultural considerations, but is he convincing? Suppose you are a guest at a friend's house and he is having pepperoni pizza for supper. Is it wrong to eat a slice?
2. You have a cold and a bowl of hot chicken soup will make you feel better. Is eating the soup wrong, all things considered? What would Curnutt say? What do you think?
3. Do animals have welfare interests as they are described by Feinberg? For example, do they have an interest in "the absence of groundless anxieties and resentments" or a interest in social intercourse?

William F. Baxter

People or Penguins: The Case for Optimal Pollution

William F. Baxter is William Benjamin Scott and Luna M. Scott Professor of Law at Stanford University. The reading is taken from his book People or Penguins: The Case for Optimal Pollution *(1974).*

Baxter formulates four goals that he thinks should be used as criteria for testing any position on pollution and the treatment of animals. All these goals relate to human benefits such as freedom, satisfaction, dignity, and equal treatment. In Baxter's anthropocentric view, the natural environment, including animals, counts only as a means of producing human benefits; it is not an end in itself and has no value apart from humans.

A "Good" Environment: Just One of the Set of Human Objectives

I start with the modest proposition that, in dealing with pollution, or indeed with any problem, it is helpful to know what one is attempting to accomplish. Agreement on how and whether to pursue a particular objective, such as pollution control, is not possible unless some more general objective has been identified and stated with reasonable precision. We talk loosely of having clean air and clean water, of preserving our wilderness areas, and so forth. But none of these is a sufficiently general objective: each is more accurately viewed as a means rather than as an end.

With regard to clean air, for example, one may ask, "how clean?" and "what does clean mean?" It is even reasonable to ask, "why have clean air?" Each of these questions is an implicit demand that a more general community goal be stated—a goal sufficiently general in its scope and enjoying sufficiently general assent among the community of actors that such "why" questions no longer seem admissible with respect to that goal.

If, for example, one states as a goal the proposition that "every person should be free to do whatever he wishes in contexts where his actions do not interfere with the interests of other human beings," the speaker is unlikely to be met with a response of "why." The goal may be criticized as uncertain in its implications or difficult to implement, but it is so basic a tenet of our civilization—it reflects a cultural value so broadly shared, at least in the abstract—that the question "why" is seen as impertinent or imponderable or both.

I do not mean to suggest that everyone would agree with the "spheres of freedom" objective just stated. Still less do I mean to suggest that a society could subscribe to four or five such general objectives that would be adequate in their coverage to serve as testing criteria by which all other disagreements might be measured. One difficulty in the attempt to construct such a list is that each new goal added will conflict, in certain applications, with each prior goal listed; and thus each goal serves as a limited qualification on prior goals.

Without any expectation of obtaining unanimous consent to them, let me set forth four goals that I generally use as ultimate testing criteria in attempting to frame solutions to problems of human organization. My position regarding pollution stems from these four criteria. If the criteria appeal to you and any part of what appears hereafter does not, our disagreement will have a helpful focus: which of us is correct, analytically, in supposing that his position on pollution would better serve these general goals. If the criteria do not seem acceptable to you, then it is to be expected that our more particular judgments will differ, and the task will then be yours to identify the basic set of criteria upon which your particular judgments rest.

My criteria are as follows:

1. The spheres of freedom criterion stated above.
2. Waste is a bad thing. The dominant feature of human existence is scarcity—our available resources, our aggregate labors, and our skill in employing both have always been, and will continue for some time to be, inadequate to yield to every man all the tangible and intangible satisfactions he would like to

have. Hence, none of those resources, or labors, or skills, should be wasted—that is, employed so as to yield less than they might yield in human satisfactions.
3. Every human being should be regarded as an end rather than as a means to be used for the betterment of another. Each should be afforded dignity and regarded as having an absolute claim to an evenhanded application of such rules as the community may adopt for its governance.
4. Both the incentive and the opportunity to improve his share of satisfactions should be preserved to every individual. Preservation of incentive is dictated by the "no-waste" criterion and enjoins against the continuous, totally egalitarian redistribution of satisfactions, or wealth; but subject to that constraint, everyone should receive, by continuous redistribution if necessary, some minimal share of aggregate wealth so as to avoid a level of privation from which the opportunity to improve his situation becomes illusory.

The relationship of these highly general goals to the more specific environmental issues at hand may not be readily apparent, and I am not yet ready to demonstrate their pervasive implications. But let me give one indication of their implications. Recently scientists have informed us that use of DDT in food production is causing damage to the penguin population. For the present purposes let us accept that assertion as an indisputable scientific fact. The scientific fact is often asserted as if the correct implication—that we must stop agricultural use of DDT—followed from the mere statement of the fact of penguin damage. But plainly it does not follow if my criteria are employed.

My criteria are oriented to people, not penguins. Damage to penguins, or sugar pines, or geological marvels is, without more, simply irrelevant. One must go further, by my criteria, and say: Penguins are important because people enjoy seeing them walk about rocks; and furthermore, the well-being of people would be less impaired by halting use of DDT than by giving up penguins. In short, my observations about environmental problems will be people-oriented, as are my criteria. I have no interest in preserving penguins for their own sake.

It may be said by way of objection to this position, that it is very selfish of people to act as if each person represented one unit of importance and nothing else was of any importance. It is undeniably selfish. Nevertheless I think it is the only tenable starting place for analysis for several reasons. First, no other position corresponds to the way most people really think and act—i.e., corresponds to reality.

Second, this attitude does not portend any massive destruction of nonhuman flora and fauna, for people depend on them in many obvious ways, and they will be preserved because and to the degree that humans do depend on them.

Third, what is good for humans is, in many respects, good for penguins and pine trees—clean air for example. So that humans are, in these respects, surrogates for plant and animal life.

Fourth, I do not know how we could administer any other system. Our decisions are either private or collective. Insofar as Mr. Jones is free to act privately, he may give such preferences as he wishes to other forms of life: he may feed birds in winter and do with less himself, and he may even decline to resist an advancing polar bear on the ground that the bear's appetite is more important than those portions of himself that the bear may choose to eat. In short my basic premise does not rule out private altruism to competing life-forms. It does rule out, however, Mr. Jones' inclination to feed Mr. Smith to the bear, however hungry the bear, however despicable Mr. Smith.

Insofar as we act collectively on the other hand, only humans can be afforded an opportunity to participate in the collective decisions. Penguins cannot vote now and are unlikely subjects for the franchise—pine trees more unlikely still. Again each individual is free to cast his vote so as to benefit sugar pines if that is his inclination. But many of the more extreme assertions that one hears from some conservationists amount to tacit assertions that they are specially appointed representatives of sugar pines, and hence that their preferences should be weighted more heavily than the preferences of other humans who do not enjoy equal rapport with "nature." The simplistic assertion that

agricultural use of DDT must stop at once because it is harmful to penguins is of that type.

Fifth, if polar bears or pine trees or penguins, like men, are to be regarded as ends rather than means, if they are to count in our calculus of social organization, someone must tell me how much each one counts, and someone must tell me how these life-forms are to be permitted to express their preferences, for I do not know either answer. If the answer is that certain people are to hold their proxies, then I want to know how those proxy-holders are to be selected: self-appointment does not seem workable to me.

Sixth, and by way of summary of all the foregoing, let me point out that the set of environmental issues under discussion—although they raise very complex technical questions of how to achieve any objective—ultimately raise a normative question: what *ought* we to do. Questions of *ought* are unique to the human mind and world—they are meaningless as applied to a nonhuman situation.

I reject the proposition that we *ought* to respect the "balance of nature" or to "preserve the environment" unless the reason for doing so, express or implied, is the benefit of man.

I reject the idea that there is a "right" or "morally correct" state of nature to which we should return. The word "nature" has no normative connotation. Was it "right" or "wrong" for the earth's crust to heave in contortion and create mountains and seas? Was it "right" for the first amphibian to crawl up out of the primordial ooze? Was it "wrong" for plants to reproduce themselves and alter the atmospheric composition in favor of oxygen? For animals to alter the atmosphere in favor of carbon dioxide both by breathing oxygen and eating plants? No answers can be given to these questions because they are meaningless questions.

All this may seem obvious to the point of being tedious, but much of the present controversy over environment and pollution rests on tacit normative assumptions about just such nonnormative phenomena: that it is "wrong" to impair penguins with DDT, but not to slaughter cattle for prime rib roasts. That it is wrong to kill stands of sugar pines and build housing for the poor. Every man is entitled to his own preferred definition of Walden Pond, but there is no definition that has any moral superiority over another, except by reference to the selfish needs of the human race.

From the fact that there is no normative definition of the natural state, it follows that there is no normative definition of clean air or pure water—hence no definition of polluted air—or of pollution—except by reference to the needs of man. The "right" composition of the atmosphere is one which has some dust in it and some lead in it and some hydrogen sulfide in it—just those amounts that attend a sensibly organized society thoughtfully and knowledgeably pursuing the greatest possible satisfaction for its human members.

The first and most fundamental step toward solution of our environmental problems is a clear recognition that our objective is not pure air or water but rather some optimal state of pollution. That step immediately suggests the question: How do we define and attain the level of pollution that will yield the maximum possible amount of human satisfaction?

Low levels of pollution contribute to human satisfaction but so do food and shelter and education and music. To attain ever lower levels of pollution, we must pay the cost of having less of these other things. I contrast that view of the cost of pollution control with the more popular statement that pollution control will "cost" very large numbers of dollars. The popular statement is true in some senses, false in others; sorting out the true and false senses is of some importance. The first step in that sorting process is to achieve a clear understanding of the difference between dollars and resources. Resources are the wealth of our nation; dollars are merely claim checks upon those resources. Resources are of vital importance; dollars are comparatively trivial.

Four categories of resources are sufficient for our purposes: At any given time a nation, or a planet if you prefer, has a stock of labor, of technological skill, of capital goods, and of natural resources (such as mineral deposits, timber, water, land, etc.). These resources can be used in various combinations to yield goods and services of all kinds—in some limited quantity. The quantity will be larger if they are combined efficiently, smaller if combined inefficiently. But in either event the resource stock is limited, the goods and services that they can be made to yield are limited; even the most efficient use of them will yield less than our population, in the aggregate, would like to have.

If one considers building a new dam, it is appropriate to say that it will be costly in the sense that it will require x hours of labor, y tons of steel and concrete, and z amount of capital goods. If these resources are devoted to the dam, then they cannot be used to build hospitals, fishing rods, schools, or electric can openers. That is the meaningful sense in which the dam is costly.

Quite apart from the very important question of how wisely we can combine our resources to produce goods and services, is the very different question of how they get distributed—who gets how many goods? Dollars constitute the claim checks which are distributed among people and which control their share of national output. Dollars are nearly valueless pieces of paper except to the extent that they do represent claim checks to some fraction of the output of goods and services. Viewed as claim checks, all the dollars outstanding during any period of time are worth, in the aggregate, the goods and services that are available to be claimed with them during that period—neither more nor less.

It is far easier to increase the supply of dollars than to increase the production of goods and services—printing dollars is easy. But printing more dollars doesn't help because each dollar then simply becomes a claim to fewer goods, i.e., becomes worth less.

The point is this: many people fall into error upon hearing the statement that the decision to build a dam, or to clean up a river, will cost $X million. It is regrettably easy to say: "It's only money. This is a wealthy country, and we have lots of money." But you cannot build a dam or clean a river with $X million—unless you also have a match, you can't even make a fire. One builds a dam or cleans a river by diverting labor and steel and trucks and factories from making one kind of goods to making another. The cost in dollars is merely a shorthand way of describing the extent of the diversion necessary. If we build a dam for $X million, then we must recognize that we will have $X million less housing and food and medical care and electric can openers as a result.

Similarly, the costs of controlling pollution are best expressed in terms of the other goods we will have to give up to do the job. This is not to say the job should not be done. Badly as we need more housing, more medical care, and more can openers, and more symphony orchestras, we could do with somewhat less of them, in my judgment at least, in exchange for somewhat cleaner air and rivers. But that is the nature of the trade-off, and analysis of the problem is advanced if that unpleasant reality is kept in mind. Once the trade-off relationship is clearly perceived, it is possible to state in a very general way what the optimal level of pollution is. I would state it as follows:

People enjoy watching penguins. They enjoy relatively clean air and smog-free vistas. Their health is improved by relatively clean water and air. Each of these benefits is a type of good or service. As a society we would be well advised to give up one washing machine if the resources that would have gone into that washing machine can yield greater human satisfaction when diverted into pollution control. We should give up one hospital if the resources thereby freed would yield more human satisfaction when devoted to elimination of noise in our cities. And so on, trade-off by trade-off, we should divert our productive capacities from the production of existing goods and services to the production of a cleaner, quieter, more pastoral nation up to—and no further than—the point at which we value more highly the next washing machine or hospital that we would have to do without than we value the next unit of environmental im-

provement that the diverted resources would create.

Now this proposition seems to me unassailable but so general and abstract as to be unhelpful—at least unadministerable in the form stated. It assumes we can measure in some way the incremental units of human satisfaction yielded by very different types of goods. The proposition must remain a pious abstraction until I can explain how this measurement process can occur. But I insist that the proposition stated describes the result for which we should be striving—and again, that it is always useful to know what your target is even if your weapons are too crude to score a bull's eye.

REVIEW QUESTIONS

1. Baxter gives four goals to be used as criteria in testing any environmental position. What are they?
2. According to Baxter, what are the implications of these criteria for animals and the environment?
3. Why does he think that the natural environment (including animals) represents only means and not ends?

DISCUSSION QUESTIONS

1. Baxter says that penguins are important only because humans like to look at them. The implication is that if humans derived no benefit or satisfaction from them, penguins would not be worth preserving. Do you agree? Explain your position.
2. Is the production of human benefit the only relevant moral consideration? If not, then what else should be considered?

William Godfrey-Smith

The Value of Wilderness

William Godfrey-Smith teaches philosophy at Australian National University (Canberra, Australia).

Godfrey-Smith explores two kinds of justification for wilderness preservation: an instrumental justification and a holistic one based on the intrinsic value of the wilderness. He finds that the instrumental justifications for conservation—saving the wilderness because it is a cathedral, a laboratory, a silo, or a gymnasium—all fail to provide a satisfactory rationale. Instead he suggests a holistic conception of nature where we think of humans and nature together forming a moral community, and where we must engage in cooperative behavior for the sake of the whole community.

Wilderness is the raw material out of which man has hammered the artifact called civilization.[1]

Aldo Leopold

The framework that I examine is the framework of *Western* attitudes toward our natural environment, and wilderness in particular. The philosophical task to which I shall address myself is an exploration of attitudes toward wilderness, especially the sorts of justification to which we might legitimately appeal for the preservation of wilderness: what grounds can we advance in support of the claim that wilderness is something that we should *value*?

There are two different ways of appraising something as valuable. It may be that the thing in question is good or valuable *for the sake* of something that we hold to be valuable. In this case the thing is not considered to be good in

From William Godfrey-Smith, "The Value of Wilderness," *Environmental Ethics* (1979). Reprinted with permission of *Environmental Ethics* and the author.

itself; value in this sense is ascribed in virtue of the thing's being a *means* to some valued end, and not as an *end in itself.* Such values are standardly designated *instrumental* values. Not everything that we hold to be good or valuable can be good for the sake of something else; our values must ultimately be *grounded* in something that is held to be good or valuable in itself. Such things are said to be *intrinsically* valuable. As a matter of historical fact, those things that have been held to be intrinsically valuable, within our Western traditions of thought, have nearly always been taken to be states or conditions of *persons,* e.g., happiness, pleasure, knowledge, or self-realization, to name but a few.

It follows from this that a very central assumption of Western moral thought is that value can be ascribed to the nonhuman world only insofar as it is good for the sake of the well-being of human beings.[2] Our entire attitude toward the natural environment, therefore, has a decidedly anthropocentric bias, and this fact is reflected in the sorts of justification that are standardly provided for the preservation of the natural environment.

A number of thinkers, however, are becoming increasingly persuaded that our anthropocentric morality is in fact inadequate to provide a satisfactory basis for a moral philosophy of ecological obligation. It is for this reason that we hear not infrequently the claim that we need a "new morality." A new moral framework—that is, a network of recognized obligations and duties—is not, however, something that can be casually conjured up in order to satisfy some vaguely felt need. The task of developing a sound biologically based moral philosophy, a philosophy that is not anthropocentrically based, and that provides a satisfactory justification for ecological obligation and concern, is, I think, one of the most urgent tasks confronting moral philosophers at the present time. It will entail a radical reworking of accepted attitudes—attitudes that we currently accept as "self-evident"—and this is not something that can emerge suddenly. Indeed, I think the seminal work remains largely to be done, though I suggest below the broad outline that an environmentally sound moral philosophy is likely to take.

In the absence of a comprehensive and convincing ecologically based morality we naturally fall back on *instrumental* justifications for concern for our natural surroundings, and for preserving wilderness areas and animal species. We can, I think, detect at least four main lines of instrumental justification for the preservation of wilderness. By *wilderness* I understand any reasonably large tract of the earth, together with its plant and animal communities, which is substantially unmodified by humans and in particular by human technology. The natural contrast to *wilderness* and *nature* is an *artificial* or *domesticated* environment. The fact that there are borderline cases that are difficult to classify does not, of course, vitiate this distinction.

The first attitude toward wilderness espoused by conservationists to which I wish to draw attention is what I shall call the "cathedral" view. This is the view that wilderness areas provide a vital opportunity for spiritual revival, moral regeneration, and aesthetic delight. The enjoyment of wilderness is often compared in this respect with religious or mystical experience. Preservation of magnificent wilderness areas for those who subscribe to this view is essential for human well-being, and its destruction is conceived as something akin to an act of vandalism, perhaps comparable to—some may regard it as more serious than[3]—the destruction of a magnificent and moving human edifice, such as the Parthenon, the Taj Mahal, or the Palace of Versailles.

Insofar as the "cathedral" view holds that value derives solely from human satisfactions gained from its contemplation it is clearly an instrumentalist attitude. It does, however, frequently approach an *intrinsic value* attitude, insofar as the feeling arises that there is importance in the fact that it is there to be contemplated, whether or not anyone actually takes advantage of this fact. Suppose for example, that some wilderness was so precariously balanced that *any* human intervention or contact would inevitably bring about its destruction. Those who maintained that the area should, nevertheless, be preserved, unexperienced and unenjoyed, would certainly be ascribing to it an intrinsic value.

The "cathedral" view with respect to wilderness in fact is a fairly recent innovation in Western thought. The predominant Greco-Christian attitude, which generally speaking was the predominant Western attitude prior to eighteenth- and nineteenth-century romanticism, had been to view wilderness as threatening or alarming, an attitude still reflected in the figurative uses of the expression *wilderness,* clearly connoting a degenerate state to be avoided. Christianity, in general, has enjoined "the transformation of wilderness, those dreaded haunts of demons, the ancient nature-gods, into farm and pasture," [4] that is, to a domesticated environment.

The second instrumental justification of the value of wilderness is what we might call the "laboratory" argument. This is the argument that wilderness areas provide vital subject matter for scientific inquiry that provides us with an understanding of the intricate interdependencies of biological systems, their modes of change and development, their energy cycles, and the source of their stabilities. If we are to understand our own biological dependencies, we require natural systems as a norm, to inform us of the biological laws that we transgress at our peril.

The third instrumentalist justification is the "silo" argument, which points out that one excellent reason for preserving reasonable areas of the natural environment intact is that we thereby preserve a stockpile of genetic diversity, which it is certainly prudent to maintain as a backup in case something should suddenly go wrong with the simplified biological systems that, in general, constitute agriculture. Further, there is the related point that there is no way of anticipating our future needs, or the undiscovered applications of apparently useless plants, which might turn out to be, for example, the source of some pharmacologically valuable drug—a cure, say, for leukemia. This might be called, perhaps, the "rare herb" argument, and it provides another persuasive instrumental justification for the preservation of wilderness.

The final instrumental justification that I think should be mentioned is the "gymnasium" argument, which regards the preservation of wilderness as important for athletic or recreational activities.

An obvious problem that arises from these instrumental arguments is that the various activities that they seek to justify are not always reconcilable with those of the ordinary vacationist. Still more obvious is the conflict between the recreational use of wilderness and the interests of the miner, the farmer, and the timber merchant.

The conflict of interest that we encounter here is one that it is natural to try and settle through the economic calculus of cost-benefit considerations. So long as the worth of natural systems is believed to depend entirely on instrumental values, it is natural to suppose that we can sort out the conflict of interests within an objective frame of reference, by estimating the human satisfactions to be gained from the preservation of wilderness, and by weighing these against the satisfactions that are to be gained from those activities that may lead to its substantial modification, domestication, and possibly even destruction.

Many thinkers are liable to encounter here a feeling of resistance to the suggestion that we can apply purely economic considerations to settle such conflicts of interest. The assumption behind economic patterns of thought, which underline policy formulation and planning, is that the values that we attach to natural systems and to productive activities are commensurable; this is an assumption that may be called into question. It is not simply a question of the difficulty of quantifying what value should be attached to the preservation of the natural environment. The feeling is more that economic considerations are simply out of place. This feeling is one that is often too lightly dismissed by tough-minded economists as being obscurely mystical or superstitious; but it is a view worth examining. What it amounts to, I suggest, is the belief that there is something *morally* objectionable in the destruction of natural systems, or at least in their wholesale elimination, and this is precisely the belief that natural systems, or economically "useless" species do possess an *intrinsic* value. That is, it is an attempt to articulate the rejection of the anthropocentric view that all value, ultimately, resides in *human* interests

and concerns. But it is a difficult matter to try to provide justification for such attitudes, and this is, for reasons that are deeply bound up with the problems of resolving basic value conflict, a problem that I have discussed elsewhere.[5]

The belief that all values are commensurable, so that there is no problem *in principle* in providing a satisfactory resolution of value conflict, involves the assumption that the quantitative social sciences, in particular economics, can provide an *objective* frame of reference within which all conflicts of interest can be satisfactorily resolved. We should, however, note that in the application of cost-benefit analyses there is an inevitable bias in the sorts of values that figure in the calculation, to wit, a bias toward those considerations that are readily quantifiable, and toward those interests that will be staunchly defended. This is a fairly trivial point, but it is one that has substantial consequences, for there are at least three categories of values and interests that are liable to be inadequately considered, or discounted altogether.[6] First, there are the interests of those who are too widely distributed spatially, or too incrementally affected over time, to be strongly supported by any single advocate. Second, there are the interests of persons not yet existing, to wit, future generations, who are clearly liable to be affected by present policy, but who are clearly not in a position to press any claims. Third, there are interests not associated with humans at all, such as the "rights" of wild animals.[7]

This last consideration, in particular, is apt to impress many as ludicrous, as quite simply "unthinkable." It is an unquestioned axiom of our present code of ethics that the class of individuals to which we have obligations is the class of humans. The whole apparatus of rights and duties is in fact based on an ideal of reciprocal contractual obligations, and in terms of this model the class of individuals to whom we may stand in moral relations—i.e., those with whom we recognize a network of rights, duties, and obligations—is the class of humans. A major aspect of a satisfactory ethic of ecological obligation and concern will be to challenge this central anthropocentric assumption. I return to this point below.

Even restricting our attention to the class of human preference havers, however, we should be wary of dismissing as simply inadmissible the interests of future generations. The claims of posterity tend to be excluded from our policy deliberations not, I suspect, because we believe that future generations will be unaffected by our policies, but because we lack any clear idea as to how to set about attaching weight to their interests. This is an instance of the familiar problem of "the dwarfing of soft variables." In settling conflicts of interest, any consideration that cannot be precisely quantified tends to be given little weight or, more likely, left out of the equation altogether: "If you can't measure it, it doesn't exist." [8] The result of ignoring soft variables is a spurious appearance of completeness and precision, but in eliminating all soft variables from our cost-benefit calculations, the conclusion is decidedly biased. If, as seems plausible, it is *in principle* impossible to do justice to soft variables, such as the interests of posterity, it may be that we have to abandon the idea that the economic models employed in cost-benefit calculations are universally applicable for sorting out all conflicts of interest. It may be necessary to abandon the economic calculus as the universal model for rational deliberation. [9]

Another category of soft variable that tends to be discounted from policy deliberations is that which concerns economically unimportant species of animals or plants. A familiar subterfuge that we frequently encounter is the attempt to invest such species with spurious economic value, as illustrated in the rare herb argument. A typical example of this, cited by Leopold, is the reaction of ornithologists to the threatened disappearance of certain species of songbirds: they at once came forward with some distinctly shaky evidence that they played an essential role in the control of insects. [10] The dominance of economic modes of thinking is again obvious: the evidence has to be economic in order to be acceptable. This exemplifies the way in which we turn to instrumentalist justifications for the maintenance of biotic diversity.

The alternative to such instrumentalist justifications, the alternative that Leopold advocated with great insight and eloquence, is to widen the boundary of the moral community to include animals, plants, the soil, or collectively *the land*. [11] This involves a radical shift in our conception of nature, so that land is recognized not simply as property, to be dealt with or disposed of as a matter of expediency; land in Leopold's view is not a commodity that belongs to us, but a community to which we belong. This change in conception is far-reaching and profound. It involves a shift in our metaphysical conception of nature—that is, a change in what sort of thing we take our natural surroundings to *be*. This is a point that I would like to elaborate, albeit sketchily.

The predominant Western conception of nature is exemplified in—and to no small extent is a consequence of—the philosophy of Descartes, in which nature is viewed as something separate and apart, to be transformed and controlled at will. Descartes divided the world into conscious thinking substances—minds—and extended, mechanically arranged substances—the rest of nature. It is true that we find in Western thought alternatives to the Cartesian metaphysical conception of nature—the views of Spinoza and Hegel might be mentioned in particular [12]—but the predominant spirit, especially among scientists, has been Cartesian. These metaphysical views have become deeply embedded in Western thought, which has induced us to view the world through Cartesian spectacles. One of the triumphs of Descartes' mechanistic view of nature has been the elimination of occult qualities and forces from the explanation of natural events. The natural world is to be understood, in the Cartesian model, in purely mechanistic terms. An unfortunate consequence of the triumph, nevertheless, has been a persistent fear among some thinkers that the rejection of Cartesian metaphysics may lead to the reinstatement of occult and mystical views of nature.

An important result of Descartes' sharp ontological division of the world into active mental substances and inert material substances, has been the alienation of man from the natural world. Although protests have been raised against Cartesian metaphysics ever since its inception, it has exercised a deep influence on our attitudes toward nature. Descartes' mechanistic conception of nature naturally leads to the view that it is possible in principle to obtain complete mastery and technical control over the natural world. It is significant to recall that for Descartes the paradigm instance of a natural object was a lump of wax, the perfect exemplification of malleability. This conception of natural objects as wholly pliable and passive is clearly one that leaves no room for anything like a network of obligations.

A natural corollary of the mechanistic conception of nature, and integral to the Cartesian method of inquiry, is the role played by reductive thinking. In order to understand a complex system one should, on this view, break it into its component parts and examine them. The Cartesian method of inquiry is a natural correlate of Cartesian metaphysics, and is a leitmotif of our science-based technology.

It should be stressed that a rejection of the Cartesian attitude and its method of inquiry need *not* involve a regression to occult and mystical views about the "sacredness" of the natural world, and the abandoning of systematic rational inquiry. It must be conceded, however, that the rejection of the view that nature is an exploitable commodity has, unfortunately, frequently taken this form. This sort of romantic nature mysticism *does* provide a powerful exhortation for exercising restraint in our behavior to the natural world, but it carries with it a very clear danger. This is that while prohibiting destructive acts toward the natural world, it equally prohibits constructive acts; we surely cannot rationally adopt a complete "hands off" policy with respect to nature, on the basis of what looks like the extremely implausible—and highly cynical—a priori assumption that *any* attempt to modify our surroundings is bound to be for the worse.

It may, however, be that advocates of the "sacredness" of nature are attempting to do no more than articulate the idea that natural systems have their own intrinsic value, and adopt this manner of speaking as a convenient way of rejecting the dominant anthropocentric morality. If *this* is all that is being claimed, then I have no quarrel with it. And it may be inevitable that this mode of expression is adopted in the absence of a developed ecologically sound alternative morality. But I think we should be wary of this style of justification; what is needed, as Passmore has nicely expressed it, is not the spiritualizing of nature, but the naturalizing of man.[13] This involves a shift from the piecemeal reductive conception of natural items to a *holistic* or systemic view in which we come to appreciate the symbiotic interdependencies of the natural world. On the holistic or total-field view, organisms—including man—are conceived as nodes in a biotic web of intrinsically related parts.[14] That is, our understanding of biological organisms requires more than just an understanding of their structure and properties; we also have to attend seriously to their inter-relations. Holistic or systemic thinking does not deny that organisms are complex physicochemical systems, but it affirms that the methods employed in establishing the high level functional relationships expressed by physical laws are often of very limited importance in understanding the nature of biological systems. We may now be facing, in the terminology of Thomas Kuhn,[15] a shift from a physical to a biological paradigm in our understanding of nature. This seems to me to be an important aspect of the rejection of Cartesian metaphysics.

The limitations of the physical paradigm have long been accepted in the study of human society, but the tendency has been to treat social behavior and human action as quite distinct from the operations of our natural surroundings. The inappropriateness of the physical paradigm for understanding *human* society seems to me to be quite correct; what is comparatively new is the post-Cartesian realization that the physical paradigm is of more limited application for our understanding of *nature* than was previously supposed.

The holistic conception of the natural world contains, in my view, the possibility of extending the idea of community beyond human society. And in this way biological wisdom does, I think, carry implications for ethics. Just as Copernicus showed us that man does not occupy the physical center of the universe, Darwin and his successors have shown us that man occupies no *biologically* privileged position. We still have to assimilate the implications that this biological knowledge has for morality.

Can we regard man and the natural environment as constituting a community in any morally significant sense? Passmore, in particular, has claimed that this extended sense of community is entirely spurious.[16] Leopold, on the other hand, found the biological extension of community entirely natural.[17] If we regard a community as a collection of individuals who engage in cooperative behavior, Leopold's extension seems to me entirely legitimate. An ethic is no more than a code of conduct designed to ensure cooperative behavior among the members of a community. Such cooperative behavior is required to underpin the health of the community, in this biologically extended sense, *health* being understood as the biological capacity for self-renewal,[18] and *ill-health* as the degeneration or loss of this capacity.

Man, of course, cannot be placed on "all fours" with his biologically fellow creatures in all respects. In particular, man is the only creature who can act as a full-fledged moral agent, i.e., an individual capable of exercising reflective rational choice on the basis of principles. What distinguishes man from his fellow creatures is not the capacity to *act,* but the fact that his actions are, to a great extent, free from programming. This capacity to modify our own behavior is closely bound up with the capacity to acquire knowledge of the natural world, a capacity that has enabled us, to an unprecedented extent, to manipulate the environment, and—especially in the recent past—to alter it rapidly, violently, and globally. Our hope must be that the capacity for knowledge, which has made ecologically hazardous activities possible, will lead to a more profound understanding of the delicate biological interdependencies that some of these actions now threaten, and thereby generate the wisdom for restraint.

To those who are skeptical of the possibility of extending moral principles in the manner of Leopold, to include items treated heretofore as matters of expediency, it can be pointed out that extensions have, to a limited extent, already taken place. One clear—if partial—instance, is in the treatment of animals. It is now generally accepted, and this is a comparatively recent innovation,[19] that we have at least a *prima facie* obligation not to treat animals cruelly or sadistically. And this certainly constitutes a shift in moral attitudes. If—as seems to be the case—cruelty to animals is accepted as intrinsically wrong, then there *is* at least one instance in which it is *not* a matter of moral indifference how we behave toward the nonhuman world.

More familiar perhaps are the moral revolutions that have occurred within the specific domain of human society—witness the progressive elimination of the "right" to racial, class, and sex exploitation. Each of these shifts involves the acceptance, on the part of some individuals, of new obligations, rights, and values that, to a previous generation, would have been considered unthinkable.[20] The essential step in recognizing an enlarged community involves coming to see, feel, and understand what was previously perceived as alien and apart: it is the evolution of the capacity of *empathy.*

I have digressed a little into the history of ideas, stressing in particular the importance of the influence of Descartes.[21] My justification for this excursion is that our present attitudes toward nature, and toward wilderness, are very largely the result of Descartes' metaphysical conception of what nature is, and the concomitant conception that man has of himself. Our metaphysical assumptions are frequently extremely influential invisible persuaders; they determine the boundaries of what is thinkable. In rejecting the Cartesian conception the following related shifts in attitudes can, I think, be discerned.

1. A change from reductive convergent patterns of thought to divergent holistic patterns.
2. A shift from man's conception of himself as the center of the biological world, to one in which he is conceived of as a component in a network of biological relations, a shift comparable to the Copernican discovery that man does not occupy the *physical* center of the universe.
3. An appreciation of the fact that in modifying biological systems we do not simply modify the properties of a substance, but alter a network of relations. This rejection of the Cartesian conception of nature as a collection of independent physical parts is summed up in the popular ecological maxim "it is impossible to do only one thing."

4. A recognition that the processes of nature are independent and indifferent to human interests and concerns.
5. A recognition that biological systems are items that possess intrinsic value, in Kant's terminology, that they are "ends in themselves."

We can, however, provide—and it is important that we can provide—an answer to the question: "What is the *use* of wilderness?" We certainly ought to preserve and protect wilderness areas as gymnasiums, as laboratories, as stockpiles of genetic diversity, and as cathedrals. Each of these reasons provides a powerful and sufficient instrumental justification for their preservation. But note how the very posing of this question about the *utility* of wilderness reflects an anthropocentric system of values. From a genuinely eccentric point of view the question "What is the *use* of wilderness?" would be as absurd as the question "What is the *use* of happiness?"

The philosophical task is to try to provide adequate justification, or at least clear the way for a scheme of values according to which concern and sympathy for our environment is immediate and natural, and the desirability of protecting and preserving wilderness self-evident. When once controversial propositions become platitudes, the philosophical task will have been successful.

I will conclude, nevertheless, on a deflationary note. It seems to me (at least much of the time) that the shift in attitudes that I think is required for promoting genuinely harmonious relations with nature is too drastic, too "unthinkable," to be very persuasive for most people. If this is so, then it will be more expedient to justify the preservation of wilderness in terms of instrumentalist considerations, and I have argued that there *are* powerful arguments for preservation that can be derived from the purely anthropocentric considerations of human self-interest. I hope, however, that there will be some who feel that such anthropocentric considerations are not wholly satisfying, i.e., that they do not really do justice to our intuitions. But at a time when *human* rights are being treated in some quarters with a great deal of skepticism it is perhaps unrealistic to expect the rights of nonhumans to receive sympathetic attention. Perhaps, though, we should not be too abashed by this; extensions in ethics have seldom followed the path of political expediency.

Endnotes

1. Aldo Leopold, *A Sand County Almanac* (New York: Oxford University Press, 1949), p. 188.
2. Other cultures have certainly included the idea that nature should be valued for its own sake in their moral codes, e.g., the American Indians (cf. Chief Seattle's letter to Present Franklin Pierce of 1854, reprinted in *The Canberra Times*, 5 July 1966, p. 9), the Chinese (cf. Joseph Needham, "History and Human Values," in H. and S. Rose, eds. *The Radicalization of Science* [London: Macmillan, 1976], pp. 90–117), and the Australian Aborigines (cf. W. E. H. Stanner, *Aboriginal Man in Australia* [Sydney: Angus and Robertson, 1965], pp. 207–237).
3. We can after all *replace* human artifacts such as buildings with something closely similar, but the destruction of a wilderness or a biological species is irreversible.
4. John Passmore, *Man's Responsibility for Nature* (London: Duckworth, 1974; New York: Charles Scribner's Sons, 1974), p. 17; cf. ch. 5.
5. In "The Rights of Non-humans and Intrinsic Values," in M. A. McRobbie, D. Mannison, and R. Routley, eds. *Environmental Philosophy* (Canberra: Australian National University Research School of Social Services, forthcoming).
6. Cf. Laurence H. Tribe, "Policy Science: Analysis or Ideology?" *Philosophy and Public Affairs* 2 (1972–3): 66–110.
7. I should mention that I am a skeptic about "rights"; it seems to me that talk about rights is always eliminable in favor of talk about legitimate claims for considerations, and obligations to respect those claims. Rights-talk does, however, have useful rhetorical effect in exhorting people to recognize claims. The reason for this is that claims pressed in these terms perform the crucial trick of shifting the onus of proof. This is accomplished by the fact that a *denial* of a right appears to be a more positive and deliberate act than merely refusing to acknowledge an obligation.
8. Laurence H. Tribe, "Trial by Mathematics: Precision and Ritual in Legal Process," *Harvard Law Review* 84 (1971): 1361.
9. Of course, in practice cost-benefit considerations *do* operate within deontic constraints, and we do *not* accept economics unrestrictedly as providing the model for rational deliberation. We would not accept exploitative child labor, for example, as a legitimate mode of production, no matter how favorable the economics. This is not just because we attach too high a cost to this form of labor; it is just unthinkable.
10. Aldo Leopold, "The Land Ethic," in *A Sand County Almanac*, p. 210.
11. Cf. Aldo Leopold, "The Conservation Ethic," *Journal of Forestry* 31 (1933): 634–43, and "The Land Ethic," *A Sand County Almanac*.

12. Cf. John Passmore, "Attitudes to Nature," in R. S. Peters, ed., *Nature and Conduct* (London: Macmillan, 1975), pp. 251–64.
13. Ibid., p. 260.
14. Cf. Arne Naess, "The Shallow and the Deep, Long-Range Ecology Movement," *Inquiry* 16 (1973): 95–100.
15. T. S. Kuhn, *The Structure of Scientific Revolutions* (Chicago: University of Chicago Press, 1962).
16. Passmore, *Man's Responsibility for Nature*, ch. 6; "Attitudes to Nature," p. 262.
17. Leopold, "The Land Ethic."
18. Ibid., p. 221.
19. Cf. Pasmore, "The Treatment of Animals," *Journal of the History of Ideas* 36 (1975): 195–218.
20. Cf. Christopher D. Stone, "Should Trees Have Standing? Toward Legal Rights for Natural Objects," *Southern California Law Review* 45 (1972): 450–501.
21. Here I differ from the well-known claim of Lynn White ("The Historical Roots of Our Ecological Crisis," *Science* 155 [1967]: 1203–7) that the Judeo-Christian tradition is predominantly responsible for the development of Western attitudes toward nature.

REVIEW QUESTIONS

1. Distinguish between instrumental value and intrinsic value.

2. How does Godfrey-Smith define wilderness?
3. What is the cathedral view?
4. Explain the laboratory argument.
5. What is the silo argument?
6. What is the gymnasium argument?
7. What problems arise for these instrumental justifications for preserving wilderness areas?
8. What is the dominant Western conception of nature?
9. Explain the holistic conception of the natural world.

DISCUSSION QUESTIONS

1. Is the holistic conception of the natural world acceptable? Defend your position.
2. Should human beings frustrate important interests to preserve the natural environment? Defend your answer.

Christopher D. Stone

Should Trees Have Standing? Toward Legal Rights for Natural Objects

For biographical information on Stone, see his reading in Chapter 7.

Stone argues that natural objects such as trees should be given legal rights and represented by legal friends who protect their interests. He admits

With permission of Christopher D. Stone; the essay quoted from appears in "Should Trees Have Standing? and Other Essays on Law, Morals, and the Environment" by Christopher D. Stone (Oceana Publishers, 1996).

that this is a radical idea, but he thinks it is no more radical than was the idea of women's rights in the past. The practical benefit would be that environmentalists could more easily protect the environment. Also it could produce a revolutionary way of viewing humans' relation to nature. Instead of seeing nature as something separate to be used, humans would see themselves as part of nature.

Throughout legal history, each successive extension of rights to some new entity has been, theretofore, a bit unthinkable. We are inclined to suppose the rightlessness of rightless "things" to be a decree of Nature, not a legal convention acting in support of some status quo. It is thus that we defer considering the choices involved in all their moral, social, and economic dimensions. And so the United States Supreme Court could straightfacedly tell us in *Dred Scott* that Blacks had been denied the rights of citizenship "as a subordinate and inferior class of beings, who had been subjugated by the dominant race. . . ." [1] In the nineteenth century, the highest court in California explained that Chinese had not the right to testify against white men in criminal matters because they were "a race of people whom nature has marked as inferior, and who are incapable of progress or intellectual development beyond a certain point . . . between whom and ourselves nature has placed an impassable difference." [2] The popular conception of the Jew in the thirteenth century contributed to a law which treated them as "men *ferae naturae,* protected by a quasi-forest law. Like the roe and the deer, they form an order apart." [3] Recall, too, that it was not so long ago that the foetus was "like the roe and the deer." In an early suit attempting to establish a wrongful death action on behalf of a negligently killed foetus (now widely accepted practice), Holmes, then on the Massachusetts Supreme Court, seems to have thought it simply inconceivable "that a man might owe a civil duty and incur a conditional prospective liability in tort to one not yet in being." [4] The first woman in Wisconsin who thought she might have a right to practice law was told that she did not, in the following terms:

The law of nature destines and qualifies the female sex for the bearing and nurture of the children of our race and for the custody of the homes of the world. . . . [A]ll life-long callings of women, inconsistent with these radical and sacred duties of their sex, as is the profession of the law, are departures from the order of nature; and when voluntary, treason against it. . . . The peculiar qualities of womanhood, its gentle graces, its quick sensibility, its tender susceptibility, its purity, its delicacy, its emotional impulses, its subordination of hard reason to sympathetic feeling, are surely not qualifications for forensic strife. Nature has tempered woman as little for the juridical conflicts of the court room, as for the physical conflicts of the battle field. . . . [5]

The fact is, that each time there is a movement to confer rights onto some new "entity," the proposal is bound to sound odd or frightening or laughable. This is partly because until the rightless thing receives its rights, we cannot see it as anything but a *thing* for the use of "us"—those who are holding rights at the time. In this vein, what is striking about the Wisconsin case above is that the court, for all its talk about women, so clearly was never able to see women as they are (and might become). All it could see was the popular "idealized" version of *an object it needed.* Such is the way the slave South looked upon the Black. There is something of a seamless web involved; there will be resistance to giving the thing "rights" until it can be seen and valued for itself; yet, it is hard to see it and value it for itself until we can bring ourselves to give it "rights"—which is almost inevitably going to sound inconceivable to a large group of people.

The reason for this little discourse on the unthinkable, the reader must know by now, if only from the title of the paper. I am quite seriously proposing that we give legal rights to forests, oceans, rivers, and other so-called "natural objects" in the environment—indeed, to the natural environment as a whole. . . .

TOWARD RIGHTS FOR THE ENVIRONMENT

Now, to say that the natural environment should have rights is not to say anything as silly as that no one should be allowed to cut down a tree. We say human beings have rights, but—at least as of the time of this writing—they can be executed. Corporations have rights, but they cannot plead the fifth amendment; *In re Gault* gave fifteen-year-olds certain rights in juvenile proceedings, but it did not give them the right to vote. Thus, to say that the environment should have rights is not to say that it should have every right we can imagine, or even the same body of rights as human beings have. Nor is it to say that everything in the environment should have the same rights as every other thing in the environment. . . .

For a thing to be *a holder of legal rights* something more is needed than that some authoritative body will review the actions and processes of those who threaten it. As I shall use the term, "holder of legal rights," each of three additional criteria must be satisfied. All three, one will observe, go towards making a thing *count* jurally—

to have a legally recognized worth and dignity in its own right, and not merely to serve as a means to benefit "us" (whoever the contemporary group of rights-holders may be). They are, first, that the thing can institute legal actions *at its behest;* second, that in determining the granting of legal relief, the court must take *injury to it* into account; and, third, that relief must run to the *benefit of it.* . . .

The Rightlessness of Natural Objects at Common Law

Consider, for example, the common law's posture toward the pollution of a stream. True, courts have always been able, in some circumstances, to issue orders that will stop the pollution. . . . But the stream itself is fundamentally rightless, with implications that deserve careful reconsideration.

The first sense in which the stream is not a rights-holder has to do with standing. The stream itself has none. So far as the common law is concerned, there is in general no way to challenge the polluter's actions save at the behest of a lower riparian—another human being—able to show an invasion of *his* rights. . . .

The second sense in which the common law denies "rights" to natural objects has to do with the way in which the merits are decided in those cases in which someone is competent and willing to establish standing. At its more primitive levels, the system protected the "rights" of the property owning human with minimal weighting of any values. . . . Today we have come more and more to make balances—but only such as will adjust the economic best interests of identifiable humans. . . .

Thus, we find the highest court of Pennsylvania refusing to stop a coal company from discharging polluted mine water into a tributary of the Lackawana River because a plaintiff's "grievance is for a mere personal inconvenience; and . . . mere private personal inconveniences . . . must yield to the necessities of a great public industry, which although in the hands of a private corporation, subserves a great public interest."[6] The stream itself is lost sight of in "a quantitative compromise between *two* conflicting interests."[7]

The third way in which the common law makes natural objects rightless has to do with who is regarded as the beneficiary of a favorable judgment. Here, too, it makes a considerable difference that it is not the natural object that counts in its own right. To illustrate this point let me begin by observing that it makes perfectly good sense to speak of, and ascertain, the legal damage to a natural object, if only in the sense of "making it whole" with respect to the most obvious factors. The costs of making a forest whole, for example, would include the costs of reseeding, repairing watersheds, restocking wildlife—the sorts of costs the Forest Service undergoes after a fire. Making a polluted stream whole would include the costs of restocking with fish, water-fowl, and other animal and vegetable life, dredging, washing out impurities, establishing natural and/or artificial aerating agents, and so forth. Now, what is important to note is that, under our present system, even if a plaintiff riparian wins a water pollution suit for damages, no money goes to the benefit of the stream itself to repair *its* damages. . . .

None of the natural objects, whether held in common or situated on private land, has any of the three criteria of a rights-holder. They have no standing in their own right; their unique damages do not count in determining outcome; and they are not the beneficiaries of awards. In such a fashion, these objects have traditionally been regarded by the common law, and even by all but the most recent legislation, as objects for man to conquer and master and use—in such a way as the law once looked upon "man's" relationships to African Negroes. Even where special measures have been taken to conserve them, as by seasons on game and limits on timber cutting, the dominant motive has been to conserve them *for us*—for the greatest good of the greatest number of human beings. Conservationists, so far as I am aware, are generally reluctant to maintain otherwise. As the name implies, they want to conserve and guarantee *our* consumption and *our* enjoyment of these other living things. In their own right, natural objects have counted for little, in law as in popular movements.

As I mentioned at the outset, however, the rightlessness of the natural environment can and should change; it already shows some signs of doing so.

TOWARD HAVING STANDING IN ITS OWN RIGHT

It is not inevitable, nor is it wise, that natural objects should have no rights to seek redress in their own behalf. It is no answer to say that streams and forests cannot have standing because streams and forests cannot speak. Corporations cannot speak either; nor can states, estates, infants, incompetents, municipalities, or universities. Lawyers speak for them, as they customarily do for the ordinary citizen with legal problems. One ought, I think, to handle the legal problems of natural objects as one does the problems of legal incompetents—human beings who have become vegetable. If a human being shows signs of becoming senile and has affairs that he is de jure incompetent to manage, those concerned with his well being make such a showing to the court, and someone is designated by the court with the authority to manage the incompetent's affairs. . . .

On a parity of reasoning we should have a system in which, when a friend of a natural object perceives it to be endangered, he can apply to a court for the creation of a guardianship. . . .

The potential "friends" that such a statutory scheme would require will hardly be lacking. The Sierra Club, Environmental Defense Fund, Friends of the Earth, Natural Resources Defense Counsel, and the Izaak Walton League are just some of the many groups which have manifested unflagging dedication to the environment and which are becoming increasingly capable of marshalling the requisite technical experts and lawyers. If, for example, the Environmental Defense Fund should have reason to believe that some company's strip mining operations might be irreparably destroying the ecological balance of large tracts of land, it could, under this procedure, apply to the court in which the lands were situated to be appointed guardian. As guardian, it might be given rights of inspection

(or visitation) to determine and bring to the court's attention a fuller finding on the land's condition. If there were indications that under the substantive law some redress might be available on the land's behalf, then the guardian would be entitled to raise the land's rights in the land's name, *i.e.*, without having to make the roundabout and often unavailing demonstration . . . that the "rights" of the club's members were being invaded. . . .

One reason for making the environment itself the beneficiary of a judgment is to prevent it from being "sold out" in a negotiation among private litigants who agree not to enforce rights that have been established among themselves. Protection from this will be advanced by making the natural object a party to an injunctive settlement. Even more importantly, we should make it a beneficiary of money awards. . . .

The idea of assessing damages as best we can and placing them in a trust fund is far more realistic than a hope that a total "freeze" can be put on the environmental status quo. Nature is a continuous theatre in which things and species (eventually man) are destined to enter and exit. In the meantime, co-existence of man and his environment means that *each* is going to have to compromise for the better of both. Some pollution of streams, for example, will probably be inevitable for some time. Instead of setting an unrealizable goal of enjoining absolutely the discharge of all such pollutants, the trust fund concept would (a) help assure that pollution would occur only in those instances where the social need for the pollutant's product (via his present method of production) was so high as to enable the polluter to cover *all* homocentric costs, plus some estimated costs to the environment *per se,* and (b) would be a corpus for preserving monies, if necessary, while the technology developed to a point where repairing the damaged portion of the environment was feasible. Such a fund might even finance the requisite research and development. . . .

A radical new conception of man's relationship to the rest of nature would not only be a step towards solving the material planetary problems; there are strong reasons for such a changed consciousness from the point of making us far better humans. If we only stop for a moment and look at the underlying human qualities that our present attitudes toward property and nature draw upon and reinforce, we have to be struck by how stultifying of our own personal growth and satisfaction they can become when they take rein of us. Hegel, in "justifying" private property, unwittingly reflects the tone and quality of some of the needs that are played upon:

A person has as his substantive end the right of putting his will into any and every thing and thereby making it his, because it has no such end in itself and derives its destiny and soul from his will. This is the absolute right of appropriation which man has over all "things." [8]

What is it within us that gives us this need not just to satisfy basic biological wants, but to extend our wills over things, to object-ify them, to make them ours, to manipulate them, to keep them at a psychic distance? Can it all be explained on "rational" bases? Should we not be suspect of such needs within us, cautious as to why we wish to gratify them? When I first read that passage of Hegel, I immediately thought not only of the emotional contrast with Spinoza, but of the passage in Carson McCullers' "A Tree, a Rock, a Cloud," in which an old derelict has collared a twelve-year-old boy in a streetcar cafe. The old man asks whether the boy knows "how love should be begun."

The old man leaned closer and whispered:

"A tree. A rock. A cloud."

"The weather was like this in Portland," he said. "At the time my science was begun. I meditated and I started very cautious. I would pick up something from the street and take it home with me. I bought a goldfish and I concentrated on the goldfish and I loved it. I graduated from one thing to another. Day by day I was getting this technique.

. . . "For six years now I have gone around by myself and built up my science. And now I am a master. Son. I can love anything. No longer do I have to think about it even. I see a street full of people and a beautiful light comes in me. I watch a bird in the sky. Or I meet a traveler on the road. Everything, Son. And anybody. All stranger and all loved! Do you realize what a science like mine can mean?" [9]

To be able to get away from the view that Nature is a collection of useful senseless objects is, as McCullers' "madman" suggests, deeply involved in the development of our abilities to love—or, if that is putting it too strongly, to be able to reach a heightened awareness of our own, and others' capacities in their mutual interplay. To do so, we have to give up some psychic investment in our sense of separateness and specialness in the universe. And this, in turn, is hard giving indeed, because it involves us in a fight backwards, into earlier stages of civilization and childhood in which we had to trust (and perhaps fear) our environment, for we had not then the power to master it. Yet, in doing so, we—as persons—gradually free ourselves of needs for supportive illusions. Is not this one of the triumphs for "us" of our giving legal rights to (or acknowledging the legal rights of) the Blacks and women? . . .

The time may be on hand when these sentiments, and the early stirrings of the law, can be coalesced into a radical new theory or myth—felt as well as intellectualized—of man's relationships to the rest of nature. I do not mean "myth" in a demeaning sense of the term, but in the sense in which, at different times in history, our social "facts" and relationships have been comprehended and integrated by reference to the "myths" that we are co-signers of a social contract, that the Pope is God's agent, and that all men are created equal. Patheism, Shinto, and Tao all have myths to offer. But they are all, each in its own fashion, quaint, primitive, and archaic. What is needed is a myth that can fit our growing body of knowledge of geophysics, biology, and the cosmos. In this vein, I do not think it too remote that we may come to regard the Earth, as some have suggested, as one organism, of which Mankind is a functional part—the mind, perhaps: different from the rest of nature, but different as a man's brain is from his lungs.

Endnotes

1. *Dred Scott* v. *Sanford,* 60 U.S. (19 How.) 390, 404–05 (1856).
2. *People* v. *Hall,* 4 Cal. 399, 405 (1954).
3. Schechter, "The Rightlessness of Mediaeval English Jewry," 45 *Jewish Q. Rev.* 121, 135 (1954) quoting from M. Bateson, *Medieval England* 139 (1904).

4. *Dietrich* v. *Inhabitants of Northampton* 138 Mass. 14, 16 (1884).
5. *In re Goddell*, 39 Wisc. 232, 245 (1875).
6. *Pennsylvania Coal Co.* v. *Sanderson*, 113 Pa. 126, 149, 6 A. 453, 459 (1886).
7. Hand, J., in *Smith* v. *Staso Milling Co.*, 18 F.2d 736, 738 (2d Cir. 1927) (emphasis added).
8. G. Hegel, *Hegel's Philosophy of Right*, 41 (T. Knox transl. 1945).
9. C. McCullers, *The Ballad of the Sad Cafe and Other Stories*, 150–51 (1958).

REVIEW QUESTIONS

1. In Stone's analysis, what is required for something to be a holder of legal rights?

2. Stone says that common law makes natural objects rightless in three ways. What are they?
3. How should the law treat natural objects in Stone's view?
4. According to Stone, how should humans relate to nature?

DISCUSSION QUESTIONS

1. Should trees have legal rights? What do you think? Should they also have moral rights?
2. Stone compares the present status of natural objects to the past status of women and blacks. Is this an acceptable comparison? Why or why not?

Karen J. Warren

The Power and the Promise of Ecological Feminism

Karen J. Warren is associate professor of philosophy at Macalester College in St. Paul, Minnesota. She is the author of Ecological Feminism *(1994) and edited a special issue of the journal* Hypatia *on ecological feminism.*

As Warren explains it, ecological feminism (or ecofeminism) sees important connections between the domination of women and the domination of nonhuman nature. She argues that both are the result of an oppressive patriarchal conceptual framework characterized by what she calls the logic of domination. The promise and power of ecofeminism is in the development of an environmental ethic that spells out the connections— historical, symbolic, theoretical—between the

From Karen J. Warren, "The Power and Promise of Ecological Feminism," *Environmental Ethics* 12, no. 2 (1990): 125–146. Reprinted by permission of the author and the publisher. [Some of the footnotes have been renumbered—Ed.]

domination of women and the domination of nonhuman nature.

Ecological feminism is the position that there are important connections—historical, symbolic, theoretical—between the domination of women and the domination of nonhuman nature. I argue that because the conceptual connections between the dual dominations of women and nature are located in an oppressive patriarchal conceptual framework characterized by a logic of domination, (1) the logic of traditional feminism requires the expansion of feminism to include ecological feminism and (2) ecological feminism provides a framework for developing a distinctively feminist environmental ethic. I conclude that any feminist theory and any environmental ethic which fails to take seriously the interconnected dominations of women and nature is simply inadequate.

INTRODUCTION

Ecological feminism (ecofeminism) has begun to receive a fair amount of attention lately as an alternative feminism and environmental ethic.[1] Since Francoise d'Eaubonne introduced the term *ecofeminisme* in 1974 to bring attention to women's potential for bringing about an ecological revolution,[2] the term has been used in a variety of ways. As I use the term in this paper, ecological feminism is the position that there are important connections—historical, experiential, symbolic, theoretical—between the domination of women and the domination of nature, an understanding of which is crucial to both feminism and environmental ethics. I argue that the promise and power of ecological feminism is that *it provides a distinctive framework both for reconceiving feminism and for developing an environmental ethic which takes seriously connections between the domination of women and the domination of nature.* I do so by discussing the nature of a feminist ethic and the ways in which ecofeminism provides a feminist and environmental ethic. I conclude that any feminist theory *and* any environmental ethic which fails to take seriously the twin and interconnected dominations of women and nature is at best incomplete and at worst simply inadequate.

FEMINISM, ECOLOGICAL FEMINISM, AND CONCEPTUAL FRAMEWORKS

Whatever else it is, feminism is at least the movement to end sexist oppression. It involves the elimination of any and all factors that contribute to the continued and systematic domination or subordination of women. While feminists disagree about the nature of and solutions to the subordination of women, all feminists agree that sexist oppression exists, is wrong, and must be abolished.

A "feminist issue" is any issue that contributes in some way to understanding the oppression of women. Equal rights, comparable pay for comparable work, and food production are feminist issues wherever and whenever an understanding of them contributes to an understanding of the continued exploitation or subjugation of women. Carrying water and searching for firewood are feminist issues wherever and whenever women's primary responsibility for these tasks contributes to their lack of full participation in decision making, income producing, or high status positions engaged in by men. What counts as a feminist issue, then, depends largely on context, particularly the historical and material conditions of women's lives.

Environmental degradation and exploitation are feminist issues because an understanding of them contributes to an understanding of the oppression of women. In India, for example, both deforestation and reforestation through the introduction of a monoculture species tree (e.g., eucalyptus) intended for commercial production are feminist issues because the loss of indigenous forests and multiple species of trees has drastically affected rural Indian women's ability to maintain a subsistence household. Indigenous forests provide a variety of trees for food, fuel, fodder, household utensils, dyes, medicines, and income-generating uses, while monoculture-species forests do not.[3] Although I do not argue for this claim here, a look at the global impact of environmental degradation on women's lives suggests important respects in which environmental degradation is a feminist issue.

Feminist philosophers claim that some of the most important feminist issues are *conceptual* ones: these issues concern how one conceptualizes such mainstay philosophical notions as reason and rationality, ethics, and what it is to be human. Ecofeminists extend this feminist philosophical concern to nature. They argue that, ultimately, some of the most important connections between the domination of women and the domination of nature are conceptual. To see this, consider the nature of conceptual frameworks.

A *conceptual framework* is a set of *basic* beliefs, values, attitudes, and assumptions which shape and reflect how one views oneself and one's world. It is a socially constructed lens through which we perceive ourselves and others. It is affected by such factors as gender, race, class, age, affectional orientation, nationality, and religious background.

Some conceptual frameworks are oppressive. An *oppressive conceptual framework* is one that explains, justifies, and maintains relationships of domination and subordination. When an oppressive conceptual framework is *patriarchal*, it explains, justifies, and maintains the subordination of women by men.

I have argued elsewhere that there are three significant features of oppressive conceptual frameworks: (1) value-hierarchical thinking, i.e., "up-down" thinking which places higher value, status, or prestige on what is "up" rather than on what is "down"; (2) value dualisms, i.e., disjunctive pairs in which the disjuncts are seen as oppositional (rather than as complementary) and exclusive (rather than as inclusive), and which place higher value (status, prestige) on one disjunct rather than the other (e.g., dualisms which give higher value or status to that which has historically been identified as "mind," "reason," and "male" than to that which has historically been identified as "body," "emotion," and "female"); and (3) logic of domination, i.e., a structure of argumentation which leads to a justification of subordination.[4]

The third feature of oppressive conceptual frameworks is the most significant. A logic of domination is not *just* a logical structure. It also involves a substantive value system, since an ethical premise is needed to permit or sanction the "just" subordination of that which is subordinate. This justification typically is given on grounds of some alleged characteristic (e.g., rationality) which the dominant (e.g., men) have and the subordinate (e.g., women) lack.

Contrary to what many feminists and ecofeminists have said or suggested, there may be nothing *inherently* problematic about "hierarchical thinking" or even "value-hierarchical thinking" in contexts other than contexts of oppression. Hierarchical thinking is important in daily living for classifying data, comparing information, and organizing material. Taxonomies (e.g., plant taxonomies) and biological nomenclature seem to require *some* form of "hierarchical thinking." Even "value-hierarchical thinking" may be quite acceptable in certain contexts. (The same may be said of "value dualisms" in non-oppressive contexts.) For example, suppose it is true that what is unique about humans is our conscious capacity to radically reshape our social environments (or "societies"), as Murray Bookshin suggests.[5] Then one could truthfully say that humans are better equipped to radically reshape their environments than are rocks or plants—a "value-hierarchical" way of speaking.

The problem is not simply *that* value-hierarchical thinking and value dualisms are used, but *the way* in which each has been used *in oppressive conceptual frameworks* to establish inferiority and to justify subordination.[6] It is the logic of domination, *coupled with* value-

hierarchical thinking and value dualisms, which "justifies" subordination. What is explanatorily basic, then, about the nature of oppressive conceptual frameworks is the logic of domination.

For ecofeminism, that a logic of domination is explanatorily basic is important for at least three reasons. First, without a logic of domination, a description of similarities and differences would be just that—a description of similarities and differences. Consider the claim, "Humans are different from plants and rocks in that humans can (and plants and rocks cannot) consciously and radically reshape the communities in which they live; humans are similar to plants and rocks in that they are both members of an ecological community." Even if humans are "better" than plants and rocks with respect to the conscious ability of humans to radically transform communities, one does not *thereby* get any *morally* relevant distinction between humans and nonhumans, or an argument for the domination of plants and rocks by humans. To get *those* conclusions one needs to add at least two powerful assumptions, viz., (A2) and (A4) in argument A below:

(A1) Humans do, and plants and rocks do not, have the capacity to consciously and radically change the community in which they live.

(A2) Whatever has the capacity to consciously and radically change the community in which it lives is morally superior to whatever lacks this capacity.

(A3) Thus, humans are morally superior to plants and rocks.

(A4) For any X and Y, if X is morally superior to Y, then X is morally justified in subordinating Y.

(A5) Thus, humans are morally justified in subordinating plants and rocks.

Without the two assumptions that *humans are morally superior* to (at least some) nonhumans, (A2), and that *superiority justifies subordination,* (A4), all one has is some difference between humans and some nonhumans. This is true *even if* that difference is given in terms of superiority. Thus, it is the logic of domination, (A4), which is the bottom line in ecofeminist discussions of oppression.

Second, ecofeminists argue that, at least in Western societies, the oppressive conceptual framework which sanctions the twin dominations of women and nature is a patriarchal one characterized by all three features of an oppressive conceptual framework. Many ecofeminists claim that, historically, within at least the dominant Western culture, a patriarchal conceptual framework has sanctioned the following argument B:

(B1) Women are identified with nature and the realm of the physical; men are identified with the "human" and the realm of the mental.

(B2) Whatever is identified with nature and the realm of the physical is inferior to ("below") whatever is identified with the "human" and the realm of the mental; or conversely, the latter is superior to ("above") the former.

(B3) Thus, women are inferior to ("below") men; or, conversely, men are superior to ("above") women.

(B4) For any X and Y, if X is superior to Y, then X is justified in subordinating Y.

(B5) Thus, men are justified in subordinating women.

If sound, argument B establishes *patriarchy*, i.e., the conclusion given at (B5) that the systematic domination of women by men is justified. But according to ecofeminists, (B5) is justified by just those three features of an oppressive conceptual framework identified earlier: value-hierarchical thinking, the assumption at (B2); value dualisms, the assumed dualism of the mental and the physical at (B1) and the assumed inferiority of the physical vis-à-vis the mental at (B2); and a logic of domination, the assumption at (B4), the same as the previous premise (A4). Hence, according to ecofeminists, insofar as an oppressive patriarchal conceptual framework has functioned historically (within at least dominant Western culture) to sanction the twin dominations of women and nature (argument B), both argument B and the patriarchal conceptual framework, from whence it comes, ought to be rejected.

Of course, the preceeding does not identify which premises of B are false. What is the status of premises (B1) and (B2)? Most, if not all, feminists claim that (B1), and many ecofeminists claim that (B2), have been assumed or asserted within the dominant Western philosophical and intellectual tradition.[7] As such, these feminists assert, as a matter of historical fact, that the dominant Western philosophical tradition has assumed the truth of (B1) and (B2). Ecofeminists, however, either deny (B2) or do not affirm (B2). Furthermore, because some ecofeminists are anxious to deny any ahistorical identification of women with nature, some ecofeminists deny (B1) when (B1) is used to support anything other than a strictly historical claim about what has been asserted or assumed to be true within patriarchal culture—e.g., when (B1) is used to assert that women properly are identified with the realm of nature and the physical.[8] Thus, from an ecofeminist perspective, (B1) and (B2) are properly viewed as problematic though historically sanctioned claims: they are problematic precisely because of the way they have functioned historically in a patriarchal conceptual framework and culture to sanction the dominations of women and nature.

What *all* ecofeminists agree about, then, is the way in which *the logic of domination* has functioned historically within patriarchy to sustain and justify the twin dominations of women and nature.[9] Since *all* feminists (and not just ecofeminists) oppose patriarchy, the conclusion given at (B5), all feminists (including ecofeminists) must oppose at least the logic of domination, premise (B4), on which argument B rests—whatever the truth-value status of (B1) and (B2) *outside of* a patriarchal context.

That *all* feminists must oppose the logic of domination shows the breadth and depth of the ecofeminist critique of B: it is a critique not only of the three assumptions on which this argument for the domination of women and nature rests, viz., the assumptions at (B1), (B2), and (B4); it is also a critique of patriarchal conceptual frameworks generally, i.e., of those oppressive conceptual frameworks which put men "up" and women "down," allege some way in which women are morally inferior to men, and use that alleged difference to justify the subordination of women by men. Therefore, ecofeminism is necessary to *any* feminist critique or patriarchy, and, hence, necessary to feminism (a point I discuss again later).

Third, ecofeminism clarifies why the logic of domination, and any conceptual framework which gives rise to it, must be abolished in order both to make possible a meaningful notion of difference which does not breed domination and to prevent feminism from becoming a "support" movement based primarily on shared experiences. In contemporary society, there is no one "woman's voice," no *woman* (or *human*) *simpliciter:* every woman (or human) is a woman (or human) or some race, class, age, affectional orientation, marital status, regional or national background, and so forth. Because there are no "monolithic experiences" that all women share, feminism must be a "solidarity movement" based on shared beliefs and interests rather than a "unity in sameness" movement based on shared experiences and shared victimization.[10] In the words of Maria Lugones, "Unity—not to be confused with solidarity—is understood as conceptually tied to domination."[11]

Ecofeminists insist that the sort of logic of domination used to justify the domination of humans by gender, racial or ethnic, or class status is also used to justify the domination of nature. Because eliminating a logic of domination is part of a feminist critique—whether a critique of patriarchy, white supremacist culture, or imperialism—ecofeminists insist that *naturism* is properly viewed as an integral part of any feminist solidarity movement to end sexist oppression and the logic of domination which conceptually grounds it.

ECOFEMINISM RECONCEIVES FEMINISM

The discussion so far has focused on some of the oppressive conceptual features of patriarchy. As I use the phrase, the "logic of traditional feminism" refers to the location of the conceptual roots of sexist oppression, at least in Western societies, in an oppressive patriarchal conceptual framework characterized by a logic of domination. Insofar as other systems of oppression

(e.g., racism, classism, ageism, heterosexism) are also conceptually maintained by a logic of domination, appeal to the logic of traditional feminism ultimately locates the basic conceptual interconnections among *all* systems of oppression in the logic of domination. It thereby explains at a *conceptual* level why the eradication of sexist oppression requires the eradication of the other forms of oppression.[12] It is by clarifying this conceptual connection between systems of oppression that a movement to end sexist oppression—traditionally the special turf of feminist theory and practice—leads to a reconceiving of feminism as *a movement to end all forms of oppression.*

Suppose one agrees that the logic of traditional feminism requires the expansion of feminism to include other social systems of domination (e.g., racism and classism). What warrants the inclusion of nature in these "social systems of domination"? Why must the logic of traditional feminism include the abolition of "naturism" (i.e., the domination or oppression of nonhuman nature) among the "isms" feminism must confront? The conceptual justification for expanding feminism to include ecofeminism is twofold. One basis has already been suggested: by showing that the conceptual connections between the dual dominations of women and nature are located in an oppressive and, at least in Western societies, patriarchal conceptual framework characterized by a logic of domination, ecofeminism explains how and why feminism, conceived as a movement to end sexist oppression, must be expanded and reconceived as also a movement to end naturism. This is made explicit by the following argument C:

(C1) Feminism is a movement to end sexism.
(C2) But Sexism is conceptually linked with naturism (through an oppressive conceptual framework characterized by a logic of domination).
(C3) Thus, Feminism is (also) a movement to end naturism.

Because, ultimately, these connections between sexism and naturism are conceptual—embedded in an oppressive conceptual framework—

the logic of traditional feminism leads to the embracement of ecological feminism.[13]

The other justification for reconceiving feminism to include ecofeminism has to do with the concepts of gender and nature. Just as conceptions of gender are socially constructed, so are conceptions of nature. Of course, the claim that women and nature are social constructions does not require anyone to deny that there are actual humans and actual trees, rivers, and plants. It simply implies that *how* women and nature are conceived is a matter of historical and social reality. These conceptions vary cross-culturally and by historical time period. As a result, any discussion of the "oppression or domination of nature" involves reference to historically specific forms of social domination of nonhuman nature by humans, just as discussion of the "domination of women" refers to historically specific forms of social domination of women by men. Although I do not argue for it here, an ecofeminist defense of the historical connections between the dominations of women and of nature, claims (B1) and (B2) in argument B, involves showing that within patriarchy the feminization of nature and the naturalization of women have been crucial to the historically successful subordinations of both.[14]

If ecofeminism promises to reconceive traditional feminism in ways which include naturism as a legitimate feminist issue, does ecofeminism also promise to reconceive environmental ethics in ways which are feminist? I think so. This is the subject of the remainder of the paper. . . .

ECOFEMINISM AS A FEMINIST AND ENVIRONMENTAL ETHIC

A feminist ethic involves a twofold commitment to critique male bias in ethics wherever it occurs, and to develop ethics which are not male-biased. Sometimes this involves articulation of values (e.g., values of care, appropriate trust, kinship, friendship) often lost or underplayed in mainstream ethics.[15] Sometimes it involves engaging in theory building by pioneering in new directions or by revamping old theories in gender sensitive ways. What makes the critiques of old theories or conceptualizations of new ones

"feminist" is that they emerge out of sex-gender analyses and reflect whatever those analyses reveal about gendered experience and gendered social reality.

As I conceive feminist ethics in the prefeminist present, it rejects attempts to conceive of ethical theory in terms of necessary and sufficient conditions, because it assumes that there is no essence (in the sense of some transhistorical, universal, absolute abstraction) of feminist ethics. While attempts to formulate joint necessary and sufficient conditions of a feminist ethic are unfruitful, nonetheless, there are some necessary conditions, what I prefer to call "boundary conditions," of a feminist ethic. These boundary conditions clarify some of the minimal conditions of a feminist ethic without suggesting that feminist ethics has some ahistorical essence. They are like the boundaries of a quilt or collage. They delimit the territory of the piece without dictating what the interior, the design, the actual pattern of the piece looks like. Because the actual design of the quilt emerges from the multiplicity of voices of women in a cross-cultural context, the design will change over time. It is not something static.

What are some of the boundary conditions of a feminist ethic? First, nothing can become part of a feminist ethic—can be part of the quilt—that promotes sexism, racism, classism, or any other "isms" of social domination. Of course, people may disagree about what counts as a sexist act, racist attitude, classist behavior. What counts as sexism, racism, or classism may vary cross-culturally. Still, because a feminist ethic aims at eliminating sexism and sexist bias, and (as I have already shown) sexism is intimately connected in conceptualization and in practice to racism, classism, and naturism, a feminist ethic must be anti-sexist, anti-racist, anti-classist, anti-naturist and opposed to any "ism" which presupposes or advances a logic of domination.

Second, a feminist ethic is a *contextualist* ethic. A contextualist ethic is one which sees ethical discourse and practice as emerging from the voices of people located in different historical circumstances. A contextualist ethic is properly viewed as a *collage* or *mosaic,* a *tapestry* of voices that emerges out of felt experiences. Like any collage or mosaic, the point is not to have *one picture* based on a unity of voices, but a *pattern* which emerges out of the very different voices of people located in different circumstances. When a contextualist ethic is *feminist*, it gives central place to the voices of women.

Third, since a feminist ethic gives central significance to the diversity of women's voices, a feminist ethic must be structurally pluralistic rather than unitary or reductionistic. It rejects the assumption that there is "one voice" in terms of which ethical values, beliefs, attitudes, and conduct can be assessed.

Fourth, a feminist ethic reconceives ethical theory as theory in process which will change over time. Like all theory, a feminist ethic is based on some generalizations.[16] Nevertheless, the generalizations associated with it are themselves a pattern of voices within which the different voices emerging out of concrete and alternative descriptions of ethical situations have meaning. The coherence of a feminist theory so conceived is given within a historical and conceptual context, i.e., within a set of historical, socioeconomic circumstances (including circumstances of race, class, age, and affectional orientation) and within a set of basic beliefs, values, attitudes, and assumptions about the world.

Fifth, because a feminist ethic is contextualist, structurally pluralistic, and "in-process," one way to evaluate the claims of a feminist ethic is in terms of their *inclusiveness*: those claims (voices, patterns of voices) are morally and epistemologically favored (preferred, better, less partial, less biased) which are more inclusive of the felt experiences and perspectives of oppressed persons. The condition of inclusiveness requires and ensures that the diverse voices of women (as oppressed persons) will be given legitimacy in ethical theory building. It thereby helps to minimize empirical bias, e.g., bias rising from faulty or false generalizations based on stereotyping, too small a sample size, or a skewed sample. It does so by ensuring that any generalizations which are made about ethics and ethical decision making include—indeed cohere with—the patterned voices of women.[17]

Sixth, a feminist ethic makes no attempt to provide an "objective" point of view, since it assumes that in contemporary culture there really is no such point of view. As such, it does not claim to be "unbiased" in the sense of "value-neutral" or "objective." However, it does assume that whatever bias it has as an ethic centralizing the voices of oppressed persons is a *better bias*— "better" because it is more inclusive and therefore less partial—than those which exclude those voices.[18]

Seventh, a feminist ethic provides a central place for values typically unnoticed, underplayed, or misrepresented in traditional ethics, e.g., values of care, love, friendship, and appropriate trust.[19] Again, it need not do this at the exclusion of considerations of rights, rules, or utility. There may be many contexts in which talk of rights or of utility is useful or appropriate. For instance, in contracts or property relationships, talk of rights may be useful and appropriate. In deciding what is cost-effective or advantageous to the most people, talk of utility may be useful and appropriate. In a feminist *qua* contextualist ethic, whether or not such talk is useful or appropriate depends on the context; *other values* (e.g., values of care, trust, friendship) are *not* viewed as reducible to or captured solely in terms of such talk.[20]

Eighth, a feminist ethic also involves a reconception of what it is to be human and what it is for humans to engage in ethical decision making, since it rejects as either meaningless or currently untenable any gender-free or gender-neutral description of humans, ethics, and ethical decision making. It thereby rejects what Alison Jaggar calls "abstract individualism," i.e., the position that it is possible to identify a human essence or human nature that exists independently of any particular historical context.[21] Humans and human moral conduct are properly understood essentially (and not merely accidentally) in terms of networks or webs of historical and concrete relationships.

All the props are now in place for seeing how ecofeminism provides the framework for a distinctively feminist and environmental ethic. It is a feminism that critiques male bias wherever it occurs in ethics (including environmental ethics) and aims at providing an ethic (including an environmental ethic) which is not male biased—and it does so in a way that satisfies the preliminary boundary conditions of a feminist ethic.

First, ecofeminism is quintessentially anti-naturist. Its anti-naturism consists in the rejection of any way of thinking about or acting toward nonhuman nature that reflects a logic, values, or attitude of domination. Its anti-naturist, anti-sexist, anti-racist, anti-classist (and so forth, for all other "isms" of social domination) stance forms the outer boundary of the quilt: nothing gets on the quilt which is naturist, sexist, racist, classist, and so forth.

Second, ecofeminism is a contextualist ethic. It involves a shift *from* a conception of ethics as primarily a matter of rights, rules, or principles predetermined and applied in specific cases to entities viewed as competitors in the contest of moral standing, *to* a conception of ethics as growing out of what Jim Cheney calls "defining relationships," i.e., relationships conceived in some sense as defining who one is.[22] As a contextualist ethic, it is not that rights, or rules, or principles are *not* relevant or important. Clearly they are in certain contexts and for certain purposes.[23] It is just that what *makes* them relevant or important is that those to whom they apply are entities *in relationship with* others.

Ecofeminism also involves an ethical shift *from* granting moral consideration to nonhumans *exclusively* on the grounds of some similarity they share with humans (e.g., rationality, interests, moral agency, sentiency, right-holder status) *to* "a highly contextual account to see clearly what a human being is and what the nonhuman world might be, morally speaking, *for* human beings."[24] For an ecofeminist, *how* a moral agent is in relationship to another becomes of central significance, not simply *that* a moral agent is a moral agent or is bound by rights, duties, virtue, or utility to act in a certain way.

Third, ecofeminism is structurally pluralistic in that it presupposes and maintains difference—difference among humans as well as between humans and at least some elements of nonhuman nature. Thus, while ecofeminism denies the "nature/culture" split, it affirms that humans are both members of an ecological community (in some respects) and different from it (in other respects). Ecofeminism's attention to relationships and community is not, therefore, an erasure of difference but a respectful acknowledgement of it.

Fourth, ecofeminism reconceives theory as theory in process. It focuses on patterns of meaning which emerge, for instance, from the story-telling and first-person narratives of women (and others) who deplore the twin dominations of women and nature. The use of narrative is one way to ensure that the content of the ethic—the pattern of the quilt—may/will change over time, as the historical and material realities of women's lives change and as more is learned about women-nature connections and the destruction of the nonhuman world.[25]

Fifth, ecofeminism is inclusivist. It emerges from the voices of women who experience the harmful domination of nature and the way that domination is tied to their domination as women. It emerges from listening to the voices of indigenous peoples such as Native Americans who have been dislocated from their land and have witnessed the attendant undermining of such values as appropriate reciprocity, sharing, and kinship that characterize traditional Indian culture. It emerges from listening to voices of those who, like Nathan Hare, critique traditional approaches to environmental ethics as white and bourgeois, and as failing to address issues of "black ecology" and the "ecology" of the inner city and urban spaces.[26] It also emerges out of the voices of Chipko women who see the destruction of "earth, soil, and water" as intimately connected with their own inability to survive economically.[27] With its emphasis on inclusivity and difference, ecofeminism provides a framework for recognizing that what counts as ecology and what counts as appropriate conduct toward both human and nonhuman environments is largely a matter of context.

Sixth, as a feminism, ecofeminism makes no attempt to provide an "objective" point of view. It is a social ecology. It recognizes the twin dominations of women and nature as social problems rooted both in very concrete, historical, socio-economic circumstances and in oppressive patriarchal conceptual frameworks which maintain and sanction these circumstances.

Seventh, ecofeminism makes a central place for values of care, love, friendship, trust, and appropriate reciprocity—values that presuppose that our relationships to others are central to our understanding of who we are.[28] It thereby gives voice to the sensitivity that in climbing a mountain, one is doing something in relationship with an "other," an "other" whom we can come to care about and treat respectfully.

Lastly, an ecofeminist ethic involves a reconception of what it means to be human, and in what human ethical behavior consists. Ecofeminism denies abstract individualism. Humans are who we are in large part by virtue of the historical and social contexts and the relationships we are in, including our relationships with nonhuman nature. Relationships are not something extrinsic to who we are, not an "add on" feature of human nature; they play an essential role in shaping what it is to be human. Relationships of humans to the nonhuman environment are, in part, constitutive of what it is to be a human.

By making visible the interconnections among the dominations of women and nature, ecofeminism shows that both are feminist issues and that explicit acknowledgement of both is vital to any responsible environmental ethic. Feminism *must* embrace ecological feminism if it is to end the domination of women because the domination of women is tied conceptually and historically to the domination of nature.

A responsible environmental ethic also *must* embrace feminism. Otherwise, even the seemingly most revolutionary, liberational, and holistic ecological ethic will fail to take seriously the interconnected dominations of nature and women that are so much a part of the historical legacy and conceptual framework that sanctions the exploitation of nonhuman nature. Failure to make visible these interconnected, twin dominations results in an inaccurate account of how it is that nature has been and continues to be dominated and exploited and produces an environmental ethic that lacks the depth necessary to be truly *inclusive* of the realities of persons who at least in dominant Western culture have been intimately tied with that exploitation, viz., women. Whatever else can be said in favor of such holistic ethics, a failure to make visible ecofeminist insights into the common denominators of the twin oppressions of women and nature is to perpetuate, rather than overcome, the source of that oppression.

This last point deserves further attention. It may be objected that as long as the end result is "the same"—the development of an environmental ethic which does not emerge out of or reinforce an oppressive conceptual framework—it does not matter whether that ethic (or the ethic endorsed in getting there) is feminist or not. Hence, it simply is *not* the case that any adequate environmental ethic must be feminist. My argument, in contrast, has been that it *does* matter, and for three important reasons. First, there is the scholarly issue of accurately representing historical reality, and that, ecofeminists claim, requires acknowledging the historical feminization of nature and naturalization of women as part of the exploitation of nature. Second, I have shown that the conceptual connections between the domination of women and the domination of nature are located in an oppressive and, at least in Western societies, patriarchal conceptual framework characterized by a logic of domination. Thus, I have shown that failure to notice the nature of this connection leaves at best an incomplete, inaccurate, and partial account of what is required of a conceptually adequate environmental ethic. An ethic which *does not* acknowledge this is simply *not* the same as one that does, whatever else the similarities between them. Third, the claim that, in contemporary culture, one can have an adequate environmental ethic which is *not* feminist assumes that, in contemporary culture, the label *feminist* does not add anything crucial to the nature or description of environmental ethics. I have shown that at least in contemporary culture this is false, for the word *feminist* currently helps to clarify just *how* the domination of nature is conceptually linked to patriarchy and, hence, how the liberation of nature, is conceptually linked to the termination of patriarchy. Thus, because it has critical bite in contemporary culture, it serves as an important reminder that in contemporary sex-gendered, raced, classed, and naturist culture, an unlabeled position functions as a privileged and "unmarked" position. That is, without the addition of the word *feminist,* one presents environmental ethics as if it has no bias, including male-gender bias, which is just what ecofeminists deny: failure to notice the connections between the twin oppressions of women and nature *is* male-gender bias.

One of the goals of feminism is the eradication of all oppressive sex-gender (and related race, class, age, affectional preference) categories and the creation of a world in which *difference does not breed domination*—say, the world of 4001. If in 4001, an "adequate environmental ethic" is a "feminist environmental ethic," the word *feminist* may then be redundant and unnecessary. However, this is *not* 4001, and in terms of the current historical and conceptual reality the dominations of nature and of women are intimately connected. Failure to notice or make visible that connection in 1990 perpetuates the mistaken (and privileged) view that "environmental ethics" is *not* a feminist issue, and that *feminist* adds nothing to environmental ethics.[29]

CONCLUSION

I have argued in this paper that ecofeminism provides a framework for a distinctively feminist and environmental ethic. Ecofeminism grows out of the felt and theorized about connections between the domination of women and the domination of nature. As a contextualist ethic, ecofeminism refocuses environmental ethics on what nature might mean, morally speaking, *for* humans, and on how the relational attitudes of humans to others—humans as well as nonhumans—sculpt both what it is to be human and the nature and ground of human responsibilities to the nonhuman environment. Part of what this refocusing does is to take seriously the voices of women and other oppressed persons in the construction of that ethic.

A Sioux elder once told me a story about his son. He sent his seven-year-old son to live with the child's grandparents on a Sioux reservation so that he could "learn the Indian ways." Part of what the grandparents taught the son was how to hunt the four leggeds of the forest. As I heard the story, the boy was taught, "to shoot your four-legged brother in his hind area, slowing it down but not killing it. Then, take the four legged's head in your hands, and look into

his eyes. The eyes are where all the suffering is. Look into your brother's eyes and feel his pain. Then, take your knife and cut the four-legged under his chin, here, on his neck, so that he dies quickly. And as you do, ask your brother, the four-legged, for forgiveness for what you do. Offer also a prayer of thanks to your four-legged kin for offering his body to you just now, when you need food to eat and clothing to wear. And promise the four-legged that you will put yourself back into the earth when you die, to become nourishment for the earth, and for the sister flowers, and for the brother deer. It is appropriate that you should offer this blessing for the four-legged and, in due time, reciprocate in turn with your body in this way, as the four-legged gives life to you for your survival." As I reflect upon that story, I am struck by the power of the environmental ethic that grows out of and takes seriously narrative, context, and such values and relational attitudes as care, loving perception, and appropriate reciprocity, and doing what is appropriate in a given situation—however that notion of appropriateness eventually gets filled out. I am also struck by what one is able to see, once one begins to explore some of the historical and conceptual connections between the dominations of women and of nature. A *re-conceiving* and *re-visioning* of both feminism and environmental ethics, is, I think, the power and promise of ecofeminism.

Endnotes

1. Explicit ecological feminist literature includes works from a variety of scholarly perspectives and sources. Some of these works are Leonie Caldecott and Stephanie Leland, eds., *Reclaim the Earth: Women Speak Out for Life on Earth* (London: The Women's Press, 1983): Jim Cheney, "Eco-Feminism and Deep Ecology," *Environmental Ethics* 9 (1987): 115–45; Andrée Collard with Joyce Contrucci, *Rape of the Wild: Man's Violence against Animals and the Earth* (Bloomington: Indiana University Press, 1988); Katherine Davies, "Historical Associations: Women and the Natural World," *Women & Environments* 9, no. 2 (Spring 1987): 4–6; Sharon Doubiago, "Deeper than Deep Ecology: Men Must Become Feminists," in *The New Catalyst Quarterly*, no. 10 (Winter 1987/88): 10–11; Brian Easlea, *Science and Sexual Oppression: Patriarchy's Confrontation with Women and Nature* (London: Weidenfeld & Nicholson, 1981); Elizabeth Dodson Gray, *Green Paradise Lost* (Wellesley, Mass.: Roundtable Press, 1979): Susan Griffin, *Women and Nature: The*

Roaring Inside Her (San Francisco: Harper and Row, 1978); Joan L. Griscom, "On Healing the Nature/History Split in Feminist Thought," in *Heresies #13: Feminism and Ecology* 4, no. 1 (1981): 4–9; Ynestra King, "The Ecology of Feminism and the Feminism of Ecology," in *Healing Our Wounds: The Power of Ecological Feminism,* ed. Judith Plant (Boston: New Society Publishers, 1989), pp. 18–28; "The Eco-feminist Imperative," in *Reclaim the Earth,* ed. Caldecott and Leland (London: The Women's Press, 1983), pp. 12–16, "Feminism and the Revolt of Nature," in *Heresies #13: Feminism and Ecology* 4, no. 1 (1981): 12–16, and "What is Ecofeminism?" *The Nation,* 12 December 1987; Marti Kheel, "Animal Liberation Is A Feminist Issue," *The New Catalyst Quarterly,* no. 10 (Winter 1987–88): 8–9; Carolyn Merchant, *The Death of Nature: Women, Ecology and the Scientific Revolution* (San Francisco, Harper and Row, 1980); Patrick Murphy, ed., "Feminism, Ecology, and the Future of the Humanities," special issue of *Studies in the Humanities* 15, no. 2 (December 1988); Abby Peterson and Carolyn Merchant, "Peace with the Earth: Women and the Environmental Movement in Sweden," *Women's Studies International Forum* 9, no. 5–6. (1986): 465–79; Judith Plant, "Searching for Common Ground: Ecofeminism and Bioregionalism," in *The New Catalyst Quarterly,* no. 10 (Winter 1987/88): 6–7; Judith Plant, ed., *Healing Our Wounds: The Power of Ecological Feminism* (Boston: New Society Publishers, 1989); Val Plumwood, "Ecofeminism: An Overview and Discussion of Positions and Arguments," *Australasian Journal of Philosophy,* Supplement to vol. 64 (June 1986): 120–37; Rosemary Radford Ruether, *New Woman/New Earth: Sexist Ideologies & Human Liberation* (New York: Seabury Press, 1975); Kirkpatrick Sale, "Ecofeminism—A New Perspective," *The Nation,* 26 September 1987): 302–05; Ariel Kay Salleh, "Deeper than Deep Ecology: The Eco-Feminist Connection," *Environmental Ethics* 6 (1984): 339–45, and "Epistemology and the Metaphors of Production: An Eco-Feminist Reading of Critical Theory," in *Studies in the Humanities* 15 (1988): 130–39; Vandana Shiva, *Staying Alive: Women, Ecology and Development* (London: Zed Books, 1988); Charlene Spretnak, "Ecofeminism: Our Roots and Flowering," *The Elmswood Newsletter,* Winter Solstice 1988; Karen J. Warren, "Feminism and Ecology: Making Connections," *Environmental Ethics* 9 (1987): 3–21; "Toward an Ecofeminist Ethic," *Studies in the Humanities* 15 (1988): 140–156; Miriam Wyman, "Explorations of Eco-feminism," *Women & Environments* (Spring 1987): 6–7; Iris Young, " 'Feminism and Ecology' and 'Women and Life on Earth: Eco-Feminism in the 80's'," *Environmental Ethics* 5 (1983): 173–80; Michael Zimmerman, "Feminism, Deep Ecology, and Environmental Ethics," *Environmental Ethics* 9 (1987): 21–44.

2. Francoise d'Eaubonne, *Le Feminisme ou la Mort* (Paris: Pierre Horay, 1974), pp. 213–52.

3. I discuss this in my paper, "Toward An Ecofeminist Ethic."

4. The account offered here is a revision of the account given earlier in my paper "Feminism and Ecology: Making Connections." I have changed the account to be about "oppressive" rather than strictly "patriarchal" conceptual frameworks in order to leave open the possibility that there may be some patriarchal conceptual frameworks (e.g., in non-Western cultures) which are *not* properly characterized as based on value dualisms.

5. Murray Bookshin, "Social Ecology versus 'Deep Ecology'," in *Green Perspectives: Newsletter of the Green Program Project,* no. 4–5 (Summer 1987): 9.

6. It may be that in contemporary Western society, which is so thoroughly structured by categories of gender, race, class, age, and affectional orientation, that there simply is no meaningful notion of "value-hierarchical thinking" which does not function in an oppressive context. For purposes of this paper, I leave that question open.

7. Many feminists who argue for the historical point that claims (B1) and (B2) have been asserted or assumed to be true within the dominant Western philosophical tradition do so by discussion of that tradition's conceptions of reason, rationality, and science. For a sampling of the sorts of claims made within that context, see "Reason, Rationality, and Gender," ed. Nancy Tuana and Karen J. Warren, a special issue of the American Philosophical Association's *Newsletter on Feminism and Philosophy* 88, no. 2 (March 1989): 17–71. Ecofeminists who claim that (B2) has been assumed to be true within the dominant Western philosophical tradition include: Gray, *Green Paradise Lost;* Griffin, *Woman and Nature: The Roaring Inside Her;* Merchant, *The Death of Nature;* Ruether, *New Woman/New Earth.* For a discussion of some of these ecofeminist historical accounts, see Plumwood, "Ecofeminism." While I agree that the historical connections between the domination of women and the domination of nature is a crucial one, I do not argue for that claim here.

8. Ecofeminists who deny (B1) when (B1) is offered as anything other than a true, descriptive, historical claim about patriarchal culture often do so on grounds that an objectionable sort of biological determinism, or at least harmful female sex-gender stereotypes, underlie (B1). For a discussion of this "split" among those ecofeminists ("nature feminists") who assert and those ecofeminists ("social feminists") who deny (B1) as anything other than a true historical claim about how women are described in patriarchal culture, see Griscom, "On Healing the Nature/History Split."

9. I make no attempt here to defend the historically sanctioned truth of these premises.

10. See, e.g., Bell Hooks, *Feminist Theory: From Margin to Center* (Boston: South End Press, 1984), pp. 51–52.

11. Maria Lugones, "Playfulness, 'World-Travelling,' and Loving Perception," *Hypatia* 2, no. 2 (Summer 1987): 3.

12. At an *experiential* level, some women are "women of color," poor, old, lesbian, Jewish, and physically challenged. Thus, if feminism is going to liberate these women, it also needs to end the racism, classism, heterosexism, anti-Semitism, and discrimination against

the handicapped that is constitutive of their oppression as black, or Latina, or poor, or older, or lesbian, or Jewish, or physically challenged women.

13. This same sort of reasoning shows that feminism is also a movement to end racism, classism, age-ism, heterosexism and other "isms," which are based in oppressive conceptual frameworks characterized by a logic of domination. However, there is an important caveat: ecofeminism is *not* compatible with all feminisms and all environmentalisms. For a discussion of this point, see my article, "Feminism and Ecology: Making Connections." What it *is* compatible with is the minimal condition characterization of feminism as a movement to end sexism that is accepted by all contemporary feminisms (liberal, traditional Marxist, radical, socialist, Blacks and non-Western).

14. See, e.g., Gray, *Green Paradise Lost;* Griffin, *Women and Nature;* Merchant, *The Death of Nature;* and Ruether, *New Woman/New Earth.*

15. This account of a feminist ethic draws on my paper "Toward an Ecofeminist Ethic."

16. Marilyn Frye makes this point in her illuminating paper, "The Possibility of Feminist Theory," read at the American Philosophical Association Central Division Meetings in Chicago, 29 April–1 May 1986. My discussion of feminist theory is inspired largely by that paper and by Kathryn Addelson's paper "Moral Revolution," in *Women and Values: Reading in Recent Feminist Philosophy,* ed. Marilyn Pearsall (Belmont, Calif.: Wadsworth Publishing Co., 1986) pp. 291–309.

17. Notice that the standard of inclusiveness does not exclude the voices of men. It is just that those voices must cohere with the voices of women.

18. For a more in-depth discussion of the notions of impartiality and bias, see my paper, "Critical Thinking and Feminism," *Informal Logic* 10, no. 1 (Winter 1988): 31–44.

19. The burgeoning literature on these values is noteworthy. See, e.g., Carol Gilligan, *In a Different Voice: Psychological Theories and Women's Development* (Cambridge: Harvard University Press, 1982); *Mapping the Moral Domain: A Contribution of Women's Thinking to Psychological Theory and Education,* ed. Carol Gilligan, Janie Victoria Ward, and Jill McLean Taylor, with Betty Bardige (Cambridge: Harvard University Press, 1988); Nel Noddings, *Caring: A Feminine Approach to Ethics and Moral Education* (Berkeley: University of California Press, 1984); Maria Lugones and Elizabeth V. Spelman, "Have We Got a Theory for You! Feminist Theory, Cultural Imperialism, and the Women's Voice," *Women's Studies International Forum* 6 (1983): 573–81; Maria Lugones, "Playfulness"; Annette C. Baier, "What Do Women Want In A Moral Theory?" *Nous* 19 (1985): 53–63.

20. Jim Cheney would claim that our fundamental relationships to one another as moral agents are not as moral agents to rights holders, and that whatever rights a person properly may be said to have are relationally defined rights, not rights possessed by atomistic individuals conceived as Robinson Crusoes who do not exist essentially in relation to others. On this view, even

rights talk itself is properly conceived as growing out of a relational ethic, not vice versa.

21. Alison Jaggar, *Feminist Politics and Human Nature* (Totowa, N.J.: Rowman and Allanheld, 1980), pp. 42–44.

22. Henry West has pointed out that the expression "defining relations" is ambiguous. According to West, "the 'defining' as Cheney uses it is an adjective, not a principle—it is not that ethics defines relationships; it is that ethics grows out of conceiving of the relationships that one is in as defining what the individual is."

23. For example, in relationships involving contracts or promises, those relationships might be correctly described as that of moral agent to rights holders. In relationships involving mere property, those relationships might be correctly described as that of moral agent to objects having only instrumental value, "relationships of instrumentality." In comments on an earlier draft of this paper, West suggested that possessive individualism, for instance, might be recast in such a way that an individual is defined by his or her property relationships.

24. Cheney, "Eco-Feminism and Deep Ecology," p. 144.

25. One might object that such permission for change opens the door for environmental exploitation. This is not the case. An ecofeminist ethic is anti-naturist. Hence, the unjust domination and exploitation of nature is a "boundary condition" of the ethic; no such actions are sanctioned or justified on ecofeminist grounds. What it *does* leave open is some leeway about what counts as domination and exploitation. This, I think, is a strength of the ethic, not a weakness, since it acknowledges that *that* issue cannot be resolved in any practical way in the abstract, independent of a historical and social context.

26. Nathan Hare, "Black Ecology," in *Environmental Ethics,* ed. K. S. Shrader-Frechette (Pacific Grove, Calif.: Boxwood Press, 1981), pp. 229–36.

27. For an ecofeminist discussion of the Chipko movement, see my "Toward an Ecofeminist Ethic," and Shiva's *Staying Alive.*

28. See Cheney, "Eco-Feminism and Deep Ecology," p. 122.

29. I offer the same sort of reply to critics of ecofeminism such as Warwick Fox who suggest that for the sort of ecofeminism I defend, the word *feminist* does not add anything significant to environmental ethics and, consequently, that an ecofeminist like myself might as well call herself a deep ecologist. He asks: "Why doesn't she just call it [i.e., Warren's vision of a transformative feminism] deep ecology? Why specifically attach the label *feminist* to it . . . ?" (Warwick Fox, "The Deep Ecology-Ecofeminism Debate and Its Parallels," *Environmental Ethics* 11, no. 1 [1989]: 14, n. 22). Whatever the important similarities between deep ecology and ecofeminism (or, specifically, my version of ecofeminism)—and, indeed, there are many—it is precisely my point here that the word *feminist* does add something significant to the conception of environmental ethics, and that any environmental ethic (including deep ecology) that fails to make explicit the different kinds of interconnections among the domination of nature and the domination of women will be, from a

feminist (and ecofeminist) perspective such as mine, inadequate.

REVIEW QUESTIONS

1. What is feminism according to Warren, and what counts as a feminist issue?
2. How does Warren explain oppressive conceptual frameworks?
3. What is naturism? How is it supposed to be related to sexism?
4. According to Warren, what are the main features (the boundary conditions, as she calls them) of a feminist ethic?
5. How does Warren explain ecofeminism?

DISCUSSION QUESTIONS

1. Does ecofeminism itself involve an oppressive conceptual framework as Warren defines it?
2. Can the vague word "oppression" be defined? If so, how would you define it? Does it make sense to say that rocks are oppressed or dominated on your definition? Who does the oppressing or dominating? Is it humans, or men, or just white men, or just those who are powerful (including some women), or some other group?
3. What is your reaction to the story about the Sioux way to hunt deer? Isn't wounding the deer and looking into his eyes to see his suffering cruel and wrong? What would Singer and Regan say? What do you think?

PROBLEM CASES

1. Killing Chickens. Suppose a farmer raises chickens on his farm. They are well fed, they have plenty of room, they have a comfortable place to sleep; in short, they are well cared for. Each year the farmer kills the oldest chickens, the ones that will die of disease or old age; he kills them quickly and with little or no pain. Then he thanks the chickens for their bodies; he is a religious man and believes the chickens have eternal souls that blissfully unite with the Great Spirit after death and that killing them does not harm the eternal souls. That done, he carefully prepares the chicken meat and eats it with great relish. He replaces the chickens he kills with new chickens so that the chicken population remains stable. Does this farmer do anything that is morally wrong? Explain your position.

2. The Draize Test. The Draize eye test is used by cosmetic companies such as Revlon and Procter & Gamble to test the eye irritancy of their products—cosmetics, hair shampoos, and so on. The substance to be tested is injected into the eyes of rabbits; more specifically, 0.1 milligrams (a large volume dose) is injected into the conjuctival sac of one eye of each of six rabbits with the other eye serving as a control. The lids are held together for one second and then the animal is released. The eyes are examined at 24, 48, and 72 hours to see if there is corneal damage. Although the test is very painful, as you can imagine, anesthetics are not used. The eyes are not washed. Very large doses are used (often resulting in permanent eye damage) to provide a large margin of safety in extrapolating for human response. Should companies continue to test

their new products in this way or not? What is your view?

3. Mechanical Mothers. (These experiments were mentioned in *Newsweek*, December 26, 1988). Researchers at the Primate Research Center in Madison, Wisconsin, have been conducting experiments to gauge the effects of child abuse on monkeys. One experiment involves putting baby monkeys with mechanical surrogate mothers who eject sharp brass spikes when the babies try to hug them. Another experiment consists of impregnating females who have been driven insane by social isolation. When given their babies, the mothers crush their skulls with their teeth. Are these experiments justified or not?

4. Guerrilla Warfare in Cathedral Forest. (Reported in *Esquire*, February 1987). Cathedral Forest in Oregon is one of the last large stands of virgin forest remaining on the North American continent. The forest is called old growth because the trees (Douglas firs) are among the oldest and biggest on the planet. Old growth constitutes an almost infinitesimal percentage of forested lands in the United States. Even though there is no commercial demand for the timber, the United States Forest Service has made the harvesting of the last of the old trees a priority. The Forest Service has sold Cathedral Forest to Willamette Industries, a large wood-products company.

To prevent the forest from being cut down, radical environmentalist Mike Roselle has resorted to an illegal guerilla action called tree spiking. He has driven long nails into trees in a spiral pattern.

Chain saws and saw blades will shatter when they hit the buried nails. Roselle hopes that the spiked trees will prevent Willamette from cutting down the forest. Is this tree spiking morally justified or not? What is your view?

5. *The Burning of Amazon Rain Forests.* (See the cover story in *Time,* September 18, 1989.) Farmers and cattle ranchers in Brazil are burning the rain forests of the Amazon River to clear the land for crops and livestock. According to the article in *Time,* an estimated 12,350 square miles have been destroyed so far, and the burning continues. Conservationists and leaders of rich industrial nations have asked Brazil to stop the destruction. They claim that if the Amazon rain forests are destroyed, more than one million species will vanish. This would be a significant loss of the earth's genetic and biological heritage. Furthermore, they are worried about changes in the climate. The Amazon sys-tem of forests plays an important role in the way the sun's heat is distributed around the earth because it stores more than seventy-five billion tons of carbon in its trees. Burning the trees of the Amazon forests will produce a dramatic increase in the amount of carbon dioxide in the atmosphere. The trapping of heat by this atmospheric carbon dioxide—the greenhouse effect—will significantly increase the global warming trend.

Brazilians reply that they have a sovereign right to use their land as they see fit. They complain that the rich industrial nations are just trying to maintain their economic supremacy. Brazilian President José Sarney argues that the burning is necessary for Brazilian economic development, particularly when Brazil is struggling under an $111 billion foreign debt load.

Should Brazil continue burning the Amazon rain forests? If not, then what should rich industrial nations do to help Brazil?

SUGGESTED READINGS

1. Leslie Pickering Francis and Richard Norman, "Some Animals Are More Equal Than Others," *Philosophy* 53 (October 1978), pp. 507–27, agree with Singer and others that it is wrong to cause animal suffering, but they do not think that this requires us to adopt vegetarianism or abandon animal experimentation.

2. Roger Crisp, "Utilitarianism and Vegetarianism," *International Journal of Applied Philosophy* 4 (1988), pp. 41–49, argues that Utilitarianism morally requires us both to abstain from eating the flesh of intensively reared animals and to eat the flesh of certain nonintensively reared animals. He calls this the Compromise Requirement View.

3. R. G. Frey, *Interests and Rights: The Case Against Animals* (The Clarendon Press, 1980), argues that animals have neither interests nor moral rights.

4. Joel Feinberg, "The Rights of Animals and Unborn Generations," *Philosophy and Environmental Crisis,* ed. William T. Blackstone (University of Georgia Press, 1974). In this important paper, Feinberg analyzes the concept of a right and contends that humans and animals have rights, but rocks and whole species do not. Future generations have rights, but only contingent on their coming into existence.

5. H. J. McCloskey, "Moral Rights and Animals," *Inquiry* 22 (Spring–Summer 1979), pp. 25–54, attacks Feinberg's analysis of the concept of right and presents his own account. According to McCloskey, a right is an entitlement to something and not a claim against someone. In his view, animals do not have rights.

6. James Rachels, *Created From Animals: The Moral Implications of Darwinism* (Oxford University Press, 1990), defends animal rights.

7. Carl Cohen, "The Case for the Use of Animals in Biomedical Research," *The New England Journal of Medicine* 315 (October 2, 1986), defends speciesism and the use of animals in biomedical research; he attacks both Singer and Regan. He argues that speciesism is not analogous to racism and sexism and that animals have no rights.

8. *Animal Rights and Human Obligations,* ed. Tom Regan and Peter Singer (Prentice-Hall, 1989), is a collection of articles on animals that includes discussions of animal rights, the treatment of farm animals, and the treatment of animals in science.

9. Barbara F. Orlans, *In the Name of Science: Issues in Responsible Animal Experimentation* (Oxford University Press, 1993), gives a detailed and informed discussion of the issues raised by animal experimentation.

10. William K. Frankena, "Ethics and Environment," *Ethics and Problems of the 21st Century,* ed. Kenneth Goodpaster and K. M. Sayre (University of Notre Dame Press, 1979), pp. 3–19, defends sentientism as an adequate basis for environmental ethics.

11. Alastair S. Gunn, "Why Should We Care about Rare Species?" *Environmental Ethics* 2, no. 1 (Spring 1989), pp. 17–37, argues that the extermination of a rare species is wrong because each species (as well as the ecological whole) has intrinsic value.

12. Aldo Leopold, "The Land Ethic," *A Sand County Almanac* (Oxford University Press, 1966), pp. 217–41. This is the classic presentation of Leopold's Land Ethic. As he puts it, "The land ethic simply enlarges the boundaries of the community to include soils, waters, plants, and animals, or collectively, the land."

13. J. Baird Callicott, "The Search for an Environmental Ethic," *Matters of Life and Death,* third edition, ed. Tom Regan (McGraw-Hill, 1993), pp. 322–81, argues that ecocentrism, a conceptually developed version of Leopold's land ethic, is the most satisfactory environmental ethic.

14. J. Baird Callicott, "Animal Liberation: A Triangular Affair," *Environmental Ethics* 2 (Winter 1980), pp. 311–38, discusses the conflict between animal rights advocates and environmentalists. For example, Singer thinks that hunting and killing animals is wrong, but Aldo Leopold did not think that the land ethic forbids hunting, killing, and eating animals. In fact, Leopold was an enthusiastic hunter and meat-eater.

15. John Passmore, *Man's Responsibility for Nature* (Charles Scribner's Sons, 1974), thinks that we should not sacrifice art, science, or other human interests for the sake of conservation.

16. Paul W. Taylor, *Respect for Nature: A Theory of Environmental Ethics* (Princeton University Press, 1986), develops a theory of respect for nature that is similar to the ethical theory based on respect for persons. It requires us to see other living things as having an inherent worth that is equal to our own, and a denial that humans have a higher worth.

17. *Earthbound: New Introductory Essays in Environmental Ethics,* ed. Tom Regan (Random House, 1984), is a collection of original essays, including Alastair S. Gunn, "Preserving Rare Species," Annette Baier, "For the Sake of Future Generations," and Mark Sagoff, "Ethics and Economics in Environmental Law."

18. *Ethics and the Environment,* ed. Donald Scherer and Thomas Attig (Prentice-Hall, 1983), is a collection of readings on specific environmental problems and the general question of defining an environmental ethic.

19. *Radical Environmentalism: Philosophy and Tactics,* ed. Peter C. List (Wadsworth Publishing Co., 1993), is a collection that includes articles on radical environmental views such as ecofeminism and deep ecology. As it is explained by Arne Naess in two articles, deep ecology starts with the view called holism in the readings but goes on to recommend a mystical vision of the whole of nature as the Self (a teaching found in the Upanishads). Also covered are the tactics of radical environmental groups like Earth First! that engage in nonviolent resistance (called monkey wrenching, a term from Edward Abbey's book *The Monkey Wrench Gang*) and the Sea Shepherd Society that takes action to save marine animals such as whales.

20. *Environmental Ethics,* ed. Louis P. Poman (Jones and Bartlett Publishers, Inc., 1994), is a comprehensive collection of readings on topics related to animals and the environment such as animal rights, biocentric ethics, ecocentric ethics, deep ecology, the Gaia Hypothesis, the greenhouse effect, and so on. Of special interest is Margarita Levin's critique of Warren's ecofeminism.

Chapter Nine

WAR AND VIOLENCE

Introduction

Conventional and Nuclear War   In this chapter we will concern ourselves with conventional war, as distinguished from nuclear war. Recent history provides us with many examples: the Korean War, the Vietnam War, the war in Afghanistan, the invasion of Grenada, the Gulf War, and most recently, the war in Bosnia. World War II started as a conventional war but ended as a nuclear war with the destruction of Hiroshima and Nagasaki in August of 1945. World War II was the first and, it is hoped, the last nuclear war.

Perhaps it is premature to say that we have seen the last nuclear war. But it has been more than fifty years since two atomic bombs were dropped on two undefended cities in Japan, and even today there is debate about whether killing hundreds of thousands of civilians was justified. Of course there are thousands of such weapons in different countries today, but as yet nobody has used them. Why? There are different answers. One is that their use is irrational: The dangers of retaliation, escalation, and radioactive fallout are too great for the use of nuclear weapons to be in any country's best interest. Another answer is that it is immoral to use them because too many innocent noncombatants are killed or injured; this is one of the objections to their use on Hiroshima and Nagasaki.

Still it is always possible that an accident, an act of terrorism, or some irrational dictator could touch off a nuclear war. But whatever the prospects for nuclear war, it seems clear that the more urgent concern today is conventional war. According to Barbara Harff in the reading, it is likely that a multitude of ethnic conflicts will develop in the former Soviet

527

Union, wars like the one in Bosnia. This war started in 1992 when Serbian nationalists and the Yugoslav Army attacked Muslims and Bosnia and Herzegovina in a campaign of ethnic cleansing that assumed the proportions of genocide, at least according to Harff. The Serbs laid siege to Sarajevo, the capital, but the city's Muslim defenders held out with food relief from the United Nations. In January of 1993, the situation became even more complicated when the Croatian Army launched an assault to retake territory in southern Croatia. Violence escalated between Croats, Muslims, and Serbs, with each group fighting the other two. Now hundreds of thousands of people have been killed, and millions have been displaced by the war.

Two Issues   The readings address two main issues raised by conventional wars like the one in Bosnia: When, if ever, is war justified? And what methods are legitimate in fighting a war? In the case of the war in Bosnia, Harff argues that the United States and other nations have a moral obligation to intervene to stop crimes against humanity, and indeed in December 1995, President Clinton ordered 20,000 U.S. soldiers to Bosnia to ensure that the Dayton peace agreement is kept. But is this military intervention justified? What should the soldiers do if fighting breaks out again? Should the U.S. forces start bombing Serbian positions? What should they do if snipers start killing noncombatants, as they have done in Sarajevo? Should they attack combatants or merely defend themselves?

Pacifism   One important position on these issues is pacifism. In the first reading for the chapter, Douglas P. Lackey distinguishes between universal pacifism, private pacifism, and antiwar pacifism. Universal pacifism either opposes all killing or all violence. Albert Schweitzer, an example of the first type, opposed all killing because life is sacred, whereas Mohandas Gandhi, an example of the second type, opposed all violence. One problem with both these views, as Lackey points out, is that sometimes killing or violence seems to be required to save lives. Private pacifism is the

view that personal violence is always wrong but political violence is sometimes morally permissible. This view is attributed to St. Augustine. But it runs into the problem of self-defense; most people believe that personal violence is justified in defense of one's life or property. The kind of pacifism that Lackey defends is antiwar pacifism; this is the view that personal violence is sometimes morally permissible, for instance in self-defense, but war is always morally wrong because it involves the killing of soldiers and civilians. The burden of this view is to show that war can never be a means to some great moral good such as political freedom. Certainly wars such as the Revolutionary War in America are defended in this way.

Just War Theory   Another important view on war is Just War Theory. Medieval Christian theologians called Scholastics originally formulated the theory, and it has been discussed ever since. The theory distinguishes between the two questions about war mentioned above. First is the question of the right to go to war (called *jus ad bellum* or "right to war"): What are the conditions that justify going to war? Second is the question of the right conduct in war (called *jus in bello* or "right in war"): How should combatants conduct themselves in fighting a war?

As William V. O'Brien explains it in the second reading, then, the theory has two components, one concerned with the right to go to war and the other with the conduct of war. There are three conditions that have to be met in order to establish the right to go to war: (1) the war must be declared by a competent authority; (2) there must be a just cause; and (3) there must be a right intention that ultimately aims at peace. The principles governing the conduct of a just war concern proportion (which compares the good achieved by the war with the evil it produces) and discrimination (which prohibits direct, intentional attacks on noncombatants).

The principle of discrimination requires us to make a distinction between combatants and noncombatants. But how do we make this distinction? According to Jeffrie G. Murphy, this distinction cannot be drawn using the concepts of innocence and guilt. Instead, he suggests that combatants are those engaged in an attempt to destroy you, provided your belief is reasonable. Noncombatants are those for whom the belief is not reasonable.

Gregory S. Kavka raises more problems for Just War Theory, problems that arise when we try to apply the theory to the recent Gulf War. The first two criteria for a just war were satisfied Kavka says, but when it comes to the criterion of right intention there are problems. Do we look at the intentions of the individuals involved, or was there a collective intention to be found? And how do we determine what these intentions were? Can we believe what the political leaders said? Furthermore, how do we determine if the criteria of proportionality and last resort were satisfied? (O'Brien puts these as specific conditions under the general criterion of just cause.) To see if the criterion of proportionality was satisfied, we have to show that the good produced outweighed the bad effects of the war. But as Kavka points out, there are difficulties in doing this. First, there is the factual problem of determining the actual effects of the war. Second, we have to decide whether we are looking at actual outcomes or merely those intended by the combatants. Third, there is the perplexing task of comparing the actual outcomes of the war with those that might have been obtained if the war had not occurred. That is, we have to consider counterfactual situations, and this is hard to do. Turning to the condition or criterion of last resort, how do we decide that all available peaceful alternatives were exhausted? Kavka suggests that there were peaceful alternatives; for example, the Soviets attempted a diplomatic solution. The upshot is that the Gulf War, a war that many people think was justified, turns out to be problematic when Just War Theory is applied to it.

Holy War   Just War Theory and pacifism have dominated discussion of war in Western thought. Both of these developed in the tradition of Christianity. There is, however, another important doctrine about war that comes from Islam, a doctrine that comes up in discussions of the Gulf War. (See the problem case on the Gulf War.) This is the Islamic doctrine of jihād or holy war. As Majid Khadduri explains it, jihād literally means exertion in Allah's path. A believer may do this with the heart, the tongue, the hands, or the sword. It is only in the last case that jihād means holy war. Holy war is the only kind of war allowed, and no distinction is made between offensive and defensive war. A holy war must be commanded by the Imām, the religious head of state, and as such it is considered to be commanded by Allah who rewards those who participate with eternal life in paradise.

Douglas P. Lackey

Pacifism

Douglas P. Lackey is professor of philosophy at Baruch College and the Graduate Center of the City University of New York. He is the author of

Moral Principles and Nuclear Weapons (1984) and The Ethics of War and Peace (1989), from which our reading is taken.

Lackey distinguishes between various types of pacifism: There is the universal pacifist view that all killing is wrong, the universal pacifist view that all violence is wrong, private pacifism that condemns personal violence but not political violence, and antiwar pacifism that allows personal violence in some cases, but condemns all wars because of the killing of soldiers and civilians. Lackey discusses objections to all these views, but he defends antiwar pacifism. Or more accurately,

From *The Ethics of War and Peace* by Lackey, Douglas P., pp. 6–24, © 1989. Reprinted by permission of Prentice-Hall, Inc., Upper Saddle River, NJ.

speaking on behalf of the antiwar pacifist, Lackey provides an answer to every objection to antiwar pacifism, leaving the reader with the impression that he supports this view.

1. VARIETIES OF PACIFISM

Everyone has a vague idea of what a pacifist is, but few realize that there are many kinds of pacifists. (Sometimes the different kinds quarrel with each other!) One task for the student of international ethics is to distinguish the different types of pacifism and to identify which types represent genuine moral theories.

Most of us at some time or other have run into the "live and let live" pacifist, the person who says, "I am absolutely opposed to killing and violence—but I don't seek to impose my own code on anyone else. If other people want to use violence, so be it. They have their values and I have mine." For such a person, pacifism is one life style among others, a life style committed to gentleness and care, and opposed to belligerence and militarism. Doubtless, many people who express such commitments are sincere and are prepared to live by their beliefs. At the same time, it is important to see why "live and let live" pacifism does not constitute a moral point of view.

When someone judges that a certain action, A, is morally wrong, that judgment entails that no one should do A. Thus, there is no way to have moral values without believing that these values apply to other people. If a person says that A is morally wrong but that it doesn't matter if other people do A, then that person either is being inconsistent or doesn't know what the word "moral" means. If a person believes that killing, in certain circumstances, is morally wrong, that belief implies that no one should kill, at least in those circumstances. If a pacifist claims that killing is wrong in *all* circumstances, but that it is permissible for other people to kill on occasion, then he has not understood the universal character of genuine moral principles. If pacifism is to be a moral theory, it must be prescribed for all or prescribed for none.

Once one recognizes this "universalizing" character of genuine moral beliefs, one will take moral commitments more seriously than those who treat a moral code as a personal life-style. Since moral principles apply to everyone, we must take care that our moral principles are correct, checking that they are not inconsistent with each other, developing and adjusting them so that they are detailed and subtle enough to deal with a variety of circumstances, and making sure that they are defensible against the objections of those who do not accept them. Of course many pacifists do take the business of morality seriously and advance pacifism as a genuine moral position, not as a mere life-style. All such serious pacifists believe that *everyone* ought to be a pacifist, and that those who reject pacifism are deluded or wicked. Moreover, they do not simply endorse pacifism; they offer arguments in its defense.

We will consider four types of pacifist moral theory. First, there are pacifists who maintain that the central idea of pacifism is the immorality of killing. Second, there are pacifists who maintain that the essence of pacifism is the immorality of violence, whether this be violence in personal relations or violence in relations between nation-states. Third, there are pacifists who argue that personal violence is always morally wrong but that political violence is sometimes morally right: for example, that it is sometimes morally permissible for a nation to go to war. Fourth and finally, there are pacifists who believe that personal violence is sometimes morally permissible but that war is always morally wrong.

Albert Schweitzer, who opposed all killing on the grounds that life is sacred, was the first sort of pacifist. Mohandas Gandhi and Leo Tolstoy, who opposed not only killing but every kind of coercion and violence, were pacifists of the second sort: I will call such pacifists "universal pacifists." St. Augustine, who condemned self-defense but endorsed wars against heretics, was a pacifist of the third sort. Let us call him a "private pacifist," since he condemned only violence in the private sphere. Pacifists of the fourth sort, increasingly common in the modern era of nuclear and total war, I will call "antiwar pacifists."

2. The Prohibition against Killing

(a) The Biblical Prohibition

One simple and common argument for pacifism is the argument that the Bible, God's revealed word, says to all people "Thou shalt not kill" (Exod. 20:13). Some pacifists interpret this sentence as implying that no one should kill under any circumstances, unless God indicates that this command is suspended, as He did when He commanded Abraham to slay Isaac. The justification for this interpretation is the words themselves, "Thou shalt not kill," which are presented in the Bible bluntly and without qualification, not only in Exodus but also in Deuteronomy (5:17).

This argument, however, is subject to a great many criticisms. The original language of Exodus and Deuteronomy is Hebrew, and the consensus of scholarship says that the Hebrew sentence at Exodus 20:13, "Lo Tirzach," is best translated as "Thou shalt do no murder," not as "Thou shalt not kill." If this translation is correct, then Exodus 20:13 does not forbid all killing but only those killings that happen to be murders. Furthermore, there are many places in the Bible where God commands human beings to kill in specified circumstances. God announces 613 commandments in all, and these include "Thou shalt not suffer a witch to live" (Exod. 22:18); "He that blasphemeth the name of the Lord . . . shall surely be put to death, and all the congregation shall stone him" (Lev. 24:16); "He that killeth any man shall surely be put to death" (Lev. 24:17); and so forth. It is difficult to argue that these instructions are like God's specific instructions to Abraham to slay Isaac: these are general commandments to be applied by many people, to many people, day in and day out. They are at least as general and as divinely sanctioned as the commandment translated "Thou shalt not kill."

There are other difficulties for pacifists who pin their hopes on prohibitions in the Hebrew Bible. Even if the commandment "Thou shalt not kill," properly interpreted, did prohibit all types of killing, the skeptic can ask whether this, by itself, proves that all killing is immoral. First,

how do we know that the statements in the Hebrew Bible really are God's word, and not just the guesses of ancient scribes? Second, even if the commandments in the Bible do express God's views, why are we morally bound to obey divine commands? (To say that we will be punished if we do not obey is to appeal to fear and self-interest, not to moral sentiments). Third, are the commandments in the Old Testament laws for all people, or just laws for the children of Israel? If they are laws for all people, then all people who do not eat unleavened bread for Passover are either deluded or wicked. If they are laws only for the children of Israel, they are religious laws and not moral laws, since they lack the universality that all moral laws must have.

Finally, the argument assumes the existence of God, and philosophers report that the existence of God is not easy to demonstrate. Even many religious believers are more confident of the truth of basic moral judgments, such as "Small children should not be tortured to death for purposes of amusement," than they are confident of the existence of God. For such people, it would seem odd to try to justify moral principles by appeals to religious principles, since the evidence for those religious principles is weaker than the evidence for the moral principles they are supposed to justify.

(b) The Sacredness of Life

There are, however, people who oppose all killing but do not seek justification in divine revelation. Many of these defend pacifism by appeal to the sacredness of life. Almost everyone is struck with wonder when watching the movements and reactions of a newborn baby, and almost everyone can be provoked to awe by the study of living things, great or small. The complexity of the mechanisms found in living bodies, combined with the efficiency with which they fulfill their functions, is not matched by any of the processes in nonliving matter. People who are particularly awestruck by the beauty of living things infer from these feelings that life is sacred, that all killing is morally wrong.

Different versions of pacifism have been derived from beliefs about the sacredness of life.

The most extreme version forbids the killing of any living thing. This view was allegedly held by Pythagoras, and is presently held by members of the Jain religion in India. (Those who think that such pacifists must soon starve to death should note that a life-sustaining diet can easily be constructed from milk, honey, fallen fruit and vegetables, and other items that are consumable without prior killing.) A less extreme view sanctions the killing of plants but forbids the killing of animals. The most moderate view prohibits only the killing of fellow human beings.

There is deep appeal in an argument that connects the sacredness of life with the wrongfulness of taking life. Even people who are not pacifists are often revolted by the spectacle of killing, and most Americans would be unable to eat meat if they had to watch how the animals whose flesh they consume had been slaughtered, or if they had to do the slaughtering themselves. Most people sense that they do not own the world they inhabit and recognize that they are not free to do with the world as they will, that the things in it, most especially living things, are worthy of respect and care. Seemingly nothing could violate the respect living things deserve more than killing, especially since much of the taking of human and nonhuman life is so obviously unnecessary.

But with the introduction of the word "unnecessary" a paradox arises. Sometimes—less often than we think, but sometimes—the taking of some lives will save other lives. Does the principle that life is sacred and ought to be preserved imply that nothing should ever be killed, or does it imply that as much life should be preserved as possible? Obviously pacifists take the former view; nonpacifists, the latter.

The view that killing is wrong because it destroys what is sacred seems to imply that killing is wrong because killing diminishes the amount of good in the world. It seems to follow that if a person can save more lives by killing than by refusing to kill, arguments about the sacredness of life would not show that killing in these circumstances is wrong. (It might be wrong for other reasons.) The more lives saved, the greater the quantity of good in the world.

The difficulty that some killing might, on balance, save lives, is not the only problem for pacifism based on the sacredness of life. If preserving life is the highest value, a value not comparable with other, non-life-preserving goods, it follows that any acts which place life at risk are immoral. But many admirable actions have been undertaken in the face of death, and many less heroic but morally impeccable actions—driving on a road at moderate speed, authorizing a commercial flight to take off, and so forth—place life at risk. In cases of martyrdom in which people choose death over religious conversion, life is just as much destroyed as it is in a common murder. Yet, on the whole, automobile drivers, air traffic controllers, and religious martyrs are not thought to be wicked. Likewise, people on life-sustaining machinery sometimes request that the machines be turned off, on the grounds that quality of life matters more than quantity of life. We may consider such people mistaken, but we hardly think that they are morally depraved.

In answering this objection, the pacifist may wish to distinguish between *killing other people* and *getting oneself killed,* arguing that only the former is immoral. But although there is a genuine distinction between killing and getting killed, the distinction does not entail that killing other people destroys life but getting oneself killed does not. If life is sacred, life, including one's own life, must be preserved at all cost. In many cases, people consider the price of preserving their own lives simply to be too high.

(c) The Right to Life

Some pacifists may try to avoid the difficulties of the "sacredness of life" view by arguing that the essential immorality of killing is that it violates the *right to life* that every human being possesses. If people have a right to life, then it is never morally permissible to kill some people in order to save others, since according to the usual interpretation of rights, it is never permissible to violate a right in order to secure some good.

A discussion of the logic of rights in general and the right to life in particular is beyond the scope of this book. But a number of students of this subject are prepared to argue that the possession of any right implies the permissibility of defending that right against aggression: if this were not so, what would be the point of asserting the existence of rights? But if the possession of a right to life implies the permissibility of defending that right against aggression—a defense that may require killing the aggressor—then the existence of a right to life cannot by itself imply the impermissibility of killing. On this view, the right to life implies the right to self-defense, including violent self-defense. It does not imply pacifism.

3. UNIVERSAL PACIFISM

(a) Christian Pacifism

Universal pacifists are morally opposed to all violence, not just to killing. Many universal pacifists derive their views from the Christian Gospels. In the Sermon on the Mount, Christ taught:

Ye have heard that it hath been said, An eye for an eye, a tooth for a tooth:
  But I say unto you, that ye resist not evil: but whosoever shall smite thee on the right cheek, turn to him the other also . . . .
  Ye have heard it said, thou shalt love thy neighbor, and hate thine enemy. But I say unto you, Love your enemies, bless them that curse you, do good to them that hate you. . . . that ye may be the children of your father which is in heaven: for he maketh the sun to rise on the evil and on the good, and sendeth the rain on the just and the unjust. (Matt. 5:38–45)

In the early centuries of the Christian era, it was widely assumed that to follow Christ and to obey His teaching meant that one should reject violence and refuse service in the Roman army. But by the fifth century, after the Roman Empire had become Christian and after barbarian Goths in 410 sacked Rome itself, Church Fathers debated whether Christ really intended that the Empire and its Church should remain undefended. The Church Fathers noticed passages in the Gospels that seem to contradict pacifism:

Think not that I am come to send peace on earth: I came not to send peace, but a sword.

For I am come to set a man at variance against his father, and the daughter against her mother, and the daughter-in-law against her mother-in-law. (Matt. 10: 34–35)

And there are several instances in the Gospels (for instance, Matt. 8:5–10) in which Jesus encounters soldiers and does not rebuke them for engaging in an occupation that is essentially committed to violence. Rather, he argues, "Render unto Caesar the things which are Caesar's; and unto God the things that are God's" (Matt. 22:21). This would seem to include military service, or at least taxes to pay for the army.

A thorough analysis of whether the Gospels command pacifism is beyond the scope of this book. The passages in the Sermon on the Mount seem to be clearly pacifist; yet many eminent scholars have denied the pacifist message. A more interesting question, for philosophy, if not for biblical scholarship, is this: If Jesus did preach pacifism in the Sermon on the Mount, did He preach it as a *moral* doctrine?

Jesus did not view his teaching as replacing the moral law as he knew it:

Think not that I am come to destroy the law, or the prophets: I am come not to destroy, but to fulfill. . . .
  Till heaven and earth pass, one jot or tittle shall in no wise pass from the law, till all be fulfilled. (Matt. 5:17–18)

Perhaps, then, the prescriptions of the Sermon on the Mount should be interpreted as rules that one must obey in order to follow Christ, or rules that one must follow in order to obtain salvation. But it does not follow from this alone that everyone has an obligation to follow Christ, and it does not follow from this alone that everyone has an obligation to seek salvation. Even Christians will admit that some people have refused to become Christians and have led morally admirable lives nonetheless; and if salvation is a good, one can nevertheless choose to reject it, just as a citizen can neglect to hand in a winning lottery ticket without breaking the law. If so, the prescriptions of the Sermon on the Mount apply only to Christians seeking a Christian salvation. They are not universally binding rules and do not qualify as moral principles.

(b) The Moral Exemplar Argument

Many people and at least one illustrious philosopher, Immanuel Kant, believe that morally proper action consists in choosing to act in such a way that your conduct could serve as an example for all mankind. (It was Kant's genius to recognize that moral conduct is *essentially* exemplary.) Some universal pacifists appeal to this idea, arguing that if everyone were a pacifist, the world would be a much better place than it is now. This is the argument that Leo Tolstoy (1828–1910) used to support the Gospel prescription not to resist evil:

[Christ] put the proposition of non-resistance to evil in such a way that, according to his teaching, it was to be the foundation of the joint life of men and was to free humanity from the evil that it inflicted on itself. (*My Religion*, Ch. 4) Instead of having the whole life based on violence and every joy obtained and guarded through violence; instead of seeing each one of us punished or inflicting punishment from childhood to old age, I imagined that we were all impressed in word and deed by the idea that vengeance is a very low, animal feeling; that violence is not only a disgraceful act, but also one that deprives man of true happiness . . . .

I imagined that instead of those national hatreds which are impressed on us under the form of patriotism, instead of those glorifications of murder, called wars . . . that we were impressed with the idea that the recognition of any countries, special laws, borders, lands, is a sign of grossest ignorance. . . .

Through the fulfillment of these commandments, the life of men will be what every human heart seeks and desires. All men will be brothers and everybody will always be at peace with others, enjoying all the benefits of the world. (*My Religion*, Ch. 6)

Few would deny that if everyone were a pacifist, the world would be a better place, perhaps even a paradise. Furthermore, since the argument is essentially hypothetical, it cannot be refuted (as many nonpacifists believe) by pointing out that not everyone will become a pacifist. The problem is whether this argument can establish pacifism as a moral imperative.

One difficulty with the argument is that it seems to rely on a premise the truth of which is purely verbal. In what way would the world be a better place if people gave up fighting? The most obvious way is that the world would be better because there would be no war. But the statement "If everyone gave up fighting, there would be no war" is true by definition, since "war" implies "fighting." It is difficult to see how a statement that simply relates the meanings of words could tell us something about our moral obligations.

A deeper problem with Tolstoy's argument is that "resist not evil" is not the only rule that would yield paradise if everyone obeyed it. Suppose that everyone in the world subscribed to the principle "Use violence, but only in self-defense." If everyone used violence only in self-defense, the same consequences would follow as would arise from universal acceptance of the rule "Never use violence." Consequently, pacifism cannot be shown to be superior to nonpacifism by noting the good consequences that would undeniably ensue if everyone were a pacifist.

(c) Gandhian Pacifism

Certainly the most interesting and effective pacifist of the twentieth century was Mohandas Gandhi (1869–1948). Though a devout Hindu, Gandhi developed his doctrine of nonviolence from elementary metaphysical concepts that are by no means special to Hinduism:

Man as an animal is violent but as spirit is nonviolent. The moment he awakes to the spirit he cannot remain violent. Either he progresses towards *ahimsa* [nonviolence] or rushes to his doom. (*Nonviolence in Peace and War,* I, p. 311)

The requirement not to be violent seems wholly negative; sleeping people achieve it with ease. But for Gandhi the essential moral task is not merely to be nonviolent but to use the force of the soul (*satyagraha,* "truth grasping") in a continual struggle for justice. The methods of applied *satyagraha* developed by Gandhi—the weaponless marches, the sit-downs and sit-ins, strikes and boycotts, fasts and prayers—captured the admiration of the world and have been widely copied, most notably by Martin Luther King, Jr., in his campaigns against racial discrimination. According to Gandhi, each person, by engaging in *satyagraha* and experiencing suffering on behalf of justice, purifies the soul from pollution emanating from man's animal nature:

A *satyagrahi* is dead to his body even before his enemy attempts to kill him, i.e. he is free from the attachments of his body and lives only in the victory of his soul. (*Nonviolence in Peace and War,* I, p. 318) Nonviolence implies as complete self-purification as is humanly possible. (*Nonviolence in Peace and War,* I, p. 111)

By acting nonviolently, pacifists not only purify their own souls but also transform the souls of their opponents: "A nonviolent revolution is not a program of seizure of power. It is a program of transformation of relationships, ending in peaceful transfer of power" (*Nonviolence in Peace and War,* II, p. 8)

Though in most places Gandhi emphasizes the personal redemption that is possible only through nonviolent resistance to evil, the spiritually positive effect of nonviolence on evil opponents is perhaps equally important, since "The sword of the *satyagrahi* is love" (*Nonviolence in Peace and War,* II, p. 59).

Gandhi, then, is far from preaching the sacredness of biological life. What matters is not biological life but the condition of the soul, the natural and proper state of which is *ahimsa*. The evil of violence is that it distorts and disrupts this natural condition of the soul. The basic moral law (*dharma*) for all people is to seek the restoration of their souls to the harmony of *ahimsa*. This spiritual restoration cannot be achieved by violence, but only by the application of *satyagraha*. Disharmony cannot produce harmony; violence cannot produce spiritual peace.

The "sacredness of life" defense of pacifism ran into difficulties analyzing situations in which taking one life could save many lives. For Gandhi, this is no problem at all: taking one life may save many biological lives, but it will not save souls. On the contrary, the soul of the killer will be perverted by the act, and that perversion—not loss of life—is what matters morally.

The system of values professed by Gandhi—that the highest human good is a harmonious condition of soul—must be kept in mind when considering the frequent accusation that Gandhi's method of nonviolent resistance "does not work," that nonviolence alone did not and could not force the British to leave India, and that nonviolent resistance to murderous tyrants like Hitler will only provoke the mass murder of the innocent. Perhaps the practice of nonviolence could not "defeat" the British or "defeat" Hitler, but by Gandhi's standards the use of military force would only produce a greater defeat, perverting the souls of thousands engaged in war and intensifying the will to violence on the opposing side. On the other hand, the soul of the *satyagrahi* will be strengthened and purified by nonviolent struggle against British imperialism or German Nazism, and in this purification the Gandhian pacifist can obtain spiritual victory even in the face of political defeat.

India did not adopt the creed of nonviolence after the British left in 1948, and it is hardly likely that any modern nation-state will organize its international affairs along Gandhian lines. But none of this affects the validity of Gandhi's arguments, which indicate how things ought to be, not how they are. We have seen that Gandhi's principles do not falter in the face of situations in which taking one life can save lives on balance. But what of situations in which the sacrifice of spiritual purity by one will prevent the corruption of many souls? Suppose, for example, that a Gandhian believes (on good evidence) that a well-timed commando raid will prevent a nation from embarking on an aggressive war, a war that would inflame whole populations with hatred for the enemy. Wouldn't a concern with one's own spiritual purity in such a situation show an immoral lack of concern for the souls of one's fellow men?

Another problem for Gandhi concerns the relationship between violence and coercion. To coerce people is to make them act against their will, for fear of the consequences they will suffer if they do not obey. Coercion, then, is a kind of spiritual violence, directed against the imagination and will of the victim. The "violence" most conspicuously rejected by Gandhi—pushing, shoving, striking with hands, the use of weapons, the placing of bombs and explosives—is essentially physical violence, directed against the bodies of opponents. But if physical violence against bodies is spiritually corrupting, psychological violence directed at the will of opponents must be even more corrupting.

In his writings Gandhi condemned coercion. Yet in practice he can hardly be said to have renounced *psychological* coercion. Obviously he would have preferred to have the British depart from India of their own free will, deciding that it was in their own best interest, or at least morally necessary, to leave. But if the British had decided, in the absence of coercion, to stay, Gandhi was prepared to exert every kind of nonviolent pressure to make them go. And when Gandhi on occasion attempted to achieve political objectives by a "fast unto death," his threat of self-starvation brought enormous psychological pressure on the authorities, who, among other things, feared the riots that would ensue should Gandhi die.

The Gandhian pacifist, then, must explain why psychological pressure is permissible if physical pressure is forbidden. One possible answer is that physical pressure cannot transform the soul of the opponents, but psychological pressure, since it operates on the mind, can effect a spiritual transformation. Indeed, Gandhi characterized his terrifying fasts as acts of education, not coercion. But the claim that these fasts were not coercive confuses the noncoercive intention behind the act with its predictable coercive effects; and if education is the name of the game, the nonpacifist will remark that violence has been known to teach a few good lessons in its day. In many spiritual traditions, what matters essentially is not the kind of pressure but that the right pressure be applied at the right time and in the right way. Zen masters have brought students to enlightenment by clouting them on the ears, and God helped St. Paul to see the light by knocking him off his horse.

In addition to these technical problems, many people will be inclined to reject the system of values from which Gandhi's deductions flow. Many will concede that good character is important and that helping others to develop moral virtues is an important task. But few agree with Gandhi that the development of moral purity is the supreme human good, and that other goods, like the preservation of human life, or

progress in the arts and sciences, have little or no value in comparison. If even a little value is conceded to these other things, then on occasion it will be necessary to put aside the project of developing spiritual purity in order to preserve other values. These acts of preservation may require physical violence, and those who use violence to defend life or beauty or liberty may indeed be corrupting their souls. But it is hard to believe that an occasional and necessary act of violence on behalf of these values will totally and permanently corrupt the soul, and those who use violence judiciously may be right in thinking that the saving of life or beauty or liberty may be worth a small or temporary spiritual loss.

4. PRIVATE PACIFISM

Perhaps the rarest form of pacifist is the pacifist who renounces violence in personal relations but condones the use of force in the political sphere. Such a pacifist will not use violence for self-defense but believes that it is permissible for the state to use judicial force against criminals and military force against foreign enemies. A private pacifist renounces self-defense but supports national defense.

(a) Augustine's Limited Pacifism

Historically, private pacifism developed as an attempt to reconcile the demands of the Sermon on the Mount with the Christian duty of charity. The Sermon on the Mount requires Christians to "resist not evil"; the duty of charity requires pity for the weak who suffer the injustice of the strong. For St. Augustine (354–430), one essential message of the Gospels is the good news that this present life is as nothing compared with the life to come. The person who tries to hold on to earthly possessions is deluded as to what is truly valuable: "If any man will sue thee at the law, and take away thy coat, let him have thy cloak also" (Matt. 5:40). What goes for earthly coats should go for earthly life as well, so if any man seeks to take a Christian life, the Christian should let him have it. On this view, the doctrine "resist not evil" is just an expression of contempt for earthly possessions.

But according to Augustine there are some things in this world that do have value: justice, for example, the relief of suffering, and the preservation of the Church, which Augustine equated with civilization itself. To defend these things with necessary force is not to fall prey to delusions about the good. For Augustine, then, service in the armed forces is not inconsistent with Christian values.

One difficulty for theories like Augustine's is that they seem to justify military service only when military force is used in a just cause. Unfortunately, once in the service, the man in the ranks is not in a position to evaluate the justice of his nation's cause; indeed, in many modern nations, the principle of military subordination to civilian rule prevents even generals from evaluating the purposes of war declared by political leaders. But Augustine argues that the cause of justice cannot be served without armies, and armies cannot function unless subordinates follow orders without questioning the purposes of the conflict. The necessary conditions for justice and charity require that some men put themselves in positions in which they might be required to fight for injustice.

(b) The Problem of Self-Defense

Many will agree with Augustine that most violence at the personal level—the violence of crime, vendetta, and domestic brutality, for example—goes contrary to moral principles. But most are prepared to draw the line at personal and collective self-defense. Can the obligation to be charitable justify participation in military service but stop short of justifying the use of force by private citizens, if that force is exercised to protect the weak from the oppression of the strong? Furthermore, the obligation to be charitable does not exclude acts of charity toward oneself. For Augustine, violence was a dangerous tool, best kept out of the hands of the citizens and best left strictly at the disposal of the state. Beset with fears of crime in the streets, the contemporary American is less inclined to worry about the anarchic effects of private uses of defensive force and more inclined to worry about the protection the police seem unable to provide.

For these worried people, the existence of a right to self-defense is self-evident. But the existence of this right is not self-evident to universal or private pacifists; and it was not self-evident to St. Augustine. In the Christian tradition, no right to self-defense was recognized until its existence was certified by Thomas Aquinas in the thirteenth century. Aquinas derived the right to self-defense from the universal tendency to self-preservation, assuming (contrary to Augustine) that a natural tendency must be morally right. As for the Christian duty to love one's enemy, Aquinas argued that acts of self-defense have two effects—the saving of life and the taking of life—and that self-defensive uses of force intend primarily the saving of life. This makes the use of force in self-defense a morally permissible act of charity. The right to self-defense is now generally recognized in Catholic moral theology and in Western legal systems. But it can hardly be said that Aquinas's arguments, which rely heavily on assumptions from Greek philosophy, succeed in reconciling the claims of self-defense with the prescriptions of the Sermon on the Mount.

5. ANTIWAR PACIFISM

Most people who believe in the right to personal self-defense also believe that some wars are morally justified. In fact, the notion of self-defense and the notion of just war are commonly linked; just wars are said to be defensive wars, and the justice of defensive war is inferred from the right of personal self-defense, projected from the individual to the national level. But some people reject this projection: they endorse the validity of personal self-defense, but they deny that war can be justified by appeal to self-defense or any other right. On the contrary, they argue that war always involves an inexcusable violation of rights. For such anti-war pacifists, all participation in war is morally wrong.

(a) The Killing of Soldiers

One universal and necessary feature of wars is that soldiers get killed in them. Most people accept such killings as a necessary evil, and judge the killing of soldiers in war to be morally acceptable. If the war is fought for the just cause, the killing of enemy soldiers is justified as necessary to the triumph of right. If the war is fought for an unjust cause, the killing of enemy soldiers is acceptable because it is considered an honorable thing to fight for one's country, right or wrong, provided that one fights well and cleanly. But the antiwar pacifist does not take the killing of soldiers for granted. Everyone has a right to life, and the killing of soldiers in war is intentional killing, a deliberate violation of the right to life. According to the standard interpretation of basic rights, it is never morally justifiable to violate a basic right in order to produce some good; the end, in such cases, does not justify the means. How, then, can the killing of soldiers in war be morally justified—or even excused?

Perhaps the commonest reply to the challenge of antiwar pacifism is that killing in war is a matter of self-defense, *personal* self-defense, the right to which is freely acknowledged by the antiwar pacifist. In war, the argument goes, it is either kill or be killed—and that type of killing is killing in self-defense. But though the appeal to self-defense is natural, antiwar pacifists believe that it is not successful. First of all, on the usual understanding of "self-defense," those who kill can claim the justification of self-defense only if (a) they had no other way to save their lives or preserve themselves from physical harm except by killing, and (b) they did nothing to provoke the attack to which they are subjected. Antiwar pacifists point out that soldiers on the battlefield do have a way of saving themselves from death or harm without killing anyone: they can surrender. Furthermore, for soldiers fighting for an unjust cause—for example, German soldiers fighting in the invasion of Russia in 1941—it is difficult to argue that they "did nothing to provoke" the deadly force directed at them. But if the German army provoked the Russians to stand and fight on Russian soil, German soldiers cannot legitimately claim self-defense as a moral justification for killing Russian soldiers.

To the nonpacifist, these points might seem like legalistic quibbles. But the antiwar pacifist has an even stronger argument against killing soldiers in war. The vast majority of soldiers who die in war do not die in "kill or be killed" situations. They are killed by bullets, shells, or bombs directed from safe launching points— "safe" in the sense that those who shoot the bullets or fire the shells or drop the bombs are in no immediate danger of death. Since those who kill are not in immediate danger of death, they cannot invoke "self-defense" to justify the deaths they cause.

Some other argument besides self-defense, then, must explain why the killing of soldiers in war should not be classified as murder. Frequently, nonpacifists argue that the explanation is found in the doctrine of "assumption of risk," the idea, common in civil law, that persons who freely assume a risk have only themselves to blame if the risk is realized. When a soldier goes to war, he is well aware that one risk of his trade is getting killed on the battlefield. If he dies on the field, the responsibility for his death lies with himself, not with the man who shot him. By assuming the risk—so the argument goes— he waived his right to life, at least on the battlefield.

One does not have to be a pacifist to see difficulties in this argument. First of all, in all substantial modern wars, most of the men on the line are not volunteers, but draftees. Only a wealthy nation like the United States can afford an all-volunteer army, and most experts believe that the American volunteer ranks will have to be supplemented by draftees should the United States become involved in another conflict on the scale of Korea or Vietnam. Second, in many cases in which a risk is realized, responsibility for the bad outcome lies not with the person who assumed the risk but with the person who created it. If an arsonist sets fire to a house and a parent rushes in to save the children, dying in the rescue attempt, responsibility for the parent's death lies not with the parent who assumed the risk but with the arsonist who created it. So if German armies invade Russia, posing the risk of death in battle, and if Russian soldiers assume this risk and fight back, the deaths of Russians are the fault of German invaders, not the fault of the defenders who assumed the risk.

These criticisms of German foot soldiers will irritate many who served in the armed forces and who know how little political and military decision making is left to the men on the front lines, who seem to be the special target of these pacifist arguments. But antiwar pacifists will deny that their aim is to condemn the men on the battlefield. Most antiwar pacifists feel that soldiers in war act under considerable compulsion and are excused for that reason from responsibility for the killing they do. But to say that battlefield killings are *excusable* is not to say that they are morally *justified*. On the contrary, if such killings are excusable, it must be that there is some immorality to be excused.

(b) The Killing of Civilians

In the chronicles of ancient wars, conflict was total and loss in battle was frequently followed by general slaughter of men, women, and children on the losing side. It has always been considered part of the trend toward civilization to confine the destruction of war to the personnel and instruments of war, sparing civilians and their property as much as possible. This civilizing trend was conspicuously reversed in World War II, in which the ratio of civilian deaths to total war deaths was perhaps the highest it had been since the wars of religion in the seventeenth century. A very high ratio of civilian deaths to total deaths was also characteristic of the war in Vietnam. Given the immense firepower of modern weapons and the great distances between the discharges of weapons and the explosions of bullets or shells near the targets, substantial civilian casualties are an inevitable part of modern land war. But it is immoral to kill civilians, the antiwar pacifist argues, and from this it follows that modern land warfare is necessarily immoral.

Few nonpacifists will argue that killing enemy civilians is justifiable when such killings are avoidable. Few will argue that killing enemy civilians is justifiable when such killings are the *primary* objective of a military operation. But what about the deaths of civilians that are the unavoidable results of military operations directed to some *other* result? The pacifist classifies such killings as immoral, whereas most nonpacifists call them regrettable but unavoidable deaths, not murders. But why are they not

murder, if the civilians are innocent, and if it is known in advance that some civilians will be killed? Isn't this an intentional killing of the innocent, which is the traditional definition of murder?

The sophisticated nonpacifist may try to parry this thrust with analogies to policies outside the arena of war. There are, after all, many morally acceptable policies that, when adopted, have the effect of killing innocent persons. If the Congress decides to set a speed limit of 55 miles per hour on federal highways, more people will die than if Congress sets the speed limit at 45 miles per hour. Since many people who die on the highway are innocent, the Congress has chosen a policy that knowingly brings death to the innocent, but no one calls it murder. Or suppose, for example, that a public health officer is considering a national vaccination program to forestall a flu epidemic. He knows that if he does not implement the vaccination program, many people will die from the flu. On the other hand, if the program is implemented, a certain number of people will die from allergic reactions to the vaccine. Most of the people who die from allergic reactions will be people who would not have died of the flu if the vaccination program had not been implemented. So the vaccination program will kill innocent people who would otherwise be saved if the program were abandoned. If the public health officer implements such a program, we do *not* think that he is a murderer.

Nonpacifists argue that what makes the action of Congress and the action of the public health officer morally permissible in these cases is that the deaths of the innocent, although foreseen, are not the intended goal of these policies. Congress does not want people to die on the highways; every highway death is a regrettable death. The purpose of setting the speed limit at 55 miles per hour is not to kill people but to provide a reasonable balance between safety and convenience. Likewise, it is not the purpose of the public health officer to kill people by giving them vaccine. His goal is to save lives on balance, and every death from the vaccine is a regrettable death. Likewise, in war, when civilians are killed as a result of necessary military operations, the deaths of the civilians are not the intended goal of the military operation. They are foreseen, but they are always regretted. If we do not accuse the Congress of murder and the Public Health Service of murder in these cases, consistency requires that we not accuse military forces of murder when they cause civilian deaths in war, especially if every attempt is made to keep civilian deaths to a minimum.

Antiwar pacifists do not condemn the Congress and the Public Health Service in cases like these. But they assert that the case of war is different in a morally relevant way. To demonstrate the difference, antiwar pacifists provide an entirely different analysis of the moral justification for speed limits and vaccination programs. In their opinion, the facts that highway deaths and vaccination deaths are "unintended" and "regretted" is morally irrelevant. The real justification lies in the factor of consent. In the case of federal highway regulations, the rules are decided by Congress, which is elected by the people, the same people who use the highways. If Congress decides on a 55-mile-an-hour speed limit, this is a regulation that, in some sense, highway drivers have imposed upon themselves. Those people who die on the highway because of a higher speed limit have, in a double sense, assumed the risks generated by that speed limit: they have, through the Congress, created the risk, and by venturing onto the highway, have freely exposed themselves to the risk. The responsibility for these highway deaths, then, lies either on the drivers themselves or on the people who crashed into them—not on the Congress.

Likewise, in the case of the vaccination program, if people are warned in advance of the risks of vaccination, and if they nevertheless choose to be vaccinated, they are responsible for their own deaths should the risks be realized. According to the antiwar pacifist, it is this consent given by drivers and vaccination volunteers that justifies these policies, and it is precisely this element of consent that is absent in the case of the risks inflicted on enemy civilians in time of war.

Consider the standard textbook example of allegedly justifiable killing of civilians in time of war. Suppose that the destruction of a certain bridge is an important military objective, but if the bridge is bombed, it is very likely that ci-

vilians living close by will be killed. (The civilians cannot be warned without alerting the enemy to reinforce the bridge.) If the bridge is bombed and some civilians are killed, the bombing victims are not in the same moral category as highway victims or victims of vaccination. The bombing victims did not order the bombing of themselves through some set of elected representatives. Nor did the bombing victims freely consent to the bombing of their bridge. Nor was the bombing in any way undertaken as a calculated risk in the interest of the victims. For all these reasons, the moral conclusions regarding highway legislation and vaccination programs do not carry over to bombing of the bridge.

Nonpacifists who recognize that it will be very difficult to fight wars without bombing bridges may argue that the victims of this bombing in some sense assumed the risks of bombardment by choosing to live close to a potential military target. Indeed, it is occasionally claimed that all the civilians in a nation at war have assumed the risks of war, since they could avoid the risks of war simply by moving to a neutral country. But such arguments are strained and uncharitable, even for those rare warring nations that permit freedom of emigration. Most people consider it a major sacrifice to give up their homes, and an option that requires such a sacrifice cannot be considered an option open for free choice. The analogy between the unintended victims of vaccination and the unintended civilian victims of war seems to have broken down.

(c) The Balance of Good and Evil in War

It is left to the nonpacifist to argue that the killing of soldiers and civilians in war is in the end justifiable in order to obtain great moral goods that can be obtained only by fighting for them. Civilians have rights to life, but those rights can be outweighed by the national objectives, provided those objectives are morally acceptable and overwhelmingly important. Admittedly, this argument for killing civilians is available only to the just side in a war, but if the argument is valid, it proves that there can *be* a just side, contrary to the arguments of antiwar pacifism.

Antiwar pacifists have two lines of defense. First, they can continue to maintain that the end does not justify the means, if the means be murderous. Second, they can, and will, go on to argue that it is a tragic mistake to believe that there are great moral goods that can be obtained only by war. According to antiwar pacifists, the amount of moral good produced by war is greatly exaggerated. The Mexican War, for example, resulted in half of Mexico being transferred to American rule. This was a great good for the United States, but not a great moral good, since the United States had little claim to the ceded territory, and no great injustice would have persisted if the war had not been fought at all.

The Revolutionary War in America is widely viewed as a war that produced a great moral good; but if the war had not been fought, the history of the United States would be similar to the history of Canada (which remained loyal)—and no one feels that the Canadians have suffered or are suffering great injustices that the American colonies avoided by war. Likewise, it is difficult to establish the goods produced by World War I or the moral losses that would have ensued if the winning side, "our side," had lost. Bertrand Russell imagined the results of a British loss in World War I as follows:

The greatest sum that foreigners could possibly exact would be the total economic rent of the land and natural resources of England. [But] the working classes, the shopkeepers, manufacturers, and merchants, the literary men and men of science—all the people that make England of any account in the world—have at most an infinitesimal and accidental share in the rental of England. The men who have a share use their rents in luxury, political corruption, taking the lives of birds, and depopulating and enslaving the rural districts. It is this life of the idle rich that would be curtailed if the Germans exacted tribute from England. (*Justice in War Time*, pp. 48–49)

But multiplying examples of wars that did little moral good will not establish the pacifist case. The pacifist must show that *no* war has done enough good to justify the killing of soldiers and the killing of civilians that occurred in the war. A single war that produces moral goods sufficient to justify its killings will refute the pacifist claim that *all* wars are morally un-

justifiable. Obviously this brings the antiwar pacifist head to head with World War II.

It is commonly estimated that 35 million people died as a result of World War II. It is difficult to imagine that any cause could justify so much death, but fortunately the Allies need only justify their share of these killings. Between 1939 and 1945 Allied forces killed about 5.5 million Axis soldiers and about 1 million civilians in Axis countries. Suppose that Britain and the United States had chosen to stay out of World War II and suppose that Stalin had, like Lenin, surrendered to Germany shortly after the invasion. Does avoiding the world that would have resulted from these decisions justify killing 6.5 million people?

If Hitler and Tojo had won the war, doubtless they would have killed a great many people both before and after victory, but it is quite likely that the total of *additional* victims, beyond those they killed in the war that *was* fought, would have been less than 6.5 million and, at any rate, the responsibility for those deaths would fall on Hitler and Tojo, not on Allied nations. If Hitler and Tojo had won the war, large portions of the world would have fallen under foreign domination, perhaps for a very long time. But the antiwar pacifist will point out that the main areas of Axis foreign domination—China and Russia—were not places in which the citizens enjoyed a high level of freedom *before the war began*. Perhaps the majority of people in the conquered areas would have worked out a *modus vivendi* with their new rulers, as did the majority of French citizens during the German occupation. Nor can it be argued that World War II was necessary to save six million Jews from annihilation in the Holocaust, since in fact the war did *not* save them.

The ultimate aims of Axis leaders are a matter for historical debate. Clearly the Japanese had no intention of conquering the United States, and some historians suggest that Hitler hoped to avoid war with England and America, declaring war with England reluctantly, and only after the English declared it against him. Nevertheless, popular opinion holds that Hitler intended to conquer the world, and if preventing the conquest of Russia and China could not justify six and one-half million killings, most

Americans are quite confident that preventing the conquest of England and the United States does justify killing on this scale.

The antiwar pacifist disagrees. Certainly German rule of England and the United States would have been a very bad thing. At the same time, hatred of such German rule would be partially fueled by hatred of foreigners, and hatred of foreigners, as such, is an irrational and morally unjustifiable passion. After all, if rule by foreigners were, by itself, a great moral wrong, the British, with their great colonial empire, could hardly consider themselves the morally superior side in World War II.

No one denies that a Nazi victory in World War II would have had morally frightful results. But, according to antiwar pacifism, killing six and one-half million people is also morally frightful, and preventing one moral wrong does not obviously outweigh committing the other. Very few people today share the pacifists' condemnation of World War II, but perhaps that is because the dead killed by the Allies cannot speak up and make sure that their losses are properly counted on the moral scales. Antiwar pacifists speak on behalf of the enemy dead, and on behalf of all those millions who would have lived if the war had not been fought. On this silent constituency they rest their moral case.

REVIEW QUESTIONS

1. Characterize universal pacifists (there are two types), private pacifists, and antiwar pacifists.

2. Why doesn't Lackey accept the appeal to the Bible, or the sacredness of life, or the right to life as a good reason for accepting pacifism?
3. What is Christian pacifism and Tolstoy's argument used to defend it? Why doesn't Lackey accept Tolstoy's argument?
4. Explain Gandhi's pacifism, including *satyagraha*. What problems does Lackey raise for this view?
5. Explain Augustine's so-called limited pacifism. What problems does this view have according to Lackey?
6. State the position of antiwar pacifism. Why do antiwar pacifists believe that all wars are wrong? According to Lackey, what are the objections to antiwar pacifism, and how can antiwar pacifists reply?

DISCUSSION QUESTIONS

1. Is Gandhi's view a defensible one? Why or why not?
2. Does the antiwar pacifist have a good reply to all the objections Lackey discusses? Are there any good objections that he does not discuss?
3. Many people think that World War II was morally justified. What does the antiwar pacifist say? What do you think?
4. According to Lackey, no great moral good was produced by the Revolutionary War in America. If America had lost this war and remained under British rule, then its history would be like that of Canada—and Canada has not suffered, he says. Do you agree? Explain your answer.

William V. O'Brien

The Conduct of Just and Limited War

William V. O'Brien is professor of government at Georgetown University, Washington, DC. He is the author of War and/or Survival *(1969),* Nu-

clear War, Deterrence and Morality *(1967), and* The Conduct of Just and Limited War *(1981), from which our reading is taken.*

*O'Brien divides the Just War Theory into two parts. The first (*jus ad bellum*) states conditions* *that must be met in order for a state to have a right to go to war. The second (jus in bello) gives principles limiting conduct in war. There are three main conditions of jus ad bellum. The war must be declared by a competent authority for a public purpose. There must be a just cause. (This condition is subdivided into the substance of the cause [e.g., self-defense], the form of pursuing it [e.g., defensive war], the requirements of proportionality, and the exhaustion of peaceful means.) Finally, there must be a right intention that aims at peace and insists on charity towards enemies.*

The jus in bello gives two principles regulating conduct in war. The principle of proportion balances the total good produced from war against the total evil. The principle of discrimination prohibits intentional attacks on noncombatants and nonmilitary targets.

The original just-war doctrine of St. Augustine, St. Thomas, and other Scholastics emphasized the conditions for permissible recourse to war—the *jus ad bellum*. To this doctrine was added another branch of prescriptions regulating the conduct of war, the *jus in bello*. . . .

The *jus ad bellum* lays down conditions that must be met in order to have permissible recourse to armed coercion. They are conditions that should be viewed in the light of the fundamental tenet of just-war doctrine: the presumption is always against war. The taking of human life is not permitted to man unless there are exceptional justifications. Just-war doctrine provides those justifications, but they are in the nature of special pleadings to overcome the presumption against killing. The decision to invoke the exceptional rights of war must be based on the following criteria: there must be competent authority to order the war for a public purpose; there must be a just cause (it may be self-defense or the protection of rights by offensive war) and the means must be proportionate to the just cause and all peaceful alternatives must have been exhausted; and there must be right intention on the part of the just belligerent. Let us examine these criteria.

Insofar as large-scale, conventional war is concerned, the issue of competent authority is different in modern times than it was in the thirteenth century. The decentralized political system wherein public, private, and criminal violence overlapped, as well as the state of military art and science, permitted a variety of private wars. So it was important to insist that war—in which individuals would be called upon to take human lives—must be waged on the order of public authorities for public purposes. This is not a serious problem in most parts of the world today. Only states have the material capacity to wage large-scale, modern, conventional war. Two other problems do, however, exist in connection with the conditions of competent authority. First, there may be disputes as to the constitutional competence of a particular official or organ of state to initiate war. Second, civil war and revolutionary terrorism are frequently initiated by persons and organizations claiming revolutionary rights.

Most states today, even totalitarian states, have specific constitutional provisions for the declaration and termination of war. If an official or state organ violates these provisions, there may not be a valid exercise of the sovereign right to declare and wage war. In such a case the first condition of the just war might not be met. This was the charge, implicitly or explicitly, against President Johnson in the Vietnam War. Johnson never requested a declaration of war from Congress with which he shared warmaking powers. War critics asserted that the undeclared war was illegal. A sufficient answer to this charge is to be found in congressional cooperation in the war effort and in the refusal of the courts to declare the war unconstitutional. . . . At this point it is sufficient to raise the issue as illustrative of the problem of competent authority within a constitutional state.

In this connection a word should be said about declaring wars. Any examination of modern wars will show that the importance of a declaration of war has diminished greatly in international practice. Because of the split-second timing of modern war, it is often undesirable to warn the enemy by way of a formal declaration. Defense measures are geared to react to hostile behavior, not declarations. When war is declared it is often an announcement confirming a condition that has already been established. Nevertheless, if a particular state's constitution does require a formal declaration of war and one is not forthcoming, the issue of competence is raised. If a public official exceeds his authority in mobilizing the people and conducting war, there is a lack of competent authority.

The second problem, however, is by far the greatest. Today, rights of revolution are frequently invoked by organizations and individuals. They clearly do not have the authority and capacity to wage war in the conventional sense. However, they do wage revolutionary war, often on an international scale. Indeed, international terrorism is one of the most pervasive and difficult problems facing the international community.

All major ideologies and blocs or alignments of states in the international system recognize the right of revolution. Usually their interpretations will emphasize the rights of revolution against others, not themselves.... Logically, there should be an elaborate *jus ad bellum* and *jus in bello* for revolutionary war, but development of such a doctrine has never been seriously attempted. As a result, the issues of revolutionary war tend to be treated on an ad hoc basis as special cases vaguely related to the regular categories of just war....

The differences between conventional war waged by states and revolutionary war waged by rebels against states are profound. Given the formidable power of most modern governments, particularly in regard to their comparative monopoly of armed force, revolutionary rights can be asserted mainly by covert organizations waging guerrilla warfare and terrorism. The option of organizing a portion of a state and fighting a conventional civil war in the manner of the American, Spanish, or Nigerian civil wars is seldom available.

The covert, secret character of modern revolutionary movements is such that it is often hard to judge their claims to qualify as the competent authority for oppressed people. There is a decided tendency to follow the Leninist model of revolutionary leadership wherein the self-selected revolutionary elite decides on the just revolutionary cause, the means, and the circumstances of taking the initiative, all done in the name of the people and revolutionary justice. As a revolution progresses, the task of certifying competent authority continues to be difficult. Support for the revolutionary leadership is often coerced or given under conditions where there is not popular acceptance of the revolutionary authority of that leadership or its ends and means. Recognition by foreign powers of belligerency—or even of putative governmental powers—is an unreliable guide given subjective, politicized recognition policies.

To complicate matters, individuals and small groups take up revolutionary war tactics, principally terrorism in the form of airplane hijacking, hostage kidnapping, assassination, and indiscriminate bombing attacks. These acts are performed in the name of greatly varying causes, some of which could not be considered revolutionary. Sometimes the alleged justifications are political or ideological, but, on investigation, the real motivation turns out to be personal and criminal. Since most revolutionary movements manifest themselves in behavior difficult to distinguish from that of cranks and criminals, the task of sorting out revolutionaries entitled to acceptance as competent authorities is excruciating.

Two issues need to be resolved concerning revolutionary activity. First, insofar as treating revolutionaries as belligerents in a war and not as common criminals is concerned, the ultimate answer lies in the character, magnitude, and degree of success of the revolutionaries. If they can organize a government that carries on their war in a controlled fashion (assuming a magnitude requiring countermeasures that more resemble war than ordinary police operations), and if the conflict continues for an appreciable time, the revolutionaries may have won their right to be considered a competent authority for purposes of just war. Beyond this enumeration of criteria it seems unprofitable to generalize.

Second, concerning the authority of rebel leaders to mobilize the people by ordering or coercing individuals to fight for the revolutionary cause, the conscience of the individual takes precedence. Lacking any color of authority to govern, the rebels cannot of right compel participation in their cause. Needless to say, they will very probably compel participation by intimidation.

JUST CAUSE

... Authorities vary in their presentation of just cause, but it seems to break down into four subdivisions: the substance of the just cause, the forms of pursuing just cause, the requirement of proportionality of ends and means, and the requirement of exhaustion of peaceful remedies.

The substance of the just cause must, in Childress's formulation, be sufficiently "serious and weighty" to overcome the presumption against killing in general and war in particular. In Childress's approach, with which I am in essential agreement, this means that there must be a "competing prima facie duty or obligation" to "the prima facie obligation not to injure and kill others."[1] Childress mentions as "serious and weighty" prima facie obligations the following: (1) "to protect the innocent from unjust attack," (2) "to restore rights wrongfully denied," (3) "to re-establish a just order."

This is an adequate basis, reflective of the older just-war literature, for discussing the substance of just cause. Indeed, Childress is more explicit than many modern commentators who simply state that there should be a just cause. Still, it is only a beginning. It is unfortunate that modern moralists have generally been so concerned with the issue of putatively disproportionate means of modern war that they have neglected the prior question of the ends for which these means might have to be used (that is, just cause). In practical terms, this task of evaluating the substance of just cause leads inescapably to a comparative analysis of the characteristics of the polities or political-social systems posed in warlike confrontation. . . .

Even more difficult for those who would answer in the affirmative is the question whether the United States should intervene to protect a manifestly imperfect political-social order (South Korea, South Vietnam or, perhaps, that of a state such as Jordan, Saudi Arabia, or Pakistan). . . .

By comparison, the substantive just causes of the older just-war literature are almost insignificant. In the modern world the just cause often has to do with the survival of a way of life. Claims that this is so can be false or exaggerated, but they are often all too legitimate. They must be taken seriously in assessing the substance of just cause in modern just-war analyses.

However, passing the test of just cause is not solely a matter of positing an end that is convincingly just, although that is the indispensable starting point. It is also necessary to meet the tests posed by the other three subdivisions of just cause.

The forms of pursuing just cause are defensive and offensive wars. The justice of self-defense is generally considered to be axiomatic. Just-war doctrine, following Aristotle and St. Thomas as well as the later Scholastics, places great importance on the state as a natural institution essential for man's development. Defense of the state is prima facie of an essential social institution. So strong is the presumption in favor of the right of self-defense that the requirement of probable success, to be discussed under proportionality, is usually waived.

Offensive wars raise more complications. In classical just-war doctrine, offensive wars were permitted to protect vital rights unjustly threatened or injured. Moreover, in a form now archaic, offensive wars of vindictive justice against infidels and heretics were once permitted. Such wars disappeared with the decline of the religious, holy-war element as a cause of and rationale for wars. Thus, the forms of permissible wars today are twofold: wars of self-defense and offensive wars to enforce justice for oneself. As will be seen, even the second is now seemingly prohibited by positive international law. But in terms of basic just-war theory it remains an option. A war of vindictive justice wherein the belligerent fights against error and evil as a matter of principle and not of necessity is no longer condoned by just-war doctrine. . . .

Turning from the forms of just war we come to the heart of just cause—proportionality between the just ends and the means. This concerns the relationship between *raison d'état* (the high interests of state) and the use of the military instrument in war as the means to achieve these interests. This concept of proportionality at the level of *raison d'état* is multidimensional. To begin with, the ends held out as the just cause must be sufficiently good and important to warrant the extreme means of war, the arbitrament of arms. Beyond that, a projection of the outcome of the war is required in which the probable good expected to result from success is weighed against the probable evil that the war will cause.

The process of weighing probable good against probable evil is extremely complex. The balance sheet of good and evil must be estimated for each belligerent. Additionally, there should be a balancing of effects on individual third parties and on the international common good. International interdependence means that international conflicts are difficult to contain and that their shock waves affect third parties in a manner that must be accounted for in the calculus of probable good and evil. Moreover, the international community as such has its international common good, which is necessarily affected by any war. Manifestly, the task of performing this calculus effectively is an awesome one. But even its successful completion does not fully satisfy the demands of the just-war condition of just cause. Probing even further, the doctrine requires a responsible judgment that there is a probability of success for the just party. All of these calculations must be concluded convincingly to meet the multidimensional requirement of just cause.

Moreover, the calculus of proportionality between probable good and evil in a war is a continuing one. It should be made before the decision to go to war. It must then be reviewed at critical points along the process of waging the war. The best informed estimates about wars are often in error. They may need revision or replacement by completely new estimates. The *jus ad bellum* requirement of proportionality, then, includes these requirements:

There must be a just cause of sufficient importance to warrant its defense by recourse to armed coercion.

The probable good to be achieved by successful recourse to armed coercion in pursuit of the just cause must outweigh the probable evil that the war will produce.

The calculation of proportionality between probable good and evil must be made with respect to all belligerents, affected neutrals, and the international community as a whole before initiating a war and periodically throughout a war to reevaluate the balance of good and evil that is actually produced by war.

These calculations must be made in the light of realistic estimates of the probability of success. . . .

There is an important qualification to the requirement of probability of success. A war of self-defense may be engaged in irrespective of the prospects for success, particularly if there is a great threat to continued existence and to fundamental values. . . .

The last component of the condition of just cause is that war be employed only as a last resort after the exhaustion of peaceful alternatives. To have legitimate recourse to war, it must be the ultima ratio, the arbitrament of arms. This requirement has taken on added significance in the League of Nations–United Nations period. It was the intention of the nations that founded these international organizations to create the machinery for peace that would replace self-help in the form of recourse to war and limit the need for collective security enforcement action to extreme cases of defiance of international law and order. There are certainly adequate institutions of international negotiations, mediation, arbitration, and adjudication to accommodate any nation willing to submit its international disputes to peaceful settlement. Indeed, the existence of this machinery for peaceful settlement has prompted international lawyers and statesmen to adopt a rough rule of thumb: the state that fails to exhaust the peaceful remedies available before resorting to war is prima facie an aggressor. . . .

RIGHT INTENTION

Among the elements of the concept of right intention, several points may be distinguished. First, right intention limits the belligerent to the pursuit of the avowed just cause. That pursuit may not be turned into an excuse to pursue other causes that might not meet the conditions of just cause. Thus, if the just cause is to defend a nation's borders and protect them from future aggressions, but the fortunes of war place the just belligerent in the position to conquer the unjust nation, such a conquest might show a lack of right intention and change the just war into an unjust war. The just cause would have been realized by a war of limited objectives rather than a war of total conquest.

Second, right intention requires that the just belligerent have always in mind as the ultimate object of the war a just and lasting peace. There is an implicit requirement to prepare for reconciliation even as one wages war. This is a hard saying. It will often go against the grain of the belligerents' disposition, but pursuit of a just and lasting peace is an essential characteristic of the difference between just and unjust war. Accordingly, any belligerent acts that unnecessarily increase the destruction and bitterness of war and thereby endanger the prospects for true peace are liable to condemnation as violations of the condition of right intention.

Third, underlying the other requirements, right intention insists that charity and love exist even among enemies. Enemies must be treated as human beings with rights. The thrust of this requirement is twofold. Externally, belligerents must act with charity toward their enemies. Internally, belligerents must suppress natural animosity and hatred, which can be sinful and injurious to the moral and psychological health of those who fail in charity. Gratuitous cruelty may be as harmful to those who indulge in it as to their victims.

Right intention raises difficult moral and psychological problems. It may well be that its tenets set standards that will often be unattainable insofar as the thoughts and feelings of belligerents are concerned. War often treats individuals and nations so cruelly and unfairly that it is unrealistic to expect them to banish all hatred of those who have afflicted them. We can, however, more reasonably insist that just belligerents may not translate their strong feelings into behavior that is prohibited by the rule of right intention. A nation may feel tempted to impose a **Carthaginian peace**, but it may not exceed just cause by giving in to that temptation. A nation must have good reason for feeling that the enemy deserves the full force of all means available, but the requirement to build for a just and lasting peace prohibits this kind of vengeance. The enemy may have behaved abominably, engendering righteous indignation amounting to hatred, but the actions of the just belligerent must be based on charity.

Lest this appear to be so utterly idealistic as to warrant dismissal as irrelevant to the real world, let it be recalled that the greatest enemies of the modern era have often been brought around in the cyclical processes of international policies to become trusted allies against former friends who are now viewed with fear and distrust. If war is to be an instrument of policy and not, in St. Augustine's words, a "vendetta," right intention is a counsel of good policy as well as of morality. . . .

THE *JUS IN BELLO*

In the *jus in bello* that emerged rather late in the development of just-war doctrine, two basic limitations on the conduct of war were laid down. One was the principle of proportion requiring proportionality of military means to political and military ends. The other was the principle of discrimination prohibiting direct, intentional attacks on noncombatants and nonmilitary targets. These are the two categories of *jus in bello* limitations generally treated by modern workers on just war. . . .

The Principle of Proportion

In the preceding [discussion] the principle of proportion was discussed at the level of *raison d'état*. One of the criteria of just-war *jus ad bellum* requires that the good to be achieved by the realization of the war aims be proportionate to the evil resulting from the war. When the principle of proportion is again raised in the *jus in bello,* the question immediately arises as to the referent of proportionality in judging the means of war. Are the means to be judged in relation to the end of the war, the ends being formulated in the highest *raison d'état* terms? Or are intermediate political/military goals, referred to in the law-of-war literature as *raison de guerre,* the more appropriate referents in the calculus of proportionality as regards the conduct of a war?

There is no question that the ultimate justification for all means in war lies in the just cause that is a political purpose, *raison d'état*. But there are difficulties in making the ends of *raison d'état* the sole referent in the *jus in bello* calculus of proportionality. First, relation of all means to the highest ends of the war gives little rationale for or justification of discrete military means. If all means are simply lumped together as allegedly necessary for the war effort, one has to accept or reject them wholly in terms of the just cause, leaving no morality of means. The calculus of proportionality in just cause is the total good to be expected if the war is successful balanced against the total evil the war is likely to cause.

Second, it is evident that a discrete military means could, when viewed independently on the basis of its intermediary military end (*raison de guerre*), be proportionate or disproportionate to that military end for which it was used, irrespective of the ultimate end of the war at the level of *raison d'état*. If such a discrete military means were proportionate in terms of its military end, it would be a legitimate belligerent act. If it were disproportionate to the military end, it would be immoral and legally impermissible. Thus, an act could be proportionate or disproportionate to a legitimate military end regardless of the legitimacy of the just-cause end of *raison d'état*.

Third, there is the need to be realistic and fair in evaluating individual command responsibility for belligerent acts. The need to distinguish higher political ends from intermediate military ends was acute in the war-crimes trial after World War II. It is the law of Nuremberg, generally accepted in international law, that the *raison d'état* ends of Nazi Germany were illegal aggression. But the Nuremberg and other war-crimes tribunals rejected the argument that all military actions taken by the German armed forces were war crimes per se because they were carried out in pursuance of aggressive war. The legitimacy of discrete acts of German forces was judged, inter alia, in terms of their proportionality to intermediate military goals, *raison de guerre*. This was a matter of justice to military commanders accused of war crimes. It was also a reasonable way to evaluate the substance of the allegations that war crimes had occurred.

The distinction is equally important when applied to a just belligerent. Assuming that in World War II the Allied forces were fighting a just war, it is clear that some of the means they employed may have been unjust (for example,

strategic bombing of cities and the two atomic bomb attacks). It is not difficult to assimilate these controversial means into the total Allied war effort and pronounce that total effort proportionate to the just cause of the war. It is much more difficult and quite a different calculation to justify these means as proportionate to discrete military ends. Even in the absence of war-crimes proceedings, a just belligerent ought to respect the *jus in bello* standards by meeting the requirement of proportionality of means to military ends.

To be sure, it is ultimately necessary to transcend concern for the responsibility of individual military commanders and look at the objective permissibility of a military means. Thus, it may be possible and necessary to absolve a commander from responsibility for an action taken that is judged to have been disproportionate but that appeared to him to be a proportionate, reasonable military action in the light of his imperfect estimate of the situation. . . .

It would appear that analyses of the proportionality of military means will have to take a twofold form. First, any military means must be proportionate to a discrete, legitimate military end. Second, military means proportionate to discrete, legitimate military ends must also be proportionate to the object of the war, the just cause. In judging the moral and legal responsibility of a military commander, emphasis should be placed on the proportionality of the means to a legitimate military end. In judging the ultimate normative permissibility, as well as the prudential advisability, of a means at the level of *raison d'état,* the calculation should emphasize proportionality to the just cause.

The focus of normative analysis with respect to a means of war will depend on the place of the means in the total pattern of belligerent interaction. Means may be divided roughly according to the traditional distinction between tactical and strategic levels of war. Tactical means will normally be judged in terms of their proportionality to tactical military ends (for example, the tactics of attacking or defending a fortified population center will normally be judged in terms of their proportionality to the military end of taking or holding the center). Strategic means will normally be judged in terms of their proportionality to the political/military goals of the war (for example, the strategy of attacking Japanese cities, first conventionally and then with atomic bombs, in order to force the surrender of Japan will be judged in terms of its proportionality to the just cause of war).

It remains clear, however, that the two levels overlap. A number of tactical decisions regarding battles for population centers may produce an overall strategic pattern that ought to enter into the highest calculation of the proportionality of a just war. The strategic decisions, on the other hand, have necessary tactical implications (for example, strategic conventional and atomic bombing of Japan was an alternative to an amphibious invasion) the conduct of which is essentially a tactical matter. The potential costs of such a tactical invasion strongly influenced the strategic choice to seek Japan's defeat by strategic bombing rather than ground conquest.

Insofar as judgment of proportionality in terms of military ends is concerned, there is a central concept appearing in all normative analyses of human behavior—the norm of reasonableness. Reasonableness must always be defined in specific context. However, sometimes patterns of behavior recur so that there are typical situations for which common models of reasonable behavior may be prescribed. In domestic law this norm is concretized through the device of the hypothetically reasonable man whose conduct sets the standard to be emulated by law-abiding persons. The reasonable commander is the counterpart of the reasonable man in the law of war. The construct of the reasonable commander is based upon the experience of military men in dealing with basic military problems.

Formulation of this experience into the kinds of working guidelines that domestic law provides, notably in the field of torts, has not advanced very far. Its advancement is one of the purposes of this book. We do, however, have some instances in which this approach was followed. For example, the U.S. military tribunal in the *Hostage* case found that certain retaliatory means used in the German military in occupied Europe in World War II were reasonable in view of the threat to the belligerent occupant posed by guerrilla operations and their support by the civilian population. On the other hand, in the *Calley* case a court comprised of experienced combat officers found that Lieutenant Calley's response to the situation in My Lai was altogether unreasonable, below the standard of reasonableness expected in combat in Vietnam.[2]

The difficulty with establishing the standards of reasonableness lies in the absence of authoritative decisions that can be widely disseminated for mandatory emulation. In a domestic public order such as the United States, the legislature and the courts set standards for reasonable behavior. While the standards have supporting rationales, their greatest strength lies in the fact that they are laid down by authority and must be obeyed. With the very rare exception of some of the post-World War II war-crimes cases, authoritative standards for belligerent conduct are found primarily in general conventional and customary international-law prescriptions. . . .

The Principle of Discrimination

The principle of discrimination prohibits direct intentional attacks on noncombatants and nonmilitary targets. It holds out the potential for very great, specific limitations on the conduct of just war. Accordingly, debates over the meaning of the *principle of discrimination* have become increasingly complex and important as the character of war has become more total. It is in the nature of the principle of proportion to be elastic and to offer possibilities for justifications of means that are truly necessary for efficacious military action. However, it is in the nature of the principle of discrimination to remain rigidly opposed to various categories of means irrespective of their necessity to success in war. It is not surprising, then, that most debates about the morality of modern war have focused on the principle of discrimination.

Such debates are vastly complicated by the opportunities afforded in the defiance of the principle of discrimination to expand or contract it by interpretations of its component elements. There are debates over the meaning of *direct intentional attack, noncombatants,* and *military targets.*

In order to discuss the problem of interpreting the principle of discrimination, it is necessary to understand the origins of the principle.

The most fundamental aspect of the principle of discrimination lies in its direct relation to the justification for killing in war. If the presumption against killing generally and war in particular is overcome (in the case of war by meeting the just-war conditions), the killing then permitted is limited to the enemy combatants, the aggressors. The exceptional right to take life in individual self-defense and in war is limited to the attacker in the individual case and the enemy's soldiers in the case of war. One may not attack innocent third parties as part of individual self-defense. In war the only permissible objects of direct attack are the enemy's soldiers. In both cases, the overriding moral prescription is that evil must not be done to obtain a good object. As will be seen, however, the literal application of the principle of discrimination tends to conflict with the characteristics of efficacious military action necessary to make the right of just war effective and meaningful.

However, it is important to recognize that the principle of discrimination did not find its historical origins solely or even primarily in the fundamental argument summarized above. As a matter of fact, the principle seems to have owed at least as much to codes of chivalry and to the subsequent development of positive customary laws of war. These chivalric codes and customary practices were grounded in the material characteristics of warfare during the medieval and Renaissance periods. During much of that time, the key to the conduct of war was combat between mounted knights and supporting infantry. Generally speaking, there was no military utility in attacking anyone other than the enemy knights and their armed retainers. Attacks on unarmed civilians, particularly women and children, would have been considered unchivalric, contrary to the customary law of war, and militarily gratuitous.

These multiple bases for noncombatant immunity were fortified by the growth of positive international law after the seventeenth century. In what came to be known as the Rousseau-Portalis Doctrine, war was conceived as being limited to what we could call today "counterforce warfare." Armies fought each other like athletic teams designated to represent national banners. The noncombatants were spectators to these struggles and, unless they had the bad fortune to find themselves directly on the battlefield, immune in principle from military attack. Attacks on noncombatants and nonmilitary targets were now prohibited by a rule of positive international law. Here again, the principle of discrimination was grounded in material facts, the state of the art and the limited nature of the conflicts, that continued to make possible its application. Moreover, the political philosophy of the time encouraged a separation of public armed forces and the populations they represented. All of these military and political supports for discrimination were to change with the advent of modern total war.

At this point it is necessary to clarify the status of the principle of discrimination in just-war doctrine as interpreted in this chapter. It is often contended that there is an absolute principle of discrimination prohibiting any use of means that kill noncombatants. It is further contended that this absolute principle constitutes the central limitation of just war and that it is based on an immutable moral imperative that may never be broken no matter how just the cause. This is the moral axiom mentioned above, that evil may never be done in order to produce a good result. In this formulation, killing noncombatants intentionally is always an inadmissible evil.

These contentions have produced two principal reactions. The first is pacifism. Pacifists rightly argue that war inevitably involves violation of the absolute principle of discrimination. If that principle is unconditionally binding, a just war is difficult if not impossible to envisage. The second reaction to the claims of an absolute principle of discrimination is to modify the principle by some form of the principle of double effect whereby the counterforce component of a military means is held to represent the intent of the belligerent, whereas the countervalue, indiscriminate component of that means is explained as a tolerable, concomitant, unintended effect—collateral damage in contemporary strategic terms.

Paul Ramsey is unquestionably the most authoritative proponent of an absolute principle of discrimination as the cornerstone of just-war *jus in bello*. No one has tried more courageously to reconcile this absolute principle with the exigencies of modern war and deterrence. [But] neither Ramsey nor anyone else can reconcile the principle of discrimination in an absolute sense with the strategic countervalue nuclear warfare that is threatened in contemporary deterrence. It is possible that Ramsey's version of discrimination could survive the pressures of military necessity at levels below that of strategic nuclear deterrence and war. But the fate of Ramsey's effort to reconcile an absolute moral principle of discrimination with the characteristics of modern war should indicate the grave difficulties inherent in this effort. . . .

The question then arises whether such heroic efforts to salvage an absolute principle of discrimination are necessary. As observed above, the principle of discrimination does not appear in the just-war *jus in bello* as a doctrinally established deduction from theological or philosophical first principles. Rather, it was historically the product of belligerent practice reflecting a mixture of moral and cultural values of earlier societies. Moreover, it is significant that in the considerable body of contemporary Catholic social teaching on war, embracing the pronouncements of Pope Pius XII and his successors and of Vatican II, the principle of discrimination is not prominent in any form, absolute or conditional. When weapons systems or forms of warfare are condemned, deplored, or reluctantly condoned, the rationales are so generalized that the judgments appear to be based on a mixed application of the principles of proportion and discrimination. If anything, these pronouncements seem more concerned with disproportionate rather than indiscriminate effects.

It is a curious kind of supreme, absolute principle of the just-war doctrine that slips almost imperceptibly into the evolving formulations of the authoritative texts and then is omitted as an explicit controlling rationale in contemporary judgments by the church framed in just-war terms. Moreover, the persistent reiteration by the contemporary church that legitimate self-defense is still morally permissible should imply that such defense is practically feasible; otherwise the recognition of the right is meaningless. But, as the pacifists rightly observe, self-defense or any kind of war is incompatible with an absolute principle of discrimination.

It is my contention that the moral, just-war principle of discrimination is not an absolute limitation on belligerent conduct. There is no evidence that such a principle was ever seriously advanced by the church, and it is implicitly rejected when the church acknowledges the continued right of legitimate self-defense, a right that has always been incompatible with observance of an absolute principle of discrimination. Accordingly, I do not distinguish an absolute, moral, just-war principle of discrimination from a more flexible and variable international-law principle of discrimination. To be sure, the moral, just-war understanding of discrimination must remain independent of that of international law at any given time. But discrimination is best understood and most effectively applied in light of the interpretations of the principle in the practice of belligerents. This, after all, was the principal origin of this part of the *jus in bello,* and the need to check moral just-war formulations against contemporary international-law versions is perennial.

Such a position is in no sense a retreat from a position of maximizing normative limitations on the conduct of war. In the first place, as Ramsey's brave but ultimately unsuccessful efforts have demonstrated, attachment to an absolute principle of discrimination leads either to a finding that all war is immoral and the demise of the just-war doctrine or to tortured efforts to reconcile the irreconcilable. Neither serves the purposes of the *jus in bello.* Second, the rejection of an absolute principle of discrimination does not mean an abandonment of efforts to limit war on moral grounds. The principle of discrimination remains a critical source of both moral and legal limitations of belligerent behavior. As Tucker has observed, there are significant points of limitation between the position that no injury must ever be done to noncombatants and the position that there are no restraints on countervalue warfare. The interpretations that follow here . . . will try to balance the need to protect noncombatants with the need to recognize the legitimate military necessities of modern forms of warfare. In this process one may err one way or the other, but at least some relevant, practical guidance may be offered belligerents. Adherence to an absolute principle of discrimination usually means irrelevance to the question of limiting the means of war or unconvincing casuistry.

In search of such practical guidance one may resume the examination of the principle of discrimination as interpreted both by moralists and international lawyers. Even before the principle of discrimination was challenged by the changing realities of total war, there were practical difficulties with the definition of *direct intentional attack, noncombatants,* and *nonmilitary targets.* It is useful, as a starting point for analysis, to recall a standard and authoritative exposition of the principle of discrimination by Fr. Richard McCormick.

It is a fundamental moral principle [unanimously accepted by Catholic moralists] that it is immoral directly to take innocent human life except with divine authorization. "Direct" taking of human life implies that one performs a lethal action with the intention that death should result for himself or another. Death therefore is deliberately willed as the effect of one's action. "Indirect" killing refers to an action or omission that is designed and intended solely to achieve some other purpose(s) even though death is foreseen as a concomitant effect. Death therefore is not positively willed, but is reluctantly permitted as an unavoidable by-product.[3]

An example that is frequently used in connection with this question is the use of catapults in medieval sieges of castles. The intention—indeed, the purpose—of catapulting projectiles over the castle wall was to kill enemy defenders and perhaps to break down the defenses. If noncombatants—innocents as they were called then—were killed or injured, this constituted a "concomitant effect," an "undesired by-product."

The issues of intention, act, and multiple effects are often analyzed in terms of the principle of double effect, which Father McCormick's exposition employs without invoking the concept explicitly. After centuries of inconclusive efforts to apply the principle of double effect to the *jus in bello,* Michael Walzer has proposed his own version, which merits reflection and experimental application.

The intention of the actor is good, that is, he aims narrowly at the acceptable effect; the evil effect is not one of his ends, nor is it a means to his ends, and, aware of the evil involved, he seeks to minimize it, accepting costs to himself.[4]

It is probably not possible to reconcile observance of the principle of discrimination with the exigencies of genuine military necessity without employing the principle of double effect in one form or another. However this distinction between primary, desired effect and secondary, concomitant, undesired by-product is often difficult to accept.

It is not so hard to accept the distinction in a case where the concomitant undesired effect was accidental (for example, a case where the attacker did not know that noncombatants were present in the target area). There would still remain in such a case, a question as to whether the attacker ought to have known that noncombatants might be present. Nor is it so hard to accept a double-effect justification in a situation where the attacker had reason to believe that there might be noncombatants present but that this was a remote possibility. If, however, the attacker knows that there are noncombatants intermingled with combatants to the point that any attack on the military target is highly likely to kill or injure noncombatants, then the death or injury to those noncombatants is certainly "intended" or "deliberately willed," in the common usage of those words.

Turning to the object of the protection of the principle of discrimination—the innocents or noncombatants—another critical question of interpretation arises. How does one define noncombatants? How does one define nonmilitary targets? The assumption of separability of military forces and the populations they represented, found in medieval theory and continued by the Rousseau-Portalis Doctrine, became increasingly less valid after the wars of the French Revolution.

As nations engaged in total mobilization, one society or system against another, it was no longer possible to distinguish sharply between the military forces and the home fronts that rightly held themselves out as critical to the war effort. By the American Civil War this modern phenomenon had assumed critical importance. The material means of supporting the Confederate war effort were attacked directly and intentionally by Union forces. War in the age of the Industrial Revolution was waged against the sources of war production. Moreover, the nature of the attacks on noncombatants was psychological as well as material. Military forces have always attempted to break the will of the opposing forces as well as to destroy or scatter them. It now became the avowed purpose of military forces to break the will of the home front as well as to destroy its resources for supporting the war. This, of course, was to become a major purpose of modern strategic aerial bombardment.

To be sure, attacks on the bases of military forces have historically often been an effective strategy. But in the simpler world before the Industrial Revolution, this was not such a prominent option. When the huge conscript armies began to fight for profound ideological causes with the means provided by modern industrial mobilization and technology, the home front and consequently the noncombatants became a critical target for direct intentional attack.

The question then arose whether a civilian could be a participant in the overall war effort to such a degree as to lose his previous noncombatant immunity. Likewise, it became harder to distinguish targets that were clearly military from targets, such as factories or railroad facilities, that were of sufficient military importance to justify their direct intentional attack. It is important to note that this issue arose before the great increase in the range, areas of impact, and destructive effects of modern weaponry, conventional and nuclear. What we may term *countervalue warfare* was carried out in the American Civil War not because it was dictated by the weapons systems but because the civilian population and war-related industries and activities were considered to be critical and legitimate targets to be attacked.

In World War I this kind of attack was carried out primarily by the belligerents with their maritime blockades. Above all, these blockades caused the apparent demise of the principle of noncombatant immunity in the positive international law of war. Other factors in this demise were developments that revealed potentials not fully realized until World War II (for example, aerial bombardment of population centers and unrestricted submarine warfare). In World War II aerial bombardment of population centers was preeminent as a source of attacks on traditional noncombatants and nonmilitary targets. By this time the concept of total mobilization had advanced so far that a plausible argument could be made that vast segments of belligerent populations and complexes of industry and housing had become so integral to the war effort as to lose their noncombatant immunity.

In summary, well before the advent of weapons systems that are usually employed in ways that do not discriminate between traditional combatants and noncombatants, military and nonmilitary targets, the distinction had eroded. The wall of separation between combatants and noncombatants had been broken down by the practice of total societal mobilization in modern total war and the resulting practice of attacking directly and intentionally that mobilization base. Given these developments, it was difficult to maintain that the principle of discrimination was still a meaningful limit on war. Those who clung to the principle tended to reject modern war altogether as inherently immoral because it inherently violates the principle. In the international law of war, distinguished publicists were reduced to stating that terror bombing of noncombatants with no conceivable proximate military utility was prohibited, but that the rights of noncombatants to protection otherwise were unclear. . . .

Endnotes

1. James F. Childress, "Just War Theories," *Theological Studies* vol. 39 (1978), pp. 428-435.
2. [For a description of the My Lai Massacre, see the Problem Cases.]
3. "Morality of War," *New Catholic Encyclopedia* 14 (1967), p. 805.
4. Michael Walzer, *Just and Unjust Wars* (New York: Basic Books, 1977), p. 155.

REVIEW QUESTIONS

1. O'Brien states three conditions for permissible recourse to war. What are they?
2. What problems arise in trying to satisfy the first condition?
3. How does O'Brien explain the four subdivisions of the just cause condition?

4. What are the elements of the concept of right intention according to O'Brien?
5. Explain the principles of proportion and discrimination.

DISCUSSION QUESTIONS

1. O'Brien says that offensive war remains an option in Just War Theory. When, if ever, would an offensive war be justified?

2. (According to O'Brien) right intention insists that charity and love exist even among enemies. Are charity and love compatible with killing people?

3. O'Brien thinks that the bombing of Hiroshima and Nagasaki was allowed by Just War Theory. What do you think? Didn't this violate the principle of discrimination?

Jeffrie G. Murphy

The Killing of the Innocent

Jeffrie G. Murphy is a member of the philosophy department at Arizona State University.

Murphy argues that the legal and moral concepts of guilt and innocence do not apply in the context of war. The concern in Just War Theory about protecting the innocent is really a concern to protect noncombatants. Murphy defines noncombatants as those who are not engaged in an attempt to destroy you, from the viewpoint of the one claiming self-defense.

Murder, some may suggest, is to be defined as the intentional and uncoerced killing of the innocent; and it is true by definition that murder is wrong. Yet wars, particularly modern wars, seem to require the killing of the innocent, e.g., through antimorale terror bombing. Therefore war (at least modern war) must be wrong.

The above line of argument has a certain plausibility and seems to lie behind much philosophical and theological discussion of such problems as the Just War and the nature of war crimes.[1] If accepted in full, it seems to entail the immorality of war (i.e., the position of pacifism) and the moral blameworthiness of those who participate in war (i.e., warmakers and uncoerced soldiers are all murderers). To avoid these consequences, some writers will challenge some part of the argument by maintaining (a) that there are no innocents in war or (b) that modern war does not in fact require the killing of the innocent or (c) that war involves the suspension of moral considerations and thus stands outside the domain of moral criticism entirely or (d) that contributing to the death of innocents is morally blameless so long as it is only foreseen but not intended by those involved in bringing it about (the Catholic principle of the Double Effect) or (e) that the prohibition against killing the innocent is only prima facie[2] and can be overridden by even more important moral requirements, e.g., the defense of freedom.

In this paper I want to come to terms with at least some of the important issues raised by the killing of innocents in time of war. . . .

THE CONCEPT OF INNOCENCE

The notions of innocence and guilt seem most at home in a legal context and, somewhat less comfortably, in a moral context. Legally, a man is innocent if he is not guilty, i.e., if he has not engaged in conduct explicitly prohibited by rules of the criminal law. A man may be regarded as morally innocent if his actions do not result from a mental state (e.g., malice) or a character defect (e.g., negligence) which we regard as morally blameworthy. In any civilized system of criminal law, of course, there will be a close connection between legal guilt and innocence and moral guilt and innocence, e.g., murder in the criminal law has as one of its material or defining elements the blameworthy mental state (*mens rea*) of "malice aforethought." But this close connection does not show that the legal and moral concepts are not different. The existence of strict liability criminal statutes is sufficient to show that they are different. Under a strict liability statute, a man can be guilty of a criminal offense without having, at the time of his action, any blameworthy mental state or character defect, not even negligence.[3] However, the notion of strict *moral* responsibility makes little sense; for an inquiry into moral responsibility for the most part just is an inquiry into such matters as the agent's motives, intentions, beliefs, etc.[4] Also, the issue of legal responsibility is much more easily determinable than that of moral responsibility. For example: It is noncontroversial that negligence can make one legally responsible. Anyone who doubts this may simply be given a reading assignment in any number of penal codes.[5] But whether or not negligence is a mental state or a character defect for which one is *morally* responsible is a matter about which reasonable men can disagree. No reading assignment or simple inquiry into "the facts" will lay this worry to rest.[6]

Now our reasonably comfortable ability to operate with these concepts of guilt and innocence leaves us when we attempt to apply them to the context of war. Of course, the legal notions will have application in a limited number of cases, i.e., with respect to those who are legally war criminals under international law. But this will by no means illuminate the majority of cases. For example: Those who have written on the topic of protecting innocents in war would not want to regard the killing of an enemy soldier engaged in an attack against a fortified position as a case of killing the innocent. He is surely, in the right sense (whatever that is), among the guilty (or, at least, among the non-innocent) and is thus a fitting object for violent death. But he is in no sense *legally* guilty. There are no rules of international law prohibiting what he is doing; and, even if such rules were created, they would surely not involve the setting up of a random collection of soldiers from the other side to act as judges and executioners of this law. Thus the legal notions of guilt and innocence do not serve us well here.

What, then, about moral guilt or innocence? Even to make this suggestion plausible in the context of war, we surely have to attempt to narrow it down to moral innocence or guilt *of* the war or *of* something within the war—not just immoral innocence of guilt *simpliciter*. That is, we surely do not want to say that if a bomb falls (say) on a man with a self-deceiving morally impure heart who is a civilian behind the lines that this is not, in the relevant sense, a case of killing an innocent. Similarly, I think it would be odd for us to want to say that if a soldier with a morally admirable character is killed in action that this is a case of killing an innocent and is to be condemned on those grounds. If we take this line, it would seem that national leaders should attempt to make some investigation of the motives and characters of both soldiers and civilians and kill the unjust among both classes and spare the just. (Only babes in arms would be clearly protected.) Now this sort of judgment, typically thought to be reserved for God if for anyone, is surely a very disquieting thing if advocated for generals and other war leaders. Thus the notions of moral innocence and guilt *simpliciter* must be dropped in this context.

Suppose, then, we try to make use of the notions of moral innocence *of the war* or moral guilt *of the war* (or of something within the war). Even here we find serious problems. Consider the octogenarian civilian in Dresden who is an avid supporter of Hitler's war effort (pays taxes gladly, supports warmongering political rallies, etc.) and contrast his case with that of the poor, frightened, pacifist frontline soldier who is only where he is because of duress and who intends always to fire over the heads of the enemy. It seems reasonable to say that the former is much more morally guilty of the war than the latter; and yet most writers on the topic would regard killing the former, but not the latter, as a case of killing an innocent.

What all this suggests is that the classical worry about protecting the innocent is really a worry about protecting *noncombatants*. And thus the distinction between combatants and noncombatants is what needs to be illucidated. Frontline soldiers are clearly combatants; babes in arms clearly are not. And we know this without judging their respective moral and legal guilt or innocence. And thus the worry, then, is the following: Under what circumstances is an individual truly a combatant? Wars may be viewed as games (terrible ones of course) between enemies or opponents. Who, then, is an enemy or opponent?

One suggestion for defining a combatant might be the following: Only soldiers engaged in fighting are combatants. But this does not seem adequate. For if killing an enemy soldier is right, then it would also seem to be right to kill the man who *orders* him to the frontline. If anything, the case for killing (say) a general seems better, since the soldier is presumably simply acting in some sense as his agent, i.e., the general kills *through* him. Perhaps the way to put the point, then, is as follows: The enemy is represented by those who are *engaged in an attempt* to destroy you.[7] And thus all frontline combat soldiers (though not prisoners, or soldiers on leave, or wounded soldiers, or chaplains, or medics) are enemies and all who issue orders for destruction are enemies. Thus we might try the following: Combatants are those anywhere within the *chain of command or responsibility*—from bottom to top. If this is correct, then a carefully planned attack on the seat of government, intended to destroy those civilians (and only those) directing the war effort, would not be a case of killing noncombatants or, in the relevant sense, innocents.

But what is a chain of command or responsibility? It would be wrong to regard it solely as a causal chain, though it is *at least* that. That is, the notion of responsibility has to be stronger than that expressed in the sentence "The slippery pavement was *responsible* for the accident." For to regard the chain here as solely causal in character would lead to the following consequence: If a combatant is understood solely as one who performs an action which is a causally necessary condition for the waging of war, then the following are going to be combatants: farmers, employees at a city water works, and anyone who pays taxes. Obviously a country cannot wage war if there is no food, no management of

the basic affairs of its cities, and no money to pay for it. And of course the list of persons "responsible" for the war in this sense could be greatly extended. But if all these persons are in the class of combatants, then the rule "protect noncombatants" is going to amount to little more than "protect babies and the senile." But one would, I think, have more ambition for it than that, e.g., one would hope that such a rule would protect housewives even if it is true that they "help" the war effort by writing consoling letters to their soldier husbands and by feeding them and providing them with emotional and sexual relief when they are home on leave. Thus I think that it is wrong to regard the notion of chain here as merely causal in character.

What kind of chain, then, is it? Let us call it a *chain of agency*. What I mean by this is that the links of the chain (like the links between motives and actions) are held together logically and not merely causally, i.e., all held together, in this case, under the notion of who it is that is *engaged in an attempt* to destroy you. The farmer qua farmer is, like the general, performing actions which are causally necessary conditions for your destruction; but, unlike the general, he is not necessarily engaged in an attempt to destroy you. Perhaps the point can better be put in this way: The farmer's role bears a contingent connection to the war effort whereas the general's role bears a necessary connection to the war effort, i.e., his function, unlike the farmer's, is not logically separable from the waging of war. Or, following Thomas Nagel,[8] the point can perhaps be put in yet another way: The farmer is aiding the soldier qua human being whereas the general is aiding the soldier qua soldier or fighting man. And since your enemy is the soldier qua soldier, and not qua human being, we have grounds for letting the farmer off. If we think of a justified war as one of self-defense,[9] then we must ask the question "Who can be said to be *attacking* us such that we need to defend ourselves against him?" Viewed in this way, the farmer seems an unlikely candidate for combat status.

This analysis does, of course, leave us with borderline cases. But, since there *are* borderline cases, this is a virtue of the analysis so long as it captures just the right ones. Consider workers in a munitions factory. Are they or are they not combatants? At least with certain munitions factories (making only bombs, say) it is certainly going to be odd to claim that their activities bear only a contingent connection to the war effort. What they make, unlike food, certainly supports the fighting man qua fighting man and not qua human being. Thus I should be inclined to say that they are properly to be regarded as combatants and thus properly subject to attack. But what about workers in munitions factories that only in part supply the war effort, e.g., they make rifles both for soldiers and for hunters? Or workers in nonmunitions factories that do make some war products, e.g., workers in companies, like Dow Chemical, which make both Saran Wrap and Napalm? Or workers in ball bearing factories or oil refineries, some of their product going to war machines and some not? Here, I submit, we do have genuine borderline cases. And with respect to these, what should we do? I should hope that reasonable men would accept that the burden of proof lies on those claiming that a particular group of persons are combatants and properly vulnerable. I should hope that men would accept, along with the famous principle in the criminal law, the principle "noncombatant until proven otherwise" and would attempt to look at the particular facts of each case as carefully and disinterestedly as possible. I say that I hope this, not that I expect it.

Who, then, is a combatant? I shall answer this question from the point of view of one who believes that the only legitimate defense for war is self-defense.[10] It is, in this context, important to remember that one may legitimately plead self-defense even if one's belief that one's life is being threatened is false. The only requirement is that the belief be *reasonable* given the evidence that is available. If a man comes to my door with a toy pistol and says, pointing the pistol at me, "Prepare to meet your Maker for your time has come," I act in my self-defense if I kill him even if he was joking so long as my belief was reasonable, i.e., I had no way of knowing that the gun was a toy or that he was joking. Thus: combatants may be viewed as all those in the territory or allied territory of the enemy of whom it is reasonable to believe that they are engaged in an attempt to destroy you.

What about our Dresden octogenarian? Is he a combatant on this analysis? Since he does not act *on authority,* it is at least prima facie odd to regard him as part of a chain of command literally construed—the concept of command being most at home in a context of authority. He does not, of course, have much to do with the war effort; and so we might find his claim that he is "helping to defeat the Americans" quaint on purely factual grounds. And yet none of this prevents its being true that he can properly be said to be engaged in an *attempt* to destroy the enemy. For people can attempt even the impossible so long as they do not *know* it is impossible. Thus I am prepared to say of him that he is, in fact, engaged in an attempt to destroy the enemy. But I would still say that killing him would count as a case of killing a noncombatant for the following reason: that the concept of attempt here is to be applied, not from the agent's point of view, but from the point of view of the spectator who proposes to plead self-defense in defense of his acts of killing. Combatants are all those who may *reasonably* be regarded as engaged in an attempt to destroy you. This belief is reasonable (though false) in the case of the frontline soldier who plans always to shoot over the heads of the enemy and unreasonable (even if true) in the case of our octogenarian. It would be quite unreasonable to plan a bombing raid on a nonmilitary and nonindustrial city like Dresden and say, in defense of the raid, that you are just protecting yourself or your country from all those warmongering civilians who are attempting to destroy you. For making such a judgment imposes upon you a burden of proof which, given the circumstances of war, you could not satisfy. You probably could not get *any* evidence for your claim. You certainly could not get what the law calls a "preponderance of the evidence"—much less "proof beyond a reasonable doubt."

Combatants, then, are all those of whom it is reasonable to believe that they are engaged in an attempt at your destruction. Noncombatants are all those of whom it is not reasonable to believe this. . . .

Endnotes

1. "Murder," writes Miss Elizabeth Anscombe, "is the deliberate killing of the innocent, whether for its own

sake or as a means to some further end" ("War and Murder," p. 45). Deliberate killing of the innocent (or noncombatants) is prohibited by the Just War Theory and is a crime in international law. A traditional account of the Catholic Just War Theory may be found in Chapter 35 of Austin Fagothey's *Right and Reason: Ethics in Theory and Practice* (St. Louis: C. V. Mosby Co., 1963). A useful sourcebook for inquiry into the nature of war crimes is the anthology *Crimes of War,* ed. by Richard A. Falk, Gabriel Kilko, and Robert Jay Lifton (New York: Random House, 1971).

2. By "prima facie wrong" I mean "can be overridden by other moral requirements"—*not,* as a literal translation might suggest, "only apparently wrong."

3. For example: In the criminal offense of statutory rape, the defendant is strictly liable with respect to his knowledge of the age of a girl with whom he has had sexual relations, i.e., no matter how carefully he inquired into her age, no matter how reasonable (i.e., nonnegligent) his belief that she was of legal age of consent, he is liable if his belief is in fact mistaken. For a general discussion of such offenses, see Richard Wasserstrom's "Strict Liability in the Criminal Law," *Stanford Law Review,* 12 (July 1960).

4. In discussion, Richard Wasserstrom has expressed skepticism concerning my claim that there is something unintelligible about the concept of strict moral responsibility. One could regard the *Old Testament* and *Oedipus Rex* as containing a strict liability conception of morality. Now I should be inclined to argue that the primitiveness of the *Old Testament* and of *Oedipus Rex* consists in these peoples not yet being able to draw a distinction between legality and morality. However, I am prepared to admit that it might be better to weaken my claim by maintaining simply that no *civilized* or *enlightened* morality would involve strict liability.

5. In California criminal law, for example, vehicular manslaughter is defined as vehicular homicide "in the commission of an unlawful act, not amounting to felony, with gross negligence. . ." (*California Penal Code,* 192, 3, a).

6. For an excellent discussion of moral and legal responsibility for negligence, see H. L. A. Hart's "Negligence, *Mens Rea* and Criminal Responsibility," in his *Punishment and Responsibility: Essays in the Philosophy of Law* (Oxford: Oxford University Press, 1963).

7. I say "engaged in an attempt" rather than "attempting" for the following reasons: A mortar attack on an encampment of combat soldiers who happen to be sleeping is surely not a case of killing noncombatants even though persons who are asleep cannot be attempting anything. Sleeping persons can, however, be engaged in an attempt—just as sleeping persons can be accomplices in crime and parties to a criminal conspiracy. Being engaged in an attempt, unlike attempting, is not necessarily a full time job. I am grateful to Anthony Woozley for pointing this out to me.

8. Thomas Nagel, "War and Massacre," *Philosophy and Public Affairs,* 2 (Winter 1972). In the same issue, Richard Brandt replies to Nagel in his "Utilitarianism

and the Rules of War." I am grateful to Professors Nagel and Brandt for allowing me to read their articles prior to publication.

9. For reasons of simplicity in later drawing upon important and instructive principles from the criminal law, I shall use the phrase "self-defense." (I shall later want to draw on the notion of *reasonable belief* in the law of self-defense.) However, what I really want to focus on is the concept of "defense" and not the concept of "self." For it seems to me that war can be justified, not just to defend oneself or one's nation, but also to defend others from threats that transcend nationality, e.g., genocide. If one wants to speak of self-defense even here, then it must be regarded as self-defense for the *human,* not just national, community. The phrase "self-defense" as it occurs in what follows should always be understood as carrying this qualification. And, of course, even clear cases of self-defense are not always necessarily justified. Given the morally debased character of Nazi Germany, it is by no means obvious that it acted rightly in trying to defend itself near the end of World War II (i.e., after it had ceased to be an aggressor).

10. Remember that this carries the qualification stated in note 9. For a survey of the law of self-defense, the reader may consult any reliable treatise on the criminal law, e.g., pp. 883 ff. of Rollin M. Perkins's *Criminal Law* (Brooklyn, N. Y.: Foundation Press, 1957). The criminal law is a highly moralized institution, and it is useful (though by no means always definitive) for the moral philosopher in that it provides an accumulated and systematized body of reflection on vital moral matters of our culture. For my purposes, I shall in what follows focus upon the *reasonable belief* condition in the law of self-defense. Other aspects of the law of self-defense (e.g., the so-called "retreat requirement"), have, I think, interesting implications for war that I cannot pursue here.

REVIEW QUESTIONS

1. How does Murphy explain the concepts of innocence and guilt?
2. According to Murphy, why don't these concepts apply in the context of war?
3. How does Murphy define "combatant"? Who is a combatant and who isn't in his view?

DISCUSSION QUESTIONS

1. Murphy thinks that workers in a munitions factory are combatants. What do you think?
2. By Murphy's account, the pacifist soldier who intends not to kill anyone is still a combatant. Is this right?

Gregory S. Kavka

Was the Gulf War a Just War?

Gregory S. Kavka is professor of philosophy at the University of California, Irvine. He is the author of Hobbesian Moral and Political Theory *(1986) and* Moral Paradoxes of Nuclear Deterrence *(1987).*

Was the Gulf War a just war? Kavka answers that it clearly satisfied the criteria of being authorized by a competent authority and being fought for a just cause. But he finds that there are problems in trying to decide if the criteria of right intention and proportionality were satisfied. As for the conduct of the war, Kavka tentatively argues that it might have satisfied the two principles of Discrimination and Proportionality.

In the early months of 1991, the United States—in alliance with a number of other nations—fought a large scale air and ground war to evict Iraq's occupying army from the emirate of Kuwait. In this paper, I will consider the question of whether this U.S. military campaign was a just war according to the criteria of traditional just war theory[1]—the only developed moral theory of warfare that we have.[2] My aim, however, is not so much to reach a verdict about the morality of the Gulf War, as it is to identify relevant moral issues, and to reveal certain serious problems of application that are inherent in just war theory itself.

Just war theory divides into two parts concerning, respectively, the question of whether or not to fight a particular war (justice of war), and the question of how the war is conducted (justice in war). I begin by considering whether it was just, according to the justice of war criteria, for the U.S. to fight the Gulf War at all. I then turn

From Gregory S. Kavka, "Was the Gulf War a Just War?" *Journal of Social Philosophy* 22, no. 1 (Spring 1991).

to the question of whether the way the war was conducted satisfied the criteria of justice in war.

SHOULD THE WAR HAVE BEEN FOUGHT?

To be a just war, a military campaign must satisfy each of four criteria: it must be authorized by *competent authority*, fought for a *just cause*, motivated by the *right intentions*, and must not cause harms that are out of *proportion* with the goods achieved. I think it is fairly clear that the first two criteria were satisfied in the case of the Gulf War. Although there was never a declaration of war by the U.S. Congress, the passage of resolutions by both houses of Congress—and the United Nations security council—which authorized the use of force to expel the Iraqi army from Kuwait, meant that U.S. President George Bush was acting as a competent authority in ordering U.S. troops into battle.[3] And the vindication of the rights of self-protection and self-determination of the Kuwaitis against the occupying Iraqi forces is a paradigm of a just cause. When we turn to the criteria of Right Intention and Proportionality, however, things get considerably more complicated.

Right Intention

The criterion of Right Intention concerns the subjective motivations of the war-making entities. One general difficulty with just war theory is that it is usually collective entities, like nations, that fight wars and there are two competing philosophical accounts of the nature of the motives and intentions of such collective entities. According to the *individualist account*, statements about the motives and intentions of collective entities are merely convenient abbreviations for more complex statements about the motives and intentions of the particular individual members of those entities. But the competing *collectivist account* says that motives and intentions can be attributed to corporate entities themselves if the actions of the entities' members express corporate policy and flow from corporate decision-procedures. As Peter French, a prominent collectivist, puts it: "[A] Corporation's Internal Decision Structure . . . licenses the prediction of corporate intentionality . . . [W]hen the corporate act is consistent with, an instantiation or an implementation of established corporate policy, then it is proper to describe it as having been done for corporate reasons, . . . as corporate intentional."[4] As we shall see, both the collectivist and individualist accounts pose serious problems of application when applied to a concrete situation such as U.S. actions in the Gulf War.

Consider first the collectivist account. Assuming that proper U.S. procedures were used in authorizing the war, the key question is what U.S. policy or policies the Gulf War implemented or instantiated. Doubtless there were many U.S. policies this war may be said to have implemented, and this fact points immediately to two sorts of problems. First, of the various policies implemented, must they *all* be morally good (or at least morally neutral) policies if the Right Intention criterion is to be satisfied? Or must this be true of only the majority of them, or of the most important ones? Second, at what level of specificity are the policies to be described and evaluated? U.S. policies, described at the most general levels (e.g., "do the right thing," "help friendly nations in trouble," "protect the national interest") are likely to be morally good or morally neutral. More specific descriptions of these policies that imply their immorality are likely to be controversial. Thus, while all might agree that "protect Middle East oil supplies to the West" was one policy implemented by the Gulf War, critics and friends of U.S. foreign policy are likely to disagree whether the implicit clause in the policy says "by any means necessary" or "by any proper means." The answer to this question is vital in determining the morality of the policy, and hence of the collective intention which implements it according to the collectivist account.

How, in principle, are such questions (about what the *real* collective policy is) to be answered? Presumably by looking at three sorts of evidence: past behavior of the collective, the nature of the collective's decision-procedures and the sorts of considerations that carry weight in

that procedure, and the particular descriptions of policy that influenced decision-makers in the case at hand. The inclusion of the first two elements suggests that, according to the collectivist account, we cannot give a proper account of U.S. motives in the Gulf War without a more general determination of the morality of U.S. behavior in international relations, and the influence various considerations (including moral ones) have within the foreign-policy decision-making apparatus of the U.S. Since these matters are far beyond the scope of this paper, I turn instead to the individualist account which focuses exclusively on the third element: how the decision-makers involved thought of what they were doing and why they did it.

According to the individualist account, "collective motives and intentions" are simply agglomerations of individual motives and intentions among the collectives' members. Unfortunately, we have no good account that tells us how to determine (or accurately describe) the motives of a collective when the motives of its various members are diverse and various, as they typically are. Even among a small leadership group—say a head of state and her small circle of advisors—there are likely to be a variety of motives for embarking on a military campaign. Indeed, even if we focus on a single decision-maker like President Bush, there may be a number of motives present, and even the individual in question may not know what they all are and which are the most important ones. And even if we put aside epistemological questions about knowing people's motives, just war theory gives us no guidance as to how to deal with the multiplicity of motives. Whose motives count? Must they all be morally legitimate ones, or only the majority of them, or most of the important ones, or most of the important ones of the most influential decision-makers? In the absence of answers to these questions, we cannot—on the individualist account—really apply the criterion of Right Intention with great confidence.

Let us sidestep these problems in applying the individualist account to the Gulf War, together with epistemological problems about determining people's real motivations, by making two assumptions. First, it is the motives of President Bush and his top advisors that matter, and second, their publicly stated intention of promoting a new world order is really what motivated their actions in the gulf crisis. I am far from convinced that the second assumption is correct. But it would be wrong to dismiss it out of hand, on the grounds that some have, namely that previous U.S. failures to intervene militarily in situations as bad as the Kuwaiti one show that our leaders' motives in the Gulf War were imperialistic (control of the gulf), economic (cheap oil), or privately political (re-election). Just war theory, or any other plausible account of international morality (e.g., a rule-utilitarian one), does not require nations to intervene militarily in all situations of international injustice or aggression. It is perfectly permissible, indeed wise and desirable, for nations to limit their interventions to situations in which grave aggressions need to be prevented or reversed, the nation possesses the means to reliably bring this about, and the nation's interests would be significantly adversely affected if it did not do so. The mere fact that a nation picks and chooses its interventions to coincide with feasibility and national interest does not mean its motives are bad, nor that it has no concern for halting aggression. This is not to say that patterns of intervention may not constitute *evidence* about the motivations of a nation's leadership. It just says that a history of selective intervention, in itself, is no evidence of impure motives when there is an intervention, and we may not dismiss the second assumption solely on the grounds that the U.S. has failed to intervene when less oil-laden states have been the victims of aggression.

Similar points apply to two other common objections against U.S. intentions being proper in the gulf situation: that the U.S. has fought clearly unjust wars in the past (from the conquest of the American Indians to the recent invasion of Panama), and that previously it armed and encouraged the aggressors in this very war—the Saddam Hussein regime in Iraq. At most, on the individualist account, these facts form part of a complex pattern of evidence about U.S. motives and intentions in the current situation. They do not in themselves show that these motives and intentions are bad ones. As regards the first argument, in particular, it must be remembered that just war theory is designed

to evaluate particular wars and the way they are conducted, it does not attempt to characterize a nation's history of involvement in wars in general. (Thus, the theory allows that just as a person of bad character may, on occasion, perform a right action, so a nation whose foreign policy is normally immoral may sometimes engage in just wars.) And while the second argument about our prior support for Iraq does have moral implications, they point toward—rather than away from—U.S. involvement in the Gulf War. For if the U.S. negligently created a danger by its prior coddling of the Iraqi regime, and the Kuwaitis suffered grievously as a result, the U.S. might bear a special responsibility to repair the effects of its negligence. On this line of reasoning, what would otherwise be a moral option for the United States—evicting the Iraqi army from Kuwait militarily—would become a moral responsibility or duty.[5] . . .

Proportionality

The criterion of Proportionality says that the good aimed at in fighting a war must outweigh the bads involved in, and caused by, the war itself.[6] There are three general difficulties with applying this criterion that make it difficult to determine whether the criterion was satisfied in the case of the Gulf War.

First, and most familiarly, there are enormous empirical difficulties in determining the effects of a war, even when it is over, together with possible disagreements about the scheme of value to be used in assessing the war and its consequences. Even if we waive the latter issue, the question about effects will remain largely unanswered for a very long time, since almost everyone agrees that it is the long-term effects on peace and stability in the Middle East that are most important, and they are not yet evident (if they ever will be).

Second, it is unclear whether we should apply the Proportionality criterion with respect to actual outcomes or what the agents involved reasonably believed at the time they made their decisions.[7] The latter alternative has the advantage of taking the just war theory as a practical, action-guiding theory that is designed to help statesmen and citizens guide their deliberations about going to war, rather than a set of abstract formulas usable only by outsiders to praise or condemn after the fact. We would normally think of the subjective "reasonable belief" version of the criterion of Proportionality as being easier on decision-makers: it does not expect them to be prescient and does not subject them to Monday morning quarterbacking. But, in this case, using the "reasonable belief" version of the criterion may make it *harder* for the war in question to satisfy that criterion. For at least as regards the immediate effects, the Gulf War was shorter and involved fewer casualties (on both sides) than was reasonably expected ahead of time by top U.S. officials.

Third, evaluating a war in terms of its good and bad upshots is more complicated than simply observing its actual effects in the world. We must also compare the war and its effects to what the world would have been like had the war not occurred, i.e., to a *counterfactual* situation. But we cannot observe what would have happened, but did not; we can only hypothesize it based on what the world was like and our limited ability to identify and extrapolate trends.

Further, it is not obvious *which* counterfactual situation we are to consider in making our comparison: the one resulting from the nation in question doing nothing,[8] from its doing what it would most likely have done if it did not fight, or from its doing what (besides, possibly, fighting) would have maximized utility. This last way of identifying the relevant alternative may be too strong: it turns the Proportionality criterion into a requirement to maximize utility. But the first way seems too weak: it allows fighting when negotiations (or threats) would achieve the same ends more cheaply.[9] And the middle way can set the baseline of comparison too low. Suppose, for example, a nation would most likely turn its army to slaughtering a domestic minority if it did not fight the war in question. Then even a costly and unnecessary war might satisfy the Proportionality criterion.

Unable to solve this problem of picking out the relevant alternative in a satisfactory way, I will henceforth simply *assume* that the relevant alternative in the gulf situation was to continue the policy actually pursued prior to the outbreak of fighting: military defense of Saudi Arabia combined with economic sanctions against Iraq. Even given this assumption, however, and even if all the data were in about future actual developments in the region, we would not know for sure whether the war produced a favorable balance of good over evil. For we would not know what *would have happened* had the alliance not fought the war. Perhaps continuation of the economic sanctions would have worked to force Iraq from Kuwait or Saddam Hussein from power. Though I doubt this is likely to have occurred, if it had, it would have set a marvelous precedent for a new world order: cancellation of aggressive gains by united diplomatic and economic action rather than war. A more likely possibility is that a purely defensive force in Saudi Arabia would have sufficed to control Iraq's military ambitions, while Kuwaiti oil riches paid off Iraqi debts and provided the Iraqis with a new interest in regional stability. This outcome, sad as it would have been for Kuwait, would not necessarily have been intolerable for the world as a whole, nor worse than the actual consequences of the gulf conflict.

The fair conclusion to draw, I think, is that we do not know whether the Gulf War satisfied the criterion of Proportionality and may never know. This is due less to the peculiarities of the Gulf War, than to general problems concerning applicability of the Proportionality criterion: potential disagreement about values, factual uncertainty and complexity, necessity of comparison with indeterminate counterfactual situations, and ambiguity between "actual outcomes" and "reasonable belief" interpretations of the criterion.[10] But even this agnostic conclusion suggests that the Gulf War fares better than most wars as regards proportionality. Most wars have clearly cost much and achieved little in terms of human well being. Supporters of the Gulf War can claim, without absurdity, that something humanly significant (the liberation of Kuwait and the removal of the Iraqi military threat) has been achieved at a reasonable cost.

Last Resort

Some interpretations of just war theory require, as a separate criterion, that all available peaceful alternatives be exhausted before a war can be justified.[11] I prefer to view this principle as a powerful rule of thumb to be used in applying the Proportionality criterion. Given the enormous costs of war, it is highly unlikely that it is proportionate to go to war before pursuing all peaceful alternatives for settling a dispute. But in the odd case where it is proportionate to fight before trying all alternatives that might conceivably work—for example, when an aggressor will use any extra time to make his military position unassailable—a nation is justified in doing so.

Though I do not endorse the last resort idea as a separate criterion that must be satisfied for a war to be just, I think it is instructive to look briefly at whether the U.S. went to war in the gulf as a last resort. Many members of the U.S. Congress apparently thought not; they voted in favor of continuing economic sanctions rather than going to war. But suppose the administration was right and the economic sanctions would not have been sufficient to force Iraq from Kuwait. (This view is credible in view of the fact that a tremendous air war did not suffice to make the Iraqis withdraw.[12]) Did the Bush Administration go the last mile for peace, as it claimed, by offering—and having—direct talks with Iraq at the highest level in order to prevent war?[13] Their apparent aim was to get Iraq to withdraw by credibly threatening to fight without actually fighting.[14] In this they failed.

But there was an alternative, potentially more effective, way of carrying out this strategy for avoiding war that was not attempted. The war occurred because the two Presidents—Bush and Hussein—looked at different precedents and drew different lessons. Bush looked at World War II, and saw Hussein as a Hitler-like tyrant who had to be stopped by superior military force.[15] Hussein looked at Viet Nam and the barracks-bombing in Lebanon and concluded that the U.S. would not sustain a military operation in which it suffered heavy casualties.[16] To get Iraq out of Kuwait without fighting, it was necessary to erase that conclusion from Hussein's mind, other than by verbal threats that he simply would not believe.

Suppose, however, that President Bush had publicly declared that he would not run for re-election in 1992 unless the Iraqi army was out of Kuwait and the original Kuwaiti government restored to power. This announcement would

constitute the kind of precommitment to fight to the end in Kuwait that Hussein—a high political leader who is assumed to value political power above all else—would both believe and understand. If he had any doubts about the determination of top American leadership to drive him from Kuwait by force if necessary, this simple public act would have erased them. It would also erase any illusions that once the war began and there were casualties, American leaders would be inclined to pull back or compromise.

This course of action would have had its moral downside. If this last resort were tried but failed, the administration would have incentives to continue a stalemated war past the point of diminishing returns. Nonetheless, if President Bush had wished to walk the last mile for peace by maximizing his chances of expelling Iraq from Kuwait by threats rather than war, this is a policy he might have been well-advised to pursue. Whether his failure to do so renders the subsequent war "disproportionate" depends upon whether this maneuver would have significantly increased the chances of a peaceful settlement. One may reasonably doubt this if one believes that Iraq's behavior during the war indicates that nothing short of decisive military defeat would have driven them from Kuwait.

There is a further issue concerning satisfaction of the Last Resort criterion in the Gulf War. Just prior to the start of the coalition's brief and decisive ground campaign, the Soviet Union was apparently making some headway toward brokering a diplomatic solution that would involve Iraqi withdrawal from Kuwait. If the Last Resort criterion is regarded as a separate criterion that must be satisfied for war to be just, the gulf *ground* war would turn out to be unjust simply because the U.S. and its coalition partners passed up this opportunity to settle the dispute with Iraq without fighting a ground war.

On the other hand, if—as suggested above— we interpret the last Resort criterion as a rule-of-thumb falling under the Proportionality criterion, the status of the ground war is harder to determine. Beneficial and legitimate objectives were achieved by the ground campaign: weakening of the dangerous Iraqi military, Iraq's commitment to paying reparations and its renunciation of its annexation of Kuwait, and strengthening of the "new world order" principle of nonaggression against one's neighbors. And casualties (especially civilian and coalition casualties) were light, because of the swiftness and one-sidedness of the campaign. Thus, unless we assume a "reasonable belief" interpretation of the Proportionality criterion, and suppose that U.S. decision-makers expected much heavier casualties from the ground war even just before it commenced, the ground war might well satisfy the Proportionality criterion, despite the fact that the U.S. failed to pursue the Soviet peace initiative.

WAS THE WAR CONDUCTED IN A JUST MANNER?

The analysis of the previous section does not rule out the possibility that the Gulf War was a just one. Do the principles of Discrimination and Proportionality, which limit how a nation may fight a war (even one it is just to undertake) rule out that possibility? The principle of Discrimination requires not making civilian populations the object of attack. It allows the killing of civilians only as unintended (though possibly foreseen) consequences of attacking legitimate military targets.[17] Coalition policies of targeting only military assets, and ordering their pilots to withhold dropping their bombs when they could not hone in on assigned targets, taken together with the "relatively light" (given the amount of bombing) casualties suffered by Iraqi civilians, indicate general compliance with the principle of Discrimination by the coalition during the Gulf War.

Nonetheless, given the enormous number of powerful bombs dropped, and the targeting of military assets located in and near cities, there were still large numbers of civilian casualties—"collateral damage" in the euphemism used by the military briefers. These foreseeable Iraqi civilian casualties may not have been enough to render the entire war disproportionate. But the principle of Proportionality *within war* says that each operation or tactic must be proportionate, in terms of its costs and benefits (including, of course, the benefits of making overall victory more likely for the side fighting for justice).

This raises problems concerning the coalition's successful military strategy of postponing the ground war until the air war had reduced the effective capacity of resistance by the Iraqi military. This strategy was explicitly motivated by a legitimate desire to minimize coalition casualties. But even if Iraqi soldiers are eliminated from the calculations of Proportionality due to being considered "guilty aggressors,"[18] Iraqi civilians cannot be eliminated from those same calculations. Their deaths may have only been unintended side-effects of the bombing of military targets, but to the extent that they were foreseeable, they must be included—at least on a par with coalition military deaths—in applications of the principle of Proportionality.

Now it is possible that both civilian and military casualties were minimized by the coalition policy of continuing the air war for over a month before commencing the ground campaign. Perhaps a shorter air war would have led to a longer and fiercer ground war, with more casualties—civilian and military—on both sides. (At least their quick defeat on the ground allowed many Iraqi soldiers to surrender or flee. Even fewer might have survived a longer ground war.[19]) But if this is so, it is probably a lucky accident—there is no guarantee that it had to be so. The just war criterion of Proportionality in war implies that coalition war planners should have aimed at minimizing something different than they apparently did: innocent casualties (where this includes at least Iraqi civilians and neutrals caught on the field of battle) rather than simply coalition casualties.

CONCLUSION

Was the Gulf War a just war? The answer provided by the analysis of this paper is a resounding "maybe." It pretty clearly satisfied the criteria of Competent Authority, Just Cause, and Discrimination. It may or may not have satisfied the two Proportionality criteria and the Right Intention criterion. The difficulties with determining whether it did are not so much specific to this particular war, but are generic ones associated with applying just war theory in any real world situation. These include characterizing the nature of collective intentions, determining what the relevant motives and intentions of relevant decision-makers were, designating a scheme of value to evaluate outcomes, and making complex factual—and counterfactual—determinations about the effects of large-scale actions (like fighting a war) and their alternatives.

The fact that, after careful scrutiny, it remains at least possible that the Gulf War was a just war (according to the just war theory criteria), leaves that conflict in pretty select company. Even the Allies' effort in World War II, often taken as a paradigm of a moral war, clearly failed to satisfy at least one of the just war theory criteria: the principle of Discrimination. And it is not clear that World War II fares better than the Gulf War on the overall Proportionality criterion.

This is not (despite the analogy drawn in one of President Bush's speeches) because Saddam Hussein is another Hitler. He has not carried out a large-scale program of genocide justified by a racist ideology, nor—as the leader of Iraq—did he ever pose the threat to the world that was posed by Hitler astride the powerful German state. Nonetheless, in a space of a decade, he invaded—with aggressive intent—two neighboring states in a volatile and vital area of the world. Stopping him in a war with a few hundred thousand casualties may not have been disproportionate compared to stopping Hitler in a world conflict with tens of millions of casualties. Indeed, if over the next decade, the Middle East is more peaceful and stable than before the Gulf War, so that it seems likely that the war was after all a proportionate one, we may expect to see the Gulf War join (or even replace) World War II in common lore as the paradigm of a just war. If the analysis of this paper—based on traditional war theory—is correct, this would not necessarily constitute a mistake.[20]

Endnotes

1. There is no single canonical version of just war theory. The criteria used here to define that theory represent an attempt to distill the main elements of just war theory as portrayed in the recent philosophical literature.
2. The main alternative theories that are frequently applied to these issues are pacifism, which regards all wars as immoral, realism, which is a theory that denies the applicability of moral criteria to war, and utilitarianism, which is a general moral theory not specifically designed to deal with moral issues surrounding warfare.
3. Even the leaders of non-democratic allied nations were "competent authorities" in the relevant sense for just war theory, which is intended to rule out uses of force by private groups and individuals.
4. Peter A. French, "The Corporation as a Moral Person," in Peter A. French, ed., *The Spectrum of Responsibility* (New York: St. Martin's Press, 1991), pp. 298, 302.
5. This conclusion might not hold if, as some people suspect, the U.S. deliberately enticed Iraq into invading Kuwait in order to have an excuse to destroy its military power. But I do not find that suspicion very credible, despite the conflicting reports about what the U.S. Ambassador told Saddam Hussein in their July 25, 1991 meeting. (For one account, see Tom Mathews, "Road to War," *Newsweek*, January 28, 1991, pp. 54, 56.) U.S. diplomacy just prior to the invasion is better explained as bureaucratic fumbling and listening to the advice of the other Gulf states to appease Saddam, than it is by conspiracy theories. Nor does the fact that the U.S. government saw Saddam and his military as extremely dangerous *after* the invasion of Kuwait imply they saw them in the same light prior to that action.
6. The Proportionality criterion takes account of probabilities: in the presence of uncertainty, good and bad effects are to be weighted by their probabilities. So, in principle, a particular good outcome (e.g., restoration of a legitimate government) may justify a small risk of causing a certain number of casualties, but not a large risk of causing the same number of casualties.
7. The notion of "reasonable belief" used here is intended to mean more than "beliefs that are reasonable given the agent's evidence." There are ways of being unreasonable in gathering evidence, such as deliberately avoiding evidence that might shift one's beliefs in an inconvenient way. Satisfying the "reasonable belief" version of the Proportionality criterion requires having beliefs about outcomes that are "reasonable" in this strict sense.
8. Early in the crisis, President Bush apparently discussed the alternative of "doing nothing" with his top advisors. See Mathews, "The Road to War," p. 58.
9. This problem might be solved if, in contrast to what I propose below, we treat the Last Resort criterion as a separate criterion rather than a useful rule-of-thumb falling under the Proportionality criterion.
10. Of course, many of the same problems apply to competing theories that are consequentialist or have significant consequentialist elements, e.g., utilitarianism, patriotism (utilitarianism with one's scope of concern restricted to fellow citizens of one's country), and normative realism ("nations should act to best promote their own interests").
11. "Last Resort" is listed as a separate criterion, for example, in the American Catholic Bishops' famous

pastoral letter on nuclear war. See U.S. Bishops, "The Challenge of Peace: God's Promise and Our Response," *Origins* 13 (May 19, 1983), pp. 10–11.

12. The fact that the air war was not sufficient to drive the Iraqis from Kuwait is strong, but not conclusive, evidence that sanctions alone would not have worked. It is not conclusive evidence because the air war may have stiffened resistance (or affected internal politics) so as to eliminate the withdrawal option for the Iraqis in ways sanctions would not have.

13. Here I assume, at least for the sake of argument, that the offer of direct talks was more than a play for domestic political support. Cf. Mathews, "The Road to War," p. 64.

14. Mathews, "The Road to War," pp. 63–65.

15. Mathews, "The Road to War," p. 64.

16. In the notorious July 25th meeting with U.S. Ambassador to Iraq, April Glaspie, Hussein is reported to have said, "Yours is a society which cannot accept 10,000 dead in one battle." (Mathews, "The Road to War," p. 56.)

17. It thus presupposes the problematic doctrine of double-effect, which ascribes enormous moral significance to the distinction between causing the deaths of innocent people intentionally and doing so non-intentionally. Whatever we may think of that doctrine, it is a central aspect of just war theory, and I will apply it here without questioning its validity.

18. It is unclear whether just war theory ascribes equal status to enemy soldiers under the Proportionality criterion, for the notion of proportioning "good" to "evil" could include within it the idea that harm to the "innocent" counts more, where "innocence" is not moral innocence (which many Iraqi conscripts may have shared with their coalition counterparts), but innocence of participating in an unjust and threatening aggression. On the two notions of innocence, see e.g., G. E. M. Anscombe, "War and Murder," in Richard Wasserstrom, ed., *War and Morality* (Belmont, CA: Wadsworth, 1970), pp. 42–53.

19. An alternative view is that the mass surrenders show the Iraqi would have surrendered as soon as attacked in any case. If this is so, the air war was an unnecessary, and therefore disproportionate, tactic.

20. An earlier version of this paper was presented on March 28, 1991, to a meeting of the Concerned Philosophers for Peace at the American Philosophical Association Pacific Division Meetings in San Francisco. I am grateful to the audience on that occasion, and to Edwin Curley, Peter French, Paul Graves, Ron Hirschbein, and Jeff McMahan for helpful discussion and suggestions.

REVIEW QUESTIONS

1. According to Kavka, what are the problems in trying to establish the criterion of right intention for the Gulf War?

2. Kavka says there are three difficulties in applying the criterion of proportionality to the Gulf War. What are they?

3. What is the last resort criterion? Did the Gulf War satisfy this criterion in Kavka's view?

4. Was the Gulf War conducted in a just manner? What is Kavka's answer?

DISCUSSION QUESTIONS

1. Some critics of the Gulf War claimed that the primary motive of the U.S. leaders was to protect a major source of cheap oil for the United States. Does this motive satisfy the criterion of right intention?

2. The month-long air campaign in the Gulf War produced civilian casualties. Did this violate the principle of discrimination?

3. Compare the Gulf War to the more controversial Vietnam War. Was the Vietnam War a just war? Was the Gulf War a just war? (See the Problem Cases at the end of the chapter for more information about these wars.)

Majid Khadduri

The Doctrine of Jihād

Majid Khadduri taught international studies at Johns Hopkins University and other schools; he is currently director of research at the Middle East

Institute, Washington, DC. He is the author of several books including War and Peace in the Law of Islam *(1955),* The Gulf War *(1988), and* The

From Majid Khadduri, *The Islamic Conception of Justice* (Baltimore/London: The Johns Hopkins University Press, 1984), pp. 164–170. [Some of the footnotes have been renumbered—Ed.]

Islamic Conception of Justice (1984), *from which our reading is taken.*

Jihād, as Khadduri explains the term, has a broad sense in which it means exertion in Allah's path, and a narrower sense in which it refers to holy war against unbelievers and enemies of the Islamic faith. It does not include secular war. Jihād as holy war is justified because it enforces God's law or stops transgressions against it. All other war, that is, war fought for nonreligious reasons, is prohibited.

The instrument with which Islam sought to achieve its objectives was the jihād. Islam prohibited all kinds of warfare except in the form of jihād. But the jihād, though often described as a holy war, did not necessarily call for fighting, even though a state of war existed between the two dārs—**dār al-Islam** and **dār al-Harb**—since Islam's ultimate goals might be achieved by peaceful as well as by violent means.

Strictly speaking, the word "jihād" does not mean "war" in the material sense of the word. Literally, it means "exertion," "effort" and "attempt," denoting that the individual is urged to use his utmost endeavors to fulfill a certain function or carry out a specific task.[1] Its technical meaning is the exertion of the believer's strength to fulfill a duty prescribed by the Law in "The path of God" (Q. LXI, 10-13), the path of right and justice. Thus the jihād may be defined as a religious and legal duty which must be fulfilled by each believer either by the heart and tongue in combatting evil and spreading the word of God, or by the hand and sword in the sense of participation in fighting. Only in the latter sense did Islam consider the jihād a collective duty (fard al-kifāya) which every believer was bound to fulfill, provided he was able to take the field. Believers who could not take to the field nor had the means to do so were expected to contribute in weapons or supplies in lieu of fighting with the sword. Participation in the jihād in one form or another was a highly-prized duty and the believer's recompense, if he actually took to the field, would be the achievement of salvation and reward of Paradise (Q. LXC, 10-13) in addition to material rewards.[2] Such war, called in Western legal tradition "just war" (*bellum justium*), is the only valid kind of war. All other wars are prohibited.

The jihād was the just war of Islam. God commanded the believers to spread His word and establish His Law and Justice over the world (Q. IX, 5). The dār al-Islam was the house of the believers where Law and Justice were given practical expression, and the dār al-Harb was the house of the unbelievers and an object of the jihād. Religion, however, was and still is to be carried out by peaceful means, as there should be no compulsion in the spread of the word of God (Q. II, 257). The expansion of the state, carried out by the jihād, was an entirely different matter. Thus the jihād, a duty prescribed by Religion and Law, was surely as pious and just as *pium* and *justum* in the way described by St. Augustine and St. Thomas and later by Hugo Grotius.

In early Islam, the scholars like Abū Hanīfa (d. 150/768) and Shaybānī (d. 189/804) made no explicit declarations that the jihād was a war to be waged against non-Muslims solely on the grounds of disbelief. On the contrary, they stressed that tolerance should be shown unbelievers, especially the **scripturaries** (though not idolators and polytheists), and advised the **Imām** to wage war only when the inhabitants of the dār al-Harb came into conflict with Islam. It was Shāfiī (d. 204/820), founder of the school of law bearing his name, who laid down a framework for Islam's relationship with non-Muslims and formulated the doctrine that the jihād had for its intent the waging of war on unbelievers for their disbelief and not only when they entered into conflict with the Islamic state.[3] The object of the jihād, which was not necessarily an offensive war, was thereby transformed into a collective obligation enjoined on the Muslim community to fight unbelievers "wherever you may find them" (Q. IX, 5), and the distinction between offensive and defensive war became no longer relevant.

The reformulation of the jihād as a doctrine of just war without regard to its defensive or offensive character provoked a debate among Shāfiī's contemporaries and led to a division of opinion among Hanafī jurists. Some, like Tahāwī (d. 321/933), adhered more closely to the early Hanafī doctrine that fighting was obligatory only in a war with unbelievers;[4] but Sarakhsī (d. 483/1101), the great commentator on Shaybānī, accepted Shāfiʿī's doctrine of the jihād that fighting the unbelievers was a "duty enjoined permanently until the end of time." [5] Scholars who came afterwards, until the fall of Baghdad at the hands of the Mongols in the thirteenth century, accepted the jihād as just war without regard to its offensive or defensive character.

Should the Caliph, head of the State, be obeyed if he invoked the jihād in a situation considered contrary to justice, it may be asked? According to the Orthodox doctrine of the Imamate, not to speak of Shiʿī doctrines, the Imām had to be obeyed even if he were in error. But on matters of foreign conduct of the state, the Caliph's powers were often questioned. In a war with the Byzantines, the Caliph Harūn al-Rashīd (d. 193/809) seems to have decided to use violence against the Banū Taghlib, a Christian community near the Byzantine borders, and to revoke their treaty with Islam on the grounds of their alleged sympathy with the Byzantines. Shaybānī, who was consulted on the matter, said in no uncertain terms that the Banū Taghlib did not violate the treaty and that an attack on them was unjustified, although he did not necessarily imply that if the Caliph issued an order, his order should not be obeyed.[6] Later when Islamic power was threatened, the scholars were dubious about the Imām's conduct if he violated his undertakings with the unbelievers, but Ibn Taymīya (d. 728/1328) spoke openly his mind in defense of Christian claims to protection when they were discriminated against even at the most critical time of danger to Islam. . . .

THE JIHĀD AS DEFENSIVE WAR

The classical doctrine of the jihād made no distinction between defensive and offensive war, for in the pursuance of the establishment of God's Sovereignty and Justice on Earth the difference between defensive and offensive acts was irrelevant. However, although the duty of the jihād was commanded by God (Q. LXI, 10–13), it was considered to be binding only when the strength of the believers was theirs (Q. II, 233). When Islamic power began to decline, the state obviously could no longer assume a preponderant attitude without impairing its internal unity. Commentators on the jihād as a doctrine of permanent war without constraints began to reinterpret its meaning in a manner which underwent a significant adjustment to realities when conditions in the dār al-Islam changed radically. Some scholars, though still adhering to the principle that the jihād was a permanent state of war, argued that the mere preparation for the jihād would be a fulfillment of its obligation.[7] Not only did Islam become preoccupied with problems of internal security, but also its territorial integrity was exposed to dangers when foreign forces (the Crusaders and Mongols) from the dār al-Harb challenged its power and threatened its very existence.

In those altered circumstances, scholars began to change their position on the question of whether the jihād, used against believers on the grounds of their hostility to Islam, was just. The doctrine of the jihād as a duty permanently imposed upon the community to fight the unbelievers wherever they might be found retained little of its substance. Ibn Taymīya, a jurist-theologian who was gravely concerned with internal disorder, understood the futility of the classical doctrine of jihād at a time when foreign enemies (Crusaders and Mongols) were menacing at the gates of dār al-Islam. He made concessions to reality by reinterpreting the jihād to mean waging a defensive war against unbelievers whenever they threatened him. Unbelievers who made no attempt to encroach upon the dār al-Islam, he asserted, were not the objective of Islam nor should Law and Religion be imposed upon them by force. "If the unbeliever were to be killed unless he becomes a Muslim," he went on to explain, "such an action would constitute the greatest compulsion," a notion which ran contrary to the Revelation which states that "no compulsion is prescribed by Religion" (Q. II, 257). But unbelievers who consciously took the offensive and encroached upon the dār al-Islam would be in an entirely different position.[8]

No longer construed as a war against the dār al-Harb on the grounds of disbelief, the doctrine of the jihād as a religious duty became binding on believers only in the defense of Islam. It entered into a period of tranquillity and assumed a dormant position, to be revived by the Imām whenever he believed Islam was in danger. It is true that the Ottoman sultans in their conquest of European territory often invoked the jihād, but in their actions they were neither in a position to exercise the rights of the Imām nor were their ways always religious in character.[9] Moreover, at the height of their power, the sultans came to terms with the unbelievers and were prepared to make peace on the basis of equality and mutuality with Christian princes, contrary to precedents. Elated by their victories against the unbelievers of Europe, they turned to eastern Islamic lands and brought them under their control when the **Shīa** seized power in Persia at the opening of the sixteenth century, thus threatening internal unity. The Ottoman Sultan, though unable to subjugate Persia, provided leadership to Islamic lands under his control until World War I.

JUST WAR AND SECULAR WAR

In theory only the Imām, enthroned to exercise God's Sovereignty on Earth, has the power to invoke the jihād and call believers to fulfill the duty. Unless the Imām delegates his power to a subordinate, nobody has the right to exercise it without prior authorization from him. Were the jihād to be proclaimed by the governor of a province without authorization of the Imām, it would be a "secular war" and not a valid or just war. If a dissident leader, whether belonging to an orthodox or to a heterodox group, claimed the right to declare a jihād, his action would be considered disobedience to the Imām and a rebellion against the legitimate authority (Q. XLIX, 9).[10] Neither the leader nor the persons who take part in such a jihād would be rewarded with Paradise, which is granted only to those who participate in a jihād declared by the Imām.

Endnotes

1. See Zabīdī, *Tāj al-Àrūs,* ed. Hārūn, VII, 534-39.
2. The promise of eternal life in Heaven, where believers attain Divine happiness and justice, is granted to all who fulfill the basic duties, but none would enable the believer to gain Paradise as surely as martyrdom in the jihād. See Sarakhsī, *Sharh Kitāb al-Siyar al-Kabīr li . . . al-Shaybānī,* ed. Munajjid (Cairo, 1957), I, 24-25. The material reward for the jihād is a share in the spoils.
3. Shāfi'ī, *Kitāb al-Umm,* IV, 84-85.
4. Abū Ja'far al-Tahāwī, *Kitāb al-Mukhtasar,* ed. Abū al-Wafā al-Afghānī (Cairo, 1320/1950), p. 281.
5. Sarakshī, *Kitāb al-Mabsūt* (Cairo, 1324/1906), X, 2-3.
6. Khadduri, *Islamic Law of Nations,* pp. 34-35.
7. See Ibn Hudhayl, *Kitāb Tuhfat al-Anfus Wa Sukkān al-Andalus,* ed. Mercais (Paris, 1936), p. 15.
8. Ibn Taymīya, "Qā'ida fī Qitāl al-Kuffār," Majmū 'at Rasā'il, ed. Hamīd al-Fiqqī (Cairo, 1368/1949), pp. 115-46; and *al-Siyāsa al-Sha'ir'ya,* ed. Nashshār and Atīya (Cairo, 1951), pp. 125-53.
9. Cf. Fuād Köprülü, *Les Origines de l'Empire Ottoman* (Paris, 1935), chap.3.
10. See Shaybānī's *Siyar,* trans. Khadduri, *op. cit.,* pp. 230–31.

REVIEW QUESTIONS

1. According to Khadduri, what does the word "jihād" mean?
2. Explain the classical doctrine of jihād as permanent war against unbelievers.
3. How was this classical doctrine modified?
4. What is the role of the Imām in jihād as holy war?

DISCUSSION QUESTIONS

1. Compare the doctrine of jihād with the just war theory. How are they similar, and how different?
2. Saddam Hussein declared the Gulf War a jihād. Was this really a jihād or merely a secular war?
3. Is the doctrine of jihād acceptable? If not, then state and explain your objections.

Barbara Harff

The Need for Humanitarian Intervention: Bosnia and Somalia

Barbara Harff is associate professor of political science at the U.S. Naval Academy in Annapolis. She is the co-author (with Ted Robert Gurr) of Ethnic Conflict in World Politics *(1994).*

Harff makes a case for humanitarian intervention in countries where crimes against humanity occur. The three main examples she discusses are Bosnia, Somalia, and Iraqi Kurdistan. In Bosnia, ethnic cleansing has assumed the proportions of genocide. In Somalia there is mass starvation resulting from a complete disintegration of political order. In Iraq the regime in Baghdad is using deadly force including poison gas against civilian Kurds suspected of rebellion. In cases such as these, Harff argues, the international community has a moral obligation to take actions to prevent the crimes against humanity. She makes a number of suggestions about possible actions; these range from early warning assessments to collective military intervention and long-term occupation.

Many legal scholars favor intervention against states that perpetrate massive human rights violations; their arguments are based upon moral principles and international standards of justice. But at present, policymakers and government leaders often allow their political interests to outweigh these other considerations. In affirming respect for the sovereignty of states, they fail to acknowledge that sovereignty is not necessarily absolute, and they ignore other provisions of in-

ternational law that in some situations should be given priority. This short-sighted position has prevented the United States and Western Europe from mounting an effective cooperative effort to deal with the Bosnian conflict.

A number of newspaper columnists have contributed to the paralysis. Aware that the crisis in Bosnia has reached a point where a military commitment would be required to end the campaign of ethnic cleansing, they evoke the image of young Americans dying for the sake of nebulous policy objectives. But the sensible way to meet this concern is not to rule out intervention, but rather to insist that it combine precise policy goals, clear strategic objectives, and tactics that are suited to the desired end-state of the military involvement. It is illogical to conclude on the basis of an extreme case requiring an extensive military commitment that all forms of intervention are misguided in principle or are someone else's responsibility. If a coherent strategy for intervention had been in place from the beginning, the Bosnian crisis might never have assumed the proportions of genocide.

A multitude of ethnic conflicts may develop in the former Soviet Union and elsewhere in the next decade. Responses to these conflicts will, in turn, set the stage for the twenty-first century. In the early phases of ethnic conflict, will global leaders stand idly by while would-be dictators fight to expand their power base by killing their citizens, crossing internationally recognized boundaries, inflaming irredentist passions, and implementing ideologies of ethnic superiority?

It may prove to be a costly mistake if the last superpower and its friends (and sometime allies) become isolationist paper tigers once again. Explosions of ethnic passion rarely remain internal affairs. From a strategic perspective, it is clear that a future diffusion of ethnic passion, hatred, and rebellion will eventually call for much greater military measures than a maximum collective show of force with a minimum use of weapons in Bosnia. Failure to exert our capabilities may mean that we will lose our chance to build a world free from the forces that create global instability. From a cost-benefit perspective—as abhorrent as that may seem, when we consider the loss of lives in Bosnia and similar theaters—early warning measures, a clear policy position, and a strategy with civil and military components are the best guarantees to forestall adventurers of the caliber of Saddam Hussein and Radovan Karadzic. From an American perspective, to be able to intervene with the knowledge that the United States is proceeding on a clearly plotted course that is strategically sound, morally correct, legally justified and internationally supported makes the task easier for the young men and women who have joined the military in order to fight for their country's just cause. Indeed, the more clearly designed the policy and tactical objectives are, the greater the likelihood that few if any American lives will be lost—provided action is taken swiftly in response to early signs of impending disaster.

The Legal Foundations of Humanitarian Intervention

Hersch Lauterpacht, one of the great scholars of international law, once asked whether law can promote the "realization of socially obtainable justice." My own answer is a qualified yes. We can achieve minimum standards of justice by affirming such essential goods as the right to live, and by enforcing sanctions against those who deprive people of those essential goods. Mass murder is unacceptable in all national legal systems and, in principle, states should apply their domestic laws to their own and others' external behavior. In other words, foreign policy should reflect the standards of national morality defined by domestic law.

In accordance with this principle, the Genocide Convention forbids governments to take steps to destroy any distinct national, ethnic, or religious group. Article 3 of the Universal Declaration of Human Rights asserts that "everyone has the right to life, liberty, and security of person." The large number of signatories to the human rights and genocide conventions attests to the fact that international morality in regard to the protection of fundamental human rights coincides with national moralities. These treaties constitute, as Lauterpacht writes, "a recognition of fundamental rights superior to the law of the sovereign State."

Thus, when basic rights are violated to the degree we see at present in Somalia and Bosnia, international responses should follow, under the leadership of a United Nations that asserts and, ideally, enforces codified standards of morality. The most common argument against such action is based on Article 2, paragraph 7 of the U.N. Charter, which prohibits intervention in matters that are within the domestic jurisdiction of any state. In contrast, Article 34 identifies a competing principle by empowering the Security Council to investigate disputes that cause international friction, while Article 51 and Chapter VIII of the Charter offer regional organizations the legal justification for collective intervention.

The Bosnian situation is illustrative. If one accepts Bosnia's claim to being an independent state (as the U.N. did when it granted Bosnia a seat in the General Assembly), then under Article 51, the Bosnians have the right of self-defense, including the right to ask for outside help and to invite intervention by individual states, regional organizations, or the U.N. If one denies that Bosnia is an independent state (as does what remains of the federal Yugoslav government), then the situation is one of civil war between a state and a secessionist region. In this circumstance, the Security Council is empowered to execute collective measures, on the grounds that the situation is causing widespread abuse of human rights and international friction. Accordingly, in response to Serbian atrocities in Bosnia and Croatia, the first act of the General Assembly in the fall 1992 session was to deny membership to Serbia/Montenegro as the successor state to Yugoslavia.

Once it is established that international standards of human rights are being violated, the right to impose such standards should prevail over assertions of national sovereignty. But the path that leads from recognizing that a crime against humanity is being committed to the prescription of appropriate responses and sanctions is fraught with political difficulties. In principle, the U.N., as a collective body representing the great majority of states, is the entity that should delegate authority for any kind of intervention to willing and capable member states. Ideally, all full members would bear both the responsibility and the costs of the actions undertaken, even if the burden of action fell to the United States as perhaps the only country presently able to take a strong stand on such matters. Specific actions to be taken would be decided by the Security Council with the assistance of the Military Staff Committee (see Article 46).

The targets of international sanctions can be expected to complain that they are being victimized by a new brand of imperialism under the guise of the new world order. Given the archaic structure of the Security Council, in which the former imperial powers play a larger role than other states, such claims may have some prima facie plausibility. But such a claim by weaker states at no time and in no place mitigates the crimes of mass political murder, ethnic cleansing or complicity in mass starvation of ethnic rivals.

What has been lacking, time and time again, on the part of states with the capacity to act is the political will to take a strong stand and accept the consequences of boldness. Standards of international morality and order are not achieved through timidity; precedent is never set through inaction. Violent ethnic conflicts in the Third World have steadily increased in frequency and intensity since the 1960s, as Ted Robert Gurr has demonstrated in a study tracking some 200 minorities during the entire postwar period. The disintegration of the Soviet, Yugoslav, and Ethiopian states has released the evil genies of nationalist xenophobia and ethnic hatred in vast new areas. Genocides—directed against people on the basis of their ethnic, racial, or social identity—and politicides—directed against people on the basis of their political beliefs—often follow war and revolution in poor countries. In my own work, I have identified more than forty such episodes since 1945 and have shown that they caused greater loss of life than all the wars fought *between* states during that period. For this reason, it is essential to demonstrate that building states on mass graves violates the moral standards of global society, and must lead with some certainty to sanctions proportional to the crimes.

In the absence of a formal international authority to monitor and police the human rights performances of states, communal and nationalist contenders seeking territory or autonomy often press their claims by force. Intimidation of opposing forces within states and assaults on less powerful neighbors are becoming more common, most acutely so in Eastern Europe. Yugoslavia in particular has regressed to a nineteenth-century mentality. Myths and memories of old injustices are invoked to mobilize young Serbs and Croats for war against one another, and together against Muslims. The territorial ambitions of the contenders take no account of Yugoslavia's carefully balanced heterogeneity; a resurgent nationalism calls instead for the creation of fictive homelands, purified of "alien peoples." The claims being made by the most militant of Serbs are reminiscent of Nazi ideology, and one can well imagine that in the future, nationalist Serbs, if unchecked, will assert their racial and cultural superiority over competing ethnic groups in a greater Serbia extending from Macedonia to Austria.

CIVIL WARS, REBELLION, REPRESSION

Bosnia, Somalia, and Iraqi Kurdistan exemplify three distinct types of crimes against humanity in which the international community has a legal and moral imperative to intervene. Bosnia is a case that combines elements of civil and international war. On the civil side, Bosnia-Hercegovina's declaration of independence provoked uprisings by Bosnian Serbs concerned with their status in the new state. On the international side, they were armed by and acted as agents of "greater Serbian" nationalists. Recent events offer clear evidence of direct Serbian military support through air strikes and artillery barrages. The states of the European Community face a double responsibility, first because they helped precipitate the civil war by granting what many observers thought was premature recognition of Bosnian independence, and second because they have ample capacity to act. Yet EC leaders have largely behaved like bystanders, offering verbal condemnation and sending inadequate relief. It is clear that most European leaders find it politically more acceptable to condemn the participants and to talk about eventual war-crimes trials than to risk military casualties by trying to stop the war while it is still in progress.

Meanwhile, new civil wars and acts of aggression tragically similar to events in Bosnia are already under way or imminent in Macedonia, Moldova, the Caucasus, and some of the new republics of Central Asia. The international community has a compelling legal right and obligation to defend the civilian victims of such conflicts, not merely to provide them with minimal humanitarian assistance. The situation in Bosnia is all the more urgent because actions there will send a message to ambitious and potentially ruthless nationalists in all the states of the former Soviet bloc and elsewhere.

In Somalia, mass starvation is the result of the complete disintegration of political order. The process began in 1988 with a north-south civil war and massacres of northern civilians that attracted virtually no international attention. Since then, feuding clan leaders and warlords have made most of the country into a deadly wasteland in which humanitarian assistance, belatedly supplied, is seized at gunpoint. International pressure and diplomacy might have forestalled the crisis at an early stage. The immediate task must be to protect civilians against mass starvation, followed by restoration of critical elements of the transport infrastructure and preparation of the groundwork for an interim government. None of these tasks can be accomplished unless peacekeeping forces are authorized to use force. Somalia is a member of two regional organizations with the potential, in theory, to respond more forcefully: the Organization of African Unity and the Islamic Conference. Neither has acted decisively.

A similar situation existed in Lebanon and has now emerged in Liberia. The Liberian case is instructive: a West African peacekeeping force, operating under international auspices, temporarily stabilized the country and facilitated negotiations among the principal factions. The West African precedent for international intervention has been marred by the recent renewal of fighting in Liberia, but the peacekeeping effort undertaken so far appears preferable to the belated and inadequate international response to the Somali conflict. Other weak African states are at risk of similar crises.

Iraq exemplifies a more common kind of humanitarian crisis. Since the 1960s the Ba'athist regime in Baghdad has repeatedly used deadly force, including poison gas, against civilian Kurds suspected of rebellion. In the aftermath of the Gulf War, the Kurds revolted again and the Allies eventually responded with humanitarian aid in a Kurdish zone protected by Allied air cover. But for many Kurds, the response came too late. Allied leaders did not act until they were pressured by domestic and regional political considerations. Media coverage of atrocities mobilized public outrage in Western countries, and the Turkish government expressed its concern about the destabilizing effect of a flood of Kurdish refugees on its own Kurdish minority.

The main precedents for humanitarian intervention to end gross human rights violations like those in Iraq are unilateral ones: India in East Pakistan, now Bangladesh, in 1971; Vietnam in Cambodia, in 1978; and Tanzania in Uganda, in 1979. The intervenors' motives in these cases were politically suspect, but, on balance, unilateral action in each instance was better than inaction: it helped to end the killings and, except in Uganda, led to the establishment of regimes with a greater respect for human rights. The establishment of a security zone in Iraq was more easily achieved because it was done under international auspices in a pariah state that had lost credibility and clout in the Arab world; two previous decades of Iraqi abuse of Kurdish villagers had no significant international consequences.

Many future conflicts are likely to require international responses of the kind offered in Iraq. Chronic warfare and repression persist in Sudan and Myanmar (Burma); Ethiopia is at serious risk of renewed warfare that could be forestalled by international action. More distant crises can also be anticipated in such large Third World countries as Nigeria and Pakistan, where there are deep regional cleavages.

AN AGENDA FOR PEACE: RESPONDING TO INTERNATIONAL CRISES

The need for a more active role by the U.N. in such conflicts has been explicitly recognized by the new Secretary General, Boutros Boutros-Ghali. His *Agenda for Peace,* issued on June 17, 1992, focuses attention on threats to international security arising from "ethnic, religious, social, cultural or linguistic strife." The Agenda outlines four kinds of responses: preventive diplomacy, peacemaking, peacekeeping, and post-conflict peace-building. "Peace-building" refers to policies that address the root causes of conflict: "economic despair, social injustice and political oppression." The case of the Iraqi Kurds highlights the need to organize such responses to gross human rights violations at an early stage rather than wait for news of atrocities to create political pressures for action. The more quickly the U.N. acts, the less devastation communal conflicts will cause, whereas the longer that effective responses are delayed, the more difficult and costly peacekeeping and peace-building will be.

Let me conclude by examining the kinds of actions that the international community has at its disposal for responding to civil wars, repression, and anarchy that threaten the human rights and lives of large numbers of people. All have been used selectively to remedy past violations. The first are lowest in cost, and pose the least challenge to sovereignty. The last constitutes the revocation of a state's sovereignty. Military occupation and trusteeship are, or should be, the ultimate sanctions for states and local leaders that will not desist from mass killings.

1. Issue early-warning assessments of impending or escalating conflicts; send fact-finding missions and widely publicize their results. Establish a U.N.-sponsored news bureau with instant access to satellite telecommunications to assure global distribution of news and reports (a CNN for peace). These policies are particularly appropriate to civil wars and repression in their early stages. Fact-finding reports issued after six months of deadly and widely publicized conflict, as in Bosnia now, are little more than empty gestures.
2. Call on governments and their opponents to seek accommodation, provide international mediation and arbitration, offer political and material incentives to encourage contenders to reach agreements. These actions are well suited for the early and middle stages of civil wars.
3. Condemn putative violations of international law, issue formal warnings of impending sanctions, set deadlines for corrective action by the perpetrators. Such responses may help restrain states from gross human rights abuses. They are less likely to influence contenders in civil wars, especially those (like the Bosnian Serbs) whose moral and political ties to the international community are weak. More important, these symbolic acts help set the legal and political stage for more forceful international action.
4. Withdraw diplomatic recognition, apply sanctions, embargo military goods, energy supplies, and other commodities that prolong fighting. These actions can be applied to all armed contenders in civil wars and against state perpetrators of gross human rights violations. Of these options, embargoes are the most likely to be effective but are also the most difficult to enforce consistently. Implementing them is likely to require higher-order responses.
5. Use limited shows of force such as overflights by military aircraft, the stationing of warships offshore, and the introduction of moderately armed peacekeeping forces with sufficient firepower to defend themselves if attacked. These actions convey strong messages to belligerents and position international forces to respond more forcefully if warnings are not heeded.
6. Begin selective applications of force such as interdiction of military movements, air strikes on strategic targets, and the capture and disarming of combatants (individually or in small units). These actions require the international community to "take sides," which is politically feasible when one state or party is clearly the aggressor or perpetrator, as in Bosnia, but which may be impossible in other civil war situations. Selective use of force also poses risks of escalation that may worsen and prolong conflict.
7. Use collective military intervention with the objectives of separating forces, disarming

contenders, protecting neutral areas, and establishing secure procedures and zones for delivering and distributing humanitarian aid. This is the most decisive and costly form of international response, and seems to be the only one that might remedy the current situation in Bosnia and Somalia. The key is to use all means necessary to establish secure and defensible zones in which civilians can be supplied and protected. This is an interim strategy that must be complemented by diplomatic and political initiatives aimed at bringing about a political settlement. There is no denying the high-risk nature of such undertakings, but the consequences of inaction will ultimately lead to far greater cost and injustice.

8. Establish interim, internationally sponsored trusteeships, rebuild civil administration and basic services, provide material and technical assistance, supervise free elections. This form of wholesale intervention is equivalent to Allied policies in occupied Germany after 1945 and current U.N. actions in Cambodia, and is appropriate to Somalia's situation today. It requires a costly long-term commitment. Peacekeeping units must remain in place and be authorized to use force until authority can be transferred to elected local leadership.

COLLECTIVE RESPONSIBILITY

The international community has a wide range of options for responding to emerging communal conflicts and humanitarian crises. The choices are not restricted to passivity on the one hand and total war on the other. There are diverse and graduated responses that can be tailored to fit specific circumstances. Many of these responses have had demonstrably constructive effects in the recent past: belligerents have been separated by peacekeeping forces, abusive governments have been discouraged or prevented from continuing gross human rights abuses, humanitarian assistance has been delivered to victims of ongoing civil wars.

The central issue for timely and effective response is political will. The responses can be carried out under the direct auspices of the U.N. itself or under the authority of regional organizations. If international organizations default on their legal obligations to respond because of political paralysis, and if regional organizations are unable to act, then a strong argument can be made that individual states have the right to act unilaterally. But unilateral military intervention should not be used unless and until all collective remedies are exhausted. The intervenor must prove necessity and proportionality: military intervention has to be shown to be imperative and should remain the last resort.

International law provides the justification for all such actions. The U.N. was not founded so that it could impede progress by doggedly clinging to standards of absolute sovereignty. Instead, it was founded to limit the arbitrary rule of "sovereigns" and to imbue the world's citizens with a sense of collective responsibility for one another and for the survival of the species. The official *History of the United Nations War Crimes Commission* includes an appendix which is as compelling today as it was in 1948. After observing that "the idea of sovereignty paralyses the moral sense of humanity," the author points out that periods of growth in international law coincide with world upheavals. "The pressure of necessity stimulates the impact of natural law and of moral ideas and converts them into rules of law deliberately and overtly recognized by the consensus of civilized mankind." The humanitarian crises of the post–Cold War world point to the compelling necessity of translating international consensus into prompt and effective collective action.

REVIEW QUESTIONS

1. According to Harff, why should the United States intervene in Bosnia?
2. Harff says that Bosnia, Somalia, and Iraqi Kurdistan exemplify three distinct types of crimes against humanity. What are these three types of crimes?
3. According to Harff, how should the international community respond to these crimes against humanity? (She lists eight different possible actions.) Why should the United States and other countries intervene?

1. Harff rejects the idea that nations have an absolute sovereignty such that it is wrong to intervene in their affairs; instead she believes that the world's citizens are responsible for each other. Do you agree? Are the citizens of the United States or Canada morally responsible for people in Bosnia or Somalia or Tibet?

2. U.S. forces were withdrawn from Somalia after fighting between U.S. soldiers and local warlords broke out. Was this the right thing to do?

3. In December 1995, President Clinton sent 20,000 U.S. soldiers to Bosnia-Herzegovina to ensure that the Dayton peace accord would be kept. Was this the right course of action?

PROBLEM CASES

1. Gandhi. (Gandi's life is beautifully portrayed in the movie *Gandhi* [1982], directed by Richard Attenborough, with Ben Kingsley as Gandhi. Gandhi's views on war are collected in *Nonviolence in Peace and War,* edited by Mahadev Desai, 2 vols. [Ahmedalbad: Navajivan Press, 1945].)

Mohandas Gandhi (1869–1948) was the most famous and effective pacifist of the twentieth century. After achieving reforms in the treatment of Hindus and Muslims in South Africa, he returned to India where he campaigned against British rule, resulting in the departure of the British in 1948, the same year that Gandhi was killed by an orthodox Hindu.

Gandhi was a Hindu who practiced ahimsa (nonviolence) towards all living things. (He was considered unorthodox, however, because he rejected the caste system and did not accept everything in the Vedas.) The concept of ahimsa originated in Jainism and was accepted by both Buddhism and Hinduism. In those religions, ahimsa is understood as not harming any living being by actions of body, mind, or speech. In Jainism, ahimsa is practiced even with respect to plants, whereas in Hinduism and Buddhism, plants are not included, but animals are.

The most original aspect of Gandhi's teaching and methods was what he called satyagraha (literally, truth force). Satyagraha involves ahimsa and austerities such as fasting. It is supposed to purify one's soul and transform the souls of those it is used against. In practice, the methods of satyagraha developed by Gandhi included marches, sit-ins, strikes, boycotts, fasts, and prayers. These nonviolent and passive methods worked well against the British and have been widely admired and copied. In the United States, Dr. Martin Luther King, Jr. (1929–1968) used similar tactics in the civil rights struggles of the 1950s and 1960s.

Gandhi's nonviolent tactics worked against the British, but would they have been effective against someone like Hitler who was not afraid to kill millions of innocent people? Is nonviolent resistence an acceptable alternative to war? What do you think?

2. The Gulf War. (For a book-length treatment of the Gulf War, including the view of it as jihād, see Kenneth L. Vaux, *Ethics and the Gulf War* [Boulder, CO: Westview Press, 1992].) In August 1990, the Iraqi army invaded and occupied Kuwait. Although the United States had received warnings, officials did not take them seriously. Saddam Hussein believed the United States would not intervene and apparently had received assurances to that effect. Hussein claimed that the invasion was justified because Kuwait had once been part of Iraq and because the Kuwaitis were exploiting the Rumaila oil field which extended into Iraq. The immediate response of the United States and its allies was to begin a ship embargo against Iraq. President George Bush, citing atrocities against the Kuwaitis, compared Hussein to Hitler. For his part, Hussein declared the war to be jihād and threatened the mother of all battles (as he put it) if the Americans dared to intervene. Iran's Ayatollah Khomeini, certainly no friend of the United States, seconded the claim of jihād adding that anyone killed in battle would be a martyr and immediately go to paradise, the Islamic heaven.

In the months that followed, Iraq ignored repeated ultimatums to leave Kuwait. But Iraq did try to stall for time, following the Quranic teaching of "withholding your hand a little while from war." (This passage is quoted by Vaux, p. 71.) Thousands of foreign prisoners were released, and Iraq responded positively to French and Soviet peace initiatives. At the same time, Saddam Hussein continued to call it a holy war, saying that the United States was a Satanic force attacking the religious values and practices of Islam.

On January 16, 1991, after a U. N. deadline had passed, the allied forces (American, British, French,

Saudi, and Kuwaiti) launched a massive night-and-day air attack on military targets in Iraq including the capital city of Baghdad. The forty days of air war that followed was very one-sided. The allied forces were able to bomb targets at will using advanced technical weapons such as radar-seeking missles, laser-guided bombs, stealth fighters that avoided radar detection, and smart cruise missles that could adjust their course. The Iraqi air force never got off the ground, but hid or flew to Iran. The Iraqi Scud missles killed twenty-two American soldiers sleeping in Saudi Arabia and civilians in Israel but were mostly unreliable and ineffective. Finally, the ground war (Operation Desert Storm) lasted only one hundred hours before the allied forces liberated Kuwait City. The Iraqis had more than 200,000 casualties (according to American estimates) while the allied forces sustained less than 200 casualties.

Can this war be justified using the Just War Theory? Carefully explain your answer. Keep in mind that some religious leaders at the time said that it was not a just war.

Was this a jihād, as Saddam Hussein and the Ayatollah Khomeini said? Remember that Kuwait and Saudi Arabia were also Muslim countries.

Oil presented another consideration. Kuwait had about 20 percent of the world's known oil reserves. Some said the war was really about the control and price of oil and maintained that if Kuwait had no valuable resources, the United States would not have intervened. (For example, the United States did nothing when China invaded and occupied a defenseless Tibet in 1949.)

3. The Invasion of Grenada.

On November 1, 1983, United States military forces invaded and occupied the Caribbean island of Grenada with only minimal resistance. The Marines captured the Pearls airport, the only usable airstrip on the island, while the Army took an uncompleted airstrip at Point Saline on the southern tip of the island. The troops came to free some 1,000 American citizens, mostly medical students, who were trapped on the island after a military coup had toppled the leftist regime of Maurice Bishop.

There were objections to the operation. The military leaders of the coup insisted the American citizens were in no danger. Some of the medical students agreed, saying they did not need or want to be rescued. Furthermore, if the purpose of the invasion was to rescue people, why was it necessary to occupy the airstrips and take over control of the country? Why not just rescue the people and leave?

In his address to the nation, President Ronald Reagan claimed that Grenada was a military threat to the United States; the new airstrip was going to be used to attack the United States. To prove his point, President Reagan said that a cache of Cuban and Soviet weapons had been found and that Cuban military personnel were there. "We got there just in time," he said.

Can this invasion be justified using the Just War Theory? Why or why not? Explain your answer.

History provides us with various examples of invasion: Iraq invaded Kuwait, the Soviets invaded Afghanistan, China invaded Tibet, and American-supported Cuban exiles tried and failed to invade Cuba in the Bay of Pigs Invasion. If you think the invasion of Grenada was justified, then what do you think about these other invasions?

4. The My Lai Massacre.

(The best movie about Vietnam is *Platoon* [1986], directed by Oliver Stone. This movie shows an attack on a village that is similar to the My Lai Massacre. There are numerous books about Vietnam, too many to mention here. Douglas P. Lackey gives a fairly brief account of the My Lai Massacre in *The Ethics of War and Peace* [Englewood Cliffs, NJ: Prentice-Hall, 1989], pp. 82–85.)

The town of My Lai is located in the northern part of South Vietnam. On March 16, 1968, two platoons of American soldiers, under orders from Captain Ernest Medina, attacked the village—first by air, and then on the ground. The first platoon of twenty-five men was commanded by Lieutenant William Calley; the second platoon was under Lieutenant Steven K. Brooks. Both platoons advanced through the village, threw hand grenades into huts, shot anyone who emerged, and rounded up everybody else. The second platoon rounded up about twenty women, made them sit in a circle, and then blew them up with hand grenades. The first platoon gathered together a larger group of about 150 women, children, and old men. (There were no young men of fighting age; presumably they were away fighting or had already been killed.) This large group was put in a ditch on the south side of the village. Lieutenant Calley and the members of the first platoon then shot everyone in the ditch except a few small children (who survived because they were shielded by their mothers' bodies). One small child tried to crawl away, but the soldiers shot him and threw him back in the ditch. After the shooting stopped, more than four hundred people from the village lay dead. There was one American casualty, a private who deliberately shot himself in the foot in order to avoid further duty.

Only Lieutenant Calley was court-martialed for this incident. His defense was that he was following orders and that he could not distinguish combatants from noncombatants in Vietnam.

Under international law, it is illegal to kill noncombatants in war. Thus if Captain Medina ordered Lieutenant Calley to do this (and it was never clear just what the orders were), then the orders were illegal. Should a soldier disobey illegal orders? What if an order is legal but a soldier considers it immoral? Should a soldier disobey orders he considers to be immoral? In general, what are the limits of obedience for soldiers?

Besides the problem of determining if and when to disobey orders, there is the problem of identifying combatants. Surely babies are never combatants, but what about young children, women, and old men? Is it allowable to kill them if one believes they are combatants? What about those who are already injured? Can they be killed too?

Lieutenant Calley was convicted and sentenced to life in prison, but his sentence was reduced and he only served three years. The other soldiers and officers were not punished at all. Should they have been court-martialed too?

5. Torture. (The best philosophical article on torture is Henry Shue's "Torture," *Philosophy and Public Affairs* 7, no. 2 [Winter 1978], pp. 124–143.) Most people consider torture to be wrong; it is prohibited in all the relevant international laws of war. Yet according to Amnesty International, torture is widespread and growing, even in civilized countries. Can torture be justified in some cases? Shue thinks so. To use his example, suppose a fanatic has set a hidden nuclear bomb to explode in the heart of Paris. Wouldn't it be allowable to torture the fanatic to find out where the bomb is hidden so that it could be defused? Surely this is a better alternative than letting the bomb explode.

Shue's example, however, is a case of terrorism, not war. Can interrogational torture, torture for the purpose of extracting information, be justified in war? Consider this hypothetical example. Suppose that towards the end of World War II, when the Allied forces are fighting near Berlin, Hitler is captured trying to escape disguised as an ordinary German soldier. (We are imaging that Hitler did not commit suicide with Eva Braun in the bunker in Berlin; that was just a story made up to deceive people.) After his capture, Hitler tries to commit suicide, but he is prevented from doing so. He has valuable information about Nazi plans that could save hundreds of lives on both sides if known before the Allies' final assault on Berlin. Hitler does not want to reveal this information; he wants the Germans to fight to the death, to kill as many of the enemy as possible before being defeated. He knows, of course, that the war is lost. However, he doesn't care about loss of life; he wants the defeat to be costly for both sides. Time is short; the Allied interrogators must act quickly. They have only twenty-four hours to get the information before beginning the attack on Berlin. Why not torture Hitler to get this life-saving information? Isn't this justified by the principle of proportionality? What do you think?

SUGGESTED READINGS

1. Immanuel Kant, *Perpetual Peace* (Liberal Arts Press, 1957). In a classic discussion, Kant maintains that war must not be conducted in a way that rules out future peace. Perpetual peace results when democratic countries let the people decide about going to war; Kant believes that the people will always vote for peace.

2. Albert Schweitzer, *The Teaching of Reverence for Life,* trans. Richard and Clara Masters (Holt, Rinehart, Winston, 1965), argues that all taking of life is wrong because all life is sacred.

3. Leo Tolstoy, *The Law of Love and the Law of Violence,* trans. Mary Koutouzow Tolstoy (Holt, Rinehart, and Winston, 1971), explains his Christian pacifism.

4. Mohandas K. Gandhi, "The Practice of Satyagraha," *Gandhi: Selected Writings,* ed. Ronald Duncan (Harper & Row, 1971), presents his argument for nonviolent resistance as an alternative to violent war.

5. *The Critique of War,* ed. Robert Ginsberg (Henry Regnery Co., 1969), is a collection of readings that includes a discussion of Gandhi's methods by R. Balasurbramanian and an article on the Hindu view of peace by Swami Nikhilananda.

6. T. R. Miles, "On the Limits to the Use of Force," *Religious Studies* 20 (1984), pp. 113–20, defends a version of pacifism that is opposed to all war but not to all use of force. This kind of pacifism would require one to refuse to serve in the military but would not rule out serving as a police officer.

7. William Earle, "In Defense of War," *The Monist* 57, no. 4 (October 1973), pp. 561–69, attacks pacifism (defined as the principled opposition to all war) and then gives a justification for the morality and rationality of war.

8. Jan Narveson, "In Defense of Peace," in *Moral Issues,* ed. Jan Narveson (Oxford University Press, 1983), pp. 59–71, replies to Earle. He does not defend pacifism; instead, he argues that whenever there is a war, at least one party is morally unjustified.

9. Jan Narveson, "Morality and Violence: War, Revolution, Terrorism," in *Matters of Life and Death: New Introductory Essays in Moral Philosophy,* ed. Tom Regan (McGraw-Hill, 1993), pp. 121–59. Narveson covers many different issues in this survey article: the nature and morality of violence, the right of self-defense, pacifism, Just War Theory, and terrorism.

10. *War and Morality,* ed. Richard A. Wasserstrom (Wadsworth Publishing Co., 1970), is a collection of articles on the morality of war and other issues. Elizabeth Anscombe discusses the doctrine of double effect as it applies to war. Wasserstrom's article "On the Morality of War: A Preliminary Inquiry" argues that the fact innocents are inevitably killed in modern wars makes it very difficult to justify them.

11. *War and Moral Responsibility,* ed. Marshall Cohen, Thomas Nagel, and Thomas Scanlon (Princeton University Press, 1973). This collection of articles has two parts. The first part examines restrictions on the goals and methods of war; the second part covers issues related to World War II and the Vietnam War.

12. Robert L. Phillips, *War and Justice* (University of Oklahoma Press, 1984), defends Just War Theory. He accepts two principles of this theory: the principle of Proportionality and the principle of Discrimination. The latter principle, however, in turn rests on the doctrine of double effect which distinguishes between intending to kill and merely foreseeing that something will die as an unintended effect of an action.

13. James Johnson, *Just War Tradition and the Restraint of War* (Princeton University Press, 1981), explains the historical development of Just War Theory from the Middle Ages to the present.

14. Michael Walzer, *Just and Unjust Wars: A Moral Argument with Historical Illustrations* (Basic Books, 1977), develops and defends Just War Theory and applies the theory to numerous historical cases—for example, the Six-Day War, the Vietnam War, the Korean War, and World War II. He argues that the Vietnam War can be justified as assistance to the legitimate government of South Vietnam and as counterintervention in response to military moves by the North Vietnamese.

15. Paul Ramsey, *The Just War: Force and Political Responsibility* (Charles Scribner's Sons, 1968). This book is a collection of articles on Just War Theory, all written by Ramsey. He is a Christian who defends a version of Just War Theory that has an absolute principle of discrimination against any killing of noncombatants. Yet having accepted this principle, he goes on to claim that the war in Vietnam was justified, even though it involved killing many noncombatants, producing an appearance, at least, of inconsistency.

16. Paul Christopher, *The Ethics of War and Peace* (Prentice-Hall, 1994). This is a useful textbook that covers the just war tradition, the international laws on war, and moral issues such as war crimes, reprisals, and nuclear, biological, and chemical weapons.

17. David Luban, "Just War and Human Rights," *Philosophy and Public Affairs* 9, no. 2 (Winter 1980), pp. 160–81, argues that the morality of war should be judged in terms of human rights. A just war defends human rights, and an unjust war subverts them.

18. George I. Mavrodes, "Conventions and the Morality of War," *Philosophy and Public Affairs* 4, no. 2 (1975), discusses the moral rule of war that noncombatants should not be intentionally killed. He suggests that this rule is not an independent moral rule, but rather part of a convention setting up an alternative to war. As such, it creates a special obligation not to kill innocent people.

19. Dilip Hiro, *Holy Wars: The Rise of Islamic Fundamentalism* (Routledge, 1989), explains the development of Islam from the prophet Mohammed to the Islamic fundamentalism found today in Iran

and Afghanistan where Islam has emerged as a radical ideology of armed resistance.

20. Ayatollah Ruhollah Khomeini, "Islam Is Not a Religion of Pacifists," in *Holy Terror,* ed. Amir Taheri (Adler & Adler, 1987), gives a clear statement of the Islamic doctrine of holy war. According to the Ayatollah Khomeini, Islam says: "Kill all the unbelievers just as they would kill you all!"

21. R. Peters, "Jihād," in *The Encyclopedia of Religion* (Macmillan Press, 1989), gives a scholarly account of the Islamic concept of jihād and its application to war.

22. A. Maalory, *The Crusaders Through Arab Eyes* (Schochen Books, 1985), covers two centuries of hostility and war between Muslim Arabs and Christian Crusaders from the West (called Franks) starting with the fall of Jerusalem in 1099; it is a sad story of invasion, counterinvasion, massacres, and plunder.

23. Jean Bethke Elshtain, *Women and War* (Basic Books, 1987). What is the feminist view of war? According to Elshtain, some feminists are pacifists working for world peace, whereas others want to reject the traditional noncombatant role of women and become warriors. As a result of the second position, the United States now has a higher percentage of women in the military than any other industrialized nation: 10 percent of the overall force of 2.1 million.

PHILOSOPHICAL GLOSSARY

Acts and Omissions Doctrine   The doctrine that there is an important moral difference between acts and omissions (or failures to act): An act can be wrong, but an omission with the same effect is not wrong. As it is applied to killing and letting die, the doctrine says that killing an innocent person is wrong but letting the person die may not be wrong, or perhaps is less wrong. The application of the doctrine to euthanasia is attacked by Rachels in the reading in Chapter 3. Glover discusses and rejects the doctrine and its application to euthanasia in Chapter 7 of his book *Causing Death and Saving Lives*. A limited defense of the doctrine as it is applied to killing and letting die can be found in Foot's "Euthanasia" and Ladd's "Positive and Negative Euthanasia" (see the Suggested Readings for Chapter 3).

Ad hoc device   A device made for a specific purpose. In science and philosophy, an ad hoc hypothesis (or device) is one added to a theory to save it from being falsified. A well-known example is the addition of epicycles to the astronomy of Ptolemy.

Ahimsa   Literally, nonviolence. The concept of ahimsa originated in Jainism, an Indian religion, and was adopted by Hinduism and Buddhism. In Jainism, one is supposed to not harm any living being, including insects and plants. In Hinduism and Buddhism, it is usually applied only to conscious or sentient beings, where this includes animals but not plants. Negatively, it means not killing or harming beings in thought, word, or deed. Positively, it means loving beings in thought, word, and deed. In Buddism, this is expressed by the wish "May all beings be happy and free of suffering!"

Altruism   The view that we should give moral consideration to others for their own sake and not because of any self-interested reason. By contrast, Egoism says that we should consider only ourselves and that any consideration of others is based on self-interest.

A priori   Known independent of experience, as distinguished from a posteriori, known from experience. "No statement can be both true and false" is known

a priori, whereas the statement "Some crows are black" is known a posteriori.

Argumentum ad hominem   A Latin phrase meaning, literally, "argument to the man." In logic, the fallacy of personally attacking one's opponent instead of responding to the opponent's arguments or claims.

Begging the question   Begging the question is a fallacy of reasoning where one assumes what one is trying to prove. For example, the claim that the Bible proves that God exists assumes that the Bible is the revealed word of God, and this assumes that God exists. Such reasoning is sometimes said to be circular.

Carthaginian peace   Carthage was an ancient city completely razed by the Romans. A Carthaginian peace, therefore, is an ironic way of talking about total destruction.

Categorical Imperative   In his moral theory, Kant distinguishes between a hypothetical imperative and a categorical imperative. One follows a hypothetical imperative when one seeks a "material end" dependent on desires, for example, eating food in order to feel satisfied. In Kant's terminology, the end of eating food is conditional on the desire to feel satisfied; it is not an unconditional end like the fulfillment of duty. A categorical imperative is a command in the form "Do X" (as distinguished from a hypothetical command of the form "If you want X, do Y") that has an unconditional end, namely, the fulfillment of duty. This end is not dependent on desires or inclinations, but is based on pure reason alone (as Kant puts it). Kant formulates the Categorical Imperative in several different ways, but he seems to think that there is just one such imperative. The standard version is that one should act only in accord with those maxims that can be consistently willed as universal laws; this is something that is supposed to be impossible for maxims aimed at mere material ends, such as drinking beer.

Ceteris paribus   A Latin phrase meaning "other things being equal." A ceteris paribus clause is often used as a hedge or qualification to a claim to indicate that there may be exceptions or that it might be false in certain circumstances or given certain factors.

Consequentialists   Those who believe that the moral rightness or wrongness of an act is determined by its consequences rather than some other feature such as motive or God's commands. Both utilitarians and egoists are consequentialists.

Criterion   (pl. *criteria*) A standard that provides a conclusive way of determining whether something exists or whether a word is used correctly. In the abortion controversy, writers have tried to establish a criterion for the fetus being a person, that is, the feature that provides logically conclusive evidence that the fetus is a person. Often a criterion is formulated in terms of a necessary and sufficient condition. (See *necessary conditions* and *sufficient conditions*.)

Cultural Relativism   A theory of moral values that holds that values are relative to society. If a society or culture approves of a certain action, then it is right; and if it disapproves of an action, then it is wrong. (This theory should not be confused with Anthropological Relativism, the factual thesis that different societies have different moral codes.) If Cultural Relativism is true, then it follows, supposedly, that there are no universal moral values that hold in all societies at all times and there are no objective moral values that hold independent of society. Cultural Relativism has been popular with sociologists and anthropologists, but not many philosophers have adopted it. Philosophers insist (with some support from anthropologists) that there are universal moral values; for example, caring for children is morally approved in all known societies. Philosophers also want to criticize societies and reform them; this means that societies have made moral mistakes in the past and present. If so, then practices such as slavery that were previously approved by a society may be objectively wrong, and acts disapproved by a society (such as allowing women in combat) may be objectively right.

Dār al-Harb   Literally, the territory of war. The land of the enemy or land not controlled by Muslims.

Dār al-Islam   Literally, the territory of Islam. The land ruled by Muslims.

Deontological theories   Deontological theories determine the rightness or wrongness of an act by something other than its consequences—for example, by God's commands or moral intuition. They differ from teleological theories such as Utilitarianism, Egoism, and Altruism, which hold that the rightness or wrongness of an act is determined by its consequences.

Dharma   In Hinduism a comprehensive term that includes the lawful order of the universe and the foundation of religion. In Buddhism dharma can refer to the teachings of the Buddha, the cosmic law underlying our world, or the moral law of karmically determined rebirth.

Distributive justice   The problem or theory of how to allocate or distribute goods and services in a society. Should there be equal distribution, or should some people be allowed to have more goods and services than others?

Divine Command Theory   In its standard form, the Divine Command Theory says that an act is right if it is commanded by God and wrong if it is forbidden by God. This theory has been defended by a few philosophers, but it faces various difficulties, some of which are discussed by Arthur in the reading. One way of defending the theory is to hold that the divine commands are "written in one's heart" and discovered by using one's conscience. This avoids some of the difficulties raised by Arthur, but it would not satisfy those who insist that God's commands are only found in the Bible or the Koran.

Doctrine of Double Effect   This Roman Catholic doctrine distinguishes between two effects of an action: an intended effect and an unintended but foreseen effect. The doctrine says that an action that has a bad effect that is foreseen but unintended is allowable provided it is motivated by the intention to produce a good effect. Sometimes the qualification is added that the good effect must outweigh the bad effect or that the good effect must be "proportional" to the bad effect. This principle can be used to defend abortions and euthanasia. A famous application of the principle was to the atomic bombing of Hiroshima and Nagasaki. It was argued that the good intention to end the war with Japan justified this action despite the fact that hundreds of thousands of innocent people were killed.

Empirical truths   Truths based on experience, for example, "It is cloudy outside." They are also called contingent truths. Empirical or contingent truths are distinguished from logical or necessary truths discovered by reasoning, for example, "It is either cloudy or it is not cloudy."

Ethical Egoism   The standard formulation of the theory is that everyone ought to act in his or her self-interest. My act is right if it is in self-interest, and wrong if it is not. Your act is right if it is in your self-interest, and wrong if it is not. This version of the theory is called Universal Ethical Egoism because it is supposed to apply to everyone equally. Another possible version of Egoism is Personal Ethical Egoism where I say that I ought to do those actions that most benefit me, but I have nothing to say about your actions. This is not really an ethical theory, but more like a personal philosophy of life. Still another version is Individual Ethical Egoism where I say that you and I both ought to do what is in my self-interest. This view involves a strange asymmetry: You ought to always help me, but I should never help you, unless that benefits me. None of these views should be confused with Psychological Egoism, the theory that everyone, in fact, is motivated by self-interest. Obviously, this is not an ethical theory, but a factual claim about how people act.

Ethnocentrism   The belief that one's own race or ethnic group is superior to other races or ethnic groups.

Fallacy of affirming the consequent   A fallacy of reasoning committed by arguments having the logical form "P implies Q; Q; therefore P," where P and Q are statements that are true or false. In the conditional statement "P implies Q," Q is called the consequent and P the antecedent. For example, consider this argument: If the fetus is a person, then the fetus is conscious. The fetus is conscious after the eighth week. So the fetus is a person after the eighth week. Here is an argument with the same logical form, only it is about Fido the dog: If Fido is a person, then Fido is conscious. Fido is conscious when barking; therefore, Fido is a person when barking.

Free-rider's principle   A free rider is one who obtains or attempts to obtain a benefit without paying, for example, a worker who receives the benefits of a union contract without becoming a member of the union. Advocates of the free rider's principle maintain that one should be allowed to do this.

Free will   According to the traditional theory of free will, acts that are produced by a special mental act of the will, and not by some external event, are said to be free, that is, not caused by anything else, either mental or physical. The standard example of an act of free will is the mental act of choosing between two

things. The theory of free will is highly controversial; it is rejected by scientists and philosophers who believe that everything is caused, including human mental and physical acts.

Hedonism   The theory saying that only pleasure is good. The theory is usually explained in terms of a distinction between intrinsic and instrumental goodness. Something is intrinsically good if it is good in itself, considered apart from anything else, whereas something is instrumentally good if it is a means of getting something else. Hedonism claims that only pleasure is intrinsically good, but it allows that other things such as beauty and power can be instrumentally good. Hedonists typically make a further distinction between types of pleasures. Mill, for example, held that intellectual pleasures (e.g., the pleasure one gets from reading or writing) are better than physical pleasures (e.g., the pleasure one gets from eating). As Mill puts it, "It is better to be a human being dissatisfied than a pig satisfied."

Ideal Utilitarianism   This is a nonhedonistic form of Utilitarianism that accepts other things besides pleasure as being good. In the version adopted by the British philosopher G. E. Moore (1873–1958), knowledge and beauty are considered to be intrinsically good, and some pleasant states of mind can be intrinsically bad.

Imām   A leader of the people. The Imām is also referred to as the Caliph and is supposed to be a successor to Mohammed, e.g., Ali.

Imperfect duty   See *perfect duty.*

Infinite regress   A series of events that continues without end—usually with the implication that this is impossible. A vicious infinite regress is one that is impossible, whereas a benign infinite regress is not impossible.

Instrumental value   See *intrinsic value.*

Intrinsic value   Sometimes the term "intrinsic value" is used to mean intrinsic goodness, but strictly speaking, intrinsic value includes both intrinsic goodness and intrinsic badness. Something has intrinsic value if it is good or bad in itself apart from its use or consequences. By contrast, something has *instrumental value* (or extrinsic value) if it is good or bad depending on how it is used. Kant used the phrase "good without qualification"; this seems to mean roughly the same thing as intrinsically good.

Intuitionism In general, Intuitionism is the view that knowledge can be found using a special kind of apprehension called intuition that is neither sense-perception nor inferential reasoning, but a kind of mental vision where a truth is directly and clearly seen to be true. In ethics, Intuitionism is the view that certain moral judgments are self-evident and that any normal person will agree. For example, Ross thought it self-evident that one has a duty to keep a promise. Other than saying that this is self-evident, in a way similar to the self-evidence of axioms and postulates of mathematics and geometry, no further justification can be given or is needed.

Lex talionis The law of retaliation. It can be interpreted to mean exact retaliation, as in the biblical saying "an eye for an eye, a tooth for a tooth, a life for a life," or it can be interpreted to mean simply that the punishment should be appropriate for the crime—a severe punishment for a serious crime, and a lesser punishment for a less serious crime.

Logically necessary A proposition is said to be logically necessary if its denial is a self-contradiction. For example, "Triangles are three-sided" is logically necessary given the ordinary meaning of the word "triangles." Sometimes properties are said to be logically necessary if it is impossible for an object to exist without the property in question. For example, it is claimed that being human is a logically necessary property of Socrates because Socrates could not exist without being human. By contrast, Socrates could have existed without being snub-nosed, it is claimed, so being snub-nosed is not a logically necessary property or essential property of Socrates. The view that objects have logically necessary properties or essential properties is called Essentialism, and it remains controversial. Essentialists make a distinction between de dicto necessity (necessity applied to propositions) and de re necessity (necessity applied to objects in the world), but there is debate about the distinction and how it should be used. For one thing, essentialists explain the distinction by appealing to the notion of an infinite number of possible worlds, and some philosophers find this idea problematic.

Metaphysical Relating to metaphysics, the branch of philosophy that answers questions about reality. In Glover's article, however, metaphysical means something transcendental or beyond the sensible world.

Mirabile dictu Amazing or wonderful to say.

Natural kind A category of entities that belong together, usually with the implication that this is a matter of necessity. For example, if Socrates is a member of the natural kind "human being," then he is necessarily a human being. Some philosophers argue that science in fact uses natural kind terms (like "water") that imply necessity.

Natural law The term "natural law" usually refers to prescriptive moral laws that are derived from human nature (as distinguished from descriptive laws of nature such as those found in chemistry and physics). For example, it is claimed that the natural purpose of sexual intercourse is reproduction and that it is wrong to interfere with this natural process.

Necessary conditions A necessary condition for something is one without which the thing would not exist or occur. The presence of oxygen is a necessary condition for human life. Being age thirty-five or older is a necessary condition for being the president of the United States. A *sufficient condition* for something is one such that its occurrence or presence makes the thing exist or occur. Prolonged absence of oxygen is a sufficient condition for human death. Being a United States senator is a sufficient condition for being a person. Something can be a necessary condition and not a sufficient condition and vice versa.

Nirvana Literally, "blowing out" or "extinction." In Theravada Buddhism, Nirvana is usually defined as the cessation of the defilements of greed, hatred, and delusion. As such it can be attained while one is still living, as the Buddha is said to have done at age thirty-five when he attained the supreme, unexcelled enlightenment. Parinirvana is the final Nirvana, literally the Nirvana that goes beyond; it is usually understood to be the indescribable state the Buddha or an arhat (a disciple who has attained the cessation of defilements) enters into after physical death. It is not total annihilation—such a view is rejected as nihilism; rather it is a state of consciousness comparable to a vast ocean. In Mahayana Buddhism and Tibetan Buddhism, still another type of Nirvana is recognized, the "Nirvana without fixed abode." Buddhas or other beings (called bodhisattvas or "enlightenment beings") who have attained this Nirvana are able to appear and disappear in any of the six realms of birth and death (that is, the realms of devas, asuras, humans, animals, ghosts, or hell-beings) or to abide in a special Buddha realm. They do not remain "fixed" in Parinirvana but appear and disappear in order to help those who have not attained Nirvana or enlightenment. Nirvana is not the same as enlightenment although they are sometimes equated. In Mahayana Buddhism, bodhisattvas can attain enlightenment without the cessation of the defilements, that is, without attaining Nirvana and without entering into the Parinirvana; this distinguishes them from Buddhas who attain both enlightenment and Nirvana. Also, Buddhas who are enlightened may renounce Nirvana; when they do this they are technically no longer Buddhas but bodhisattvas. For example, Manjushri, the Bodhisattva of Perfect Wisdom, is said to have been a perfect Buddha innumerable world-eons before our universe. He vowed to manifest himself as a disciple of all Buddhas in all world systems so that he could mediate between the Buddhas and humans.

Normative propositions   Propositions or statements containing value terms such as "ought," "right," and "good." For example, "You ought to love your neighbor as yourself," or "Pleasure is good."

Perfect duty   In Kant's ethical theory, a perfect duty is an action that we should always perform or abstain from performing without exception. For example, Kant thought that the duty not to lie is a perfect duty that admits no exceptions. Another example is the duty not to kill an innocent person. An imperfect duty, by contrast, asks us to promote certain goals such as the welfare of others, but we are not required always to do this. We can choose when and how to fulfill an imperfect duty. For example, one person might give money for famine relief, while another gives money to help the homeless; but both are fulfilling the imperfect duty to help others. A person who does nothing at all to help others, however, would fail to satisfy the imperfect duty to help others.

Positive and negative duties   Positive duties tell us what we are morally required to do, whereas negative duties tell us what we are morally forbidden to do. Some moral philosophers have held that negative duties such as the duty not to kill innocent people are stronger than positive duties such as the duty to help others, but this remains controversial.

Positive and negative duties are often correlated with positive and negative rights. A positive right implies that others have a positive duty to do something. The right to life, for example, if interpreted as a positive right, requires others to give food and other necessities for life. By contrast, a negative right implies that others have a negative duty not to do something. They are sometimes called rights of non-interference. Thus the right to life, if interpreted negatively, implies that one has a negative duty not to interfere with another's life.

Positivism   A philosophical position developed by Comte in nineteenth-century France, and adopted by many philosophers, that is characterized by hostility to theology and metaphysics and optimism about the use of the scientific method to obtain knowledge about the world. In the twentieth century, logical positivists dismissed statements in religion, ethics, and metaphysics as factually meaningless because they could not be empirically verified. To do this, they adopted a verifiability principle saying that a statement is factually meaningful if and only if it can be empirically verified. This principle was criticized as self-defeating (when applied to itself, the verifiability principle is itself factually meaningless) and too narrow (it excludes many meaningful sentences such as commands and exclamations). Because of these difficulties, logical positivism was replaced by a movement called linguistic or conceptual analysis that attempts to explain the meaning of language in terms of its use and pays close attention to the vagueness and ambiguity of language. The articles by Mary Anne Warren and Jane English in Chapter 2 illustrate this method of doing philosophy.

Preference Utilitarianism   This is a nonhedonistic form of Utilitarianism holding that satisfaction of one's desires is what is good, rather than just pleasure, and not having one's desires satisfied is bad. Peter Singer is the main proponent of this theory.

Prima facie duty   In Ross's terminology, a prima facie duty is a duty or obligation one has unless it is overridden by some other duty. Prima facie means literally "on the face of it." The basic idea is that one prima facie duty can override another prima facie duty. For example, suppose Jane promises to meet Mary for lunch, but she cannot get anyone to care for her two small children. Jane breaks her promise to meet Mary because she feels her duty to care for her children overrides her duty to keep her promise. A duty that is not overridden by any other duties becomes an absolute duty.

Prima facie rightness   Literally, rightness at first glance. To say that an act is prima facie right means that its rightness can be overridden by other moral considerations. For example, it is prima facie right to keep a promise. But suppose that doing this will produce a great harm. If that is the case, then the rightness of keeping a promise would be overridden by a more important moral consideration. Or at least that is what Ross and his followers would say. (See *prima facie duty*).

Principle of Equal Consideration of Interests Peter Singer's principle that we ought to give equal consideration to everyone's interests, including those of nonhuman animals. Singer argues that racism, sexism, and speciesism all violate this principle.

Principle of Universalisability Kant's principle that an act is right if you are willing to have everyone do it, that is, if you are willing to universalize it, and wrong if you are not willing to have everyone do it, if you are not willing to universalize it.

Prisoner's dilemma A problem in game theory that applies to situations where people must cooperate. The problem is usually stated in terms of two prisoners, say John and Jane. Both John and Jane are offered the same deal: If one of them confesses and the other does not, the one who confesses will go free and the one who does not confess will get a stiff prison sentence. If both confess, then both will get moderate prison sentences. If both refuse to confess (and thus cooperate with each other), then both will get light prison sentences. So there are four possible outcomes:

1. John confesses and goes free, and Jane does not confess and gets a stiff sentence.
2. Jane confesses and goes free, and John does not confess and gets a stiff sentence.
3. Both confess and get moderate sentences.
4. Neither confesses and both get light sentences.

Now assume that (1) is the best outcome for John and (2) is the best outcome for Jane and that the next best outcome for both is (4). The worst outcome for both is (3). What should they do? Each will reason as follows: "The other one will either confess or not confess. If the other one confesses I must confess too in order to avoid the sucker's outcome—a stiff sentence for me and the other one goes free. If the other one doesn't confess, then I must confess to get the best outcome for me. Thus no matter what the other one does, I must confess." If both reason in this way, both will confess, producing (3) instead of (4): that is, they produce the worst possible outcome for both instead of the best one for both.

This sort of problem seems to arise in many situations of cooperation and conflict between persons. For example, suppose there is a public good that we all want, say clean air. Clean air can only be produced by cooperative collective action. But to produce this public good, each individual must make a sacrifice (say by driving less often), and this gives each one a reason to not cooperate. So each person

might reason as follows: "Other people will either act to produce clean air or they will not. If they do, then I can get clean air without sacrificing (the best option for me). If they do not, then why should I be a sucker and sacrifice without getting the benefit? So in any event, I should do nothing." If everyone reasons in this way, then we will never get clean air.

Propositional attitude A psychological attitude that takes a proposition as its object, for example, believing that the sun will rise tomorrow, or hoping that there is survival of death.

Retributivism A theory of punishment holding that punishment is done to correct an inequity or moral imbalance the offense has created, and not because it produces any good consequences—as in the utilitarian theory of punishment. Retribution or "paying back" the criminal is sometimes thought of as personal revenge or getting even, but it can also be perceived as a kind of impersonal correction of a moral imbalance.

Satyagraha The term "satyagraha" (literally, "truth force") was coined by Mohandas K. Gandi to express the force Indians used in South Africa and later in India to oppose unjust laws. As practiced by Gandi and his followers, it requires nonviolence (ahimsa) toward all living beings but permits breaking unjust laws, provided the lawbreaker accepts the legal punishment for breaking the law. In practice, the activities employed included fasting, marches, strikes, boycotts, and so on. To give a specific example, in South Africa Gandi burned his identity card identifying him as "colored"; for doing this he was beaten by the police and imprisoned. By accepting the punishment, Gandi showed respect for the law as such. Also, the passive and nonviolent resistance was supposed to be done with humility and lack of anger toward one's opponents.

Semantics The study of the meaning of signs and symbols, as distinguished from syntactics, the study of the grammatical arrangement of signs and symbols in order to convey meaning.

Shìa A branch of Islam composed of sects that are the followers of Ali and who uphold Ali's leadership after Mohammed. Distinguished from the Sunni who appeal to the sunna (custom or tradition) to determine correct behavior rather than to the Imams or leaders. The Sunni are usually considered to be Orthodox Muslims.

Slippery slope argument   In general, an argument that one cannot draw a line or avoid certain consequences. For example, a slippery slope argument is that if one allows some sick people to be killed, then one must allow all sick people to be killed (and slide down a "slippery slope" of killing). In the abortion controversy, one finds the argument that if an infant is a person, and the development of the infant from the zygote is a slippery slope, that is, a smooth continuous curve of development without any sharp breaks or discontinuities so that no lines can be drawn, then the zygote is a person too. This argument is attacked by Thomson in the readings.

Social Contract Theory   The basic idea of Social Contract Theory is that morality arises from an agreement or contract made by people that enables them to live together. In his book *Leviathan*, the British philosopher Thomas Hobbes (1588–1679) says that people living in a state of nature apart from society would find life "solitary, poor, nasty, brutish, and short." To avoid such a life, people live together in a society. But social life is possible only if people agree to follow moral rules such as "Don't murder" and "Don't steal." Another philosopher who is associated with this theory is Jean-Jacques Rousseau (1712–1778). In his work *The Social Contract,* Rousseau asserts that humans living in a state of nature are stupid animals; they become intelligent beings only when they live together in a civilized society. The British philosopher John Locke (1632–1704) made an important contribution to Social Contract Theory in his work *Two Treatises of Government*. He argues that in the state of nature humans are free and equal, but this does not mean that they can do anything they want. There is a law of nature, established by God, that gives each person certain natural rights—a right to life, a right to liberty, and a right to property. But to enjoy these rights, humans must live together under a social contract which establishes a government to protect these rights and settle disputes. Without a government, humans in a state of nature would infringe on each other's rights.

Statism   Control and planning of a nation's economy by a centralized government, as distinguished from free market capitalism.

Subjectivism   A theory of moral values holding that values are relative to a person's subjective feelings or emotions. If a person approves of an action, then it is morally right; and if the person disapproves of an action, then it is morally wrong. This theory should not be confused with the factual thesis that different people have different feelings about moral values. No doubt this factual thesis is true, but it does not follow that moral values are different for different people. An act might be right even if a person disapproves of it; and an act might be wrong even though a person approves of it. This is simply to say that people can be mistaken about what is right or wrong. If such mistakes are possible, and most philosophers insist that they are, then Subjectivism cannot be true. Another standard criticism of Subjectivism is that it fails to recognize the fact that there are genuine moral disagreements. Pro-life and pro-choice advocates disagree about the wrongness of abortion, but this disagreement is not just a disagreement in feeling or emotion. Both sides could emotionally disapprove of abortion, yet disagree about its wrongness in some cases, say pregnancy due to rape.

Sufficient conditions   See *necessary conditions*.

Supererogatory   An act is supererogatory if it is morally good but beyond what is morally required, such as giving all your money to the needy.

Tao   Literally, the way or path. In the *Tao Te Ching,* the phrase "eternal Tao" is used to refer to the indescribable, ultimate reality that is the Mother of the ten thousand things, that is, all individual things that exist. Sometimes, the word "tao" refers to the manifestation of the eternal tao in nature. In Confucianism and Taoism, the word "tao" is also used to refer to the moral path that leads to goodness (jen) or to a good life or, in religious Taoism, to immortality.

Teleological theories   Teleological theories determine moral rightness or wrongness by looking at consequences of actions. The standard teleological theory in ethics, as we can see in the readings, is Utilitarianism. Utilitarianism takes different forms, depending on what view about the good is adopted (for example, Hedonism or some nonhedonistic view), but all versions agree that the consequences for everyone should be considered. Unlike Utilitarianism, Ethical Egoism is a teleological theory that only considers the consequences for the agent and ignores the consequences for others. A third teleological theory is Altruism; it considers consequences for others but not for the agent. More teleological theories can be formulated, depending on who is given moral consideration. One might only be concerned, say, with one's family or one's religious group.

Teleological theories are usually contrasted with deontological theories, which do not look at consequences in determining moral rightness or wrongness. Kant's theory and the Divine Command Theory are examples of deontological theories. Another example is situation ethics where one is supposed to decide what is right or wrong in concrete situations without using abstract rules for guidance. Appeals to conscience or moral intuition would also be classified as deontological.

Theory of Instantaneous Ensoulment   The medieval doctrine that God puts the soul into the fertilized egg at the moment of conception and not afterward. This is a standard Roman Catholic belief that is sometimes used to defend the conservative prohibition of abortion.

Utilitarianism   A standard theory in ethics that uses the Principle of Utility to determine whether an act is morally right or wrong. This principle is formulated in different ways, but a standard version is this: Everyone ought to act so as to bring about the greatest good for the greatest number. Utilitarians do not agree about what is good or bad. Some of them, called hedonists, think that only pleasure is intrinsically good (good in itself) and that only pain is intrinsically bad (bad in itself). For example, the classical utilitarians Jeremy Bentham (1748–1832) and John Stuart Mill (see the reading in Chapter 1) were hedonistic utilitarians. Other utilitarians believe that satisfaction of one's desires is what is good and not having them satisfied is bad. They are called preference utilitarians. (See *Preference Utilitarianism.*) Still another version is Ideal Utilitarianism which holds that other things are good besides pleasure, such as beauty. The British philosopher G. E. Moore (1873–1958) held this theory, and it is discussed by W. D. Ross in the reading in Chapter 1. (See *Ideal Utilitarianism.*)

INDEX